SECOND EDITION

Organizational Behaviour

Dedicated to
Valerie, Jeffrey, Richard and Shona
and to the memory of Flo

SECOND EDITION

Organizational Behaviour

John Martin

The University of Hull

THOMSON
™
LEARNING

Australia • Canada • Mexico • Singapore • Spain • United Kingdom • United States

Organizational Behaviour – 2nd edition

Copyright © 2001 John Martin

The Thomson Learning logo is a registered trademark used herein under licence.

For more information, contact Thomson Learning, Berkshire House, 168–173 High Holborn, London WC1V 7AA or visit us on the World Wide Web at:
http://www.thomsonlearning.co.uk

British Library Cataloguing-in-Publication Data
A catalogue record for this book is available from the British Library

ISBN 1-86152-583-4

First edition 1998, reprinted 2000
This edition 2001

Text design by Design Deluxe
Typeset by Saxon Graphics Ltd, Derby

Printed in Italy by G. Canale & C.

Contents

Part 1 Management and organizational behaviour 1

Part II   Individuals within organizations   73

Part III   Groups within organizations   165

Part V Processes within organizations 351

Part VI   The structure and design of organizations   483

Part VII The management of organizations 629

List of Figures

List of Tables

List of Management in Action panels

Preface

This preface locates the major themes of the second edition of this book in the management and organizational context within which much human behaviour takes place. It also provides an introduction to the key features and structure of the book, along with suggestions on how students and lecturers might make use of the content. Another important feature of this book available to both lecturers and students is the accompanying web site, which is also described in this preface.

This book is intended for those people who seek to gain an insight into the world of humans and their association with organizations. Organizations are an integral part of human experience. Most people are either employed within or own an organization. It is human beings who consume the outputs produced by organizations. This book is therefore intended to appeal to anyone who seeks to better understand this important aspect of human life. Topics included in the book include:

+ A reflection on the nature of organizations and management.
+ Consideration of those aspects of individuals and groups that form the human face of organizations.
+ The nature of work and its relationship to the technology used by organizations.
+ A review of processes such as motivation, learning, communication, decision making and negotiation that takes place within organizations.
+ The structure and design of organizations.
+ Organization culture.
+ Management and leadership.
+ Ethical perspectives within organizations.
+ Managing change.
+ Power and control, conflict and organizational politics.
+ Stress.

This book will appeal to a wide range of people including:

+ Practising managers who seek to develop an academic understanding of the topics through which to interpret their experience, perhaps as part of a diploma or degree programme.
+ A second category of reader would be those with an academic background in either business or management who, having gained some management experience, have returned to higher education to further their development through an MBA or other masters programme.

✦   A third group of readers would include those without formal management experience, but perhaps with some employment experience, who are studying aspects of human behaviour and management within an organizational context, perhaps as part of a degree programme.

✦   A fourth category of reader would have an academic background in either the social sciences or one of the science disciplines, and have some subsequent organizational experience. Such individuals would be likely to study this book in seeking to further their studies in the business, organizational or management fields through one of the many masters programmes intended to achieve this objective.

✦   Another category of reader would include those individuals studying for the professional qualifications offered by the professional associations and who inevitably include aspects of organization, management and behaviour within the syllabus.

The blend of theory, critical perspective and practical application is balanced throughout the book in an accessible and engaging writing style. This will appeal to the wide cross-section of individuals indicated offering challenges to each, without oversimplification or obfuscation, in each case seeking to further the understanding of the individual in this challenging and exciting field.

Organizational behaviour and management

Organizations in their many forms represent a fundamental part of the human experience. They provide the goods and services that form an essential part of human life in the twenty-first century. They also provide the employment from which individuals and families draw the money that allows them to acquire the goods and services essential for life. Organizations also pollute the world in which we and future generations live and cause untold harm to the people who work in them. They are a 'double-edged sword' in every sense of the term. In short, they are a fascinating social creation, interesting both to study and to work within.

Individuals who aspire to achieve success in the formal organization within which they seek to carve out their careers need to develop an understanding of many specialist disciplines. There is a need to understand marketing, accounting and those aspects associated with product manufacture and service design and delivery. However, in addition to developing these technical skills, there is a need to develop competence in understanding how an organization functions as a collective endeavour involving people with the full range of human qualities without which no organization could function. This is the realm of organizational behaviour.

There are many constituent parts of any organization. There are the functions and departments that undertake the work to be done. There are the owners, directors, managers and workers who comprise the hierarchy. There are the stakeholder groups (suppliers, customers, trade unions, government etc.) within and around the organization that can influence its activities. There are the formal and informal groups that exist within the organizations as individuals undertake their duties and socialize with each other. All of these constituents of an organization have a degree of influence on how it will function in the complex and dynamic environment of the marketplace.

The individuals and groups that form the basis of human activity within an organization must have their behaviour directed and channelled if it is to stand any chance of achieving its objectives. This text teases out and illuminates the major forces that shape and control this dynamic activity. It is inevitable, given the relatively brief history of the study of organizations and management, that there is considerable argument and contradiction among all of the perspectives discussed in this book. At the moment there is no formula or 'one best way' of managing or organizing that will guarantee success. Real success in managing organizations comes from this recognition and through being equipped to understand the strengths, weaknesses and limitations of the many perspectives offered. The understanding and flexible adaptation of the perspectives offered represent the only path for those aspiring to run organizations effectively. The complexity of organizational behaviour demands nothing less.

Objectives of the book

It is human beings who both design organizations and work within them. Human beings, therefore, determine both what is done and how it is to be achieved. Against this background the purpose of this book is to develop an understanding of the most important aspects of this aspect of human experience, including:

✦ What defines organizations and management.

✦ The nature and impact of individuality on work activities.

✦ The ways in which groups form and interact as they carry out much of the work undertaken within organizations.

✦ The influence of technology on work organization.

✦ The nature of processes such as motivation and decision making on the functioning of organizations.

✦ The design and structural determinants of organizational form.

✦ Management issues such as leadership, ethics and change.

✦ The power, political and control dimensions of organizational activity.

✦ The nature and impact of stress on the people employed by organizations that can result from working in them.

Specifically in relation to this purpose, the text sets out to achieve a number of objectives:

✦ Provide an introduction to organizational behaviour. While offering an up-to-date and reflective perspective, the text does not seek to be of interest only to expert readers seeking to advance their already considerable knowledge. It is intended to be of interest to those readers who need to develop the breadth and depth of their understanding of what makes an organization function. Such readers may be practising managers, experienced in the ways of organizational life, who are seeking to develop a basis for reflecting upon that experience and developing cognitive frameworks for understanding and explaining human aspects of their experience. This may be through self-study or as part of a formal degree or development programme. Such readers will find that the clearly presented theoretical material, supported by the applied illustrations, will meet their development needs. Other readers may lack direct organizational experience and be undergoing some form of structured development (such as undergraduate students, professional qualification students, or master students with no background in this area) that requires the inclusion of organizational, managerial and behavioural dimensions. These readers will gain both an understanding of the theoretical material on which organizational behaviour is grounded and also an insight into the realities and complexities of organizational life which the academic material seeks to inform.

♦ Include a critical perspective. In addressing the first objective the text goes beyond the purely descriptive and introduces a critical perspective to the material, by seeking to recognize the embedded nature of much theory and the underlying power dimensions to management activity. However, it does not seek to become a critical text in its own right. The critical perspective suggests that knowledge as well as organizations are grounded in the social context that created them and any real understanding must take that into account. This text seeks to achieve that perspective while not losing sight of the other objectives.

♦ Demonstrate an applied relevance. To be of any value the study of organizational behaviour needs to retain a relevance to actual organizations and the experience of those within them. This is achieved in a number of ways, including the incorporation of applied research studies, the Management in Action panels, and through some of the Research activities at the end of each chapter.

♦ Provide a basis for further study. The Reference sources used as well as the Further and Key reading are intended to provide a basis for readers to take their interest in particular topics further. This is an objective that can also be achieved through the use of the links indicated in the web pages associated with this book.

♦ Provide a student-centred perspective. There are a number of student-centred devices that have been used in the text as an aid to encouraging learning. These include the Chapter summary and Learning objectives at the start of each chapter, frequent headings and key point markers in the text, the Management in Action panels and the Discussion questions and Research activities at the end of each chapter.

♦ Encourage students to develop research as well as practical and theoretical understandings. The use of Research activities as well as Discussion questions will encourage students to become actively involved in their own learning in relation to the subject matter. It will also help them to understand the difficulties of carrying out field and desk research as a necessary part of creating understanding in the management an organizational field.

♦ Interactive approach to learning. The use of group activities as part of the Research activities for each chapter allows students to develop collaborative skills in seeking to explore relevant features of the subject matter.

♦ Learning support. The web site at www.thomsonlearning.co.uk provides students and lecturers with extensive support material directly linked to topics in the text.

The audience

There are a number of groups for whom this book would be appropriate. Human behaviour occurs in every organization, irrespective of size, location and industry. There are many courses and degree programmes that contain aspects of organization, management or perspectives on the human issues associated with running public or private sector businesses. These can include undergraduate programmes in management and business studies or those degrees with management as a minor component, as well as postgraduate degrees and other post-experience qualifications such as the Diploma of Management Studies, MA and MBA programmes. There are also the many professional qualification schemes in management, accountancy, engineering and related disciplines that include behavioural, managerial and organizational modules, for whom this book would be an important contribution. Such courses are invariably offered on both a full- and part-time basis and many self-study or distance learning approaches to these routes to personal development also exist. This book together with the associated support material is designed (based on the author's considerable experience in teaching the subject to all of these groups and using each of the forms of delivery indicated) to be a valuable asset in the delivery of the subject.

To cater for this breadth of audience, the material is presented as both academic and practical in nature. It is also presented in a way which encourages students to interact with the material and to seek out applications from live organizations. For students studying alone, perhaps on a distance learning programme, the web site should be particularly useful in helping to offset the feeling of isolation that often accompanies such study patterns.

The structure of the book

Each chapter is essentially self-contained, unless it specifically forms part of a sequence. However, it is inevitable that there is considerable interaction between the material. For example, the groups that form part of every organization are made up of individuals, they are also part of the organizational hierarchy and there will be some degree of organizational politics displayed within them. However, for ease of research, study and book organization these issued have to be compartmentalized. Students should recognize that much of the richness and complexity of organizational behaviour arises from the multiple elements active in any particular situation. This should be come evident as students work through the book and it is reinforced through the Management in Action panels throughout the text and the Research activities at the end of each chapter.

For a proper understanding of this subject it is necessary to reflect on the history of the material included as it did not arise within a vacuum. Organizations have existed for many thousands of years. Many of the ideas currently used within modern organizations can trace their origins back many years, centuries in some cases. I have included a flavour of this evolutionary perspective, without allowing the text to become a historical review. Suggested further reading sources provide additional material in this respect.

Chapters 1 and 2 serve as an introduction to the study of management and organizations along with an overview of the evolutionary development of management across history. This material places the subsequent chapters into a framework based on the:

- Individuals within organizations.
- Groups within organizations.
- Work design and technology.
- Processes within organizations.
- Structure and design of organizations.
- Management of organizations.
- Dynamics of the work environment.

Key features

- Chapter summary. Each chapter begins with a brief outline of the content which provides a clear indication of the range of material covered. It effectively sets the scene for study of the chapter content.
- Learning objectives. The learning objectives for each chapter provide a clear statement of what students should expect to master by the end of their work on that material. Progress in achieving the objectives can be assessed by individuals through the work that they undertake on the discussion and research questions, as well as the stop and consider topics associated with many of the Management in Action panels.
- Key readings. At the end of each chapter a range of key readings is identified. These are all taken from the same book and are important, being extracts from the original work of leading thinkers.
- Further reading. These suggestions provide students with additional sources of material on aspects of the material discussed within each chapter.
- Discussion questions. A range of questions that could be used as the basis of discussion, essays or exams is provided to allow students to test and further their understanding of the material covered.
- Research activities. These are designed to further students' understanding of the material through library, Internet and field research activities. These should be used to further a student's understanding of, and practice in, research in this field.
- Management in Action panels. These are included to provide an indication of aspects of organizational behaviour as experienced by managers in a real organizational context. They also provide the basis for Stop and Consider activities as a means of reflecting upon the material in some depth and also identifying alternative perspectives and links with other concepts.
- Web site. This represents an innovative feature for this book and provides extensive online support for lecturers and students. Figure 0.1 lists the resources in full.

How to use the book

Everyone has their own preferred way of studying. Most courses differ in the way in which they approach a topic and the emphasis given to particular perspectives. It is, therefore, not practical to offer precise advice on how to use this book and the available support material for every situation. Chapter 9 specifically addresses the subject of training and development and introduces a number of perspectives on different learning strategies. This material could usefully be reviewed as an aid to making the most of the material available to you.

There are, however, a number of general pointers that may be of use in seeking to gain maximum advantage from this book and your study of organizational behaviour. They include:

✦ Recognizing that this book is not attempting to provide you with a formula through which to manage other people or guarantee organizational success. That 'holy grail' does not exist; individuals and situations are too complex and dynamic for that type of simplistic approach to be credible.

✦ Evolution of knowledge is occurring all the time. New ideas, perspectives and interpretations are emerging almost every day. The study of organizational behaviour is not a fixed event. It is for that reason that monitoring appropriate sections of the business press and the management and academic journals and magazines pays dividends. This is also the value of the web site for this book in that it is updated regularly indicating current articles and items of interest from both the academic and practitioner worlds.

✦ Resources exist to be used in support of your study. This book is not a novel, but it does represent a major resource for your journey of discovery in organizational behaviour. The learning objectives and chapter summaries are intended to guide you in your travels. Also the Discussion questions, Research activities, Key and Further reading act as pointers, maps and travel guides to help you gain the maximum benefit from the minimum effort enroute. They are there as a help, not a hindrance or a chore; do use them. During your course you will be examined or tested in some way. The resources provided through this book are attempting to prepare you for that process as well as ensure a fuller understanding of the subject. For example, the Discussion questions at the end of each chapter are designed to assist in your development of a breadth and depth of understanding of the theoretical material as well as the practical implications of it. Through discussion with other people of your collective views about these questions you will become better able to develop your understanding of them along with the ability to address any assignment or examination questions.

✦ Personal experience. Every student reader has had direct experience of organizational behaviour in some capacity. It may have been extensive through working in organizations as a paid employee or even a manager. It could have been a vacation job as a student. However, it may also have been through school, or membership of a sports or youth club. The important thing to keep in mind throughout your study of this book is that you will have seen many of the concepts in practice, whether you realize it or not. Consider for a moment a primary school and the way the total activity is organized (structure), the way teachers lead the learning process (leadership, management and control) and the interpersonal behaviour of the children (individuals, groups, power etc.). Reflect on your experience and its ability to enhance and illustrate this subject.

✦ Networking is an important aspect of any manager's experience. The same is true in your study of organizational behaviour. Every student will know many people who have been or are currently involved in organizations. Parents, grandparents, family members, friends, other students and lecturers are all likely to have had direct experience of a wide range of organizations across a considerable period of time. These are all valuable sources of material, examples and illustrations of organizational behaviour in practice. The Research activities associated with each chapter should encourage you to begin to make effective use of these resources in support of your learning experience.

✦ When studying each chapter consider the integrated nature of human behaviour. It is not possible to consider each chapter as an isolated 'chunk' of material than can be ignored once it is finished. Look for and consider the links between ideas and concepts as you work through the book.

✦ Confidence in managing comes through experience and learning. Use the opportunities provided by the book and its treatment of organizational behaviour to experiment with ideas, test them out and to interact with other people to enable you to develop your own perspectives on human behaviour in a work context.

Support material

Accompanying text of key readings

Clark, H, Chandler, J and Barry, J (1994) *Organizations and Identities: Text and Readings in Organizational Behaviour*, Thomson Learning, London.

The text of the Key reading referred to at the end of each chapter is intended to support this book through the provision of a wide range of original sources. It is not often that students have the opportunity of reading such a diverse range of original material in one book. To search out appropriate material from each of the authors identified would take an inordinate amount of time and effort.

Organizational Behaviour *web site*

The supporting web site for the new edition of *Organizational Behaviour* is at www.thomsonlearning.co.uk. This comprehensive resource provides open access learning materials to students of *Organizational Behaviour*, including chapter overviews, links to the home pages of companies discussed in the cases, extra essay-style questions and a full list of organizational behaviour definitions from the Thomson Learning Pocket IEBM (*International Encyclopedia of Business and Management*). Students and lecturers can contact John Martin through the site to post their comments and queries about the book and the web site.

The lecturers' area of the site is password protected and the password is available to lecturers who recommend the book on their courses. Please register through the web site for your password. There will be no printed manual provided with this edition but all resources which previously appeared in the printed manual will now be provided online. The extensive lecturer resources include teaching notes, PowerPoint™ slides, extra case materials, and suggested course outlines.

The web site is a totally optional resource. Use of the book is not dependent in any way on the web site. Full value can still be obtained through the many excellent features included in the book. However, the Internet provides an opportunity to enhance the level of support and understanding in ways not available though the medium of the printed

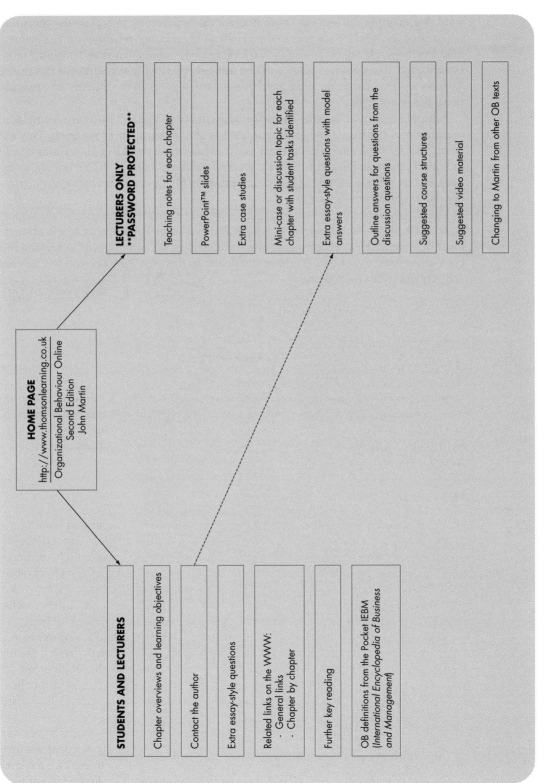

FIGURE 0.1 *The Organizational Behaviour* web site.

word. For example, the web site offers students the opportunity to explore the enormous potential of the World Wide Web in their study of organizational behaviour. The primary links have been selected because of their relevance to the subject matter and potential interest to readers. The web site resource will be regularly updated so that it retains its value to students and lecturers as the most appropriate starting point on the Internet for organizational behaviour topics.

A further benefit of the web site is the opportunity to update illustrative examples of organizational behaviour and learning materials after publication of the book. This will ensure that the book retains its currency and freshness throughout its life – a major benefit to both lecturers and students. Users can send comments back to the author about the book and the web site, as well as interesting examples of organizational behaviour in practice that they have encountered.

The *Organizational Behaviour* web site is a valuable resource that highlights the importance of *Organizational Behaviour* as a book and as a subject at the heart of the management of organizational endeavour. It also demonstrates the commitment to keeping this book at the forefront of both teaching and debate in this area. Why not visit the web site and experience this for yourself?

Acknowledgements

Any organizational activity inevitably reflects the efforts of a great many people. Writing a book is no exception. It is not possible specifically to mention everyone who played a part in helping to create this text.

The following people were particularly generous with their time and talent in reviewing material and offering advice on the content of the first edition of this book.

+ Professor Michael Brimm, Professor of Organizational Behaviour at INSEAD (Fontainebleau, France).
+ Professor Gordon C Anderson, Principal of Caledonian College of Engineering, Sultanate of Oman and Visiting Professor of Business, The Philips College, Nicosia, Cyprus.
+ Professor Derek Torrington, Emeritus Professor of Human Resource Management, UMIST.
+ Professor Eugene McKenna, Professor Emeritus, University of East London, Chartered Psychologist and Director of Human Factors International Ltd.
+ Professor Dave Tromp, Professor of Industrial Psychology and Chairperson of Industrial Psychology, University of Stellenbosch, South Africa.
+ Dr Jim Barry, Reader in Organization Studies, University of East London.

The contribution of the above people played a significant part in making the first edition of the book the success it was which helped to create the opportunity to develop this second edition. In addition, may I offer my deepest thanks to the panel of anonymous reviewers who offered their time and talent in reviewing the first edition along with the proposals for the second edition. Their comments were both helpful and appropriate. The end result can only be described as a considerable improvement as a consequence of their efforts. I can but hope that they feel justified in devoting the time that they did when they inspect the finished second edition. The responsibility for any mistakes, errors and omissions remain, however, firmly my own.

At Thomson Learning a number of people have been supportive of the whole project and of invaluable help in attempting to steer the work in appropriate directions. Worthy of particular note in this context are Mark Wellings, who first persuaded me of the challenge in writing the first edition of the book; Maggie Smith and Jenny Clapham subsequently attempted to cajole and encourage me into producing the second edition manuscript in a reasonable time and of a high quality; Fiona Freel and Paula McMahon ensured that the results of the production process were excellent and timely; Anna Faherty took over editing responsibilities in the latter stages of the process, never an easy objective to achieve, but she did it with style. Without them this edition would never have happened.

There are many academics, managers, bosses, subordinates and colleagues with whom I have had the pleasure and sometimes pain of working over the course of my career. Individually and collectively these have all played a considerable role in shaping my fascination with, and views on, organizational life and behaviour. The benefits and effects of their impact on me are in no small way reflected in the views and perspectives offered in this book.

Finally, and by no means least, I would like to place on record the support and interest of my wife, family and friends, who tolerated the time spent on the project as well as continually showing interest in how it was progressing.

I would also like to place on record my appreciation to the many copyright holders who have given permission to use material for which they hold the rights. Every effort has been made to identify and contact all copyright holders, but if any have been inadvertently omitted the publisher will be pleased to make the necessary arrangement at the earliest opportunity.

PART I

Management and organizational behaviour

CHAPTER 1

Management and organizations

CHAPTER SUMMARY

This chapter introduces the concepts of organization and management. This is followed by consideration of research in the social sciences, how it differs from the natural sciences and the concept of an organization as a social construction. Management is then introduced as a specific category of activity within an organization. Organizational behaviour and other perspectives are also introduced. The chapter concludes with a consideration of the applied perspectives on these topics.

LEARNING OBJECTIVES

After studying this chapter and working through the associated Management in Action panels, Discussion questions and Research activities, you should be able to:

✦ Understand the evolution of organizations as social structures intended to contribute to human society.

✦ Describe the distinction between research in the natural and in the social sciences.

✦ Explain the particular difficulties involved in studying and developing theories in the area of management.

✦ Outline some of the ways in which organizations change and evolve over time.

✦ Assess the relative merits of the differing theoretical traditions in the study of organizations.

✦ Appreciate that the concept 'organization' incorporates many different forms.

✦ Discuss the nature of management and its relationship to the organization within which it is practised.

✦ Detail how the study of organizational behaviour can contribute to an understanding of management.

Introduction

Organizations are an inescapable feature of modern social experience for all human beings. From the remotest village high in the Himalayan foothills to life in a large metropolis, organizations impact on all aspects of the human experience. The work activities and responsibilities referred to as management are also inextricably linked to the functioning of organizations and form a parallel theme of study in this introduction.

A first look at organizations

When asked to describe what is meant by the term *organization*, most people indicate the many public and private sector bodies that provide the goods and services necessary for life and employment. However, there are many bodies that bear a strong similarity to commercial organizations but which are undeniably different in function or purpose. For example, is the Church of England (or any other religious grouping) an organization in the same way that IBM is? Is a trade union, a students' union or a sports club an organization in the same sense of the term as a university or hospital?

No two commercial organizations are the same. Figure 1.1 identifies some of the major variables that influence the physical manifestation (profile) of individual organizations.

A number of the variables identified in Figure 1.1 are relatively obvious, others less so. Although there is a degree of interrelationship between the variables, there is scope for management choice. For example, it is not unusual for some owners to restrict the growth of their organization deliberately in order to retain direct involvement in running the business. Taking each variable in turn:

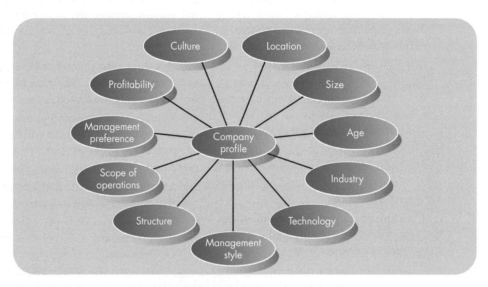

FIGURE 1.1 Determinants of organizational form.

✦ Size. The physical size of an organization is a major determinant of how it appears. The small corner shop selling a range of grocery items and sweets, employing two people would be vastly different in appearance from a large national supermarket chain with many thousands of employees. The size of an organization could also influence many of the other variables, such as the level of technology that it is able to support.

✦ Age. There is an apparent stability and security that comes from the appearance of age – financial institutions deliberately create this image. The age of an organization could also be expected to impact on many structural and functional issues.

✦ Industry. The nature of the product or service from which the organization derives its income is another primary determinant of its form. A company engaged in quarrying minerals would be expected to differ in many ways from a bank of roughly similar size and age.

✦ Technology. The type and level of technology used by an organization is another variable that is both influenced by and influences the organization. The use of robotic assembly processes has reduced human involvement in the assembly of products such as motor vehicle and other consumer goods, thereby driving up productivity as well as influencing the profile of the organization.

✦ Management style. The dominant style of management within the organization also influences the appearance that it presents to the outside world. The use of hierarchical control through layers of supervision and management produces a tall, thin organizational form. This can be contrasted with the approach to management that relies on self-managed work teams and which would provide a flatter organization as a consequence.

✦ Structure. The functional approach to organizational activity in which departments are organized around job expertise such as personnel, finance and production provides a very different appearance to one which is based upon product groupings with mixed operational teams.

✦ Scope of operations. A wholesaler of children's toys is acting as a distributor within the supply chain. Such an organization would appear very different to another organization in the children's toy industry which made some toys and retailed a much wider range directly to customers.

✦ Management preference. The application of the same set of principles across every organization is doomed to failure because of the *situational variety* experienced in practice. Managers exercise a degree of preference and choice in designing their organizations.

✦ Profitability. The larger the monetary resource available the greater the degree of elaboration possible. The scale of finance available provides an opportunity to influence the form that individual organizations take.

✦ Culture. Issues such as the degree of individuality and formality influence work preferences and the way in which work is undertaken within an organization. There is an inevitable tension within large international organizations between the need for a global corporate identity and the dominant culture within local operating environments.

✦ Location. There are cultural, legislative and dominant business practice issues that vary across the world and which shape organizations within each national border. Aspects such as communications and transportation also influence activities signifi-

MANAGEMENT IN ACTION 1.1

Implementing Japanese management methods

Yuasa Battery was set up in the early 1980s in Wales to make sealed lead-acid batteries. It fell to the Japanese Managing Director, Kazuo Murata, to build and establish the factory as a viable operation. Two important lessons were learned from the experience of opening Yuasa Battery:

✦ Do the simple things right.

✦ Create conditions for improvement.

In seeking to establish the company a number of problems endemic to western companies were identified. They included:

✦ Worker attitude to the wage – work bargain.

✦ Lack of the strict application of company rules.

✦ Workers not involved in determining improvements in productivity and working practice.

✦ Individualism emphasized within western culture.

The Managing Director of Yuasa Battery, Kazuo Murata, began the process of unlearning the 'bad habits' and creating the improvement necessary. This included:

✦ Fairness. The strict application of rules, procedures and standards in a fair manner resulted from this strategy. Rules are intended to benefit the organization and they should be applied consistently and fairly if they are to have any value.

✦ Discipline. Consider a sports team or a military force. Each must exercise a disciplined approach to its task if it is to be successful. This implies a controlled approach to work and getting the basics right.

✦ Improvement. The two earlier points are the basics of good organization, but to become a world-class organization continuous improvement is also necessary. Everyone must feel challenged by this necessity every working day. This implies critical self-examination and the development of better ways of working.

Based on: Harrison, A (1994) Implementing Japanese management methods, *Professional Manager*, January, pp 10–12.

cantly. For example, mining operations are frequently carried out far from the location of the users of the extracted minerals and the company head office.

Management in Action 1.1 demonstrates some of these issues as identified by a Japanese company setting up business in the UK.

Stop | Consider   *To what extent does the approach adopted by Kazuo Murata at Yuasa Battery provide an effective means of managing an organizational change process?*

Variables such as the type of people employed, job design, control processes and patterns of employment also influence how any specific organization will manifest itself.

So far the discussion has not provided a clear differentiation of the parameters of an organization. How can a commercial organization be differentiated from a social club? The ultimate answer is that there is no clear distinguishing criterion as all forms of social grouping contain elements of similarity in terms of purpose, structure, people and systems.

A number of writers offer definitions of an organization that offer broad similarities, including:

A. 'Organizations are collections of people working together in a coordinated and structured fashion to achieve one or more goals' Barney and Griffin (1992, p 5).

B. 'Organizations are social arrangements for the controlled performance of collective goals' Huczynski and Buchanan (1991, p 7).

C. Organizations are 'consciously created arrangements to achieve goals by collective means' Thompson and McHugh (1995, p 3).

Each of these definitions is able to differentiate the more obvious non-organizational forms such as friendship groups, but what of other organizations such as youth clubs? A club with specific goals for the social development of members could easily fall within these definitions and yet would be of little interest to management and organizational researchers. Yet to incorporate terms such as *profit*, *budget* or *commercial* into the definition would cut out many non-profit organizations that do form a legitimate focus of study. The short answer is that there is no single definition that tightly draws a boundary around the notion of an organization. Different research activity is addressed at aspects associated with slightly different categories of the concept. This is just one level of complexity in attempting to understand organizations, the managers who run them and the employees who work.

A first look at management

Managers are, by definition, the individuals that organize and control the organizations that employ them. In a small company they may actually own the organization itself, but usually they run an organization on behalf of the people to whom the organization legally belongs. It is the task of the management of the organization to ensure that the objectives of the beneficial owners are achieved. They are required to *operationalize* the objectives of the beneficial owners. It is from that perspective that their decision-making function and power originates.

However, even in that simple paragraph there are a number of assumptions that when surfaced create complexity in the research into management. For example, it assumes that it is the *beneficial* owners of an organization who should have the primary say (or influence) on issues such as how the company is run. That is a viewpoint that can be questioned from many different perspectives. A Marxist point of view would fundamentally bring into doubt the idea of capitalism, suggesting in turn that common ownership requires that everything is owned by the state in trust for the people. Consequently, a different approach to the determination of primacy in decision perspective must apply.

Equally it could be argued, from a capitalist perspective, that in seeking to maximize returns to shareholders in the long run it is necessary to gain the highest levels of commitment from all employees. In so doing, if their interests are not put first, then the best returns will not be forthcoming. It is this latter approach that has led to the *stakeholder* approach, defined as any group or individual who can affect, or is affected by, the performance of the organization (Freeman, 1984). The best levels of success can only be achieved by balancing the needs and contributions from each of the possible stakeholder groups, of which the shareholders represent only one category. For example, Henry Ford was famous for developing the assembly line approach to manufacturing motor cars in the early 1900s. His efforts achieved considerable success in developing production technology, cheap mass appeal products and profits for the company. However, in 1913 labour turnover was 380%. In order to keep 15,000 positions filled management had to recruit 50,000 people each year. In order to achieve a net increase of 100 people in the factory they had to recruit 963 people, because so many would not be able to stand the pace and conditions of work on the assembly lines (Losey, 1999). Management did not integrate the worker group as a significant stakeholder in their planning of the process.

It is only over recent years with the delayering of organizations that managers have seen their own position come under threat. Prior to that form of cost cutting, managers tended to have a much higher degree of job security than other categories of employee. They also enjoyed higher pay, better benefits and career opportunities. As a consequence, their primary loyalty was to the absentee owner, from whom these benefits accrued. However, in the search for ever higher levels of productivity and cost efficiency senior managers (and owners) found that, having reduced the numbers of employees significantly, the only areas left within which to seek dramatic cuts in cost were the previously protected management areas. This trend was also fuelled by the desire of organizations to 'get closer to the customer' by seeking to become more horizontal and less vertical. This *delayering* process created a situation in which managers began to experience high levels of stress and job insecurity, the result being the emergence of feelings of alienation and an increase in trade union membership among managerial employees. In short, they were recognizing the need to find ways of looking after their own interests in response to the *employer* not being willing to do so.

Management is a strange type of work in that it is an activity in which an employee, no different in principle from any other employee, is expected to act in *loco parentis* for the owner. As such it is expected by all concerned that the manager should act in ways that may be to their own disadvantage in pursuit of the objectives of the owner. The delayering of organizations is a clear result of this requirement of managerial activity. It is because managers have traditionally become so personally and closely aligned with the objectives of the *beneficial owner* that the implications of delayering and related forms of cost saving have been such a traumatic shock. Managers are paid by the owners of the organization to act on their behalf; they forget that contractual relationship at their peril!

There is an inherent conflict of interest in terms of the expectations and requirements of the owners and those of the manager as an employee. It is for that reason that it is difficult in practice for the stakeholder concept in running an organization to be fully implemented. While the rhetoric may be evident in the sense of talking partnership etc. the dominance of hierarchical thinking and shareholder dominance is deeply engrained.

In addition, it is diffcult to be precise about management in theoretical or practical terms because it does not represent a homogeneous activity. There are two major differences identifiable in management activity:

✦ Level. There are many different ways to describe the level of management activity, the most common being a reflection of seniority. For example, director, senior manager, junior manager and supervisor. While that approach provides a useful basic reference criterion, it also contains considerable ambiguity. For example, simply knowing that an individual is a chief executive provides no clue to the level of responsibility involved. The company might employ ten people in one location or many thousands in locations throughout the world.

✦ Job. The second major difference in managerial activity refers to the work of the individual. A manager might be responsible for the work of a personnel department, an engineering department, an accounting department, or a production department. They might even be a general manager, responsible for the work of several functions and having specialist managers reporting to them. In this last case the manager will be responsible for activities in which they have no direct experience, which in itself creates complexity.

Figure 1.2 reflects these two variables and their impact on jobs.

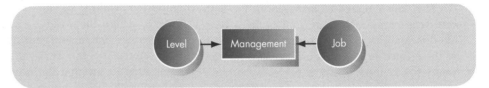

FIGURE 1.2   Major influences on management activities.

In addition to the two determinants of management activity just described, many of the variables described in Figure 1.1 also impact on management work. For example, the industry is a significant factor in this respect. Consider the very obvious differences between the job of a branch manager of a major bank and the job of a departmental manager in a manufacturing company. Both are responsible for the operational aspects within a defined part of the business, yet in other respects the jobs are very different as a result of the manufacturing/service nature of the organization.

Management preference is another major influence on the actual job of a manager. In many management jobs there is a high level of opportunity to shape the actual work undertaken by the individual holding that position. A personnel manager has some degree of freedom to determine what tasks to delegate and which to retain for their personal attention. They also have considerable latitude to practise a style of management that they as individuals feel comfortable with, which can influence their own job activities and those of their subordinates.

The conclusion from this first look at management is that the practice of management reflects a complex process involving level, job, personal and professional variables. This process is carried out in a complex organizational environment. The result being that it is not possible to talk of either organization or management as single entities. Management in Action 1.2 reflects one person's view of the skills needed by future generations of managers.

Stop | Consider   *Do you agree with Karen Clarke's analysis that the roles she describes reflect different skills from those required in the past?*
  Or do they represent the same skills but expressed in a different social context?

Natural and social science research

The discussion so far has provided an introduction to the concepts of *organization* and *management* that suggests a high degree of complexity as well as high levels of interdependence. This provides a fertile basis for research activity as well as the opportunity for the parallel existence of competing explanations.

MANAGEMENT IN ACTION 1.2

Survival skills for a new breed

The manager of the future will need different skills, it was argued by Karen Clarke in the essay that won first prize in an Institute of Management competition.

The skills required of managers in the past were decision making, expert (in their field), boss and director. This is progressively being replaced by three roles as organizations prepare for the twenty-first century. They are:

✦ Leader. The person setting the future direction for the business and concentrating on the wider picture (not day-to-day activity). The role of the leader becomes one of ensuring that progress towards the goal is maintained.

✦ Coach. The job of a coach is one of encouragement and of ensuring that everyone is pulling in the same direction. It is a process which allows empowerment and change to flourish.

✦ Facilitator. This is the process of identifying continuous improvement and encouraging a self-critical evaluation of work activity and performance.

It is argued by Clarke that it is now essential to achieve strategic positioning and operation of the business through the effort and ability of the staff employed within it. In order to achieve the world-class service and manufacturing levels increasingly necessary for survival, staff must be committed to meeting the needs of customers. Consequently, delegation and empowerment are key factors in employee work activities of the future.

The desirability for managers to be the decision makers is increasingly being questioned. In the face of global competition there is simply not the time for employees to pass decisions back in the system for someone else considered more appropriate to determine. It is employees who are closest to the needs of customers and they must be allowed to operate as the customers' representative within the organization.

Adapted from: Clarke, K (1993) Survival skills for a new breed, *Management Today*, December, p 5.

In attempting to understand organizations as entities in their own right and management as one form of human activity within that context, it is necessary to be able to offer explanations that stand up to critical evaluation and replication. The natural sciences have developed mechanisms over many centuries that are able to meet that need. However, the primary difficulty for organization or management research is that it is not possible to isolate the key variables and replicate organizational functioning in the laboratory. Study of these phenomena therefore rests firmly within the social science arena.

It is frequently suggested that the study of organizations and management provides many competing theories but is unable to offer clear guidance to practitioners. For example, there are many theories of motivation, but on what basis should a manager choose between them? It is only within the last 100 years that writings in management encompassed more than a reflection of the experience of practitioners offering their own recipes for success or an intuitive analysis of organizational functioning. It is hardly surprising that the study of management and organizations is still comparatively unsophisticated and crude in its ability to offer comprehensive explanations.

The study of people and organizations is different from the study of the physical properties of metal or chemical reactions. However, that does not mean that it is impossible to apply the principles of scientific enquiry into social areas. For example, there are many psychologists working at the micro level of human behaviour that provide *robust scientific explanations* for aspects of it. Theories developed in this way are frequently based on laboratory studies in which much care is taken over the control of variables and other conditions. The difficulty comes from the need to extrapolate adequately from laboratory conditions to the *complexity* and *richness* of human experience within an organizational concept.

Consider as an example a laboratory experiment in which decision-making strategies among managers were to be investigated. Variables such as the decision-making topic, characteristics of the individuals concerned, restrictions on extraneous factors and time limits could all be controlled and accounted for. Equally, the measurement of the process could take a number of forms. For example, the actual decision made, time taken to reach a decision, individual interaction patterns and information used in the process. However, it is difficult to be certain what such an experiment indicates about decision making by *real* managers in *real* organizations in *real* time and, perhaps more important, dealing with *real* problems with *real* outcomes. There are so many additional variables that can influence decision making in practice. Power, control, politics and the dynamics of organizational experience are not accounted for in a laboratory experiment.

The experience of the world around each and every human being is dependent upon their ability to undertake three activities:

+ Detect. It is first necessary to be aware of the objects and situations outside the individual that provide the form for *reality*. This requires the input of information to the individual through the senses of hearing, sight and so on. However, the human senses are not aware of all possible stimuli available. For example, we cannot detect radio waves or see very well in the dark.

+ Interpret. Having detected the existence of *things* around the individual it is then necessary to impose meaning onto them. As a simple example consider the act of seeing a motor car. The reality of its being a motor car comes from the ability of the individual to add meaning and significance to the visual image from past experience and learning. The problems and consequences of this inability to apply an existing *frame of reference* to reality has been the basis of many science fiction books and films.

+ Predict. Having perceived a motor car then the implications arising from it can be predicted. For example, if the individual is attempting to cross a busy street then it should be avoided, as it could do great harm to them. So it is necessary (or at least sensible) to wait for a more appropriate time to cross. Without prior knowledge and experience of the object it would not be possible accurately to predict possible outcomes or develop an appropriate behavioural response.

From that basis it is clear that reality is not something that exists in a purely physical form outside the individual, but as a social construction experienced within the mind of each individual. The physical objects may be identical for all individuals in that situation, but their experience of them may be very different. Figure 1.3 illustrates this point by showing that two people looking at the same solid object will experience very different representations of it. Each person has only partial insight into the whole.

One of the most frequently referenced works in this field is that of Berger and Luckmann (1967) in which they explore the sociology of knowledge. Much of the possible

variation in interpretation of stimuli is eliminated by the education and socialization processes to which all human beings are subjected as they develop within a particular society.
In effect, we are *conditioned* how to see and *interpret* the world around us. This forms the
justification for induction courses which provide new employees with the *organization's*
preferred ways of *seeing* the world.

When social scientists attempt to theorize about the world inhabited by human beings
they are, to a very real extent, researching themselves as well. When attempting to understand an interpretation of the social world offered by a researcher it is important to consider their perspective in relation to it. But this is able to offer only a partial insight of the
perspective of the individual in question. Figure 1.4 attempts to illustrate this phenomenon
by showing that it is never possible fully to understand another's perspective because in
observing it only a partial view of the target person's perspective is provided.

The scientific process that forms the basis of the natural sciences is described in Figure
1.5, adapted from Wallace (1971). It demonstrates a circular process that allows for
hypotheses to be developed from existing theory (or understanding of the world). In turn,
these must be operationalized and subjected to some form of testing in order to verify or
refute the theory being examined. A cyclical process of identifying and testing hypotheses
leads to more generalizations about the world, which leads to the development of more
theory.

The process reflected in Figure 1.5 is frequently described as the positivist approach to
research or, more accurately, logical positivism (Remenyi *et al.*, 1998, p 32). In this
paradigm the researcher would hold the view that the observable social reality existed and

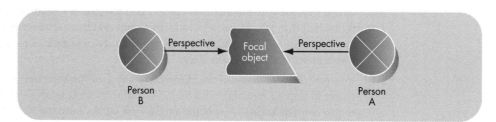

FIGURE 1.3   Different perceptions of the same focal object.

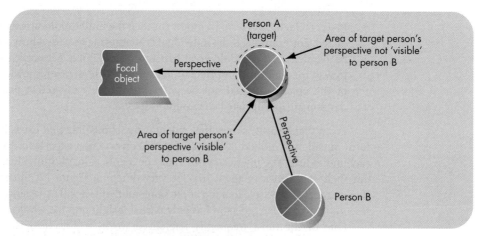

FIGURE 1.4   Understanding the perspectives of others.

that the end product would be the creation of law-like generalizations, applicable in every organizational and human context. This is the perspective that suggests that the real world exists outside each human being and the laws that govern the social world are simply out there, waiting to be discovered. The researcher is, therefore, 'an objective analyst and observer of a tangible social reality' (p 33).

This can be contrasted to the paradigm that holds that the real world exists only in the mind of the individuals perceiving it. This is the phenomenology perspective and holds that the social world is different for each person experiencing it, as they will interpret their perceptions of it in line with their internal schemas, based on past experience, socialization, education etc. In that sense there will be considerable degrees of overlap in understanding between some individuals in the same situation, but there will be considerable degrees of difference. For example, the workers' view of a proposed 5% pay rise would probably not be the same as their bosses'. 'To the phenomenologist the researcher is not independent of what is being researched but is an intrinsic part of it' (Remenyi *et al.*, p 34). The world is socially constructed and meaning can only be identified in terms of the understandings of the actors in that situation. Experiments and the attempt to create law-like generalizations simply will not work in this paradigm.

The debate between these two paradigms can get acrimonious at times as the protagonists view research (and the world in which it functions) from diametrically opposing positions. The debate is not just academic in essence, although that is the arena in which it is carried out. For if either side of the debate is ultimately correct, in the sense that the other is wrong, then a significant aspect of research becomes inappropriate and of no value in helping to explain or run organizations. The debate also impacts on the choice of research approach that could and should be adopted. For example, the positivist tends to favour the use of scientific method based on hypothesis and a deductive research process (Gill and Johnson, 1997, p 28). The deductive approach is based on the development of conceptual and theoretical structures before testing begins as a process of empirical observation through questionnaires, surveys and experiments etc. By comparison, induction moves from observation to the provision of explanation. It reflects the ethnographic, case study and participative enquiry (Reason, 1994) approaches to research methodology.

Another important feature of social science research is the *level* at which it is being carried out. Essentially, the level in this context can be described as a scale running from macro to micro issues. There are five levels as follows:

✦   Individual. This represents the micro level and takes as its focus of attention the

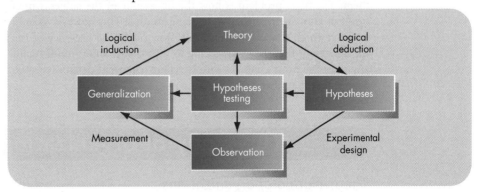

FIGURE 1.5   Scientific research processes (*adapted from*: Wallace, W (1971) *The Logic of Science in Sociology*, Aldine-Atherton, Chicago)

individual within an organizational setting. This field is predominantly based on the work of psychologists. Issues such as perception, attitude formation, individual difference and motivation are common topics under this heading.

✦ Group. Most human behaviour within an organization takes place in a group. It is important therefore to understand how groups form and perform the work expected of them.

✦ Managerial. Managers are individuals and they operate in groups just like other employees. However, there are a number of distinctive features associated with management activities that make it worthy of special categorization. For example, the nature, act and process of managing others are major areas of study.

✦ Organizational. Typically, this would seek to address issues such as job design, structural frameworks and technology.

✦ Societal. Issues such as power, control, politics, conflict and change fall under this umbrella heading. They represent part of the dynamic of the ways in which organizations function as a small-scale version of society. They also reflect the environmental forces that act upon any organization and within which it must function.

In addition to the obvious differences between the natural and social sciences there is the ethical issue of carrying out research on human subjects. Any of the research fields which involve human beings are faced with ethical problems. See for example Finch (1993) in relation to the ethics and politics of undertaking qualitative research on women from the perspective of the feminist tradition. From another field, chemists working in the field of new drug treatments invariably reach a point at which they must be tested on human beings, which inevitably raises ethical issues.

There are research guidelines on how human beings should be studied and by which researchers must abide if they are to attract funding and recognition for their work (see, for example, the Bristish Sociological Association, 1973). The primary difficulty presented by such requirements is that research subjects should knowingly participate and should not be subjected to risk, harm or damage in any way as a result of the process. The challenge for researchers under these conditions is to develop and test theory (or otherwise create understanding) in such a way that it is not affected by the subjects knowing that they are being studied or at the very least that they give their informed consent to the process. Reason (1994, p 1) goes so far as to suggest that research should be carried out *with* people, not *on* them. The basic problem is how the behaviour of the subjects might have changed as a result of knowing that they were being studied. This however is only one of the problems in the research process. For example, how might the presence of the researcher influence the behaviour that they are seeking to record and understand? Again, to what extent does any response from a subject simply reflect what that person feels the researcher wishes to hear, rather than their true opinion?

The study of organizations

The evolution of organizations

Organizations have always existed in one form or another. When human beings began to develop collective activity as a means of improving their chances of survival and the quality of life, the basis of the social organization was formed. This form of activity is still evident today in the many thousands of small family businesses (Bork, 1986). There is evidence of early forms of organization not based upon the family unit being used by the Sumerian people who settled around the River Euphrates approximately 3500 years BCE (McKelvey, 1982). Of course, many organizations during that period continued to be family run. For example, the leadership of the state was based upon dynastic family groupings. By the time of the Roman Empire (around 300 BCE) there was a significant banking and insurance industry in existence to support international trade and commerce.

With the fall of the Roman Empire the large organizations that had existed to facilitate trade disappeared. Smaller, more locally focused organizations emerged. During the Middle Ages the *guild* became a significant force in controlling organizational activity. Craftsmen from a particular trade would band together and regulate entry to that trade, the number of people allowed to practise the craft and other aspects of the work such as pricing. In that sense they were the early forms of the trade unions and trade associations found today.

The emergence of the factory system during the Industrial Revolution again changed the nature of organizational activity. Large-scale factory-based production became the normal working experience for many people. The creation of factory-based systems of production required different types of job to be designed for the workers and the development of new forms of hierarchical management and technical specialism. This approach formed the basis for most modern large-scale organizations.

The *bureaucratic* approach to organizational activity emerged as a result of the need to have large-scale administrative structures to run both commercial and public sector organizations. This was necessary in the days before computer technology. The bureaucratic form of organization began to be expensive to run, slow to respond and unable to meet the needs of customers effectively. Consequently, over recent years many organizations have developed alternative structural forms in an attempt to make themselves cheaper to run and more responsive to ever changing consumer demand. This process is creating circumstances that allow small organizations to flourish, as large companies outsource much of their activity (Wood, 1989). However, some of the challenges facing small organizations in today's competitive world are outlined in Management in Action 1.3.

Stop | Consider

What is it that might make the challenges facing small organizations more difficult and complex than those facing large organizations?

To what extent is it the challenges that differ with the size of organization rather than the capability within the organization to deal with them that creates the difference?

The distinction has already been made between family-owned and commercial organizations. This is not the usual distinction that would be made between organizations. The main distinction that would be made between organizations is that between those in the *private* and *public* sectors. Private sector organizations are those that exist for the commercial benefit of their owners. The owners can be any group of individuals, a family, partnership or shareholders. Public sector organizations are not run directly as commercial organizations but are the public service and local government institutions that are necessary for the effective functioning of society.

MANAGEMENT IN ACTION 1.3

The big challenge facing small firms

About one-third of all jobs are in firms with fewer than 20 employees and one-half are in firms of fewer than 100 employees. However, many small firms have a relatively short lifespan. The Institute of Directors estimates that four out of five go under within six years.

In attempting to survive, small businesses are faced with many of the same requirements placed upon much larger organizations. There are requirements covering tax returns, employment legislation, health and safety requirements and local authority planning requirements to name just a few. These areas of demand on a company can make the difference between life and death for a small company that might not have the technical or financial capability to absorb the costs and time involved.

The abolition of maximum awards for compensation in sex and race discrimination cases could result in costs of £30,000 in some cases, which would be difficult enough for most companies to absorb, but could result in the closure of a small one. The industrial tribunal system has become increasingly legalistic over the past few years and it is not uncommon to find both parties to an unfair dismissal claim being represented by

a solicitor. Under these circumstances it is frequently cheaper for a company to settle out of court for (say) £400 rather than pay the legal costs even if the case is won. This sends a wrong signal to employees and can encourage frivolous claims with little of substance to support them.

Over recent years the development of national training and other initiatives such as National Vocational Qualifications and Investors in People have been introduced as a means of encouraging improvements in business. The schemes themselves frequently contain significant levels of bureaucracy (for a small firm) and they find it difficult to find the financial resources to pay for the introduction. However, evidence suggests that, if undertaken effectively, the changes that come about as a result of changes to communication and training of employees can help to reduce cost and encourage employee commitment to the survival of the business.

Based upon: Thatcher, M (1996) The big challenge facing small firms, *People Management*, July, pp 20–5.

Another way of classifying organizations is in relation to the *profit* or *non-profit* nature of their activities. Over the past few years there has been a significant development in non-profit organizations that either run on commercial lines or interest group organizations that exist on a network basis. An example of the former would be a co-operative, the latter a community group running an allotment and selling the produce to its members at cost price as a means of providing work experience and an interest for local people.

The discussion so far has emphasized a western perspective on organization and the developments in management. In Asia there were parallel developments from quite a different tradition. The Confucian perspective in China emerged around 500 BCE and has produced a different basis for running organizations and society (see, for example, Chen, 1995).

Challenges facing organizations

The world is constantly changing. Some of this change is *evolutionary* and other *revolutionary*. For example, the development of computer technology is subject to continual refinement. This is something that is evolutionary in nature. A change process experienced as a series of small frequent (incremental) amendments to the existing situation. Considering this type of change on a daily basis would offer no noticeable difference, but over the period of years considerable change is achieved.

Revolutionary change, in comparison, is a sudden and dramatic process that fundamentally alters the situation. One example of this is the arrival of the out-of-town shopping and leisure complex. Over a relatively short period of time town centres have become deserted as people find it more convenient to be able to drive to one of these centres. The effect has been to force many town centre businesses either to relocate to a new complex or to close down altogether.

Change has always been a part of life. It has been argued by many writers that the pace of change impacting on organizations is occurring ever more rapidly. So much so that one catch-phrase over recent years has been an exhortation to innovate or die! This carries the clear implication that unless change becomes institutionalized the organization will not stay in business for long.

There is a counter-argument to this view which suggests that by forcing change into an organization, managers are creating the very instability that can inhibit their ability to survive. Inevitably, change within an organization impacts on all the people within it. Managers themselves are no longer exempt from this, as Management in Action 1.4 demonstrates.

Stop	Consider

To what extent do the ideas contained in MiA 1.4 reflect changes in the design of management jobs and to what extent do they reflect an approach to delayering, involving sharing out the remaining work in a more structured way?

There are many ways of categorizing change. Johnson and Scholes (1993) describe a *PEST analysis* process that provides a systematic basis for considering the environmental influences surrounding an organization:

+ Political/legal. Influences impacting on the organization from political and legislative sources.

+ Economic. These reflect the economic conditions and trends that can influence the environment within which the organization must operate.

+ Social/cultural. Changes to the populations (customer and workforce) surrounding the organization can also have a significant impact on its functioning. For example, in Europe there is an expectation among employees that they are entitled to increasing levels of involvement in company decision making.

+ Technological. The changes to the technology available to organizations affects both the products and services available and also the ways in which companies operate.

Figure 1.6 is taken from the Johnson and Scholes (1993) text and identifies some of the more important PEST issues that present challenges to be addressed by the organization.

The factors identified in Figure 1.6 represent a very rational view of change as it influences organizations. In addition to the processes identified there are the political reasons that lead managers to seek change within their organizations. For example, new managers often seek to make change in order to demonstrate a clear break with what existed previously. Equally, managers can attempt to enhance their own career prospects by seeking to be regarded by senior managers as proactive in pursuing change.

MANAGEMENT IN ACTION 1.4

Metamorphosis of the manager

There has been a process of cutting back, down-sizing, delayering and rightsizing going on for many years now. It has had many titles and most have attempted to hide the brutality of the process – that of cutting thousands of jobs. For example, General Electric (GE) shed more than 100,000 jobs during the 1980s. However, a new phenomenon has been detected over recent years, that of title cuts, rather than job cuts.

A job cut simply means that human beings lose their jobs (perhaps in their thousands). This is a process largely separate from that of a consideration of the structure of the organization or the design of jobs within it. Factories can be closed and work reallocated without actually changing the nature of the jobs within the remaining parts of the business.

A title cut implies that the work of the organization is being reviewed and that as a result job design issues will be raised. The work being done within the organization will be reallocated and distributed differently from the past and so it is 'jobs' that become surplus to requirement. What happens to the people in those jobs then becomes the second phase of the process. Title cuts imply a fundamental review of the hierarchy, compartmentalization, structure and design of the way in

which the organization goes about its business. To indicate the significance of these ideas, GE 'promised' a third fewer managers by the year 2000.

Networking is the process being suggested as the management approach of the future in an attempt to eliminate titles and to transform organizations into the rapid-response, customer-sensitive entities necessary for global competition. There are many examples of these networks evolving in practice. For example, Du Pont removed four layers of management and gave employees more power to act faster and more decisively. Business managers were brought in lower down the organization in an attempt to provide hands-on managers with the opportunity to win orders. WT Gore & Associates abolished all job titles and termed everyone an associate, expected to work towards the best interests of the company. With Apple Computers speed of response and development is vital and managers must now seek out opportunities and then find the necessary support for their proposals.

Adapted from: Lester, T (1992) Metamorphosis of the manager, *Management Today*, August, pp 72–5.

1 What environmental factors are affecting the organization?
2 Which of these are the most important at the present time? In the next few years?

Political/legal
Monopolies legislation •
Environmental protection laws •
Taxation policy • Foreign trade regulations
• Employment law • Government stability

Economic
Business cycle • GNP trends • Interest rates •
Money supply • Inflation • Unemployment •
Disposable income • Energy availablity and cost

Socio-cultural
Population demographics • Income distribution • Social mobility • Lifestyle changes • Attitudes to work and leisure • Consumerism • Levels of education

Technological
Government spending on research •
Government and industry focus of technological effort • New discoveries/development • Speed of technology transfer • Rates of obsolescence

FIGURE 1.6 'PEST' analysis (*source*: Johnson, G and Scholes, K (1993) *Exploring Corporate Strategy*, 3rd edn, Prentice Hall, Hemel Hempstead).

People within organizations

Organizations do not *exist* in any real sense of the word. They might be described as legal and financial entities on paper, but it is the people within them that breathe life into the documents. Management in Action 1.5 illustrates some of these people perspectives in the context of the introduction of business process re-engineering.

Stop | Consider

Is business process re-engineering (BPR) yet another attempt to find the elusive formula that would guarantee the success of a company?

If BPR were to be successful would every company follow it and therefore find the same solutions to the question of minimal cost with maximal customer focus?

If that were to happen how would companies be able to compete against each other – as presumably all would have the same approach to organization and work? Might the answer to this question imply that the formula approach to improvement can never work in the long run?

The earlier discussion on management stated that the manager is acting on behalf of an absentee owner. This view is usually referred to as an *agency* perspective – the manager acting as an agent of (on behalf of) the owner. From a different perspective, as early as 1964, Cyert and March were writing about *coalitions* and Rhenman was writing about *stakeholders* in the running of organizations. Networks and coalitions formed between the many internal and external stakeholder groups linked with the organization is implied by these views. Figure 1.7 illustrates some of the primary stakeholder groups that can be identified in relation to any organization.

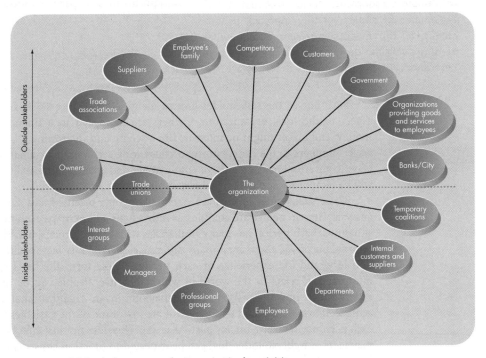

Figure 1.7   Major influences on the organization's activities.

MANAGEMENT IN ACTION 1.5

Cut out the middlemen

The techniques and formulas that are used as the basis of seeking out the best way of working and the lowest cost of operation are often silent on the human impact of their activity. At best these approaches assume a rationality in the human dimension and imply that communication can overcome any unwillingness on the part of employees to accept the need to produce more for less.

Business process re-engineering is the latest in a long line of approaches to attempt to ensure that organizations become truly efficient. Michael Hammer is one of the leading gurus in this field and insists that it is a process that is about eliminating work, a process that should not be considered as the same as eliminating people (simple downsizing). The net result, however, is the same, but it is argued that by concentrating on the fundamental redesign of the business process an effective organization will then result and one into which the people can be accommodated. The major area of impact for this approach to efficiency is the middle manager levels, what Hammer calls the 'death zone'. Re-engineering he describes as a process intended to replace the

organizational forms that emerged during the Industrial Revolution when workers needed to be closely supervised for many reasons, including low levels of trust.

In the re-engineered company teams are essential and a customer rather than boss focus is required. This invariably leads to the notion of self-managed teams with a much reduced role for managers in the traditional sense of the job. Management becomes a role requiring lead-and-enable skills rather than those of command and control. It also reduces the ratio of managers required from approximately 1:7 to anything approaching 1:50. As an indication of the impact of re-engineering, Taco Bell moved from 350 area supervisors for its 1800 fast food outlets in 1988 to 100 market managers responsible for 2300 outlets a few years later. The effect on sales was an increase (on average) of 22% per year and profits by 31% per year.

Based on: Flood, G (1994) Cut out the middlemen, *Personnel Today*, 22 March, p 36.

Each one of the stakeholder groups identified in Figure 1.7 has an interest in some aspect of the focal organization. Owners are interested in a financial return for their money; employees might be interested in a secure and interesting job that pays a realistic wage; suppliers in the opportunity to create long-term strategic alliances for commercial benefit; government as a source of employment and taxation. Internally some of the groups will be temporary and seek to achieve limited goals.

These stakeholder groups are essentially people oriented and so provide a basis for analysis. Human beings are complex as individuals and perhaps even more so in collective situations. Each person has many similarities with other humans, but, critically for organizational purposes, also a great many differences. Personality factors differ as do the education level and life experience of each person. These form the basis of how individuals interpret and relate to the world in which they live. People can be unpredictable to an extent which makes consistency of behaviour in an organizational setting difficult to achieve. Illness, mood and temperament are just some of the variables that can affect how each person will behave on any particular day. This does not just affect employees, it affects managers as well. No individual can be expected to function consistently and at peak performance all day, every day – even if business process re-engineering (or any other model) assumes that they can or should.

It is the predictable consistency in operation provided by computer-based technology that makes it such an attractive option in most work settings. It is not possible for human beings to match the unfailing and relentless consistency of performance achieved by robots in a factory, for example. However, human beings do have some advantages over computer technology. They are adaptable, flexible and can demonstrate a level of initiative beyond that available through any computer. Consequently, there is still a need to employ, and a benefit to be gained from, that unpredictable but fascinating beast of burden – the human being. Call centres represent a modern organizational development in which new patterns and forms of work are emerging based on computer and telecommunications technology. As such new ways of work are evolving in these environments and as a consequence some people refer to these as the modern-day equivalent of the 'sweatshops' of old, with demands for high work rates over extended periods, work of a low level and highly repetitive, constant management monitoring of work and high labour turnover. During November 1999 the first major strike of employees in call centres was organized by the Communications Workers' Union in the UK over what were described as an 'oppressive management style' and 'persistent under resourcing' (Lamb, 1999). This action demonstrates the difficulty facing managers in effectively blending together the opportunities available through new technology and human beings. Management in Action 1.6 reflects some of the issues surrounding the introduction of another aspect of computer-based technology – teleworking – which allows individuals to work from home using a fax, telephone and other computer-based technologies.

Stop | Consider

Could universities use the principles and technology involved in the teleworking approach to work for the delivery of undergraduate and postgraduate degree programmes?

What would be needed to be able to operate effectively in such a way?

To what extent would the lack of opportunity to live away from home for an extended period of time, together with the ability to interact with lecturers and other students diminish the level of personal development actually achieved through a teleworking-based degree?

It is people who create organizations, either as a source of income or in response to a perceived social, political or personal need. It is people who operate the organization, taking decisions and physically arranging to produce the products or services. It is yet more people who regulate the organization in terms of safety, taxation, financial matters and fraud. Even more people are the suppliers and customers of the organization. Within the organization, careers are worked out and living standards are determined, individuals seek to advance their own position and status at the expense of others. On occasions they also seek revenge for some real or imagined slight from the past. In short, the human aspect of organizations is the story of human life and experience plus that of society, albeit writ small!

Human behaviour also influences the perception and understanding of organizations themselves. Morgan (1986) and Gharajedaghi and Ackoff (1984) both describe organizational activity in terms of the differing *metaphors* that can be employed by people to understand it. They represent the ways in which an individual interprets an organization, which determines the characteristics that will be attributed to it and assumptions about how it functions. For example, considering an organization in metaphorical terms as a brain or as a machine bestows on it qualities associated with those structures. The

MANAGEMENT IN ACTION 1.6

Flexible working with IT

Estimates vary as to the level of teleworking that actually exists. One study by the Henley Centre for Forecasting suggests that around 1.2 million people are engaged in teleworking in the UK, which represents about 4% of the workforce. It also suggests that about 70% of large and medium-sized organizations intend to introduce teleworking over the next few years.

The potential benefits to organizations can make the introduction of teleworking a very attractive option. The reduced costs of running company premises (heat, light, insurance and so on); the reduced levels of stress and absence for staff who do not have to experience commuting each day; and the part-time employment of specialists who might otherwise need office accommodation being among the more obvious benefits. In addition, there can be the benefits for business as a result of the distributed nature of work and information. For example, if there were to be a serious fire in the head office, not all information and equipment would be lost and a rapid recovery would be more likely. For employees the reduced cost of work activity (travel, clothing and so on) as well as the opportunity to be flexible when they actually perform the necessary tasks represent some of the potential benefits.

There are, however, a number of disadvantages. There is the reliability of technology to be considered; the security of sensitive or confidential data; employees may not work the hours expected of them; employees may not like to be isolated from co-workers all of the time or to be at home constantly. Equally, there are occasions when face-to-face contact is an important part of management and organizational functioning.

The use of teleworking has not developed as quickly as some writers anticipated but the use of technology to transfer work to remote locations is a trend likely to continue. Some companies have begun to relocate whole operations through the technology opportunities available. For example, London Underground has its timetables created by IT experts in Bangalore in India and American Airlines has moved its ticketing operations to Barbados.

Adapted from: Baron, A and Hutchinson, S (1995) Flexible working with IT, *Consultants' Conspectus*, January, p 31; and Littlefield, D (1995) Remote working has pleasures and perils, *People Management*, 30 November, p 13.

metaphor adopted also conditions how individuals will assume that an organization works. The decisions and expectations of individuals in relation to the organization are also influenced by the metaphor adopted.

The study of organizations

The study of organizations as institutions takes many different forms. Accountants, lawyers, economists and strategists all have research interests in organizations. Marketing specialists, human resource management, operations management are all management disciplines that attempt to offer some insight into the functioning of organizations. Sociologists, psychologists and critical thinkers from various traditions also have an interest in attempting to theorize about organizations. It is difficult to be specific when describing what defines the study of organizations; it means many different things depending upon who uses the phrase and for what purpose they use it.

However, simply because something is complex does not mean that it could not or should not be studied. Indeed, it is that very complexity that makes situations attractive from a research point of view. Thompson and McHugh (1995) provide a means of defining what they term as the *mainstream* and *critical* approaches to the development and interpretation of organizational theory. The main domain assumptions made in each tradition are identified in Table 1.1.

The assumptions identified in Table 1.1 from the mainstream approach to the study of organizations emphasize a very rational view of the attribution of the qualities indicated: in short, the application of scientific method in the search for explanation and a more valid *science of organizations.*

The critical tradition, in contrast, requires approaches to the study of organizations to be:

✦ Reflexive. This implies that any approach to the study of organizations should attempt to ensure that the values, practices, knowledge and expectations are not taken for granted.

✦ Embedded. This element insists that organizations need to be considered as one part of a total environment. They are *embedded* in a context and that context needs to be understood and incorporated into any explanation.

✦ Multi-dimensional. The people dimension of an organization needs to be explained in terms of the multi-dimensional nature of human beings. Individual behaviour is embedded in a contextual and family setting.

✦ Dialectical and contradictory. There are many inherently contradictory and inconsistent patterns of organizational functioning. For example, control of operational activity is a necessary aspect of managerial activity. However, this directly impacts on employee behaviour either in the form of work regulation or social control. In either case it is likely that employees will resist attempts to prescribe levels of control that they find unacceptable. This inevitably leads to attempts to increase the level of control and so a cycle of reciprocal behaviours is set up.

✦ Socially transforming. Critical theory is part of the creation of an attempt to *empower* all members of an organization, the beginnings of a notion (sometimes referred to as praxis) that individuals can be encouraged to see beyond the existing constraints and to be able to reflect on and engineer a reconstruction of their 'reality'.

Domain assumptions of mainstream approaches	Domain assumptions of critical approaches
Organizations as goal seekers	Reflexivity
Search for rational-efficiency-based order and hierarchy	The embeddedness of organizations
	Multidimensionality
Managerialism	Dialectics and contradiction
Search for organizational science	Social transformation

TABLE 1.1 Domain assumptions of the mainstream and critical approaches to the study of organizations (*source*: Thompson, P and McHugh, D (1995) *Work Organizations*, Macmillan, London)

The management of organizations

Why organizations need managers

Managers plan, organize and control the acquisition, disposal and application of resources within the organization in pursuit of the goals determined by the owners. That view reflects the classical model described by Fayol (1916). From that perspective management is a very rational process and one category of employment within the organization. As such it requires someone to undertake specific duties associated with *managing*, just as a cleaner in a factory undertakes that particular job. One implication of this view is that being a manager confers no special status or rights over any other form of employment. Yet in practice (as was suggested earlier) one of the major functions of management is to act *in loco parentis* for the absentee owner, which implies going beyond the wage/work bargain that forms the basis of most paid employment relationships.

There are other fundamental differences between the jobs of managers and those of most employees. Most employees are engaged to undertake a range of duties associated with the creation of the product or service that forms the rationale for the existence of the organization. Even employees who act as a support to the creation process contribute in a very necessary way by preventing the waste of productive resource. Managers, by the same token, do not do that. They are specifically tasked to direct, organize and control the activities of others. They represent the most indirect of all operational jobs. It is this remoteness from direct operational activity and their agency function that sets them apart from other employees.

The type of work expected of managers is different from that of other employees. The impact of management's activities on other employees fundamentally influences the relationship with them. For example, it is management that decides who to recruit and who to dismiss. The power to take away someone's job is a particularly powerful weapon, right or responsibility, irrespective of how it is defined. It is such a potent tool that it is a right not usually given to every level of management. Managers are able to direct, channel and change the organizational experience for employees. Employees are not able to impact on managers in the same way. That is not to suggest, however, that employees are powerless within the organizational context.

Why managers need organizations

Perhaps a more interesting question to ask is why do managers need organizations? At first it would appear to be a nonsensical question based on the assumption that organizations created the need for managers. However, there are a number of issues that suggest that the relationship between management and organizations is more complex than would at first appear to be the case.

One common joke in management circles suggests that there are only two skills in management. One is to create enough problems to justify the need for the job to exist. The second is not to create more problems than make for an easy life. This may be a cynical view of managerial activity but it does reflect aspects of the power and influence that managers have. This view of management can be reinforced by the shock that was experienced by many managers as organizations began to downsize and delayer. Up to that time redundancy was something that happened to other employees, not managers. The trauma experienced by many managers resulted in increased levels of alienation and lower levels of commitment among that group. The justification for the trauma being that employers (in effect, more senior managers) could not be trusted to consider individual managers or protect them from the effects of change. The basis of the psychological contract between employer and managers had been fundamentally changed. The basis of the 'old contract' was that managers put their best efforts to work in furthering the interests of the capital owner in return for a career and the appropriate status. Frequently the best efforts willingly contributed by managers involved long working hours with no additional payment, taking work home and generally putting the job before family.

Worrall and Cooper (1999) report from the *Quality of Working Life* survey (the third year of a five-year tracking study) a number of interesting results that suggest that managers are changing their working patterns in response to the new business enviornment. They are beginning to move away from a reliance on the company as the source of all things and in some cases see the need for a better balance between home the work lives. Some of the relevant results are included in Table 1.2

So what are the significant factors that create a reciprocal need between managers and organizations?

✦ Career. Individual managers expect to have a career. Organizations need managers for more senior positions. Performance appraisal systems, career development and succession planning all provide a basis for career development. However, there is a wide diversity of opportunity available within organizations, as indicated in Management in Action 1.7.

Stop | Consider

To what extent are the initiatives illustrated in MiA 1.7 a reflection of the recognition by organizations of a need to build a different psychological contract with managers?

✦ Status/power. With a managerial position comes status and power. The ability to have other people do what the individual manager wants is heady wine! Being considered as a significant member of the local community can also reflect the status of a manager.

✦ Work preference. Being a manager gives the individual some degree of choice in their work activities. They can delegate aspects of their work. They are able to shape events and the direction of work under their control.

Working hours reduce	1997	38% work more than 50 hours a week
	1999	32% work more than 50 hours a week
Working weekends	1997	13% always work weekends
	1999	8% always work weekends
Relationshps with children	1999	41% of junior managers express concern
Balance between work and home lives	1997	25% feel work is less important than home
	1999	30% feel work is less important than home

TABLE 1.2 Managers' changing attitudes (*source*: Worrall, L and Cooper, CL (1999) *The Quality of Working Life: The 1999 Survey of Managers' Changing Experiences*, Institute of Management and UMIST, London)

MANAGEMENT IN ACTION 1.7

Ticket to ride or no place to go?

In days gone by there was a degree of certainty in career path direction and development opportunities. It was rather like buying a ticket for a train journey. Once the journey was planned, the ticket could be bought and the ensuing ride would provide a predictable form of transport towards a known destination. The changes that are being experienced in many organizations these days has largely destroyed that certainty and introduced a need to identify alternative career development practices.

One early response to this was the attempt to introduce self-development and career planning. Early experience, however, tended to be disappointing with this approach for a number of reasons, including:

✦ Frequent changes to the career development process by HR departments.

✦ Small (and downsized) HR departments cannot sustain such initiatives over time.

✦ Limited scope and support for career development in totality. For example, comparatively limited capability to support lateral career moves.

✦ Limited ability of line managers to direct and manage career development programmes.

✦ General company processes. For example short-term business objectives limit the scope for career planning to be taken seriously.

Research by the Institute for Employment Studies suggests that there is a trend back towards company involvement through a partnership approach to career development. The basis being the need for role adaptation, teamworking and lateral job movement rather than vertical job promotion, the intention being to create flexibility in the workforce and an ability to cope with continual change, supported by development. In achieving these ideals, three issues need to be addressed in order to give any career development strategy credibility:

✦ An appropriate and honest message. Any message from the organization about career development has to be credible in the eyes of those to whom it is intended to apply.

✦ Workable career development processes. Whatever the process of career development it has to add value to the experience and needs of the business.

✦ Real intention to deliver. It is also necessary to intend to deliver the career development promised and to follow through with the purposes behind it.

Adapted from: Hirsh, W and Jackson, C (1996) Ticket to ride or no place to go?, *People Management*, 27 June, pp 20–5.

✦ Professionalization. There is an increasing trend to *professionalize* management. The professional associations to which managers belong and the educational establishments offering management training are making efforts to raise the status of the job, thereby making it more attractive as a career option. It is not just the law and accountancy that can now lay claim to be a profession.

✦ Self-interest. Management is a political process as much as it is a decision-making one. There are few managers who are as quick to take responsibility when something goes wrong as there are when accolades are being handed out. The question to be answered is not does self-interest feature in management practice but to what extent will a manager put self-interest ahead of other criteria in any given situation.

✦ Lifestyle. A higher salary, better benefit package, and so on, generate a whole range of lifestyle differences. Not that all managers earn more than those whom they supervise.

Frequently, for first-line managers the opposite is true as a result of the loss of bonus or overtime payments. However, there are differences in the social groupings with which people mix and the leisure activities that they undertake that create a raft of lifestyle differences.

✦ Expectation. Individuals are conditioned to expect differences as a result of becoming a manager. They expect respect, a higher income and greater freedom to influence events around them. Consequently, having tasted these fruits the result is an expectation (and desire) that they continue, leading to a need to perpetuate such positions. For example, it is not in the interests of most managers to see too many management jobs disappear or for radical alternatives in the form of self-managed teams to be developed. It would simply eliminate much of the opportunity and potential benefits available and require individuals to seek other forms of employment.

Many of these issues are generalizations which interlink and reinforce each other. For example, career and expectation are strongly linked together, as are the status and lifestyle benefits that result from promotion. The line of argument here is not that management originally created organizations because they needed them but that once in existence management perpetuates a need for organizations to exist in order to continue to fulfil their needs.

The study of management

Prior to the twentieth century the management literature tended to be based around the writings of individuals who brought to the attention of a wider audience their own perspectives. For example, Babbage (1832), a mathematician by training, attempted to offer ideas on how to improve the efficiency of operational activity. One of the first teachers of management topics was one Andrew Ure who taught in Glasgow in the early seventeenth century (Wren, 1987). However, it was not until the beginning of the twentieth century that the study of management began to feature systematically as a major activity in its own right.

Just as with the study of organizations described earlier the study of management can be broken down into two broad classification types. They are the *mainstream perspectives* and the *critical perspectives* (Alvesson and Willmott, 1996). Griffin (1993) identifies a number of what could be described as the mainstream perspectives to management theory (see Table 1.3).

Not every writer would agree with every entry in Table 1.3. For example, it could be argued that the inclusion of operations management is wrong because it represents a particular function within management – the management of production or service activities. Equally, some systems theorists would argue that they go beyond the mainstream perspective and attempt to incorporate a critical perspective into their work.

Not every approach identified in Table 1.3 will be discussed in this book. Elements of those approaches appropriate to the study of organizational behaviour will be incorporated. The mainstream perspectives (Alvesson and Willmott, 1996, pp 10–11) are limited in their ability to offer a comprehensive explanation of management because they ascribe to it the qualities of a *technical activity* which underplays the *social relations* and *political dimensions* involved. They describe the critical perspective on the study of management as incorporating the following characteristics (pp 38 and 39):

Classical perspectives

✦ Scientific management. Concerned with the systematic evaluation of work and the search for higher productivity

✦ Administrative management. A forerunner of the systems approach, attempting to identify ways of managing the whole organization

Behavioural perspectives

✦ Human relations. An approach to management based upon the importance of groups and the social context

✦ Organizational behaviour. A holistic approach to managing organizations incorporating individual, group and organizational processes

Quantitative perspectives

✦ Managment science. The development of mathematical models as the basis of decision making and problem solving

✦ Operations management. That areas of management attempting to produce the goods or services more effectively

Integrating perspectives

✦ Systems theory. A range of approaches to the study of organizations and management that attempt to cast these issues as an interrelated set of elements which are able to function as a whole

✦ Contingency theory. An approach which views the behaviour in any given context as a function of a wide set of contingent factors acting upon that situation

Contemporary

✦ Popularism. This reflects the wide variety of fads and fashions that gain rapid credence and just as quickly fade into obscurity. Only a few approaches in this category ever last longer than a few years or become a sustainable basis for actual managerial behaviour

TABLE 1.3 Mainstream management perspectives (*adapted from*: Griffin, RW (1993) *Management*, 4th edn, Houghton Mifflin, Boston, MA)

✦ Management is a social practice. The evolution of management reflects a practice that emerged within a social, historical and cultural context. It cannot be separated from that context if it is to be understood properly.

✦ Tensions exist in management practice. The experienced reality of management as a political and social process is different from that postulated in the mainstream perspectives as a rational process seeking to apply impartial and scientific techniques to the problems of managing.

✦ Critical studies are themselves embedded. Although critical studies attempt to acknowledge the existence of the tensions inherent in management, they are themselves embedded in a particular context. Consequently, they need to incorporate a measure of reflexivity in them.

✦ Critical studies seek to illuminate and transform power relations. Critical studies attempt to transform the practice of management as well as illuminate it.

✦ Critical theory contains an emancipatory intent. One of the purposes of critical theory is to provide a basis for individuals within organizations to become emancipated from the constrictions implicit in mainstream views.

✦ Critical analysis is concerned with the critique of ideology. It is implied that modern forms of domination are maintained through the theories and ideologies that underpin and inform the running of society and organizations. The questioning of received wisdom on how things should be provides a basis for liberation and emancipation.

✦ Critical theory implies more than a reconstruction of mainstream perspectives. Critical thinkers seek to achieve fundamental change in the essentially power-based nature of management.

The study of management is a complex process and there are many different perspectives that could be adopted towards it. Yet, for all the research that has been undertaken into management, we are no more able to practise it effectively than in years gone by. As Mant (1979) said: 'We do not, it seems to me, require one penny more spent on fundamental research into the "unknown", but to understand why we are so bad at putting to use what we already know' (p 207, quoted in Watson, 1994, p 11).

The emergence of organizational behaviour

It is implied in Table 1.3 that *organizational behaviour* can be considered as providing a mainstream perspective on management. From that position it is clear that it has strong links with the human relations school which emerged after the *Hawthorne Studies* directed by Elton Mayo during the late 1920s and early 1930s. It was these studies that first highlighted the complexity of human behaviour in an organizational setting. This led to a recognition of the importance of the social context within which work occurred and of group dynamics as a significant influence on individuals.

However, organizational behaviour incorporates many more features than might be considered at first glance appropriate to a behavioural approach to human activity within an organization. The study of organizational behaviour involves two distinct features:

1. Interdisciplinary. There are many areas of study that can be integrated into organizational behaviour. It involves aspects of psychology, sociology, anthropology, political science, philosophy, economics and the systems sciences. To this wealth of base material can be added a critical theory perspective on the embedded nature of much mainstream literature. Critical theory seeks to emancipate people from existing constraints and power relationships. Yet in so doing it invariably imposes another reality, albeit a different one, on the situation.

2. Explanatory. Organizational behaviour sets out to offer *explanations* of the relationships between variables. It does not provide an intention to *prescribe* the relationships or interactions between variables. When dealing with human behaviour at the macro level one is concerned with probability rather than certainty.

The study of organizational behaviour can be most easily reflected in a diagram (see Figure 1.8).

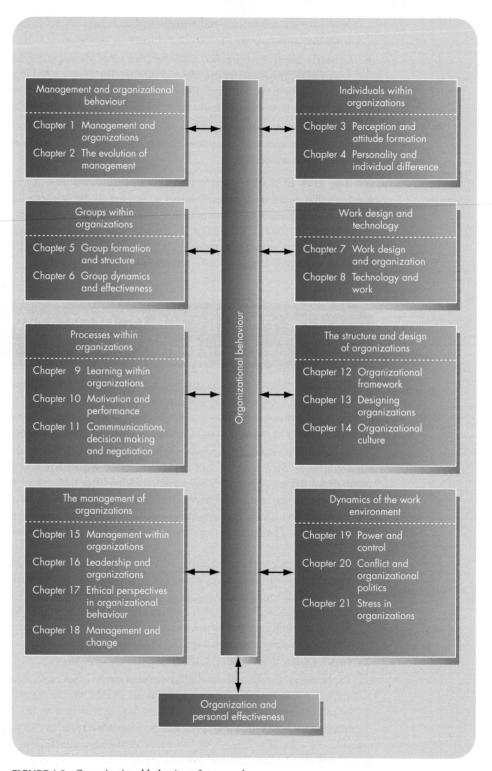

FIGURE 1.8 Organizational behaviour framework.

Each section within this book takes as its focus one aspect of organizational behaviour. Compartmentalization is a convenient means of considering complex material from a teaching and learning perspective. However, the reality of organizational behaviour is that there are considerable and significant interdependencies and interrelationships between all the topics discussed. Rather than make Figure 1.8 look a complete mess with lines going in every direction, this has been shown as two-way lines between individual boxes and the linking theme box of organizational behaviour.

Management and organizations: an applied perspective

Organizations are the entities that require the roles and skills that managers possess. Management can therefore be described in terms of three main functions:

1. Direction. Before any work can be done there is a need for a plan of action. It is necessary for management to decide what the organization should do and how it should achieve that objective. Once done at the level of the organization, this process can be broken down into the strategies and goals to be achieved by each sub-unit within the company. For example, once a chocolate manufacturer has decided that it will make Easter eggs in particular varieties and sizes, it is then the job of the various section managers to set about determining the production schedule and other operational parameters so that the sales and profit objectives can be met.

    In practice, this *top-down* approach is much too simplistic as there may well be constraints in the system that limit the ability to achieve the overall objective. For example, the chocolate company may not have the warehouse capacity to store the volume of Easter eggs produced. So the development of strategy at any level of the organization is based on an iterative process and also contains elements of *bottom-up* determination.

2. Resources. Another important function of management is to provide the resources to enable the task to be achieved. There are many resources necessary, including money, organization structure, job design, technology, procedures, systems and appropriately skilled people.

3. People. In all but the very smallest of organizations managers do not physically make whatever it is they are responsible for. One way of conceptualizing management is to think of it as a series of subcontracting arrangements. The board of directors is subcontracted by the owners to run the company. The board of directors in turn subcontracts the departmental work to line managers. This process cascades down to the people who actually make the products. This demonstrates that managers achieve their objectives through the efforts of other people. Therefore, in order to achieve their goals, managers find themselves in the position of having to manage the people rather than the process.

Having determined that management can be considered as a set of functions it is necessary to consider how managers *manage* in that context. Recognizing the existence of *levels in the hierarchy* and *specialisms in area of expertise* within management, there are two variables in management activity:

1. Role. This view of management suggests that each manager adopts a particular role in performing the duties associated with their job. Just as an actor plays a part in a play and in doing so adopts appropriate behaviour patterns, managers are expected to adopt particular patterns of behaviour in doing their job. Mintzberg (1975) identified ten management roles which he grouped into three categories. Figure 1.9 identifies each role.

    Role theory does not effectively explain all management activity as at any point in time a manager might be engaged in a number of roles at the same time. For example, at a meeting they might be a *spokesperson* representing their department's view, *disturbance handler* attempting to find a compromise between two opposing points of view and *leader* seeking to provide direction and leadership to the meeting.

2. Skill. Over recent years there has been an emergence of the notion of competency as the basis of identifying the abilities needed to perform specific jobs (Armstrong, 1991). Katz (1987) provides one list of the management competencies necessary to undertake a job in this field (see Table 1.4).

Not all management jobs require equal measures of each of the three skill areas. It will vary with seniority and function. There are many other writers who have claimed to identify the competencies necessary for particular managerial jobs. For examples of other competency lists see Dulewicz (1989) and Woodruffe (1990). Management in Action 1.8 illustrates how the effectiveness of directors within the AA (Automobile Association) was improved using a competency-based approach.

| Stop | Consider |

Identify the advantages and disadvantages to the company of the AA's approach to developing its senior managers described in MiA 1.8.

One of the other major aspects of organizational activity that managers are having to come to terms with is the effect of globalization. Even very small companies are experiencing some form of global activity. This might include selling products made by the company through a sales agent in another country. At the other end of the spectrum it could involve a very large organization operating across several national boundaries and with a truly multinational workforce and global perspective on its operations.

Category	Role	Example
Interpersonal	Figurehead	Represent company on trade delegation
	Leader	Chair department meeting
	Liaison	Co-ordinate activities with another department
Informational	Monitor	Check weekly production figures from department
	Disseminator	Write report on monthly production for directors
	Spokesperson	Attend board meeting to speak about expansion plans
Decision making	Entrepreneur	Design productivity improvement scheme
	Disturbance handler	Resolve argument with another department
	Resource allocator	Allocate budget to section heads
	Negotiator	Agree new budget with boss

FIGURE 1.9 Mintzberg's management roles.

MANAGEMENT IN ACTION 1.8

Tuning up for life in the fast lane

The AA (Automobile Association) is a diverse group providing a wide range of motoring services commercially and on behalf of its members. It is made up of six business areas covering commercial services, retail operations, membership services, insurance services, business services and financial services. Each business is headed by its own board of directors, which in turn reports to the group board. Senior management development is a long-standing item on the agenda of the main board and one such discussion led to a consideration of the value of creating the role of internal non-executive directors.

Following the request by another group to allow one of the senior managers from the AA to become a non-executive director a review of company practice was undertaken. As a result, an opportunity to enhance both management development practices and performance of the separate businesses within the AA group was recognized. The creation of the role of internal non-executive director was a novel way of gaining multiple benefits. Retaining the talent of senior managers within the group was seen as one of the major benefits to be gained, along with the availability of more knowledgeable (in company terms) non-executive directors and the potential to develop board level skills among senior managers. The period of office for the non-executive director was fixed at two years. The aim of the role was to contribute to the business by:

+ Taking a strategic perspective and identifying issues and implications, applying past experience in a creative and constructive way.

+ Probing the facts, challenging assumptions and providing counter-arguments, using the benefit of wider experience and knowledge.

+ Being alert to the need for change and supporting new initiatives, policies and practices.

+ Helping to make sure that AA values are safeguarded.

+ Evaluating the performance of the business in wider context.

+ Acting as an adviser or sounding-board to the business.

The launch was in the summer of 1994 and initial reviews suggest that the process has benefited both the organization and the individuals involved. It led to the creation of business development opportunities between individual businesses and also opened up career moves for the individuals on the programme into areas of the business for which they have gained experience as internal non-executive directors.

Adapted from: Bennett, H (1996) Tuning up for life in the fast lane, *People Management*, 132, June, pp 34–5.

Organizations need to develop an expertise in operating in locations that may have cultural and operating conditions very different from those prevailing at home. Individual managers need to develop the skills and ability to deal with governments, customers, suppliers, employees and colleagues from different countries.

There are recruitment and career-pathing implications resulting from being involved with international operations that do not exist in single-country situations. For example, in seeking to open up a new operation in a foreign country should the management team be recruited in that country and trained in company operations, or should they be company people who are sent on assignment to the new country? Only after the event when the success of the venture is being judged against the original plan can any evaluation of the original recruitment decision be made.

Interpersonal skills	necessary to communicate with other people in such a way as to facilitate operations
Conceptual skills	necessary to provide a basis to think in ways that solve problems creatively
Diagnostic skills	necessary in identifying cause-and-effect relationships and problem solving

TABLE 1.4 Management skills

There are many ethical issues that arise as a result of operating globally. For example, business practice around the world varies in relation to the giving of gifts, provision of hospitality and the offering of inducements in order to acquire orders. Company policy is needed to provide guidance for employees at all levels in relation to these issues.

Some of the large multinational organizations are bigger in financial terms than many of the countries in which they operate. This gives them considerable power – in terms of the potential to be able to influence the economic health, political processes and legislation in those countries. Managers need to be able to deal with these situations and an understanding of organizational behaviour can assist with the development of appropriate competencies.

Managers have a clear self-interest in the study of both organizations and management itself. With increasing knowledge and understanding comes an increased ability to control. This oversimplifies the arguments involved as issues such as company politics, prestige and an ability to fight off competition and so remain in business are also part of the process. However, from a management perspective running an organization is not just about the technology or techniques. It is about the personal, interpersonal, social, power and political aspects associated with the process.

Conclusions

This chapter has introduced the concepts of both organization and management which form the basis of much of the emphasis in the rest of this book. It has also included some of the research orientations and approaches adopted to the study of these issues in the real world and by real people.

The purpose of this chapter has been to set the scene for much of the later work in the book. It also set out to provide readers with some background to the research issues and approaches that are used to inform thinking in this and other areas of the study of management and organizations.

Discussion questions

1. Define the following key terms used in this chapter:

    PEST analysis   Organization   Guild
    Agency   Management   Organizational behaviour

Stakeholder	*Frame of reference*	*Bureaucracy*
Embeddedness	*Natural science*	*Critical theory*
Metaphor	*Social science*	*Professionalization*

2. Should a company recruit locally or appoint a home country team to start up an operation in a new country? Justify your answer.

3. 'It is not possible to generate robust social science theories because there are so many variables at work. It requires the development of a totally new science.' To what extent would you agree with this statement and why?

4. 'There is no such thing as a typical organization or management job therefore it is pointless attempting to theorize about them.' To what extent would you agree with this view? Justify your answer.

5. 'Managers need organizations.' To what extent do you agree with this view and why?

6. To what extent does critical theory offer an improved way of thinking and theorizing about organizations?

7. 'Management decision making is a complex activity as differing rationalities can be applied to the expenditure of resources.' What do you think is meant by this statement?

8. Why do you think that individual human beings seek jobs as managers?

9. 'The study of organizational behaviour enables managers to become more effective at their job.' Discuss this statement.

10. Change can be equated with challenges facing organizations and managers. Is this a valid comparison to make? Examine both sides of the argument and justify your own point of view.

Research activities

1. With a group, arrange to interview about ten managers from a range of type and size of organization. Select managers from different job areas, different levels of seniority, of different ages and include both men and women. Find out why they became managers, how they learned what the job involved, what they consider the job to be about and how they define an organization. Compare the results from the different people in your sample with each other. What conclusions can you draw from your research and how does it compare and contrast with the material in this chapter?

2. Repeat Research activity 1, but this time interview a range of non-management employees and compare their views on management and organizations with those collected from among the management population. What differences and similarities between the two sets of responses emerge and why? What does this tell you about conducting research into management and organizational areas?

3. In the library use books, magazines, journals, newspapers and any other resource that you can find to identify as many different types of management job and type of organization. From this information (and by using your own knowledge) what distin-

guishes management from non-management jobs and what differentiates a social group from an organization? To what extent do you consider that these differences are meaningful from a research point of view?

Key reading

From Clark, H, Chandler, J and Barry, J (1994) *Organization and Identities: Text and Readings in Organizational Behaviour*, International Thomson Business Press, London:

- ✦ Kumar, K: Specialization and the division of labour, p 13. This extract attempts to rationalize the transformations that took place during the Industrial Revolution.
- ✦ Kumar, K: Secularization, rationalization, bureaucratization, p 17. This extract considers a number of organizational and work-related changes in a broader social context.
- ✦ Friedman, AL: Marx's framework, p 25. This article introduces the work of Marx on the capitalist system and its effects on society.
- ✦ Foucault, M: Docile bodies and panopticism, p 35. This extract considers the nature of control and the role of surveillance in achieving it.
- ✦ Foucault, M: The subject and power, p 43. This considers the nature of power in relation to organizational and social activity.
- ✦ Campbell, B *et al.*: The manifesto for new times, p 49. This article suggests that change is not something from history and that society is in a continually evolutionary state.
- ✦ Fundamental list: Modern times and new times, p 57. This list provides a number of terms, people and products from the recent past and from more current times.

Further reading

Burrell, G and Morgan, G (1979) *Sociological Paradigms and Organisational Analysis: Elements of the Sociology of Corporate Life*, Ashgate. Aldershot. A classical review of the different ways of seeing things in organizational theorizing.

Chisholm, A and Davie, M (1992) *Beaverbrook: A Life*, Hutchinson, London. This book reflects the life history of one of the more colourful characters and adventurers in the twentieth century. It reflects many facets of organization and management.

Clegg, SR and Palmer, G (eds) (1996) *The Politics of Management Knowledge*, Sage, London. This text explores the relationship between management knowledge, power and practice within an increasingly global organizational environment.

de la Billière, General Sir P (1994) *Looking For Trouble*, HarperCollins, London. An autobiography of a senior military officer, this book provides an insight into the nature of leadership as well as military organization.

Gunn, C (1993) *Nightmare on Lime Street*, 2nd edn, Smith Gryphon, London. This book provides a perspective on the possibility of malpractice in Lloyds of London. It reflects the possibility that not all employees can be trusted to act in the best interests of the owners.

MacGregor, I with Tyler, R (1986) *The Enemies Within*, Collins, London. This is the story of the miners' strike in the British coalfields during 1984 and 1985 written from the perspective of the Chairman of the then National Coal Board.

McClintick, D (1982) *Indecent Exposure: A True Story of Hollywood and Wall Street*, Columbus Books, London. This book provides a number of insights into the way in which some people operate in search of personal advantage within an organizational framework.

Mills, AJ and Murgatroyd, SJ (1991) *Organizational Rules*, Open University Press, Milton Keynes. This text introduces the existence of the formal and informal rule frameworks that guide much of the human activity within organizations.

Potter, J (1996) *Representing Reality*, Sage, London. This book provides a review of various constructionist views of scientific knowledge as well as providing examples from conversations and other interactions.

References

Alvesson, M and Willmott, H (1996) *Making Sense of Management: A Critical Introduction*, Sage, London.

Armstrong, M (1991) *A Handbook of Personnel Management Practice*, 4th edn, Kogan Page, London.

Babbage, C (1832) *On the Economy of Machinery and Manufactures*, Charles Knight, London.

Barney, JB and Griffin, RW (1992) *The Management of Organizations: Strategy, Structure, Behaviour*, Houghton Mifflin, Boston, MA.

Berger, P and Luckmann, T (1967) *The Social Construction of Reality*, Penguin, Harmondsworth.

Bork, D (1986) *Family Business, Risky Business*, AMACOM, New York.

British Sociological Association (1973) *Statement of Ethical Principles and their Application to Sociological Research*, London.

Chen, M (1995) *Asian Management Systems: Chinese, Japanese and Korean Styles of Business*, Routledge, London.

Cyert, RM and March, JG (1964) *A Behavioural Theory of the Firm*, Prentice Hall, New York.

Dulewicz, V (1989) Assessment centres as the route to competence, *Personnel Management*, November.

Fayol, H (1916) *General and Industrial Management*, trans C Storrs (1949), Pitman, London.

Finch, J (1993) It's Great to have Someone to Talk to: Ethics and Politics of Interviewing Women. In

Hammersley, M (ed.) *Social Research: Philosophy, Politics and Practice*, Sage, London.

Freeman, R E (1984) *Strategic Management: A Stakeholder Approach*, Pitman, London.

Gharajedaghi, J and Ackoff, RL (1984) *Mechanisms, Organisms and Social System*s. Reprinted in Tsoukas, H (1994) *New Thinking in Organizational Behaviour*, Butterworth-Heinemann, Oxford.

Gill, J and Johnson, P (1997) *Research Methods for Managers*, 2nd edn, Paul Chapman, London.

Griffin, RW (1993) *Management*, 4th edn, Houghton Mifflin, Boston, MA.

Huczynski, AA and Buchanan, DA (1991) *Organizational Behaviour*, 2nd edn, Prentice Hall, Hemel Hempstead.

Johnson, G and Scholes, K (1993) *Exploring Corporate Strategy*, 3rd edn, Prentice Hall, Hemel Hempstead.

Katz, RL (1987) The skills of an effective administrator, *Harvard Business Review*, September–October, pp 90–102.

Lamb, J (1999) Oppressive management behind call centre strike, *People Management*, 25 November, 13.

Losey, M (1999) Address at the 51st Annual Society for Human Resource Management Annual Conference. Reported in *People Management*, 15 July, 18.

Mant, A (1979) *The Rise and Fall of the British Manager*, Pan, London.

McKelvey, W (1982) The Evolution of Organizational Form in Ancient Mesopotamia. In *Organizational Systematics*, University of California Press, Los Angeles, CA, pp 295–335.

Mintzberg, H (1975) The manager's job: folklore and fact, *Harvard Business Review*, July–August, 49–61.

Morgan, G (1986) *Images of Organization*, Sage, Newbury Park, CA.

Reason, P (ed.) (1994) *Participation in Human Inquiry*, Sage, London.

Remenyi, D, Williams, B, Money, A and Swartz, E (1998) *Doing Research in Business and Management: An Introduction to Process and Method*, Sage, London.

Rhenman, E (1964) *Industrial Democracy and Industrial Management*, Tavistock Institute, London.

Thompson, P and McHugh, D (1995) *Work Organizations: A Critical Introduction*, 2nd edn, Macmillan, Basingstoke.

Wallace, W (1971) *The Logic of Science in Sociology*, Aldine-Atherton, Chicago, IL.

Watson, TJ (1994) *In Search of Management*, Routledge, London.

Wood, S (1989) The Transformation of Work. In Wood, S (ed.) *The Transformation of Work*, Unwin Hyman, London.

Woodruffe, C (1990) *Assessment Centres*, Institute of Personnel Management, London.

Worrall, L and Cooper, CL (1999) *The Quality of Working Life: The 1999 Survey of Managers' Changing Experiences*, Institute of Management and UMIST, London.

Wren, D (1987) *The Evolution of Management Theory*, 3rd edn, John Wiley, New York.

CHAPTER 2

The evolution of management

CHAPTER SUMMARY

This chapter begins with an outline of the early history of management activity and gradually travels forwards in time to the twentieth century. It is only over the past 100 years that the research, theory development and teaching of management has become a significant part of organizational and academic activity. Consequently, this chapter will introduce a number of the major themes that have contributed to the field throughout history. This will be followed by a brief introduction to some of the newer approaches to the study of management and organizations, before concluding with an applied perspective on the topics introduced.

LEARNING OBJECTIVES

After studying this chapter and working through the associated Management in Action panels, Discussion questions and Research activities, you should be able to:

✦ Understand that there is no one perspective, approach or model of organization or management that totally explains the concepts.

✦ Describe the significance of a historical perspective in developing an appreciation of management as an activity.

✦ Explain the significance of the scientific and administrative management approaches to managing an organization.

✦ Outline the systems approaches to the study of management.

✦ Assess the relative contribution towards an understanding of management from each of the different perspectives described in this chapter.

✦ Appreciate that management theory is continually changing and that researchers adapt and develop their ideas over time.

✦ Discuss the significance of some of the more recent perspectives on management, including modernism and postmodernism.

✦ Detail the main themes associated with the human relations and quantitative schools of thought.

Introduction

This chapter is intended to continue the introductory perspectives begun in Chapter 1. In this chapter a number of ideas, theoretical perspectives and models will be introduced that will be explored in greater detail in later chapters. The purpose of this chapter is to establish a historical and evolutionary perspective to the development of management and organizational theory. Management and the organizations that employ them are not a new or recent phenomenon; they have both been around for many thousands of years. Many of the ideas that we think of as modern and recent innovations have their origins far back in the mists of time. The purpose of this chapter is to introduce this perspective.

Many academics in the business and management area prefer to emphasize recent work, ignoring the historical perspective. For example, it is not uncommon to hear history teachers saying that the only thing people learn from history is that people learn nothing from history. That approach does have its advantages in that it encourages the view that what is current is all that matters and allows a veil to be drawn over the past. In some ways it also allows human beings to forget their mortality by emphasizing the current and ignoring any cyclical life patterns. However, there are also disadvantages that arise from not exploring the past and considering how ideas and practices develop over time.

In research terms concentrating on relatively recent times obscures just how little published work is really new and innovative. The pressure on researchers is to publish volume rather than quality in order to meet institutional, publication and personal career targets. The targeting of research funds in 'value for money' areas tends to channel research in safe and predictable ways. In the rush for conformity that naturally follows from this there is little time to stand back and reflect. This chapter attempts to do just that – to reflect on where management and organizations originated from and by what routes they arrived at the present day practices that are taken for granted in managing. In doing so, it is also possible to give due recognition to some of the considerable achievements from the past and the people who provided the tools and techniques in use today.

Management and organizational theory is continually evolving, albeit at a slow rate. An acknowledgement of that process provides a context against which to judge the contribution of writers on the subject and a basis against which to evaluate the achievements of the many managers at work every day.

Early management practice

The study of early management activity is difficult in that there are few specific writings or records that have survived on the subject or the practices engaged in. Archaeologists and historians still argue about how the pyramids in Egypt were actually constructed and so it is equally as difficult to understand how the work was organized and managed. Very often the understanding of how management was practised in ancient times comes from scraps of writing about events, society or trade practices in general. It is therefore included as either an incidental description or as part of the general background context to the main activity. Management in ancient times does not seen to have commanded the special place in either academic or social circles to warrant the separate and detailed consideration evident today.

Most texts in the business field provide the distinct impression that management as an activity and topic of interest originated around the turn of the twentieth century with the emergence of FW Taylor and scientific management. While this may be true in terms of the volume of activity in developing the subject for study, it is far from the truth in terms of the practice of management. This section is therefore intended to provide a general and chronological introduction to the practice of management prior to the twentieth century.

Management in the ancient world

The first point to be made in this section is that the ancient world chronologically covers many thousands of years and geographically the entire world. It embraces the evolving nature of society from the food-gathering Mesolithic family groupings, moving around with the seasons, to the great Roman Empire, covering much of the then known world. Parallel developments were also taking place in China, India and other parts of the world.

Even in those very early, and by today's standards primitive, days knowledge and information passed between locations and civilizations. Trade and people movement was taking place in an increasingly sophisticated manner. With this movement some cross-fertilization of thinking and ideas was inevitable. However, this was very limited by today's standards and probably occurred across restricted geographical areas: a form of incremental development over time and space. Over the course of the generations covered by this section of this chapter it is possible to detect an ever increasing complexity of organization, functioning and managerial practice. Much of this development would seem to be based upon the trial and error methods driven by organizational need and previous failure, rather than theory development and formal training.

Table 2.1 identifies some of the major developments identified during the ancient times covered by this discussion.

Approximate year	Individual or group	Contribution
5000 BCE	Sumerians	Written documents, records, taxation
4000 BCE	Egyptians	Planning, control, organizing
2600 BCE	Egyptians	Decentralization
1800 BCE	Babylonians	Business, law, minimum wage, responsibility
1600 BCE	Egyptians	Centralization
1500 BCE	Hebrews	Management by exception, chain of command
1100 BCE	Chinese	Planning, organizing, directing, controlling
600 BCE	Nebuchadnezzar	Production control and wage incentives
500 BCE	Chinese	Job specialization
400 BCE	Xenophon	Recognition of management as separate activity
175 BCE	Cato	Job descriptions
900 CE	Alfarabi	Traits of leader
1100 CE	Ghazali	Traits of manager

TABLE 2.1 Selected management concepts in ancient times (*source*: George, CS (1971) *The History of Management Thought*, 2nd edn, Prentice Hall, Englewood Cliffs)

There are a number of striking elements incorporated into Table 2.1. Many of the contributions indicated in it would be familiar in management circles today. For example, the circular events of centralization and decentralization identified by the Egyptians over some 600 years or more is indicated, with the system of government in the empire being decentralized in the early years and then becoming centralized as the administrative weaknesses and consequent threats to the rulers were identified. The same cycle of centralization and decentralization is evident in many organizations in modern times.

The argument in relation to the existence of cycles of centralization and decentralization within an organization runs approximately thus. As a company grows in size from its very small beginnings, it tends to be organized in a centralized way, that is, under the close control of the central manager or perhaps a small team of managers. However, this eventually leads to slow decision making, high central administrative costs and lack of innovation in the sub-units of the company. So in response to this tendency to lethargy and high cost, a decentralization process begins in which freedom of action and responsibility for results is delegated down the organization to unit managers or section supervisors. However, over time this too begins to create problems in that duplication of effort can arise (every sub-unit lays claim to require its own accounting function in the search for better and more timely pricing and cost-control data for example). Restrictions in the ability to take advantage of opportunity as a result of the need to compete for resources with the other sub-units also arises.

In extreme circumstances this can lead to the break-up of the organization as managers seek to buy out their sub-units in the belief that they could do better as an independent company. As a consequence of the duplication of effort and lack of ability to tap into the opportunity for synergies within the organization cost begins to increase and the need for increased efficiency emerges and becomes ever stronger as learner and fitter competitors gain advantage in the marketplace. Inevitably, the pressure to centralize grows in order to capture the benefits of administrative cost reduction and co-ordinated operational activity. So the cycle begins once again. This process has also been seen over recent years in the political sphere with the attempts to break up the Soviet Union, as the individual countries within it sought to become independent and therefore responsible for their own destiny.

The realization that neither centralization or decentralization offers the perfect form of organization was recognized by the leaders in ancient Egypt as they experienced the realities of running their vast country. It is a lesson that has had to be learned anew by every generation of managers since then. This perhaps justifies the view that humans learn very little from history. It is also justification in itself for looking back to see just how much progress has been made in understanding organizations and management practice across the centuries.

Organizational control during the *ancient world* period tended to take the form of the direct control of labour and the passing on of advice from father to son. For example, the Egyptians had laws preventing tradesmen from practising any trade other than that passed down by parents or from engaging in political activity (Wilkinson, 1842).

It was recognized by the Babylonians by around 1800 BCE. that although work can be delegated, responsibility cannot. Contenau (1954) describes the building of a canal around that time in which it was made clear in a letter from the king that if the work was not acceptable the supervisor would be punished, not the workers. This is another aspect of ancient organizational life that finds many examples today. The captain of a ship is held responsible for any accident, even if he is not on the bridge at the time. However, it is a responsibility that not every manager is keen to accept. It is not uncommon to find that

MANAGEMENT IN ACTION 2.1

Babylonian management practice

The following extracts from the Code of Hammurabi, originating from around 1800 BCE, demonstrate many management concepts as familiar today as they were at the time that the were written:

♦ Minimum wages:

'If a man hire a field labourer, he shall pay him 8 gus of grain per year.'

♦ Control:

'If a merchant give to an agent grain, wool, oil or goods of any kind which to trade, the agent shall write down the value and return the money to the merchant. The agent shall take a sealed receipt for the money which he gives to the merchant. If the agent be careless and do not take a receipt for the money which he has given to his merchant the money not receipted for shall not be placed in his account.'

♦ Responsibility:

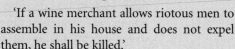

'The mason who builds a house which falls down and kills the inmate shall be put to death.'

'If a wine merchant allows riotous men to assemble in his house and does not expel them, he shall be killed.'

'If a doctor operates on a wound with a copper lancet, and the patient dies, or on the eye of a gentleman who loses his eye in consequence, his hands shall be cut off.'

Adapted from: George, CS (1971) *The History of Management Thought*, 2nd edn, Prentice Hall, Englewood Cliffs.

individual managers are only too willing to accept responsibility when things go well and praise is being handed out, but they can be very quick to seek a culprit if something goes wrong! Management in Action 2.1 identifies a number of Babylonian management practices that retain a modern parallel.

Stop | Consider

Compare and contrast the issues identified in MiA 2.1 with modern management practice.

To what extent do you consider that the concepts and practices described are essentially the same across the centuries, but that it is the social context within which they are carried out that changes?

What does your answer to the previous question imply about the understanding and practice of management today?

About 500 BCE Sun Tzu wrote a military textbook on the *Art of War*. It set out the basis of military campaigning and, in the process, identified many key management tactics. Described from a military perspective are issues such as planning, control, directing and military tactics intended to win battles. As a book it has recently been rediscovered and now appears in new translations and amplified form, Griffith (1971), Clavell (1983) and Wee (1991) being just some of them. There are even texts which bring together a number of the ancient military writings from China in an attempt to illustrate and understand what are thought to be different ways of thinking about leadership and management. (See, for example, *The Seven Military Classics of Ancient China*, Sawyer, 1993.) By about 1 CE it is thought that China had developed a factory-based system of production with departments

MANAGEMENT IN ACTION 2.2

Sun Tzu – The art of war or management

The following extracts reflect the views of a Chinese military leader writing about 500 BCE:

◆ The establishment of an effective military leadership depends upon five *spheres*:
  ◆ Leadership – causes people to follow their superiors willingly; therefore, following them in death and in life, the people will not betray the leader.
  ◆ Cyclical natural occurrences – include yin and yang, cold and heat and the seasons and lunar periods.
  ◆ Geographic factors – are the high and low, the wide and the narrow, the far and the near, the difficult and the easy, the lethal and the safe.
  ◆ Commandership – requires wisdom, credibility, benevolence, courage and discipline.
  ◆ Rules – are in regulations for mobilization, official duties and the management of material.
◆ All generals have to learn about these five *spheres* in their entirety. To know them is to be victorious, those who do not know them will fail.
◆ Each of the five *spheres* is evaluated through

survey (research and planning).

◆ Military leaders who do not understand the five *spheres* and who do not heed the surveys will fail and should be dismissed.

It does not take much imagination to make the switch from the military leadership described above to the commercial practice of management. The need to understand and plan in relation to the market, customer needs, employee requirements and the use of rule and procedures to control the business are all as evident today as they were 2500 years ago. Equally, the need to train and evaluate leaders (managers) in relation to the role expected of them and to remove inefficient people are also described in graphic detail. It would appear from the translation used that Sun Tzu considers leadership and commandership to be related processes but consisting of different facets as described above. Perhaps similar to the distinctions between leadership and management as the terms would be used today.

Adapted from: Huang, JH (1993) *Sun Tzu: The New Translation*, Quill, William Morrow, New York, pp 38–40.

reflecting the specialization of labour involved (Collons, 1971). Management in Action 2.2 illustrates a small range of Sun Tzu's ideas, taken from another source than that just identified.

| Stop | Consider | *To what extent do you agree with the view expressed in MiA 2.2 that leadership and comandership in ancient military times can be equated with the distinction in modern organizations between leadership and management?* |

Ancient Greece and Rome saw yet more aspects of management develop that would be familiar in today's organizations. Socrates suggested, for example, that management skills were transferable between public and private sector organizations. The only difference, he claimed, being one of scale. Aristotle was also recorded as saying that before becoming a leader an individual should first learn how to take orders. In Rome there existed the regulation of many aspects of organizational activity to prevent a threat to the government's influence and control over society, as well as to protect the stability of society. These form part of the legal and organizational legacy handed down over the centuries to today. For example, the emergence of a joint stock company in which capital was raised from private individuals to make goods for sale was limited in size to that necessary to supply the government under a specific contract. However, the government introduced several aspects that were beneficial to management activity. For example, the guaranteeing of weights and coins helped trade flourish (Wren, 1994).

Management in the medieval world

After the fall of Rome and during the *dark ages* that followed there is little recorded material on the subject of management. Of the few sources available, two of the more notable are identified in Table 2.1, concerning the characteristics of leaders and managers in 900 and 1100 CE respectively. The dark ages are characterized as a period when *feudalism* was the predominant form of social organization with most people being forced into working on the land owned by other people. The *tithe* system forced a significant part of the production of agricultural labour to be used in support of the lifestyle for the church and secular rulers over some 400 years from about the time of the fall of the Roman Empire. A tithe is a form of taxation that requires a proportion of the goods made, cash earned, or food grown to be handed over to the feudal lord or local church.

Table 2.2 identifies some of the key contributions that occurred during what can loosely be described as the medieval period, which followed the dark ages.

The Crusades from Europe began as a religious enterprise to retake Jerusalem but which ended in failure. However, what did emerge was a recognition of organizational differences between Europe and the Muslim-centred Middle East. There was also, in many ways, a grudging recognition of a superiority in the ways of doing things in the Middle East. New trade routes and opportunities were also opened as a result of the two centuries of military activity in the name of Christian superiority.

In parallel with these activities, Marco Polo had been exploring the Far East,

Approximate year	Individual or group	Contribution
1340	Venetians	Double entry bookkeeping
1395	Francisco Di Marco	Cost accounting practice
1410	Soranzo brothers	Journal entries and ledgers
1436	Venetians	Assembly line production techniques, inventory and cost control, personal management
1468	Friar Johannes Nider	Rules of trade, business ethics
1500	Sir Thomas More	'Sin' of poor management, job specialization
1525	Machiavelli	Politics and power in achieving control, mass consent, leadership qualities

TABLE 2.2   Selected management concepts in the medieval period (*source*: George, CS (1971) *The History of Management Thought*, 2nd edn, Prentice Hall, Englewood Cliffs; and Wren, DA (1994) *The Evolution of Management Thought*, 4th edn, John Wiley, Chichester)

comprising China, India, Tibet and Burma. As well as the new trade routes that opened as a result of his travels, in the last years of the thirteenth century he brought back to Venice information on how organizations operated in the places to which he travelled. For example, one piece of information that he provided was in relation to how the armies that he had seen were organized using the principle of a unit of ten at every reporting level. This created a workable hierarchy in which no manager needed to control and integrate the activities of more than ten subordinates.

Across Europe in the Middle Ages trade was split into two broad categories of activity. There were the *craft guilds*, which were responsible for the manufacture of goods, and the *merchant guilds*, which were responsible for the sale and trade in goods. The craft guilds were the groups of people from a particular craft who organized the work and running of that craft in order to protect it from dilution or erosion. They determined the number of people who could practice a craft in a particular place, how many apprentices could be trained and the boundaries between crafts. The merchant guilds were the buyers and sellers who facilitated trade and production. They would buy raw material for sale to producers (both craft guilds and *domestic producers*) and they would then buy the finished goods for sale in markets both at home and abroad.

Domestic producers were the forerunners of the factory production system. They were based on a family unit and worked in their own home. Raw materials would be delivered to them, the family would produce goods from the material supplied (using their own tools) and the completed articles would be collected by the supplier when more raw material would be left. Typical examples of this type of work would be weaving and spinning. Domestic production is also known as *outworking*, *putting-out* or *homeworking* and is still found today. Addressing envelopes for mass mailing and advertising is one example that can be seen today.

The Venetians were well placed to take advantage of the opportunities that became available for trade in the Middle Ages. By the early 1300s a form of double-entry bookkeeping had been developed, which was published by Pacioli in 1494. A sophisticated approach to the merchanting process had also been developed with the widespread use of the joint venture and partnership as a way of increasing capital and spreading risk. The use of selling agents was also common during this time. The process involved the merchant selling goods to an agent who had the rights to sell those goods to particular markets in return for either a share in the profit or, more latterly, a percentage of the value of the transaction (Lane, 1944).

Among the most fantastic aspects of Venetian management practice are those found in the records from the *Arsenal of Venice*. This was a government-owned shipyard, operational from about 1436. Its purpose was to build naval ships in order to protect the merchant fleet operating out of Venice at that time. Lane (1934) provides a detailed review of the running of the Arsenal and this is summarized in George (1971).

The ships built were perhaps small by most standards. They were about 106 feet long and approximately 20 feet wide. Each ship was divided into three sections: fighting platform at the front, space for the oars down the centre and a command centre at the stern. The purpose of the Arsenal was not just to build the ships but to make arms and other military equipment, to store such equipment and ships until needed and to refit ships as necessary. To do so required a workforce of some 2000 people and a site of around 60 acres.

George (1971) identifies seven main points from the Lane (1934) text that are worthy of mention (pp 36–41). To this can be added the management requirements of the operation, making eight in all. They are as follows:

◆ Management. The political and commercial importance of the Arsenal required that the state be involved in the management of it. In addition, the sheer size of the operation required a sophisticated form of management control. Many of the issues discussed in the following paragraphs form part of the management activities associated with the running of the shipyard. The structure of the operation was officially headed by three lords of the Arsenal, who reported to the commissioners – the link between the Arsenal as an operational unit and the Venetian Senate.

   Reporting to the lords of the Arsenal were the foremen and technical experts responsible for aspects of the production and design process. Among the specialist support functions available to the lords of the Arsenal were the bookkeepers and pages who had the responsibility of creating and reconciling the financial aspects to the running of the shipyard.

◆ Warehousing. Because of the need to be able to store and repair ships as well as build them it was necessary to have available a wide range of components that could be found and used at short notice. Components held in warehouses included rudders, benches, oars, pitch (for sealing joints in the wooden ships) and masts. These were held in specified quantities in specific locations so that they could be found, used and replaced quickly. It took several years to be able to introduce an equivalent system for raw material such as timber. This control of raw material became necessary because of the high cost involved in sorting through the vast stocks of timber scattered throughout the shipyard before appropriate pieces could be found for the particular use intended.

◆ Assembly. In order to be able to complete ships quickly a system of assembly line-based production tasks were instituted. Ships in reserve were not held in a completed state but required the joints to be made watertight (caulking) and fitting out to be done. The hull of a ship, once in the water, was towed along a canal past warehouses which would pass over the designated components (oars, masts, stores, weapons etc.) until at the end it was ready for active service. Management in Action 2.3 describes the report of one visitor in 1436 who saw at first hand the assembly line technique associated with the finishing of a galley.

Stop | Consider

The assembly line approach to building ships must have been an impressive sight. Why then do you suppose that it was approximately another 350 years before Henry Ford developed the idea into the factory approach as we would recognize it today?

   It was not unknown for important visitors to be treated to a spectacular event in having a ship 'built before their very eyes'. For example, Henry III of France visited Venice in 1574 and during dinner one evening saw a vessel built, finished and armed within one hour.

◆ Personnel. A number of modern personnel practices can be found to have been used from the records of the Arsenal of Venice. Recruitment was controlled in key crafts with admission tests being required before young people could become apprentice carpenters, for example. Wages and quality were also closely controlled in the manufacturing and assembly shops. Both piecework and day rates were used in appropriate situations. The making of oars was based on piecework with credit being given only for those finished pieces that were acceptable to the supervisor. Day wage (non-

MANAGEMENT IN ACTION 2.3

The Arsenal of Venice

The following quotation provides some insight into what must have been a truly magnificent sight. The clear description of an early assembly line in which the galley was towed past several work stations, each adding to the completion of the ship until by the end of the process it was ready to sail:

> And as one enters the gate there is a great street on either hand with the sea in the middle, and on one side are windows opening out of the houses of the Arsenal, and the same on the other side, and out came the galley towed by a boat, and from the windows they handed out to them from one cordage, from another the bread, from another the arms, and from another the balistas and mortars, and so from all sides everything which was required, and when the galley had reached the end of the street all the men required were on board, together with the complement of oars, and she was equipped from end to end. In this manner there came out ten galleys, fully armed, between the hours of three and nine.

Written by Pero Tafur in 1436 after visiting the Arsenal. Taken from Lane, FC (1934) *Venetian Ships and Shipbuilders of the Renaissance*, Johns Hopkins Press, Baltimore. *Quoted by*: George, CS (1971) *The History of Management Thought*, 2nd edn, Prentice Hall, Englewood Cliffs, pp 37–38.

incentive based) were paid to those employees who could not be encouraged to produce faster – for example employees engaged on fitting exposed timbers to the hull. Each year a merit review of the master craftsmen was undertaken in order to evaluate performance and other contributions as the basis of wage determination and advancement.

Starting and finishing times were also tightly managed as was the potential theft of timber or other useful components from the shipyard. Individual managers were able to delegate some of their duties (such as discipline and record keeping) so that they could concentrate on the major issues such as volume of production, cost and quality. Employees were also entitled to a number of wine breaks each day (5 or 6) in order to allow some recovery of energy and to maintain productivity.

✦ Standardization. In order to be able to mass produce anything a high degree of standardization is required. The Venetians recognized this and decreed that aspects of the design and manufacture of ships should be capable of standardization. Bows were to be of a standard design and size so that all arrows would fit them. The stern of each ship was to be identical so that rudders could be mass produced and fitted with ease to any ship, without the need for personalization. Deck fittings and rigging was also to be standardized in order to allow uniformity and pre-manufacture of appropriate components, ropeworks, sails and other parts. This created the first true fleet rather than a collection of individual ships sailing as a fleet.

✦ Accounting. The control of the operation required a strict accounting of the money involved in building the ships. This involved an accounting of money, material and time. By 1370 the accounts comprised two journals and one ledger. One journal was kept by the lord of the Arsenal responsible for cash transactions. The chief accountant kept a ledger from a journal produced by his deputy. At frequent intervals the journal kept by the lord of the Arsenal responsible for cash transactions was reconciled against the ledger produced by the chief accountant. Every year the account books were balanced and sent to the treasurer's office for storage and audit.

Several accounting innovations were introduced by the managers of the Arsenal over the years. For example the notion of splitting accounts into fixed expenses, variable expenses and extraordinary expenses was introduced during 1564.

✦ Inventory control. There were a number of inventory control procedures implemented within the Arsenal. Some have already been implied in that effective warehousing required a system that recorded the number and location of items. In addition, the control of inventory requires the recording of withdrawals and of quality. The quality and quantity of raw material and purchased components arriving at the Arsenal was checked by inspectors who reported back to the lords of the Arsenal on how actual arrivals compared with purchase intentions. These same inspectors were also responsible for inspecting finished goods to ensure that they were of an acceptable standard.

Goods leaving the Arsenal were the responsibility of doorkeepers whose duties were to prevent anything leaving without the proper authorization.

✦ Cost control. It became apparent to the managers of the Arsenal that not all aspects of the operation were as tightly controlled as others. For example, the cost of finding an appropriate log was found to be three times as expensive as the log itself was worth. This formed the basis of a management initiative to improve the ability of the shipyard to store, retrieve and process wood. It seems that piles of wood were searched before appropriate pieces could be found and that the wood itself was left lying around the shipyard basically getting in the way of smooth operations. Stacks of timber even had to be moved from the slipways before ships could be launched. A clear waste of time and money. This example illustrates the attempt at problem solving through the application of cost-control techniques.

Machiavelli is a character of whom few people will never have heard. Indeed, his name is synonymous with the mischief and evil doings by people in power or those intent on achieving it. The truth about him is, as is ever the case, more complex. In a recent review of his life and work De Grazia (1989) finds him to be a character in search of how to justify to both the leader and the led the need for a new statecraft in a changing world. Perhaps not quite the Machiavelli of old. George (1971), quoting from the first edition of Jay (1967) identifies four main themes identified by Machiavelli (pp 45–46):

1. Mass consent. Machiavelli recognized that ultimately power rested with the masses. Princes, kings and other leaders may enforce their own will on the people for a while, but if they are to achieve effective control the masses must support them. This is a very early expression of the acceptance theory of power. In practice, power flows from the bottom up, not from the top down. Managers who lose the confidence and active support of their subordinates find themselves in a very awkward position. It is very difficult to achieve any reasonable level of efficiency or effectiveness under such circumstances. The subordinates inevitably adopt an instrumental approach to their work and minimize the contribution they make. He went so far as to suggest that given a choice of acceding to power through the support of the people or through the nobles, a prince should always choose the support of the people.

2. Cohesiveness. There exists an organizational and state need for unified operations and continuity of management and government. Machiavelli argues that a prince should

'manage' his subordinates and friends in a positive way in order to retain their support in running the organization or state. This can be interpreted as a form of manipulation in seeking to exercise control over those governed. It was the job of the prince to provide clear leadership and guidance in letting everyone know what policies, laws and practices were to be followed. A lack of clarity in these matters would lead to demoralization and lack of control. For example, the punishment should always fit the crime without fear or favour being exercised.

3. Leadership. Machiavelli recognized two forms of leader: the first was a natural leader who enjoyed an instinctive ability to exercise control and rule. The other type of leader had to learn the skills necessary to be able to undertake their duties effectively. There are several characteristics of good leadership identified by Machiavelli, including the need to mix with subordinates, but not to the extent of losing dignity or compromising authority. Another area of advice offered is in the use of incentives to encourage citizens to contribute to society to the maximum extent possible in terms of skill and ability. An effective leader should be adaptable, being sensitive to the changing moods and wishes of the people and society.

4. Survival. Every organization, be it state, church, department of state or commercial organization, appears to have an inbuilt desire to survive. In this context the end justified the means. A leader had a duty to ensure the survival of state and as such had the responsibility to seek out and deal decisively with all threats to it. Similarly, a manager has a duty to ensure the survival of the organization for which they are charged with responsibility.

Although Machiavelli was writing about the affairs of state and of the tasks of rulers in the political context his ideas have many parallels in the commercial world of management. It was, however, for later generations to identify these similarities between the task of running a country and that of running a business.

Management during the Industrial Revolution

The emergence of Protestantism as conceived by such individuals as Luther and Calvin created a new situation in which it was possible for scientific enquiry to flourish. It has been argued by writers such as Weber (1905) that it was the possibilities available through the Reformation period that allowed the emergence of the *Protestant work ethic* and so encouraged the rapid development of capitalism. Equally, his critics have argued the opposite, that capitalism was the creator of Protestantism (Tawney, 1926). Whichever way round the relationship happened, major developments occurred during this period that further developed organizational and managerial practice.

The essential line of argument in support of the Protestant work ethic was the rejection of the Roman Catholic church's insistence on subsistence standards of living and aspiration to the monastic style of life. This was replaced by the Protestant notion of stewardship and responsibility for maximizing the contribution from each individual and unit of resource. This, it was argued, provided the basis for the development of the capitalist ideology and forms of organization. Each Protestant had a moral and God-given responsibility to work hard in the pursuit of maximizing their skill and return on capital employed, whether that capital be money skill or some other resource. The counter-argument was that capitalism had already emerged before the Reformation and that having done so it laid the groundwork for individuals to seek to change the dominant religious beliefs to those supportive of commercial reality.

Whatever the truth, the emergence of the Protestant religions paved the way for a number of other changes over time. For example, Locke wrote about political theory in 1690 which formed part of the intellectual basis of the later revolution in England. This in turn was followed by many other writers, most notably Adam Smith's *Wealth of Nations* in 1776. This work argued that the *invisible hand of the market* ultimately determined the most efficient utilization of resources. The application of self-interest at a personal level produced a situation (multiplied up by the number of people exercising that right) in which everyone gained as resources would automatically follow higher prices and better rewards. Smith recognized the benefits of allowing the free market to determine economic and business activity, but he also recognized some of the potential problems. Part of his approach was to encourage the specialization of work, while recognizing that taken to extreme and for too long it would have a deleterious effect on the worker.

Up to the beginning of the 1700s the guild system had been the predominant system of manufacturing, supported by the domestic production of the goods and food necessary for personal use. The development of the *putting-out* system was introduced prior to the Industrial Revolution as another way of producing goods for sale. It required families to use their own equipment, tools and skill to work on components provided to them by manufacturer and merchants who then paid for the completed work when it was picked up. While such practices were attractive they also had many drawbacks. Quality control was difficult as the agent had no direct control over the way the work was undertaken and only saw the finished products. Equally, agents could not control the pace of work as the piece-based payment system encouraged the family to fit such jobs around other work. Unless the agent provided the tools and equipment there was also considerable variation in the ways in which the work was undertaken and hence standards of completed work. As the workers were very vulnerable to price fixing by the agent it was not uncommon to find the theft of components from an agent in order to sell them to others in order to gain a better income.

Equally, the use of forced labour in various forms was prevalent prior to the Industrial Revolution. The use of slavery and forms of compulsory labour on behalf of a feudal lord such as the practice of serf labour in England has been common across much of history and in most parts of the world. Even during the Industrial Revolution slavery managed to continue until the mid-1800s in the deep south of the United States of America. However, forced labour has still not been completely eliminated in all its forms and has recently been identified by the International Labour Organization to exist even now in parts of the modern economies of India, Pakistan and Peru (reported in Nolan, 1999). However, it was with the development of factory-based production systems that such labour practices began to diminish.

It was the opportunities possible through the engineering developments in machinery manufacture and range of application, as well as the perceived need for tighter control of operational activity that encouraged the introduction of factory-based production. These reasons for the development of factory-based operations are in addition to the deficiencies identified in the putting-out system described earlier.

Table 2.3 identifies some of the leading contributions made in the management and organizational areas from the late 1700s to mid-1800s.

Wren (1994) brings together a number of sources and identifies various problems that arose in the early factory system and which had not been encountered previously. They were:

✦ Labour. With the introduction of the factory system it was necessary to find appropriate labour to operate the machinery and prepared to adopt the regulated working practices necessary to obtain the best return from the investment. This was not easy as

Approximate year	Individual	Contribution
1767	Sir James Stewart	Source of authority and impact of automation
1776	Adam Smith	*Wealth of Nations*, specialization, control
1799	Eli Whitney	Scientific method, quality control, span of management
1800	James Watt	Standard operating procedures
	Matthew Boulton	Planning, work methods, incentive wages
1810	Robert Owen	Personnel management, training, workers' housing
1820	James Mill	Human movement at work
1832	Charles Babbage	Scientific approach to work organization
1835	Marshall Laughlin	Relative importance of management aspects of work

TABLE 2.3   Selected management concepts from the Industrial Revolution (*source*: George, CS (1971) *The History of Management Thought*, 2nd edn, Prentice Hall, Englewood Cliffs)

many people were drifting into the cities from the rural areas and found the new ways of life difficult to adjust to. Many skilled workers were not prepared to give up their craft and guild-based work security for employment in a factory. Such employment inevitably required the worker to engage in a narrow range of tasks repeated at high frequency over long periods of time and under close supervision when compared with that previously existing under the guild system. With the development of new machinery came the need for new skills and these were inevitably in short supply. Those with scarce skills could easily transfer allegiances to other employers for higher wages or better conditions. In short, it was a period with unstable workforce conditions in which there was considerable social as well as employment-based change.

✦   Training. Having obtained people the employer was faced with the problem of how to ensure that they did the necessary jobs. This created a training need of considerable proportion. It has already been indicated that engineering skills were in short supply as it was an emerging area of technology. Even within the factory it was difficult for managers to achieve the consistency of work necessary for factory operations. In small workshops or individual craft-based work individualism is acceptable, indeed something to be encouraged. However, in a factory in which standardization and uniformity are essential ingredients in being able to mass produce goods to an acceptable and identical quality this poses severe difficulty. Employers found it necessary to begin to educate employees in the very basic mathematical and reading skills necessary to interpret orders and drawings. This was extended by the application of job simplification processes in creating specialized work activities to simplify the job instruction necessary to achieve the output desired.

✦   Discipline and motivation. For workers unused to the routines demanded of factory-based operations the strictures of regular attendance and controlled work activity came very hard. Absence was a regular feature of the work pattern of many employees as they sought to exercise some degree of control over their lives by taking time off work to celebrate holidays and feast days. Employers attempted to counter this by institutionalizing holidays and by offering company outings and feast days.

Sabotage was another common problem in factory operations. Employees would smash a piece of machinery in response to attempts to increase the rate of production or to the proposed introduction of more efficient work practices. The *Luddite* movement came to epitomize these machinery-destroying episodes. The causes of these events appear to be many and varied, not always linked to the threatened introduction of new equipment intended to raise productivity and therefore thought to cause unemployment. It is also apparent that there was not a single movement of Luddites but isolated and separate incidents that have been linked together under a common title. Several episodes of Luddite behaviour resulted in the perpetrators being hanged for murder around 1812. It is hardly surprising that it soon died out for lack of any leadership prepared to organize a systematic revolt.

Motivation appears to have been based upon three broad categories of activity (much as today). The first represents the use of positive reinforcement and inducement to encourage particular behaviours (the so-called carrot approach). The second involves the opposite approach – the stick is applied if something not desired occurs. This is negative reinforcement and is intended to reduce the likelihood of something happening as a result of the application of punishment. The third approach involved the attempt to win over the hearts and minds of employees so that they supported the aims and objectives of management. This approach attempts to internalize management values in the minds of employees so that they adopt a management perspective towards their work. The use of various incentive options in support of these approaches appears to have been common across many factories. Piecework plans to encourage higher output, corporal punishment of child labour and fines for adults also appear to have been widespread. In support of changing the moral ethos of workers, the call to regular church attendance and to avoid the pitfalls of drink etc. appear to have featured highly.

✦ Management. The introduction of new factory methods of work created a need for a new breed of worker – the manager. The ability of the owner of a business to directly manage every aspect of it became less viable as the *Industrial Revolution* progressed. The scale of operations as well as the complexity involved required the delegation of part of the responsibility for managing a factory to other specializts. Wren (1994) suggests (p 45) that the people appointed to these positions were generally illiterate workers who demonstrated a high degree of loyalty and ability to perform the job for which they were to be responsible. Pay was not much better than it was for the workers and the motivation in seeking out such positions was the opportunity to exercise nepotism in recruiting family to positions and thus enhance their own standard of living. Owners tended to employ family members in positions of power, presumably on the basis of trustworthiness, protecting the family fortune and to develop business expertise for future generations of owner.

There were few opportunities to learn about management from books, even if people in the target market could read, and the experiences of others tended to be handed down from person to person within a very restricted number of people. Problems were very much new (as was the whole factory system) and so there was little by way of precedents to help in solving them and so it was a time of experiment and, effectively, making it up as they went along. The first guides to management were produced for the spinning trades in about 1832 by a man called Montgomery. So much was he in demand that he moved to the United States of America and was able to undertake a comparison between British and American management practices which was published in 1840.

MANAGEMENT IN ACTION 2.4

The Soho Foundry

The Soho Foundry was among the first major applications of scientific management in England. It took place about 100 years before Taylor began his work in America. The factory began operations to make the steam engines designed by James Watt and by 1800 it had been taken over by the sons of the two founders. Expansion of the business inevitably required larger factory premises and considerable effort went into its development. Among the ideas incorporated into the new factory were:

✦ Product forecasting and production planning. Sales intelligence was systematically gathered both at home and abroad so that production plans could be made.

✦ Machine speeds were calculated and systematically varied according to the job being performed.

✦ Production processes were broken down into small parts and specialization of components introduced as well as job specialization among workers.

✦ A mixture of piecework and day rates was

used as appropriate to the type of work involved. The use of standard job times was introduced as the basis of output evaluation.

✦ Entertainment was provided for employees on special occasions. Christmas gifts were given to workers and their families. Wage rises were also applied at Christmas time.

✦ Housing was provided for workers and considered as part of their wage.

✦ Overtime wages were paid for excess hours worked each day. Working conditions were considerably improved by such initiatives as frequent painting of the walls to make the foundry clean and pleasant to work in.

✦ The company also set up a Mutual Assurance Society – a form of insurance scheme for the workers – largely administered by the workers.

Adapted from: George, CS (1971) *The History of Management Thought*, 2nd edn, Prentice Hall, Englewood Cliffs, pp 59–62.

With the generally improving standards of education and organizational practice, the standard of manager began to rise during the Industrial Revolution and it became easier to find suitable candidates prepared to take up the challenge. George (1971) describes in some detail an early factory operation in 1800 which demonstrates that the foregoing discussion of factory operations was by no means universal. Originally established by James Watt and Matthew Boulton to make steam engines in Soho, in London, it provides a model example of its day in the application of planning, organizing, cost control, work study and employee welfare programmes to achieve a factory-based production of steam engines. Management in Action 2.4 illustrates some of the initiatives adopted by Watt and Boulton.

Stop | Consider

To what extent might it be that the employment practices described in MiA 2.4 were different from the norm at the time rather than because they represent good practice that provided the benefit to both workers and managers? Justify your views.

There are many other issues that could be introduced in the discussion of the introduction of the factory system during the Industrial Revolution. The use of child and female labour, living conditions, education standards and some of the pioneers of early human relations applications through the Quaker movement such as Rowntree and Cadbury. However, space precludes consideration of the vast amount of social, economic and organizational material available.

Scientific and administrative management

The application of science to the running of organizations can be found in some of the very early sources identified in Tables 2.1, 2.2 and 2.3. The development of scientific management as an approach to the exercise of management responsibilities is widely credited to FW Taylor (1856–1915), who lived in America. However, as with many other aspects of management theory, the reality is more complex. This section begins with an introduction to scientific management and concludes with a review of another approach grounded in a similar intention, that of administrative management.

Scientific management

It has already been implied that the seeds of *scientific management* were sown long before FW Taylor brought together several strands of thinking into a single methodology for applying scientific principles to the design and organization of work. However, he did more than any other person or group to bring together a number of themes associated with the approach and progress them into a workable system.

The scientific management approach advocates the use of work study techniques to the systematic investigation of work and the subsequent matching of worker to job requirements. The basis of this perspective had existed for many centuries in one form or another. For example, there is evidence of the use of time study to determine the length of time needed to undertake tasks within factory operations well before Taylor used it. Currie (1963) indicates that a Frenchman (Perronet) was using time study as early as 1760 to record the length of time needed to make pins. He also records the application of similar techniques in England around 1792.

The approach to scientific management as developed by Taylor involved the systematic identification of what each job involved in terms of the demands made on the individual worker, the design of appropriate tools and equipment, the selection and training of appropriate employees capable of doing the job, the encouragement of high productivity throughout the use of incentive-based wage structures and the appropriate management of work. Taylor began to apply his ideas on work that was routine and repetitive. The example always quoted is the loading of iron slabs that each weighed 92 pounds onto railroad trucks. This was carried out within the Bethlehem Iron Company, in which he had been employed to improve output. Through the systematic study of what was involved in the work, Taylor identified what he termed as the 'one best way' of performing the task. He then recruited men with the appropriate physical characteristics to undertake the heavy transportation task, taught them exactly what was required of them and paid them on a piecework basis. Piecework is an incentive wage system that pays a sum of money for each unit of output produced. The higher the output achieved, the higher the wage earned. By using this combination of factors he was able to increase the daily output by a factor approaching 400%.

There is also evidence that other people were interested in the application of work study techniques at about the same time that Taylor was developing his ideas. For example, in England, Jevons (1888) describes the use of different sizes of spade for different material densities and the effects on worker effort, fatigue and productivity. Babbage (1832) also pre-dates Taylor with many ideas on the application of systematic methods to understand work activities and the application of a strict division of labour, the use of incentive payments to encourage higher productivity and many other elements of scientific management.

There were many organizational and economic factors in existence in the USA at the time that Taylor was working and which increased the impact of his ideas over those that had existed before. It is not possible to know just how much Taylor knew of the work of the other people who had been involved in early scientific management types of application. It is likely, however, that he was significantly influenced by Henry Towne, who in 1886 deliv-ered a paper to the American Society of Engineers setting out his own approach to modern management within the Yale and Towne Manufacturing Company. Whatever the true extent of Taylor's use of other people's ideas he was keen to claim originality for his views. He was also responsible for making the most systematic and significant impact in the appli-cation of scientific management principles to industry.

It was an approach not without its critics and the strict application of its tenets was not possible in many situations. Industrial unrest and management hostility both conspired to undermine the basis of its potential contribution to what Taylor claimed was his intention – the creation of a more harmonious employment environment in which managers and workers co-operated in achieving mutual gain. However, press stories of the time suggested that high unemployment would follow the application of his ideas. A number of strikes were recorded following the application of scientific management principles and the method was eventually banned from use in the American defence industry during World War I.

It was left to the people who followed in Taylor's footsteps to develop his ideas and approaches so that implementation could be achieved. Names such as Gantt and Gilbreth are among the most famous who developed aspects of his work and formed the basis of much modern industrial engineering practice. However, Taylor's ideas found support in the fledgling Soviet Union as the country sought to develop the centralized approach to the mass production of goods and utilities with little by way of skilled labour to call on. Scientific management is a topic that will reappear in several chapters of this book. It has obvious relevance to topics such as motivation, job design and management practice for example.

Administrative management

Another stream of thinking emphasized the view that management as an activity involved the undertaking of tasks relative to the running of the organization as a whole. Individuals such as Weber, Fayol and Barnard would be considered to fall within this general category. Many terms have been used to classify this approach to management thinking and the one preferred here is *administrative management*. The other major title used in this area is *clas-sical management*, reflecting a view of what has been described as a traditional perspective on organizational functioning.

In combining the ideas of the three writers just indicated, there is no attempt to suggest that they collaborated with each other or that they were even aware of each other's work. The justification for grouping them together is that the ideas that they were discussing offer a broadly similar perspective on aspects of organizational activity. They were separated in time, by language and by location. Weber was writing in Germany and publishing around 1905. Fayol was French and publishing around 1916, while Barnard was in America writing around 1938. The English translations of Weber and Fayol did not appear for many years after the original publication of their work. For example, Fayol did not appear in English until 1930 although it was not widely published until another translation appeared in 1948 (Wren, 1994, p 182).

The ideas developed by these writers is discussed in greater detail in subsequent chapters and so will not be covered in depth here. Weber's ideas on *bureaucracy* were developed at a time when size and complexity of organizations were increasing rapidly and there was no computer-based technology to assist with the routine processing of administrative work. Fayol identified functions such as planning, organizing and controlling associated with the management process. He also indicted 14 principles of management which, if applied in a very much common sense manner, could be beneficial to the managing activity. He also suggested that management could be taught in the classroom in order to improve the exercise of it in practice.

Barnard was a practising manager (like Taylor, Fayol and many of his predecessors) and his contribution to management and organizational thinking was to describe an organization in terms of a co-operative system. In this view he was hinting at much of what was to follow in the *human relations movement* in which the people aspects of the organization feature more strongly. It is also an early recognition of the *systems view* of organizational thinking in which the integrated nature of many aspects of organization and environment are postulated to form an integrated interactive and mutually dependent framework.

The human relations and quantitative schools

There is a very strong emphasis on the *task* aspects of organizational functioning in much of the earlier work already discussed, particularly scientific management thinking. Plus there was the general unrest among workers and managers that followed from the direct attempts to direct and control worker activity. It is hardly surprising, therefore, to find a reaction and a countertrend emerging. This developed with the *human relations* approach to understanding behaviour within an organization. Equally, the emphasis on the *soft issues* associated with people and work relationships was followed in time by the emergence of a *hard* approach based on numbers and data – the *quantitative school*.

The human relations school

Early research on the *human relations* aspects of work activity revolved around the nature of groups and the interactive functioning of group effort. There were two broadly parallel initiatives underway, one in England, the other in America. In England towards the end of the World War I a series of studies was set up by the Industrial Fatigue Research Board into aspects of working conditions. One report from that research programme, published in

1928, identified the existence of a slight benefit when operatives worked in groups (Huczynski and Buchanan, 1991, p 154).

In America during 1921 a Christian-based church group held a conference on human relationships with a special reference to industry. This led to a research process involving the examination of the effects of groups in a work setting. Due to financial difficulties this work ended in 1933. At about the same time sociometry was developed (a mechanism for recording, analyzing and determining group composition) thus providing a research technique appropriate to group activity (Wren, 1994, p 276).

The Hawthorne Studies are widely claimed to be the forerunner of the *human relations movement*. But, as we have just seen, there were other research activities involving groups going on at around the same time. The Hawthorne Studies gained the widest recognition as the most significant research base on group activity within an organizational setting. The studies are discussed in greater detail in a number of later chapters and so will only be introduced here. They began in 1924 with the simple objective of discovering the effects of illumination on worker productivity and ended in 1933 with research output describing the importance of groups and group-based behaviour on activity at work. The Gillespie (1991) book identified in the Further reading section in this chapter is strongly recommended as an authoritative source on both the research itself and the organizational, social and academic conditions under which it was undertaken. From a reading of this work it is quite clear that it is difficult, if not impossible, to separate research and the interpretation of its output from the organizational, social, political and personal surroundings in which it takes place.

The result of the Hawthorne Studies was to fuel many other initiatives in an attempt to understand individual and group behaviour in an organizational setting. Developments in motivation theory and group dynamics are just two of the areas that emerged as a consequence of this work.

The quantitative school

The quantitative school approach attempted to define management problems in numbers terms and sought to find ways of modelling relationships so that causal relationships could be identified and predictions made. World War II provided a significant impetus to the development of this approach with the creation of many operations research techniques in Britain and which spread to America shortly after the war. The military need to move vast quantities of people, equipment, military supplies, food, and clothing was a large-scale problem not encountered before on the same scale. The development of mathematical models which allowed the variables involved to be qualified and set into relationships with each other helped to plan and execute these logistical necessities. The development of consulting practice as a means of adding to the problem-solving expertise and management capabilities of an organization became widespread during and after this period and the creation of operations research techniques aided this development.

The techniques developed under the management science umbrella impacted significantly on issues such as quality control through the introduction of statistical process control methods. This allowed the establishment of systematic methods of measuring product quality and of identifying acceptance and rejection criteria for product management. Production-planning techniques emerged during this period as did forecasting methods and scenario planning. Scenario planning allowed (once the computer technology was available) the setting up of operational models that could have their parameters systematically varied in order to evaluate different decision options.

Systems approaches to management

The systems approaches to management developed from early work in the biological sciences. Ludwig von Bertalanffy introduced the phrase *general systems theory* as part of his view that there were common characteristics of a *system* that were identifiable in all the sciences. In management terms, this perspective was adapted by the 1960s to reflect the view that the earlier perspectives (introduced earlier in this chapter) were lacking in being able to offer comprehensive explanations of management and organizational phenomena. This can be simplified in recognizing the general limitations offered by the main approaches as follows:

✦ Scientific management. Concentrated on the tasks necessary in pursuit of the objectives to be achieved and how to control employee activity in that process. As such it ignored the social and organizational factors associated with work and the people employed within it.

✦ Administrative management. Emphasized the structure and design of organizations together with the needs of the management process in running them. It generally ignored the people, job and task aspects of organizational activity.

✦ Human relations. This concentrated on the people aspects of work, the social conditions under which it was undertaken and the group dynamics involved. It paid scant attention to the organizational aspects relevant to work and ignored the job design and environmental circumstances surrounding the work. It also ignored the technological and economic issues surrounding work and organizational functioning.

The systems approach led to a recognition of the existence of a continuum of complexity in systems development, from the very simple biological organizms through to the complex social systems such as an organization. The approaches adopted attempted to capture an understanding the breadth of factors and influences impacting upon the system under enquiry. These included aspects of the environment with which a system needed to interact in order to survive. This led to the description of an organization as an *open system*. In this context, an open system implies one that is integral to and dependent upon the environment of which it is part for its very existence. This conception of an organization implies that it is not just a collection of individuals or groups that meet together for particular purposes. It is a social structure that is part of the environment around it and that needs the environment as both recipient of output and provider of input.

There are several systems approaches to management and some of the ideas originated from studies during the 1940s on coal-mining practices in England. Originally coal mining was a team-based activity in which groups of men would share the work and arrange the rewards accordingly. With the introduction of coal-cutting technology productivity improvements were possible but the consequence was a fundamental change to the existing working practices. Men became tied to specific mechanically paced jobs and less opportunity for social interaction existed. Increased accident and absence rates resulted and these became a focus for study. As a consequence, Trist and Bamforth (1951) described the sociotechnical nature of effective job design. In this approach, the social as well as the technical aspects surrounding the work were combined into a design of the work activities. In turn this formed an early stimulus to the further development of the systems approaches to management and work organization.

One of the difficulties in attempting to apply systems ideas to organizational and management issues is in defining the system under investigation. A system is composed of many subsystems and is itself part of a larger system. Consider, for example, a school class. It is probably made up of family and friendship groups, teacher and pupil groups and ability groups. However, it is also part of a school, which in turn is part of the education system and a town and a country, and so on. Therefore, a network of systems exists in an exceedingly complex interactive and mutually dependent set of relationships.

In addition, the environment is also very difficult to define in relation to any system. Consider the school class just introduced. The environment consists of family members, friends, other classes, teachers, educationalists, employers, government officials (national and local), building and equipment suppliers, taxpayers, media providers, authors and so on. The short answer is that a system and its environment can only be defined in the particular circumstances in which it is being considered. There is not just one system or environment in existence in any specific context. As an approach this has both advantages and disadvantages. It avoids the problems of generalizing and it allows a personalized approach to particular situations. But, by way of contrast, it makes communication difficult as it is not possible to offer general observations and can therefore sound trite and crass when attempting to suggest that everything depends upon the circumstances!

This foregoing discussion could imply the existence of a considerable degree of uncertainty and ambiguity within the systems approaches. They frequently claim to offer an emancipatory perspective to analysis and decision making through the involvement of stakeholders in creating an analysis of the system and the forces acting on it. It can, however, be argued that as an approach, systems thinking also provides a manipulative opportunity to managers. It is the people who define and control analysis about the systems in focus who are creating the reality within which others must function and these are, by definition, managers. Conversely, it can be argued that systems thinking is something that everyone can become involved in and that everyone can therefore assist in constructing the reality, analysis and the subsequent action plans. In the end it is predominantly managers who have most to gain commercially from these interventions and they control the information and the access to it that can create the reality understood as a system. Involvement can be used as a means of persuading employees towards a management agenda and viewpoint, thereby providing a means of control through absorption and reframing the reality within which employees work (Townley, 1994).

Sociological and other perspectives on management

As a discipline sociology adopts a different perspective to the study of management and organizations compared to the other specialisms that express an interest in those subjects. Sociologists take as the focus of attention the behaviour and interactions between groups, societies and the structures developed to maintain control and order within them. They have a particular interest in the relationships and mechanisms of control and order within social groupings. Psychologists, being the other major discipline interested in people, are more interested in the behaviour patterns of individuals. They focus on what it is that creates behaviour differences among individual people even if they are 'behaving' in a group context.

There are other disciplines that have an interest in the study of management and organizations. For example, anthropology, political science and economics have a degree of interest in these subjects. The contribution of each of the disciplines can produce contradictory interpretations and perspectives on particular items of interest. For example, in studying management the disciplines indicated might emphasize the following factors and influences:

✦ Psychology. The personality and other characteristics of effective leaders, decision-making styles and communication patterns.

✦ Sociology. Might concentrate on aspects of the results of management decision making in terms of the impact on power and control relationships in the workplace. For example, the effects of technology on the reinforcement of managerial status in relation to subordinates. They might also analyze the structures and ideological basis of control mechanisms introduced by managers.

✦ Political science. Researchers from this background might well take an interest in the strategies and tactics that managers and trade unions engage in as they attempt to achieve their objectives.

✦ Anthropology. These specialists might consider aspects of culture and how managers seek to create (or change) an organizational culture. They might also examine the symbols, roles and rituals that are used by managers to reinforce the cohesiveness of the organization.

✦ Economics. Economists have as their sphere of interest the working of the organization as a medium of exchange and of the application of market principles. They might well examine the efficiency of management decision making in terms of established economic theory and its possible impact on the future well-being of the organization. They would also take an interest in issues such as pay-bargaining strategies and outcomes, as well as product-pricing policies on profitability etc.

Each of these disciplines is offering a series of perspectives on the topics of organizations and management, and yet they do not, of themselves, provide a complete explanation. It was suggested in Chapter 1 that any individual perspective offers only a restricted understanding of the focal object and this is an issue that will arise in every subsequent chapter of this book. The advantage of a sociological perspective to organization and management is that it introduces a critical perspective to the otherwise individual perspective of psychology. It considers the context in which the behaviour takes place, not just the behaviour itself. In reflecting upon the context, sociology takes account of the history of social organizations and of the structures of control under capitalism and other economic systems.

Marcuse (1964) provides a seminal work in the field of analyzing the unfolding of modern capitalist society and the implications for organizations and the people living in such a society. He demonstrates the possibility that the use of certain terminologies and practices associated with such concepts as 'freedom' and 'democracy' can, in reality, repress individuality and disguise exploitation. The changes in terminology from boss and owner to bureaucrat, manager and company hide the nature of the control of the masses by masking domination and encouraging the creation of 'false needs'. These false needs are what would now be called consumerism in the search to create ever more products and services that add little to life, yet are sought after as necessary items and symbols of achievement and meaning.

In a much later work Reed (1989, Chapter 1), identifies three strands of sociological perspective on management that have evolved over the course of the twentieth century:

1. Technical perspective. A means-oriented approach to management in which it is regarded as a rationally designed 'tool' intended to achieve objectives through the co-ordination of social action.

2. Political perspective. Regards management as a social process intended to resolve conflict and difference between interest groups in order to allow the achievement of particular objectives.

3. Critical perspective. This approach regards management as a mechanism of control and domination. Management is the representative of the owner and as such is intended to achieve a return and result beneficial to that group. It is therefore an instrument of the owners in pursuit of their own interests.

New thinking about organizations and management

The application of sociological- (or the other discipline already introduced) based perspectives to thinking and theorising about organizations does not embrace every possible way of considering management and organizational issues. As Jacques (1996) points out there are no business problems in academic study and teaching, there are only finance problems, human resource management problems and organizational behaviour (OB) problems. However: 'Nobody in business has an OB problem. There is an OB aspect to every problem, but there is also an accounting aspect, a policy aspect and so forth' (p x). He then goes on to explain the *realities* of academic experience in creating the framework within which business and management is studied and taught, which he at one point describes as producing the, 'emotionally laden fault lines in academia' (p xii).

Part of the reason behind the compartmentalization of the study of management and organizations is the need to teach the wealth of subject matter involved. Another represents the need to identify research issues that can be isolated and examined in detail in order to control the variables and to allow the creation of theory. There is also a degree of carry-over from the business world evident in the compartmentalization found in the ways in which it is actually arranged. Most organizations are arranged around functional specialism and most careers are organized similarly. One is trained as an accountant or an engineer. It is only much later in a career that someone will encounter responsibilities for functions or areas of expertise other than the one for which they originally trained.

The growing recognition of the difficulties and relative artificiality created by compartmentalization has created a number of multidisciplinary initiatives. Within many large organizations the use of cross-functional project groups provides exposure to other ways of thinking and interpreting issues at a relatively early stage in careers. At the university level and in terms of professional development there is usually some inclusion of modules in which the individual is exposed to other ways of thinking, interpreting and developing action plans. The use of multifunctional case study analysis would be one example of this approach. However, this approach is still in its early days of development and most people feel more comfortable in compartmentalized surroundings. It leads to a security in the certainty that one can develop a high degree of expertise and specialization in a relatively small area of knowledge. Emerging from it are the advantages (and disadvantages) of job specialization found in factory environments. The advantages lie in the realms of productivity, skill level and training time. The disadvantages arise in the lack of ability to map research, knowledge and expertise onto the experience of real organizational functioning and human experience.

There are individuals and groups who recognize the relative limitations in the traditional way of constructing an understanding of management (and organizational theory). Jacques (1996), for example, sets out to describe and analyze the history of management in America using a variety of perspectives and seeks to evaluate it in historical and predictive terms. Thompson and McHugh (1995) provide an excellent review of the trends over recent years in theorizing about organizations and management (their Chapter 12) and in so doing recognize that the activities within the organization are carried out in a particular social context. Managers are free to shape their organizations in any ways they feel necessary, but freedom in any context is restricted by the conditions and prevailing norms of the day.

Thompson and McHugh (1995) identify a number of themes across time that in large part run parallel with each other. In doing so they identify a number of themes and approaches that will be dealt with either later in this chapter or elsewhere in the book. They introduce *modernism* and *postmodernism* as alternative formulations of social reality. Modernism is the representational aspects of the 'grand narrative, a coherent story about the development of the social and natural, revealed through the application of reason and science' (p 378). Postmodernists, in comparison, reject that cohesion, arguing that reality is made up of a differing range of realities and that it is constructed by our ability to express (or formulate) it. It is a view that holds that the 'truth is a product of language games' (p 379).

Watson (1994) argues that there will never be a single overall organization theory and that every practitioner, researcher, teacher and consultant will create their own, based upon a distillation of ideas from learning and experience. He goes on to suggest that the lack of a single theory does not mean that individuals cannot develop shared interpretative schemes containing common elements. So there are many new ways of thinking and theorizing about organizations and management emerging as time goes by. Management in Action 2.5 describes how the board of directors might look in the not too distant future.

Stop | Consider

How realistic is the view of the future of the board of directors in MiA 2.5?

Search out the article that it is based on and read the complete piece. Now formulate your own view of what the future might hold and compare it with the views of other students. Discuss the differences and similarities in each other's ideas, exploring the reasons for any variations. What does this tell you about the future of management?

Postmodernism

In attempting to understand organizations and provide theoretical frameworks many different approaches have been developed. These are frequently given titles as an attempt to both differentiate them from other perspectives and to encapsulate some of the intrinsic essence of the underlying thinking. Another way of considering titles is as simplifying devices, intended as a form of shorthand to compress meaning into *bite-size chunks* of information. For example, *scientific management* and *Fordism* are two terms used to

MANAGEMENT IN ACTION 2.5

Beam yourself up to the boardroom

The future of management is something that is of interest to many people, not least managers themselves. With the development of technology and globalization moving ahead at an ever faster pace it is possible to consider what might be available only a few short years from now. Lynn does just that in considering how a board of directors might operate in the year 2020.

The starting point for the review is to note that a board of directors still exists and has broadly the same responsibilities as today. It is largely the ways in which they function that change as well as the people themselves. For example, face-to-face meetings are rare, the virtual meeting house being the norm, based on the Internet ability to telecommute using electronic imaging. In the mythical company created by Lynn to illustrate his view of the future, the use of 'flesh time' (the term for a meeting between human beings actually in the same physical space) is regarded as an eccentricity by the young career executives and perhaps something that would be phased out. It is also regarded as a potential risk to the company as the need to travel across the world for meetings is dangerous as the volume of sky traffic is rocketing with the associated accident rate.

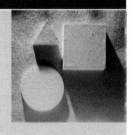

Equally the need for 'real' meetings is unnecessary as at least one of the directors is said to be technically dead. However, the ability of computer systems to simulate a particular human being's thinking processes is used to retain the value of that particular individual for the board. Equally the company has been able to scale down much of its administration functions as a result of the opportunity to base itself on a space station out of earth orbit. Technically, therefore, it is not liable to the requirements of the earth's legal and taxation systems. One of the key items for discussion is the issue of the possible cloning of the group's star salesperson. Given that cloning becomes permissible under certain conditions, for example not being able to find an equivalent person without it, it is a viable option as a means of company growth.

Adapted from: Lynn, M (1999) Beam yourself up to the boardroom, *Management Today*, May, 61–5.

describe approaches to organization that are based upon work fragmentation, deskilling, machine-paced work and alienated labour. This level of categorization is rather specific but there are terms which attempt to stand further back from the specific. Carter and Jackson (1993) for example use the terms *pre-modern*, *modern* and *postmodern* to describe epochs of tendency in dominant approaches to what defines rational. The typical basis of organizational rationality in each epoch is identified in Table 2.4.

Pre-modern	Modern	Postmodern
Diagnostic rationality based on theo-logic	Objective rationality based on scientific logic	Subjective rationality based on mytho-logic

TABLE 2.4 Epochs of organizational rationality (*source*: Carter, P and Jackson, N (1993) Modernism, postmodernism and motivation, or why expectancy theory failed to come up to expectation. In Hassard, J and Parker, M (eds) *Postmodernism and Organizations*, Sage, London)

The trend evident in the epochs identified in Table 2.4 is in essence one of an increasing reluctance to accept the given and assumed natural order of things, towards one of uncertainty and an acceptance of a rule of thumb rather than formula management.

It is important to recognize that these epochs or trends are intended to represent indications of how organizations function and how researchers theorize about them. Research as well as organization is an integral part of the broader social milieu and is as much influenced by, as influencing within it. *Postmodernism*, therefore, is meaningful in terms of its juxtaposition with *modernism* and it is useful to begin by attempting to provide an indication of the modernist view. Gergen (1992, p 211), identifies modernism as being characterized by:

✦ Reason and observation. The basis of understanding and survival emanate from an ability critically to observe, develop testable hypothesis and refine knowledge.

✦ Fundamentalism. That there are underlying principles and rules governing the universe and everything in it.

✦ Universal design. That there is a growing ability to master the universe through the identification of fundamental principles. Through this improved control will emerge better organizations, societies and standards of life.

✦ Machine metaphor. Take any machine and consider it as a system. It requires *inputs* of power and raw material, then *transforms* that input into some useful activity or product and spews out the end product (*output*) back into the environment. It also wastes some of the input during the process. Organizations can be described in similar terms, as can people. Therefore, if a machine system provides a useful model through which to represent other entities, this metaphor can be taken further and regarded as an essential building block of how things should be.

This rather simplistic view of the universe and how to discover it has been brought into question. For a number of writers the use of language to describe the observations from a modernist perspective became problematic. Even if the *things* being observed and described formed the basis of the essentials of the universe, the language used to articulate them did not. It is the actual pen that creates the writing not the term pen. The term pen conveys nothing about the nature of writing, communication or the intended purpose of the individuals involved. So if there is a distinction between *thing* and *symbol*, how accurate can the symbols be and how accurate can any inferences and conclusions be that are based upon them? Reality and the language used to construct it are, in effect, separate entities.

Hassard (1993) brings together the work of a number of writers in order to identify the distinguishing features of postmodernism as a basis for understanding organizations. They are:

✦ Representation. Rather than reflecting facts though language and forming ever clearer understandings, research is suggested to represent several different agendas. For example, it reflects the pre-existing knowledge base used to create understanding and it represents the professional standing of the people involved. Language reflects social, political, personal, access/exclusion and control purposes as well as descriptive needs.

✦ Reflexivity. The requirement to reflect on the assumptions made as part of the creation of knowledge. If language is not the slave of facts then its use must be questioned on every occasion.

◆ Writing. It could be assumed that the use of language was to be considered 'as a sign system for concepts which exist in the object world' (p 13). This is not so: postmodernism would see writing as a means by which the symbols of language can be separated from the objects themselves yet remaining linked through the spatial and temporal reality of experience for individual people.

◆ Difference. This concept is related to the need to both separate and join. In postmodernism it is necessary to *deconstruct* knowledge. In the foregoing discussion it is apparent that knowledge is *constructed* from the social context and by the language used. In attempting to create *real* understanding it is first necessary to *deconstruct* these issues.

◆ De-centring the subject. Most of the knowledge created takes as its basis and perspective the individual. It is the human perspective and interpretation that contain the significant focal direction. That should not be the case, according to postmodernism. Lying on the floor and looking at the world from a child's height would give some impression of a different world from that of the adult, for example.

Using this thesis, *postmodernism* sets about questioning the place of reason and 'methodological unity' (Hassard, 1993, p 1). From its origins as a perspective on culture and art this perspective has been used in an attempt to provide meaningful interpretation on organizations as they exist in real time and space. Postmodernism would suggest that it is only by facing up to the paradoxes that exist that the otherwise hidden assumptions begin to emerge.

However, not everyone would support the basic approach suggested by postmodern thinking. It may be interesting to question rationality and to engage in deconstruction, but some experiences are very real, no matter how they are described. For example, as Tsoukas (1992) argues:

> It is because actions are not taken and voices not uttered in a vacuum that not all accounts are equally valid. No matter how much I shout at my bank manager he is not likely to lend me money if I am unemployed. This is not a figment of my imagination. Others also tell me they have had similar experience. (p 644)

The point being that this experience is common to many people and that as part of organizational activity and the human experience it cannot be explained away as simply a figment of imagination or language symbolism.

Management theory: an applied perspective

The issues of a historical perspective is frequently regarded as irrelevant by many managers and, indeed, academics. The world is vastly different from what it was only a few short years ago and therefore the experiences of bygone years (history) has little to offer, it is argued. For example, the application of technology in organizations has changed the nature of work out of all recognition, just as it has introduced new products and services. The social conditions are also different today and this influences people's expectations of the role of work in their lives and the ways in which individuals relate to work and its requirements.

There is a marked tendency in organizations and academic life to consider the recent past only when looking forward. In the rush towards the future and progress the past gets left behind at an increasingly rapid rate. To this is added the marketing pressures that every human being is constantly subjected to, which attempt to persuade consumers that what is new is better, improved and superior to that which existed only yesterday. Just how many times can a washing powder become 'new and improved' and be able to get clothes 'whiter, brighter and with an even fresher smell'? This question is never asked – at least in polite circles! This dash towards the new and an ever more consumer-oriented society leads some individuals to decry anything older than yesterday as past its ability to function effectively, old fashioned, out of date and no longer relevant.

To this general social milieu add the organizational changes over recent years that have resulted in *delayering, downsizing, rightsizing, re-engineering* or any one of the other names for driving up productivity, reducing cost and cutting jobs. Among the consequences of this has been the dramatic reduction in the number of older employees and managers within organizations and the rapid rise of younger executives with less experience, but with a high drive to succeed. The stage is thereby set within organizations for young senior executives to decry the claims of older, more experienced managers that history might repeat itself and to consider past experience as important in the drive towards a 'brighter' or at least new future.

Within academic business circles there is pressure for improved productivity and part of this impacts on research output. Gone are the days when an individual could report something because it was interesting and they felt that they wished to share their knowledge with others. The situation today is that university staff are expected to have something to say and are required to make that available for public consumption. Research ratings, career progression and reputation depend to a significant extent on the volume of output.

Attempts are made to measure the quality of output from university research material, the funding councils require it. However, the system tends to influence individuals into recycling ideas rather than creating new ones. Another successful career plan is to latch onto the latest fad in management and to become among the first into print in that area. The socialization of new academic staff into the ways of career implied by the description just given is briefly described by Jacques (1996, p xi). Other forms of constraint in the academic process are evident in the Gillespie (1991) text included in the Further reading section in this chapter. Research and the creation of knowledge are not always a neutral process intended simply to develop new knowledge.

Against this background it is hardly surprising that in both business-related, academic and organizational circles there is a tendency to look forwards rather than backwards. Even when looking backwards it tends to be a relatively recent glance. In most contexts, the interest in the study of management and business begins around 1900 with FW Taylor. Prior to that time organizations and management are commonly thought to have nothing of relevance worth noting or if it had it was only of limited value.

There is also a great temptation to regard life today as more complex and difficult than anything that has gone before. In many ways that is true. Consider the instability of the financial markets and the ease with which a problem in one country can influence interest rates and economic factors in another. This undoubtedly creates more opportunities for complex interaction than existed before the application of communication and computer technology created the current situation. However, that simple analysis does not take into account the risk associated with the days before such technology was available. Consider the merchants in Venice seeking trading opportunities with China after the return of

Marco Polo in 1295. They would fund and organize the purchase of goods and their transportation over vast distances. Once it had set off on its journey the goods would be largely out of contact and control until the agent returned with more goods for sale, perhaps several months or even years later.

It might be argued that even with the high levels of uncertainty that existed in history things were easy when compared with the problems of today. But that tends to assume current knowledge and resource availability. The world appears to be a much smaller place and global communications much easier than in years gone by. The problems faced by the merchants in Venice were very difficult and taxing to them with their knowledge and experience base at that time, just as is the case today with the benefits of what we know and take for granted in dealing with business issues. In other words, life never gets any easier it is just that the problems and solutions change as do the tools, technology and circumstances prevailing at the time. A problem is still a problem if it cannot be solved. It would have been just as complex and risky for Marco Polo to prepare and undertake a journey in his day as it would be to arrange for a satellite to be built and launched today. Totally different, but equally difficult problems.

The purpose of this chapter is to place modern management and organizational activity into an evolutionary context. Many of the ideas, techniques, problems and practices that are taken for granted in today's world have a much longer history than might at first be thought. There are several implications that emerge from this. First, it demonstrates a continuity across time in the ways in which organizations have been managed and the difficulties faced by those organizing them. Second, it demonstrates that we have not progressed as far as we might like to think we have. The circumstances might have changed but the underlying issues relating to the management of people and organizing of business are remarkably stable. Third, it implies that it *should* be possible to learn from history and that we should not be surprised when, for example neither centralization nor decentralization offers by itself a perfect mechanism for the design of the organization. The Egyptians discovered that some 1600 years BCE! Fourth, it demonstrates that even though research into management has existed for less than 100 years it has come a long way in teasing out some of the issues for discussion and begun to develop theory, albeit tentatively on what management is and how it functions within the complex social structure known as an organization.

The job of managing an organization now is probably just as difficult as it was in the times of the ancient Egyptians or Chinese. Imagine the enormity of the task of being told that you were to be in charge of building a pyramid or the Great Wall of China. The sheer complexity involved as well as the scale of the operation must have given the managers responsible many sleepless nights. With no computers available and with only a limited range of tools, techniques and specialists to assist in the process these feats of construction represent a marvel of management as well as one of construction. Similar perhaps to the difficulty of running a financial organization today when interest rates around the world are constantly changing and individuals, companies and governments can move vast sums of money instantaneously by electronic means. A real nightmare, 24 hours each day, 365 days each year.

The purpose of taking a historical perspective on management is to demonstrate that there are few new or truly novel ideas around today. Armed with some insight of that perspective, modern managers are in a much stronger position to judge and evaluate the many fads and fashions that emerge every year. Just as the Egyptians found some 1600 years BCE there are no perfect answers to running and managing organizations (or empires). The formula approach does not provide long-term solutions to problems. Organizations are dynamic social structures, full of dynamic individuals who behave in ways that are not always predictable or understandable. Customers and other stakeholder groups are fickle and unpredictable, too, as is the general environment around each organization. There is little choice other than to be ready, willing and able to manage accordingly, adopting a flexible and creative approach to the problems and situations encountered. That much can be deduced from adopting a historical perspective.

Conclusions

This chapter has considered in some detail the historical origins of management. It briefly reviewed some of the major themes emerging over many thousands of years, attempting to demonstrate that management has a much longer tradition than is frequently implied. It was also the intention of this chapter to introduce the notion that many so called modern management ideas and problems can be traced back into history.

This chapter also attempted to introduce some of the general themes that will be considered in much greater detail later in this book and which form much of the substance of the organizational behaviour approach to the study of management and organizations. A historical perspective to the subject matter places the reader in a stronger position to evaluate more critically and effectively much more recent material and perspectives.

Discussion questions

1. Define the following key terms used in this chapter:

Craft guilds	*Arsenal of Venice*	*Industrial Revolution*
Merchant guilds	*Protestant work ethic*	*Open system*
Domestic producers	*Luddite*	*Administrative management*
Feudalism	*Scientific management*	*Putting-out system*
Systems theory	*Human relations*	*Quantitative school*
Modernism	*Postmodernism*	*Reflexivity*

2. To what extent would an improved historical perspective on the researching and teaching of management and organizational subjects improve the performance of practising managers?

3. 'The only thing that people learn from history is that people learn nothing from history.' To what extent does this explain why some of the issues identified from history are still relevant today?

4. If research is a social process fixed in time and space by the prevailing accepted beliefs and norms, can history ever be effectively understood and incorporated into a theoretical framework for management and organizations?

5. How can the knowledge that the ancient Egyptians found that neither centralization or decentralization on its own allowed them to effectively manage the empire help evaluate organization design today?

6. Is the functional approach to managing, teaching and research in the organizational field a practical and effective option for dealing with the real world? Justify your answer.

7. To what extent does the postmodern perspective demonstrate that the idea of progress in society and life in general is an illusion?

8. To what extent is there a trend apparent in the unfolding of an understanding about management from that based on scientific management, followed by an emphasis on administrative (process) issues to the systems perspectives that attempt to incorporate a broader range of perspectives?

9. 'Death is the price that the human species pays for progress.' Reconcile this statement with the view that many organizational and management problems have existed for many thousands of years.

10. Given that our understanding of historical events comes from a modern interpretation of circumstances which we can never experience, to what extent can the interpretation of history ever become objective?

Research activities

1. From the library collect examples of history books and books from the archaeological field. Look for material on trade, social life, government, military and organizational activity. To what extent does your research confirm the general view in this chapter that much management thinking appeared at a very much earlier date than otherwise thought? If your research does not lead to that conclusion, why not?

2. Seek to speak to a number of practising managers and identify the extent to which they have a knowledge or understanding of the historical perspective on management. In your interviews with them consider whether they feel that they might benefit from a better understanding of the history of management thinking. If so, in what ways and, if not, why?

3. Prepare a time capsule about management theory and practice today. It should seek to inform future generations about what you know about management and what you have learned about its history. It would be intended to be locked away for some hundreds of years and to give those who find it a clear picture about management today and in the past. What might you seek to put into such a time capsule and why? Compare your answers with those of other groups of students.

Key reading

From Clark, H, Chandler, J and Barry, J (1994) *Organization and Identities: Text and Readings in Organizational Behaviour*, International Thomson Business Press, London:
   ✦ Kumar, K: Specialization and the division of labour, p 13. An introduction to the evolution

of organizations and society. The context in which management emerged as a significant activity.

◆ Kumar, K: Secularization, rationalization, bureaucratization, p 17. Introduces the perspectives adopted by Weber in the creation of the bureaucratic notion of organizing.

◆ Friedman, AL: Marx's framework, p 25. This extract introduces the ideas on social organization, capitalism and exploitation developed by Marx. The role of management is critical in the achievement of capitalist objectives in this model.

◆ Coyle, K: Postmodernism, p 58. Considers the essence of postmodernism in the context of a critique of post-Fordism.

◆ Whyte, WH: The organization man, p 149. Considers how organizations seek and mould 'appropriate' people to work in the organization.

◆ MacKenzie, G: Class, p 189. Introduces the nature of class as an evolving social structure in order to meet the needs of manufacturing industry as it developed.

◆ Nichols, T and Beynon, H: The labour of superintendence: managers, p 192. Introduces material that reflects worker views of managers and the nature of management activity itself.

◆ Perkin, H: The rise of professional society: England since 1880, p 204. Considers the impact of the increase in 'professionalisation' over the past 100 years.

◆ Illich, I: Disabling professions, p 207. This extract introduces some idea of the power that the creation of professional status gives to those individuals that hold it. As such it can provide an insight into the negative power that can be exercised by professional groups.

Further reading

Chen, M (1995) *Asian Management Systems*, Routledge, London. This text considers the similarities and distinguishing features between the approaches to management in Chinese, Japanese and Korean businesses. As such it provides a balancing perspective with the western-based views adopted by most textbooks.

Gillespie, R (1991) *Manufacturing Knowledge: A History of the Hawthorne Experiments*, Cambridge University Press, Cambridge. The Hawthorne Studies represent the most famous and often quoted large-scale research carried out this century. It began the human relations movement and spawned many later initiatives into worker motivation and group working. It therefore represents an important piece of management history. This book looks behind the scenes at the research process and critically examines it, bringing out a number of political and ideological features that shaped the conduct and interpretation of the research. It is therefore about the process of creating knowledge in the real world by real people.

Jones, G (1996) *The Evolution of International Business: An Introduction*, Routledge, London. Management is increasingly carried out in an international context. This text introduces readers to the study of how organizations have evolved internationally since the nineteenth century. As such it provides a background to the context within which management is carried out on an international scale.

Stewart, R and Barsoux, J-L (1994) *The Diversity of Management: Twelve Managers Talking*, Macmillan, Basingstoke. This book offers an interview-based perspective on what being a manager involves. As such it provides a perspective to be compared with the insights gained from theory development and other research approaches.

Watson, TJ (1994) *In Search of Management: Culture, Chaos and Control in Managerial Work*, Routledge, London. This book draws on participative research techniques to identify the reality of management in one organization. It reflects in depth how managers attempt to control their own lives while at the same time shape the direction of organizational activity.

Wilson, JF (1995) *British Business History, 1720–1994*. Manchester University Press, Manchester. This text concentrates on the history of British manufacturing industry over the past three centuries.

In this analysis the author argues that organizational culture is the most important component in business organization and management practice during that period.

References

Babbage, C (1832) *On the Economy of Machinery and Manufactures*, Charles Knight, London.

Carter, P and Jackson, N (1993) Modernism, Postmodernism and Motivation, or Why Expectation Theory Failed to Come up to Expectation. In Hassard, J and Parker, M (eds), *Postmodernism and Organizations*, Sage, London.

Clavell, J (1983) *Sun Tzu: The Art of War*, Delacorte Press, New York.

Collons, RD (1971) Factory production – 1 AD *Academy of Management Journal*, **14**, 2, pp 270–273.

Contenau, G (1954) *Everyday Life in Babylon and Assyria*, Edward Arnold, London.

Currie, RM (1963) *Work Study*, 2nd edn, Sir Isaac Pitman, London.

De Grazia, S (1989) *Machiavelli in Hell*, Princeton University Press, Princeton.

George, CS (1971) *The History of Management Thought*, 2nd edn, Prentice Hall, Englewood Cliffs.

Gergen, KJ (1992) Organization Theory in the Postmodern Era. In Reed, M and Hughes, M (eds), *Rethinking Organization: New Directions in Organization Theory and Analysis,* Sage, London.

Gillespie, R (1991) *Manufacturing Knowledge: A History of the Hawthorne Experiments*, Cambridge University Press, Cambridge.

Griffith, SB (1971) *Sun Tzu: The Art of War*, Oxford University Press, New York.

Hassard, J (1993) Postmodernism and Organizational Analysis: An Overview. In Hassard, J and Parker, M (eds), *Postmodernism and Organizations*, Sage, London.

Huczynski, AA and Buchanan, DA (1991) *Organizational Behaviour: An Introductory Text*, 2nd edn, Prentice Hall, Hemel Hempstead.

Jacques, R (1996) *Manufacturing the Employee: Management Knowledge from the 19th to 21st Centuries*, Sage, London.

Jay, A (1967) *Management and Machiavelli*, Holt, Rinehart & Winston, New York.

Jevons, WS (1888) *The Theory of Political Economy*, Macmillan, New York.

Lane, FC (1934) *Venetian Ships and Shipbuilders of the Renaissance*, Johns Hopkins Press, Baltimore.

Lane, FC (1944) *Andrea Barbarigo: Merchant of Venice (1418–1449)*, Johns Hopkins Press, Baltimore.

Marcuse, H (1964) *One Dimensional Man*, Routledge & Kegan Paul, London.

Nolan, P (1999) Prior engagement, *People Management*, 16 December, 29–33.

Reed, MI (1989) *The Sociology of Management*, Harvester Wheatsheaf, Hemel Hempstead.

Sawyer, RD (1993) *The Seven Military Classics of Ancient China*, Westview Press, Boulder, CO.

Tawney, RH (1926) *Religion and the Rise of Capitalism*, John Murray, London.

Thompson, P and McHugh, D (1995) *Work Organizations: A Critical Introduction*, 2nd edn, Macmillan, Basingstoke.

Townley, B (1994) *Reframing Human Resource Management: Power, Ethics and the Subject at Work*, Sage, London.

Trist, EL and Bamforth, KW (1951) Some social and psychological consequences of the longwall method of coal getting, *Human Relations*, vol. 4, p 3–38.

Tsoukas, H (1992) Postmodernism, reflexive rationalism and organization studies: a reply to Martin Parker, *Organization Studies*, **13**, 643–49.

Watson, T (1994) Towards a Managerially Relevant but Non-managerialist Organization Theory. In Hassard, J and Parker, M (eds). *Towards a New Theory of Organizations*, Routledge, London.

Weber, M (1905) *The Protestant Ethic and the Spirit of Capitalism*, trans by T. Parsons, (1958) Charles Scribner's Sons, New York.

Wee, Chow Hou (1991) *Sun Tzu: War and Management*, Addison-Wesley, New York.

Wilkinson, Sir G (1842) *Manners and Customs of Ancient Egyptians*, 2nd edn, John Murray, London.

Wren, DA (1994) *The Evolution of Management Thought*, 4th edn, Wiley, New York.

PART II

Individuals within organizations

CHAPTER 3

Perception and attitude formation

CHAPTER SUMMARY

This chapter considers the concepts of perception and attitude. It begins by describing the general significance of perception, then moves to an in-depth review of the process together with each of the stages. This is followed by the introduction of the concept of attitude as a major determinant of behaviour also during the process, demonstrating the links with perception. An introduction to the topic of impression management follows this as an aspect of perception and attitude formation at an interpersonal level. This is followed with a discussion of the organizational implications of human perception and attitudes. The chapter concludes with a review of the applied and practical perspectives on perception and attitude formation.

LEARNING OBJECTIVES

After studying this chapter and working through the associated Management in Action panels, Discussion and Research questions, you should be able to:

✦ Describe the processes of perception and attitude formation.

✦ Detail the perceptual framework model.

✦ Explain the links between perception, attitude and subsequent behaviour in an organizational context.

✦ Understand what it is about perception and attitude formation that makes it difficult for managers to utilize them in managing people.

✦ Discuss the practical and ethical dilemmas facing managers in their attempts to shape perceptions and attitudes.

✦ Appreciate the links between perception, attitudes and other management activities.

✦ Outline the impression and image management concepts and their relationship with perception and attitude formation.

✦ Assess the significance of the behaviour of others being subject to interpretation through the perceptual filters within managers.

Introduction

Perception can be considered as a process of *simplification*. There are a vast range of stimuli impacting upon the human senses all the time, even when we sleep. Because of this volume and range it is not possible for anyone to pay attention to every stimulus and still be able to cope with the most simple of tasks. Imagine for example, trying to cross a busy street in the centre of a major city while listening intently to every sound, smelling every odour, feeling the clothes worn press onto the body and watching every other person etc. A sure scenario for an accident! In addition to this volume-based need for *simplification*, human beings need to be able to classify the sensations that are experienced in order to make them meaningful to us. The classification of a particular visual image as being a motor car is necessary to be able to identify the benefits and hazards associated with it.

Two concepts related to perception are those of attitude and impression management. Human beings have attitudes about all manner of things and these impact on behaviour in relation to the focal object. These attitudes are partly formed by the perceptual process which begins the focus of this chapter. Equally, the attitudes that a human being holds will influence the perceptions about the focal objects to some extent. This circular process between attitude and perception is evident in many aspects of human behaviour, not least discrimination between particular groups of people. Impression management reflects a deliberate attempt by one individual (or a group) to seek to convey particular perceptions to other people. For example, in a job interview the applicant would seek to convey a 'good' impression to the interviewer in order to improve their chances of being appointed. Good impression in that context refers to the desire to appear to be the type of person that the company is seeking. Children seek to give a particular impression to their friends by having the latest toy or clothes and so in marketing terms they 'pester' their parents to buy the desired articles. In essence, children seek to be perceived in a particular way by their friends thereby creating particular attitudes towards themselves and gaining higher status within the group.

The significance of perception

In acting out their lives every human must become aware of what is *out there*; the vast range of 'things' that are external to the person themselves. They must then be able to decide what is significant in any particular context and in what way 'it' is significant. This is necessary before the individual can then determine how to respond to the 'it' that has been perceived. This is the basis of the process referred to as *perception*. Most of the time people are not aware of the psychological process of perception. They simply become aware of the things going on around them that attract their attention. The process is generally *subconscious*. The following list contains some of the main human *senses* representing the detection systems for external stimuli to impact people and in which some form of perception occurs:

✦ Vision.
✦ Temperature.

+ Sound.
+ Taste.
+ Pain.
+ Touch.
+ Smell.

In addition there is an eighth sense: an ability to be aware of spatial relationships. For example, a blindfolded individual could probably find their way around a familiar room without too much difficulty. A *mental map* of the room exists in the person's head indicating where 'things' are normally to be found, thus providing an indication of the relative spatial relationships between the objects.

The significance of perception within organizations lies in the nature of it as the basis for action on the part of the people involved. For example, management may *perceive* the introduction of empowerment through a total quality management initiative as the delegation of decision making. The stated purpose being to engage employees in the operational activities of the organization to a much higher level than before and therefore to improve productivity and customer service. Employees, by the same token, may *perceive* the initiative as an attempt to reduce the total number of jobs and workers as well as providing a means to make remaining staff work harder. There is no certainty that any two people (or groups of people) will perceive the same stimulus in exactly the same way. The easiest illustration of this is to put half a litre of liquid in a one litre bottle and ask people what they see. There will be at least two different replies – a half-empty bottle, or a half-full bottle. There are also many other ways in which the raw stimulus could be perceived and described.

The perceptions that people hold are formed throughout life as a result of *experience* and *socialization*. Similar observations can be made in relation to the development of *attitudes*. Some attitudes are deeply held and as a consequence probably difficult to change. Other attitudes are perhaps less entrenched and liable to change in line with experience. For example, attitudes towards fashion are notoriously fickle and liable to change quickly. There are obvious and strong links between perception and the attitudes that people hold. Attitudes are formed on the basis of perceived information. Perceptions are interpreted in the light of experience and attitudes. Management in Action 3.1 provides examples of these links.

Stop | Consider *Is the situation described in MiA 3.1 inevitable as a result of the likely perception and attitudes of people in that situation?*

Could the problems have been anticipated and how might the situation have been dealt with in order to avoid some if not all of them?

A model of perception

Perception as a process can be described as a sequence of events from the receipt of a stimulus to the response to it (see Figure 3.1). The following sections of this chapter will consider each of the elements from the model in Figure 3.1 in greater detail.

There is a process of learning built into the model of perception to account for the

MANAGEMENT IN ACTION 3.1

Attitudes and perceptions in times of change

The organization in question was going through a significant period of change. As part of this, the personnel department was expected to manage many aspects of the process and a number of new appointments were made in order to strengthen the ability of the function to achieve these objectives. This involved the recruitment of a number of experienced personnel specialists from outside the industry, training and industrial relations being two examples of the additional expertise sought.

The process also involved the reallocation of a number of the existing personnel staff to new duties. One of the existing personnel staff perceived that the newly appointed specialists were a threat to their standing within the organization and began to engage in hostile behaviour towards them. The situation became extremely political and resulted in many additional problems for the organization until the personnel director was able to stabilize the situation.

Interpretation of this story from an attitudes and perception perspective suggests several things:

◆ The existing personnel specialist held a number of attitudes that led him to perceive the new people from outside as having skills that were more valued by the organization. This led him to interpret this as a threat to his future career and position within the organization. This resulted in attitudes and behaviour that were openly hostile to the people involved and anything suggested by them.

◆ The new personnel specialists had been brought in to supplement the existing resources of the organization. They arrived with a set of attitudes that implied that the organization was not unique in the process that it was going through and that adopting their previously learned skills  would enable it to achieve its objectives. Resistance from the established specialists was at first seen as a minor irritation and inevitable. However, the continued display of hostile behaviour led to a deterioration in the working relationship between the people involved. The new staff began to interpret this behaviour at a personal level and as a slight on their skills. Consequently, the negative attitudes of the existing specialists produced an increasingly negative response from the new staff.

◆ In effect a 'doom loop' of deteriorating attitudes, fuelled by perceptions of other people's behaviour, was happening. This led to appeals to higher authority to resolve the perceived problems (by removing the 'other' people). Several conflict-resolving sessions were held and one or two of the new specialists left of their own accord. Some three years later the situation is not completely resolved and a form of uneasy truce exists between the individuals concerned.

This case study illustrates many different aspects of human behaviour in a work context, not just perception and attitudes. It can be interpreted from the perspectives of management control, politics, group dynamics and the management of change, for example. It is introduced here in order to illustrate the circular relationship between attitudes and perceptions.

feedback present in many experiences. For example, human beings quickly learn to identify which sounds are the most significant in any particular context. Traffic sounds have a particular importance when attempting to cross the road and are therefore attended to, yet may be totally ignored when sitting at home.

Humans are constantly bombarded with stimuli from a variety of sources. It is a necessary part of survival that humans are able to differentiate between trivial and important events. Imagine attempting to cross a busy street while concentrating only on the insects that crawl on the surface of the road!

It is often assumed that as individuals we all perceive the *reality* of the world around us in the same way. However, a glance at a range of newspapers covering political stories or industrial relations should provide adequate support for the view that there are always at least two points of view in any situation. This reflects something that has been acknowledged by psychologists for some considerable time. Look at Figure 3.2. What do you see? Now ask one or two of your friends.

Do you see a young woman or an old woman in the picture? Does everyone you ask see the same? It is the individual who interprets the *raw material* serving as the visual

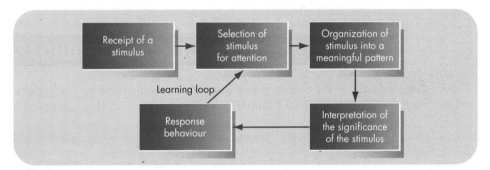

FIGURE 3.1   The perceptual process.

FIGURE 3.2   Ambiguous figure (originally published by Hill, WE (1915) *Punch*, 6 November).

stimulus, in the light of a range of internal and external influences. There has been some suggestion that younger people tend to see the young woman, whereas older people tend to see the old woman. Whatever the case, there are two possible interpretations of the same stimulus and it is not possible to state with absolute certainty that one perception is right and the other wrong. It has already been suggested in this chapter that individual experience and socialization are likely to impact on how stimuli are interpreted by individuals. Given that perception represents a simplifying process intended to allow (among other things) individuals to screen out insignificant issues, previous experience in defining what is significant for the individual plays an important role. As the life experience for every individual is different in some way or other, it is hardly surprising that perceptions of stimuli would also differ. Parents, friends, location, relative wealth are just some of the factors that might be expected to play a part in developing the experience and socialization of individuals and hence their perceptions.

It is easier to illustrate the many aspects of the perceptual process using visual examples. Readers should understand, however, that similar perceptual processes are at work in all the human senses.

Receipt of a stimulus

Each of the human senses has its own mechanisms for the registration of stimuli. For example, Figure 3.3 illustrates an experiment in which a pair of coiled but separate tubes

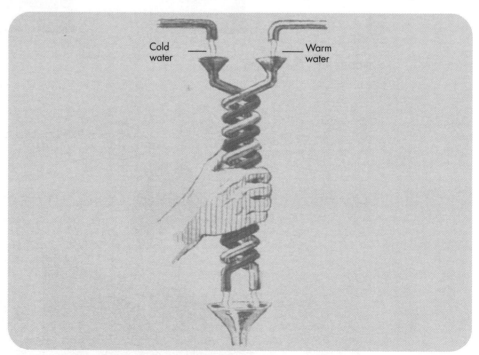

FIGURE 3.3 Perception of 'hot' as a result of the simultaneous stimulation of warm and cold receptors (*source*: Hilgard, ER, Atkinson, RC and Atkinson, RL (1971) *Introduction to Psychology*, 5th edn, Harcourt Brace Jovanovich, New York).

have cold water passed through one and warm water passed through the other. If the temperature of the cold water is between 0–5° Centigrade and the warm between 40–44° Centigrade a subject taking hold of the coil will experience a hot, burning sensation. It is thought that the perception of this sensation occurs as the result of the simultaneous stimulation of warm and cold sensation receptors in the skin. This example illustrates a feature common to all sensory receptors: that raw data, or energy from the environment, impact on one or more of our senses and stimulate a physical reaction within that particular location.

That the perceptions from our senses can play tricks on us has already been established in the experiment illustrated in Figure 3.3. This is more apparent in the world of visual illusion. Indeed, magicians rely on just this phenomenon to amaze audiences during stage and television performances. Another aspect of this is demonstrated in the impossible figure, which at one and the same time exists and yet cannot exist. Figure 3.4 is an example.

In this particular case, the difficulty lies with the ability of the eye to *see* two dimensions from the image presented and the *perceptual system's* ability to construct three dimensions from that data. Most of the time the perceptual processes work consistently in creating meaning for the individual, but in this particular example the two systems provide contradictory messages and *reality* breaks down. That is what the stage magician depends upon in creating the illusion sought. In human terms, when such contradictions arise they force a slowing down in the ability to process information, while clarification is sought and the ambiguity resolved. While this might be acceptable in watching a stage performance it could be dangerous if, say, the pilot of a passenger aircraft has to take valuable time to resolve conflicting images presented to them at a critical moment during a flight.

Selection of stimuli for attention

The selection of which of the many simultaneous stimuli impacting on the senses to pay attention to allows the individual to identify the most significant events: those that need to be attended to or those that are of most interest. This is a decision-making process. A function of three main elements: the circumstances, internal and external factors.

The circumstances

Circumstances can have a direct impact on the selection of the stimuli to which attention

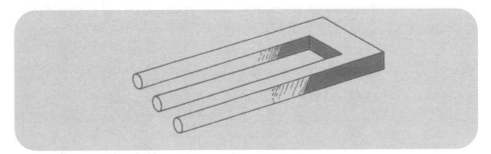

FIGURE 3.4   An impossible figure (*source*: Hilgard, ER, Atkinson, RC and Atkinson, RL (1971) *Introduction to Psychology*, 5th edn, Harcourt Brace Jovanovich, New York).

will be directed. Senior managers of a company experiencing financial difficulties could be expected to pay more attention to the justification for every item of expenditure than when a healthy profit was being made.

Within the same organizational context different perceptual principles can operate. People in expensive business suits walking around a factory floor can create a wide variety of rumours because they stand out as different from the normal person in that context. By comparison in a head office environment it would be people walking about in boiler suits who would attract attention because they would be different from most others in that context.

An individual trapped on a small island in the middle of a rapidly rising river would be paying close attention to the behaviour of any nearby people on the bank of the river. The trapped individual would be concentrating on the opportunity and likelihood of rescue and would be seeking to determine that their own shouts for help had been heard and that a rescue was being attempted. They would not particularly be paying attention to any birds that happened to be singing in a nearby tree or fish swimming in the river.

Factors external to the individual

There are a number of factors external to the individual that can impact on the selection of a stimulus for attention. The circumstances just discussed are an obvious example of things that are external to the individual. However, there are also features associated with the stimuli themselves that influence the process. Certain features of a particular stimulus might make it more likely to stand out from those around it and therefore attract attention, including:

✦ Repetition. The more often something is repeated the more likely it is that the message gets through to the level of consciousness. Advertising often applies this principle to increase the awareness of a particular product or brand name. However, repetition can lead to the senses turning off from the awareness of the presence of a stimulus. This is called *habituation*. This can create hazards in a working environment if individuals frequently ignore warning signs that are always present for example. Regular drivers frequently become lazy in their driving habits because of the relative infrequency of accidents involving them. Driving is perceived as a safe activity during which chances can be taken.

✦ Size. It is perhaps obvious, but the larger a particular stimulus is, the more likely it is that it will attract attention.

✦ Contrast. The relative features of the foreground compared with the background can influence a perception. For example, consider Figure 3.5.

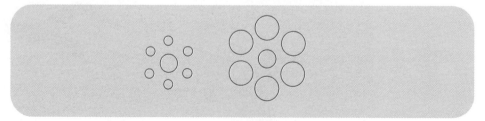

FIGURE 3.5   Contrast effect on perception (*source*: Hilgard, ER, Atkinson, RC and Atkinson, RL (1971) *Introduction to Psychology*, 5th edn, Harcourt Brace Jovanovich, New York).

Do you see:

A. Two figures, one a large circle surrounded by small ones, and a small circle surrounded by large ones

B. Two figures, each with a same size of circle in the centre but surrounded by different sizes of circle?

Option B is a more accurate reflection of the two diagrams. However, many people report that option A is correct! The relationship between foreground and background circle sizes influences the perception of the figures.

+ Novelty. The presence of the unusual (in a particular context) tends to attract attention. This aspect of perception is also used by marketing specialists in designing advertising campaigns.

+ Intensity. The brighter or louder a particular stimulus the more likely it is to attract attention.

+ Motion. Something which moves is more likely to attract attention than something which is stationary. Predatory animals use this feature in being able to move very slowly to get close when hunting their prey.

+ Familiarity. For example, humans find it very easy to spot a familiar face among a crowd of strangers.

Factors internal to the individual

There are a range of factors internal to the individual that influence which stimuli are likely to be attended to (see Figure 3.6).

Taking each factor in turn:

+ Personality. The personality characteristics of individuals influence the way that they predispose themselves to seek information from the environment (Witkin *et al.*, 1954).

+ Learning and past experience. Young children and animals become aware of relevant stimuli very early on. Figure 3.7 shows the hesitation of a toddler faced with a visual cliff. The same pattern is used for the 'ground' on both sides of the central island. Both sides are covered with thick glass, however, the 'cliff' side is much lower. Although it would be perfectly safe for the infant to crawl out over the 'cliff' it is reluctant to do so, yet it will crawl happily onto the 'shallow' side. This suggests that depth perception develops very quickly after the infant begins to move around (Gibson and Walk, 1960).

In an organizational context Oliver and Wilkinson (1992) provide a detailed

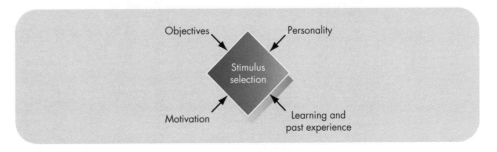

FIGURE 3.6   Internal factors influencing stimulus selection.

review of Japanese management practices, including the emphasis on *socialization* and *training*. Through these processes employees are *tuned into* the issues that management consider important. Their perceptions and attitudes are effectively being shaped by management. Of course, there is a debate about the extent to which employee perceptions and attitudes are actually being shaped by these processes or whether they are superficially complying with the requirements of the job.

✦ Motivation. Both the physical and social needs that are influential for an individual at any point in time will affect the environmental stimuli to which attention will be given. For example, an employee paid a bonus based on the number of units of output is likely to change their perception of, and attitude to, work in seeking out ways of increasing production.

✦ Objectives. People seek out those things and situations which are of value to them. Individuals have goals, intelligence and ability which they utilize to advantage in interacting with their environment. Consequently, stimuli which offer a synergy, or which may be otherwise relevant within that framework will be scanned for relevance before being rejected or processed further. For example, an individual with shares in a particular company may well scan the newspapers for any snippet of information which might suggest a potential change in the share price.

Organizing stimuli into meaningful patterns

Infants are born with no direct experience of the world. Their experience is based on the genetic material which they inherit from their parents and their experience while in the womb. The process of grouping the stimuli from the environment into meaningful patterns is one that develops in the child through early experience. The most important aspects of this process appear to be:

✦ The figure – ground principle. This principle is all about the process of perceiving a stimulus in a background context. Figure 3.8 illustrates the principle. Do you see a

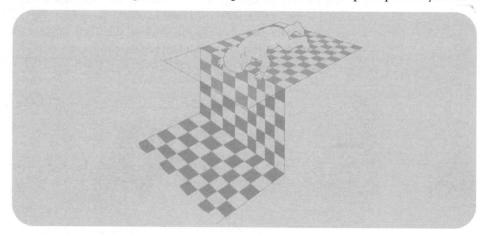

FIGURE 3.7 The visual cliff.

chalice or two faces in profile? Whichever you perceive depends upon what you identify as background and what as foreground. This particular example also illustrates another facet of perception, that of cultural influences. The use of a chalice in Figure 3.8 is only meaningful in those cultural contexts where such drinking vessels are known. In other situations, the drawing might have to be changed to that more resembling a vase to have any significance. In other cultural situations the illusion might not work at all.

✦ The principle of continuity. This relates to the tendency to detect continuous patterns in groups of individual stimuli. However, a row of numbers may be just that, they may not be related in a meaningful way. The daily sales returns from each of the outlets of a national retail company may not be related in any way, yet management frequently attempt to *identify patterns* from such data.

✦ The principle of proximity. Proximity refers to the perceptual process of creating association simply on the basis of nearness. For example, Figure 3.9 indicates how lines could be assumed to be associated, yet with a little more information a different relationship is suggested.

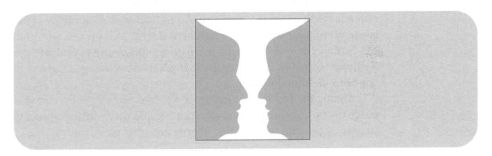

FIGURE 3.8 Reversible figures.

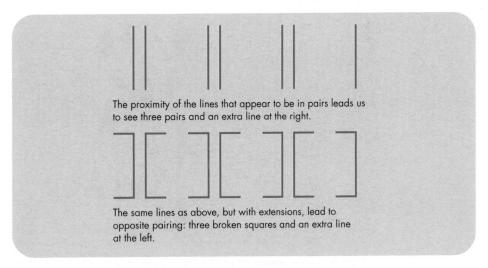

The proximity of the lines that appear to be in pairs leads us to see three pairs and an extra line at the right.

The same lines as above, but with extensions, lead to opposite pairing: three broken squares and an extra line at the left.

FIGURE 3.9 The principle of proximity (*source*: Hilgard, ER, Atkinson, RC and Atkinson, RL (1971) *Introduction to Psychology*, 5th edn, Harcourt Brace Jovanovich, New York).

◆ The principle of closure. The principle of closure is all about making a whole out of the parts available. Figure 3.10 is a series of dark shapes, what does it suggest to you?

Perhaps it appears to you to represent a dog? If it does, then it is doing so not because of the actual drawing, but because your perceptual system is seeking to draw together the available information and enclose it into a known and familiar image.

◆ The principle of similarity. This concept relates to the grouping together of stimuli on the basis of similar characteristics. For example, all workers are lazy might be the view of a particular manager. Consequently, such a manager seeing a worker standing around and not working might not recognize that the individual could be waiting for a machine to be repaired and therefore is not able to work.

Interpreting the significance of a stimulus

The significance of a particular stimulus will be judged against a range of criteria. For example, it will depend upon the physical and mental state of the individual at the time and also as a result of prior experience. An individual feeling thirsty is likely to become more aware of stimuli that have a refreshment theme. This process within the perceptual model can be thought of as a *filtering* mechanism attempting to evaluate the significance of any particular stimulus. It is a process that is subjective and *goes beyond* the information contained in the stimulus itself.

Among the factors that influence the interpretation of a stimulus are the use of language in creating contextual understanding and therefore perceptual shaping. It is to a discussion of this and some of the other factors that we now turn.

FIGURE 3.10   The closure principle (*source*: Coon, D (copyright © 1985, 1991) West Publishing Company. By permission of Brooks/Cole Publishing Company, Pacific Grove, CA, a division of Thomson Publishing Inc.).

Language and perception shaping

The interpretation of a particular stimulus is dependent on many factors including prior understanding. This is sometimes also referred to as the individual's *frame of reference*. There are many possible illustrations that can be used to demonstrate the need for a high degree of contextual understanding before meaning can be understood. For example, if you watch television or a movie in a language that you do not understand it is very difficult to follow the story. Your attempts to interpret what you see and hear can only be based on what you already know. Tone of voice, the behaviours of the actors and the background scenes are all that you have to base a judgement on. Under these circumstances it is difficult to be sure of the story as the information available to you is only partial. Your frame of reference does not exactly match that of the stimuli presented.

Equally, imagine a situation in which an individual were able to travel back or forwards in time. The sites and scenes experienced would be truly shocking as the individual would not have the prior knowledge on which to function effectively in what would be an alien context. The reaction to and implications arising from a person living some 2000 years ago seeing an aeroplane for the first time can barely be imagined. Their perceptual framework would be based on completely different understandings. Part of the creation of understanding in any context in the modern world is based on the use of language.

Language is a form of communication and creates meaning for the users through the signals and information that it contains. However, language contains many levels of communication within it, it is not just the words and their associated meaning. There is the associated tone of voice and body language signals which accompany the spoken words. Equally in the written form of language a skilled writer can create word pictures to convey additional meaning to the readers. The role of language in creating perceptions for people has long been recognized. For example, there is an interesting review of the work of Max Weber in relation to the discussion of the Protestant ethic in Ray and Reed (1994, pp 23–32), in which the use of language to create perceptions of heaven and hell within Protestantism and its role in relation to the development of capitalism is explored.

Lothian (1978) reviewed the use of language in relation to understanding the published accounts of companies. He concluded that the difficulty for private shareholders in understanding published accounts lay with the accountants who used complex professional language to explain non-complex ideas. He goes so far as to suggest that much of the accountancy profession's language was bogus and intended to impress the innocent and unwary, while drawing a boundary around the members of the profession. Another way in which perception and language are strongly linked is discussed in Whitmore (1994). In her review Whitmore discusses the ability of a university researcher to interact effectively with socially excluded groups. She was seeking to study groups of people in receipt of welfare payments and who were always worried about being reported to the authorities for some breach of the rules. She reports that:

> 'In spite of the fact that I was acutely aware of talking in 'academese' and tried not to use jargon or big words, my small words were often their big words. What I assumed was 'normal talk', they saw as 'professor words' … The way we organized our thinking, how we expressed ourselves, both cognitively and emotionally, were different. The verbal and non-verbal meanings were simply not understood in the same way. (p 95)

In this review Whitmore is describing how the perceptions of both groups (researcher

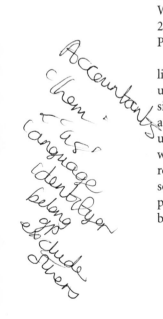
Accountants
them
use
language
identifier
belong
exclude
others

and subjects) were linked with the language used and the interpretation of the other group's actions and words as a way of creating and reinforcing meaning. Therefore, language created a perceived group differentiator, based on existing perceptual frameworks and experience. These guided the future actions of the group members towards perceived outsiders.

Perceptual errors

Perceptual errors reflect the mistakes that can occur during the process of making sense of perceptual information. They can be mistakes of judgement or in understanding. One form of perceptual error has already been introduced in the form of visual illusion. Figure 3.8 for example can be interpreted in two distinct ways and therefore the possibility of error in interpretation exists. Of course, the use of the term error in this context is interesting in that it depends on the intention of the provider of the stimulus, not the perceiver. So if the provider of the drawing in Figure 3.8 intended a chalice to be seen then the 'error' would arise if the perceiver saw two faces.

In an organizational context the fact that it is possible to experience errors in perception can be problematic from several perspectives. Perceptual error could be accidental. For example, management might keep repeating the mantra that the 'customer is king' in seeking to focus employee attention on providing the highest standards of customer service. However, employees might interpret the intention as being a clear signal that market forces dominate management thinking and therefore future employment is far from secure. Employee reaction to the management intentions might be negative, not what was intended at all.

However, perceptual error can be used with more sinister intent. In the situation just described management might actually be thinking in terms of market forces and cutting the workforce, but be seeking to achieve this by indirect means. In other words, they might be seeking to hide their real intentions behind a subterfuge, deliberately seeking to use the positive image of customer service to achieve particular employee perceptions of the situation and minimizing the dangers from the revealing of their true intention. Previous experience of the actions of managers by many employees leads them to the conclusion (perception) that future actions should be regarded as hostile towards the benefit of employees. Therefore this forms a significant part of the perceptual framework through which stimuli from that source will be judged.

There are a number of categories of perceptual error, some of which have already been introduced and others will be introduced later. Areas of perceptual error not already introduced include (the last two are discussed in greater detail later in this chapter):

+ Expectancy. The expectations that exist prior to an event can significantly influence behaviour relative to that event. Being told that a new boss is temperamental and a stickler for accuracy will lead to a different reaction and perception of their actions to being told that they are friendly with an informal style.
+ The halo effect.
+ Stereotyping.
+ Perceptual defence mechanisms.

Halo and horns effect

The *halo effect* is the bias introduced when attributing all the characteristics of a person (or object) from a single attribute. For example, a person who is a good timekeeper may be claimed to be a high-performing employee in all other respects. This has obvious dangers in forming judgements and actions in relation to other people. In seeking to reduce the number of employees, managers deciding who should stay on the basis of perceptions formed only from attendance records might result in a loss of more highly skilled and productive workers who have a less 'perfect' attendance record.

The opposite of the halo effect is sometimes referred to as the *horns effect*. This takes the view that everything about a person is bad simply on the basis of a single instance. It is equally biased in its view as that formed under the halo effect and can be just as damaging to individuals and organizations in practice.

Attribution and perception

Attribution theory attempts to provide a model that accounts for the way in which we make sense of other people's behaviour. Using the ideas in relation to perception it can be envisaged how we attribute various characteristics to other people. We also interpret their behaviour in comparison with others and in terms of past experience. This forms the basis of attribution theory. It is about the causes of behaviour in others, as perceived by ourselves. Management in Action 3.2 illustrates these experiences in a newly appointed first-line manager.

| Stop | Consider | *To what extent does the situation described in MiA 3.2 reflect perception in action or simply poor management? Justify your views.* |

What does this tale suggest in the context of attribution theory? It is clear that the new manager's manager adjusted his perception of the causes of staff behaviour in the department. This was the result (attribute) of their complaints over his head to the director. Kelley (1973) is credited with developing the theory of attribution. The central principle is that of *covariation*. A causal relationship is said to exist between two events if they occur together. If a particular outcome occurs only when a specific situation exists, then the situation is said to *covary* with the effect. For example, on a car assembly line good quality output is observed to occur when supervisors are walking the line; it is also noted that when they are absent from the line (say, at meetings) an increase in quality defects occurs. In this situation it would be natural to suggest (attribute) that close supervision is the cause of good quality output.

Kelley suggests that individuals attempt to identify covariance relationships through a number of devices. The criteria used include:

✦ Distinctiveness. If the particular event is not distinctive then it becomes pointless to imply a specific attribution as its cause. For example, a manager considered it her responsibility to improve the standard of English in reports produced by her staff. On one occasion a report was allowed to be issued without being vetted. That was distinctive behaviour in that context and therefore worthy of further consideration by staff as to the cause of the change.

MANAGEMENT IN ACTION 3.2

The new manager's tale

The manager had been in post for about three months at the time of the interview. He was in his early twenties and it was his first managerial appointment. He had been employed by the organization for about two years prior to the interview and had been working in an administrative capacity during that time. The individual had been promoted to the new position from within the team that he was to manage. The office was small with about six people working in it. The main activities within the office were the administration associated with sales planning and customer service on an international scale. As a result there was a considerable amount of information and paperwork flowing through the office at any one time. Customer records had to be kept up to date as had the information flow to other departments and sections within the organization. A considerable proportion of the time was spent in liaison with customers and dealing with their queries. This process was made more difficult because of the different time zones involved.

During the interview it became clear that the quality of administrative systems was not of the highest order, in terms of records, accuracy and information content. The department had grown very quickly and the previous manager had not been thorough in ensuring that the systems introduced were adequate. Also staff had been recruited without any previous experience in that type of work, neither had they been trained adequately in customer care and the work of the department. Consequently, a 'slack' attitude to work existed and the unit creaked along rather than playing its full part in progressing the aims of the company. As might be expected, a crisis occurred and senior management had been forced to take action by replacing the previous manager. The new manager was judged to be capable of making the changes necessary to the operational frameworks of the department. Unfortunately, he was resented by the other staff, who saw him as a threat to their old, easy-going ways.

The new manager suggested that his boss considered that senior management would not wish him to take a hard line with the staff in order to implement change, that things would eventually calm down and that the other staff were good at their job (if they were given good procedures to work within and so on). Consequently, pressure was put on the new manager to make the situation work. Unfortunately, the staff became more entrenched in their views and openly hostile towards him – at one point saying to his face that he was the problem in the office and that they hated him. Repeated requests to his boss for help produced little action. By this time the new manager was of the view that even if the other staff were capable of doing the work, they were not acceptable to him. This inevitably made the situation even worse.

The more senior manager would not take action against the other staff, neither would he take action against the new manager. After a couple of months the staff went over the head of the more senior manager to the director responsible and complained that the new manager was no good and that the more senior manager was showing favouritism by supporting the new manager. They claimed to have no confidence in either manager. When the more senior manager found out that the other staff had gone to his boss (the director) without telling him first he was furious. At that time his view of them changed and they suddenly became less than acceptable for the work within the department. What was previously the result of inadequate staff training and system design was now the fault of the staff themselves. He was attributing the behaviour of the staff to particular causes, they did not want to co-operate with management and were trying to hide incompetence. Previously, his view was that they felt threatened by the situation and needed help to provide the expected service.

+ Consensus. If the particular event produces the same effect on other people then a degree of consensus is said to exist. If a manager who is always rude and bad tempered is suddenly friendly, and if other people are also more friendly than usual, then there is consensus between reactions. This implies that something common to both reactions exists.

+ Consistency. The *sameness* of reaction and behaviour over time and situations. If a manager is always rude and bad tempered it would not seem to suggest anything unusual if they are abusive in a particular context. However, if the same manager were to praise, thank, or be pleasant on a particular occasion then it would become inconsistent behaviour and worthy of further consideration.

Arriving at the attributions for particular behaviours is an important process as the subsequent responses depend upon how individuals interpret the original causes. In the instance just described when the manager returned a report marked up for correction it did not cause offence or a problem. The reaction would be different where demands for reworked reports were the exception. Weiner (1975) developed a framework for determining a classification for different types of attribution and therefore appropriate response behaviours (see Figure 3.11).

The diagram is designed assuming that the purpose is to identify the attributions of, and provide a response to, a subordinate's performance. The diagram is built up from two axes, *location* and *stability*. Location can be determined from the perceived source of the behaviour:

+ Internal. Based on the attributes of the individual in terms of ability, motivation, skill and effort for example.

+ External. Based on the factors outside the individual, such as family circumstances, company policies and the attitudes of managers.

Stability is determined on the basis of the perceived degree of permanence of the attribute:

+ Permanent. This reflects an enduring feature, something that is ongoing and which will remain a force in the future.

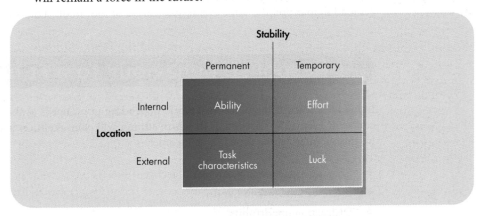

FIGURE 3.11   Attributions and response determinants (*source*: Weiner, W (1975) *Achievement, Motivation and Attribution Theory*, General Learning Press, Morristown, NJ).

✦ Temporary. A transient feature, something that is likely to change over time. An example would be someone who is late for work one morning as a result of their car breaking down.

Each of the four cells in the matrix has been given a title that represents the underlying characteristics of behaviour that fall into that area. Consequently, the response to the attributions implied by those concepts will also differ:

✦ Ability. This implies that there is an underlying problem with the person themselves and their ability to do what is expected of them. If a subordinate were to make a serious mistake in a situation that implied this cell of the matrix, then retraining might be appropriate.

✦ Effort. This implies that the subordinate is capable of doing what is expected of them, but did not apply themselves adequately to the job. Under these circumstances, a telling off or some other punishment might be considered.

✦ Task characteristics. This implies that the subordinate had little direct control over what happened, therefore putting it right would also be beyond their control. Consequently, an appropriate response might be to seek ways of improving their ability to deal with the situation in future.

✦ Luck. There are occasions when things do not go according to plan. The subordinate in question may have experienced difficulties in obtaining information from another department because they were busy or short staffed. Whatever the attribution, the appropriate approach will be to overcome the problem quickly. For the future, any lessons should be learned to try and prevent reoccurrence.

Attribution theory does not identify the actual cause of behaviour. What it does provide is the perceiver's view of the cause of the behaviour. This provides the essential foundation for what is called the fundamental attribution error (Harvey and Weary, 1984). This holds that there is a tendency to see others' behaviour as the result of stable, internal characteristics while one's own behaviour is a function of temporary, environmental forces. In a work context this implies that managers tend to see employees' behaviour as a reflection of the underlying characteristics of the person (good or bad). Contrariwise, employees tend to interpret the same events as a feature of the circumstances at the time.

Response behaviour to a stimulus

Individuals react to the perceptual world depending upon needs at the time. In the usual course of events the decision as to which stimuli will gain attention is dependent on the balance of forces at the time. These include:

✦ Pressure to achieve a particular objective.
✦ Interest in the task in hand.
✦ Distraction opportunity.
✦ Consequences of failure to achieve the end result.

✦ Physiological state.

The actual behavioural responses to a perceived stimulus can fall into one of two main categories. They are:

✦ Internal behaviour shapers. These response categories are not observable behaviours themselves. They are, however, the motivations, attitudes and feelings that help to determine much of the observable behaviour in people.

✦ Observable behaviour. This refers to the actual behaviour that would be seen by other people. It is the tangible and physical expression of the underlying behaviour shapers. It is the reactions such as leaving a building when the fire alarm sounds, or work activity following job instructions from a supervisor.

Perceptual defence

Perceptual defence provides a measure of protection against information, ideas or situations that are threatening to an existing perception or viewpoint. It is a process that encourages the perception of stimuli in terms of the known and familiar. For example, a manager having taken the decision to introduce a new product into the company is likely to search out information that reinforces the validity of the decision and also interpret information received in a favourable light. Information that is contradictory to the validity of the decision is likely to be seen as a challenge requiring the decision to be proved correct rather than negating the decision itself. This partially reflects the view behind the often heard statement that problems are opportunities in disguise.

The learning loop

The role of *learning* on the perceptual process itself is something that the model described in Figure 3.1 recognizes as *feedback*. This is intended to indicate that individuals learn from experience. The person involved will perceive the consequences of their behaviours and as a result adjust their subsequent behaviour and perceptual frameworks. An individual who is disciplined by their manager for being late for work will, hopefully, change their future behaviour and arrive punctually. Similarly, an employee praised for good work will be more likely to continue to repeat it in the future.

The effect of learning on the perceptual process can be demonstrated through a number of illusions. Figure 3.12 is the Müller–Lyer visual illusion (named after the originators) which, it has been suggested, has a basis in the prior learning of individuals. Which

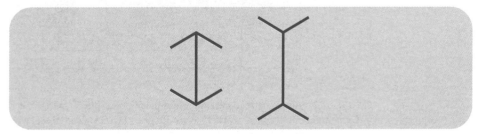

FIGURE 3.12   The Müller–Lyer illusion.

of the two vertical lines is the longer? In practice, they are the same length. It can be suggested that this illusion of differing line length arises in certain people because of an association with rooms and buildings with corners based on these models. Individuals, therefore, attempt to place a perspective or context onto the shapes as a result of their prior learning.

Person perception

Person perception is of particular interest in organization behaviour because of the significance of interpersonal interaction within a work setting. How individuals perceive managers, subordinates, fellow workers is the basis of the effectiveness of any organization. Much of the day-to-day activity in employee relations is concerned with the management of perceptions and subsequent attitudes relative to the work setting. Warr (1971) offers a schematic model of person perception (see Figure 3.13).

The model comprises five sets of components, all linked together in a complex array of information flow and interdependency. They are:

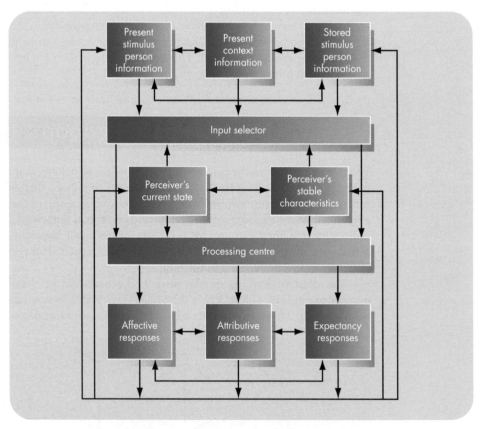

FIGURE 3.13   A schematic representation of person perception (*source*: Warr, PB (1971) Judgements about people at work. In Warr, PB (ed.) *Psychology at Work*, Penguin, Harmondsworth).

- ✦ The person and context information base. These provide the current and previously acquired information on the target person and the context within which the perception is set.

- ✦ Input selector. This refers to the process by which the vast array of current and previously obtained information is to be sifted, the assumption being that it is not possible to process all available information and that a filtering device is needed to weed out unnecessary information.

- ✦ The perceiver's state. This is intended to provide for the variable effect on perception of the perceiver. Their current physical, psychological and emotional state will influence their perceptions, as will their underlying personality characteristics.

- ✦ The processing centre. This is a series of decision rules built up from experience of interacting with people over time. It therefore allows a form of probability output from the available data. This is reminiscent of the mechanisms involved in the attribution theory discussed earlier.

- ✦ The response level. Having developed a profile of the target person in terms of the attributes and expectations, the perceiver will develop an appropriate response. This will not just be in terms of actual behaviour, but will include liking, respect and interest, for example. These judgmental facets to person perception all feed back to the other components as the process is cumulative. The stored information is updated by current events and is interactive in real time.

A simplified form of person perception is to envisage it as a three-factor process, involving the characteristics of the perceiver, the characteristics of the perceived and the situational variables. Figure 3.14 illustrates the main features of this approach to person perception.

The model of person perception reflected in Figure 3.14 has strong links with attribution theory. Taking each determinant from the model in turn:

- ✦ Perceiver characteristics. Those internal aspects of an individual that determine perceptual selection and attribution. For example, personality, motivation, objectives,

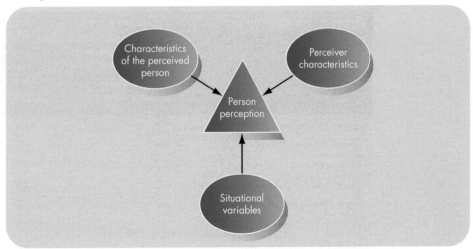

FIGURE 3.14   Person perception: a simplified model.

learning, past experience and the individual's value system. Working with someone from another culture is a useful way of experiencing the scope of a value system on person perception as new ways of thinking about people and their characteristics and traits emerge through the exposure.

✦ The characteristics of the perceived person. When we meet someone, there are a wide variety of clues available. Their physical appearance, skin colour, gender, age, general appearance, voice, behaviour and apparent personality all provide information to the perceiver's sensory receptors (DePaulo *et al.*, 1987). Although the characteristics of the perceived person can make a positive contribution to the process of person perception, there is also a danger that it may lead to stereotyping.

✦ Situational variables. Meeting someone for the first time in the company of either a friend, or someone that you dislike, would be likely to influence the initial perception of the new individual. A social, business or general context with their differing degrees of formality are also likely to influence initial perceptions. The room in which a meeting takes place, its standard of decoration and the general atmosphere all produce stimuli which influence person perception. The impression of the surroundings are linked or associated with the person in them and therefore the perception of them.

Table 3.1 provides an illustration of person perception in action. It reflects the perceptions of supervisors and subordinates about each other. The perception that was being examined related to the views that each group held about the other in terms of recognition for good performance.

Table 3.1 indicates a clear difference in perceived behaviour between the two groups. Supervisors perceive that they provide a much more positive response to good performance than do their subordinates. The difference between the two groups is startling, not just marginal. The perceptions of the subordinates about the supervisors is clearly different from the supervisors' perception of their own behaviour. One implication of this is that managers in general need to be much more aware of the signals that they give out if they are to avoid misunderstandings.

Hastorf and Cantril (1954) studied the reaction to an American rules football game

Types of recognition	Frequency with which supervisors say they give various types of recognition for good performance (%)	Frequency with which subordinates say supervisors give various types of recognition for good performance (%)
Gives privileges	52	14
Gives more responsibility	48	10
Gives a pat on the back	82	13
Gives sincere and thorough praise	80	14
Trains for better jobs	64	9
Gives more interesting work	51	5

TABLE 3.1   Person perception in the context of recognition behaviour (*adapted from*: Likert, R (1961) *New Patterns in Management*, McGraw-Hill, New York

between two university teams. The subjects of the research were students from the universities concerned, Princeton and Dartmouth. General reports about the game suggested that both teams had engaged in rough play, but that Dartmouth had been the more aggressive. From a film of the game both sets of students were asked to score the number of fouls committed by each side (see Table 3.2).

The Princeton students saw a much larger number of fouls being committed by the Dartmouth team than the Dartmouth students did. They perceived the situation in a different light, based on their attitudes towards their own team. However, this would not explain why the Princeton students did not significantly underreport their own team's performance.

There are many possible explanations for this result, including the extreme behaviour of the Dartmouth team, causing the need to *sanitize* their misdeeds by their supporters. This implies a group reaction to the result, the game being the same perceptual stimulus for each observer, the stimulus being interpreted in the light of the attitudinal model. It would also be possible to argue that the attitudinal frameworks influence the perception itself, making the game different for each observer. The observer would therefore *see* only that which had meaning and significance for that individual. It is in this form that the significance for organizations becomes apparent. Individual perceptions and attitudes are informed through group interaction and therefore managers need to function at both levels in shaping appropriate behaviours.

Stereotyping and projection

Stereotyping is the tendency to attribute everyone (or thing) in a particular category with the characteristics from a single example, for instance, the stereotype that suggests that all people of the Jewish faith are shrewd business people, because a small number are successful. This is a factor of person perception that is most frequently seen in the area of race relations, but also has very direct links to the organizational world. For example, some managers would claim that all workers are lazy and some workers would claim that all managers search for ways to exploit workers. These can be clear perceptual stereotypes in which every member of a category of employee or manager is being described in the terms found only in a small number of individuals.

Not all information perceived could be expected to be either supportive or contradictory towards a particular stereotype. For example, an employee might find that not all managers were seeking to exploit them. This apparently contradictory information must somehow be dealt with by the recipient. It has been suggested that information which supports a particular stereotype is processed more intensively that information which is inconsistent with it (Bodenhausen, 1988). This builds on an earlier study which demonstrated that various denial or protection devices were adopted by students presented with

	Average fouls committed by	
	Princeton team	Dartmouth team
Dartmouth students (48)	4.4	4.3
Princeton students (49)	4.2	9.8

TABLE 3.2 Observed fouls in the Princeton and Dartmouth football game

contradictory information in relation to a stereotype (Haire and Grunes, 1950), the aim being to protect the original stereotyped image of the target, rather than accept the disconfirming evidence provided.

The apparent benefits of stereotyping are associated with its ability to allow categorization of people into groups. This could, assuming that the basis of stereotyping were correct, be a simplifying process. It could significantly reduce the need for mental processing of people as individuals and allow capacity to be free to deal with more important issues. However, in doing so there is a real danger of missing important aspects of individuality within the people being stereotyped. For example, sex, race, disability and age discrimination are commonplace in the organizational world. But, for example, adopting the common stereotype that older people are less skilled and flexible than young people fails to take into account the potential benefits arising through experience.

Projection implies that others possess the same characteristics as ourselves. In other words, we tend to assume that everyone thinks in the same way that we do. Also that others will behave in the way that we would in a particular situation. This is a potentially dangerous assumption for managers to make in relation to their employees. Managers invariably express surprise when employees react in a way that was not anticipated or when they refuse to agree with management's point of view. However, there is no reason why employees should perceive the world the same way that managers do, that much should be obvious from the discussion in this chapter so far. Equally, a manager who describes the behaviour of other managers as power and politically motivated might actually be inclined to behave in such ways themselves and be seeking to protect themselves by projecting these characteristics onto other people.

Body language and perception

Body language is a form of communication parallel to the spoken word. It includes a wide range of features associated with the ways in which people interact with each other. For example, posture, tone of voice, gestures and facial expression are common examples. Each of these aspects of communication provides signals along with the spoken words that are uttered by an individual. It is from the wealth of information available through body language that perceptions are formed about what a person has actually said. It is possible for a person to lie easily, but it is very difficult for them to be able to eliminate from their body language the signals that would allow another person to be at least suspicious.

Morris (1982, pp 160–71) describes situations in which people engage in the process of lying or otherwise attempting to deceive other people. Examples that he quotes include the defendant in a murder trial who knows that he is guilty yet seeks to maintain his innocence, another example being that of a bereaved mother seeking to 'put a brave face' on things for the sake of the children. In discussing these and other situations, Morris refers to the body language evident from the principle actors as *non-verbal leakage*, in other words, the means through which the individual's true feelings leak out into the observable domain.

In the case of the bereaved mother, the 'brave face' must not be too convincing or she would be accused of being unfeeling, but equally it must be apparent or she would be accused of lacking courage and control. Morris describes this as *pseudo-deception* as compared with the attempts to deceive totally on the part of the murderer seeking acquittal. In that example, the body language must seek to reinforce the verbal lies.

Morris suggests that it is possible to control some aspects of body language such as smiling, frowning and other facial expressions, but that some body posture, hand gestures and leg movements will be directly controlled to a lesser degree. Therefore, these are more likely to provide clues as to the true feelings of the individual, hence the term *non-verbal leakage*. The individual is not able totally to prevent clues about their true feelings emerge. However, other people have to be able to read the clues available. In both these illustrations attempts are being made by the actors to influence other people's perceptions of them and their feelings or truthfulness.

There are a number of cultural aspects associated with body language. For example, Pease (1984) draws attention to a number of hand gestures which have different meanings in different cultural context, including the thumbs-up sign, the OK ring and the V sign. For example the thumbs-up sign usually refers to an OK signal in English-speaking countries, but can reflect an obscene response in Greece for example (pp 12–3). In pages 23–6, Pease reflects on cultural differences in preferred spatial zones between people. He describes his observation of a Japanese and an American slowly moving around a room as they conversed. In Japan it is normal to operate on a 25-centimetre 'intimate' zone for conversations, but the American was more comfortable with a 46-centimetre zone and so kept backing away, only to be followed by the Japanese colleague seeking to get closer. Clearly, such events can influence people's perceptions of each other. Invasions of personal space can be interpreted as threatening and illustrations of a desire for an intimate relationship. They are signals that can be easily misinterpreted.

Self-perception

Having introduced a number of features associated with the perception of other people, there is one further aspect that is important in the process. That is the perception of the self. In Figure 3.14, there is the variable of the perceiver's characteristics which are suggested to impact on the perception of other people. However, these characteristics tend to be classified in physical terms or as experience, motivation, personality etc. Just as important to the process of perceiving other people is the self-perceptions of the individuals themselves. Each person thinks of themselves in particular ways, they hold a perception of themselves. For example, an older person might consider that they are mature, successful, affluent, sociable, knowledgeable, worthy of respect, a pillar of the community, youthful and able to relate to young people. That defines their self-perception and it will to some extent impact on various aspects of that person's behaviour, including their perceptions of other people.

Attitude formation

The term *attitude* has entered everyday usage in that people are occasionally said to have an 'attitude problem'. At work, managers frequently look for a 'good attitude' in potential recruits. So it clearly reflects a potent force in dealing with people. Management in Action 3.3 provides an illustration of how attitudes to work can change, even in Japan, where it has often been assumed that society actively seeks to retain its traditional values.

MANAGEMENT IN ACTION 3.3

More than the job's worth

In Japan it is the devotion to duty of the salaryman that is responsible for much of the economic growth that turned the country into an economic superpower since World War II. In return for devotion to the interests of the employer the salaryman was guaranteed both a career and a job for life.

However, there was a high price to pay for the lifetime job protection and it is increasingly being called into question by the very people who were thought to be most benefiting from it. There are an estimated 10,000 deaths each year from *karoshi*, literally meaning sudden death from overwork. There is a growing willingness to take employers to court over infringements of employee treatment and human dignity. There exists a recognition of the lack of appropriate values in managing people by large employers. For example Mr Haruo Kawaguchi sued his employer (Teikoku Hormone Manufacturing) for compensation for a six-year separation from his family as a result of a job transfer to another location.

Employees are slowly beginning to rethink their perceptions about the nature of work and its role in their lives. In a poll of 1600 executives the values that made Japan successful such as efficiency, growth and competition were thought to be least important to the future of society. Creativity, fairness and symbiosis were identified as the most important qualities for the future development of society. Individuals are also beginning to shun the pursuit of career progression in favour of performing an interesting or worthwhile job. For example, Mr Tetsuro Handa moved from being a high-flying section manager

in the export department with Mitsubishi to their environmental affairs department because he felt that it would be more important and rewarding in his life irrespective of promotion opportunity.

This shift in perception is being fuelled by the worst recession in Japan for 20 years and by the early retirement or semi-redundancy among salarymen. During the recession in the early 1990s Japanese companies had to make strenuous efforts to cut back on labour costs, putting the notion of lifetime employment for salarymen under threat. To get round the difficulties that would have resulted from dismissing many thousands of such employees a number of measures were introduced by companies. These included unpaid (or reduced pay) leave, enforced holidays, early retirement and compulsory transfers to remote satellite operations. It has been estimated that there are about 1 million surplus workers on the books of Japanese companies as a result of this recession. One of the consequences to emerge is an adverse impact on the health of individuals. Increased incidence of mental health problems (such as depression and loss of confidence) and being afraid to tell their families of their true position are common examples. Under these conditions, it is hardly surprising that traditional loyalties are being questioned and a new perception of the way that life and work interact is being formed.

Adapted from: Dawkins, W (1993) More than the job's worth, *Financial Times*, 16/17 October, p 9.

Stop | Consider   *Does the situation in MiA 3.3 suggest that it is possible to have too much of a 'good' attitude towards work? Argue the case from both management and employee points of view.*

The basis of attitudes

Attitudes are linked with many other aspects of behaviour. They have traditionally been considered to be relatively stable dispositions to behave in particular ways towards objects, institutions, situations, ideas or other people. They are also usually considered to develop as a result of experience. In other words they influence an individual's response to something or someone. All people have attitudes towards things – school, university, parents, work, politics, sport, religion and other people. Some attitudes are deeply held and difficult to change, while others are more superficial and easy to drop or amend.

In one approach to the study of attitudes (Rosenberg, 1960) suggests that to change an attitude it is necessary to change either the underlying feelings or beliefs. This approach relies on a model of attitudes based on that shown as Figure 3.15.

Looking at each of the three components in turn:

✦ Cognitive component. This refers to the beliefs and values that the individual holds perhaps in terms of support for a football club, say Sunderland AFC. One belief related to support for the club might be that it is the best football club in England. A related value underlying support for the club would perhaps be that it is important to the individual supporter to have something from their home town that provides a source of pride. The important points to note from this analogy are that beliefs are evaluative in nature, for example the 'best' football team. Values, by the way of contrast, tend to be the judgmental criteria against which beliefs are measured. For example, an individual may *need* something from their roots to cling onto as a way of providing meaning in their life. The football team may or may not serve these purposes, depending upon its success.

✦ Affective component. The feelings and emotions that make up the affective component arise from an evaluation between the two elements within the cognitive component. A supporter of the football club just mentioned could be expected to develop feelings and attitudes according to the success of their team related to the underlying beliefs and values about it. The *affective component* of an attitude tends to be socially

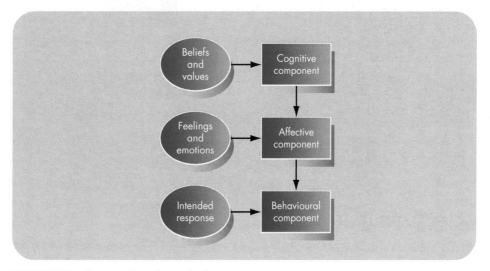

FIGURE 3.15 Construction of an attitude

learned. We acquire the ability to express our reaction to the balance between the cognitive elements in ways that align with our social environment.

✦ Behavioural component. This reflects the outcome of the process. It is the actual or intended behaviour. In the case of support for a football team that is not performing well, an individual could continue support and hope for better results in future, change their allegiance to another club or give notice that if losses continue they will stop supporting them. The behaviour resulting from the affective component would also be influenced by the importance of the attitude for the individual and the degree of intensity with which it was held.

The description of attitudes provided so far assumes a dispositional perspective. This approach assumes that an attitude is a relatively stable disposition to act in particular ways towards objects or people, and that it is based on experience. Another approach from Salancik and Pfeffer (1977) suggests that attitudes develop from the social frameworks and experiences encountered. In diagrammatic form this process would be as shown in Figure 3.16.

By means of the socially derived cues and markers the individual is sensitized to the prevailing attitudes and behaviours in particular contexts. The pressure is then on the individual to reach an accommodation between their previously held attitudes and behaviour norms and those expected in the current context. From this perspective attitudes are suggested to be situation specific rather than reflecting underlying frameworks within the individual.

Of course, the two approaches are not necessarily mutually exclusive. In some contexts it is necessary to suppress one's own feelings and values if continued acceptance by the group is to be maintained. For example, in a work context employees are primarily employed to undertake the tasks demanded by management. From that point of view the personal beliefs and values of the individual have to be subjugated to those of management if the individual is to be accepted into the organization.

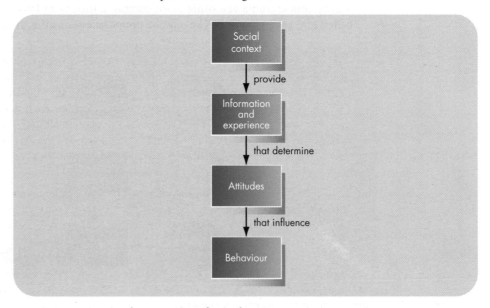

FIGURE 3.16   Situational construction of attitudes

Attitudes and perception

There is a twofold relationship between attitudes and perception. First, individuals perceive the attitudes of other people. They do this through the receipt and interpretation of a range of stimuli, visual, speech, body language, dress etc. People then *classify* the people they perceive around them based on the clues detected. For example, a group of young males all with very short hair and outlandish clothing perhaps torn and covered with studs and chains might be interpreted by an old person as likely to be violent thugs looking to beat up and rob some innocent individual. In that example, the perceiver is not experiencing the real attitudes of the group of young people, they are observing a number of stimuli and drawing conclusions from them about the attitudes and intentions of the group. In turn, their own behaviour will be influenced by their presumptuous interpretation of the signals.

Second, individuals seek to give out particular perceptions through the management or their attitudes and other signals. For example, a group of young people dressed as just indicated might be seeking to convey a particular image of themselves as a group or followers of a particular fashion. Equally, it would not be expected that a bank manager would dress casually in jeans and sweater for an important business meeting as to do so would give completely the wrong impression (or perception) to the clients.

Attitudes and behaviour

Attitudes have an influence on behaviour, but it is a complex relationship. Katz (1960) suggests that attitudes serve four main functions:

1. Adjustment. This allows the individual to adapt to the environmental circumstances that they encounter. It contains elements of rationalization and justification by the individual for the behaviours in which they engage.
2. Ego defensive. By adopting particular attitudes individuals allow themselves to protect their self-esteem from potentially threatening situations or knowledge. For example, that 'fact' that an employee was sacked from their job was nothing to do with their incompetence, but was because the manager hated them personally.
3. Value expressive. This allows the individual to externalize the important values that they hold. Young people frequently express their rebellion from the control of older people by adopting individual and sometimes shocking clothing styles. Johnson (1999) reports a survey indicating that only 8% of employees in the UK felt that their values and those of their employers were very similar, only 14% felt that they were very proud of their organization and only 30% felt any strong loyalty towards it. All these data reflect clear attitude patterns expressing the underlying values associated with work.
4. Knowledge. This allows the individual to provide a structure to the world around them. It allows the individual to group together facets of the world into a common category each with attitude-based response patterns for ease of working within a complex environment.

Festinger (1957) and Festinger *et al.* (1958) developed the concept of *cognitive dissonance* to explain behaviour in situations where conflicts existed between attitude components. It contains three main elements:

1. There may exist dissonant or 'non-fitting' relations among cognitive elements.

2. The existence of dissonance gives rise to pressures to avoid any further increases in it and actively to seek reductions in the level experienced.

3. Manifestations of the operation of these pressures include behaviour changes, changes of cognition and circumspect exposure to new information and new opinions.

Essentially, Festinger describes a mechanism that seeks to provide consistency between perceptions, attitudes and actions. A feeling of anxiety is produced when there is a contradiction or incongruity between the components of an attitude and behaviour. An employee may hold an opinion that they are a good worker and indispensable to the organization. The manager of that same individual may perceive that the person is a poor employee and barely acceptable. If the manager tells the employee of their opinion then the employee will be in possession of two sets of contradictory information. In order to deal with the dissonance created by that knowledge and to be able to rationalize the discrepancy the individual may adopt a number of strategies. These could include working as the manager expected, suggesting that the manager does not have the knowledge to form a correct judgement or implying that they were simply biased and unreasonable.

Management in Action 3.4 illustrates the concept of dissonance. Japanese graduates find that employment with foreign companies does not provide the same benefits available from a Japanese company. Consequently, the dissonance is reduced by *labelling* the foreign organizations and by not seeking to join them.

Stop | Consider
Is the example used in MiA 3.4 an illustration of cognitive dissonance or is it an example of a lack of knowledge creating negative attitudes? Justify your view.

Another area in which attitudes and behaviour are linked emerges through the spiritual side of human nature. Attitudes towards the role of spirituality within organizations varies tremendously. However, there is a developing awareness that it is not possible to keep driving for ever higher performance from each individual without some negative consequences. A feeling is growing that there is a role for organized religion, poetry, yoga etc. to offer opportunities for people to find peace within themselves, together with an improved balance between the various components of life, including work. Welch (1998) provides one example of a Benedictine monk offering residential weekends on meditation and discussions on spirituality as a way of helping individual's search for meaning in their lives. Another example refers to a firm of solicitors which recruited a poet in residence. As well as writing officially for the company as part of the process, they hosted workshops for all staff on poetry writing as a way of creating connections between individuals. The basis of this type of initiative is the recognition of a need for balance in life and the development of sustainable values, attitudes and beliefs in relation to work if sustained success is to be achieved.

Impression management

So far in the discussion, perception has been described as a phenomenon in which the individual learns to make sense of the world in which they live. This is a unidirectional view of

MANAGEMENT IN ACTION 3.4

Foreign company jobs lose allure

Working for a foreign company creates additional perceptual consequences compared to working for one that originates in the same national environment as the employee. There are the very obvious differences in loyalty that might be expected to exist. For example an American company operating in Britain could be expected to have a higher level of commitment to its American operations than those in Britain. If problems were to emerge it could reasonably be expected that the British operations would be cut back first. Equally there are cultural differences to be considered. Would an American company operating in the UK be expected to treat (in all respects) its employees in ways identical to British companies?

There are problems and perceptions that have had an impact on the perception of employment in foreign companies by Japanese employees. Students leaving university in Japan tend to be channelled into careers and companies by several factors, just as they would be in any country. These include the preferences of professors, networks of contacts and the 'play-safe' views of parents. Considering foreign employers in Japan as a source of employment for jobs creates particular difficulties for the potential recruits. There has been considerable public reporting and comment on the actions of several large US

companies in Japan as they attempt to cope with recession. Large companies such as Eastman Kodak, Northwest Airlines, NCR and IBM have undertaken a range of measures as they cut back recruitment levels and cancel agreements to hire fresh graduates. Even though a number of Japanese companies adopted similar strategies the adverse media coverage created a climate of hostility for the foreign (predominantly American) companies.

Western companies are perceived as having a much more aggressive attitude towards employees and to be much more likely to dismiss them than are Japanese employers. For many potential employees the security of lifetime employment and the flexible career patterns adopted by Japanese companies are much more attractive than the benefits offered by overseas employers. Working life in a foreign-owned company is perceived as likely to be brief and unpredictable. Mr Thomas Lynch, a partner at KPMG Peat Marwick advises foreign companies in Japan to face up to the problem and emphasize the benefits available to Japanese employees in order to offset the negative perceptions created by the negative publicity.

Adapted from: Thomson, R (1993) Foreign company jobs lose allure, *Financial Times*, 19 March, p 3.

the topic. Recognizing that humans undertake a judgmental and categorized evaluation of people and events around them provides an opportunity for individuals to present a particular image to the world around them and so encourage a desired response.

Impression management is something that all actors and politicians become very familiar with in the course of their work. An actor has to be credible in the part they are playing and they use a variety of techniques including make-up, lighting, costume and set design to create the illusion that they are *in reality* the character they are playing. Politicians similarly must present themselves as credible, honest and trustworthy if they are to be elected or hold one of the offices of state. The use of public relations experts and media consultants can assist with the development of particular images and impressions of the individuals concerned. Marketing specialists use many of the same techniques in attempting to position the goods or services of an organization in the perceptions of potential customers.

Within an organization there are several aspects associated with impression management in addition to the marketing and public relations perspective indicated earlier, including:

✦ Career strategies. In order to enhance prospects of promotion and limit the likelihood of demotion it is necessary to create particular impressions to those able to deliver the desired development. Giacalone (1989) identifies a number of what he describes as *demotion-preventing* and *promotion-enhancing* strategies. These include being associated with the right people at the right time and providing plausible excuses for particular courses of action.

✦ Public image. The use of corporate identity symbols can include a badge or logo of some description, but it can also be taken further through the design of company premises and staff dress codes. Many fast food chains have a house style for their restaurants that allows instant recognition anywhere in the world. Rafaeli and Pratt (1993) developed a basis for the comparison of organizations based on requirements for dress codes among employees.

✦ Managerial. In industrial relations situations it is necessary for the management team to present a unified front and to create an *impression* of the organization that supports the public stance adopted during negotiations. Attempts to hold down pay increases by suggesting that bankruptcy is a danger, while at the same time allowing managers to continue to spend heavily on entertainment is unlikely to be accepted by the workforce.

There is some evidence that a new form of impression management is emerging within organizations, a management-imposed requirement for particular appearance characteristics. In some ways this is not a new phenomenon. For example, a number of airlines have recruited only young attractive people to work as cabin staff for many years. However, this is now beginning to resurface in a number of ways that has led researchers at Strathclyde University to coin the term *aesthetic labour* to describe requirement to have the management-determined mix of appearance, age, weight, class and accent characteristics. The researchers describe the trend using the example of a hotel seeking to project a total image concept, with the hotel building representing the hardware and the staff the software. Once recruited staff would also experience pressure to mould themselves into the desired characteristics in order to provide the total experience sought by managers (Lamb, 1999). In the same article it is reported, by way of example, that three teenage girls were dismissed from a night club for being too ugly and were replaced by 'models'.

Perception within an organizational context

Perception, attitudes and organizations

Organizations have many aspects of perception and attitudes to contend with:

A. **The attitudes and perceptions of actual customers.** A considerable proportion of company marketing effort goes towards encouraging particular attitudes and perceptions in their customers. The effort of organizations to achieve this are not restricted to an advertising or marketing approach. The results that a school achieves in examinations taken by its pupils will do much to encourage parents to send their children to it. The cartoon included as Figure 3.17 provides an illustration of the negative attitudes and perceptions of customer care which organizations attempt to prevent, yet is all too familiar to the customer, which is why the humour works.

B. **The attitudes and perceptions of potential customers.** This category within the environment are the people who do not currently buy the product or service offered by the organization. Much organizational effort goes into attempting to understand the characteristics of these people and consequently how to influence their attitudes and buying habits.

C. **The attitudes and perceptions of the wider community.** This is where public relations emerges as the discipline involved with the presentation of the organization's perspective. This can be in response to either a negative situation (bad publicity) or it can be an attempt to optimize the positive value from an organization's activities.

D. **The attitudes and behaviours of employees.** Management in Action 3.5 illustrates the management reactions to an employee who developed what could be described as deviant behaviour patterns, deviant, that is, in terms of the norms expected by managers and delivered by most employees in that situation.

Stop | Consider *Which attitudes were wrong in MiA 3.5 and why?*
    On what basis did you form your answer to the first question and why is that the best basis for deciding between the attitudes expressed?

E. **Supplier attitudes and perceptions.** The purpose of seeking to influence the attitudes and behaviours of suppliers is to provide the organization with a favourable basis for trading. This could involve obtaining extended credit terms, rapid and frequent delivery patterns or improved quality at a reduced price.

FIGURE 3.17 Attitudes and perception.

MANAGEMENT IN ACTION 3.5

Have long holiday, will travel nowhere in job

The perception and attitude towards work in Japan is noticeably different to that in the west. Employees are expected to place the interests of the employer above personal interest. This is taken to such a level that it is not uncommon to find that individuals introduce themselves in terms of their company first. For example (and using a British illustration) a typical greeting might be 'Hello, I'm Hull University's Mr John Martin'. The same level of dedication applies to the time spent at work and the taking of holiday. The director of one government ministry retired after 35 years' service and proudly announced that he had never asked for any time off work other than for public holidays and that he had accumulated two years' worth of time off, which he could not now take as he was retiring!

One employee of the Ministry of Health dared to break this unofficial code of honour and his story became a best-seller as a popular book. However, it did nothing for his career prospects. Mr Masao Miyamoto lived and worked in America for 11 years after initially studying medicine in Japan. On moving to America he undertook postgraduate work at Yale University and subsequently practised psychiatry. Upon his return home he was appointed to a position in the Ministry of Health. He found the work culture and attitude of long hours spent at the office difficult to accept after living in America for so long. It was common for staff not to leave before 7 pm, even if there was no work to do; they would not seek more than about four days' holiday; and would work for seven days each week.

Each year a holiday request chart was circulated and junior staff were expected to apply for holidays for that year by filling in the desired spaces on the form. No one ever applied for their

full allowance and people always applied for less holiday than their superior. Mr Miyamoto applied for two weeks' holiday and began a controversy that sabotaged his career and resulted in his being exiled to a menial job checking sailors for cholera in Yokohama. Mr Miyamoto's immediate boss attempted to persuade him to withdraw his application but after much long debate (and *sake* drinking) agreed with his holiday request. However, the director of the section was less amenable and although the holiday was eventually agreed, Mr Miyamoto was accused of selfishness, causing disruption and of dishonouring his position. It was also suggested that he might like to resign rather than remain in such a difficult position.

However, it was only after Mr Miyamoto applied for a holiday the next year to visit Tahiti that he was transferred to Yokohama. It was at that point that he wrote his book poking fun at the bureaucratic nonsense that he perceived around him. This further infuriated his superiors and some of his colleagues, but others quietly began to voice some measure of support for his personal stand. His bosses still find ways of undermining his confidence and of pointing out that he does not fit in, even in his choice of clothes. Even in a suit and tie, just like his colleagues, it is pointed out to him that he does not dress in a way that conforms to the dress code usually adopted within the Ministry. A high price for taking a holiday, to which by law he was entitled.

Adapted from: McCarthy, T (1993) Have long holiday, will travel nowhere in job, *The Independent*, 12 August, p 11.

F. **The organization's competitors.** These must also be encouraged to consider the organization as a 'solid' market player. If the organization is to be taken seriously in an industry it is necessary to generate an image that encourages that view. Competitors will ignore or even worse attempt to destroy a competitor considered weak or a threat.

G. **Regulators.** The power of regulators to control organizational activity through legislation and other rules tends to make them subject to attempts at influence by many pressure groups. This is done in an attempt to channel the future direction of legislation and policy. This is usually an area shrouded in mystery and behind-the-scenes activity, rather than direct intervention. Study tours, lectures, seminars, reports and fact-finding visits are just some of the 'tools' adopted by the professional lobbyist.

H. **Shareholders.** These are, technically, the owners on whose behalf managers run the organization. In the public sector it is the members of the general public, through parliament, who are the *owners*. There is a need for organizations to develop approaches to the presentation of shareholder information in such a way that the individuals and institutions involved are encouraged to maintain their investments. In the financial markets, a considerable number of analysts are employed to get behind the public output from organizations and identify the true position. It is, therefore, a game of cat and mouse with the stock market value of the organization being the prize.

Perception, attitudes and control

Whatever the ownership structure of the organization, managers find themselves having to achieve objectives through other people. Therefore, managers need to shape the behaviour of other people in order to direct them towards the goals sought. In order to control behaviour within the organization, managers have to either:

✦   order others to carry out management wishes or

✦   persuade individuals willingly to undertake what is required of them.

The first option implies force and coercion by managers while the second implies rationality linked to the exercise of free will on the part of the employee. In practice, managers utilize a mixture of both approaches. The use of excessive force and direct orders is unlikely to produce a willing response among those subject to them. Neither is it likely to produce the high levels of productivity required of organizations these days. Perception and attitudes provide the concepts through which managers can control the behaviour of employees. If successful, this should encourage employees to be more compliant in doing management's bidding. Also, employees would be encouraged to see themselves as stakeholders in the organization, thereby, through association and commitment, encouraged to invest in positively helping management to further its objectives.

Garrahan and Stewart (1992) provide a review of Japanese management practices in a new car assembly plant, in which the whole question of participative management practice as a control process is explored. From that discussion it becomes apparent that careful initial selection of employees to join the company is reinforced through subsequent employee training and management practice. The effect being that employees have their perceptions and attitudes towards work and the organization *shaped* to a management preferred model. However, being in an area of high unemployment there is inevitably an unanswered question as to the degree of success in actually shaping employee perception and attitude as compared to producing a *compliance response* based on the lack of alternative work options. Employees who need the job might be expected to adopt whatever attitudes are expected in order to earn a wage.

Information (or perceptual stimulus) is influenced through the attitudinal frameworks held by the individual. This reinforces the view that managers and employees do not simply register and respond to the 'facts out there'. It is a more complex process and potentially leads to errors in the assessment of a situation that can be wrong and damaging to any of the stakeholders or the organization itself.

Perception and attitude formation: an applied perspective

The world is constantly changing and managers must manage in that dynamic situation. Perceptions are a constant source of information to each individual as they attempt to make sense of the world in which they live. As a continuous process, perception is potentially amenable to adjustment in the light of new information through attitude changes. For example, finding out that a previous attitude about certain people is wrong could change future perceptions about them. Part of the purpose of perceptual and attitudinal mechanisms is to introduce the familiar into an uncertain world. It allows the individual to filter out the unnecessary and concentrate on significant aspects. That implies that either perceptions and attitudes change in the light of experience or that behaviours become increasingly detached from appropriate interaction with the experienced world.

Perception is a truly personal experience. Employees and managers are not likely to interpret the *facts* in the same way or even in a consistent way across time. It is these dual aspects of *uniqueness* (each person is different) and *variable interpretation* (of the same stimuli) of the familiar that creates the difficulties for managers. Managers attempt to operate in a three-dimensional world in this context (see Figure 3.18).

Taking each dimension in turn:

✦   Time. Managers are constrained by events of the past. The size, culture and organization of the company were all determined in the past. Managers are working in the present time in attempting to ensure that the organization is able to meet its present commitments. They are also working in the future in order to provide an ability to survive over time.

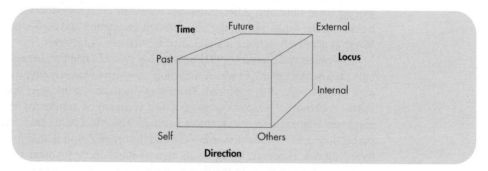

FIGURE 3.18   Three-dimensional view of management activity.

◆ Locus. Managers deal with internal and external events. The *locus of emphasis* can either be internal or external (or both) depending upon the circumstances. For example, a hostile takeover in the City will force an external perspective as managers attempt to fight off the raiders. Of course, much of the impact of the action will be felt within the organization as costs are cut in an attempt to win the support of existing shareholders through improved returns on their investment.

◆ Direction. This dimension in the model attempts to reflect the degree of introspection in the process. Managers will be forced to consider either their own perspective or that of others, not necessarily within the organization. Managers can either operate according to their own agenda or can find it necessary to function according to the dictates of others. In seeking to defend against a hostile takeover, the agenda is largely determined by the raiders.

Managers attempt to extract the maximum utility from these concepts in *manipulating* the perceptions and attitudes of others. Many managers might find the use of the word *manipulation* in this context difficult to accept. It is a word with connotations that imply an unacceptable approach to making people do things against their will. However, efficiency can only be achieved if employees and managers work in unison towards the same objectives and with the same vigour. It is in achieving that particular synergy that Japanese organizations have been particularly successful (Oliver and Wilkinson, 1992). The needs of the organization are determined by managers largely as a result of their interpretation (or perception) of the situation (see Figure 3.19).

From Figure 3.19 it can be seen that managers receive a great many stimuli from a variety of sources, all of which are interpreted through the process within the managers' psychological make-up. The result is a response set that directs subsequent action in the running of the organization. If a manager interprets the business environment as hostile,

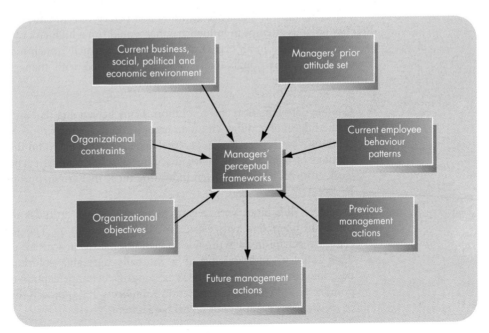

FIGURE 3.19   Managers' perceptions and the impact on subsequent actions.

they may well use the situation to exert additional pressure to force changes or concessions from an otherwise unwilling labour force.

It is the formal role that managers play within an organization that make their perceptions of particular importance. Managers are charged with the responsibility of running companies, therefore their perceptions and attitudes, linked to their subsequent behaviours, influence the direction of the organization and the manner through which it is achieved. That is not to suggest that employees have no influence on the process, simply to state that the ultimate influence rests with managers. It is they who take the credit for success and they who must also accept responsibility for failure.

Part of the perceptual selectivity process directs individuals to give credence to information provided from sources that are regarded as authoritative. This helps to explain why employees in some organizations do not believe management when they attempt to communicate particular points of view. Previous management messages may not have been reliable therefore employees come to rely on more credible sources. This demonstrates the concept of *perceptual set*, or the predisposition to perceive what we expect to perceive. Employees expect to see a management that is consistent with previous experience. They respond accordingly. They may receive the signals telling them how desperate the situation is, but simply read the signals as more of the same, and therefore safe to ignore.

This phenomenon also influences how men perceive women. Deaux and Emswiller (1974) demonstrated that men interpreted competence in women as the result of luck rather than skill. Given that most managers are male, this approach provides a mechanism to inhibit the progress of females by attributing any success to chance factors. It also provides an opportunity for men to reinforce the solidarity of their male identity by maintaining a perceived superiority over women. Ragins and Sundstrom (1990) studied the perceived power of male and female managers by their subordinates. They found that generally there were no differences between the sexes in this context, although women managers were suggested to display higher levels of expert power than men.

Direct attempts to influence attitudes and perceptions are not common. Clearly, any direct or obvious attempt to influence either would run a high risk of failure. The process of *influence* adopted in an organizational context is usually much more subtle. It can be detected indirectly through many activities associated with management control and authority, including:

✦ Conflict determination and resolution. Many behaviours that are considered deviant or the subject of conflict within an organization have their roots in attitudes and perception. What is perceived as acceptable behaviour is based on the attitudes and perceptions of managers. By taking disciplinary action against particular behaviours or work attitudes a signal is given indicating those that are inappropriate or should not be repeated.

✦ Employee difficulties with regard to management's attitudes and behaviours can usually be referred to a grievance procedure for resolution. The purpose of these procedural mechanisms is to provide an institutionalized process for exploring the immediate problem and arriving at a mutually agreeable solution. Another way of describing this process would be as arriving at a better perception of the other person's point of view. Management in Action 3.6 reflects this approach through the provision of mechanisms dealing with sexual harassment.

MANAGEMENT IN ACTION 3.6

American sailors see red over sex

The issue of sexual harassment creates many difficulties for managers attempting to identify and deal with issues of unwelcome or unacceptable behaviour. This is particularly true in the armed forces. Until recently men and women had separate categories of activity within the military environment, which kept the opportunity for offensive conduct between the sexes to specific environments and of manageable proportion. However, over recent years, with a growth in the combat role of women, along with other opportunities for mixed-sex work activity, harassment has been forced high up on the military agenda.

There have been a number of high-profile instances over recent years where military personnel have been held accountable for their actions in this area. One such case was the 1991 Tailhook scandal, when American navy pilots went on the razzle at their annual party. This involved what has been described as a drunken sexual rampage and created a situation which the navy could not ignore. One consequence of this was the development of a code of conduct intended to provide guidance on acceptable and unacceptable behaviour between the sexes. Although generally welcomed it raised a number of comments and issues about how the military manages its personnel.

The code provides for three levels of behaviour between the sexes, each colour coded. Green light behaviour could include putting a hand on someone's elbow or making reference to appearance, provided it refers to their uniform. It reflects behaviour that would be acceptable. The amber light is intended to indicate behaviour that could be interpreted as sexual harassment, even if this was not intended. It includes whistling, lewd jokes, staring and violating personal space. The red light level indicates those behaviours that would always be interpreted as sexual harassment and which would result in punitive action if

continued. This category includes offensive letters, grabbing, forced kissing, fondling, sexual assault and rape.

The problem for military authorities is that it is not possible to categorize social behaviour in the neat and precise way necessary for most military purposes. Most military commands and training are based around short, precise instructions that are not capable of misinterpretation. However, in the field of sexual harassment this is not possible. There are examples in behaviour in the green light category of the naval code of conduct that would, in a particular context, place it in the red light area. For example, the phrase, 'My, what a nice set of epaulettes you have', said in a particular tone of voice and with the emphasis on part of the phrase could be directly intended as harassment. Equally, there are examples of amber category behaviour that could be either green or red in nature depending upon the context. There is also a view that suggests that it is worrying that someone in the navy might hold the view that rape would not automatically be classed as unacceptable behaviour.

The US Navy stands by its approach on the basis that it represents a step in the right direction and provides clear guidance on acceptable behaviour. Rear Admiral Kendell Pease supported its use saying that in an age of sound-bite communications and bumper-sticker mentality the code was a means of grabbing people's attention and forcing them to take account of the issues. It was aimed at young people in the navy who are very familiar with motor cars and traffic signals as a way of controlling behaviour. Therefore it was hoped that the same approach to behaviour between the sexes would improve standards.

Adapted from: Macintyre, B (1993) American sailors see red over sex, *South China Morning Post*, 22 June, p 16.

Stop | Consider

To what extent do you consider that the approach described in MiA 3.6 would actually change the perceptions and attitudes of the people involved?

How would you seek to influence attitudes about sexual harassment in an organizational context?

✦ Culture is another area with which perception and attitudes are strongly associated. If culture is defined as broadly 'the way that we do things around here' then it should be apparent how particular perceptions and attitudes could support it. Equally, it also suggests why 'inappropriate' attitudes and perceptions might be seen as hostile to management's intentions and defined as such.

✦ Communications. The communications frameworks of the organization can educate, inform and persuade and so influence attitudes and subsequent perceptions. It is for this reason that managers can find themselves at odds with trade unions over who has the right to communicate directly with employees. Communication is much more than the actual words used to convey the message.

✦ Management style. The way in which managers go about their tasks provides a clear signal to everyone as to what is regarded as important. This provides clear insights or clues to employees on what management is seeking so that an appropriate reaction can be determined. A workforce that perceives a management which pushes for higher worker productivity while enjoying long lunch breaks itself will generate a cynical attitude base.

✦ Work organization, job design and satisfaction. The way in which work is organized, planned and designed also provides a clear signal to employees about the professionalism of managers and the degree to which they are serious about the business. Job satisfaction is an important attitude indicator, employees who perceive that their work is boring, menial and of little worth are likely to react accordingly.

✦ Participative management. Such practices provide for the perceptions of employees to be taken into account in the decision-making processes of the organization. This not only provides a clear signal on what is seen as important within the organization, but it allows the differing perceptions to be taken into account. It also provides the opportunity to influence attitudes and perceptions through discussion.

✦ Power and control. Managers assume the right to manage and, therefore, to control the activities of others. This task is made much easier if the individuals to be controlled are compliant and amenable to the process. To achieve this requires that their perceptions and attitudes are shaped accordingly. Another aspect of this particular dimension is found when the search for power over another leads to bullying. An attitude that says that an individual has the right to make another do their will through the application of force, violence or intimidation. Research by NOP found that 10% of people had actually been bullied at work and that the majority of the cases were within management and professional groups (Walsh, 1998). Non-management employees tended not to be bullied as often.

✦ Reward structures. Pay is the most obvious reward. Basic wages or salary are often supplemented with bonus payments for extra output or performance. In addition, promotion, access to development opportunities and praise or punishment are all elements of the reward structures available for managers to use in encouraging appropriate behaviour. It can, however, be argued that reward structures do not produce

MANAGEMENT IN ACTION 3.7

On the shelf at 45

There has been a debate over the last few years about the perceived value of older workers. It has become apparent during recent recessions and productivity-enhancing initiatives such as delayering, downsizing, rightsizing or whatever it might be called that it has been the older, longer serving employee who has been cast aside in favour of a younger person. There are many reasons for this trend including the relative cost advantage of younger employees and a perception that they are easier to train, more adaptable and willing to change. The older worker has, however, begun to fight back.

In a letter to the *Financial Times*, a researcher from the Institute of Manpower Studies indicated that the perception of employers about age-related performance was based on inaccurate stereotypes. The correspondent goes on to quote research findings that older people tend to have lower turnover rates, less frequent absence for sickness, better commitment and time-keeping habits than younger people. Even with this type of research finding employers still tend to discriminate against older people with research from Industrial Relations Services showing that almost one-third of all job adverts contained an age bar. This represented an increase from the level of one-quarter of adverts four years earlier. In addition to those specifying an age bar, four out of five wanted someone under the age of 45.

Examples exist in a wide range of industries of the application of the perception that younger people are better. For example, Simone Kesseler from Cornhill Publications expressed views that their kind of business (telesales) attracted younger people (between mid-20s and early 30s) for management positions, although it was not a formal company policy. Roger Steare, a director of Jonathan Wren, a City recruitment consultancy, explained that in the dealing rooms it was de

rigueur that new entrants to the derivatives markets were under 35. In the computer industry age can be closely aligned with experience. Russell Clements, director of the IT recruitment consultancy Computer Futures, suggested that with seniority comes a limitation in being able to demonstrate practical experience with the most recent computer systems. This creates difficulties for older managers in seeking jobs at a lower level following redundancy.

Reed employment agencies attempted to influence the attitudes of employers by offering a discount of 50% on their fee to employers taking on workers over 50 years of age. Some employers are beginning to recognize that with age comes experience and that this forms an important asset to the organization in many situations, according to Chris Trott from Chusid Lander, a career consultancy. Subsequent to an article in the *Financial Times* there was a small flurry of letters in support of the older worker and in praise of their qualities. However, it was also pointed out that the same newspaper frequently printed job adverts and articles generally supportive of the ageist stance. Another letter pointed out that certain pension schemes made it prohibitively expensive for employers to take on older workers. So the issue of being too old to work is far from being resolved and is largely based on the perceptions and attitudes of employers.

Adapted from: Summers, D and Milton, C (1993) On the shelf at 45, *Financial Times*, 19 March, p 12. In addition, extracts from the letters pages of the same newspaper as follows: Older people often make better workers than the young, 17 March 1993, p 16; The over 45s: possessed of wisdom but rejected in advertising, 24 March 1993, p 20; No ignoring the actuarial facts of age, 26 March 1993, p 18.

fundamental shifts in attitudes or perceptions. It is possible to achieve the desired reward through compliance behaviour, an instrumental approach. In other words, employees deliver what is expected without changing the underlying attitudes or perceptions. Rambo and Pinto (1989) demonstrate the complex interactions between variables in the creation of perceptions about a pay increase. In reaching this perception, it is not just the scale of money that is taken into account, many other variables influence the decision, future promotion opportunities and size of the current salary being just two.

Perceptions are not directly observable and are usually inferred through the behaviour or attitudes of individuals. One form that these links take is in the discriminatory behaviour adopted by managers towards categories of employee. Sex and race discrimination are the main forms that have a legislative basis to their intended elimination and control. Management in Action 3.7 is about age discrimination. It is clear from the discussion that a number of facts, attitudes and opinions are used to support or oppose the practice of using age as a job selection criterion.

Stop | Consider

MiA 3.7 discusses age discrimination. There are many other forms of discrimination that exist within an organizational setting. Based on your understanding of perception and attitudes as discussed in this chapter, to what extent do you consider that it will ever be possible to eliminate discrimination from within organizations? Or will other forms of discrimination emerge as circumstances change?

Conclusions

The subjects of perception and attitude formation are key aspects of management. They raise issues of ethics as a result of the potential for managers to seek to influence others in an attempt to manipulate events. They are also processes that involve every individual all the time. They are dynamic processes and are of value in helping to simplify the complexity of the world as it is experienced. Unfortunately, by so doing they also make people vulnerable to mistakes in classification by creating illusions and encouraging other errors.

The challenge facing managers is to make positive use of these concepts while not becoming so cynical and manipulative that individuals simply become pawns in the game of life, there to be manipulated at the whim of the master. Perception is one of the fundamental ways in which attitudes are formed and it provides the basis of creating the perceptions of the self by others.

Discussion questions

1. Define the following key terms used in this chapter:

Perception	*Halo effect*	*Figure–ground principle*
Attitude	*Covariation*	*Projection*
Attribution	*Perceptual set*	*Person perception*
Contrast effect	*Stereotyping*	*Stimulus*

2. Describe the perception process.

3. To what extent are the attributions that we make about the consequences of our behaviour more important than the consequences of that behaviour?

4. Do attitudes depend on perceptions, or the other way around?

5. Provide an explanation for the expression, 'Beauty is in the eye of the beholder.'

6. Why is perception described as an active process rather than a passive one?

7. Why might different people interpret the same situation differently? Provide examples from your own experience.

8. Can managers influence the attitudes and perceptions of their subordinates? How could they set about doing so?

9. Why is it that attitudes cannot be directly measured?

10. What is perceptual selection and how does it link with the other stages in the perceptual process?

Research activities

1. Arrange to speak to a manager and a shop floor worker about a situation that they have experienced. Perhaps they have just completed the annual pay negotiations or are undertaking some form of change. If it is not possible to speak to two people from the same organization then make whatever arrangements you can. Discussion issues should centre around how each person perceives a management issue of the day that they have both experienced. What conclusions can you draw from this exercise about perception and attitudes?

2. In the library search out ten research papers from different journals on the subject of perception and ten more on attitudes. Summarize the information obtained and identify in what ways the material supports or refutes the material presented in this chapter. Develop an argument to justify the different viewpoints identified.

3. Along with a friend identify a third person known to you both. Provide independent descriptions of the third person. Use the simplified model of person perception included as Figure 3.14 in this chapter and attempt to account for the different descriptions obtained.

Key reading

Taken from: Clark, H, Chandler, J and Barry, J (1994) *Organization and Identity: Text and Readings in Organizational Behaviour*, International Thomson Business Press, London:

◆ Eysenck, HJ: The rat or the couch?, p 82. This identifies the basis of psychological inquiry, how it developed together with its contribution to understanding phenomena such as perception.

- ◆ Mead, GH: The self, p 99. Of historical interest. As such it illustrates some of the value gained by individuals from perceiving the world around them in the creation of the self.
- ◆ Milgram, S: Conformity and independence, p 132. Considers the effects of social pressure on the perceptions and behaviour of people.
- ◆ Friedan, B: The forfeited self, p 124. This reflects on the gender aspects of theory development.
- ◆ Labov, W: The logic of nonstandard English, p 178. Language as a basis of group identity and as a means of communication is part of the creation of the perceptual world.
- ◆ Mackenzie, G: Class, p 189. The perception of social differences between individuals and groups within society is the basis of control and power within that context.

Further reading

Ajzen, I and Fishbein, M (1980) *Understanding Attitudes and Predicting Social Behaviour*, Prentice Hall, Englewood Cliffs, NJ. A thorough review of the attitude literature and its implication for social behaviour.

Bromley, DB (1993) *Reputation, Image and Impression Management*, John Wiley, Chichester. A social psychological review of the subject of impression management in a variety of forms.

Cialdini, RB (1985) *Influence: Science and Practice*, HarperCollins, London. An interesting and readable text covering the psychology of influence and related behaviours. As such it covers many of the issues relevant to the behavioural consequences of attitudes and perception.

Pease, A (1981) *Body Language: How to Read Others' Thoughts by Their Gestures*, Sheldon Press, London. A practical guide on the interpretation of body language. Not an academic book but it does offer a wide-ranging review of areas that form a significant stimulus input to the perceptual system.

Segall, MH, Dasen, PR, Berry, JW and Poortinga, YH (1990) *Human Behaviour in Global Perspective: An Introduction to Cross-cultural Psychology*, Allyn & Bacon, Needham Heights. Offers a broad review of the subject matter. There are a number of references to attitudes and perception, but Chapter 4 is of particular relevance.

References

Bodenhausen, GV (1988) Sterotypic biases in social decision making and memory-testing process models of sterotyping use, *Journal of Personality and Social Psychology*, 55, 726–37.

Deaux, K and Emswiller, T (1974) Explanations of successful performance on sex-linked tasks: what is skill for the male is luck for the female, *Journal of Personality and Social Psychology*, 24, 30–85.

DePaulo, BM, Kenny, DA, Hoover, CW, Webb, W and Oliver, PV (1987) Accuracy of person perception: do people know what kinds of impression they convey?, *Journal of Personality and Social Psychology*, 52, 303–15.

Festinger, L (1957) *A Theory of Cognitive Dissonance*, Harper & Row, New York.

Festinger, L, Riecken, HW and Schacter, S (1958) When prophecy fails. In (eds) Maccoby, E, Newcombe, T and Hartley, EL, *Readings in Social Psychology*, Methuen, London.

Garrahan, P and Stewart, P (1992) *The Nissan Enigma; Flexibility at Work in a Local Economy*, Mansell, London.

Giacalone, RA (1989) Image control: the strategies of impression management, *Personnel*, May, 52–5.

Gibson, EJ and Walk, RD (1960) The visual cliff, *Scientific American*, 202, 64–71.

Haire, M and Grunes, WG (1950) Perceptual defences: processes protecting an original perception of another personality, *Human Relations*, **3**, 403–12.

Harvey, JH and Weary, G (1984) Current issues in attribution theory and research, *Annual Review of Psychology*, **35**, 431–2.

Hastorf, AH and Cantril, H (1954) They saw a game: a case study, *Journal of Abnormal and Social Psychology*, **49**, 129–34.

Johnson, R (1999) Home truths, *People Management*, 28 October, 65–7.

Katz, D (1960) Determinants of attitude arousal and attitude change, *Journal of Personality*, **24**, p 81.

Kelley, HH (1973) The process of causal attribution, *American Psychologist*, February, 107–28.

Lamb, J (1999) Face values gains credence in 'unwritten' HR policies, *People Management*, 25 November, 14–15.

Likert, R (1961) *New Patterns in Management*, McGraw-Hill, New York.

Lothian, N (1978) Bad language in financial reports, *Accountancy*, November, 42–6.

Morris, D (1982) *The Pocket Guide to Manwatching*, Triad Grafton, London.

Oliver, N and Wilkinson, B (1992) *The Japanization of British Industry: New Developments in the 1990s*, 2nd edn, Blackwell, Oxford.

Pease, A (1984) *Body Language: How to Read Others' Thoughts by their Gestures*, Sheldon, London.

Rafaeli, A and Pratt, MG (1993) Tailored meanings: on the meaning and impact of organizational dress, *Academy of Management Review*, January, 32–55.

Ragins, BR and Sundstrom, E (1990) Gender and perceived power in manager–subordinate relations, *Journal of Occupational Psychology*, **63**, 273–88.

Rambo, WW and Pinto, JN (1989) Employees' perception of pay increases, *Journal of Occupational Psychology*, **62**, 135–46.

Ray, LJ and Reed, M (1994) *Organizing Modernity: New Weberian Perspectives on Work, Organization and Society*, Routledge, London.

Rosenberg, MJ (1960) A structural theory of attitudes, *Public Opinion Quarterly*, Summer, 319–40.

Salancik, G and Pfeffer, J (1977) An examination of need-satisfaction models of job attitudes, *Administrative Science Quarterly*, **22**, 427–56.

Walsh, J (1998) Macho culture blamed for rise in workplace bullying, *People Management*, 15 October, 13.

Warr, PB (1971) Judgements about people at work. In Warr, PB (ed.), *Psychology at Work*, Penguin, Harmondsworth.

Weiner, B (1975) *Achievement, Motivation and Attribution Theory*, General Learning Press, Morristown, NJ.

Welch, J (1998) Creed is good, *People Management*, 24 December, 28–33.

Whitmore, E (1994) To Tell the Truth: Working with Oppressed Groups in Participatory Approaches to Inquiry. In Reason, P (ed.) *Participation in Human Inquiry*, Sage, London.

Witkin, HA, Lewis, HB, Hertzman, M, Machover, K, Meissner, PP and Wapner SS (1954) *Personality Through Perception*, Harper & Row, New York.

CHAPTER 4

Personality and individual difference

CHAPTER SUMMARY

This chapter introduces the concept of individual difference, also termed personality. We begin with a description of what individual difference is and how it is defined. This leads into a consideration of how it has been dealt with in a number of the leading research traditions, in the process reviewing a number of the major theories. The major contextual and other determinants of individual differences are then introduced. The measurement of individual difference and the development of psychometric tests is then integrated into the discussion, along with an introduction of graphology. The use of individual difference is analyzed in the context of an organization and its interaction with people. The chapter concludes with a review of the management perspectives on individual difference.

LEARNING OBJECTIVES

After studying this chapter and working through the associated Management in Action panels, Discussion questions and Research activities, you should be able to:

+ Outline the concept of individual difference.

+ Describe the major theoretical approaches to the study of personality.

+ Appreciate the links between personality and other aspects of individual difference.

+ Understand the strengths and weaknesses of each of the major theories of personality.

+ Detail the relevance of individual difference for other levels of analysis within an organizational setting.

+ Discuss the basic process involved in the development of psychometric tests.

+ Explain the distinction between psychometric tests and the projective approach to personality measurement.

+ Assess the significance of individual difference as a basis for taking decisions relating to people within organizations.

Introduction

Human beings as individuals are unique, every person is different from every other person. Psychologists have long sought to explain what it is that makes each person different. The psychological construct that has been used to embrace the features of individual difference is that of *personality*. The concept of individual difference has a long tradition within psychology and can be traced back to the early Greeks. Theophrastus was a philosopher, who 2000 years ago, asked why it was that with a common culture and education system people displayed different characteristics (Eysenck, 1982).

Personality is about the characteristics that people have that account for *individual difference*. Each human being has the potential to behave in similar ways, yet they do not. Individuals find themselves attracted to some people and repelled by others. Some of the reasons are based on the perception and attitude factors discussed in Chapter 3. However, friendship (or enmity) can also be based upon personality. The sayings that particular individuals are 'too much alike to be friends' or that 'opposites attract' imply that there are *characteristics* that make it more (or less) likely that two people will 'get along'.

Personality eludes precise definition. Allport (1937) identified about 50 different interpretations of the concept. Since then many writers have attempted to define personality through areas of study implied by the term. Hall and Lindzey (1970) suggest that the definition of personality preferred by each writer reflects the theoretical perspective adopted by that person, rather than any common underlying conceptual insights. In other words, the definition of personality used by a particular writer becomes apparent through the description and justification of a particular theory.

The study of individual difference

The problem underlying the level of ambiguity in definition arises because it is not possible to observe psychological phenomena. Personality (as the assumed psychological construct that defines individual difference) cannot be directly observed. Some of the ways in which individual's differ can be observed and described through obvious characteristics such as height, weight etc. However, people differ in other, less tangible ways, for example intelligence, which are much less clear in terms of meaning. Equally, some descriptions of people involve superficial, detectable differences and indicate nothing about the underlying nature and causes of variety between them. Consequently, inferences must be drawn about the underlying psychological structures (of personality) from what can be seen.

The construct of the personality is a convenient way of grouping together a number of characteristics relevant to describing the ways in which people differ from each other. Consider for a moment two friends and how they differ from each other. Perhaps a description would include some of the following:

✦ Physical description. Height, weight, build, hair length and colour.

✦ Emotional description. Gushing, withdrawn, nervous or manipulative.

✦ Sociability description. Friendly, generous, giving, likeable and 'nice'.

MANAGEMENT IN ACTION 4.1

Down with superegos

There are many examples of individuals with very large egos. They exist in the acting profession and the arts as well as the media and other areas of public life. They are the larger than life individuals who frequently make the headlines and demand everything just as they prefer it, irrespective of other considerations. In the entertainment business, sport and other forms of public life such superegos can be a positive asset in creating publicity, filling theatres and attracting attention for fashion designers. Examples are frequently said to include Dustin Hofman, John McEnroe, Naomi Campbell and Armand Hammer.

Superegos are also to be found in business and commercial life and can make life very difficult for the smooth running of a company. Robert Maxwell was a famous example of a superego in this category. It is when such individuals reach the top of the organization that they find most opportunity to express the ego they possess.

At the lower levels of an organization the superego manager might be able to make life difficult, if not impossible for a subordinate or even a group of people, but they would be unlikely to impact on the whole organization. Manfred Kets de Vries (from Insead, a business school in France) argues that individuals need a degree of narcissism to become a business leader, but that when such an individual gets to the top strange things begin to happen. Because of seniority it is frequently necessary for subordinates and colleagues to find ways of containing the effects of the ego and of coexisting with it. Only rarely does a superego find themselves in a position of subordinates engaging in open revolt and of attempting to oust the individual before they bring the whole organization down. The situation is made worse if the superego is the owner of the company as they are able to exercise a greater degree of control over direction and their own activities in relation to it.

Based on child-rearing practice it has been suggested that two basic options exist for dealing with superegos within an organization. The first involves the practice of kow-tow, going along with the superego for a quiet life. This according to Peter Honey (a management consultant) involves  bowing, scraping, following orders and tugging the forelock. As an approach it can work in situations where contact is irregular. For example one literary agent who deals with difficult authors accepts their little quirks and attempts to anticipate the issues that each will pick on and deal with them before they become problems.

The second approach is to directly take the superego on. However, according to Honey this needs to be done carefully if it is to have any effect on the situation. Facing up to a superior with a superego could simply result in dismissal and so it becomes essential to pick the times, places and issues over which to stand fast. Manfred Kets de Vries suggests that in large public companies the only option in many situations is for the subordinate to seek alternative work if they find it impossible to cope with a boss with a superego. The option to approach another executive with the problem might appear attractive, but might also create problems for the whistleblower.

Gerrard Egan from Loyola University in Chicago suggests that organizations need to allow managers to develop appropriate skills in managing others and in being able to capture the benefits of mentoring and the use of confidantes who will tell an individual when they are going too far. The inclusion of subordinate and peer appraisal assessment should also provide an opportunity to contain the effects of the superego within an organization. According to Manfred Kets de Vries the successful leaders are those who are able to put their narcissism to good use rather than simply allowing it free reign.

Adapted from: Kellaway, L (1993) Down with superegos, *Financial Times*, Monday 11 October, p 12.

All these and the many more factors not indicated reflect ways in which people can be differentiated from each other. However, they are not all aspects of personality. Some are aspects of ability or physical characteristics, others are probably a reflection of transient emotional states. Management in Action 4.1 describes how a number of famous people behave and discusses how (as employees) they might be dealt with by their managers.

Stop | Consider   *Do ego and narcissism as described in MiA 4.1 form part of personality? How, if at all do these concepts differ? Justify your answer.*

There is no single definition of personality that would be accepted by all theorists. In one common view, personality is considered to represent those personal characteristics that result in consistent patterns of behaviour (Burger, 1986). This rather loose definition provides some insight into the concept, but leaves many issues undecided. For example, an individual has many characteristics (say, the ability to drive a motor car) which provide the basis for a wide range of behavioural activities, yet they would not usually be regarded as personality characteristics. Also ignored in this definition is any reference to the source of personality. Is personality something that each individual is born with, or does it develop over time with experience? The answer is, probably, both. The relationship between these variables is shown in Figure 4.1.

Taking each element in turn:

A. **Genetic influences.** It is not absolutely clear how much of the personality is determined by the genetic inheritance of the individual. In common expression there are many examples of heredity being used to justify behaviour. For example: 'That [particular behaviour] is just like your father [or mother].' However, an equally strong case has been put forward for the lack of genetic determination of personality, suggesting that it develops through interaction with people and events. This is the so-called nature–nurture controversy.

More recently it has been suggested that both nature (genetics) and nurture (environment) play a part to varying degrees in the determination of personality. For example, that genetics determine the range of possible development for a particular characteristic, but that environmental influences determine the actual extent achieved (Pervin, 1984). There is also some recent evidence from studies on twins by Holden (1987) that the genetic determinants of personality are more significant than previously thought.

B. **Environmental influences** include:
  ✦ Family. When we are born we become part of a family. In our early years we are socialized into a family group and by that family group into the wider society. Parents and siblings all have parts to play in introducing the individual to the behaviour patterns accepted within those cultures. Family in this context also

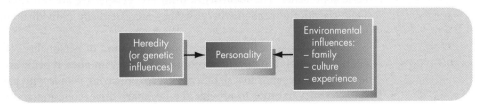

FIGURE 4.1   Relationship between the determinants of personality.

includes grandparents, aunts, cousins and so on, as all have a part to play in establishing behaviour patterns in the child.

There are many ways in which the family influences the development of the individual's personality. They include:

✦   The process of interaction with children which will encourage particular behaviour patterns.

✦   Older members serving as role models for the younger members to imitate.

✦   The circumstances surrounding the family, including family size, economic status, religion and geographic location.

✦   Culture. The culture that an individual is born into has a considerable influence on the behaviour norms to which they are exposed. For example, western cultures tend to emphasize individual characteristics while Asian cultures tend to emphasize collective values. Consequently, appropriate personality characteristics will be encouraged (through socialization) in individuals within each culture. One of the difficulties with the concept of culture is that it can lead to the assumption that all individuals within a specific context will display the same characteristics. The concept of culture is an ideal type. That is, the characteristics implied by a specific culture will be found to a greater or lesser extent in each individual within that context.

✦   Experience. The friendship and other groups to which individuals belong and the general experiences of life all have an effect on behaviour. For example, the experience of being shunned by other children in the infant school playground can have a significant influence on the personality and self-esteem of a child (Bradshaw, 1981).

There are a number of ways in which the subject of personality has been studied. The two major types of theory can be classified as nomothetic and idiographic approaches. *Nomothetic theories* offer an approach to the study of personality based upon the identification and measurement of characteristics. This is achieved through the application of personality tests and tends to assume that the genetic determinants of personality are the most significant.

Idiographic approaches, in contrast, claim that it is necessary to take into account the uniqueness of each individual in describing their personality. It is also claimed that tests are of limited value in measuring personality when as a construct it is defined in terms of the self-concept of the individual. As such within the idiographic tradition, personality is largely a function of the dynamic interaction between the individual and the environment in which they live.

As with many other areas of psychological research, this classification scheme does not account for all the theories that have been developed. There is a third approach to the understanding of personality that combines elements of both the idiographic and nomothetic approaches. The approaches from this perspective are not easy to integrate into a single classification scheme because they are essentially individual contributions to the field.

One challenge in the organizational application of personality refers to the desire to identify which of its many dimensions are the relevant ones. It being argued that organizational success depends to a significant degree on having people with particular personality characteristics in order to provide the necessary drive, cohesion and cultural blend. It is assumed, for example, that intelligence is necessary for success, but is it? Management in

MANAGEMENT IN ACTION 4.2

How do you rate on the common sense scale?

Common sense is an illusive quality that is popularly claimed to be widespread and yet is difficult to identify, particularly in management activities. It is something that recruiters look for in aspiring applicants, particularly potential managers. Einstein defined common sense as the collection of prejudices that people have accrued by the age of 18. Victor Hugo claimed that it was acquired in spite of, rather than because of, education.

However, as Furnham points out there are three major problems with the notion of common sense as a management characteristic. First, the tenets of common sense are frequently contradictory. Consider for example: 'Clothes make the man' and 'You can't make a silk purse out of a sow's ear'. They can't both be right in every situation. Second, if successful management is the application of common sense then no failure can be attributed to faulty reasoning by the individuals concerned. Third, if successful management reflects common sense, and most people have (supposedly) this characteristic, why is there so much disagreement on the issues, processes and procedures associated with the practice of management?

Furnham provides the following true/false quiz to allow you to test yourself on how much common sense you possess. Perhaps you would like to try it for yourself? Remember, however, that it is just for fun!

1. If you pay someone for doing something they enjoy, they will come to like the task even more.   True/False

2. Most people prefer challenging jobs with a great deal of freedom and autonomy.
   True/False

3. Most people are more concerned with the size of their own salary than with the salary of others.   True/False

4. In most cases, workers act in ways that are consistent with their attitudes.
   True/False

5. In bargaining with others, it is usually best to start with a moderate offer – near to the one you desire.   True/False

6. In most cases, leaders should stick to their decision once they have made it, even if it appears they are wrong.   True/False

7. When people work together in groups and know their individual contributions cannot be observed, each tends to put in less effort than when they work on the same task alone.
   True/False

8. Even skilled interviewers are sometimes unable to avoid being influenced in their judgement by factors other than an applicant's qualifications.   True/False

9. Most managers are highly democratic in the way that they supervise their people.
   True/False

10. Most people who work for the government are low risk takers.   True/False

11. The best way to stop a malicious rumour at work is to present convincing evidence against it.   True/False

12. As morale or satisfaction among employees increases in any organization, overall performance almost always rises.   True/False

13. Providing employees with specific goals often interferes with their performance: they resist being told what to do.   True/False

14. In most organizations, the struggle for limited resources is a far more important cause of conflict than other factors such as interpersonal relations.   True/False

15. In bargaining, the best strategy for maximizing long-term gains is seeking to defeat one's opponent.   True/False

16. In general, groups make more accurate and less extreme decisions than individuals.
                                    True/False

17. Most individuals do their best work under conditions of high stress.   True/False

18. Smokers take more days sick leave than do non-smokers.   True/False

19. If you have to reprimand a worker for a misdeed, it is better to do so immediately after the mistake occurs.   True/False

20. Highly cohesive groups are also highly productive.   True/False

Furnham offers the following advice for interpreting the results:

◆ Score 5 or fewer right answers – try early retirement.

◆ Score between 6 and 12 right answers – consider taking an MBA degree.

◆ Score between 13 and 15 right answers – pretty average, but no room for gloating.

◆ Score 16 or over – you do appear to have that most elusive of qualities: managerial common sense.

Answers

True = answers 6, 7, 8, 9, 10, 18, 19.

False = answers 1, 2, 3, 4, 5, 11, 12, 13, 14, 15, 16, 17, 20.

Taken from: Furnham, A (1993) How do you rate on the common sense scale?, *Financial Times*, 5 May, p 14.

Action 4.2 might be taken to imply that common sense is a far more important issue from an organizational point of view.

Stop | Consider   *Having undertaken the exercise in MiA 4.2, what do you think about common sense? Is it a feature of personality or some other aspect of human nature?*
    Is common sense more or less significant (than other aspects of personality) to the achievement of individual's success within an organization?

Nomothetic perspectives

The *nomothetic* approach concentrates on the identification and measurement of those dimensions that are generally considered to be the common characteristics of personality. This approach is based on the analysis of data obtained from research carried out on large numbers of individuals, the purpose of the research being to develop measurement scales reflecting each of the identified characteristics of personality. Once developed this approach allows the measurement and comparison of personality profiles between individuals. So for example, person X has Y level of the introversion characteristic, a score which is similar to the vast majority of the population of which person X forms a part. There are many personality tests of this type, but the best known were those developed by Eysenck and Cattell.

Eysenck and the study of personality types

As far back as Galen, the so-called classical temperaments of *sanguine, phlegmatic, melancholic* and *choleric* were being used to describe personality types (Eysenck, 1965). Quoting a source first published in 1798, Eysenck described the four temperaments as follows:

✦ Sanguine. A person 'carefree and full of hope; attributes great importance to whatever he may be dealing with at the moment, but may have forgotten about it the next. … He is easily fatigued and bored by work but is constantly engaged in mere games – these carry with them constant change, and persistence is not his forte.'

✦ Phlegmatic. A person who displays a 'lack of emotion, not laziness; it implies a tendency to be moved neither quickly nor easily but persistently. … He is reasonable in his dealing with other people and usually gets his way by persisting in his objectives while appearing to give way to others.'

✦ Melancholic. A person who will 'attribute great importance to everything that concerns them. They discover everywhere cause for anxiety and notice first of all the difficulties in a situation, in contradistinction to the sanguine person. … All this is not so because of moral considerations but because interaction with others makes him worried, suspicious, and thoughtful. It is for this (reason) that happiness escapes him.'

✦ Choleric. A person 'said to be hot-headed, is quickly roused, but easily calmed down if his opponent gives in; he is annoyed without lasting hatred. Activity is quick but not persistent. He loves appearances, pomp and formality; he is full of pride and self-love. He is miserly; polite but with ceremony; he suffers most through the refusal of others to fall in with his pretensions. In one word the choleric temperament is the least happy because it is most likely to call forth opposition to itself.'

Eysenck was a prolific writer and produced many books and papers over the years. His 1967 and 1971 texts provide a good overview of the development of his work. His research approach to the study of personality involved both the rating of individuals by skilled raters and the completion of questionnaires by subjects. Eysenck carried out his research on people in the UK, USA and Europe. The results of his vast quantity and range of research data were subjected to a factor analysis in order to identify the underlying dimensions of personality. Factor analysis is a statistical 'technique used to locate and identify fundamental properties underlying the results of tests or measurements and which cannot be measured directly' (Remenyi *et al.*, 1998, p 222). It therefore identifies the presence of underlying relationships between test results. The outcome of the factor analysis was the identification of two dimensions along which personality could be said to vary:

✦ Extroversion. Measured on a scale running between the extremes of *extroversion* and *introversion*. The extrovert likes excitement, is sociable and lively. The introvert, by way of contrast, has a quiet and retiring aspect to their personality.

✦ Neuroticism. This implies a scale running from *neurotic* to *stable* in personality characteristics. The neurotic person tends to worry, is anxious, moody and unstable. The stable person tends to be calm, even tempered, carefree and reliable.

The two personality dimensions identified by Eysenck and the relationship between these and the much older temperaments is reflected in the main axes and quadrants of

Figure 4.2. This figure also indicates the main characteristics of each of the 'types' of personality in the words around the perimeter of the outer circle. For example, someone who was *unstable* would also score highly on tests measuring the concepts of touchy, moody etc. These also reflect the concepts upon which the factor analysis indicated earlier was carried out. The angle between the basic characteristics (passing through the centre point of the circle) is a reflection of the relationship between them. For example, there are about 90° between the characteristics of 'sober and rigid' and 'aggressive and excitable', implying that there is little or no correlation between them. Between the characteristics of 'sober and rigid' and 'lively and easygoing', however, there are 180°, implying a negative correlation. More of 'sober and rigid' means less of the opposite characteristics.

Assessment of the theory   Eysenck claims that the two main personality dimensions are linked to physiological functioning of the human body. For example, neuroticism is (he suggests) positively linked with those aspects of the autonomic nervous system that control body temperature, heartbeat etc. He has attempted to use his theory to explain criminal behaviour and mental illness. For example, criminals are said to be highly extroverted, which, he claims, means that they are slow to condition and any conditioned behaviour is quickly extinguished. Essentially, *conditioning* represents a process of linking stimuli and responses as a basis of acquiring patterns of human behaviour. For example, employees generally do not absent themselves from work for long periods without good reason as they learn from experience that it leads to disciplinary action being taken against them and a loss of income. (Conditioning is discussed more fully in Chapter 9 in relation to learning.)

In linking extroversion with conditioning in the way he does Eysenck is suggesting that

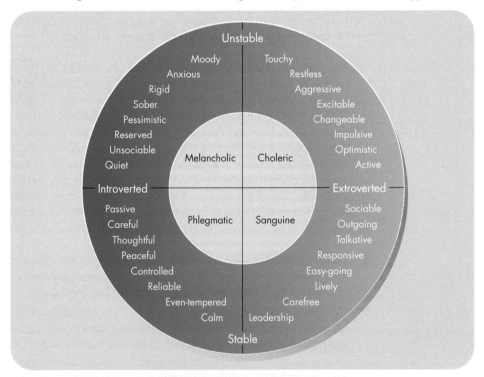

FIGURE 4.2 Eysenck's model of personality (*source*: Eynsenck, HJ (1965) *Fact and Fiction in Psychology*, Penguin, Harmondsworth).

criminals are not conditioned into the patterns of behaviour that would be expected in normal society. The extrovert continually seeks novelty and stimulation which can be achieved through the criminal experience. However, there must be many extroverts who do not become criminals. Equally, it could be argued that much criminal behaviour reflects a conditioned response as the individual gains rewards from it in some way.

There have been many criticisms of Eysenck's work, including the role that nature and genetics is said to play in the development of personality. Also, that having a theory based on just two dimensions is overly simplistic when considering the complexity of human personality and behaviour. However, his work has been based on a considerable amount of detailed research and so has strength. Eysenck himself does not claim that there are only two dimensions associated with personality, simply that they account for most of the published research. By implication, therefore, they are the most significant in the description and understanding of personality and individual difference.

Cattell and personality characteristics

Cattell (1965) developed a test known as the *Sixteen Personality Factor Questionnaire*, (*16PF*). Just as with Eysenck he used factor analysis to sample the variables in what he refers to as the *personality sphere*. His research process in identifying the 16 personality factors was as follows:

1. Trait elements were identified. This was achieved through a dictionary search for all words that described behaviour.

2. Initial research. Synonyms were taken out from the initial pool of words. A small sample of students was intensively studied over a six-month period and rated (by trained observers) on each of the remaining trait elements.

3. Analysis. The results of the initial research were subjected to a cluster analysis. This statistical process identifies relationships (clusters) within the base data. In Cattell's research this was applied to the ratings obtained from the student studies. Fifty clusters were identified and named as *surface traits*. These were then subjected to a factor analysis.

4. Identification of *source traits*. The factor analysis of the surface traits produced the 16 personality factors or *source traits*. It is claimed that because the source traits are determined from the surface traits, which in turn were identified from the trait elements, they account for the whole personality. In short, the trait elements represent all the words developed to account for behaviour, so they must between them embrace every aspect of it, so the research that follows must therefore define individual difference.

In developing the theory Cattell made use of three sources of information:

✦ **L-Data.** This refers to information, or ratings, obtained through the use of trained observers. The 'L' stands for life. For example, the initial research programme of student rating described earlier.

✦ **Q-Data.** This refers to questionnaire responses. An example of these would be the 16PF. He also developed tests of personality for other groups, including:
  ✦ child's personality quiz (CPQ), for children aged from 6 to 11 years
  ✦ high school personality questionnaire (HSPQ), for young people aged between 12 and 15 years.

✦   **T-Data.** This refers to data obtained through test applications. The results are obtained from the performance on tasks specifically designed to measure personality. These objective tests, as Cattell referred to them, were carried out when the subject had no knowledge of their true purpose. Cattell and Warburton (1967) describe over 200 such devices, including:

✦   a chair that recorded the movement of anyone sitting in it, the purpose being to record the 'fidget' score for each person.

✦   as part of a paper and pencil test the inclusion of two sets of identical questions, separated by a few pages. Included in the second presentation was some visually distracting material (say, cartoons). The difference in time to complete the two sets of questions measured the person's distractibility score.

The 16 factors used by Cattell in the 16PF questionnaire (the source traits) are as shown in Figure 4.3.

The first 12 factors have been identified in L-data-based research as well as through Q-data research. The last four items have been found only in Q-data. That is why they have been given a reference designation beginning 'Q', rather than following on from the previous alphabetical designation. The scale for each bipolar factor ranges from one to ten, thus allowing each individual completing the questionnaire to have their results plotted onto the score sheet. The actual questionnaire used by someone completing the 16PF test

Scale		Scale of measurement	
A	Reserved, detached, critical, aloof	1 ↔ 10	Outgoing, warm-hearted, easy-going
B	Less intelligent, concrete thinking	1 ↔ 10	More intelligent, abstact thinking
C	Affected by feelings, easily upset	1 ↔ 10	Emotionally stable, calm, mature
E	Humble, mild, conforming	1 ↔ 10	Assertive, competitive
F	Sober, prudent, taciturn	1 ↔ 10	Happy-go-lucky, enthusiastic
G	Expedient, disregards rules	1 ↔ 10	Conscientious, moralistic
H	Shy, timid	1 ↔ 10	Socially bold
I	Tough-minded, realistic	1 ↔ 10	Tender-minded, sensitive
L	Trusting, adaptable	1 ↔ 10	Suspicious, hard to fool
M	Practical, careful	1 ↔ 10	Imaginative, careless
N	Forthright, natural	1 ↔ 10	Shrewd, calculating
O	Self-assured, confident	1 ↔ 10	Apprehensive, troubled
Q1	Conservative, respects established ideas	1 ↔ 10	Experimenting, radical
Q2	Group dependent, good 'follower'	1 ↔ 10	Self-sufficient, resourceful
Q3	Undisciplined, self-conflict	1 ↔ 10	Controlled, socially precise
Q4	Relaxed, tranquil	1 ↔ 10	Tense, frustrated

FIGURE 4.3   Catell's 16 PF factors (*adapted from*: Catell, RB, Eber, HW and Tasnoka, MM (1970) *Handbook for the Sixteen Personality Factor Questionnaire (16PF)*, Institute for Personality and Ability Testing, Champaign, IL).

contains a number of questions appropriate to each of the factors. After completion by the individual the results for each question are converted to a score on the scale of one to ten by comparison with published norms for the population to which the subject belongs. The individual scores for each factor can be plotted on the scale to provide a profile of the individual's personality. To illustrate this point, Figure 4.4 shows the 'average' profile of managing directors obtained by Cox and Cooper (1988). The test result for a specific managing director could be calculated in comparison with the average for that population and shown on the chart.

Cattell subjected his 16 source traits to another round of factor analysis. From that he identified eight second-order factors. Of these there are only four that are of major concern. Two of the others are not clearly defined and the other two are very close to the existing source traits of intelligence (B) and conscientiousness (G). The four factors were called:

✦ Anxiety. Defined in terms of worry over problems and difficulties, feelings of guilt and tenseness.

✦ Exvia. Defined at one extreme as outgoing, uninhibited and a good mixer. At the other extreme a shy, self-contained person.

✦ Radicalism. Measures the degree of aggression, independence and self-direction within the individual.

✦ Tendermindedness. Defined in terms of sensitivity, liability to frustration and emotionally controlled conduct.

Scale		Scale of measurement	
A	Reserved, detached, critical, aloof	1 2 3 4 5 6 7 8 9 10	Outgoing, warm-hearted, easy-going
B	Less intelligent, concrete thinking	1 2 3 4 5 6 7 8 9 10	More intelligent, abstact thinking
C	Affected by feelings, easily upset	1 2 3 4 5 6 7 8 9 10	Emotionally stable, calm, mature
E	Humble, mild, conforming	1 2 3 4 5 6 7 8 9 10	Assertive, competitive
F	Sober, prudent, teciturn	1 2 3 4 5 6 7 8 9 10	Happy-go-lucky, enthusiastic
G	Expedient, disregards rules	1 2 3 4 5 6 7 8 9 10	Conscientious, moralistic
H	Shy, timid	1 2 3 4 5 6 7 8 9 10	Socially bold
I	Tough-minded, realistic	1 2 3 4 5 6 7 8 9 10	Tender-minded, sensitive
L	Trusting, adaptable	1 2 3 4 5 6 7 8 9 10	Suspicious, hard to fool
M	Practical, careful	1 2 3 4 5 6 7 8 9 10	Imaginative, careless
N	Forthright, natural	1 2 3 4 5 6 7 8 9 10	Shrewd, calculating
O	Self-assured, confident	1 2 3 4 5 6 7 8 9 10	Apprehensive, troubled
Q1	Conservative, respects established ideas	1 2 3 4 5 6 7 8 9 10	Experimenting, radical
Q2	Group dependent, good 'follower'	1 2 3 4 5 6 7 8 9 10	Self-sufficient, resourceful
Q3	Undisciplined, self-conflict	1 2 3 4 5 6 7 8 9 10	Controlled, socially precise
Q4	Relaxed, tranquil	1 2 3 4 5 6 7 8 9 10	Tense, frustrated

FIGURE 4.4 16 PF profile of managing directors (*source*: Cox, CJ and Cooper, CL (1988) *High Flyers*, Basil Blackwell, Oxford).

Exvia is a neologism, not found in an ordinary dictionary. It is an example of one of many words coined by Cattell in an attempt to define the dimensions used in his theory.

Assessment of the theory   The approach adopted by Cattell depends very much on the first step in his research process. If he has been able to identify all the possible trait elements in the personality sphere, then the rest must follow. The statistical tests carried out on his findings are such that the surface and source traits must account for the variation in behaviour. The basis of the claim is that because the behaviour exists, a verbal label is necessary to describe it. If no label exists then the behaviour cannot exist. This, of course, raises many questions relating to behaviour, language and the way in which personality interacts with both.

Words are used to describe ideas and feelings as well as behaviour, needs and wants. Consequently, the words identified might not reflect individual difference characteristics alone. There is also a complex relationship between the observable behaviour of individuals and the underlying personality characteristics that help to shape that behaviour. The links between what is observable, the words used to describe it and the associated psychological structures are far from clear.

Idiographic perspectives

The *idiographic* perspective emphasizes the development of the self-concept aspects of personality rather than concentration on the measurement of common characteristics. There are difficulties for the test-based approach of Eysenck and Cattell as a result of the imposition of the researcher's own frame of reference on data collection and analysis. Eysenck and Cattell reflect the *positivist* approach to epistemology in research. Epistemology is the branch of philosophy that debates the ways in which individuals begin to understand the world and communicate that knowledge to others (Burrell and Morgan, 1979, p 1). *Positivists* hold that the social world consists of cause and effect relationships, just like the world of the natural sciences and that the role of social science is to discover these causal connections (Kolakowski, 1993). Inevitably, therefore, positivists tend to follow the experimental and scientific tradition in the search for underlying regularities laws that create the social world.

However the *interpretivist* tradition takes the opposing perspective and suggests that the social world is fundamentally different from that of the natural sciences. Therefore, the underlying laws implied by *positivists* do not exist as such. *Interpretivists* hold that the social world is created (or given meaning and substance) within the minds of the people who live in it. Consequently, there will be differences in how individuals conceptualize the social world in which they live. Therefore, understanding the individual and their view of the social world is necessary in seeking to understand behaviour.

In relation to individual difference, idiographic theorists argue that in order to understand unique personality characteristics it is first necessary to understand how the individual relates to the world in which they live and the individual qualities that make each person different from every other person.

Cooley, an American psychologist, introduced the concept of the *looking-glass self* to the debate on personality. He draws attention to the interactive nature of much behaviour and the development of self-image as a result of this process. We begin to see ourselves as others see us through the responses that we generate from others. This is the *looking-glass*, or mirror, that reflects a perspective back to us. Through the interactions with the people around us we come to understand who we are and so learn to adapt our personality to accommodate our environment.

Mead (1934) added to this approach through the concept of the *generalized other*. This concept is intended to reflect the existence of two components in the 'self'. They are:

✦ I. The unique, spontaneous and conscious aspects of the individual.

✦ Me. The internalized norms and values learned through experience within society.

The *generalized other* refers to the understanding that the individual develops of the expectations that society have of them. It is in the *me* element of the 'self' that this evaluation takes place. The *I* component is the aspect of personality that attempts to ensure that the individual meets their own expectations, rather than becoming a creature totally of the *me* component. It also allows the opportunity to provide for evolution in society through the adaptation of social norms to meet the needs of the individuals within it.

Rogers (1947) proposed that the main objective of personality is a desire fully to realize one's potential. Like Mead, he also used the two components of *I* and *me* in describing the self-concept. His view of the linkages between *I*, *me* and the *self-concept* is illustrated in Figure 4.5.

One implication of this model of the self-concept is that the personality will be subject to change as the underlying personal self and social self change due to experience. This linkage is demonstrated in the model by the connections between the elements and the relationship implied by them. If this change did not occur then a tension would be created which could lead to the emergence of personality disorders within the individual.

Erikson (1980) considered the personality to be continually developing throughout life. His view was that as the individual passed through the various life stages tensions and conflicts arise which have to be dealt with. For example Erikson's fifth life stage covers the years from 12 to 18 years of age when an individual experiences tensions between identity and role confusion. In dealing with these conflicts the individual who successfully negotiates a resolution achieves healthy personality growth, whereas unresolved conflicts can lead to problems in later life. In this model there is a clear link between the concept of individ-

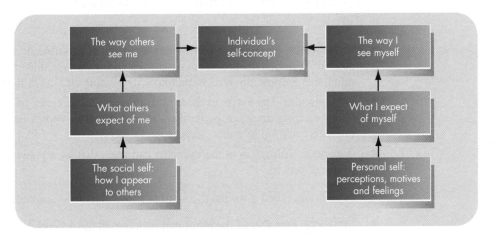

FIGURE 4.5 Rogers' view of the 'I' and 'me'.

ual difference and the development of the *self-concept* in a dynamic and ongoing relationship over time.

Other perspectives on individual difference

Freud and psychoanalysis

Sigmund Freud lived from 1856 until 1939 and spent most of his life in Vienna. He trained as a physician and then specialized as a neurologist. He originally worked with Josef Breuer who specialized in the use of hypnosis in the treatment of hysteria. In 1895 Freud and Breuer published a book called *Studies on Hysteria*. However, by the time of its publication Freud was beginning to use *free association* for the treatment of hysteria. In doing so he was moving away from an emphasis on hypnosis and had also stopped working with Breuer. This use of *free association* was the critical step in the development of psychoanalysis.

Free association is a process that begins with an item of emotional significance for an individual. The initial task of the psychoanalyst is to identify these items of significance through discussion with the patient. Freud suggested that dreams were a potent source of items of emotional significance with which to begin the process. The individual is then encouraged to talk about their ideas and thoughts in relation to these items of emotional significance until for whatever reason they stop. In technical terms they *break off from the chain of association*. This process is then repeated for other items of significance for the individual.

The points at which the individual broke off the thought chain were held to be major points of psychological resistance. Freud claimed that this occurred when the individual's internal psychological processes attempted to protect them from bringing out into the open those things which the individual wished to be protected from. It was these resistance points that became the focus for Freud's research and the development of psychotherapy.

Freud was a prodigious writer and his collected papers amount to some 24 volumes (Strachey, 1953–66). His theorizing was complex and covered many aspects of life, from cannibalism to the choice of career. According to Freud, there are three levels of mental activity:

✦ Unconscious. This refers to mental activity that is inaccessible, deeply hidden and only accessible through the process of psychoanalysis. Although hidden from the conscious mind, this unconscious level of mental activity motivates much human *behaviour*.

✦ Pre-conscious. This refers to those ideas that are unconscious, but unlike the unconscious category, they can be recalled when necessary. People's names and telephone numbers often fall into this category.

✦ Conscious. This refers to the thoughts and ideas that we are aware of in the normal course of activity.

In addition, Freud classified the mind as consisting of three areas:

✦ Id. The *id* is the area of the mind that contains all the inherited information available to the individual. It is the cauldron of our very being. It is the part of our mind that follows the pleasure principle in seeking immediate gratification and satisfaction regardless of the consequences.

✦ Ego. The *ego* develops during childhood and serves to balance the demands of the *id*. In doing so the *ego* follows the reliability principle in assessing the consequences of behaviour originating in the demands of the *id*.

✦ Superego. This becomes the internalized version of parents. The *superego* becomes the observer of the ego and controls it through the same devices as would be adopted by the parents. Freud claimed that the *superego* had developed by about the age of five.

According to Freud, detectable behaviour in an individual is a balance between these three components of the mind. A well-adjusted individual will be controlled by their *ego*, a neurotic (driven by anxiety about the imposition of external control) through their *superego*, and the psychopath (driven by their own desires) through the *id*. The intention of psychotherapy as used by Freud is to restore the *natural* balance between the three components of the mind and so produce a 'healthy' individual in terms of personality.

In terms of individual difference, Freud described a process of development lasting from birth through to early adult life. The development of personality was the outcome of internal struggles and involved passing through a number of stages:

✦ Oral. The initial stages of life lasting from birth to about the age of two years. It reflects the importance of feeding, pleasure achievement and bonding with the mother.

✦ Anal. Lasting from about two years of age until four. It reflects the focus of attention shifting from the 'input' to the 'output' aspects of life.

✦ Phallic. At about the age of four the child enters the final stage of development which ends with puberty. This reflects the development of the individual in terms of the growing initial awareness of genital significance in subsequent sexual activity.

It is through the *id, ego* and *superego* that adults manage their interaction with the world around them. Freud described a number of defence mechanisms adopted by the ego in order to maintain the balance between the id and superego. Defence mechanisms protect the individual from the 'damage' that could result from unresolved internal conflict. The main forms of *ego defence mechanism* are:

✦ Sublimation. This allows the desires emerging from the id to be expressed in an acceptable manner. For example, pottery making and painting can be described as a sublimation for the anal drives to handle and smear faeces.

✦ Repression. This describes a process where the existence of something is deliberately kept hidden from the conscious thinking level because it might be too painful.

✦ Denial. This is a defence mechanism similar to repression, except that the ego alters the perception of the situation in order to maintain the balance.

✦ Projection. The transmission of feelings and motives to other people. A manager might seek to justify their own political activity on the basis that others began such behaviour first.

✦ Reaction formation. This produces the opposite feelings and behaviour at the conscious level to those held at the unconscious level. So for example, unrequited love can become hate.

✦ Regression. The avoidance of problems between the id and superego through the adoption of patterns of behaviour that once produced satisfaction. For example, an older child may suck its thumb when being scolded by its parents.

✦ Isolation. This results in a separation of feelings and emotions from the experiences that normally produce them.

✦ Undoing. This attempts to 'undo' something that is thought to have happened. The obsessional washing of hands, over and over again, could reflect a person attempting to cleanse themselves in a deeper way.

Assessment of the theory

Freud's approach to personality is not a single theory as such. It is a complex model, including aspects of intellectual and sexual development, training, education, mental structure, social process and the dynamics of interaction. As such it is difficult to offer specific criticisms and equally difficult to defend it against any that are raised. Eysenck (1953) sets out the major objections to the theory, essentially on the basis that it was not scientific:

✦ Lack of data and statistical analysis. The data were not subjected to the processes considered acceptable by psychologists trained in the 'scientific method'.

✦ Sample base. The sample for his theory were mostly private patients, middle class and female. Furthermore, they put themselves forward for his treatment of their neurosis. They are not a representative sample and claims for a theory developed on such a population must be open to question.

✦ Inadequate definition of terms used. The terms used to define Freudian theory are ill defined and consequently it is not possible to be absolutely certain of the meaning or even of their existence.

✦ Lack of 'testability'. Because of the 'richness', and complexity of Freudian theory it is not possible to falsify it. The scientific method involves a reductionist approach. Freud adopted a holistic model and attempted to reflect the complexity of life in a complex model.

The arguments raised by Eysenck are those that would be expected from a positivist when commenting on the work of an interpretivist (see, for example, the discussion in Henwood and Pidgeon, 1993 on this type of debate). The exponents from these two traditions talk past each other in deciding what offers an acceptable basis for explaining the social world. They therefore criticize each other's work largely because it does not fit into their preferred paradigm.

Other arguments against Freud's work include that it offered circular arguments to support the ideas in it and that by emphasizing early childhood it produces a model that is deterministic and ignores the possibility of subsequent individual development (see, for example, the work of Erikson outlined earlier). However, Freud's model offers a 'richness' in attempting to encompass the whole of personality in a grand theory. Parts of the theory have been subjected to a more rigorous form of testing with some success (Kline, 1972).

At a practical level much of Freud's work led on to other research and subsequent thinking on the complexity of personality. Freud was interested in understanding the whole person and the part that early development played in the formation of the adult personality. The theory can be seen in some behaviour at work, for example, employees and managers often display 'temper tantrums' when things do not go according to plan, perhaps reflecting the ego defence mechanism of regression at work.

Jung and the cognitive approach

Jung was a close associate of Freud for a while, but the relationship was destined not to last for long and they parted company in 1913. Jung developed an approach to personality based on Freudian theory, but which incorporated aspects of the future goals held by an individual rather than simply emphasizing the past (Jung, 1968). It postulated three levels of personality:

✦ A conscious level. This aspect of personality allowed for reality to be incorporated as a result of the everyday experience of the individual.
✦ An unconscious level. This makes up the individuality of each person and is composed of the complexes and facets within individual difference.
✦ A collective unconscious. This is the pool of inherited and socially derived universal experience that each person carries with them inside their personality.

Personality differences were reflected by a number of dimensions within Jungian theory, including the use of the extroversion and introversion. Another dimension was that of cognitive style, reflecting four different approaches to information gathering and evaluation:

✦ Sensing. People who prefer to deal with hard information in a structured context.
✦ Intuiting. People who dislike routine activities, but who prefer to deal with possibilities rather than certainty.
✦ Thinking. People who prefer the use of logic and rationality as the basis of problem solving, without the feelings of others entering into the process.
✦ Feeling. People who prefer to have social harmony around them, get along with others and have sympathy for those around them.

From this description it might be apparent that there are two dimensions involved in this framework: *sensing* and *intuiting* are at opposing ends of a continuum as are *thinking* and *feeling*. This is reflected in Figure 4.6.

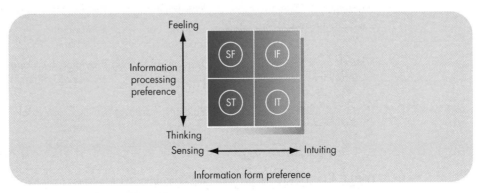

FIGURE 4.6 Jung's cognitive styles.

The main personality characteristics for each cell in the matrix shown in Figure 4.6 are described in Table 4.1. This indicates the application of Jung's theory in differentiating personality and in describing the consequences of that approach for job preferences.

Assessment of the theory   The theory developed by Jung lends itself more easily to testing than that of Freud. The Myers–Briggs Personality Indicator (referred to as the MBTI) is based on Jung's view of personality, to which was added a dimension reflecting lifestyle (Myers–Briggs, 1987). This is now a well-established psychological test and is widely used by organizations as an assessment tool and by researchers interested in occupational choice, personality and management style.

However, the work of Jung has not gone without criticism. Eysenck (1965) claims that the concepts of extroversion and introversion were already in existence. However, it must be remembered that Eysenck offers a theory of personality based on the scientific method and that he is generally dismissive of approaches based on a holistic perspective.

Murray and personology

Murray was another writer who attempted to reflect the whole individual in the theoretical model. Indeed, he preferred the term personology to psychology as a description of his work. He emphasized the study of personology as a 'science of men taken as gross units' (1938). Murray worked intensively with a small number of subjects. The potential advantage of this was a fuller understanding of each individual person, with, potentially, generalizable theory resulting from the in-depth analysis.

Murray identified a total of 44 variables in his approach to individual difference, including:

✦   Needs. These form the main motivating factor in behaviour. He identified 20 *manifest* and eight *latent* needs. Manifest needs he described in familiar terms, for example, play, achievement, understanding and autonomy. Latent needs he described as being inhibited and usually expressed in fantasy rather than overt behaviour.

| | Jung's cognitive style | | | |
	Sensing/thinking (ST)	Intuiting/thinking (IT)	Sensing/feeling (SF)	Intuiting/feeling (IF)
Prefers	Facts	Possibilities	Facts	Possibilities
Personality	Pragmatic, down-to-earth	Logical, but ingenious	Sympathetic, sociable	Energetic, insightful
Work preferences	Technical skills	Theoretical solving problem	Providing help and services to others	Understanding and communicating with others
	Physician, accountant, computer programmer	Scientist, corporate planner, mathematician	Salesperson, social worker, psychologist	Artist, writer, entertainer

TABLE 4.1   Differences between Jung's cognitive styles (*adapted from*: Vecchio, RP (1991) *Organizational Behaviour*, 2nd edn, Dryden Press, Hinsdale)

◆ Presses. These are the external determinants of behaviour. *Presses* operate on the needs of the individual, depending upon the circumstances. For example, successful organizations are able to create environments and cultures which in turn encourage an achievement orientation and behaviour among individual employees.

◆ Internal states. Murray identified four *internal states* that are capable of influencing behaviour, for example the ego ideal. The ego ideal refers to an aspect of personality that reflects an unrealized achievement drive based on a high level of, as yet unmet, aspiration.

◆ General traits. Murray listed 12 of these, including anxiety, emotionality and creativity. They are intended to embrace the broad characteristics that influence much behaviour. They can be seen as qualifiers to the other variables. For example, a person with a high level of anxiety will respond differently to the need for play than will a highly creative person.

Murray developed his theory over a number of years, through the application of a range of measurement devices. He tested his subjects on 24 different test applications in a single 36-hour period. This inevitably placed his subjects under considerable strain. Among those tests were:

◆ Autobiographies. Subjects wrote about their lives and this was analyzed to identify any of the 44 variables already described. Particular emphasis was placed on childhood events.

◆ Interviews. Murray and his team interviewed each subject about issues such as their memories of childhood, family relationships and problems currently being experienced.

◆ Experiments. A number of tests were used to measure specific aspects of the theory. For example, one test required subjects to print words quickly using a hand-printing set.

◆ Projective tests. A projective test is an ambiguous stimulus and subjects are asked to describe what is happening. The interpretation of the picture is considered to reflect something about the individual's life and inner thinking processes. Figure 4.7 is similar to those used by Murray in that the events in the picture could be interpreted in many different ways. The description provided by the subject is therefore based on their elaboration of the limited (and ambiguous) information provided.

Assessment of the theory   Murray drew heavily on the work of Freud and Jung as his inspiration, but he provided a broad range of measurement to support his work. Eysenck (1959) claimed that there is almost no validity for the projective technique and that testers do not agree with each other on the interpretation of test protocols. He goes on to claim that projective tests are the vehicles for the riotous imagination of clinicians.

Murray was not the first to use the projective test as a means of gaining insight. Leonardo Da Vinci was the first person to record that paint smudges tended to be interpreted differently depending upon occupation and experience (Rabin, 1958). In more recent times we have the Rorschach test, named after the Swiss psychiatrist who developed the approach. They are also frequently referred to as 'inkblot' tests, as they are created from a series of shapes formed from inkblots. Figure 4.8 is an example of an inkblot shape as used in this type of test.

The type of projective test used by Murray differed from the Rorschach test in that he required subjects to create a story from an ambiguous drawing, rather than responding to a shape such as Figure 4.8. He went further than many of his contemporaries in providing a scientific basis for his work. However, it is still susceptible to the claim that it is weak in the level of scientific method adopted.

Kelly's personal construct theory

Kelly suggested that every human being was effectively a scientist in the way in which they developed the ability to interact with the environment (Kelly, 1961). This view implies that

FIGURE 4.7 Ambiguous picture.

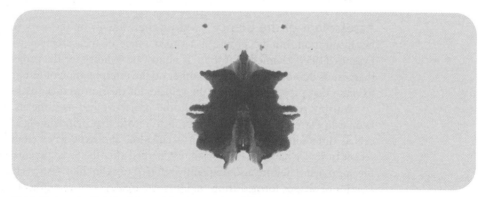

FIGURE 4.8 An 'inkblot' figure like that used in the Rorschach test.

human beings are essentially predictive in their approach to identifying appropriate behaviour within a particular environmental context. The scientific process involved in determining behaviour patterns reflects a process of reformulating hypotheses about the world in the light of new information and seeking to adjust the behavioural repertoire accordingly.

Human beings develop a series of constructs through which to view the world around them. These form the basis of the ability to categorize the similarities and differences in events as they occur in the environment. A construct in this context is a bipolar continuum of extremes. For example, happy–sad; I am now–I would like to be; friendly–hostile; work I enjoy–work I hate. These are illustrations of constructs defined by Kelly and the constructs are arranged into a complex internal mental framework as the individual's *personal construct system*. It is described as a hierarchical network as they interlink in a web of expectation and relationship. For example, an individual classified as trustworthy will be expected to display many other related behaviours such as honesty, reliability, friendliness and so on. For Kelly, the personality reflects the way in which the individual develops a framework for, and experiments with, their world.

There are a number of characteristics relating to the way in which individuals utilize their network of constructs and the dynamics associated with the process, including:

✦ Individuals develop a personal prediction model for future events based on the identification of a replication of patterns in past events.

✦ Individuals differ in the networks of constructs that they develop. One of the consequences of this is that it produces a relatively unique interpretation basis within each person.

✦ The constructs that people develop have a limited range of application. Every construct contains a field of relevance for its application. This is psychologically based and meaningful only for the individual concerned.

✦ Construct systems are dynamic. They are essentially a basis for effective functioning in the future. The frameworks are liable to modification in the light of the feedback obtained from the responses to particular behaviours.

This approach to the study of personality implies that the personal construct theory accounts for individual difference. It allows for two individuals to respond differently to the same situation. The hierarchy and network of constructs is unique for each individual, therefore the experience of a situation is different for each individual exposed to it.

Kelly developed the 'repertory grid' as a means of identifying and measuring the constructs utilized by an individual. The process for developing a repertory grid is as follows (Kelly, 1961):

✦ The individual is asked to identify an important way in which two significant people (to the testee) are similar, but differ from a third. These two opposing features are the construct dimension underlying the channel of thought used by the individual.

✦ This process is repeated (not necessarily based on the same people) until between 20–30 separate distinguishing features are identified.

✦ A matrix is formed with the significant names along the top and the constructs identified listed down the side.

✦ A binary number (zero or one) would be entered in each cell of the matrix, based on the subject's assessment of whether each named person was more like one extreme of the construct or the other.

✦ The completed matrix can then be factor analyzed to identify the similarities and differences between the constructs identified. The cell entries can be examined to identify patterns among relationships. Figure 4.9 is an example of a repertory grid indicating the basic appearance of the matrix and constructs identified.

Assessment of the theory   The personal construct approach to personality allows the development of an understanding in terms that are meaningful for the individual. The repertory grid mechanism allows the identification of how the individual construes the world and how they set about interacting with it. From this perspective it is grounded in a broader interpretation of personality than many of the other theories. Kelly suggests that personal construct theory is relevant to an understanding of an individual's perceptual frameworks and attitudes as well as personality and its development. It is a theory concerning the way in which an individual makes sense of their world and experiments with it.

This notion of experimenting with the world has lead to some criticism of the theory. It is often assumed by scientists that they are the people who experiment and that only they are in a position to utilize the scientific method effectively. But, of course, this need not be the only definition of experimentation. Young children experiment with the world around them when they are engaged in play activities. They are learning the skills needed to manipulate aspects of their environment and how to behave towards it. This approach continues in adult life according to Kelly, reflecting a form of life and behavioural experimentation.

The theory provides an explanation of personality that takes the whole person into account. It provides a means of developing an understanding of personality in a way that is relevant to the individual being studied. It does not force the person into a framework developed on other people. The theory provides an approach to the study of personality that does not pre-judge the form of personality; it is defined by the individuals being studied.

		Significant people					
		Self	Father	Mother	Brother	Friend A	Friend B	
Constructs	Loving	1	1	1	0	0	1	Cold
	Friendly	1	0	1	1	0	1	Unfriendly
	Trustworthy	1	1	1	1	1	1	Untrustworthy
	Helpful	1	0	1	0	1	0	Unhelpful
	Like me	1	0	0	0	1	1	Not like me

FIGURE 4.9   Simplified repertory grid.

The social and situational context in individual difference

Human beings live in a social world. Individual difference is one way in which that collectivity can be varied and allow individuals to survive and cope with life. There is therefore an implicit assumption that emerges from this view of the social value of individual difference, that there will exist a degree of reciprocal influence between the individual and the social context. In terms of the personality this is further supported through the nature–nurture debate alluded to earlier. A young child is relatively helpless and does not display the full range of personality characteristics apparent in adulthood. These develop and become more apparent over time.

One aspect of this development process reflects the *socialization* concepts already introduced. In growing, the child is introduced into the family unit and learns much of their behaviour patterns from that context and the environment which surrounds the primary grouping. Part of this process is about learning to be male or female. Boys are given different toys to play with than girls and they are also treated differently by their parents. It has been argued that this leads to boys developing the stereotypical aggressive behaviours of being tough and not crying. Girls, by the same token, are encouraged to develop different characteristics.

Another way in which the context and individual difference links together is through the notion of an *internal* or *external locus of control*. Individuals vary in the degree to which they consider that they are subject to control by forces internal or external to themselves. This does not refer to the direct control of behaviour or thoughts through hearing voices etc. It simply indicates the degree to which an individual considers that they are in charge of their own destiny. In many ways this is based around the individual's expectations. Human beings are predictive organisms in that we tend to learn from experience and predict future events based upon them. Individuals tending towards an internal locus of control would rely more heavily on their own capabilities and behaviour in seeking success. Kuratho and Hodgetts (1989) for example, suggest that successful business leaders fall into this category, relying on a belief in success being created by their personal ability to control events, not through the contribution of others.

Measuring personality and individual difference

Psychometrics

Personality measurement is an area of considerable interest in psychology. Several ways in which personality characteristics can be measured have been introduced earlier in this chapter. For example, the 16PF personality inventory. This could be described as a *hard systems* approach to the measurement of personality. However, the use of the idiographic or psychoanalytical method allows much more richness to be taken into account in developing an understanding of the whole person and their personality. These could be described as soft *systems* approaches to the study of individual difference. A combination of hard and soft systems is used in the work of Murray and Kelly as they attempt to utilize qualitative and quantitative approaches to the understanding of personality.

A psychological test is usually defined as a set of tasks presented in a standard form and which produce a score as the output, usually in numerical form allowing for comparison with population norms. This is called *psychometrics* or the process of mental measurement.

There are two main reasons that psychometric tests are used. The first is to undertake scientific research into behaviour and an understanding of people. The second is to enable decisions relating to people to be made. For example, who to appoint to a particular job and for the purposes of identifying appropriate career development advice. In both of these examples there is a need for accurate information in relation to those aspects of people that are of interest to the purpose. There are many tests available that can offer insights into a wide variety of the many aspects of individual difference. They include tests of particular skills, abilities, intelligence, aptitudes, job preferences, psychological functioning and extroversion/introversion. Test batteries such as the 16PF introduced earlier seek to test a broad range of dimensions of individual difference within the one instrument.

There are three ways in which tests can measure individual difference:

1. Comparison of performance against a standard. Response times to undertake a particular task being one example.
2. Norm-referenced measurement. This compares an individual's performance on a test with that of a peer group.
3. Criterion-referenced measurement. This compares performance on a test with an 'ideal' result.

The basis of a psychometric test is that the responses given by the testee can be interpreted as an indication of an underlying characteristic. Therefore, a test is claimed to be *valid* if it measures what it claims to measure. That does not mean, however, that there is a direct link between the test question and the underlying characteristic. The question asked may bear no apparent relationship to the characteristic itself. It is, however, necessary that the question elicit responses that can discriminate between those people with the underlying characteristic and those without it. In addition a test needs to be *reliable* in consistently producing the same result (individual profile) over time. There are different forms of *validity* and *reliability*, including:

✦   Face validity. This refers to the degree to which a test appears as if it ought to measure what it sets out to measure.

✦   Predictive validity. This form of validity reflects the ability of tests to predict future events. A test would have predictive validity if high-scoring individuals were successful, while low-scoring individuals performed badly in the job for which the test was being used as a selection aid.

✦   Construct validity. This refers to the extent that a test can be related back to a theory.

✦   Test/retest reliability. This reflects the ability of a test to produce the same score when it is administered on two different occasions.

✦   Alternative form reliability. Some tests are developed in two or more different forms. All the forms available should produce the same score or individual profile.

✦ Split half reliability. This reflects the internal consistency within a particular test. Splitting the test up and comparing the results from the various combinations of questions or activities within it is a means of measuring this form of reliability.

The application and interpretation of psychometric tests is a skilled job. Over recent years the British Psychological Society, the professional body representing psychologists, has developed and introduced a series of training programmes and qualification levels for those people seeking to use psychometric tests. This was done in response to a widespread concern that anyone could use, or more accurately misuse, these tests and in so doing inflict considerable damage to individuals, organizations and the psychology profession.

Developing psychometric tests

Psychometric tests go through a considerable development process before being accepted as usable for release and general application. The process of test development can be summarized as follows:

✦ **Step 1.** The initial ideas for a test often emerge from a practical need, for example, assisting personnel managers to identify the most appropriate job applicants. Tests can also originate from a theoretical need to measure some characteristic of individual difference as part of the development of theory.

✦ **Step 2.** The development of appropriate test items is a creative process. Many items generated will be unsuitable for any number of reasons, chiefly that they do not contribute to measuring the intended characteristics. It takes a considerable amount of time and ingenuity to identify an appropriate range of test items suitable for eventual use.

✦ **Step 3.** The final forms of the test are developed and the administration arrangements designed. Attempts to prevent 'faking' an answer are built into the test. As far back as 1956 William H Whyte was offering advice on 'How to cheat on personality tests' (see Management in Action 4.3).

Stop | Consider

MiA 4.3 implies that it is easy to 'fake' test results in the sense of being able to present a particular image of the 'self' in an attempt to conform to the management desired profile. Do you think this is possible? Does it matter as long as the individual demonstrates that they can, if necessary, display the desired characteristics? What might this imply?

✦ Step 4. The 'standardization' and 'norming' process. The populations for whom the test is intended to be used must be identified and statistically valid test scores collected for them. These results are used to calculate the standard scores or profiles against which a particular individual will be compared. These provide the basis of comparison between an individual and the general population of which they form part. For example, Figure 4.4 demonstrated the 16PF profile of managing directors, against which particular managing directors could be compared. This stage provides the basis (once the test is published) for conclusions to be drawn about an individual. These ultimately lead to courses of action being identified, perhaps recruitment to a particular job or further training being given.

MANAGEMENT IN ACTION 4.3

How to cheat on personality tests

There are many organizations that make use of psychometric tests in the search for the perfect match between the organization, work and worker. This is nothing new: as early as 1956 one author was offering the following advice on how to make the best of having to take a personality test, the output from such tests being a comparison of the individual taking the test with the population of which they are part. They are premised on the view that while there are some tests in which a high score would be beneficial to the individual, many require the individual to demonstrate that they are broadly similar to everyone else. So, for example, if the test were intended to identify who would make a 'good chemist' then a high score in comparison with the population at large would be beneficial to the career prospects of the testee. By way of contrast, in a test of personality, it would be beneficial to find that the test results indicate that the individual displays 'normal' characteristics in common with the bulk of the population.

To quote specifically from the advice offered by the author when taking personality tests:

> By and large, however, your safety lies in getting a score somewhere between the 40th and 60th percentiles, which is to say, you should try to answer as if you were like everyone else is supposed to be. This is not always easy to figure out, of course [...] When in doubt, however, there are two general rules that you can follow: (1) when asked for word associations or comments about the world, give the most conventional, run-of-the-mill, pedestrian answer possible. (2) To settle on the most beneficial answer to any question, repeat to yourself:

(a) I loved my father and my mother, but my father a little bit more.

(b) I like things pretty well the way they are.

(c) I never worry much about anything.

(d) I don't care for books or music much.

(e) I love my wife and children.

(f) I don't let them get in the way of company work.

The rationale behind this advice is that psychometric tests are intended to identify the presence of those characteristics desired by organizations. The feeling emerging from the above quotation is that the individual so described would be an 'organization man' of the highest order. Someone who would not think much and would not be distracted from the task in hand. Performing the tasks identified by management in a way which would not question them or pose a threat to the position of management. The human equivalent of the computer – after all remember this was written before the computer was used within organizations. It was also offered at a time when the masculine choice of words would have not seemed out of place – because there were so few women in career positions within management. However, the main point that emerges from considering these words of advice are that tests are intended to identify those characteristics deemed important by the test creators. That is as true today as it was when they were first written.

Taken from: Whyte, WH (1960) *The Organization Man*, a Penguin special, Penguin, Harmondsworth.

MANAGEMENT IN ACTION 4.4

Personality tests: the great debate

The debate about the value of personality tests has been going on for many years and is still far from being resolved. The basis for the use of such tests within organizations is quite simple. It is argued (by the supporters of tests) that there are in existence a number of personality characteristics that can be measured. Furthermore, certain personality characteristics are of value in the execution of particular jobs. Put simply, a sales job is assumed to require a high degree of extroversion. Therefore, if organizations can identify the personality requirements associated with particular jobs and then measure the existence of these same characteristics within job candidates a good match can be made. The result being higher individual and company performance. There are also indirect benefits possible in that training needs can be identified and individual work satisfaction could be improved through the analysis of test results.

The counter-argument is that the test results do not match the predictions made in terms of increased organizational performance. In short they do not deliver high performance compared with organizations and individuals that do not use tests as the basis of decision making. It is argued that the normal experience of work for an individual is very complex and rich in terms of events and interaction with other people. Consequently, there are many other variables active in the dynamic achievement of performance than implied by a personality test.

Given that the value of tests is evaluated through the use of statistics the debate is frequently likened to the old saying about, 'lies, damned lies and statistics'. Without a sophisticated understanding of the use of statistical analysis and the implications of test design and evaluation an extreme view is likely to be taken towards test use. Most professional test designers would not claim to provide the ultimate ability to understand individuals and make decisions about them. They would argue, as does D Mckenzie Davey, a chartered psychologist, that tests should be used in the same way in which a physician would use data on blood counts. Temperature and pulse rate would be used along with observation in order to reach a diagnosis and before deciding on a treatment plan based on discussion with the patient.

The debate is perhaps a futile one in that not all aspects of work are personality based and intuitive methods of determining job opportunities are also limited in their ability to predict subsequent performance accurately. Perhaps both approaches are needed, but caution should be exercised in interpreting the results of tests, just as it should with the opinions of human beings about other human beings. Training in the use of tests and their interpretation is as necessary as it is in other areas of decision making and management.

Adapted from: Fletcher, C (1991) Personality tests: the great debate, *Personnel Management*, September, pp 38–42.

✦ **Step 5.** At this stage, the data will be subjected to the various reliability and validity analyses described earlier. This is done in order to establish the credibility and value of the test for the user markets.

At this point the test becomes available for use and enters the commercial market. However, it is not the end of the process. Norms for other populations may be developed if the test were thought to be useful for purposes or groups than those for which it was originally designed. Also the test could be subjected to criticism from other test designers, academics or users. Management in Action 4.4 illustrates the strength of the debate about the use and validity of psychometric tests for the measurement of personality.

Stop | Consider

Given what was said earlier about the different epistemological perspectives on the nature of knowledge in the social world, is the debate outlined in MiA 4.4 futile and impossible to resolve?

Intelligence

Intelligence is a common term that is frequently associated in everyday use with the achievement of academic success; people who can pass exams are frequently described as being of high intelligence. But is that what the concept refers to and if so how does it relate to individual difference? Phares (1987) defines intelligence in terms of an ability to adapt to a variety of situations both old and new, a capacity for learning and the ability to make use of a wide range of symbols and concepts in relating to the world. From that perspective the concept of intelligence represents a broad range of factors and embraces many aspects of what would be classed as individual difference.

There are many theoretical approaches to the study of intelligence. These have included the development of the IQ concept in which the mental age of the testee was calculated from an intelligence test and compared with their physical age to give a scale of relative intelligence. So someone of average intelligence would score a mental age equivalent to their actual age and someone of higher than average intelligence would generate a test result showing a greater age than their true one. In comparison, Thurstone (1938), for example, developed a model that suggested the notion that intelligence was based on a number of primary mental abilities such as verbal comprehension, word fluency, numbers ability and perceptual speed.

More recently, Guilford (1967) proposed a model of intelligence consisting of three dimensions (contents, products and operations). Each of these dimensions comprises a number of different abilities (4, 6 and 5 respectively). The model can be drawn as a cube with each of the three dimensions representing one of the three principle dimensions (length, height and depth) of the cube. Each of the individual intelligence abilities within the now three-dimensional model would intersect with the others, creating a total of 120 variations in intelligence variation (4x6x5). The three dimensions within the model are:

✦ Contents. The four elements within this dimension reflect the base information on which subsequent actions are formed. For example, the semantic and symbolic meaning of numbers.

✦ Products. The six elements within this dimension reflect the form in which information is processed. For example, the relationship between the weight and price of goods in a supermarket.

✦ Operations. The five elements within this dimension reflect what the person actually does. For example, solve a problem or evaluate alternative courses of action.

Sternberg (1985) proposed an information processing-based theory of intelligence. In this model it was proposed that there exists three ways in which intelligent behaviour is evident:

✦ Components. This aspect reflects the analytical abilities possessed by an individual and would find expression in test results.

✦ Experiences. This aspect reflects the creative abilities that an individual has in being able to combine the things that they experience into novel patterns.

✦ Context. This aspect reflects the ability of an individual to be aware of contextual circumstances and to exhibit an ability to utilize the environment to their own advantage.

It has long been recognized that the conventional measures of intelligence have enjoyed only limited success in being able to predict success in job terms. John D Mayer and Peter Salovey first developed a theory of emotional intelligence during the 1980s which Mayer defines as, 'the ability to perceive, to integrate, to understand and reflectively manage one's own and other people's feelings' (Pickard, 1999, pp 49–50). This was not directly intended to address the issue of organizational success as it originally emerged from an interest in how emotion and cognition could be used to influence individual thinking processes. It was Goleman (1996) who first popularized EQ (as emotional intelligence has become known) as an aid to organizational functioning. This has been expanded by a number of writers including Dulewicz and Higgs from the Henley Management College who have developed a model consisting of three main components and a total of seven elements of EQ in relation to organizational success. Their model is as follows:

✦ The drivers. The two traits of motivation and decisiveness are responsible for energizing individuals to achieve their goals.

✦ The constrainers. The two traits of conscientiousness and integrity, and emotional resilience perform the function of modifying the potential of the drivers to push to excess or in the wrong direction.

✦ The enablers. The three traits of sensitivity, influence and self-awareness help to ensure that the other traits operate in the social context involving the individual and other people.

Dulewicz and Higgs (as described in Pickard, 1999) argue that for organizational success to be achieved it is also necessary for an individual to have what they describe as intellectual intelligence (creativity and external awareness, for example) and managerial intelligence (delegating and business sense, for example) in addition to EQ. It has been shown that men and women have different EQ profiles with women displaying stronger interpersonal skills, with men showing higher levels of independence and a sense of self (Lucas, 2000).

A number of organizations have used the EQ concept to review individual difference profiles among work groups and claim to have some success in changing behaviour patterns at work. It is, however, early days for this relatively new model in terms of its replacement for conventional models of intelligence.

Graphology

Graphology refers to the study of handwriting. It is one of a number of alternative forms of personality assessment with a long, if not scientific tradition. For example, there is the study of the shape of the so-called bumps on the head, in practice the shape of the bones forming the skull and face. This was called phrenology and examples of the assumed significance of the various 'bumps' can still be found on pottery busts with the areas of the head marked in terms of which aspects of personality they were thought to influence. Graphology takes as its area of interest the writing of an individual and subjects it to analysis by a trained person. Supporters of graphology would claim that it is a branch of behavioural psychology, with no connections with astrology or intuition. Opponents would ague that it has no basis as a reliable form of assessment (Klimoski and Rafael, 1983).

Among the qualities 'extracted' from a sample of handwriting would be the size, slant, pressure, spacing of letters and words and the beginnings and endings of words. For example, it is argued that someone who leaves a wide spacing between the lines of writing is an independent person who prefers to limit their contact with other people. As a technique for assessing the personality characteristics of people graphology might not gain the support of many psychologists but there is evidence that even during the 1980s just under 3% of the top 1000 UK companies always used it for the assessment of management recruitment as reported in a survey by Robertson and Makin (1986).

Individual difference, perception and attitudes

The previous chapter discussed the topics of perception and attitude in considerable depth. It should have been clear from that discussion that individuals vary in the way in which they interact with the world around them as expressed through their perceptual and attitudinal frameworks. Consequently, there are also links between these two topics and individual difference.

Perception

There exist at least two ways in which perception and individual difference could be associated. First, perceptions could be influenced by factors located within the personality. Second, personality could at least in part be formed by the ways in which people perceive and interact with the world around them.

As an example of the first possibility, Figure 4.10 (which we have already seen as Figure 3.14) reflects a simplified model of person perception. One of the factors influencing the perception of other people is indicated as the perceiver's characteristics. In other words, who we are influences the ways in which we relate to and interpret other people.

Another way in which individual difference and perception are linked is through what Witkin (1965) defined as *field dependence*. This concept reflects the degree to which an individual is influenced in their perceptions through the surroundings associated with a particular stimulus. The field-independent individual has the capability to separate the background from the stimuli more effectively and so interprets events in a clear, detailed and organized way. Such individuals also have a clear perspective of their own characteristics, beliefs and needs and how they differ from other people. Through the notion of *field dependence* the links between perceptual and individual difference frameworks become apparent. The perceptual impact of the concept of field dependence has been studied through an embedded figures test in which figures are hidden within another picture and

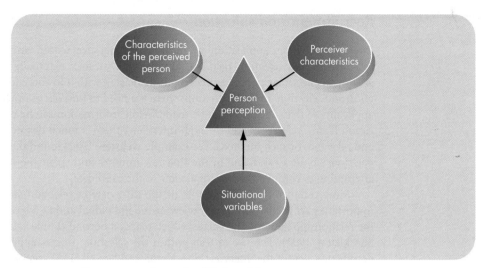

FIGURE 4.10   Person perception: a simplified model.

the individual has to find them. Through these tests the concept became associated with cognitive style and so personality.

Attitudes

Attitudes are also influenced by individual difference factors. It has been suggested that extroversion or introversion creates a disposition favourable or unfavourable towards the acceptance of attitudes (McKenna, 1994, p 256). This same source also quotes the work of Eysenck who demonstrated that introverts are more susceptible to socialization and the acceptance of the dominant values of society (and hence the associated attitudes) than are extroverts. There is also evidence that those with an authoritarian personality are likely to have attitudes that display subservience to superiors at the same time as hostility towards inferiors.

Organizational applications of individual difference

The study of personality has tended to concentrate on providing mechanisms for describing the characteristics that separate individuals from each other. However, there is an interesting paradox involved in this. The measurement process provides a basis of comparison for the individual against a group of others, a population. This very approach allows a subtle shift in emphasis in the organizational application of personality measurement away from the identification of individuality, towards the identification of appropriateness or suitability, the identification of individuals with characteristics that are acceptable or desirable to management.

Recruitment and selection

The most obvious application of individual difference within an organization is the recruitment and selection field. In advertising a vacancy externally the organization is seeking to encourage people not currently associated with it to come forward for consideration and selection. In such situations there is a need to find out as much as possible about applicants so that a decision can be made. While information can be obtained from application forms, references and through interviews there is much debate about the accuracy and relevance of such methods. For example Webster (1964) found that interviewers made decisions about a candidate in the first few minutes and spent the rest of the interview attempting to confirm their original view of the candidate.

More recent reviews of the role of the interview in selection suggest that it has an important part to play as a final review of the individual and as a basis for negotiation of the relationship between the parties which places it beyond simple validity (Anderson and Shackleton, 1993). The use of tests within the selection process appears to be increasing despite this view of the interview. Shackleton and Newell (1991) report that the use of personality tests had increased to 37% from 12% over a five-year period.

At one time personality tests were used for management positions and ability or aptitude tests were the preserve of manual jobs. This is now being questioned in some quarters. Some managers feel that the use of personality tests provides the opportunity to identify individuals who will 'fit' more effectively into the organization. In effect, these managers argue that they can achieve organizational objectives more easily if they can identify individuals with the 'approved' characteristics. Research by Newell and Shackleton (1994) would seem to support this trend, at least in respect of management level jobs, in that they report levels of test use in approximately 75% of managerial jobs, but only 20% of manual jobs. Management in Action 4.5 provides a review of the appropriateness of personality and other tests for manual jobs.

Stop | Consider

In situations where many times the number of applicants come forward than there are vacancies available, is it conceivable that only a few individuals will have the necessary skills and abilities sought by management?

In such situations to what extent could tests be used as a cheap mechanism for cutting down the number of suitable applicants and providing a defendable basis for such decisions, rather than as a process to identify the most suitable applicants?

Development

Psychometric tests can be used for recruitment purposes, but they can also be used to provide a profile of the people already in the organization. This can be used to provide a basis of control through access to promotion, development and related organizational 'rewards'. People with 'approved' characteristics, or prepared to develop (or adopt) them (assuming that is possible) will be the ones who find advancement within the organization. Thus management may be able to achieve its objectives more easily as employees align themselves with the managerially preferred behaviours.

The development of technical specialists and managers is another area where testing has been used as the basis of reflecting personality characteristics. Tests such as the Occupational Personality Questionnaire (the OPQ) have been developed by Saville and

MANAGEMENT IN ACTION 4.5

Put to the test down the line

Most tests are developed for white-collar, professional and managerial level jobs. Even if computerized, they tend to be of the paper and pencil type, requiring high levels of literacy and numeracy. However, for blue-collar jobs this approach might be inappropriate and not tap into appropriate characteristics and abilities. A worker on an assembly line needs a different range of skills from those of an office worker or manager. They are manipulators of tangible things rather than data, information or records. They make the goods that are sold by the company and so require the physical and mental characteristics that are appropriate to those activities rather than the personality and aptitude skills of the professional engineer or manager. The language barrier can be a major hurdle for minority ethnic groups and those people with a lower education level than required for most professional jobs.

Companies faced with recruitment decisions in the blue-collar areas are faced with a potential problem. They can either seek out the most appropriate existing test and hope for the best or they can commission the design of an appropriate test for their own circumstances. The first option carries with it the possibility of inappropriateness and the second the high development cost as well as the time delay in developing the test. However, with the high levels of unemployment over recent years the recruitment process has become difficult for many companies. It is not uncommon to find many thousands of applications for just a few jobs. A major sifting process which is effective becomes essential not just desirable. For example, when Toyota opened a new production unit in Derbyshire some 19,000 applications were received for about 950 jobs; when Motorola built a two-way radio and pager factory in Dublin it

tested about 2000 people for about 150 jobs; Nissan opened a car factory in Sunderland and received about 11,500 applications for about 300 jobs, while a later expansion involving a rolling programme of 1500 vacancies attracted some 32,000 applications.

Toyota commissioned the development of a specific test to identify the ability of potential recruits to work in the flexible assembly environment that they were creating. The test involved the individual going through a 90-minute procedure based on a video approach to learning a range of spurious tasks and then being tested on the ability to do the work described. By concentrating on practical skills this approach removed any possible bias in the results based on ability to understand the language used or from inappropriate characteristic identification.

Other companies such as Motorola in Dublin were more cautious about the use of tests but envisaged that there could be a role for them. Nissan used a variety of aptitude tests for mechanical, verbal and numerical comprehension and a practical skills test aimed at dexterity and hand–eye co-ordination. This was in addition to the usual interview and site visits as part of the selection process.

It has been suggested that the costs and time involved in developing new tests for blue-collar jobs is so high that there are many existing tests that might be applied as an alternative. However, the fairness and objectivity of the test for the particular circumstances should be the prime concern in taking such decisions.

Adapted from: Ring, T (1992) Put to the test down the line, *Personnel Today*, 30 June, pp 21–4.

Holdsworth (a firm of occupational psychology consultants) to enhance this very objective. It utilizes a series of 30 dimensions, or scales, to reflect the profile of an individual's personality. Examples from the OPQ questionnaire are shown in Table 4.2.

This particular test can be used in a number of ways including management selection and/or development. In selection terms it could be used as a means of providing the profile of an individual, which could then be used to make a decision, or as recommended by the professional associations, used as the basis of an informed discussion. The profile, or score of the individual on each of the 30 scales, would be compared against the *ideal* profile for the job for which they were being considered. The OPQ can also be used for determining a development programme for individuals. Based on the results of the test the individual would be offered advice and support in undertaking any training or development to change their work performance and/or career options. The test could also be used where jobs were expected to change significantly. The intention being to identify appropriate training for the individuals concerned or to identify alternative job opportunities.

As with all instruments that measure personality, the OPQ as a single instrument does not intend that it should be the only basis of a decision in relation to selection and development. Indeed, research by Blinkhorn and Johnson (1990) using three of the most widely used psychometric tests (including the OPQ) found little evidence of a long-term relationship between test results and performance at work. There are other factors to be taken into account, and there is no substitute for seeking a variety of information inputs to a decision.

Assessment centres were first used during World War II as a means of selecting officers for the military. Since then they have evolved to the point where many organizations use them for selection and development purposes. Assessment centres are events that are made up of a range of different activities, requiring solo and group performance. Individuals are observed by assessors and scored on their performance on each activity. At the end of the process the scorers pool all the information gained from the activities and decide on the outcome. The justification for this assessment being that the tasks can be designed to reflect real work activity. Performance is assessed in a live situation, multiple measures of personality and performance are obtained and the results are the combined effort of a number of trained assessors. Management in Action 4.6 provides an indication of assessment centres and how they could be designed.

Persuasive	negotiates, enjoys selling, convincing with arguments
Controlling:	takes charge, directs, manages, organizes
Competitive:	plays to win, determined to beat others, poor loser
Decisive:	quick at conclusions, may be hasty, takes risks
Traditional:	prefers proven orthodox methods, conventional
Practical:	down to earth, likes repairing and mending things
Artistic:	appreciates culture, shows artistic flair
Critical:	good at probing facts, sees disadvantages, challenges

TABLE 4.2 Examples from the SHL® Occupational Personality Questionnaire (OPQ)® (SHL and OPQ are registered trade marks of SHL Group plc. © SHL Group plc.)

MANAGEMENT IN ACTION 4.6

How to plan an assessment centre

Assessment centres are widely used as the basis of selection, promotion and career development decisions within organizations. They offer improved decision making as a result of the incorporation of a wider range of test and evaluation opportunities into the process, compared with reliance on a single measure such as an interview.

The basis of an assessment centre is that a small group of participants undertake a series of tests and exercises in order to allow the evaluation of their skills, competencies and general suitability for specific roles within the organization. They can also be used as the basis of career development planning through the possibility of identifying training needs and particular preferences for types of work. The evaluations of participants are made during the assessment centre by a number of specially trained staff. An assessment centre replicates a number of features of the organization and work, which allows informed judgements about the strengths and weaknesses of the participants to be made.

There are three main types of assessment centre used by organizations. They are graduate recruitment, job selection (usually managerial or technical specialist) and for internal or development purposes. Each is different and requires a specific design of assessment centre. For example, graduate recruitment would need to assume much lower levels of company knowledge and work experience than a centre designed for internal promotion purposes.

The key features in the design of an assessment centre are:

♦ Skills and competencies. It is necessary to begin with a clear idea of the important skills and competencies being sought. For example one organization assumed that sociability was a key quality required among sales personnel. Only later was it discovered that this was irrelevant and that independence and persistence were much more significant qualities in relation to success.

♦ Tests and techniques. Given that most assessments last about two days a variety of techniques and tests is common. They might include structured interviews, self-assessment questionnaires, psychometric tests, in-tray exercises, group discussion, group problem-solving exercises, job simulation exercises and job-related role play.

♦ The assessment process. In designing an assessment centre there are three main elements to consider. First, the qualities and competencies being sought and how they are to be measured. Second, the weighting to be applied to each element of the process. For example, should the psychometric tests be more highly rated in the overall result than the group discussion? Third, the form of assessment used in order to ensure consistency of judgement between raters and the avoidance of discrimination or stereotyping of participants.

♦ Assessors. The selection of assessors can be difficult in that a mix of specific training and experience is often needed. Specialist training is required in the application and scoring of psychometric tests, for example. Line managers have the experience in work practicalities but might not have the ability to rate individuals on group discussions consistently. Generally, a mix of assessors is used in a centre and training provided for them as necessary.

♦ Feedback. Decisions need to be made about the level and form of any feedback to participants. Clearly, the more participants the more difficult and costly in time and money it is to provide detailed feedback. However,

MANAGEMENT IN ACTION 4.6   continued

delegates frequently appreciate some indication of their strengths and weaknesses. If a development centre is being run then its whole purpose is to provide feedback to individuals on their future needs. There is always a difficult area in relation to the creation of management reports from assessment centres. Participants frequently feel uneasy at the thought of managers being provided with information about them, particularly if this is not released to the participant.

✦ Validation. Any assessment centre is only as good as its ability to contribute to the

effectiveness of the people working within the organization. There is little point in undertaking lengthy and costly procedures if they add little to the quality and performance of staff. Consequently, a process of monitoring and evaluating the assessment centre needs to be developed so that the impact on the business can be reviewed and corrective action taken as necessary.

Adapted from: Fowler, A (1992) How to plan an assessment centre, *PM Plus*, December, pp 21–4.

Stop | Consider

Think about your future career. Design an assessment centre intended to identify your strengths and weaknesses in relation to your plans.

Who would you seek to be the assessors and fellow subjects of the centre and what skills would you expect the assessors to have?

On what basis would you be able to integrate more than yourself as a subject in the process and what effect would that have on your original design of the centre?

Marketing

Marketing specialists are always seeking to understand consumers so that they can present the organizational offerings more appropriately. Equally, of course, an improved understanding of the consumer should allow for the design of more appropriate products and services. From those perspectives individual difference is an important concept in the marketing vocabulary.

Several studies have been conducted over the years which seek to determine how potential customers perceive the characteristics of individuals who actually purchase particular items. One early study (Haire, 1950) compared the responses of housewives in describing the type of people who might have one of two variations of shopping list. The difference between the shopping lists was the inclusion of either ground or instant coffee. Some 48% of housewives indicated that the shopper who bought instant coffee was a lazy person who did not plan ahead, whereas only 12% of the people who bought ground coffee were described in the same way. This study has been repeated several times over the years with some moderate support.

Another aspect of individual difference in marketing is the ascription of personality factors to brands. Branded products contain both the physical properties that make up the product and its symbolic meaning for the direct consumer and wider population. For example a Rolls-Royce is not just another form of personal transport. It makes a statement about the owner in terms of wealth, lifestyle and status. These factors have significance for both the consumer and among the wider community. They allow other people to 'know' who the driver is and to encourage a particular impression to flow from those connections (real or imagined).

To 'know' the characterisitcs of people in the intended market for products and services is to enable organizations to provide offerings that will gain acceptance quickly. Consequently, considerable effort goes into defining the profile of consumers and what defines their individual preferences.

Discrimination

Discrimination occurs in many forms. Women, ethnic minority groups, older people, younger people, religious groups, gay men and lesbians represent just some of the people who have found themselves discriminated against throughout history. Discrimination is associated with the attitudes (usually negative) of one group of people towards another. For example, women find it difficult to break through the 'glass ceiling' and obtain the highest positions within organizations. Studies of the influence of personality factors on negative attitude formation have a long history. For example, Adorno *et al.* (1953) demonstrated that people displaying the highest levels of prejudice towards other groups also had strongly authoritarian personalities.

Stress

Stress exists in many jobs and arises from a number of sources. One of the causes of the susceptibility to stress in people is the nature of the individual. Rosenman *et al.* (1964) considered the possible relationship between personality characteristics and tendency to experience heart disease. They concluded that people with Type A personalities are more at risk from coronary problems. Type A people place a high emphasis on work at the expense of other aspects of their lives, frequently work at home and are less interested in exercise, for example. This finding has been substantiated a number of times over the years, more recently by Friedman and Booth-Kewley (1987).

Another aspect of stress at work arises through the phenomenon of bullying. Bullying has probably always existed, although there is a growing recognition that it is becoming more significant in its impact both on people and on organizations. Cooper (1999) reports a survey indicating that 18% of respondents had been bullied during the previous year, while a total of 61% had either been bullied or witnessed it over the same period. Adams (1992) draws attention to bullying in all its forms as found within any organization. The case studies that she provides also give clear indications of the stressful impact of the experiences for the individuals so victimized. Also included is a review of a number of the components of individual difference that contribute to the exercise of bullying (or victim) behaviour by individuals.

The testing business

Another organizational effect of personality is the growth of an industry around the measurement of it. There are a considerable number of psychologists and consultancies that offer services to organizations based on the existence of personality and the measurement of it. Naturally, it is in the business interests of those practitioners to ensure that the opportunities for the application of personality is brought to management's attention. This includes the training of company staff to use and interpret particular instruments, the development of new tests and the application of the techniques in organizational activity. The difficulties that can arise from poorly trained individuals applying psychometric tests has long been recognized and has lead the British Psychological Society to introduce formal accreditation training. In addition the Institute of Personnel and Development has introduced a Code of Practice on Psychological Testing.

Individual difference: a management perspective

Managers are supposed to have particular personality characteristics in order to be successful; intelligence and initiative are often quoted as examples. In Management in Action 4.7, one management trainer using ideas from *Gestalt psychology* explains an attempt to influence how managers function. This includes the utilization of personality concepts.

Stop | Consider

Observe the behaviour of some of your friends in a social context. Could you classify the behaviour under the categories indicated in MiA 4.7? Equally, seek to classify your own response to such behaviour.

Does your analysis support the suggestions made in the panel that it is necessary to adopt appropriate personality modes in order to influence the behaviour of others?

Managers can also be affected by the application of personality testing through the development and promotion opportunities that they provide. Within an organizational setting the concept of personality is inseparable from the opportunities that it provides. It is not that the identification of personality is an interesting activity in its own right, but that it allows managers to take decisions about other people. However, it also allows managers to take decisions about other managers. It is a concept that serves a *gatekeeper* function. The idea that individual difference can be defined in terms of certain characteristics and that some of these characteristics are helpful to managers leads naturally to the conclusion that if the *right* characteristics can be identified then the *best* candidates can be selected. Consequently, who is selected as management material in the first place and how far they progress in the management hierarchy can be strongly tied to the various forms of testing available. In addition, it is also influenced by the willingness of an individual to take action based on the results of a test. For example, being prepared to accept the offered definition of their personality and accepting the need for particualr development.

The process of testing allows managers to specify the characteristics that they consider as important in employees of the organization. It is therefore a process of *social engineering*. A model employee is identified and individual candidates measured against that particular standard. This could relegate into second place the ability to perform the job by the individual as the managers seek individual difference *fit* with their ideal employee. In an extreme situation this would allow managers systematically to manipulate the shape and form of the organization in terms of the people characteristics. This approach is taken to its logical conclusion in the view that recruitment should be based on 'organizational fit' not just the job requirements (Bowen *et al.*, 1996).

Change is a natural part of organizational life. This can include personnel changes,

MANAGEMENT IN ACTION 4.7

Finding the child inside the manager

Trainers frequently claim that much of the training they provide for managers is wasted because the classroom activity is not effectively transferred back to the workplace. They are constantly seeking ways to increase the level of impact of the training message and of improving the transfer of learning to the workplace. Abe Wagner, a psychologist from the USA, has attempted to find new ways of getting managers to improve their ability to communicate effectively by adapting the principles of transactional analysis.

Wagner claims that every adult is made up of six personality states:

1. The natural child.
2. The adult.
3. The nurturing parent.
4. The rebellious child.
5. The compliant child.
6. The critical parent.

He argues that the first three of these personality states are helpful in communicating and managing effectively. The second three are unhelpful in these respects and should be resisted personally and in others. He provides training for managers in how to make use of these ideas in their work.

The personality mode can be identified from the behaviour and verbal expressions of the individual. For example, an autopsy following the failure to clinch an important sale can often be a reflection of the critical parent mode. It concentrates on identifying the inadequacies in others involved in the process. Wagner suggests that the best way to deal with these situations is to articulate the thoughts about the situation and recognize which mode is dominant from them and then allow the adult mode to take over through a pep talk with oneself.

He also suggests that recognizing the dominant personality state in others allows effective

response strategies to be developed. For example, imagine a subordinate in a rebellious child mode, with negative attitudes, being generally obstructive and working badly being the observed behaviour patterns. The worst approach to attempting to improve the behaviour and performance of that person would be to adopt the critical parent mode. The criticism of the behaviour and attitudes in the subordinate would be likely to reinforce their rebellious child personality state. Wagner recommends that the best way of encouraging appropriate personality modes in others is to adopt the adult or nurturing parent behaviour patterns oneself.

On occasions it could be more effective to adopt the same personality mode as another person in order to influence their behaviour. Wagner quotes the example of an employee playing a child by refusing to work on a Saturday. If the manager adopts a child perspective in response they might be able to appeal to emotions within the employee and persuade them to work. Being an adult and appealing to their sense of responsibility would be unlikely to work.

Managers have a natural tendency to function, look and talk like parents, reinforced and encouraged by employees who perform in the child mode. This situation Wagner describes as leading to a co-dependency of personality modes between managers and workers. The training of managers usually emphasizes how to make changes involving others, ignoring the need to change the manager first. For this reason most training courses fail to deliver their intended objectives. Wagner argues that to be successful, managers should allow the natural child within them to come out and his training courses are designed to allow that to happen.

Adapted from: Kellaway, L (1993) Finding the child inside the manager, *Financial Times*, 7 April, p 12.

product changes, market changes, economic changes and legal changes. Among the consequences of change are the influences on the people employed. As the organization changes so do the jobs within it and the people performing those jobs. Part of this process influences the personality characteristics actually present (assuming that it is the people that are changing), and the characteristics valued and therefore sought by the organization.

There are a number of situations where the application of personality concepts could be of value within an organization. For example, there are obvious links between extroversion and jobs which require a high level of interpersonal activity, such as sales, hospitality and public relations. There are also links between aspects of personality and organizational objectives. For example, as managers seek to improve effectiveness through initiatives such as employee empowerment, there is a need to tap into different human attributes than if employees are simply regarded as a 'pair of hands'.

Conclusions

The concept of individual difference is a difficult one for managers to deal with. It operates at many different levels within the organization and has a number of different theoretical roots along with many different measurement mechanisms (over 5000 are available). At a common sense level personality is something that most people, including managers, would claim to recognize. It reflects how people get on with each other and features such as sociability, intelligence and so on. It is only when an attempt is made to be more precise in the definition of individual difference and its measurement, followed by establishing specific links with work activities that the real difficulties emerge. The links between personality and particular jobs are an area where managers might be expected to show interest, but there is little by way of agreement about the precise nature of that relationship.

Discussion questions

1. Define the following key terms used in this chapter:

Personality	*Nature–nurture debate*	*Repertory grid*
Psychoanalysis	*Psychometrics*	*Ambiguous figure*
Idiographic	*Personality dimension*	*Rorschach test*
Nomothetic	*Construct*	*Assessment centre*

2. To what extent does personality explain individual differences between people?

3. Describe the genetic and environmental origins of personality. Which do you consider the most important to the development of adult personality? Why?

4. Would it be desirable for all the employees within an organization to have similar personality characteristics? Why, or why not?

5. To what extent do you consider that it might be possible to use graphology to understand the personality characteristics of an individual?

6. In what ways might personality and perception be linked?

7. Can personality be measured accurately by any form of psychometric test? Why or why not?

8. It has often been suggested that Freudian theory tells us more about Freud than it does about personality. Discuss.

9. Kelly's personal construct theory provides a useful theory of personality. However, it is not practical to use the repertory grid technique in an organization as it is too complicated. Discuss.

10. 'Any organization needs "different"' people within it in order to optimize performance and effectiveness through the unique contribution of each individual.' Discuss.

Research activities

1. In the library, seek out ten books and journal articles that discuss personality theory and/or its application to organizational activity. Include at least one article that reviews personality test results as a means of providing 'norms' against which to compare individual results. What do these views of personality contribute to your understanding of personality and its organizational value?

2. In a group of three people, each person write down a description of the personality of the other two. After you have done this compare notes. Are the two descriptions of each person similar or different? Why? Each person should use an ambiguous drawing to create a story. Are there any points of similarity between the way in which an individual described the picture and the personality description provided by the two other people? Why or why not?

3. Obtain a piece of A4 paper and fold it in half lengthways. With a fountain pen, poster paint or something similar put five random 'blots' on one side of the paper. Fold the paper to create a mirror image of the 'blots'. Let it dry and then look at it, letting your imagination create meaningful pictures from what you see. What might this tell you about your personality?

   It is important to understand that you are not a trained psychologist, or an expert in the field of personality. Therefore, the exercises described here are not to be taken seriously. They are intended to provide you with some experience of working with personality concepts. You are not able to offer professional or meaningful advice from them, neither should any information obtained be interpreted as providing a meaningful or accurate picture of any individual's personality.

Key reading

From Clark, H, Chandler, J and Barry, J (1994) *Organization and Identities: Text and Readings in Organizational Behaviour*, International Thomson Business Press, London:
   ✦ Freud, S: The dissection of the psychical personality, p 71. This introduces the basis of Freud's approach to psychoanalysis.

◆ Eysenck, HJ: The rat or the couch?, p 82. Introduces the debate between behaviourism and psychology.

◆ Mead, GH: The self, p 99. Introduces another perspective into the development of the human personality.

◆ Merton, RK: Bureaucratic structure and personality, p 144. This examines the relationship between personality development and the need to work within an organizational framework.

◆ Whyte, WH: The organization man, p 149. This considers the implications for individuals of having to work within commercial organizations.

◆ Kanter, RM: Men and women of the corporation, p 152. This considers the process organizations use in 'moulding' individuals into a form which meets the requirements of management.

Further reading

Bartram, D (1992) The personality of UK managers: 16PF norms for short-listed applicants, *Journal of Occupational and Organizational Psychology*, **65**, 159–72. This is a study which examines the 16PF test results of 1796 managers applying for jobs. From the analysis the 'norms' are developed, against which to compare individual manager's test results. As such it provides the basis for interpretation of the results for UK managers.

Cook, M (1988) *Personnel Selection and Productivity*, Wiley, Chichester. In concentrating on selection it has several chapters that are relevant to the subject of personality and psychometric tests.

Deary, IJ and Matthews, G (1993) Personality traits are alive and well, *The Psychologist*, July, 299–311. This review provides strong support for the view that traits provide a basis for predicting and explaining behaviour.

Heriot, P (ed.) (1989) *Assessment and Selection in Organizations: Methods and Practice for Recruitment and Appraisal*, Wiley, Chichester. This text covers many aspects of the application of personality, tests and assessment centres.

Robertson, IT and Kinder, A (1993) Personality and job competencies: the criterion-related validity of some personality variables, *Journal of Occupational and Organizational Psychology*, **66**, 225–44. This is a classic example of a research paper which examines the issue of the validity of psychometric tests.

Toplis, J, Dulewicz, V and Fletcher, C (1987) *Psychological Testing: A Practical Guide for Employers*, Institute of Personnel Management, London. As the title implies this is intended to provide guidance to employers on the nature and use of various forms of test.

Woodruff, C (1992) *Assessment Centres; Identifying and Developing Competence*, Institute of Personnel Management, London. This is intended for the practitioner market, but does provide an excellent insight into the assessment centre process, as used in selection and development.

References

Adams, A (1992) *Bullying at Work: How to Confront and Overcome it*, Virago Press, London.

Adorno, J W, Frenkel-Brunswick, E, Levinson, DJ and Sandford, RN (1953) *The Authoritarian Personality*, Harper & Row, New York.

Allport, G (1937) *Personality: A Psychological Interpretation*, Holt, Rinehart & Winston, New York.

Anderson, N and Shackleton, V (1993) *Successful Selection Interviewing*, Blackwell, Oxford.

Blinkhorn, S and Johnson, C (1990) The insignificance of personality testing, *Nature*, **348**, 671–2.

Bowen, DE, Ledford, GE and Nathan, BR (1996) Hiring for the organization, not the job. In Billsberry, J (ed.), *The Effective Manager: Perspectives and Illustrations*, Sage, London.

Bradshaw, P (1981) *The Management of Self-esteem*, Prentice Hall, Englewood Cliffs, NJ.

Burger, JM (1986) *Personality: Theory and Research*, Wadsworth, Belmont, CA.

Burrell, G and Morgan, G (1979) *Sociological Paradigms and Organisational Analysis: Elements of the Sociology of Corporate Life*, Heinemann, London.

Cattell, RB (1965) *The Scientific Analysis of Personality*, Penguin, Harmondsworth.

Cattell, RB and Warburton, FW (1967) *Objective Personality and Motivation Tests*, University of Illinois Press, Urbana, IL.

Cooper, C (1999) In my opinion, *Management Today*, June, p 14.

Cox, CJ and Cooper, CL (1988) *High Flyers*, Basil Blackwell, Oxford.

Erikson, EH (1980) *Identity and Life Cycle*, Norton, New York.

Eysenck, HJ (1953) *Uses and Abuses of Psychology*, Penguin, Harmondsworth.

Eysenck, HJ (1959) The Rorschach Test. In Buros, OK (ed.) *Fifth Mental Measurements Yearbook*, Gryphon Press, New Jersey.

Eysenck, HJ (1965) *Fact and Fiction in Psychology*, Penguin, Harmondsworth.

Eysenck, HJ (1967) *The Biological Basis of Personality*, Thomas, Springfield, CT.

Eysenck, HJ (1971) *Readings in Extraversion and Intraversion*, Vols 1, 2 and 3, Staples Press, London.

Eysenck, HJ (1982) *Personality, Genetics and Behaviour*, Prager, New York.

Friedman, HS and Booth-Kewley, S (1987) The disease-prone personality: a meta-analytic view of the construct, *American Psychologist*. June, pp 539–55.

Goleman, D (1996) *Emotional Intelligence: Why It Can Matter more than IQ*. Bloomsbury, London.

Guilford, J P (1967) *The Nature of Human Intelligence*, McGraw-Hill, New York

Haire, M (1950) Projective techniques in market research, *Journal of Marketing*, 14, 649–56.

Hall, CS and Lindzey, G (1970) *Theories of Personality*, Wiley, New York.

Henwood, KL and Pidgeon, NF (1993) Qualitative Research and Psychological Theorizing. In Hammersley, M (ed.) *Social Research: Philosophy, Politics and Practice*, Sage, London.

Holden, C (1987) Genes and behaviour: a twin legacy, *Psychology Today*, September, 18–19.

Jung, CG (1968) *Analytical Psychology: Its Theory and Practice*, Routledge & Kegan Paul, New York.

Kelly, G (1961) *The Abstraction of Human Processes. Proceedings of the 14th International Cognitive Psychological Conference*, Copenhagen, pp 220–9.

Klimoski, RJ and Rafael, A (1983) Inferring personal qualities through handwriting analysis, *Journal of Occupational Psychology*, 56, 191–202.

Kline, P (1972) *Fact and Fantasy in Freudian Theory*, Methuen, London.

Kolakowski, L (1993) An Overall View of Positivism. In Hammersley, M (ed.) *Social Research: Philosophy, Politics and Practice*, Sage, London.

Kuratho, DF and Hodgetts, RM (1989) *Entrepreneurship: A Contemporary Approach*, The Dryden Press, Fort Worth, TX.

Lucas, E (2000) EQ: how do you measure up?, *Professional Manager*, January, pp 10–12.

McKenna, E (1994) *Business Psychology and Organisational Behaviour: A Students' Handbook*, Lawrence Erlbaum, Hove.

Mead, GH (1934) *Mind, Self and Society*, University of Chicago Press, Chicago, IL.

Murray, HA (1938) *Explorations in Personality*, Oxford University Press, New York.

Murray, HA (1943) *Thematic Apperception Test*, Harvard University Press, Cambridge, MA.

Myers–Briggs, I (1987) *Introduction to Type*, Oxford Psychologists Press, Oxford.

Newell, S and Shackleton, V (1994) The use (and abuse) of psychometric tests in British industry and commerce, *Human Resource Management Journal*, 4, 1.

Pervin, LA (1984) *Current Controversies and Issues in Personality*, 2nd edn, Wiley, New York.

Phares, EJ (1987) *Introduction to Personality*, 2nd edn. Scott Foresman. Glenview, IL.

Pickard, J (1999) Sense and sensitivity, *People Management*, 28 October, pp 48–56.

Rabin, AI (1958) Projective Methods: An Historical Introduction, In Rabin, AI (ed.), *Projective Techniques in Personality Assessment*, Springer, New York.

Remenyi, D, Williams, B, Money, A and Swartz, E (1998) *Doing Research in Business and Management: An Introduction to Process and Method*, Sage, London.

Robertson, IT and Makin, PJ (1986) Management selection in Britain: a survey and critique, *Journal of Occupational Psychology*, **59**, 45–58.

Rogers, CR (1947) Some observations on the organization of personality, *American Psychologist*, **2**, 358–68.

Rosenman, RH, Friedman, M and Strauss, R (1964) A predictive study of CHD, *Journal of the American Medical Association*, **189**, 15–22.

Shackleton, V and Newell, S (1991) Management selection: a comparative survey of methods used in top British and French companies, *Journal of Occupational Psychology*, **64**, 23–36.

Sternberg, RJ (1985) *Beyond IQ: A Triarchic Theory of Human Intelligence*, Cambridge University Press, New York.

Strachey, J (1953–66) *The Standard Edition of the Complete Psychological Works of Sigmund Freud*, Volumes I–XXIV, Hogarth Press/Institute of Psychoanalysis, London.

Thurstone, LL (1938) Primary mental abilities, *Psychometric Monographs, Number 1*, University of Chicago Press, Chicago.

Webster, EC (1964) *Decision Making in the Employment Interview*, Industrial Relations Centre, McGill University.

Whyte, WH (1956) *The Organization Man*, Simon & Schuster, New York.

Witkin, HA (1965) Psychological differentiation and forms of pathology, *Journal of Abnormal and Social Psychology*, **70**, 317–36.

PART III

Groups within organizations

CHAPTER 5

Group formation and structure

CHAPTER SUMMARY

This chapter begins with a consideration of the concept of a group. It then goes on to review the ways in which groups are used within an organization and the significance of groups in that context. The distinctions between formal and informal groups as they relate to the different stakeholders within the organization are then introduced. A short review of the main research into group working will follow before outlining a number of approaches to the study of how groups are formed and structured. This will be followed by a discussion of role theory and job design in terms of how groups function within organizations. The chapter will conclude with a critical review of the ideas discussed along with some indication of their relevance to management and organizations.

LEARNING OBJECTIVES

After studying this chapter and working through the associated Management in Action panels, Discussion questions and Research activities, you should be able to:

✦ Outline the concept of a group as distinct from a collection of individuals.

✦ Understand the differences between formal and informal groups.

✦ Describe the Hawthorne Studies and their significance in understanding the nature of groups.

✦ Discuss the different approaches to the study of how groups form, are structured and the value of role theory.

✦ Appreciate the links between the group level of analysis within organizational behaviour and the individual and organizational levels.

✦ Detail some of the links between group formation and structure and job design, organization design and motivation.

✦ Explain the difficulties facing managers in attempting to manage both formal and informal groups.

✦ Assess the organizational and managerial implications of group activity.

Introduction

Groups form a significant part of the everyday experience of people. There are many different types of group that exist and most can be categorized under one of three distinct headings:

✦   Organizational. These groups are established by an organization in order to meet its own needs. Examples would include the production and finance departments.

✦   Self-interest. People form or join a number of groups as a means of protection, or to further their plans and objectives. Examples would include trade union groups and industry pressure groups formed to lobby government to adopt particular policies.

✦   Affinity. These groups offer members the opportunity to meet the basic human need to 'belong'. Examples would include sports teams, social groups and family groups.

This approach provides for the classification of a group according to the purpose that it serves. But what is a group? Would every collection of human beings constitute a group? Superficially, the answer is yes. How else could a collection of people standing on a railway platform waiting for a train be described? But are they a group in any deeper meaning of the term? Is there any reason or purpose behind their *togetherness*, other than a need (or desire) to travel on the same train? Perhaps some of the individuals will be travelling together as a group, for example, a school outing. Other people will be travelling to work as individuals and may not know their fellow travellers, indeed they may not want to know or associate with them other than as commuters.

Definition of a group

Shaw (1981) suggests that a *group* consists of two or more people who interact with each other in such a way that each influences and is influenced by the others. Schein (1988) suggests that a group can be any number of people who interact with each other, are *psychologically aware* of each other and think of themselves as a group. Although different in emphasis, both of these definitions have a number of features in common, including:

✦   More than one person is involved. It is not possible to have a one-person group.

✦   Interaction must take place. The people waiting on the railway platform are not a group unless they interact with each other. This may occur in some situations, for example if the train is late in arriving the individuals may begin to talk to each other and collectively protest to the railway staff.

✦   Purpose or intention. Schein suggests that the individuals involved must perceive themselves to be a group. This implies a purpose or intention behind the *collectivization* of people.

✦   Awareness. It implies that the individuals take cognizance of each other in their psychological processes. It is part of the interaction and influence process as described by Shaw.

Groups and organizations

Large organizations are made up of many groups. It would not be possible to achieve the objectives of such organizations without the existence of groups. The scale and complexity of activity requires that it be broken down into manageable chunks of activity. For example, sales-related work forms a convenient subgrouping of the overall organizational activity and one that can usefully be separated from the manufacturing processes. However, such groupings tend to focus the attention of members inwards on the activities, needs and perspectives of their group rather than the overall objectives of the organization. As a result of the creation of such segmented activity centres (groups) it is necessary to also provide integration arrangements in order to ensure that the organization is able to function effectively. An example would be the need for a production planning process to ensure that sales intentions can be realized by the production department.

Even quite small organizations require groups to be formed. Perhaps the only organization that does not require a grouping-based arrangement of activity is one of fewer than three or four people. Even such very small organizations are likely to have some form of compartmentalization within them, if only between the owner/manager and the workers. Frequently with organizations of five or six people there is a demarcation between administrative and operational activity beginning to emerge. As organizations grow and evolve the need to create the means of specialization through grouping together the available human resource into convenient units also develops.

There are many types of group that function formally within an organization. Some of the more obvious are indicated as follows:

✦ Hierarchical differentiation. The split of an organization into management, staff and manual worker categories. This can be further subdivided into senior, middle and junior management levels. This form of grouping represents the seniority and status-based organization of work. It reflects the decision-making and responsibility scope of work activity commonly used as the basis of payment and reward within organizations.

✦ Specialism groupings. The collection of people into the work teams within a function. An example would be the recruitment team within the personnel department or the electricians within the maintenance department. This form of grouping reflects the collection of common activities and responsibilities into a single unit in order to enhance performance and concentrate expertise.

✦ Activity groupings. These are the means through which much organizational activity is co-ordinated, the most common examples being committees and working parties. They could include the remuneration committee of the board of directors or the regular meeting of a quality circle within one of the departments. This category of group represents one of the primary means of counteracting the functional grouping approach to work. Activity groups typically reflect an attempt to break down the insularity of functional groups; cover activities not specifically the responsibility of one group; ensure that appropriate perspectives are brought together in dealing with particular issues and monitor the performance of the organization.

✦ Boundary spanning. In this category, groups are typically formed to span the boundary between one organization and another. One example would be a customer liaison group, intended to provide an interface between customers and the organization. Another would be the regular meetings between senior managers and the organization's bankers to review aspects of company finances. There are internal examples of boundary-spanning groups within organizations, but many would also be classified as activity groups already described.

✦ Professional. This could involve the grouping of professionals within the organization into an appropriate work-based group, perhaps even a professional institute or similar association if the company is large enough. It reflects a particular type of work-based grouping commonly found among accountants, engineers, lawyers, doctors and other professional groups.

The approach adopted within an organization to the grouping of people is increasingly being recognized as a basis of competitive advantage. Traditional organizational hierarchies are focused on functional groupings and hierarchical management responsibility. However the customer experience of an organization is not hierarchical, it is horizontal. Consider shopping at a supermarket, conducting your personal banking or purchasing new equipment for your company. In each of these transactions the customer will encounter the lower level staff who process orders, sales and define the customer experience with the supplying organization. In meeting the needs of customers a cross-functional approach is needed within a traditional, functional organization. It is hardly surprising, therefore, that such organizations have difficulty in providing excellent customer service. The boundaries between the various functional groups can act as fences or friction points, preventing a seamless customer-focused experience. In addition the senior managers tend to become remote from the experience of customers as they spend more time 'managing cost' rather than 'doing customer activity' within the organization. This conflicting model of customer experience and organizational functioning is reflected in Figure 5.1.

Likert (1961) developed the idea that organizations should be considered as a collection of groups, rather than individuals. In his view individuals would inevitably belong to more than one group and consequently the groups would overlap. This he described as a *linking pin* process and it is shown as Figure 5.2.

While Figure 5.2 is a simplistic representation of the nature of groups within an orga-

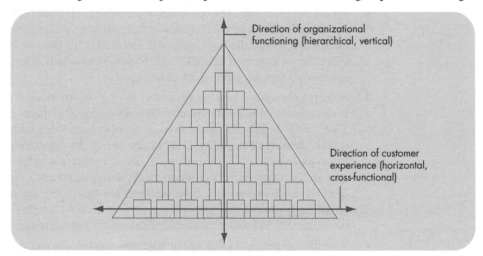

FIGURE 5.1   The hierarchical/customer conflict.

nization, it is useful as a means of describing the overlapping memberships of individuals as part of the formal organization structure. Likert recognized that this basic model underestimated the true level and complexity of group activity within an organization. Any individual belongs to many groups at one and the same time. For example, a library assistant in a university library may belong to the issue desk team, the copyright monitoring team, the book repair team, the student debts working group as well as the service development working group. In addition they may have supervisory responsibilities for a number of other staff and be part of a number of friendship and social groupings.

The linking pin model also ignores the *instrumental value* of groups to individual members. For example, Handy (1993) argues that individuals join and use groups for a number of purposes, including meeting social and affiliation needs and gaining support for their objectives. Groups in organizations are not just imposed on people from above. Individuals create groups and vary their level of participation in groups depending upon a range of personal and organizational factors.

In an organizational setting groups are frequently described as teams and Management in Action 5.1 reflects the importance of these to Reuters, the financial and information services company.

Stop | Consider

Use Figure 5.1 to explain the process adopted within Reuters.
What does this suggest about the nature of groups within organizations?

The significance of groups

Looked at from a top-down perspective, groups are designated by the higher levels of the hierarchy within an organization. It is senior managers who decide on the form that the organization will take and in doing so they also designate the formal groupings that will be created to achieve the perceived operational needs. The group structures within the organization therefore represent a *given* for most people. Group structures are created and people recruited into the team for which their skills and experience have prepared them. The formation of formal groups is therefore a process of *selection* and *socialization*.

In circumstances in which new recruits are chosen to join existing organizations part

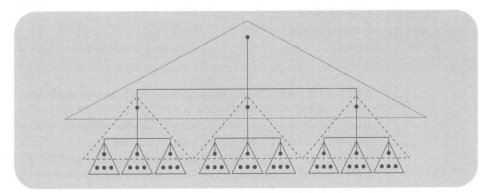

FIGURE 5.2 Likert's linking pin model of organizational groups (*source*: Likert, R (1961) *New Patterns of Management*, McGraw-Hill, New York).

MANAGEMENT IN ACTION 5.1

Restoring order from chaos

In the words of John Parcell, from Reuters:

> By the late 1980s it [Reuters] had acquired a reputation for poor service and arrogance. Many orders were handled wrongly, late or not at all. So customers got angry and often refused to pay their bills.

John Parcell and Geoffrey Sanderson were brought into the UK operations of Reuters as managing director and deputy to apply re-engineering principles. What they found was that customers would have to wait between three and six months for new hardware and services and even two weeks if only services were involved. Once the order had been met it took another two months to send the bill and another three or more to collect payment. Even simple orders would go through a dozen departments and five computer systems. The sales staff and engineers who formed the direct interface with customers did not know each other.

Parcell and Sanderson identified, with the assistance of management consultants, a process which included:

✦ The creation of four geographic divisions. This focused the company on customer location.

✦ These divisions were organized into multifunctional account teams of about six people. Each team was responsible for the business of about 50 customers.

✦ The customer order, delivery, installation, billing and follow-up system (the order life-cycle) was totally redesigned. The number of 'hand-offs' between people was reduced from about 24 to four.

✦ Performance criteria were identified indicating when the order stages had to be completed.

✦ Training and change management assisted the transition and ensured that everyone knew what was expected of them and possessed the necessary skills.

Two years after the initial change it has been reported that the multifunctional teams are working well and are beginning to press for more autonomy in dealing with customers. It is reported that employees find the working atmosphere one of mutual help and covering for each other. In excess of 95% of all orders are now installed on time. Those involving hardware and services are operational between three and four weeks after orders are placed and less than one day for services. Bills are also more than 98% accurate. Surveys have shown that customer dissatisfaction has dropped to less than 10%.

Adapted from: Lorenz, C (1993) Restoring order from chaos, *Financial Times*, 2 June, p 11.

of the process is the *fit* between the existing people and the applicant. Once inside the organization the individual is subjected to an extended process of *socialization* into the organization and the groups to which they will become affiliated. It is more common to find situations in which a new person joins an existing group than for a group to be formed from nothing. Project teams, company reorganizations and the creation of special task forces are common examples of circumstances in which new groups may be formed within an existing organization.

The significance of groups within an organizational setting arises from two main factors:

✦ Necessity. This reflects the need for an organization to arrange for the work that has to be done to actually get done. It is not physically possible for the chief executive of a large company personally to undertake the full range of work needed. Consequently, devices have to found which allow the range, scale and volume of work that needs to be done to be undertaken by a large number of people in the most cost-effective way possible. While there are many different ways in which this can actually be achieved they all involve some form of grouping of people.

✦ Dynamic. This aspect reflects the nature of groups themselves. This aspect will form a significant part of the topic to be covered in the next chapter and so will only be introduced briefly here. The definition of a group introduced earlier in this chapter makes it apparent that as a social framework it contains a measure of 'togetherness'. Being a member of a group confers personal and social benefits as well as organizational benefits. There is also a personal cost associated with group membership in that individuals have to align their behaviour (or otherwise conform) to the norms of the groups to which they belong. Groups tend to develop a life of their own in that the very 'togetherness' sought from the existence of a group creates a unity that can subvert the formally intended purpose. Management in Action 5.2 reflects just such a situation.

Stop | Consider

What does MiA 5.2 illustrate about the significance of groups for organizations and the individuals that work within them?

The significance of groups in terms of the organizational context is that they are necessary to the achievement of the desired objectives and can provide competitive advantage. But at the same time the creation of groups can lead to other behaviours emerging and because they develop a degree of independence from the organization that created them they can be difficult to direct and control. In extreme cases, they can even become hostile to management and seek to frustrate attempts to direct them.

Equally, from an individual point of view groups are also significant. Human beings belong to many different groups based on family, friendship, location, social grouping and work activities. There are many advantages to being in a group. Sharing responsibility, friendship, support with problems, a feeling of value and comfort in times of distress are just some of them. As many animals find, there is relative safety in numbers. However, there are also individual costs associated with group membership. It is not possible to be an individual within a group. The very essence of a group implies 'togetherness', 'unity' and 'commonality'. From that point of view each member must give up something to become and remain a member. A member who cannot or will not adopt the necessary norms of behaviour and otherwise accept the requirements of membership will probably find themselves subjected to some degree of sanction or, in extreme cases, expulsion. Group membership reflects a social process of give and take, not just take and sometimes the requirement to give (or conform) can outweigh the benefits obtained for the individual.

Formal and informal groups

The emphasis in the discussion so far has been on those groups that exist as part of the formal activities within an organization. Such groups are established by management and

MANAGEMENT IN ACTION 5.2

Fiddles in the bonus scheme

This is a true story based on an experience I had a number of years ago. Only some of the details have been changed to prevent the possibility of identifying the organization and the individuals involved.

The maintenance department of the local authority of a major city in England was responsible for all building repairs on civic buildings, public housing and other areas for which the authority was responsible such as roads, schools etc. The management of the authority was determined to raise the level productivity among the maintenance workers as part of the drive to reduce the cost of public services. Consequently, they introduced a time-saved bonus scheme for all maintenance workers. The system was in essence very simple. Work study engineers (known as bonus surveyors) were recruited and developed job times for the work that was done by staff in the maintenance department. Once the list of job times was developed they were given to the supervisors who then produced a job card for each job that needed to be done and gave it to the individual worker.

The worker then knew what the job was, where it was and how long it should take to complete. Once the job was completed the worker would fill in how long it had taken to do, sign the job card and hand it back to the supervisor. At the end of the week all the job times that each worker had earned were added up, as was the actual time taken to do them. If there was any time saved (the worker had earned more hours than they had actually worked) this was converted to money and paid to the worker as a bonus.

The system was not complicated as far as bonus schemes are concerned and everyone soon became used to how it should operate. However, the workers also quickly found that it was very easy to fiddle the scheme. Consider for a moment the type of work undertaken by the maintenance department. It tended to involve individual

tradespeople working alone and away from their base (a depot in which the administrative staff, materials and equipment were kept). Also supervisors had large geographic areas to cover and could not  monitor work activities closely. Equally, the nature of maintenance work is uncertain and can involve having to undertake tasks that were not originally intended. Take for example the need to repair a door lock that is not working properly and which might involve any or all of the following tasks:

+ Resiting the lock itself on the door or the keep in the frame.
+ Taking the lock off the door, stripping it down, cleaning it, lubricating the surfaces, putting it back together and refitting it to the door.
+ Taking the lock off the door and replacing it with a new one.
+ Replacing the lock and making repairs to the door if another type of lock has been fitted.

Naturally, each of these variations required times to be worked out and some of the tasks took longer than others to complete. Inevitably, it did not take the workers long to discover that they could make more bonus if they claimed that the job had been very complex and needed more work than was actually necessary. The level of bonus paid out began to increase as word spread on how to fiddle the system. This was not helped when recognition dawned that supervisors were generally unable to check any of the work, even if they wanted to. Consequently, management decided that in order to ensure that the bonus scheme achieved its original objectives they would employ a number of people as bonus checkers. These people would specifically take a sample

(10%) of the previous day's job cards, visit each job and check to ensure that what had been claimed had actually been done.

This was a boring job and guaranteed to catch many workers out as by this time most were fiddling the bonus scheme to some degree. In some cases it was a deliberate attempt to gain more bonus than the worker was entitled to claim, in others it was done in error in an attempt to reflect the tasks that had actually been necessary as not every combination of task could be covered by the work standards available. Workers caught fiddling the bonus were subjected to formal disciplinary investigation and some were dismissed for major acts of cheating. The bonus checkers soon became bored with the process and also began to find ways of fiddling the system to their own advantage.

They did so as follows. As individuals they were required to sign in at the depot each morning and afternoon, which they dutifully did. They would then go to the office and collect the required 10% sample of job cards and report any problems found during the previous working period. The supervisor would then make arrangements to follow up on any problems and deal with the disciplinary hearing if necessary. Having completed any office work individual bonus checkers would then get into their cars and drive off the site to begin the necessary checking for that morning or afternoon.

However, what the bonus checkers would actually do is drive to a cafe on the other side of town to the main maintenance depot and all meet up. The group would then spend a couple of hours drinking coffee and chatting as well as signing off most of the 10% sample of job cards without looking at the work. Having become bored with chatting to each other they would all set off to look at a couple of jobs, selected to maximize mileage claims and to be near to home for lunch. Inevitably there was a very high probability of finding a fiddle on a job card and this one would be brought to management's attention on the next visit to the office.

This approach to seeking to operate bonus schemes within the maintenance department of the authority lasted for about four years until the entire system was changed. Everyone involved continued to fiddle the bonus to some extent for as long as it lasted. Eventually both workers and bonus checkers came to an uneasy truce in that both knew of the fiddles perpetrated by the others but neither group went out of its way to make real problems for the other.

function according to management's rules and standards. From that point of view they are not a naturally occurring social structure. They are designed and imposed by managers on the workforce as a way of achieving the desired objectives in a controlled manner. They also represent an attempt to impose *social control* on the workforce in encouraging certain behaviours and discouraging others through adopted (or imposed) norms, without the need for large numbers of management 'enforcers'.

It is possible to differentiate between types of formal group within an organization on the basis of purpose. Based on the work of Argyle (1989) it is possible to identify formal groups involved in the following activities:

◆ Teams. These are frequently project or activity groups. They are usually given a high degree of freedom in terms of deciding on the processes to be used to achieve the objectives set.

◆ Tasks. The nature of the objectives to be achieved are more clearly set out for this type of group and so there is little discretion available in terms of activity and method to be adopted. Most work groups would fall under this heading.

◆ Technology. The nature of this classification is that the *technology* or *process* dictates the work *activities* and *methods* involved. There exists little opportunity for the group to exercise discretion in either of these areas. In practice it forms a special type of *task* category (point 2 in this list).

◆ Decisions. Much management time is taken up with meetings (a form of group activity) associated with decision making. Of course, this form of group activity is not restricted to managers as many specialist and administrative staff would also be involved.

◆ Management. In addition to decision making, management must collectively plan, guide and monitor organizational activity.

Informal groups exist within all organizations. It is also true that within most formal groups there exist a number of informal ones. Informal groups serve a number of functions both positive and negative. It is usual to describe informal groups in either friendship or interest terms. Membership of an informal group is voluntary and the significance of their existence is frequently understated. In most organizations *things get done* on the basis of the informal groups and networks that exist. Hofstede (1984) draws attention to the concept of a *marketplace bureaucracy* in his analysis of culture and structure. The essence of this concept is that individuals depend more on personal relationships than formal reporting relationships to get things done. The facilitation in this form of bureaucracy is achieved through the trading of support for mutual advantage. It is based on the unstated assumption of, 'You help me this time and I will help you in future', hence the term marketplace. Hofstede suggests that it would be commonly found in Scandinavian countries, the UK and Ireland.

However, the negative role of informal relations and networks in excluding women from management positions was also demonstrated by Cooper and Davidson (1982). In response to this form of discrimination there have been moves towards the formation of women-only groups or networks. The purpose being to enhance the ability of women to progress in the male-dominated professions, including management. Management in Action 5.3 illustrates some of the difficulties facing women in attempting to progress into senior positions.

Stop | Consider   *How might the situation described in MiA 5.3 be changed when this can only be achieved by persuading men to change their attitudes and organizational practice, thereby allowing more women through the 'glass ceiling'?*

Friendship groups form on the basis of relationships within an organization. They are not restricted to level or functional area within the company and frequently act as information channels. In practice much friendship group activity has a social basis and becomes a process of mutual *looking out for each other*. If friendship groups become too strong, they may attempt consciously to influence events in their favour, perhaps through clandestine means. Consequently, there is a danger of friendship groups working against the interests of management. It is also possible for such groups to form the basis of resistance to change. It is at this point that friendship groups become interest groups. Interest groups could also form as a response to a perceived threat. For example, comments from senior managers that a delayering exercise were being considered might encourage junior managers to form a group (or join a trade union) in order to protect their jobs by seeking to influence or frustrate management's intentions.

MANAGEMENT IN ACTION 5.3

Men's room only

The first women's colleges were opened in Oxford a century ago yet the representation of females among the higher levels of academic staff is still relatively small.

In 1993 when this material first appeared in print it was reported that only six out of 178 professors and four out of 69 readers at Oxford were women. It was argued that this couldn't be due to a shortage of potential applicants as women represent about 13% of university lecturers, 27% of college lecturers and 42% of undergraduates. Nationally, the Association of University Teachers, the trade union representing academic staff in universities, claimed that the position of women was not much better with only about 5% of professors in the 'old' universities being women. Two-thirds of female professors have been appointed since the late 1980s.

It has been suggested that universities suffer from the existence of a 'glass ceiling', a phenomenon evident in many organizations and professions. It represents an invisible barrier to promotion. Women in an organization or profession reach a certain level within the hierarchy, to find that they can see the senior levels above them but that they are unable to reach these positions.

At Oxford University a group of academic staff were determined to challenge the decision to allocate money available for promotion to fund additional professorships rather than readerships. The argument being that this approach reinforced

the position of men as professors because few women had the status allowing them to be successful in seeking promotion to that rank. However, if the promotions were to be concentrated at the level of readerships then more women would be likely to be successful because of the greater number that would be eligible for promotion. The justification for the decision, put forward by Oxford University, was that in terms of international status and recognition of its work, the title professor would be of greater benefit to both the individuals and the institution.

Oxford claim that they are making good progress from what was a very low base in the promotion of women. Until 1979 only one-third of colleges accepted women. Those seeking to enhance the position of women claim that the predominantly male culture of British universities is generally intimidating to women and that this needs to be addressed. As one student explained:

> The problem is that the system has been built around men for 750 years. Are we prepared to change ourselves to reflect the diversity we now have?

Adapted from: Authers, J (1993) Men's room only, *Financial Times*, 18 May, p 17.

The existence of informal groups is something that is frequently seen as a matter of concern by managers. Indeed, some writers on the subject refer to them as *shadow organizations* (Stacey, 1996), the clear implication being something sinister and potentially damaging to the host organization. However, as has already been implied, there is a degree of inevitability about their existence and they can be of value to management. The *grapevine* can be a useful means through which to communicate with individuals in the organization according to Dalton (1959).

Adler *et al.* (1989) report that 66% of their respondents in the People's Republic of China indicated that it was only infrequently necessary to bypass the hierarchical line in order to achieve efficient work relationships. In an earlier study Laurent (1983) found that only 22% of respondents in Sweden responded similarly, but that 75% of Italians did so.

The results indicated clearly that there are national difference in the degree to which informal lines of communication would be used. However, it is never possible to be certain of the degree to which respondents reply to questions of this type in terms of what they think would be an acceptable or desirable answer rather than reflecting actual practice. Katz (1973) also suggests that informal groups can assist the integration of employees into the organization by blurring the distinction between work and non-work activities.

Informal groups form the lifeblood of most organizations in that they depend on a level of mutual need and dependency among the members for their existence. Informal groups form because the individuals wish to *band together*, perhaps for protection against a management decision; perhaps because they enjoy similar leisure interests; or perhaps because there is a work-related dependency. Whatever the reason for the existence of an informal group many of them contribute to the effective running of the organization. It is the ability of one employee to speak directly with another and discuss work-related events and problems that is mutually beneficial and keeps things running smoothly. Standard operating procedures provide guidance on what should be done, people in their working relationships actually make this happen. However, as discussed earlier, Hofstede (and others) suggest that this 'bending' of the hierarchical formalities would only be expected to arise in certain cultural circumstances.

Many of the recent attempts to increase levels of employee commitment can be interpreted as attempts to tap into already existing informal processes. Management in Action 5.4 provides an indication of the processes involved in reorganizing people into teams and the associated training required.

Stop | Consider

To what extent do you consider that it is possible for management to capture aspects of informal relationships and group membership and formalize them within working practices?

Would such attempts to formalize the informal simply lead to the creation of different forms of informal grouping as individuals seek to exert some control over their organizational experience?

Why groups form

In an organizational context there are two major reasons why groups are a significant factor for both employers and employees. First, it is necessary to use groups or teams of individuals to achieve the organization's objectives. Second, most humans prefer to associate with other people. The main reasons that groups form include:

✦ The need to have more than one person to undertake the work. In organizations of more than one person it is necessary to separate the activities to be done and to allocate people into teams.

✦ The need to incorporate the expertise of a number of people in order to achieve the end result. For example, a project team set up to design a new product may need the skills of designers, engineers, accountants, production and marketing specialists.

✦ The need for organizations to match complexity in the environment through the provision of internal operating methods and arrangements. Ashby (1964) termed this as the *law of requisite variety*. He suggested that only variety could destroy variety. In

MANAGEMENT IN ACTION 5.4

Sense of involvement

Du Pont's printing and publishing business introduced an annual hours work system in 1992 and as a result moved from four- to six-shift working. The 750 workers were organized into 30 self-managed teams. Within the teams employees are trained in all tasks performed by the group, some retaining a core skill function. Each team is responsible for every aspect of the process, including production, costing, productivity, quality, safety and work allocation. This is achieved through a weekly pre-shift meeting supported by one training day every six weeks. The gains achieved are tangible and Pat Tunney, the personnel manager at Du Pont, indicated that productivity rose by 36% in the first year of operation and he predicted a 25% rise the following year.

Team building can be achieved in many different ways. Sue Bradshaw, the dealer development manager with Peugeot, described their approach. In pursuit of accreditation to the BS5750 quality standard an improvement cycle was identified thorough which continuous change could be made within the dealer network. The company introduced a 'team builder' programme which began with a PC-based questionnaire to generate information for the individual's team profile. This was used to discuss role preferences and team communication style with each

individual before a two-day team development workshop. This led naturally into ongoing discussions by the team about how to improve the performance of the business.

Other companies opt for outdoor training as the means to encourage understanding and develop the trust and confidence between individual members. Rank Xerox CSD manager for human resources, Christine Hands, indicated that:

> Group members need mutual trust and respect for each other's skills, knowledge, opinions and commitment. They need to communicate freely and easily with each other.

The team training available to Rank Xerox was provided by a US company and was described by Hands as a mini-Olympics in the following way:

> It went down as a lot of fun. Their style was very un-English – it took some people a while to come to terms with it. But by the end of the week no one wanted to leave.

Adapted from: Haughton, E (1993) Sense of involvement, *Personnel Today*, 29 June, pp 26–30.

other words, only organizational complexity could match and offset environmental complexity. Among the implications of this is that the creation of teams can encourage synergy, creativity and innovation through group membership.

✦ The opportunity to allow employees to minimize the worst aspects of their work by sharing it out or rotating it among the group. This should enhance satisfaction or, at the least, minimize dissatisfaction.

✦ Groups provide for the social needs of individuals. Friendships provide a form of social significance for the individual within the work setting. It allows the individual to be more than just a number or a means of production. Such networks and relationships allow for the support of the individual in the work setting by other workers.

✦ The groups to which an individual belong provide a basis for socialization into the *norms* of behaviour within the organization. This includes the extent to which official rules are followed and the way in which employees maintain the balance between management demands and employee preference.

✦ Group membership also provides the individual with a measure of protection from outside threat. It has been argued that employment conditions and protection have only been improved across Europe as a result of the high levels of trade union membership.

✦ Groups also emerge as a result of the nature of the work to be undertaken within an organization. This can be to acquire information; seek clarification of that already obtained; pass work on (or obtain it); cross-reference something; or elicit help in undertaking something. The result is that mutual dependency is formed with people either helping (or hindering) each other.

The discussion on groups reflects the complexity in organizational activity. The concept of *variety* has already been introduced as a useful means of reflecting this state of affairs. Management in Action 5.5 reflects how one organization attempted to deal with this notion of variety.

Stop | Consider   *Does the approach described in MiA 5.5 reflect an attempt to encourage the rapid development of groups which, of necessity, change frequently? Or does it reflect an organizational need to cope with a complex environment? Does this distinction matter?*

Formal groups are created by the organization of which they form part. However, the informal groups that exist are created by the people within the host organization. They both feed off and interact with the formal groups around them. Informal groups come into existence for a number of reasons, including:

✦ The nature and form of the formal organization. The way in which the formal organization operates can influence the way that individuals organize themselves and interact.

✦ The need for human beings to function in a social environment and to form relationships of their own choosing. Schein (1956) describes the manipulation of prisoners of war by the Chinese Communists during the Korean War. The use of rank was dispensed with and groups were reorganized when it became apparent that something approaching an effective structure was emerging.

✦ The voluntary nature of many informal groups offsets the involuntary nature of many formal, organizational groups.

✦ The approach adopted by managers to the running of the organization will also influence the formation of informal groups.

✦ The need to run the organization. Organization structures and procedures are the mechanisms that determine what should be done where and when. However, procedures cannot cater for the interpersonal and dynamic nature of organizational activity. Organizational functioning depends to a significant extent on individuals co-operating in a reciprocal network of activity. Inevitably, in such situations self-help networks of mutual dependency (informal groups) form. In some cultures informal groups may form for other reasons. For example, cohorts of students recruited by a single organization at the same time may 'keep in touch' during the course of their careers and offer mutual support and advice to each other.

MANAGEMENT IN ACTION 5.5

Construction on a united front

MW Kellogg is an international construction company employing some 4000 skilled workers. The UK operation specializes in petrochemical design and construction projects that can last from a few weeks to several years. Each project requires a dedicated team of anything up to 100 people from a range of professions and disciplines. Project teams can also involve individuals and groups that are not directly employed by MW Kellogg. This situation can create many difficulties as people have to work effectively together and at the same time look after the interests of the organization they represent. Add to this the cultural, language and professional differences that exist when operating internationally and it is surprising that any project is completed.

Angela Freddi, senior personnel officer for MW Kellogg, attempted to find ways of encouraging the creation of effective teams in this context. Purpose-designed courses were introduced with the help of an outside training company, Arete. The process for each project group follows a similar pattern:

✦ Once the project group is selected Arete visits each member in order to identify potential problem areas.

✦ This information is discussed with the personnel department and a three-day course is designed to address the issues identified and create a team.

✦ Courses have a common theme to them. The first two days are intended to break down barriers and to build team spirit. The third day focuses on issues relevant to the project that the team is to undertake.

✦ Non-company people who will be part of the project team are encouraged to attend the course.

✦ Members of the project group will be taken off their current job in groups to go through the course. Participants on each course are from a range of the disciplines and professions represented on the project.

Another aspect of these courses worthy of note is the use of either indoor or outdoor activity, depending upon the background and experience of the participants. These activities involve the solving of problems, where every member of the team has to experience being a team leader and operating at the lowest level. This is intended to provide individuals with the experience of what it is like to allow someone else to have the lead role as well as to reflect on their own strengths and weaknesses.

Adapted from: Simons, C (1992) Construction on a united front, *Personnel Today*, 30 June, pp 33–4.

Research approaches

One of the earliest research activities into group activity was reported by Triplett (1897). Triplett observed that racing cyclists performed better when accompanied by a pacemaker than when they were alone. Table 5.1 indicates the results that he observed for two leading racing cyclists to cover a one-mile training 'race'.

The gain from having a pacemaker was an improvement in performance of approximately 20%. This in itself was an interesting result as the experiment was not carried out in a competitive situation. Triplett interpreted these findings in terms of the arousal of the competitive instinct from the presence of the other cyclist. This became known as *social facilitation*, the presence and involvement of others in an activity producing an enhanced performance in an individual.

These co-action effects (changes in behaviour through the presence of others) have been observed in a wide range of species. Table 5.2 has been developed from Zajonc (1965) and demonstrates this.

Another form of social facilitation is referred to as the *audience effect*, the mere presence (rather than the active participation) of others producing an enhancement in behavioural activity.

The British experience

During World War I the British government established a committee to study the relationship between working conditions, fatigue and output. After the end of the war this committee changed its focus and in 1918 came under the control of the Medical Research Council and became the Industrial Fatigue Research Board. Initially, the board concentrated on issues surrounding the nature of work and its effect on people. The board eventually published some 33 research studies relating to aspects of the employment of people.

Commissioned by the Board, Wyatt *et al.* (1928) reported a study carried out in a number of organizations. It concentrated on women performing a number of jobs, including wrapping soap, folding handkerchiefs, making bicycle chains, weighing and wrapping tobacco, making cigarettes and making rifle bullets. Among the conclusions drawn from their work was that the social conditions within which the work was done held significant consequences for the people. Also, boredom was less likely to arise when people worked in groups rather than on their own.

In the USA work was underway at the same time that, when linked with the ideas from

| | Time to cycle one mile | | |
	Paced	Unpaced	Gain for pacing
Person X	99.6 seconds	123.8 seconds	+19.5%
Person Y	102.0 seconds	130.0 seconds	+21.5%

TABLE 5.1   Racing times for one mile

Harlow (1932)	Laboratory rats ate more if fed together than when fed alone
Chen (1937)	A species of ant worked harder at nest building when working in a group than when alone
Rasmussen (1939)	Thirsty laboratory rats would drink more when in the presence of other rats than when alone
Tolman and Wilson (1956)	Repeated the Harlow (1932) findings but with chicks rather than rats

TABLE 5.2   Social facilitation in non-human species

the research activity already described, was to lead to the development of the human relations movement. The significance of the social aspects of work on productivity emerged as a major alternative to the task emphasis in work organization prevalent up to that point.

The Hawthorne Studies

The Western Electric Company in the USA had begun a series of investigations at its Hawthorne Works in 1924. The studies were initially carried out by staff within the company, as it was intended to identify productivity improvements of practical value. In 1927 researchers from the Harvard Business School became involved in the research and the names of Mayo, Roethlisberger and Dickson are now the most closely associated with it.

It is Mayo who is credited with the leadership of the research team from Harvard. He was an Australian by birth and spent time during and after World War I working with disabled military personnel. It is hardly stretching credibility to imagine that such an experience would have a major impact on his thinking about people, work, organizations and life in general. The significance of people in a collective setting was a predominant theme of the Hawthorne research and the subsequent interpretation of the results.

The studies within the Hawthorne works can be separated into four stages:

✦ The illumination experiments.
✦ The relay assembly test room study.
✦ The interview programme.
✦ The bank wiring observation room study.

We now look briefly at each stage of the research in turn. The research process will be discussed in some detail as it represents one of the most detailed and comprehensive studies into the nature and impact of group working to date.

The illumination experiments   The intention of these experiments was to identify the relationship between levels of light and output. The experiment was undertaken by splitting the workers into experimental and control groups. The experimental group was subjected to situations in which the level of illumination was systematically varied and the output monitored. The control group continued in conditions of normal levels of light and the levels of output recorded.

The results of the experiments were inconclusive in that production levels did not appear to vary in relationship to the level of light. The level of output increased even when the level of light was very poor. Output also increased in the control group; which had no change in lighting. The highest level of output recorded was when the experimental group returned to their normal working conditions.

This unexpected set of findings led to the conclusion that worker output was in practice influenced by many factors. This prompted the subsequent research in an attempt to identify the range and degree of impact of these factors.

The relay assembly test room study   The work in this room involved female workers assembling a number of small components to make the relay switches used in telephone equipment. The very nature of this work is highly repetitive and boring. To conduct the research, a group of six women were selected from among the regular workforce. Two of the women (who were friends) were selected by the research team. These two women then selected the other four workers. The six women to be studied were transferred to a special room designated for the research study.

Working conditions in the normal department were replicated in the experimental room. The experiment began with a period during which the work practices were identical to those in the normal department. For example, a 48-hour working week with no rest breaks, or provision of refreshment. The normal output on assembling relays was 50 per hour worked. This level of output allowed the research team to detect even relatively small changes in productivity. There followed a research period of almost two years, in which a number of variables associated with the work arrangements were systematically varied (see Table 5.3).

The researcher was located in the room with the women workers and by noting all that happened created the records that were used in the subsequent analysis. The women were generally kept informed about the experiment and consulted about events that were to take place. The observer also tried to maintain a friendly atmosphere in the room through his general approach to the staff and the recording of data.

Output increased under each of the experimental manipulations during this phase of the research. Output even increased when the experiment was ended and the women went back to the normal working arrangements operated in the main department. The main reasons put forward as an explanation for the results obtained included:

✦ The special status accruing to the women as a result of having been selected for

Duration of experiment (weeks)	Experimental condition
8	Incentive introduced to reward increased individual effort
5	A morning and afternoon rest period of five minutes allowed
4	Rest periods extended to 10 minutes each
4	Introduction of six five-minute rest periods
11	Introduction of 15-minute morning and 10-minute afternoon rest periods with the company providing refreshments
7	In addition to the two rest periods immediately above finish work at 4.30 pm (30 minutes early)
4	As previous rest periods but finish work at 4.00 pm (60 minutes early)
9	Saturday working eliminated, plus one 15-minute and one 10-minute rest period allowed each day
11	Introduction of 15-minute morning and 10-minute afternoon rest periods with the company providing refreshments
7	In addition to the two rest periods immediately above finish work at 4.30 pm (30 minutes early)
4	As previous rest periods but finish work at 4.00 pm (60 minutes early)
9	Saturday working eliminated, plus one 15-minute and one 10-minute rest period allowed each day

TABLE 5.3 Examples of the experimental conditions used in the relay assembly test room

involvement in the experiment resulted in an increased motivation to co-operate and perform at their best.

✦ The influence of being consulted and kept informed by the experimenter enhanced output as a result of the increased level of participation.

✦ Morale improved as a result of the general friendliness of the observer and conditions of the experiment.

✦ The management approach to supervision during the experiment was different from that experienced normally. The increased freedom experienced by the women within the work setting reduced stress and encouraged higher output.

✦ The group was self-selected, thereby allowing the better than normal relationships to create a climate of mutual dependence and support appropriate to group working.

The results of this stage of the experiment encouraged the researchers to seek out the social and other variables operating in the work setting through an extended interview programme.

The interview programme   More than 20,000 interviews were conducted in this phase of the research. Among the earlier findings was the suggestion that output and productivity were related to supervision and working conditions. The interview programme was designed to identify employee attitudes and feelings towards these issues using structured questions. However, it quickly became apparent that workers wanted to talk about other aspects of their work. As a response, the process was changed, involving open-ended and non-directive questions. This allowed interviewees to discuss things that they considered important.

There were a number of findings that emerged from the analysis of this vast amount of research data. Employee views about management in general, the company, even society as a whole were obtained. Indications were also obtained that there was a network of informal groups in existence within the organizationally based work teams. These groups were the primary means by which supervisors and leading employees controlled the productive activities and behaviour of other employees within departments. The techniques developed in this stage of the research programme played a significant part in the subsequent introduction of counselling and attitude surveys as part of human resource management practice.

The existence of informal groups within the formal ones, in effect the existence of a organization within an organization, led to the final stage in the research programme, the bank wiring observation room study. This was intended to discover how these informal groups functioned and exercised control.

The bank wiring observation room study   This stage of the research consisted of the direct observation of 14 men employed in the department. The men were organized into three teams each consisting of three wirers and a supervisor. In addition, there were two inspectors checking the work of the department as a whole.

The observation of this department also identified the existence of two informal groups. These groups did not coincide with the formal structures within the department. Figure 5.3 reflects the composition of these groups, and is based on Roethlisberger and Dickson (1964, p 504). In this figure it can be seen that one supervisor, one wirer and one inspector were not affiliated to either informal group. In addition, two wirers were only partially integrated to the groups. This suggests that not everyone joins (or is allowed to join) an informal group and that the boundaries of such groups are also somewhat fluid.

The two informal groups were found to have developed their own behaviour standards or *group norms* as they came to be called. These norms covered a number of features of the work of the department, including the levels of output to be achieved by each person. Much of the activity of the informal groups was intended to control the behaviour of members with the aim of protecting the group from interference by management while maintaining group cohesion.

These informal groups became adept at being able to 'manage' management by providing an impression of activity within the department that met the expectations of managers. Output was reported as being constant over the week, even if it had varied on a daily basis. The overall level of output was correctly reported, but the pattern of production was smoothed out. Managers expect consistency (and to achieve what they anticipated) in work activity. Deviation from this expectation becomes a focus of attention and investigation. By 'meeting' that expectation, employees retained effective control over their day-to-day working environment.

The norms of behaviour under which the informal groups operated consisted of a number of rules in which individual workers would be named according to the following criteria:

✦ Chisler. A person who turned out too little work. Someone who was not doing their fair share of work.

✦ Rate buster. A person who produced more than a reasonable volume of work.

✦ Squealer. A person who reported anything to a supervisor that could be to the detriment of a fellow worker.

One rule in the department was that inspectors and supervisors should become part of the informal group structure and not act as part of management. This included an

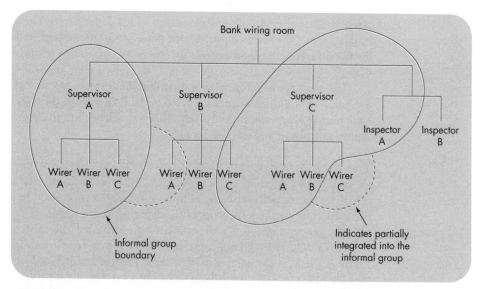

FIGURE 5.3   Formal structure and informal groups within the bank wiring observation room.

expectation of co-operation with the group in enforcing its norms and not acting in an officious manner.

The informal groups were reducing the opportunity for members to earn at their maximum level, or at their personally preferred level, in favour of the maintenance of group cohesion. In practice, the group looked after the collective interest of the members, but the price was a loss of individualism and earnings potential.

Within the bank wiring room the group norms and control were enforced through a hierarchy of negative sanctions. These began with light-hearted comments about an individual's output level. If this was not successful in bringing the individual back into line, or a more serious breach of the norms occurred the comments would become more pointed. This could also include physical contact in the form of tapping on the upper arm, referred to as *binging*. The inspector who was not part of an informal group in Figure 5.3 considered he was superior to the wirers and generally acted in an officious manner. The workers played tricks on him with equipment, they ostracized him and generally applied so much social pressure that he asked to be transferred to another department.

There are a number of key findings that emerged from the Hawthorne Studies, including:

✦ Informal groups inevitably form within formally designated groupings.

✦ Informal groups will not always match the groupings designated by management.

✦ Individuals at work are not simply motivated by pay and other tangible benefits.

✦ Informal groups will attempt a form of bottom-up management in order to influence their working environment.

✦ The rewards that an individual gains from membership of an informal group may be more significant and meaningful to that individual than any benefit that can be obtained from management.

✦ Informal groups may seek to frustrate management's intentions and objectives.

✦ The groups to which an individual belong will have a significant influence on their behaviour and attitudes towards work.

✦ First-line managers and supervisors are subjected to strong and competing pressures for their affiliations from those above and below.

✦ Management has little or no influence on the establishment and form or membership of informal groups within the organization.

✦ Informal groups can engage in competitive activities that are against the interests of the organization as a whole.

As society changes so too do the forms of control that can successfully be applied. Early approaches to managing relied heavily on coercion and force. This continued, with a small number of notable exceptions, until the time of the Hawthorne Studies, which began a more concerted move towards the humanization of work. The human relations movement, as it became known, was interested in how to adopt a social dimension to work organization and motivation.

Another way of thinking about this notion of humanization of work is to consider it as an attempt by managers to maintain control within a changing social environment. It had become apparent that social attitudes and structures were beginning to change and that existing methods of control were not producing levels of output and quality required at an acceptable price. This, if nothing else, had been demonstrated by Taylor in his application of *scientific management* principles. However, given the adverse reaction that his approach generated, alternative ways were needed to achieve improvements in productivity and retain control. The human relations approach offered an opportunity for managers to achieve the desired objectives but in a different, more acceptable (at least to the workers) way.

The Hawthorne Studies have been very influential in providing ideas and theory relating to groups within an organizational setting. Management in Action 5.6 provides an illustration of how one organization attempted to combine formality and informality into its teamwork activities.

Stop | Consider   *To what extent can initiatives such as that described in MiA 5.6 ever truly reflect the nature of informal groups and therefore capture the potential benefits available?*

Group formation and development

Groups do not simply come into existence automatically. If the individuals concerned do not know each other then it is hardly likely that they will be willing or able immediately to perform effectively within the collective context implied by being a member of a group. People need to get to know each other and to determine how they should work together before they can begin to tackle the issues facing the group. This section seeks to review the ways in which groups form and begin to develop the ability to work effectively.

Group formation

Homans (1950) proposed that any group (he used the term *social system*) existed within an environment consisting of three elements:

✦ Culture. The norms, values and goals that make up the shared understandings within which the group will function.

✦ Physical. The geographical context, involving the actual location and its tangible characteristics, within which the group will operate.

✦ Technological. This relates to the facilities etc. that the group will have access to in pursuing its activities.

Homans argued that this three-element environment imposed a range of *activities* and *interactions* on the individuals and groups within the system. As a consequence of these impositions, a variety of *emotions* and *attitudes* are engendered among the members towards the environment and the other participants. This Homans called the *external system*. He also suggested that frequent interaction between people would lead to a more positive attitude and a better relationship between them. The converse was also true, that is, better attitudes lead to a higher frequency of interaction. This chain of events and reactions leads to the formation of a group (as shown in Figure 5.4).

With an increased level of interaction Homans observed a tendency for individuals to develop attitudes and emotions not dictated by the external system. This led to the

MANAGEMENT IN ACTION 5.6

Working as a team member

Sherwood Computer Services set about changing itself. Kevin Crane, the personnel director, explained the rationale:

> Every software house can provide the software and systems the client wants. It is the efficiency with which the client is handled that makes the difference and that comes down to the way we are organized.

Dramatic losses had shaken the company and many costs were cut, including the number of staff (to below 500). Having identified that changes in work organization were needed, Crane brought together two teams of ten employees to work out how the company should be organized. Staff from Ashridge Management College facilitated progress. The results of these groups were circulated around the company and applications were invited for places on ten task forces to review aspects of reorganization.

Six weeks later each task force reported its findings to the board. Not surprisingly the range of views covered all eventualities from do nothing to eliminate the structure completely. The new structure created managerless client teams of about 15 people and a business team of 14 senior managers reporting to the three members of the board of directors. Each team was to be responsi-

ble for all client activity. Potential internal competition for clients was controlled through the creation of market co-ordination groups covering the major areas of business.

Each client team was responsible for managing its own efforts and work activities. Each client team determined its business plan and agreed it with senior management, performance being monitored against that plan. The team assessed the performance of its members through peer assessment of the personal, professional and technical skills as identified by those with whom individuals most closely interacted. Sherwood introduced a pay system in which additional pay was obtained through the acquisition of additional skills of value to the client team.

In moving to the new structure it was the middle and junior managers who needed most convincing because their jobs were disappearing and they had most to lose. Senior managers spent considerable amounts of time talking to small groups of managers in order to convince them of the ultimate benefit to themselves as well as the company.

Adapted from: Carrington, L (1991) Working as a team member, *Personnel Today*, 22 January, pp 38–9.

development of new *frames of reference* and *norms* emerging between the individuals concerned. In turn these embellishments produced new activities not specified by the external system. This Homans called the *internal system*, in effect the development of informal groups within the system.

Homans suggested a number of features of these external and internal systems:

✦ The external and internal systems are mutually dependent. A change in one will produce a change in the other. For example, a change in work structure (formal group) can change the patterns of interaction between individuals (informal group). Conversely, attitudes in the internal system can influence the way in which work gets done.

✦ The two systems and the environment are mutually dependent. Individuals will mould and adapt work activities to suit themselves. Multidisciplinary project teams are an example of this process, incorporating the opportunity to tap into the internal system as well as the external.

Homans' theory is an important view of how groups are formed for two reasons. First, it stresses the mutual dependency between the many elements associated with the existence of groups. Second, it exposes the distinction between behaviour required by the environment and external system and the emergence of behaviour not required by the formal system, but equally as significant.

Group development

The existence of a group is no guarantee that it will be an effective or meaningful arrangement for either the organization or individual members. Groups do not automatically become effective at meeting their objectives and satisfying the needs of the individuals concerned.

Consider for a moment an organization that you have encountered. This could be your university or a company that you have worked for. Reflect on the groups that you were part of. It should quickly become apparent that within an organization a number of different groups and collections of individuals exist. For example:

✦   There exist a number of units within an organization that would not qualify as a group. Just because individuals work on similar activities and are classified as part of the same department does not qualify them as a group. For example, it is not uncommon in universities for some lecturing staff in the same department never to meet or even know each other if their academic interests and work commitments never require them to interact.

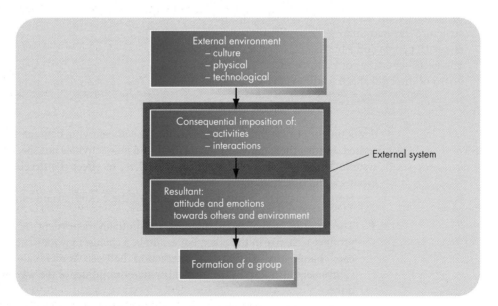

FIGURE 5.4   Homans' explanation of group formation.

+ Within formal units in an organization there may exist a number of smaller, formal and informal groups. For example, a large department may contain a number of sub-sections.

+ Within organizations there will exist a number of informal groups. Friendship group-ings and task-dependent networks across formal boundaries are common examples.

+ Some groups (formal and informal) will be relatively permanent. For example, a project group may be formed to design a new product and see it through to the market or a standing committee on remuneration policy might meet twice each year but change membership frequently as people leave the company or are promoted into other jobs.

+ Some groups (formal and informal) will be transient. Such formal groups are widely used within organizations as project teams, task forces or problem-solving groups. Informal groups in this category tend to form in response to particular events. For example, employees who feel threatened by a management proposal may form a pres-sure group.

Each of these situations presents different behavioural situations. It is therefore impos-sible to present a single comprehensive theory of how all groups develop. In some cases it is the existing members of a group who must adapt to new circumstances. In other cases it is individuals who must become part of an existing group. In other situations it is a new collection of individuals who must become a group to undertake a new task. In this area there are two approaches that offer an insight as to how groups develop.

Bass and Ryterband (1979) identify a four-stage model of group development:

+ Initial development of trust and membership. Individuals coming together for the first time need to learn to trust each other and to feel confident enough to contribute to the activities within the group.

+ Beginning of communication and decision making. Once trust begins to develop and the individuals are able to communicate more easily mutual dependence emerges. This allows decisions to be made and problems to be solved.

+ Performance improvement. In the previous stage conflicts can arise between individ-uals as the group norms are being developed. In this third stage, these teething prob-lems have been largely overcome and the effectiveness of the group improves. Individuals focus on the work of the group and become collectively motivated to achieve the objectives.

+ Ongoing maintenance and control. At this stage individuals have become accustomed to working together on routine group activities. Consequently, there is a degree of independence between members and flexibility in adapting to new situations.

This model has a number of similarities to the better known work of Tuckman, who in 1965 described a four-stage model of group formation. Tuckman and Jensen (1977) sub-sequently added a stage to the basic model. The five stages are as follows:

Stage 1 Forming. This stage occurs when the individuals first come together. It involves each individual getting to know the others, their attitudes, personalities and back-grounds. Individuals use this stage to make a personal impact within the group. It is also likely that anxiety is felt by the individuals as they attempt to define their position within the group. This process also begins to define the hierarchy and roles that will exist within the group.

Stage 2 **Storming.** As a formal structure begins to emerge and individuals begin to feel more confidence in their position within the group, conflict arises. Individuals begin to bring to the group their own agenda. Issues begin to emerge as the group *storms* its way towards the next stage. If successfully handled this stage leads to a more focused group in terms of relationships between the members and the ease with which it can achieve its goals. Not all groups successfully negotiate their way through this stage and lingering problems can continue to inhibit progression. In extreme cases groups can collapse at this stage.

Stage 3 **Norming.** This stage reflects the process of establishing the norms to be operated within the group. This includes the behavioural standards among members, for example to allow (or prevent) jokes and other diversions. Also the procedural rules that provide the group with its operating framework are developed. Someone with a hidden agenda may also seek to bring in items that allow them to achieve their objectives. Norming is a process that goes on within a group and as such management has only limited opportunity to influence it.

Stage 4 **Performing.** Only when the group has successfully completed the three previous stages can it make significant progress in its work. In that sense the group is now mature and able to operate effectively.

Stage 5 **Adjourning.** This stage involves the leaving of a group by individuals or the complete dissolution of one having achieved its objectives. Frequently, at this stage a period of reflection and reorientation is undertaken as individuals consider past glories and anticipate future success.

In practice, a group may not successfully negotiate itself through one of these five stages. Any unresolved difficulties carried forward will result in problems in subsequent stages. For example, a lack of clarity on humour is likely to result in frustration as some people tell jokes while others resent the diversion. The ability of individuals to progress and achieve items from a hidden agenda can be another major source of difficulty and friction for a group if it is not dealt with effectively. The consequences of these factors being a reduction in the level of effectiveness or member satisfaction within a group.

Group norms are the means through which a group regulates the behaviour of its members. The norms of behaviour become internalized by the individuals and institutionalized in the accepted patterns of behaviour. They provide a powerful group mechanism through which to release time and energy in order to concentrate on important issues. Imagine if a group had to establish behaviour standards and codes of conduct every time it convened. The goals would never be met. Conversely, the workings of a group can become overly concentrated on establishing norms and regulating the behaviour of its members. Some committees fall into this trap by concentrating on procedural matters and minutes, losing sight of the objectives to be achieved.

Feldman (1984) suggests that groups will adopt a satisficing approach to regulating individual behaviour, unless:

✦   Group survival is at risk. If the behaviour of an individual threatens the group, then they will be dealt with.

✦ Lack of clarity in the expected behaviour of group members is creating problems in group activity or performance.

✦ By taking action the group can avoid bringing into the open things that it would be embarrassing or difficult to resolve.

✦ The central values held by the group are being threatened. If by allowing something to continue the status of a group might be compromised then action would be taken.

In this section we have described how groups develop to the point that would allow them to function effectively. But that is only one aspect of a group that needs to be considered. All groups have a structure within them. There exists a number of roles within the group. Formal groups have formal structures, the chair, the secretary and so on. Informal groups have informal roles within them. They are the dominant individuals who lead the activities and direction of the informal group.

Role theory and group structure

In formal groups the structure of the group may be dictated by the situation. For example, a department (or project team) will be created, designed and the members designated by management. The individual members have little direct say in who will be appointed to the team and what role they will perform. In other situations, particularly informal groups, the membership is self-selected and members have a greater influence on both structure and roles. Many groups within an organization are comprised of representatives of other groups or departments, perhaps even from outside the organization itself. Consequently, these representatives are subject to report back requirements and direction from their sponsoring groups. This can often create conflict between personal and group loyalty for the individuals concerned.

There are a number of ways of considering group structure. For example, Huczynski and Buchanan (1991) identify a number of dimensions on which the structure of a group is dependent:

✦ Status. The reflection of the value placed upon particular positions within the group. It can also be seen as a reflection of the value of a particular person in the eyes of other people.

✦ Power. The ability to influence other people. This can either be a function of the position of a person or a reflection of personal influence.

✦ Liking. The personal affiliations among members of a group. It is inevitable that individuals will prefer the company (and ideas) of people they like at a personal level and distance themselves from people that they do not like. This affects the patterns of communication within the group.

✦ Role. This concept refers to the behaviours that accompany a particular function or position within a group. The roles that exist, or that people identify for themselves, determine to a significant extent the behaviour patterns that they engage in.

✦ Leadership. The style adopted by the leader of a group can also have a distinct influence on events within that group.

Belbin (1993) identifies nine team roles that, it is suggested, determine the performance of a group. While detailed consideration of this will be held over until the next chapter, it is appropriate to introduce the ideas here because they contain a relevance to the structural aspects of group activity. The roles themselves (see Table 5.4) cover the main requirements of group structure and also provide, according to Belbin, for the achievement of high performance.

It should be apparent that in addition to role definitions, structural issues (as indicated in the Huczynski and Buchanan framework) can be detected in the Belbin views on how a group will function. The Belbin roles also identify the primary weaknesses common within each role. These he describes as allowable weaknesses that are inevitable but can be controlled or tolerated. The Belbin model also allows for the possibility of a mismatch between formal organizational status and group membership role. Management in Action 5.7 includes a review of the Belbin model and how it can be incorporated into a team development approach.

Rolls and descriptions – team role contribution	Allowable weaknesses
Plant: Creative, imaginative, unorthodox. Solves difficult problems	Ignores details. Too preoccupied to communicate effectively
Resource investigator: Extrovert, enthusiastic, communicative. Explores opportunities. Develops contacts	Over-optimistic. Loses interest once initial enthusiasm has passed
Co-ordinator: Mature, confident, a good chairperson. Clarifies goals, promotes decision making, delegates well	Can be seen as manipulative. Delegates personal work
Shaper: Challenging, dynamic, thrives on pressure. Has the drive and courage to overcome obstacles	Can provoke others. Hurts people's feelings
Monitor/evaluator: Sober, strategic and discerning. Sees all options. Judges accurately	Lacks drive and ability to inspire others. Overly critical
Teamworker: Co-operative, mild, perceptive and diplomatic. Listens, builds, averts friction, calms the waters	Indecisive in crunch situations. Can be easily influenced
Imlementer: Disciplined, reliable, conservative and efficient. Turns ideas into practical actions	Somewhat inflexible. Slow to respond to new possibilities
Completer: Painstaking, conscientious, anxious. Searches out errors and omissions. Delivers on time	Inclined to worry unduly. Reluctant to delegate. Can be a nit-picker
Specialist: Single-minded, self-starting, dedicated. Provides knowledge and skills in rare supply.	Contributes on only a narrow front. Dwells on technicalities. Overlooks the 'big picture'

TABLE 5.4 The nine Belbin team roles (*source*: Belbin, M (1993) *Team Roles at Work*, Butterworth Heinemann, Oxford)

MANAGEMENT IN ACTION 5.7

How to build teams

Based on the work of Belbin, Fowler suggests that ten is a satisfactory number of members in a management or project team. For a complex topic involving intensive work on a clear issue, six members represents a good number. Over 12 members and groups tend to subdivide. With only three or four members any group is unlikely to have the range of team skills necessary and may be dominated by a single personality. Naturally there are many varied and practical reasons why a group may not adhere to these principles. For example, a management group will consist of as many members as report to the chief executive, irrespective of size. The role that specific members adopt in a group will also be determined to a significant extent by their purpose in that group. For example, in a negotiating group a trade union representative is there to represent the interests of members, not to help managers to find ways of meeting their objectives.

The work of Belbin on team roles offers one way of helping to ensure that there is a balance of skill within the group. Managers should be able to display some flexibility in team roles. In some team situations they will be expected to take a lead role, whereas in others they will be subordinate to more senior managers. This requires team training if team membership is to be effective. Fowler identifies two forms of team training:

- ✦ Team theory training. This involves the training of individuals in recognizing their own team style and that of others. It would also involve an understanding of team dynamics. This type of training is an individual approach and need not involve a particular team being trained at the same time.

- ✦ Team-building training. This type of training should involve the entire team. It attempts to create a team from a group of individuals. It should also be specific to the project or purpose for which the group has been established. This approach frequently uses outdoor or simulation training as a means of putting teams into situations in which they must learn to depend on, support and encourage each other.

Team training is not simply restricted to the start of a project; it is something that should be ongoing if the group is to avoid becoming stale. For example, a long-standing management group might take time out every few months to review how well it is performing as a group, perhaps with the support of a skilled consultant.

Adapted from: Fowler, A (1992) How to build teams, *PM Plus*, March, pp 25–7.

Stop | Consider

Identify the implications of the Belbin model for the recruitment, selection, training, development and career progression issues within an organization.

What might your analysis of the first question imply about the ability or even desirability of seeking to design groups?

Another way of looking at the notion of roles within an organizational context is to consider the implications in terms of the individual concerned. For most people their primary role within an organization is defined by the job description. This document sets out what tasks and responsibilities are *expected* from the postholder. The job description therefore defines the *expected role* for the individual, at least as far as the organization, customers, suppliers and other employees are concerned. For example, to know that someone holds a job with the title of personnel manager would immediately convey a range of expectations about what that person should do at work.

However, that is not the end of the matter, because individuals are not simply a function of other people's expectations. Each individual will interpret the expected role in terms of their personality characteristics and a range of other factors such as past experience, beliefs and intentions. In effect they must perceive the expected role and interpret it for themselves. This has been referred to as the *perceived role* in which the individual brings to the job their own understanding of it. Finally, there is the *enacted role*, which reflects what the individual actually does in carrying out the tasks for which they are responsible. It reflects their actual behaviour on the job.

According to Handy (1993) role theory consists of a number of components. They include:

✦ Role set. This reflects the people, or more accurately the other roles, surrounding the individual forming the basis of the analysis. For example, the role set for a university lecturer might contain the roles and people reflected in Figure 5.5.

✦ Role definition. This is based on the role expectation discussed earlier and sets out what the role of the focal person should be. Job descriptions and common knowledge were introduced as the basis of role expectations but they are not the only *signals* used to define a particular role. Uniforms, badges of rank, office location, style and equipment are all signals of the *expected role* of the person occupying the role.

✦ Role ambiguity. This reflects the degree of ambiguity in the minds of the role set as to exactly what their respective roles should be at any point in time. For example, a subordinate going to a meeting with an unpredictable boss might not know their role until the boss makes clear what their respective roles should be on this particular occasion. On one occasion the subordinate might be expected to be humble, contrite and accept that the boss was not happy with something and to be prepared to be told off without question. On other occasions they might be expected to be outgoing, jovial

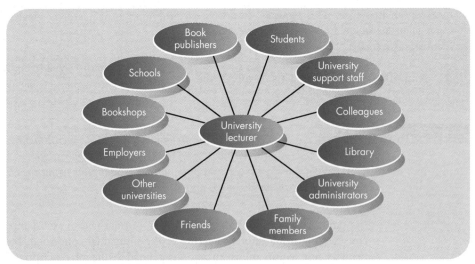

FIGURE 5.5   Role set of a university lecturer.

and prepared to join in the fun that the boss has decided to engage in. Clearly to engage in inappropriate role behaviour (the *enacted role*) would cause many problems for both parties to the encounter.

✦ Role incompatibility. This reflects incompatible expectations between members of the role set about their respective roles. It reflects an aspect of the *perceived role* discussed earlier. A manager might expect subordinates to accept their every word and instruction without question, whereas the subordinates might expect to have a much higher degree of freedom over their work activities. These two expectations are clearly incompatible and need to be resolved if conflict is to be avoided.

✦ Role conflict. This arises as a result of the conflicting role requirements acting on an individual at the same time. For example, a manager is expected to both support and help subordinates as well as achieve objectives with a finite level of resources. Clearly, these two realities come into conflict on occasions. A subordinate may be experiencing personal or medical problems and not be able to perform at full capacity during a prolonged period. However, the manager may not have the budget to allow additional staffing to maintain the output objectives and so need to pressure the individual to do more work, which will conflict with their desire to help the person.

✦ Role overload/underload. These situations arise when an individual is either faced with too many roles, each competing for pre-eminence, or they do not have enough role demand placed upon them for their existing capability. Many managers (particularly women) faced with the competing demands of work and home roles find that they cannot achieve a satisfactory balance between them and so they experience role stress and other problems. Similarly an individual who considers themselves to be underloaded becomes bored and frustrated because they feel underutilized and undervalued.

✦ Role stress. Each of the role concepts discussed can lead to stress under certain circumstances. It is generally considered that a certain degree of stress is necessary if effective performance is to be achieved. There is an old saying in organizations that if you want something done give it to a busy person. The logic being that busy people have to be organized and that they develop a level of efficiency which a person who is not busy does not achieve. However, what is not clear is the desirable level of stress either for efficient working or to allow an individual to be able to cope without danger to themselves or others. Equally, it is not clear if the appropriate level of stress (if it could ever be identified) remains constant for each individual or whether it changes depending upon a variety of circumstances. What is clear, however, is that role stress can result in poor performance, health problems and a host of other problems for both individuals and organizations. Stress is a topic which will be covered in detail in a later chapter.

Job design, technology and groups

Usually jobs are thought to be the preserve of an individual, as reflected in the job description. However, that need not always be the case. There is a specific chapter in this text devoted to the topic of job design and so it will not be explored in detail here. However, group working comes in many different forms and can be found in many different situations. There are many reasons why groups can be used in job design including the reality that in many situations more than one person does the same job and, therefore, it may make sense to group such teams together. Also it may be used as part of a specific organizational design process. For example, management may create multidisciplinary work teams focused on particular customer groups or categories, rather than employ the traditional functional structure.

Teamworking is most frequently described in terms of *autonomous work groups*. This form of team activity is based around the ideas that a group would accept responsibility for a specific part of the overall task to be undertaken and would then have the freedom to organize its internal activities based on the wishes of the members. This freedom can include the sequencing of activity, the pace of work, the arrangement of rest periods, responsibility for supervision and quality monitoring together with the appointment and training of new members. The most famous examples of autonomous work groups in practice are the applications in the motor industry by companies such as Saab and Volvo. Valery (1974) indicates that there were some 1000 different attempts by Swedish organizations to introduce novel forms of work organization intended to improve productivity and job satisfaction.

Another form of teamworking is to be found in the motor industry in the UK. Garrahan and Stewart (1992) describe the approaches to teamworking in the Nissan car factory in Sunderland. In this approach production teams do not have the opportunity to design the work of the team, but they are expected to co-operate strongly in producing a dynamic and self-regulating group intended to produce at the highest levels of productivity and quality. Within the production groups each member is expected to accept responsibility for the work of other team members and to point out the errors and faults produced by team members in a process of continual improvement.

Of course, there are many forms of simple teamworking that do not go as far as requiring the specific redesign of existing single-person jobs. For example, many lecturers work as part of a course team. The team might meet to design a degree programme jointly and to determine who should teach which modules. Thereafter, the team members would go their separate ways in designing and delivering each module, only coming together as a group to review progress, solve particular problems and to standardize marks. In a medical context, there are likely to be many professionals involved in developing the treatment plan for a specific patient. They will inevitably function as a group in the process of the determination of the plan, but will function as individuals in delivering specific aspects of the treatment.

Technology is another area in which job design and teamworking is influenced. In many cases the introduction of technology to a work situation fundamentally changes the design of the jobs that people undertake. It also frequently relegates the role of many people to machine minders and monitors of automatic processes. In doing so it can often be a team of people who are given the responsibility to operate a range of equipment and to function as a group in deciding upon the balance of work activity between members.

Group formation and structure: an applied perspective

Groups are of particular significance to both managers and organizations as well as the individuals who belong to them. There are a number of reasons for this, including:

✦ The process of management involves the management of groups. This could be a section, a team, a factory, or even a whole organization made up of many groups. Yet managers cannot directly manage all of the groups for which they are responsible. Delegated authority provides for subordinates to take responsibility for the management of specific committees or defined area of work activity for example.

✦ Managers must be part of some of the groups that they manage. Recall the Hawthorne Studies. There were supervisors working in the sections within which the research was being conducted. The group pressure on them to conform to group norms placed the individuals in a difficult position because of the potential for divided loyalties. This is a pressure still found in all first-line supervisory jobs today. It is very common for first-line supervisors to be titled team leaders today. However, their importance is frequently undervalued by senior managers as they are frequently not regarded as properly part of the management team. Neither do the workforce regard them as full members of their groups, but they do recognize the ability of first-line managers to act as a filter between the workers and management. This was recognized by the Hawthorne workers in their behaviour towards supervisors.

✦ Managers are part of a management group in addition to any others to which they belong.

✦ There are moves towards managers empowering employees. This is usually described in terms of pushing decision making and responsibility down to the lowest level possible within the organization. Often this is part of a business process re-engineering or downsizing exercise. One form of this process is the self-managed team. However, it is a movement that demands different approaches to control, and can lead to new difficulties between groups and managers.

✦ Individuals spend a considerable proportion of their lives within organizations and much of this time and energy is spent in some form of group activity. Consequently individuals invest heavily in the organizations and groups to which they belong. Not surprisingly individuals do not like to feel that they are wasting their time and energy and so seek to achieve some return on their investment, whether this be through the formal or informal groups that exist depends upon the situation and the individual.

It is not uncommon for individuals to seek out personal or career benefits from group membership. Such behaviour is political in that the individual is attempting to manipulate events to their advantage. Promotion opportunities can be enhanced by membership of the 'right' committees and by being seen to be active on successful projects. It is perhaps cynical, but essentially true, that once it becomes apparent that a project is likely to be successful, people previously not involved suddenly want to be associated with it. Conversely, if there is a danger of the failure of a project, people actively begin to distance themselves from it.

Management is a political process. Managers are continually in competition with other managers for resources, influence and recognition. Promotion, and in times of recession (or delayering) continued employment frequently depends on being able to deliver objectives with reduced resources. The ability to squeeze additional productivity out of subordinates is a prized ability. It is from this perspective that the ability to manipulate the use of groups (both formal and informal) to achieve objectives within an organizational setting gains significance.

The significance of formal groups is self-evident, in that some form of compartmentalization of activity is necessary to carry out the work of an organization. Indications are that informal groups are also an inherent part of organizational life. They also exist irrespective of management intentions on the subject. In situations where management is not trusted by employees, the emergence of a *shadow organization* might more directly challenge the ability of managers to manage. Managers therefore need to develop an understanding of the importance of groups within an organization as well as an insight into issues such as how they form and function as well as how they can go wrong, a topic for the next chapter.

Within an organization the groups that exist are constantly subject to change. New people join a department; existing members leave or are transferred to other duties; existing groups are reformulated as the tasks for which they were established change; and new groups are created as new tasks emerge. It is within this constantly changing milieu that managers must provide a framework of consistency and stability. Of course, not everything is changing all the time. But there is a steady flow of people- and task-related change, sufficient to create instability and lack of security, particularly in large organizations. It is partly for these reasons that the autonomous work group has significance as it contains the ability to effectively delegate a significant degree of organizational functioning to the teams, thereby reducing the load on managers.

It is in an attempt to provide stability within an otherwise changing environment that groups have a significant part to play. Rather like the individual strands of a spider's web the relationships formed within a group can help to provide strength in times of difficulty. If the individual strands in a spider's web become broken, then all is not lost, the damage can quickly be overcome and normality restored. Similarly, within an organization the groups that exist can provide task and personal support to individual members as well as continuity of operational activity.

Managers find themselves in a number of different groups as part of their work. They also manage many groups in order to meet the objectives of their position. It is not uncommon to find that managers ignore the formation and structural aspects of the teams that they create. It is often assumed that the roles within formal groups will naturally overcome any difficulties and deliver what is expected of them. Informal groups are frequently ignored as nothing to do with the organization, irrelevant, an inconvenience, or of little practical impact. Clearly most of these assumptions are questionable, or even false.

The challenge for managers is to provide the formal groupings within the organization that will allow the necessary activities to be undertaken while at the same time retaining some control or influence over the informal groups. Given the nature of informal groups as they have been described in this chapter, it should be apparent that their very nature makes this an impossible objective. Under these circumstances how can managers expect to control the activities and formation of these informal groups? It could be argued that the very existence of these informal groups is a function of management's attempt to maintain control. In other words, an informal group is an employee response to ensure a degree of independence from the all-pervading management domination in what can be otherwise described as a coercive employment relationship. The freedom of employees is severely constrained within most organizational situations. They are appointed to particular positions, with a job description that defines the *expected role*. Consequently the informal group provides a counterbalance to that externally defined behaviour control.

It can be suggested that the informal group is therefore a mechanism through which individuals seek to achieve a personal level of social meaning in a context where so much of the contact and activity is dictated by others. The individual usually has little opportunity to influence events in the working environment and the emergence of social arrangements that meet the needs of the individuals involved more effectively is hardly surprising. For example, the nature of the job to be done is prescribed by management; the colleagues with whom one works are appointed by management; the physical working environment is designed and provided by management; and the standards of performance are set by management. Consequently, the formation of informal groups provides the opportunity for individuals to display a little of themselves in what is a largely prescribed situation.

Perhaps, therefore, the challenge facing managers is not one of how to control both the existence and formation of formal and informal groups, but how to direct the energies of the groups that exist in the interests of the organization. In the formal groups that exist management should consider the features of the group that might be expected to influence the outcome. In the context of this chapter, this could include the purpose, composition and other group formation issues discussed. If the formal groups are to be effective in achieving their objectives then issues such as the Belbin team roles and the Tuckman and Jensen stages of group development need to be taken into account in order to ensure that the potential for success is provided.

In the case of informal groups, managers can to a small extent utilize their existence to the benefit of the organization without appearing to exert covert control. For example, the provision of social facilities for employees can provide an opportunity for interaction among employees that can offset the *givens* within the organization. The use of group working as the basis of task achievement can also provide an appearance of lack of management control, which if linked with appropriate socialization and training can direct employees' behaviour in company preferred directions.

The difficulties facing many managers in terms of how to provide for control has lead to particular problems in some family organizations. Management in Action 5.8 illustrates these problems from a number of public disagreements in India over structure, control and related issues.

Stop | Consider   *What does MiA 5.8 suggest about the role and functioning of family groups at a senior level within organizations?*

Would it ever be possible to prevent such family disputes from arising in an organization?

MANAGEMENT IN ACTION 5.8

Portraits of families at war

With economic reform in India changing the way in which business is run, a number of splits in large family-run business groups have emerged. One of the added complexities in running family businesses in India is that the principle of primogeniture does not exist and potential heirs will squabble for years over what constitutes a fair share from an estate.

Wagstyl indicates:

Even after a family has launched companies on the stock market and diluted ownership to 20% or less, family members usually dominate management. Directorships, chairmanships and even whole companies are created to accommodate personal whims.

In the mid-1980s one group's interests in sugar, oil, chemicals, textiles and engineering were divided between Mr Ram, his two sons and his brother. In the shareout Mr Ram had control of Jay Engineering, a maker of sewing machines. It performed badly and so Mr Ram turned to his son Mr Shriram for help; he agreed, providing he was given a free hand. Mr Ram promised to hand over the chairmanship to Mr Shriram, but failed to do so. It is suggested by people who know the company that the real problem is the favour that

Mr Ram has shown to a senior manager within Jay Engineering, giving him substantial blocks of shares and suggesting publicly that Mr Shriram could learn from this 'favoured' individual. Naturally Mr Shriram would not take such advice easily and so a public dispute resulted.

Arguments around the cement, textiles and chemical businesses owned by the family of Mr Kedar Nath Modi are also interesting. Mr Modi divided his business interests between his three sons over a decade ago. In the late 1980s he insisted on a redistribution of these businesses and wealth as his middle son was making considerably more money than his other two. Having reluctantly agreed to the redistribution Mr Yogendra Modi subsequently repeated his success and proved better at making money than his two brothers. His father attempted to impose a second redistribution of the family businesses and wealth on Mr Yogendra Modi, but this was resisted. A former cabinet minister who was called upon to find a solution to this dispute was unable to do so.

Adapted from: Wagstyl, S (1993) Portraits of families at war, *Financial Times*, 25 October, p 18.

Conclusions

This chapter has considered the research into the significance of groups along with the effects of group membership on organizational activity. It is clear that groups, both formal and informal, are significant in terms of organizational activity, employee and management functioning. However, there are still many areas of research to be explored in defining how groups function across all the variables involved. The existence of groups within organizations is closely associated with the need for managers to exercise control over the processes for which they are responsible. It could be argued that informal groups are a natural reaction to that situation. That groups are formed and have structure has been established in this chapter. It is now appropriate to go on to consider issues such as group dynamics and performance in the next chapter.

Discussion questions

1. Define the following key terms used in this chapter:

   Formal group   *Social facilitation*   *Homans' theory*
   Informal group   *Group norms*   *Group structure*
   Psychological group   *Frame of reference*   *Bass and Ryterbrand's*
   Tuckman and Jensen's model   *The Hawthorne Studies*   *model*

2. Groups within organizations are different from groups in other contexts. Discuss this statement.

3. Is the distinction between the concept of formal and informal groups a useful one?

4. Explain the results obtained by Triplett (when he studied the performance of racing cyclists) with reference to the concepts of a group introduced in this chapter.

5. The bank wiring room observations demonstrate that employees can effectively manage managers without their being aware of it. Give and justify your own views on this statement.

6. Should management do everything it can to prevent informal groups from forming in the organization? Justify your answer.

7. Describe the group development stages identified in this chapter. Distinguish between the theoretical models offered as an explanation of this process.

8. What is the relevance of role theory as applied to how groups function within an organization?

9. To what extent is the creation of formal groups within an organization an attempt to provide managers with the means of social control?

10. The management team within an organization cannot be considered as a single group. Discuss this statement, justifying your answer.

11. Should individuals be trained in the theories of group formation and structure in order to ensure that they can become effective contributors to group activities? Why or why not?

12. The Hawthorne Studies show that it is important for managers to take an active interest in all aspects of their subordinates' lives if organizations are ever to be truly successful. Discuss.

Research activities

1. Search through the library stock available to you for about ten journal or magazine articles relating to group formation and structure. Summarize the points made by the writers and compare and contrast those ideas with the material contained within this chapter.

2. In a group of which you are a member, work with some of the other members and attempt to identify the individuals within that group who fall into the roles identified by the Belbin model of team roles. Do this individually at first and then compare your answers with the others in the group. Do you all agree with the roles allocated to each person? Explain any differences.

3. In this chapter it has been suggested that managers should attempt to ensure that informal groups within their organization are, at the very least, sympathetic to management's goals. Is this possible and how might this be achieved? In attempting to address these issues discuss the issues with a manager, trade union officer and an employee. Incorporate their thoughts and ideas into your work and reflect on the implications for both theory and practice.

Key reading

Clark, H, Chandler, J and Barry, J (1994) *Organization and Identities: Text and Readings in Organizational Behaviour*, International Thomson Business Press, London:
  ✦ Mayo, E: The work group and 'positive mental attitudes', p 237 and Roethlisberger FJ and Dickson WJ: Group restriction of output, p 247. Both of these extracts provide the opportunity to read original material from the researchers involved in the Hawthorne Studies in which they reflect and conclude from the process.
  ✦ For material relevant to a consideration of the nature of the sexual division of work and the continuance of the male group dominance, see for example: Kanter, RM: Men and women of the corporation, p 152 and Dex, S: The sexual division of work, p 177.

Further reading

Armstrong, P (1984) Competition between the Organizational Professions and the Evolution of Management Control Strategies. In Thompson K (ed.) *Work, Employment and Unemployment*, Open University Press, Milton Keynes. This text considers how professional groups attempt to 'engineer' access to decision making through restrictions on the interpretation of information and what can be described as hostile strategies towards other groups.

Belbin, M (1993) *Team Roles at Work*, Butterworth-Heinemann, Oxford. This is the latest edition of the text in which Belbin reviews his work on the subject of teams and the roles within them. It covers a wide range of issues relevant to both this chapter and the next one.

Bensman, J and Gerver, I (1973) Crime and Punishment in the Factory: The Function of Deviancy in Maintaining the Social System. In McQueen, DR (ed.) *Understanding Sociology Through Research*, Addison-Wesley, Reading, MA. This text provides an insight into sociological research in general. However, the specific reading indicated describes the use of informal practices within the assembly operations of an aircraft factory. Essentially, 'illegal' practices were condoned by supervisors and inspectors as part of complex web of control and group behaviour. It is therefore worth reading from this perspective alone.

Gillespie, R (1991) *Manufacturing Knowledge: A History of the Hawthorne Experiments*, Cambridge University Press, Cambridge. As the title suggests, this work looks at the intellectual and political dynamics of this famous collection of research into work activity. In doing so this work examines the way that scientific knowledge itself is produced.

Leavitt, H (1972) *Managerial Psychology: An Introduction to Individuals, Pairs and Groups in*

Organizations, 3rd edn, University of Chicago Press, Chicago, IL. Develops the theme of how groups control individual members. This point was initially discussed in relation to the Hawthorne Studies. Leavitt develops a formal framework of escalating pressure points to be applied to 'deviant' members.

Markham, SE, Dansereau, F and Alutto, JA (1982) Group size and absenteeism rates: a longitudinal analysis, *Academy of Management Journal*, December, 921–27. This paper considers a number of features associated with the size of groups, particularly the absence rates of members.

Smith, KK and Berg, DN (1987) *Paradoxes of Group Life*, Jossey-Bass, San Francisco, CA. This text discusses the conflicts that exist for the individual as a result of group membership. Some cultures have a cultural orientation towards the group, others lean towards an emphasis on the individual. In either context, the individual must forgo certain freedoms once within the group. This text introduces the main issues surrounding this debate.

References

Adler, NJ, Campbell, NC and Laurent, A (1989) In search of appropriate methodology: looking from outside the People's Republic of China, *Journal of International Business Studies*, Spring, pp 61–74.

Argyle, M. (1989) *The Social Psychology of Work*, 2nd edn, Penguin, Harmondsworth.

Ashby, RW (1964) *An Introduction To Cybernetics*, Methuen, London.

Bass, BM and Ryterband, EC (1979) *Organizational Psychology*, 2nd edn, Allyn & Bacon, Boston, MA.

Belbin, M (1993) *Team Roles At Work*, Butterworth-Heinemann, Oxford.

Cooper, C and Davidson, M (1982) *High Pressure; Working Lives of Women Managers*, Fontana, London.

Dalton, M (1959) *Men Who Manage*, John Wiley, New York.

Feldman, DC (1984) The development and enforcement of group norms, *Academy of Management Review*, **9**, 47–53.

Garrahan, P and Stewart, P (1992) *The Nissan Enigma: Flexibility at Work in a Local Economy*, Mansell, London.

Handy, CB (1993) *Understanding Organizations*, 4th edn, Penguin, Harmondsworth.

Hofstede, G (1984) *Culture's Consequences: International Differences in Work-related Values*, Sage, Beverley Hills.

Homans, G (1950) *The Human Group*, Harcourt Brace, New York.

Huczynski, AA and Buchanan, DA (1991) *Organizational Behaviour: An Introductory Text*, 2nd edn, Prentice Hall, Hemel Hempstead.

Katz, FE (1973) Integrative and adaptive uses of autonomy: worker autonomy in factories. In (eds) Salaman, G and Thompson, K, *People and Organizations*, Longman, London.

Laurent, A (1983) The cultural diversity of western conceptions of management, *International Studies of Management and Organization*, **13**, 1–2, pp 75–96.

Likert, R (1961) *New Patterns of Management*, McGraw-Hill, New York.

Roethlisberger, FJ and Dickson, WJ (1964) *Management and the Worker*, John Wiley, New York.

Schein, EH (1956) The Chinese indoctrination programme for prisoners-of-war, *Psychiatry*, **19**, 149–72.

Schein, EH (1988) *Organizational Psychology*, 3rd edn, Prentice Hall, Englewood Cliffs, NJ.

Shaw, ME (1981) *Group Dynamics: The Dynamics of Small Group Behaviour*, 3rd edn, McGraw-Hill, New York.

Stacey, R (1996) *Strategic Management and Organizational Dynamics*, 2nd edn, Pitman Publishing, London.

Triplett, N (1897) The dynamogenic factors in pacemaking and competition, *American Journal of Psychology*, **9**, 503–33.

Tuckman, B and Jensen, N (1977) Stages of small group development revisited, *Group and Organizational Studies*, **2**, 419–27.

Valery, N (1974) Importing the lessons of Swedish workers, *New Scientist*, **62**, 892, 27–8.

Wyatt, S, Fraser, JA and Stock, FGL (1928) The Comparative Effects of Variety and Uniformity in Work. Medical Research Council, Industrial Fatigue Research Board, Report No. 52. HMSO, London.

Zajonc, RB (1965) Social facilitation, *Science*, **149**, 269–74.

CHAPTER 6

Group dynamics and effectiveness

CHAPTER SUMMARY

This chapter begins with a consideration of the communication and behavioural issues surrounding group activity. We then move on to consider the ways in which groups influence and control the behaviour of members. This is followed by a review of the decision-making aspects of group activity as well as the dynamics of the interaction within and between groups. Organizational requirements for effectiveness in group activity and the associated member satisfaction are the next areas for consideration. This is followed by a critical review of groups within an organizational context and an introduction to the applied perspectives of group working.

LEARNING OBJECTIVES

After studying this chapter and working through the associated Management in Action panels, Discussion questions and Research activities, you should be able to:

✦ Outline the nature of the dynamic processes that occur within and between groups.

✦ Describe the concept of effectiveness as applied to group activities.

✦ Explain how decisions are made in groups and the difficulties that can be encountered in reaching agreement.

✦ Understand how control can be achieved within groups through such mechanisms as socialization and authority.

✦ Discuss the similarities and differences between models of how groups can be made more effective.

✦ Appreciate the complex relationships that exist between the groups to which individuals belong.

✦ Detail some of the links between groups and communications, negotiation, group formation and organizational design.

✦ Assess the implications of issues such as groupthink and the risky shift phenomena on group functioning.

Introduction

The previous chapter introduced the basis of group activity within an organizational setting. It discussed, among other important topics, what defines a group and its significance within organizations. How groups go through the process of forming, the application of role theory and some of the major research in the field were also introduced. It should be clear from the discussion in the previous chapter that formal groups have purpose within an organizational context. They are part of the managerially determined approach to achieving the desired objectives. Informal groups develop for other reasons and frequently serve the needs of the workforce for a degree of influence in an otherwise managerially created reality. This chapter develops the review of group activity further and seeks to consider how groups function in practice. It will begin with a consideration of the communication processes within group activity and then go on to review a number of the other influences on the ability of a group to achieve its objectives and provide a degree of member satisfaction.

All groups, particularly those within organizations, function within a broader *environment*, containing other groups and individuals. Figure 6.1 reflects a simplified view of part of the environment surrounding the human resource department of a large bank.

The existence of groups within an environment, as reflected in Figure 6.1, carries with it a number of implications for the functioning of any group, including:

✦ That a need for communication and interaction between the members of a group will exist.

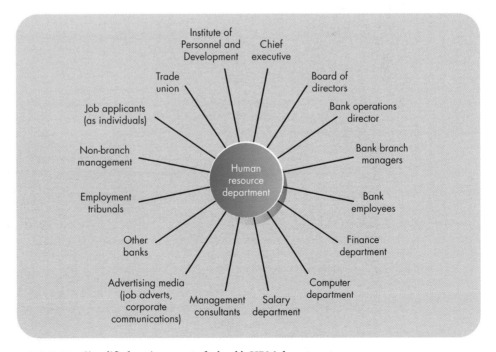

FIGURE 6.1   Simplified environment of a bank's HRM department.

✦   There will be a need for a group to engage in communication and interaction with other groups both inside and outside the organization.

✦   There exists a need for the group to achieve the objectives set for it.

✦   That groups invariably cannot achieve the desired objectives without the co-operation and support of other individuals and groups.

✦   That in order to achieve the desired objectives there exists a need to channel and control the activities of members within the group.

✦   For a group to be successful at both a personal and organizational level there should be the provision of a means through which to meet the social needs and aspirations of group members.

✦   There exists a need to take account of the potential impact of the social and political dimensions surrounding the activities of a group.

Each of these issues and more will be discussed in the exploration of group functioning in the remainder of this chapter.

Communications within groups

For any group to function at even the most basic level it is necessary for the members to interact with each other to some degree. This inevitably takes the form of communication. There are different patterns of communication that can be identified within a group, each of which has implications for the behaviour of individuals. Figure 6.2 indicates the major

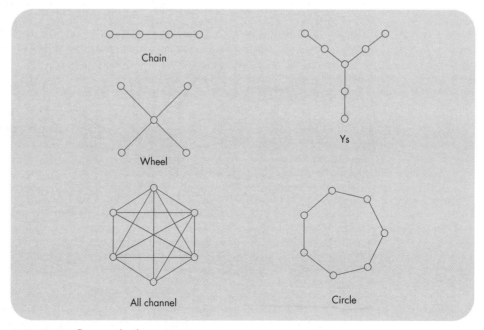

FIGURE 6.2   Communication patterns.

communication linkages based on the work of a number of writers, including Bavelas (1948), Leavitt (1978) and Shaw (1978).

Each of these communication networks has implications for a number of group features. For example, the style of leadership adopted and the ability of individuals to contribute to group decision making. Consider the wheel and Y patterns of communication and the implications for both the flow of communication and group leadership. In both examples there exists a focal person through whom the essentially linear communication patterns pass. Such a person might either be a very strong and directive leader seeking to exert total control over the activities of a group or they might be a dominant individual within the group who in practice has taken control of the process. Clearly, such patterns of communication have significant implications for the work of the group, the degree and quality of debate within the group and the ways in which any decisions would be taken. Compare these implications against the patterns of communication displayed in the chain, channel and circle patterns of communication none of which contains a dominant individual.

In organizational group activity not all tasks are equally complex. For example, consider the difference in complexity faced by the production management team within a factory making internal doors for domestic houses when they have to determine:

A. If they should make pattern Z before pattern Y when there are enough of both patterns in stock to cover one month's sales.

B. If they should accept a one-off order from a large customer which would require considerable development and tooling costs and from which there would be no repeat business.

In both examples there are different issues and factors to be taken into account in reaching the decision, each with different possible consequences for the organization, group, production function and individuals. The differences in decision requirement inevitably impacts on the complexity of the process of seeking to integrate the perspectives of each part of the production function in taking the necessary decisions. This decision complexity is also impacted upon through the patterns of communication adopted by the group.

Baron and Greenberg (1990) suggest that where simple tasks are involved the wheel pattern of communication could produce an effective result. The task could be undertaken by the central person alone with the necessary information provided by the peripheral members. They also suggest that the all-channel pattern of communication would produce a poor result in such situations because the flow of information circulates all around the group with no single person collating it in terms of the decision necessary. Baron and Greenberg also point out that for complex problems the outcome of both patterns of communication would be reversed. In complex decision situations it is necessary to have the flow of communication around the group to encourage 'richness' in analysis and debate as well as limiting the demands placed on the leader of the group to find a personal solution.

Analyzing behaviour within groups

Indicating what the most common patterns of communication are within a group context does not of itself identify the actual interaction patterns within a particular group at a particular point in time. A number of techniques have been developed to allow the patterns of interaction between the members of a group to be charted and analyzed.

Moreno (1953) developed the *sociogram* as a means of charting preferences and interactions between group members. It is based on the positive and negative feelings of individuals towards other members of the group. To construct a *sociogram* each member of the group is required to express preferences (usually up to three) for other group members in specific situations. For example, who would you most (or least) prefer to work with? The results are displayed in diagrammatic form, illustrating the *relationships* involved, in Figure 6.3.

A solid line between two individuals indicates that a two-way preference has been identified, a dotted line, that a one-way choice has been expressed – in the direction of the arrow. Examination of Figure 6.3 indicates that there are three subgroups (or *cliques*) within the overall group. Person A is a *star* in that they are a frequent preference among other members, person B however is comparatively isolated, with few preferences being indicated by other members. Sociograms are not without their critics, however. The patterns indicated on a sociogram are not necessarily patterns of interaction, since they merely represent patterns of preference. The actual behaviour within a specific group context may be completely different from what might be predicted from the preference charts. Relative preference might influence the patterns of communication and the manner of any expression, but the links are tenuous. For example an individual within a group may tend to reject another member, but in a particular group meeting may feel it necessary to interact and support that person against another member over a particular issue.

Another approach to describing group activity was that of Bales (1958) who developed *interaction analysis*. He used small group activities such as committees to study how patterns of interaction developed during decision making. He identified 12 categories of activity clustered together under four headings. Table 6.1 reflects the Bales' categories.

Bales' work indicates that there are two significant aspects to group activity:

✦ The task to be undertaken and the solution being sought. This is referred to as the *task function*.

✦ The group atmosphere and member feelings. This is referred to as the *maintenance function*. It describes behaviour intended to preserve relationships, maintain cohesion and minimize the harmful effect of conflict among members.

In addition there is the *political dimension* to the behaviour of individuals within groups. Individuals may have many reasons for seeking to pursue their own objectives rather than those of the group: a sponsor may have laid down 'things' to be achieved by an individual group member, for example the industrial relations manager of a company might be given specific pay targets to achieve in negotiations with the trade unions, or they

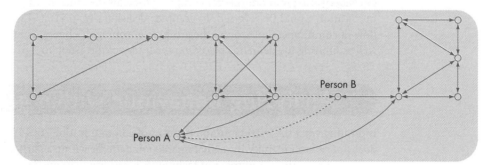

FIGURE 6.3 Example of a sociogram.

might be told what they cannot concede. In that sense they are not completely free to nego-tiate within the context of a joint management and trade union group. Promotion oppor-tunity could also be enhanced by an individual seeking to be 'noticed' within a particular group – an example of *self-interested* behaviour.

A well-balanced group will display the three functions (task, maintenance and politi-cal) in proportion appropriate to the purpose of the group, the individuals forming it and the context surrounding its existence. Management in Action 6.1 suggests that team activ-ities are important to organizations but that there are problems facing managers as they attempt to gain the advantage available.

Stop | Consider

To what extent does MiA 6.1 imply that it is not possible to create groups of any signifi-cance within western organizations?

How might Bales' work lead to overcoming some of the weaknesses in group activity implied by MiA 6.1?

Controlling behaviour within groups

When the members of a group come together they invariably engage in what would be classed as a meeting. In other words, interaction and communication between the members takes place. Whatever the cause of the gathering it will have purpose, unless it is a chance encounter and interaction is restricted to an exchange of pleasantries. The actual purpose might be social, perhaps arranging a night out at the cinema, or it might be

A	**Socio-emotional: positive reactions**
1	Shows solidarity, raises others' status, gives help, reward
2	Shows tension release, jokes, laughs, shows satisfaction
3	Agrees, shows passive acceptance, understands, concurs, complies
B	**Task: attempted answers**
4	Gives suggestion, direction, implying autonomy for others
5	Gives opinion, evaluation, analysis, expresses feeling, wishes
6	Gives orientation, information, repeats, clarifies, confirms
C	**Task: questions**
7	Asks for orientation, information, repetition, confirmation
8	Asks for opinion, evaluation, analysis, expression of feeling
9	Asks for suggestion, direction, possible ways of action
D	**Socio-emotional: negative reactions**
10	Disagrees, shows passive rejection, formality, withholds help
11	Shows tension, asks for help, withdraws out of field
12	Shows antagonism, deflates others' status, defends or asserts self

TABLE 6.1   Bales' categories of interaction

MANAGEMENT IN ACTION 6.1

Reaping the benefits of teamwork

No chief executive as an individual can produce all that the organization makes and administer the company as well. Other people are needed and so working in groups and teams is a necessity. The predominant culture in the west is based on the achievement of the individual and that of the east (Japan and other Asian countries) on the collective efforts of groups. It is argued, therefore, that if western businesses are to emulate the success of those from the east then more effort to generate effective teamworking is needed.

As Furnham points out groups are a natural part of life experience in the west and that:

> We are, however, loyal to some groups: usually those we have been forced to join, or with whom we have endured hardship and difficulty. The family, school class-mates, fellow military conscripts do often command our loyalty. But, because we don't have jobs for life and find it easier to get promotion by moving between organizations, we rarely stay long enough in a team to be really part of it.

There are many implications that emerge from these words for the ways teams are formed

and how they function within organizations. For example, given the move for individuals to take more responsibility for their own career development how can teams be superimposed in the work setting? Equally, most performance management procedures and practice within companies place a heavy emphasis on individual effort and achievement, not contribution to team activities. In recruitment situations most of the emphasis is placed on the job-related skills of the individual. Only subsequently are the organizational and colleague 'fit' aspects considered.

So deciding that teamworking is a good thing for both the organization and the individual is one thing. But actually carrying through the implications that follow from that perspective would create many effects within the organization. Teamworking should not to be taken lightly, regarded as a fad or quick-fix solution to an organization's ills!

Adapted from: Furnham, A (1993) Reaping the benefits of teamwork, *Financial Times*, 19 May, p 14.

formal, perhaps a new product development group meeting to discuss design options. The intended purpose will dictate the intentions of the members, but the actual behaviour will need to be channelled if the purpose is to be achieved. Consequently, there are many parallels between the control of behaviour within formal group situations and the control of meetings. However, it is not just a question of the effective development of an agenda, good leadership and sticking to the point in discussion. There are many other ways in which the behaviour of group members is directed and we will now review some of these.

Perception and attitudes

Groups have the ability to influence the behaviour of the individuals within them by helping to shape the perceptions and attitudes held by members. For example, Sherif (1936) demonstrated that for two- and three-person groups, individuals could be influenced by the other person(s) present. Subjects were placed in a darkened room and given the task of tracking a light source. The light was stationary, but subjects perceive it to move, an illusion referred to as the *autokinetic phenomenon*. There was a wide variation in the movement reported by individuals 'seeing' this effect. Figure 6.4 shows the results obtained by Sherif.

There were four trials in the experiment. The first trial recorded the amount of movement reported by each subject independently. Successive trials were reported in the knowledge of the other subjects' responses. The results indicated that knowledge of the opinion of others influenced subject judgement. Once established the *norm* became the basis of subsequent judgement for individuals. It was also noted that few subjects tested were aware that their judgement was being influenced.

This study clearly demonstrates that the groups of subjects developed norms of behavioural response in the common task and that they were generally unaware of the process taking place. From the previous chapter you will recall discussion of the Tuckman and Jensen (1977) model of *group development*. In this model stage 3 specifically reflected the process of groups engaging in a process of establishing *norms* of behaviour. Interestingly, the much earlier Sherif work would seem to suggest that although the process of creating *norms* exists, it occurs much earlier in group development than implied by Tuckman and Jensen. They suggest that it occurs as part of a sequential process leading towards group performance. Sherif's work implies either that this stage-based group development process occurs very quickly (by the fourth trial) or that the collective shaping of perceptions begins right at the start of the development process.

Individuals in a group clearly place themselves in a situation in which acceptance by other members is important. A group by definition cannot be a collection of individuals; there is a degree of *conformity* implicit in any group setting. The group norms that become accepted help to specify the areas of collectivity. However, it is for each member to take steps to become a member of the group or to remain on the fringes and only partially connected. To become a full member of a group it is necessary for both the individual and the other members to instigate acceptance. One way to become accepted by other people is to become like them or at least to be someone that they would wish to associate with. While there are many dimensions to this compatibility process such as personality and the potential to contribute a benefit, one of the key aspects is that of attitude. Behaving in accordance with the expectations of others (largely displaying approved attitudes and behaviour patterns) is a key aspect of gaining their acceptance and so membership of the group. From that perspective developing particular *attitude sets* that reflect those of the rest of the group is one way of gaining acceptance. It also reflects one way in which the group controls the

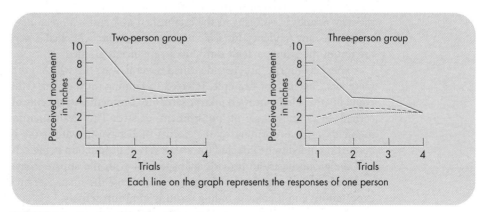

FIGURE 6.4 Results of the Sherif experiment.

behaviour of members. It does this by creating a membership which displays particular attitudes supportive of group objectives.

So far the discussion has ignored the opportunity for the potential 'deviant' group member to seek to change the attitudes of the rest of the group towards their position. This possibility introduces *political* and *negotiation* perspectives into group behaviour. Factional activity and conflict are possibilities when an individual decides to 'fight back' or 'resist' conformity to group-imposed norms. Observation of this aspect of the control mechanisms active in group situations can most clearly be seen in politics and industrial relations when attempts are made to 'do a deal' involving groups compromising on previously held positions. Frequently, the positions adopted by groups (or individual members) are publicly stated positions and therefore more difficult to contradict or change. This complicates the possibilities of being able to reconcile any deal achieved and the public positions of the individuals engaged in the process. In practice, this arises because of the representative nature of such groups and therefore the need for all parties to negotiate with at least two sets of stakeholders, these being as a minimum the other parties in the negotiation forum and the group from which the representatives originate.

For example, a trade union must effectively represent its members to management and in doing so it needs a strong mandate from the members. Inevitably, the expectations that a very good deal can be struck is frequently raised among the members in the process. However, the members are not party to the actual negotiations between management and the trade union. So a separate process then ensues in which the differences between management and the trade union positions are reconciled and a deal agreed. This deal must then be 'sold' to the members. This frequently causes problems for the union negotiators as they will undoubtedly have compromised on some of their initial claims during the negotiation, which the employees may not be happy with. This leads to the need to incorporate the ability to manipulate perceptions and attitudes among the constituents as part of the underlying processes.

Socialization

Socialization takes place when new people join an existing group and are faced with a process of learning how 'things' are done. Many groups exist for long periods of time and it is individual members who join and leave. An example would be an existing work group with a new employee replacing someone who has left the company. That person is joining an existing set of relationships and interactive networks. The group will seek to ensure that the new member conforms to the established *task* and *maintenance* requirements. At the same time, any tendency for *self-interested* behaviour will elicit a negative response from the rest of the group, at least until full acceptance is granted.

The Hawthorne Studies identified several ways in which groups controlled their members. *Binging*, for example, referred to tapping on the arm. Other sanctions applied could involve a light-hearted joke or sarcastic comment and ridicule of the individual concerned. In effect, a scale of 'punishment' existed. The clear intention being to *socialize* members into conforming to the norms of behaviour within the work group. In that context it tended to be directed towards levels of production being achieved by individuals and the group desire to provide management with the apparent levels of output that it expected. A clear attempt by the group to manage the managers by conforming to their expectations and thereby avoiding scrutiny of group activity.

Alvesson and Willmott (1996; 103) describe socialization as: 'The process through which humans acquire, and identify with, the values, customs and aspirations of the social groups in which they live.' They also describe it as *social doping* within an organizational context as:

> Employees are told – more or less explicitly – how they must perceive and relate to the established organizational reality, and how they should participate in organizational rites where the 'correct' values, virtues and ideals are communicated. (p 103)

This view clearly sets out the role of *socialization* as a basis of control within the group context of organizations.

Authority

One feature of decision making within groups (to be discussed next) is the degree to which the group can ensure consistency in the views of the members. This can be achieved either through conforming to the norms of the group or by following the lead of the authority figures within it. Asch (1951) describes an experiment in which subjects were asked to decide upon the relative length of a number of lines. To do this they were presented with a diagram similar to that in Figure 6.5.

The subjects were asked to judge which of the three lines (A, B or C) was the same length as line D. The experiment was carried out in groups of about seven people, only one of whom was a true subject. The order of giving the individual judgement was also fixed so that the real subject was near the end of the process and so would be aware of the judgement announced by the others. The 'plants' were instructed to select the wrong answer. Most subjects (about 80%) displayed agreement with the opinions of the rest of the group. Asch suggested three reasons why subjects would adjust their opinions:

✦ Perceptual movement. Subjects changed their judgements as the result of what they felt to be group pressure. They perceived the majority to be right.

✦ Judgement movement. Although this category knew that they were reporting incorrectly they believed that their judgement was wrong.

✦ Action movement. This category simply went along with the majority, but were aware of what they were doing.

Milgram (1974) also considered response orientation based upon the influence of an authority figure. This experiment involved a simple memory test, the stated intention being to measure the effect of electric shock on memory. A correct response by the subject resulted in the progression to another question in the test. Failure to give a correct response

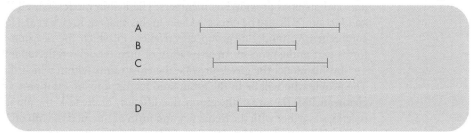

FIGURE 6.5 Diagram similar to that used by Asch.

resulted in an electric shock being administered and the question was repeated. After each electric shock the voltage was increased for the next repetition of the question. The equipment was clearly marked with a scale of electric shock magnitude. At the top end of the scale was a danger warning, indicating that if it were applied it would be fatal for the subject.

The experimenter in this process was, in fact, the subject for the experiment, although they were not aware of it at the time. The equipment for the experiment was not connected to the subject. The supposed subject was strapped into a chair and electrodes were fixed to their body (the experimenter helped to do this), but the electrodes were not wired up to the electric shock generator. The supposed subject for this experiment was 'in' on the subterfuge and deliberately responded to the questions incorrectly. The shock generator was wired up to an electric light and the 'subject' was instructed to respond with increasing cries of pain when it was illuminated and as the voltage increased. The 'subject' was in a separate room and could not be seen by the experimenter.

When the 'experimenter' began to show signs of resistance to the continuation of the experimental process they were encouraged to go on by Milgram or other research confederates. Most of the 'experimenters' continued with the experiment to the point where harm would have been done to the 'subject'. Milgram concluded that the power of an authority figure was able to pressure individuals to exhibit extreme behaviour. In the group variation of this experiment, it was noted that the reaction of the group tended to determine the reaction of the individual. If the group were rebellious the true subject would be as well, if compliant they tended to react in the same way.

Management in Action 6.2 was found pinned to the wall in a personnel department and it is something that reflects both the positive and negative aspects of group formation and activity.

Stop | Consider *What does MiA 6.2 suggest about the role of authority and politics in relation to the use of groups in organizations?*

Decision making within groups

Many groups within an organization have a major decision-making aspect to their purpose. This applies whether the group is a manufacturing department seeking ways to assemble toasters, or a board of directors seeking to develop a business strategy. The *team roles* identified by Belbin, introduced in the previous chapter, are an attempt to provide an effective basis for decision making within the group through the appropriate mixture of personal qualities provided by members. The Belbin model, as well as that of Margerison and McCann will also be discussed later in this chapter. Kretch *et al.* (1962) describe a more comprehensive model of group effectiveness in which the decision-making component forms part of the process. An adaptation of their model is reflected in Figure 6.6.

In this model the *givens* provide the constraints within which the group must work. The people who will be in the group and its purpose are examples. Other environmental factors include the size of the group, the difficulty of the task, the physical setting for group meetings together with the frequency and form of interaction with other groups. The *intervening factors* reflect the *decision-making* process which includes motivation and the leaders' approach to running the group. The level and type of member participation in the

MANAGEMENT IN ACTION 6.2

Teams and progress

We trained hard but it seemed that every time we were beginning to form up into teams we would be reorganized.

I was to learn later in life that we tend to meet any new situation by reorganization and a won- derful method it can be for creating the illusion of progress while producing confusion, inefficiency and demoralization.

Petronius Arbiter, 210 BCE.

group decision-making process is another aspect of the intervening factors at work in any given context.

That the quality of group output is of importance to organizations has long been recognized. In seeking to achieve this, it is often suggested that incentive schemes encourage groups to take 'more effective' decisions. Management in Action 6.3 indicates how senior managers can benefit from such arrangements. It also indicates the natural reactions of other groups who do not perceive that they receive the same benefit for their efforts.

Stop | Consider

In relation to the incentive scheme described in MiA 6.3 explore the likely perspectives of:
A the chief executive of LWT
B an ordinary employee of LWT.
Can these different perspectives be reconciled and if so how?
What do these different perspectives imply about the nature and role of groups within organizations?

During World War II, the US government was attempting to encourage the consumption of cheaper cuts of meat among the general population. Lewin argued that the decision on meat purchase was based on group norms, rather than an individual decision at the

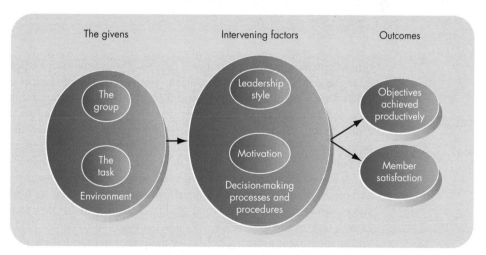

FIGURE 6.6 The determinants of group effectiveness (*source*: Kretch, D, Crutchfield, RS and Ballachey, EL (1962) *Individuals in Society*, McGraw-Hill, New York).

MANAGEMENT IN ACTION 6.3

LWT managers likely to receive £55m payout

London Weekend Television introduced an executive share option scheme as part of a capital restructuring programme during 1989. Managers in post at that time were able to purchase unlisted management shares at 83.2p each. The management shares could be converted into ordinary shares over time according to a sliding scale based on the price of the quoted shares.

The maximum conversion rate for the management shares was 4.048 ordinary shares for each management share, providing the quoted share price was an average of 278p over the 20 business days following the announcement of the half-year results in September 1993. On 6 May 1993 the quoted share price was 392p and predicted as a good prospect to rise further.

There was little doubt about the improvement in company performance since it had retained its ITV franchise. The share price on 6 May 1993 was a reflection of the market's view of that performance, together with an anticipation of continued growth in television advertising.

The board and senior management team of 44 people had been given the right to apply for the special management shares under the scheme. One of the key purposes of the scheme was to tie

senior managers to the company during the period of the franchise. This was in addition to the desire to motivate them to enhance the market value of the company. Other employees did not receive special payments or share schemes as a consequence of the franchise deal. There was, however, a company profit-sharing scheme to which all employees belonged.

It was predicted by the trade union representing employees in the broadcasting industry that the special share scheme would pay out £55m to the management team. In sharing out the money it would create 15 millionaires. The chairman of the station stood to gain a gross profit from the deal of in excess of £7m, the chief executive, sales director and the former chairman were also set to receive more than £5.3m each. The lowest gross profit for an individual within the scheme was calculated by the trade union as £73,750, which also described the scheme as obscene.

Adapted from: Snoddy, R (1993) LWT managers likely to receive £55m payout, *Financial Times*, 7 May, p 18.

time of purchase. In 1943 a number of groups of housewives were exposed either to a lecture or engaged in a group discussion on the relative benefits of cheaper cuts of meat (Lewin, 1958). One week after the experiment 32% of those who engaged in the group discussion had tried a cheaper cut of meat, compared with only 3% who had attended the lecture. The group discussion was significant in setting the group norms which encouraged the desired behaviour and in turn influencing actual future behaviour. This experiment demonstrates the power of group decision making in directing the future behaviour of members.

It is clear that in modern management practice the use of teamwork is highly favoured as a means of improving company performance. Indeed, they are held to be central to the success of such initiatives as total quality management (TQM) according to Wilkinson (1993). One of the ways of encouraging managers to recognize the benefits of teamwork and of adopting appropriate behaviour patterns is to expose them to situations where they are forced to take collective decisions in hostile environments. Outdoor training is one such environment and it is reviewed in Management in Action 6.4.

MANAGEMENT IN ACTION 6.4

Dispelling the macho myth

Outdoor training frequently has a macho image based on individual, generally unfit executives being forced to undertake silly exercises in the cold and damp. It has also been suggested that the people who provide such courses are either over-grown boy scouts, taking pleasure in the pain and discomfort of others or they are professional trainers who have a particular set of development skills that can be useful to organizations.

The advocates of outdoor training suggest that it represents a vehicle for the learning process and has particular relevance in the areas of leadership, communication, teamworking and the management of change. Not all outdoor training is based on mountain climbing, white-water rafting or potholing. Some involve problem solving such as rescue simulation and bridge building, linked to classroom discussion and analysis of the activity itself. Management supporters of this form of training claim that it takes individuals out of the usual company or classroom environment and therefore leaves many of the restrictions behind that might inhibit effective learning. It also allows individuals to fail in an environment which is safe in that it does not contain the status and 'baggage' associated with the normal organizational context.

A number of women on an appreciation course run by one such training provider considered that the approach offered a good opportunity for women. It was felt, however, that situations in which individuals (of either sex) were forced into situations causing excessive mental or physical stress should be avoided as they were likely to be counterproductive.

There is a wide range of outdoor training courses available involving a gamut of approaches to the topic. Raleigh International (previously known as Operation Raleigh) has used this type of activity as part of its selection of young people for a long time. It has now broadened its scope and markets its schemes to employers as management development tools. Employers can use the selection weekend scheme for junior personnel or graduate trainee level staff as a means of building leadership and confidence in the individual. It also encourages teamworking skills as part of the group activities involved.

Adapted from: Dickson, T and Milton, C (1993) Dispelling the macho myth, *Financial Times*, 30 June, p 19.

Stop | Consider

To what extent can the experience of group activity provided by outdoor training be transferred back to the workplace?

MiA 6.1 suggested (among other things) that groups within which the members experience hardship develop loyalty and commitment. Is this the real benefit of outdoor training for the generally unfit executive?

Whyte (1956) argues, however, that in most cases a group does not produce the best decision. Groups tend, in his words, to *mediocrity*:

In your capacity as a group member you feel a strong impulse to seek common ground with the others. Not just out of timidity but out of respect for the sense of the meeting you tend to soft-pedal that which would go against the grain. And that, unfortunately, can include unorthodox ideas. (p 53)

Group dynamics

Group dynamics refers to the patterns of behaviour and interaction that actually emerge within a group context. Patterns of communication and related analysis techniques were discussed earlier, but that of itself does not explain what actually takes place when human beings interact across time within a group. It might only explain what could happen if particular communication patterns are followed. There are many other aspects of group dynamics that impact on the experience of groups for the members as they interact in a dynamic sequence of interlocking behaviours.

Cohesion

According to Piper *et al.* (1983) *cohesion* refers to the attractiveness of a group to its members, reflected in their motivation to be a part of it, and the degree of resistance to leaving it. In real terms *cohesiveness* represents the strength of the feelings of togetherness among the members of a group. This can apply to both formal and informal groups. It can be represented as a scale of measurement running from strong to weak.

A group with a weak level of *cohesion* is effectively a loose combination of people, each person with little or no commitment to the other members or the intended objectives of the group. Conversely, a group with a strong level of *cohesion* is likely to display behaviour patterns that are tightly focused on the objectives to be achieved and support for each member of the group. Keller (1986) found that cohesive groups more frequently met their objectives. Shaw (1981) suggested that members of cohesive groups displayed more energy (than members of low-cohesion groups) in pursuit of group objectives. The strength of feeling among individual members towards the group is also likely to be evident in the level of commitment shown towards the group and its activities as reflected in levels of attendance at meetings, creating problems within the group etc. (Hodgetts, 1991).

There are a range of factors which contribute to the level of *cohesion* developed within a group. They are (see also Figure 6.7):

✦ Environmental factors. These can include perceived threats to the group and the desire to achieve available rewards.

✦ Organizational factors. These can include the nature of the task to be achieved, the perceived status of the group and the importance of the task to the organization.

✦ Group factors. These can include the size and composition of the group, the personality characteristics of the leader, frequency of interaction and the timescales for achieving the objectives of the group.

✦ Individual factors. These can include the desire (or needs) of individual members to be part of a cohesive group, the level of commitment held by individuals to group objectives, the perception of the other members' intentions and the perception of the other forces acting upon the situation.

From a management point of view it would be very useful if all the formal groups within the organization were strongly cohesive, as long as they were supportive of the management-determined objectives. There is some research evidence that such groups deliver the highest levels of productivity (Berkowitz, 1954). However, there is a real danger for managers in the existence of strongly cohesive groups that are hostile to their intentions. Such groups can become an organization within an organization or a *shadow organization* as some writers would describe them. They can be very resistant to the intentions of management if these are perceived to be against the interests of the group. Management in Action 6.5 illustrates this type of situation in graphic terms.

Stop | Consider   *Was it inevitable that the factory described in MiA 6.5 would close or could it have been saved?*

How might you have sought to save the factory if you were the production director? What problems might you have encountered in doing so and how would you have dealt with them?

Risks and group decisions

Stoner (1961) suggested that groups take decisions that involved greater risk than an individual alone would be prepared to take. This became known as the *risky shift* phenomenon and has been identified in a number of different countries and among different groups of subjects. Essentially, the experiment involved the administration of a choice dilemma questionnaire. There were 12 situations described in the questionnaire, all of which required a dilemma to be resolved and a decision to be made. A sample of one of the dilemmas to be addressed is included as Figure 6.8.

The research process involved three stages and two experimental conditions. This is most easily shown as a diagram (Figure 6.9).

Experiments of this type are known as *repeated measures* experiments and for the *risky shift* reveal that individuals tend to make more risky decisions after group discussion and that groups tend to make more risky decisions than individuals. A number of explanations have been put forward for this, including:

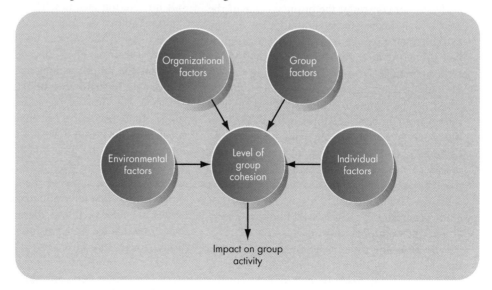

FIGURE 6.7 Determinants of group cohesion.

MANAGEMENT IN ACTION 6.5

The anti-management workforce

This is a true story told from the perspective of the production director of the company concerned. Some of the details have been changed to disguise the actual company and the people involved.

The organization was a manufacturing company, based in the north of England. It employed about 300 people in the manufacture and sale of industrial containers made from woven polypropylene fabric. Essentially the production process involved cutting the fabric into lengths determined by the design of the container, printing any customer logo or design on them, sewing the components together to form the container and then packing bundles together according to the customer order quantity. The majority of the workforce were female and had been with the company since it was formed about eight years earlier. Wages for the factory employees were based on a piecework system of negotiated prices.

The company had always had a difficult financial time in terms of cashflow and the quality of management had never been high in terms of leadership or control of the business. One of the 'tricks' that management used to play on the workforce on a regular basis was that if cashflow had been bad in a particular week one of the senior managers would 'go missing' on a Thursday. As a consequence the wages cheque could not be signed to enable staff to withdraw money from the bank and make up the wages – so the workers would not be paid on a Friday. Essentially, the company did not have enough money in the bank (or borrowing capability) to pay the wages and used the absence of the cheque signatory as an excuse. This became part of employee folklore as one aspect of how managers abused the workforce.

Because job times were negotiated, rather than being set by the use of time study, attempts were always being made by managers to cut the

price of a job. This was resented and caused many arguments and much employee disgruntlement over the years. The production director who told me this story had been appointed after his predecessor had been hospitalized with a nervous breakdown. The final straw had been when the trade union representatives wanted to see him and had kicked his office door off its hinges when he had asked them to make an appointment to see him. This manager had been in post for about one year before being taken ill and had been transferred from a similar post elsewhere in the group. He had replaced the previous production manager who had been sacked because he was thought to be incompetent and the cause of many of the problems with the shopfloor employees.

The shopfloor workers were a very close group, led by some very strong and dominant personalities. Over the years they had come to distrust management and they had learned that they had to fight for every concession. Even for the provision of a canteen room with a water boiler, but no catering facilities. The piece rates were a constant source of conflict and any new product was refused by the workers unless they were paid average earnings. Then they delayed agreeing a price for the job for as long as possible, years in some cases. In such cases the actual time taken to complete jobs on average earnings was much longer than necessary, but no employee would break with the group norms of working at a very low pace. Even the piece rates that were agreed were very slack; one job could be actually be done in less than a quarter of the allowed time. So employees on that job could make a decent week's wages in one day. It was the agreement of this piece rate that led to the dismissal of the production manager indicated above.

A new production director was recruited from outside the company, the appointed person being very experienced in industrial relations issues. He was also known by the workforce as he had been engaged in consultancy activity within the company over a couple of years. The task was clear. Get away from the traditions of the past, form new working relationships with employees and improve productivity. In short and in financial terms, turn the company around and make it profitable. The appointed production director had the necessary skills and some credibility among the workforce and things began well. He was welcomed into the company at all levels and began to draw up a plan of action, including the design of training programmes, new wage systems and communication with the workers.

Early on in the process it was found that one of the supervisors was taking bribes from employees for the handing out of jobs which would allow them to make high wages. The production director held a disciplinary investigation and the person concerned was dismissed. However, when the individual went to court to seek compensation for unfair dismissal the shopfloor workers wrote a letter in support of his claim. This stated that the director had been unfair in his treatment of the individual, who was in practice a good supervisor. Fortunately, the court disregarded the letter in the face of overwhelming evidence to the contrary and the dismissal was upheld. When the shopfloor representatives were subsequently asked to explain their actions, they replied that the supervisor was a valued member of their group and that managers should not be allowed to victimize individuals. The fact that he had been taking bribes from their members was acceptable to them to the extent that it had actually been done!

The production director interpreted this response as an indication that the employees were beginning to worry that their ability to control events through the strength of the group was being threatened. Attitudes towards the new production director also began to harden among the workforce and the negotiations over revised working practices and wage systems began to stall.

A few redundancies were declared, including a supervisory post. However, things did not change fundamentally. The finances of the company slowly began to improve and the breakeven point was reached after about six months. Radical solutions began to be considered by both company and group boards.

Eventually it was decided that the problems were simply too great ever to be totally overcome with the workforce employed. It was decided to sell the company, but not as a going concern. The proposal of the company board was to close the company and sell the assets and this was agreed by the group board. It was considered that no one would buy the company as a going concern for a realistic price. Consequently, the chief executive and production director called a factory meeting of all employees and announced the closure, along with the redundancy of all employees.

The workforce cheered! Cries and shouts of 'We have finally beaten management' and 'They have finally had to admit that we are stronger than them' and 'We have shown them that they cannot force us to accept change' were heard from among the employees. The atmosphere among the workforce in those first few days after the announcement was euphoric. Smiles were everywhere and production levels were higher than had ever been achieved before. Employees no longer wanted to work on average earnings jobs and have an easy time. They all wanted to maximize their earnings as this would directly influence the level of redundancy pay to which every employee would be entitled.

However, as the day of closure drew ever nearer one or two people began to recognize that things were not as good as they at first thought. For example, talk of a workers buyout fell apart after one meeting because the trade union would not put up the money and said that employees would have to find the money themselves. Also agreement could not be reached on how many company cars the employees should provide once they owned the company and, more significantly,

MANAGEMENT IN ACTION 6.5   continued

who would be given one. Equally, there were no other jobs in the area that would offer the same rates of pay as employees had been earning, without demanding much higher levels of effort.

A few employees began to talk to the production director and suggest that the real problem with the workforce was that a few hard cases had effectively bullied everyone else into agreeing with them. It was also suggested that if these individuals were sacked everyone else would be willing to accept more reasonable work and pay arrangements. It was also said that employees had not believed that the company was actually in a diffi-

cult financial position and that the way employees had behaved was not really that bad and had only been intended as fair industrial relations tactics. Had they known how serious things were they would have gone along with management's intentions, it was said. Management took the view that these were empty promises as the individuals concerned had been only too willing to go along with the previous practices and views of the very cohesive workgroup. The factory was closed and the assets sold to new owners. The assets were relocated to another part of the country and a new factory opened.

Mr E is president of a light metals corporation in the United States. The corporation is quite prosperous, and has strongly considered possibilities of business expansion by building an additional plant in a new location. The choice is between building a new plant in the United States where there would be a moderate return on the initial investment, or building a plant in a foreign country. Lower labour costs and easy access to to raw materials in that country would mean a much higher return on the initial investment. On the other hand, there is a history of political instability and revolution in the foreign country under consideration. In fact, the leader of a small minority party is committed to nationalization, that is, taking over all foreign investments.

Imagine that you are advising Mr E. Listed below are several probabilities or odds of continued political stability in the foreign country under consideration. Please tick the lowest probability that you would consider acceptable for Mr E.'s corporation to build in that country.

☐   The chances are 1 in 10 that the foreign country will remain politically stable.

☐   3 in 10

☐   5 in 10

☐   7 in 10

☐   9 in 10

☐   Please tick here if you think Mr E's corporation should not build a plant in the foreign country, no matter what the probabilities.

FIGURE 6.8   Choice dilemma questionnaire, sample questions (*source*: Kogan, N and Wallach, MA (1967) Risk taking as a function of the situation, person and the group. In Newcombe, TM (ed.) *New Directions in Psychology*, Vol. III, Holt, Rinehart & Winston, New York.

✦ Responsibility diffusion. It is argued that within a group there is less individual responsibility. Consequently, individuals can avoid personal responsibility for any failure. Comments such as, 'I knew that it would not work, but the others insisted on adopting that approach', are all too familiar in most groups. However, this does not seem to be the only possible explanation. Nordhoy (1962) re-examined the original data and found that some of the original questions included consistently produced group responses that were more cautious than individual ones. Perhaps the phenomenon produces an exaggeration effect, rather than a one-way shift in risk taking.

✦ Cultural values. Perhaps the phenomenon can be explained in terms of the cultural values surrounding the group. If a group is composed of individuals for whom risk is a normal part of life, then perhaps they will tend to favour that approach in their joint decisions.

✦ Rational decision making. It is possible that in attempting to reach a decision, any group is able to utilize the talents of the members in the discussion process. This increases the opportunity of the group to assess the arguments fully and make a better and more fully informed decision than an individual would be capable of.

✦ Majority decision making. If a group relies upon simple majority voting then it is possible for minority views to be overruled. This in turn minimizes the opportunity for full discussion of the points raised, hence limiting consideration of all the necessary aspects, so encouraging more risky decisions.

✦ Polarization. Moscovici and Zavalloni (1969) suggest that groups function in a way which tends to move individual attitudes towards extreme positions. This they describe as a function of the values within the group and an increase in commitment to the decision brought about by discussion.

Groupthink

Janis (1982) reviewed a number of foreign policy decisions involving military planning within the US government and, as a result, coined the word *groupthink*. His research included studying the Bay of Pigs disaster (when the USA invaded Cuba, ignoring information that the Cuban military was able to defend the landing area) and the Vietnam war.

Condition	Stages in the experiment		
	1st test (individual)	2nd test (group)	3rd test (individual)
Experimental group	Subjects complete questionnnaire as individuals	Group completes same questionnaire (concensus decision)	Individual completes questionnaire (being told that it is a personal decision and to disregard previous group decision)
Control group	As above	No activity	Repeat individual completion of questionnaire

FIGURE 6.9 The research process for the risky shift experiment.

As a result, he concluded that such effects were the result of concentrating on harmony and morale to the exclusion of other points of view. In other words highly *cohesive groups*, particularly those involving very hierarchical memberships such as might be found in the military, were likely to create the very conditions that prevented the full discussion and critical evaluation of important issues. Inevitably, this engendered situations which encouraged agreement at any price, unquestioning acceptance of the perspectives of senior members and a lack of critical evaluation of information, thereby encouraging very poor decision making. Janis identified a number of symptoms which might signify that a group was likely to be suffering from *groupthink*:

✦ Invulnerability. The group becomes overly optimistic and convinced of its own invulnerability. In the Bay of Pigs fiasco, the US military planners could not envisage that with the military capability at their disposal they could be beaten by Cuba, a country which was much smaller in both physical and military terms, and generally less well developed than the USA.

✦ Rationalization. Such groups find ways to rationalize any evidence or opinion that might suggest an opposing point of view. For example, the Cubans might be defending their homeland, but on this occasion this will not matter because … followed by a range of reasons offered in support of the viewpoint.

✦ Morality. A fundamental belief in the moral correctness of any proposed action. The USA was morally right to seek to overthrow the 'wicked' regime in Cuba – according to the planners.

✦ Values. Individuals with opposing points of view are frequently stereotyped as weak, stupid or evil. Any evidence or information from these sources is therefore automatically disregarded as irrelevant, contaminated or simply of no value.

✦ Pressure. Direct pressure can be used with great subtlety in order to provide an appearance of free speech while preventing active consideration of the views expressed. For example, it is not uncommon in meetings to hear a certain type of chairperson state that they are seeking the full agreement of all members for a particular proposal and that they will take silence to indicate willing support. This strategy effectively requires any individual with doubts to speak out and possibly signal opposition to the chairperson. Any individual would have to feel very strongly about an issue to speak out under such circumstances. Equally, of course, direct pressure can also be used to control individuals through such suggestions as promotion prospects being dependent on 'playing the game' in an approved way and being openly supportive of organizational objectives.

✦ Self-censorship. Members of the group develop a means of self-censorship in order to hide any doubts and to protect the group cohesion. Such a strategy can also be used to the personal advantage of an individual seeking to be viewed by the senior members of a group as supportive of them and their ideas.

✦ Unanimity. A carefully orchestrated unanimity with the equally careful exclusion of divergent views. As indicated earlier silence can be taken as a clear signal that all members are in agreement with the decision, creating an impression of unanimity through pressure.

✦ Mindguards. The creation of informal mindguards to filter information flows and to protect the group from adverse comment. Collective responsibility is invoked as a justification for supporting the decision and to marginalize any dissent.

Janis also suggested a number of mechanisms through which groups could guard against *groupthink* (Figure 6.10). They included encouragement for individuals to voice any doubts: the use of subgroups to broaden the search for ideas and to serve as a cross-check on ideas and analysis; encouraging self-criticism among the group and ensuring that junior members are allowed to speak first.

The mechanisms suggested by Janis are intended to offer a group the opportunity to explore different and possibly divergent or contradictory perspectives before beginning collectively to focus on workable solutions to the problem under review. It is premised on the view that it is the junior members of any group who are likely to hold alternative viewpoints and be less conservative in their approach to problems. However, such individuals are also subject to the social control and dynamic of the organizational and group hierarchy and this can work to the disadvantage of the group in certain situations.

The role of the *devil's advocate* in this process is based on the idea that someone should be specifically appointed within the group to explore an opposing point of view. It is based on the approach used within the Roman Catholic church during the process of investigating individuals for elevation to the status of saint. In that process evidence is actively collected that the person is worthy of this high status. The role of the devil's advocate, in contrast, is to search out information that would demonstrate that the person had not led a pure life. In short, to prove that the person was not worthy of elevation to sainthood. The same concept is suggested as a means of preventing a group from simply going along with the accepted case by being forced to consider alternative perspectives.

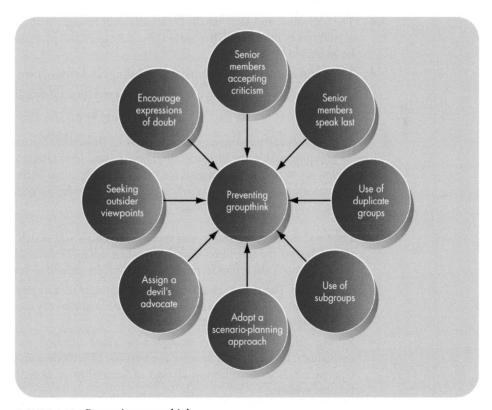

FIGURE 6.10 Preventing groupthink.

Freud, psychotherapy and group dynamics

Groups must come to terms with their own internal functioning before they can effectively address the tasks facing them. Freud was among the first to address these issues (Strachey, 1953–66) and provided the basis for much of the later work on *group dynamics*. For Freud, group activity is based on the libidinal impulses of the individual which become transformed through group membership. It is the libidinal (or sexual) impulses that create the links between people and which help to maintain the group.

There are other aspects of the group dynamics that Freud seeks to explain. The competition between group members he explains as ambivalence towards the leader who, in effect, becomes a substitute parent. The members compete for supremacy in an attempt to become a new leader. Whatever the views about the value of Freud's work, it does draw attention to the *emotional power* present in group activity. The ability of a group to create powerful forces in favour of conformity, and indeed rebellion, is without question. Freud's work also points to the clear existence of both a conscious and unconscious level of behaviour in relation to group activities.

Bion (1961) developed a psychotherapy model that relied upon the dynamics of group activity to create changes in individual behaviour. He developed this approach while treating soldiers suffering breakdowns during World War II. As with Freud, Bion was part of the process which he was describing and so his results do not carry the 'weight' of experimentation. Bion concluded that much group experience was the result of conflict between three aspects of group life:

✦ The individual and their needs. Each individual brought with them their needs and aspirations to the group. They would also have an expectation that their needs would be addressed by the group.

✦ The group mentality. This related to the feelings and atmosphere within the group.

✦ The group culture. This Bion described as the need for structure and leadership within the group.

The conflicts and tensions experienced between these three features produces a *second level* of grouping within the *primary* one. These second level groupings, or *basic assumption groups*, act to resolve the tensions for the individuals. It has been suggested that these mechanisms are particularly active when the group is under pressure to achieve results. These effects can be dealt with through:

✦ Fight and flight responses. In this mode, individuals will switch between attack and retreat against the identified threat depending upon the circumstances, the purpose being to protect the group from a threat that might cause it to break up.

✦ Dependency. The group defends itself by increasingly turning inwards upon itself. For example, rather than face up to the issue at hand, a group may concentrate on the procedural aspects of what it is doing.

✦ Pairing. This involves pairing through a ritualized approach to interaction between individuals. It would seem to serve the purpose of providing an alternative leader or objective. It is a metaphorical change in leadership or objectives when problems become evident.

The Tuckman and Jensen model was earlier introduced as a way of describing the stages of *group development*. This model provides a framework for understanding the process of forming and defining the purpose of a group. It should be apparent that there are points of similarity between the discussion of Freud and Bion and the Tuckman and Jensen material on group development. Both represent an attempt to explain the influences on human behaviour that people bring with them to a group setting and the processes that they need to go through in seeking to achieve the objectives set for the group.

Group dynamics – another view

Another way of describing the dynamic processes within a group is shown in Figure 6.11. This attempts to bring together a number of the elements associated with the internal behaviour of groups.

Within Figure 6.11 there are multiple interactions between the elements in the *group behaviour* box. For example, the style of leadership will influence the process of decision making and the characteristics of the individual members will influence the style of leadership that will be most effective. There is a feedback loop between the *outcome* boxes and the other elements within the model. This is because the group will receive feedback on its progress during its life. For example, if a group produces minutes of meetings, there is likely to be a response from the people who see them. Equally, dissatisfied members are likely to make their dissatisfaction apparent to group leaders in ways that cannot be missed at some point in time.

Taking each of the elements within Figure 6.11 in turn:

✦ Size. The larger the group the more complex the communication process. Within a group there are a number of trade-offs in relation to the number of participants involved in the process. The larger the number of participants the broader the range of experience that can be brought to bear on the task. By the same token, the more people involved the smaller the contribution any individual can make. Other considerations associated with size of a group include the need for rules and procedures, the

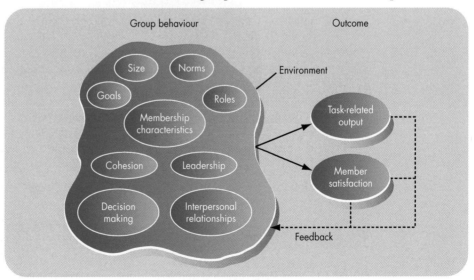

FIGURE 6.11 Determinants of dynamic activity within groups.

potential domination of a group by a subgroup, the time to reach a decision increases with size and there is a tendency for factions (or subgroups) to form within a group.

✦ Norms. Sanctions can be imposed by the group on those individuals who do not abide by the norms operated by the group. This was clearly demonstrated in the *Hawthorne Studies*. Some groups can also develop *anarchic* norms of behaviour, compared to the normal behaviours encountered in a particular setting.

✦ Goals. Group output is made up of two components: the objectives set for the group and the satisfaction level of members (the *outcome* boxes in Figure 6.11). In most group activity both of these are necessary for success. Imagine a situation where a negotiating group is given the task of agreeing a new pay deal on behalf of workers. If the deal is presented by management as a 'take-it-or-leave-it' situation, the workers may accept it, but morale among members of the negotiating group is likely to drop, along with the morale and productivity of the workforce.

✦ Member characteristics. Individuals differ along a wide range of dimensions, including problem-solving style. A preponderance of one problem-solving style within a group may make it more likely that a result is achieved rapidly, but there are dangers through such issues as the *risky shift* and *groupthink* phenomena.

✦ Roles. The Belbin model of group roles have already been introduced along with a discussion of role theory in the previous chapter. Another model was developed by Margerison and McCann (1990) and is called the *Team Management Wheel*. It is reproduced as Figure 6.12 and attempts, according to the authors, to go beyond the Belbin

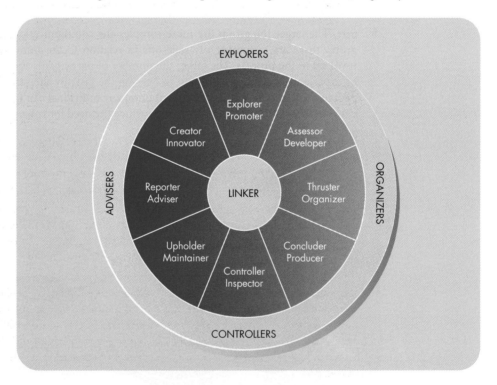

FIGURE 6.12 The Margerison–McGann Team Management Wheel (© Prado Systems Ltd. Reproduced by kind permission of TMS Development International Ltd. Tel 01904 641640).

model by, 'show[ing] that people have particular work preferences that relate to the roles they play in a team'. This model will be discussed in more detail later in this chapter.

There are a number of other role frameworks that attempt to define what happens within a group. Hoffman (1979) provides the following framework clustered around three categories:

✦ Task roles. These roles encourage the achievement of the objectives of the group. Specific roles include initiator, information givers and seekers, co-ordination and evaluation.

✦ Relationship roles. These roles help to maintain the team while it is functioning. Examples include encouragement, gatekeeper, follower, standard setter and observer.

✦ Individual roles. These concentrate on the needs of the individuals within the group. Examples include blocker, dominator, recognition seeker and avoider.

The main difference between this last classification and those of Belbin and Margerison–McCann is that Hoffman is describing what *may* exist rather than what *should* exist in order to achieve an effective team.

✦ Cohesion. This refers to the degree to which a group feels itself to be a group. At an individual level it is reflected in the desire to stay as part of the group. There is a relationship between *cohesion* and *conformity*. For example, a group containing a norm of low conformity to group norms might be high in cohesion if the norms were only loosely structured and enforced. Such an example would be a group that would be unlikely to achieve objectives, but would be high in member satisfaction.

✦ Leadership. The approach of the leader is important in setting the pattern of behaviour within a group. Informal leaders can emerge over time and tend to be influential in an indirect way. Alternatively, they can directly challenge the nominal leader if that person is weak or seen not to be meeting the needs of members or the objectives being sought.

✦ Decision making. The way in which a group goes about taking decisions can also have an effect on the outcome. Clearly, a group that spends its time talking and arguing without any real sense of purpose is unlikely to produce meaningful results.

✦ Interpersonal relationships. The way in which the individuals relate to each other within a group can also have a major impact on it. For example, members of a working party who do not like each other at a personal level are less likely to co-operate effectively. The art of sabotaging an 'enemy' within a committee can be carried off with some finesse and become a great source of personal pleasure, even if it is counterproductive in terms of the objectives being sought!

✦ Environment. All of these features are carried out within a particular organizational environment. Every organization has its own culture and ways of working. In some instances, group activity is seen as very informal and a means of solving problems. In other cases, it is seen as a formal process of communication and decision making. Some groups may even be seen as a mechanism for agreeing to decisions actually taken elsewhere.

Dynamics between groups

Groups invariably function within a world of groups. Take as an example a joint management trade union negotiating committee. Although this would be a group in itself, it must interact with a number of other groups, which in turn will interact with other groups. Figure 6.13 attempts to reflect this complex situation.

In Figure 6.13, the trade union negotiators have no choice other than to consult with the employee group. Similarly, management representatives must consult with the senior managers of the company. Other interactions will be less formal and some only evident as influencing forces. For example, all participants will interact with their family groups and some influence could be expected as a consequence. Interaction with professional or occupational groups could also be expected to have some influence on the primary group's activity. The influences that could be expected to operate between groups is shown in Figure 6.14.

The model reflected in Figure 6.14 assumes that there are several intervening variables

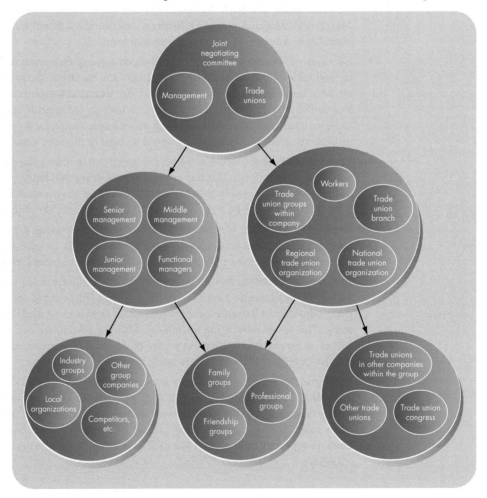

FIGURE 6.13   The group hierarchy.

that interact on the relationships that exist between groups. Not all of these variables will function all of the time, neither will they have equal potency. The dynamic of the relationship between groups and the behaviours that result are, however, affected by them. Taking each of the factors identified in Figure 6.14 in turn:

✦ Objectives. The *objectives* that each group have may well differ. This affects the relationship between the groups depending how each group *perceives* its own and the others' objectives. Within an organization it would be the ideal for all groups to perceive their objectives as part of the overall company objectives. The nature of conflict between groups is strongly influenced by the perception of the objectives that exist.

✦ Task competition. Groups that are strongly linked together because of the nature of the work are more likely to develop a *power* basis to the relationship. A typical example of this would be employees joining a trade union to reduce their dependency on management. At the other extreme groups can function independently of each other.

✦ Resource competition. Where groups must compete for resources then they could be expected to seek ways of gaining an advantage over the others. Two departments may put forward bids for additional resources to improve productivity, but there may be a limit to the finance available. Under these circumstances the two departments can either begin a 'war', or find ways of reaching a compromise.

✦ Uncertainty. There is often little opportunity for a group to be certain about another group's motives or intentions. Among the consequences of uncertainty are a lack of trust and an increase in political behaviour towards other groups.

✦ Inter-group relations. Previous experience of interaction with other groups can determine future behaviour. A management that is found to have lied to its workforce will find future interactions tainted by that experience.

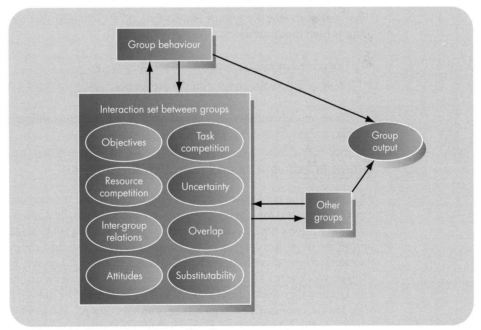

FIGURE 6.14 Influences on group behaviour.

✦ Attitudes. Frequently, inter-group relations are based on attitudes established over many years. McGregor's theory X and theory Y are examples of how the attitudes of individual managers can form the basis of stereotypical inter-group behaviour.

✦ Overlap. Over the past 200 years many trade unions came into existence in the UK, largely based on occupational groupings. As a consequence, overlap in their claims to represent particular groups of workers arose. Consequently, a set of rules were agreed between the trade unions as the basis of regulating competition for members.

✦ Substitutability. The opportunity to bypass or circumvent another group provides an opportunity to exercise a degree of control over that group. The threat of alternative suppliers is a classic way for one organization to pressure another into conceding lower prices.

A number of the issues raised from this section can be identified in Management in Action 6.6. This considers the frequently subtle ways in which male dominance of organizations can be maintained accidentally – or is it deliberately?

Stop | Consider

Form two groups, one comprised of men the other of women. Explore MiA 6.6 in terms of the material provided on group dynamics between groups. Each group should present its analysis and then collectively explore the reasons for any differences in perspective. Do these differences reflect group dynamics or gender?

Is it possible to determine if gender discrimination is accidental or deliberate. Does this distinction make any difference? If so to what?

Group effectiveness and satisfaction

What makes an effective group? Figures 6.6 and 6.11 suggest that there are two different outputs from group activity:

✦ The achievement of objectives in a productive way.

✦ Member satisfaction level with the experience.

These models imply that effectiveness should be measured against both of these criteria.

Group effectiveness and member satisfaction

A group could be *productive* and achieve its objectives, but the members may not enjoy the experience or feel that it was satisfactory for them personally. Conversely, the individuals could have a good time through the group experience, but fail to achieve anything in relation to the objectives set. For example, one manager described during an interview that they worked in an organization where the management style was very autocratic and senior managers took very little notice of their subordinates. Morale among middle managers was very low and they felt 'driven' in their work. Labour turnover among this group was quite high, but the company paid high salaries and was very profitable. This example falls quite clearly into the category of group success (among the management) measured by financial results, but with low personal satisfaction.

MANAGEMENT IN ACTION 6.6

Old boys' network

In October 1992 the Institute of Manpower Studies published a report into the merit pay systems used by four organizations. The work was funded by the Equal Opportunities Commission (EOC). In one case the report found that within a performance-based pay system bosses gave different targets to men and women. Men were expected to demonstrate intelligence, energy, dynamism and assertiveness. Women, however, were measured against organizational ability, honesty and dependability. It was also discovered that in comparing men and women of similar job level and performance ranking, the men were more likely to have been offered training and promotion. As deputy chairwoman of the EOC, June Bridgeman noted: 'Employees, especially women, need to be aware they may lose out in pay and promotion if appraisal and merit pay is adopted.'

In another report, the Institute of Management, supported by Bhs (the large retail organization) found that women were pessimistic about promotion opportunities, feeling that they were held back by their mainly male employers. Only 20% of women expected internal promotion as their next move, compared with 36% of men.

Again, almost 50% of women managers felt that childcare responsibilities had adversely affected their careers, whereas only 16% of men in equivalent managerial jobs felt that children had held their careers back. Career breaks for women can also work against individuals. In this study, 29% of respondents had taken a career break, of which 39% had returned to work at a lower level. As high a figure as 74% of women strongly agreed that women managers brought positive skills to the workplace, but only 33% of men expressed the same view.

One woman respondent indicated: 'If you leave work to have a child, you effectively lose all skills in the employer's eyes and have to start again.' Another indicated that in her view: 'Old boy's networks are alive and strong.' Yet another said: 'There is a subtle way in which we are never given quite the full authority, never quite the full credit, never quite the full respect.'

Adapted from: Lowe, K (1992) Old boy's network, *Personnel Today*, 10 November, p 14.

Conversely, a community association was established in a particular village with the aim of ensuring that a bypass was built to divert through traffic away from the houses and shops. Most active in the association were the retired people who had most free time to devote to the aims and objectives of the group. However, everything was done with such precision, elaboration and over such a long period of time that the bypass is still not built. The individuals concerned continue to express commitment to the objectives and approach the task with considerable enthusiasm. Effectively, the community association helps to provide a sense of social worth and value to the individuals active in it. This seems to provide a clear example of individual satisfaction but limited achievement of the *stated* objectives.

These examples raise the question of just how group effectiveness should be measured. Should it only be a reflection of the achievement of objectives or should it reflect the individual perspective? It also raises the question of dependency between the two elements. Is it possible for a group to be totally effective in achieving its objectives if the individuals are not *satisfied* in any meaningful way? Conversely, does the achievement of objectives create its own satisfaction?

Results from the Hawthorne Studies suggest that both factors of achieving results and member satisfaction interact in the dynamic of the workplace and that satisfaction has a significant effect on output. However, for most groups it is impossible to know what the degree of relationship is because it is not possible to run experiments where the variables are systematically manipulated and results measured. Also what about the objectives being sought? Do they represent what could be achieved or the 'best' possible outcome, or do they simply reflect what is being sought? In any particular context it is never certain if the objectives set for a group reflect that which could be achieved (optimally) or simply some defined change to a current situation (for perhaps rational reasons) that gives the appearance of progress in some general way. In crude terms do the shareholders of a company care that they do not achieve the highest returns possible on their investment, as long as the next dividend is the same or better than the previous one, the share price does not buck the trend and the board offers a plausible justification?

McGregor (1960, p 228) describes the concept of *unity of purpose* to explain the way that some managerial groups perform effectively. By this term he draws attention to the commitment of individuals to the group and to the achievement of the objectives. He goes on to describe the features that differentiate *effective* from *ineffective* groups. The main features of his ideas are included as Table 6.2.

Dimension	Effective group	Ineffective group
1 Atmosphere	Informal, comfortable, relaxed	Indifference, boredom, tension
2 Discussion	Participative, pertinent to task	Dominated by a few people, drifts off point
3 Objectives	Understood and accepted by all	Lack of clarity, not fully accepted by individuals
4 Active listening	Members listen to each other, contribution to debate and ideas	Pushing of own ideas, no evidence of building on others, talking for effect
5 Disagreement	Brought into the open and resolved or accepted	Not resolved, suppressed by leader, perhaps warfare domination is the aim
6 Decision making	By consensus	Premature decisions and actions before full examination. Simple majority voting
7 Criticism	Frank but not personal	Embarrassing, tension producing. Involves personal hostility, destructive approach
8 Feelings	Expressed on group activity as well as ideas. Few hidden agendas	Hidden, not thought appropriate to group activity
9 Action	Clear allocation and acceptance	Unclear in allocation, lack of commitment to achieve result
10 Leadership	Not chair dominated, 'experts' lead depending on circumstances, no power struggles	Chair dominated
11 Reviews	Self-consciousness about present operations, frequent reviews	No discussion of group maintenance issues

TABLE 6.2   Features of effective and ineffective groups (*adapted from*: McGregor, D (1960) The *Human Side of Enterprise*, McGraw-Hill, New York)

The ideas contained in Table 6.2 could be used to record the way in which a particular group functions. This in turn would allow the members to review their own approach and improve the level of group effectiveness achieved. It does not, however, address the issue of what could be achieved. It simply allows a review in terms of what exists.

The two *team systems* already introduced in the context of groups seek to define the requirements for a balanced set of abilities and preferences among the members, if success is to be achieved. These ideas were the Belbin model and that of Margerison and McCann. Both of these models also have significant implications for group effectiveness and member satisfaction. It is now to a more detailed consideration of these two approaches that we turn.

Belbin's team roles

Belbin's team roles were outlined in Table 5.4 in Chapter 5, taken from Belbin (1993). These roles are:

+ The plant.
+ The resource investigator.
+ The co-ordinator.
+ The shaper.
+ The monitor evaluator.
+ The teamworker.
+ The implementer.
+ The completer.
+ The specialist.

For Belbin, each of these roles has an important part to play in achieving an effective group process in terms of the objectives to be achieved. It is the balance between the contributions of each role that delivers the opportunity for the group to make 'good' decisions through allowing the dynamic between individuals to form a complementary process, not a destructive one. In his 1981 book, Belbin describes what he considers to be the attributes of successful and unsuccessful teams. These conclusions are based upon his work associated with the application of the *team roles model* in training and research contexts. According to Belbin unsuccessful teams display the following characteristics:

+ Morale. There was only a tenuous link between the level of morale among the individuals and degree of success in achieving group objectives. In other words, groups with a high level of morale are just as likely to fail as those with low morale.
+ Mental ability. This proved to be a critical factor in that without someone of high ability in a creative or analytical sense, failure was relatively certain.
+ Personality. Organization culture creates a tendency to encourage the recruitment and promotion of people with a preponderance of particular personality traits. The consequence of this *cloning* or *clustering* is a negative impact on group decision-making effectiveness.
+ Team composition. Some groups will fail because of organizational deficiencies rather

than anything specific to the group. For example, senior management may fail to act on the recommendations of one of its specialist functions. However, unless a balance of team roles is achieved within that function then the group is likely to be ineffective in operation.

✦ Individuals with no team role. Belbin identified about 30% of the managers tested as having no clearly defined team role profile. The consequences of the inclusion of such individuals into a team are effectively to destabilize what could otherwise be an effective group.

✦ Unknown factors. Between 10–15% of managers failed to take the tests that would determine their team role. This might suggest that individuals that avoid being tested tend to associate with ineffective groups more frequently than would be expected.

✦ Corporate influences. Few groups operate in isolation (as illustrated in Figure 6.13). There are constraints and political influences active in all situations. There is also a lack of information, and the existence of imperfect information on occasions which can impact on the quality of any decision. Among the consequences of this are that groups can be *channelled* in particular directions during their deliberations and suffer *interference* in their activities, which may result in a poor quality output in objectives terms. For example, Bray (2000) reports that Qantas (the Australian airline) is to raise its domestic fares by an average of 3.5% just as cut-price competition is about to grow significantly with the entry of Virgin Atlantic into the market and the rapid expansion of an existing local carrier. A price war looks more likely than the opportunity to raise prices. Only time will tell if the decision to raise prices by Qantas will be sustainable, but the signs are not favourable.

✦ Role reversal. Occasionally Belbin found that individuals who displayed a particular team role profile would switch and adopt another role, less suited to their abilities. This switch produced a negative effect on the group activity.

Successful or *winning teams*, as Belbin prefers to call them, display the following characteristics:

✦ An individual in the chair who could make use of the role to ensure an effective process. A person with an ability to work with the talent available within the group.

✦ A strong plant, essentially a creative and clever person, within the group. Someone able to make an effective contribution.

✦ A good range of mental ability spread across the individuals within the group in such a way that complemented the team roles present.

✦ Wide team role coverage within the group. The key team roles within a group provides a basis for effective interaction and balanced decision making.

✦ A match between team roles and personal attributes. In many groups activity is allocated on the basis of past experience rather than team role profile. Successful teams were able to achieve a balance in these features.

✦ The ability of the team to compensate for role imbalances. This refers to the ability of a team to compensate for its own weaknesses.

The Margerison–McCann Team Management Wheel

Margerison and McCann (1990) use the analogy of a wheel to describe their team management system (Figure 6.12). Their approach to effective teams is also based on research. The authors claim that they span the psychological and sociological traditions and go further than Belbin in providing an explanatory and practical model. Figure 6.15 reflects the relationship between the Team Management Wheel and other approaches.

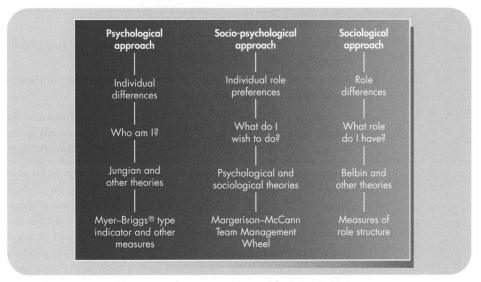

FIGURE 6.15 Different approaches to understanding teams (© Prade Systems Ltd. Reproduced by kind permission of TMS Development International Ltd. Tel 01904 641640)

The model is based around the *Team Management Profile Questionnaire*, which is a forced-choice normative questionnaire. It measures individual work preferences on four dimensions:

✦ Relationships. The approach to relationships is measured on an extroversion–introversion scale.

✦ Information. Measured in terms of the preferences in the way in which information is gathered and used by the individual in analyzing situations.

✦ Decisions. Measured in terms of the approach adopted by the individual to taking decisions.

✦ Organization. Measured in terms of structure or flexibility preferences of the individual in approaching tasks to be achieved.

The information collected provides a profile of the individual in terms that can be translated onto the 'Wheel'. The profile identified falls into the segments on the Wheel, each of which implies the following characteristics:

✦ Creator–Innovators. These individuals are independent and likely to challenge the present ways of doing things. They can generate new ideas.

✦ Explorer–Promoters. Individuals who explore new ideas and sell them to other people.

+ Assessor–Developers. Individuals good at linking the creative and operational sides of a team. They are good at taking an idea in principle and making it work in practice.

+ Thruster–Organizers. The people who can get things done. They can organize resources and people to achieve results.

+ Concluder–Producers. These people can ensure that results are achieved and that the work of the team is effective and efficient.

+ Controller–Inspectors. These individuals ensure that the details are correct and the output is 'up to standard'.

+ Upholder–Maintainers. Good at providing support and stability to a team. They support and advise the team.

+ Reporter–Advisers. The data collection and interpretation specialists. They are the experts in the field and collectors of information.

+ Linker. This activity is not seen as a preference as such, but as a skill that can be developed by any manager. This activity is central to team activity in that it performs a *connecting* role in ensuring that the team operates in an effective manner.

The concept of effectiveness in this model is defined in terms of a balance of individuals across the preferences in the Wheel. Most importantly, the writers claim that different situations and team objectives require different combinations of roles from the Wheel. In other words the team composition should be designed to meet the needs of the situation. This implies that the current profile of every manager should be available when the composition of a team is considered and that profile, not just status, politics or function, should be taken into account. What the authors term a 'high-performing team' should:

+ Accept that all team members have a responsibility to undertake the linking role.

+ Have high expectations and set high targets.

+ Gain high levels of job satisfaction.

+ Experience high levels of co-operation.

+ Provide team managers who lead by example.

+ Develop teams that have a balance of roles matched to skills.

+ Experience high degrees of autonomy.

+ Learn quickly from mistakes.

+ Develop teams that are 'customer' oriented.

+ Display good problem-solving skills and review group performance.

+ Be motivated to perform.

The reasons that teams fail, according to Margerison and McCann, include:

+ A lack of balance across the team roles.

+ A lack of effective linking between the roles.

+ A lack of effective relationship management within the team.

+ A lack of effective information management within the team.

+ The existence of impoverished decision-making processes.

+ The tendency to want to take decisions too early in the process.

MANAGEMENT IN ACTION 6.7

New plant puts GM in the fast lane

The Eisenach plant of General Motors (GM) is located in what was East Germany and originally built Wartburg cars. In those days the output statistics of the plant were about 100,000 cars built by 10,000 people. Following the reunification of Germany and the acquisition of the plant by GM it now produces 125,000 cars with only 2000 people. An increase in productivity of over 500%.

It takes 18.3 hours to manufacture a car in Eisenach compared to 30 hours in the GM factories elsewhere in Germany and Spain and 25 hours in the UK. Quality is also better than other GM plants with only six faults per completed car in Eisenach, compared with 20 defects per car elsewhere in Germany and 14 in Britain.

To achieve this revolution in productivity and quality the company introduced so-called lean production processes and teamworking. Just-in-time working methods require minimal stocks of raw material and work in progress between processes as buffer protection to cover breakdowns. It is not uncommon in conventional manufacturing to find considerable levels of stock held between stages in the process to allow production to continue if a breakdown occurs. For example, Bochum (a GM plant in Germany) would have 365 underbodies in stock to be able to keep the assembly lines running should production in the

body shop be halted. In Eisenach the same figure is ten underbodies. This level of buffer converts to 20 minutes of production time to fix a problem before the whole factory comes to a standstill, compared with six hours at Bochum.

Team and flexible working practices have also been introduced. For example, there are ten skilled maintenance people per shift compared with 300 in Bochum. In Eisenach, if a breakdown occurs, the assembly line workers help the maintenance personnel to rectify the problem, rather than simply sit and wait for it to be fixed.

The plant at Eisenach is being used as a testbed for new managerial ideas in production and for the training of prospective senior managers for other locations, the intention being to export the advantages of lean production and teamworking to other parts of the company. However, a new factory is in a completely different position to one that has been part of GM for many years and which will have a history and tradition of particular working practices. Thus existing factories will require a different management of change approach.

Adapted from: Parkes, C (1993) New plant puts GM in the fast lane, *Financial Times*, 9 June, p 2.

That effectiveness in group activity is a key factor in organizational success is demonstrated in Management in Action 6.7. This extract not only demonstrates the need for work group effectiveness, but also stresses the importance of the people/technology interface.

Stop | Consider

To what extent does MiA 6.7 demonstrate that for groups to be truly effective appropriate operational processes and structures need to exist as well?

In seeking to export the ideas from the Eisenach plant to existing GM locations how would you make use of either the Belbin or the Margerison and McCann models of group composition and effectiveness?

Groups and organizations

The Hawthorne Studies provide the most frequently cited basis for thinking about groups within an organization. However, it has been implied that the studies were 'rigged' in that it has been suggested that the process did not achieve the standard of objectivity necessary to be able to isolate the dependent and independent variables. For example, employees were required to participate in the experiments and the researchers became counsellors not only by collecting information but also by seeking to direct employee dissatisfactions as well (Thompson and McHugh, 1990, p 78). The same authors draw attention to the views of Mayo on issues such as trade unions and conflict (p 80) (see also Gillespie (1991) for a review of the context). The design of the research and interpretation of the evidence was to a significant extent a function of the individual researchers' attitudes, beliefs and values.

Research in real organizations is not like research in the controlled conditions found in a laboratory. It involves people interacting and behaving in real time and factors not under experimental control impacting on the process. For example, the mood and feelings of people can change depending on a wide range of factors both inside and outside the work setting. Also the researchers are not physically able to observe and record every aspect of behaviour, its determinants and consequences within a multi-person group. There is simply too much going on. Equally, there is always an issue of how much the researcher under-stands of what is actually going on. Within any situation there is a physical behaviour level of observable activity. That is, the actual movements of the people, their spoken words and other observable events. However, there is also a shared meaning level of behaviour present that allows the participants to interpret the gross behaviour activity in terms of what it means within the particular group setting. This level of meaning is not easily gained by the researcher and can readily be missed. In some situations deliberate attempts can be made by a group to provide a researcher with the wrong interpretation of events, a problem common among early anthropological studies. So there are many practical and academic difficulties in seeking to achieve what Maslow (1966, p 50) described as 'spectator knowledge'.

However, the same criticisms could be made of most research endeavours. In addition to the points already raised, when analysing the data available, a researcher is looking for pat-terns, associations and trends. It is inevitable that links will be identified that are not relevant and perhaps do not stand up to subsequent critical scrutiny. This process of research, publi-cation and critical evaluation is all part of the process of creeping forward in the creation of new knowledge. In knowledge terms the Hawthorne Studies are a comparatively recent event. It is hardly surprising that the results are still being questioned and re-examined by modern researchers critically evaluating what the original research team actually did.

As the Hawthorne Studies illustrate, groups can have a significant effect on the behaviour of their members. The balance between output and effort by members of the group described in the bank wiring room study illustrates the power of groups to shape the behaviour of individual members. Other studies, for example, those of Asch, illustrate the ability of groups to produce conformity. Yet, conversely, the same experiment, repeated in the UK by Perrin and Spencer (1981) did not produce a compliance effect. This suggests that such effects demonstrated by Asch could be a function of culture, social or experi-mental conditions at the time, ignoring the possibility that it was a function of the experi-mental design (as that was common to both experiments).

In a study of informal group practices in maintaining output and control, Bensman and Gerver (1973) studied assembly in an aircraft factory. Company policy stated that if wing parts were not in alignment disassembly and complete rebuilding should follow. This inevitably resulted in a long delay and a loss of production. The 'informal' practice was to use a hard steel screw to force the components together, thus saving time. The company did not allow employees to acquire such screws and anyone found in possession of one was liable to instant dismissal. However, all employees carried one 'for emergencies'. Supervisors and inspectors knew of the practice and would turn a 'blind eye' as long as it was not used too frequently. By allowing specific infringements of the rules a balance of power was maintained which allowed for acceptable outcomes for all parties through tolerance of this *focused deviancy*.

Many groups are influential in the general milieu of organizational life. Interest groups such as trade unions, government and environmental groups have the potential to influence management. The gathering of information about the various interest groups that might impact on operational or business activity is becoming an issue of priority for managers. In a television documentary (BBC 2, 1994) it was reported that during the 1985 British miners' strike the government and coal industry managers employed *agents* to collect a wide range of information in relation to the underlying views of employees from the various trade union areas. This resulted in management and government initiatives to encourage the formation of groups that were prepared to go through the picket lines and work normally.

The models of Belbin and Margerison and McCann could provide managers with the ability to *design* teams through the selection and training of individuals. Naturally, such a process could not offer a guarantee that individuals will perform in totally predictable ways. That is why the Margerison and McCann model is specifically intended to be used for development purposes only and not as part of the recruitment or selection process. However, it could allow organizations to review the balance of individual preferences needed or available in particular team contexts, perhaps improving the probability of success (as defined by management) through balance between preferences. It is also likely (assuming that the underlying theory is valid) that such groups will produce a more satisfying experience for the individuals. In some ways this can be described as a form of *social engineering*, control of group activity and hence corporate results achieved through indirect means. This should be compared with a random *natural selection* in group membership (within the normal constraints of how group membership is designated) that would allow individuals to apply themselves to the random dynamic of situations that they experience. All management decision making is *manipulative* in that it seeks to influence events and behaviour in pursuit of particular objectives. So perhaps attempts to make groups more effective through the application of the models available should be described as a form of *subtle manipulation*, in principle no different from any other form of management.

Training is an attempt by managers to *shape* the behaviour and attitudes of employees in appropriate ways. Appropriate, that is, as defined by managers. Such an approach attempts to *infuse* a management-determined perspective and value set throughout the organization. Group working as a means of continuing to reinforce that perspective is a useful means of providing follow-up and *reinforcement* of the original *socialization*. The *institutionalization* of inter-group and intra-group ways of working and interacting can provide an effective means by which corporate *standards* can be continually reinforced. The term *esprit de corps* takes on a new depth of meaning when considered in this light. Initiatives such as the introduction of total quality management (TQM) and customer-focused group working depend for their success to a significant degree on the individual groups accepting delegated responsibility to act with minimal control and direction from above. In other words, the groups must act in a form of *loco parentis* on behalf of management and so have absorbed the management perspective.

However, there is always another side of the coin to consider. Recall the earlier discussion in relation to cohesion within groups. If a particular group (or groups) develop very strong levels of cohesion and they do not support the management agenda then this could present major difficulties. Management in Action 6.5 describes one such situation. When management set out to introduce widespread use of customer-focused group working (for example) within an organization they are undertaking a process that will fundamentally change the balance of power and require management to engage in behaviours that actively create and maintain employee support. The old adage of divide and rule becomes much less sustainable in an organization dependent on groups with delegated power.

In order to achieve the objectives of an organization, two main conditions are necessary:

✦ There must exist appropriate subgroupings. This includes the use of groups designed to meet the operational needs of the business and those necessary to ensure co-ordination of resources in pursuit of the common objective.

✦ Within individual groups there needs to be appropriate mechanisms to meet the purposes set for them. This includes the provision of an appropriate composition for the group and also the control of the dynamics of how it will operate in order to achieve its objectives.

The informal groups within an organization should not be hostile to the intentions of management if success is to be achieved. If there is hostility towards the objectives being sought by management, it is unlikely that they will be achieved. Even if they are achieved it will not be done easily, effectively or efficiently. Consequently, the ability of a manager to put together a team of people who are likely to produce the best outcome for both the organization and the individual is equally as important as ensuring that the interactive processes between groups function in a positive way. However, there remains a fundamental difficulty for managers in seeking to control or influence the informal groups that exist in any organization. Any direct attempt to influence such groups would be strongly resisted, yet they cannot be ignored (as they are on any organizational chart). In many ways such groups emerge as a reaction to the imposed groupings forced upon employees by managers and so deliberately resist any attempts to direct or control them. They can also be supportive of management in certain conditions.

Group dynamics and effectiveness: an applied perspective

In the previous chapter it was suggested that groups are in an almost constant state of flux as people leave and join, new groups are formed and the objectives for existing groups are subject to change. This affects the way in which groups operate as well as the processes through which they go in undertaking their allotted tasks. Because of the significance of groups within an organization managers need to develop the ability to make effective use of groups. This includes an understanding of how groups function and the process of achieving the desired level and form of outcome from group activity. The failure to understand these issues or make effective use of them in managing group activity is likely adversely to influence the outcome.

The influences arising from the dynamic nature of the environment create a situation for organizations in which both *uncertainty* and *risk* are high. For example, employees may have accepted a wage rise below the rate of inflation for the past five years on the basis that it helped to preserve jobs within the company. However, that is no guarantee that they will agree to do so in future. Circumstances change and the range of influences acting upon the situation and individuals involved may well create a shift in collective attitude. Consider the links providing a basis for interaction and influence between the networked groups illustrated in Figure 6.13 in this context. So although groups can be used to collectivize things and so reduce uncertainty and risk, they do not eliminate it. Equally, as a result of issues such as *cohesion*, *risky shift* and *groupthink* they can introduce other forms and levels of risk into a situation.

Because of the risk and uncertainty that remain for an organization from the application of group activity it is tempting to suggest that surplus capability is required within a group in order to be able to deal with crises. For example, members of a group may be unexpectedly taken ill or new developments may come to light which make the task of the group more difficult or complex. In other words, on average any group should be operating at a sub-optimal level. Indeed in an interview with Tyler (1999) Luttwak (a leading consultant) argues that a little inefficiency is inevitable and to be welcomed within organizations as part of the human experience. The surplus capability available at times could be used to absorb some of the variety from the environment. However, this runs counter to much of the received wisdom on organizational efficiency, in which the pressure is to minimize. In practice, the approach to this issue depends very much on the purpose for which the group was established and the nature of its operations. In a formal organizational group (say a department) there is frequently a structural means of limiting the dangers from risk. For example, a manager may appoint a deputy to act in his/her absence, thereby minimizing the potential of the department grinding to a halt if the manager is away for any length of time. Groups will make different provision for the need to deal with uncertainty and risk, depending upon the perceived risk and its possible consequences.

Groups can be used by individuals towards their own ends. Management is a *political* process as well as being a decision-making one. The achievement of objectives through competitive forces is a necessary feature of organizational life. For example, no company has unlimited supplies of money for expansion and other projects. The allocation of funds to those activities that can provide the best return is more of an art than a science. There are a number of quantitative techniques that exist to make the decision easier, but each requires the inclusion of assumptions about the financial returns possible, future interest rates etc. The competitive nature of the process of selecting the 'best' activity for investment means that all participants have a vested interest in attempting to make their project the most attractive. This process can colour the way that groups function in decision making, presentational, interactive and political terms, while preparing and presenting such cases.

If groups are a key aspect of organizational life then management has a duty to ensure that they perform well, just as there is a responsibility to ensure that other resources are effectively utilized. From that point of view, how groups take decisions, interact and the roles that individuals adopt for themselves are all important issues. The models provided by Belbin and Margerison and McCann seek to assist significantly with this process. A more recent development in seeking to gain effective team results is the creation of the *virtual team*. The use of technology in communicating across time and space, supported by team

MANAGEMENT IN ACTION 6.8

How incentives can drive teamwork

Having invested heavily in new technology during the 1980s senior management of AA Roadside Services wanted to retain the essential people focus of the business. For example, ten layers of management were reduced to four and the 5500 staff (including patrol staff, emergency operators and fleet maintenance staff) were reorganized into 250 teams of between 20 and 30 staff, each led by a team leader. There was considerable emphasis on team-building activities at all levels in the new structure. Other initiatives introduced included a total quality action programme intended to empower the teams in changing the business and improving customer service.

There were a number of incentive schemes in existence prior to the introduction of teamwork. One paid a bonus to staff within a geographic area based upon the achievement of lower monthly expenditure compared to the budget. While this type of scheme is comparatively easy to run, it encourages people not to do things (spend money), rather than actually doing something positive (provide good customer service). Clearly this form of incentive was not in sympathy with the ethos of the teamwork-based organization.

In seeking to identify a new approach more in keeping with the team concept a staff survey was undertaken, which indicated, among other things, that staff valued recognition as much as money. A specialist consultancy, Integra Business Solutions, was brought in to assist with the design of new incentive arrangements. The scheme designed was given the title 'Teamwork Pays'. There are two main components in the scheme. The first is business performance related. This produces a sliding scale of incentive payment

depending upon improvement in business performance. The second element is related to the achievement of local operational performance by each team. To encourage effort at a local level the 350 teams are split into 18 leagues and so each team is effectively in competition with about 20 others. The rewards for this incentive element provide recognition for the achievement of the winning team and involve prizes given out at award ceremonies.

For both of the incentive elements there are sub-factors that measure contribution. For example, business performance is measured by a combination of quality and financial targets. About 2500 pieces of information have to be supplied each month to the consultancy administering the scheme on behalf of AA Roadside Services. This is needed to provide feedback to the teams and management on performance achieved, and so on, as well as the calculation of bonus and league tables. The scheme is being supported by an expenditure of approximately £3m per year on direct rewards. The key factor in the design of the incentive scheme was to find a way of reinforcing the teamwork operating culture and AA Roadside Services feel that they have achieved that. Changes to the management performance-related pay scheme have also been introduced to reinforce at a senior level the 'Teamwork Pays' approach.

Adapted from: Pickard, J (1993) How incentives can drive teamwork, *Personnel Management*, September, pp 26–32.

membership without the need to be physically present in the same room defines the *virtual team*. Young (1998) demonstrates how several organizations have gained advantage from the application of these ideas. The key feature of the virtual team for Young is the ability to use technology to create and support collaboration at a distance.

That organizations perceive an operational advantage from the application of teamwork should be obvious. The difficulty facing managers is how to ensure that they can realize the potential. Within the complex web of organizational activity it is all too easy to create a situation where forces are acting in opposition to each other. One common example is the encouragement of teamwork in operational activity, but reward being determined by individual effort, the pressure on individuals being to maximize individual results in order to optimize their earnings levels. Management in Action 6.8 is an example where this danger was recognized and management attempted to align the various components involved in support of the teamworking objectives.

Stop | Consider	*With some 2500 pieces of information being used to calculate performance is it likely that individuals will be able to impact on performance in overall terms?*

With some 2500 pieces of information being used to calculate performance is it likely that individuals will be able to impact on performance in overall terms?

*   One argument against team-based incentives is that it encourages the 'convoy' effect in that individuals can sit back and let everyone else in the team work hard and earn the bonus. This inevitably leads to resentment and a slowing down of individual contribution, because ultimately a convoy of ships (people in this case) can only move at the speed of the slowest. How would you seek to prevent such effects in the scheme outlined in MiA 6.8?*

Conclusions

In this and the previous chapter we have considered how it is that groups set about structuring themselves; how they function and take decisions. The groups that are relevant to an organization are many and varied, both internally and externally. It is in making effective use of the ideas contained within these chapters that management can attempt to ensure that internal effectiveness is enhanced and external threats from even more effective groups minimized. It is also a means through which some of the social needs of individuals can be provided for within a work setting.

Groups, both formal and informal, are an important part of organizational life. Informal groups within organizations present a particular challenge for managers as they are essential, unavoidable and largely unmanageable. They represent the grease on the wheels of the formal organization as people help, or hinder, each other in practice and frequently outside the formal organization frameworks. As the pressure on managers to produce ever higher rates of return from ever fewer resources increases, the significance of achieving a form of self-management within the organization becomes apparent. Group working and the more effective use of groups generally represent ways of seeking to achieve this objective. In this chapter we have introduced some of the main issues surrounding the ways in which groups operate and achieve success. As managers seek to improve the performance of their organizations the levels of effectiveness of the groups within them becomes a more critical factor.

Discussion questions

1. Define the following key terms used in this chapter:

Groupthink	*Belbin's team roles*	*Team Management Wheel*
Risky shift	*Communication patterns*	*Hoffman's model*
Group dynamics	*Group cohesion*	*Milgram's experiment*
Virtual team		

2. What is a sociogram? How might you use it as a means of analyzing group interactions and the dynamics between individual members?

3. Explain in your own words the team roles described by Belbin along with their significance in group activity.

4. Describe the different patterns of communication that might be found in groups and suggest how each might influence subsequent decision making by the group.

5. Define in your own words the team management role preferences described by Margerison and McCann and their significance in group activity.

6. Much has been made of the existence of informal groups within an organization. As a manager how might you seek to understand the informal groups that exist within your organization and to what extent might you seek to manage or influence them?

7. What are the factors that might be used by managers to influence and control the behaviour found in organizational groups? How successful would you expect such mechanisms to be and why?

8. What is group cohesiveness? How does it relate to group conformity?

9. In your own words distinguish between the features of effective and ineffective groups as described by McGregor in Table 6.2.

10. What determines the dynamics within a group?

11. Figure 6.13 describes a hierarchy of group interrelationships. Describe such a hierarchy for a tutorial group to which you belong.

12. Explore the reasons why managers should be concerned with member satisfaction as a feature of group outcome.

Research activities

1. Prepare a 5-minute presentation on the advantages and benefits to be gained from using the Margerison and McCann Team Management Wheel to develop more effective study and tutorial groups within your university or college. Your presentation should include consideration of the process that would need to be undertaken in adopting and using the model as well as why it might be an improvement over the present arrangements for organizing study groups and tutorials.

2. In an earlier section, the ideas of McGregor in the area of group effectiveness were introduced to you. These were summarized in Table 6.2 and it was suggested that this could form the basis of profiling the operation of a group.

This activity requires you to draw up a profiling chart from Table 6.2, using a scale of 1–5 between the extreme points. Identify a group of which you are a member and carry out an analysis using the sheet that you have designed. As this could be a sensitive activity, it would be best advised to carry this activity out on your tutorial group. Having drawn up the profile of the group in question, what are your conclusions regarding the level of effectiveness suggested by the profile as compared to your intuitions? What do other team members feel about your analysis? Is it similar to theirs? What would you suggest as ways to improve the effectiveness of the group studied?

3.   For a group of which you are a member, draw a sociogram. What conclusions can you draw from this about how that group operates, the decision-making process and the general level of effectiveness? How would you recommend that the group improved its level of effectiveness?

Key reading

From Clark, H, Chandler, J and Barry, J (1994) *Organization and Identities: Text and Readings in Organizational Behaviour*, International Thomson Business Press, London:

◆   Milgram, S: Conformity and independence, p 132. An extract from the classic studies of group pressure on member decision making.

◆   Kanter, KM: Men and women of the corporation, p 152. Considers the ways in which male-dominated organizations function in attempting to maintain a consistent approach to dealing with women.

◆   Oakley, A: Myths of woman's place, p 169. Introduces a perspective on how men retain the dominant position within organizations.

◆   Dex, S: The sexual division of work, p 177. This article looks at the division of work and its ability to retain the dominant position of the male 'group'.

◆   Cockburn, C: Male dominance and technological change, p 197. Introducing an employee and trade union perspective on the gendered aspects of organization.

◆   Perkin, H: The rise of professional society: England since 1880, p 204. This extract introduces a class-based perspective on how the professions have been able to influence events over the past 100 years.

◆   Illich, I: Disabling professions, p 207. This piece describes some of the negative implications of allowing some groups to become overly dominant.

◆   Mayo, E: The work group and 'positive mental attitudes', p 237. An extract from the classical Hawthorne Studies.

◆   Roethlisberger, FJ and Dickson, WJ: Group restriction of output, p 247. Similarly an indication of what the researchers from the Hawthorne Studies wrote about their work.

◆   Coch, L and French, JRP: Overcoming resistance to change using group methods, p 260. This piece reviews how change can be achieved through an emphasis on group problem-solving approaches.

◆   Janis, IL: Groupthink and poor quality decision making, p 279. An extract from this classic review of group influence on decision making.

◆   Needham, P: The 'autonomous' work group, p 310. A perspective on group work in an organizational setting.

◆   Hyman, R: The power of collective action, p 322. The power of the various groups to influence events is crucial to an understanding of how industrial action achieves its purpose and Hyman reviews this.

Further reading

Adair, J. (1983) *Effective Leadership*, Pan Books, London. Reviews group activities from a leadership perspective. It clearly indicates the inter-relatedness of many aspects of group activity.

Cartwright, D and Zander, A (1968) *Group Dynamics: Theory and Research*, 3rd edn, Tavistock, London. Although quite old now, this is a research-based text which gives an insight into how these issues can be studied.

Gregory, M (1994) *Dirty Tricks: British Airways' Secret War Against Virgin Atlantic*, Little, Brown, London. An interesting review of some of the main features of the campaign of BA against Virgin. It shows how the perception of the activities of groups can form a basis for future action. It also highlights how 'lobbying' can be used to influence decision making in groups.

Hackman, JR and Walton, RE (1986) Leading Groups in Organizations. In Goodman, PS (ed.) *Designing Effective Work Groups*, Jossey-Bass, San Francisco, CA. Part of a larger text (all of which has something to offer) this work considers the group and contextual issues that influence activity.

Shaw, ME (1976) *Group Dynamics*, McGraw-Hill, New York. Covers a number of issues relevant to how groups function and behave in the collective activities.

Zander, A (1983) *Making Groups Effective*, Jossey-Bass, San Francisco, CA. A good review of the subject and related topics.

References

Alvesson, M and Willmott, H (1996) *Making Sense of Management: A Critical Introduction*, Sage, London.

Asch, SE (1951) Effects of Group Pressure upon the Modification and Distortion of Judgements. In Guetzkow, H, (ed.) *Groups, Leadership and Men*, Carnegie Press, New York.

Bales, RF (1958) Task Roles and Social Roles in Problem Solving Groups. In Maccoby, EE, Newcomb, M and Hartley, EL (eds) *Readings in Social Psychology*, 3rd edn, Holt, Rinehart & Winston, New York.

Baron, RA and Greenberg, J (1990) *Behaviour in Organizations*, 3rd edn, Allyn & Bacon, London.

Bavelas, A (1948) A mathematical model for group structures, *Applied Anthropology*, 7, 19–30.

BBC Television (BBC 2) (1994) Close up north, 10 March.

Belbin, M (1981) *Management Teams: Why they Succeed or Fail*, Butterworth-Heinemann, Oxford.

Belbin, M (1993) *Team Roles At Work*, Butterworth-Heinemann, Oxford.

Bensman, J and Gerver, I (1973) Crime and Punishment in the Factory: The Function of Deviancy in Maintaining a Social System. In McQueen, DR (ed.) *Understanding Sociology Through Research*, Addison-Wesley, Reading, MA.

Berkowitz, L (1954) Group standards, cohesiveness and productivity, *Human Relations*, 7, 4, 509–19.

Bion, WR (1961) *Experiences in Groups*, Tavistock, London.

Bray, R (2000) Travel update, *Financial Times*, London, 1 May, p 12.

Gillespie, R (1991) *Manufacturing Knowledge: A History of the Hawthorne Experiments*, Cambridge University Press, Cambridge.

Hodgetts, R M (1991) *Organisational Behaviour: Theory and Practice*, Macmillan, New York.

Hoffman, LR (1979) Applying experimental research on group problem solving to organizations, *Journal of Applied Behavioural Science*, 15, 375–91.

Janis, IL (1982) *Victims of Groupthink: A Psychological Study of Foreign Policy Decisions and Fiascos*, 2nd edn, Houghton Mifflin, Boston, MA.

Keller, R T (1986) Predictors of the performance of project groups in research and development organisations, *Academy of Management Review*, 11, 4, 715–26.

Kogan, N and Wallach, MA (1967) Risk taking as a function of the situation, person and the group. In Newcombe, TM (ed.) *New Directions in Psychology*, Vol III, Holt, Rinehart & Winston, New York, pp 111–278.

Kretch, D, Crutchfield, RS and Ballachey, EL (1962) *The Individual in Society*, McGraw-Hill, New York.

Leavitt, HJ (1978) *Managerial Psychology*, 4th edn, University of Chicago Press, Chicago, IL

Lewin, K (1958) Group decision and social change. In Maccoby, EE, Newcombe, M and Hartley, EL (eds) *Readings in Social Psychology*, 3rd edn, Holt, Rinehart & Winston, New York.

Margerison, C and McCann, D (1990) *Team Management: Practical New Approaches*, Mercury Books, London.

Maslow, AH (1966) *The Psychology of Science: A Renaissance.* Harper & Row, New York.

McGregor, D (1960) *The Human Side of Enterprise*, McGraw-Hill, New York.

Milgram, S (1974) *Obedience to Authority*, Tavistock, London.

Moreno, JL (1953) *Who Shall Survive?*, Beacon House, London.

Moscovici, S and Zavalloni, M (1969) The group as a polariser of attitudes, *Journal of Personality and Social Psychology*, **12**, 125–35.

Nordhoy, F (1962) Group interaction and decision making under risk. Unpublished Master's thesis, School of Industrial Management, MIT, Cambridge, MA.

Perrin, S and Spencer, C (1981) Independence or conformity in the Asch experiment as a reflection of cultural and situational factors, *British Journal of Social Psychology*, **20**, 205–9.

Piper, WE, Marrache, M, Lacroix, R, Richardson, AM and Jones, BD (1983) Cohesion as a basic bond in groups, *Human Relations*, **26**, 2, 93–108.

Shaw, ME (1978) Communication networks fourteen years later. In Berkowitz, L (ed.) *Group Processes*, Academic Press, New York.

Shaw, M (1981) *Group Dynamics: The Psychology of Small Group Behaviour*, McGraw-Hill, New York.

Sherif, M (1936) *The Psychology of Social Norms*, Harper, New York.

Stoner, JAF (1961) A Comparison of Individual and Group Decisions Involving Risk. Quoted in Brown, R (1965) *Social Psychology*, The Free Press, New York.

Strachey, J (ed.) (1953–66) *The Complete Psychological Works of Sigmund Freud*, Vol I–XXIV, Hogarth Press, London.

Thompson, P and McHugh, D (1990) *Work Organization: A Critical Introduction*, Macmillan, Basingstoke.

Tuckman, B and Jensen, N (1977) Stages of small group development revisited, *Group and Organizational Studies*, 2, 419–27.

Tyler, C (1999) Why a little inefficiency does you good, *Financial Times*, Weekend, July 17/18, p vii.

Whyte, WH (1956) *The Organization Man*, Simon & Schuster, New York.

Wilkinson, A (1993) Managing Human Resources for Quality. In Dale, BG (ed.) *Managing Quality*, 2nd edn, Prentice Hall, Hemel Hempstead.

Young, R (1998) The wide-awake club, *People Management*, 5 February, pp 46–9.

PART IV

Work design and technology

CHAPTER 7

Work design and organization

CHAPTER SUMMARY

This chapter introduces a number of perspectives and approaches to the design of work within an organization. The range of tasks to be performed as part of the organization's activities must (taking a management stance) be combined into jobs in such a way as to minimize cost and maximize productivity. At the same time the design adopted should ensure that the individuals employed have something meaningful to contribute and should encourage a feeling of committed to the organizational objectives. Failure to recognize these aspects in the organization of work inevitably leads to employees feeling alienated and so withdrawing from effective engagement with the employer's objectives. The forces impacting on the organization of work will be reviewed in this chapter as will the ways in which working patterns and practices can contribute to the value of work for both employees and managers.

LEARNING OBJECTIVES

After studying this chapter and working through the associated Management in Action panels, Discussion questions and Research activities, you should be able to:

✦ Understand the nature of job design as it impacts on organizational structure and employee perception of the value of work.

✦ Describe the main approaches to the design of work within an organizational setting.

✦ Explain how work study attempts to influence job design activities and how changing the design of jobs can be a difficult process.

✦ Outline the interrelationship between technology and work organization.

✦ Assess the contribution of the quality of working life movement and the use of quality circles as an influence on work organization.

✦ Appreciate how issues such as flexibility and the pattern of work activity can influence the design of the jobs to be done within an organization.

✦ Detail the Fordist and post-Fordist approaches to work organization.

✦ Discuss how the use of groups within organizations can influence the design of the jobs that people undertake.

Introduction

It is inevitable that the structural framework of an organization will determine to a significant degree the types of jobs that exist within it. The configuration of activity into personnel, finance, marketing and production departments determines the broad area of specialism in the work to be performed. However, the structure of an organization does not of itself fully prescribe the nature of jobs that will be created within it. For example, within a personnel department it would be possible to arrange for the work to be undertaken by generalists (individuals being involved with all personnel activity) or to split activity into a range of specialist groups (a recruitment team, an industrial relations team etc.). Also issues such as technology, culture and the pattern of work activity could all be expected to have an impact on the ways in which work is actually organized within any particular context.

The design of jobs is frequently based on what has always existed in that situation, the traditional work arrangements simply being perpetuated. However, increasingly the formal design of jobs is being seen as a means of improving levels of employee motivation, quality and commitment to the objectives of the organization. This chapter brings together much of the work and thinking around these ideas in a review of how work is organized, together with the influences active in the process and the possible consequences from the choices made.

The nature of a job

It may seem obvious what a job is. People hold jobs, careers are made up of jobs and jobs form the basis of many stories on television, in films and in books. It is widely understood what the job of a police officer or doctor involves. However, not all police officers do the same job, some specialize in traffic duties, others in the detection of crime, while others patrol the streets or manage the service. In short, there are many different forms of police officer job. In much of the academic literature there is discussion of *management* as a job (a discrete set of activities) without any real recognition that there are many different types and levels of management job. For example, the job of an engineering manager is different in many respects from the job of an accounting manager. Equally, the job of a first-level production manager is completely different from the job of the chief executive.

Add to this the opportunity for individuals to adapt jobs to their own preferences and jobs can become unique, even if they are performed by many people. For example, Roy (1960) identified the use of informal breaks and playing 'games' with fruit as a means of coping with the high level of monotony in the production tasks within a particular factory. Through these informal practices employees maintained some influence over their work activities and were therefore able to reduce the level of boredom and monotony. It has even been suggested that the concept of work as we know it is a relatively new one. Management in Action 7.1 reflects the views of Professor Alain Cotta on this.

| Stop | Consider |

To what extent (and why) do you agree with Cotta's view that three groups of people (or classes) will emerge based on their relationship to work?

If you disagree with his analysis, to what extent and how (and why) do you consider that the nature of work in society is changing over time?

MANAGEMENT IN ACTION 7.1

Why not simply stop working?

Professor Alain Cotta from the Dauphine University in Paris argues that the idea of work being an edifying pastime carrying social status is only about 200 years old. Before the Industrial Revolution only people with no other option worked. The more an individual worked, the lower their social status. The Industrial Revolution changed the social standing of work and introduced a meritocracy based upon work having moral value. The change in the perception of work created a situation in which people became part of a new type of 'machine state'. Order was achieved through the direction and control of the work process by the new hierarchy.

Cotta builds on the ideas of Elias Canetti, a Nobel Prize winner who predicted that the machine would replace muscle. Cotta refers to this as the 'neuron prosthesis'. It is based on the reality that:

> More than half of the people are now employed in sectors where they create, release, transfer, receive and utilize information. The crossing of the frontier between muscle and neuron may have as many consequences as the rise of industry.
>
> People are now looking forward to filling their time instead of producing. Man is trying to free himself from the original painful constraints of work.

Cotta points out that arguments against work today tend to focus not so much on the duration, but on the subordination of individuals to orders. However, as Donkin points out, delayering and

empowerment over the past few years have in practice had a major impact on management in that the middle ranks see themselves as having been emasculated and the influence of the senior levels as having been challenged.

Cotta describes the emergence of three groups within society, differentiated by their relations with work:

✦ Middle class. Defined as those for whom work remains to be endured as their only way to make a living.

✦ Excluded from work. Excluded as a result of the ever rising skills needed. Also includes those individuals who have retired, have a private income or voluntarily absent themselves.

✦ Those who choose to work. They include the professions and other forms of work that an individual opts into without the need to.

Cotta does not have a category for the traditional working class. Equally, he asks whether progress will create extremes in the approach to work, exclusion and predilection. The pressure on the middle class as their need to work is challenged by technology might well be simply to give up work and opt out. The alternatives being: 'The sentence to death of work or the assertion that it can be the reason for living.'

Adapted from: Donkin, R (1994) Why not simply stop working?, *Financial Times*, 16 November, p 14.

It is now appropriate to consider what defines a job in general terms. A *job* can be considered to be a collection of tasks brought together as a practical *chunk* of activity for people to undertake. The work of an organization has to be broken down into the tasks to be achieved, which then have to be grouped together and allocated to an appropriate number of people in a set of arrangements referred to as jobs. There is nothing sacrosanct about a job; it is a social construction created and adapted by people, for people. However, within an organization the beneficiary is management, not necessarily the job holder as it is managers who design the jobs to be done. Therefore the designs of jobs serve particular interests.

While it is generally true that managers are the main beneficiaries of the particular job design adopted, there are examples where jobs have been designed for the benefit of the job holder. Examples include the professions such as the law and medicine. Traditionally, it has been argued by the bodies representing the interests of the professions that entry to these jobs should be carefully controlled in order to ensure the perpetuation of the superior status (and often income levels) associated with these areas of work. Such bodies have similar objectives to the trade unions which represent other classes of employee, but they are able to exercise effective levels of control over jobs through different means.

The design of jobs reflects a series of compromises in practice that create benefits and problems for both managers and employees. If a manager decides to create a new type of job within their organization (by grouping together the tasks to be done in a novel way) then it is unlikely that they will find an employee already having those skills and the company will be forced to train everyone. This will inevitably increase the cost of operations and will also make it more difficult to recruit new people quickly. It also means that the employer becomes vulnerable to problems if they do not ensure that they 'keep their employees happy'. Employees would not be easy to replace if they left. Alternatively, by using the same basis of job design as commonly found in society employers do not gain competitive advantage from the opportunity effectively to link work organization to the specific company situation. However, using standard jobs labour is more likely to be readily available, training costs would be reduced and an increased clarity of what everyone should be doing within the organization would exist.

From an employee's perspective both approaches to job design have advantages and disadvantages. Having skills that are widely used means that it becomes easier to find alternative work, but it is more likely that the jobs will be repetitive. A higher level of uniqueness in job skill, by way of contrast, might attract higher wages and provide more interesting work. However, such employees would be more vulnerable to competition from those prepared to accept lower pay for greater transferability of skill and hence a greater chance of work.

How do jobs vary? Jobs are usually described as varying in two dimensions, vertical and horizontal (see Figure 7.1).

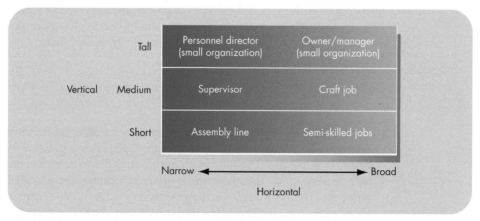

FIGURE 7.1   Job dimensions.

Taking each dimension of Figure 7.1 in turn:

✦ Vertical. This dimension reflects the *responsibility* incorporated into a job. For example, an assembly line job with no responsibility for checking work quality, completing production records and requisitions would contain very little *vertical responsibility*. Contrariwise, the job of an owner–manager in a small company incorporates considerable vertical loading as the person concerned would be involved at every level of the organization all of the time. One moment they may be helping to pack an order, the next they may be dealing with the bank concerning overdraft facilities.

✦ Horizontal. This dimension reflects the *breadth of activity* in a job. Jobs with a narrow range of tasks are limited in scope, highly routine and boring. Jobs with a broad range of tasks incorporated into them have *task variety* which can minimize levels of monotony and boredom. At the narrow end of the spectrum simple repetitive assembly line jobs would be found. At the other extreme would be a craft job, where a joiner, for example, may undertake the full range of tasks from the design through to the completed manufacture of a single piece of furniture.

A job is not something that is static and incapable of being manipulated by either management or the job holder. Jobs are *things* that can be consciously designed, providing managers with a vehicle through which they can control employees and harness *energy* in pursuit of their objectives. They are also something that provides employees with a basis for protecting a defined area of work, thereby gaining a degree of power in a defined context. Also day-to-day influence over work activity provides employees with an opportunity to relieve the boredom of control.

Management in Action 7.2 illustrates the benefits gained by both parties through the introduction of multiskilling. Multiskilling is an approach to designing work that involves the provision of additional skills to employees that would traditionally span a number of craft and semi-skilled areas. For example, production workers may be trained to undertake minor mechanical repairs to the machines used in their jobs, eliminating the need to call for the assistance of a trained maintenance employee on every occasion. Multiskilling is frequently claimed to reduce cost, increase job satisfaction, career development and increase productivity. In short to provide benefits to everyone.

| Stop | Consider |

MiA 7.2 outlines the nature of multiskilling in one company. How might the introduction of such an approach actually reduce cost and improve productivity as claimed in the panel?

How might those employees already with the higher levels of skill be expected to respond to multiskilling, as they might expect to see an encroachment by only partly trained workers into their field of work? How would you persuade such employees to accept multiskilling?

Work study, ergonomics and job analysis

Work study

In an attempt by managers better to understand the detailed work that individuals and groups undertake and to be able to arrange for jobs to be designed in the most efficient

MANAGEMENT IN ACTION 7.2

Clear benefits of multiskilling

Pilkington Glass employed some 1200 people in its two UK factories in 1991. The company specialized in making 'float glass', made by floating a ribbon of heated ingredients on a bed of molten tin to produce clear flat glass panels. Each week the two factories produced about 11,000 tonnes of glass on production lines half-a-mile long. The prospect looked bleak for the company due to a reduction in demand for its products and lower profit levels. The company determined to address its problems from three directions:

✦ Creating one business out of two sites. One of the factories was over 100 years old, the other 10 years old. Each ran as a separate business with separate accounting, management and administrative functions. This was rationalized into one business with two sites and so duplication was largely eliminated.

✦ Reducing the number of people employed. This was reduced from 1200 to about 900, with plans to further reduce to about 800 being in place.

✦ Introducing multiskilling for the remaining employees. As a consequence of the first two changes the need for people to tackle more than one job became very important.

During the 1980s Pilkington had introduced two classes of craft job, either mechanical or electrical. In 1991 this was taken further by incorporating all maintenance within one job. Individuals concentrated on a few skill areas, but they were expected to demonstrate a reasonable ability to deal with any craft area. In the administrative areas these same principles have been introduced, with staff being expected to deal with all areas of clerical work from personnel to finance.

Clearly, training was necessary to ensure that all employees had the necessary skills to be able to undertake their new responsibilities. A training programme was developed by Glyn Davies, production services manager, and his training team that was linked to the NVQ national training structures. It was necessary to develop 1300 training modules in total to embrace all the needs of the staff. However, most staff needed only one module to provide them with the necessary skills. About 25% of employees needed two or three modules to equip them to do their new jobs.

The introduction of multiskilling was reinforced by a pay rise for accepting the new working practices. This was further reinforced by the payment of a higher wage when the full level of job flexibility was achieved. Employee reaction to the training process ranged from those who did not enjoy it, to those who found it beneficial and a contribution to improved job satisfaction. Supervisors were also trained as assessors and this improved the quality of supervision provided, according to Davies. The results of the multiskilling exercise also percolated into the output of the factories which doubled, with a higher yield of finished product from raw material.

Adapted from: Littlefield, D (1995) Clear benefits of multiskilling, *People Management*, 9 March, p 37.

way, the techniques that fall under the heading of *work study* have been developed over the years. *Work study* is commonly thought to have emerged through the work of FW Taylor in developing *scientific management* in the early years of the twentieth century. The search by Taylor for the *one best way* produced techniques used to analyze and define the work methods and pace of work that should be expected from employees. He encouraged the acceptance of and compliance with these requirements by employees through the payment of output-based bonuses. However, the study of work has a much longer tradition. For example, there is some evidence that medieval monks used job times to determine the duration of monastery- and cathedral-building projects. Currie (1963, p 2) also describes an extract from an employment contract in which an individual undertook secretly to time jobs in a factory and report the outcome to the owner:

> I Thomas Mason, this 22nd day of December, 1792 solemnly pledge myself to use my utmost caution at all times to prevent the knowledge transpiring that I am employed to use a stop watch to make observation of work done in Mr. Duesbry's manufactory; and to take such observations with the utmost truth and accuracy in my power and to give the results thereof faithfully to Mr. Duesbry.

It was Adam Smith (1776) who was first credited with coining the phrase *division of labour* in the context of the study of work. The term described the detailed job design used to increase the output of pins per person achieved by breaking up the overall task into specialized and smaller activities. This represents the essence of work study. The study of work activity in order to identify the component parts involved, then to critically evaluate them in order to identify the most efficient methods of work that could be used and subsequently determine the time to undertake these duties. Essentially, work study contains as its core activity two distinct elements: method study and work measurement. The contribution associated with each is reflected in Figure 7.2.

Taking each aspect in turn:

✦ Method study. There are a range of techniques that enable work methods to be described and analyzed in great detail. Essentially, the process requires the movement of both employee and material to be charted in such a way as to facilitate critical examination. In undertaking this systematic process a job is designed in terms of the tasks required of the employee being studied.

✦ Work measurement. The measurement of work is essentially based upon the use of timing techniques to identify how long particular tasks should take to perform. Having identified the time to undertake the allotted tasks the determination of levels of output as well as of numbers employees and work/rest periods would also be identified.

The extract from the employment contract just quoted provides some indication of

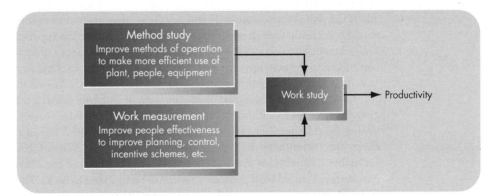

FIGURE 7.2   Work study (*adapted from*: Currie, RM (1963) *Work Study*, Pitman, London).

the secrecy with which work study activity had to be undertaken. It can be assumed from the tone of the document that employees in the late 1700s did not generally respond positively or with enthusiasm to having their jobs studied. By the time Taylor had developed his *scientific management* techniques at the turn of the twentieth century this had changed little, leading to the following criticisms of it being presented to a commission on industrial relations in the USA (Hoxie, 1915):

✦ That it formed the basis of a cunningly devised speeding-up and sweating system.

✦ That it furthered the trend towards task specialization.

✦ That it condemned the worker to monotonous and routine work activities.

✦ That it transferred to managers the traditional knowledge, skill and judgement of the workers.

✦ It emphasized quantity at the expense of quality.

✦ That it placed at management's disposal a wealth of information that could be used unscrupulously to the detriment of workers.

✦ That it allowed ever tighter control and discipline of worker activity, beyond a level at which this should be necessary.

The application of *work study* techniques to job design provides management with an opportunity to control not only the design of work but also its delivery. This is part of what Torrington and Hall (1992) identify as the disciplinary aspect of management. Management ensuring they are satisfied that the employee is delivering what is expected under the contract of employment. One way of achieving compliance is through the threat of sanction unless behaviour is appropriate. However, that relies upon negative reward – punishment for a failure to do that which is required. A more effective approach is to reward positive behaviours in which the delivery of appropriate behaviours gains the employee benefits – perhaps a bonus payment for increased output. This is what *scientific management* attempted to achieve. That it failed to do so was largely because of the negative reaction to being *spied* upon and *controlled* – as workers perceived it. This was often with some justification as such initiatives were frequently followed by job cuts, demands to work harder for less pay (or at least without a proportional increase) and a generally tighter control of work activity.

Discipline in the sense of control over behaviour is most effective if the underlying values are internalized by the individuals involved. If employees could be persuaded to adopt the same values, standards and norms as management then the job of management would become that much easier. Employees would require less supervision and would naturally function in ways that were supportive of management's objectives. They would be committed to the management and organizational objectives. That was what Taylor sought to achieve through *scientific management*, but he completely missed the point.

Compliance can be required, but *commitment* is an individual level response and in the gift of employees to withhold if they wish to do so. *Compliance* involves the employee following the rules precisely, for which they cannot be punished. But equally the rules cannot cover every eventually in precise detail, so failure (or systems breakdown) is almost inevitable. *Commitment* involves the employee going beyond the contract and doing what management would wish them to do without being asked to do so. The control system that can ensure that employees give full *commitment* against their will to an organization has not yet been developed. Torrington and Hall identify three levels of discipline active within an organization that reflects this progressive internalization of discipline, as indicated by Figure 7.3.

The lowest level of discipline within an organization is that imposed by management. This equates with the imposition of a particular job design and rule framework by management. The highest level of discipline is associated with self-discipline. If the internalized standards and norms coincide with those of management then the result would be to their advantage. This encourages managers to seek to align employee *frames of reference* to their own. There are approaches to job design that attempt to encourage employee involvement to achieve higher levels of *appropriate* internalization – appropriate to management that is. It has been argued that these *softer* approaches are little more than attempts to achieve the same objectives as *work study*, but to disguise the objective by providing for the achievement of control through an acceptable appearance and *socialization* processes.

Ergonomics

Ergonomics is frequently defined as the human–machine interface. It sets out to identify how the human being interacts with the work-based physical environment, particularly the equipment to be used in the jobs being studied. It then seeks to design the equipment in such a way as to have minimal impact on the people using it, thereby allowing maximal efficiency with minimal effort and stress being experienced by workers.

Ergonomics is one of a range of specialist areas including physical anthropology which specializes in seeking to develop anthropometric profiles of human beings. So, for example, it has been found in America that 25% of the population has an arm reach of less than 21 inches. Therefore 75% have a reach longer than 21 inches (Kennedy and Filler, 1966). Other specialist fields include work physiology and biomechanics both of which seek to understand the actual impact of work on the human body. For example, jobs which require considerable energy expenditure perhaps need more rest periods built into them or the design of specialized mechanical handling equipment to take away the strain on muscles and joints.

Job analysis

Job analysis is a systematic approach to the identification of the content of a job. It can be used to support a wide range of activities, including:

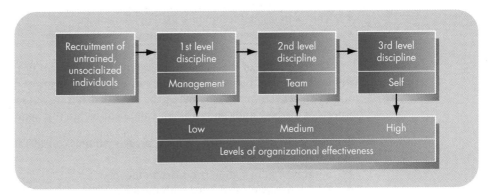

FIGURE 7.3   Organizational discipline (*adapted from*: Torrington, D and Hall, L (1993) *Personnel Management*, 2nd edn, Prentice Hall, Hemel Hempstead).

✦ Resourcing. A detailed knowledge of the jobs to be undertaken within the organization provides the basis for human resource planning in terms of the numbers employed, succession and career development. Knowing the skills being sought provides a means of being able to identify the most suitable candidates. In a *downsizing* exercise it is essential (to management) to retain the most competent employees; a job analysis would enable the skills required to be identified and matched against the profile of existing employees.

✦ Training. Knowing the content of jobs allows the skills required to be matched against employee capability. This allows training plans to be developed to ensure that employees are competent to deliver the tasks expected of them.

✦ Career development. Knowing the jobs that people have done (and the content) allows career development paths to be identified. Career moves can be planned to provide additional experience and responsibility in order to ensure the appropriate development of senior staff.

✦ Payment. Job analysis provides the information required for the preparation of a *job description*. A job description is a document that sets out the duties and other requirements associated with a job. These can then be used to determine the relative magnitude of jobs through a *job evaluation scheme*. The rank order (or scale) of jobs produced through job evaluation in turn can form the basis of a pay structure.

✦ Performance evaluation. Knowing the tasks that are to be performed by an employee provides a basis for understanding how much work should be produced by an *average* worker. Both of these pieces of information are necessary to determine the performance of an individual employee.

✦ Equality. The systematic analysis of a job provides a basis for decision making about jobs and people that is not dependent on gender, race or any other irrelevant criteria. One definition of equality is inappropriate decision making and this is much easier to perpetuate and justify without clear information. *Job analysis* forces attention onto the tasks and activity involved in a job, rather than who undertakes the work.

There are two main approaches to job analysis according to Ivancevich (1992):

✦ Functional job analysis. This approach requires consideration of four aspects of the work:
   ✦ Employee activities relevant to data, people and other jobs.
   ✦ The methods and techniques used by the worker.
   ✦ The machines, tools and equipment used by the worker.
   ✦ What outputs are produced by the worker.
   The first three of these categories require an assessment of the tasks undertaken within the job and how they are achieved. The fourth involves the type and level of output expected from the employee to be identified. It is easy to see the two *work study* aspects of method study and work measurement within this approach to job analysis.

✦ Position analysis questionnaire. This approach requires consideration of six aspects of the work:
   ✦ Sources of information necessary to the job.
   ✦ Decision making associated with the job activity.
   ✦ Physical aspects associated with the job.
   ✦ Interpersonal and communication necessary to the job.

✦ Working conditions and their impact on the job.
✦ Impact of work schedules, responsibility etc.

In addition to issues surrounding the work to be done, the position analysis question-naire incorporates an assessment of the people dimension of the work.

Job analysis plays a significant part in the identification of what tasks should be con-tained within a job. It is, however, only one part of the process. Figure 7.4 reflects the nature of work as a function of both organizational and individual factors.

Although Figure 7.4 is largely self-explanatory, two points are worth highlighting. First, *management intentions* are indicated as an influence on both job analysis and job design. This is intended to reflect the iterative nature of decision-making aspects of man-agement's involvement. For example the *job analysis* of an existing job may raise questions in relation to the design of a particular job that leads to a further round of job analysis and job design. Second, whatever the nature of a job as defined on paper, employees *perceive* and *interpret* the work expected of them and respond accordingly. This process is further *filtered* by such forces as motivation, training etc. For example, a workforce suffering from low levels of morale is unlikely to undertake the full range of expected duties with enthu-siasm or attention to detail. This will inevitably lead to inefficiencies somewhere in the operational system and problems for management.

Approaches to designing jobs

The tasks to be undertaken in an organization need to be combined into specific jobs that make sense for people to undertake. In most situations job design is about changing jobs that already exist. The design of totally new jobs (perhaps for opening a new factory or department) does exist but to a lesser extent than the redesign or change of existing ones. The reasons for job redesign can be many. For example, the adaptation of work to new equipment. It could also reflect an attempt to improve quality or productivity or as the

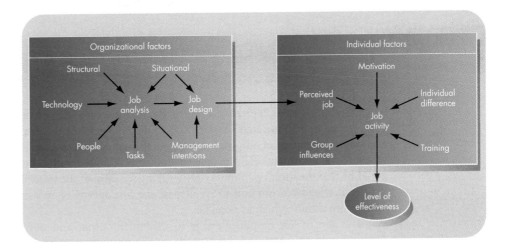

FIGURE 7.4 Job analysis and job effectiveness.

result of high labour turnover or other signs of employee dissatisfaction. It can also reflect the desire of management to cut cost by reallocating tasks (or sharing out the work to be done) in a different way. There are a number of standardized approaches to the ways in which jobs have been designed and these will be reviewed in the following sections.

Simplification and job engineering

Historically, jobs were based around whole activities and craft-based skill. Families would engage in furniture or clothes making or farming etc. With the introduction of the factory system this process began to be eroded as opportunities emerged for increasing the output per worker through the *division of labour* that could be applied to work carried out in factory environments. The application of the *division of labour* was observed by Babbage (1832) to reduce training times, increase skill through constant repetition of a small range of tasks and also reduce waste as a result of the higher skill level achieved. Fewer tool changes and machine set-ups were also required as a result of the *batch* nature of production and the specialized nature of equipment to support it.

It was FW Taylor who introduced the *scientific management* approach to job simplification. Taylor considered that methods of work and equipment should be carefully designed before employees were *scientifically* selected. This approach to job design is referred to as *job specialization*, *job engineering* or *job simplification*, job specialization because that was the work study aim. Job engineering introduced an engineering metaphor to the process – engineering the one best way of maximizing output and minimizing labour input. The application of scientific management to work produced considerably simplified jobs – hence the third title.

Job simplification involves combining a set of tasks into the smallest size to make an *efficient* contribution to the overall process. It is seen in many production jobs and assembly line processes. In assembly line approaches to production the workers stay in a fixed position and the item being made moves down the line until it is completed. The number of workstations and workers must be carefully balanced to provide an efficient assembly process with minimal idle time. The assembly of motor vehicles is the most obvious example of this process in action. Management in Action 7.3 provides an illustration of job simplification as applied to the slicing and packing of bacon.

| Stop | Consider | *In practice the process described in MiA 7.3 was not very efficient. It did not prove possible to balance the line effectively so that each workstation was fully occupied and each machine fully utilized. How might the jobs have been more effectively designed?* |

Using work measurement techniques the number of operators (and tasks) needed at each workstation illustrated in MiA 7.3 would be determined in order to produce the highest possible levels of output. In the bacon slicing case it is suggested in the diagram that a balanced line contains eight people (including one shared with other lines). However, it could be that the slicer operator is only working for 50% of the time. Under these circumstances it would be common to recalculate the line speeds or redesign the jobs to keep worker utilization as high as possible.

The aim of job simplification is to maximize output and minimize labour input. Consequently, this approach lends itself to the application of technology in seeking to match human activity to the needs of production. The difficulties associated with job

MANAGEMENT IN ACTION 7.3

Job simplification on a slicing line

The overall job involves the slicing and packing of bacon, including the following tasks:

+ A side of bacon needs to be cut into slices.

+ The slices need to be collected and stacked together in the pack quantity.

+ The individual stacks of bacon need to be placed into a packing machine.

+ The packing machine needs to be set up for the type of pack to be produced and needs to be operated during the packing process.

+ The packed bacon needs to be weighed, priced and labelled.

+ The packs need to be checked for presentation, label accuracy and quality.

+ Individual packs of bacon need to be put into cardboard boxes ready for cold storage and despatch to customers.

+ The cardboard boxes need to be labelled with the contents and customer details.

The layout below represents the work study approach to the work using a simplification approach.

The simplified tasks in this job involved:

1. Slicing. One person responsible for obtaining the bacon, setting and cleaning the slicing machine and pacing the slicing processes to keep the other workstations fully utilized.

2. Stacking. Four people working on either side of a conveyor belt splitting the cut bacon into stacks of the right quantity as it passes them by. The conveyor belt speed and rate of slicing pace the work for these operators.

3. Packing. One person responsible for setting the machine, placing individual stacks of bacon into it and generally ensuring a smooth operation. They would also monitor the quality of the packed product.

4. Pricing and boxing. One person responsible for setting the automatic weighing and pricing machine, boxing the packs of bacon, sealing and labelling the boxes, stacking the cartons on a pallet ready for transport to the cold store. This person would also monitor pack quality, rejecting faulty packs and stopping the line to reset the machine if necessary.

5. Transport. Someone else would remove loaded pallets and bring in empty ones as part of a similar job for other packing stations.

In addition to these direct production activities there would be a need to keep records of output and quality. Also to ensure that the whole process worked smoothly with individuals working as a team.

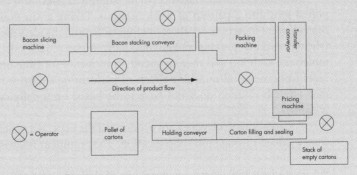

simplification were recognized very early. It can be argued that the founding of the human relations movement was a direct consequence of the dehumanizing effect of such work. As far back as 1952 Walker and Guest identified the type and level of dissatisfactions found among car factory assembly workers, including:

✦ Lack of control over the pace of work required by the management-determined speed of the assembly line.

✦ Repetitiveness (short cycles) of the work being undertaken.

✦ Low skill levels required to undertake the jobs on the line.

✦ Limited social interaction with fellow workers because of the physical spacing between workstations and pace of work required.

✦ No employee control over the tools used or the methods of work adopted on the line.

✦ No involvement in a total product, employees only ever see and work on part completed goods passing down the line.

This approach to job design is not restricted to work in factories. It can also be found in administrative jobs. For example, in accounting departments, someone has to open the post, sort the invoices from the payments and enter the details into a computer system. Such jobs bear all the classic symptoms of job simplification, including monotony, boredom, high labour turnover, alienation and lack of commitment. The same is true in education in which the job of teachers and lecturers is being ever more closely prescribed through national and local initiatives in schools and universities. This is usually justified in the name of providing quality and consistency in educational experience for students. However, in the process, the opportunity for the exercising of professional judgement and work determination at an individual level is increasingly minimized, just as it is for an assembly line worker in a factory.

Job rotation

Job rotation as an approach to work organization accepts that simplified jobs provide the most efficient methods of work. However, it also recognizes shortcomings that limit the opportunity to achieve the full potential. For example, the effects of boredom and monotony on employee commitment levels. The solution to this dilemma is for job designers to seek to limit the adverse effects of job simplification while retaining the benefits of specialization.

The simplest solution to this (so the argument goes) is to combine two (or more) simplified jobs into a pattern of work rotation. Taking as an example the jobs indicated in Management in Action 7.3, there are four different jobs identified in the bacon slicing team (slicing, stacking, packing and boxing). *Job rotation* requires that each person be trained to undertake each job and then to spend a proportion of time on each. This provides some relief from the mind-numbing effects of performing a narrow range of tasks all day, every day. The job rotation does not have to be based on a daily cycle, it could be weekly or monthly.

The rotation of jobs does not produce all the expected benefits and can reduce the efficiency gained through job simplification. The argument follows thus:

✦ Employees must learn a wider range of skills in order to undertake a broader range of tasks. This increases training time and the cost of labour. Also employees claim that their responsibilities and skills are higher than required to undertake a simplified job alone and so claim more pay.

+ With the reduced practice opportunity as a result of the rotation employees do not build up the same level of skill, speed or proficiency as when performing single, simplified jobs.

+ Rotation round a series of simplified jobs does not change the fact that the work is basically mundane, boring and monotonous.

Conversely, *job rotation* can provide a benefit through the ability of employees to take on a wider range of duties at short notice. This provides management with an increased degree of flexibility in labour utilization and an opportunity to cope with unforeseen situations.

Job enlargement

Job enlargement adopts a slightly different approach to job design in that it seeks to build up a job by adding more tasks into it to form a larger job. In effect it seeks to move a job along the *horizontal* axis in Figure 7.1 towards the *broad* end of the scale. It adds a wider *range* of similar duties into the enlarged job.

The potential advantages to be gained though job enlargement is that the perceived meaningfulness of the work is increased for the employee as a result of the broader range of tasks involved. It is argued that although productivity may not be as high on paper as for simplified jobs, overall it may be higher as employees are likely to be motivated and to have a higher interest in their work. In effect, the utilization of labour is likely to be higher and, consequently, output could also therefore be higher.

It is not always easy to introduce enlarged jobs into a factory as it requires a different approach to the pattern of interaction between machines and people to be adopted. As an approach this can conflict with the *purist* view of *work study* as to what should be happening at a task level of work. Work study attempts to eliminate or control activity considered to be irrelevant or unnecessary to the main purpose of the job. In many situations this is unrealistic, but it can be difficult to change the desire for close and tight control among managers. Hence the persistent drive to keep trying to apply the principles of work study. Imagine, for example, how you could enlarge the jobs described in Management in Action 7.3 without totally changing the layout of machines and processes.

Conant and Kilbridge (1965) provide an early description of the application of job enlargement to the assembly of water pumps in washing machines. The assembly of the pump had been done on a production line with each worker adding components as the pump body went past. After redesign the enlarged job allowed each worker to assemble the entire pump, but still on an assembly line with no loss of productivity. The major problem with enlargement as a design option is that it is frequently restricted to simple assembly line jobs, which even when enlarged remain relatively small jobs. Consequently, the benefits to employees quickly dissipate and the job becomes monotonous once again.

Job enrichment

Job enrichment requires that activity and responsibility be added to a job in a *vertical* direction (as defined in Figure 7.1). It is a process intended to integrate responsibility and control over the tasks performed by the employee. Herzberg (1968, 1974) identified six forms of enrichment that designers should seek to include in jobs:

+ Accountability. Provide a level of responsibility and support for employees that allows them to accept accountability for their actions and performance.

+ Achievement. Provide employees with an understanding and belief in the significance of their work.

+ Feedback. Superiors should provide feedback to employees on their performance and work activities.

+ Work pace. Employees should be able to exercise discretion over the pace of work that they adopt and be able to vary that pace.

+ Control over resources. Employees should have high levels of control over the resources needed to perform their duties.

+ Personal growth and development. Opportunities should be found to encourage employees to acquire and practice new skills and develop themselves through their work.

Another approach to *job enrichment* was developed by Hackman and Oldham (1980). They suggest that there are five core job dimensions, which in turn combine and produce psychological responses, which in turn produce work and personal outcomes (Figure 7.5). This they termed the *job characteristics model* of job enrichment.

Taking each of the core job dimensions in turn:

+ Skill variety. This element reflects the idea that a job should contain a wide range of different skill requirements. In addition, the job should contain a wide range of activities and require a broad range of talents from the employee. The broader the range of skill required the more significant the job will be to both the employee and employer.

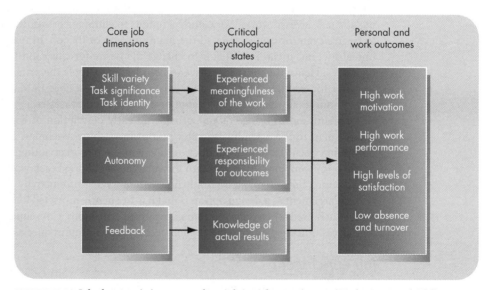

FIGURE 7.5 Job characteristics approach to job enrichment (*source*: Hackman, J and Oldham, R (1980) *Work Redesign*, Addison-Wesley, Reading, MA).

This is because it will have a longer training period and ensure that the individual is considered as a major contributor to the organization. Individuals vary in their need or ability to cope with skill variety and it is necessary to create balance in the degree provided and the employee's ability to cope. Too little variety will produce boring and monotonous work; too much will produce fragmented work activity with stress and uncertainty of output for the employee.

✦ Task identity. This element is about the degree of *wholeness* in a job. It reflects the degree to which the employee undertakes a complete job. If the employee only undertakes a small number of tasks on part of a whole product then they are unlikely to think about the finished article. Neither are they likely to think that they are engaged in a meaningful part of the operation.

✦ Task significance. The importance of the job being done is of significance to the employee. This aspect is usually reflected through the degree of impact on the lives or work of other people. Very few people would be satisfied with their job if it was felt to be of no consequence to anyone.

✦ Autonomy. This is a reflection of the degree of freedom that the individual has to schedule and adapt their work methods. A closely prescribed job – working on an assembly line – has very little scope for autonomy compared with the job of a sculptor, who has considerable freedom to choose subject, tools and the artistic interpretation of the subject. Autonomy provides the individual with responsibility for their actions thus providing a sense of *ownership*.

✦ Feedback. This allows an employee to know how well they are doing in the eyes of others; it also provides an indication of how effectively they fit into the organization. This can be achieved through a number of routes from making employees responsible for whole jobs to formalized meetings with managers to discuss performance etc. The purpose is to provide a learning opportunity for the individual in terms of performance, quality, integration and contribution.

The first three core job dimensions are linked together in Figure 7.5 because they lead to a feeling of relative *meaningfulness* in the job. Hackman and Oldham developed a means of being able to measure the level of job enrichment present in any job, the *motivating potential score* (MPS). This name recognizes the links between job enrichment and motivation as indicated in the model.

The score produced through the application of the MPS is essentially a subjective response by the job holder, based upon their ability to compare with other jobs that they have experienced. It is a useful, although not altogether objective measure. There is evidence of general empirical support for the MPS, although not strong support for the causal linkages suggested by it (Wall *et al.*, 1985).

Based on a social information-processing view of job design, Salancik and Pfeffer (1978) argue that the assumptions behind the *job characteristics* approach were open to question. Individuals have basic and stable needs that can be met through work and jobs display stable characteristics that people respond to in evaluating work. They argue that the process of evaluating the value of work for an individual is a more complex process than previously thought or recognized by the Hackman and Oldham model. It is a process based upon the social reality of work experience for the individual and as a consequence dependent upon a personal perspective of each individual. Management in Action 7.4 reflects some of the debate surrounding job enrichment in car production.

MANAGEMENT IN ACTION 7.4

Steering the middle road to car production

The early approach of FW Taylor to the design of jobs was heavily criticized. Experiments by both Volvo and Saab in Sweden in the 1970s to introduce teamworking (called long-cycle dock assembly) into car production have now been largely abandoned. More recently the introduction of 'lean production' methods by Japanese car manufacturers are also being criticized. So what should managers do as they seek to achieve higher productivity and quality levels and prices that can compete with the lowest cost producers in the industry?

Wickens argues for a middle way involving a synthesis of teamwork, flexibility, continuous improvement and ownership of change as the basis of high efficiency, high-quality work and jobs. All work contains two elements – prescribed and discretionary activities. The prescribed aspects of work are those over which the employee has no freedom of choice or action. They are activities that must be done in a specific way at a specific point in time, in a specific place. Discretionary aspects of work are those over which the employee has considerable freedom to choose how, when and where the jobs are done. A senior manager might have 95% of their time classified as discretionary, whereas an assembly line worker might only have 5% of the same category. Wickens argues that the challenge facing job design is to make the work experience as meaningful as possible for those who have only 5% of discretionary activities available to them.

The paradox of production described by Wickens is the need for top-down control of the production process at the same time as achieving commitment from the workforce. In his article he states:

> The mistake is to believe that the production system itself gives the results. What counts is the relationship of people with the process. A controlled Taylorist process need not alienate if the workers are able to contribute, and long-cycle dock assembly will not satisfy if that is all there is (nor will it last if it cannot compete). What we must aim for is lean, people centred volume production.
>
> The big challenge is the integration of new technology, new management practices and the people in the new flat organizations. No company has yet got it right. But if we are to have lean production, it must be managed by people who care about people. A synthesis between higher efficiency and higher quality of work and jobs is possible.

Adapted from: Wickens, P (1993) Steering the middle road to car production, *Personnel Management*, June, pp 34–8.

Stop | Consider   *Wickens argues that: 'A synthesis between higher efficiency and higher quality of work and jobs is possible.' How and to what extent might these ideas be applied to the bacon slicing operations described in MiA 7.3?*

Technology and work organization

Technology influences the organization of work through a number of routes. There is the technology used in the work itself. There are the administrative and procedural technologies that must be complied with. There are the social technologies that influence how people become integrated with the other technologies while undertaking their work. In addition, there is the impact of new technology on the range of products and services that can be provided, hence allowing the creation of new job and organizational arrangements. Management in Action 7.5 provides an insight into one aspect of this, namely the relationship between people and the advanced manufacturing technology increasingly appearing in factory operations.

Stop | Consider

Speculate on the future impact of technology on work organization. To what extent is it likely that technology can eliminate the need for most people to do jobs as we currently understand the term?

What are the arguments (for and against) that suggests that technology should be restricted if it begins to impact on the ability of society to maintain reasonably high levels of employment?

The four areas of impact of technology just indicated combine to produce the form that jobs and organizations take. For example:

✦ Equipment. This category includes the machines, tools and work methods required by the process itself. To extract ore from a deep mine requires tunnelling equipment, conveyor methods of removing the ore and crushing/filtering equipment to extract the minerals. It is not possible to operate a mine with the equipment required for building aircraft. There will however, be some common equipment in most organizations. For example, fork lift trucks exist in almost all organizations. In addition, the relative cost of labour is an influence on the technology that can be justified, as is the need for high volume, consistent quality and the business that the organization is in.

✦ Administrative. Every organization needs procedures to identify and control the operational processes and cost. Although there are legal and professional standards to follow in many accounting and employment fields, there is considerable freedom of choice in how these are implemented in practice. Developments such as *just in time* seek to eliminate much of this administrative process, substituting instead a needs-based *pull system* with flows activated according to a previous plan. Considerable savings in physical stock, time, space and money have been reported by such methods (see for example, Evans *et al.* (1990), pp 712–13, 715–19). Such approaches directly influence the design of jobs for the workers who administer and manage organizations as well as manual employees.

✦ Social. With the influences of these two forces indicated a considerable degree of the constraint in the design process is established. However, there are opportunities for influencing the actual design of jobs through the ways that people are *fitted in* around these constraints. Examples include the use of teamwork and job sharing. The history of the organization and the way that it has used its employees in the past influences both the choices available for the future and employee preferences. For example, employees who perceive a history of employer exploitation are more likely to be suspicious of new initiatives.

✦ New activity. As technology changes over time so the need for some jobs disappears and new jobs and organizations are created. Such cases are not restricted to the arrival of a new technology itself, even new technologies change as they become more accessible and integrated. For example with the arrival of the computer on a commercial

MANAGEMENT IN ACTION 7.5

Matching AMT jobs to people

The starting point for considering the design of jobs involving advanced manufacturing technology (AMT) is the level of human intervention necessary. Many systems designers attempt to eliminate the use of human intervention in the running of systems, but this has not been completely successful. There are two forms of human intervention with AMT:

✦ Production intervention. This is a necessary part of the production process. It involves such tasks as changing tools, loading and unloading materials. These occur at predictable times and are necessary because it is not cost effective to automate a process fully.

✦ Corrective intervention. This is necessary because the system may make a mistake during the production process. These can be machine faults, human error, programming faults or material problems. These categories of fault are impossible to predict and so the impact on automatic processes is difficult to define. Hence the need for human intervention, skill and flexibility.

It is in the field of corrective interventions that most scope for job design exists. When a fault arises there are essentially two options available. First, call a specialist to diagnose and correct the fault. Second, allow the operator to deal with some or all of the implications of the problem. Each option has its own advantages and disadvantages. For example, allowing operators to deal with problems may result in a lower downtime, but no operator could be expected to be expert in

all aspects of the process and technology. Equally, the need to call out an expert wastes time and the problem may be easily rectified by the operator. To design a two-stage process of allowing the operator to diagnose and rectify if possible, only calling for support if necessary, might save time in some cases but could considerably lengthen delays in others.

In one case where many corrective interventions were necessary a working party identified changes to the jobs which improved overall efficiency. Breakdowns reduced by about 40% and machine downtime reduced by about 28% after the changes to the job design. This demonstrated that allowing operators greater control over corrective interventions had a direct impact on performance.

In another case the process had a much higher level of reliability. In this instance, poor communications and low involvement in the planning of work caused problems for the workers. Regular communication meeting were introduced and workers were given responsibility for planning daily work priorities. Following some resistance from technical staff and supervisors the changes began to pay dividends in higher productivity and job satisfaction. Senior staff were freed from routine decisions and were thus more able to think and plan ahead, while the workers concentrated on achieving the objectives for the current work period.

Adapted from: Martin, R and Jackson, P (1988) Matching AMT jobs to people, *Personnel Management*, December, pp 48–51.

scale in the early 1960s came the job of a punched card operator. In those days the only way to input information in significant volume was to first create a card with the data punched into it as a series of holes. Batches of these cards were then fed into a card reader and the computer could then process the data. Such jobs were in high demand and commanded high salaries. However, with the next stage of computer development and keyboard input etc., such jobs disappeared almost overnight. Similar examples of new jobs and organizations appearing can be seen in the so-called 'dot.com' organizations of today.

The relationship between the first three of these forms of technology and job design can be shown as a diagram (see Figure 7.6).

Groups and work organization

The work of the Tavistock Institute brought together the Taylorist tradition and the human relations movement into a single perspective on job design. Trist and Bamforth (1951) studied the impact of the mechanization of coal mining on the work of miners. Traditionally, cutting coal had been undertaken by small groups of skilled miners, supported by a number of labourers. Coal was extracted from short *faces* (a seam of coal being worked on) by teams of miners working in groups. The introduction of machines and conveyor belts allowed much longer faces to be worked (referred to as the longwall method). Jobs had to be changed to allow the machines to be used efficiently. The small teams were combined into larger groups organized around the machinery and with a new hierarchical structure. As a consequence a number of other non-work behaviours changed as well. These included a deterioration in the quality and effectiveness of communications between workers across shifts and jobs; an increase in the blaming other shifts for problems; increased absenteeism; increased number of accidents; increased stress; and a generally deteriorating industrial relations situation.

Through their research activity Trist and his colleagues demonstrated that it was possible for a particular technology to support different types of work structure. They also demonstrated that the social and technical aspects of work needed to be integrated into a unified interactive socio-technical system. In addition the work also needed to be undertaken in an economically viable way. The Tavistock Institute has been involved in many similar studies and has reinforced the application of the *open systems* model of an organization (Figure 7.7) and job design in achieving effective operations. The *open systems* view seeks to introduce into the concept of an organization the dynamic, interactive and dependent nature of its relationship with the environment.

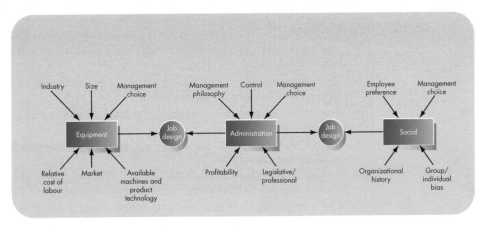

FIGURE 7.6 Technological influences on job design.

Autonomous work groups are an extension of the socio-technical approach to job design. The job to be done is effectively *contracted* to a work group which then decides for itself how to undertake it. It essentially becomes responsible to management for the output and cost of operations. This allows control to remain within the group for job design, work allocation, work rates and work schedules. There have been a number of variations of the basic autonomous work group concept. For example, the group can either have a leader appointed by management or it can elect its own leader as a permanent or rotating job. Emery and Thorsrud (1976) suggest that it is not only a question of linking the physical aspects of the tasks into the desired social organization that needs to be taken into account. The psychological job demands of human beings should also be taken into account. Table 7.1 reflects a number of the psychological demands identified as essential if job design were to be effective.

The most famous application of these ideas on job design have been in the Kalmar plant of Volvo, the Swedish car maker. It began operations in 1974 and used teams of between 15–20 people in car-building activities. Socio-technical job design is also associ-

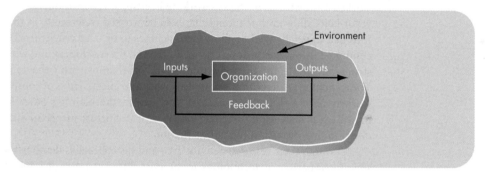

FIGURE 7.7 Open systems model of an organization.

+ Optimal level of work cycle – to avoid short cycle, repetitive activity
+ The inclusion of supplementary tasks in relation to the main job
+ The inclusion of opportunity to determine own performance in terms of quality and quantity of output
+ The job should contribute to the value of the product as far as the customer is concerned
+ There should be provision for job rotation and involvement in a broad range of facets of the overall job
+ Provision of communication opportunities so that employees' requirements can be incorporated into job and product design
+ The job should consist of a meaningful pattern of tasks providing a feeling of a complete whole
+ The job should comprise degrees of skill, knowledge, care or effort that is worthy of respect in society
+ Wherever possible, jobs that interlock should be grouped to allow for teamwork

TABLE 7.1 Psychological job demands (*adapted from*: Emery, F and Thorsrud, E (1976) *Democracy at Work*, Martinus Nijhoff, Leiden)

ated with concepts such as the quality of working life. Management in Action 7.4 reflects some of the more recent ideas on the integration of teamwork in the car industry.

Organizational influences on work organization

The discussion so far has explored a number of different perspectives associated with the organization and design of work. In addition to these influences there are a number of forces acting on the situation that emerge from the organization itself. It is the intention of this section to review a number of these forces and to explore the links with the ways in which work is organized and jobs designed. However, some of this discussion will inevitably involve consideration of organization structure, frameworks and culture as topics. These issues will be discussed more fully in Chapters 12, 13 and 14 of the book. In this context they are being introduced as relevant as influences on the way in which work may be organized.

Bureaucracy

Bureaucracy is a term used to describe an approach to organizational design that is particularly relevant to large-scale public and private sector organizations. Weber (1947) is the earliest and most frequently quoted source of material in relation to the notion of *bureaucracy*. Weber was a sociologist working at Heidelberg University in Germany at the turn of the last century. He was interested in the concepts of power and authority, how they differed and found expression within society. He concluded that the nature of authority changed as society developed and that what he termed as *rational–legal* authority was emerging. This was based on the creation of formal written rules which enjoyed a legal status within the organization. These rules governed the appointment of those empowered to lead as well as the way in which their leadership was allowed to be exercised. For example, we follow the instructions of more senior managers because we accept that they have the legal power to exercise authority over us.

At the time Weber was writing he was surrounded by organizations that were growing rapidly in size, complexity and sophistication. International trade was developing rapidly as was the public sector and the growth in domestic consumption. There was no computer-based technology to assist with the running of the large-scale organizations and all records, documents etc. had to be produced by hand. This required armies of people to undertake the range of duties involved, all of whom had to be organized and channelled in their work activities. *Bureaucracy* was therefore regarded by Weber as providing the principles forming the best way to organize activity in order to achieve the objectives necessary. The main principles of *bureaucracy* as set out by Weber are included in Table 7.2.

In this type of organizational arrangement Weber was describing the application of impersonality and rationality as guiding principles. In other words he was suggesting that as an *ideal type* of organization such an organization would be run in the best interests of its customers and according to rational rules. Authority would be exercised according to these principles and not based on whim, nepotism or favouritism.

In using the term *ideal type*, Weber was recognizing that this may not be found in precise form in specific organizations, but that the general principles would be found in most organizations to a greater or lesser extent. Other writers have criticized this notion and suggested that rules do not necessarily create order and stability. Gouldner (1954), for example, draws attention to the fact that within organizations rules are created by managers and that employees usually do not have any say in the development. In short, rules are drawn up for the benefit of those creating them. In his analysis, Gouldner identified different classes of rules, each of which elicited a different response from those subjected to them.

Having said that, the concept of bureaucracy has been very influential over the years in providing the basis upon which organizations should arrange their activities and design the jobs to be undertaken. While *bureaucracy* should, if followed closely, allow for the design of jobs which all fit together into a cohesive organizational framework it does have certain drawbacks. For example it does not allow for the employee to be able to exercise judgement in the course of their work. They are required (or forced, depending how the concept of rules is to be interpreted) simply and unthinkingly to follow the rules. Any exceptions should be referred to a higher authority for resolution. In a very real sense the human employee exists within the organization as a substitute for a machine. They are there to follow set procedures mechanistically and channel their energies as directed by the *rationally–legally* appointed superior. Creativity, ingenuity and individuality are all to be eschewed, if not forced out of the organization. It is an approach to organization that encourages a compliance response from employees, not the high commitment demanded in today's environment.

Taylorism

F W Taylor developed his views on work organization, which he termed *scientific management*, during his working life as a manager in the steel industry in the USA during the late 1800s and early 1900s. His approach was very much *task* oriented and he used work study techniques to explore the actual working methods being used and identify the *one best way* of performing each task. He set out to achieve three main objectives through his approach to work organization:

✦ High productivity. Through the identification of the *one best way* of doing each task and applying the use of monetary incentives workers would be encouraged to produce

✦ Specialization. Each job specializes in a particular set of tasks
✦ Rules. That rules should govern the conduct of business and the tasks being undertaken
✦ Hierarchy. That there should be an ordered system of reporting relationships
✦ Impersonality. The duties of each office should be conducted without fear or favour
✦ Appointed officials. Individuals should be appointed based on qualification and capability
✦ Full-time officials. The job should be the main occupation of the individual
✦ Career officials. Promotion should be based on merit
✦ Private–public split. The private life of an employee has no part to play in the job

TABLE 7.2 Bureaucratic principles

efficiently. This would benefit both company and employee financially and in other ways.

✦ Standardization of work activity. Through the application of work study techniques the one best way would be identified and each employee would be carefully selected to match the needs of the task. This would standardize both work activity across employees and the performance they achieved (through the application of incentive payments).

✦ Discipline at work. He also attempted to introduce an improved hierarchical approach to authority which would allow the decisions of managers to be effectively cascaded throughout the organization. This would allow a more effective control of workforce activity, channelling it in the desired directions which the scientific management designed jobs would then covert into a highly cost-effective output.

As with Weber he was working in a particular social context and responding to the needs of management as he perceived and understood them. For example, workers were liable to engage in what he termed *systematic soldiering*, a deliberate restriction on the amount of work done by employees to protect their jobs and income levels, given the relatively low level of education at the time as well as the lack of an industrial ethos among the workers (many factory workers were immigrants to America with limited language skills and predominantly from an agricultural and rural background). As he saw it he was seeking to organize work around the limitations that existed at the time through the development of a *science of work* and the introduction of an appropriate distinction between management and worker responsibilities.

As with many attempts to introduce work study techniques as the basis of work organization since his day he encountered significant problems. The workers resisted his attempts at the close control of activity, managers resisted the attempts to reorganize their jobs as well and eventually Taylor was dismissed by the company. During World War I the American government became so concerned at worker hostility to *scientific management* as a way of designing jobs and work output (following a strike) that they banned it from use in the defence industry.

However, the widespread use of the approach to determine how jobs should be designed and the level of output that should be expected from each worker has continued across the world. For example, Pean (1989) describes the results of applying work study to eye surgery carried out in a Moscow hospital. The procedure was studied and broken down into five discrete workstations, each staffed by a medically qualified person. The patient is laid out on a bed attached to a conveyor belt, has the anaesthetic given to them and then moves automatically between workstations where the surgeon performs the specific tasks appropriate to that stage of the surgery. By the end of the ten minutes 'processing' time the patient leaves the operating theatre conveyor belt as one of the 15 per hour who can be treated in this way.

Classical management view

Although the main name in this context is that of Fayol a number of other individuals have been influential in developing the approach to organizing that became known as the classical management view. Essentially the classical view holds that there are a number of guiding principles that should be followed in creating an organization and the jobs within it. It was Lussato (1976) who brought together the ideas that reflected the general thrust of the ideas within the classical model (see Table 7.3).

The application of these principles would create a basis of the way to organize work within the organization. However, as with the other approaches introduced it relies upon the application of rules etc. to be able to function. Just like the other approaches it ignores several important aspects associated with human nature at work within any organization. It assumes that the application of rules and authority and so on creates order and predictability. It ignores the very human qualities that make up the people employed in the organization and does not allow for the application of individuality or creativity in the exercise of work responsibility. In brief, it is represents a *top-down* approach to how work should be organized.

Contingency view

The contingency view of organization essentially holds that its structure and the design of the work within it should be driven by the circumstances that the organization finds itself in. From that perspective the external and internal forces acting upon the organization would be interpreted by management and appropriate working arrangements created. Figure 7.8 reflects the contingency chain of events leading to the design of work activity within the organization.

The advantage of the contingency view of organization is that it specifically allows for the existence of variation between organizations. The sum total of the circumstances impacting on any two organizations, even of similar size, location and industry is never completely identical. Therefore the application of contingency principles would recognize this and allow for the development of different organizational responses. The difficulty with the concept of contingency is that it relies heavily on the ability and/or willingness of managers to acknowledge the existence and significance of the forces acting upon the

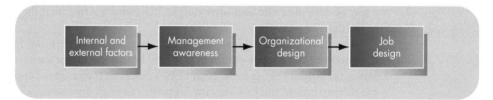

FIGURE 7.8   Contingency approach to work organization.

- ✦ Scalar concept. This literally means the hierarchy or chain of command
- ✦ Exception. Only exceptions to the norm should be referred upwards. This encourages delegation and management by exception
- ✦ Span of control. The number of subordinates reporting to any boss should not be excessive, as this causes work overload and management and communication problems
- ✦ Specialization. The specialization of work principle should also be applied to management jobs
- ✦ Unity of command. Each person should have only one boss

TABLE 7.3   Classic management principles

situation. Equally, it depends on their being prepared and/or able to take action on the work organization factors as part of a response strategy.

Culture

One aspect of the relationship between culture and work organization was identified by Spender (1989). He described organizations as bodies of knowledge, used and created by managers. He also considered that each body of knowledge was specific to a particular industry. They constitute the received wisdom of each industry and comprised the shared beliefs, judgements and underlying knowledge about the nature and functioning of the industry, its markets and networks. Spender termed this common understanding the *industry recipe*. In that sense his views are very close to the Deal and Kennedy (1982) view of culture as 'the way we do things around here'. Spender was working at the level of the industry commonalities that impact on how organizations function through the inherited recipes. In that sense one aspect of the recipe would be an understanding of how to arrange the organization's work-based resources to be able to function effectively in a particular industry.

At an organizational level one of the earliest studies of the transfer of working practices between cultures was that carried out by Rice (1958). A new weaving technology developed in Britain had been exported to an existing textile mill in Ahmadabad in India. The new machinery, designed and built in Britain, was based around western conceptions of how jobs should be created to support the operation of the machine. This required a complete change to the ways in which weaving jobs had been undertaken previously in the Indian factory. Twelve specialized jobs with a total of 29 operators were necessary to run the machine, whereas with the previous machines each worker would have had a specific job to undertake. The new arrangement of work required completely different job structures to be introduced. This caused confusion among the workers and productivity and quality both suffered as a consequence. The result was not a function of low morale or poor management–worker relations, which had all been good previously. It was simply that the culture of the organization within its national context was not in alignment with the cultural basis of the job design as built into the machine. In seeking to overcome the difficulties it was decided to develop a group approach to work organization, thus allowing teams to develop and design job structures that they would feel most suitable. This was adopted and found to impact positively on both quality and productivity.

In Chapter 14 a range of models of organizational culture will be introduced. Each of the models of culture discussed there has an implication for the organization of work. For example, Handy (1993) describes four manifestations of organizational culture. In this model work organization could be influenced as follows;

✦ Power culture. In this form of culture there is a strong central person who directs everything and through whom everything most go. Commonly found in the smaller owner/manager, entrepenural organizations, although examples in specific departments can be found in larger organization. Such a culture is dependent on the central person and jobs in that context tend to be fluid in content, dependent on the whim and changing moods of the individual at the centre of activity. Jobs are regarded very much as a support to that person.

✦ Role culture. This culture is typically found in large organizations and bureaucracies. It is based around the notion of functional responsibility and, therefore, the jobs within it tend to be highly structured with clear boundaries and responsibilities.

✦ Task culture. This form of culture is essentially team based as the work of the organization needs to be tightly focused on the objectives of to be achieved. It is the individuals and their capabilities that form the inherent strength of the organization. Jobs tend to be skill oriented with a premium on flexibility of actual task undertaken as individuals and groups of employees adapt to the immediate needs of the business.

✦ Person culture. This culture is predominantly based around the individual and their capabilities. Typical examples would be a management consultancy or legal chambers. Jobs tend to be organized around the skills of the people involved, with new people being brought into the organization as circumstances and the need for new expertise change.

Each of the models of culture could be reviewed in a similar manner to explore the relationship with work organization. When studying Chapter 14 reflect on the connections with the design and organization of work that are implicit in the models discussed.

Fordism and post-Fordism

The terms *Fordism* and *post-Fordism* reflect application of *scientific management* principles to the running of manufacturing and other organizations, largely developed and refined by Ford in the early years of the twentieth century.

Fordism

It was the fledgling motor car industry in which the ideas and principles which became known as *Fordism* were first developed. At the turn of the twentieth century motor cars were traditionally made by teams of craftsmen. The process of manufacture was so detailed that it could take anything up to 13 weeks to complete each vehicle. Even in volume car production there was much skilled work. Partly assembled vehicles remained in one position while teams of workers moved around the factory building up the product as they went. This process was relatively inefficient.

Early attempts to increase productivity included building vehicles on a trestle that could be pushed between teams. This ad hoc process was refined into a simple production line in which employees remained in one position and the vehicles moved between workstations. Early attempts required the workers to push each vehicle to the next workstation as they completed their task. This left control over the pace of work to the employee. It was Henry Ford who made a breakthrough in the early years of the twentieth century by mechanically driving an assembly line at a speed determined by management. The breakthrough took three forms. First, mechanically driving the assembly line. Second, the continuous movement of the line removed control of activity from workers. Third, the pace of the line became an integral part of the job design process.

The combination of mechanically paced assembly lines, scientific management-based job design and piecework payment was the mixture that managers had been seeking in order to control production. Because of the pivotal role of Henry Ford and the Ford Motor Company in this process it has become known as *Fordism*. In employee terms, it is frequently associated with alienated workers with no interest whatsoever in the end product of their labours performing boring tasks. An indication of the benefits of assembly line technology can be found within data published by Ford itself (see, for example, Table 7.4 taken from Ford Motor Company (1918)).

It did not take long for the benefits of Fordism to become established across a wide range of industries and countries. The principles were introduced to the manufacturing of a wide range of household goods, including radios and vacuum cleaners. The River Rouge factory of Ford in the USA became the biggest factory in the world, employing some 80,000 people in the assembly of the Model 'T' car. The factory received raw material in the form of metal, rubber and wood and through its own foundries, tyre factories, machine shops and assembly lines a new car was spewed out every few seconds.

However, not everything was perfect. Many employees were not able to tolerate the noise, pace of work, boredom and sheer scale of operation, consequently, labour turnover was very high. The response of Ford was to raise wages, thereby retaining labour and allowing employees to become consumers of the goods being produced. It was possible to save for a new Ford through a company savings scheme. Money was used as a *golden handcuff* in an attempt to lock the employee into the company. Ford also engaged a private police force to ensure that workers were committed and did not form or join trade unions. It was in principle and practice very much a *top-down* process with decisions and policies being formulated by managers. Employees were regarded as an extension of the machines that were used to drive the factory system.

Managers were not able to realize the full potential from the *Fordist* approach. The relentless pressure of an assembly line introduced an additional cause of stress into a delicately balanced system. Supervisors were continually pressed for increases in line speed, jobs were deskilled to the level of the banal and the opportunity for social interaction eliminated. The human dimension of the organization was something that Ford actively discouraged: 'A big business is really too big to be human. It grows so large as to supplant the personality of the man' (Ford, 1923, p 263). So conscious was Ford of the need to maintain order and control that several unique features were present in the factories. Under the influence of the sociological department within the company great emphasis was placed on the 'quality' of the working environment. Walls and roofs of factory buildings at the River Rouge factory were painted regularly and windows washed, by the team of 700 cleaners and painters. Welfare provision included a school, a hospital, cut price shops and a newspaper. However, there was a strong element of paternalism and attempts to achieve control over workers' lives through this provision.

Industrial disputes began to emerge as employees found ways of resisting the inevitable control and alienation of work on an assembly line. In structuring production into a stream of activity greater output and reduced cost had been achieved at the expense

Pre-assembly line	Post-assembly line
1100 men assemble 1000 car engines in a 9-hour day	1400 men assemble 3000 car engines in an 8-hour day
Each engine = 9.9 labour hours	Each engine = 3.37 labour hours
	A reduction in labour content of 6.17 hours or 62.3%

TABLE 7.4   The effect of an assembly line on car engine production (*source*: Ford Motor Company (1918) *Facts from Ford*)

of vulnerability. A break in any part of the production process brought the entire system to a standstill. This placed a considerable degree of power in the hands of employees. Blauner (1964) describes it thus:

> The social personality of the auto worker, a product of metropolitan residence and exposure to large, impersonal bureaucracies, is expressed in a characteristic attitude of cynicism toward authority and institutional systems, and a volatility revealed in aggressive response to infringement on personal rights and occasional militant collective action. Lacking meaningful work and occupational function, the automobile worker's dignity lies in his peculiarly individualistic freedom from organizational commitments. (p 177)

Goffee and Scase (1995) summarize a number of weaknesses associated with the Fordist model (pp 78–9), including:

✦ Alienation. The organizational consequences of alienation can include high labour turnover, absenteeism, the production of poor quality products and even sabotage.

✦ Product change. The original Ford model depended on a single product with no variation. However, with increased competition and customer ability to exercise choice this becomes difficult to sustain in practice.

✦ Managing and doing distinction. Taylor envisaged a strict distinction between managerial and operational activity. The danger of this view is that it separates parts of the organization that need to co-operate, creating low trust relationships.

✦ Inhibition of creativity. The imposition of managerial control can actively inhibit levels of creativity and desire for change, even among those charged with pursuing them.

✦ Potential not fully realized. Because of the need to plan ahead for specific levels of capacity in production, variation in market demand can frequently lead to an under-utilization of resource. In addition, many of the issues discussed also have the effect of reducing output

These difficulties soon became apparent and led initially to tighter control of the process and work methods in an attempt to *manage* out the undesirable influences. Considerable effort was put into method study and other technique-based approaches in seeking out the problems and solutions.

The post-Fordist model

There are immense benefits to be gained from the application of scientific management to the running of an organization. However, there are a number of forces that conspire to offset these benefits and they are one-off by definition. Once the workers produce a car engine in 3.73 hours instead of 9.9 hours this becomes the *norm* in successive years. Eventually, different approaches become necessary to obtain the *next generation* of leaps in productivity.

Post-Fordism attempted to retain the advantages of *Fordism*, but to overcome the major weaknesses. There are three areas in which post-Fordism sought to address the difficulties identified:

✦ Market. Marketing trends demand increasingly fragmented product ranges, updated products and new products, introduced at regular intervals.

✦ Methods. The clearest illustration of just how adaptability can be incorporated into production processes comes from the motor car industry. For example, any of the large car makers can produce a large number of end product variations within the basic body shell design for any particular model.

✦ Management. In attempting to overcome the Fordist problems it is managers who must decide what must be done. They need to be prepared to change their own practices to more effectively capture the potential from employees. Ford tried paying higher wages to *handcuff* employees to his factory. This worked for a while, but what was prized and special yesterday does not always work today. It does not take long for the new conditions to become the norm against which comparisons are made, as well as becoming ordinary by virtue of familiarity. So a circular process is established in which *treats* are necessary on a regular basis to maintain interest. Early work from the Human Relations School and the Tavistock Institute began to suggest that employees could usefully become more involved in the activities in which they were engaged. Developments such as empowerment (delegation of responsibility), delayering and downsizing (reducing the number of levels and people) began to follow as organizations attempted to make more effective use of the *human resources* at their disposal.

Figure 7.9 reflects the phasing process between Fordism and post-Fordism with the three forces just outlined.

There are a number of forces that produce a reticence in moving away from the principles embedded in the Fordist approach. As an *ideal type*, the efficiencies available through Fordism retain their attraction. The difficulty is it cannot be achieved in its pure form in the long run. Humans are not machines and there are reactions to being controlled by the inflexible assembly line. Roy (1960) describes the rituals and routines of four factory workers over the course of a working day as they attempt to cope with the demands of production. Fordist managers would regard such behaviour as deviant and as creating a loss of

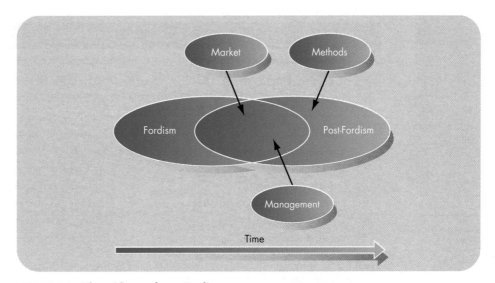

FIGURE 7.9   The evidence of post-Fordism.

efficiency for the system and therefore to be eliminated. The underlying problem is that it is not possible to separate the individual completely from the human.

Other pressures in the environment also tend to encourage the retention of Fordist principles, including:

✦ Risk. Every person within a Fordist organization is familiar with their role and the types of problem that will be encountered. To introduce change carries with it risk associated with any change and a lower certainty that the events can be dealt with effectively or quickly.

✦ Training. The training and experience of most managers have been in organizations which originate and espouse the Fordist perspective. Managers make use of what they know and believe in running organizations. It takes time for new ideas, thinking and knowledge to filter through and become an accepted part of their skill base.

✦ Systems. The systems and procedures adopted within organizations tend to reinforce the status quo. Many organizations reward executives based upon short-term financial gains rather than long-term measures of corporate performance.

✦ Preference. Managers with careers to develop are not likely to deliver things not valued by those in a position to allocate rewards. Also, as Kanter (1989) points out, management skills have developed in specific organizational settings and to change these makes many of these skills redundant. The maintenance of the distinction between managed and manager could also be brought into question if radical organizational change were to be pursued.

Goffee and Scase (1995) identify a number of distinguishing features which the authors describe as paradigm shifts in management, reflecting the evolution of organizations from Fordist to post-Fordist models (see Table 7.5).

From: Fordist	To: Post-Fordist
✦ Precisely-defined job roles	✦ Broadly-defined job roles
✦ Specialist skills	✦ Transferable skills
✦ Tight control	✦ Loose control
✦ Bounded responsibilities	✦ Autonomy and discretion
✦ Rules and procedures	✦ Guidelines for behaviour
✦ Closed communication	✦ Open/fluid communication
✦ High status differences	✦ Low status differences
✦ Low-trust relationships	✦ High-trust relationships
✦ Prevailing custom and practice	✦ Innovation and change
✦ Colleagues as individuals	✦ Colleagues as team members
✦ Invisible management	✦ Visible leadership

TABLE 7.5 Paradigm shifts in management (*source*: Goffee, R and Scase, R (1995) *Corporate Realities*, Routledge, London)

Flexibility, empowerment and patterns of work

The notion of the flexible firm will be introduced in a subsequent chapter in relation to organization structure. However, as an approach to work organization it also contains a strong association to job design. Taking a broad view of an individual's perception of their job then it could be expected that many experiences at work would influence the process. Equally the approach to flexibility adopted by the organization could be expected to significantly impact on the way that jobs were arranged within the organization. For example:

+ Flexibility. There are a number of forms that flexibility can take. Flexibility could be *job flexibility*, *location flexibility* or *temporal flexibility*. The opportunity to undertake a different job can help to develop the individual by introducing them to new skills, or old skills in a new setting or it can simply introduce a fresh location to add variety to an otherwise predictable work routine. Temporal flexibility refers to changing the times of work. Management in Action 7.6 provides a survey indicating many forms of flexibility and some indication of their value.

Stop | Consider

MiA 7.6 reports that 44% of organizations reported management resistance and 24% reported trade union resistance to flexibility. Identify the reasons that might lead to this level of resistance as well as how they might be overcome.

The report on which MiA 7.6 is based is largely silent on the employee perspective on the use of flexible working practices. Identify what you believe different categories of employee might think about these approaches. For example, a new graduate just starting work, a single mother with two children, a junior manager aged 48 years old etc. What does this add to your understanding of the advantages and disadvantages associated with flexible working and its impact on work design, from both management and employee perspectives?

+ Empowerment. Employee involvement in decision making is generally described as a form of *empowerment*. It could incorporate, at its lowest level, consultation with a trade union over issues of common concern or, at the other end of the spectrum, worker representatives on the board of directors. Whatever the particular form, the purpose is to involve employees in decisions relating to the direction of the organization and in allowing them to take more decisions on operational issues. If nothing else, empowerment should provide employees with a stronger view of the whole picture and their part in it. It should also encourage a closer connection between the employee and the customer as the employee is frequently *empowered* to take the necessary actions to satisfy the needs of the customer. These represent most of the core job dimensions identified by Hackman and Oldham (1980) (Figure 7.5).
+ Patterns of work. There are many different patterns of work. For example, shiftwork as compared to a daytime-only pattern. Curson (1986) identifies a broad range of alternative patterns. Among the options are:
  + Annual hours. Based on variable hours worked each week, accumulated towards an annual total.

MANAGEMENT IN ACTION 7.6

Juggling act

Personnel Today and Plantime conducted a survey to find out more about flexible working. Among the practices identified from the research were part-time working, annualized hours, flexible hours, job sharing, telecommuting and home-working.

Earl's Court Olympia, an exhibitions and catering company, has a number of flexible practices and systems in order to be able to meet the needs of its clients. Jim Black, group personnel director, points out that many exhibition facilities are used out of normal working hours and clients frequently make many last-minute demands. So the company needs the maximum level of flexibility possible. For example, within the catering division of the company a database of all staff skill areas and work location and hours preferences is held to allow managers to match individuals to the tasks in hand. The maintenance department uses an annualized hours system (which allows for peaks and troughs in work demand within a total working time for the year) to allocate staff to particular projects.

Some of the findings from the survey include:

✦ 90% of organizations use part-time working.

✦ 50% of organizations use flexitime.

✦ 26% of organizations use job sharing.

✦ 14% of organizations use annualized hours.

✦ 11% of organizations use telecommuting.

The advantages of flexible working include:

✦ 40% of organizations report it helps to recruit and retain certain staff.

✦ 39% of organizations report that it improves the ability to deal with peaks and troughs in demand.

✦ 34% of organizations report that it improves flexibility from a management perspective.

✦ 31% of organizations report that it reduces company costs.

✦ 28% of organizations report that flexibility improves morale and is popular among staff.

✦ 16% of organizations report that it reduces overtime costs.

Some of the barriers to introducing flexibility include:

✦ 44% of organizations report management resistance.

✦ 30% of organizations report administrative difficulties.

✦ 24% of organizations report trade union resistance.

✦ 24% of organizations report employee resistance because of fears over remuneration.

✦ 18% of organizations report the costs of introducing flexibility.

✦ 15% of organizations report practical problems such as fragmented workforce locations.

The results of the survey show that organizations are using a wider range of flexible working practices in their attempts to provide a better match between customer, business and employee needs.

Adapted from: Hall, L (1994) Juggling act, *Personnel Today*, 8 February, pp 21–4.

✦ Compressed week. This provides for a smaller number of working days to be worked, but of longer duration. For example, four days at ten hours compared to five days at eight hours.

✦ Overtime restrictions. This can be achieved by providing time off as an alternative to pay, flexing working hours or simply restricting overtime working.

✦ Temporary and part-time working. Allows individuals to choose the amount of time that they want to devote to a particular employer (or job). Of course, there is an argument that employers gain an unfair advantage through pay and legislative limitations on protection for such workers.

✦ Job sharing and homeworking. Job sharing allows two (or more) people to share a specific job, by agreement taking a proportion each. Homeworking allows individuals to work at home utilizing computer-based technology to communicate with clients or other employees. In both the employee is able to balance work with other commitments.

✦ Sabbaticals and career breaks. This approach allows individuals to balance the various aspects of their life though compartmentalizing activity. For example, university lecturers may apply for a sabbatical in order to undertake some research that would otherwise be difficult to complete. Career breaks can provide a means of an employee with prime career responsibilities to retain a career while meeting their other obligations.

The links between each of these aspects of work experience and job design are not direct. Each could influence the ways in which tasks are combined into jobs. More likely they are an influence on how the job is interpreted by the employee. For example, employees in a supportive environment in which they have some opportunity to adapt their work and balance their commitments are more likely to interpret a boring job in a positive light because of the overall context. Management in Action 7.7 provides an insight into how one organization used *teleworking* and *flexiplace* working to the benefit of customers, employees and the organization.

| Stop | Consider |

In the situation described in MiA 7.7 to what extent do you consider that it is the novelty of being different from the other design groups or the personal benefits from having the flexibility opportunity that creates the benefits?

Would you expect the same level of benefit to be achieved after, say, ten years when these forms of flexibility might have become the norm? Why or why not?

Changing the design of jobs

Change is the subject of a detailed review in Chapter 18 and so will not be explored in depth here. However, much of the change activity within organizations is intended to impact on the way in which work is undertaken. The approach to changing in the design of jobs within the organization will depend on many factors, many of which are indicated in Figure 7.10.

In certain situations the use of work study techniques would be used in order to carry out a method study of the work in question and to develop alternative job content. This

MANAGEMENT IN ACTION 7.7

Flexible work comes of age

Teleworking conjures up all sorts of images, most of them inaccurate. At the Basingstoke offices of Digital Equipment it was found that some employees occupied their desks for only about 40% of the day. Flexible working was seen as a way of retaining key employees and cutting some of the operational costs.

Ian Christie, deputy head of Digital's business design group, spends about half his time at the Basingstoke office. The rest of the week he is either visiting clients, working from home or visiting other Digital locations. Telephone calls are automatically diverted to his home, his car phone or any other location that he specifies. Teleworkers frequently keep papers and other items normally found around an office at home or in the car. Some members of the 13-strong business design team spend more time in the Basingstoke office than others. The choice is theirs. Each has telephone, computer and e-mail systems provided by the company. When working at the company offices an individual would use one of the six desks allocated to the team. The only 'must attend' requirement is a monthly meeting for the whole group, which can last a full day and provides the only forum for the team to discuss plans, etc.

The team has a group secretary, Barbara Prowse, who acts as a traditional secretary, but also undertakes a liaison and co-ordination role for the team. This is not always easy as the individuals can be at any one of a number of locations across the country. Staff are paid a basic salary with an individual performance element (dependent upon reaching targets). In this environment it is up to individuals to determine their own working hours as necessary for the jobs being done. Health and safety is an issue for staff working from home. For those with 'homeworking' contracts the company undertakes a safety inspection, provides a fire extinguisher and the individual is cautioned about the need for breaks when undertaking repetitive tasks such as sitting at a computer.

The result of the introduction of flexible working in the business design group at Digital has been a reduction in the operating costs of between 25–50% with a doubling of business handled in comparison with other groups.

Adapted from: Merrick, N (1993) Flexible work comes of age, *Personnel Management Plus*, October, pp 22–3.

would perhaps then form the basis of a negotiation between management and trade unions representing the job holders about the nature of the new job, appropriate rates of pay etc. In more coercive organizational situations it could involve the manager deciding that a change was in order and what form it should take. This new requirement would then be given to the employee as an instruction on the basis of comply or be dismissed. Clearly, there could be employment legislation in existence that might have a bearing on the ability of management either to get away with such actions or which would allow the employee to claim a measure of compensation if they were dismissed, but that is outside the scope of this discussion. Equally, there could be a legal restriction on management in terms of the degree of freedom to change the content of a job. For example, it is not possible (to take a silly example) for me to take on the job of diagnosing medical conditions and prescribing drugs as part of my responsibilities to students. I am not a medically qualified or legally certified doctor.

The approach adopted by management in seeking to change the design of jobs within an organization will inevitably have a major impact on the response generated from the employees. An imposed job change on employees is at best likely to generate a compliance response from the employees. A response hardly likely to engender a spirit of co-operation or high levels of productivity, quality or customer service. However, when the senior managers of organizations decide that they need to downsize in some form or other in order to reduce cost, then little can be done to make the wholesale job losses and work reorganization palatable to everyone. Early retirement and voluntary severance deals give people some degree of financial protection or compensation for the loss of their job. For those who remain inside the organization after such major upheavals, it is sometimes a case of having to go along with more work and longer hours for the same money or leave.

Taking large numbers of people out of an organization without also simplifying the operational processes and procedures simply means that fewer people must do more work. This was the essence of the *business process re-engineering* (BPR) concept which sought to encourage managers to go back to first principles and redesign the organization from the ground upwards (Hammer, 1990). The demand fundamentally to redesign all aspects of work organization as well as cutting numbers employed is perhaps a significant reason why BPR has been less than successful in achieving the intended widespread recognition and success originally expected.

Alienation, satisfaction and productivity through work organization

Job design and productivity are both organizational imperatives and both feature as management drivers. Job design is about grouping the tasks that need to be undertaken into

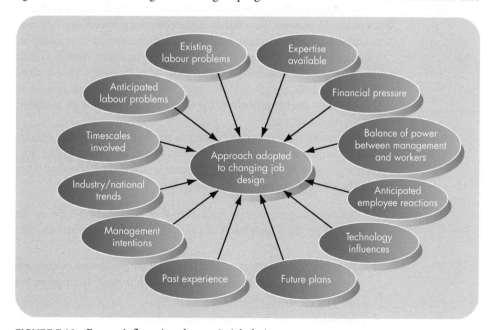

FIGURE 7.10   Factors influencing changes in job design.

convenient *chunks* of work. The basis of this decision can be subject to a number of forces including organization structure, historical job structure, employee or managerial preference. Productivity is a reflection of conversion efficiency and therefore cost. Hence, a concept strongly tied to the nature of work organization within the company. The continued existence of an organization is largely a function of its relative productivity within the competitive environment.

The search for productivity and control leads naturally to the job simplification approach to job design, based on the machine metaphor of organizational functioning. This view ignores the perhaps rather obvious *truth* that people are not machines. The recognition of this *truth* led to the adoption of other job design approaches in the search to capture the most effective way to organize work. In the service industries, for example, the nature and level of contact between employees and customers is a particular feature of the design of both jobs and the service encounter itself. Considerable training effort in most service companies goes into trying to drum into staff the desired (as defined by management) form of customer greeting and processing procedures. What much of this ignores is that most customers are aware of the relative insincerity of these trained-in exchanges and are not taken in by them. This is for many reasons including the fact that most people have experienced such processing technologies supporting very poor real customer care. Indeed, many customers will work in other organizations that preach customer care but cannot deliver it and so employees become cynical about such programmes.

Alienation represents a concept that emerged in the work of Marx and describes, 'the condition of humanity under capitalism' (Sims *et al.*, 1993, p 228). It originally reflected the inevitable (for Marx) separation between the worker as a human being and the person with the skill to provide the capitalist with the means of production; from a specific connection with the actual end product, other people and any control over the application of their labour. Sims *et al.* go on to point out that the meaning of the term *alienation* has changed over the years and now is generally taken to infer frustration and separation. Blauner (1964) suggested that as organizations moved towards mass production the level of alienation would increase, but that as high-technology operations began to take over the level would reduce as the human being became the master of technology and drudgery became a thing of the past. Not surprisingly this view has been heavily criticized for being overly simplistic and a reflection of the view of technology at the time (see for example, Thompson, 1989, pp 19–23). However, the concept of *alienation* forces a consideration of the design of work, particularly the way in which technology is integrated into it, and the impact on the worker.

A number of job design approaches attempt to incorporate *satisfaction* into work. This is based on the assumption that workers contribute more if they are happy and feel that they are contributing something of value to something of value. There are three possible links between performance and satisfaction (Petty *et al.*, 1984):

✦ Satisfaction generates performance. This would reflect the view that job design should aim to produce high levels of satisfaction as this in turn will optimize worker performance.

✦ Performance generates satisfaction. The converse view is that achievement generates satisfaction. Therefore, every effort should be made to improve performance as this in turn will increase satisfaction.

✦ Satisfaction and performance link indirectly. This holds that the two are linked, but only under certain conditions. Intervening variables such as management style, pressure, personality factors, job design, equity and rewards are examples of the factors that could mediate between the two. Figure 7.11 illustrates this relationship.

In his book on motivation, Vroom (1964) provides a clear indication that a satisfied worker is not automatically a high performer. It could be that at one extreme a very happy worker is enjoying work so much that they spend most of their time socializing, while at the other extreme a productive worker hates the job so much that working hard makes the time pass quicker. The relationship between satisfaction and productivity is less direct, more complex and a function of forces from a variety of sources acting upon the situation (Bassett, 1994). These include the individual, the job, working environment, management and the personal relationships involved.

Quality of working life and quality circles

The quality of working life (QWL) movement emerged from a belief in the need to improve the experience of work for all employees. There is no single definition of QWL but one which captures the breadth of the approach is Kopelman (1985, p 239):

> A philosophy of management that enhances the dignity of all workers, introduces changes in an organization's culture, and improves the physical and emotional well-being of employees.

Implicit in this definition is a broad approach to work activity, including job design and the other factors identified in Figure 7.9. It attempts to integrate both organizational needs for a productive workforce and the late twentieth-century expectations that individuals have in relation to work. James (1991, p 16) describes QWL as being composed of:

✦ A goal. The creation of more involving, satisfying, effective jobs and work environments at all levels.

✦ A process. Achievement of the goal through employee involvement. Bringing together the needs and development of people with the needs and development of the organization.

✦ A philosophy. Viewing people as assets to be released and developed, rather than costs to be controlled.

FIGURE 7.11   Relationship between performance and satisfaction.

QWL activity tends to be concentrated into eight areas of working life experience (Walton, 1973):

✦ Compensation. The rewards for work should be above a minimum standard for life and should also be equitable.

✦ Health and safety. The working environment should reduce the adverse effects of pollution that can impact on the physical, mental and emotional state of employees.

✦ Job design. The design of jobs should be capable of meeting the needs of the organization for production and the individual for satisfying and interesting work.

✦ Job security. Employees should not have to work under a constant concern for their future stability of work and income.

✦ Social integration. The elimination of anything that could lead to individuals not identifying with the groups to which they belong. This includes the elimination of discrimination and individualism, while encouraging teams and social groups to form.

✦ Protection of individual rights. The introduction of specific procedures aimed at guaranteeing the rights of employees at work.

✦ Respect for non-work activities. Respect for the activities that people engage in outside work. Recognize the impact of work activities on private life.

✦ Social relevance of work. Initiatives to increase the understanding among employees of the objectives of the organization and the importance of their part in them.

QWL initiatives have enjoyed mixed results, partly as a result of the complexity of the issues involved. There are external forces that influence how employees react to company initiatives. For example, the economic climate can either be hostile or favourable to the security of employment aspects of QWL. The activities of other organizations can also influence the perceptions of employees about the actions of their own employer, for example, being seen as simply following a trend. The wider social environment and attitudes can also influence events. For example, sex discrimination is a function of the prevailing social attitudes among predominantly male power holders which no longer match the changing social expectations of gender roles.

From the perspective of QWL, job design is an important part of the overall experience of individuals at work. It should be undertaken to ensure that the other seven aspects are not compromised. The use of quality circles has been associated with attempts at continuous improvement. While not part of job design as such, circles can play a significant part in shaping peoples experience of work. A quality circle is described as (Department of Trade and Industry, 1985):

> A group of four to 12 people coming from the same work area, performing similar work, who voluntarily meet on a regular basis to identify, investigate, analyse and solve their own work-related problems. The circle presents solutions to management and is usually involved in implementing and later monitoring them.
>
> The particular effectiveness of circles depends on these few key features which combine to give them a special character quite different from other proven forms of group working such as task forces. They are not always called circles but it is convenient to use this general term for descriptive purposes. The precise design too will vary from place to place but all circle-like groups follow an essentially standard pattern of approach to problems.

Quality circles originated in the USA but gained wide acceptance in Japan during the 1960s, since when they have been re-exported to the west as a result of their success in improving quality, commitment and productivity. For circles to be successful the members need to be trained in problem solving, communication and teamworking. They also need to be seen to be taken seriously by managers. There has been some hostility to the concept from trade unions, managers and employees for a number of reasons, including a perceived erosion of power, the need to give up free time and that it was a management attempt to reduce cost.

In introducing quality circles management need to demonstrate their commitment as well as recognizing that by allowing employees to solve problems, a shift in control takes place. A quality circle approach to QWL can be suggested to impose a parallel set of structures onto the existing formal hierarchy (Bushe, 1988; Goldstein, 1985). These dual frameworks can become a problem if commitment to the quality circle begins to take precedence over commitment to the formal organization. Potentially becoming a struggle for power, circle members seek to increase their influence over their working life and managers to retain power over both activity and agenda.

Work organization: an applied perspective

Not all jobs are in the gift of managers to design. The professions including the law, medicine etc. ensure through qualification schemes, training and work demarcation that individuals are prepared in a nationally, or even internationally, consistent way. This limits the ability of managers to change these jobs or impose their own structure on them within particular organizational settings. Even with non-professional jobs, the more a particular organization *personalizes* its jobs (designs jobs without reference to what is generally the case in society) the more it is necessary to train employees to do the work. This increases the cost of recruitment, training and wages which would need to be offset by productivity improvement if commercial disadvantage were to be avoided.

Boring and mundane aspects of work cannot be completely eliminated. They can be simplified, automated, incorporated into other activities or simply reduced in volume, but they are a certain aspect of organizational life. One difficulty with such activities is that personal preference plays a significant part in their definition. What is boring and mundane to one person is not so to another. Some people are able to cope with such jobs in a way which minimizes the negative impact of them. Every job becomes boring at some point in time. No matter how much an individual enjoys their work there are times when it is undertaken less than willingly and a change welcomed. These issues further complicate the design process as it is not possible to say that any particular job design will be 'good' for every person all the time.

Managers also have multiple objectives to achieve which influences the design of the jobs for which they are responsible. Cost reduction, efficiency and City expectation all tend to push managers towards job simplification in the search for high work rates at minimal cost. Yet the need to provide excellent levels of customer service demand different approaches. Management in Action 7.8 provides an insight into how two organizations used work sharing linked to pay reductions thereby saving jobs, while attempting to maintain service levels.

MANAGEMENT IN ACTION 7.8

Cutting wages to preserve jobs

Arkin describes two very different organizations that used job sharing as a means of coping with a reduced volume of work. Sheffield City Council experienced a number of financial crises as a result of government spending limits and its own grandiose capital investment projects. Volkswagen found itself with a reducing demand for its cars and the resultant need to cut costs.

Employees at Sheffield City Council agreed to accept seven days extra paid leave in return for a pay cut of 3.25%. All employees including the chief executive were affected, apart from teachers and those earning less than £90 per week. This was one form of work sharing. Trade union officers were able to agree the arrangement with council managers as a one-off process, but were reluctant to attempt the same again. It was felt that employees would not be prepared to accept further reductions in pay or work. It is interesting to note that in the case of Sheffield City Council there was no diminution in the volume of work needing to be done, just the ability to raise enough money to pay for the level of services. The deal struck did allow £7m of savings to be made without creating more unemployment in the city.

Volkswagen had agreed with the engineering union, IG Metall, and a smaller staff association on the works council that in return for pay cuts of between 10 and 12% a reduction in the working

week from 36 hours to 22.8 hours would be implemented. Some departments would work a four-day week while others might have found it necessary to work five days but fewer hours each day. Equally, it was not envisaged that the reduction in working hours would apply to managers. They would find it necessary to put in a full week. Equally, a company spokesman suggested that some people may be required to work longer hours to be able to ensure that the shorter hours worked smoothly. As with Sheffield City Council, the company was keen to find ways of avoiding large-scale layoff or redundancy of workers.

In the case of Sheffield, managers were able to avoid about 1400 redundancies through the effect of the longer holidays. Volkswagen was able to avoid about 30,000 people becoming unemployed through the reduced working week. Both organizations argue that this approach allowed individuals to remain economically active, they retained a degree of self-worth, kept the areas in which they lived alive and retained the skills needed within the organizations. So everyone gained from an otherwise difficult situation.

Adapted from: Arkin, A (1994) Cutting wages to preserve jobs, *Personnel Management Plus*, January, pp 18–19.

Stop | Consider

Consider the approaches adopted by both organizations in MiA 7.8. Do these represent one-off changes to work organization that could not be repeated by the same organizations? Why or why not?

The VW example makes it clear that the changes did not apply to managers and that some people would have to work longer hours. To what extent do such changes in work organization function on the basis that as long as more people gain than lose everything will be OK? Or does it imply that managers were simply being protected from pay cuts? What does this imply might happen to morale etc. among those adversely impacted on in some way or other?

To persuade managers to divert employee time from productive activity to the use of quality circles as an aid to subsequent improvement is not always easy, particularly if the result is to be an erosion of managerial decision making, control and power. The Taylorist notion that managers *think and decide* and workers *labour* is still evident in many operational situations. Many managers are less than comfortable with the notion that employees can and should be empowered to organize themselves through such initiatives as self-managed teams. The use of such approaches can be seen to bring into question the very need for managerial existence. What it specifically does introduce, however, is an issue regarding the design of management jobs. There tends to be an assumption in much of the discussion of this topic that job design is about the work of workers other than managers. However, managerial jobs also need to be designed and created. A significant aspect of such initiatives as quality circles, delayering, downsizing and business process re-engineering calls into question the traditional view of what management work should be about and how it should be exercised. In the language of metaphor, perhaps the job of management should be seen as conducting an orchestra, not policing a football crowd. This is perhaps what differentiates management from leadership.

In deciding what combination of activities should define a particular job there are a number of factors to be taken into account:

+ Operations. These are the operational objectives to be achieved. Building domestic appliances or providing legal services for example define to a significant extent the types of jobs that will exist within the particular organizations.

+ Philosophy. These are the guiding philosophies of the organization. Approaches to empowerment and quality of working life, for example, will impact on the way in which work is viewed and therefore organized.

+ Technology. The level and type of technology available within the organization influences the form that the jobs required to support it take.

+ Market. A service industry company will inevitably place significant store on the impact of employees on the customer experience. This influences the design of the jobs in question as well as the standards of behaviour expected. Equally, education and training prior to employee entry to the labour market (and in-company provision) influence the skills and abilities that recruits can be expected to bring with them. Organizational deviation from *standard* jobs carries with it implications for training and cost.

+ History. The evolution of the company and how it has approached job design and generally managed its employee relations in the past will influence what is likely to be achieved in the future. This influences both management and employee perceptions and expectations.

+ Creativity. The ability to create jobs that are interesting, stimulating, rewarding and enable high levels of productivity to be achieved is a function of the *creativity* of the people involved. It is too easy to adopt a *follower* approach to the design of jobs and seek to adapt other organizations' ideas without thinking them through in relation to the specific context. Equally, there is never a clean sheet on which to create something new and original on every occasion. Inevitably, therefore, job design becomes a balancing process between these two extremes.

+ Political. Managers can use job design as a political tool in defining the control of employee activity. It can be used to reinforce the rights and status of managers or it can be used to attempt to capture the commitment of employees. For example, it can be argued that by empowering employees in ways defined by managers, control is achieved through less direct and more acceptable means (to employees).

✦ Profitability. The level of profit within an organization determines the level of *slack* within the system. A highly profitable organization has the ability to direct resources towards experimentation and the development of alternative ways of working. An organization with little money available will have less freedom to concentrate on anything other than survival. There is an interesting paradox here because it is organizations with little spare money that actually need the best response from everyone to maximize the chance of survival. Situations of scarcity require the highest ability and creative responses from managers and employees in order to break the cycle of crisis. Yet this is usually when it is least visible.

✦ Work patterns. Patterns of work such as job sharing and shiftwork also have an influence on the design of jobs. It is not uncommon in factories to find shiftworkers being trained to undertake minor repairs to equipment in order to reduce the total number of engineers required during the working week.

✦ Preference. If the particular design of a job does not sit comfortably with either managers or workers then something will happen. Managers can specifically initiate a redesign process. Employees can simply adapt their work activity informally or they can formally press for change. Employees can also resign, seek alternative work, the level of quality could drop or there may be increased industrial relations problems. The existence of any of these reactions might signal underlying job design problems.

✦ Risk. The level of risk aversion is also a factor in the job design process, just as it is in many other aspects of decision making. With any new idea there is a risk of failure. A new job design may deliver the anticipated benefits or it may not. It may even make some things worse. The attitude of the decision maker to risk determines how far away from the *tried and tested* they will move.

These influencing factors impact on the design of jobs in both direct and indirect ways. They also act on the process in subtle ways that are not always recognized by the participants. Figure 7.12 summarizes the impact of these factors on job design.

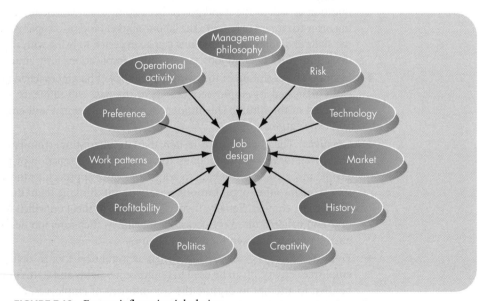

FIGURE 7.12   Factors influencing job design.

Conclusions

Job design is something that influences a considerable range of aspects of work, not just the physical carrying out of the necessary tasks. It can influence the way in which the organization approaches the very nature of employment within it. Job design can reflect a belief about the rights of employees to high level involvement in the activities of the company or it can reflect a basic view of workers being simply flexible (or necessary) alternatives to machines.

Job design is also something that can be used to draw out from employees additional commitment to the objectives of management without any reward other than job satisfaction. In other words, it is a facet of management that can be used to reflect the moral values and beliefs of the people involved or it can be a form of cynical manipulation. The difficulty lies in being able to identify the proportion of each of these reasons at work in any given context. Anyone who is seeking to manipulate employee commitment for commercial or personal gain is unlikely to admit it.

Consequently, a high level of trust is required if radical approaches to job design are to be adopted: trust that managers are not going to abuse employee commitment; trust that employees will not abuse the additional power that they would be given to self-determine work activities (if that were the option chosen). Trust is something that is hard to gain but easy to lose. Unfortunately, managers generally do not have a good track record maintaining trust – at least as far as employees perceive it.

Discussion questions

1. Define the following key terms used in this chapter:

Job design	*Empowerment*	*Job satisfaction*
Work study	*Autonomous work groups*	*Job rotation*
Quality of working life	*Job simplification*	*Patterns of work*
Quality circle	*Job enlargement*	*Fordism*
Job enrichment	*Socio-technical job design*	*Post-Fordism*
Flexibility		

2. Why should managers be concerned with job design?

3. What is a job and why is job design such a complex concept?

4. If job design is a function of the many factors identified in Figure 7.11 how can work study techniques offer any real value in identifying the most effective design?

5. Compare and contrast the Hackman and Oldham job characteristics approach to job enrichment with the ideas associated with the socio-technical perspective.

6. Why would a satisfied employee not be the most productive?

7. Identify ways in which the job dimensions model (Figure 7.1) can be related to the organizational discipline model (Figure 7.3).

8. How does technology influence the organization of work?

9. In the section 'Quality of working life and quality circles' it was suggested that the introduction of quality circles introduced a 'parallel organization' onto the existing hierarchy. Explain why this might be so, identify the consequences of this for management and suggest how the problems can be overcome.

10. Describe the main organizational influences on work organization and explain how each would impact on the design of jobs.

Research activities

1. Along with a group of about six or eight fellow students imagine that you are a quality circle within your university or college. Identify some aspect of your work as student that is causing you problems. Identify the causes of the problems and develop ways of solving them. What implications do your proposed solutions have for:

    ✦ Your 'job' as students.
    ✦ The 'job' of lecturers.
    ✦ The 'job' of tutorial or teaching assistants.
    ✦ The 'job' of university administration staff.
    ✦ The 'job of any other people whom you identify as having an impact on your problems?

2. For the work that you identified in Research activity 1 put together a plan of action for selling your ideas to the people whom you identified as needing to change their jobs in order to help solve your problems. How would you seek to gain their agreement to help you change their jobs in order to help you? Discuss your ideas with some of the people involved and identify what factors may limit their ability to do what you would wish them to do. What lessons for job design do you draw from this?

3. Talk to about four people you know who work in different organizations and at different levels. Find out how their jobs were designed. For managers, how do they review the design of those jobs for which they have responsibility? Compare what you find out with, and explain it in terms of, the material contained in this chapter.

Key reading

From Clark, H, Chandler, J and Barry, J (1994) *Organization and Identities: Text and Readings in Organizational Behaviour*, International Thomson Business Press, London.

✦ Kumar, K: Specialization and the division of labour, p 13. Reviews the way in which work is structured within society.
✦ Bell, D: Work and its discontents, p 44. Considers some of the parallels between the views of work and of religion.
✦ Dex, S: The sexual division of work, p 177. Introduces the gendered nature of work and the reinforcement of male domination.
✦ Cockburn, C: Male dominance and technological change, p 197. Reviews the gendered aspects of work and technology in the printing industry.

- ✦ Perkin, H: The rise of professional society: England since 1880, p 204. Reviews the nature of the professions as they emerged as dominant forces in society.
- ✦ Illich, I: Disabling professions, p 207. Examines the power of the professions and attempts to neutralize that effect.
- ✦ Thompson, EP: Time and work – discipline, p 216 This describes a historical review of work patterns and time intended to control worker activity.
- ✦ Herzberg, F: Motivation through job enrichment, p 300. An extract from the classic text by Herzberg looking at the links between motivation and the enrichment of work.
- ✦ Needham, P: The 'autonomous' work group, p 310. A case study-based review of the introduction of autonomous work groups in a factory setting.
- ✦ Atkinson, J: The flexible firm, p 337. An introduction to the notion of flexibility at an organizational level, which has clear implications for job design.
- ✦ Pollert, A: The flexible firm: a model in search of reality, p 343. This forms a response to the concept of the flexible firm described above.
- ✦ Hirst, P and Zeitlin, J: Knowing the buzz word is not enough, p 345. Reviews the application of flexibility practices in the UK.
- ✦ Bradley, K and Hill, S: What quality circles are, p 364. An introduction to the concept of quality circles.
- ✦ Hill, S: Quality circles in Britain, p 366. As the title implies, this extract provides a brief review of the approach to quality circles in Britain.

Further reading

There are a number of occasional papers published by the ACAS Work Research Unit that have relevance to the ideas contained in this chapter. For example:

- ✦ No. 27 December 1983. Effective and satisfactory work systems, Geoff White.
- ✦ No. 29 February 1984. Employee involvement in work redesign, Geoff White.
- ✦ No. 43 May 1989. Quality circles – a broader perspective, Sean Russell and Barrie Dale.
- ✦ No. 46 July 1990. Self-regulating work groups, David Grayson.
- ✦ No. 50 November 1991. Quality of working life and total quality management, Graham James.

Handy, CB (1993) *Understanding Organizations*, 4th edn, Penguin, Harmondsworth, pp 318–34. Provides a concise review of the topic of job design in broad terms.

Barling, J (1994) Work and Family: In Search of More Effective Workplace Interventions. In Cooper, CL and Rousseau, DM (eds) *Trends in Organizational Behaviour*, John Wiley, Chichester. Considers the links between family and work roles and examines the assumptions surrounding the interrelationship between job design on family 'well-being'.

Whitaker, A (1992) The Transformation in Work: Post-Fordism Revisited. In Reed, M and Hughes, M (eds) *Rethinking Organizations: New Directions in Organization Theory and Analysis*, Sage, London. This chapter reviews much of the debate surrounding the notion of post-Fordism in its broader social and organizational context.

References

Babbage, C (1832) *On the Economy of Machinery and Manufactures*, Charles Knight, London.

Bassett, G (1994) The case against job satisfaction, *Business Horizons*, May–June, 7, 3, 67.

Blauner, R (1964) *Alienation and Freedom*, University of Chicago Press, Chicago.

Bushe, GR (1988) Developing co-operative labour–management relations in unionized factories: a multiple case study of quality circles and parallel organizations within joint quality of work life projects, *Journal of Applied Behavioural Science*, **24**, 129–50.

Conant, H and Kilbridge, M (1965) An interdisciplinary analysis of job enlargement: technology, cost, behavioural implications, *Industrial and Labor Relations Review*, **18**, 377–95.

Currie, RM (1963) *Work Study*, 2nd edn, Pitman, London.

Curson, C (ed.) (1986) *Flexible Patterns of Work*, Institute of Personnel Management, London.

Deal, T and Kennedy, A (1982) *Corporate Cultures: The Rights and Rituals of Corporate Life*, Penguin, Harmondsworth.

Department of Trade and Industry (1985) *Quality Circles*, National Quality Campaign, Department of Trade and Industry, London.

Emery, F and Thorsrud, E (1976) *Democracy at Work*, Martinus Nijhoff, Leiden.

Evans, JR, Anderson, DR, Sweeney, DJ and Williams, TA (1990) *Applied Production and Operations Management*, 3rd edn, West Publishing, St Paul, MN.

Ford, H (1923) *My Life and Work*, Heinemann, London.

Ford Motor Company (1918) *Facts From Ford*, Detroit, MI.

Goffee, R and Scase, R (1995) *Corporate Realities: The Dynamics of Large and Small Organizations*, Routledge, London.

Goldstein, SG (1985) Organizational dualism and quality circles, *Academy of Management Review*, **10**, 504–17.

Gouldner, AW (1954) *Patterns of Industrial Bureaucracy*, The Free Press, New York.

Hackman, JR and Oldham, GR (1980) *Work Redesign*, Addison-Wesley, Reading, MA.

Hammer, M (1990) Re-engineering work: don't automate, obliterate, *Harvard Business Review*, July–August.

Handy, CB (1993) *Understanding Organizations*, 4th edn, Penguin, Harmondsworth.

Herzberg, F (1968) One more time: how do you motivate employees?, *Harvard Business Review*, January–February, 53–62.

Herzberg, F (1974) The wise old Turk, *Harvard Business Review*, September–October, 70–80.

Hoxie, R F (1915) *Scientific Management and Labour*, D. Appleton, London.

Ivancevich, JM (1992) *Human Resource Management*, 5th edn, Richard D Irwin, Homewood, IL.

James, G (1991) *Quality of Working Life and Total Quality Management*, ACAS Work Research Unit, Working Paper No. 50.

Kanter, RM (1989) The new managerial work, *Harvard Business Review*, **67**, 6.

Kennedy, KW and Filler, BE (1966) Apperture Sizes and Depth of Reach for One- and Two-handed Tasks. Report No AMRL-TR-66–27, Aerospace Medical Research Labs, Wright Patterson Air Force Base.

Kopelman, RE (1985) Job redesign and productivity: a review of the evidence, *National Productivity Review*, Summer.

Lussato, B (1976) *A Critical Introduction to Organization Theory*, Macmillan, London.

Pean, P (1989) How to get rich off Perestroika, *Fortune*, 8 May, pp 95–6.

Petty, MM, McGee, G and Cavender, J (1984) A meta-analysis of the relationship between individual job satisfaction and individual performance, *Academy of Management Review*, October, 712–21.

Rice, A K (1958) *Productivity and Social Organization: The Ahmedabad Experiment*, Tavistock, London.

Roy, DF (1960) Banana time: job satisfaction and informal interaction, *Human Organization*, **18**, 158–68.

Salancik, GM and Pfeffer, J (1978) A social information processing approach to job attitudes and task design, *Administrative Science Quarterly*, **23**, 224–53.

Sims, D, Fineman, S and Gabriel, Y (1993) *Organizing and Organizations: An Introduction*, Sage, London.

Smith, A (1776) *An Inquiry into the Nature and Causes of the Wealth of Nations*.

Spender, JC (1989) *Industry Recipes*, Basil Blackwell, Oxford.

Thompson, P (1989) *The Nature of Work: An Introduction to Debates on the Labour Process*, 2nd edn, Macmillan, Basingstoke.

Torrington, D and Hall, L (1992) *Personnel Management: A New Approach*, 2nd edn, Prentice Hall, Hemel Hempstead.

Trist, EL and Bamforth, KW (1951) Some social and psychological consequences of the longwall method of coal getting, *Human Relations*, **4**, 3–38.

Vroom, VH (1964) *Work and Motivation*, John Wiley, New York.

Walker, CR and Guest, R (1952) *The Man on The Assembly Line*, Harvard University Press, Cambridge, MA.

Wall, TD, Clegg, CW and Jackson, PR (1985) An evaluation of the job characteristics model, *Journal of Occupational Psychology*, **51**, 183–96.

Walton, RE (1973) Quality of working life: what is it?, *Sloan Management Review*, **15**, 11–21.

Weber, M (1947) *The Theory of Social and Economic Organization*, trans by MA Henderson and T Parsons, Oxford University Press, New York.

CHAPTER 8

Technology and work

CHAPTER SUMMARY

This chapter is based on the notion that technology inevitably influences both the nature of work undertaken by people within organizations and also the purpose of that work. It begins with a review of the meaning of the term which will be followed by introduction to the evolution of technology. This provides a basis for understanding the social context within which technology is utilized. This will be followed by the consideration of a number of aspects of technology as it is used within organizations, such as the range of different perspectives on it, the politics associated with its use and its links with alienation. This leads naturally into a review of the impact of technology on a range of organizational aspects, such as structure, job design and change. The chapter will conclude with a review of the applied connotations of technology.

LEARNING OBJECTIVES

After studying this chapter and working through the associated Management in Action Panels, Discussion questions and Research activities, you should be able to:

✦ Understand what is meant by the term technology and how it influences both the organizational context and jobs that people undertake.

✦ Describe how new technology influences the operational and support activities found within organizations.

✦ Explain the relationship between technology and the managerial

perspectives on organizational functioning.

✦ Assess the links between technology and change.

✦ Outline the relationship between technology, politics and rationality in managerial decision making.

✦ Discuss the notion of diversity and the potential conflict between uniformity through technology and differentiation.

✦ Detail the relationship between technology and control.

✦ Appreciate how the application of technology can result in alienation and the degradation of labour.

303

Introduction

The concept of *technology* is most frequently associated with the application of computers and automation to work activities. However, there are other perspectives about the notion of technology and how it impacts upon the operation of organizations that are important to consider. In the past, technology literally referred to the machines and the methods of production associated with them. However, today it can be regarded as a rather vague term which alludes to a broad spectrum of organizational influences, together with the related social connotations. It is appropriate to begin this chapter by attempting to examine the meaning of technology a little more closely.

Technology – a definition

Technology is a broad term incorporating social and procedural issues as well as equipment aspects. From a historical perspective technology reflects a process in which human endeavour is oriented towards solving real problems, experimenting with new ways of doing familiar things or simply finding out new knowledge.

This outline of *technology* is based on the work of Winner (1977) who points out clearly the changing view of the concept. According to his analysis technology has gone from being a relatively precise term with little significance to a rather vague term with a considerable degree of importance in terms of its value to organizations and society. Winner (p 10) further identifies three general applications of the term technology:

✦ Apparatus. This category of technology refers to the *physical apparatus* or *materials* that are necessary for the achievement of tasks. It includes the tools, machines and instruments needed to undertake work either in support of people's actions or as an automatic means of producing goods and services.

✦ Technique. This refers to the purposive aspects of human activity through the application of *skills*, *methods*, *procedures* or *routines* as a means of achieving objectives.

✦ Organization. This use of the term refers to *social arrangements* including factories, bureaucracies and teams established to achieve particular goals. It is the framework within which the *apparatus* and *techniques* are practised.

Fox (1974) introduces an attempt to define technology from the perspective of the industrial sociologist, and distinguishes between:

✦ Material technology. This refers to the tangible aspects of technology that can be seen, touched or heard.

✦ Social technology. This refers to the social and behaviour shaping devices of structure, control, co-ordination, motivation and reward systems. In other words it is the means though which individuals are managed to ensure that the desired objectives are achieved.

The *material technology* described by Fox clearly aligns with the *apparatus* concept as identified by Winner. The *social technology* of Fox would also match the *organization* category described by Winner. However, the *technique* classification identified by Winner is not so easy to incorporate into the work of Fox. It could be argued that the purposive nature of *technique* makes it part of the *material technology* described by Fox. A similar argument would be based on the physical aspects of skill etc., which can be expressed and therefore experienced by others. However, the execution of skill requires routines and procedures to be followed in achieving the set objectives and therefore it could also be classed as a *social* aspect from Fox's classification.

The problem with both of these definitions of technology is that any specific example studied is likely to contain elements of each classification. For example, the introduction of new equipment in a factory is likely to influence both the techniques used and the social organization within which it is carried out, as well as being a physical piece of apparatus itself. In terms of Fox's classification scheme there is also likely to be an interaction between the 'hard' aspects of the material technologies and the 'soft' aspects of social order and behaviour within which the tangible aspects will be operated.

Clark *et al.* (1988) introduced an alternative approach, based on the notion of an engineering system. Their definition offers a relatively narrow view of technology, but adds complexity and sophistication through the incorporation of engineering principles. Their definition begins with a view of technology based on the notion of hardware, software, engineering principles and the functional configuration of components. Such a system is composed of:

✦ Primary elements. The two elements within the primary category are the *architecture* (design and structure) and the *technology* (hardware and software).

✦ Secondary elements. The two elements within the secondary category are the *dimensioning* (adaptation for specific use) and *appearance* (ergonomic and aesthetic features).

This approach has the advantage of overcoming the potential conflicts inherent in the earlier definitions because of the inclusion of variability within it. The earlier definitions saw the significance of technology as a function of its attributes. Not all examples found can be fitted neatly into this framework. The model of Clark *et al.* incorporates a wider number of variables into a single model. Consequently, additional richness and complexity can be accommodated without violating the essential unity of the framework. Within this model it is easy to accommodate the findings that there are both *imperatives* and *constraints* that exist and which operate on the choice of technologies used:

> First, they [the technologies] eliminate or reduce the amount of complex tasks requiring manual skills and abilities; second, they generate more complex tasks which require mental problem-solving and interpretative skills and abilities and an understanding of system interdependencies; third, in order that many tasks can be performed effectively, tacit skills and abilities associated with the performance of work with the old technology are still required; fourth, they involve a fundamentally different relationship between the user and the technology compared to [older] technologies. (McLoughlin and Clark, 1988, pp 116–17)

In order to understand technology and the impact of it in an organizational context the approach of Clark *et al.* has much to commend it. It adopts a clear view of technology as being the hardware and the software associated with the physical representation of it. However, it allows for the introduction of the contextual and social dimensions through the other dimensions of *architecture, dimensioning* and *appearance* as part of a single model.

The actual approach adopted to the study of technology will depend on the purpose to which it is being considered. For example, engineers are concerned with the equipment aspects; industrial engineers with the efficiency of use; product designers with the implications for the physical end result; managers with control, levels of throughput and cost; and social scientists with the social, political and control aspects of it. Braverman (1974) incorporated these into two broad categories of approach to technology:

+ Engineering approach. Regards technology as a representation of machines and equipment. Emphasizes the internal relationships between them and concentrates on the physical aspects.

+ Social approach. Considers technology from the perspective of the associated labour and views it as a social construction serving the needs of particular groups within society. This is an issue that will be developed further in the subsequent discussion of alienation.

This approach to technology is very much a function of whether it is considered to be a collection of hardware or as part of the social ordering and structure of society. The particular *metaphor* adopted will significantly influence the subsequent view of its impact. What does emerge from this review of the definition of technology is that it reflects much more than simply machine- and computer-based approaches to work. Management in Action 8.1 demonstrates the *broad impact* nature of the subject by providing a view of the technological impact on the future lives of stereotypical individuals.

Stop | Consider

Given that 2004 is a lot closer than when the forecasts in MiA 8.1 were developed, how valid and useful are they?
What benefits do such predictions have in terms of the impact of technology?

The evolution of technology

Technology is not static. The ability of the ancient Greeks to provide an automatically opening temple door when a particular altar fire was lit must have seemed like pure magic to the people of the day (Klemm, 1959). It was certainly an example of a new technology in its time. There would appear to be four major implications that emerge from a historical perspective on technology:

+ Experience. All technology is *new technology* at some point. What we refer to as new technology today will not be so classified in the future.

+ Loss. Political, military, religious and social events can conspire to *lose* a particular technology. The Roman occupiers of Britain (around 200 CE) had central heating for their houses. Because such systems would be operated by slaves some of the aboriginal inhabitants would have developed appropriate skills in utilizing that technology.

MANAGEMENT IN ACTION 8.1

Real lives in media's 2004

The world of technology is constantly changing. It is vitally important for the many companies that need to develop products and services for future consumption to understand these trends. Indeed their very existence depends on understanding future consumer behaviour in relation to technology.

The Henley Centre, the UK forecasting group, has attempted to identify how people will actually lead their lives around the year 2004 and what this might mean for consumer behaviour. In addition, the changes in media as a result of technology development and their impact on marketing communications also formed part of the study.

In broad terms the study predicts that a polarization will evolve between the technology haves and the have-nots. The forecasters point out that there is a real danger of product and service providers generalizing an assumed access to and use of technology across consumer groups. Conventional media will still have a significant role in society. For example, it is predicted that mass market terrestrial television will still account for the majority of viewing, but that the audience will be more 'downmarket' than at present. Many viewers will continue to use television as a form of companionship, entertainment and relaxation because they will not be able to afford the other forms of leisure and media available to them.

The Henley Centre study identified four distinct groups of consumers in relation to technology and media developments:

✦ Technophiles. This category is estimated at 24% of the population. Enthusiastic about technology with considerable interest in the application of new technology. In age they are likely to be under 35, more likely to be male and from social group C1.

✦ Aspirational technophiles. This category is estimated at 22% of the population. Are

'excited' by technology in a general sense, but less interested in its application. They are more likely to be male and from the AB social group.

✦ Functionals. This category is estimated at 25% of the population. Not particularly interested in technology, but sympathetic to its application where it can enhance existing services. More likely to be female and aged over 45.

✦ Technophobes. This category is estimated at 28% of the population. It is hostile to technology in all its forms and also sceptical about its ability to offer anything new. They are more likely to be female and aged over 60. They are also likely to be evenly distributed across the social groups.

As an example of the impact of technology and media development in the year 2004, the study describes a day in the lives of a number of people. The following is an extract of one of these descriptions:

Lesley is a 23-year-old part-time student and a technophile. The study provides her with a deliberately androgynous name because there are fewer gender differences in attitude and behaviour among younger people than were evident in the past.

She wakes to the sound of a small, independent radio station, then reads the newspaper while eating her breakfast. She could have downloaded articles from her personal computer but feels insufficiently awake. Conventional newspapers continue to play an important role: most are read over breakfast as few kitchens have terminals to access online versions. Lesley then checks her e-mail and links up with the university's online teaching system. She has access to most databases and published material through the Supernet, the upgraded Internet system introduced in 1999. She needs to go to college only one day a week and works in a restaurant most evenings. Before going to work, she watches television with her flatmates, surfing 100 channels and sometimes stopping to participate in an interactive advertisement. In spite of growth in personalised media, people still like to watch, listen and play together – to be social and keep up with their peers. At work, the radio is on in the kitchen; the giant TV screens that used to be in the dining area were too intrusive. Back home, Lesley unwinds with a book – even for a technophile, the book will continue to be a source of escapism, relaxation and entertainment.

Adapted from: Summers, D (1995) Real lives in media's 2004, *Financial Times*, 30 March, p 14.

However, when the Romans left Britain, the use of central heating died out, not to become widely available until the mid-1900s.

✦ Erratic. The development of technology does not follow a smooth or continuous pattern across time and location. Military need plays a significant role in technological advancement. One of the effects of the end of the Cold War – the peace dividend – has been a reduction in size of defence-sponsored development as well as the military itself.

✦ Human. Decisions relating to technology are taken by people and it can support their objectives. The development of a machine-based factory technology could be used to replace human labour and reduce the power of trade unions. Conversely, the higher skills needed to operate and maintain sophisticated technology increases the power and value of the remaining employees.

There are a number of perspectives that could be adopted in reviewing the evolution of technology. It appears from even the most cursory reading of the history of the subject that there was a considerable movement of technology around the world even in ancient times. For example, the windmill appears to have been brought to the Islamic cultures of the Middle East from countries in the Far East before the tenth century and into the parts of Europe by the twelfth century. The following sections will attempt to provide a brief insight into the evolution of technology from a predominantly European perspective, based on Klemm (1959).

Ancient history

Cave drawings in southern France dating from the later Palaeolithic period (Stone Age) indicate the use of traps for catching bison and mammoth. Examples of the very first machines were based on a lever to release a fall of tree trunks onto the trapped animal. The use of stone implements was slowly replaced with those made from copper and bronze and by around 1000 BCE. with iron. During the later part of this period the great works of Egypt, in the building of the pyramids and civil engineering works to harness river flood waters were being effected through the ability of the state to organize and control the necessary resources. In ancient Greece and Rome manual labour was looked down on as something that was generally appropriate for slaves to be engaged in, very much subordinate to philosophical and intellectual pursuits. Much of the technological activity during this period seems to have been driven by a small range of forces:

+ Subjugation of nature. In this context the main purpose of technology was to overcome the difficulties and problems that nature appeared to present in controlling the world in which people lived. For example, understanding and explaining the principles of leverage in general and as used to row a ship in particular. The use of screw mechanisms to drain water from mines was something that the Romans had achieved in Spain before 200 CE.

+ Religious and political representations. The building of the pyramids, temples and the use of technology to open doors automatically when particular sacrificial fires were lit are examples of the ingenuity to which technology could be put. The use of aqueducts to carry water to cities was an example of politically based civil engineering feats used for the benefit of citizens.

+ Military. The need for weapons of defence or attack was a significant driver to the application of technology in this period. The slingshot, catapult and other engines of war were developed as the understanding of maths, geometry and proportion grew alongside an ability to work with the best raw materials in wood, rope and metal.

+ Curiosity. The simple exercise of curiosity and the resultant development of mechanical devices and amusements for the citizens of the day created more technological development. A water organ and water pump are but two examples of this form of mechanical artwork.

It is worth noting that the Romans had an understanding of the water wheel and its potential in grinding corn etc. However, the ready availability of slaves made it an uneconomic and unnecessary proposition at the time. This and the earlier point about the presence of central heating in Roman houses, which was 'lost' for almost 2000 years illustrate the *relative* nature of technology – its development depends significantly on its perceived value *relative* to other options. This clearly illustrates the social and contextual influences on technology.

The Middle Ages

Klemm summarizes the achievements of this period as, 'utilizing the elemental forces of beast, water and wind to a far greater degree than was possible for Antiquity' (p 79). The development of sailing technology through the introduction of the stern rudder and improved rigging arrangements allowed for more effective transport of goods and people over larger distances. In military terms the development of the gun as a piece of hardware based on a better understanding of gunpowder and metalworking provided an opportunity for both improved defence and attack activity.

The Renaissance

This period of history is typified by the recognition that developments in the future could be based on an understanding of what had gone before. Social development went hand in hand with technological development. The success of the craft and commerce basis of much activity at the time had begun to break down the privilege, ownership and power of the feudal lords. The ability of various craft-based occupations (builders, stonemasons, sculptors, goldsmiths etc.) to create ever more sophisticated results was largely a function of the development of rules for their work, based on an analysis of what had gone before, rather than the application of rules of thumb. In essence, the evolution of the scientific method. The image conjured up by the mention of the work of Leonardo da Vinci would typify this period. His careful analysis of such things as anatomy, architecture and flight provide the clearest picture possible of the new spirit of development and a desire to understand the workings of nature.

The continuous development of ways to improve the effectiveness of work became the focus of activity. The result of this broad combination of humanism with an attempt to understand and control nature through technology was the basis for developments in many of the arts and crafts. In many ways this period can be described as a time of consolidation in areas of mechanics (leverage, pulleys etc.) and attempting to harness and develop the results more effectively.

The baroque period

The formalization of research is what typifies this period of history. The emergence of scientific instruments such as the microscope and the calculating machine are examples which created the opportunity for systematic and scientific research to develop. The emergence of the first scientific societies and journals led to the possibility of the exchange of knowledge and the testing/replication of conclusions. The application of technology, was directed towards increases in the volumes of production through the division of labour and improved organization of work activity.

The development of an effective ability to protect the interests of those individuals who developed new ways of doing things and inventions was crucial to the further development of technology. Allowing individuals to reap the benefits for their inventions was a means not only of encouraging the creation of a high number of new technologies but of allowing the commercial exploitation of them.

The age of rationalism

This period saw the transformation from small-scale industrial operation based on craft to the industrialization model found in the Industrial Revolution. Improvements in the design of the steam engine by Watt in the middle of the eighteenth century were the basis for developments in mining, metal processing and manufacturing. This went hand in hand with the development of machines and chemicals for the textile industry. In essence, this period saw the emergence of the skilled engineer as the person capable of converting the *new technology* into practical applications through a mixture of theory and practice.

In terms of trade this period saw the publication (in 1776) of *The Wealth of Nations* by Adam Smith in which the notion of free trade and competition as the basis of a strong economy were first put forward, ideas which further encouraged the development of technology as an aid to competitive advantage supported by the free market. Indeed, it can be said that the division of labour described by Smith set the scene for the later work of Taylor and *scientific management*. In France the Polytechnic was opened in Paris in 1794 as an institution for the scientific study and the teaching of technology.

The period of industrialization

Continuous improvements to the ability of engines to meet the power needs of the emerging factory system typified the early part of this period. The development of the railway engine also allowed the rapid and easy movement of people and goods, further allowing markets and industry to develop. It was during this period that the first claims that machines were replacing workers appeared. It was said that 150,000 people operating factory-based spinning machines could produce more yarn than 40 million people using the old-fashioned hand wheel (Baines, 1835).

The machine pacing of work in a factory and its effects on jobs also emerged at the same time (Ure, 1835). This aspect of technology began to make a more direct appearance in the thinking of the day with a number of writers of the period making reference to the dismal conditions for the workers, low pay, grinding pace of work and the emergence of the trade unions, strikes and riots. However, by the middle of the nineteenth century improvements in technology and organization were seen as the main means of increasing output.

During the latter part of the nineteenth century and the early years of the twentieth century the technologies developed in the western world were transported to other countries, noticeably America, Japan and Russia. The development of the internal combustion and diesel engines allowed the introduction of more efficient forms of machine and transport. It was in the early years of that century that Henry Ford began to experiment with mass production methods in the assembly of motor vehicles. This signalled the introduction of production-based technology on a large scale and was grounded in the availability of electrical power, dating from the 1880s.

Since the early years of the last century there have been many more technological developments that have contributed to the world as we know it today. For example, flight, computers, radio and television, the nuclear industry and medical technology are all examples of recent and significant developments. The development of such technologies has led many people to argue that the world has entered a post-industrial or information era.

Perspectives on technology

The impact of technology on an organization has been studied from a number of different perspectives and based on a differing view of what technology actually is. There are six different approaches that are worthy of specific review in this context.

Woodward and production technology

In a study of 100 manufacturing organizations in the electronics, chemical and engineering industries Woodward (1965) defined technology in terms of the approach to production adopted by the companies. This she split into:

✦ Unit or small batch. This indicates that items are made in very small quantities, perhaps even being made individually, specifically to a customer order.

✦ Large batch or mass production. This reflects the manufacture of large quantities, perhaps on an assembly line as in the manufacture of motor cars.

✦ Continuous process. This reflects operations where the raw material is taken from its initial state and subjected to a continuous sequence of processes until it is in its final form ready for sale. Typical examples are oil refineries and chemical plants.

Woodward found that there was a definite tendency for a number of organizational characteristics to vary depending upon the classification of the production process. Table 8.1 indicates some of the primary findings from this study.

Although there were differences between the organizations in the sample there was a clear tendency for the production technology to influence a number of aspects of structure. It also became apparent that those organizations that were the most commercially successful were closer to the norm for their particular production technology than those firms that were less successful. Given that the definition of production technology used in this study is very broad, there are many significant differences between operations in large batch and mass production environments. For example, it has been argued that the categories adopted were simplistic and may not have reflected technological complexity but degree of continuity in the process (Bedeian, 1984).

Burns and Stalker – stability and change

From their study of electronics and traditional manufacturing organizations (1961) they identified:

✦ Mechanistic structures. Close definition of jobs and procedures to be followed. Clear lines of authority and levels within the hierarchy. Best suited to stable environments with a slowly changing technology.

✦ Organismic structures. Lack of definition of jobs and hierarchy. Continuous adaptation of hierarchy and jobs as the prevailing technology undergoes change.

Technology in the context of the Burns and Stalker study is one of the factors that make up the environment within which the organization operates. It is, therefore, something to which the organization must adapt itself if it is to harness the technology to advantage. This view was supported by the work of Lawrence and Lorsch (1967), but has been criticized by writers such as Hughes (1985) who claim that political activity and government policy also play a significant part in the success of organizations.

Unit or small batch	Lowest number of levels of management and span of control of chief executive Highest ratio of direct to indirect staff and total labour cost
Large batch or mass production	Lowest number of verbal communications and skilled employees Highest number of written communications, sanction procedures and span of control of supervisors
Continuous process	Lowest number of written communications and span of control of supervisor Highest number of levels of management and ratio of managers to other staff

TABLE 8.1   Conclusions from Woodward's study

Perrow – a continuum from routine to non-routine

A slightly different approach to the notion of technology was introduced by Perrow (1967, 1970). He created a view of technology that was based on a continuum from routine to non-routine in terms of the approach to operational activity. This view allowed the concept to be applied to organizations other than the manufacturing companies so far described. Used in this way technology is an integral part of the processes involved in the work of the organization. It relates to the ways that problems (or exceptions to the normal routine) are dealt with and the integrative approaches to functional interdependence. In this way the notion of technology is broadened into a concept that reflects social, structural, procedural, relationship perspectives as well as the hardware associated with machines and production processes.

Thompson – resource and technology matching

In this view it is argued that the organization attempts to arrange its resources and processes in such a way as to allow it to match its natural technological tendency. Thompson (1967) identified three categories of technology:

✦ Long linked. This approach describes the sequential processes most obviously found in assembly line factory operations. The technologies used in this type of process are designed to ensure that each part of the process fits together effectively in producing the end result.

✦ Mediating. This form of operational technology seeks to bring together (mediate) what would otherwise be independent activities or needs. For example, a bank brings together borrowers and lenders, the human resource department within a company seeks to ensure that the needs of both management and workforce can be met as far as possible. In this form the process begins with a classification of *need*, then an identification of appropriate transactions. The technology in this context comprises the operating procedures, rules etc. that allow the encounter to be effectively executed.

✦ Intensive. This definition of technology revolves around skill. It attempts to provide a personal level of service within a standardized framework. Typical examples include a medical treatment, where the doctor will need to personalize the treatment regime within a standard process of consultation and care. Similarly, a university attempts to provide individual learning experiences for each student within a structured framework of courses, lectures, tutorials and assessment.

This view of technology reflects organizational attempts to achieve broad objectives as described in the three categories, with an ability to deal effectively with problems and at minimal operating cost. Features of this approach include the structure and design of the organization in which, for example, a warehouse can help absorb some of the variability in sales levels or the human resource function can assist in resolving some of the people problems quickly or train employees to a high level of skill and proficiency.

The Aston studies

In terms of technology these studies utilized three categories:

✦ Operations. This type of technology reflected the nature of the transformation process, the techniques used.

◆ Materials. This aspect of technology reflected the nature and characteristics of the things that were being processed. For example, different metals have different properties and need to be processed differently. Equally, in a service organization each customer's needs are slightly different (the various patients visiting a doctor) and therefore the processing (treatment) would differ accordingly.

◆ Knowledge. This reflects the skill and ability required to undertake the tasks necessary to achieve the objectives. For example, a nuclear power station would not be capable of operating at full capacity unless the employees, specialists and managers were trained and skilled at the tasks expected of them.

Blumer and industrialization

In a work published after his death, Herbert Blumer considered the nature of *industrialization* (the application of technology to a particular context) and its influence as an agent of social change (Maines and Morrione, 1990). In this work Blumer suggests that the term *industrialization* is frequently used in a way which conjures up the stereotypic image of the development of the factory system, urbanization of residence, the use of machines, the dilution of skilled work and the formation of a managerial class etc. To this framework is added an emotional veneer as the result of, 'inadequate study, partisan interests, doctrinaire concerns, and agitation on behalf of social reforms' (p 15). To Blumer this view of industrialization emerged largely from Great Britain as a reflection of the particular historical process.

Blumer makes several points of distinction between industrialization and technological change, including (pp 18–20):

◆ Non-industrial technological change. There are a number of technological developments that have no impact on the level of industrialization. For example, the introduction of the steel axe as a replacement for the stone axe is an example of technological development that need not directly impact on the level or type of industrialization within which it is used.

◆ Industrialization as one form of technological development. Industrialization brings with it many changes other than those based on the technology. For example, the increased use of female labour, the arrival of a managerial class, factory-based work disciplines, the development of organized labour are just some of the consequences of industrialization that are not, of themselves, technologically based.

◆ Transplanted industrialization. It does not automatically follow that technology evolves as part of the process of industrialization. Many of the developing countries of the world have received what could be classified as transplanted technology. However, this is frequently a package of industrialization, including the appropriate technology.

◆ Causal relationships. In the discussion of the impact of technology on society it is frequently implied that there is a direct link between the two. For example, it can be suggested that the introduction of high technology creates social problems in society through increased levels of alienation. This approach tends to underestimate the complexity of the relationships and chain of events involved.

◆ Ambiguity. The term technological development contains a higher level of ambiguity in terms of its interrelationship with social change than does the concept of industrialization. In other words, technology contains a wide variety of meaning which it is difficult to restrict in attempting to tease out the social implications.

In terms of the relationship between the terms industrialization and technology Blumer is approaching the question from the perspective of social change. In dealing with social science concepts it is inevitable that definitions will not have the precision of the natural sciences. In terms of how these two concepts impact on social change it is apparent that for Blumer there are differences between them. They can be considered to be overlapping circles in a Venn diagram. On occasions, they will meet and be very similar, but on other occasions they will differ. In his work Blumer does not spell out in detail his idea of technology, but it is clear from this discussion that he adopts a mechanical view rather like the *apparatus* concept identified by Winner.

Each of the six approaches to technology discussed contains different perspectives on the subject. Whatever approach to the concept is adopted it is clearly much too simplistic to consider technology as equivalent to computers and automation. From the studies reviewed it is clear that there are links between technology and structure, work organization, hierarchy, people management, customer needs, operational strategy and organizational success. In addition there is also the suggestion that with some forms of technology there are opportunities to become more sensitive and adaptive to the environmental pressures surrounding the organization. In being able to adapt to the changing environments surrounding the organization there is assumed to be a greater likelihood of commercial success in the short term and survival in the long term. Clearly, therefore, a view of technology that generally provides an opportunity to support managerial objectives is emerging from these studies.

Japanization, technology and work

That organizations reflect the broader social context in which they exist cannot be denied. The difficulty is in delineating the extent of the relationship. These relationships become even more complex when cross-cultural perspectives impinge on the situation. This was highlighted with particular force during the late 1970s and early 1980s when the impact of Japanese manufactured goods suddenly became apparent throughout the western world. The quality and reliability of Japanese products and the perceived value for money decimated the market share of many long-established producers. For example, by 1986 Japanese manufacturers held 84% of the world market for 35 mm cameras, 71% of microwave ovens and 55% of motorcycles (BBC/OU, 1986). Oliver and Wilkinson (1992) provide many similar statistics which indicate the significance and magnitude of the Japanese threat. Table 8.2 is a summary of some of these data.

	Japan	West	America	Toyota
Set-up time (hours)*			6.0	0.2
Number of set-ups per day*			1.0	3.0
Sales per annum per employee†	$150K	$85K		

*Based on the work of Burbridge (1982)
†Based on the work of Parnaby (1987)

TABLE 8.2 Japanese and western productivity comparisons (*adapted from*: Oliver, N and Wilkinson, B (1992) *The Japanization of British Industry: New Developments in the 1990s*, 2nd edition, Blackwell, Oxford)

The threat to jobs and even whole industries quickly became apparent and a search for an explanation undertaken. The original view was that there had to be a new way of managing to provide such impressive results. It was thought to be a reflection of the Japanese culture and religion as well as the emphasis on the group rather than individual prowess. Oliver and Wilkinson (1992) identify a number of features of Japanese production methods that collectively provide the scale of benefit achieved, including:

✦ Quality. The view that quality is integral to the entire production process and reduces the cost of operations was generated by US consultants during World War II. There was very little interest in these ideas in the west, but Japanese managers adopted the principles during the rebuilding of the economy in the 1950s. The view of quality in the west was that it was *inspected into* a product after it was made. The quality was checked and repairs carried out if necessary. In Japan, quality was seen as a feature of the manufacturing process and reflecting the level of control within the organization. One of the ways that this can be achieved is by solving problems as they arise rather than tolerating them.

✦ Just in time. This approach requires the elimination of inventory, items needed in production arriving at the point of use *just in time*. Inventory is regarded as unnecessary and a means of hiding problems. The traditional western approach to planning is to *push* items into the system in the belief that if all the parts are available production flow will be maintained. Just in time operates on the basis that the needs of assembly should dictate when components are *pulled* forward into the production process. Small frequent deliveries as and when needed is the basis of production in this approach. Operating under just-in-time conditions requires inventory levels to be deliberately and progressively reduced. It also requires the problems resulting from the lack of inventory to be dealt with so that they do not continue to restrict operational activity.

✦ Continuous improvement. The need to improve quality and solve problems associated with just-in-time production require specific programmes. It is never possible to achieve perfection, improvements can always be achieved. This is the philosophy behind continual improvement. It is also part of this approach that improvement can be best identified by the people most directly involved in the work. In the west employees do not traditionally expect to be involved in solving problems and to have their opinions sought by managers. In Japan a culture that expects individuals to participate in these activities (usually in their own time) is the norm. Failure to do so to an acceptable level would be held against an individual in pay and promotion terms.

✦ Work organization. The use of cellular manufacturing methods and U-shaped production lines allows for greater employee flexibility as well as improved control of the product and process. According to Gaither (1992, p 294) the benefits of a cell approach to production are:
  ✦ Machine changeovers are simplified.
  ✦ Training periods for workers are shortened.
  ✦ Materials-handling costs are reduced.
  ✦ Parts can be made faster and shipped more quickly.
  ✦ Less in-process inventory is required.
  ✦ Production is easier to automate.

  A cell becomes a micro production unit dedicated to the production of a small range of products, thereby allowing a high level of expertise, flexibility and efficiency to develop.

U-shaped assembly lines are assembly lines that have been shaped to encourage a team commitment to develop. In straight assembly lines the linear approach ties workers to specific workstations and their only contact would be with adjacent work activities. U-shaped assembly lines simply bend the straight line to create involvement opportunities. Figure 8.1 shows a U-shaped production line, based upon the principles developed by Toyota.

Teams provide an opportunity for people to work together, help each other with a social perspective to their work. In the Japanese approach this is taken much further. Oliver and Wilkinson (1992) quote Sayer (1986) who indicates that one Toyota worker performed 35 different jobs in one day and walked six miles. Another view of these types of work practice is also quoted by Oliver and Wilkinson referring to Domingo (1985) who suggests that the system deliberately introduces tension into the system which turns every day into a challenge. A negative view of teamwork is provided by Garrahan and Stewart (1992). They describe a control and conflictual perspective on team-based production methods. They suggest that it provides a more effective level of management control and in practice sets one worker against another in the drive to find problems and seek continual improvement. Each worker is expected to report quality problems immediately. Failure to do so makes the individual liable to punishment rather than the 'creator' of the problem.

✦   Structure and system. Japanese organization structure was researched by Lincoln and Kalleburg (1990) who show that they generally contained more hierarchical levels and incorporated a greater measure of formality. Oliver and Wilkinson describe the Japanese approach to accounting as providing a strong market focus. The approach adopted being essentially an *outside-in* perspective of identifying a market price and then managing costs within that constraint. The western approach tends to be based on identifying costs and then attempting to ensure that price can cover these needs, an *inside-out* approach. Similar strengths in product development activities can also be identified. Smaller teams, with greater power and forced by the system to face up to the

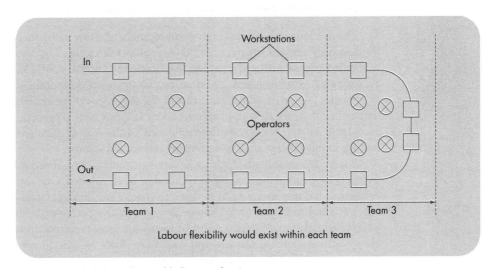

FIGURE 8.1   'U'-shaped assembly line production.

requirement to *get it right first time* are able to respond more quickly to changing market forces.

The relationship between buyers and suppliers has been frequently described as an adversarial one in the west. Buyers would frequently have many suppliers and would play one off against the other in terms of price and delivery. The Japanese approach is based upon co-operation and long-term relationships with a small number of suppliers. This leads to an inevitable development of dependence relationships. Neither party can afford to abuse the relationship. The location of suppliers is frequently adjacent to the customer so that just-in-time principles can be better applied, with transport distances being minimized and automated. It is common to find companies part owning their suppliers.

✦ Personnel practice. There are many features of personnel practice that have been suggested to differ between the west and Japan. Practices such as lifetime employment; high levels of company welfare benefit; selection for employment based on degree of *fit* with company values and norms; promotion and reward based upon seniority and service; and excessively long working hours have all been identified as major points of distinction. However, the experience of employment in Japan would appear to be somewhat more complex. Lifetime employment has not been available to all workers and organizations have made use of large numbers of temporary or short-term contract workers.

✦ Social, political and economic factors. Organizations and management practice emerge in a specific context, therefore it should not be surprising to discover differences in how organizations are structured and function. It could be argued that much of current management thinking is dominated by western ideas and that we should not expect to find that these insights offer the only explanations. That said there are a number of features of the Japanese environment that are worthy of note. It is not uncommon to find executives in a Japanese company who have spent time as union officials in that same company as part of their career. The education system is very competitive and forces very young people to study extremely hard for long periods of time. Entrance to the best universities is very competitive and demands considerable sacrifice on the part of students and their families.

The need to work effectively in teams is another feature of Japanese life that is fostered from an early age and which is carried over into working life. The role of the government, particularly the Ministry of International Trade and Industry (MITI), has been crucial in encouraging organizations to develop strategic programmes of overseas trade. Information, financial, administrative and research support are available for particular initiatives involving the development of markets and products, a process that has led to many complaints of state subsidy and manipulating of the market. Companies who do not co-operate in this process are also activity discriminated against.

Fuelled by the inroads made by Japanese products into home markets western manufacturers have found it necessary to respond or be eliminated. One way of responding is to emulate. It has not always been possible to change working practices quickly (or successfully) as employees and trade unions have sometimes perceived initiatives as a threat to established rights and benefits. Most of the major motor manufacturers have experienced years of frustration, negotiation and dispute in order to introduce some of the Japanese practices into UK factories (see, for example, Giles and Starkey, 1987; Turnbull, 1986).

In order better to serve their export markets and to placate any suggestion of unfair competition, Japanese producers began to build factories in the west. Garrahan and Stewart (1992) describe this process in general terms, with particular emphasis on the role of the decision of Nissan to build a car assembly plant in Washington, near Sunderland. In this situation there was an opportunity to import Japanese management methods by Japanese companies and to impose them onto *greenfield* sites. The term *greenfield* is used to describe a new location as compared to a *brownfield* site, which already contains an operational unit. Clearly, in a greenfield location there are no established practices to change and management have a free hand to set their own agenda without hindrance. This must, of course, be tempered with the knowledge that there will be the established norms, expectations and behaviour patterns that exist in the surrounding environment. The Garrahan and Stewart text provides a very vivid description of this process and is a useful point of comparison with the authorized management views expressed by Wickens (1987). Wickens was at the time the head of personnel and administration at the company and the first British appointment to be made in the UK operation.

The arrival of Japanese companies in the UK provided an opportunity to observe some of the ideas on Japanese management at first hand. Of course, many Japanese home country practices could not be translated directly but many of the others were. Essentially, the notion of a flexible workforce committed to teamwork and getting it right first time were introduced along with single union agreements (the nearest form of enterprise unions that could be achieved in the UK). There is the suggestion that transplanted Japanese operations are little more than warehouses (screwdriver factories) and that the full transfer of all manufacturing activity is far from the intention (Williams *et al.*, 1992). This also has a major impact on the work activities and approach to management adopted by such organizations.

The work reviewed so far clearly reflects that Japanese companies have found ways of organizing themselves that produce very effective organizations. However, there are a number of questions that emerge out of a consideration of this approach to management. First, it is necessary to consider whether or not Japanization reflects an approach to management that is fundamentally different from *Fordism* and *scientific management*, or whether it simply reflects a high degree of refinement of those principles. Second, it raises a question about the purpose of effectiveness. In whose benefit is effectiveness being pursued and why? This in turn leads to a consideration of the purpose of organizations and the goods and services that they produce. Whose benefit are they intended to serve and why? Also emerging are questions related to the purpose of work itself.

It is clear that the purpose of the Japanese approach to management is not intended to be the benefit of the employees. It has been suggested already that stress is a common experience among Japanese workers, to the extent that death is becoming a recognized result. The references already identified indicate the low levels of satisfaction of Japanese workers compared with western counterparts. The pressure to conform to the needs of the group are considerable and individuality is not encouraged and indeed considered a threat to group cohesion. Therefore one is left with the conclusion that Japanese management practices are grounded in the same principles of power and control as Fordism, but that they are a considerable degree of sophistication more effective from the perspective of management.

Assumptions about technology

There are a number of commonly held assumptions that relate to the nature of technology, its impact on organizational functioning and operation:

✦ Neutrality. The first assumption is the view that technology is a neutral process. That is not so. It is management who determine the organizational objectives that are being sought and the way that they will be *operationalized through technology*. Technology is, therefore, something that is part of the design and achieve aspects of management and can be used and, indeed, abused by managers in an attempt to control and direct employees. It can also be used to ensure that the entire organizational process works to a management-determined agenda. In that sense, technology is under the control of management, to use as they consider appropriate.

✦ Impact. Taking a very limited view of technology, it is frequently asserted that it is only in the production areas of an organization that technology has any impact. This may be where technology has its most obvious impact, but it is not the only, or even major area of involvement. For example, administrative and accounting procedures, control reports, quality-control data are just some of the specialist areas where technology has made an impact. In addition the opportunity to integrate islands of manufacturing activity or stages in service delivery have also been evident over the past few years. These approaches take a broader view of technology and incorporate the people, material, flexibility, adaptability and political aspects into the concept.

✦ Modernism. There is a general tendency to see new things as *better* than those that went before. Nowhere is this more evident than in advertising of consumer products. Television and static advertising campaigns are forever attempting to persuade customers that a reformulated product such as a cleaning agent is a considerable improvement over the previous product. The same is true of many aspects associated with technology. Components produced by computer-controlled machines are said to be more accurate, reliable and better than those produced by skilled employees. While this may be true in some circumstances, not everything can be so easily fitted into this perspective. It is very difficult for example, to claim customized qualities for a mass produced standard product.

✦ De-skilling. It is often assumed that the introduction of higher levels of technology will allow the level of skill required from employees to be reduced. This should provide two main benefits for management. First, reduced labour cost as skill is positively correlated with pay. Second, reduced training times and cost as it is quicker and cheaper to train people to a lower level of skill. However, offsetting these claimed advantages are the higher skill levels needed to operate more complex equipment and processes as well as the new jobs created as a result of the different technologies adopted. It is also apparent that this assumption is based upon a relatively narrow definition of technology in that not all forms provide for de-skilling among employees.

✦ Structure. The studies described earlier tend to emphasize the structural and framework aspects of technology. This is not the only area of impact for technology. It also affects the control processes, it reinforces the dominance of managers and technical specialists over general employees, it is part of the political process of management and provides the opportunity for new products and services. Structure is also influenced by technology in very complex ways that tend to be understated by the earlier theories.

✦ Efficiency. It is assumed that the application of technology will increase productivity and efficiency in operational activity. While his may hold true in a very narrow sense, it does depend how broad a measure of efficiency and productivity is used. For example, the cost of the acquisition of the technology, retraining the workforce, the cost of the new jobs created are just some of the additional costs to take into account in determining the *balance of benefit*. This approach is also based upon a narrow conception of technology and from the implications referred to earlier, efficiency could be one of the least important variables involved in the adoption of technology. For example, the application of new process technologies as a means of demonstrating to customers a commitment to consistent and high quality as well as a means of forcing change in working practices can have many benefits in addition to efficiency. In addition when a new technology is introduced into an organization it is not unusual to find additional work being created as the organization learns to deal with the new situation.

The politics of technology

Among the many professional facets to management activity it is also a political process. Individual managers are in competition with each other for scarce resources, there is never enough money to fully invest in each department or function. Managers also seek to achieve personal, professional and functional significance within their organizations in order to develop their careers. Management is also political in that the pursuit of objectives requires interaction and co-operation with many other stakeholders who may have conflicting objectives. For example, employees may want much higher pay and the manager may want to reduce labour costs. Part of this process involves using technology as a political tool in order to achieve control or influence. For example, the power to dictate work routines in bank branches by a head office administrative department can be neutralized by the introduction of computer systems with data entry and information access directly undertaken by branch staff.

There is another form of people control achieved through the political use of events and activities that engage with their lives. It is this form of control to which Braverman (1974) refers when he began what became known as the labour process debate. Essentially, this debate turns on the use to which human labour is put in the transformation of raw material into commodities for capitalist markets and the part played by managers in the organization of that work. It is management that determines the nature of any technology in any given context. Consequently, it is a management agenda that determines the use of technology and how human labour will be accommodated around it. The application of technology can provide managers with a number of direct benefits including tighter control over the work process, pace of work, skill levels required and the design of work. All of these lead to a reinforcement of the dominant position of managerial control over organizational functioning and lower costs of operational activity.

This debate revolves around the degree of *malice aforethought* that managers use in taking those decisions. Is it done to control labour and reinforce management's position or is it done to further the commercial business objectives of the organization? One of the key problems in researching in this area is that of being able to find out the true causes of particular managerial actions. A manager who is attempting to manipulate workers is unlikely to admit it! Many writers prefer to limit consideration of decision making to a form of rationality. Schon (1994) for example talks of a *technical rationality* (p 243) in which the search for solutions to instrumental problems follows a logical pattern and competence can be measured through the degree to which the intended effects are achieved. Also Child (1985) argues that social and organizational aspects of such decisions are generally subordinate to the financial imperatives. He goes as far as suggesting that the broader aspects are essentially consequences of the financial perspectives, not objectives in their own right.

Technology and alienation

At a common sense level *alienation* is a form of switching off. In a work context that would be the equivalent of not feeling part of (connected to) the department or the organization and not engaging with anything on a significant level. In a very real sense, leaving one's brain at home each morning because the employer simply requires the benefit of a pair of human hands. It can be argued that the only reason organizations employ human beings is that there are some tasks for which an effective machine has yet to be developed. Looked at from this perspective then, people are simply a substitute for machines. This is, of course, too simplistic an argument as it ignores the social, political and economic aspects associated with human work. It does however, provide a very stark introduction to the nature of *alienation*.

Thompson (1989) provides a definition of alienation as follows:

> Work performed under conditions in which the worker is estranged from his or her own activity in the act of production, though the sale of labour power and the subordination of skills and knowledge to the capitalist, or other external social forces. (p xiii)

This definition picks up a number of aspects from the earlier sociological viewpoints of writers such as Blauner, Braverman and Marx. Essentially attempting to assess the nature of work within the context in which it is carried out, the *labour process debate* brings together a number of traditions in considering issues such as the degradation of work and de-skilling. It is within this paradigm that the notion of *alienation* as defined earlier is set.

Alienation is about separation, ownership and the rights of workers as stakeholders. It is argued that alienation occurs as an inevitable reaction to the control of work by managers and that technology plays a significant part in the support that process. It has already been suggested that technology is not neutral, it is utilized by managers as part of their attempts to achieve business objectives. Blauner (1964) made this assertion in relation to continuous process industries on the basis of his research in a number of different (technologically speaking) industries. In doing so, his approach to alienation was based on the *feelings* of workers formed in response to the specific dominant technology. It was defined in terms of:

+ Powerlessness. A lack of control or influence over the pace and methods of work, as well as the general working conditions and the processes involved in carrying it out.

+ Meaninglessness. A feeling of being a very small part of a large process and that the individual's contribution had little real significance in terms of the finished product or service.

+ Isolation. A lack of belonging, or of a feeling of not being part of a team or group.

✦ Self-estrangement. A reduced feeling of self-worth as a consequence of being reduced to a number within a crowd and a lack of work being a significant focus for life.

The degree to which continuous process technologies can achieve the type of work envisaged by Blauner must be open to question from a number of perspectives, at least in the short term. For example, the number of jobs available in continuous process operations tends to be much smaller than in most other forms of technology applications. Not all products and services are amenable to continuous process technologies, a hospital can never function like a chemical factory. It does, however, have its own version of continuous process technology – it functions 24 hours a day and for 365 days a year and it contains some highly skilled personnel. As such a hospital should be a *low alienation* environment containing high skill, high discretion jobs in a human-based caring environment.

Alienation is clearly an aspect of the human experience of work in some contexts and as such technology impacts on that experience. There are clearly differences in the way that alienation can be experienced and therefore the impact of technology can be expected to be different for each variation. However, what is not in question is that the two concepts are linked and that alienation can adversely affect behaviour with the organization. It can be argued that a significant aspect of some of the features of more recent approaches to job design are attempts to reintroduce elements of ownership and reduce the feelings of separation arising from the use of technology. Perhaps an attempt by managers to balance the people issues with the procedural, production and machine technologies available in the search for efficiency from their investment.

Determinism, rationality and control

There are compelling arguments that technology, particularly new technology, is independent of any particular organizational context and universally applied. However, Friedman and Cornford (1989) use the term *autogenerative* to suggest that computer innovations are as much a function of the user as they are the original designer. Taken in isolation, this view could support the deterministic perspective in that the development of technology is part of a cyclical relationship with the designer and user both developing the technology for each other's benefit. However, it can also be used to support the opposing point of view. If the user can influence the innovation process they are in a position to shape it and can control it to a significant extent. The economic imperative provides organizations with a basis for attempting to match (or better) competitor activity in the search for competitive advantage and so seek the maximum capability that technology can provide.

Management objectives play a significant part in the way in which the environment is perceived and interpreted. The objectives that management seek also colour the way in which the situation is interpreted and decisions taken. Decision making is a political process and can be used for reasons other than the benefit of the organization. For example, the director in charge of a computer department may seek to ensure that the company takes decisions that enhance the reputation and standing of the department. In that sense it is more effective to consider not a technological imperative as such, but to see things in terms of cause and effect, with technology being a major determinant of the options available. Figure 8.2 reflects this situation, and reflects the role of technology as a driver of options as well as being a feature of managerial interpretation.

This view is perhaps closer to the conclusion reached by McLoughlin and Clark (1988) in which they argue for a complex definition of determinism rather than the simple linear process suggested by many writers. So far rationality has been assumed. This suggests that managers take decisions based on a rational process in the best interests of the organization. That is a major assumption. The word rational might be implied in many decisions, but rational from whose point of view? Rationality is an illusive concept and is not necessarily obvious or apparent to everyone. It depends on the points of view and perceptions of the individuals involved.

The justification of new technology is frequently based upon improvements in control in one form or another. Control of cost, control of a process, control of employees being among the most commonly used. Control can become a self-perpetuating process of management finding ways to improve control over employees, leading to adverse employee reaction, confirming the need for ever tighter control. Clegg and Dunkerley (1980) describe this as a *vicious cycle of control* (see Figure 8.3).

The application of any technology can be easily justified in control terms as it ensures a consistency of operation not possible through human beings. In addition, it is easier to fit people around the technology than adapt the technology to the people. Conversely, even sophisticated new technology is comparatively stupid by human standards. It is not very flexible in that it can only operate within program parameters and certain narrow climatic conditions. It has been argued that the 'office of the future' is being significantly held back

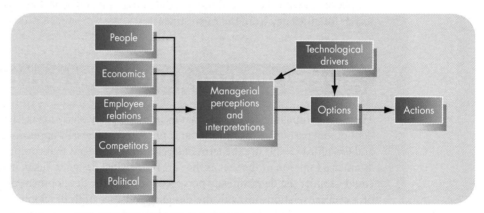

FIGURE 8.2   Technological change and decision making.

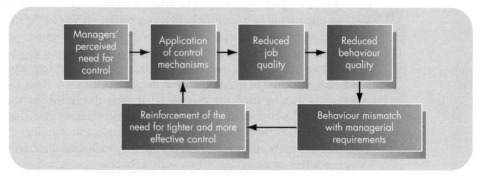

FIGURE 8.3   The vicious cyle of control (*adapted from*: Clegg, S and Dunkerley, D (1980) *Organization, Class and Control*, Routledge & Kegan Paul, London).

because of poor new building design and the limited availability of appropriate facilities in existing buildings (air conditioning and cable ducts etc.). People, by way of contrast, are flexible, they can adapt to changes in circumstances and are capable of solving problems for which they have not been *programmed* or trained. Even with the development of expert systems, computers are not as adaptable as people. It is this constriction in the way in which computers operate that provides the control possibilities through structuring the time, space and activities of the humans with whom they come into contact.

There are several aspects to the relationship between control and technology. For example:

✦ Adoption. It is a management decision which technologies are introduced into an organization. This provides managers with the opportunity to target particular technologies, particular applications or particular intentions. Each of these objectives provides a basis to reinforce the control aspects of management through an agenda-setting process.

✦ Development. The majority of technological development (at least as far as organizations are concerned) is funded by management for purposes identified by them. This allows control of the organizational environment to be exercised through channelling and directing the evolution of technology.

✦ Access. It is again a management decision to whom and how access to technology should be granted. For example, in using computer-controlled machines in a factory the design of the computer programming could be the responsibility of the machine operators or it could be done by a separate group of specialists. Which option is chosen is a management decision in which control of the skill levels and hence power are part of the process.

✦ Application. The application of technology provides a very clear illustration of control. There are always more opportunities to apply technology than there is money available to fund it. This requires management to ration its resources and therefore it must select which parts of the organization have access to which technologies. This allows management to target selectively parts of its operations for the application of technology. This *threat* of having technology introduced (or developed) is part of the *control balance* in any context. It also allows for people problems – as defined by management – to be solved by the application of technological solutions, a form of direct control. For example, poor quality of work on an assembly line (perhaps as a result of boring, monotonous jobs of very short duration and at a constant pace) can be improved by the application of robot technology to replace the people.

✦ Intention. Most of the issues discussed so far in relation to control have an indirect link with technology. In other words, control is achieved largely as a byproduct of the main or stated purpose. By its intention, management as a policy can use technology to increase its control over events and people. This comes through the justification of the technology, overt or covert. Frequently, technology is justified on the basis of a reduced cost of operation for a specified quality and quantity. Through covert *intention* management can seek to achieve objectives which improve its control as a first priority and subordinate cost to an incidental benefit. For example, an improved level of quality achieved through the application of technology provides management with improved control of the process (and indirectly the people operating it).

The impact of technology

Structure

Technology can affect structure in a number of ways. The impact will depend upon management discretion and the ways in which the technology is used within the organization. The impact influences three areas of structural design:

- Scale. Technology can impact on the number of jobs provided by an organization. The large-scale introduction of computers in an office or robots in a factory can be used to cut the numbers employed. Organization structure is a means of compartmentalization based upon the need to manage human activity. If the operation is automated a significant rationale for the existing structure also changes.

- Function. The introduction of a new technology produces a need to accommodate new jobs or even functions within a structure. Also it is not unusual to find new jobs springing up within existing departments, for example, computer accountant, a job responsible for seeking ways of using computer technology in accounting.

- Integration. The integration of technology into existing jobs also influences the structure. For example, the use of CAD/CAM allows the integration of designers with production, logistics and marketing specialists. Under such operating circumstances it becomes increasingly difficult to justify the traditional separation of activity into functional compartments. This can be used as the justification for reviewing the structure of an organization.

Where new technology has been integrated into an organization to the extent that it dominates operational activity, Mintzberg (1983) describes the emerging structure as an *adhocracy*. This form of structure is typified by:

- Few levels of management.
- Little formal control.
- Decentralized decision making.
- Few rules, policies and procedures.
- Specialization of work function.

This form of structure can be particularly useful when the nature of the work facing the organization does not fall into regular patterns and the work itself is complex. Typical areas where this form of organization might be seen are in a hospital casualty area or a consultancy organization where no two client problems are identical or amenable to the same solution. The introduction of expert systems is an attempt to harness some of the decision rules and diagnostic skill involved in such situations.

Job design

New jobs are created by technology; computer programmer is a job that did not exist 40 years ago, for example. Some jobs have also disappeared from organizations. For example, punched card operator was an essential job with early data-processing computers. It came into existence with a particular technology and existed only as long as direct keyboard entry was not possible. At that time the only way to enter information was to convert data into machine-readable punched cards. Many thousands of these were required for every processing operation. A change in the technology eliminated the need for this job to be done and it disappeared virtually overnight.

Other jobs have been changed as a result of the application of technology to the work. For example, secretaries, 'as a group, have been affected by the introduction of word processing and their jobs look set to change further with the spread of computer systems offering electronic mail, diary management, graphics, spreadsheets and desk-top publishing' (Thompson, 1989, p 1). This source goes on to examine a number of options for the ways in which the job of a secretary could be changed to make use of technology in becoming a personal assistant. In effect, receiving delegated authority to act on their own initiative on behalf of the superior.

Job performance has been changed through the application of new technology to the training of individuals. Management in Action 8.2 indicates the impact of simulation machines on the training of pilots, ships' officers and power engineers.

Stop | Consider   *Given that every trainee in a simulator knows that it is not for real, can such training ever replace real experience?*

Managerialism

Managerialism refers to the ability of managers to maintain control of the organization through the imposition of their perspective on every aspect of activity. It is management that determines the technology that will be used by the organization and how it will be utilized. There are organizational differences in the degree to which new technology is utilized. Some organizations pride themselves on being at the forefront of technological applications, others prefer to be followers, allowing the cost and risk of development to be carried by others.

Management also decides the degree of employee involvement in determining the human interface with new technology. There are a range of options from full involvement in the design and selection of new technology to simply being told what employees will be expected to do. Terry Molloy, the Deputy General Secretary of the Banking, Insurance and Finance Union, writing on behalf of the trade union movement in a government report in 1984 is quoted (Thompson, 1985, p 5) as saying:

> To get the maximum benefit from IT, it is necessary to involve the workforce. This is not only right in principle, but right in practice, since the people who perform the tasks that will be changed by IT understand the practicalities better than any systems analyst or departmental manager. In our recommendations we lay great stress on the need for proper consultative mechanisms when introducing IT, and indeed, for consultation to start at the earliest planning stage.

Thompson goes on to illustrate the problems for management if they do not take into consideration the employee point of view. Also demonstrated is the crucial effect of the attitudes of middle managers. A case study regarding the implementation of a new computer system to the freight operations of British Rail (undated but presumably during the

MANAGEMENT IN ACTION 8.2

Tournament of the skies and other simulations

In Japan, Ishikawajima-Harima Heavy Industry (IHI) developed a simulator that reproduced a ship's bridge and could be used from the safety of a warehouse. To adapt the £6m simulator to any location all that is needed is a set of images and data about local tides and currents. The simulator screens stretch 225°, providing realistic day or night visual imagery. Sound equipment reflects engine vibrations through the floor as well as noises such as metal tearing on impact. The performance of trainees is monitored for later feedback and analysis. In addition to its training use, the simulator can be used to recreate accidents, allowing an investigation team the opportunity to understand what happened.

In the UK electricity supply industry coping with emergency situations that disrupt power distribution is an important requirement. Staff controlling the system can work for many years without experiencing an emergency and so never develop the expertise in handling crises. They have to rely on general training, skill and manuals to assist in dealing with emergencies. With the introduction of a simulator realistic situations can be created that provide exposure to the more likely events. In the north this may be the effects of snow and in the south the effects of a power failure from France or high winds from the channel.

The Royal Air Force has introduced a simulator that can replicate battles. It is impossible to obtain and use the aircraft of possible enemies for practice work in the sky. The development of a combat simulator called 'Joust' was intended to be able to replicate many different flying situations and aircraft types. It is possible to train pilots how to fly in battle conditions and in different flying circumstances without the risk of losing planes or pilots. The increase in skill, reaction times and the ability to fly planes creatively in battle could make the difference between life and death for a pilot facing hostile action. Multiple aircraft can be simulated at the same time, pitting pilots against the machine or other pilots in group flying and bomber protection duties, etc.

Flight simulators are being used not just to train pilots but to examine how they interact with the technology. Monitoring the use of flight controls, reactions to equipment layouts and the medical consequences of flying are all possible with the new £15m simulator shared by Lufthansa and Berlin University's Institute of Aerospace.

Adapted from: Thomson, R and Fisher, A (1994) All at sea from the safety of a warehouse. The human factor. Collapsing the system without getting the sack, *Financial Times*, 3 February, p 12; and Boggis, D (1995) Tournament of the skies, *Financial Times*, 10 March, p 17.

early 1970s) illustrates the problems. A top-down approach was adopted, with middle managers and employees given a new system to operate with very little involvement. All was well in the early stages until it became apparent that with implementation would come job loss and change. Resistance to implementing the system meant that only after ten years was significant change beginning to happen.

This case clearly illustrates the exercise of *negative power*. Management have a controlling interest and can determine to a significant extent the form and direction of the agenda. They also have the resources to provide a higher than chance probability of success. However, they are vulnerable to the withdrawal of co-operation in achieving their intentions. That is one reason why the trade union movement is always sensitive to the removal of the right to strike or take industrial action. Ultimately, the withdrawal of labour or co-operation is the most powerful weapon in employee relations. This is the exercise of negative power – not doing something with the intent to influence.

Technology, innovation and diversity

Innovation is about creating new things or creating new ways of doing existing things. New technology is, by definition, an innovation. Technology can also help organizations to innovate in the design of new products and it can assist in improving existing operations. Betz (1987) describes innovation as falling into one of three categories (see Table 8.3):

✦ Radical. This is the initial development of a technology. It represents the major breakthrough that allows the subsequent transformation of an industry or the creation of a new one. The development of the first computer during the 1940s is an example. The highest level of risk is associated with this type of innovation as much cost and time is needed. Many ideas are developed but most do not achieve commercial realization.

✦ System. This represents the commercialization of a technology. A computer by itself is simply a calculating and storage machine. However, linked to a typewriter it can develop into the multifunction workstation of today. The level of risk is lower than the radical level as it tends to involve the combination of existing technologies, rather than the creation of something completely new.

✦ Incremental. This represents the least risk of the three levels and is a process of refinement. It represents the upgrading of a computer system through the miniaturization of components or improvements to a word-processing package. It is the level of innovation that aims to extract the maximum capability and potential out of a particular technology.

There are many ways in which innovation occurs. There are the research activities in universities that create many of the first radical versions of a particular technology. For example, my own university, in Hull, played a pioneering role in the development of the liquid crystal, now an essential element of calculators and other forms of display screen. There are military laboratories specifically looking at technology from that context. There are science parks located near to universities intended to encourage the transfer and exploitation of pure research through commercial expertise. Within large organizations there is frequently research and development activity engaged on projects spanning the three categories we have examined. Management in Action 8.3 provides an insight into how a number of organizations innovate as part of their survival activities.

Category	Example
Radical	Development of computer
System	Linking computer to typewriter technology
Incremental	Improvement in word-processing package

TABLE 8.3 Categories of innovation

MANAGEMENT IN ACTION 8.3

Innovators keep on the ball

The Wellcome Cancer Research Campaign Institute in Cambridge believes that social interaction between researchers is one of the best ways of encouraging the flow of ideas. With a £3m annual research budget the institute undertakes innovative research. The building was purpose built in 1992 and has laboratories around the outside to maximize daylight in the workplace. Chemicals and research equipment are kept in communal areas to force staff to meet others. Journals are kept in individual's rooms so staff are encouraged to interact when they need information. People are free to come and go as they please. Dr John Gurdon, chairman of the Institute, said: 'There is an exceptional amount of movement here, people going around talking to others, sharing equipment. We believe time is saved by talking to people before doing something.'

Hewlett-Packard spends about £100m a year on long-range research at its laboratories in Japan, California and Bristol. In Bristol the research staff dress informally and are encouraged to spend 10% of their time on any activity that interests them, using laboratory facilities. Irreverence, humour and tolerance are encouraged. Every idea is regarded as having some merit until it is shown to be otherwise.

In non-research organizations which need creativity similar ideas are catching on. Hunt Thompson Associates, a London architects' practice with 61 employees, uses lunchtime once a week as the space for swapping ideas. Each week one of the architects presents their work as either the basis of a discussion or simply to bring the others up to date on a project, the intention being to create an atmosphere of informality and encourage interaction and innovation through the involvement of as many people as possible.

Mitsubishi Heavy Industries sought some fresh ideas for its European marketing strategy by holding a series of brainstorming sessions with undergraduates from Pembroke College, Cambridge. Although many of the ideas were unrealistic they were thought provoking, radical and stimulating, according to Mr Henry Anderson, the European general manager of planning and development for the company.

In a recent survey, some 80% of American companies thought that innovation was important for their business, but only 4% thought that they were good at it. The job cuts, recruitment freezes and other downsizing/delayering exercises of recent years all sap the morale of existing employees as well as reduce the inflow of new people and ideas. The trend to decentralization can also see the break-up of central research departments and the lowering of morale among research staff, with a consequent loss of creativity and innovation.

The existence of an innovative capability does not guarantee success for the organization. Xerox failed to exploit some of the pioneering work from its own research laboratories on the personal computer during the 1970s. Senior management priorities at the time were in securing the future of its core business areas. Both creativity and the will to exploit the ideas must be present for the benefits to be realized.

Adapted from: MacKenzie, A (1995) Innovators keep on the ball, *Financial Times*, 1 May, p 11; and Houlder, V (1995) Caught in a brainstorm, *Financial Times*, 1 May, p 11.

Stop | Consider   *Consider how technology could be used to influence the process of innovation as described in MiA 8.3.*

Organizations require conformity. Products and services must consistently conform to the appropriate specification. One of the major benefits of technology is that it can produce conformity to a much higher level than human beings. The use of company uniforms, dress codes, rules and training are all part of the process of *engineering* (or socializing) the behaviour of people. Herriot and Pemberton (1995) argue uniformity is a weakness and through diversity comes strength.

They argue that uniformity leads to situations where inappropriate decisions are taken. The Bay of Pigs (Janis, 1972) is one of many decisions used to illustrate the point. This decision was about a group of people being so close in type and perspective that they could not entertain any different points of view. The result was military failure and embarrassment for the American government. By encouraging difference and establishing learning processes based on its incorporation into normal decision making higher levels of innovation are encouraged. In turn a higher success rate will be achieved. They link their argument to the Myers–Briggs indicator of personality to create balanced teams. You will recall the Belbin and Margerison and McCann team roles introduced in an earlier chapter. These provide a similar perspective on the need for a balance of personality and work preference if a team is to be successful.

Technology and change

Major differences between old and new technologies will inevitably create more change than if the differences are relatively small. Another aspect of the relationship between new technology and change is the nature of the cause and effect process. Does the process of change exist irrespective of a technological input, perhaps driven by the need to change the product or service or reduce costs? If so, then the development of technology is a function of change, rather than the other way round. If change already exists then the search for technological solutions to problems is what generates the process, not the development of a technology followed by a search for applications.

The relationship between technology and work is not just experienced at a work level. There are other levels of impact, for example:

+ Employment. To build cars using manual labour obviously provides more jobs than would be the case if a fully automated process were employed. However, if cars made on an automated assembly line are of a higher quality and cheaper to purchase, then the organization may be able to employ more people as a result of increased sales. Equally, there will be employment opportunities that emerge as a result of the new technology itself. So some employment opportunities will disappear and others will emerge.

+ Careers. Some careers change as technology changes the jobs within them. For example, to be a senior maintenance engineer today demands a working knowledge of computer-based equipment and electronics, as well as the traditional electrical and mechanical specialisms. Other career paths will disappear as the traditional types of work are replaced by computers. Careers will emerge out of the new work opportunities that are created by the adoption of a technology. For example, computer specialisms have emerged over the past 30 years as that form of technology has evolved.

+ Products and services. New products and services emerge as technologies change and develop, for example, the building and selling of robot machines and computers. In the service sector the introduction of ATMs has provided a completely new range of service opportunities to banking customers. This provides for the creation of two distinct forms of new product and service. First, those associated with the technology itself. Second, the products and services that can be developed as a consequence of the technology.

- ✦ Economic activity. Economic activity is both influenced by and influences technology. Companies not profitable enough to raise capital are in a difficult position when they need to invest in new technologies, which in turn may affect their chances of survival. The economic health of nations also influences the ability to be able to acquire new technologies.

- ✦ Risk. Every new venture carries with it an element of risk. With the introduction of new technology comes particular risk as so much of the processing is obscured from view. Earlier in this chapter it was argued that one of the benefits of information technology was the *visibility* that it provided. Managers are able to *see* in great detail (through reports and systems) what is going on. However, before that is possible much information processing takes place within the computer systems and is, therefore, not observable. It is the end result rather than the process that is visible. Lengthy commissioning and debugging processes are necessary in order to ensure that the system delivers what is required. Apocryphal stories are legion about new computer systems that send the wrong products to customers or that keep sending an order over and over again.

- ✦ Internationalism. Companies of all sizes and types now compete for international markets for their products and services. New technology plays a significant part in this process. There is also the international trade in high technology itself. Companies and governments are constantly seeking ways to capture new developments for the benefit of their organizations or citizens. Companies buy competitors' products and services and deconstruct them to learn about new manufacturing processes etc. on a global scale.

- ✦ Fashion. Inevitably what significant organizations are doing becomes the norm for many others. This is one means by which risk can be reduced. The first adopters of a particular technology will encounter and solve most of the problems. Following also gives managers confidence (real and political) that something will work and produce benefits. Conversely, there is an element of avoiding thinking and of being less than creative as a result of simply following what others do. By simply following the trend and not working things out for themselves managers can be missing opportunities. The trick, if there is one, is to achieve an effective balance between following and innovating.

- ✦ Transition. It is never possible to move from one state to another instantaneously and without consequence. Change takes time to achieve. In implementing a new technology there is a series of time lags between the initial idea and creation of the equipment and systems capable of meeting the need. There is also a time lag between installing equipment and being able to make full operational use of it. The transition period involved can be fraught with problems and difficulties. It is a time of running with two systems while a phased changeover takes place. Figure 8.4 reflects this transition period.

There are the cost, space and process-based implications associated with the need to keep old and new systems running in parallel. There are also people-related problems associated with technology change. Frustration is a common experience as replacement technologies begin to encroach on the work of employees. Employees who consider that they have no future in the new order are less likely to willingly co-operate in solving the problems that emerge. They are more likely to engage in *Luddite* behaviour and further slow the change process.

✦ Limitations. New technology is not always capable of living up to its image or the claims of its designers and salespeople. Neither is it always the best solution to every operational need. An electric typewriter (or handwriting) can be a quicker way of producing a short letter than a word processor. Perhaps speaking directly to a colleague could be a more effective way of dealing with a problem than exchanging e-mail. Therefore a combination of old and new technologies integrated into a well thought out partnership can offer the most effective combination of options.

Information technology

Forester (1987) suggests that it is high (computer-based) technology that allows the development of new techniques that impact directly on work. Much of the computer-based technology is intended to provide improvements in the ability of organizations to process information in one form or another.

Information technology, argues Zuboff (1988), differs from the technology used in the nineteenth century in one respect only: it combines the replacement of people with machines *and* it provides a higher level of transparency through the ability of computer technology to process information. 'Activities, events, and objects are translated into and made visible by information when a technology *informates* as well as *automates*' (p 10). It is the control potential from the transparency achieved via the technology that is the *new* dimension to the technology. It brings employee activity into the public domain. With knowledge comes the opportunity for control.

Buchanan and Boddy (1983) suggest four aspects of information-handling capabilities that differentiate computer systems from other forms of technology:

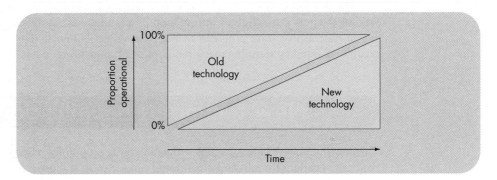

FIGURE 8.4 Technology transfer.

◆ Capture. Computer systems are able to capture data passively or actively in a number of ways. The collection of vehicle density through sensors placed on a road reflects an active collection of data.

◆ Storage. There are two types of storage in computer systems. First, the program that governs the activities of the machine itself. Second, the information captured by the system as directed by the program.

◆ Manipulation. Computer systems are capable of manipulating the information captured and stored. A production line computer system could capture volume and dimension data on items passing across a sensor. It could then automatically calculate a range of quality-control data for the production batch.

◆ Distribution. The information collated can be automatically distributed to anyone with access to the system and entitled to the information. In the case of a quality-control analysis, the results could be displayed on a monitor at the worksite for all to see.

Management in Action 8.4 reflects the application of information technology to the computer needs of the Royal Navy, illustrating the Buchanan and Boddy framework.

Stop	Consider	*Explain how the approach described in MiA 8.4 illustrates the Buchanan and Boddy framework.*

It has been argued (Konsynski and Sviokla, 1994) that the failure by management to obtain the full value and potential from information technology is a consequence of the continued use of outdated paradigms of organizational functioning. They claim that *cognitive reapportionment* is necessary if managers are to obtain full advantage. The new paradigm sees organizations as *bundles* of decisions: decision making being based on an appropriate allocation of *bundles* between humans, systems or a combination of the two.

Information technology is not restricted to computer applications. The portable telephone has made an impact on a number of job functions. Sales staff can be in constant contact with the office and can phone orders directly into a computer system or fax it directly from their car. Compact discs store vast quantities of data for subsequent retrieval and analysis. Electronic mail (e-mail) can eliminate the need for the traditional memo and provide immediate access for senior managers to all employees, bypassing the normal hierarchy. This last point has a number of connotations for open door management policies.

The development of neural networks, imitating human brain functioning, leads the way for the next generation of information processing. For example, the development of expert systems that solve problems in ways that reflect human activity can help to detect credit card fraud by scanning many thousands of transactions on a daily basis.

New technology applications

The growth in new technology jobs within emerging economies reflects a process that has major implications for jobs and organizations in the west, as illustrated by Management in Action 8.5.

MANAGEMENT IN ACTION 8.4

Charting a course on high-tech seas

The Royal Navy has about 60,000 employees, all of whom must be paid each month. There exists a need for constant information flows from each of the Navy's ships and shore establishments on the status and movement of personnel. One key area of complexity is that of allowances. There are rules that cover entitlements such as lodging allowances (21 different categories covering London allowances, married personnel and even the use of a houseboat) and service-at-sea bonuses. It has been estimated that these rules are about ten times more complex than in most commercial organizations.

Documents arrive daily at HMS *Centurion* (the central pay and personnel office) from 111 locations around the world. These locations include 42 ships, 12 mobile units, 19 reserve units and 38 shore establishments. Typically, the operational personnel staff are a petty officer and a couple of ratings, known as writers. On board ship (or other establishment) this team looks after pay, allowances, leave, travel, foreign currency, cash and provides advice on promotion and so on. Each of these 'transactions' requires a record to be made and sent to HMS *Centurion*. This might be relatively infrequent if a ship is on an operational mission.

At HMS *Centurion* the data would be 'input' to the computer system and the accuracy of claims checked against the rule framework. About 90% of errors are identified at this point and the

original form referred back to its source for checking and amendment, causing delay and additional expense. Frequent changes to the allowance rules caused the system to malfunction on a regular basis.

To address the problems an 'expert system' was introduced via a task force headed by Commander Angus Ross. Writers at all locations were given PC terminals and enabled to input information to HMS *Centurion* directly via modem or satellite link. The system was able to check the accuracy of data before transmission and so improve the quality of information.

The system forces local units to ensure the accuracy of information before they send it, allowing staff at HMS *Centurion* to concentrate on exceptions and the overall management of the pay system. The benefits in financial terms are anticipated to be reductions in the cost of paying each employee from about £125 a year to around £55 a year and an improved level of service. This figure is still high compared to an average of £25 a year per employee found in commercial organizations. However, given the complexity of the pay and allowances in the Navy and the nature of its operations, achievement of this level would be unlikely.

Adapted from: Ross, A (1995) Charting a course on high-tech seas, *People Management*, 9 March, pp 38–41.

Stop | Consider *Does the process described in MiA 8.5 reflect similar processes to that applicable to the transfer and globalization of technologies in the past? Why or why not?*

The approach for the following discussion is to examine the major organizational classifications of manufacturing and service, with a section on administration. Few organizations are purely manufacturing or service, most contain elements of both. A theatre falls firmly within the service sector. However, within this sector groups of people will be engaged in *manufacturing* scenery, costumes and the preparation of food for the

MANAGEMENT IN ACTION 8.5

Jobs for all in the global market?

Various predictions have been offered about the high-tech future. Sir James Goldsmith argued that some 4 billion people had recently entered the world labour markets from China, India, Indochina, Bangladesh and the countries that originally formed the Soviet Union, the labour cost being typically 90–95% less than that in Europe. Peter Jay suggested that high-tech development in India was not costing jobs in the UK, but that companies such as BA, BT, and IBM were using staff in developing countries to undertake technical jobs with the results being transmitted back to the UK via satellite.

Crabb reviewed developments in India to find out more about the possible impact on jobs within the UK. India has relaxed its closed economy, tariffs have fallen dramatically and returning graduates with experience of working in the USA have brought a new focus back with them. Salaries for highly skilled new graduates are very low by comparison with the west. For example, software engineers can start on as little as £1000 per year. At about five hours' time difference there is sufficient overlap time to be able to engage in telephone communication with clients. There is also a sufficient period of non-overlap to allow uninterrupted access to computer systems on the client's premises. The level of business between the west and India has risen from about $39 million in 1986/87 to $14,200 million in 1993/4.

There are typically three routes for software developed in India to arrive in the west:

+ Outsourcing. Western companies outsourcing some or all of their IT operations to India. This route is the basis of the scenario that predicts the wholesale loss of IT jobs to India. Companies using this approach include Swissair and Lufthansa.

+ Joint venture. A variation of exporting with products developed by 'partners' being taken back to home locations. Examples include Mahindra–British Telecom, Tata–Unisys, IBM–Tata and Fujitsu– ICIM (ICL).

+ Exporting. The normal exporting of software products to the west by Indian companies. For example, London Underground commissioned CMC in India to develop a new train scheduling, signalling and timetabling system. Priced at around £200,000, the 18-month project cost was well below that proposed by European suppliers.

Perhaps Robert Reich in his 1991 book *The Work of Nations* sums up the situation and implications of high-tech development in countries such as India by suggesting that there are three types of worker in the modern world:

+ Routine production worker. The person whose job is moving to ever cheaper parts of the world.

+ In-person servers. Retail workers, domestic helpers, security guards, etc. This category of worker finds that they are being squeezed in wage terms due to competition for jobs and the application of technology to their work.

+ Symbolic analyzers. In the UK these workers would be referred to as 'knowledge workers'. This category are the real winners according to Reich. 'If you are well educated, if you have skills, if you are a problem solver, you have a larger and larger market within which to sell your problem-solving skills. International trade is working to your advantage.'

Adapted from: Crabb, S (1995) Jobs for all in the global market?, *People Management*, 26 January, pp 22–7.

restaurant. Hill (1983) describes manufacturing as being about the production of goods for purchase and *subsequent* consumption. Service, by comparison, involves the production of intangibles consumed at the time of provision, with the customer taking away the benefit of the service.

Manufacturing

Manufacturing is about making tangible items for subsequent sale. Motor cars, washing machines and toasters are obvious examples. New technology has impacted onto this type of operation in a number of ways. Machines can now process information and therefore demonstrate a relatively low level of thinking ability. This takes many forms and leads to more integration of activity as computers *talk* to each other.

Robots with the ability to pick up, move and position items began to appear in the 1960s. They were used predominantly for paint spraying, spot welding and stacking operations. Automatic trains could also follow a predetermined path around a factory collecting and delivering pallets of components or finished goods. These driverless trains followed a magnetic strip buried in the floor and as computer technology developed were able to integrate a broader range of functions such as self-loading. From these early days there are many apocryphal stories of managers being pinned against walls or run over by runaway trains or robots. These stories, usually told by shopfloor employees, often demonstrate that even the robots and computers have an *attitude* towards management. Management in Action 8.6 reflects the trend in the development and use of robots over recent years.

Stop | Consider   *What does MiA 8.6 imply about the way in which technology spreads and becomes accepted within manufacturing operations?*

With the incorporation of vision- and touch-sensitive devices robots can be used for a wide range of tasks within the manufacturing process. For example, the quality and quantity of glass bottles can be determined as they travel down a conveyor belt and pass an electronic eye (sensor) linked to a computer. The dimensions of the bottles can be checked against a model held in the memory of the computer and the quality of the glass can be reflected in light patterns passing through the glass and checked against the norms anticipated. Pass/fail decisions can then be made by the computer about individual bottles and they can be channelled to either packing or recycling accordingly. In addition, records and analysis of quality data can be generated for subsequent interpretation by management.

Advanced manufacturing technologies (AMT) and flexible manufacturing systems (FMS) have also incorporated the computer to create more flexible and consistent products. The purpose of such systems is to link together a number of machines so that items can be automatically transferred between them in successive stages of production. They also allow groups of machines to be linked together so that smaller batches of product can be made efficiently. These systems attempt to replicate the economy of large-scale production but for small quantities. Small batch sizes with frequent deliveries is a function of what began as a very low technology approach to production, just in time.

The design of manufactured items has also been subjected to computer technology. Designs can be drawn directly onto a computer screen through a mouse, drawing palette, etc. These can be interpreted by the computer and converted into three-dimensional representations, parts lists, detailed drawings etc. The combination of computer-aided design

MANAGEMENT IN ACTION 8.6

Reaching further into industry

Before 1980 the use of robot technology was considered by many to be expensive, the performance of machines fell short of both expectation and claims and the standard of service was frequently low. Countries with labour shortages and a relatively inflexible workforce tended to adopt robot technology much more rapidly than countries with low labour cost and plentiful labour. For example, by 1993 the USA had about 30 robots per 10,000 people employed in industry, compared to Japan with about 320 robots per 10,000 workers. Germany had about 62 robots per 10,000 workers compared to about 29 in France and 19 in the UK.

Poor robot programming and design frequently created collisions with surrounding buildings and equipment. Poor product design in relation to the use of robots also created difficulties. It is also possible to automate production processes without the involvement of robot technology. For example, the European 'white goods' industries (washing machines, refrigerators, etc.) have been able to achieve high levels of efficiency and automation without the extensive use of robots. Small production batches did not justify robot use according to Professor Arthur Collie from the University of Portsmouth. Very large

batches tend to be moved to locations with cheap labour, in turn offsetting any potential advantage from the technology.

Changes within the robotics industry mean that the sphere of application for the technology is wider than at any time in its history. Low-cost robots for use in light assembly are being developed. The automotive industry (the highest user of robot technology) is subcontracting more of its work and pressing suppliers for cost savings that encourage the application of robot technology. Robots are being improved in functionality and ease of programming. The range of functions that can be undertaken by a robot is being increased to allow faster movement, greater reach and heavier load-carrying capacity. All of which should allow for a greater range of potential applications. Robot manufacturers consider that the small and medium-sized enterprise (SME) market is the one with most potential growth for the new breed of robot.

Adapted from: Baxter, A (1995) Reaching further into industry, *Financial Times*, 6 June, p 13.

(CAD) with computer-aided manufacture (CAM) provides a very powerful approach for technology to create and produce products automatically. This can be totally amalgamated into computer integrated manufacture (CIM). However, this is very difficult and has yet to be achieved on a significant scale with any degree of success.

Evidence concerning the impact of new technology on work in manufacturing organizations is not consistent. Forester (1987, Chapter 6) reviews a number of texts and reports from Europe, the USA and Japan that reflect this ambiguity. The major perspectives include:

✦ Take-up. The adoption of high technology has not been as dramatic as might be expected. In the USA in 1983 only 4.7% of machine tools were numerically controlled – remember these were the first generation new technology machines!

◆ Cost. Integrated systems are expensive to develop and install. Organizations that have opted for high levels of new technology have not generally enjoyed significant financial benefit over other organizations. However, there are some amazing results claimed: Normalair-Garrett in the UK achieved some very significant cost savings using FMS – labour down from £400,000 to £150,000; output per worker up from £70,000 to £210,000; work in progress held at any time reduced from £690,000 to £90,000.

◆ Reliability. Very high levels of reliability are required within integrated production systems as the failure of a single component can stop a whole assembly line or island of production. Production systems become more vulnerable than if they consist of individual machines not linked together.

◆ Government policy. Governments in the major industrialized nations adopted different policies towards new technology. In the UK a form of passive facilitation is the best description of the approach adopted up to 1981, at which time the crisis in the machine tool industry as a consequence of Japanese penetration of the market became impossible to ignore. The result was a more positive encouragement of the adoption of high technology through conferences, grants and consultancy support.

◆ Employee impact. There can be a considerable saving on labour with the adoption of new technology. Yamazaki (a Japanese machine tool manufacturer) claim that 12 day workers plus a night watchman using FMS can produce as much as 215 workers and four times as many machines using traditional methods. Also, lead times (time to make the product) reduced from three months to three days. In the west the reduction of job opportunities as companies cut back in an attempt to slash costs concentrated the minds of both managers and employees on the need for high technology. It was claimed that humans would be replaced by automation. While this has been true to a significant extent it does not reveal the complete picture. New jobs *are* created by technology. In addition, different types of jobs are created within organizations adopting high technology, for example computer programmers. Also some jobs change as a result of the application of technology.

◆ Managerialism. Part of the lower take-up of high technology in the USA and Europe could be the result of low levels of technological expertise among managers. They fail to understand the complexity involved and resist adopting new systems. It is also suggested that where new technology is adopted the full benefit is not achieved because western managers do not understand how to obtain maximum flexibility from it. An emphasis on short-term results also mitigates against the introduction of integrated technology which requires long time frames to become fully operational.

◆ Social factors. The social factors associated with high technology influence general attitudes towards it. For example, the management perspective on control. Braverman (1974) discussed *alienation* and the managerial imperative for control over workers. Shaiken (1985) introduces similar arguments in connection with work in a high-technology factory and the demeaning effect on people's lives. The evidence is somewhat contradictory, some studies reporting employee satisfaction with CNC equipment.

Forester argues the negative arguments are not proved because of positive comments and engineers design systems to achieve tasks, not control desires. There are three weaknesses in this argument. First, engineers design systems to a management agenda – they never have a completely free hand as management funds the process and demands influence over it. Second, opinion surveys can be unreliable – is an employee seeing many fellow workers made redundant likely to be critical of new technology provided by management? If so, they may be regarded as unreliable or uncommitted. Also there is no way of knowing that what interviewees say is what they actually believe. The third weakness is that technology can be neutral in principle, but biased in practice. It is managers who decide how new technology will be used to meet their needs. The political, power and control justifications may never be articulated, but that does not mean that they do not exist.

Service

The effect of new technology on employment in services has been noticeably different from that in manufacturing. Although there has always been a service sector, for example, doctors and market traders, it was just beginning to develop in scale and significance when computer technologies arrived. The rapid growth of the service sector was largely enabled because of the release of labour from manufacturing as a result of the use of technology in that sector. People also had the money to spend on more than the essentials of life. Jobs have not been obviously lost in the service sector, growth having outstripped this tendency.

There is an unevenness in the effect of new technology on different categories and levels of job across the service sector (Reed, 1989). For example, the history and control of work within the medical profession gives practitioners a much greater say in the application and job impact of new technology than would be available to the staff in a bank. Some occupational groups are more able to control the impact on their jobs and working conditions than others.

Administrative

Forester (1987) indicates that a 1985 UK survey showed that less than 50% of office workers had direct access to any electronic equipment other than a phone or calculator. By the early 1960s most large companies had a mainframe computer undertaking routine processing of accounting and payroll information. Most computer departments began as data-processing departments, often within the accounting section.

The development of new technology in the office has concentrated on three main areas:

✦ Convergence. Much of the technology available began as separate pieces of equipment with different functions. This distinction is disappearing with the inclusion of microprocessors in such equipment. The multimedia workstation is rapidly making an entry as the major application of new technology.

✦ Visibility. The use of networks and data-analysis packages allows greater visibility of information among managers. Once the raw data are entered into the system it can be analyzed and reported on much more quickly. It is also possible for managers to *experiment* with the information available to them. Considering questions such as: 'If we reduced the expenditure on x, what would the consequences be?'

✦ Integration. Integration is not the same as convergence. Convergence is the bringing together of technological difference. Integration is about creating an office system as a single set of processes not a separate set of tasks. It is about being able to undertake several activities at the same time, accessing information sources as necessary to achieve the objective. It might be a budgetary control system as a single process, being able to access, analyze and extrapolate historical records, current information and future plans, all this being carried out at a single electronic workstation, perhaps even remotely as a teleworking exercise.

The effects of new technology on work in the office can be summarized under four headings (Forester, 1987):

✦ Employment. In any reduction in the overall numbers of administrative jobs it is difficult to separate out the effects of technology, economic downturns and cost cutting. There is also the need to take into account the creation of jobs in the computer and systems areas.

✦ Job quality. There is a common view that most jobs in high technology involve sitting at a computer screen, typing information into the system for hours. This view sees people being required only because the technology has not developed to the extent that they can be eliminated altogether. While this view of technology is true to an extent, previously armies of clerical staff would have sat at rows of desks making entries in ledgers all day long. It is not clear which job would have the lower *quality* in job design terms. Data-entry duties can often be automated thus releasing time for analysis, interpretation and action at a lower level in the organization.

✦ Health and safety. There have been fears expressed about the impact of prolonged use of computers on the health of workers. This has included the effects of radiation from the computer screen; the impact of constant use of a keyboard on joints and muscles and back problems from continually sitting in one position. Research into these issues is ongoing. The problems can be resolved to a significant extent by the use of correct seating and lighting, the introduction of regular breaks away from screens or through keyboard design and usage techniques (see Management in Action 8.7).

Stop | Consider   *Can you think of any other areas of life that could offer benefits to computer users? If so, what are they and how might they be used?*

✦ Social relations. Communication with or through a computer systems inevitably reduces or eliminates the opportunity for people to interact with each other at work. There are, however, organizational benefits to be gained from human interaction, problem solving and innovation being among the obvious. A lack of human interaction can be used as a form of control – the divide and rule principle – leading to alienation and lack of commitment. The relationship between technology and the way in which it is used is not automatic, managers ultimately determine how the technology will be integrated with employees.

Technology: an applied perspective

In this chapter technology has been introduced as a broad ranging concept, not just the application of computer technology to operational activity. This breadth of meaning provides one of the major benefits to managers as they seek to run organizations, that of

MANAGEMENT IN ACTION 8.7

Piano gives a lesson for the workplace

The use of computer keyboards has dramatically changed the nature of much work within organizations. It has also increased the risk of injury for those using a keyboard inappropriately. Tenosynovitis, tendinitis and carpal tunnel syndrome are just some of the injuries that can be found in this context. Stephanie Brown, a New York-based professor of piano, noted similar injuries among those piano players who did not develop effective keyboard skills. She first noted these problems in relation to computers when she began to use a computer keyboard for the first time. She commented: 'It's well known that certain positions and motions can cause injury in practically every sport. Everyone has had the experience of watching someone swing a tennis racquet or golf club and think "ouch!". It just looks wrong. Using a computer keyboard is no different. It's a vigorous micro-athletic workout for the hands and fingers. Do it wrong and you're asking for trouble.'

Brown published a book, *The Hand Book*, to

publicize 14 lessons in how to avoid some of the pitfalls to which she gave names such as the 'the cobra', 'the spider' and 'the Flying Pinky'. Athletes warm up before a race and so should computer users.

There are also issues associated with injury, such as workstation adjustment, that are given recognition in her book. Some of the dos and don'ts when using a computer keyboard identified in her book include:

✦ Keep the natural wrist line.
✦ Let the wrists float.
✦ Let the elbows hang free.
✦ Relax the ring and little finger.
✦ Don't squeeze the mouse.
✦ Rest the hands when not keying.

Adapted from: Boyling, J (1994) Piano gives a lesson for the workplace, *Financial Times*, 12 January, p 21.

control. With the introduction of computer-based technologies management control has been developed further through automation and integration of activity. Technology in its broadest sense provides a number of potential benefits to the management of any organisation:

✦ Control of process. Management is able to control the design of operational layouts, machine configurations and the methods of work.

✦ Control of work. Management is able to control the design of jobs and issues such as work rate, quality and product design. Through these aspects management is also able to control social relationships at the workplace. For example, Garrahan and Stewart (1992) describe the so-called Japanese assembly line technologies as an attempt to achieve high quality by forcing employees to report the mistakes of others in the team.

✦ Control of people. Management is able to more closely define and control the activities and behaviour of the people in the workplace through the application of technology. This can be through the subordination of people to machine processes, the application of administrative technologies or the application of scientific management-based technologies. Each of these opportunities restricts the freedom of influence over, and ownership of, their work by individuals.

✦ Control of cost. Management is able to control the cost of operations through a number of technologically based devices. They control the design of the work itself through decisions relating to the type of technology adopted. They control the pace of work through the speed of machines and the sequencing of activities. These are the obvious consequences of technology. However, through the development of administrative technologies and procedures there is an improved level of visibility among managers about how costs are influenced and, therefore, how they can be managed.

✦ Control of agenda. Management is able to control the technological agenda within the organization, within society and among competitors. It is management that decides on the technology to be used and on its preferred options for future developments. It is this decision-making and channelling capability that ensures that the technological agenda can be significantly influenced by managers. Management also shape the future of much pure research through funding assistance.

✦ Control of resistance. Management is able to control the level of resistance to the use of technology through a number of routes. The creation of jobs, career opportunities and fashion creates a view of technology that can become attractive to those seeking to create a future in organizational life. The threat of the loss of work can reduce resistance (particularly if jobs are scarce). The use of *people technologies* can encourage employees to become an active part of the *process* itself. For example, employee involvement, matrix structures, teamwork and profit share options are just some of the ways in which employees are encouraged to identify with management's objectives.

✦ Control of skill. Management is able to control the level and type of skill that exist through the design of jobs and the nature of technology itself and how it is adopted within the organization.

✦ Control of organization. Management is able to control the design of the organization itself through the use of technology. The number of people employed, the type of work, the compartmentalization of activity are all amenable to the influence of technology. These issues influence the size and shape of the organization's hierarchy, structure and approach to bureaucratization/formality etc.

✦ Control of location. Management is able to control the location of an organization as a result of the ease with which activity can be transferred between locations. For example, Management in Action 8.8 reports how one publishing organization in Singapore dealt with a labour shortage by transferring some of its activities to other parts of the world.

Stop | Consider   *Identify some of the problems that might be expected in setting up operations as described in MiA 8.8. How might they be overcome?*

It is easy to understand how and why organizations are tempted to rush into adopting new technology if it improves control, thereby reducing a number of existing operational problems and the perceived level of risk. However, there are broader considerations that need to be taken into account regarding the application of technology. During the transition period associated with the emergence of a new technology there are usually significant labour imbalances. Individuals with the old skills are displaced from the opportunity to

344 Technology and work Part IV

MANAGEMENT IN ACTION 8.8

Singapore dials long distance to find staff

The island of Singapore has an enviable growth rate of approximately 10% per year. The island is booming and jobs are easy to find. This poses problems for many employers who find it necessary to recruit labour from overseas in order to be able to function efficiently. Another way of attacking this issue using technology has been developed by the island's main newspaper publishers, Singapore Press Holdings (SPH).

Mr Cheong Yip Seng, an editor-in-chief at SPH, indicated that about 80% of the graduate intake to SPH has left by the end of their fourth year, to earn higher wages in stockbroking and other professions. Recruitment teams have been sent as far afield as South Africa in an attempt to recruit sub-editors and business writers. About 17% of the staff at SPH are from overseas. Mr Cheong commented: 'We have never been able to bring our staffing levels up to full strength. Journalists, subs, photographers, graphics people – we just can't find enough of them.'

In a unique experiment in newspaper publishing a proportion of the sub-editing, layout and graphics work is being undertaken by satellite offices in Sydney and Manila. In Sydney, there is a team of 12 people, about six of whom are Singaporeans and Malaysians who had settled in Australia. These staff provide the sub-editing and

layout expertise for sections of the *Straits Times* (the main SPH English-language newspaper). The Asian employees provide the local knowledge about style and related aspects to ensure that the paper retains a local feel and conforms to local needs. In Manila there are five graphic artists who feed artwork between Singapore and Sydney on a regular basis. Only about 5% of the *Straits Times* is 'subbed' offshore in this way. Plans exist to extend that to about 40% over time, if the experiment is successful.

One of the difficulties experienced in the experiment is that Sydney is two hours ahead of Singapore and consequently it is not possible to leave the later aspects of the newspaper to be produced there. The group are considering opening offices in Bombay, because it is two hours behind Singapore time and many good journalists live there. However, communication links with India remain a difficulty in getting the project off the ground. The telephone lines must be of top quality to ensure the best transmission between the two locations.

Adapted from: Cooke, K (1995) Singapore dials long distance to find staff, *Financial Times*, 31 May, p 3.

work and there is a shortage of people with the new skills. This creates difficulties for organizations, governments, trade unions and individual workers. Removing employees with outdated skills results in organizations having to meet redundancy costs. At the same time the cost of labour with scarce skills increases. Inevitably, the level of employment in an economy reduces, with a reduction in revenue for a government at a time when state benefits may be needed to support the displaced employees and to *pump prime* training initiatives to equip people with the emerging skills. The trade unions also face a loss of members as individuals leave jobs and perhaps move into other areas of work. They also face difficulties as members (or potential members) question the value of bodies that claim to represent their interests but who find it difficult to prevent job losses and change being forced upon workers.

Risk of failure is one of the problems that technology brings. It is developing at such a rapid rate that no sooner has a particular technology been introduced than it has been superseded, the danger here being that competitors adopt the next generation of new technology and steal an advantage. The cost of the adoption of a particular technology can be prohibitive and is not something that can be undertaken every year. Flexibility and keeping future options open is a key requirement of new technology. However, technology suppliers make this very difficult by seeking to *lock* customers into their own product range in order to protect future business. Variations in product and technology standards prevent the easy switching from one supplier to another. Consequently, the successful adoption of new technology comes not so much from the technology itself but from its effective integration with other work activities and existing technologies.

Very few managers have an in-depth understanding of the technologies available. In progressing their careers managers progressively move away from the operational levels of activity. Increasingly, technology becomes something that other people use regularly. Managers inevitably rise through a particular discipline, accounting, personnel or production for example. They will have some knowledge of new technology applications within their own areas of expertise but less in other areas. At some point in their careers, managers have to take responsibility for disciplines of which they have no direct experience. Inevitably, when this happens, technology continues to develop within their original profession beyond that with which they were familiar and they have responsibility for activities within which they have little experience, the danger being that managers become reactionary and resist technology applications, or they become prey to the claims of vested interests. In most organizations senior managers have enough experience to be able to tread this line with some considerable skill, but it is a danger that continues to exist. Effective measures are needed to ensure that senior managers are not left behind in understanding new technology.

Another element of new technology for managers is the effect on jobs and employees within the organization. It is easy to see technology as an end in itself rather than a means to an end. Technology is not capable of running a company without input and support from that most capable and flexible of all technologies (an old technology at that), the human being. The true success of new technology comes from the effective integration of these two totally different expressions of creativity. After all it is technology that is intended to support people not the other way round!

Buchanan and McCalman (1988) studied the effects of computerized information systems in hotels and concluded that they offered a number of advantages, which they describe as a visibility theory:

+ Sharing. Computer-based systems encouraged managers to share information more readily than manual systems.

+ Confidence. The more widely available information encouraged and motivated managers, thus increasing confidence levels.

+ Pressure. The wider and timely availability of information as a result of computerization puts pressure on managers to react quickly and effectively in pursuing business objectives.

+ Visibility. Improved information flows bring into the open the relative performance of individual managers.

+ Co-operation. These four previous elements combined produce a situation where managers find it easier to work together and reduce levels of conflict generally.

Conclusions

This chapter has served to introduce the concept of technology in its broadest sense as it impacts on organizations and those who work in them. It has shown that technology has been evolving for as long as people have been attempting to improve their ability to survive and raise living standards. In doing so technology as it impacts on that most fundamental of social structures, an organization, has a particular part to play. It influences both the way in which employees experience work and the rewards that they accrue from it, also, the level, cost and type of goods and services that are available to be acquired by consumers. In that way humans are both victim and creator of the beast that enslaves them.

This chapter has also reviewed a number of the new technology applications within organizations and the impact of these on how people operate. New technology was also considered in terms of decision making, rationality and as part of a change process. It is inevitable that any discussion of new technology will quickly become dated as suppliers and innovators create new technologies and different applications for existing ones. The risk associated with new technology is that it begins to take a predominant position in organizational thinking and diverts attention away from human capabilities and diversity as an important element in survival.

Discussion questions

1. Define the following key terms used in this chapter:

   Informates   *Vicious cycle of control*   *Visibility*
   New technology   *Industrialization*   *Rationality*
   Social technology   *Technology*   *Adhocracy*
   Japanization

2. What is new technology and how does it differ from previous technologies?

3. Identify the ways in which new technology has influenced the traditional ways of exercising control within organizations.

4. How are technology, diversity and innovation linked together?

5. Does technology manage managers or do managers manage technology? Justify your answer.

6. What effect does technology have on structure and job design within organizations?

7. Managers are as much victims of technology as those employees with skills that are superseded by technology. Comment on this statement.

8. Discuss the notion that understanding how technology has unfolded across history provides an improved picture of its benefits and problems today.

9. Technology supports the values of the prevailing rulers of society. Discuss.

10. Does technology inevitably lead to alienation? Justify your answer.

11. The main reason for managers to seek to utilize technology is to increase their control over the processes for which they are responsible. Technology is, therefore, a political tool in the service of capital. Discuss this statement.

Research activities

1. In the library seek out ten journal articles that describe the impact of new technology on work. What similarities and differences are contained in that set of papers and this chapter? Why might that be so?

2. Speak to a manager you know (or one who is prepared to discuss the subject) and ask them to define what they understand technology to be, its value to them and the way in which they decide upon its application. Seek out a trade union officer and ask the same questions, but this time in relation to their experience of how managers/organizations use technology. What conclusions do you draw from the differences and similarities in views expressed?

3. It could be argued that western technology originally emerged in different religious as well as social and cultural conditions. Seek out literature that may be expected to offer an insight into this aspect of technological development and assess the arguments for yourself.

Key reading

From Clark, H, Chandler, J and Barry, J (1994) *Organization and Identities: Text and Readings in Organizational Behaviour*, International Thomson Business Press, London.

✦ Bell, D: Work and its discontents, p 44. Considers the notions of efficiency and rationality in the context of work and technology.

✦ Campbell, B *et al.*: The manifesto for new times, p 49. This describes the evolution of Britain over the past 20 years or so. Its purpose is to provide one perspective of the context within which technology develops.

✦ Coyle, K: Postmodernism, p 58. This provides a critique of the postmodernist perspective on the evolution of the capitalist society.

✦ Dex, S: The sexual division of work, p 177. Reviews the gendered nature of work, including the role of technology in this process.

✦ Cockburn, C: Male dominance and technological change, p 197. Explores the gendered nature of work and the part played by technology in this process.

✦ Brunsson, N: The virtue of irrationality – decision making, action and commitment, p 294. Considers the conflicting nature of decision rationality and action rationality and the inclusion of irrationality into the process.

✦ Hobsbawm, EJ and Rude, G: Early forms of worker resistance – swing riots, p 317. Reflects on the nature of worker resistance and its manifestation in agricultural machine breaking and rioting together with the response of the courts.

✦ Taylor, L and Walton, P: Industrial sabotage, p 321. A more recent review of worker resistance.

✦ Braverman, H: The degradation of work, p 385. Considers one aspect of technology – the compartmentalization of work.

✦ Marx, K: Alienated labour, p 387. The classic review of alienation from the Marxist perspective.

✦ Fromm, E: Alienation, p 391. Considers the notion of alienation from an individual point of view in its effect on how work is perceived.

♦ Mills, CW: The cheerful robot, p 396. This extract argues for individuality and a significant role for human beings as a response to alienation.

Further reading

Clark, J (ed.) (1993) *Human Resource Management and Technical Change*, Sage, London. This text does not consider specifically the organizational behaviour issues associated with new technology, but it does reflect on the nature of technical change in its broadest sense and the human resource issues that emerge.

Forester, T (1987) *High-tech Society*, Basil Blackwell, Oxford. Provides a very readable review of the evolution and technicalities of technology. It also develops a number of themes associated with the application of technology in a work and social context.

Haydu, J (1988) *Between Craft and Class: Skilled Workers and Factory Politics in the United States and Britain, 1890–1922*, University of California Press, Berkeley. Considers the reaction of skilled metalworkers to the economic changes surrounding them as a result of new production methods emerging in the early twentieth century. The author places this process in the context of the emergence of different approaches to collective effort as a means of attempting to achieve greater influence on management decision making.

Inkster, I (ed.) (1985) *The Steam Intellect Societies*, Department of Adult Education, University of Nottingham. This series of essays reflects on the emergence and development of what would now be regarded as post-experience technical education. It emerged as a result of the increasing sophistication of technology and the need to have the workforce trained and educated to a higher level in order to ensure that the machinery was maintained in good working order. However, this need also provided an opportunity for those individuals inclined to seek upward mobility through further education and development.

Maines, DR and Morrione, TJ (eds) (1990) *Industrialization as an Agent of Social Change: A Critical Analysis by Herbert Blumer*. Aldine de Gruyter, New York. This text takes a critical sociological approach to the notion of industrialization (including the role of technology) and its function moulding society. As the editors point out it was an unfinished work at the time of the author's death, and having been reworked several times it was clearly something with which he was not satisfied. It is therefore interesting to read it critically as a piece of scholarship that was partly complete.

Thompson, P (1989) *The Nature of Work: An Introduction to Debates on the Labour Process*, 2nd edn, Macmillan, Basingstoke. As the title suggests, this text takes a detailed look at the labour process concept, its origins and implications. as such it elaborates the political and social context within which work exists.

References

Baines, E (1835) *History of the Cotton Manufacture in Great Britain*, London.

BBC/Open University (1986) Strategies for change: the task force. PT 611: The structure and design of manufacturing systems. Open University/BBC production, course film.

Bedeian, AG (1984) *Organizations: Theory and Analysis*, 2nd edn, Dryden Press, Hinsdale.

Betz, F (1987) *Managing Technology*, Prentice Hall, Englewood Cliffs, NJ.

Blauner, R (1964) *Alienation and Freedom: The Factory Worker and His Job*, University of Chicago Press, Chicago.

Braverman, H (1974) *Labour and Monopoly Capital: The Degradation of Work in the Twentieth Century*, Monthly Review Press, London.

Buchanan, DA and Boddy, D (1983) *Organizations in the Computer Age: Technological Imperatives and Strategic Choice*, Gower, Aldershot.

Buchanan, DA and McCalman, J (1988) Confidence, visibility and pressure: the effects of shared information in computer aided hotel management, *New Technology, Work and Employment*, **3**, 38–46.

Burns, T and Stalker, GM (1961) *The Management of Innovation*, Tavistock, London.

Child, J (1985) Managerial Strategies, New Technology and the Labour Process. In Knights, D, Willmott, H and Collinson, D (eds) *Job Redesign: Critical Perspectives on the Labour Process*. Gower, Aldershot.

Clark, J, McLoughlin, I, Rose, H and King, R (1988) *The Process of Technological Change: New Technology and Social Choice in the Workplace*, Cambridge University Press, Cambridge.

Clawson, D (1980) *Bureaucracy and the Labour Process: The Transformation of US Industry, 1860–1920*, Monthly Review Press, New York.

Clegg, S and Dunkerley, D (1980) *Organization, Class and Control*, Routledge & Kegan Paul, London.

Domingo, R (1985) 'Kanban': crisis management Japanese style, *Euro-Asia Business Review*, **4**, 22–4.

Forester, T (1987) *High-tech Society*, Basil Blackwell, Oxford.

Fox, A (1974) *Man Mismanagement*, Hutchinson, London.

Friedman, AL and Cornford, DS (1989) *Computer Systems Development: History, Organization and Implementation*, John Wiley, Chichester.

Gaither, N (1992) *Production and Operations Management*, 5th edn, Dryden Press, Fort Worth, TX.

Garrahan, P and Stewart, P (1992) *The Nissan Enigma: Flexibility at Work in a Local Community*, Mansell, London.

Giles, E and Starkey, K (1987) From Fordism to Japanisation: Organizational Change at Ford, Rank Xerox and Fuji Xerox. Paper presented at a conference on the Japanization of British Industry, UMIST.

Herriot P and Pemberton C (1995) *Competitive Advantage Through Diversity: Organizational Learning Through Difference*, Sage, London.

Hill, T (1983) *Production and Operations Management*, Prentice Hall, London.

Hughes, M (1985) Debureaucratization and Private Interest Government: The British State and Economic Development Policy. In Streeck, W and Schmitter, PC (eds) *Private Interest Government: Beyond Market and State*, Sage, London.

Janis, IL (1972) *Victims of Groupthink: A Psychological Study of Foreign Policy Decisions*, Houghton Mifflin, Boston.

Klemm, F (1959) *A History of Western Technology*, George Allen & Unwin, London.

Konsynski, BR and Sviokla, JJ (1994) Cognitive Reapportionment: Rethinking the Location of Judgement in Managerial Decision Making. In Heckscher, C and Donnellon, A (eds) *The Post-bureaucratic Organization: New Perspectives on Organizational Change*, Sage, Thousand Oaks.

Lawrence, PR and Lorsch, JW (1967) *Organization and Environment*, Harvard University Press, Cambridge.

Lincoln, JR and Kalleburg, AL (1990) *Culture, Control and Commitment*, Cambridge University Press, Cambridge.

Maines, DR and Morrione, TJ (eds) (1990) *Industrialization as an Agent of Social Change: A Critical Analysis by Herbert Blumer*, Aldine de Gruyter, New York.

McLoughlin, I and Clark, J (1988) *Technological Change at Work*, Open University Press, Milton Keynes.

Mintzberg, H (1983) *Structure in Fives: Designing Effective Organizations*, Prentice Hall, Englewood Cliffs, NJ.

Oliver, N and Wilkinson, B (1992) *The Japanization of British Industry: New Developments in the 1990s*, 2nd edn, Blackwell, Oxford.

Perrow, CB (1967) A framework for the comparative analysis of organizations, *American Sociological Review*, April, pp 194–208.

Perrow, CB (1970) *Organizational Analysis: A Sociological View*, Tavistock, London.

Reed, M (1989) *The Sociology of Management*, Harvester Wheatsheaf, Hemel Hempstead.

Sayer, A (1986) New developments in manufacturing: the just-in-time system, *Capital and Class*, **30**, 43–72.

Schon, DA (1994) Teaching Artistry through Reflection-in-action. In Tsoukas, H (ed.) *New Thinking in Organizational Behaviour*, Butterworth-Heinemann, Oxford.

Shaiken, H (1985) *Work Transformed: Automation and Labor in the Computer Age*, Holt, Rinehart & Winston, New York.

Thompson, JD (1967) *Organizations in Action*, McGraw-Hill, New York.

Thompson, L (1985) New Office Technology: People, Work Structures and the Process of Change. WRU Occasional Paper No. 34, April. ACAS Work Research Unit, London.

Thompson, L (1989) New Office Technology: The Changing Role of the Secretary. WRU Occasional Paper No. 44, January. ACAS Work Research Unit, London.

Turnbull, PJ (1986) The Japanisation of British industrial relations at Lucas, *Industrial Relations Journal*, **17**, 193–206.

Ure, A (1835) *Philosophy of Manufactures*, London.

Wickens, PD (1987) *The Road to Nissan*, Macmillan, London.

Williams, K, Haslem, C, Williams, J, Adcroft, A and Johal, S (1992) Factories or Warehouses: Japanese

Manufacturing Foreign Direct Investment in Britain and the United States. Occasional Papers on Business, Economy and Society, No. 6, University of East London.

Winner, L (1977) *Autonomous Technology: Technics-out-of-control as a Theme in Political Thought*, MIT Press, Cambridge.

Woodward, J (1965) *Industrial Organizations: Theory and Practice*, Oxford University Press, London.

Zuboff, S (1988) *In the Age of the Smart Machine: The Future of Work and Power*, Heinemann, Oxford.

PART V

Processes within organizations

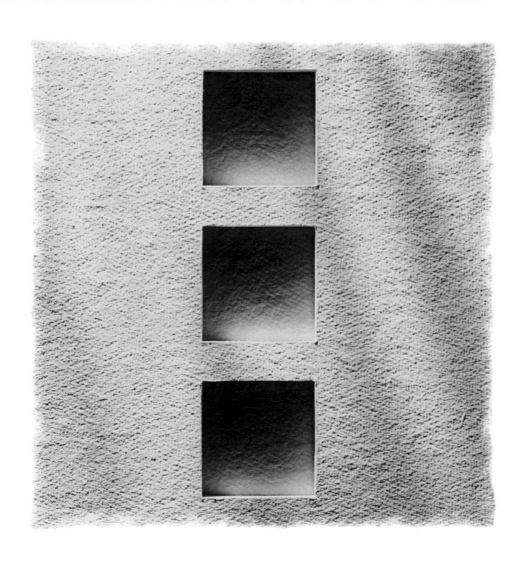

CHAPTER 9

Learning within organizations

CHAPTER SUMMARY

This chapter begins with the introduction to a number of concepts associated with learning in an organizational context. This is followed by a review of a number of learning theories that not only reflect how human beings learn, but also underpin much of the training activity within organizations. This leads naturally into a review of how the learning interacts with major aspects of organizational functioning, including training and development. Following this will be a consideration of the application of the concepts, introduced from a management perspective.

LEARNING OBJECTIVES

After studying this chapter and working through the associated Management in Action panels, Discussion questions and Research activities, you should be able to:

✦ Outline and differentiate between the concepts of learning, training, development and education.

✦ Describe the major theoretical approaches to the study of learning.

✦ Understand the concept of a learning organization.

✦ Appreciate the links between learning and individual difference.

✦ Discuss the links between concepts such as socialization and learning to the control of people within organizations.

✦ Detail the relevance of knowledge management for an organization.

✦ Assess the organizational implications of learning.

✦ Explain why the styles of learning are relevant to understanding how people learn.

Introduction

Learning is a major activity within society as a whole, not just organizations. Children spend a considerable number of years in the formal school system and many go on to advanced academic or vocational study. Employees need to learn how to do the jobs that they will be expected to undertake within organizations and will also need to learn many new skills over the course of their working life.

Within an organizational setting learning most frequently finds expression in the form of training and development activities. Organizations are faced with trading and economic situations that require flexibility from existing workers and so find that it is necessary continually to train and retrain employees in order to retain organizational viability. In some locations skill imbalances exist, with unfilled vacancies coexisting alongside high unemployment. This leads to a range of (usually) government sponsored initiatives to retrain unemployed workers thereby enabling them to meet the skill requirements of the available jobs. In some countries or job sectors skill shortage and high employment levels coexist which can create high labour turnover as employees 'job-hop'. In this context, learning through training and development has an important role to play in helping to retain staff who might otherwise leave.

The opportunity for personal and professional development are important 'weapons' in management's attempt to attract and retain good staff, as well as the means of enhancing organizational performance. There are also benefits to be garnered in terms of improved levels of control (achieved through socialization) that management gain from the application of training and development processes. Governments are also interested in training and development for economic, political and social reasons, in addition to their role as a very large employer. A healthy economy (as a result of many factors including training and development) frequently reflects political and social stability which is to the benefit of both individual citizens and the dominant political rulers.

Clearly, the processes supported by learning have considerable significance for individuals, managers, governments and society. It is therefore useful to begin this chapter with an in-depth review of the similarities and differences between the main concepts to be discussed.

Learning, training and development

It is perhaps useful to begin with a brief review of the concepts that are supported by a learning process. The terms training and development are often used in practice as if they were interchangeable. Education is another term that is commonly used and which has a strong association with training and development. The *Oxford Dictionary* defines these three concepts in the following way:

+ Develop. To unfold more fully, to bring out all that is potentially contained within.
+ Educate. To bring up so as to form habits, manners, intellectual and physical aptitudes.
+ Train. To instruct and discipline in or for some particular art, profession, occupation or practice; to make proficient by such instruction and practice.

From these definitions the obvious similarities and differences between the concepts and their application to an organizational setting become apparent. The concept of *education* would seem to be a general process representing the basic preparation for adult life in a specific environment. In an organizational setting, this would equate with the *socialization* or *induction* process for new employees to a company, examples of which would include meeting appropriate managers and colleagues, and learning about the basic rules, procedures and product range of the company.

Training is described as a job-specific form of education. It could either be organization specific or general. For example, a company might train its staff for the particular word-processing package that it uses. This training would be specific to that particular organization, but could also be transferable to other companies (if they use the same package). In December 1993 a national initiative by the then UK government attempted to place work-based training on a par with academic qualifications in order to enhance its value, transferability and perceived significance (Wood, 1993).

Development reflects a less specific activity which relates to potential. Development is about the future. It does not necessarily relate to the job an individual presently undertakes. It could be a set of experiences that provide the individual with a basis for future career moves. It could also be used to enhance the skill levels of an individual in anticipation of future change in the nature of work or products. For example, the planned introduction of high-technology equipment is frequently preceded by introductory courses for those affected. The content might deal with computers in general and specifically the equipment being considered, together with applications and familiarization with keyboards and screens. Development as an activity has traditionally been reserved for managers. However, it is being increasingly used to describe the full range of training and development activity, the argument being that it is a less restrictive term than training, does not preclude the use of training activities within its sphere of influence and is more easily associated with the concepts of individual and organizational growth. This approach is often associated with the notion of *human resource development,* in which individual, career and organizational development are brought together as an integrated approach to mutual benefit (Beardwell and Holden, 1997).

Each of the terms education, training and development assumes that some form of *learning* takes place within the individual. This can be reflected as a mutually dependent set of relationships as shown in Figure 9.1.

The *Oxford Dictionary* defines the term *learn* as to 'get knowledge of or skill in by study, experience or being taught'.

In other words, the individual is affected in some way or other as a result of the process. Learning can also be defined as the relatively permanent change in behaviour or potential behaviour that results from direct or indirect experience (Hulse *et al.,* 1980). The major elements in these definitions are that:

✦ Learning implies change. The acquisition of a new skill suggests that the individual will be different by comparison with 'before'. For example, if an employee learns a new skill, that person can undertake a different range of tasks. The difference becomes more difficult to detect, however, when the learning is cognitive in nature. For example, how will you be changed as a result of reading this chapter? You will have increased your level of understanding in the organizational behaviour field. In that sense *you* will have changed. But such *changes* might not be easily detectable as behaviour.

✦ Learning implies sustained change. The definitions of learning suggested earlier imply a long-lasting change consequence. Conversely, anything that produces a short-term effect is not true learning. So, for example, a student who *learns* the appropriate material for an exam and then puts it from memory has not *learned* anything.

✦ Learning influences behaviour. In some instances this is comparatively easy to see. For example, acquiring the skill of being able to drive a car. In other cases, the individual is learning to influence future behaviour. Your course in organizational behaviour is intended to introduce you to the behavioural and other issues associated with the human dimensions of organizations and consequently to influence your future management style and decision-making abilities (always assuming that you become – or are already – a manager).

✦ Learning results from experience. Some form of direct experience is necessary in order to produce learning. In the case of learning to drive a car, it is necessary at some point actually to get behind the steering wheel and drive on public roads. Indirect experience leads to vicarious learning. For example, an employee cheating on their time sheet and so earning more bonus will frequently be following the example of other employees.

The learning process is outlined in Figure 9.2. This indicates the relationship between the learning process itself and the purpose to which it is being put. Equally, the impact on learning of past learning events is recognized in the model through the feedback loop. So for example, bad experiences in the formal school education system might negatively

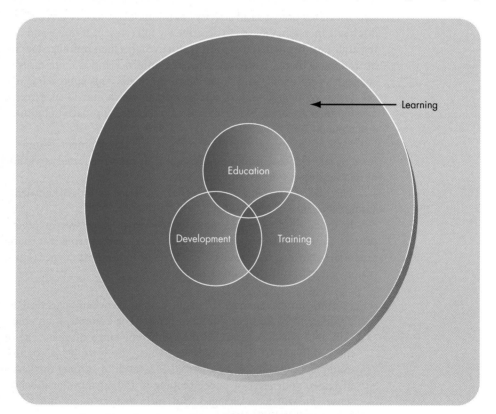

FIGURE 9.1   Learning, education, training and development.

impact on an individual's willingness to expose themselves to learning opportunities in the future.

Also indicated in the model are those elements that precede learning, but which influence it:

✦ External factors. For example, the pressure placed on individuals to undergo learning. Children must by law be educated in an approved manner.

✦ Internal factors. For example, mood, intelligence, ability, personality and motivation all influence the learning process.

✦ Learning experience. A poorly designed learning event may result in the trainees not learning that which they were intended to learn.

Management in Action 9.1 provides an insight into some of the links between success and how to acquire (or learn) it.

Stop | Consider

To what extent is it possible to learn to be successful, or is it a question of having the right family and connections with a large degree of luck? Justify your views on this issue.

The process by which people learn has long been an area of interest in psychology. There are three main approaches that have emerged over time, each one adding to the

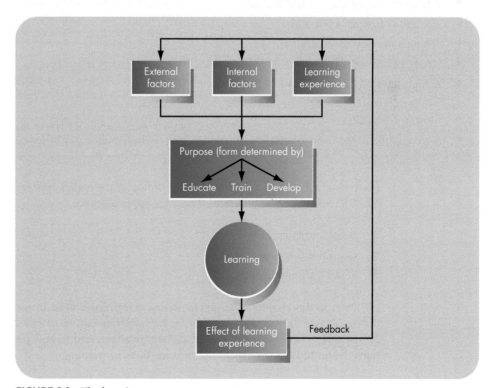

FIGURE 9.2   The learning process.

MANAGEMENT IN ACTION 9.1

Take it from the top

The Performance Group, a Norwegian management consultancy, spent two years talking to 40 'world-class performers' in order to tease out the secrets of success at the top. They included a Brazilian archbishop, a French chef, an Australian marathon runner, a Russian conductor, the manager of the Los Angeles Dodgers and the chief of an Native American tribe. The researchers claim that the results identified that all high performers have a number of characteristics in common and that how to succeed can be learned by anyone.

The common characteristics among the top performers interviewed included:

✦ A sense of compelling purpose.

✦ A greed for knowledge.

✦ The ability to learn from their mistakes.

✦ The ability to learn from others.

✦ Strong powers of concentration.

✦ Strong personal discipline.

✦ A high level of intensity in what they were doing.

✦ Most had integrity.

✦ A recognition of the need to motivate others.

✦ A recognition of the value of relaxation.

✦ A recognition of delegation.

✦ A competitive streak.

The Performance Group argues that each one of these characteristics can be learned and used to enhance the performance of both the individual and the organization that they work for. However, some of the interviewees suggested that they believed that some of their success was due to inborn gifts. For example, Valery Gergiev suggested that the key feature was the abilities each individual was born with, that could subsequently be developed by training and experience. Many of the interviewees indicated that their fathers were the most important influence in their lives, mothers were hardly mentioned. Some even inherited their position from their fathers. So perhaps success at the top is not just a question of learning the key qualities after all.

Adapted from: Kellaway, L (1993) Take it from the top, *Financial Times Weekend*, 23/24 October, p 9.

understanding of the process by building on top of the earlier approaches and accounting for different learning experiences. The three approaches are:

✦ Behaviourist theories.

✦ Cognitive theories.

✦ Social learning theories.

Later in this chapter other perspectives on learning will be introduced together with the concepts of the *learning organization, knowledge management* and *strategic training and development*. These will be discussed as they are all relevant to how people (and organizations) learn through the experience of some form of training.

Behaviourist theories of learning

The behaviourist school of psychology has enjoyed a long and illustrious tradition. The two best-known names from this field of psychology are Pavlov, who developed the theory of *classical conditioning*, and Skinner, who developed the theory of *instrumental conditioning* as an approach to learning.

Pavlov and classical conditioning

Pavlov carried out his research in Russia. He was concerned with the learning experienced by dogs in relation to their natural reflexes. Pavlov noticed that whenever his laboratory dogs were given food they salivated (1927). This was a natural reaction in the dogs, to which he gave the term *unconditioned response*. This became the first step in the conditioning process. The second step was to link what Pavlov termed the *unconditioned stimulus* (food) with a *conditioned stimulus* (the ringing of a bell). This was done by ringing the bell on each occasion on which food was presented. Pavlov was trying to get the dogs to learn that the sound of the bell was associated with the appearance of food. After several repetitions the dogs salivated automatically when the bell was rung. This was the third step in the conditioning process, the *conditioned response*. A direct link between the stimulus (bell sound) and the response (salivation) had been made. This series of steps can be shown as a diagram (see Figure 9.3). In the *classical conditioning* model, the salivation was conditioned to occur as a result of the previously established association between the bell and the food.

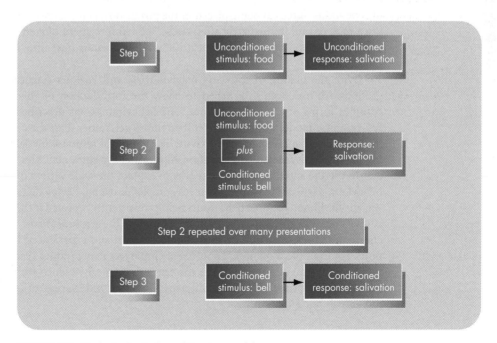

FIGURE 9.3 Pavlov's classical conditioning model.

Discussion of the stimulus–response model

This conditioned response is a relatively simple reaction when compared with the behaviour of humans, particularly in a social setting. The theory was able to explain some of the simpler forms of learning but the *conditioned response* quickly died away if it was not frequently reinforced. This feature of the model was referred to as an *extinction response* and makes it more difficult to explain how *classical conditioning* could build *learning* opportunities from the spontaneous, dynamic and random nature of much human interaction and experience. Pavlov was also able to make his experimental dogs respond to a wide range of bell-related variables, so demonstrating a generalizable stimulus dimension which might help explain some of the links with real experience.

The work of Pavlov was running in parallel, although independently, with a number of American theorists. They included Watson, who coined the term *behaviourism* to describe the emphasis on observable behaviour rather than the introspective approaches common in psychology at that time. Watson believed that learning in the environment was responsible for almost all development, ability and personality in the growing child. He introduced into the field of behaviourism the concept of stimulus–response associations (*conditioning*) as the basis of much human behaviour (Watson, 1924). The routine behaviour reflected in *stimulus–response* patterns can provide an explanation of some individual behaviour from life in general and organizations in particular. For example, a manager who shouts at employees to ensure that instructions are followed might discover after a while that employees do not respond to any instruction not given with a shout.

Thorndike built on this stimulus–response model through his studies of the ability of cats to escape from puzzle boxes (1932). From these observations he concluded that the cats could learn by *trial and error* (slow learning). Thorndike suggested that what was happening was a slow strengthening of the stimulus–response connection through a number of repetitions of the cat being placed in the puzzle box, being allowed to escape and receiving a food reward immediately afterwards. The reinforcement offered by the food made it more likely that the cat would repeat the same behaviour next time it was placed in the puzzle box.

With the linking of the early behaviourists and Pavlov's classical conditioning the groundwork had been established to allow the introduction of this approach to more complex forms of learned behaviour. The behaviour so far described within the stimulus–response model was generally at the reflex level, rather than the conscious purposeful forms reflected in much human activity. The stimulus–response model is good at explaining the simple cause and effect relationships evident in some activities. However, it is difficult to use the stimulus–response model to explain the wide variety of observable human behaviour, particularly when it involves complex learning. Pavlov demonstrated that there was the likelihood of some behaviours being consistently repeated if the stimulus–response connection was adequately reinforced. However, the *classical model* does not allow for choice in the response options available to humans and experienced in everyday interactions. For example, a manager shouting at employees may produce reactions ranging from rapid compliance at one end of the spectrum to physical violence at the other. The actual behavioural responses occurring will depend upon a wide variety of factors acting on the individuals and situation.

Skinner and instrumental conditioning

Skinner is associated with the *instrumental* approach to conditioning, but he was not the first person to be associated with it. Instrumental in this context refers to behaviour being 'instrumental' in producing an effect. For example, a hungry rat can be conditioned to press a lever to obtain food. Pressing the lever (behaviour) releases the food and allows feeding (the effect). The pressing of the lever is therefore *instrumental* in obtaining food.

Skinner put forward a distinction between two types of behaviour, *respondent* and *operant* (1953). *Respondent* behaviour was said to be under the direct control of a stimulus. This was the stimulus–response relationship in classical conditioning. For example, salivation in response to food presentation. *Operant* behaviour, contrariwise, was seen in terms of spontaneity, with no direct or obvious cause. A stimulus controlling operant behaviour is referred to as a *discriminative stimulus*. An example would be the knocking on your front door, which tells you that someone is trying to see you for some purpose, but does not force you to answer the door. It might be hard to ignore the knocking, but you can choose to do so. In this way the concept is synonymous with the term *instrumental* in that the behaviour (answering the door) is instrumental in producing an effect (finding out why someone was knocking on it). It is for this reason that the term *instrumental conditioning* is used to describe this form of learning.

The best-known experiments in this area involve laboratory rats being placed in a *Skinner box*, named after the designer. There are many variations of this type of experiment and so only a simple generalized account will be provided here. Imagine a small cage, bare except for a feeding tray, a lever and a light source. Figure 9.4 is a schematic diagram of such a Skinner box.

A hungry rat is placed in the box and left to explore its new surroundings under the watchful eye of the experimenter. As the rat approaches the lever in the box a pellet of food

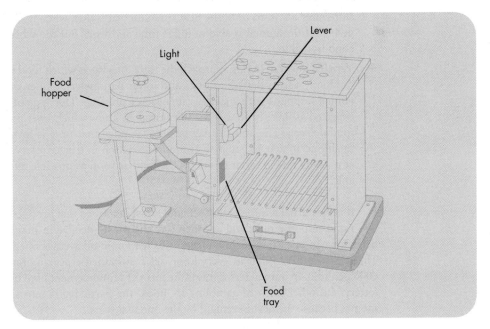

FIGURE 9.4   A Skinner box.

will be made available in the food tray. After a few repetitions of this, the rat may accidentally touch the lever and again food will be made available. From then on, only touching the lever will produce a food pellet. Eventually, this is also replaced with the actual pressing of the lever being required to obtain food. The lever pressing is *reinforced* by the presentation of food. There are an enormous range of variations that can be introduced to this basic process and it has been used on a wide range of animals. Pigeons have been taught to 'recognize' colours and play table tennis, whales and dolphins trained for wildlife shows and dolphins trained to plant mines on enemy ships in a military context. All of these created using *instrumental conditioning* as the basis of learning the desired behaviour.

The process of *reinforcement* is used to *shape* the behaviour pattern desired. Over many cycles of repetition only behaviours closer and closer to the desired outcome will be rewarded until the actual behaviour presented matches that desired by the trainer. Once established, it is not necessary to reinforce every occurrence of the desired behaviour in order to maintain it. There are four types of *reinforcement* schedule that can influence the level and rate of continued repetition of the desired behaviour. They are:

✦ Fixed ratio. Reinforcement takes place after a fixed number of repetitions of a particular activity. For example, one pellet of food every 20 lever presses. This tends to produce a rapid and consistent rate of response in order for the respondent to be able to maximize the reward.

✦ Variable ratio. This also provides reinforcement after a number of repetitions of the desired behaviour. However, unlike the fixed ratio, this time the number of repetitions required to produce the reward is randomly varied. This produces a rapid rate of response as the respondent (rat in a Skinner box) has no way of predicting which response (lever press) will produce the pellet of food.

✦ Fixed interval. This approach produces a reinforcement following the first appropriate behaviour after a set time interval. The behaviour pattern under this regime almost stops after a reward until the next time interval is due, when it starts again. This suggests that the animal is able to judge time and work out the schedule that it is being conditioned to.

✦ Variable interval. In this approach the time interval at which food becomes available is randomly varied between upper and lower parameters. Under these conditions, the animal responds with a steady rate of lever pressing. This type of response would be expected as there is no way for the animal to know which lever press will activate the food delivery. The animal may be able to judge that time is involved, but it will be unable accurately to gauge the random variation in trigger intervals. It must respond at a steady rate in order to obtain the food as soon as possible after it becomes available.

It is the partial reinforcement schedules just described that produce the most sustained and rapid response rates and are therefore the most effective in maintaining the desired behaviour. In one experiment a pigeon was *reinforced* on average once every five minutes. That equates to 12 times in every hour. Yet it sustained a pecking rate of approximately 6000 per hour. In human terms this is the form of reinforcement used by gaming machines, lottery and other form of gambling to 'hook' the participants into spending their stake money, because the next bet might be the one that wins.

So far in the discussion we have described only *positive reinforcement*. That is, the subject being rewarded for doing something that the designer of the conditioning programme seeks. Other *reinforcement* options available include:

✦ Negative reinforcers. This refer to an unpleasant event that precedes behaviour and which is removed when the subject produces appropriate behaviour. For example, a torturer may stop beating up a prisoner if they confess to a crime.

✦ Omission. This refers to the stopping of reinforcement. Naturally, it leads to a reduction and eventually the extinction of the particular behaviour. For example, employees who do an excellent job may stop doing so if managers do not reinforce the behaviour by acknowledging the contribution.

✦ Punishment. This relates to an unpleasant reward for particular behaviours. The slap on the leg of a child who does something wrong would be an example. This form of reinforcement decreases the occurrence of the behaviour in question.

The relationship between these four forms of reinforcement are shown in Figure 9.5.

Many experiments have been carried out on the conditioning of human behaviour. For example, Verplanck (1955) carried out a reinforcement exercise during an informal conversation with a student. The student was not aware of the reinforcement process being carried out. It is worth noting that the experiment as described would not meet the ethical standards required today and so would need to be designed differently. The reinforcement schedule designed required the experimenter to reward all statements of opinion made by the student. These included phrases such as, 'I believe', 'It is my opinion', 'I think', when used by the student within the conversation. The reinforcement was in the form of positive feedback to the student through the experimenter using phrases such as, 'I agree', 'You are right', 'That is so'. The use of this verbal reinforcement increased the number of statements of opinion used by the student. In another part of the same experiment, extinction was also demonstrated. This was achieved by the experimenter failing to reinforce any statement of opinion (by remaining silent) when the student made one. Not surprisingly, the use of these statements by the student reduced under this regime.

Discussion of instrumental conditioning

The process of *instrumental conditioning* has a wider application than the classical approach. It provides for the shaping of behaviour into particular patterns. It has also been

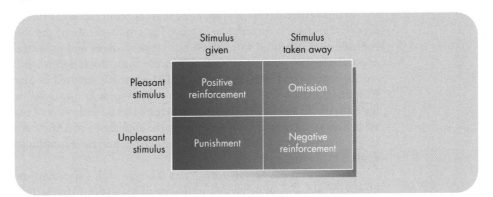

FIGURE 9.5   Reinforcement framework.

used to account for many of the beliefs and superstitions that pervade human life. Examples include blowing on the dice to make them lucky; putting on a particular item of clothing before an exam in order to guarantee success; and never watching a favourite football team live on television to improve their chance of winning. That instrumental conditioning can explain much of human behaviour has been established over many years. The difficulty arises in being able to explain how *reinforcement* operates in the everyday exposure to multiple and random experience. The experiment described earlier might explain how one lecturer can influence the behaviour of one student. But is it adequate in explaining how an entire (and probably) large class learn successfully or perhaps conversely fail to learn as intended? The answer is clearly no.

If reinforcement is delayed then it may become associated with other behaviour by default. For example, a company profit share scheme that rewards employees with a bonus if higher profits are achieved would usually be paid about three months after the financial year end. However, the 'behaviour' of the employees in increasing productivity would have covered a full year, beginning some 15 months before the payment would be received. Such indirect links between behaviour and reward stretch the *conditioning* principle beyond credibility. Under such circumstances it is more likely that employees will interpret any profit share payments received as a random event by an arbitrary management, selecting a level of payment that underrepresents their true effort over the preceding year. In addition to any reinforcement issues active in such situations there are also factors such as perception and memory to take into account as dynamic processes that also impact on how individual's interpreted situations.

The conditioning approach to learning cannot explain all thought and behaviour patterns evident in people. Individuals have objectives and purpose behind many of their behaviours which do not easily fit into a model based on the principles of conditioning. However, instrumental conditioning does have a place in the management of people as Management in Action 9.2 demonstrates. This case illustrates the complexity in the real world and how instrumental conditioning can be used to influence behaviour.

Stop | Consider

If you were the new domestic supervisor described in MiA 9.2 how would you have gone about establishing your credibility with your staff? How would you set about carrying out your new responsibilities in such a management job?

Would your approach contain any degree of conditioning in it? Why or why not?

In this particular case, it is apparent that the reinforcement process was combined with many other aspects in order to achieve the requirements of the job. The management control issues, the need to work within set procedures and guidelines together with the opportunity for operational managers to use some discretion when interpreting policies are all incorporated into the approach. The approach adopted in Management in Action 9.2 is an informal version of what has generally become known as *behavioural modification*, the basis of the approach being that managers should seek ways of maximizing appropriate behaviours among employees through the application of a range of reinforcement principles. Figure 9.6 is a representation of the behavioural modification process as it might be applied by a manager.

The model is self-explanatory in that it begins with a systematic review of the requirements and actuality of behaviour in the specific situation. This is then followed by a decision-making process which results in the identification of the appropriate reinforcement

MANAGEMENT IN ACTION 9.2

The domestic supervisor and conditioning

The domestic supervisor in a university hall of residence had been appointed to the job following the retirement of the previous incumbent, who had held the job for approximately ten years. With the change in personnel, management had decided to restructure the duties of the post and take the opportunity to increase the level of direct supervision of the domestic staff working in the hall. At the same time the job title was changed from housekeeper to domestic supervisor. Previously, direct supervision of the domestic staff had fallen under the responsibilities of a supervisor who looked after two halls specifically for these activities.

The new domestic supervisor described how she was initially concerned about how to approach the job to ensure that she obtained a positive response from the staff. It was necessary to increase the level of direct supervision of the staff, which inevitably meant increased levels of work inspection. Given that the staff had all been in the same jobs for many years and worked under a different regime, this could become a problem.

The new domestic supervisor had held supervisory jobs previously and at one time ran her own business. Calling on this wealth of experience she decided on the following course of action. The first stage was to let the existing staff get to know her and that 'things' would inevitably change. This involved several actions, including the provision of a bag of sweets on the desk from which all could help themselves, 'for a bit of energy to start the day'; frequent visits to each worksite to get to know the job and meet the staff on their own territory; only gradually over the period of a couple of weeks to begin to offer advice and suggestions on what needed to be done. This was usually done in terms of 'Would it not be easier to try it this way?' or 'Why not do this job when you have finished that one?'. The 'suggestion' would only become more like an

instruction if the individual would not enter into the spirit of the process and 'did not take the hint'.

This approach began to create a team in which the individual employee did not feel threatened. This was important as a number of them had applied for the domestic supervisor's job when it was advertised and felt some resentment at being rejected. They began by resisting the approach. Not in a serious way, but by finding excuses for not doing things that the domestic supervisor wanted doing, or doing them in the old way. This required the most tact on the part of the domestic supervisor as she attempted to change the behaviour patterns of the staff. The approach adopted was to keep a 'light touch' in the way that issues were raised by making a joke or a light-hearted comment about something. For example, it was pointed out to the staff, while laughing, that they should clean the light fittings on their way to their longer than strictly allowed tea break as they had said that they did not have time to do this job. The point was made in such a way that it could not be seen as a direct order, given in an offensive manner. But it was a clear signal of what was expected and the possible next step and penalty if it was not implemented. This was followed by frequent and obvious checks on that particular job, with comment on the result. Praise if it had been done, a jocular, 'Not had time to do these yet?' if it had not.

This reflects the application of instrumental conditioning in shaping the behaviour of the employees. This was not done deliberately by the domestic supervisor. It was, however, described as common sense in achieving the objectives necessary without causing problems. The staff are apparently unaware that their behaviour had been shaped. They considered that they have gone through a period of 'getting used to working with a new boss'.

approach to be adopted. Once selected and operational, the results of the reinforcement approach would then be regularly monitored and any remedial or follow-up action taken. Among the criticisms of this type of approach to the *organization* of human behaviour is that it is managers who decide what defines appropriate behaviour (presumably in support of particular objectives) and it therefore forms part of a *social engineering* or control process.

Cognitive approaches to learning

The basis of cognitive theories of learning are that an individual develops internal (*cognitive*) frameworks that allow them to interact more effectively with the environment around them. Therefore this approach creates a need to study the working of the mental processes involved in learning.

The early work in this field was carried out on animals and was based on the behavioural model already introduced. Kohler describes an experiment in which a

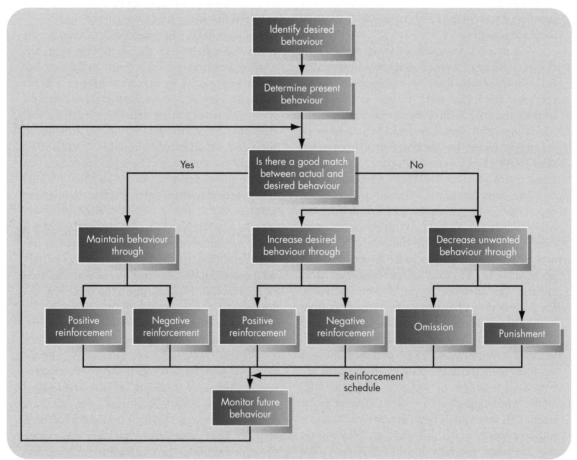

FIGURE 9.6 Behavioural modification (*adapted from*: Lunthans, F (1985) *Organizational Behaviour*, 4th edn, McGraw-Hill, New York).

chimpanzee demonstrated insight as a learning process (1925). Sultan (the name of the chimpanzee) was placed in a cage and given a short stick. A piece of fruit was placed outside the cage and beyond the range of the short stick. A longer stick was also placed outside the cage, but within range of the short stick. After a few attempts at obtaining the fruit by using the short stick, Sultan began to seek other ways of obtaining the fruit. After a number of false starts, he paused for a lengthy period and just looked around him. Suddenly, he jumped up, used the short stick to pull the long stick into range and thereby obtain the fruit. This suggested to Kohler that the chimpanzee was using *cognitive processes* to create *insights* into the problem and how it could be solved, in effect learning through problem solving. This approach to learning would seem to differ from the trial and error process described by Thorndike in that a sudden insight is apparent in finding a solution to the problem of obtaining the fruit.

This led to a number of other approaches to the development of cognitive learning. Essentially, this approach assumes that people are actively involved in the process of learning. They are not simply at the mercy of outside forces and internal drives. A simplified way of thinking about this cognitive approach is shown in Figure 9.7.

A more recent approach to the cognitive perspective on learning is based on information processing as a psychological process. According to Fitts and Posner (1967) the three primary characteristics of skilled performance are:

✦ Organization.
✦ Goal directedness.
✦ Utilization of feedback.

The process of providing feedback enables the individual more effectively and quickly to achieve the goal being sought. There are many obvious examples of feedback in action. Central heating and air conditioning systems function through feedback, based on the thermostat. The most easily understood form is negative feedback. Negative feedback allows the system being controlled to remain on target (see Figure 9.8).

Essentially, negative feedback reduces the gap between the current and intended situations. So, in a central heating system, the feedback process measures the actual room temperature, compares it with the desired temperature and switches the boiler on if the room is too cold. In an organizational setting, a manager will usually receive monthly financial reports setting out actual expenditure against the budgeted level. This form of feedback is more commonly referred to as a budgetary control system. If the manager is spending more money than is provided for under the budget, they will be able to seek ways of

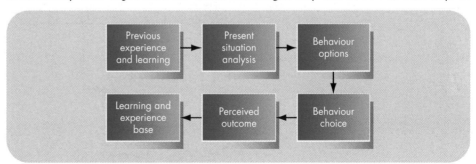

FIGURE 9.7 A cognitive model of learning.

reducing future expenditure, the intention being to utilize the principles of negative feedback to ensure that actual costs do not exceed the planned level over the year.

Feedback within the cognitive model of learning can originate either from within the individual or from the environment around the individual. For example, a child learns from the pain suffered that touching hot objects is dangerous; while budgetary control systems are usually managed by finance departments on behalf of line managers. Feedback can also arrive at the same time as the originating event, for example, a room thermostat constantly responds to room temperature. It can also be delayed, as in the case of the financial information that is published after the end of the reporting period. Delayed feedback is of no value in maintaining current performance, but can be of value in influencing future behaviour. By the time the financial reports reach a manager the money is spent, nothing can change that situation. However, the manager can adjust spending in future financial periods and in that sense learn about financial management and to anticipate expenditure patterns.

Feedback, as described, is a useful means of controlling activity and providing learning opportunities in the dynamic world in which we live. However, it is rare in behaviour that a simple chain of events is the major determinant of behaviour. Take, for example, driving a car. This involves a co-ordinated set of feedback loops (visually searching the road around the car, listening to noise from the engine, sensing the feel of the road, judging speed and direction and so on) arranged into a framework which allows priority to be given to particular behaviours. This prioritization process can produce braking at one moment, accelerating at another, steering etc. all included in the dynamic activity that we call driving. This much simplified description of driving reflects the concept of prioritization and the hierarchical notion of response habits within the stimulus–response model. One way that the concept of feedback has been combined with the hierarchical notion of response habits is in the application of a *TOTE* unit.

TOTE refers to a **t**est, **o**perate, **t**est, **e**xit sequence and was first described by Miller *et al.* (1960). The *TOTE* model is shown in Figure 9.9. In essence the test phase of the model reflects a feedback loop in that if a mismatch between plan and goal is detected then the operate phase is activated. This sequence is repeated until a match between actual and goal is identified, when the cycle ends and that particular behaviour also ends.

The benefit of the TOTE unit is that it can be used to describe a series of hierarchically organized behavioural sequences. The example used by Miller is hammering a nail into a piece of wood. One phase is the identification of the position of the nail, the goal being to make it flush with the surface of the wood. The second phase is the hammer position

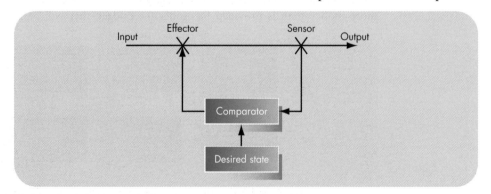

FIGURE 9.8   Negative feedback.

(lifting or striking). The process of hammering the nail, then, consists of a TOTE model that is reflected in Figure 9.10.

In describing this process Miller *et al.* (1960) say:

> If this description of hammering is correct, we should expect to see the sequence of events to run off in this order: test nail. (Head sticks up) test hammer. (Hammer is down) lift hammer. Test hammer. (Hammer is up) test hammer. (Hammer is up) strike nail. Test hammer. (Hammer is down) test nail. (Head sticks up) test hammer. And so on, until the test of the nail reveals that its head is flush. Thus the compound of TOTE units unravels itself simply enough into a co-ordinated sequence of tests and actions, although the underlying structure that organises and co-ordinates the behaviour is itself hierarchical, not sequential.

The TOTE unit so described is made up of sub-units. But the hammering of a nail into a piece of wood may in itself be part of a much larger set of goals. For example, the

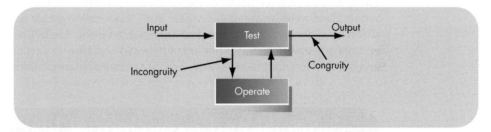

FIGURE 9.9   TOTE unit (*source*: Miller, GA, Galanter, E and Pribram, KH (1960) *Plans and the Structure of Behaviour*, Holt, Rinehart & Winston, New York).

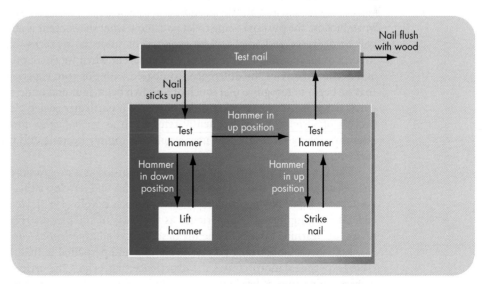

FIGURE 9.10   TOTE model of hammering a nail (*source*: Miller, GA, Galanter, E and Pribram, KH (1960) *Plans and the Structure of Behaviour*, Holt, Rinehart & Winston, New York).

particular nail might be part of a tree house for a child or it may be part of the construction of a house for a family. As such the person doing the hammering may be an employee and have as a goal the need to earn bonus in order to pay for a summer holiday or it may be a manager checking that employees have done their job correctly.

Discussion of cognitive learning

The notion of learning based on *feedback* is central to the cognitive approaches to learning. Take, for example, attempting to learn all the subject matter from your course without any *feedback* from lecturers before your final exams. The process of linking feedback into a dynamic hierarchical framework provides an important basis for understanding how learning fits into a cognitive-based model. It is also vital underpinning for the practice of performance management within organizations. For example, appraisal systems rely on the provision of feedback on the performance of individuals as a means of identifying training needs, development and career opportunities, as well as future salary or bonus levels. Handled well, feedback can be of significant mutual benefit to the individual and organization. Handled badly, or not undertaken at all, it can lead to people not doing those things which need to be done or personal underachievement. Ineffective feedback can also encourage people to do things that are unnecessary (because they are not told not to do so) and can therefore lead to inefficiency and, in extreme cases, organizational failure.

Social and experiential learning approaches

The social environment (or culture) within which learning takes place is a major influence on the process. Infants are *socialized* into a family unit, young people are *socialized* into various friendship and affinity groups. Often the first lecture in a course is designed as an introduction, the purpose being to let you know what the content is about, how the course will be delivered and what will be expected of students, a process of socialization. The process of *socialization* also becomes very apparent when we encounter a different *culture* and become aware of the differences compared with our own experiences. It is only then that we begin to recognize that much of our own behaviour and understanding is based on particular views of the world and the norms of a particular society. In organizations, the process of *socialization* is frequently referred to as an *induction* programme, the main intentions being to ensure that new employees rapidly become effective and (hopefully) stay with the company.

The process of socialization can also be regarded as a programmed period of experience. Social learning attempts to embrace this idea and develop a theoretical base from it. Perhaps the best-known exponent of this approach is Kolb (1985). He proposed a *learning cycle* of learning linked to experience as the basis of the process (Figure 9.11). For that reason the learning cycle is frequently described as an *experiential learning* approach.

Kolb views the learning process as circular and perpetual in that the output from one cycle (experimentation) creates the experience that begins the cycle over again. It firmly locks learning into a developmental cycle in which individual behaviour and its consequences for the individual form the basis of the process. It implies a process of continual adaptation as actual behaviour is followed automatically by reflection and generalized testing out in new situations of the lessons learned. Looking briefly at each stage of the model:

✦ Concrete experience. This refers to an experience of some description which could either be planned or unplanned in nature. In an organizational context this could be an employee being praised by a manager for a job well done.

✦ Reflective observation. This stage in the cycle relates to the cognitive process of thinking about the experience that began the process. This might include the cause of the experience along with the implications of it. For example, how did the employee feel about the praise from the manager? What caused it and was it justified? Was it an unusual event and why?

✦ Abstract conceptualization and generalization. This stage is about the conclusions that emerge from the review process. Issues including the identification of when it may happen again and under what circumstances and so on would be considered. In the example given, would the employee like to be praised in future for good work, and what form of work might trigger the praise?

✦ Experimentation in new situations. For example, transferring the experience to other job situations. In effect, this becomes the basis of new experiences to begin the cycle all over again. In the example given, the employee might seek to change their work behaviours in other situations to see if that also triggered praise from the manager or created other rewards etc.

The Kolb model has many implications for training and development activities within organizations and is the most frequently found basis of course design in that context. For the learning process to be fully effective each of the four stages needs to be provided in a training programme design. Individuals need to have the opportunity to reflect on and generalize about the experience (the training itself) if they are to be able to internalize and make future use of the learning points being taught in the classroom. If this is not done adequately then the transfer of learning to the workplace behaviour will not happen and much of the potential benefit lost. For example, learning to drive only on a simulator would not prepare an individual adequately for city and motorway driving in practice. Work in the simulator needs to be developed ('experimented' on) by practice on the roads. The Kolb model also paves the way for other forms of structured 'on-the-job' learning approaches.

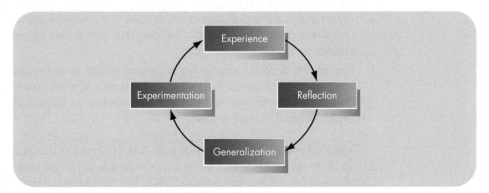

FIGURE 9.11   The Kolb learning cycle.

Through *discussion*, *coaching* and *mentoring* based on the principles of the Kolb model individuals can be encouraged to identify learning and development opportunities in everyday work activity. As a process it should also assist individuals adapt to the ever changing world in which we live as it implies continuous development.

Discussion of social and experiential learning

Social learning is a process which emphasizes the individual in the learning process. In this model, learning is not possible without the active involvement of the individual in reflecting and concluding about the experiences encountered. That is why it is frequently referred to as *experiential learning*. It places the responsibility for learning on the ability of the individual to establish links between behaviour and experience through evaluation. External forces can only facilitate and encourage the process through provision of experience and encouragement of reflection. This is why the transfer of knowledge from the classroom to the workplace (or from any training not done at the work site) is difficult to achieve in practice and without specific actions to encourage it. It also implies that those individuals who are more willing or able to develop this strategy towards learning will actively seek out developmental opportunities and therefore become the more highly skilled employees. The differential access to self-development opportunities provided by some jobs also influences the process and the relative success of some job holders.

The concept of *continuous development* implied by the social learning model has been utilized as a major theme within individual and organizational development. For example, the need to foster an *organizational culture* which values continuous development has been identified as significant to its success. Wood *et al.* (1990) suggest a five-stage process of continuous development:

✦ Integration of learning and work. The use of continuous development as a mechanism of incremental work improvement.

✦ Self-directed learning. The identification by the individual of their own development needs.

✦ Emphasis on process rather than techniques. The acquisition of what can be referred to as generalized skills rather than specific task-oriented skills. In other words, to develop understanding, potential and commitment.

✦ Continuous development as an attitude. This reflects the approach to learning through the development of appropriate attitudes to reflection and experience rather than simply technique or skill acquisition. It seeks to develop the attitude that sees learning and development opportunities in everyday events and situations rather than a reliance on formal training events.

✦ Continuous development for organizations as well as individuals. The objective of continuous development is to achieve organizational objectives through the recognition of the links between learning and performance. As individuals develop, so do the organizations that employ them.

These approaches tend to provide a model of learning that, although strongly tied to the social setting within which the individual functions, are isolationist in practice. Learning as a process is a very personal affair. It is the individual that experiences, reflects and develops as a consequence of the opportunity to experiment with their behaviour patterns. However, individuals are invariably in an interactive relationship with other people and their environment and learning is also influenced by those variables, a point made by Stuart (1986).

Other approaches to learning within organizations

Socialization and learning

Some aspects associated with *socialization* and learning have already been discussed in the previous section in relation to experiential learning. In historical terms one of the most frequent forms of training achieved through the social learning process was that which came to be called the '*sitting-by-Nellie*' approach. This expression originated in factory environments where a large number of women were employed, hence the use of the name Nellie. This form of training was very simple and essentially relied on one employee who had developed a particular skill teaching it to another person by demonstration. In practice, the employee to be trained was sent to sit beside Nellie (the employee who already had the particular skill) to watch and learn through what might be classed as structured tutoring. However, as the employee with the skill invariably received no training in how to train, it was a very uncertain and inefficient process. Equally, of course, the process assumed that the skilled employee wanted to pass on the skills and also that what the trainee employee would learn was what management wanted them to learn. Such approaches provided an ideal opportunity for *socialization* into the employee groups and prevailing practices to be achieved. However, this provided a means through which to reinforce the existing status quo, rather than mould behaviour and attitudes in the way in which management might have wished. Management in Action 9.3 describes one job from my own career experience that demonstrates the effects of employee-dominated socialization linked to the sitting-by-Nellie approaches to training.

| Stop | Consider | *What factors introduced in your OB course (other than learning by socialization) can you identify in MiA 9.3? You might begin by reviewing MiA 5.2 in the context of groups when thinking about this exercise.*
What would you do (and why) had you been me in the situation described in MiA 9.3? |

Learning styles

Another question to consider in relation to learning as an individual process is why it is that not everyone is equally successful at all forms of learning that they are exposed to. For example, not everyone achieves the same marks in an examination yet they will have studied the same course and been taught by the same teacher. Not everyone learns to drive a motor vehicle at the same speed, some individuals learn very quickly while others take a very long time and many lessons before they are able to pass the driving test. There are many aspects to the answer to this question, age, motivation, the nature of the relationship with the teacher, interest in the topic and prior experience being just some of them.

MANAGEMENT IN ACTION 9.3

Who checks the checkers?

This is a true story based on an experience I had a number of years ago. Only some of the details have been changed to prevent the possibility of identifying the organization and the individuals involved. (This experience is described in greater detail in MiA 5.2.)

Some years ago I had the misfortune to be made redundant from my then employer who decided to disband the industrial engineering department. Consequently, I was forced to seek alternative work and was offered the opportunity to become a bonus checker with the housing maintenance department of a local council. This job was obtained through the good offices of a friend who already worked as a bonus checker in the council and recommended me to his boss. I duly became part of the bonus team (about ten people in total) and started work on the appointed day. I was not given any induction training or other guidance on what was expected of me and simply introduced to the others in the team and 'given' to my friend to be shown the duties and responsibilities.

Essentially, the duties of the job required bonus checkers to take a 10% sample of completed job cards from the previous day and physically to go into the houses in which repair work had been done and check to see if the maintenance worker had actually done what the job card indicated. The maintenance people were all on a work-measured bonus scheme which paid bonus providing they 'earned' more hours than they had worked. Each job to be done had a set hours allowance available, but, of course, if more work were necessary more time would be given. So for example, if a lock were broken and had to be changed the allowed time was (say) one hour, but if the door also needed repairing an additional time of (say) two hours would be added. Naturally the maintenance people worked away from close supervision and they were frequently tempted to overclaim the work that had been nec-

essary in order to earn more bonus. The job of the bonus checker was intended to prevent that from happening by 'policing' the system.

However, bonus checking was boring and guaranteed to catch many maintenance employees out, as most of them were 'fiddling' the times claimed on their completed job cards to some extent. The existing bonus checkers had slipped into a system which meant that they collected the stated sample of 10% of the previous day's job cards and then they all disappeared to a cafe to drink coffee, eat burgers, share the sample of job cards out between themselves and chat all morning. This process was then repeated in the afternoon, having gone home for lunch in between! Naturally the sample of job cards would be signed by the bonus checkers to indicate that they had been checked and then handed in at the end of the day. In order to maintain some control a very small sample of jobs was checked and a few maintenance workers were caught cheating and disciplined. The daily routine for the bonus checkers was varied over the course of the week by going to the pub occasionally or by driving around the car showrooms to look at new cars (and even test drive them), engaging in any one of a wide range of diversions available as an alternative to work or by simply driving into the countryside if it was a nice day.

This routine was already established before I joined the section and it was this method of work that I was socialized into by my friend and other colleagues. Management never checked to ensure that I (or any of the others) was doing what was expected of us; the system was apparently being followed. Job cards were being signed as having been checked and a few people were caught cheating, so everyone was happy. At first I enjoyed this job, it was easy to learn what was required and the entire team were able to please ourselves what we did most of the time. No one in the council was particularly bothered about what we did as, at least superficially, everything was normal and as expected. However, I quickly became bored and could see no chance of development from the job I was in and so left after a month. The bonus checking section continued as described for about

another two years and then it was restructured and changed as part of a local government reorganization. In the new structure it was not possible for the bonus checkers to continue in the way that they had done as their jobs were also changed.

Kolb added to this discussion by suggesting that individuals have a preference for activity at one of the four stages in the learning cycle. This, he claimed, reflected the preferred *learning style* for that individual. Honey and Mumford (1992) further developed the ideas originated by Kolb and produced their own version of his learning styles questionnaire. Using their questionnaire it is possible to determine one's preferred learning style as being one of the following:

✦ Activist. An individual who prefers action, new experiences and will try anything at least once.

✦ Reflector. An individual who prefers to think about things and understand what they are trying to achieve or do before they actually take action.

✦ Theorist. An individual who prefers to understand the linkages and relationships between ideas and events before taking action.

✦ Pragmatist. An individual who prefers to see and understand the how and what related to that which they are expected to do before they take action or decide what to do.

There is a clear implication in this approach to learning styles that individuals may not always complete the full cycle of four stages of learning if they allow their preferred style to dominate. To so restrict the cycle of learning would be likely to restrict the learning actually acquired. For example, a *theorist* might become so locked into thinking about the relationships between variables etc. involved that they keep putting off changing their actual behaviour on the pretext of not knowing enough to justify a variation in thier usual actions. Consequently, it is one of the responsibilities of trainers to encourage individuals with a dominant style to experience the other styles as part of effective learning based on the Kolb cycle.

Studies of personality have also been used to explore the relationship with learning. The results have suggested that personality factors such as extroversion and introversion have an impact on how individuals will respond to aspects such as punishment and reward in learning processes. For example, extroverts respond better to rewards and prefer short-term material than do introverts. Other studies have shown the effect of the personality of the trainer on the evaluation of trainee performance. For example, extrovert trainers more positively evaluate extrovert trainees. Studies such as these demonstrate the complexity involved in the technical process of learning and also the variety of the interpersonal, process and situational forces acting upon learning as an activity.

Talent, skill and competency

Based on some 120,000 hours of taped interviews with managers collected over many years, Buckingham (1999) suggests that successful managers seek to build on the innate *talents* that individuals possess rather than simply seeking to develop *skills* or apply *competency* models. The author identifies a clear distinction between skills and knowledge (which can be taught) and talent which he describes as, 'the grooved highways of the mind' (which cannot be taught). *Competency* is frequently defined as the behavioural dimensions that lead to performance and in that way is strongly aligned with skill. Boyatsis (1982, p 21) defines a competency in terms of, 'an underlying characteristic of a person which results in effective and/or superior performance in a job'. This view of competency views it as something that delivers extra performance, in short the ability to demonstrate superior skill levels. The proponents of the competency concept would strongly argue in support of a distinction with skill, but it is far from clear specifically how they differ. The most common explanation is that competency is a broader notion than is skill. Certainly, assuming the Boyatsis definition, it could be argued that personality aspects and motivation level are all competencies.

Buckingham argues that managers should seek to capitalize on the innate talents of individual employees by, first, seeking to recruit on the basis of high levels of talent. Second, by recognizing that individual difference is important and that it is the end result that is of value, not the process or procedures used to achieve it. Third, that the necessary skills and knowledge can and should be trained. Fourth, that individuals should be encouraged to use their innate talents in finding their own path to the desired outcome. It is argued that so much of the training done in organizations is intended to create a learning environment in which cloning is the desired outcome, rather than improved performance per se. Individual difference and talent should be a cause for celebration, not restriction.

Action learning

Action learning refers to a form of organizational and individual learning that is also cyclical and experiential in nature. Reavans progressively became disenchanted with management education and suggested that managers did not need education but the ability to be able to solve problems (1972). Action learning generally falls within the OD (*organization development*) perspectives on organizational functioning and change. From that perspective *action learning* can be defined in terms of: 'a form of action research in which the focus is helping organizations to learn from their actions how to create entirely new structures, processes and behaviours' (Cummings and Worley, 1993, p 683). Action learning therefore reflects an approach which relies upon the abilities of individuals and the organization to *learn* how to deal with problems and situations through developing an understanding of them and then creating change. Change is then followed by reassessment and further adaptation as necessary based on the new *learning* achieved. It is in practice learning through action, a form of continuous development. In individual learning terms an approach very much dependent on the same experiential learning process described by Kolb. *Action learning* also has very strong association with the concept of the learning organization (to be discussed next).

Culture

The *culture* of an organization is also a significant determinant of its approach to learning. Some organizations consider that they gain a competitive advantage by engaging in training and development to a considerable extent. They perhaps feel that it makes the company seem more attractive to potential employees and therefore eases possible recruitment problems by encouraging high-quality applicants. Equally, individuals keen to learn are generally considered to be keen to apply what they have learned to the benefit of the employer and to be prepared to accept lower salary levels in return for development opportunities. Other companies regard such activities as an unnecessary expense, something which simply encourages employees to seek promotion and better paid positions elsewhere. *Culture* is an imprecise concept, but there are distinct differences in how learning is viewed across organizations and between individual managers which are also related to aspects of the term.

Culture is also something that some would claim could be created or changed through learning activity. New employees will be socialized into the existing culture through the formal and informal induction and training processes they experience. A management decision to seek to change an existing culture will usually be accompanied by considerable quantities of training activity as the new behaviours, values etc. are explained and taught to employees. Brown (1995) provides a review of a number of the learning-based aspects associated with culture change which demonstrates this breadth of association between culture and learning.

The learning organization

Pedler *et al.* (1989) identify the notion of a *learning organization*. They describe it in terms of the facilitation of learning for all employees and the constant transformation of the organization in response to that new knowledge and ability. In essence, the discussion of learning so far in this chapter has taken the perspective that it is something that people as individuals become involved with. The concept of the *learning organization* suggests that organizations can also adapt to new circumstances, therefore they can undertake a learning process just as effectively as people. The concept of human learning in an organizational context implies that people should adapt (learn appropriate skills) as determined by managers on behalf of the organization. The *learning organization* concept suggests that organizations should also adapt to accommodate the humans within it. Mumford (1989) suggests that the main characteristics of a *learning organization* include:

+ Encouragement for managers to accept responsibility for the identification of their own training needs.
+ Encouragement for managers to set challenging learning goals for themselves.
+ The provision for all employees of regular performance reviews and feedback on learning achieved.
+ Encouragement for managers to identify learning opportunities in jobs and to provide new experiences from which employees and managers can learn.
+ Encouragement of a questioning attitude to the accepted ways of doing things within the organization.

✦ The acceptance that, when learning, some mistakes are inevitable, but that individuals should learn from them.

✦ Encouragement of on-the-job training and other learning activities.

The notion of the learning organization with its constant renewal and adaptation to employees as they continually develop themselves is of fundamental importance in creating a modern, flexible and adaptable organization. It reflects an approach that allows the organization more effectively to meet the needs of all the *stakeholder groups* associated with it and is important in the strategic human resource management perspective adopted by many organizations today (Mabey and Salaman, 1995).

Knowledge management

That knowledge is power has long been understood. *Knowledge*, although invisible, is a commodity, just like any other. It can be stored, sold, bought, traded and stolen. It can also be grown, developed and harvested just like any crop from the world of agriculture. Organizations contain much information within them and in addition have access to a vast range of information from outside sources. With the development of computer-based technology, such as database systems and the Internet over recent years, the opportunity to capitalize on the information available has never been greater. What has this to do with the concept of learning, you might ask? Put quite simply, organizations and the individuals within them have now to *learn* much more than was the case just a few years ago and also they have to *learn* how to make effective use of the knowledge that they have actual or potential access to. In short, knowledge is now a significant part of the strategic and competitive activities of any organization.

There is another dimension to the concept of *knowledge management*. That is the growing realization that management objectives can be more effectively achieved if managers seek to ensure that employees are trained to absorb management's values and norms in addition to having their technical and job skills upgraded. This often finds expression through training and development being driven by business objectives and solidly grounded in the workplace. For example the creation of so-called universities within companies such as Motorola and Unipart (Pickard, 1995) all deliver high-quality learning opportunities but as part of the organization's strategic intentions to enhance its own performance. In other words, the development process being firmly dictated by, and intended to support the objectives of, management.

There are different forms of knowledge that exists within a company. For some organizations knowledge represents the purpose for existence as they specialize in selling knowledge to others. There is also the practical knowledge that exists in relation to the products and services provided by the company, there is the business-related knowledge related to the industry and how to actually function within it. There is also the wider knowledge in relation to what might be called market intelligence or understanding what is going on in the world that might be relevant to the organization. In addition, there is the accumulated knowledge and experience of the people who work within the organization in how to make it all work relatively smoothly. This last category of knowledge is rarely, if ever, documented in any form and is dependent on the accumulated experience of the people working in the organization. Nonaka (1996) called this aspect *tacit knowledge* and suggested that it is just as important to organizational success as the formally classified and captured forms of knowledge.

With the practice of delayering, downsizing or rightsizing, which has become the way of life for many organizations, many of the middle ranks in organizations have been removed. Among the effects of that is the loss of much of the stored, unrecorded (*tacit*) knowledge of the company. The practice of delayering in its many forms provides a situation in which management must ensure that employee groups are supportive of the business objectives, as without the previous levels of operational management employees have much greater freedom of action and responsibility. Consequently, if they are not effectively integrated into the business, or feel alienated, there exists a real danger of significant problems or even organizational failure in extreme cases.

Information flows around an organization in ways that are not reflected in any organization chart or other formal document or policy. There are obviously the predictable information paths that are determined by policy and business practice. For example, financial data are collected and disseminated according to set rules and reporting requirements. Customer orders are processed in a way that ensures that orders and invoices are paid as appropriate. However, these forms represent only a small proportion of the total information circulating within a company at any point in time. There will be information about planned orders, proposed new products that some but not everyone, in the organization will be aware of. In addition there will be information about job vacancies, forthcoming training courses and problems that are in the process of being resolved between departments or sections. On top of all of that information there will be the inevitable gossip, rumour, idle chit-chat and thousands of other pieces of relevant and indeed irrelevant information (and misinformation) that circulate in every workplace. In every sense of the phrase information spreads around the organization as its very lifeblood carrying with it all manner of necessary items of value (and occasionally malevolent, evil rubbish that can easily do harm) to every corner.

Under these circumstances, with *knowledge* carrying with it such a diverse range of meanings and implications with it for organizations, it is hardly surprising that management seek to control it and easy to understand why it is so difficult an area to control. It is for that reason that Nonaka (1996) argues that those organizations that will be commercially successful in the future are those that have effectively managed both *explicit* and *tacit* aspects of their knowledge. It is also easy to understand under these circumstances why learning as a process becomes vital to encourage commitment, acceptance and internalization of management's objectives among employees. The rationale for company universities and other initiatives to create a basis for forms of knowledge management follow as management seek to embrace the workforce and channel it in predetermined ways.

According to Lloyd (1999) knowledge management strategies need to be grounded in the concept of *wisdom*. In that context, he defines wisdom as knowledge with a long shelf-life, whereas data are information with a very short shelf-life. In that sense, wisdom in how to manage the control aspects of knowledge forms an important dimension to the development of any effective strategy. This view also supports the view that experience and age are of value to an organization, always assuming that wisdom develops with experience etc. Rightsizing, delayering and other cost-cutting processes that remove experience can be a danger to the organization if *wisdom* is also eliminated.

Knowledge management is not just restricted to internal company activities. These days there is a distinct tendency for organizations to form strategic alliances with a wide variety of other organizations. This can take the form of supply chain management (Slack *et al.*, 1998) in which customers and suppliers form stronger and closer commercial arrangements, often linked together through mutual information systems. Supply chain management can also involve potential competitors working together on common projects to support a particular development, for example the development of industry standards. Each form of collaboration carries with it potential dangers for each partner if mutual respect is not part of the relationship.

Mintzberg *et al.* (1998, p 357) describe future successful organization as *amoebas*. Such simple creatures are among the most successful on earth as they constantly change shape and adapt to their environment. Their semi-permeable cell walls define them in terms of separation from the environment around them and yet they also allows the relative free movement of 'things' into and out of the amoeba. Using that as an analogy for organizations, it is clear that the free flow of information, skill and capability and so on forms part of the future as envisaged by Mintzberg and his colleagues, processes that will require ever more effective knowledge management strategies.

Learning within an organization

Learning through training

Much of the learning within an organization is carried out under the guise of training. Training courses are organized for employees on many topics, usually intended to deliver some benefit to the organization in the form of a capability to undertake a range of tasks more efficiently or productively. Most of this form of training is based around the notion of the *learning curve*. It reflects the idea that performance is a function of time and experience, in other words, practice makes perfect. The curve in Figure 9.12 is a very simplified one and should be considered as an *ideal type*.

In practice, the effectiveness of the training will influence the rate of increase in performance, as will the ability of the trainees along with the impact of situational and emotional factors. Some skills require substantial periods of reinforcement or practice before any increase in performance can be made. In other cases, performance improvement is categorized by a series of jumps and plateaux.

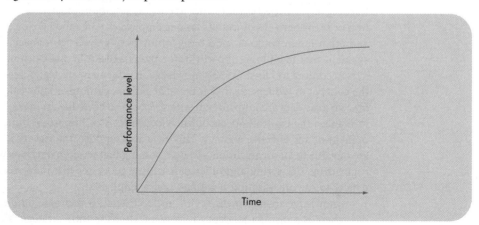

FIGURE 9.12   The learning curve.

The training process in learning

There are many forms of training used within organizations. They are usually used on the basis of meeting an identified need. *Training needs* can be identified from a number of sources. For example, a performance appraisal, the existence of low productivity or quality, the introduction of new products or technology, the carrying out of a formal skills audit. What these all have in common is a gap or difference between what is expected and what currently exists (Figure 9.13).

Once the gap has been identified, appropriate mechanisms can be designed to meet the need. Training programmes designed to meet a specific need should be planned around the following issues:

✦ Training objectives. The objectives should provide a target for measuring performance (or the level of success in training). An example might be: 'On completion of the course the trainee will be able to type at 75 words per minute, with no more than 1% error rate.'

✦ Training content. The content should have been determined by the previous analysis and be a means to close the identified gap.

✦ Duration. The length of the training programme should be determined by the range of material to be covered and the amount of practice required to achieve the effective closure of the identified training gap.

Learning event design

The means through which to deliver an effective *learning event* will be dependent on a wide range of issues including the preferred style of the trainees, the task to be learned etc. The options available for the design of training programmes include:

A. **Demonstration.** This refers to being shown how to do something and then allowed to get on with it. It is a commonly used approach but is relatively inefficient as it does not provide structure or feedback to improve performance effectively.

B. **Coaching.** This provides an interactive, encouragement-based approach to training. Consider the coaching process for a sports team as an example. It includes practice, feedback, reflection, structure and motivational perspectives.

C. **Discovery training.** This assumes that people learn more effectively if they discover 'it' for themselves. Consequently, it aims to provide this through an experiential

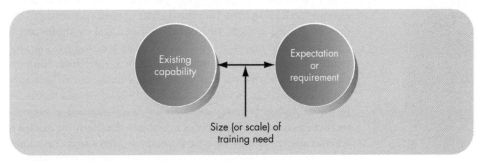

FIGURE 9.13 The training need.

environment. It needs very careful planning so that the 'right' learning is acquired. Managers are frequently exposed to discovery learning. They are put into situations and expected to sink or swim, developing solutions to problems as they go. In a structured form this would be referred to as action learning.

D. **Job rotation, secondments and special assignments.** These provide for training by systematically moving people between jobs, activities or projects in order to give them experience. These may be permanent changes or of limited duration. While this may provide employees with additional skills, together with a broader experience of the context around the work, it can lower productivity as extensive learning occurs. Also, if employees do not then get the opportunity to practice the full range of skills acquired, there is little practical benefit to either the organization or the individual.

E. **Action learning.** Typically a team would be established and expected to solve a specific problem perhaps with the help of an external facilitator. Several masters degrees are based upon these principles. Students are expected to work in groups on research topics and problem-solving issues (often within their own organizations) and then submit a dissertation on the process and the learning achieved through it.

F. **Job instruction.** This is the systematic application of learning theory to skill acquisition. It involves setting objectives and by demonstration, coaching, practice and feedback allowing trainees to become skilful in the task. This approach is frequently based explicitly on the principles of the Kolb model discussed earlier.

G. **Lecture.** The process of delivering information with little or no direct involvement from the audience.

H. **Talks and discussion.** Informal lectures with higher participation levels and for smaller groups.

I. **Case studies.** The use of predetermined situations to provide opportunities for analysis and presentation of solutions without the risk of failure inherent in 'live' situations.

J. **Role play and simulation.** These allow the participants to act out situations as if they were real. Much of the basic training for police officers is based on role play, reflecting situations that they will encounter. Pilots spend a considerable amount of time in flight simulators in order to gain flying experience in a safe environment. Doctors now practice techniques such as keyhole surgery on patient simulators to gain the skills necessary to operate on real people with higher levels of success.

K. **Computer-based and programmed learning.** For example, learning to type on a computer with a typing programme built into it. The computer provides the instruction and tests ability before moving on to more difficult skills. Interactive video can also be used to provide film-quality graphics to a computer-based training programme. An example could be a bank training its staff in customer care and dealing with customer queries. Filmed sections of information and real examples can be interspersed with computer-based questions and scoring of understanding. The ability to provide experience in this way allows individuals to pick their own route through the learning package at their own pace. A recent review of the use of this approach is included in the Management in Action 9.4. Schank (1999) proposes that before any form of what he terms online training can become truly effective a major rethink of teaching methods is needed. He proposes a *goal-based scenario* approach to learning based on a better understanding of how human memory builds new knowledge. In short, he claims that the individual must create a personal journey through the new knowledge and that the technology must be supportive of this process.

MANAGEMENT IN ACTION 9.4

On the right lines

The use of technology in training first appeared in the early 1980s and has since developed rapidly. The ability of staff to make use of computer-based technology at or near their place of work introduces many benefits not available through other training methods. For example, it allows the employee to work at their own pace and to concentrate on those aspects of a programme that are of interest and value to them. It also allows training to be done at a time appropriate to both the local line manager and the trainee, rather than at a time chosen by the training department. Neil Walker, senior technology-based training designer for the TSB Retail Banking and Insurance Division suggests that:

> Historically, the role of trainers has been to run training courses … now it is to discuss with the line manager what the training needs of the individual are and then make suggestions, which could be anything from technology-based training to short, off-the-job courses.

At Abbey National, a leading finance organization, CD technology has been added to desktop computers within the branch network. This makes it easier for branch managers to keep track of student training and performance as well as improving the administration of distance learning activities. John Buttriss, manager of the distance learning unit within the bank, describes the system as follows:

There is rather a shopping list approach with 70 courses on the CD that is out at the moment. Theoretically, what we would like to do is keep the shopping list but make the computer come up with a suggested training log for each individual. That way, you are empowering the student to provide the line manager with the necessary information.

British Airways has used self-directed courses for its 10,000 cabin staff in preparation for the annual safety equipment examination. Staff who fail the test are prevented from working and this causes individuals severe stress before the exam and difficulties for managers should they fail. Tim Dyer, BA's training services manager, indicated that:

> A multi-media training application was developed with the AimTech Corporation which enables employees to study for the test at their own pace. … The possibility of using the application with a video information system which connects into the back of a television is being researched. If we deliver this application on the visual information system, it can be installed in each cabin crew hotel room in major cities like New York, Johannesburg and Tokyo, allowing crew members to prepare for the test during their down-time.

Adapted from: Sheppard, G (1993) On the right lines, *Personnel Today*, 9 November, pp 22–4.

Stop | Consider *How easy would it be to design degree programmes using the principles indicated in MiA 9.4?*
To what extent would such an approach substitute for a degree programme which included interaction between students and students and lecturers?

L. **Distance learning.** This is a varied form of activity. It now embraces a wide range of programmes from basic skills acquisition to higher degrees. The process of distance learning includes a variety of instructional approaches, the written word, television, video, audio, electronic, and residential periods offering face-to-face contact. In addition to academic courses, many organizations adopt this approach for in-house programmes as do the professional institutes for membership qualifications.

Training evaluation

Evaluating the benefits of any training is a difficult process. Ultimately, it is an attempt to measure the degree of the *transfer of learning* to the organizational context. However, there are many complications involved in judging the degree to which this might have happened. For example, trainees can enjoy the training event and therefore judge it to be a success, yet in practice they may gain little practical job-related benefit from it. Conversely, trainees may not enjoy the experience and yet subsequently find the job relevance high. There may be other change initiatives active at the same time as a *learning event* which restricts the ability to demonstrate that training was the only (or major) source of improvement. It might also take a considerable period of time for any tangible benefits from training to filter through to a measurable benefit.

However, training needs to be evaluated if it is to achieve its objectives and be regarded as a resource of value to the organization and employees. It could never be certain that learning as intended has taken place unless some form of evaluation occurs. According to Hamblin (1974) evaluation takes place at a number of levels:

+ Reaction. This refers to the immediate responses of the trainees on issues such as the perceived benefits, feelings towards the experience and content. It is one form of judging success, on the assumption that if the people subjected to the learning event feel that have not enjoyed the process or gained from it, that is probably true.

+ Learning. This reflects the actual benefit taken away from the training event. It is the degree to which the training has been internalized by the trainees in the form of new skills etc. This is frequently reflected in the end of course test and is intended to reflect the exit capability of the people who have been trained. This does not guarantee, however, that they acquired these capabilities through the learning event or that they will actually utilize the new skills in the workplace.

+ Job behaviour. In an organizational context, learning is usually designed to impact on the job that the individual is expected to perform. So seeking to determine if the actual job behaviour of individuals experiencing the learning event changes subsequent to the process is one way of attempting to judge both the transfer of knowledge to the workplace and the impact of such changes.

+ Organization. At the organizational level training is intended to improve effectiveness in terms of productivity, quality, output, customer relations and so on. Consequently, the need to justify training in terms of a positive effect at the organizational level is crucial. It might be possible to quantify aspects of this level of evaluation, but it will probably include a significant degree of qualitative evaluation of judgement. The evaluation of this level is usually restricted to a senior management overview of the impact of training over an extended period.

+ Ultimate value. This refers to the intangible benefits that the organization gains from any training activity. This could be its ability to survive in a hostile market, profitability or even its contribution to society as a whole.

Three features are apparent from a consideration of these evaluation levels:

✦ Measurement. This becomes increasingly less certain and vague as one moves from the immediate reaction to the ultimate value level. It is relatively easy to assess individual reactions to a particular *learning event*. It is, however, more difficult to quantify the extent to which a particular event impacts on the whole organization.

✦ Time. This is another variable in the list. Reactions from trainees tends to be determined immediately after the event. Assessment of the impact on the organization as a whole can only be determined after some considerable time has elapsed. By the time organizational value can be determined, other variables will have invariably 'contaminated' any cause and effect links that might have existed.

✦ Hindsight. The initial assessment of trainees reaction to a particular *learning event* is an important evaluation measure, but would the reaction be the same, say, six months later when the opportunity to take a broader perspective has evolved, or when other factors change in the context?

The evaluation of training is not a precise science and this results in difficulties for both managers and trainers in identifying the justification for such interventions. Management in Action 9.5 indicates one approach to this issue.

Stop | Consider	*The approach described in MiA 9.5 utilizes a questionnaire to assess the value of training. Make a case in support of this approach to evaluation.*
	Having identified the benefits of such an approach consider now what the disadvantages of a questionnaire approach might be?

Development

Development can be applied to any category of employee and the term *employee development* is increasingly finding favour over that of training. It is a process that allows potential to be realized. As such, it places a higher level of responsibility on the individual. The individual must want to be developed and must be prepared to co-operate in development activities. Because of the longer timeframes implicit in development the return is not likely to become apparent for many years. For these reasons organizations are tending to make use of the concept of *development centres*, which broadly consist of the same type of activity as an assessment centre (Rodger and Mabey, 1987), the emphasis being to identify strengths and weaknesses as the basis of individual and organizational development activity.

Learning: a management and organizational perspective

Learning is an important part of organizational activity. It impacts on all aspects of the employment of people, from the induction of new employees to the development of future generations of directors. Unless individuals are exposed to learning opportunities they cannot be expected to undertake the duties that are expected of them, even if they know what they are. The workforce is traditionally male dominated at a senior level and there

MANAGEMENT IN ACTION 9.5

Measuring the gains from training

Many companies and training specialists have struggled with the attempt to justify training activity. To misquote a well-known saying: 'Many employers suspect that half the money they spend on training is wasted – the problem is, they don't know which half.' In some cases the evaluation of training benefit is relatively easy to measure. For example, consider the provision of a training course intended to increase the proficiency of typing within the organization. It would be possible to measure the cost of typing both before and after the training course and to demonstrate the savings made.

The level of difficulty in measuring any gain increases dramatically when considering the area of management development. The fruits of such training activity may not become apparent for many years, by which time other things will have changed dramatically. As Bickerstaffe suggests:

> Most human resource specialists are forced to rely on more or less unscientific methods of evaluating training. Usually this involves visiting programmes and providers, debriefing participants and tracking the career development and promotions of managers and employees after they have attended training courses.

Sundridge Park Management Centre has developed a performance improvement process (Pip) in an attempt to measure the effectiveness of the training that it provided on behalf of clients. Bickerstaffe describes the system:

> Pip is based on a system of questionnaires, designed to elicit an indication of a person's knowledge on key areas, their attitudes and styles of work and to trace how these change over the duration of the course and in the longer term.

To an extent the system is competency-based, but each questionnaire is tailored to the particular course being evaluated and to the needs of the organization.

The first questionnaire is completed by both the delegate and boss before the course. After the course each delegate completes another questionnaire. This should demonstrate an increase in the knowledge acquired as a result of the course. After three months both delegate and boss complete another questionnaire which is intended to reflect the retention of knowledge and the application of skills in the workplace. There have been several conclusions that have emerged from early applications of the Pip approach. The Prudential financial services group was among the first to use the system and identified a number of interesting results. These include an increased understanding of the importance of self-development among managerial employees and the need to regard change as a bottom-up process rather than top-down. Also, training should involve whole departments, not just individuals or groups.

Plans are already in hand to create a database of results from Pip findings in order to allow organizations to profile themselves and form comparative judgements about their training effectiveness.

Adapted from: Bickerstaffe, G (1993) Measuring the gains from training, *Personnel Management*, November, pp 48–51.

have been a number of learning initiatives to enhance the development of women and thereby improve their access to these positions. Management in Action 9.6 introduces the debate about the value of separate training for women in this context.

Individuals per se are not totally responsible for achieving organizational goals. It is the various groups and teams within the organization that achieve objectives. Therefore, it

MANAGEMENT IN ACTION 9.6

Trial separation

Given that the workforce in most organizations is male dominated it has been argued by many that special training courses for women provide the kick-start necessary to both meet their needs and boost confidence. However, it has also been argued that women-only training can be counter-productive in advancing their position in the workplace.

Opportunity 2000, an employer-led campaign to boost the status of women, has prompted many large employers to establish action plans to achieve this objective. Companies such as Barclays and Midland banks, the BBC, Lucas and BP have incorporated women-only training into their equal opportunity programmes. Others such as United Biscuits, British Airways and Rank Xerox have not given this type of approach such a high priority within their equal opportunity development.

Among those organizations that provide women-only training it is claimed that such courses provide benefits both to the individual and the organization. For example, Ashridge Management College has provided for many years a one-week intensive programme called Business Leadership for Women. From a survey of former students approximately half had subsequently been promoted and more than 90% thought such training was essential. It is not just the career and professional categories of women that have benefited from the provision of such training. Springboard, as a training organization, has developed courses for women at the lower levels

of the organization. It reports that individuals perform better after attending their programme and that they frequently take on more responsibility, even if they do not seek promotion.

Among those organizations that have not specifically provided single-sex courses it is suggested that women themselves do not want to be segregated. For example, United Biscuits conducted a survey in one of its divisions that produced a 70% response rate. One of the findings was that if women wanted training it was of a more general nature, not special single-sex courses. However, a similar survey within another division found that women wanted special courses. This suggests that people and circumstances vary and perhaps change over time. As a special needs category it is not appropriate to assume that women will automatically want such provision. Other companies have found that attempting to tackle issues such as organization culture and individual training need determination from both men and women but that this is a more effective route to influence the role and position of women in the workplace. As the campaign director for Opportunity 2000 said when interviewed, the best time to provide women-only training is when women themselves want it.

Adapted from: Tchiprout, G (1993) Trial separation, *Personnel Today*, 9 February, pp 32–3.

Stop | Consider   *To what extent (and why) is the provision of women-only training a good thing?*

is a necessary part of organizational life to be able to work as part of a team. Within organizations trainers spend a considerable amount of time on team-building exercises and courses to enhance employee and management ability in this area. Because organizations rely heavily on groups to perform much of the activity, they form a significant focus of attention for managers. Training in group formation and dynamics can provide a basis for shaping the behaviour of groups and so influence the level of effectiveness achieved.

Training and development are usually regarded as internal activities. However, most organizations are in a position to need to influence the external environment as well. Customers need to be persuaded to buy products and services from the organization. Suppliers need to be persuaded that the organization is a good credit risk. Government needs to be convinced to follow one set of policies rather than another. The influencing process used to achieve these objectives reflects a form of training. One party seeks to ensure that another party *learns* certain 'facts' or a particular point of view that the other party would wish it to learn. Much of the purchasing, marketing and lobbying activity engaged in by organizations utilizes approaches that are based on the underlying concepts and principles discussed in this chapter.

The challenge facing managers and organizations is how to make cost-effective use of learning within the organization. There are limitless opportunities for the utilization of the principles of learning in the training and development activities carried out in most organizations. If the degree of benefit achieved were the only criterion for success involved, then there would be no decision to take. Unfortunately, there is always a cost associated with the provision of learning activity and the benefits are not always easy to identify or quick to materialize. Managers are therefore required to exercise judgement in determining the best area for the application of learning, just as with any other resource.

Human beings are naturally adaptive and creative in the ways that they approach events around them. Consequently, if no training or development were to take place in the formal sense of the term, individuals would simply 'muddle through'. This is frequently relied upon in times of financial hardship, when organizations cut back on training and development in order to save money in the short term. People are the most flexible, adaptable resource available to an organization and can cope in the short term without clear direction, unlike machines and most computers.

Learning is also a process that is part of the management *control* process within an organization. For example, it is the training provided by management that signals to employees the behaviour considered appropriate within the organization. Employees are *socialized* into the company and jobs that they undertake. In that sense, management is shaping the behaviour of employees just like Skinner shaped the responses of his laboratory animals. Another dimension of the control aspect associated with learning is control through access. Only those employees who are regarded as a worthy investment will have access to the many development opportunities available through their companies. Consequently, a clear reward for being classified as a good employee is the opportunity to be developed. This also encourages employees to deliver compliant behaviour and acceptable performance to management in return for an appropriate classification and development. However, as with all human behaviour the links between learning and control are not as certain as might be implied from the discussion so far. Individuals do have the freedom of choice to ignore the intentions of managers and indeed to react against these wishes if they so desire. An individual may not value development or may not wish to adopt particular behaviour patterns in response for the returns potentially available.

It is easy to imagine that more training and development activity would solve all management's problems and produce an optimally effective organization. As with many organizational activities, that is too simplistic to be credible. The challenge is, therefore, one of finding the appropriate level of activity commensurate with organizational requirements in the short, medium and long term. Management in Action 9.7 describes how one organization sees its role in this context.

Organizations are subjected to change in many forms. People join and leave an

MANAGEMENT IN ACTION 9.7

Quick on the uptake

Motorola, the giant electronics company, has begun to reach future generations of employees and customers through a number of innovative training programmes. It became concerned that in the USA the education system was developing children who lacked the sophistication to use its products. It viewed the US education system as teaching children that to collaborate with others was to cheat and that success was a function of being able to memorize facts and to be able to recite them at will. Consequently, it ran a series of week-long summer camps for the 12–15-year-old children of employees to explore the world of science and technology.

The company also provided classes for parents intended to show them how to manage their children's education and compare it with similar provision in China and Taiwan, the argument being that future competition for jobs will be from those countries and that to retain job opportunities in the USA it is necessary to ensure that US children are able to perform at a high level.

In the UK and many other countries local Motorola companies have begun similar initiatives to get close to education. In Scotland, for example, a drive is on to encourage girls to take an interest in engineering subjects and to see it as a career option.

In the USA retired employees are invited back to tell stories about the history of the company. This is intended to provide a depth of understanding among current employees about present activity in the context of company history as well as indicating how things have been dealt with in the past. It is a form of developing a continuity of culture, tradition and life pattern, thereby enabling current employees to regard themselves as part of an ongoing, dynamic process and as guardians of the future.

Adapted from: Williams, M (1993) Quick on the uptake, *Personnel Today*, 12 October, p 31.

Stop | Consider   *To what extent is the process described in MiA 9.7 about learning and to what extent is it about employee control and a recognization of the need to offset the consequences of delayering and downsizing, perhaps even a need to train future consumers to adopt company products?*

---

organization for many reasons. The nature of activity within the organization is subject to change as technology impacts different aspects of operations and products or services are subject to development. Consequently, there is a permanent background of training activity to ensure present and anticipated needs are met. There is also the natural career progression movement for individuals, necessary to meet the future need for senior specialists and managers. The failure of many organizations to meet these basic requirements has been a source of criticism in many reports and investigations into the subject. In the determination of an appropriate level of *learning* activity, management face a dilemma in the need to balance the costs and benefits. Too often in the past the benefits derived from learning activity have been undervalued by managers, particularly the potential to socialize employees into management preferred behaviours. Over recent years in many countries there have been a number of major initiatives attempting to improve the impact and level of training and development at all levels within organizations.

For the training specialist in the real world of organizations, these are not just interesting issues for debate. Managers under pressure for cost-effective output in the short term and being asked to divert employee time to training activities need to be convinced of the value. Organizations also need to be convinced of the value of the activity, particularly in times of economic stringency. Yet, as has already been indicated, there is no single theory or approach to learning that will guarantee commercial success. Equally, the determination and evaluation of any benefits accruing from any learning event are difficult to ascertain and disentangle from other variables. Managers must therefore work things out for themselves, taking into account the variables active in the particular situation.

It is an unfortunate fact of commercial life that when economic stringency is necessary, training activity is often the first to suffer cutbacks. There is still a considerable amount of persuasion to be done in convincing senior managers of the commercial necessity of training and development. The potential of learning to contribute significantly to the control and shaping of behaviour, together with its motivational properties, has already been suggested in this chapter. Therefore managers ignore the value of it at their peril. Management in Action 9.8 provides a review of how training specialists are coming to grips with the political as well as the technical dimensions of their work.

Stop | Consider

To what extent does the view of the future role of trainers described in MiA 9.8 reflect the view of learning outlined in this chapter?

To what extent is the management of training a political process rather than a technical one?

Within organizations learning has many applications. They include:

✦ Induction of new employees. The purpose here is to enable new employees to become effectively integrated into the organization in the shortest possible time.

✦ Initial job training. Not all new employees will possess the necessary skills to perform the tasks expected of them.

✦ Subsequent job training. Over the course of employment the jobs that individuals perform will change. New equipment, new products etc. all produce a need to acquire new skills.

✦ Training on transfer or promotion. When moving to another job within the same organization different skills will be required. This is particularly true in the case of a first appointment to supervisory or management positions.

✦ Training for special groups. There are a variety of special groups for whom particular training provision needs to be made. They include disabled people, women returning to work following a career break, individuals from ethnic minority groups, employee representatives and employees with responsibility for dealing with customers.

✦ Development. It can be argued that as a distinct activity development has little relevance for most employees, as their responsibilities are tied to the present time. Management has the responsibility for the future and so requires development. Conversely, it can be argued that the commitment of employees is enhanced through development opportunity and that they are therefore more likely to adopt a positive

MANAGEMENT IN ACTION 9.8

A new role for trainers

The context in which training is carried out within organizations has changed over recent years for two reasons. First, organizations contain more complex training needs. Second, the nature of personnel activity within the organization is also changing. With the evolution of the human resource approach to the function and the downsizing and delayering of structures has come an empowerment of line managers. One of the consequences of this is a need to see the training specialist as a facilitator of the process, rather than a provider of training activity.

Sloman argues that the new role for trainers is reflected in a model that comprises two linked propositions:

A The training function
   ✦ Modern training practice requires the articulation of a clear training strategy with clear targets, clear control and accountability.
   ✦ The training resource thus makes a significant and distinctive contribution to the process of skills enhancement to allow the organization to function at the strategic, tactical and operational levels. It should also assist in the capture of wider human resource benefits through the development of people.
   ✦ One of the ways in which this is achieved is by developing an appropriate training culture for the organization in which all play an active part in achieving business plans.
B The trainer's role
   ✦ The role of the training professional is to develop and articulate the training strategy and promote a training culture.

   ✦ This is achieved by defining appropriate relationships with all managers to achieve the maximum leverage for the training resource. It requires the adoption of a proactive role in presenting options and alternatives to line managers. It also requires the development of appropriate information and appraisal systems that can meet the perceived needs of managers and employees as they perform their duties.

In order to achieve this role, Sloman argues that trainers need to become strategic facilitators and to develop a number of new skills including:

✦ Strategic awareness. The ability to acquire and translate business strategy information into action plans and options for managers as well as providing an assessment of the training implications.
✦ Diagnostic capacity. The ability to offer appropriate expertise in skill analysis, training needs analysis and of methods of skill enhancement.
✦ Influencing skills. The ability to influence the organization in seeking to capture the value potential of training and achieve a training culture. This is likely to require the individual to achieve influence beyond their formal status within the organization.

Adapted from: Sloman, M (1994) Coming in from the cold: a new role for trainers, *Personnel Management*, January, pp 24–7.

attitude towards work, to the benefit of the individual, management and the organization.

✦ Professional development. Many employees undertake work in which job training is related to professional development. For example, accountants are trained by following a course of study leading to membership of one of the accounting bodies.

✦ Specialist career development. Within many of the specialist areas of an organization there are occupational hierarchies. Examples are common among engineers, computer specialists and accountants. Progression within these jobs often depends on technical competence rather than managerial responsibility. However, their development can be of critical importance to the success of their organizations.

✦ Managers' career development. Managers need to be developed in terms of their own specialism, in order to ensure that they keep up to date. They also need development in the management areas of their responsibilities, the intention being to develop individuals for more senior responsibility as well as for improved performance in their present job.

✦ Development for directors and senior managers. The nature of senior management work is dramatically different from that of more junior managers. It is not unusual to find separate senior management programmes within large organizations, intended to meet these needs. Indeed, the Institute of Directors now runs a training programme so that new directors can learn about their new responsibilities.

✦ Job termination training. Every person recruited leaves the organization at some point in time. It could be that they find alternative work; or that they retire; or that they die while in service; they may be dismissed by the company; or they may be made redundant if their job disappears. In some of these cases, the organization may consider providing counselling or training to help the individual adjust to their new circumstances.

✦ Special initiative training and development. Organizations frequently engage in a particular activity that generates a training or development need. Examples include the development of a new product, the need to improve productivity or quality and the introduction of new equipment.

The importance of learning gains increasing significance from the inclusion of a more obvious strategic perspective to the management of the human resource within organizations. Figure 9.14 illustrates the stakeholder approach to strategic training and development (Mabey and Salaman, 1995). It attempts to link together the main elements of the process while reflecting its fluid nature. This model also recognizes that business direction is determined through the stakeholder process and forms part of the generally negotiated balancing between agendas and priorities for the groups involved. It also has many features that would suggest an affinity with the concept of the learning organization.

Conclusions

Learning is an activity that continues during the entire life of every individual. Human behaviour is also influenced in many ways by the experiences that are encountered in daily life. Psychologists have attempted to understand and explain the processes involved in this phenomenon and in doing so have developed a number of models associated with learning, training and development. Organizations need trained people in order to achieve objectives and they need to develop the talents of individuals in order to make provision for the future. The strategic human resource approach practised by many organizations today places a high priority on the development of employees in order to capture the benefits of the learning organization.

Discussion questions

1. Define the following key terms used in this chapter:

   Training   *Social learning*   *Technology-based training*
   Operant conditioning *TOTE system*   *Development*
   Behaviour modification *Education*   *Strategic training and development*
   Reinforcement   *Feedback*   *Learning*
   Learning organization

2. Kolb describes learning as a circular process (Figure 9.11). Identify an occasion when

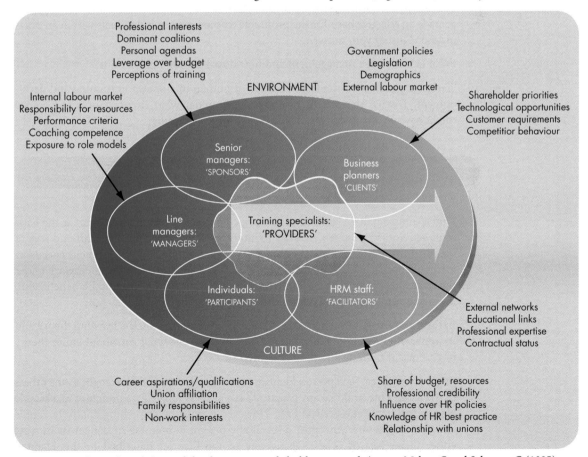

FIGURE 9.14 Strategic training and development: a stakeholder approach (*source*: Mabey, C and Salaman, G (1995) *Strategic Human Resource Management*, Blackwell, Oxford).

you learned something and explain the process using Kolb's model. What conclusions about training can you draw from the process?

3. 'Each individual should accept responsibility for their own training and development. It is not up to organizations to provide more than essential job-related training.' Discuss.

4. 'Training and development are nothing more than elaborate mechanisms for ensuring worker compliance with management's wishes.' Discuss.

5. How can the effectiveness of any learning event provided by management be evaluated? Justify your answer.

6. How would you recommend to your lecturers that they keep attendance at lectures high and ensure that work is handed in on time? Justify your views based on material presented in this chapter.

7. Describe behavioural modification as an approach to conditioning human behaviour. To what extent does this model provide for a social engineering approach to management control that is doomed to fail because human beings are not animals?

8. Can the notion of the learning organization and strategic training and development provide an effective basis for the profitable employment of individuals within an organization? Justify your answer.

9. What is knowledge management and how does learning impact on it?

10. 'Technology can never replace the value of human interaction in training and development.' Discuss this statement and identify under what circumstances technology might have an advantage over traditional forms of training.

Research activities

1. Find a company that claims to use strategic human resource management as the basis of its activities in this area. Arrange to interview some of the training staff and seek to identify how they differentiate between strategic training and development and other forms of approach. What do they see as the benefits and problems for their work under the strategic perspective? Do they consider the strategic approach to be beneficial to the trainees, managers and organization. If so, why and, if not, why not?

2. In the library, seek out ten books and journal articles that discuss learning theory and its application within organizations. What do these views tell you about either theory or practice of training and development?

3. In groups of three, each person identify a simple task that could be taught to the others in the team. This could be any practical task, such as repairing a puncture in a bicycle tyre or making home-brewed beer. However, it must be something relatively simple and completely safe, you must not put the person in any risk of danger or hurting either themselves or others. Using one of the theories described in this chapter, develop a training programme to enable one of the other team members to undertake the task. Train that person how to do the job. Discuss with the trainee and the third

member (an observer) the effectiveness of the programme along with the relevance of the theory used. What general conclusions emerge?

Key reading

From Clark, H, Chandler, J and Barry, J (1994) *Organization and Identities: Text and Readings in Organizational Behaviour*, International Thomson Business Press, London:
- ✦ Eysenck, HJ: The rat or the couch?, p 82. This considers some of the behavioural aspects of training in the context of a review of psychology and psychoanalysis.
- ✦ Vroom, V: Motivation: a cognitive approach, p 125. This piece previews the next chapter but in a way which has relevance to training as a cognitive process.
- ✦ Labov, W: The logic of nonstandard English, p 178. This introduces the distinction between formal education and an ability to function effectively in a particular social context.
- ✦ Bowles, S and Gintis, H: Schooling in capitalist America, p 185. This material addresses the purpose and results of education and suggests a bias in the process towards a particular end result.
- ✦ Fiedler, FE: Leadership – a contingency model, p 272. By introducing the least preferred co-worker scale, the material provides an insight into the training of managers.

Further reading

Clark, FA (1992) *Total Career Management*, McGraw-Hill, Maidenhead. Although this text concentrates on career issues, there are many links with training and development.

Cohen, MD and Sproul, LS (eds) (1996) *Organizational Learning*, Sage, Thousand Oaks, CA. As an edited work, this text allows the perspectives of a number of leading researchers on organizatioanl learning to be brought together.

Gilley, JW and Eggland, SA (1989) *Principles of Human Resource Development*, Addison-Wesley, Reading, MA. This work reviews many aspects associated with the development of individuals within an organizational setting. It is intended to meet the needs of a wide variety of readers and is not specifically an 'academic' text.

Harrison, R (1992) *Employee Development*, Institute of Personnel Management, London. A textbook on the subject of training and development intended for personnel practitioners. It is a comprehensive review of the practice and theory of the subject. This book also includes numerous examples and case studies.

Institute of Personnel Management/Incomes Data Services European Management Guides (1993) *Training and Development*, Institute of Personnel Management, London. This is a practical book that reviews the training and development practices in member states of the European Union.

Nilsson, WP (1987) *Achieving Strategic Goals Through Executive Development*, Addison-Wesley, Reading, MA. This text sets out to provide a justification for a link between strategic management and development.

Patrick, J (1992) *Training: Research and Practice*, Academic Press, London. A comprehensive review of the training debate. It takes a psychologist's perspective and concentrates on an in-depth review of the topic.

Senge, P (1990) *The Fifth Discipline*, Doubleday, London. A book that encourages a systems- and holistic-based approach to managing change as well as encouraging the notion of continuous development and the application of the learning organization concept.

References

Beardwell, I and Holden, L (eds) (1997) *Human Resource Management: A Contemporary Perspective*, 2nd edn, Pitman Publishing, London.

Boyatsis, RE (1982) *The Competent Manager*, John Wiley, New York.

Brown, A (1995) *Organisational Culture*, Pitman Publishing, London.

Buckingham, M (1999) Clone free zone, *People Management*, Institute of Personnel and Development, London, 30 September, **5**, 19, 42–5.

Cummings, TG and Worley, CG (1993) *Organization Development and Change*, 5th edn, West Publishing Company, St Paul, MN.

Fitts, PM and Posner, MI (1967) *Human Performance*, Brooks-Cole/Prentice Hall, Belmont, CA.

Hamblin, AC (1974) *Evaluation and Control of Training*, McGraw-Hill, Maidenhead.

Honey, P and Mumford, A (1992) *The Manual of Learning Styles*, 3rd edn, P. Honey, Maidenhead.

Hulse, SH, Deese, J and Egeth, H (1980) *The Psychology of Learning*, 5th edn, McGraw-Hill, New York.

Kohler, W (1925) *The Mentality of Apes*, Harcourt Brace Jovanovich, New York.

Kolb, DA (1985) *Experiential Learning: Experiences as the Source of Learning and Development*, Prentice Hall, New York.

Lloyd, B (1999) Does knowledge have any value without wisdom?, *Professional Manager*, Institute of Management Foundation, Corby, **8**, 4, 6.

Mabey, C and Salaman, G (1995) *Strategic Human Resource Management*, Blackwell, Oxford.

Miller, GA, Galanter, E and Pribram, KH (1960) *Plans and the Structure of Behaviour*. Holt, Rinehart & Winston, New York.

Mintzberg, H, Quinn, JB, and Ghoshal, S. (1998) *The Strategy Process*, revised European edn, Prentice Hall, Hemel Hempstead.

Mumford, A (1989) *Management Development: Strategies for Action*, Institute of Personnel Management, London.

Nonaka, I (1996) The Knowledge Creating Company. In Starkey, K (ed.) *How Organizations Learn*, International Thomson Business Press, London.

Pavlov, IP (1927) *Conditional Reflexes*, Oxford University Press, New York.

Pedler, M, Boydell, T and Burgoyne, J (1989) Towards the learning company, *Management Education and Development*, **20**, part 1.

Pickard, J (1995) Learning that is far from academic, *People Management*, Institute of Personnel and Development, London, 9 March.

Reavens, RW (1972) Action learning – a management development programme, *Personnel Review*, Autumn.

Rodger, D and Mabey, C (1987) BT's leap forward from assessment centres, *Personnel Management*, July, 32–5.

Schank, R (1999) Courses of action, *People Management*, Institute of Personnel Management, London, 14 October, **5**, 20, 54–7.

Skinner, BF (1953) *Science and Human Behaviour*, Macmillan, New York.

Slack, N, Chambers, S, Harland, C, Harrison, A and Johnston, R (1998) *Operations Management*, 2nd edn, Pitman Publishing, London.

Stuart, D (1986) Performance Appraisal. In Mumford, A (ed.) *Handbook of Management Development*, Gower, Aldershot.

Thorndike, EL (1932) *The Fundamentals of Learning*, Teachers College, New York.

Verplanck, WS (1955) The control of the content of conversation: reinforcement of statements of opinion, *Journal of Abnormal and Social Psychology*, **51**, 668–76.

Watson, JB (1924) *Behaviourism*, University of Chicago Press, Chicago, IL.

Wood, L (1993) TECS hail work training scheme, *Financial Times*, 1 December, 26.

Wood, S, Barrington, H and Johnson, R (1990) An Introduction to Continuous Development. In Wood, S (ed.) *Continuous Development*, Institute of Personnel Management, London.

CHAPTER 10

Motivation and performance

CHAPTER SUMMARY

In this chapter we consider the topics of motivation and performance. We begin the discussion with a review of the major theories in this field. This is followed by a consideration of the organizational and management perspectives relevant to the topic. The social context within which work is carried out means that there is a continual reappraisal of the role and meaning of work in people's lives. It is against this backdrop that managers must achieve business and organizational objectives by motivating employees and managing their performance.

LEARNING OBJECTIVES

After studying this chapter and working through the associated Management in Action panels, Discussion questions and Research activities, you should be able to:

✦ Describe the major motivation theories.

✦ Outline the relationship between motivation and employee performance.

✦ Explain why motivation is a concept of considerable significance to managers.

✦ Understand what makes the study of motivation difficult.

✦ Discuss the dilemmas facing managers in applying motivation theory to a work setting.

✦ Appreciate the links between motivation and activities such as performance management, pay determination, employee participation and job design.

✦ Detail the various ways in which motivation theories can be classified.

✦ Assess the significance of classifying motivation theories.

Introduction

The term *motivation* is a familiar one. Reflect on any team sport: the players spend considerable time and effort on the field in attempting to exhort the other players to *perform* more effectively. In other words, to *motivate* individuals to produce better results. Within organizations, managers are constantly seeking ways to improve *performance* at every level of the business, in order to raise *productivity* and reduce cost. A major element in this process is the application of practices assumed to contain the necessary motivational properties. Clearly, all these terms are closely related and of considerable significance to each of the stakeholder groups associated with organizations.

The *Pocket English Dictionary* defines motive as: 'What impels a person to action, e.g. fear, ambition, or love.' This, however, is only part of the richness of the concept as it would be used in organizational behaviour terms. The same source defines perform as: 'Carry into effect … do (great things, wonders, &c).' It also contains what is an unfortunate definition of perform from a management perspective: 'Execute tricks at a public show.' Clearly, therefore, performance reflects the achievement of results that would be considered extraordinary and motivation is the key to achieving the necessary level of performance. However, the definition of performance also suggests another, darker, more menacing perspective, that of the manipulation of behaviour at the whim of another for the benefit, pleasure or entertainment of others. This alternative perspective provides a basis for much of the controversy and uncertainty surrounding the application of performance management techniques popular in current organizations.

Psychologists have long recognized the distinction between *drives* and *motives*, reflecting the distinction between unconscious physiological reactions and the social process directing controllable behaviour in people. Drives reflect those behaviour forces that are based on the physiological/biological needs of the body. For example, if we are hungry, the smell of food will tend to *push* our behaviour in the direction of eating. By the same token, a motive reflects *learned patterns of behaviour*. For example, we actively seek out situations involving interactions with other people in an attempt to socialize with them rather than spend time on our own. The basic motivational process reflecting these distinctions is shown in Figure 10.1.

Baldamus (1961) introduced the concept of *traction*, to indicate the feeling among some workers of being pulled along by the rhythm of a particular activity. This implies that

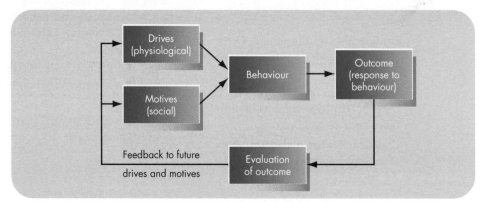

FIGURE 10.1   The basic motivational process.

a highly repetitive job is not automatically boring and could contain some motivational properties as a direct consequence of the nature and pace of the work. Motivation as an organizational concept reflects a complex process, clearly relating to the willingness or energy with which individuals address their work activities.

Management in Action 10.1 illustrates a number of recent attempts to improve the motivation of senior managers by directly linking reward to the performance of the company. When you read these examples consider the assumptions underlying the plans described. For example, what are the underlying views of motivation; the views about managers and the basis on which they work; can financial reward ensure motivation?

Stop | Consider

It is known that many managers quickly sell off shares allocated to them as a reward through share option schemes. Therefore, it is argued, they must be thinking (and acting) only in the short-term interests of themselves and their organizations. Senior managers seeking to ensure that other managers think and act in the long-term interests of the organization developed the reward strategy indicated in Management in Action 10.1 in an attempt to ensure a long-term perspective. There are a number of assumptions behind this process that are worth considering, including:

1. *That 'owners' (the City) have a longer time horizon than managers when it comes to measuring results.*
2. *That managers will be motivated and feel themselves rewarded through the acquisition of shares.*
3. *That requiring managers to purchase and hold shares will not demotivate them.*
4. *That increasing the ownership among managers will not (in time) create different, and perhaps less desirable, problems.*
5. *That the proposals will not create hostility and resentment among non-participating employees.*
6. *That managers will accept the policy in practice.*

It is interesting to note in Management in Action 10.1 that the attempt to motivate described is being applied to senior managers by even more senior, senior managers. The implication being that it is not just factory workers and junior staff employees who need to be motivated. The organizations indicated clearly believe that the best results can only be achieved if the people at the top are rewarded for the achievement of results in the long term. This is an interesting approach, particularly as the stock and financial markets are frequently criticized for forcing organizations to adopt short-term policies. More recent research carried out by an international consultancy supports this view by demonstrating that share options alone do not produce the highest performance in shareholder returns. According to the research only 30% of share movement is due to corporate performance, the remaining 70% being a function of 'market sentiment' (Patterson and Smith, 1998).

How would you react to the suggestion (and why) that executives must buy shares in their company if you were:

A. *The chief executive officer?*
B. *A senior sales and marketing manager?*
C. *The director of human resource management?*
D. *A team leader in the manufacturing department?*
E. *A trade union representative?*
F. *A factory worker?*
G. *A shareholder?*
H. *A customer?*

MANAGEMENT IN ACTION 10.1

Executives forced to buy slice of pie

It is generally accepted that managers with a significant part of their personal wealth tied up in a business will be more concerned about its performance than managers without such a stake. In the search for optimal returns a number of large multinational organizations have begun to insist that senior managers purchase nominated levels of stock in their organizations.

Union Carbide, Kodak and Xerox are among the large companies to go down this route. Organizations that have not gone as far as to require executives to buy shares, but 'encourage' them to do so include CSX, a US-based transport group. It offered loans to 160 of its top executives to buy shares at the prevailing market price.

Attempts to link the financial interests of managers to those of the shareholders is not new. Profit-share and share option schemes have existed for many years. Profit-share schemes pay a bonus to each executive, usually expressed as a percentage of salary and dependent upon the profit level achieved by the company. Executive share option schemes allow individual managers to buy shares at today's price but at some point in the future. Both forms of linking reward to profit have limitations. Profit share tends to emphasize a one-year time frame in thinking and action planning. Executive share options allow the manager to judge the 'value' between the price to be paid and current market price. If the market price has gone down the executive can refuse the option to buy. If the price has risen, the temptation to cash the shares in and take the 'profit' is high.

Brian Dunn, who specializes in executive compensation with Towers Perrin in New York, suggests that managers tend to hold less than 25% of the shares acquired under a share option scheme. The rest are sold quickly to take the profit

as cash. This supports the views expressed by Washington-based Institutional Shareholder Services who have been campaigning for a change in share option scheme rules to limit executive freedom to sell shares.

The Kodak scheme requires Kay Whitmore, the chairman, to purchase and hold shares to the value of four times his annual base salary. The more junior of the top 40 executives within Kodak will have to acquire shares over a five-year period to the value of one year's salary. Xerox requires its top 50 managers to acquire only one year's salary worth of shares, but this has to be achieved over 18 months.

The requirement to force executives to buy a specified amount of shares creates a number of dilemmas for both organization and individual alike. To resist buying shares is tantamount to arguing that a stake in the business is either undesirable or will not influence the decision making of the individual. To acquiesce is tantamount to accepting that the company has the right to determine how an executive spends their salary. It can also be argued that executives are paid a salary to take decisions in the best interests of the shareholders. Any shortcoming in that area should be dealt with through the normal company procedures and management control processes. Just how insistent can a company be and what are the rights of intrusion into an executive's financial planning if these plans become popular is the key area of debate.

Adapted from: Dickson, M (1993) Executives forced to buy slice of pie, *Financial Times*, 1 February, p 11.

Early approaches to motivation

In the pre-industrial era communities and individuals were probably motivated by the strong desire to survive and the perishable nature of much of the means of doing so. Much of the available food could not be stored for long periods and so the *need* was to adopt behaviour patterns that maintained its flow. In addition, the political and social structures were such that individuals had less freedom of choice in their lives. Slavery, bonded or enforced labour meant that individuals could be forced to perform tasks on behalf of others, frequently for a subsistence living in return. However, the discovery over recent years of elaborate and beautifully drawn cave paintings are but one example of the existence of activity beyond the demands of survival even in very ancient times, the implication being that even then life was more complex and richer than might be assumed looking back using today's perspectives, standards and values.

The issue of how much work management should expect from employees began to emerge in the Middle Ages. There are examples of the pace of work being set by management at the Arsenal of Venice in the 1400s (George, 1972, Wren, 1987) and of monks estimating the time to build churches and cathedrals at about the same time, (Currie, 1963). Management in Action 10.2 describes one early approach to this subject.

| Stop | Consider | *Would you have sought a job as a printer or a supervisor in early Korea (and why)?* |

At the beginning of the twentieth century FW Taylor was attempting to develop and introduce *scientific management* to the companies in which he was working, initially Midvale Steel (1878–98) followed by Bethlehem Iron Company (1898–1901). It involved identifying the *one best way* to carry out a job and then motivating employees to follow the work method specified through linking the payment of wages (reward) to the output achieved. His initial attempts were successful, the workers' earnings increased, productivity increased and costs reduced, as Table 10.1 (based on Taylor, 1947) indicates.

The level of production increased considerably, but the wages of employees changed very little by comparison. Table 10.2 reflects the changes resulting from the use of Taylor's scientific methods.

Looked at in this way the figures provide a clear picture of benefit for both employer and employee, but the employer gains demonstrated far outweigh those for the employee. However, Taylor's success was short lived and he was dismissed from the company in 1901 as the result of the growing hostility towards his methods from managers and workers alike.

	Pre-scientific management	Using scientific management
Earnings per employee per day (average)	$1.15	$1.88
Tons per employee per day (average)	16	59
Labour cost per ton (average)	$0.072	$0.033
Number of yard labourers	500	140

TABLE 10.1   The effect of scientific management

MANAGEMENT IN ACTION 10.2

Printing in early Korea

In sixteenth- and seventeenth-century Korea methods of printing had developed from the carving of pages of individual text to the use of a movable type. As there were literally thousands of characters in the language and the workforce were largely illiterate, good-quality and accurate printing proved to be a difficult task to achieve.

In order to circulate official documents it was necessary first to have them printed and published. Under these circumstances the composing of the printing blocks and the subsequent printing process itself was a very skilled job. In order to ensure the accurate reproduction of documents a motivation scheme was introduced for the printers and supervisors.

The scheme was based on a negative incen-

tive principle, in other words punishment for mistakes rather than reward for accuracy. The punishment was that for every mistake or unclear printed character the supervisor, compositor

and printer would be flogged 30 times. The consequence, not surprisingly, was very high quality printing, but difficulty in the recruiting and training of people as compositors, printers or supervisors. As with most incentive schemes some benefits were achieved, but other problems were created.

Adapted from: Boorstin, DJ (1983) *The Discoverers*, Random House, New York, pp 505–8.

Chester Barnard described what he saw as the major activities associated with being a senior executive in the 1930s. As a practising manager (the president of a large telephone company) he was writing from experience rather than theory. In terms of motivation he suggests that it was a balancing process:

> The net satisfactions which induce a man to contribute his efforts to an organization result from the positive advantages as against the disadvantages which are entailed. (Barnard, 1938, p 140)

He suggests in a footnote on the same page that the individual did not usually invoke a logical process in this decision-making process. Logical in this context being defined as an understandable basis for action as perceived by Barnard (as a senior manager) rather than through the frame of reference of the individual. This is a common perspective adopted by many present-day managers when designing motivational programmes. Managers

	Change as a result of scientific management	Percentage change
Earnings per employee	+$0.73	+$63.5%
Tons per employee	+43	+268.8%
Labour cost per ton	−$0.039	−54.2%
Number of yard labourers	−360	−72%

TABLE 10.2   The benefits of scientific management

frequently assume that what they would find motivating everyone else within the organization will also find motivating. This is not necessarily so. In his views Barnard was essentially adopting a human relations approach, but also anticipating some of the later theoretical and practical approaches to the question of what motivates people to deliver high performance.

The theories of motivation

There is no one theory of motivation that can be claimed to embrace the entire range of organizational and personal circumstances that exist. For example, something that motivates an individual today may not work tomorrow, yet may become viable again the day after, perhaps due to mood swings and factors outside of the work setting. Equally every individual employee is different and will respond to particular motivation processes differently. For example, the use of recognition and praise for good work may be motivational to one person, but yet have only limited effects for someone seeking to earn additional money to pay a large mortgage. Organizational circumstances also change over time which impacts on aspects of motivation practice. For example, up to recent years employees working in the British banking sector enjoyed very generous access to cheap loans for housing etc. Over time the value of this type of benefit has been significantly reduced by management, a fact recalled by many longer serving employees and often seen as evidence of an uncaring management stance.

In this chapter we will use the convention of classifying theories into *content* or *process* theories wherever possible. Content theories concentrate on identifying the motives that produce behaviour. Process theories emphasize those mechanisms that encourage (or reward) behaviour in the dynamic context. Figure 10.2 provides an overview of the way that these approaches emerged from the earlier work in this area.

Another important concept in relation to motivation at work is that of an *intrinsic motivator*. This represents a source of motivation that originates inside the individual as a response to the job itself and the circumstances surrounding its execution. For example, an architect may be motivated to produce exciting buildings because of the satisfaction gained from having the opportunity to realize their ideas and also through avenues such as professional and peer recognition of their work. An *extrinsic motivator,* by way of contrast, is one that originates outside the individual worker and which influences their behaviour. For example, Taylor was prepared to reward employees with higher wages providing they worked to his prescribed methods. Figure 10.3 reflects the relationships between extrinsic and intrinsic motivation and the resulting work activity. It also clearly demonstrates the existence of feedback in the process. If the rewards obtained by an individual do not meet their expectations either in terms of the level received or the impact on their lives then a reassessment of the rewards offered would be made and perhaps future behaviour adjusted accordingly.

Both intrinsic and extrinsic concepts can be used with some effect in designing motivational practice within organizations. The self-regulation implied through intrinsic motivation would (if successful) provide managers with the tangible benefits associated with lower cost and higher quality along with a reduced need for close supervision, than would a reliance on extrinsic motivators alone. Writers such as Foucault (1977), Hollway (1991) and Townley (1994) criticize management literature and theory, including motivation. They describe it as an attempt to seek to formulate employees as objects of knowledge and therefore subjected to theoretical attempts to locate them within a power–knowledge framework, the ultimate intention being one of making employees more manageable (Townley, p 92). Performance is delivered by employees within a reality defined and measured by managers, consequently the underlying motivational models are frequently evaluated as a reflection of this perspective.

Content theories

Content theories emphasize particular aspects of an individual's needs or the goals that they seek to achieve as the basis for motivated behaviour. The major theories falling into this classification include:

✦ Maslow's hierarchy of needs theory.

✦ Alderfer's existence, relatedness and growth (ERG) theory.

✦ McClelland's acquired needs theory.

✦ Herzberg's two-factor theory.

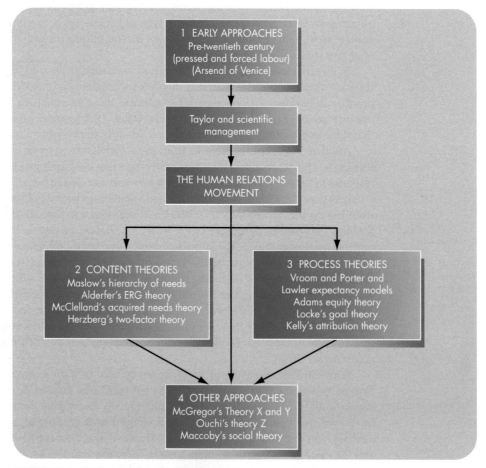

FIGURE 10.2   Evolution of motivation theory.

Maslow's hierarchy of needs

Maslow was an American psychologist who produced the idea that a hierarchy of needs could explain purposeful behaviour (Maslow, 1943, 1987). The basis of the model is that individuals have *innate needs* or *wants* which they will seek to satisfy. In addition, these needs have an in-built prioritizing system. Figure 10.4 shows the model, indicating the hierarchical nature of the innate needs.

The five levels included in this hierarchy can be defined in the following way:

✦ Physiological needs. These include the wide range of basic needs that every human body requires in order to stay alive and function normally. Examples would include the need for food, air to breathe, water to drink and sleep. In an organizational context this would also include the need for wages.

✦ Safety needs. This category incorporates needs that provide for the security of the individual in their normal environment. Examples would include the need to be free from harm and to have shelter from the elements. In an organizational context this would also include the need for job security.

✦ Social needs. From this category individuals would look to draw on social support necessary to life. Examples would include friendship and a sense of belonging. In an organizational context this might include the need to work as part of a team.

✦ Esteem needs. This would include individuals having self-respect. Also incorporated in this category are concepts of achievement, adequacy, recognition and reputation. In an organizational context this could include the formal recognition by management of useful ideas originating from employees or employee of the month awards.

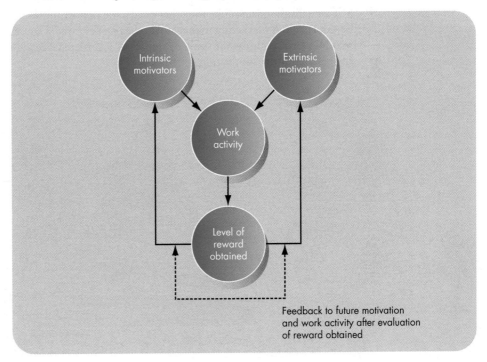

FIGURE 10.3 Intrinsic and extrinsic motivation.

✦ Self-actualization needs. This category is related to the opportunity to realize one's full potential. That is, the ability to have a significant influence over one's own life. In an organizational context this could include the freedom to organize one's job to suit personal preferences and circumstances, also to be managed on the basis of ends not means.

Maslow suggests that these elements in the hierarchy are not to be considered as a rigid framework, within which individuals move in a totally fixed and predictable way. He suggests that the hierarchy displays the following properties:

✦ A need once satisfied is no longer a motivator. For example, once employees become accustomed to being consulted by the employer on matters of company policy, it becomes the norm and therefore loses some of its motivational properties. In effect, the basis of comparison shifts.

✦ A need cannot be effective as a motivator until those before it in the hierarchy have been satisfied. For example, it would be of little value to offer employees who are currently very poorly paid the opportunity to work in teams in an attempt to increase productivity.

✦ If deprived of the source of satisfaction from a lower order need it will again become a motivator. For example, if a self-actualizing employee is given notice of redundancy, their natural reaction would be to start looking for another job (reversion to a lower level need for security).

✦ There is a innate desire to work up the hierarchy. Employees working in a team may in addition seek to plan and organize their work without management involvement.

✦ Self-actualization is not like the other needs; the opportunities presented by it cannot be exhausted. A marketing manager who has just enjoyed a successful sales campaign may also have a number of similar campaigns at earlier stages of development to form the basis of future motivation.

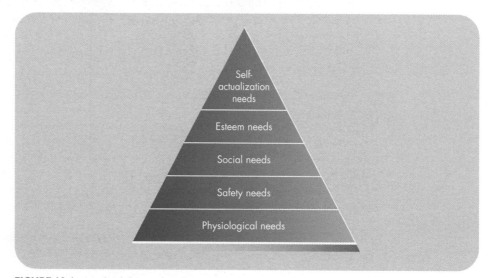

FIGURE 10.4   Maslow's hierarchy of needs.

Assessment of the theory Maslow did not specifically describe his theory as applicable to the work situation, although that is where it has gained most exposure. There are a number of difficulties in applying his theory to humans in an organizational context, including:

✦ Not everyone is motivated only by things that go on inside the organization. There are many people who self-actualize outside the work setting, running youth groups, trade unions and participating in a wide variety of other leisure activities.

✦ People at different stages of their lives will be motivated by different things. For example, a young employee saving up to buy a motor car will be motivated by factors different from an employee five years away from retirement.

✦ The amount of satisfaction needed at a specific level before a higher level need is activated is unknown.

✦ The theory cannot explain all behaviour. For example, how can it explain that many actors are prepared to endure personal hardship in order to pursue their art?

✦ To what extent can a theory developed in the USA during the 1940s, reflecting the values of that time along with the culture base of US behaviour, be relevant to today's organizations and other countries?

✦ Organizational events can impact on satisfaction at more than one level in the hierarchy. For example, money can be used to satisfy needs at every level in the hierarchy. However, the application of money as motivation is not under the control of managers, it is for the individual to determine the need and level of the hierarchy that is being met through the money given. This represents an indirect motivational process.

✦ Individuals will place different values on each need. For example, some people prefer to work in relative security but with lower pay. It is just this issue that has over recent years been creating difficulties within public sector employment. Traditionally public sector employment has been very secure and some degree of advancement almost guaranteed. However, over recent years most countries have struggled with the desire to cut public spending and have, consequently, changed the basis of the psychological contract with employees. A not surprising reaction to that situation is that public sector employees now consider themselves to be as vulnerable to high work demands and low security as those in the private sectors and are demanding higher wages and better rewards etc. in return.

Having said all that, Maslow's theory has been very influential over the years in assisting managers to prioritize elements in their attempts to motivate employees. It is an approach which encourages managers to 'get the basics' right before they attempt to undertake complex motivational initiatives. It should force managers to examine motivation from the employee perspective and to seek out how they perceive the situation. It also provides a basis for managers to reinforce what they already provide through benefit and support programmes as part of the employee reward package. For example, reminding employees of the existence and value of counselling and pension schemes.

Overall, there are many potential advantages to managers seeking to apply the Maslow model to the design of motivation within the organization – which is why it has much popularity as a topic on management courses. However, that alone does not make it a good theory. There have been studies carried out that have shown limited support for it as well as studies that have not supported the model. However, as a theory it must be seen in the context of the strong desire among managers for control of the process and outcome of work. It is in that context that, although originating outside the organizational context, it gains its significance, as suggested by Townley (1994).

Alderfer's ERG theory

Alderfer (1972) describes a three-level hierarchy, compared to the five levels proposed by Maslow. They are:

+ Existence needs. This category is grounded in the survival, or continued existence, of the person. As such it would include many of the issues covered by the physiological and safety needs identified by Maslow.

+ Relatedness needs. This category is based on the need for people to live and function in a social environment. It would embrace the need to be part of a group and belong to a valued organization. It would incorporate many of the issues covered by the safety, belonging and esteem needs described by Maslow.

+ Growth needs. This category is grounded in the need for people to develop their potential. As such it would cover the self-actualization and much of the esteem needs described by Maslow.

Assessment of the theory   Having described the Alderfer model as being strongly related to the Maslow framework, that does not imply that Alderfer merely simplified the original material. His work does contain many similarities to a simplified form of Maslow's hierarchy. For example he suggests that individuals move through the hierarchy, from *existence needs* to *relatedness needs* to *growth needs*, as each becomes satisfied. However, he does make more than Maslow of the variability inherent in all motivational situations. For example, he suggests that more than one need could be functioning at the same time; also that individuals may regress back down the hierarchy. Alderfer further postulated a *frustration–regression* mechanism that would, in effect, substitute for any growth needs as the ultimate aim of the individual if they were to be continually frustrated in achieving them.

Maslow's theory was not specifically work related. Alderfer, by the same token, contains a more direct organizational basis in grouping together categories of need into a more usable framework (at least as might be perceived by managers). It is also a stronger or more robust theory than Maslow's. It postulates that managers should seek to motivate by addressing all three levels of need, but that if one (say growth) cannot be met then additional effort will need to be put into providing for the others as they will increase in significance for the individual. However, it suffers from the same criticisms as the Maslow theory in its evident cultural positioning, underlying assumptions and managerialist perspectives.

McClelland's acquired needs theory

This theory develops a different set of needs as the basis of motivation (McClelland, 1961):

+ Achievement. He abbreviates this to nAch.
+ Affiliation. He abbreviates this to nAff.
+ Power. He abbreviates this to nPow.

To some extent these categories can be regarded as elements within the higher order needs described by Maslow. His ideas were developed by using projective psychological techniques. He also suggests that needs are acquired through the social process of individuals interacting with the environment. McClelland suggests that all people have these three needs to some extent although there is a tendency for only one of them to be dominant at any point in time. Questionnaires similar to that included as Figure 10.5 are suggested to be able to identify the existence of individual needs as well as their relative dominance.

Assessment of the theory Questionnaires have been developed that it is claimed, can be of use to managers in attempting to motivate their employees by sensitizing managers to individual needs and the associated job implications. Table 10.3 is one such attempt. It provides a work preference and job example for each category of need. One difficulty associated with such tables is the generalized nature of the preferences and examples. Also, if needs provide a basis for job suitability, how can this be linked with the fluid nature of the needs themselves? For example, nAch tends to emphasize the individual aspects associated with work, typified by the job of a sales representative. However, if a such a person classed as nAch and working as a sales representative then moves towards nAff as the dominant need this may suggest the necessity to change jobs, but there may be no

1 Do you like situations where you personally must find solutions to problems?

2 Do you tend to set moderate goals and take moderate, thought-out risks?

3 Do you want specific feedback about how well you are doing?

4 Do you spend time considering how to advance your career, how to do your job better or how to accomplish something important?

If you responded yes to questions 1–4, then you probably have a high need for achievement.

5 Do you look for jobs or seek situations that provide an opportunity for social relationships?

6 Do you often think aboput the personal relationships you have?

7 Do you consider the feelings of others very important?

8 Do you try to restore disrupted relationships when they occur?

If you responded yes to questions 5–8, then you probably have a high need for affiliation.

9 Do you try to influence and control others?

10 Do you seek leadership positions in groups?

11 Do you enjoy persuading others?

12 Are you perceived by others as outspoken, forceful and demanding?

If you responded yeas to questions 9–12, then you probably have a high need for power.

FIGURE 10.5 How to identify McClelland's needs (*source*: Steers, RM and Porter, LW (1979) *Motivation and Work Behaviour*, McGraw-Hill, New York).

suitable job opportunities available, carrying with it a variety of consequences for all concerned (from underperformance to job termination).

Herzberg's two-factor theory

The original research carried out by Herzberg involved interviews with 203 accountants and engineers from organizations around Pittsburgh in the USA (Herzberg, 1974; Herzberg *et al.*, 1959). He used the *critical incidents* approach by asking questions about what had made the individual feel good or bad about their work. The answers were then subjected to a *content analysis* which identified that those factors that led to satisfaction were fundamentally different from those issues that lead to dissatisfaction. This he labelled the *two-factor theory of motivation* and named the categories *motivators* and *hygiene* factors. The theory offers some insight into the relationship between motivation and job satisfaction.

The hygiene factors were those that, if absent, caused dissatisfaction. They are predominantly concerned with the context within which the job is carried out and other extrinsic issues. The presence of these factors will not motivate individuals as such, but their absence will serve to create dissatisfaction with the job and organization. They included:

✦ Salary.

✦ Working conditions.

✦ Job security.

✦ Level and quality of supervision.

✦ Company policies and administrative procedures.

✦ Interpersonal relationships at work.

The motivating factors were those that could motivate the individual to improve their work performance. They were primarily concerned with the content of the work, together with the way in which it formed a meaningful whole (intrinsic factors). They included:

Individual need	Work preferences	Example
High nArch	Individual responsibility Challenging but achievable goals Feedback on performance	Field salesperson with challenging quota and opportunity to earn individual bonus
High nAff	Interpersonal relationships Opportunities to communicate	Customer service representative; member of work unit subject to group wage bonus plan
High nPow	Control over others Attention Recognition	Formal position of supervisory responsibility; appointment as head of special task force or committee

TABLE 10.3 Work preferences based on McClelland's needs theory (*source*: Schermerhorn, JR, Hunt, JG and Osborn, RH (1982) *Managing Organizational Behaviour*, John Wiley, New York)

✦ Recognition.

✦ Sense of achievement.

✦ Responsibility.

✦ Nature of the work itself.

✦ Growth.

✦ Advancement.

Although Herzberg did not claim a hierarchical relationship for the two factors, it is possible to compare this theory with those of Maslow, Alderfer and McClelland. This is most easily illustrated with a diagram(see Figure 10.6).

The significance of Herzberg's model is that the two factors are not opposite ends of a continuum. Lack of positive levels in the hygiene factors does not lead to demotivation, but to dissatisfaction. High levels in the hygiene factors does not lead to motivation, but to non-dissatisfaction. High levels among the motivation factors will, as might be inferred, lead to positive motivation. However, low levels of motivating influences will reduce the overall level of motivation, but not create dissatisfaction. It would, however, create feelings of non-satisfaction. So in effect there is a non-overlapping middle ground between these two factors, as shown in Figure 10.7.

The major implication of this theory for anyone seeking to make use of it in designing motivational practices is that they need to concentrate on two sets of factors at the same time if motivation and satisfaction are to be maintained.

Assessment of the theory There have been a number of criticisms of Herzberg's work. They include:

✦ The results obtained are research method dependent. Studies which use the same research methodology as Herzberg tend to arrive at broadly similar conclusions. Research using different methods is less supportive of the conclusions.

✦ The results obtained by Herzberg are capable of different interpretations. This is the

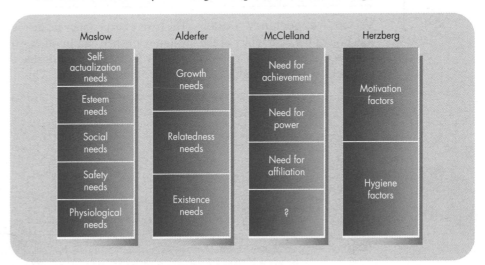

FIGURE 10.6 Comparison of the need theories.

line developed by Vroom (1964). Also, the theory is not clearly set out which has resulted in different interpretations when replicating his work (King, 1970).

✦ It does not provide for individual difference. For example, close supervision may be resented by some and yet welcomed by others.

✦ In an organizational context the application of the principles implied by the model is often restricted to manual or unskilled workers. This is surprising, given that it was developed from a research base drawn from accountants and engineers. It is often claimed that manual workers adopt an instrumental approach, concentrating on pay and security rather than the intrinsic aspects of the work. Alternatively, work by Blackburn and Mann (1979) suggests that people in low-skilled jobs adopt a wide range of work approaches, not just economic factors, a result that reinforces the traction aspects associated with highly repetitive work referred to earlier.

✦ As with all content theories the universal application of Herzberg's work has been criticized because of the underlying assumptions about people and work as well as the cultural basis of the work.

Process theories

Process theories attempt to provide a model of the interactions between the variables involved in the motivation process. The major process theories include:

✦ Vroom/Porter and Lawler expectancy models.
✦ Adams' equity theory.
✦ Locke's goal theory.
✦ Kelly's attribution theory.

The Vroom/Porter and Lawler expectancy models

Vroom's expectancy model   The basis of expectancy models is that motivation is a function of the desirability of the outcome of behaviour. In other words, if an individual believes that behaving in a particular way will generate rewards that the individual values and seeks, they will be motivated to produce those behaviours. This is also referred to as a

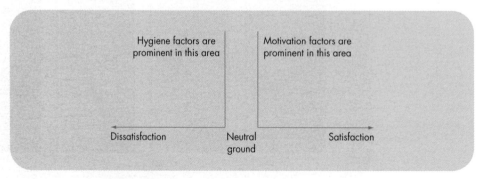

FIGURE 10.7 Satisfaction and Herzberg's two factors.

path–goal theory, because it is possible to identify a distinct path leading to particular goals (Figure 10.8).

This model implies that individual behaviour will be moulded by what is perceived as the available rewards on offer and their importance to the individual. For example, offered the opportunity to attend training courses leading to a professional qualification in return for higher performance, an employee seeking such an opportunity will be motivated. If, however, an employee was not interested in becoming professionally qualified, it would have no effect on their behaviour. Also, an offer of training would not motivate the employee even if they were interested in becoming qualified, but did not believe that the manager could or would deliver the opportunity.

Vroom (1964) was the first person to link expectancy theory to work motivation. The model contains three key elements:

✦ Valance. This refers to the importance of the outcome for the individual. Valance can either be positive or negative. It is positive if the individual wants to acquire or achieve the outcome. Negative valance clearly refers to the opposite effect. Valance should be distinguished from value. Valance is based on anticipation, value implies the satisfaction from actually possessing something. In deciding whether to work overtime, an individual may take into account the family wish to go to the cinema that night. If the individual does not want to see the film, working late will allow them to achieve that objective (the valance). Subsequently, if the individual finds that the family could not get seats and so went to a restaurant instead, the value gained (realized valance) through working overtime may be altered.

✦ Instrumentality. This concept links together the ideas of *first* and *second level* outcomes. It is necessary to become familiar with the notions of first and second level outcomes before *instrumentality* can be fully understood.

First level outcomes are those things that emerge directly from behaviour and are related to the work itself. Examples include productivity, labour turnover, absenteeism, quality and 'doing a good job'. While these results may hold valance for the individual, it is the opportunities that these first level outcomes provide that contain the highest levels of it. For example, higher levels of productivity (first level outcome) may generate a financial bonus. The bonus is a second level outcome (it is a function of the additional output produced, not the level of motivation) and as such tends to be need related. The importance of second level outcomes is that they are dependent on the

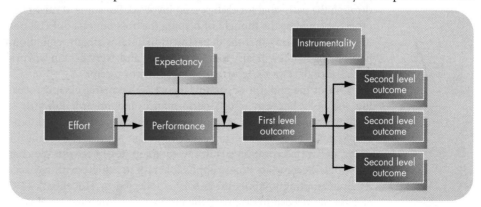

FIGURE 10.8 Vroom's expectancy model.

first level outcomes, not on the original effort. For example, working harder may increase productivity (first level outcome), but if the company did not have an incentive scheme then no financial bonus would be paid (no second level outcome). Equally, individuals are usually rewarded for actual achievements not for the amount of effort expended.

✦ Expectancy. This is about the probability that a particular first level outcome will be achieved. Machines are liable to break down, parts may not arrive when required and other workers may not work hard. The result of these and other sources of variability is that the achievement of a first level outcome may not be certain.

The model can also be described in an equation. The use of an equation has the advantage of reflecting the motivational process in the way that it would be experienced by an individual. The equation allows a wide range of forces acting on the behaviour of an individual to be identified and the positive and negative influences taken into account, also the cumulative effect of the interactions within and between forces can be determined:

$$M = \Sigma \, (E \times V)$$

where M refers to the motivational force resulting from the sum of all the expectancy and valance elements in the equation, E refers to the expectancy measure reflecting the probability that effort will result in a particular first level outcome and V refers to the valance (or attractiveness) of a particular outcome for the individual.

The Porter and Lawler extension   Porter and Lawler (1968) develop the model by attempting to link motivation and performance. In their model they draw attention to the fact that it is not just motivation that produces performance, but a range of variables such as the individual's view of work. Figure 10.9 gives a diagrammatic view of the extended model.

Assessment of the theory   According to the expectancy model, individuals always seek to optimize the return on their investment of effort. One illustration of this concept is to consider a manager faced with a crisis needing the staff to work late one night. Individuals will have completed their basic work commitments for the day and will have plans for the evening. If the manager is to achieve the objective it will be necessary to work through the path–goal for each person involved. For some, it might be the extra money, for others, it could be the thought of helping the boss out of a difficult position, for yet others, it could be ensuring that the department maintains a high reputation with customers, the point being that it will vary for every person, and every person will evaluate for themselves the balance of rewards, effort and probability of receipt.

One of the implications of this theory is that managers must seek ways of strengthening the links between effort, performance and reward. Rewards should be linked to employee values. In order to apply this approach managers need to be able to identify the employee calculus in order to be able to design appropriate arrangements. Because of the many and varied components in the equation, together with the changeable nature of it, this would become an almost impossible task to achieve with any accuracy. The complexity in attempting to apply the theory is reflected by Hollenback (1979) in which matrix algebra was needed to deal with the number and combination of variables.

Adams' equity theory

People develop strong feelings about the *relative fairness* of the treatment that they receive at work. When reaching a conclusion on fairness, individuals need a point of reference against which to judge what they actually experience. The main source of such comparisons being the perceived treatment of other people. This formed the basis of the *equity* approach to motivation (Adams, 1965), based on social exchange theory. This model suggests that individuals operate social interactions as a form of trading. In effect, a balance sheet approach in which individuals invest in relationships to the extent that they anticipate a balanced return.

Equity theory in motivation is therefore part of an evaluation and investment process. The most obvious application of these ideas lies in the field of financial reward. Every employee is paid a wage or salary together with a range of additional benefits and these provide many opportunities for comparison. Examples of the different opportunities that exist for making comparisons include other employees performing the same job, the same job in other companies, friends, neighbours and professional colleagues. Industrial relations specialists are well aware of the difficulties of equity in pay comparisons. Management in Action 10.3 reviews the concept of fairness, including equity.

Stop | Consider *Consider the productivity and office changes described in MiA 10.3. Attempt to interpret the results using each of the previous motivation theories so far discussed. To what extent can they provide equally satisfactory explanations for the behaviour of the underwriters?*

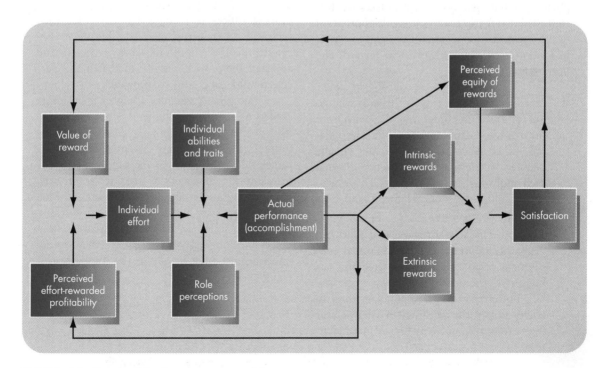

FIGURE 10.9 Porter and Lawler expectancy model.

MANAGEMENT IN ACTION 10.3

Moving tale of a fair day's work

Furnham reports the experience of a group of underwriters in the USA who were forced to move offices during a refurbishment programme. Among the group of underwriters were varying degrees of seniority, yet all performed at approximately the same level before the move. As a result of the move the reassigned work places meant that some staff moved into an office normally allocated to someone of a higher grade, some moved into offices normally inhabited by staff of a lower grade and others were allocated offices appropriate to their grade of seniority. The productivity of staff allocated lower status offices dropped dramatically. Conversely, staff allocated offices of a higher status dramatically increased their productivity. Staff allocated to appropriate office accommodation stayed at the pre-move levels of productivity.

Furnham provides one explanation for this phenomenon through the concept of 'equity'. It is suggested that there are three possible approaches to the determination of what it is 'right' to expect in relation to exchanging 'work' and 'reward'. The options are:

✦ Equality. Imagine a group of friends who go out for a meal and order what they wish from the menu and drink as they see fit. The bill at the end of the meal could be split equally between all the friends irrespective of what each individual actually 'spent'. Those who choose modestly subsidize those who have expensive inclinations.

✦ Taxation. This would suggest that food and drink consumption should be separated from payment responsibilities. The greediest (or hungriest) should order as they wish. The bill, however, would be split according to ability to pay, the wealthiest having to bear the heaviest responsibility for their contribution.

✦ Equity. This approach requires each individual to show restraint in ordering both food and drink to comply with the desires of the group to fund the evening. It is not  unusual to find an individual seeking to retain an expensive option, compared to group desires, being told to pay for themselves under this approach. Equity requires that no individual is markedly out of line compared to the others in both consumption of food and drink and payment of an equal share.

Of the three approaches the equity view tends to be the most commonly found. The taxation option is the least popular – apart from those individuals who deliberately seek advantage from a situation. In the case of the underwriters moving offices it is suggested that they each reviewed the 'rewards' received (the office allocated) for the 'input' of work expected and adjusted their work activity to match the perceived 'value' of the offices provided.

These same principles apply in many other aspects of organizational life. It is not unusual to find people who feel unfairly dealt with taking more time off work, going slow or generally being unhelpful to the work of the organization. The problem for managers is that it is for each employee to undertake the evaluation of what 'equity' means for them. Managers are not in a position to judge on behalf of employees what determines an 'equitable' situation, they cannot know against what or whom the comparison is being made.

Adapted from: Furnham, A (1993) Moving tale of a fair day's work, *Financial Times*, 24 March, p 14.

For Adams, the process of comparing can produce two possible outcomes, equity or inequity. Equity is achieved when a perceived balance between the individual and the target is achieved. Inequity arises when the balance is disturbed in either a positive or negative direction. The individual would feel that an inequitable situation existed if, for example, they were paid more than the comparator, not just if they were paid less. Figure 10.10 reflects the operation of equity theory. Which option is chosen to restore equity will depend on a number of factors active in the situation and within the individual.

Assessment of the theory   Much of the research on equity theory has concentrated on its application to pay and rewards. Dornstein (1989) examined the basis of comparison in people's judgements about the fairness of received pay and found that it changed depending on a number of factors. Research in Hong Kong by Law and Wong (1998) suggests that the use of different methodologies to explore fairness produces differing results, further clouding the issue. Consequently, it is not clear how individuals apply the principles of equity theory, neither would managers find it easy to be sure that equity were being achieved for each individual. However, more recent work in this area suggests that individuals use both instrumental and value-expressive standards when evaluating the fairness of pay procedures (Jones *et al.*, 1999), a clear implication of this being that not only does pay need to be allocated fairly, but the pay allocation procedures need to be perceived to be fair by those subject to them.

Working relationships are much less personal than those based on friendship and it is less likely that the same level of commitment to them exists (Campbell and Pritchard, 1974). Consequently, it is argued that the perception of inequity will be less in a work

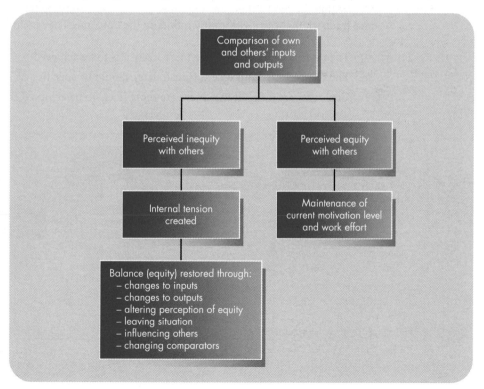

FIGURE 10.10   Adams' equity theory.

context when overpayment is involved. It is more likely that individuals will change the basis of their view of what forms an equitable payment (Locke, 1976).

Even with the possible limitations described, the model provides a useful mechanism for considering the significance of equity between employees along with the implications for motivation and performance of failing to achieve a perception of it. These points are particularly relevant to the subject of pay and other tangible rewards. The theory implies that organizations should give close attention to the comparison process when designing pay structures, incentive schemes, merit awards and even promotion, the key being that perceived equity exists for the individual, which is not the same as the actual equity. The earlier chapter on perception (Chapter 3) provides enough basis for understanding the significance of the perceptual process as a personal and largely subjective interpretation process rather than a simple registration of facts or reality.

Locke's goal theory

Locke (1968) suggested that people's intentions play a significant part in formulating their behavioural patterns. In a work context, this can be used as a mechanism to motivate desired behaviours. It is on the basis of this model that many performance appraisal systems attempt to shape behaviour and achieve improved performance. An individual needs feedback in order to gauge the extent to which their goal is being achieved. Performance appraisal systems are a formal feedback mechanism to direct employee behaviour towards the achievement of management determined objectives. A generalized model of goal theory is shown as Figure 10.11.

Within the model there are a number of issues surrounding the notion of goal setting and feedback that can significantly influence the outcome. They include:

✦   The more specific the goal the more likely it is to be achieved.

✦   The completion requirement (finish date) should be specific.

✦   Goals that are difficult to achieve are more likely to be achieved than easy ones.

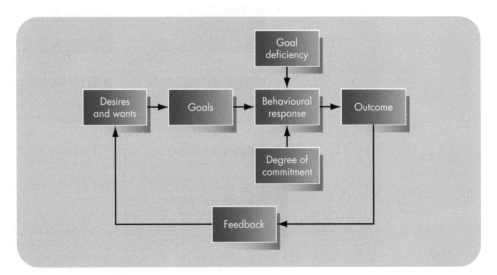

FIGURE 10.11   Goal theory.

In modern performance appraisal use these ideas have been refined into the so-called *SMART* objectives that form the basis of determining performance objectives. The acronym SMART stands for setting objectives that are specific, measurable, attainable, realistic and time bounded (Armstrong and Murliss, 1998, p 247).

Assessment of the theory   There have been a number of studies of goal-setting approaches to motivation (for example Early *et al.*, 1990; Erez *et al.*, 1985 and Shalley *et al.*, 1987). Generally the results have been supportive of the approach, but raise questions that remain unanswered. For example, what degree of subordinate involvement is required in setting goals to achieve optimal results? Another outstanding issue is the need to understand the process through which the behavioural impetus of the employee is maintained once the goals have been agreed.

Issues such as individual difference, personality, previous experience, education and training and career path are among the factors that could be assumed to have an effect on the validity of the goal-setting model. These aspects also remain to be researched in any depth. The approach is widely used as the basis of performance appraisal systems, particularly where projects, tangible results or change are features of the job. However, the model does have limitations. Some jobs are not amenable to goal setting (for example, assembly line tasks and call centre activities). With an increasingly turbulent operating environment being common for many organizations, goals are subject to frequent change. This makes it increasingly difficult for individuals to maintain performance targeted at specific goals over an extended period. Goal setting represents an individual level process, but most tasks within an organization require groups of people to co-operate in order to achieve them. This reality of organizational life means that it is frequently difficult to provide enough individual control over work activity to be certain that goal theory is effectively motivating behaviour.

Attribution theory and motivation

Attribution theory suggests that motivation is a response by the individual to a self-perception of their behaviour. Individuals decide (through perception) whether their behaviour is responding to internal or external influences. On the basis of this decision, the individual will decide whether or not they prefer to be intrinsically or extrinsically motivated. The result of this decision affects the form of motivation that will be effective for that individual (Kelly, 1971).

The effects of an intrinsically motivated individual being managed within a regime that was based on extrinsic motivation was studied by Deci (1971). He found that such individuals subsequently became extrinsically motivated. Wiersma (1992) concluded that the links between extrinsic and intrinsic motivation were complex and could work against each other in particular situations. It is argued that intrinsic motivation provides the 'best' approach to obtaining a totally effective employee, one who will perform well and take a pride in producing good quality work. However, many motivation strategies rely on incentive schemes or other extrinsic principles to motivate employees through tangible rewards. The criticism of such approaches being that they *purchase* output, generating at best an instrumental or compliance response. The earlier points made in relation to employee control by management and framing the reality within which performance is defined in this context are also pertinent to this discussion.

Additional perspectives on motivation

McGregor's Theory X and Theory Y

McGregor (1960) explicitly introduced a particular set of underlying assumptions concerning human nature into motivation when he proposed the notion of Theory X and Theory Y. His claim was that managers tend to hold beliefs that would classify employees into either a Theory X or Theory Y category. Consequently, managers operate policies and practices (including motivation) that are based on one or other of these sets of assumptions (see Figure 10.12).

In essence McGregor implies that motivational practice is in real danger of becoming a self-fulfilling prophecy as employees respond to the reality created for them, points that would be supported by the work of Deci (1971) and Townley (1994) already introduced.

Ouchi's Theory Z

Ouchi investigated the ways in which Japanese and US managers managed their subordinates. In doing so he identified a number of cultural differences between the two:

Theory X

1   The average man is by nature indolent – he works as little as possible.
2   He lacks ambition, dislikes responsibility, prefers to be led.
3   He is inherently self-centred, indifferent to organizational needs.
4   He is by nature resistant to change.
5   He is gullible, not very bright, the ready dupe of the charlatan and the demagogue.

The implications for management are:

1   Management is responsible for organizing the elements of productive enterprise – money, materials, equipment, people – in the interest of economic ends.
2   With respect to people, this is a process of directing their efforts, motivating them, controlling their actions, modifying their behaviour to fit the needs of the organization.
3   People must be persuaded, rewarded, punished, controlled, their activities must be directed.

Theory Y

1   People are not by nature passive or resistant to organizational needs. They have become so as a result of experience in organizations.
2   The motivation. The potential for development, the capacity to assume responsibility, the readiness to direct behaviour towards organizational goals, are all present in people. It is a responsibility of management to make it possible for people to reorganize and develop the human characteristics for themselves.
3   Management is responsible for organizing the elements of productive enterprise in the interest of economic ends. Their essential task is to arrange the conditions and methods of operation so that people can achieve their own goals best by directing their own efforts towards organizational objectives.

FIGURE 10.12   McGregor's Theory X and Theory Y (*source*: McGregor, D (1960) *The Human Side of Enterprise*, McGraw-Hill, New York).

- ✦ American organizations
  - ✦ short-term employment
  - ✦ explicit control processes
  - ✦ individual decision making
  - ✦ individual responsibility
  - ✦ segmented concern
  - ✦ quick promotion
  - ✦ specialized careers.
- ✦ Japanese organizations
  - ✦ lifetime employment
  - ✦ implicit control processes
  - ✦ collective decision making
  - ✦ collective responsibility
  - ✦ holistic concern
  - ✦ slow promotion
  - ✦ generalist careers.

From these profiles it is possible to identify a number of implications for motivational practice. Ouchi developed his Theory Z on motivation from the work of McGregor on Theories X and Y, suggesting that it would tend towards the Japanese profile, for example, adopting longer term employment contracts, but not as long as the Japanese (Ouchi, 1981).

Hofstede, Trompenaars and cultural influences on motivation

Hofstede (1980) introduced the impact of national culture into the debate about motivation. In his research he used the following framework to study the differences between 40 countries:

- ✦ Power distance. Reflects the degree to which a society accepts that organizational power is distributed unequally.

- ✦ Uncertainty avoidance. Reflects the extent to which a society feels threatened by uncertainty and ambiguity and actively seeks to minimize these situations.

- ✦ Individualism–collectivism. This reflects the underlying arrangement of society into a loose (everyone is responsible for themselves) framework; or an integrated, tight social arrangement involving collective responsibility.

- ✦ Masculinity. This reflects the degree of domination of society's values by 'masculine' characteristics.

In his research he put forward the idea that each of the theories of motivation reflected a particular set of cultural norms. As such they could be expected to be most effective in situations reflecting that particular cultural orientation. This introduces into the debate on motivation the notion that the wide range of theories available may not be mutually exclusive. His work has been subjected to heavy criticism recently, largely because his research was based on employees from a single company (IBM), the argument being that such an international group of people would have a high degree of commonality compared to representative members of the national groups researched. A more recent cultural perspective is offered by Trompenaars (1993) in which he offers seven different dimensions of national culture which could impact on organizational behaviour, including motivation. For example, some societies rely on achievement as a measure of success, whereas others favour ascription or favour based on age, experience etc.

Maccoby's social theory

A different approach to the concept of motivation is that offered by Maccoby (1988). He argues that the social and work environments have changed over recent years, particularly as a result of the growth of new technology. The effect of this has in practice invalidated the relevance of traditional approaches to motivation. He argues that a new motivation theory is needed, based not upon the *partial man* assumptions of Maslow, but specifically including concepts of trust, caring, meaning, self-knowledge and dignity. Emerging is a new type of worker, interested in self-development and motivated by opportunities for self-expression and career development, combined with a fair share of profit.

This approach to motivation, put more directly as getting the best out of employees, gains some credence in a review of business and management practice in *Management Today* in 1999. The main themes and arguments from that article are outlined in Management in Action 10.4.

Stop | Consider   *How would you reconcile the different points of view evident in MiA 10.4? Is the answer to utilize PR techniques in an attempt to disguise (or put a spin on) the real management purpose behind seeking to achieve high levels of motivation and performance?*

Performance management and motivation

The management of performance is a major issue for managers in the search for stable and high levels of productivity. One way of achieving this is through the achievement of a *controlled performance* from individuals. To see this in context, imagine a team sport where each member of the team played at their own speed, not delivering a consistent effort. The result would be a team that did not win many games. It is the same within organizations; managers continually seek to achieve operational *consistency*. Looked at as a model this can be seen as a process of managing a number of variables concerned with motivation, performance management and rewards (see Figure 10.13).

The model also reflects the cyclical process between motivation, reward, productivity and objectives. Taking each of the elements within the model in turn:

✦ Work environment. This refers to the physical circumstances in which the activities take place. The level of technology, methods of work used and equipment provided being examples.

✦ Ability. The skills and abilities that individual employees possess. This also reflects the organization's recruitment and selection processes along with its training and development provision.

✦ Clarity of objectives. If individuals are to be expected to achieve high levels of job performance they need to be provided with clear objectives. If the employee does not know what they are trying to achieve then anything will seem to be acceptable.

✦ Motivation to perform. This refers to the behavioural influences known as motivation.

MANAGEMENT IN ACTION 10.4

Can nice guys finish first?

The most common perspective on management is that it reflects hard-nosed, ruthless, aggressive and brutal decision making in pursuit of the highest level of profit that can be achieved. In effect business leaders are regarded as driven individuals determined to succeed at any cost. In Darwinian terms, the real survival of the fittest.

However, most chief executives when they are interviewed or provide material for research or magazine articles tend to describe their duties in terms of providing good working environments and looking after staff. For example, Peter Mead of Abbot Mead Vickers (a leading advertising agency) refused to retrench staff during the last recession and also refuses work associated with cigarette promotion. Michael O'Leary (CEO of Ryanair) gave staff share options worth £4 million when the airline was floated on the stock market. He is reported as saying that the style of a company should largely be dictated by the staff as this will ensure that they are valued, which in turn will lead to greater success (performance). The idea of 'niceness' is not new. For example in the 1970s JW Marriot, who founded the hotel chain of that name, was saying: 'You can't make happy guests with unhappy employees.'

There is even support from the sciences for the idea that niceness or co-operation between organisms could create advantage. Novak (a zoologist) and Sigmund (a mathematician) put forward the notion that doing good etc., even with no expectation of return (indirect reciprocity as they called it) could glean an advantage over more ruthless rivals. This was tested through a computer model that explored the ways in which groups developed, based on variation in co-operation and altruism levels. The model postulated that the level of 'niceness' would be reflected in the reputation of the individual among peers and consequently result in positive or negative stored goodwill. This would then be capable of being 'cashed in' at some time in the future to the

benefit (or detriment) of the individual. Those with a good reputation would gain befit. Conversely those with a bad reputation would suffer in the long run. Support for the model also comes from the animal kingdom with examples of 'niceness' among the Arabian babbler bird and the owl monkey for example.

However, there is also research that suggests that organisations need to be tough to survive. Silvestro reviewed the performance of a number of stores in a large grocery chain. She found that at individual store level, although employee satisfaction and loyalty were correlated, profitability and employee satisfaction were inversely correlated. Low employee satisfaction correlated with high profitability and vice versa. However, profit in stores is also strongly related to the size of the unit and this could also impact on a range of issues such as management style, closeness of supervision, workload, customer relationships etc, all of which would be expected to impact on expressed loyalty and 'happiness'. This research suggests even at its simplest level that commercial realities might force 'niceness' out of the situation, so that even if managers actively seek to care for employees the realities of organizational life might prevent it from happening.

Add to this the harsh effects of downsizing and delayering exercises on morale, trust and commitment, what Kakabadse refers to as the consequences of the 'survivor syndrome', and the scene is set for a real Darwinian process. Lynn refers to the resulting senior management attitude as being: 'Do what you can, but look after yourself first.' He concludes (rather cynically) with the view that perhaps the best strategy is to use public relations more effectively to bridge the gap between (or put a spin on) the two opposing *realities.*

Adapted from: Lynn, M (1999) Can nice guys finish first?, *Management Today*, February, pp 48–51.

The precise content of which depends upon the particular drivers, needs and motives active at the time.

✦ Job performance. This relates to the observable activity level delivered by the individual. It would encompass not only the pace of work but also the quality of output produced. Job performance is a function of individual level activity. This has to be linked with environmental elements (such as machines and computer systems actually working as intended) in order to produce achieved productivity.

✦ Intrinsic rewards. Intrinsic rewards are those that accrue to the individual as a direct result of the job itself. Rewards obtained in this way act as internal reinforcement. Consequently, there is a feedback loop to motivation from intrinsic rewards.

✦ Productivity. Productivity has been described as a relative term, a measure of conversion. Relative effectiveness in producing more goods for the same input of labour.

✦ Extrinsic rewards. Such rewards are generated from outside the job itself. The most obvious example being bonus schemes in which pay is based on output. These rewards are also intended to influence motivation and objectives. For an extrinsic reward system to be effective the individual must have a good knowledge of the basis of any reward, and hence clear objectives. (See Management in Action 10.5 for an example of the intention behind the use of extrinsic rewards.)

✦ Corporate objectives. The level of productivity achieved will determine to a significant extent the degree to which corporate objectives are achieved. This last element also refers to the guiding principles within the model. Consequently, motivational practices should be designed to encourage the delivery of things that are of value to the organization, based on corporate goals.

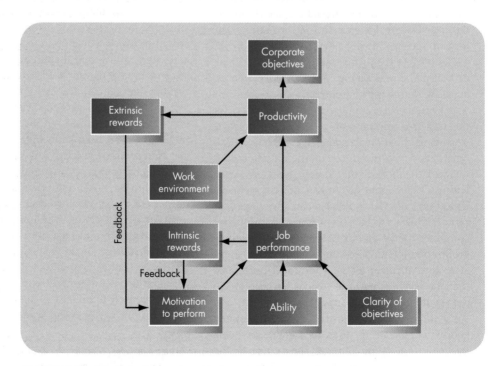

FIGURE 10.13 The links between motivation, performance and rewards.

MANAGEMENT IN ACTION 10.5

Extrinsic reward and service standards

The following quotation was taken from an insurance company report to policy holders.

Staff Developments
We believe that our staff are our most important resource and it is through their efforts that our service standards have been recognized with a plethora of awards. Using human resources effectively means recognizing and rewarding performance and we have, with this in view, introduced a performance-related pay system. Our system will reward achievement rather than awarding 'across-the-board' cost of living rises regardless of individual merit.

Taken from: Scottish Amicable policyholder's report, 1992.

Performance management as a process can be described as the links between a number of the boxes included in Figure 10.13. For example it seeks to provide feedback on actual performance achieved while impacting on factors such as ability (through the identification of development needs) and setting clear objectives about what is expected from the employee in the future (clarity of objectives). It reflects the management activities directly intended to motivate individual employees to improve their performance.

Organizations vary in the degree to which they attempt to plan for future performance. At the simplest level of planning the use of work study techniques to develop incentive schemes provides a basis for the determination of future performance. However this approach is based on the Taylorist notion of *one best way* and ignores the possibilities of *continuous improvement*. Other organizations use performance appraisal techniques in one form or another to assess individual contribution. Examples include 360° and team appraisal systems which seek to embrace a broad spectrum of measures in relation to individual or group performance. However, concern about the use of 360° feedback as part of a performance management process rather than as pure development has been expressed by writers such as Fletcher (1998).

Another approach found in many organizations over recent years is that based upon the concept of *competencies* (defined as 'behavioural dimensions that affect job performance' (Woodruffe, 1990, p 47). This approach seeks to encourage the consideration of personal development as the basis of future performance enhancement. Dulewicz (1989) indicates one set of competency clusters for middle management jobs based upon intellectual, interpersonal, adaptability and results orientation factors. Other writers suggest different competencies as the basis of what determines effective capability and performance for particular jobs. The application of competency frameworks seeks to identify and monitor the actual behaviours necessary for an individual to carry out their allotted tasks effectively. As such it retains the traditional (Taylorist) perspective of seeking to optimize the whole through optimizing the performance of the individual. Many of the motivation theories discussed in this chapter could be used in support of such approaches.

Although the competency approach has the advantage of being behaviour based it ignores much of the creative and team dimensions to many jobs. Motivation is consequently integral to the process of review and development as a means of the individual being encouraged to deliver what is expected of them. It is managers who dictate what behaviour is expected and also evaluate delivery. Subsequent access to career development opportunities is largely a function of management sponsorship, which in turn is heavily dependent upon being evaluated and documented as a 'worthy person' for such investment. As a consequence there are power, political and control (as well as performance and development) aspects to performance management processes. Figure 10.14 reflects the competency process in action along with an indication of the areas of motivational influence.

Kaplan and Norton (1996) proposed the use of a *balanced business scorecard* as the means to enable a review four major aspects of organizational performance. They are:

✦ Financial.
✦ Innovation and learning.

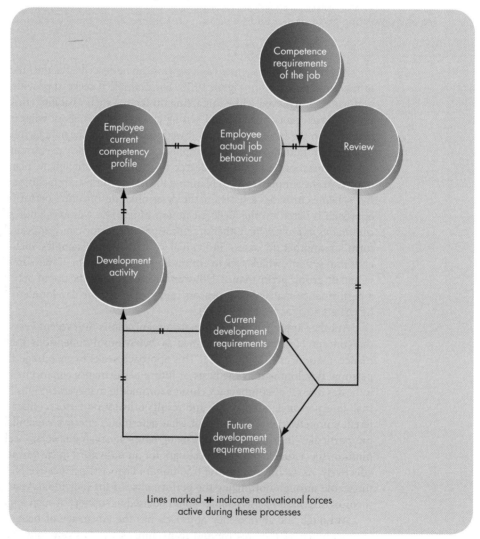

Lines marked ╫ indicate motivational forces active during these processes

FIGURE 10.14 Competency processes and motivation.

+ Internal processes.

+ Customers.

These macro level dimensions can form the basis of assessing the organization's performance relative to its objectives. This could subsequently form the basis of cascading downwards the organization level goals (with appropriate measures) and actual performance as part of the performance management process. In short, the performance of individuals needs to be seen as part of a broader process of organizational performance. This conception of performance is reinforced in recent research carried out by the Tavistock Institute which demonstrates that global pressure influences both organizational frameworks and the moves towards the need for high performance working (Stern and Somerlad, 1999). The Institute of Personnel and Development in association with the International Labour Organization (part of the UN) suggest that high performance working be defined in the following terms (Stevens and Ashton, 1999):

+ Sustained market success (or achievement of organizational objectives).

+ Innovation in quality and customer satisfaction (or product or service differentiation).

+ Customer and continuous improvement focus.

+ Use of self-managed work teams.

+ Viewing the workplace as a source of added value.

+ Clear links between training and development and organizational objectives.

+ Support for organizational and individual learning.

More recent developments in performance management systems and techniques are moving a considerable distance from the original notion of Taylor and the earlier motivation theorists. Also a richer, more complex understanding about the nature of work and what performance actually means is slowly emerging. The definition of high performance working described earlier is based on completely different assumptions about what performance means for the organization compared to that based on individual performance. The more recent work described seeks to take a more obviously *holistic* and top-down view of performance and the links with motivation. However, that in itself does not eliminate difficulties or problems. For example, improved understanding of motivation could provide managers with more control over employees, leading towards that aspect of the definition of the word *perform* introduced at the beginning of this chapter which talks of it being to 'execute tricks at a public show'!

Motivation and performance: an organizational perspective

Motivation is an individual level phenomenon. People as individuals are motivated to a particular degree on a scale running from not motivated to completely motivated (see Figure 10.15).

All motivation theories allow for the existence of cognitive processes. *Content theories* adopt the needs and wants perspective and *process theories* concentrate on the decision making that guides behaviour. The common factor with both categories is that individual behaviour is motivated towards the achievement of goals.

Motivation is based on *internal cognitive processes* that are not available for direct inspection. Consequently, in order to assess motivation inferences must be drawn from observable activity. Human beings are employed to undertake those things that the organization seeks, irrespective of personal wants or desires. This adds additional complexity to the use of the concepts of motivation and performance for a number of reasons:

✦ Managerial assumptions. Managers cannot be aware of why individuals are behaving as they are, so wrong assumptions may be made. For example, work behaviour will be subject to motivational forces from outside the organizational setting.

✦ Situational context. Employees who have never been given any degree of involvement in the organizational decision making may find participative management styles motivating. However, when memories begin to fade the basis of comparison will change. Employees will see participation as the norm and as a *frame of reference* against which to measure future events.

✦ Personal preference. Not all individuals actively seek increased levels of motivation at work. Some employees will see work as instrumental to support other aspects of their life. Lee and Lawrence (1985) suggest a four-factor model of decision-based motivation based on the goals sought, strategies adopted, coalitions formed and the power available through which to achieve the desired goals.

✦ Instrumentality. Managers can mistake instrumental behaviour for motivated behaviour. One survey showed that more than 40% of workers were worried about losing their jobs during the following 12 months (Summers, 1993). This might imply a compliant workforce, adopting an instrumental approach to work in co-operating with managers, thereby (hopefully) avoid losing their jobs.

✦ Bio-social basis of behaviour. The needs and wants held to underpin motivation are not themselves constructs that are problem free. In order to function biologically humans need certain things such as food and sleep. However, beyond these basic requirements, many needs are socially determined. For example, what type of food, how much quantity, how should it be cooked and served?

✦ Motivated to do what? What are employees being motivated to achieve? It could be argued that the organizational purpose of motivation is to *delight the customer*, but is that so? It could be argued that being completely customer focused might not be what managers seek. Consider the number of whistleblowers who have brought into the public domain aspects of unethical or even criminal activities within organizations. They are usually treated harshly by managers who would prefer to hide such activities. The customer is simply one of many stakeholders linked to an organization each with expectations and degrees of influence. Consequently, 'motivated to do what' is usually a reflection of that which has been determined by management.

FIGURE 10.15   The motivation scale.

✦ What is performance? Again this appears to be an easy question to answer, at least superficially. However, consider the university experience of students. What defines a high-performing lecturer? One who produces the highest marks among students, one who produces the most research or does performance mean something else? The answer lies in the definition of the purpose of a university. If a university exists to develop the intellectual capability of students then a different definition would emerge from that within a university which conceived its purpose as being to provide personal development for its students and different again from one which considered cutting-edge research to be its purpose. Management in Action 10.6 illustrates this point in relation to performance management within teaching.

Stop | Consider	*Is 'improvement in pupil performance' a real indicator of teacher performance as suggested in MiA 10.6? Why or why not?*
	MiA 10.6 suggests that approximately 5% of teachers are 'poor'. What might you think would be the consequences (and why) of allowing some or all of the other 95% to earn additional performance-related pay?

Society determines many aspects of life that are classified as a basic need. For example, televisions are now 'essential' to life compared with 30 years ago. A Marxist analysis would bring into question the basis of motivation grounded on '*needs*' that are socially constructed and which are then used as the basis of '*forcing*' individuals to increase their effort within the capitalist system. This, it would be argued, is a circular process in which the individual is trapped into meeting the ever increasing *needs* of the capital owners. A real *zero-sum* game! This results in the manipulation of both consumption and of work practice. It has been argued that motivation only became an organizational issue when meaning was lost from work: 'In consequence, motivation theories have become surrogates for the search for meaning' (Seivers, 1986).

It is reasonable to suggest that a motivated individual will feel a higher level of commitment to work. Indeed many recent management writers suggest that higher levels of *ownership* of the work done by employees is desirable. However, in that context ownership is taken (by managers at least) to refer to the task and a responsibility to produce high quality, not company ownership. There is, however, a problem for managers in this proposition in that individuals might claim *ownership* of the activity as a whole and attempt to divest management of its presumed right of control. Garrahan and Stewart (1992) provide a review of more recent motivational practices, such as teamworking, quality circles and company culture. These are practices frequently associated with Japanese organizations or European and US organizations attempting to emulate them. In their description, the negative impact on the individuals can clearly be identified through increased stress reported by some employees and descriptions of a take it or leave it style on management's part.

Motivation and performance: a management perspective

Increased productivity is the major management objective sought in an attempt to achieve corporate goals (at least according to the rational model of organizations). Motivation is a

MANAGEMENT IN ACTION 10.6

Could do worse

The British government has determined that it is essential for the future well-being of both the country and individual citizens for the standards of educational achievement to be raised. An excellent objective in its own right and not one that would be questioned here. However, what is of interest is the role of the teaching profession in that context and the performance management intentions that result from the basic objective.

The Chief Inspector of Schools has publicly said that in his opinion there are some 15,000 poor teachers. This represents approximately 5% of the total number of teachers employed in schools across the country. In order to impact on the basic objective of raising standards the government has determined that a significant part of the process requires an improvement in the performance of teachers. There are also other aspects of the government strategy, but these are outside the scope of this discussion. (One example, however, is a fast-track dismissal process for extreme cases of bad performance.)

The existing mechanisms of reviewing teacher performance are employee driven, in that every two years individual teachers have the opportunity to identify areas of competence that they wish to discuss. In performance management terms this represents a process of self-appraisal. To be effective the teacher carrying out the self-review would need to be prepared to interpret their own strengths and weaknesses in relation to the context in order to identify development needs. As with any form of performance appraisal such systems can work well or badly, depending upon a wide range of individual, managerial and organizational circumstances. However as Upton suggests:

> Many schools and authorities have recognised this approach to be a nonsense and have introduced performance management that includes direct observation of classroom performance. This allows the effective identifica-

tion of individuals' real training and development needs.

The proposals put forward by the government for the future performance management of teachers states that:

> We recognise that the demands on teachers are great and that most of them do a very good job. We want to be able to recognise and reward these people in ways that are not possible under the current system.

The proposed system will involve an annual appraisal of performance and target achievement. The setting of future targets will also be included, some of which will be linked to the school's objectives. In short a conventional top-down performance management system, intended to deliver what senior managers and the government define as performance. It is hoped (by Upton and others) that at least one of the objectives will be related to pupil performance in the form of 'improvement' rather than exam performance. Local school governors will be able to award additional salary increments to those producing exceptional performance (as measured across a number of criteria).

However, there are a number of underlying assumptions and traps included in such proposals that are not explicitly considered in the proposals as described. For example, what does higher educational achievement mean? Is it simply more qualifications passed or should it be measured in other ways? The annual debate about the lowering of examination standards when ever higher numbers of pupils achieve better grades is a reflection of another aspect of this debate. Some schools and teachers have been accused of giving hints or other indirect and subtle advantages to pupils simply as a way of improving 'apparent' pupil performance and hence positions in school league tables of achievement.

Another aspect of this debate concerns the application of rewards to enhance individual performance. There is the temptation to use the so-called 'sharp pencil' to falsely claim the achievement of performance when it has not actually been achieved (indirect help to pupils as described above for example), a phenomenon well understood over many years by factory managers. The term 'sharp pencil' originates from the practice of employees in factories using output-based bonus schemes to inflate the claimed level of production to receive more bonus. There are very strong individual and organizational pressures to take such actions. It is also apparent that teachers are not to be trusted to self-regulate their performance – that is why the system is being changed. So how can the dangers of manipulating performance be prevented other than through ever more complex administrative and checking procedures? These in turn produce a danger of diverting resources away from the very activity in which improvement is being sought.

Perhaps a more important dimension of this new process lies in the number of teachers eligible to be paid additional money for exceptional performance. If the new performance management system is effective then average performance should increase, eventually resulting in all teachers being regarded as exceptional and eligible for additional pay. This would cost vast sums of money and create more problems when most teachers are at the top of their pay scales. If only a proportion of teachers become eligible for an award the implication is that the threshold increases each year as performance generally improves, so making it harder to achieve each year. What happens to the performance of teachers told they have done well, but that the target has changed (or that others have done even better) and so they are ineligible for any additional money? Also can the government be sure of having the necessary money available to fund the process over the years?

Adapted from: Upton, L (1999) Could do worse, *People Management*, 25 March, p 35.

mechanism through which this is achieved and rewards are the device through which motivation can be triggered. In this way motivation can be seen as a manipulation to achieve management's goals. Management in Action 10.7 reflects the way in which many organizations see the links between corporate objectives and reward.

Stop | Consider *To what extent is profit level a reflection of a high-performance company or individuals?*

For managers there are a wide range of motivational options available. It could be argued that every aspect of the experience (real or perceived) in the workplace influences the motivation level of the people within it. Indeed this could be expanded to encompass events and situations outside the immediate working environment including:

✦ Family relationships and events. Crises at home can divert the energies of individuals for example.

✦ The local community. A win by the local football team can have beneficial effects, although the effect is far from certain, as Moreton (1993) suggests.

✦ Commercial environment. The closure of a competitor can help to secure the jobs in other organizations, as can economic effects such as changes in the exchange rate.

MANAGEMENT IN ACTION 10.7

Nice little earner

Profit sharing has been in existence for many years in one form or another. In the UK the government provided tax breaks for such schemes when it allowed up to £4000 of salary to be tax free, provided it was earned under an approved profit-related pay scheme. In the late 1980s very few schemes had been registered by the Inland Revenue, covering only about 100,000 employees. However, the popularity of such schemes grew rapidly and by 1993 approximately 1.2 million workers were covered by almost 5000 registered schemes. In the 1996 budget the government announced the phasing out over a number of years of the tax breaks associated with such schemes and so it is for the future to decide what the effect will be.

There is little doubt in the minds of many managers that an approach linking the commitment of employees to the financial interests of the company is an attractive option. Kellaway reports that in one accounting practice (Stoy Hayward) all but five of the 1000 employees indicated that they would like to participate in a profit-related pay scheme. Many other large organizations have opted to participate in these types of schemes, including Boots the Chemist, the Halifax Building Society and ASDA Property.

The original intention behind the introduction of profit-related pay schemes was that by linking pay to profit it effectively becomes a variable cost. Consequently, employees would be encouraged to work more effectively in pursuit of higher profit levels. In good times they would benefit from the additional reward. In bad times their pay would naturally fall in line with the lower profit (or even losses) achieved.

Some employers have designed schemes that pay a variable bonus (depending on the level of profit achieved) in addition to the basic salary. In

this approach the worst that can happen is that employees receive only their basic salary. No profit (or a loss) equates with no additional bonus. The other alternative, favoured by some as the way to achieve maximum impact from such schemes, is to transfer a proportion of existing pay to a profit-related basis. It is this last possibility, of allowing pay actually to fall, that has proved to be the controversial aspect of some profit-related pay schemes.

In a scheme that transfers a proportion of existing salary to a profit basis there can be attractive aspects for both parties. Assuming the scheme is designed to produce the same level of gross pay at current levels of profit then the employee will gain as a result of the tax-free nature of the profit-based pay. If profit levels rise then the employee will gain even more as the total level of pay will increase. However, should profit levels slip then the employee will find that their usual level of pay actually falls and they will take home less pay.

There are problems with the notion of profit-related pay from a number of directions. Those on low pay and with little or no tax liability would not benefit, for example. Some industries are notoriously volatile and would find it difficult to engage in the level of financial or profit planning necessary. Profit-based schemes are inevitably group in nature and in motivation terms the link between individual effort and profit level is remote in the extreme. Equally, employees can work much more efficiently, yet profits can fall due to market pressure, leading to a negative association being recognized between effort and pay.

Adapted from: Kellaway, L (1993) Nice little earner. *Financial Times*, 23 April, p 14.

Most of these would only be expected to have an indirect effect on motivation within an organization and then for only a relatively brief period. This illustrates the dynamic nature of much human behaviour, an issue not always apparent from particular motivation theories. Motivation is not something that is achieved and then fixed at that level. It is fluid, being subject to variation in the vast range of forces acting on the individual. This makes managing motivation difficult, as managers must be permanently sensitive to (and understand) their employees as individuals and adjust their own behaviour accordingly. Figure 10.16 seeks to reflect the processes involved in this circular and dynamic process. It also illustrates that managers are limited in the range of levers available to them in seeking to impact on the performance of employees.

Managers face major difficulties in attempting to motivate employees. To begin with, the construct of motivation is an abstract one. There are a number of theories offering a view on the nature and process of motivation but not all offer a realistic option for being able to motivate employees. Imagine attempting to apply the expectancy model calculation for each employee on a regular basis! Finally, managers individually do not have complete freedom to change company policy to a significant extent in order to personalize motivational opportunities. Although motivation is an individual level response, managers must maintain consistency in the treatment of employees across groups. It was to address this issue that the so-called *cafeteria* or *flexible* approach to employee *benefits* was developed, the idea being that individuals are able to pick and mix a personal benefits package, up to a set limit, from the total range available (Stock, 1992). In effect, a personalized pay

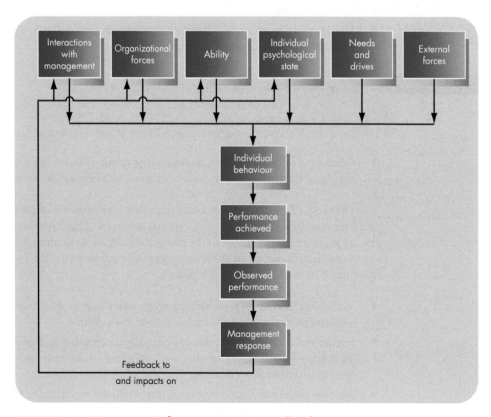

FIGURE 10.16   Management influence on motivation and performance.

package, intended to optimize the motivational effect from collective arrangements, was established.

Another difficulty facing managers is deciding which theory to follow. Each has something to offer and brings a slightly different perspective to bear on the subject. The theories discussed predominantly originate from a western (USA) culture and may not be valid in other cultural settings. The meaning of work, acceptance of ambiguity and power distance all could be expected to play a part in determining a cultural perspective to motivation, according to Hodgetts and Luthans (1990).

The options (or levers) available to managers with which to influence levels of motivation include:

✦ Pay levels and structures. Also the other terms and conditions of employment.

✦ Incentive schemes. Including monetary, gift and prizes. Hilton (1992) reviews the use of non-financial incentives as a motivation facilitator.

✦ Organizational factors. The structure, job design and the way in which employees are integrated into the business processes (for example, decision making) can be adjusted to influence motivation levels.

✦ Performance appraisal. There are many of these systems, including management by objectives – MBO techniques.

✦ Management style.

✦ Feedback, praise and punishment.

✦ Management by example. The letter in Management in Action 10.8 is an example of how one person feels about the example set by senior people.

Stop | Consider *Do you agree with the points made in MiA 10.8, and if so why?*
Would you agree with the points made if you were one of the senior managers receiving a high salary. Why or why not?

✦ Company policies. Including issues such as compassionate leave, equal opportunities, study and further education possibilities can all affect employee motivation.

The range of the motivation levers indicated is another set of issues that makes it difficult for managers to optimize motivational strategies. This basic complexity is increased further when interaction between the elements is taken into account. Managers do not have the opportunity to adjust all the levers potentially available, for the following reasons (see also Figure 10.16 in relation to this point):

✦ Availability. Not all organizations employ every option. Not every organization uses incentive schemes to reward higher output, for example.

✦ Freedom of action. Some levers are centrally determined and so individual managers do not have the freedom to alter the application. Company policies are not usually open to variation in application.

✦ Personal preference. Not every employee is equally amenable to the rewards on offer. For example, a young employee may be more interested in higher wages or career opportunities, whereas an older employee may be interested in pension benefits.

MANAGEMENT IN ACTION 10.8

Top managers should show the way in radical rethink on pay

The following letter is quoted from a national newspaper. It is clear that the writer feels strongly about the symbolism of pay levels at board and senior manager levels:

> Sir, Shares can go down as well as up, circulars from my bank and insurance company have warned me since the collapse of the 1987 financial 'bubble'. Can executive salaries do the same?
>
> I have followed the debate in your columns on the troubles of the financial sector. … Entirely missing has been the question of whether the disproportionate increase in top salaries of the early 1980s, justified on grounds of the quality of judgement of senior executives, should be reversed.
>
> I appreciate that a cut in remuneration for board members and general managers would contribute only a little to redressing the balance of bank reserves and profits. But such a signal that top management recognizes its share of the responsibility for the evident errors of the last decade, and is prepared to share in the cuts and added burdens of the 1990s as fully as it shared in the added profits of the 1980s would do much to rebuild the battered confidence of staff and customers.

> No such signal has yet been given.
>
> There is a wider point at issue. If the British economy is to hold low inflation – as bank economists exhort – attitudes to salaries throughout the economy have got to change radically.
>
> No stronger signal could be given of the acceptance of radical change than a reversal of the continuing trend for top salaries to increase.
>
> The Quaker families who laid the foundations for more than one of England's clearing banks understood the importance of gestures and symbols, and of demonstrating by the way they behaved the responsibilities they shouldered towards their fellow men. I fear that their descendants have lost sight of that sense of shared responsibility to the wider community. The impact on bank profits of a 10–20 per cent cut in board remuneration would be minimal. But think of the potential impact on the economy and on British society!

> William Wallace
> London

Taken from: Letters page in the *Financial Times*, 19 February, p 14.

◆ Variability. Employees vary each day in what will motivate them. These personal factors can be as simple as feeling unwell or perhaps feeling hostile to the organization as a result of a 'telling off' from the boss.

◆ Group norms. This and peer pressure can significantly influence the behaviour patterns of employees, irrespective of management's hopes and desires.

Management in Action 10.9 describes how one organization has attempted to link together several issues into a motivating process.

Stop | Consider

Does MiA 10.9 demonstrate that managers have a vested interest in certain types of motivation and performance management practice or does it demonstrate that they too need to be motivated? Justify your opinion.

MANAGEMENT IN ACTION 10.9

An encouraging start to employee motivation

There are many different approaches to the motivation of employees. Some companies attempt to achieve high levels of motivation through the use of payment systems and bonuses; others attempt to achieve it by encouraging staff to become involved in decision-making activities. One such company is Appor Ltd. This organization makes plastic soap dispensers, predominantly for its parent company, the Deb group.

The managing director, Martin Williamson, was himself motivated to attempt to involve and empower employees through a leadership course run by Heslegrave Gill, a firm of business consultants. The course was facilitated by the consultants who encouraged the use of discussion, business games and other activities to help groups of participants solve problems.

Back in Appor, Williamson had experienced the failure of quality circles as a result of their degeneration into 'dumping grounds' for problems. He began to develop a new approach to the way in which people worked by increasing the level of employee contribution and teamwork in pursuit of clearly understood common goals. A training strategy was developed that involved weekend residential training sessions run by Heslegrave Gill, which were open to all managers and employees who cared to attend. The intention was to demonstrate in a non-work environment that every individual had the ability to solve problems. A second weekend course was arranged that was intended to encourage the transfer of the confidence achieved at the first session into dealing with work-related issues.

Back in the factory, the progress made in the training weekends was not translated into positive action. Consequently, a specific event was organized in which the factory was stopped for one

half-day and people encouraged to identify problems that needed solving. Small teams were set up and sent away to work on the problem. Teams were allowed one hour each week to work on the problems that they were attempting to solve. The teams disbanded once the problems had been solved. If the expenditure of money was required to implement a solution approval from a line manager was necessary as they retained control of budgets.

Several other initiatives were also introduced in the company, including the circulation of company accounts and a profit-share scheme. Successful implementation of solutions by a team was rewarded by the opportunity to present their work to the whole company. All employees vote for the most innovative or successful solution and the winning team wins a small cash prize.

However, all has not been good news in the programme. The momentum generated by the scheme began to slow and managers would not always co-operate fully with the teams. Some managers felt threatened by the scheme and found it difficult to deal with empowered employees. All managers have been given training in leadership and motivation in order to encourage them to adapt to their new roles and adopt an open style of management. Some of the employees are also reluctant to participate fully as they find talking openly in teams or in public difficult. However, these problems, once identified, can be tackled through ongoing programmes intended to maintain involvement and motivation at a high level.

Adapted from: Arkin, A (1991) An encouraging start to employee motivation, *PM Plus*, April, pp 18–19.

Conclusions

Motivation is essentially an individual level response and yet managers must operate most of the time at a group level. Company policies and procedures have to be applied consistently if claims of inequity or injustice are to be avoided. This places a heavy burden on most managers as they attempt to increase the levels of performance among their employees by adopting both personal, collective and personalized collective methods.

The general conclusion, therefore, seems to be that motivation is a concept that may be intuitively attractive in explanatory terms and offer some opportunity for managers to enhance the nature and meaning of work for individuals. However, it is not possible to offer a definitive definition of the concepts of motivation or performance or how they should be used. They are social and political concepts as well as being psychological and technical in nature.

Discussion questions

1. Define the following key terms used in this chapter:

Motivation	*Maslow's theory*	*Adams' equity theory*
Drive	*Alderfer's theory*	*Attribution theory*
Extrinsic motivation	*McClelland's theory*	*Herzberg's theory*
Intrinsic motivation	*Content theories of*	*Vroom's theory*
Process theories of	*motivation*	*Porter and Lawler's*
motivation	*Locke's theory*	*theory*
Performance management		

2. Content theories of motivation offer a more realistic view of the concept in an organizational setting. Discuss.

3. If you were a manager, would you prefer to have your team extrinsically or intrinsically motivated? Why?

4. Motivation is best achieved through offering employees a monetary reward for working harder. Discuss this statement.

5. Are needs socially, physiologically or psychologically determined? What are the implications for motivation?

6. Discuss what performance means to the 'job' of being a student. If you were a lecturer how would you measure student performance and why?

7. What is motivation? Describe two theories of motivation and suggest where you think they might be most useful. Justify your answer.

8. To what extent would you agree that the concepts of motivation and performance simply reflect management processes intended to exercise more effective control over employees in support of a managerialist agenda.

9. It would be impossible for an organization fully to motivate all employees all the time. Discuss.

10. Compare and contrast one content theory of motivation and one process theory of motivation.

Research activities

1. Make arrangements to speak to a manager. This may be someone at your college or university or a friend of the family, perhaps even someone where you have worked during vacations. Find out from them what they understand about motivation and how they seek to motivate the people who work for them. Compare your findings with others in your class.

2. This is similar to activity 1, but this time based on the perceptions of a manual worker or someone who works in an office. Ask them what they understand by the term motivation. Also ask how they are motivated at work and how they would prefer to be motivated. Discuss your findings with others in your class and compare the ideas emerging with those from activity 1.

3. Return to Management in Action 10.1, 'Executives forced to buy slice of pie'. Imagine that you are the human resource manager of a large company and your managing director has just read this article. He has asked you to prepare a management report for him setting out a case for or against the adoption of this type of policy for your organization. Prepare a report that offers a conclusion and justify your views.

Key reading

From Clark, H, Chandler, J and Barry, J (1994) *Organization and Identities: Text and Readings in Organizational Behaviour*, International Thomson Business Press, London:
- Bell, D: Work and its discontents, p 44. It is against the backdrop of control that motivation forms a means of control of human activity.
- Maslow, AH: A theory of motivation, p 106. An introduction to one of the major motivation theories.
- Vroom, V: Motivation: a cognitive approach, p 125. An introduction to motivation by one of the leading researchers of his day.
- Thompson, EP: Time and work – discipline, p 216. This also provides a perspective on the organizational context within which motivation takes place.
- Taylor, FW: Scientific management, p 231. An introduction to the ideas from the pen of the original writer.
- Mayo, E: The work group and 'positive mental attitudes', p 237. This extract considers the influences within group activity that impact on output.
- Roethlisberger, FJ and Dickson, WJ: Group restriction of output, p 247. This provides another perspective on the Hawthorne research.
- Herzberg, F: Motivation through job enrichment, p 300. This provides another insight into aspects of motivation from the work of the original researcher.

Further reading

Anderson, GC (1993) *Managing Performance Appraisal*, Blackwell, Oxford. This text provides a practitioner's handbook on the subject of performance appraisal together with its links with pay, reward and development.

Flannery, TP, Hofrichter, DA and Platten, PE (1996) *People, Performance and Pay: Dynamic Compensation for Changing Organizations*, The Free Press, New York. Intended to review how pay and performnce practices can be lined up with modern organizational culture. Being practitioner oriented it does not explicitly analyze the underlying assumptions about motivation included in the discussion.

Garrahan, P and Stewart, P (1992) *The Nissan Enigma: Flexibility at Work in a Local Economy*, Mansell, London. This text reviews the establishment of a Japanese car assembly plant in the north-east of England. In doing so it provides an alternative insight into the group working activities operating within the plant. It also describes the nature of motivation, productivity and reward in that context.

Hartle, F (1995) *How to Re-Engineer your Performance Management Process*, Kogan Page, London. Seeks to explore the nature of performance management and it application across Europe and the USA as well as how to align the process with changing organizationanl frameworks and cultures. The text does not make explicit the links between motivation and performance, but assumes that the objective is to improve performance.

Sargent, A (1990). *Turning People On: The Motivation Challenge*, Institute of Personnel Management, London. Intended to be a practitioner's review of the main points associated with motivation. The book is designed to review the subject for managers and to prompt them into accepting the 'motivation challenge'. As such it is rather simplistic in its coverage of the material, but can serve as a useful summary and managers' guide.

Weiner, B (1992) *Human Motivation: Metaphors, Theories and Research*, Sage, Thousand Oaks. This text is described as a source book in the sphere of motivation theory. In that sense it incorporates a much greater level of detail than is possible in a single chapter. It offers an approach to motivation that places it in a social context.

References

Adams, JS (1965) Injustice in Social Exchange. In Berkowitz L (ed.) *Advances in Experimental Social Psychology*, Academic Press, London.

Alderfer, CP (1972) *Existence, Relatedness and Growth*, The Free Press, New York.

Armstrong, M and Murlis, H (1998) *Reward Management: A Handbook of Remuneration Strategy and Practice*, 4th edn, Kogan Page, London.

Baldamus, W (1961) Tedium and traction in industrial work. In Weir D (ed.) *Men and Work in Modern Britain*, Fontana, London.

Barnard, CI (1938) *The Functions of the Executive*, Harvard University Press, Cambridge, MA.

Blackburn, RM and Mann, M (1979) *The Working Class in the Labour Market*, Macmillan, London.

Campbell, JP and Pritchard, RD (1974) Motivation Theory in Industrial and Organizational Psychology. In Dunnette M (ed.) *Handbook of Industrial and Organizational Psychology*, Rand McNally, Chicago, IL.

Currie, R (1963) *Work Study*, Pitman, London.

Deci, EL (1971) The efforts of externally mediated rewards on intrinsic motivation, *Journal of Applied Psychology*, **18**, 105–15.

Dornstein, M (1989) The fairness judgements of received pay and their determinants, *Journal of Occupational Psychology*, **64**, 287–99.

Dulewicz, V (1989) Assessment centres as the route to competence, *Personnel Management*, **21**, 11, November, 56–9.

Early, PC, Northcraft, CL, Lee, C and Lituchy, TR (1990) Impact of process and outcome feedback on the relation of goal setting to task performance, *Academy of Management Journal*, March, 87–105.

Erez, M, Early, PC and Hulin, C (1985) The impact of participation on goal acceptance and performance: a two-step model, *Academy of Management Journal*, March, 50–66.

Fletcher, C (1998) Circular argument, *People Management*, Institute of Personnel and Development, 1 October, pp 46–9.

Foucault, M (1977) *Discipline and Punish: The Birth of the Prison*, Allen Lane, London.

Garrahan, P and Stewart, P (1992) *The Nissan Enigma: Flexibility at Work in a Local Economy*, Mansell, London.

George, CS (1972) *The History of Management Thought*, 2nd edn, Prentice Hall, Englewood Cliffs, NJ.

Herzberg, F. (1974) *Work and the Nature of Man*, Granada Publishing, London.

Herzberg, F, Mousener, B and Synderman, BB (1959) *The Motivation to Work*, 2nd edn, Chapman & Hall, London.

Hilton, P (1992) Using incentives to reward and motivate employees, *Personnel Management*, September, 49–52.

Hodgetts, RM and Luthans, F (1990) International Human Resource Management: Motivation and Leadership dimensions. In *International Human Resource Management Review*, Vol. 1.

Hofstede, G (1980) Motivation, leadership and organization: do American theories apply abroad?, *Organizational Dynamics*, Summer, 42–63.

Hollenback, J (1979) A matrix method for expectancy research, *Academy of Management Review*, **4**, 579–87.

Hollway, W (1991) *Work Psychology and Organizational Behaviour*, Sage, London.

Jones, FF, Scarpello, V and Bergmann, T (1999) Pay procedures – what makes them fair?, *Journal of Occupational and Organizational Psychology*, **72**, 129–45

Kaplan, RS and Norton, DP (1996) *The Balanced Scorecard: Translating Strategy into Action*, Harvard Business School Press, Boston.

Kelly, HH (1971) *Attribution in Social Interaction*, General Learning Press, Morristown.

King, N (1970) A clarification and evaluation of the two-factor theory of job satisfaction, *Psychological Bulletin*, **64**, 18–31.

Law, KS, and Wong, CS (1998) Relative importance of referents on pay satisfaction: a review and test of a new policy-capturing approach, *Journal of Occupational and Organizational Psychology*, **71**, 47–60.

Lee, R and Lawrence, P (1985) *Organizational Behaviour: Psychology at Work*, Hutchinson, London.

Locke, EA (1968) Towards a theory of task motivation and incentives, *Organizational Behaviour and Human Performance*, **3**, 157–89.

Locke, EA (1976) The Nature and Causes of Job Satisfaction. In Dunnette M (ed.) *Handbook of Industrial and Organizational Psychology*, Rand McNally, Chicago, IL.

Maccoby, M (1988) *Why Work: Motivating and Leading in the New Generation*, Simon & Schuster, New York.

Maslow, AH (1943) A theory of human motivation, *Psychological Review*, **50**, 370–96.

Maslow, AH (1987), *Motivation and Personality*, 3rd edn, Harper & Row, New York.

McClelland, DC (1961) *The Achieving Society*, The Free Press, New York.

McGregor, D (1960) *The Human Side of Enterprise*, McGraw-Hill, New York.

Moreton, A (1993) Linking sport with productivity, *Financial Times*, 19 February, 12.

Ouchi, WG, (1981) *Theory Z: How American Business can Meet the Japanese Challenge*, Addison-Wesley, New York.

Patterson, S and Smith, P (1998) How to make top people's pay reflect performance, *The Sunday Times, Business*, 9 August, p 12.

Porter, LW and Lawler, EE (1968) *Managerial Attitudes and Performance*, Richard D Irwin, Homewood, IL.

Schermerhorn, JR, Hunt, JG and Osborn, RN (1982) *Managing Organizational Behaviour*, John Wiley, New York.

Seivers, B (1986) Beyond the surrogate of motivation, *Organization Studies*, **7**, 4.

Shalley, C, Oldham, G and Porac, J (1987) Effects of goal difficulty, goal setting method, and expected external evaluation on intrinsic motivation, *Academy of Management Journal*, September, 553–63.

Stern, E and Somerlad, E (1999) *Workplace Learning, Culture and Organisational Performance*, Tavistock Institute/Institute of Personnel and Development. London.

Stevens, J and Ashton, D (1999) Underperformance appraisal, *People Management*, Institute of Personnel and Development, 15 July, p 31–2.

Stock, J (1992) Introducing flexible benefits, *Institute of Manpower Studies*, Report No. 231.

Summers, D (1993) Fear of unemployment still high, *Financial Times*, 4 May, 18.

Taylor, FW (1947) *Scientific Management*, Harper & Row, New York.

Townley, B (1994) *Reframing Human Resource Management: Power, Ethics and the Subject at Work*, Sage, London.

Trompenaars, F (1993) *Riding the Waves of Culture*, Nicholas Brealey, London.

Vroom, VH (1964) *Work and Motivation*, John Wiley, New York.

Wiersma, UJ (1992) The effects of extrinsic rewards in intrinsic motivation: a meta analysis, *Journal of Occupational and Organizational Psychology*, **65**, 101–14.

Woodruffe, C (1990) *Assessment Centres: Identifying and Developing Competence*, Institute of Personnel Management, London.

Wren, D (1987) *The Evolution of Management Theory*, 3rd edn, John Wiley, New York.

Communication, decision making and negotiation

CHAPTER SUMMARY

This chapter introduces the three closley related concepts of communication, decision making and negotiation. Both decision making and negotiation require communication to take place. In addition, negotiation represents a forum in which decisions are made. Most of the behaviour that takes place within an organization contains aspects of the three activties discussed in this chapter. Company objectives must be communicated to employees if they are to understand what they are to achieve; managers must decide on the priority to give to particular customer orders; managers must negotiate with other managers over budget allocations for example. The chapter begins with a review of the relationship between each of these concepts and organizations. It then moves on to consider each concept in detail. The discussion examines the nature of each concept, its theoretical basis and its significance within an organizational setting. This is followed by a critical assessment of the implications of each and the management perspectives on them.

LEARNING OBJECTIVES

After studying this chapter and working through the associated Management in Action panels, Discussion questions and Research activities, you should be able to:

✦ Outline the concepts of communication, decision making and negotiation.

✦ Describe communications, illustrating the process involved and the media options available.

✦ Explain how decision making takes place, differentiating between programmed and non-programmed decisions.

✦ Understand how communications, decision making and negotiation are linked together.

✦ Appreciate the organizational significance of communication, decision making and negotiation.

✦ Discuss how communication, decision making and negotiation link to other chapters in this book.

✦ Detail how principled negotiation is intended to achieve a satisfactory and consistent result for all parties.

✦ Assess the organizational significance of communications, decision making and negotiation.

Introduction

Communications, decision making and negotiation are fundamental aspects of everyday life for all employees and all organizations. *Communications* is a process of information and influence. One definition states that communication in an organizational context, 'is an evolutionary, culturally dependent process of sharing information and creating relationships in environments designed for manageable, goal-oriented behaviour' (Wilson *et al.*, 1986, p 6). *Decision making* as a process represents a means of selecting a particular course of action from among the many options available. *Negotiation,* by the same token, broadly reflects a process of difference reduction through agreement between individuals and groups who have mutually dependent needs and desires. Kennedy (1999) defines negotiation as, 'the process by which we obtain what we want from somebody who wants something from us' (p 14). The notion of compromise as the basis of negotiation is something that Kennedy argues against because it obscures the essential 'exchange' purpose of the process.

There are strong links between these three activities in a very particular way within an organizational context. Not every act of *communication* involves decision making or negotiation. *Decision making*, however, requires a flow of information to make it effective. Every *negotiation* also requires communication and decision making as part of the process. For example, a company may automatically communicate its annual results to employees without a specific decision being implied as a consequence. However, a production manager cannot make a decision on which orders to make without information on priority, capacity and raw material availability. During the annual wage negotiations between managers and trade unions communication between the parties on issues such as desires, expectations and ability to pay are the basis of exploring possible solutions and ultimately decisions on what will determine an acceptable agreement. The one-way hierarchical relationship between these concepts implied by this discussion is reflected in Figure 11.1

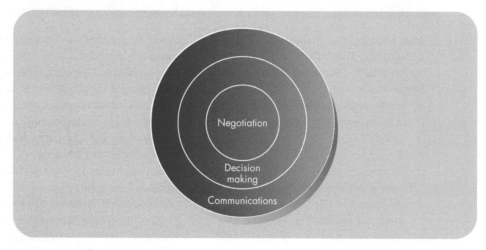

FIGURE 11.1   The one-way hierarchy.

Communications within organizations

Communication differs from the simple passing of information from one person to another in that it implies the two-way process. Sitting in front of a television set watching a news programme is not a process of communication, it reflects *information transmission* because there is no direct interaction involved. Individuals may think about, or discuss some of the news items with other people, or even shout at the television screen, but the direct link with the presenters and producers does not exist. The nature of communications within organizations is reflected in Figure 11.2.

Figure 11.2 also includes an element of external communications within the model. This reflects the actuality of communications in that individuals engage in a considerable degree of communication with organizations and groups outside of their own. For example, suppliers, government departments, customers, professional associations and competitors all have business-related communications links with an organization. In addition to the formal links implied in Figure 11.2, there exists a wide range of other *formal* and *informal communication* networks that exist both in and around any organization. For example, friendship groups within th company. In addition, all employees communicate with family members and friends and some of this interaction will contain an organizational dimension or relevance. In one form, this could involve an employee describing their feelings about work to family or friends; in another, it could involve an employee selling company secrets to a competitor. These links could also involve an employee filling in a tax return setting out their earnings from employment together with other forms of income. This combines company and private issues in a communication with an outside agency that will also receive information from the income sources identified as a verification. All of the communication links indicated may contain various degrees of association with organizations, both formal and formal. It is possible to summarize these aspects of communication in two dimensions. One relates to the degree of formality involved. This reflects the distinction between what might be termed the business need. Formal being associated with the commercial activities of the organization and informal to do with matters involving the organization but not in a business sense (expressions of attitude,

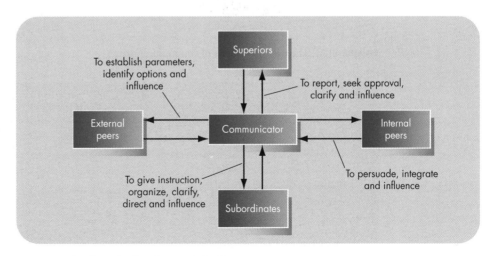

FIGURE 11.2   Organizational communications.

feeling or opinion etc.). The second dimension relates to direct and indirect aspects of the communication process. So, for example, the organization would be directly involved in communicating to its customers, but only indirectly involved with an individuals's tax affairs. These two dimensions can be reflected as a diagram (Figure 11.3) along with an illustration of what form of communication might fall in each quadrant.

Organizations are complex entities, the larger ones exceedingly so. This is reflected in many aspects of organizational activity, including communications. Complexity in communication is an exponential function of the number of people involved. Consider the possible number of interaction combinations in an organization consisting of just five people (see Figure 11.4).

There are ten channels between the five people in Figure 11.4, reflecting the number of communication possibilities. Any particular episode could be initiated by either party which increases the number of directional channels to 20. Now consider the number of channels of communication possible in a company of 2000 people, even recognizing that not every individual needs (or even desires or has the opportunity) to communicate with every other individual. In addition to the vast number of individual communication links there are the large number of groups that exist within an organization and which need to communicate with other individuals and groups. Clearly, in large organizations the communication process needs to be managed carefully if total chaos is to be avoided. There are many ways in which organizations seek to achieve this in practice, including:

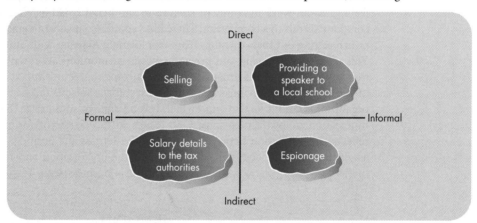

FIGURE 11.3 The two dimensions of communications.

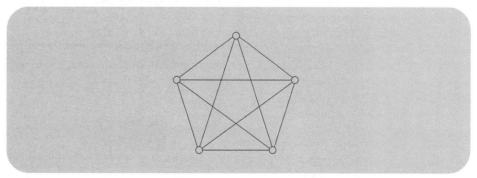

FIGURE 11.4 Communication channels.

✦ Limitation. Not every employee would be expected to interact with every other member of the company. This is achieved through a number of organizational *devices* including hierarchical and departmental structures.

✦ Procedure. The development of appropriate procedural arrangements sets out to ensure that only *appropriate* information is circulated to those individuals needing it (or with an assumed right to access it).

✦ Teamwork. The use of teams and committees attempts to simplify communications through the use of *representatives* and by *concentrating* the communications on relevant issues at specific times.

✦ Automation. The use of *electronic media* for the transmission of information increases the opportunity for easier communications.

✦ Separation. The identification of activities that require communication and those which can be *designated* as information flow. For example, employee communications is often separated into categories such as newsletters (one way) and formal meetings between employee representatives and human resource managers (two way).

Management in Action 11.1 provides an illustration of how the direct shopfloor experience of one senior manager changed a number of company policies. This example illustrates how even in large, supposedly customer-focused business such as supermarkets, the chief executive can become isolated from the experience of the staff actually delivering the customer service and, therefore, from the customers themselves. It also demonstrates the significance of informal communications at the workplace.

Stop | Consider

Do you consider it inevitable that a chief executive such as Mr Adriano cannot know the level of detail about their company that would have allowed him to have prior knowledge of the existence of the one aisle and no talking policy? Justify your answer.

Decision making within organizations

There are many areas of decision making from the minor short-term to the major long-term commitment of capital resources. Decisions are taken by all levels of employee within the organization. For example, word-processor operators have to decide upon the sequence for processing allotted tasks. At the other extreme, the board of directors will have to consider issues such as the construction of new factories and launching of new products. The major distinction between these two types of decision making being the *scale* of the decision and the *timeframe* for the impact of it.

At the lower levels within the organization, decisions tend to be focused on immediate events involving the sequence of activities and the use of current resources in order to achieve the desired daily/weekly output. For example, a supervisor in a factory will constantly monitor the flow of work in order to divert people to bottlenecks or to adjust production to achieve the best output every day. At a senior level, the directors may only review the financial results of the company every quarter. The rest of the time they may consider issues such as the implications of industry news about trends etc. on the *strategic development* of the company. However, even senior managers are involved in relatively small

MANAGEMENT IN ACTION 11.1

Back to the floor

'Back to the floor' is the name of a television programme in which chief executives are invited to work for a week on the shopfloor of their organizations, accompanied by a television crew. The experience is inevitably a difficult one for the individual chief executive as they must work alongside ordinary employees many levels below them in the hieracrchy, subordinate themselves to junior managers and perform often physical tasks for a full week. In addition, the camera crew follows every move, picking up every mistake and obvious lack of knowledge on the part of the boss. The benefits of a senior manager experiencing life at the sharp end of the business can be imagined, but why they would wish to subject themselves (and their organizations) to scrutiny (and humiliation) by television in the process must raise questions about the decision-making capabilities of such managers or at best their show-business motives.

One such programme transmitted in October 1999 by the BBC involved Dino Adriano, the chief executive of Sainsbury's (a large British supermarket chain) becoming a shelf stacker and checkout operator for a week. Among the surprises that lay in store for Mr Adriano in his new work role was finding that one company policy required each night shift shelf stacker to work in a separate aisle and not to talk to colleagues. The effect of this was to isolate each employee from other people (other than their boss) except during meal breaks. As one such worker told him: 'We are the forgotten army of the company. It can be very lonely working for ten hours a night on on your own and not being allowed to talk to anyone.' Not

surprisingly, Mr Adriano was shocked by this discovery and the policy was scrapped immediately. The point being that even with all the communication that exists between levels of management within the company and the presence of specialist personnel staff, the top boss was not aware of the existence, consequences or impact of this particular policy.

Another aspect of communications occurred as Mr Adriano ate his meals in the canteen with the ordinary staff on duty at the time. Among the general observations and comments made regarding the employee views of the company and its management, one employee asked how much he was paid. The employee then commented dryly that at £500,000 it was very large compared with their own salary at £9000. Such conversations required Mr Adriano to be skilled at communicating with the staff concerned in order both to handle the situation in the short term and maintain his credibility after the temporary secondment when he once again became chief executive. Also, with a careless comment he could have directly undermined the position of the many store and specialist managers in the company. Being the boss he could easily have changed many aspects of activity and work practice during his experience. So he had a balance to strike in order to benefit the company and improve its public relations (or at least not make it worse) while learning from the experience.

Based on: 'Back To The Floor', BBC2, 28 October 1999.

---

decisions. For example, Mr Adriano, the Chief Executive of Sainsbury's had to decide whether or not to participate in the television programme described in Management in Action 11.1. In such cases the decision to appear in public may appear small by comparison to some of the large financial decisions made, but they could have significant and fundamental consequences if they go wrong. For example, if Sainsbury's did not have any editorial influence over the making of the 'Back To The Floor' programme, it could have been used to make Mr Adriano look foolish and incompetent, perhaps adversely impacting on customer perception of the company, a loss of sales along with a steep fall in share price.

At senior levels business decision making can involve many facets and take considerable time. It is reported that Margaret Thatcher began to court Japanese business leaders in the mid-1970s, well before she became British prime minister. Her approach to them being that when (in the future) she was elected prime minister she could be trusted to create an appropriate business climate for them in Britain. It was approximately ten years after this level of approach that Nissan became one of the early Japanese companies to invest in large-scale production facilities in the north-east of England (Garrahan and Stewart, 1992).

The foregoing discussion also illustrates the third property associated with decision making within organizations, that of *risk*. Generally speaking, the larger the decision and the longer timescale involved the greater the degree of risk associated with it. For example, consider the options facing a medium-sized bank if it wants to become a large organization. Although there are many options available, the main ones are either to open a large number of new branches or to take over a competitor and gain size through the additional resources acquired. There are considerable dangers in either approach. The cost and refurbishment of new outlets will be high and training of new staff will take time. The level of additional business gained may not justify the additional expenditure, but this may not become apparent for some considerable time. With a takeover (or merger) there are also many difficulties to be resolved. For example, overlap in customers and retail outlets, duplication in management and incompatible computer systems are just some of the issues to be addressed. The end result may be that the growth achieved will not equal the business levels of the two separate organizations or the cost of the merger.

The three elements associated with decision making are reflected in Figure 11.5.

Negotiating and organizations

Many of the employees within an organization are involved in negotiations in one form or another for much of their time. Negotiations are frequently considered to be restricted to

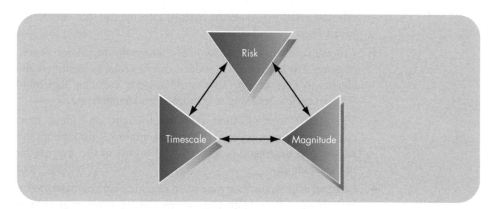

FIGURE 11.5 Dimensions of decision making.

circumstances when industrial relations problems are to be solved or commercial contracts and money are exchanged. However, if *negotiation* is defined in terms of the *resolution of difference,* the *exchange of 'something' mutually sought* by both parties and the *making of agreements*, then it assumes a much broader significance in organizational activity.

Negotiations can take place either formally or informally. The annual negotiations between managers and trade unions over rates of pay and negotiations over the terms to be included in a sales contract are typical *formal negotiations*. Informal negotiations take place every day between people at all levels within the organization. For example, the sales director of a company might seek to *persuade* the production director to change the priority on a particular order. To do so an *informal negotiation* might take place in which mutually acceptable compromises (or exchange of 'value') would be explored and agreed over a cup of coffee. Equally, two colleagues may *negotiate* informally every day over who should collect the post from the main office. Other tasks to be done over the day might be *traded* as part of the process.

Management in Action 11.2 provides an example of the scope of formal negotiations and the links with other business decisions.

Stop | Consider

> *Why does negotiation play a part in the process described in MiA 11.2? Why would managers seek to negotiate such issues with employees rather than simply decide an appropriate course of action and then communicate the decision to the staff?*

Communications

Figure 11.6 reflects the main interaction networks that form the basis of communication for managers. In addition to the work-related internal and external network reflected in Figure 11.6, managers will (in common with other employees) be part of friendship and family-based frameworks.

Communication serves four general functions within an organization:

✦ Information processing. Communication is more than the simple transmission of information. Data will be collected and turned into information that has meaning and purpose. The ability of individuals to create and share information is what generates effective activity. It is on the basis of information that decisions and planning can be undertaken.

✦ Co-ordination. Communication also allows the integration of activity within the organization. For example, if a sudden drop in sales is identified all departments can be alerted to take action. This could include reducing expenditure, cutting output, product review, speaking to customers and bankers, etc.

✦ Visioning. Communication expresses thoughts and ideas. It is a process that can convey vision, mission and strategies to employees throughout the organization. It can also help in shaping the organizational culture of the organization by creating shared understandings.

✦ Personal expression. Everyone in an organization will have their own views and opinions about work and non-work issues. These include opinions about the products and services offered, the individuals that manage the organization and how the company

MANAGEMENT IN ACTION 11.2

Unions agree to staff cuts at Aer Lingus

Decision making between senior managers and trade union officials frequently involves some tough negotiating. Events in Aer Lingus late in 1993 demonstrate this complexity very clearly. Aer Lingus is the state-run airline in the Irish Republic and had been suffering financial difficulties in the increasingly competitive and deregulated airline business. In the financial year ending March 1993 the company posted pre-tax losses of I£190.7m on a turnover of I£817m. Some progress in dealing with these problems was made and later in 1993 losses had been reduced to about I£1.2m per week.

Clearly, this situation could not be allowed to continue and steps were taken to mount a rescue plan. This involved cutting costs within the company and an injection of equity from the government. The savings within the company were to include a reduction of I£21m in the airline's payroll costs and I£15m in non-labour overheads. The equity injection of I£175m from the government was conditional on the airline achieving a total cost saving of I£50m.

In people terms this plan required the airline to reduce its headcount by 800 from a total of 5500 people. The management argued during negotiations with the trade unions that of the 800

people who had volunteered for redundancy only 300 could be released unless radical changes in working arrangements were also agreed. Mr Paul O'Sullivan, the trade union officer representing staff in the company, indicated that the negotiations were the most difficult and tough that he had been engaged in. He said that it was, 'heartbreaking' to negotiate over job losses on such a scale. He also indicated that the changes to working arrangements being asked of the workforce were vast, but that they were necessary to the survival of the company. The deal struck between the company and trade union needed to be agreed by staff through a secret ballot before it could be implemented.

To make the negotiation process even more complex there was an outstanding pay claim to be determined. As part of the proposals over job losses and work reorganization an agreement to go to arbitration was included in order to examine the management's claim that it could not afford any pay increases.

Adapted from: Coone, T (1993) Unions agree to staff cuts at Aer Lingus, *Financial Times*, 2 November, p 27.

compares with other employers. Individuals at all levels will also have opinions on the way in which the company is run. Understanding these *attitudes* and *feelings* is an important aspect of management activity. Indeed attempts to shape employee attitudes and feelings form a not insignificant focus for much internal company communications. This is the basis of the *social partnership* approach to engaging employees in a form of management–worker relationship supposedly based on mutual commitment, understanding and respect so much talked about today. For a review of this process in action within the Rover Group see Whitehead (1999). For a review of the trade union perspective on this process and the associated so-called *sweetheart deals* (in which employers select the trade union to which their employees will belong) see Walsh (1999). It has been argued that this dimension to communication and involvement is intended to provide managers with an ability to manage (or manipulate) employees more effectively rather than involve for altruistic reasons, which is why it is so much in vogue.

The methods of communication that occur within organizations include:

✦ Written. The use of memos, letters and reports are the chief means of communicating through this medium. In addition, there are the company procedures, the majority of which will be committed to writing.

✦ Oral. Individuals interact with each other in a variety of ways within organizations. Meetings to discuss important items involve considerable oral communication. Less formal interactions also take place frequently. For example, an administration assistant may telephone the accounts department to query a particular entry in the weekly budget report.

✦ Non-verbal. There are a host of non-verbal communication signals that accompany interaction and which provide interpretative information between the individuals involved. Examples include tone of voice, body posture and spatial positioning. For example, the seating arrangements can set the tone for a meeting. Sitting across the corner of the desk (Figure 11.7A) provides a less *threatening* layout than sitting across the desk (Figure 11.7B). The physical environment in which an individual works can also provide powerful clues to the authority of that particular person

✦ Electronic. With an increase in the availability and sophistication of electronic devices the opportunity to communicate in novel ways has emerged. The ability to use electronic mail instead of written memos, teleconferencing in place of face-to-face meetings and the use of the fax machine to send written information have all changed the nature of much communication. Management in Action 11.3 provides a review of the uses for electronic mail. Along with the emergence of road and other forms of rage that of *mail rage* is emerging in which individuals can find themselves being abused

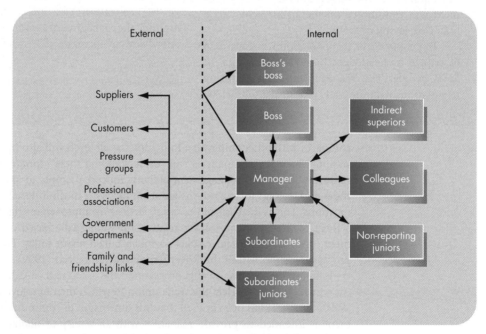

FIGURE 11.6   The manager's communication network (*adapted from*: Hellriegel, D, Slocum, JW and Woodman, RW (1989) *Organizational Behaviour*, 5th edn, West Publishing, St Paul, MN).

and threatened through e-mails. This has led some people to suggest a form of communication online that differs from conventional written communication as well as limitations on the volume of such communication in an attempt to limit the dangers.

Is the provision of more communication (as possible through the increasing use of electronic media) a good thing and, if so, from whose perspective?

The communication process

The process of communication is a social activity involving two or more people across time. Figure 11.8 reflects the essential nature of this process and it should be noted that it is circular. The process involves the sender initiating a communication sequence with the receiver responding and providing feedback to the originator, thus beginning an iterative process.

Taking each element described in the model:

✦ Source/receiver. This part of the communication process represents the originator (or group of people) who initiates an exchange. For example, in a discussion between a manager and subordinate it would be the manager's opening remarks about its purpose.

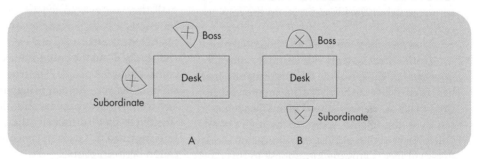

FIGURE 11.7   Seating arrangements for effect.

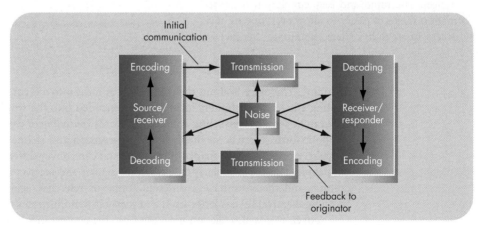

FIGURE 11.8   The communication loop (*adapted from*: Moorhead, G and Griffin, RW (1992) *Organizational Behaviour*, 3rd edn, Houghton Mifflin, Boston, MA).

MANAGEMENT IN ACTION 11.3

Secret messages

Electronic mail (e-mail) is now a very common means of communication between individuals and organizations. It is not uncommon to find 'state-of-the nation' messages from the chief executive being circulated to all employees via the e-mail system. It has also been known for individual managers to inform employees of their annual pay increase by e-mail, rather than through a face-to-face meeting.

There are many positive benefits obtainable through the application of an e-mail system. Companies can ensure that suppliers and customers have all the information necessary to achieve instantaneous and smooth operation with a satisfactory exchange of product. The rate of increase in e-mail traffic is estimated to be approximately 19% a year, based on the number of new users.

However, there are also many potential problems with e-mail systems. For example, one executive was caught spreading false information that had been deliberately placed in another executive's mailbox. He was moved to another job as a result of the 'illegal' access to another's mail. Disciplinary action against the abusers of access to e-mail files is growing in response to this type of situation. Information overload is another real danger. The rapid and easy circulation of information makes it easier to allow everyone to have access to it, rather than attempt to channel or

direct it. Many people receive information that they do not need or want in order to be able to do their work effectively. Some companies have introduced bulletin boards for less essential and general circulation information. Others have attempted to 'manage' the flow, route and timing of data in the system.

The possibilities for subordinates to communicate directly with senior managers through the e-mail represents just one of the cultural differences that has resulted from the introduction of this form of technology. Before its introduction the existence of a secretary could protect a boss from being disturbed by subordinates. With e-mail they are able to bypass these gate-keeping functions easily. Some organizations seek to restrict the use of e-mail and electronic data interchange (EDI) on the grounds that they restrict the contact between people. The true interaction possibilities between human beings are missing from any form of electronic communication and it is suggested that ultimately the organization is impoverished if it does not encourage communication between people.

Adapted from: Simon, B (1994) Secret messages, *Financial Times*, 28 February, p 13.

♦ Encoding. This stage is about the conversion of ideas into a form for transmission. In sending a letter to customers ideas must be encoded into the words on paper before they can be sent. In converting an idea into words (*encoding* or expressing the ideas in symbolic form) there is inevitably a loss of precision and richness from the original thought. Words also have shades of meaning and can convey different things to different people. This is particularly true when the sender and receiver come from different cultures and therefore have a different frame of reference against which to judge meaning. Figure 11.9 is a letter from a newspaper that illustrates this point.

Spoken words also take on meaning from the context in which they are used and the non-verbal cues that accompany them. For example, 'can I help you?' said with a sneer conveys a totally different meaning from when it is said with a smile.

◆ Transmission channel. This reflects the actual *channel* of communication chosen to convey the message from sender to receiver. In speaking it is sound waves, in written communication it is words on paper and electronically it is radio waves or electrical impulses. The choice of medium may involve more than one conversion of form. The use of the telephone involves the transmission of speech into the mouthpiece, a conversion into electrical impulses, then the conversion into sound energy in the ear piece at the other end.

◆ Decoding. This involves the receipt of signals and the application of prior experience and knowledge to their interpretation. This can be an automatic process, as when speaking to someone in a language understood by both sender and receiver; or it can require interpretation, as with the need to refer to a phrase book if translation between languages is necessary. The meaning attached to a signal by the receiver may not be that intended by the sender. For example, managers may intend that a message reassures employees by signifying that although orders are down and that costs will have to be reduced, job cuts are not planned. Employees may interpret the message in terms of costs needing to be cut now and jobs being at risk in the future. Expectation and prior experience on the part of the receiver influences the interpretation of messages just as much as the content and context of a communication.

◆ Feedback. The receiver may become a sender and provide a signal to the originator that conveys a response on how the first signal was interpreted. For example, an

Aussies did not 'run away'

AS AN AUSTRALIAN WRITER living in Malaysia, I am well aware of the sensitivities of language and language-translation.

Take the Malaysian–English expression, to 'run away' for example. Here in Malaysia I find it a rather quaint expression to leave a place in a hurry.

In Australian–English it is take far more literally and it is rarely applied to adult behaviour. There, it means to drop everything and run. If used in a military context, it would mean desertion of duty and absolute cowardice.

Unfortunately, this expression has found its way into the nightly English-language Sound and Light performance in Malacca. It is used to describe the withdrawal of British and Australian troops from Malaya to Singapore during World War II.

While that very military manoeuvre (withdrawal, recall, regrouping, etc.) is indeed a very sensitive issues in British–Australian–Malaysian historical relations it cannot be described as 'running away'. To call it that is deeply offensive to the dozens of Australian and British tourists who come to watch this show each night.

There is every chance that the older tourists that this show attracts may even have been here during the war. Almost every elderly Australian knows people who were in Changi Prison, on the Burma Railway or who died in Borneo.

On behalf of the disgruntled group that I happened to join last week, I'd like to ask the organizers to change those two words, so as not to offend the very people for whom the show is designed.

**Pauline Bruce
Kuantan**

FIGURE 11.9 Words are a different form of communication (*adapted from: New Straits Times*, Malaysia, 13 May, 1994).

employee about to step off a walkway into the path of a truck may stop walking in response to a shouted warning. It is possible that a response to a message is conveyed though body language, an expression of boredom for example. Communication without *feedback* does not allow the sender to know if the recipient has received or understood the message. Imagine a manager issuing instructions for the day's production activities without having any idea if they have been received, understood or are being actioned.

✦ Noise. This refers to the *contamination* of the signal as a result of *interference* surrounding the process. In an organizational setting it could be the background noise in a busy office that makes it difficult to hear a telephone conversation. In electronic terms is could refer to the volume of e-mails received by an employee that meant that they overlooked an important message from a customer.

Interpersonal communication

At its most basic level, interpersonal communication involves two people in a dyadic interaction utilizing all of the elements of the process described in Figure 11.8. Of the communication channels open to individuals non-verbal signals are the least obvious and yet carry much information. Table 11.1 provides a summary of the main non-verbal communication categories used to support other forms of communication.

Taking each category in turn:

✦ Body language. An individual can stop speaking but their body keeps on sending *signals*. The following example illustrates this process: 'In 20 minutes Mr. Roosevelt's features had expressed amazement, curiosity, mock alarm, genuine interest, worry, rhetorical playing for suspense, sympathy, decision, playfulness, dignity and surpassing charm. Yet he said almost nothing' (Gunther, 1950, p 22).

There are a number of features of body language that provide meaning or interpretative clues to other communication activities. They include gestures, touch, posture, facial expression and eye contact. There are also cultural differences in the meaning of many of the signals given (Pease, 1981).

✦ Paralanguage. This aspect of verbal communication conveys a number of clues and can be split into four separate areas (Trager, 1958). Voice quality (pitch, range, resonance etc.), vocal characteristics (whispering, groaning, coughing etc.), vocal qualifiers (momentary variations in volume or pitch) and vocal segregates (pauses, interruptions such as 'ah', 'um' etc.).

✦ Proxemics. This refers to the spatial needs of people and their environment. This links together communication distance and the type of message. Seeing two people physically very close, heads almost touching, would tend to suggest that a secret was being

Body language	touching, eye contact, gestures, dress, etc.
Paralanguage	voice tone, speed, pitch, etc.
Proxemics	seating arrangements and personal distance, etc
Environment	room design and facilities, etc.
Temporal	the use of time to create effect and influence

TABLE 11.1   Non-verbal communications

shared, whereas the same individuals separated by several feet could be discussing the weather.

✦ Environment. The layout of a room can have a powerful effect on the communication process. A meeting between a boss and a subordinate over a pay rise will be more likely to take place in the boss's office (or territory), a home base to give support to the boss's views. The following describes the feelings of a lawyer summoned to appear before the US Justice Department to explain why criminal proceedings should not be instituted:

They were immediately shown to the criminal division's coldly utilitarian conference room. 'It's the most perfect government room you ever saw,' Trott says. 'It's nothing but a table, some chairs, a picture of the president and the attorney general on the walls.' 'It was,' he adds, 'an icebox, a meat locker.' (Carpenter and Feloni, 1989, p 74).

✦ Temporal. The use of time to create an impression is well understood by most effective communicators. Calling all employees together for a meeting at a time which requires them to interrupt their normal work will give the message greater impact. A manager making someone wait outside their office a few minutes before a meeting creates pressure and can destabilize the person kept waiting. Management in Action 11.4 is a true story of how one manager used time to control an industrial relations situation.

Stop | Consider

Is the situation described in MiA 11.4 an example of good communication, effective communication or good or bad negotiation practice? Or does it simply reflect a pragmatic approach to issues of power and control? Justify your answers.

How would you have dealt with such situations if you were the senior manager involved?

How would you deal with such situations if you were a trade union representative?

Electronic communications

In today's organization the use of computer-based technology to communicate is widespread and becoming increasingly commonplace. The facsimile (fax) machine is now a key piece of equipment for sending messages and documents between locations. The use of copier and electronic mail systems allow information to be circulated more widely and more rapidly than ever before.

In manufacturing companies, the ability to design products on computer systems that produce parts lists and production schedules makes the task of ordering and invoicing that much easier. In service organizations the ability to call up a client file on computer allows the transaction to be more effectively tailored to client needs.

Organizations can design computer systems that allow designated individuals access to appropriate information from a database. For example, a computerized personnel system can hold information on each employee's career history, references, performance markings, pay progression, attendance record, disciplinary warnings and so forth. Access to the available information can be restricted in various ways. For example, job history, references and previous performance markings could be available to the department head but not the immediate supervisor of the person. The same principles can be applied to any of the company information systems including finance, budgets and marketing data.

As with all areas of management activity the potential of electronic communication

MANAGEMENT IN ACTION 11.4

The power of time

The industrial relations manager of a large privately owned manufacturing company told the following story, which he claimed was true. Industrial relations within the company was difficult at the best of times. For example, whenever management attempted to introduce a new machine into the factory a dispute with one or more of the trade unions would result. From a management point of view everything was an uphill battle. It was not uncommon for the senior shop stewards to refuse to accept a piece of equipment unless manning levels and outputs were agreed before it was commissioned. Not infrequently threats of strike action were also used to force management into conceding to employee demands.

In one instance (on a Friday), the shop stewards had threatened that unless a particular manning level could be agreed immediately a strike would be called. The factory finished work at 12.30 lunch time each Friday and so any strike would mean an early finish and Monday off work (effectively a long weekend). The managing director (who had decided to deal with the matter) said to the shop stewards that he had been called to a meeting with the group chief executive, but that he would be back as soon as possible. The shop stewards were asked to wait in the managing director's office and they were given coffee.

The managing director had a short meeting with his boss and sent for the industrial relations manager to meet him in the head office complex. The two managers then had lunch together at the instigation of the managing director. Protestations by the industrial relations manager that a strike was imminent drew little reaction and a leisurely lunch resulted. By this time the factory employees had gone home, having finished work, but the shop stewards were still waiting in the managing director's office. A strike

could not be called as management had not refused a meeting, so all the shop stewards could do was wait. Clearly, they became frustrated and made several attempts to contact the managing director to  press for the meeting, as they could see their original advantage slipping away. Responses from the managing director were that the senior managers were still meeting and would be back in the factory as soon as possible.

After a very leisurely lunch, that lasted until about 4.30 in the afternoon, the managing director decided that it was time to return to the factory. Not surprisingly, the shop stewards had left by then, refusing to wait any longer. Consequently, the two managers also went home for the weekend. First thing the following Monday morning the shop stewards stormed into the managing director's office to demand an explanation of the events from Friday. The response of the managing director was calm and he asked if they would have preferred him to have left the group chief executive and a discussion that could influence the future of the factory. He had the long-term interest of the factory and its employees at heart, even if they could not see beyond today. In any case, he had returned as early as he could, only to find that the shop stewards had gone home. Clearly, the problem that they wished to discuss was not important enough to make them want to give up some of their free time to solve it. There was no response from the shop stewards and the dispute ended. Management had 'won' this time, through the effect of using time to their advantage. However, this was not a tactic that could be used often as the shop stewards would find ways to counteract it. In this particular company it was a continual battle of wits between management and employees.

needs to be balanced with the other forms of communication available in order to produce an effective process at a cost that the organization can afford. This forms part of what is referred to as the *knowledge management* activities within an organization. For example, there is little to be gained from introducing teleconferencing between two locations only five miles apart when the usual communication between them is twice each year. However, with more frequent need to visit and/or seek technical support or assistance it may be justified.

Communications and the law

It has long been realized within organizations that information is a source of power and that there is unequal access to it between managers and employees. Indeed, there exists unequal access to information between levels of management and across functions. In an attempt to redress the balance slightly between employers and employees British employment legislation requires managers to communicate certain information to trade unions in specific industrial relations circumstances. This includes areas of collective bargaining and proposals to declare redundancies. Where trade unions have a need for particular types of information they can reasonably expect employers to disclose these so that they can undertake their responsibilities for representing members more effectively. Recent research has shown support for the view that consultation does help to save jobs in such situations (Edwards and Hall, 1999).

Additionally, limited liability organizations with more than 250 employees have to include a statement in their annual reports identifying any actions taken over the year to introduce, maintain or develop communication with employees.

Within the European Union there are expectations that employee participation will go further than simply being entitled to information and regular communication. The introduction of works councils is now built into the European Union's employment legislation (see Management in Action 11.5).

Stop	Consider	*Within an organizational setting to what extent can communications between employers and employees ever be less than an involvement in decision making?*
		If you were the vice chancellor of your university (or principal or chief executive) how would you seek to communciate with your employees and students and what would you see as the boundaries and objectives of such processes?

Decision making

Decision making is a major part of organizational life. It is the basis of action and of choosing between alternatives. Decisions affect every person at all levels in an organization. Directors must decide on policies and strategies aimed at long-term success, manual employees must take decisions within a much narrower set of variables and over a much shorter timeframe.

It is frequently suggested that the decision making engaged in by front-line staff (manual workers, sales assistants etc.) are short term and therefore of limited impact. That is an oversimplification of their potential to significantly influence the future well-being of

MANAGEMENT IN ACTION 11.5

Talking shop soon open for ideas

The Commission of the European Union proposed a form of works council to be established for companies operating on a European scale. These would be Europe-wide committees of about 30 management and employee representatives drawn from across the operations in member countries. Meetings would be at least once each year, although sub-committees could meet more frequently if necessary.

The trade union movement across Europe has been supportive of the works council requirement. For example, John Monks, general secretary of the British Trades Union Congress, indicated that his movement had long been in favour of the stakeholder approach to running a business. One consequence of this perspective was that employees have the right to be consulted over matters of significance to their interests. However, there exists a more sceptical view where some unions have experienced employers using the consultative process as a delaying tactic for difficult decisions. Also, by making the unions part of the decision-making process it can provide a way of embracing and therefore limiting their freedom of action over industrial relations issues. Equally, some unions point to the fact that the agenda of any works council is largely determined by a management perspective. Counter to that view Mr Brian Revell, a trade union official on the Nestlé works council, indicated that the company had been receptive to ideas that emerged, covering issues such as the promotion of more women to senior positions.

From a management perspective there were a number of companies that experienced difficulty in conforming to the requirement to have a works council at a European level. For example, British

companies were generally exempt from these requirements until the Social Chapter was signed by the Blair government in 1997. However, about 100 UK-owned companies have operations in Europe that would have qualified for works councils anyway and so they faced a dilemma as to whether to include representatives from their British operations or not. Most decided to include the UK operations in order to create a unified system and in anticipation of being required to do so.

There are, however, companies that do not have a 'European' level in their hierarchy. Guinness, for example, anticipated having to establish a new tier of management in order to comply as it did not currently organize at that level. BurgerKing faced a difficulty as it included the Middle East and Africa within its European business group.

The possibility of including an employee perspective in the decision-making processes of any organization remains an attractive option for many managers and trade unionists. However, the means by which to achieve that relatively simple objective remains as elusive as ever. Many employers argue that the approach proposed is too bureaucratic and does not match the dynamic reality of most organizational functioning. As suggested by one executive at Philips, the Dutch electronics group: 'The directive is the wrong, static approach. It will certainly slow down decision making.'

Adapted from: Goodhart, D (1994) Talking shop soon open for ideas, *Financial Times*, 20 April, p 22.

any business. It is the front-line staff of any organization who interact directly with customers or make the products that the customer will use. In doing so they are the ones who deliver (or fail to do so) the company objectives. The ability of front-line staff to decide for themselves the extent to which they will 'delight the customer' (to use an appalling phrase in current use) which can directly impact on future sales and company reputation. Recent trends in *delayering*, *downsizing* and *rightsizing* place greater emphasis on the ability of front-line staff to take decisions (*empowerment*) and thereby vastly increase the vulnerability of the organization to the actions of these staff (both positive and negative). Consequently, there exists an ever greater need for employers to communicate and engage staff effectively if they are to minimize the potential negative consequences.

Approaches to decision making

Decisions are about choice. If there were no choices then decisions would not be necessary. For example, a production manager may have had a machine out of service for two days and as a consequence be late in the delivery of orders to some customers. The choices facing the manager are to cancel some of the orders, increase the speed of the machine (when it is working again), work overtime, subcontract some of the orders, or continue to deliver late on existing work and reschedule future orders. The problem facing the manager is identifying which option provides the most appropriate course of action. Each possibility has advantages and disadvantages. Customers would seek to encourage a decision which delivers the product on time. The maintenance team would prefer a decision which is less likely to result in future damage to the equipment. The quality specialists and designers within the company would be keen to maintain product standard and the finance people would wish to see costs not exceed revenue. In addition, employees and other managers will have views that could influence the solution actually adopted. For example, the sales manager may have favourite customers that they do not want to upset. The difficulty facing the production manager is that many of these viewpoints and expectations are in conflict. For example, if employees work overtime and get paid extra for doing so, unit cost will inevitably increase. However, the customer will be happy and may provide further orders as a result of the service provided. It is finding ways to balance these competing pressures that forms the basis of decision making.

Decision making takes time, is resource demanding and carries with it a degree of risk. In situations where the *problem* has not occurred before it is necessary to work out the options and relative benefits for each before deciding which to follow. If the problem is new then there is no experience on which to judge the likely success of any course of action. The decision is taken before the result can be known. The actual chain of events that will follow from any decision cannot be fully anticipated and there are frequently extraneous factors that emerge as time passes. The D-day landings of the allied forces in France in June 1944 was the culmination of considerable planning and training activity. However, by chance a crack German armoured regiment was on exercise in the area of one of the landing zones and so was able to reinforce the defence of the area more effectively than had been anticipated. In that situation, there was no opportunity for the military commanders to take another decision in the light of the new information. It simply had to be dealt with as the landings progressed. In other words, only subsequent decisions could take account of the new situation. This perspective has led commentators to describe a *stream* of decisions rather than a single activity.

Mistakes and failure can arise if the wrong decisions are made. It is personally, commercially and organizationally dangerous to make too many mistakes. However, they can also provide an effective learning experience. The trick, if there is one, appears to be to encourage risk taking while minimizing the dangers. Coca-Cola attempted to achieve this balance by celebrating failure as an opportunity to learn. Penny Hughes is quoted as saying mistakes were actually applauded in Coca-Cola and, that people were aware that they could take a decision from a position of safety (1999, p 61).

Simon (1960) describes decisions as falling along a continuum from *programmed* to *non-programmed*. Programmed in this context refers to the existence of decision rules that lead from problem to the solution. If a photocopier stops reproducing copies part way through a run a code number on a control panel indicates the type of problem and the machine manual indicates how to clear the blockage or repair the machine. The programmed aspects of this process are created through the design of the machine, the inclusion of sensors to detect certain malfunctions and the development of an operator's manual. Similar effects can be seen in the training of airline pilots using flight simulators. The purpose is to expose the pilot to a wide variety of flying experiences and train them how to respond effectively without putting lives and expensive aeroplanes at risk. Programmed decisions, therefore, reflect a form of problem solving as a solution exists which simply needs to be determined or found.

Non-programmed decisions, however are new, cannot be anticipated or do not have pre-existing methods of resolving them. A recent example of this is the situation facing the cross-channel ferry companies on the opening of the Channel Tunnel rail links between the UK and France. Although not a rapid emergence of a new product (the tunnel took several years to design and build) the effect on the ferry companies is dramatic. The ferry companies have never experienced this situation before (at least not across the English Channel) and so they are forced to rely on their internal ability to define and solve problems intelligently. Only time will tell how successful they are in achieving this. Tom Bentley, a director of Demos, suggests that timing is the most difficult aspect of any decision. Acting too early or too late can turn an otherwise good decision into a mistake or failure. In his view the best approach to decision making combines early thought and planning with leaving the actual decision to the last moment. An approach which, in his view, provides the most flexible response capability (Bentley, 1999, p 61).

Comparing the two approaches of *programmed* and *non-programmed* decision making a number of conclusions should be apparent, including:

✦ Risk. There is less *risk* of failure in a decision which is based on the programmed approach. Decisions based on this approach are familiar, there is considerable experience of the 'behaviour' of variables and the outcome has a higher predictability as a result. In a situation requiring a non-programmed response the relationships between the variables must be worked out each time. This invariably involves anticipation, judgement and higher levels of expertise. This approach inevitably contains a higher potential for failure as a result of the increased uncertainty. The distinction between these approaches can be compared to the difference between a sporting event and a theatrical performance. In both of these situations careful planning, training and practice occurs. However, in the case of a sporting event, the intention is to beat the opposing side and that introduces the non-programmed dimension to the process. Each side will attempt to create new situations and actions in order to gain an advantage. In a theatrical performance the rehearsal is intended to produce replication for each performance. The aim is to ensure that each individual knows what they must do at every stage in the show. The risk of getting it wrong (in not producing equivalent repeat performances) is thereby greatly reduced.

✦ Cost. Reliance on non-programmed decision making incurs a higher *cost* for the organization. In a company producing designer clothing each item must be different, and tailored specifically for each client. The cost of producing each item is therefore much greater because there is no opportunity for economies of scale. Conversely, in situations where considerable effort has been applied to the development of programmed decision approaches, the cost of operations can be reduced. The cost of solving the *programmed* problem might be much higher in absolute terms, but it is a one-off cost and shared over a vary large number of the same decision situations. For example, air travel safety has been greatly increased as a result of the efforts of pilot trainers, aircraft designers, maintenance planners and air traffic control specialists to *routinize* much of the process, learn from experience and *programme* into the decision-making activities as much of this as is possible. In addition because of the lower levels of skill necessary to implement programmed decisions the training time and cost of labour is usually lower than needed for non-programmed decision situations.

✦ Performance. Measured in units of output per person, the *performance* of an organization using a high proportion of programmed decisions will be greater. Programmed decisions need less processing time and therefore individuals can take more of them. Consider, for example, the lending policies of banks and financial institutions. If a programmed decision approach is adopted the resulting 'formula' is applied to each applications and an answer produced quickly. The process can be speeded up to the extent that it becomes a marketing advantage and is used as such by a number of banks.

✦ Variety. Unique situations cannot be dealt with in a programmed mode of operation, they must be channelled out and dealt with separately. In a pure form, organizations would be faced with an 'either/or' situation, emphasizing a programmed or non-programmed approach because of the different requirements. However, as a result of technology developments it is less significant today. Motor car design and manufacture is an excellent example of the ability to combine programmed and non-programmed aspects in the one process. The designers of a motor car will begin with a small number of variations for a particular model, engine size, number of doors and body style. However, from the basic model there are a wide range of optional extras available that produce a vast number of end product variations. The use of computer technology along with process technologies such as just in time allows the appropriate components to be made available to the factory at the correct time to provide cost-effective assembly, with the illusion of relative uniqueness built into the product.

✦ Employee skill. Where non-programmed decisions are the norm, the skill level of employees must be of a higher order than required for programmed decisions.

   Programmed decisions are a process of situation recognition, identification of the appropriate decision rules and applying them to the situation. For non-programmed decisions, the employees involved must be capable of high level analysis and trained in a wide range of techniques to cope with the uncertainties inherent in the process. For example, imagine the level of knowledge and skill required to deal with a computer crash if there were no handbooks available.

✦ Organization design. The structure of the organization in terms of the number of departments and their function will be affected by the approach to decision making. The lower skill levels implied by the programmed approach to operational decision making produces the need for smaller number of specialists and a large number of people at the lower levels of the organization. For example, the design of a company specializing in designer clothing will be very different to one specializing in ready-to-wear apparel.

The approach described by Simon is one based on the need to apply differing levels of pre-planning into the process of decision making. Programmed decisions require careful thought and anticipation, but this can be separated from the events themselves. So an airline can train pilots to deal with anticipated emergencies before they actually occur. As the decision sciences evolve and develop the opportunity to include ever more complex problems in the programmed category emerges. Complex, non-programmed decisions can frequently be broken down into a network of sub-problems, many of them programmable, therefore a *simplification* process becomes available. Non-programmable decisions are frequently novel situations that can serve as a means of identifying situations that may arise again and which are worthy of capture and conversion into hierarchies of programmed decisions.

Problem-solving preferences

Another way to think about decision making is to consider the preferences that individuals have for approaching the process. In Chapter 4 the views of Jung in describing information gathering and evaluation approaches were outlined. The *information-gathering* approach is defined in terms of either *sensing* (preference for facts) *or intuition* (preference for possibilities). The *information evaluation* approach is defined in terms of *thinking* (preference for logic) or *feeling* (preference for values) in analyzing available information. This view of the individual preferences in problem solving can be reflected in a diagram (see Figure 11.10), each cell in the matrix reflecting a different approach to solving problems.

Another approach to individual problem solving is that described by Thompson and Tuden (1959). Their model is based upon two dimensions:

✦   Preferences for outcomes. This is about the goals that are being sought. It is measured along a continuum from clear to unclear. So if the end result is known (fix the photocopier) then it would fall at the clear end of the spectrum. If, however, the end result is not clear (design a new product) then a different set of choices emerge.

✦   Beliefs about causation. This is also measured along a clear/unclear continuum. It refers to the understanding that the individual has about the relationship between

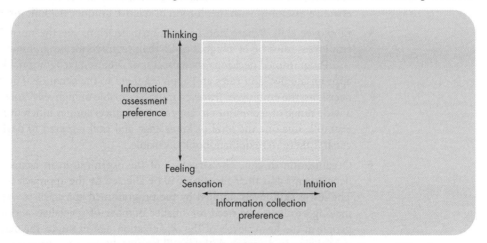

FIGURE 11.10   Problem-solving preferences (*adapted from*: Hellriegel, D, Slocum, JW and Woodman, RW (1989) *Organizational Behaviour*, 5th edn, West Publishing, St Paul, MN).

cause and effect in that specific situation. For example, in original research there can be little clarity as to how the variables will interact. Conversely, a knowledge that clearing a paper jam will allow the copier to function properly would fall at the 'clear' end of the spectrum.

This model goes further than the model described in Figure 11.10 by providing an indication of the problem-solving approaches that arise from these dimensions. Each of the four cells in Figure 11.11 implies a different approach to the problem-solving process. For example, where the outcome and the relationship between the variables is clearly understood, then a logical approach will achieve the best result. By the same token, where neither variable is clear, inspiration is the best guide to dealing with the problem.

However it is necessary to recognize that there are differences between decision making and problem solving. Jones (1999, p 71) reports on a symposium at the 1998 British Psychological Society London conference which explored aspects of decision making. One speaker (Nigel Harvey) pointed out that a good decision can still result in a bad outcome, whereas problem solving cannot. Problem solving has a right answer but decisions are frequently made in conditions where considerable uncertainty exists and the aim is to reach the 'best' or optimal decision possible. Emma Soane suggested that City traders reported that emotion played an important part in their decisions as they often carry great risk and uncertainty.

Decision-making models

There are a number of models that attempt to describe how decisions are made within organizations, including:

✦ Rational model. This assumes that decision makers always follow a *rational* approach. Actions would be based on data collection and analysis, along with evaluation of alternatives. Appropriateness of the decision would be measured against the benefit to the organization as a whole, rather than any specific group or individual (Harrison, 1987).

✦ Restricted rationality model. Although the rational model may offer an ideal or preferred model, it may even be claimed to be the basis of all decisions by many organizations. However, as a model of decision making, it ignores the 'humanness' in the

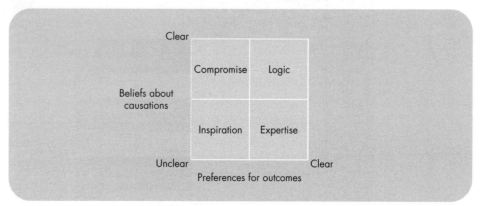

FIGURE 11.11   Two dimensions of decision making (*source*: Thompson, TE and Tuden, A (1959) *Comparative Studies in Administration*, University of Pittsburgh Press, Pittsburgh).

process. Individuals may lack the intellectual capacity or technical competence to evaluate every option rationally. Perceptual bias group dynamics and politics can also play a significant part in the decision-making process. There are many aspects of behaviour within an organization that influence how decisions are taken, not just rational aspects (March and Simon, 1958). McKenna (1994) describes this model as bounded rationality and suggests that it comprises three main processes:

✦   Sequential consideration of alternatives.
✦   Using *heuristics* (rules which guide a search) to identify the most appropriate alternatives.
✦   *Satisficing*, choosing on the basis of the identification of the first acceptable solution.

✦ Pragmatic model. Pragmatism is a means of combining both rationality and the reality of human behaviour into a systematic approach aimed at achieving the best decision in the circumstances. Figure 11.12 reflects the main elements of this approach.

✦ Political model. In this model, decision making becomes a process intended to achieve

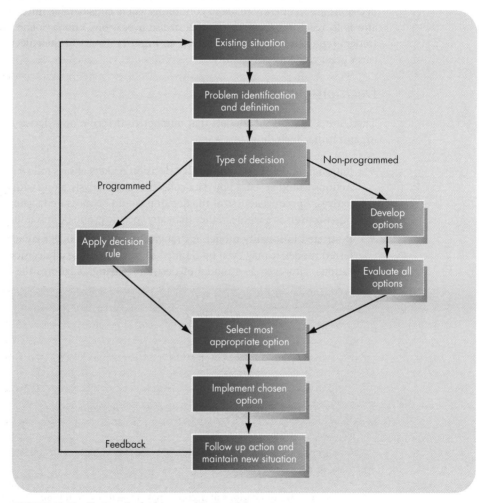

FIGURE 11.12   Pragmatic decision-making model.

personal objectives through organizational activity. As such, information becomes part of the political process, as does its interpretation. One form of this was described as a *garbage can* model by Cohen *et al.* (1972). This is based on the idea that organizations are essentially comprised of solutions looking for problems. For example, a company may purchase a number of components. The production managers may wish to bring under their direct control this subcontracted work. They are likely to continually seek ways to demonstrate that the company would be 'better off' producing the items in-house. Quality problems with suppliers' products will be highlighted, as will late delivery and so on. In effect, the solution already exists (expand the production department) all that is necessary is for the 'problem' to occur. Cohen *et al.* see the *garbage can* as a receptacle for solutions and situations, both waiting to be matched up.

Another approach to the political model describes decision making in terms of managers looking after their own short-term interests. Powell and Mainiero (1999) carried out an experiment in which managers were asked to take a decision about which employees they would allow to adopt non-standard working arrangements. Generally, the basis of the decision was that employees would be refused permission to change their working arrangements if it would cause inconvenience to the manager. Within the results four different clusters were identified representing managers who adopted different criteria to the decision. So the same decision basis is not used by every manager even though self-interest is apparent in the overall process. Management in Action 11.6 illustrates just how far the political model can be stretched in seeking personal objectives.

Stop | Consider *Once it was formulated could the reward manager's plan have been prevented and, if so, how and by whom?*

◆ Conflict model. Janis and Mann (1977) describe a model based on five assumptions. First, it is applicable to important life decisions only. Second, procrastination and rationalization are part of difficult decisions as they allow individuals to deal with stress. Third, some decisions will be wrong and that this can affect future decisions. Fourth, that alternative options will be compared against personal moral standards. Finally, individuals will be ambivalent towards the alternative decision options, making it difficult to choose between them. Figure 11.13 describes the algorithmic nature of this approach.

◆ Cycle model. This approach to decision making proposes a nine-step process based upon research carried out by Archer (1980) in which the decision-making stages used by some 2000 managers were explored. The steps identified in the process of decision making were as follows:
  ◆ *Monitor* the environment for issues that need to be decided and for feedback on the consequences of previous decisions.
  ◆ *Define* the issue(s) or problems(s) that need to be decided. Separate symptons from problems.
  ◆ *Specify* the risks, constraints and objectives for the decision.
  ◆ *Diagnose* the problem(s) more thoroughly.
  ◆ *Develop* the possible options or alternative courses of action available.
  ◆ *Establish* the criteria against which any decision will be made and success judged.
  ◆ *Appraise* the options in terms of the established criteria.

MANAGEMENT IN ACTION 11.6

Getting a better company car

This event was described to me by the chief executive of a large successful company who thought it was rather funny and demonstrated both that politics could have personal benefits and how easily senior managers can be manipulated.

Essentially, the story was as follows. The head of the reward systems department within the company decided that he wanted a bigger, more expensive company car than the existing policy allowed. Having thought about this for a while he decided upon the following course of action. In the subsequent annual review of pay and benefits for the company the reward manager proposed (having consulted with sales managers first) that it would be in the company's interest for sales staff to be given a more prestigious car. This (he argued) would, among other things, enhance their status internally, encourage customers to perceive sales staff as more senior emplyees and also motivate sales staff to sell more. The cost of the bigger cars was justified financially on the basis of additional sales, lower sales staff labour turnover etc. After some discussion the new cars were acquired and the policy changed. This was stage one of the reward manager's plan achieved.

Stage two was to wait a while (a few months) and then informally and on the quiet to 'remind' a number of head office managers and other company car drivers that junior level sales staff now had bigger cars and to ask if they were happy about this situation. Naturally, a few responded that this change to the car policy lowered their own perceived internal status by lifting the level of benefit given to sales staff. This effectively 'planted the seed' of an attitude among company car drivers that implied a problem might be emerging. The next move by the reward manager was to raise the issue more directly with the manager responsible for organizing and running the company car fleet. This was where the reward manager ran the most risk of failure as, in effect he had to pass the problem over to another

manager, who might have reported the reward manager's intentions to higher management. However, by implying that every manager (including the car fleet manager himself) could gain by a car upgrade if the 'problem' were addressed, he was soon convinced. The car fleet manager was persuaded that by carrying out a user survey among company car drivers he would soon detect significant resentment towards the new policy. Not surprisingly this was found to be the case and the car fleet manager wrote a report to his manager and the head of personnel to that effect.

The reward manager was then brought back into the 'problem' and asked to find a solution that could be accommodated within the company's overall reward strategy. This was done. The reward manager essentially proposed that as the company had enjoyed a couple of good years additional money could be made available, any change could be phased in over a number of years as company cars were replaced (which would reduce the cost) and direct pay increases could be shaved back a fraction over the whole company to reduce the overall cost. Not surprisingly, the head of personnel supported this proposed plan as the overall cost was marginal and it would avoid a morale and industrial relations problem (he would also get a bigger car as a result). The proposal was put to the chief executive who agreed with it (how surprising) and it was put it to the board (who all agreed with it). So the company car policy was changed and all managers (including the reward manager) gained by getting a bigger car.

This process was not a fast one, taking over two years from the start to the reward manager getting his new and bigger car. He did, however, manipulate the entire process to meet his particular objective.

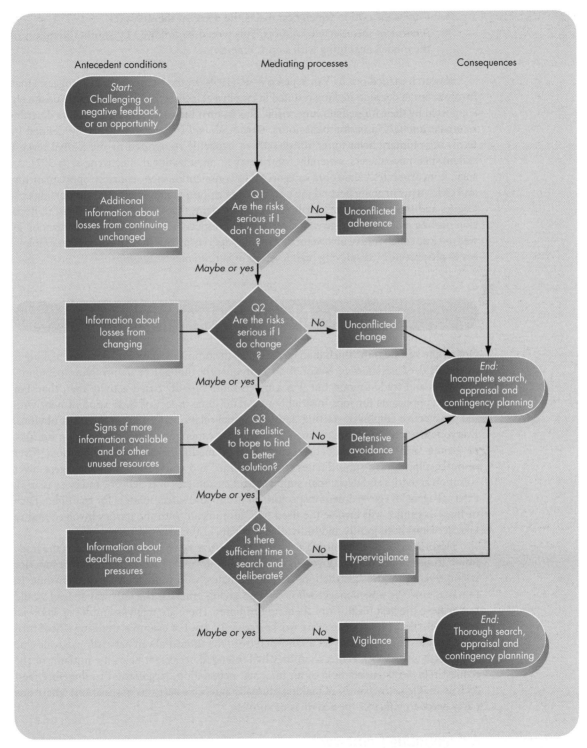

FIGURE 11.13 Conflict model of decision making (*source*: Janis, IL and Mann, L (1977) *Decision Making: A Psychological Analysis of Conflict, Choice and Commitment*, The Free Press, New York).

+ *Choose* the option which best meets the needs of the situation.
+ *Implement* the selected solution. This would be followed by another iteration of the model, beginning with step 1, *monitor*.

Research carried out by Van Y peren *et al.* (1999) in the Netherlands also suggests that involvement in decision making resulted in employees feeling that they were more positively supported by their immediate supervisor. This in turn increased what the authors describe as *organizational citizenship* behaviours. *Organizational citizenship* is generally defined in terms of voluntary behaviour, 'not directly or explicitly recognized by the formal reward system that, nevertheless, generally contributes to organizational effectiveness' (p 377). As such, it incorporates behaviours categorized as conscientiousness, courtesy, sportsmanship and civic virtue in going beyond the basic job description requirements and supporting colleagues and the organization's goals. The authors claim that through involvement in decision making employees are given a clear signal of respect by the employing organization as well as close collaborative involvement with the supervisor. This in turn encourages employees to reciprocate by displaying high levels of *organizational citizenship*.

Negotiation

One of the key areas in which managers engage in communication and decision making is in the field of *negotiation*. Negotiation is frequently thought of as involving personnel managers and trade unions, but it is a much more broadly based activity than that. For example, applicants for jobs invariably negotiate some aspect of their appointment with the prospective employer, starting date and initial salary being among the most obvious. Everyone working in organizations will frequently experience negotiation with a number of groups and individuals. These circumstance might include, with their boss (over resource allocations); subordinates (over deadlines and workrate); other managers (over common activities and decisions); suppliers and customers (over delivery and price issues); external agencies (government inspectors on health and safety matters for example). Each of these examples will involve the need to communicate with the parties involved and to take decisions both jointly and individually as part of the negotiation process.

Negotiation is often regarded as a *formal process*, as when management meets the trade union to agree rates of pay. However, it is often an informal process. Technically, a superior is empowered to give 'instructions' to subordinates, who must then carry them out. In practice, however, any manager who relied on giving orders as the only way to lead would not achieve the best result from their subordinates. There are many examples of *informal negotiations* that take place in every workplace every day. For example, deciding whose turn it is to make the coffee or to get a sandwich from the canteen. Even persuading a colleague to perform a work task earlier than they had intended because it helps the initiator or the request represents an example of an informal negotiation. Negotiation is, therefore, best seen as an *interactive process* of making mutually agreeable bargains in situations where one party needs to *influence* the activities of another.

A negotiating framework

Formal negotiation is a means through which differences can be resolved and agreement specified, thereby allowing all parties to have a record of their rights and obligations. In all relationships there is a power dimension and negotiation can be a reflection of that balance of power that exists within the relationship. For example, if a company has many suppliers of a particular raw material and each source is equivalent in terms of quality, the suppliers are individually very weak compared to the customer and it would be almost impossible for individual suppliers to raise prices. The customer would simply switch to another supplier. This process has also been apparent historically in the employment field and led to the emergence of trade unions as a means of providing a balance in the power between employers and employees. Figure 11.14 provides a framework for understanding the formal negotiation process within employee relations.

It is clear from Figure 11.14 that negotiations are a process dependent to a significant extent upon previous encounters, expectations and external forces. It should also be apparent how communications and decision making fit into this model of the process.

Negotiating tactics

There are a number of approaches to dealing with conflict that are relevant to negotiations. They include *avoidance* (simply ignoring the problem), *smoothing* (seeking to 'patch up' a rift through calming actions), *forcing* (one's own point of view onto others), *compromise* (seeking an acceptable middle ground) and *confrontation* (facing up to the differences and seeking accommodation) (Torrington and Hall, 1987).

The tactics that negotiators encounter depend on a number of features of the process itself. They include the preferred style of the individuals involved; the relative power balance between the parties; the degree of change involved; the willingness of the parties to accept change; previous encounters; environmental influences; training and experience in negotiation along with the dynamics of the process itself. Less formal negotiations will also be less likely to exhibit the clear patterns of behaviour implied by many of the tactics discussed. For

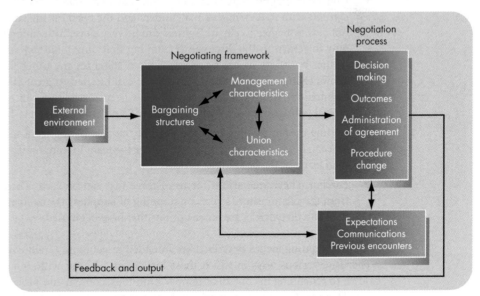

FIGURE 11.14 A negotiating framework (*adapted from*: Kochan, TA (1980) *Collective Bargaining and Industrial Relations*, Irwin, Homewood, IL).

example, deciding whose turn it is to make the coffee is likely to be treated as a bit of fun, unless someone never makes it and then the approach is likely to change significantly.

It is naive to suggest that all negotiations are a means by which both parties can discuss differences and reach mutually acceptable compromise. Many negotiations are undertaken from a *win–lose* perspective. In other words, one side must 'win', so the other must, of necessity, 'lose'. This is based upon the notion that the issues are *fixed* and can only be shared out like cutting a cake into pieces. In this analogy, a piece once cut and allocated is no longer available for the other party. In extreme cases, the tactics employed by individuals using this approach can become very aggressive. Typically, a *deep diving* approach is taken on each item to be covered until a win is recorded and then moving on to the next issue. Similar tactics include (Scott, 1981):

✦ Probing. From the outset seeking information of value, without giving anything away that may help the other side.

✦ Get/give. Seeking to gain something before conceding anything. Matching what is given to what was gained.

✦ Emotion. The use of voice tone and other body language signals to create emotion in the process. The use of anger would be a typical example.

✦ Good guy/bad guy. The 'reasonable' member follows the 'aggressive' and 'unreasonable' one and builds on the advantage gained by the threat of more to follow.

✦ Poker face. The ability to manage the body language and verbal cues allows the fighter to cloak their feelings and intentions.

✦ Managing the minutes. The person producing the minutes is in a strong position to slant the official record. The careful choice of words and phrasing can be used to great effect, as can the selective inclusion (or exclusion) of items discussed.

✦ Understanding not agreement. One side may *understand* the other's position without *agreeing* with it. A customer may understand the need for the supplier to raise prices, but may not agree to pay it. Fighters can be very clever at seeming to reach *agreement*, only to return to the discussions claiming that only *understanding* was reached and further negotiations are necessary. This destabilizes the other party and frequently allows change to be achieved. This tactic can be used to great effect at the close of a negotiation. To think that agreement has been reached and to relax, only to have a crucial point threaten the whole process is a difficult position to find oneself in.

✦ Getting upstairs. Going over the head of the negotiating team to the boss is a threat that can be used to effect. It can encourage the team to lean towards a settlement rather than bring in the boss to the process.

✦ Forcing. There are various forms of force that can be used. Threats of withdrawing from the relationship (strikes or stopping of supplies) is one form, but bribes, blackmail and dirty tricks are other options that have been used.

The fighting tactics described are intended to gain and retain control of the process. There are various ways in which these tactics can be dealt with, but essentially it comes down to remaining in control of temper, emotions, content and process.

There are few occasions in which the power balance is completely one-sided and therefore negotiation should be regarded as a joint process of identifying the best outcome for all concerned. Often this comes down to understanding what the best alternative to a negotiated agreement is. In other words, what will happen if no agreement is reached? This is a point made by Fisher and Ury (1981) in their description of *principled negotiations*. This requires negotiators to concentrate on four aspects:

✦ Separate the people from the problem. It is the issues that are important, not the people conducting them. By forcing attention onto the issues, the people involved become focused on finding mutually acceptable solutions.

✦ Focus on interests, not positions. The purpose of a negotiation is to reach agreement. All parties to the process have an interest in the final solution rather than the position from which they begin. Again, this should force an emphasis on finding mutually acceptable solutions.

✦ Invent options for mutual gain. This is the major difference from the win–lose approach. There is no single cake to be split into a fixed number of pieces. For example, in negotiations over price increases, the discussions need not be about profit, loss and cost alone. It is possible that an increase in price may be acceptable if conditions regarding delivery, quality and packaging can be met. It is up to the negotiators to seek out ways by which they can both win from the process. It is a *win–win* process.

✦ Insist on objective criteria. The means by which success and failure should be judged need to be objective and sound in the circumstances. Often a negotiation can degenerate into a horse trading event in which issues are traded so that each party wins some and loses some. 'Objective criteria' means a decision basis that is independent of either side. This approach should ensure that it is the merits of the case that decide the outcome, not pressure or trading tactics.

The authors recognized that not every negotiator operates by these principles and they include in their work a number of tactics for dealing with such situations, including knowing what the alternatives to agreement are. After all, it may be in the best interests of one party to walk away from a particular negotiation, rather than reach an unacceptable agreement.

Communication, decision making and negotiation: an applied perspective

There are many applications of communications, decision making and negotiating in the field of management. Managers must develop appropriate policies and practices with regard to these issues. For example, some organizations adopt a high profile and, consequently, court publicity at every opportunity. Other organizations adopt the opposite approach, preferring to stay out of the public eye and seeking to operate in private. There is, however, a fine line between simply avoiding publicity and actively seeking to divert attention from something that should be brought into the open. The first case is an example of not using communication to its fullest potential, the second a potentially sinister and manipulative approach in order to hide something. This latter approach provides the opportunity for corruption to develop and flourish through obscurity. It is not therefore in the long-term interest of any individual, company or society. Corruption in all its forms has a long history and has affected human behaviour in organizations in every continent, its effect being to wear down the fabric of society (Alatas, 1991). The challenge facing managers is how to achieve operational effectiveness without directly abusing the resources available to them (or encouraging such behaviour in others by default or indolence) through the unethical and inappropriate use of communication, decision making or negotiation.

Most communication within an organizational context takes place between individuals and groups. The more formal external contact tends to be restricted to specialist departments and senior managers acting on behalf of the organization. However, word of mouth and accidental communication should not be underestimated as active sources of information and influence. Employees and managers invariably talk to other people as part of their social life outside work. The views and opinions expressed in that context can have a significant impact on public perception of an organization, sales levels, its standing in the local and business community. Rumours originating from such interaction can easily build pictures that form the basis of investigative journalism and City speculation, both of which can have adverse (or positive) impacts. Not everyone is a good communicator and not all channels offer equal effectiveness in getting the message across (see Table 11.2, indicating the relative effectiveness of internal company communications).

Many of the situations relating to communication will also involve decision making and negotiation. Communications can form part of a negotiation process with trade unions, government departments, customers or banks for example. It is a management responsibility to establish who can negotiate what with whom in relation to company operations. Also, it is necessary to establish who can take what level and type of decision. Not to establish these frameworks can result in major difficulties for the organization. It is reported (Carpenter and Feloni, 1989) that a respected Wall Street financial institution had little by way of formal financial accountability at the top of the organization and so was unable to control and monitor the level of 'check-kiting' (a complex process of moving cheques around various bank accounts to obtain loans). As a result of these fundamental weaknesses in communication and decision making, together with the resulting lack of control, the organization eventually collapsed and was absorbed into another Wall Street firm. This example shows the complex interactions between communication, decision making, negotiation (local managers were free to negotiate deals with local banks), management structure, accountability and operational activity.

Poor communications (along with poor judgement and decision making) can also impact on an organization in ways that were not intended. The chief executive of a large

Team briefing	57%
Roadshows/staff meetings	11%
Newsletters	7%
Noticeboards	6%
House journal/newsletter	6%
Other	5%
E-mail	4%
Video	1%

TABLE 11.2   Effectiveness of employee communication channels (*source: Personnel Today*, 3 May, 1994)

and successful chain of discount jewellery shops in the UK found that sales dropped to nil overnight after a careless comment in an after-dinner speech was widely reported. His comment cast doubts on the quality of his company's products and, by implication, the intelligence etc. of his customers. As a consequence, most of the shops closed down and he lost his job along with many of the staff!

There is a significant difference between a manager communicating the technical features of a product to customers' and the same manager attempting to convince employees to work harder because of a reduction in the number of people employed following a delayering exercise. The intended audiences are different, as is the purpose of the message, but so is the relative power relationships that will influence subsequent events. The political nature of decision making was well described by Pettigrew (1973) in linking a hierarchy of power to control of resources.

In decision-making terms the *groupthink* phenomenon is of particular importance (Janis, 1982). The decision to establish a group to take a decision could itself be flawed. It is often assumed that a group will take a better decision than an individual, the justification being the inclusion of a range of expertise and opinions and skills. Unfortunately, this view assumes that such a group will undertake its tasks without the wide range of potential *interference* factors *corrupting* the process. There are many other pressures acting on the members of a group, even when it is made up of senior people. Many of these factors have already been introduced and include, personal, political, interpersonal and capability issues. In decision making there are number of approaches which seek to improve the creative dimensions (and hence the overall quality) of it. Of the approaches developed, those created by Edward De Bono are perhaps the best known. Management in Action 11.7 indicates some of his views on how to improve decision making.

Stop | Consider

Could you envisage using the thinking hats approach in practical decision making? Why or why not?

What do you think the effect would be if you tried it with a group of fellow students in order to decide on the answer to this activity?

How would you persuade other people to join a decision-making process based upon the thinking hats approach?

Managers are collectively and individually responsible for the actions carried out within the organization. They may not personally take a decision but they have a responsibility to ensure that those who undertake these activities do so to the highest levels of professionalism. That is not to say that perfection should be expected on every occasion, that would be unrealistic. What it does imply is that managers have a responsibility to ensure that it is done to the highest standard *in the circumstances*. There is the potential to have access to a variety of sources of information to help in decision making. As shown in Table 11.3 managers have a varying but wide access to a range of sources.

The notion of *programmed decisions* should encourage organizations to channel many of the decision-making areas towards the routine (and controlled) end of the spectrum, thereby freeing time and resources to concentrate on strategic and *non-programmed* decision areas. However, as Child (1973) points out, this approach further differentiates the organization on the basis of technical expertise as a prerequisite for access to and interpretation of information relevant to non-programmed decisions. Those who deal with programmed decisions have the *scientific management* approach to their work imposed upon

MANAGEMENT IN ACTION 11.7

Put on your thinking caps

In an interview with Lucy Kellaway, Edward De Bono, the person who developed 'lateral thinking', talked about his latest approach to creative thinking – the six thinking hats. He argues that approaches to thinking adopted in the west are too rigid and lock creative process into patterns that are no longer appropriate to the fast changing world of today. In making this claim he refers to Socrates, Plato and Aristotle as the 'Gang of Three', who developed the approach to thought still dominant today.

His latest approach to making people more effective in their lives and work is to adopt the perspectives and processes of the six thinking hats. Each hat is a different colour and represents a different thought process. The colours are:

♦ White. This hat is used to denominate the information-gathering stage of thought.

♦ Red. This hat represents the feelings and emotions towards the thought object.

♦ Black. This hat incorporates the evaluation of risk, critical appraisal and the adopting of a cautious approach to the focus issue.

♦ Yellow. This hat requires the wearer to concentrate on issues associated with the feasibility of solutions and the benefits to be gained from them.

♦ Green. This hat is the one that emphasizes the development of new ideas, options and possibilities.

♦ Blue. This hat is described as the 'meta' one. It is intended to concentrate on the total

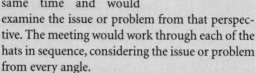

process, ensuring that the end result takes all hats into account.

In a meeting context, everyone would wear the same colour hat at the same time and would examine the issue or problem from that perspective. The meeting would work through each of the hats in sequence, considering the issue or problem from every angle.

Companies in the USA which have already used his 'six hats' approach include IBM, Rothmans, Du Pont, Federal Express and the Mormon Church. The approach has spread to other parts of the world, including Canada, Japan, South Africa, Italy and the UK.

De Bono argues that by adopting the logical and concentrated approach to creative thinking implied by the six hat approach, the chemical actions in the brain are different from when an undifferentiated approach is being used. The result is a more efficient thinking process in which each person concentrates on the same perspective at the same time thereby eliminating the political and ego-based 'contaminants' that otherwise disrupt effective thought and decision making. By everyone emphasizing the same aspect at the same time he suggests that a much more effective inclusion of each perspective occurs. He claims that meeting times can be reduced by approximately 50%, saving some executives the equivalent of about one day each week in wasted time.

Adapted from: Kellaway, L (1994) Put on your thinking caps, *Financial Times*, 17 June, p 17.

---

them. Their jobs are deskilled, routinized and generally regarded as inferior and menial. Whereas those who deal with non-programmed decisions develop a wide range of skills, are likely to have enriched jobs and be regarded as highly valuable by their employing organizations. They are also likely to be the ones who regard themselves as having careers and access to promotion to senior levels. In short, they become the 'haves' compared to the programmed decision category employees who are the 'have nots'

The view of limited rationality introduced in the context of decision-making models leads to a notion of *satisficing* rather than a selection between optimal choices. This leads to a short-term approach to control, based on frequent reviews of performance against target, rather than a strategic approach based on the longer term achievement of goals. Lindblom (1959) describes this as the *science of muddling through*. In other words, a continuous process of readjustment of actions in line with perceived deviation from a short-term objective in an attempt to achieve what Cyert and March (1963) call *uncertainty absorption*. Decision making can be a career-limiting event if the decision turns out to be wrong and costly or embarrassing for the organization. There are many ways in which individuals attempt to deal with this aspect of life, including the holding of meetings in an attempt to improve decision making and share responsibility.

Management in Action 11.8 illustrates how meetings and decisions are frequently seen by individuals.

Stop | Consider

In the light of MiA 11.8, is, 'a decision not to take a decision, actually a decision'? Justify your answer.

Decisions can be placed into one of three categories: operational, tactical and strategic. The timeframes and consequences of each vary. For example, operational decisions represent the day-to-day activities involved in meeting the immediate needs of the organization. As such they tend to be the low-cost, small impact and low-risk decisions, perhaps more akin to problem solving. At the other extreme, strategic decisions involving issues such as acquisitions and divestment of divisions or entire companies, the development of new products and new facilities tend to be at the high-cost, high-risk end of the spectrum. The decision to build a new factory may take five years from first idea to post-commissioning hand-over, by which time both the market and product may have changed considerably. Strategic decisions are expensive to correct if they turn out to be wrong.

People can experience the theories that underpin communications, decision making and negotiation through training courses and degree programmes. Experience within organizations adds to this by providing practice opportunity in live situations. The hierarchical structure of organizations can be seen as allowing experience in these skills to be gained by individuals in a structured and relatively risk-free environment. Junior staff are allowed to take comparatively small decisions and are usually monitored by supervisors or junior managers. Promotion brings with it the opportunity to become experienced in dealing with ever larger communications, decision-making and negotiation issues. One of

Newspapers, journals and magazines	98%
Word of mouth	95%
Market reports	85%
Company reports	83%
TV/radio	75%
Online information sources	59%
Microfiche	34%
CD-ROM	19%

TABLE 11.3 Source of information available to managers (*source: Personnel Today*, 3 May, 1994)

MANAGEMENT IN ACTION 11.8

On the road to procrastination

There are many light-hearted observations found on company notice boards and office walls about the benefits or otherwise of meetings. The following is not uncommon:

Are you lonely? Work on your own? Hate making decisions? Hold a meeting! You can see other people, draw flowcharts, feel important and impress your colleagues. All in work time. **Meetings** – the practical alternative to work.

It has long been established that making decisions is stressful. The well-known 'executive monkey' studies from the 1960s demonstrated that forcing the animals to decide between options, the results of which determined if an electric shock would be applied, caused the animals to become ill. There are many parallels between these experiments and the work experience of modern managers. Under pressure from many quarters to cut costs and at the same time enhance customer service it is hardly surprising that many attempt to slow down the rate of change and decision making. In his light-hearted review, Furnham draws attention to the decision-avoidance possibilities of committees and individuals.

Committees, claims Furnham, represent the most popular decision-avoidance technique. He goes on to explain that the best committees at this process are those that include individuals who prefer to do nothing who can then legitimately meet and decide that nothing can be done. At an individual level, the more popular decision-avoidance techniques are claimed to be:

✦ The temper tantrum. Adopting the behaviour typical of a spoilt two-year-old child can frequently manipulate the reactions of others to the extent that any decision becomes unnecessary or at least favourable.

✦ The hush-hush approach. Pointing out to a colleague that information exists that they could not possible be party to can effectively halt any work. It effectively means that any

progress on the problem would result in severe embarrassment or even worse at a personal or professional level.

✦ The clarification method. This approach can also be classed as elaboration. It adopts the approach that continually referring back an issue for further information or clarification or for the delineation of decision boundaries can simply exhaust the person being targeted and so halt a project.

✦ The double-talk method. This approach is much beloved of those individuals with the ability to use long words and complex sentences. It is a jargon-based approach intended to confuse others and to make them look inadequate as the basis of controlling their behaviour.

✦ The denial approach. Simply stating over and over again that no decision is necessary can frequently be used to avoid having to take one.

✦ The 'that's your problem' response. Simply handing the problem back to the originator can be an effective way of avoiding a decision. It can involve trying to make them feel that they should be adapting to a situation or be capable of taking the decision themselves without the need to refer it to other people.

Furnham finishes with two quotes demonstrating opposite perspectives on procrastination. Victor Kiam is reputed to have said that: 'Procrastination is opportunity's natural assassin.' James Thurber, by way of contrast, suggested that: 'He who hesitates is often saved.' A view which perhaps explains the popularity of decision-avoidance techniques.

Adapted from: Furnham, A (1994) On the road to procrastination, *Financial Times*, 4 May, p 17; original source for the meetings quotation unknown, but this version taken from the *Australian Family Physician*, 1992, 21, p 904.

the consequences of delayering (otherwise known as downsizing or rightsizing) of organizations over recent years has been the reduction in the amount of practice opportunity available. This is particularly evident in the opportunity for *graded* decision-making and negotiating experience, with a possible increase in the level of risk and failure for both individuals and organizations.

Essentially, the steps between levels in a delayered organization are much larger and there are fewer checks on activity (pushing decision making down the hierarchy is a prime objective of such schemes) and, consequently, there is less room for error or incremental learning.

There is a unique relationship between the three concepts of communication, decision making and negotiation that is not often found in management theory. There is a cumulative relationship between them. Communication can take place isolated from the other two. The simple exchange of information and interaction does not imply either decision making or negotiation. Decision making, however, cannot take place without communication, but it can take place without negotiation. The chief executive reviewing the financial performance of the company can decide on an appropriate course of action based upon the financial reports available and other information communicated by and discussed with senior managers. This does not necessarily require that the chief executive must negotiate with anyone over the intended course of action. Negotiation, however, can only take place in conjunction with the other two. In order to negotiate the parties must communicate and take decisions. Management in Action 11.9 provides an illustration of how communications and decision making link with negotiation to provide the basis of an effective result.

Stop | Consider

Think about the points made in MiA 11.9 and explain why you think they are significant in terms of negotiation success based upon the material in this and other chapters in this text.

Conclusions

Communications, decision making and negotiation are three of the most important aspects of managerial activity. They are interlinked in a way that makes them difficult to separate and consider in isolation. From the point of view of anyone connected with organizations they are all about the process of influencing others in some way or other. For example, communication has as one of its main features the persuasion of others to a particular point of view. Decision making has as one of its main objectives the selection of a course of action that will inevitably impact on others. Negotiation has as one of its main features the persuasion of others to reach agreement (or an exchange) on a mutually acceptable basis.

Discussion questions

1. Define the following key terms used in this chapter:

   Communication   *Non-programmed decision*   *Tactics*

MANAGEMENT IN ACTION 11.9

How clever negotiators get their way

Huthwaite Research Group has studied negotiating behaviours for over 25 years and identified a number of ways in which successful negotiators distinguish themselves:

♦ Seeking information. Skilled negotiators spend about 30% of their time in negotiations asking questions, compared to only 10% by average negotiators. This is thought to give a degree of control over the discussion and avoid direct disagreement.

♦ Testing understanding. Skilled negotiators spend twice as much time as average ones testing that they understand what the other party is saying. This aspect is about the clarity of the issues under discussion and how each party understands the other's point of view. It is about statements such as: 'Let me see if I have understood what you are saying?'

♦ Summarizing. The same can be said of summarizing the arguments as it goes along as about testing understanding. Summarizing flows naturally from testing understanding. It is about statements such as: 'Can I just take a few minutes to review where we have got to?'

♦ Behaviour labelling. This aspect of effective negotiation is about providing advance indication of what is to be said next. For example, rather than simply saying, 'What is your best discount for bulk orders?', the skilled negotiator would say first, 'Can I ask you a question? What is your best discount for bulk orders?'. It is suggested that labelling the following behaviour in this way takes some of the surprise out of the process, slows the whole process down, focuses attention on the second sentence rather than the label and so is more likely to gain a response.

Huthwaite's research also showed that successful negotiators avoid the following behaviours:

♦ Irritators. By avoiding saying unpleasant and offensive things about opponents arguments can obviously be avoided. However, average negotiators are more likely to offer favourable comments about themselves and their case. For example: 'This represents a very favourable offer.'

♦ Defend/attack spirals. By directly avoiding the use of attack or defend behaviours a spiral of deteriorating quality of discussion can be avoided.

♦ Counterproposals. Simply using counterproposals avoids the opportunity to explore the merits in the other case or to find ways for mutual benefit. Skilled negotiators make significantly fewer counterproposals.

♦ Argument dilution. Skilled negotiators use many fewer justification claims to back up their case. This runs counter to the argument that the more reasons to back up a case the stronger it becomes. However, more reasons provide more potential points of disagreement if the other party hold a different perspective. This can dilute the strength of the underlying argument.

Source material © Huthwaite Research Group. For further information, please contact Huthwaite International. Tel: 01709 710081. Web site: www.huthwaite.co.uk

Decision	*Non-verbal communication*	*Groupthink*
Principled negotiation	*Negotiate*	*Feedback*
Decoding	*Programmed decision*	*Encoding*

2. Compare and contrast programmed and non-programmed decision making, giving examples of each.

3. Describe some of the tactics used in negotiation. How would you counter some of the aggressive tactics described?

4. Describe how communications can be thought of as a perceptual process.

5. Is rationality the only basis on which decisions are taken? Illustrate your answer from your own experience.

6. Is negotiation group dynamics in a particular situation? Justify your answer.

7. Why is decision making important for an organization?

8. 'Negotiation is nothing more than a power struggle between two unequal parties.' Discuss this statement.

9. Would it be possible for managers to operate in such a way that negotiation with trade unions could be avoided?

10. 'Communication, decision making and negotiation skills are so closely linked to the personality of the individuals that they cannot be learned.' Discuss this statement.

Research activities

1. Obtain the annual reports for a range of large and small companies from the manufacturing and service industries. What can you infer about their approach to communications from the literature that you have obtained? Obtain the annual reports for a single company from a number of years. What can you infer about changes to the communication strategy adopted over time?

2. Attempt to make contact with a trade union officer and a manager and ask them to describe how they take decisions before going into an industrial relations negotiation and how they take decisions once the negotiation has begun. Ask the manager if they consider that industrial relations decisions differ from other areas of decision making, and if so why?

3. Make contact with a manager in a local organization and identify the groups with which they negotiate. In the discussion see if you can identify whether the manager uses different tactics and approaches for any of the different groups. Also identify how the planning and preparation for specific negotiations differ. How does the manager deal with difficult negotiations?

Key reading

From Clark, H, Chandler, J and Barry, J (1994) *Organization and Identities: Text and Readings in Organizational Behaviour*, International Thomson Business Press, London:

✦ Janis, IL: Groupthink and poor quality decision making, p 279. A review of the potential problems in an institutionalized environment forms the basis of this extract.

✦ Brunsson, N: The virtue of irrationality – decision making, action and commitment, p 294. This argues for an irrational perspective in decision making in order to improve effectiveness.

✦ Hyman, R: The power of collective action, p 322. This extract introduces some of the distinctions between organized and unorganized conflict in the industrial relations field.

✦ Bradley, K and Hill, S: What quality circles are, p 364. Quality circles were introduced to improve the work experience of employees and productivity. As such employees are trained in communication and problem-solving skills.

✦ Hill, S: Quality circles in Britain, p 366. This article indicates the development of quality circles in Britain and outlines some of the emerging issues.

Further reading

Checkland, P (1981) *Systems Thinking, Systems Practice*, John Wiley, Chichester. This is quite a difficult text for anyone new to systems thinking, but it offers a useful review of the hard and soft approaches to problem solving.

Cialdini, RB (1988) *Influence: Science and Practice*, HarperCollins, New York. A highly readable text on the general topic of persuasion in all its forms. It includes consideration of all three topics covered in this chapter, but from a different perspective.

Fisher, D (1993) *Communications in Organizations*, 2nd edn, West Publishing, St Paul, MN. This text considers communication from many perspectives relevant to material within the organizational behaviour field.

Fisher, R and Ury, W (1981) *Getting To Yes*, Hutchinson Business, London. This book describes the principled negotiation approach developed by the authors. The subtitle for the book is 'negotiating without giving in', and this effectively describes the approach adopted by the authors. It was followed by a second text (*Getting Past No*, W Ury, 1991, Business Books, London) which outlines how to deal with difficult people in a negotiation context.

Hickson, DJ, Butler, RJ, Cray, D, Malory, GR and Wilson, DC (1986) *Top Decisions: Strategic Decision Making in Organizations*, Basil Blackwell, Oxford. This book describes the decision-making activities across organizations ranging in size from very small to very large. Among its strengths is that it shows how the political dimension of organizations manifests itself in the decision-making process.

Kennedy, G (1999) *The New Negotiating Edge*. Nicholas Brealey, London. A recent addition to the wide range of texts on negotiation. Written by a professor at Edinburgh Business School it provides a good balance between theory qnd practice.

Scott, W (1981) *The Skills of Negotiating*, Gower, Aldershot. This is a practical 'how to' type of book which covers many of the facets of negotiating in a range of situations. It is readable and sets out to improve the capability to carry out negotiations as well as describing the process itself.

Spitzer, Q and Evans, R (1999) *Heads You Win: How the Best Companies Think*, Touchstone Books, London. Based on a specific problem-solving approach the authors review the practical implementation issues around the model. It is intended as a practitioner text and is supported by the consultancy experience of the authors.

References

Alatas, SH (1991) *Corruption: Its Nature, Causes and Functions*, S Abdul Majeed, Kuala Lumpur.

Arucher, E (1980) How to make a business decision: an analysis of theory and practice, *Management Review*, February.

Bentley, T (1999) Decide now, *Management Today*, July, Haymarket Group, London.

Carpenter, DS and Feloni, J (1989) *The Fall of the House of Hutton*, Henry Holt, New York.

Child, J (ed.) (1973) *Man and Organization*, Allen & Unwin, London.

Cohen, MD, March, JG and Olsen, JP (1972) A garbage can model of organizational choice, *Administrative Science Quarterly*, **17**, 1–25.

Cyert, RM and March, JG (1963) *A Behavioural Theory of the Firm*, Prentice Hall, Englewood Cliffs, NJ.

Edwards, P and Hall, M (1999) Remission: possible, *People Management*, 15 July, **5**, 14, Institute of Personnel and Development, London.

Fisher, R and Ury, W (1981) *Getting To Yes*, Hutchinson Business, London.

Garrahan, P and Stewart, P (1992) *The Nissan Enigma: Flexibility at Work in a Local Economy*, Mansell, London.

Gunther, J (1950) *Roosevelt in Retrospect*, Harper, New York.

Harrison, EF (1987) *The Managerial Decision Making Process*, 3rd edn, Houghton Mifflin, Boston, MA.

Hughes, P (1999) Decide now, *Management Today*, July, Haymarket Group, London.

Janis, IL (1982) *Victims of Groupthink: A Psychological Study of Foreign Policy Decisions and Fiascos*, 2nd edn, Houghton Mifflin, Boston, MA.

Janis, IL and Mann, L (1977) *Decision Making: A Psychological Analysis of Conflict, Choice and Commitment*, The Free Press, New York.

Jones, F (1999) Decision making, *The Psychologist*, **12**, 3.

Kennedy, G (1999) Negotiating a fair exchange, *Professional Manager*, May, **8**, 3, Institute of Management, Corby.

Lindblom, CE (1959) The science of muddling through, *Public Administration Review*, **19**, 79–88.

McKenna, E (1994) *Business Psychology and Organisataional Behaviour: A Students' Handbook*, Lawrence Erlbaum Associates Ltd, Hove.

March, JG and Simon, HA (1958) *Organizations*, John Wiley, New York.

Pease, A (1981) *Body Language*, Sheldon Press, London.

Pettigrew, A (1973) *The Politics of Organisational Decision Making*, Tavistock, London.

Powell, GN and Mainiero, LA (1999) Managerial decision making regarding alternative work arrangements, *Journal of Occupational and Organizational Psychology*, **72**,1, 41–56.

Scott, W (1981) *The Skills of Negotiating*, Gower, Aldershot.

Simon, HA (1960) *The New Science of Management Decision*, Harper & Row, New York.

Thompson, TE and Tuden, A (1959) *Comparative Studies in Administration*, University of Pittsburgh Press, Pittsburgh, PA.

Torrington, D and Hall, L (1987) *Personnel Management: A New Approach*, Prentice Hall, Englewood Cliffs, NJ.

Trager, GL (1958) Paralanguage: a first approximation, *Studies in Linguistics*, **13**, 1–12.

Van Y peren, NW, van de Berg, AE and Willering, MC (1999) Towards a better understanding of the link between participation in decision making and organizational citizenship behaviour: a multilevel analysis, *Journal of Occupational and Organizational Psychology*, **72**, 3, 377–92.

Walsh, J (1999) Division of labour, *People Management*, 16 September, **5**, 18, Institute of Personnel and Development, London.

Whitehead, M (1999) Rover's return, *People Management*, 16 September, **5**, 18, Institute of Personnel and Development, London.

Wilson, GL, Goodhall, HL and Waagen, CL (1986) *Organizational Communication*, Harper & Row, New York.

PART VI

The structure and design of organizations

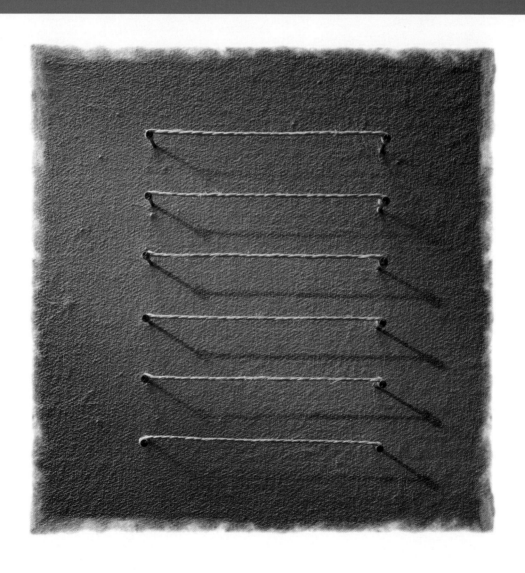

CHAPTER 12

Organizational frameworks

CHAPTER SUMMARY

This chapter begins with a consideration of the significance of an organization's structure and introduces some of the factors that influence and underpin the choices made, including bureaucracy. The organizational lifecycle concept is also introduced as an influence on the functioning of an organization as well as a factor in decision making related to design. This is followed by a discussion of the major structural variations adopted by organizations. Subsequently the notion of the flexible firm is introduced as a precursor to a discussion of the virtual and alternative organizational forms. The chapter concludes with a consideration of the applied dimensions associated with organizational design.

LEARNING OBJECTIVES

After studying this chapter and working through the associated Management in Action panels, Discussion questions and Research activities, you should be able to:

✦ Outline the main structural choices available to organizations.

✦ Explain why organizations operating internationally have more variables to take into account when deciding structural arrangements.

✦ Describe the differences in design and control implicit in the product, process and matrix, flexible and virtual structural forms.

✦ Understand the significance of the term bureaucracy in relation to organizational structure.

✦ Discuss the implications of the notion of organization as theatre.

✦ Appreciate how the work of Fayol, Weber and Foucault has informed the approaches to structure.

✦ Detail how the need to compartmentalize the work of an organization is at variance with the need to integrate activities.

✦ Assess the significance of the development of more recent approaches to structure such as the shamrock and federal organization.

Introduction

There has always existed a need to arrange the resources of an organization in such a way that will achieve the objectives set for it, in the most effective manner possible. Imagine the organization structure necessary to build the great pyramid of Cheops in Egypt. It covers an area of 13 acres and was constructed from approximately 2.5 million blocks of stone, each weighing an average of 2.5 tons. Construction is estimated to have lasted some 20 years involving a total labour force of 100,000 men (George, 1972, p 4).

Obviously, there are many differences between the way work was organized in ancient Egypt and the way in which it is organized today in modern Europe, but *organizational design* decisions had to be made even then. The framework of an organization in any age represents the way the designers interpret, in the light of prevailing models and fashion, the objectives to be achieved matched together in a particular framework with the resources available. Of course, this explanation implies that an organization is consciously designed and created from nothing. While this may be true to some extent the evolution of most organizations is based around growth, shrinkage, merger, demerger and changing commercial activities. Consequently, the opportunity open to most organizations and would-be designers is restricted to adapting that which already exists, in many ways a more complex process than creating afresh. Changing an existing organization structure requires a major effort by all concerned, particularly if it is a large and complex entity. This reflects an aspect of organizational design that will be addressed in the following chapter.

Perspectives on organizational structure

Traditional approaches to organizing emphasized the task aspects of the work being undertaken and hence the structure of the organization. In essence it represented an approach to organization which reinforced *hierarchical control* and *segmented responsibilities*. This section will explore a number of the major views in relation to the nature and significance of structure, from a range of theoretical, applied and symbolic perspectives.

Weber and bureaucracy

The essence of *bureaucracy* with its hierarchy of control, rule frameworks and task specialization was first articulated by Weber (1947). His ideas were developed in the early years of the twentieth century, a time when organizations generally were becoming much larger and more complex but did not have the benefits of technology to aid the process. The consequence was a need to develop the human equivalent of the computer in administering large organizations efficiently – the bureaucracy. Weber described this need in terms of a machine analogy. He likened the benefits available from bureaucracy to the advantages to be gained in manufacturing through the application of machines and factory-based technology.

Weber was born in Germany and was an academic all his working life. His main areas of research interest were in the sociology of religion and the sociology of economic activity. One of his major contributions was his study of the *power* and *authority relationships* within organizations. He postulated three types of organizational form differentiated through the way in which authority was legitimized within them. He described the three organizational forms as ideal types, by which he meant exemplars or typical models which would be found to a greater or lesser extent in practice. For example, any combination, or even all three might exist within parts of the same organization. The three types of organization were:

✦ Charismatic. In the *charismatic* form of organization authority is based around the personal qualities of the leader. Frequently found in religious or political movements, this type of organization might be found among small owner-managed companies in the commercial world. However, as a result of the strong reliance on the charismatic qualities and authority of the leader the issue of succession is invariably a problem that is not easy to resolve. If the succession process can be institutionalized then the organization invariably transforms into one of the two remaining categories.

✦ Traditional. The *traditional* form of organization relies on accepted precedent as the dominant form of authority. The leader in such an organization relies on tradition and accepted custom as the basis of being obeyed. It reflects a form of maintaining the status quo by continually referring back to precedent as the ultimate arbiter of the legitimacy of an instruction to follow the direction of a leader. Many family-owned organizations rely on this form of organization as leadership and authority are restricted to family members, irrespective of ability or experience.

✦ Rational–legal. The *rational–legal* notion of authority forms the basis of the *bureaucratic* form of organization according to Weber. This approach is termed rational because the organization is established to achieve specific (rational) objectives. It is also legal in the sense that it adopts a rule- and procedure-based approach to the exercise of authority. The exercise of authority in terms of who, how and to what extent is prescribed by the rule frameworks and is therefore independent of the individual postholder. Weber argued that this provided the basis of bureaucracy because it allowed for precision, speed, continuity, unity, strict subordination and the minimization of labour cost etc. Bureaucracy emerges as such a highly efficient structural approach because all the resources of the organization are effectively directed at the objectives being sought, without undue interference or whim.

It is the last of these three categories of organizational basis that is of significance in this discussion through the association with *bureaucracy*. The basis of a bureaucratic form of organization is reflected in Table 12.1, adapted from Scott (1992). The points included in Table 12.1 do not individually or collectively suggest a specific structural form in itself, but more an approach to the process of subsequently arranging and channelling resources, together with the humans that must of necessity undertake the work. If these principles and guidelines are followed whatever the framework adopted actually looks like, it will be bureaucratic in essence and approach. It reflects an attempt to provide a sound sociological and philosophical basis for a factory-based analogy to efficiency at a time when neither computer nor administrative technology was well developed. Weber also linked his ideas on bureaucracy to his views in relation to economic development and the emergence of Protestantism with its associated work ethic.

Gouldner (1954) introduced the idea that there existed different types of bureaucracy. He suggested that the three types of bureaucracy were:

+ **Mock.** The rules and procedures in a *mock bureaucracy* are largely ignored by all inside the bureaucracy, having been imposed on them by an outside agency.

+ **Punishment.** In practice the *punishment bureaucracy* represents a variant on the mock bureaucracy in that the rules are imposed on the workers inside the organization. However, the difference is that in the punishment bureaucracy it is management alone that develop the rules and procedures and then impose them on the other groups. Not surprisingly, Gouldner felt that this approach would not encourage the full commitment and support of the employees because they did not accept the legitimate basis of the authority implied under these circumstances.

+ **Representative.** In a *representative bureaucracy* the rules and procedures are generally supported by those inside the organization having been developed by managers with the involvement of the other worker and stakeholder groups.

Another view of bureaucracy is that the tight structures and procedures that are evident in the principles of it cannot eliminate the political and interactive human behaviour. Crozier (1964) studied a number of bureaucracies and described them in terms of *dynamic social systems*. He identified individuals who sought ways to achieve their own goals and position in the overall scheme of things through capitalizing on areas of uncertainty or ambiguity in the rules, procedures and responsibilities of individuals and groups within the organization.

Management in Action 12.1 shows the involvement of the Chinese military in business activities, reflecting elements of what one academic has called the bureaucratic entrepreneurlism approach to organizing on a massive scale.

Stop | Consider *Can commercial and military operations be successfully integrated under the one bureaucratic organization? Justify your views.*

A number of criticisms have been levelled at bureaucracy based on the negative impact on people. Weber himself recognized the potential negative effect of boring, routine and monotonous jobs on the people who did them, but insisted that it was the only way to

Characteristics of bureaucracy
Fixed division of labour
Clear hierarchy of positions
Postholders selected on the basis of capability
Postholders appointed and not elected
Administrative basis for keeping files and records
Separation of business and private affairs
Postholders paid by salary paid in money
Work in the organization is primary occupation of postholder
Promotion based on achievement or seniority
Rules govern work routines
Depersonalization of decision making
Disciplined approach to work required

TABLE 12.1   Bureaucratic form of organization

MANAGEMENT IN ACTION 12.1

The generals' big business offensive

The military in China is branching out into the running of commercial enterprises. This is the claim of a number of observers who specialize in the role and functioning of the military in China. China Poly Group is one such company and it is on its way to being one of the country's largest conglomerates. For example, it is working on a number of commercial ventures including the development of a freeport complex and infrastructure on the island of Hainan off the coast of Vietnam in partnership with a Japanese construction company.

There are two main categories of military/commercial link developing within China. The first category is a cluster of manufacturing, investment and trading companies under the direct control of parts of the People's Liberation Army (PLA). The second category involve the application of state-owned defence industries to the development and sale of civilian equipment and products. This category falls under the direct control of the government. John Frankenstein, from the University of Hong Kong Business School, who specializes in the topic, refers to this military involvement in private enterprise as, 'Chinese bureaucratic entrepreneurialism'.

Among the major corporations set up as part of the military and government establishments are:

✦ China Poly Group. Founded in 1984 and part of the general staff structure within the military. It was set up partly to compete with Norinco and is involved in shipping, finance, property, trading, electronics, telecommunications and construction. It also controls two companies listed on the Hong Kong Stock Exchange.

✦ Norinco. Founded before 1984 by the government and with over 157 factories under its control. It is involved with arms sales, trading, construction, real estate, finance and car manufacture.

✦ Xinxing Corporation. Is heavily associated with the logistics branch of the military and represented at most of the major military depots. It is involved with pharmaceuticals, clothing, food, construction, fuel and vehicles.

In addition to these corporations there are about 20 other companies operating within the military/state commercial enterprise framework. This also includes the police who have a company specializing in security equipment. To some extent the military is able to cover its own costs as a result of the revenue generated from these organizations. For example, the estimated cost of running the military in China is put at about two or three times the Yn52 bn official budget provided by the government.

There is, however, a degree of unease about the situation within China; the Central Military Commission established an audit commission to control possible abuses through fraud and corruption. In addition, there have been some attempts to control the further proliferation of these organizations through tighter control from the centre.

Adapted from: Holberton, S and Walker, T (1994) The generals' big business offensive, *Financial Times*, 28 November, p 19.

create efficient administrative and organizational structures. It is also the basis of work by Merton (1968) who describes the development of a bureaucratic personality as a result of being tied to the application of rules and fixed procedures. This is similar to the notion of the *organization man* phenomenon described by Whyte (1956) in which he describes in graphic detail the implications of working and succeeding in a bureaucracy.

In recent years the concept of bureaucracy has become a term of derision. This is as a result partly of the inability of bureaucracies to change with the times and partly of the frequently perceived unwillingness of staff in such organizations (at least from the customer perspective) to bend the rules and accommodate non-standard events. Equally, the notion of a bureaucratic form of organization is not appropriate to all situations. For example, organizations that operate in an industry or market in which flexibility or adaptability represent key factors for success will not do well if they are bureaucratic in structure. Also organizations that employ large numbers of professional employees (accountancy or legal practices being examples) would not get the best out of the staff if they relied on bureaucratic structuring. As Hatch (1997, p 172) suggests professionals are highly trained and socialized to adopt high standards of both work quality and performance and so rules and procedures seeking closely to direct such employees are redundant and offensive to them.

Organ and Greene (1981) carried out a study among research scientists and engineers in an attempt to measure the tension between the control inherent within a bureaucracy and the desires of such professionals to operate under *self-actualization* conditions in their work. Their conclusions suggested that bureaucratic structures can assist in the management of such professionals through the formalized structures and the resulting clarity in role expectations that exist. Also, a higher degree of clarity in the position (and contribution) of the individual in the total organizational context exists, which helps them judge their value relative to others. This has led some writers to suggest a differentiation between a *machine bureaucracy* in which the objective is to manage an administrative operation which is relatively stable and predictable and a *professional bureaucracy* in which the control processes need to be different in focus and intention in the management of professionals.

The trend of questioning the value gained from bureaucracy is increasingly becoming apparent in parallel with the increasing *professionalization of management* as a work activity. This is evident from the proliferation of management training courses and use of professional qualifications as an entry to management careers and professional associations. Also, the growth in management degrees being offered through higher education reinforces this trend. Professionally trained managers, generally of a younger age, are less willing to accept the constraints placed on them through bureaucratic frameworks and actively challenge the status quo in the search to apply their newly acquired professionalism. Consequently, attempts to cling onto bureaucracy as the dominant form of organization is perhaps doomed in the long term. However, whether the public sector can be managed effectively in a non-bureaucratic form remains to be seen. Recent attempts across the world at the privatization of large parts of the public utilities have yet to prove that they can meet the needs of society as effectively as the structures that they replace.

Fayol and classical management

Fayol was a practising manager who wrote from the perspective of his experiences in running the mining company in which he spent his entire working life, eventually becoming general manager. In his 1916 book he identified the operations necessary to run a company as:

- ✦ Technical. The production and manufacturing activities.
- ✦ Commercial. Purchasing and sales activities.
- ✦ Financial. Funding and control of capital.
- ✦ Security. Protection of goods, people and the organization.
- ✦ Accounting. Stockholding, costing and statistical information.
- ✦ Managerial. The *management process* of organizing, co-ordinating, commanding, controlling, forecasting and planning.

Fayol also identified a number of principles associated with the *management process* and which he considered impacted on the structure of the organization. They included centralization and decentralization, the division of work into compartments and the unity of command, principles still important in today's organizations. The basic approach to organizing described by Fayol has been developed by a number of people over the years and has become known as *classical management theory*. Names such as Mary Parker Follett, Oliver Sheldon, Lyndall Urwick and James Mooney are all commonly linked to these ideas. That is not to suggest that they all worked together (or even in the same country), but that their ideas were broadly similar and so common themes between them could be identified. Lussato (1976) described his views on what were the main principles associated with classical management theory (Table 12.2). In a real sense, the classical approach to organizing adapted and went beyond the administrative and control emphasis of bureaucracy and emphasized the need to consider the whole organization in structural and process terms.

The size of an organization and the complexity of operational activity creates the need for the work to be compartmentalized in order to ensure that it can be done. Kanter (1983) described this as *segmentalism* in which individuals restrict themselves to the 'boxes' implicit within bureaucratic frameworks. This she contrasted with the *entrepreneurial spirit* found in successful organizations.

In addition to this distinction, Kanter describes differences in problem solving between bureaucracies and innovative companies. She claims that innovative companies display an *integrative* approach to linking structure and culture. This point highlights the prime dilemma facing managers when they contemplate the design and structure of an organization. On the one hand, structure creates differentiation and task-based efficiency, because it *segments*, often on the basis of function. For example, the production department is separated from the personnel and marketing departments on the basis of task specialization. This represents the classic structural configuration of an organization (Figure

Scalar chain	Hierarchy of grades of seniority
Exception principle	Delegation of decision making to the lowest level possible
Unity of command	Each employee should have only one boss
Organizational specialization	Creation of appropriate departments and functions
Span of control	The achievment of an optimal number of subordinates for each boss
Application of scientific management	The application of FW Taylor's ideas in running organizations through the use of work study techniques and principles

TABLE 12.2   Classic form of management

12.1). On the other hand, following *segmentation* there is a need for the integration of activity and effort in order to be able to complete the whole product or service. The work of the marketing department must be integrated with that of the production department if the objectives of meeting customer needs and efficiency are to be met. *Segmenting* activity creates advantages through specialization, but requires specific mechanism to achieve integration. *Bureaucracy* seeks to achieve this balance through procedure and work routines, but at the cost of responsiveness and minimalism. Innovative organizations seek to avoid the dilemma by adopting other structural approaches.

The main advantage of this *classical* type of structure is that a high degree of expertise and efficiency can be achieved as a result of the opportunity for individuals to concentrate on a relatively small range of duties. The main problem with such structural arrangements is that they encourage the achievement of functional objectives as opposed to the overall objectives of the organization. This view can be identified in the research interviews carried out by Watson (1994) in which one manager reported:

> They are far more interested in steam-rollering in these new things [changes to work practices] so that they can move on in their careers than they are in trying to understand people and show them how these new ideas will advantage everybody. (p 155)

'They' in this context refers to managers who, it is suggested, function on the basis of benefit to their own careers rather than the benefit of the whole organization.

This illustrates the second need within an organization when it segments itself, namely the need to form integrative mechanisms to allow the 'segments' to work together in seeking to achieve the common objective. Not infrequently, this leads to the development of systems and procedures to ensure that all interested parties have the opportunity to contribute to the process. Watson's research demonstrates the extensive processes used to balance the forces of segmentation and integration when one of his interviewees reported that a customer order passed through 14 different pairs of hands before arriving in the manufacturing department (p 149). The relative slowness of the decision making within this type of framework, together with the potential for interfunctional conflict, is easy to envisage. Management in Action 12.2 describes how Electrolux attempted to deal with these conflicts.

Stop | Consider

Explain the situation in Electrolux in terms of the classical management theory described in Table 12.2.

Will the attempts at better integration by major international organizations such as Electrolux simply lead to ever larger and more complex administrative functions?

Will such approaches described in MiA 12.2 build into the organization the seeds of destruction through the growth of non-added value activity?

Justify your views.

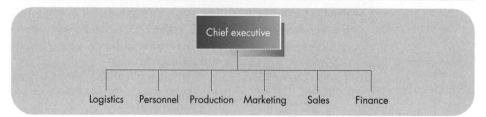

FIGURE 12.1 Functional organization structure.

MANAGEMENT IN ACTION 12.2

How to bridge functional gaps

For a considerable number of years Electrolux has pursued a strategy of growth by acquisition. Over the past decade it acquired Zanussi (Italian), Frigidaire (American) and AEG's appliances division (German). This phase has now ended and the company has begun a process of finding ways of integrating its diverse brands into cohesive operations that combine factory, sales, marketing and finance activities. In addition, there is a need to integrate the human side of the business, creating a set of shared goals and a willingness to co-operate among people, irrespective of formal reporting lines. The matrix approach to organizing did not provide the richness required from the complexity found within Electrolux and so alternative processes have been instigated to generate the 'competitive speed' sought by management.

Many multinational companies have moved over recent years towards structures based upon international product divisions or lines of business. This can provide some benefits but does ignore the other two dimensions of the matrix organization – functional and geographic management perspectives. The danger in moving too far in the international product division direction is that power begins to be concentrated at that level and also the motivation of local country managers drops. Both of these potential problems ignore the needs of local managers on whom so much depends.

Electrolux has essentially three product groups: 'hot' products, 'cold' products and 'wet' products. In late 1992 it set up pan-European industrial divisions for each of these three groups, which control product design and manufacture. A central marketing group was established for all product groups, with activity on the ground

controlled through brand 'portfolio managers' in each sales area. It was not the intention to combine these two sides of the business as the complexity would be too great. For example, there are four different brands in most countries. To attempt to integrate manufacturing with marketing under these complex conditions would create financial reporting problems and functional difficulties. Customers also expect the marketing people to be capable of dealing with the full range of products from each brand, they do not want to deal with different personnel.

The company engaged in a wide range of initiatives intended to capture the benefits of the current structure while enabling better management information to be provided. Examples included the development of a comprehensive order-to-payment system which covered the entire product cycle from manufacture to delivery to customer payment across the whole of Europe for all products and brands. Another related to the attempt to develop financial information by brand and product division. This involved the collation of much cross-border information and output of product-based end-to-end cash models. These initiatives have been supported by other measures such as management information systems and reward systems to encourage local managers to release information to allow the debate to move beyond haggling over transfer prices.

Adapted from: Lorenz, C (1994) How to bridge functional gaps, *Financial Times*, 25 November, p 14.

Foucault – power and control through structure

From a philosophical perspective Michael Foucault considers many issues associated with the need for co-ordination and differentiation within an organization. He does this through a wide range of publications not specifically associated with commercial organizations, but in such a way that pertinent themes and critical evaluations can be identified. Townley (1994) provides an insightful analysis of his work from an organizational perspective. Among the relevant features identified from his work to the nature of structure are:

✦ Enclosure. In creating an *enclosure*, boundaries are created allowing distinctions to be drawn between the distinct entities so segregated. This compartmentalization process helps to create control through pattern and order in an otherwise chaotic milieu. Examples include the enclosure that creates particular organizations (IBM is a separate *enclosure* from ICL), or the distinctions between paid labour (at work) to unpaid work (carried out at home).

✦ Partitioning. *Partitioning* refers to a vertical and horizontal differentiation of people within an enclosure. It refers to the classification of people into occupational groups and hierarchies. In recent times the distinction between core and peripheral employees is an example of partitioning. The concept of *segmentalism* discussed earlier and introduced by Kanter is an example of *partitioning*.

✦ Ranking. This relates to differentiation on the basis of a hierarchy, perhaps determined by technical skill, or experience. So, for example, *ranking* reflects the relative seniority within a sub-grouping – production manager, assistant production manager, production supervisor and trainee production manager being examples.

These concepts provide the basis for interpreting how an organization is defined in social terms and how it creates a means of being able to control its own activities. This is achieved through differentiation and the creation of a *web of meaning* and *externalization* of activity. The key implication of Foucault's description being that organization and structure are means of creating understanding among what would today be described as stakeholder groups as a precondition of the exercise of power and control.

However, in creating understanding people impose frameworks that make sense to them, the essence of all human *perception*. Understanding is created in the minds of individuals in terms of the cognitive structures that already exist. In other words, organizations are a creation of management's imagination, designed in such a way as to meet the perceived requirements of the creator. For example, worker participation in Polaroid was ended because, although successful, it was feared that it undermined the need for supervisory and managerial positions (Jenkins, 1973). Organization structure therefore derives its significance from its purpose as a mechanism of control and power on behalf of the designers (namely, management). This contrasts sharply with the earlier bureaucratic and classical view that the significance of structure is in its intention to achieve organizational objectives.

Structure as theatre

Another view of organization suggests that creating structure reflects a form of set design as might be used in the theatre. Bolman and Deal (1994, p 95), claim that it is possible to interpret organizational structure as, 'an arrangement of space, lighting, props, and costumes to make the organizational drama vivid and credible to its audience'. In making this claim the authors cite a number of studies that suggest, at least in the field of educational organizations, structure and activity are not strongly related. It is also suggested that a *symbolic logic* applies in the determination of levels of support for the organization by stakeholders through the perception of symbols, rather than through the use of any deeper measurement of value or contribution. In effect, the authors argue that the structure of an organization creates a ceremonial stage for particular performances to be carried out for the benefit of particular audiences. The symbol of structure provides the stage and other props that allow the actors within the play (organization) to act out their parts in a controlled way and within a defined script (structure, procedures and roles). The significance of structure from this perspective is that it has little direct link with commercial objectives. It is of prime relevance to the way in which the organization wishes itself to be interpreted by those who come into contact with it, together with the way that it defines the roles and actions of those within it.

Giddens and structuration theory

Giddens (1979) discussed the essence of *structuration* as a way of reflecting the creation of social structure through repeated human interaction. In his view it is the constantly repeated patterns of interaction (or lack of it) that form the basis of the feeling that structure is certain and enduring. For example, it is the routine process of individuals in the production department passing information to other individuals in the finance department that creates an understanding of the 'compartments' and structure of the production and finance departments. Just as important in the establishing of social structure are the patterns of non-interaction. For example, if the engineers hate the designers and vice versa then contact will be hostile and very limited. As a consequence that will become part of the defining features of the structure of that organization. Many attempts at business process re-engineering or other major reorganizations have failed because senior managers have not been able to change the actual patterns of social interaction at the lower levels of the company, despite dramatic changes in job function and structure.

There is an in-built contradiction with this approach to organization structure in what has been described as the *duality of structure*. This refers to the essentially circular process described in Figure 12.2.

Figure 12.2 reflects the circular and problematic process evident in the statement that

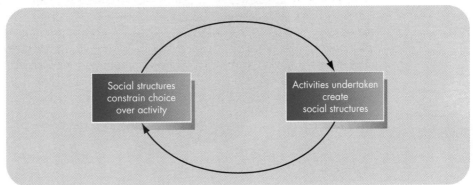

FIGURE 12.2   The duality of structure.

what humans do creates social structure, but the structures created also constrain what humans can do. 'Constrain' in this context is used not only in the sense of restrict, but also implies to channel and direct. From that perspective the social structures that exist within an organization both depend upon and create adaptations in the actual organization structure. This is because of the dynamic nature of the ever changing form, patterns and purpose of human interaction interacting with the formal and informal structural influences. In short, social structure is fluid and influences organization structure, which in turn impacts on the social structure as well.

An open systems view of structure

The open systems view of an organization is profound, yet in essence very simple (Figure 12.3) and is based on the work of Katz and Kahn (1966).

The basis of the open systems model is that a company starts life with only the essential core of the business present (along with minimal levels of support). This is essential to the creation of the organization as without it the organization could not achieve its intended purpose. It is only later, according to Katz and Kahn, that the organization begins to elaborate itself by adding adaptive or buffering functions, thereby creating more elaborate structural frameworks. These adaptive functions can include personnel, accounting, public relations, marketing and research and development for example.

The process of elaboration goes through a number of stages as follows:

✦ Activities such as purchasing and marketing become structurally separated from the core operations tasks. This forms the start of the buffering of the main operations process in order to protect it from the instability of the market and suppliers.

✦ Pressure to integrate the already established functions begins to arise in order to prevent the tendency to compartmentalize and fragment effort.

✦ The growth in the organization by this stage in its development frequently brings a number of needs not previously encountered, which must be dealt with. For example, improved equipment maintenance, the recruitment of staff and the demands of local

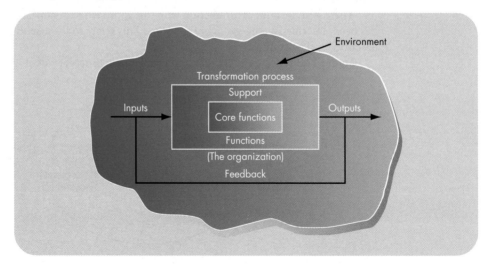

FIGURE 12.3   Open systems model of an organization.

and national government for information and tax revenues. The inclusion of these necessary activities reflect a second tier of support to the organization. They become necessary to prepare and preserve aspects of the organization's environment so that the core functions can concentrate on the main purpose of the business. The inclusion of these less direct activities is usually accompanied by the arrival of new levels of managers, some of whom supervise the work of other managers.

✦ The next stage of the organization's evolution is likely to bring with it the need to be able to deal with product diversity and increasing sales volume. There emerges a need for higher levels in the sophistication of the approach to production planning, raw materials and supplies management and customer satisfaction issues in order to protect cashflow and reputation.

✦ As the company further evolves it will encounter new situations and will inevitably respond by further elaborating itself and its social structures and organizational framework.

This last stage is likely to continue until the organization is faced with the need to take stock of its position. Perhaps this might be forced on the organization as a result of economic downturn; competitor pressure; rising cost of labour or operations generally; or perhaps the arrival of alternative products or services onto the market. Whatever the cause, the process of elaboration will cease and a redesign will be undertaken in order to take account of the new circumstances. This model is not dissimilar to the model proposed by Greiner (1972) introduced later in this chapter.

Shamrock and triple I organizations

Charles Handy (1989) introduced the idea that an organization could be represented as a *shamrock* (a small three-leaved plant). In the picture of a shamrock (Figure 12.4) are the three different categories of employee, each of whom are organized, managed and rewarded differently:

✦ Professional core. This category of employee represents the professional worker such

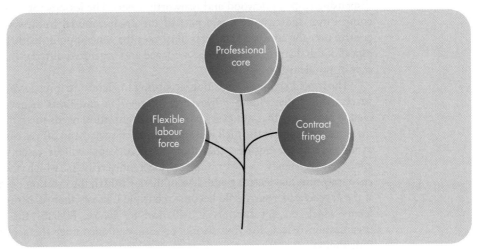

FIGURE 12.4 The shamrock organization.

as engineers, managers and specialists who direct the organization in its technical and professional endeavours.

✦ Contractual fringe. This category of worker are provided by subcontractors of various description who provide the necessary but not essential services to the host organization. Typically, such activities are paid for results and not time. Generally, much of the low-skill, boring and monotonous work in organizations has been contracted out at a substantial cost saving.

✦ Flexible labour force. This category represents the part-time, casual and freelance workers now so common in many organizations. This category reflects the ultimate form of flexibility in terms of number and skill in that they simply come and go as needed and are rewarded accordingly. It is not just the low skilled who are now part of this category of employee. For example, many university or college lecturers and management consultants are employed on a contract or casual basis providing only a limited range of services under a job by defined contract.

The purpose of the model is to encourage managers to consider their organizational purpose along with the nature of the staff relationship to the organization. As a consequence there are organizational structure implications that flow from the model in that the three categories of worker engage with the organization differently and need to be managed and integrated differently to conventional employees. For example, integration between the three main categories becomes very difficult in the short term as the working patterns vary so dramatically and are not easily changed.

In addition to the three categories of employee already discussed, Handy introduces another dimension of organizational activity that can impact on structure. That is the common practice of using the customer as a worker. This practice is more common than might at first be recognized. Consider self-service restaurants, self-assembly furniture and the wide use of automated teller machines (ATMs) by the banks for example. In each of these cases work that would have at one time been done by a company employee is now widely accepted as part of the customer's responsibility. It is interesting to note in this context the recent customer outcry to the attempts of banks to charge more widely for the use of ATMs, when they were originally introduced as a cheaper and more efficient way of dispensing cash (Littlewood and Ashworth, 1999). The lessons for management are clear: control over the customer as a part of the organizational framework is not as easy as control over the core workers. This illustrates the general point made by Handy, that each aspect of the shamrock needs to be managed and organized differently and that it is not an easy or problem-free option.

The *triple I organization* is one, according to Handy, that recognizes that in the future success will depend upon *intelligence, information* and *ideas*, hence the triple I name. Handy recognizes that not every part of the orgnization needs these three concepts in full measure, for example the mail will still need to be sorted and offices cleaned. However, it is at the core of the business that these three concepts will be essential for survival and effectiveness. Handy is describing an ideal university in which the collegiate system encourages mutual learning and development through the creation of new knowledge etc. If the *key factors for success* do become the triple I factors then structural (and leadership) forms which do not support it will lead to failure. Perhaps the *shamrock* form of organization reflects the frameworks necessary to encourage the achievement of *triple I* functioning.

Strategic management and structure

Figure 12.5 illustrates a strategic management perspective, intended to produce alignment between the organization and its identified objectives. Decisions resulting from this process have a significant impact on organizational design considerations. Structure in this context is the means by which effort is co-ordinated and through which results are achieved. Indeed, Porter (1985, p 23) argues that: 'Each generic [competitive] strategy implies different skills and requirements for success, which commonly translate into differences in organizational structure and culture.'

The strategic approach to structure begins with an intention to create understanding of the environment within which the organization is functioning. Once in an understandable form these 'data' then become amenable to manipulation through a decision-making process. Management in Action 12.3 illustrates the strategic links with structure in attempts by Volkswagen to improve its position. This involves not only reorganizing the activities within the company but replacing individuals and relationships with suppliers.

Stop | Consider

Use the Internet, company reports etc. to see if you can identify what has happened to VW since 1993 (when the crisis emerged) and seek to identify to what extent the 'medicine' prescribed by the company doctor was successful or not.

From this brief review of the significance of structure it is apparent that it is management that defines the boundaries and content of organizations. They also construct the reality which confines what other people must adapt to. This provides management with a range of benefits other than an ability to meet operational objectives.

Organizational lifecycle

It is well understood that products go through a lifecycle. A new product is designed and introduced to the marketplace. If it is successful then sales will begin to grow rapidly.

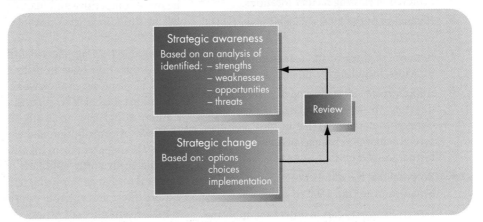

FIGURE 12.5   Strategic management approach (*adapted from*: Thompson, JL (!990) *Strategic Management Awareness and Change International*, International Thomson Publishing, London).

MANAGEMENT IN ACTION 12.3

Bitter pill from company doctors

The role of the company doctor is frequently a difficult one. Brought in to deal with a crisis, hard decisions have to be made and there is a direct and inevitable impact on people and jobs. Volkswagen (VW) found itself in need of a company doctor in attempting to get itself out of its financial crisis in 1993. Pre-tax profits had been on the slide for a number of years, dropping from about DM3bn in 1989 to a loss of DM1.25bn for the first three months of 1993. The scale of the losses was very significant for both group and country as the turnover of the company accounted for about 3% of the economic output of the reunified Germany.

Mr Ferdinand Piëch was appointed chairman of the Volkswagen group and within a few days had developed an emergency strategy. The range of measures proposed by Mr Piëch and his emergency team included:

✦ Reduction of 20,000 jobs by the end of 1993 and a further 16,000 by the end of 1997.

✦ Capital investment to be reduced by about 50% to DM6bn in 1993.

✦ New factory in Mosel to be delayed or scrapped.

✦ Productivity and output improvements to be achieved in existing factory locations.

✦ Reduction of the 1992 dividend from DM11 to DM2.

✦ Removal of three of the management board directors, including the finance director.

✦ Appointment of a new group purchasing director, Mr José Lopez, headhunted from General Motors (GM). He in turn recruited several senior purchasing specialists from his former team at GM.

✦ Proposal that the number of suppliers to VW be cut from around 1500 to about 200.

✦ Design changes to cars in order to simplify the logistics, stock and cost aspects. For example, reduction of the 16 rear-axle variations in the VW Golf to four.

✦ Change in the nature of the supply chain so the VW could concentrate on core operations and source complete sub-units from outside. For example, buying complete brake systems from pedals to brake pads as a single sub-assembly, so that they could be fitted in one go, at the lowest cost and in the fastest time.

✦ Proposal that the number of management levels be reduced from nine to three.

✦ Building on the existing performance of satellite factories, overseas investments and other marques within the group. For example, the plant in Mexico supplied volume to keep the share of the market at 32% and Škoda (also part of VW, along with Audi and Seat) in the Czech Republic increased its deliveries by about 18% in the first two months of 1993.

Every aspect of the business had been identified for 'treatment' by Mr Piëch in his role as company doctor. He intended that no stone be left unturned in the drive for lower costs and higher profits. He indicated that suppliers would have to be more competitive and that costs would have to fall to the lowest level possible without driving either the supplier or VW out or business. He promised to help suppliers identify ways to reduce their production costs in order to create a symbiosis in joint survival. Anyone not in a direct operations jobs at VW, such as central administration, would have to justify their existence on the basis of contribution and earning their keep. It was also apparent from his actions that the traditional softly softly approach of German management to change was being rejected in favour of a more direct and vigorous approach, led by individuals from other countries.

Adapted from: Parkes, C (1993) Bitter pill from company doctors, *Financial Times*, 1 April, p 21.

Eventually, the level of sales will stabilize as the product becomes mature. Thereafter, sales will decline as the market changes and newer products emerge. Eventually, the product will be withdrawn as it no longer meets the need for which it was intended. Occasionally, a new lease of life will be generated for old products based on fashion or changes in taste.

The Greiner model of organizational growth (in the following section and Figure 12.8) reflects one aspect of this lifecycle perspective. Also the Katz and Kahn discussion from earlier reflects upon this issue. But is organizational growth always followed by death or even contraction in size? The creation of large numbers of new companies each year is inevitably followed by the failure of a large number early in their existence. In that sense there is a lifecycle. However, a number of companies will change form and many will be taken over and absorbed into other organizations. Have such companies died or ceased to exist in any meaningful way? Equally, companies that go into receivership and have their assets sold, only to reappear in another guise or under new ownership could be said to have died or survived, depending upon the definition of 'death'.

Quinn and Cameron (1983) describe four organizational lifecycle phases:

◆ Entrepreneurial phase. This stage is typified by the presence of an owner/manager, little formal control and an emphasis on survival.

◆ Collectivity phase. During this phase the concerns are to increase the involvement of employees in running the business as it becomes less easy for the owner/manager to control every aspect of it. Delegation becomes a key part of the process during this phase.

◆ Formalization phase. During this phase an organization is mature and oriented towards stability and predictability. This includes the development of rules and procedures, together with structured meetings and communication between people in the company.

◆ Elaboration phase. The next phase introduces a process of differentiation into the organization as it attempts to fight the ravages of stagnation. It could include the introduction of a holding-company concept or of a divisionalized structure in an attempt to allow innovation, increase motivation and performance.

Again, the earlier work of Katz and Kahn is of relevance here. To these four stages a fifth can be added based on the work of writers such as Cameron *et al.* (1988):

◆ Organizational decline. There are two distinct forms of decline. The first is a decline in absolute terms, in other words reductions in the physical size of the organization. The second relates to what could be described as relative decline. In other words, decline through stagnation. The lethargy brought on as a result of age, size, bureaucracy and a passivity towards the competitive environment results in an inability to stay in close contact with the environment, and hence competitors begin to dominate the market.

Whetten (1980) identified four response options to decline:

◆ Generating. This response is about anticipation and continual adjustment. It begins with the identification of the need for constant adjustment of the organization to retain its relationship with the markets etc.

◆ Reacting. By reacting to the decline organizations often take the view that 'it' is a temporary change and that the basic approach should be to follow existing procedures more precisely. Unfortunately, by the time the decline is recognized as a long-term threat it is often too late to take effective action.

✦ Defending. In adopting this approach management usually attempts to match the organization to the perceived situation. This inevitably leads to cutbacks across a broad spectrum of cost. As a consequence there is a real danger of sending the company into a downward spiral of continuous cutbacks which eventually leads to total closure.

✦ Preventing. By adopting this approach an organization attempts to influence the environment. This can be done through mergers and acquisitions, marketing initiatives and by lobbying politicians in an attempt to influence trading conditions.

Clearly, the generating approach should be the most effective way for any organization to remain in an integrated relationship with its environment over a long period of time. The major difficulty of achieving such a flexible organizational framework is in managing the process. Being adaptive implies being close to the numerous different elements within the overall environment. There is simply not the time, opportunity or knowledge at the higher levels of most organizations to control and manage such complexity effectively. They must rely less on the vertical hierarchy for decisions, communication and co-operation must occur at the lowest levels possible within the organization (Toffler, 1985).

Structural frameworks

From the foregoing discussion it should be apparent that among the most important decision areas that can influence the design of an organization are:

✦ Formalization. This relates to the notion of the formality and degree of prescription involved with the way in which the organization undertakes its activities.

✦ Job design. The way individual tasks are combined together to create specific jobs influences the structure of the organization. For example, a car-manufacturing plant built around the concept of assembly lines, with each employee undertaking only a very limited number of tasks, will have a different structure than if assembly were done by teams of employees building a whole car.

✦ Height. A tall structure will have different structural frameworks from one that is relatively flat. This is frequently reflected as the size and shape of the pyramid used to diagram most organizations (Figure 12.6).

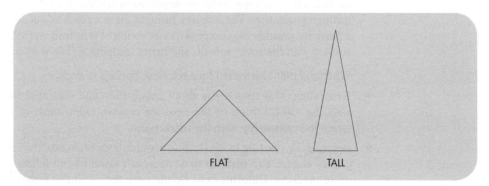

FIGURE 12.6 Organizational height.

◆ Orientation. An organization that is designed around the functional activities (personnel, finance, marketing etc.) will have different structural arrangements from one organized along product lines (all activities involved with a specific product grouped together) and differently again from a shamrock organization or one adopting the triple I concepts.

◆ Centralization. The degree to which an organization operates in a centralized or decentralized manner in terms of decision making and delegated authority will also influence the structural design. This issue is also relevant to the discussion about the federal organization discussed earlier.

◆ Co-ordination. The mechanisms for ensuring that whatever the form of segmentation within the organization the various sub-units are integrated in a way that provides a capability of contribution towards the objectives sought. The relationship between line and staff activities within an organization is also relevant to this process. Line activities are those with a direct impact on the main purpose of the business (manufacturing, sales). Staff functions are the support activities (accounting, personnel) to the main purpose operations.

Taking these points into account we now examine the most frequently found forms of organizational structure.

Entrepreneurial structures

The entrepreneurial structure is typically found in small organizations where the owner also plays an active and dominant role in running them. In the early years there may not be enough work to justify employing staff. The most simple form of an entrepreneurial structure is shown in Figure 12.7.

In running an entrepreneurial organization all decisions of any significance are taken by the owner/manager, with employees being the resource to implement them. In this form of organization the management activities are largely inseparable from the personalities and personal preferences of the owners. Decision making is very often based on personal feelings and needs, rather than those of the business. Personal relationships feature very heavily as an important feature of the activities within this type of organization. The relative lack of size together with the direct involvement of the owner creates a scenario where everyone needs to be able to work together effectively if major problems are to be avoided. Individuals typically become involved with a wide range of tasks in order to deliver the service or complete the order on time. It is not uncommon to find the owner 'rolling up

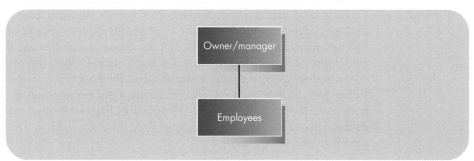

FIGURE 12.7   Entrepreneurial organization structure.

their sleeves' and undertaking the most menial tasks when necessary. In a very real sense power and authority within the organization lie with the owner/manager.

There are a considerable number of entrepreneurial organizations in both the manufacturing and service sectors. In the service sector many small partnerships exist in the field of personal services. For example, legal firms, accountancy practices, travel agencies, retail shops and restaurants. Indeed, it was part of the job creation strategy of the UK government during the 1980s to encourage the establishment of many small enterprises, the intention being to encourage unemployed people to create their own jobs and in addition to create a number of jobs for other people. The failure rate of new businesses is very high, with something like 30% going into liquidation within two years. Figures for the UK for 1994 indicated that 127,482 new businesses were formed, the highest number since 1989 (*Financial Times*, 1995).

Having survived the early difficulties associated with the start-up of a small organization, the entrepreneur is faced with the problems associated with success. Success brings with it the opportunity for growth. Increases in the volume of orders, demand for the product or service all carry with them the need for change in the organization. Growth in the volume of work in a business can be absorbed to a certain degree. Existing employees can work overtime or they can work more efficiently, new production methods can be introduced or the work can be allocated differently. However, at some point in time additional staff, new premises and equipment will be required. This poses a number of problems for the entrepreneur, but the main area for concern is often the reduced opportunity for day-to-day involvement in organizational activity. With a growth in size there is a need to manage other people who in turn do the work. It is not unusual to find entrepreneurs deliberately limiting growth in an attempt to retain personal involvement and levels of control.

The difficulties and choices facing the entrepreneurial manager and their successors were described in the work of Greiner (1972). He describes a process of having to address issues of centralization and decentralization along with differentiation and uniformity on a regular basis. Centralization creates an environment which encourages uniformity in all aspects of organizational activity. Decentralization, conversely, often originates out of a recognition that differentiation in organizational activity is necessary. Small organizations are, by definition, centralized. As they grow in size the opportunity emerges to differentiate activities through the introduction of different products and services and to open up new markets. In the early years these changes in direction can be absorbed by the existing structure and procedures, but eventually more radical and fundamental change is forced upon the organization. This forces management to deal with a series of crisis. This process Greiner demonstrates through a diagram, presented here as Figure 12.8.

It is clear that there are a number of growth strategies adopted by organizations, perhaps beginning with the creative enlargement or development of the product range. The next phase needs effective leadership to achieve growth through the integration of the volume provided by the creativity. But before that can happen, there will be a crisis of leadership, requiring the previous leader to adapt their approach to the new circumstances. Failure to do so may lead to stagnation, failure of the organization or a change in leader. It is to avoid facing up to the crises identified in Figure 12.8 that many owner/managers deliberately restrict the size of their organizations at the point at which they feel that they can retain effective control.

Product-based structures

Organization structures based on product require that the activities within the organization are categorized according to the use to which they will be put. In this approach the product or service becomes the focus for the efforts of the people and resources. Typically, each product group would be the responsibility of one manager, in effect the chief executive of a business unit within a business. The key features of this type of structure are:

✦ Product focus. The focus for the structure is the range of products or services that the organization intends to provide. In the true product structure there would be no overlap between divisions supplying the service or product, each would be dedicated to its own specific range.

✦ Single head. This type of structure creates a number of businesses in their own right. Each concentrates on its own product or service range and deals with its own customers. In that sense, each unit is a separate company. In practice, there is invariably a single manager responsible for each business unit. This type of post often carries the title of divisional director or general manager to signify the importance within the company.

✦ Limited autonomy. However the organization designs its structure within this product-based approach the divisional manager will be accountable to the head office for the running of the business unit. It does not make operational sense to have a product-based structure with a manager responsible for its activities if that person is not given the authority to undertake their duties. However, there is a need to retain an

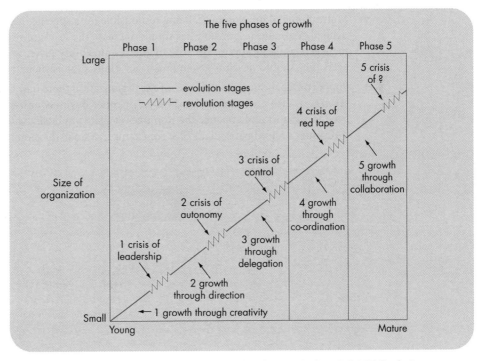

FIGURE 12.8 The growing pains of an organization (*source*: Greiner, L (1972) Evolution, revolution as organizations grow, *Harvard Business Review*, July/August).

overall consistency across the whole company. Consequently, each division will enjoy only limited autonomy. There has to be some restriction on the degree of freedom of action allowed to each division or anarchy and financial disaster could result as each attempted to become totally independent.

Product-based structures are advantageous when there is a need to get close to customers and the company offers a range of products, each serving a specific market. It is an option when there is instability in the various markets, requiring the organization to be proactive across a broad front. Splitting the product range into groups, each the responsibility of a separate business unit, provides the opportunity to concentrate on part of the overall problem. This achieves the advantages of specialization, without losing the benefits of being a large organization. An example of a product-based structure is included as Figure 12.9.

The main advantages of a product structure include:

✦ Risk. This approach spreads the risk of particular products failing and dragging the whole organization down with them. It is possible more effectively to control the overall operation because decision making can be split into the operational levels within the business unit and strategic decision making can be focused at head office.

✦ Evaluation. The decision-making process becomes clearer as a result of the compartmentalization of the business. Those products and business units that are successful will be more visible through the cost and profit evaluation processes used within the organization. Equally, problem operations are more easily detected and remedial action taken.

✦ Motivation and development. Being responsible for a specific business unit with well-defined goals and responsibilities should increase the levels of motivation among the managers and employees. Because of the responsibility given to business unit managers they should develop 'general manager' skills at an earlier stage of their careers.

✦ Support. Depending upon the size of the organization there may be a range of support services available within the head office, or other business units. These could be utilized to support and enhance the resources available in business units that experience difficulties or need particular skills. For example, a small division may not have its own

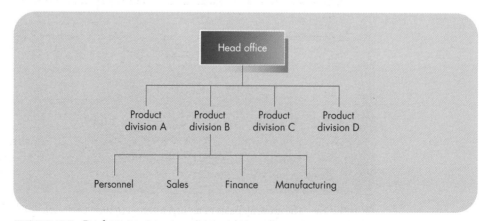

FIGURE 12.9 Product structure.

training and development specialists, but can call on the group specialist to design an appropriate course if an identified need is detected.

✦ Acquisition and divestment. The integration of acquired companies should be effected more easily if they are to be absorbed into an existing specialized structure. Even if the acquired company itself has a number of products which are to be split among separate business units, this should produce a more satisfactory result more quickly. Divestment can also be more easily achieved as the closure or sale of one complete division should have minimal impact on the others within the company.

✦ Change. It is assumed that because each business unit will be closer to its customers and the market for its products it will be more adaptable and responsive to the need for change. It would be more obviously in the interests of employees at every level to adapt and develop products, services and working practices to meet the ever changing needs of customers.

The disadvantages of a product-based structure include:

✦ Responsibility. There may be confusion or lack of clarity between the responsibilities and rights of head office to interfere with business unit activity or to instruct a unit in what it must do in particular situations.

✦ Conflict. It is likely that there will be conflict between business units as a result of competition for resources. No company can support every request for additional resources. Every manager could make use of additional resources if they became available. An organization must find some way of prioritizing requests.

✦ Short-term perspective. Depending upon the career development patterns together with budgetary and incentive arrangements, it is possible that business unit managers will concentrate on short-term results. A manager faced with the option of taking decisions which will benefit the unit in (say) five years, but who knows that he will have moved jobs by then, will be tempted to take decisions that reflect on his or her immediate performance.

✦ Relative size. Not all business units will be the same size and co-ordination between them can become difficult as a consequence, particularly if there are commercial linkages between them. Smaller units often feel forgotten and dominated by the larger ones, which can lead to frustration, underperformance and missed business opportunities.

✦ Customer confusion. It is possible that a single customer may have contact with more than one business unit. This leads to duplication and frustration for both parties.

Process-based structures

Process-based structures split the organization according to the manufacturing or service activities involved. Another way of describing this type of structure is as a functional approach. For example, the typical process-based structure of a manufacturing company would group together the resources under production activities, personnel, marketing, finance and engineering (see Figure 12.10).

Typically, process would be the structural form that an entrepreneurial organization would first evolve into when growth required change. It is also likely that the business units within a product-based structure would adopt a process orientation as the basis of grouping together the sub-tasks.

The advantages of the process-based structure are:

✦ Specialization. Categorizing in functional groupings allows individuals to develop a high level of expertise in that particular discipline. It also means that support is readily available to people in that function from the other specialists around them. The benefits of this approach should be apparent in the levels of productivity achieved and the ability of the organization to deal with crises that arise.

✦ Stability. Such structures are able to deal more effectively with circumstances in which there is a continuity across time. However, with specialization comes loyalty to the functional group rather than business objectives. With markets that are unstable, requiring frequent changes in product or service, comes the need to respond quickly and effectively. This is not easy to achieve through a process structure.

✦ Centralization. At the lower levels of process-based organizations there is little integration of activity across the functions. Consequently, it is only at the higher levels that any form of holistic picture of the organization, its objectives and strategies is possible. This inevitably leads to a centralized approach to running the organization. It is the centre of the organization that directs, controls and regulates everything that goes on. Management in Action 12.4 illustrates recent moves in a number of large complex organizations to recentralize aspects of their operations, having felt that decentralization had gone too far.

Stop | Consider

Consider the extent to which you would expect the changes described in MiA 12.4 to have any positive effect on the effectiveness of the organizations indicated. Also to what extent do they reflect the desire of the people at the top to exercise power and control?

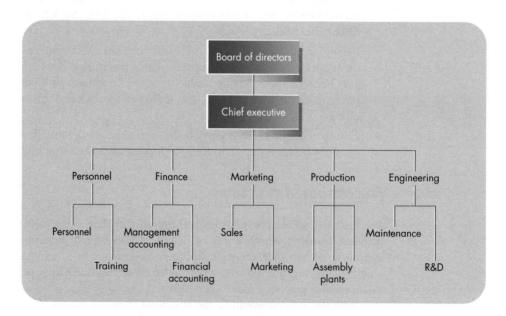

FIGURE 12.10 Process structure.

MANAGEMENT IN ACTION 12.4

Return to the centre

Many organizations are seeking to move away from the decentralized structures carefully created over the past decade or so. They are attempting to create a new unified corporate brand through seeking to provide a 'glue' to hold the entire organization together, as many have rediscovered what one of the pharaohs in ancient Egypt found (only just in time) many thousands of years ago (according to George (1972)). There is a danger that in any decentralized organization the sub-units inevitably begin to question the purpose of head office and the value obtained from it in return for the 'tax' levied on them. Equally the sub-units tend to develop their own ways of doing things, some of which may be appropriate, but many that will be done for expediency and may cut across the need for a corporate consistency in policy development and application.

In a survey carried out by the Institute of Personnel and Development among 153 chief executives from multi-site organizations employing between 500 and 5000 people, 85% were providing more leadership and direction from the centre. About 33% were also taking decision making away from divisional sub-units. These findings were equally applicable to the public as well as private sector organizations. In interpreting the findings, Professor Andrew Kakabadse from Cranfield School of Management suggests that many companies are never completely centralized or decentralized and so are in a state of semi-flux most of the time. He also made the point that the over the past decade many companies became decentralized in order to get closer to the customer. However so many organizations now do this that it is no longer a competitive advantage and so new directions have to be sought, particularly strategic advantage driven by the centre and the top levels in the organization.

For example, Hampshire County devolved personnel responsibility to individual departments during the late 1980s and early 1990s,

retaining a small central department to develop policy and support departments with specialized advice. By 1997, however, it was apparent that personnel practice across the departments was beginning to differ in significant ways. For example, some departments offered relocation expenses to new staff, while others did not. It was described by Rita Sammons (the head of personnel and training) as people with the available expertise working in silos not being available to the entire council. The solution developed involved a reduction in the number of personnel units to six, still physically located in departments but part of the central personnel function which has also been strengthened by the creation of new senior posts.

IBM has also changed its approach to personnel management through the creation of a pan-European call centre to offer guidance and support to managers across the continent. This means that the service is more consistent in its advice across a larger part of the business, but that the relationship between personnel and the operations that it serves are not as direct or human based. They are operating through telephones or electronically at a distance. The business need was to seek to orient all the front-line services of the company towards a consistent approach to customers. To do that it was argued a stronger line was needed from the centre as well as a consistency provided from the various support services. It is seeking to globalize within the company in line with the globalization of its products and customers. That needs a highly centralized approach, hence the changes. Local country personnel managers are increasingly concentrating on those issues that cannot easily be carried out on a global scale, industrial relations being the most obvious example.

Adapted from: Arkin, A (1999) Return to centre, *People Management*, 6 May, pp 34–41.

✦ Clarity. Because of the compartmentalized nature of this form of structure individuals within it are able to concentrate on just part of the overall operation. This provides a clarity of purpose. It is argued that the encouragement of this single-mindedness allows both a clarity in operational terms but also a greater degree of specialization and efficiency among the operational level of employees.

The disadvantages of the process-based structure are:

✦ Co-ordination. Specialization is also a disadvantage in that the very act of separation requires co-ordination between the functions. If co-ordination does not take place, or if it is ineffective, then the benefits of functional specialism will not be realized.

✦ Budget orientation. As a direct consequence of breaking the organization into functional units, no one group is responsible for the profitability of the organization. That responsibility lies at the level of the chief executive. Within the specialist functions responsibility is for the achievement of a budget. However, the achievement (or otherwise) of a budgeted level of expenditure does not guarantee that the profit achieved will be the best that could have been achieved.

✦ Succession. Because of the nature of the functional approach, individuals do not obtain the experience of general management until they are very senior within the organization. Functional managers are not responsible for the activities beyond their expertise. Without this experience problems can be created for career development, learning and succession planning activities for senior managers.

✦ Growth. The growth of the organization can become a problem for the process structure. As the size of the organization and the product range grows it can create problems of co-ordination and thereby restrict the performance of the organization.

✦ Political. It is likely that the emphasis on the function as the main focus of activity within the organization creates a primary loyalty to that group. This can lead to empire building and political behaviour as managers seek to enhance their importance, influence and careers within the organization.

International organizations

One of the difficulties in attempting to identify the types of structure used by international organizations is the range of size and type of such organizations. The type of involvement in international activity also creates an effect. The most commonly found forms of international activity include:

✦ Exporting. Telephone, post or the faxing of orders are the simplest means of actually initiating this form of trade. The use of the post or an international freight company is the most common means of shipping orders to the customer. Larger organizations may employ overseas representatives to sell the products made in the home country. The essence of exporting is that a company based in one country sells its products or services in other countries though sales offices or directly in response to customer orders. In the case of the service industries this could involve sending a management consultant to another country to undertake an assignment.

✦ Agents. A variation of the exporting approach is to sell through a number of agents in other countries. Typically, the agent would be self-employed, perhaps dealing with a number of suppliers across a broad range of similar products. The main advantage is that they have a better knowledge of foreign markets than the company itself. Among the disadvantages are a lack of direct control over the agent. Sales are in the hands of someone who may not be fully committed to selling the company products, particularly if they carry a portfolio of similar offerings. In addition, the organization does not build up any direct expertise in the foreign markets covered by the agent, as it is the interests of the agent to keep the company at arm's length.

♦ Licensing. This involves a company granting a licence to another company to produce and sell something the first company has exclusive rights over. In return a fee would be paid to the original company. This can be an effective means of generating money for the original company without the risks and costs of setting up in other counties. However, it is also creating an opportunity for other organizations to obtain production technologies, design specifications and market information in a way that could be damaging to the original company.

♦ Franchising. This is a process whereby the franchisee is granted a right to use a trademark in return for a payment to the franchisor. The franchisee is required to find a sum of money to start the franchise and is given help with the process. The franchisor would continue to support the franchisee in the running of the business in return for a fee. There are many franchise operations, hotel chains, fast food restaurants, business and domestic services being among the most common.

♦ Management contracts. Essentially, this form of foreign involvement is about managing an operation on behalf of another in return for a fee. In that sense it does not involve the parent company in any overseas sales of its own products or services. It is foreign involvement through the sale of its management expertise.

♦ Turnkey operations. This type of activity involves the construction of a new facility and its subsequent operation until the commissioning phase is completed. Then a fully operational facility would be handed over to the owners. This type of foreign involvement is again based upon the sale of expertise rather than the sale of products to a market.

♦ Contract arrangements. This could involve a range of activities in which one organization contracts with another to exchange goods and services. For example, the sale of military equipment to a specific country might also include the training of local staff over a number of years.

♦ Direct investment. This approach incorporates the various forms of ownership that could be found in foreign investment. This could embrace the total ownership of a company in another country or the part ownership through a joint venture or partnership. The essence being that a measure of direct control of the process is achieved through this type of involvement.

♦ Portfolio investment. This approach to international activity involves the financial involvement in operations in other countries, but not necessarily based on control of resources. It is an organizational form of investment. The parent company might hold a portfolio of investments in overseas organizations and would move its resources from location to location based upon objectives and returns. In that sense it does not reflect a business relationship in the normal sense of the term.

♦ Multinational enterprise. Often referred to as an MNE for short, such organizations engage in a truly international scale and type of operation. They engage in an integrated approach to the manufacture and marketing of products and services across a number of countries. In organizational design terms they can vary considerably in structure depending upon the nature of the business and the strategies adopted.

There are a number of ways in which international activities can be incorporated into the organization. Following is a description of the main options for dealing with international activities, at least of those organizations that have a physical presence in more than one country:

✦ International division. The creation of an international division as a separate business unit within the company is a way of coping with relatively small international activities. A simple example of an international division is shown in Figure 12.11.

   The advantages of this type of structure include a basis for concentrating the international activities and expertise within one unit which allows the development of appropriate specialisms (export credit, customs documentation etc.) within that grouping. It also allows the overseas company to be relatively small by comparison and not be swamped by the larger operations.

✦ Product-based business units. This type of structure groups together international activities by product type, thus allowing for the development of appropriate expertise within each location. Product-based expertise is also spread across the spectrum of international activity for each product group (see Figure 12.12).

   The main disadvantage of this approach to organizational structure is the potential overlap and duplication in particular locations. This can be inefficient, confusing and frustrating for the customers and staff.

✦ Geographic business units. This approach compartmentalizes operational activity by location (see Figure 12.13).

   The advantages of this type of structure include an opportunity to group together specialists in particular parts of the world. It also provides an opportunity to provide a single company in a specific country or region. The difficulties include the potential for duplication of resource availability within the company. For example, each country will have its own production, marketing, finance and personnel specialists. This can lead to duplication of effort and additional cost within the group as a whole.

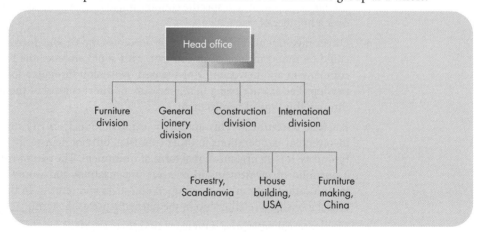

FIGURE 12.11   International operations as separate division.

◆ Functional orientation. The functional approach to international operations differentiates activity by purpose and location. For example, the personnel people wherever they are based report through their line managers to head office rather than to any specific country general manager (see Figure 12.14).

Because of the functional nature of the grouping of resources in this structural form there should be the opportunity to generate high levels of productivity and technical/professional support for the operations. The advantages allow for variability in functional presence in particular countries. For example, a marketing presence in a location without production facilities. However, the difficulties lie with the separation and functional loyalty engendered in each of the specialist groups. Because each group reports to head office through its own chain of command disputes can become a major

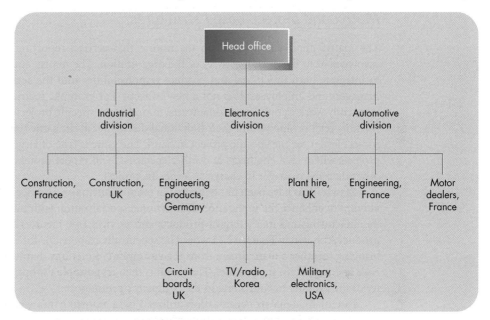

FIGURE 12.12   Product-based international operations.

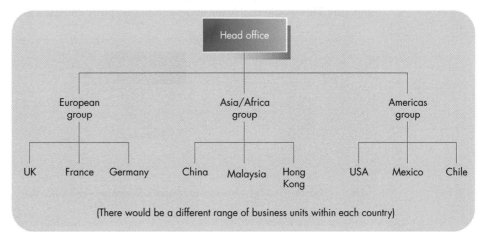

FIGURE 12.13   Place-based international operations.

hindrance to efficient operations. Integration among the specialists within each country is a major challenge for management.

✦ Matrix organization. The concept of a matrix approach to organizational design is that there are dual reporting relationships in existence. In an international context that would be the equivalent of a combination of a product and geographic approaches. The dual reporting relationships being to both a product group for technical issues and the geographic group for national and locational responsibilities.

✦ Holding company. Operating as a holding company results in the organization of the company into legally separate entities. Each then becomes responsible as a profit centre for its own activities.

Matrix and project-based structures

The matrix approach is based on the notion that vertical reporting relationships limit involvement in the overall activity of the organization. The matrix emerges as an attempt to integrate both functional and product responsibilities into the activities of individual managers and employees. It is not a new concept. For example, management consultants frequently work in multifunctional teams to undertake specific projects. Members retain a working relationship within their individual disciplines at the same time as reporting to a project leader for the specific project in hand. The same is true of large-scale construction projects where civil engineers and other specialists will report professionally to someone other than the manager in charge of a specific project.

Matrix ideas have been implemented in manufacturing and service organizations in an attempt to enhance the integration of functional specialization with more effective design, manufacturing and marketing of products and services (see Figure 12.15). The 'manager product A' shown in Figure 12.15 would be specifically responsible for that product and for bringing together a team drawn from the appropriate functions that would have an influence and impact on the product. That team is then responsible for optimizing the capability of the product to contribute to the company's profit etc.

Essentially, a matrix organization utilizes a twin reporting framework in an attempt to provide a more complex application of resource. It reflects the principles of the contingency approach to design (to be discussed in the next chapter) in that it allows a duality of emphasis. This should enable the organization to capture and use a greater amount of envi-

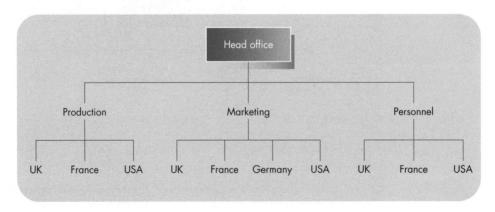

FIGURE 12.14 Functional basis for international operations.

ronmental detail in its operational activity. However, there are a number of difficulties inherent with the matrix structure, including:

✦ Complexity of operation. The introduction of a matrix structure can add complexity to what may already be a complex situation. Imagine a very large manufacturing organization employing many thousands of people across a number of locations and perhaps countries. To add a matrix dimension to such an organization would increase the complexity of operation by a considerable order of magnitude. In communication terms alone the need to involve other people in the activities associated with product groups could create havoc.

✦ Split responsibilities. In the matrix structure managers (and others) will have split responsibilities. For example, in the construction industry it is common to find that professional staff (surveyors, engineers etc.) are accountable to a site manager for the duration of a project, but to a senior professional in head office as their line manager. Responsibility for the activity of the organization is diffused across a number of people.

✦ Split accountabilities. Employees find that they have more than one superior. In the last example used, the professional engineers and surveyors would be responsible to the site manager for the actual day-to-day work that they were engaged in, but to the line manager for professional standards, career development etc. This provides an opportunity for employees to take advantage of the situation leading to operational inefficiency.

✦ Increased political opportunity. The ambiguity that emerges as a result of the com-

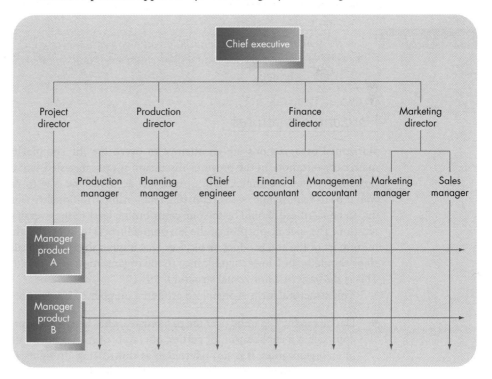

FIGURE 12.15   Matrix structure.

plexity created through the matrix approach can provide opportunities for individuals to engage in this form of behaviour. For example, it would be possible for a line manager to blame mistakes on a project team and thus avoid responsibility.

✦ Lack of clear focus. Because of the split responsibilities it is possible that a lack of focus creeps into organizational activities. Unless great care is taken in setting out individual responsibilities, it is possible that things of importance may be missed, everyone assuming that they are someone else's responsibility.

✦ Requires specific skills. Because of the need for people to work with two bosses there is a requirement for particular social skills and abilities. It is not easy to work effectively for two different people, each with different priorities and demands, particularly when accustomed to the unity of command espoused by the traditional organizations. The potential pressure on individuals is much greater in a matrix structure and they need the resilience, personality characteristics and training to be able to cope effectively.

✦ Conversion. Most organizations seeking to employ a matrix structure will already be in existence and hence find themselves needing to convert to that model. Change is very difficult to achieve when it involves a radical shift in operational activity. The process of being able to move from one framework to another, together with the time and resources involved, should not be underestimated.

One of the largest moves away from the matrix concept is described in Management in Action 12.5. Shell employed a three-dimensional matrix representing national, business divisions and functions which will be streamlined as a means of simplifying the demands on central services and co-ordination.

Stop | Consider *Can the complexity of a large multinational organization ever match the complexity of the world in which it operates and display effectiveness and contain efficient operations? Why, or why not?*

Horizontal structures

Horizontal organizations are an attempt to overcome the complexity generated by the matrix organization. In the previous discussion it was suggested that dual reporting relationships created a complexity in operational activity. One way to resolve this problem would be to remove one of the reporting relationships. Rationality would suggest that the one to be sacrificed should be the one contributing least to the overall success of the organization. The specific purpose of the horizontal links is to integrate effort across functions in support of the end product or service. This implies that the vertical reporting relationships should be of a lower significance to the organization and should be dispensed with. This is the basis of a horizontal structural form.

This structural form is organized around a number of key features, including:

✦ Flat hierarchy. The trend over the past few years has been to delayer organizations. This approach is a euphemism for cutting out layers of management, usually in the middle of an organization. It is also referred to as 'downsizing' or 'rightsizing', the effect being the same – fewer managers and organizational levels.

MANAGEMENT IN ACTION 12.5

Barons swept out of fiefdoms

The chill wind caused by flat oil prices, growing global competition and unrelenting shareholder pressure for improved financial returns has hit many of the major oil companies. Shell is no exception to those pressures. Large multinational companies must be capable of achieving several objectives at the same time. The difficulty is that these objectives contradict and conflict with each other and so a delicate balancing act is required if the organization is to survive in an ever more hostile environment. Mr Cor Herkströter, the Dutch chairman of Shell, elaborated these points by pointing out that the competing objectives included:

♦ Marshalling their resources across the globe more effectively, rapidly and flexibly.

♦ Slashing the costs of head office or the corporate centre.

♦ Retaining an ability to respond to differing market situations around the world.

♦ Retaining an ability to respond to differing competitive circumstances around the world.

These represent difficult aspects of international operations to balance. Companies have attempted to deal with these circumstances in different ways, but most involve adapting or changing the matrix approach to organizing that many international companies have adopted in the past. The major difference now is that the three-dimensional matrix of the past, in which national interest, business sectors and functions produced several layers of decision making with overlapping responsibilities, is being replaced by a simpler two-dimensional matrix structure. This was clearly the form recently proposed by the top management at Shell for a massive shake-up in its own structures.

Shell produced some impressive financial results over recent years. For example in 1994,

earnings rose by 24% and the return on capital employed was 10.4%, in double figures for the first time since 1990. A shake-out among the operating companies had seen the workforce fall by over 10,000 people, representing a reduction of about 10%. Still the company felt the need to engage in a major restructuring that would inevitably further improve performance. The justification for the change was described by Mr John Jennings, the chairman of the UK part of the group, as being a need to improve the rate of return to enable the long-term future of the company to be secured. In other words, the company, although profitable in the short term, would eventually run out of the momentum necessary to enable it to be viable in the long term.

The matrix structure of Shell had been organized around the operating companies at each location. For example, Shell Australia contained within it businesses in exploration, oil products, chemicals, gas and coal. However, above that level of organization there were the three matrix groupings associated with function, region and business sectors. In addition, there were the professional services (legal, financial, etc.) provided by head office to the rest of the group. To be able to operate such a structure effectively required considerable numbers of co-ordination activities to be carried out as well as many levels of committee to make decisions. Mr Ernst van Mourik-Broekman, the head of human resource management, indicated that the company had a committee culture that needed to be changed.

The proposed structure was based upon the five business sectors covering the main activities of the group. They are exploration and production, oil products, chemicals, gas and coal. The operating companies will report to whichever of these business sector groups is appropriate to their activities. Each business sector will be

MANAGEMENT IN ACTION 12.5   continued

headed by a committee made up of a small number of the heads of the operating companies. They will act in an investment co-ordinating and strategic capacity for the sector, leaving individual operating companies with the executive authority necessary for adapting to local conditions. Each committee will act in a collegial manner, with no formal hierarchy and members free to challenge each other on performance issues. The meetings will be chaired by a non-executive group managing director who will also report to the committee of managing directors, the most senior executive group.

The main aims of the restructuring are to focus decision making at appropriate levels within the company. For example, the operating companies need to be strongly focused on the needs of local customers and other front-line issues. The executives of these businesses need to be personally responsible for operating performance. At the business-sector level decisions are about directing resources between units in the best interests of the sector as a whole. Above that level is the group, with its need to make decisions in relation to the whole company and taking account of the interests of shareholders and other stakeholders. The proposed structure should ensure that it retains a global cohesion, while at the same time being responsive to local conditions. This should be achieved by:

◆ Retention of a dotted-line relationship between corporate headquarters and the individual operating companies, running parallel with the business reporting structures.

◆ Retention of strong country management focused on local issues.

◆ Retention of a professional service input to top management in an advisory capacity.

◆ Reinforcement of the changes through changes to management processes and mechanisms.

◆ Reinforcement of the mechanical, structural and cultural changes through training aimed at developing new skills and attitudes such as teamwork and mutual support.

Adapted from: Lascelles, D (1995) Barons swept out of fiefdoms, *Financial Times,* 30 March, p 19; and Lorenz, C (1995) End of a corporate era, *Financial Times,* 30 March, p 19.

◆ Process organization. Customers usually experience an organization horizontally, not vertically. Consider, for example, shopping at a supermarket. In the supermarket you directly 'experience' the work of the shelf stackers, the delicatessen servers and the checkout staff etc. Your experience of the supermarket is a direct function of how well those activities integrate into a complete package of services. So, the argument goes, if the customer is the driving force for the organization the structural basis for activities should be the units or processes experienced by the customer – horizontal, not hierarchical.

◆ Team activity. There are very few, if any, jobs within an organization that can be said to be individual in nature. It is almost inevitable that everyone depends upon other people for some part of their job. The cleaner requires someone to order the cleaning materials. The chief executive needs people to do the work of the organization. The sales staff require administrative support to process orders and a factory to make the products. So if group activity is inherently part of organizational life, then work groups should become the norm for organizing activity within it.

Bringing these ideas together should enable an organization to operate horizontally. Activities would be organized around the customer experience of the company and work teams ensure that all aspects of the delivery of the product or service are integrated effectively towards meeting those needs. An example of one horizontal organization is shown in Management in Action 12.6.

Stop | Consider

To what extent would it be possible to retain in the long term the horizontal design in part of the organization and conventional structures in other parts of the organization (as reflected in MiA 12.6)? Would those employees not allowed the benefits of such working resent those that were and would those differences become a source of problems?

The holding company

The holding-company framework is one in which the head office is a company in its own right and owns (fully or partly) a number of separate businesses. These in turn are legally constituted companies in their own right (see Figure 12.16).

Within each of the subsidiary companies, the structure adopted could be any one of the frameworks just described. Some holding companies keep a very tight control on the way in which each of the subsidiary organizations operates. In its pure form the holding company acts as a banker to the group. It brings together organizations that create a synergy within the group as a whole and divests those companies that do not fit with the plan or that otherwise fail to live up to profit potential and forecast. In that sense the parent company is acting as an investment house on behalf of its shareholders.

One response to the desire for size in a commercial organization is to create a structure in which integration and diversification exist at the same time. The holding-company concept can help to achieve that requirement. The existence of separate companies within the holding company provides the potential to manage according to profit (or contribution) to the parent company. This should result in the individual company's displaying the following characteristics:

✦   Objectives. Being relatively free to pursue its own objectives.

✦   Market. Being able to get closer to the markets in which it operates.

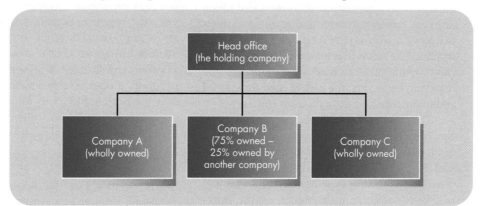

FIGURE 12.16   Holding-company framework.

MANAGEMENT IN ACTION 12.6

What a way to run a company!

Orticon is a Danish company that makes hearing aids; it employs about 1200 people. Lars Kolind has been the president of the company since 1988. The company was very traditional in its approach to the ways in which it went about its business, having been in existence for about 90 years. It had, however, lost touch with developments in technology and changes in the market. Having realized that the situation could not continue, Kolind set about changing how it functioned in order to be able to compete with its larger rivals such as Siemens and Philips. He suggested that: 'We did not have the same resources as our big competitors so we were forced to look for a different way to get ahead. We set out to create a company that doesn't work like a machine but functions like a brain.'

Out went the traditional organizational hierarchy and specific job titles. Office walls were removed and so was the right to work at a specific desk. Desks were provided for people to work at, but they were available on a first-come, first-served basis. If a junior was at a desk normally used by the boss then it would be the boss who would have to find somewhere else to work. Each person has a mobile phone and a personal trolley for their files and they tow it around with them as they go from task to task. People do whatever tasks are necessary without pre-allocation or thought of structure or status. There is also a high degree of freedom to come and go as the individual pleases, with no set hours or time-off constraints. The same degree of flexibility does not exist within the factory operations of the company, because of the higher need for control and in order to be able to produce efficiently.

The effect on the business has been dramatic. New product development has improved as a result of the greater degree of interaction between staff. Lounges, coffee bars and meeting rooms are provided to function as places for staff to mix and talk freely with each other away from the work-

place. For example, the company was able to introduce a new product that was years ahead of the competition very quickly because of the recognition that the technology already existed. The technology had been available within the company since the late 1970s but the potential had not been recognized until people began to interact in different ways following the restructuring.

Profits also increased dramatically as a result of the changes. In 1990 pre-tax profit was 13.1m Danish Kroner, the forecast for 1994 was 124.8m Danish Kroner. People have not let the team down since the introduction of the much more relaxed approach to work. People do not appear to have taken advantage of the situation. Each employee is allocated a mentor within the company who would help to guide the work and behaviour of the individual. The mentor would also be involved with salary discussions about the employee with project leaders. Salary proposals are then put to the management committee for final approval.

It is a matter of debate whether the success of Orticon could be replicated in other countries and social settings or whether it is situation specific. It is also necessary to consider the role of Lars Kolind in achieving success. He holds strong beliefs about human nature and how people function best together. Equally, the same structural and organizational flexibility is not possible in the manufacturing parts of the company. So it is not a universal panacea for achieving higher staff contribution. It does nevertheless represent a significant innovation and many large businesses and consultancies have shown interest in attempting to understand it by making visits to the company.

Adapted from: Piper, A (1994) What a way to run a company!, *The Mail On Sunday*, 11 September, pp 76–7.

+ Motivation. Management has the benefit of being responsible for a company with its own profit targets, without the risks associated with the stock market.

+ Funding. It should be possible to fund growth and development from within the group as there will be a greater level of knowledge about the risk and benefits from specific projects.

In practice, this approach to organizational design is one step further than the divisional structure referred to earlier. It attempts to provide greater opportunities for the benefits of federalism to be realized, without the constraint of too much control. Some of the problems with the holding-company approach are:

+ Support. There may not be technical or other support available from within the group when subsidiaries need it.

+ Risk. Subsidiaries are always vulnerable to the next deal. Subsidiaries are liable to be sold in order to raise capital to acquire a more attractive prospect.

+ Part owned. When two or more parents own a subsidiary (company as in Figure 12.16 for example) there is always the risk of a disagreement and a parting of the ways, the organizational equivalent of divorce. In this context the subsidiary can face uncertainty until one or other parent can buy out the others, a third party comes to the rescue or a management buyout takes place.

+ Cohesion. There may be a distinct lack of cohesion between the subsidiaries and only a limited perceived benefit or purpose behind membership in a holding company.

+ Restrictions. It may be that competition for capital from inside the group restricts the opportunity for growth in some of the subsidiaries. It is never possible to support every request for more resources. It is also possible that there may be head office restriction on some of the commercial activities that might otherwise be attractive to a truly separate company. For example, transfer pricing between companies may be determined by group policy rather than market levels and trading in some markets may be prevented if it competes with another group company.

The flexible firm

It was Ashby (1956) who first suggested the law of requisite variety. In order to ensure that the variability (variety) experienced by any system is effectively controlled, it is necessary for the controller to match the complexity of the environment. The example often used to illustrate the notion of variety is a motor vehicle. Imagine there are 5000 possible causes for a motor vehicle not starting. If a repair technician has knowledge of only 4999 of these causes and the unknown one is the actual cause of the failure on any specific occasion, then they will not be able to repair the vehicle. In that sense any form of organizational structure, but particularly the more complex forms such as the matrix, federal and shamrock, is an attempt to improve the level of requisite variety by providing a higher level of internal complexity to match more effectively that found in the environment. However, if it were that simple then the best of the available options would provide the most effective means of adding complexity to the organization in order to match that from the specific environment experienced.

The flexible firm is an idea based around the premise that employees can be trusted to do what is necessary to make the organization function effectively. It postulates that it is the horizontal perspective of an organization experienced by a customer which should determine structure. In that sense it further develops the matrix concept. It is the basis of the ideas such as the shamrock and triple I organization introduced by Handy and discussed earlier. Another approach to the notion of the flexible organization is that described by Atkinson (1984). In this approach the flexible firm could be created through:

✦ Numerical flexibility. The variability in physical size that could be achieved through a range of strategies related to security of employment. Only a small proportion of employees would be regarded as *core*. The variation in number being achieved through successive *layers* of *peripheral* employees on a short-term, part-time or subcontracted basis.

✦ Functional flexibility. This involves the ability of the organization to achieve multi-skilling and non-demarcated working practices, thus ensuring that core employees could be used across a range of jobs, reducing non-working time and the need for additional staff.

✦ Financial flexibility. This provides for expenditure variability through pay systems etc. aligned with company performance, reducing the amount of fixed cost carried by the organization.

It is the notion of flexibility in the sense of increasing the level of what might be classified as layers of progressive employee detachment from access to permanent employment that is very common today. Many organizations contain high levels of casual and temporary employees on a range of employment terms from those lasting a few weeks to a few years. It is described by many trade unions as the increasing casualization of work. However, many employees (particularly those with key and relatively transferable skills much in demand) prefer the potential benefits from becoming freelance, working for several organizations but without the ties and frustrations of working for one.

The virtual, federal and networked organization

The term virtual organization appeared towards the end of the 1980s and described a number of organizational innovations. The term originates from the computer world and the concept of virtual memory. Virtual memory is a term that reflects the appearance of more memory within a computer than actually exists. Translated into an organizational context, it is a metaphor for an organization that appears to be larger and capable of producing more than its resources would allow.

Such organizations have been in existence in some industries for many years. For example, small consultancies have operated a network, using associates to expand their ability to accept large contracts by pooling resources as a temporary measure. What makes the term more significant today is that it is being introduced into manufacturing organizations.

The basis of the virtual organization is that it is a temporary network of otherwise independent organizations for a specific purpose. It could include suppliers, customers, competitors and specialists such as designers, engineers and finance experts, the purpose being to take advantage of the particular strengths of each member of the alliance in achieving a specific objective, from which each member would benefit.

Clearly, the main advantages of the virtual organization include the opportunity to provide a response to opportunities that would otherwise be beyond the capability of the individual members. There are potential dangers with this type of approach including the risk of providing potential competitors with commercially sensitive information and expertise. Also, a failure to manage the dynamics of the relationship effectively could lead to a collapse of the venture.

In terms of the structure and design issues, there should be opportunities to reduce hierarchical frameworks to a minimum as each member of the alliance concentrates on only part of the process. However, there is a need for the integration of activity across the member organizations which would not exist in other forms of structure. Byrne *et al.* (1993) quote a number of key lessons (based on data supplied by Booz Allen & Hamilton Inc., a large consultancy practice) for organizations attempting to develop virtual relationships, including:

+ Marry well. It is necessary to identify and select the right members of the network for the right reasons. Success depends upon a high degree of trust and dependability among each of the members.

+ Play fair. Each member needs to gain from their membership or at least find that membership is in their interests. If the members cannot trust each other then important information and contributions will be held back and result in failure.

+ Offer the best. To commit the best employees to collaborative activities provides a clear signal of commitment to the project and also increases the probability of success.

+ Define objectives. It should be clear to each member of the network what the ultimate objective is and their part in it. To fail to identify the objectives will result in a lack of direction and targets against which to measure progress.

+ Common infrastructure. There needs to be an ability for each of the members to communicate with each other in a meaningful way. This requires some commonality in procedures and perhaps computer systems. Without the formality of hierarchy and clear lines of responsibility, it would be easy for communications to become confused, leading to failure.

The *federal organization* described by Handy (1989) reflects the joining together of separate groups under a common identity for a specific purpose. It seeks to reflect the need for market impact and economies of scale along with flexibility inherent in small organizations. It is fundamentally different from the notion of a decentralized organization. Decentralization implies delegated power being passed to the subordinate operational units, with the centre retaining absolute control. Federalism, by way of contrast, reflects a reverse form of delegation in which it is the individual groups which specify the limits and purpose of the overarching body, not the other way around. Handy makes much of the political analogy in describing the approach to federalism in such countries as Switzerland and the role of the president as the chairman of the co-ordinating committee. It is a simultaneous tight–loose arrangement in which the centre holds some power (perhaps to channel money into specific projects etc.) aimed at the long-term strategy of the whole organization, but the main driving force for activity comes from the individual units themselves.

In structural and decision-making terms the key aspect associated with federalism is the concept of *subsidiarity*. This is a term in common usage for those interested in the political workings of the European Union and the Roman Catholic church. It essentially reflects the notion that it is wrong for a higher authority to take unto itself a decision that could more easily and appropriately be taken by a body at a lower level. Not surprisingly, this is an issue which can cause difficulty in a federal organization if the centre seeks to take too much power or control over certain activities previously seen as a local issue.

In both the virtual and federal form of organization the need is to develop effective networks between the various levels and types of employment and partner relationships in the system. If these are not developed and operated to the benefit of the entire membership then difficulties will arise and failure result.

Alternative organizations

So far the application of the ideas within this chapter has been in terms of conventional organizations, commercial companies and public sector organizations. These are not the only types of organization that exist. Organizations are social creations and there are as many variations as human ingenuity can create. What follows is a brief introduction to some of the major alternatives that exist.

The human service organization

This type of organization has been in existence for many years. They include schools, hospitals, social work/welfare departments and public assistance providers. Notionally, they are often organized along bureaucratic lines, usually because they are part of a larger public sector organization. However, there are differences in these organizations that make them a useful starting point for consideration of non-standard organizations. Hasenfeld (1992) suggests that it is the common experience of the recipients of these services that they evoke a mixture of 'hope and fear, caring and victimization, dignity and abuse' (p 4). He goes on to propose that employees of these organizations inevitably suffer a conflict between a personal need to provide the standards of service that professional standards and norms would require and the constraints and restrictions imposed by the managers of the organization. He identifies a number of reasons that could account for this pattern of contradiction (pp 4–9):

✦ People as 'raw material'. Such organizations do not produce goods or services in the conventional sense. They do act in a very direct way upon the people who come to them for whatever purpose. This makes these organizations uniquely different from most others in achieving the transformations implicit in being an organization.

✦ Human services as moral work. Because of the nature of human services there is a moral perspective involved in the activities. It conveys messages about the 'social worth' and 'self-identity' of the people on whose behalf the service is being performed. The definition of the processing of clients as being either *objects* or *subjects* also reflects the moral dilemma facing the providers of human services. If they are objects then the professional knows best. If they are subjects then the individual should be involved in determining their own *processing*.

✦ Human services as gendered work. It is historically indisputable that the caring and nurturing activities within society have been regarded as the domain of females. It has been argued (Hasenfeld, 1992, p 7) that this *fact* creates organizations that have a tendency to reflect feminine qualities when compared to the typically male qualities that dominate commercially oriented bureaucracies. He indicates that feminist-oriented organization structures would emphasize collectivism rather than bureaucracy, together with participation rather than authority and control.

Hyde (1992) describes the functioning of a number of feminist health centres. Placing her analysis in an ideological framework, it is apparent that such organizations approach many aspects of organization differently from that of the traditional form. The analysis begins with a review of the way in which ideology influences organizational activity (Figure 12.17). Many of the elements of the analysis support the earlier comments about the distinctive qualities of human service organizations.

The co-operative and the kibbutz

The co-operative and the kibbutz are both examples of consensual organizations (Iannello, 1992, p 27). The writer quotes a definition from Rothschild and Whitt (1986) as, 'any enterprise in which control rests ultimately and overwhelmingly with the member–employees–owners, regardless of the particular legal framework through which

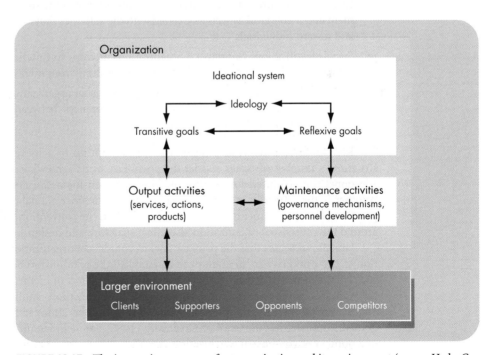

FIGURE 12.17 The interaction patterns of an organization and its environment (*source*: Hyde, C (1992) The ideational system of social movement agencies. In Hasenfeld, Y (ed.) *Human Services as Complex Organizations*, Sage, Newbury Park, CA)

this is achieved'. This work identifies the following aspects that differentiate consensual organizations:

✦ Authority. Authority in a consensual organization is retained by the collective body and is not a function of position. Authority may be temporarily vested in a particular individual but is subject to recall and control by the whole group.

✦ Rules. Within a consensual organization rules emerge from the norms and ethical values associated with the founders and members of the group. Within a bureaucratic organization the rules are designed by management to control activity in support of their objectives. Rules are therefore a 'given' in that context in that employees have less impact on and ownership of them.

✦ Social control. Unlike managerial organizations, social control in the consensual organization is based on group dynamics and the value frameworks of the individuals involved. Social control in managerial organizations is based on supervision, disciplinary sanction and the socialization of individuals.

✦ Social relations. These are also based on the values and ideals espoused by the collective. In managerial organizations they are more likely to be impersonal and professional.

✦ Recruitment and advancement. This aspect of the collective organization is based on friendship networks rather than the formalized assessment of qualification and skill. Compatibility with the ideals of the organization is a significant requirement for employment in such organizations.

✦ Incentive structures. In the consensual organization it is the social, collective involvement and ideological aspects associated with the activities that is suggested to motivate and reward individuals.

✦ Social stratification. Consensual organizations attempt to function under egalitarian principles and therefore avoid the differences resulting from hierarchical stratification.

✦ Differentiation of labour. Emphasis in the consensual organization is on integration, flexibility and contribution. Consequently, differences between jobs and between 'manual' and 'mental' work is less pronounced.

Rothschild and Whitt also imply that in attempting to achieve a non-hierarchical structure, a number of issues restrict the possibility of its achievement. They include the additional time required for decision making in a non-hierarchically structured setting. Another is the difficulty in moving away from non-democratic habits, values and work practices. The environmental constraints arising from the conventionally organized world around the consensual organization also affect structure and design.

Iannello indicates that the primary goal of consensual organizations is the humanization of the workplace in an attempt to re-establish the relationship between workers and society. The means of achieving this is to minimize the effect of hierarchy on the organization. In discussing research into this type of organization studies of the kibbutz, Yugoslavian worker organizations and the Mondragon operations in Spain are frequently quoted. Summarizing the work of Greenberg (1986), Iannello identifies the characteristic of a number of consensual organizations as:

✦ Kibbutz. Originating in Israel, the kibbutz is an attempt to combine work, social and family life into an integrated whole. Decisions are agreed at a weekly meeting of the whole organization. The leadership positions are elected and carry no special privileges or reward. Formal hierarchy is actively discouraged and control is achieved through a system of committees and the weekly meeting. Of the three types of organization described, only the kibbutz achieves any significant degree of employee influence over their sub-society. This is because the workers enjoy a high measure of control over all aspects of the productive process and social context. In the two following examples, workers set broad policy but then willingly subjugate themselves on a daily basis to a more conventional form of management control and work design.

✦ The former Yugoslavia. A national system of employee-governed organizations evolved. Legislation required organizations of more than ten people to establish a works council, its function being to determine the main company policies. The council also elected (and could remove) the management board and the plant director. It was the job of the management board to run the company on a day-to-day basis under the general direction of the works council. Given the recent major political and social upheavals in this part of the world it can only be assumed that this organizational approach has largely ceased to function and that it did not engender any depth of harmony between the peoples involved.

✦ Mondragon. This type of consensual organization originated in Spain and consists of some 80–90 individual co-operatives, employing approximately 19,000 people. Responsibility in each of the separate co-operative organizations lies with the general meeting of all members, which meets once each year. Its function is to elect the board of directors and senior managers. Managers below this level are appointed in the conventional way. The organization seeks to function on the basis of shared ownership and egalitarian principles of operation.

Organizational frameworks: an applied perspective

The relevance of the foregoing discussion for organizational design lies in the decision-making process around the options available. It is managers who make the decisions about the organization, its size and structure. It is therefore a process that is based upon the same perceptual, political and self-interest factors that exist in every other area of managerial work. That is not to suggest that there are no rational or business-related reasons for the choices that are made. It is simply to suggest that in making a choice, factors other than the 'facts' can influence decisions. Equally, this is not the place to begin to consider just how many things that are taken as 'facts' stand up to scrutiny as objective and essential influences on structure. In this context it is relevant to point out that the reasons that justify the choice of a particular design configuration are just as vulnerable to perceptual 'interpretation' as any other stimuli. However, make choices with regard to organizational design managers are required to do.

In the discussion so far the different frameworks have been introduced as discrete types. The impression is easily gained that organizations consider at frequent intervals the structure that is best suited to their circumstances and then implement that form. Rarely does the process operate in that simple way. It has been suggested earlier in this chapter that organizations evolve and change over time in response to the success achieved and the desires of the owners. This process is reflected in the Greiner model included as Figure 12.8. However, the process is less well defined and less certain than is implied by that model. For example, a company may be taken over by another and integrated into an existing operation and structure. An owner/manager may decide to restrict the size of the organization deliberately in order to retain effective control. The original partners may decide to break up the company if they find that they can no longer work together. A sudden expansion opportunity may present itself as a result of a large order. All of these situations will force some rethinking of the organizational design, but they are far from the simple and linear growth model implied in Figure 12.8.

Organizations evolve and in moving from one 'stage' to another in the lifecycle the structure tends to adjust. It is frequently only when a significant crisis occurs that a fundamental rethink of major activity, including structure, is undertaken. Radically to change the way in which work is undertaken within an organization requires time and additional resources. It also carries with it the risk of failure; lowers performance until employees become accustomed to the new patterns, practices and reporting arrangements; it may also disrupt the service to the customer as mistakes inevitably occur. Consequently, it is hardly surprising that *evolutionary change* is preferred to *revolutionary change*. However, evolution also carries significant risk, the lack of clarity in responsibilities during the gestation or transition period for example. The effect of evolutionary change in organization design produces a degree of mismatch between the structure in existence at any point in time and that desired.

The Bank of England has been in existence for over 300 years. It has changed its structure a number of times over that period in response to the changing economic and political needs of the day. Management in Action 12.7 is an indication of a recent review of its latest evolution.

Stop	Consider

To what extent does the restructuring indicated in MiA 12.7 reflect a new structure or simply the rearrangement of sections to improve aspects of the changing workload of the bank?

The technology utilized within an organization is an influencing factor in structural decisions. It is also true that technology is not a neutral factor in management activity. Management pays for the development of technology through the willingness to purchase it. The decision to use technology can be based on the desire to control activity within the organization as much as through a need to increase efficiency and reduce cost. In that context it influences both the design of jobs within the organization and the configuration of the units that make up the organization itself. Technology can be used as the justification for a change in the structure of an organization. In short, a change in structure can be deliberately brought about through the introduction, adaptation or elimination of particular technologies. From that perspective, structure is the driving force behind the technology, not the other way around.

The design of an organization is the macro level arrangement of activities and responsibilities. It is also the basis of defining the jobs done within the company. For example, the existence of a personnel department implies that there will be personnel specialists working within that function. This defines the nature of jobs undertaken within the structure. It is difficult to sustain integrated, broad job content in a highly functional structure.

MANAGEMENT IN ACTION 12.7

On a wing and a prayer

After over 300 years of existence even the Bank of England needs to review its organization structures from time to time. The world of high finance changes ever more rapidly and it is subject to increasing global influences. The requirement for the Bank of England to be able to meet its twin objectives of monetary and financial stability remains and so it must change to match the new circumstances in which it finds itself.

The project for identifying a new structure had been the responsibility of the deputy governor with the specific proposals developed by three working groups from inside the bank. Considerable consultation took place within the bank over a five-month period in drawing up the proposals. The resulting 'organogram', or diagram of the organization, reflected the two most important functions of the bank, the first wing containing those activities necessary to secure monetary stability, the second wing embracing activities relevant to financial system security. These clear distinctions were intended to replace a more fragmented set of departments and functions covering areas such as international activity, economics and banking supervision.

The proposed management structure of the Bank would retain the position of governor and deputy governor as the two senior positions within the Bank. Reporting to these positions would be four executive directors, two for each of the two wings of the Bank's activities. The functions of monetary operations and monetary analysis would be allocated to the directors within the monetary stability wing. Within the financial stability wing one of the executive directors would be responsible for regulation, supervision and surveillance with the other taking responsibility for financial infrastructure, such as financial markets, stock exchange settlement etc.

One of the concerns expressed about the proposed structure was that international aspects would no longer warrant a separate division. With some 500 foreign banks in the City and the huge financial flows passing through London, this could expose a potential weakness. The counter-argument being that international issues touch every aspect of the Bank's work and so there existed a need to involve every aspect of its operations, not just as a separate unit. In addition, a wing liaison unit was intended to be included to improve co-ordination in such areas between the various parts of the new structure.

In addition to the two wings covering the main objectives for the Bank, there would be a small number of central service units reporting directly to the governor and deputy governor. These include legal, audit and central services as well as a special investigations unit. These functions either embraced all aspects of bank activity or implied a statutory role or even a special function arising from which a direct link to the top would be necessary. The overall purpose of the restructuring was intended to make the Bank more flexible in achieving its objects of playing an effective part in running the financial matters of the country.

Adapted from: Norman, P (1994) On a wing and a prayer, *Financial Times*, 29 April, p 19.

Conclusions

This chapter reviews the major themes associated with the basis of organizational structure. It also attempts to introduce and discuss the main options for the configuration of activity within organizations. It demonstrated that there are a considerable number of options available with regard to the design of an organization and that each has advantages and disadvantages.

The structural form of an organization shapes to a considerable degree the behaviour of the individuals within it. It determines the jobs that people do as well as the nature of interaction within and outside the organization. It also determines the nature of any reporting and control relationships. At several points in the discussion in this chapter the notion of an interactive relationship with the environment has also been introduced.

Discussion questions

1. Define the following key terms used in this chapter:

Federal organization	*Product structure*	*The flexible firm*
Process structure	*International structural options*	*Fayol's management process*
Matrix structure	*Horizontal structure*	*Organizational lifecycle*
Shamrock organization	*Virtual organization*	*Bureaucracy*

2. Compare and contrast the concepts of segmentalism and integrative as described by Kanter and the concepts of centralization and decentralization in relation to organizational design.

3. One interpretation of the virtual organization is that it purports to be something more substantial than it actually is. If this represents a significant organizational form for the future to what degree should regulation be introduced to protect customers from fraud and being cheated by unscrupulous entrepreneurs?

4. Is it possible for an organization ever to be truly horizontal in structure? Why or why not?

5. 'The ultimate demise of an organization is as inevitable as the demise of the people who work in it.' Discuss this statement.

6. Is the concept of a horizontal organization the same as the matrix organization? Identify and differences and similarities. Which would you prefer to work in and why?

7. To what extent is the concept of organization as theatre of any value in understanding structural issue?

8. 'Organizations with fewer layers of management will face significant problems in the future as their managers will not have the opportunity to gain experience in major decision making before they have that responsibility.' Discuss this statement.

9. To what extent can co-ordination reduce the conflict within a functional organization?

10. Describe bureaucracy and its various forms. In what ways and to what extent does bureaucracy have a part to play in modern organizational design?

Research activities

1. Obtain a number of annual reports (or organization charts) for six different types and sizes of organization. Include some small organizations from the service and manufacturing sectors as well as some that operate internationally. Identify the different structural frameworks that they employ. How are they similar and in what ways do they differ?

2. Repeat activity 1 but this time compare two organizations across a number of years. Can you find evidence that the organizations have changed their structural form? If so why, and is there any evidence to indicate the level of success achieved as a result?

3. Seek an interview with a practising manager and ask them to consider the concept of the horizontal structural framework described earlier in this chapter. Ascertain their views about the advantages, disadvantages and appropriateness of this type of structure to their organization. What does this tell you about what may be described as a novel structure? Compare the results with other students and put together a general view based upon a variety of industries and organizations.

Key reading

From Clark, H, Chandler, J and Barry, J (1994) *Organization and Identities: Text and Readings in Organizational Behaviour*, International Thomson Business Press, London:

- ◆ Kumar, K: Specialization and the division of labour, p 13. Considers the topic from a historical and sociological perspective.
- ◆ Kumar, K: Secularization, rationalization, bureaucratization, p 17. Considers the relationships between church, state and organization as the basis of bureaucracy.
- ◆ Friedman, AL: Marx's framework, p 25. Introduces a Marxist point of view of organizations.
- ◆ Merton, RK: Bureaucratic structure and personality, p 144. Considers the relationships between bureaucracy and individual behaviour.
- ◆ Whyte, WH: The organization man, p 149. Offers some reflections on people in large organizations.
- ◆ Kanter, RM: Men and women of the corporation, p 152. Considers among other issues the gendered nature of work within organizations and the social basis of role and activity.
- ◆ Perkin, H: The rise of professional society: England since 1880, p 204. Describes the emergence of the professional as a dominant form of control in society, and hence organizations.
- ◆ Weber, M: Bureaucracy, p 225. An extract form the original work on this topic.

Further reading

Child, JA (1984) *Organization: A Guide To Problems and Practice*, 2nd edn, Harper & Row. Reviews a number of themes covered in this chapter in a very readable form.

Daniels, JD and Radebaugh, LH (1989) *International Business: Environments and Operations*, 5th edn, Addison-Wesley, Reading, MA. This text covers a considerable amount of material relevant to international operations, their finance and management. It also incorporates a broad review of the structural and design choices facing organizations.

Drucker, PF (1988) The coming of the new organization, *Harvard Business Review*, January–February. This is an article that takes a futuristic look at what is around the corner in organizational design terms.

Handy, CB (1989) *The Age of Unreason*, Arrow Books, London. This text takes a view of organizations and their relationship with the environment as its core. It explores how this relationship has changed and the potential for future design frameworks.

Mintzberg, H (1979) *The Structure of Organizations*, Prentice Hall, Englewood Cliffs, NJ. This text provides a broad review of the issues surrounding the topic of organizational design.

Toffler, A (1985) *The Adaptive Corporation*, Pan Books, London. A readable and futuristic view of how organizations need to develop in the future.

References

Ashby, R (1956) *An Introduction to Cybernetics*, Methuen, London.

Atkinson, J (1984) Manpower strategies for flexible organizations, *Personnel Management*, August 28–31.

Bolman, LG and Deal, TE (1994) The Organization as Theatre. In Tsoukas, H (ed.) *New Thinking in Organizational Behaviour: From Social Engineering to Reflective Action*, Butterworth–Heinemann, Oxford.

Byrne, J, Brandt, R and Port, O (1993) The virtual corporation, *Business Week*, 8 February, 98–103.

Cameron, KS, Sutton, RI and Whetten, DA (1988) *Readings in Organizational Decline: Frameworks, Research and Prescriptions*, Ballinger, Cambridge, MA.

Crozier, M (1964) *The Bureaucratic Phenomenon*, Tavistock Publications, London.

Fayol, H (1916) *General and Industrial Administration*, translated by C Storrs (1949), Pitman, London.

Financial Times (1995) Jump in number of new companies, 18 January, 6.

George, CS (1972) *The History of Management Thought*, 2nd edn, Prentice Hall, Englewood Cliffs, NJ.

Giddens, A (1979) *Central Problems in Social Theory: Action, Structure and Contradiction in Social Analysis*, University of California Press, Berkeley.

Gouldner, A W (1954) *Patterns of Industrial Bureaucracy*, The Free Press, New York.

Greenberg, ES (1986) *Workplace Democracy*, Cornell University Press, Ithaca, NY.

Greiner, L (1972) Evolution and revolution as organizations grow, *Harvard Business Review*, **50**, 37–46.

Handy, CB (1989) *The Age of Unreason*, Business Books, London.

Hasenfeld, Y (1992) The Nature of Human Service Organizations. In Hasenfeld, Y (ed.) *Human Services as Complex Organizations*, Sage, Newbury Park, CA.

Hatch, MJ (1997) *Organization Theory: Modern Symbolic and Postmodern Perspectives*, Oxford University Press, Oxford.

Hyde, C (1992) The Idealist System of Social Movement Agencies: An Examination of Feminist Health Centres. In Hasenfeld, Y (ed.) *Human Services as Complex Organizations*, Sage, Newbury Park, CA.

Iannello, KP (1992) *Decisions Without Hierarchy*, Routledge, London.

Jenkins, D (1973) *Job Power: Blue and White Collar Democracy*, Doubleday, Garden City, NY.

Kanter, RM (1983) *The Change Masters*, Allen & Unwin, London.

Katz, D and Kahn, RL (1966) *The Social Psychology of Organizations*, John Wiley & Sons, New York.

Littlewood, F and Ashworth, A (1999) Hole in the wall raid, *The Times, Weekend Money*, November 27, p 64.

Lussato, B (1976) *A Critical Introduction to Organization Theory*, Macmillian, London.

Merton, R K (1968) *Social Theory and Social Structure*, revised edn, Collier Macmillan, London.

Organ, DW and Greene, CN (1981) The effects of formalization on professional involvement: a compensatory approach, *Administrative Science Quarterly*, **26**, 2, 237–52.

Porter, ME (1985) *Competitive Advantage: Creating and Sustaining Superior Performance*, The Free Press, New York.

Quinn, RE and Cameron, K (1983) Organizational life cycles and some shifting criteria of effectiveness: some preliminary evidence, *Management Science*, **29**, 33–51.

Rothschild, J and Whitt, JA (1986) *The Cooperative Workplace*, Cambridge University Press, Cambridge.

Scott, RW (1992) *Organizations: Rational, Natural and Open Systems*, 3rd edn, Prentice Hall, Englewood Cliffs.

Toffler, A (1985) *The Adaptive Corporation*, Pan Books, London.

Townley, B (1994) *Reframing Human Resource Management: Power, Ethics and the Subject at Work*, Sage, London.

Watson, TJ (1994) *In Search of Management: Culture, Chaos and Control In Managerial Work*, Routledge, London.

Weber, M (1947) *The Theory of Social and Economic Organization,* trans AM Henderson and T Parsons, Oxford University Press, New York.

Whetten, DA (1980) Sources, Responses and Effects of Organizational Decline. In Kimberly, J and Miles, R (eds) *The Organizational Life Cycle,* Jossey Bass, San Francisco, CA.

Whyte, WH (1956) *The Organization Man*, Simon & Schuster, New York.

CHAPTER 13

Designing organizations

CHAPTER SUMMARY

This chapter introduces a number of aspects, including the contingency model, associated with the design of organizations. It begins by discussing a range of factors that determine the shape and form of any organization. These include the number of levels in an organization, together with the span of supervisory control and centralization and decentralization. This is followed by a discussion on how organizations can be charted and the nature of determinism, before introducing the basis of contingency theory and its major constituents. This is then followed by a review of a number of the perspectives on how organizations have sought to review structure over recent years through the VSM and BPR approaches. The chapter concludes with a review of the applied perspective on the topic.

LEARNING OBJECTIVES

After studying this chapter and working through the associated Management in Action panels, Discussion questions and Research activities, you should be able to:

✦ Describe the origins of the contingency approach to organizational design.

✦ Explain the limitations of the standard organization chart in describing activity within an organization.

✦ Understand the concept of determinism and how it relates to organization structure.

✦ Outline the dimensions which underpin the structuring of organizations.

✦ Appreciate how the use of metaphor can influence organizational design.

✦ Assess the contribution to organization design through the viable systems model.

✦ Discuss the contingency model and its relationship to structure and environment.

✦ Detail a number of alternative organizational forms and assess the degree to which they reflect a contingency approach.

Introduction

In the previous chapter the traditional approaches to designing organizations were discussed. Much of the basis for such views of design as *bureaucracy* and *classical management theory* involved a notion of the need and desirability of predictability and stability over time. These approaches to design originated when a slower pace of activity was the norm and the computer had not been invented. As a consequence the dominant philosophy was the achievement of competitive advantage through improving the ability of human workers to perform with machine-like pace, rhythm and accuracy. This is reflected in the conceptions of technical and social control as critically discussed by philosophers such as Foucault (see for example, the excellent review by Townley, 1994).

Alternative ways of organizing have existed for hundreds if not thousands of years. However, over the past 25 years competition from the developing economies and Japan has fundamentally changed the business environment in the west. The consequential shock waves forced a massive rethink among business leaders on a wide range of issues, including organizational design. It has produced the search for more effective ways of organizing in order to meet the new competitive circumstances. It is this wide-ranging and fundamental search for new ways to improve organizational design and consequential activity that differentiates today's business from that of the past. This chapter will review the concepts and processes associated with the design of organizational frameworks as the basis of the arrangement, co-ordination and control necessary to achieve desired objectives.

Management in Action 13.1 illustrates the dangers associated with a failure to change together with the difficulties associated with doing so.

Stop | Consider *Based on the argument contained in MiA 13.1 should the design of an organization be determined before activity begins, or is it important to consider structure alongside all activities within the organization?*
To what extent is this possible or practical?

Factors influencing organization design

In attempting to design an organization there are a number of departments, functions, activities or components to be fitted together within a framework. Whatever the purpose or size of the organization it is necessary to integrate these components effectively so that the desired objectives can be achieved. The structure of the organization is only one part of this integration process. Other important elements are the systems and procedures that the organization utilizes in support of its activities. For example, the use of financial reporting can help to ensure that each operational unit within the organization knows how it is contributing to the overall financial well-being of the organization. One aspect of this for large diverse or geographically spread organizations is the role and size of the corporate headquarters relative to the operating divisions. Some of the issues relevant to the role of the corporate head office in running organizations is explored in Management in Action 13.2.

MANAGEMENT IN ACTION 13.1

The gospel according to Schonberger

Making changes in a company is a difficult process and not always completely successful. BP, the international oil company, found this out in 1992. 'Project 1990' had been instigated by the new chairman, Robert Horton, to restructure the 'civil service'-style head office of the company and to introduce a new culture based on empowerment and teamwork. Among the results was a 40% reduction in the number of people working at the head office. One estimate suggested that the number of staff could reduce by as many as 10,000 by the end of the exercise. 'Project 1990' had been running for some time and rumours of morale problems had surfaced. This together with poor financial results in 1991 resulted in the share price dropping by one-third against the FT index, to its lowest level since 1989. This situation produced a new set of problems for the company to deal with.

It often takes a crisis to force a management team to seek radical change, by which time it is frequently too late. It is easier from many points of view for a company to keep going in familiar ways than actively to seek to do things differently. This approach, however, effectively ties a company up in chains of inertia and makes achieving the change necessary more difficult, even when it becomes essential to survival. Richard Schonberger, who first brought total quality management (TQM) and just-in-time (JIT) to the attention of British managers in the early 1980s, helps companies to improve themselves. He argues that it is often not the change itself that is difficult to achieve, what is lacking is the will to see things through – to deal with the vested interests that stand in the way of making the changes happen. To be effective, any change programme needs to win the battle for the hearts and minds of all employees decisively.

One company that used Schonberger's expertise to change itself was Amtico, a flooring

company and part of the Courtaulds group. As a starting point for the restructuring and change programme they arranged a two-day seminar by Schonberger for all 300 people employed by the company. Only a few people stayed at work to take phone messages and deal with customer enquiries. Everyone was to hear the same message at the same time not, as is more usual, a tiered and 'target group designed' version of the message.

The purpose of the two-day session was twofold. First, to educate the audience on the basic concepts of TQM and JIT. Second, to send clear signals of company intent and to attempt to win the commitment to the process of those attending. After the two-day seminar, the management consultants working with Schonberger then assisted Amtico to make the transformation. The process achieved considerable success over the following few months. Manufacturing time was reduced from three weeks to three days. The product flow through the factory was reduced from four miles and five departments to a few hundred yards and one manufacturing cell. Inventory levels reduced by 65% and quality improved. Further plans were put in hand to improve things even more by increasing the use of cell manufacturing techniques and improving quality.

According to Schonberger the process must be driven by the people at the top, who must 'get religion before the troops will'. The drive and commitment must then be built lower down the organization. The intention being to kick-start the change process and provide it with enough momentum to keep it from getting bogged down and grinding to a halt.

Adapted from: Wheatley, M (1992) The gospel according to Schonberger, *Management Today*, June, pp 74–6.

MANAGEMENT IN ACTION 13.2

The central question

The relationship between company head office functions, the divisions and outstationed operational activities can frequently be a strained one. One well-known reference to the style of management involved has been called 'seagull' management. This refers to senior people who fly in from head office, make a lot of noise and consume as much food and hospitality as they can squeeze out of their hosts and then fly off again, invariably leaving a considerable volume of 'droppings' on their hosts as they do so! However, over the past few years, in seeking to cut costs, the role and size of head office activity has increasingly been under scrutiny.

Foster reports a study of 100 major UK companies carried out by Michael Goold and David Young, both from the Ashridge Strategic Management Centre, in which a number of the relevant issues were identified. From the results of the survey the following information has been extracted:

◆ The largest number of staff in a head office was 2500.

◆ The smallest number of staff in a head office was ten.

◆ Thirteen companies with a total payroll size of between 10,000 and 50,000 people had head office sizes of 100 people or fewer.

◆ Five companies with a total payroll size of between 10,000 and 50,000 people had head office sizes of over 1000 people.

A number of influences impact on the size of a head office, but it is not possible to offer definitive rules that would indicate a likely number of people involved. For example, the size of an organization might be expected to have some bearing on the size of head office. However, organizational life is never that simple. Other influences on the size of head office include the industry, company

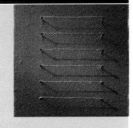

history, level of diversification within a company, the level of international operational activity and the strategic approach of the company.

One of the distinctions identified in the Ashridge study is between the obligatory functions such as financial reporting, taxation, legal and secretarial and those functions over which scope for managerial choice exists. It is in the areas over which choice exists that companies can adopt dramatically different policies towards the purpose and role of head office. In single business companies it is possible that the head office might be seen differently than in a widely diversified conglomerate. The links between head office and individual units in a single business company would be more likely to be regarded as a mixture of central services and direct support and control for the business as a whole. This would be less likely to be the case in a diversified company.

Zeneca was separated out from ICI as a fully functioning company with a solid reputation, but without a head office as such. Previous to its separation from ICI it had been part of that set of structures. At separation Zeneca had the opportunity to create its own head office. The result was the creation of the possibility for separate business units to function with the maximum freedom and so a relatively small head office was created. This consisted of about 100 people.

One of the authors of the Ashridge report concludes by stressing that the size of a head office is not overriding. Companies should not simply strive for a minimal scale in numbers of people at head office. He believes that some companies have gone too far in this respect, driven by a desire to follow the current fashion for downsizing and delayering.

Adapted from: Foster, G (1994) The central question, *Management Today*, April, pp 56–61.

Stop | Consider *The report quoted in MiA 13.2 suggests that the size of a head office should not be the only criterion on which to evaluate it. Make a case for this being so as well as a case for minimal size being the most desirable. How might these two extreme positions be reconciled?*

Integration processes to support particular organizational designs include the communication, consultative and reporting mechanisms adopted, the purpose being to ensure that separate parts of the organization keep each other informed about their activities, problems and requirements so that effective integration of effort takes place. Company policies on issues such as secondment and career development can also influence the degree of unanimity within the structure as a whole. This view of design suggests that structure alone will not guarantee the success or failure of an organization. The weaknesses and deficiencies of a particular structural configuration can be offset to a significant degree by the support mechanisms introduced by management. Naturally, the converse is also applicable, that an effective structure can be weakened through poor support *infrastructure*.

It was Mintzberg (1979, 1981) who provided a simple view of the structural components that needed to be fitted together in the design of any organization. Figure 13.1 is adapted from his work.

Each of the components has a different set of functions to perform:

✦ Senior management. Responsible for the direction of the organization and ensuring that appropriate objectives are set for the other people within the organization.

✦ Middle management. Responsible for ensuring that the resources of the organization are effectively utilized in pursuit of the objectives set by senior management.

✦ Technical support staff. The professional staff provide expertise across a number of necessary disciplines. For example, designers, engineers, lawyers and computer specialists.

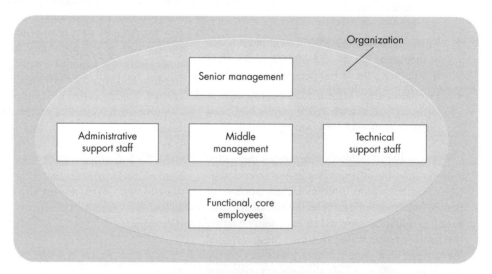

FIGURE 13.1 Organizational components (*adapted from*: Mintzberg, H (1979) *The Structuring of Organizations*, Prentice Hall, Englewood Cliffs, NJ).

◆ Administrative support staff. These are the staff who provide the indirect support in the form of clerical and administrative activities, maintenance of the production equipment and post room duties.

◆ Functional core employees. This category of employees actually work on the products and services offered by the organization. Production workers, teachers, management consultants and retail counter staff are clear examples.

A slightly different view of how to categorize organizational activity was described by Handy (1993). He adopted a classification based on the type of activity undertaken by different parts of the organization:

◆ Policy. This is the guiding policy and direction of the organization. In addition, the allocation of resources and setting of priorities are important features in this category.

◆ Innovation. This aspect is about the development of new products and services, changing the organization itself and finding new ways to meet the needs of customers.

◆ Steady state. This category describes those parts of the business that function best in a programmed mode. For example, production facilities are most efficient when they are able to plan ahead and organize their resources effectively.

◆ Crisis. This deals with unexpected events that arise in every organization at some point of time. The repair of machines that breakdown is a clear example. However, responding to the needs of a customer who in turn is experiencing a sudden upsurge in demand for their products is also an example of a crisis.

Handy stresses in his work that the 'activity types' are not the same as functional groupings. Many of the functional groups will incorporate a number of the four types of activity described here. For example, a personnel department could be described in the following terms:

◆ Policy. The senior personnel team that has the responsibility for the determination of personnel policy and the integration of personnel activities.

◆ Innovation. The development of new personnel initiatives such as the design of a new pay deal intended to encourage teamwork and flexibility.

◆ Steady state. This would be the routine processing of personnel data and statistical information. Monthly wage processing would be an example.

◆ Crisis. This could be the industrial relations section having to respond to a walkout by factory employees.

These examples indicate the complex nature of organizational activity and the difficulty in prescribing brief, although intuitively attractive descriptions of how organizations function. Handy does recognize this constraint but suggests that functions will tend towards one or the other 'activity types' as a dominant orientation.

Child (1988) suggested six components necessary for the creation of an organization structure. They included:

◆ Task. This dimension reflects the way in which the actual tasks that need to be performed within the organization are bundled together in order to create the jobs that will actually be undertaken.

◆ Reporting relationships. This dimension reflects the way in which management will be imposed on the organization. It incorporates decisions relating to the span of control and levels of authority invested in a graded hierarchy of responsibility.

◆ Clustering. This dimension reflects how the groups of activity (for example the sections, departments and divisions) will be clustered together in a recognizable organizational pattern.

◆ Procedures. This dimension reflects decisions relating to the systems, procedures, communication networks and information flows that impact on the means of integration and co-ordination both within the organization and in relation to its external stakeholders.

◆ Delegation. This dimension reflects the degree of differentiation in decision making and the exercise of discretion between the levels in the graded hierarchy. It is the responsibility factor that impacts on the scope of any job.

◆ Motivation. This dimension reflects the productivity aspect of organizational activity. This not only impacts on the number of people needed to perform the tasks necessary, but the style of management and the relationships between individual employees and managers. In the mechanisms adopted for the review of performance and allocation of reward any organization clearly signals its philosophy towards people and the way that they should work in seeking to achieve the desired objectives.

The following discussion will bring together the foregoing perspectives on organizational design in considering many of the major factors necessary to the creation of an organizational framework.

Purpose

It might seem obvious, but it needs to be clearly understood that the purpose of the organization is a major determinant of the structure that is likely to be adopted. An organization in the information technology industry is likely to arrange its resources differently compared to a hospital. However, it is more complex than that simple example might suggest. For example, a hospital that is to specialize in accident and emergency treatments will structure itself differently from one that will specialize in care of the elderly, equally a software house in the games field will organize itself differently from a software house specializing in the financial services industry.

In each case the purpose of the organization, its objectives, how it perceives its need to relate to the various internal and external stakeholder groups will impact on the way in which its structure is arranged. It is also likely that such issues will impact on how the organization sets about the design process itself.

Levels

Any organization with more than one person in it comprises a series of *levels*. This might be as simple as two if the organization consists of two people, the owner–manager and one employee. However, within organizations such as the civil service and very large private sector companies there might be many levels. In history this issue was well understood with references in the Bible to the role of leadership in the time of Moses and, of course, the Roman army was organized around the notion of units of ten soldiers and groups of ten units at a higher level. For example, in the Old Testament book *Exodus*, Chapter 18, verses 13–27 (Jerusalem Bible translation), Moses is advised by his father-in-law to ease the burden of the responsibility on himself for resolving disputes by appointing Judges to administer justice in the following words:

> The work is too heavy for you. You cannot do it alone. … Teach them [the people] the statutes and the decisions; show them the way they must follow and what their course must be. But choose from the people at large some capable and God-fearing men, trustworthy and incorruptible, and appoint them as leaders of the people: leaders of thousands, hundreds, fifties, tens. Let these be at the service of the people to administer justice at all times. They can refer all the difficult questions to you, but the smaller questions they will decide for themselves, so making things easier for you and sharing the burden with you. (verses 18–22)

This quotation clearly describes the advice of the ancient equivalent of a management consultant to create *levels* within society as the basis of organization and easing the burden on the principle leader. This is still apparent today as a guiding principle of organization. It is not usually possible, except in the smallest of organizations, for the owner–manager personally to undertake every task necessary. Equally, it is not usually possible for a chief executive directly to control every aspect of a business. Therefore, with size and complexity comes the necessity to compartmentalize an organization and to allocate responsibilities. Within any organization there are large tasks (defined in terms of high-profile, complex activities, frequently with significant cost implications) that need to be done and there are also many small tasks that need to be done. This is the basis of the division of labour (to be discussed next). However, the *levels* concept within an organization is slightly different from the concept of the division of labour in that it reflects the graded hierarchy associated with the magnitude of decision making together with responsibility for resources and areas of the business.

In effect the concept of the levels within an organization is a top-down view of how things should be. Consider the example from Moses included earlier. It is clear from that description that the idea and intention originated from the advice given to Moses himself and intended to impact directly on his role by creating jobs to undertake the duties of judge at various levels between the people and himself. However, this was not in response to pressure or need from below, but an identified need from above. Interestingly, Moses himself did not identify the need, it was his adviser. Moses appears from the story as relayed to have been happy to carry on as things were, but it was his father-in-law who pointed out the dangers to Moses of not making changes to the way in which justice was being dispensed. This represents the classic manner of senior managers designing and running an organization from the perspective of 'how things appear' at the top. One of the dangers of so doing results from detachment of senior managers, as the real work of the organization in terms of meeting the needs of the customer are carried out at the lower *levels* of the organization.

The people at the top of any organization are of necessity remote from the real experience of identifying and meeting the needs of their customers. They deal with different facets of the organization, including the long-term strategy, resource availability, political and interorganizational issues. These are, by definition, remote from the day-to-day experience of operational activity. In addition, most of the information that reaches the senior levels of any organization has been through so many *levels* within the organization before it reaches them that it has been sanitized to convey the perspectives of the *levels* who prepare the information. This represents the political dimensions of management which will be explored more fully in a later chapter.

One of the hardest jobs for any senior management team is to be able personally to understand the organization they are responsible for, as opposed to understanding the picture as presented to them by others. A recent BBC television series called 'Back To The Floor' was such compelling viewing for just that reason, putting a chief executive back on the shop, office or factory floor was inevitably a major shock as the reality was totally different compared to their perception or expectation. That is not to suggest that the people below the top levels within an organization deliberately mislead or that they are incompetent. It simply reflects the inevitable filtering and (to use a term from politics) 'spin' resulting from the jobs, responsibilities, attitudes and perspectives between the customer activity of the organization and the top levels.

Recent attempts at delayering and downsizing have sought to simplify organizational frameworks through the introduction of flatter organizations. The removal of *levels* of the organization has taken place predominantly in the middle ranks of management jobs. This is a topic that will be specifically discussed later in this chapter.

Division of labour

The *division of labour* reflects the need to group together the tasks that need to be done into the meaningful 'chunks' of activity that are called jobs. Work design was the subject of Chapter 7 and so will not be reviewed in detail here. However there are aspects associated with the *division of labour* that are relevant to the design of organizations. It has been common across history to organize work based on internal organizational factors or on the basis of the professions that claim exclusive rights to practise a defined area of work. So, for example, the medical and legal professions lay very strong claim to defined areas of work just as the craft guilds laid claim to defined areas of skilled manual work in the Middle Ages. The internal determinants of the *division of labour* are partly a consequence of the compartmentalization of work and partly the levels just discussed, in short, a top-down basis for deciding how the organization should be arranged in terms of the work to be done.

The more usual implication associated with the division of labour reflects the change in the nature of organizations during the Industrial Revolution and the introduction of the factory system. It is frequently argued that the factory system emerged as a result of the developing technology and the need to reduce the cost of production in order to meet the needs of a rapidly growing market. Writers such as Marglin (1974) argue that this is not necessarily the case and that the breaking down of work into the minute tasks associated with factory production was intended by the owners of capital to provide them with a defined role in the system in order to justify a larger share of the rewards. The division of labour was only one of the disciplines imposed on workers as a result of the new factory-based systems.

Division of labour is therefore about how work is organized and there are many ways in which that can be done. In the early years of the twentieth century F W Taylor and the followers of *scientific management* considered that it was necessary to separate out the managerial, thinking tasks clearly from the doing, manual tasks. The job of the manual worker was simply to follow orders in the grinding monotony of factory work under this system. In his 1947 text he refers to the need for a worker who handled pig iron to be so stupid and phlegmatic that their mental capacity resembled that of an ox. In this he was pointing out that an intelligent, alert person would have difficulty coping with the grinding boredom in the demands of *scientific management*. Similar negative points to those of Weber in relation to the negative impact of *bureaucracy* on workers. However, both writers considered that the approach to the division of labour implied by their 'models' was necessary and of benefit to society as a whole. In fact Taylor suggested to a special committee of the USA Senate in 1911 that his purpose was to redirect the attention of both workers and managers away from current levels of profit, towards the creation of ever larger pools of surplus until both parties could gain handsomely from the returns achieved.

While creating the division of work associated with factory operations might provide managers with greater levels of control and a basis for reducing the cost of labour, it also introduces problems through worker *alienation* and poor quality etc. More recent attempts by managers to organize the work of employees has therefore focused on the desirability of enlarging jobs as opposed to breaking them down into the smallest constituent parts. A number of initiatives have been based around the idea that workers should be encouraged to contribute to their fullest potential to the benefit of the organization and themselves. This approach has usually involved approaches to *empowerment* (allowing employees a measure of job-related decision-making responsibility), job enlargement (giving employees some degree of supervisory responsibility) and/or participation (involvement in corporate decision-making processes). However, it has been argued that these approaches reflect attempts by managers to control employees through different routes. If employees can be engaged with managers in the running of the enterprise, then, it is argued, they will become like managers and will automatically perform their allotted duties (and more) in the best interests of the capital owners, what Thompson (1989) refers to as 'the manufacture of consent' (p 159).

Centralization and decentralization

Centralization and decentralization is an old problem, as indicated from the example described in George (1972) in which one of the pharaohs of ancient Egypt decentralized the running of the country into regional governorships only to *centralize* it again when problems emerged. It remains a difficult problem today, even in the political world. Michael Heseltine (1999) reflects on the role of the British prime minister. In this discussion he points out the temptation of political leaders to centralize power and control on themselves in order to drive change in public policy, while at the same time it is impossible for the individual to cope with the demands of so doing. His advice is to delegate to competent ministers rather than to change the basic system of politics or the public sector. So, if necessary, change the ministers rather than the system if the prime minister is not able to achieve change through them.

There are advantages to *decentralization* which revolve around:

✦ The increased speed of decision making. This is because of the reduced number of levels that decision making passes through. This arises as a consequence of the need to report to head office from the perspective of a profit centre rather than simply an operational division. Equally, the focus of the local management should be more tightly directed to meeting the needs of their business unit and so place a premium on the speed of reaction to situations.

✦ Being more adaptable and flexible. *Decentralized* businesses effectively operate as businesses within businesses. As a consequence, the dynamic of each unit differs in comparison to that within a divisionalized structure. The profit motive, the tight focus on a specific business unit activity and the competition from other business units within the holding-company structure mean that local managers tend to become more flexible and adaptable in pursuit of their objectives.

♦ Closer customer focus. As a consequence of the breaking down of the company into specific business units much of the peripheral interconnectivity is removed. Because of this the focus of the business unit is more tightly and closely linked to a smaller and homogenized customer base.

♦ Improved internal competition. Across the entire group there will exist a number of separate business units. Each of these units becomes a profit centre in effect (even if profit level is not the main measure of contribution). Consequently, each business unit will consider itself in competition with the other business units. The level of competition stems from the desire of individual managers to be regarded as star performers (the basis of promotion and additional rewards) and also to be able to attract higher levels of investment from corporate headquarters. It is argued that the increased level of competition between business units would benefit the entire organization. However, issues such as transfer pricing between group members are an inevitable difficulty as they can be used to manipulate particular financial results which distort true ability to deliver results.

♦ The need for head office functions to justify their existence. The basis of *decentralization* is that each business unit becomes largely self-sufficient. One impact of this is to change the fundamental nature of head office functions. Their job changes from the need to control and direct the sub-units, to the acquisition, divestment, allocation of resources, monitoring of performance and dealing with any collective reporting or shareholder needs. It is common to find that individual business units resent the existence of head office functions and regard them as offering no value to the business. One way in which this has been addressed is to require many head office functions to pay their own way by effectively becoming consultancy suppliers to the business units. Any head office function so operating that could not cover its costs through providing added value services to the business units would be at risk of closure.

♦ Better preparation of managers for senior corporate roles. It is argued that the existence of separate business units within a group provides an improved training process for managers. A business unit is in effect a separate company in all but name. As a consequence the experience of running such organizations can provide a structured approach to accepting ever larger responsibilities, but still under the guidance of the corporate level of management. This it is suggested should deliver senior managers more capable and experienced at taking the big decisions etc. found at the corporate levels.

However, there are also disadvantages with the notion of decentralization. The main disadvantage with such approaches is that of fragmentation. It is implied in the earlier discussion that the role of head office is always under threat in a decentralized organization. That pharaoh found this to be true in ancient Egypt when the regional governors began to talk of breaking up the country in order to become the pharaoh of a smaller but independent country. Consequently, he removed the governors and reverted to a *centralized* administrative structure. This is still a major potential problem with decentralization. The senior managers of the individual business units can envisage only too easily that they (personally and in corporate terms) would be better off outside the group structure and thereby seek devolution. In addition, there is always a danger in a decentralized organization that the potential synergies available from trading between the component parts may not be fully realized, thereby failing to extract the maximum potential out of the group framework.

Centralization as a form of organization tends to have the opposite advantages and disadvantages to those discussed for decentralization. For example, the major benefits from centralization arise from the ability to integrate effort and collaboration between the subunits. It is also possible to minimize the level of duplication across the entire group through the establishment of corporate administrative and support units. The difficulty for *centralized* organizations is actually capturing these benefits. Divisional managers have a tendency to be suspicious of 'head office' functions and their contribution because they are not under divisional control and report to senior corporate level managers. There is, therefore, a tendency to duplicate activity in the local units as line managers seek better, more timely, more supportive services etc.

There is almost an inevitable circularity in the *centralization–decentralization* approach of organizational design. Over time and from whichever approach the organization starts pressure will build. In a decentralized organization, there will be pressure to seek the maximum level of in-house collaboration between units and to minimize the level of duplicated effort. Very few organizations seem able to achieve consistently over time the full potential from decentralization and this can be exacerbated through the aspirations of divisional managers who seek to advance their own position. So a natural reaction to such pressure is either to separate completely or integrate more effectively. More effective integration leads the organization towards the centralization approach to design.

Arkin (1999) reviews current organizational practice and suggests that there is a *recentralization* trend evident partly because so many companies are now 'closer to the customer' (decentralized) and so new ways of achieving competitive advantage must be found. Arkin points out the sensitivity involved in these changes as it involves a delicate balancing act involving the need to take account of the powers and responsibilities of local managers as well as the organizational politics associated with change. Professor Andrew Kakabadse from Cranfield University has studied this phenomenon and is quoted by Arkin as saying that new forms are emerging based on degrees of centralization. The Virgin group is suggested to be one such variant by adopting a semi-centralized structure in which local discretion on company care matters is supported by a centralized approach to branding and related matters.

The usual arguments in favour of centralization are the ability to cut cost and sharpen performance. Initially, this might actually be achieved to some degree, but eventually weaknesses with the centralized approach begin to surface and must be dealt with. The cost of central administration and support services begins to increase as ever greater demands are placed on them by the local units, used to close and dedicated support provided by the previous structures. Entire new career structures and reward levels are created as the providers of central services argue that they are the ones who undertake the 'biggest' jobs with most responsibility and should be paid accordingly. It eventually becomes apparent that the only way to achieve the anticipated levels of control and integration within the centralized organization is to spend ever larger sums of money on central services as every new level of control achieved raises the spectre of gaps which appear and new potential possibilities for even better control over the entire system, with more expenditure. Eventually this process itself comes under scrutiny and attempts to achieve cost control are attempted. This frequently takes the organization back towards the decentralized approach to design. Recent approaches such as business process re-engineering, downsizing (or rightsizing as it is sometimes called) frequently have this effect as organizations seek to delegate responsibility to the lowest levels possible and focus of the essential aspects of the business. It is this balancing process that Kakabadse has identified along with attempts to prevent the circularity from perpetuating itself.

Line and staff functions

One form of expression frequently encountered in an organizational design context is the term line and staff. It is perhaps unfortunate that these terms are used in two different ways which can confuse if the distinction is not clear. The first way in which the term *line* is used is to refer to a *line manager*. Every employee (and manager) has a line manager. It refers to the person to whom they report, in short their boss. So the *line manager* of a production worker might be the department supervisor. In turn, the department supervisor's line manager would be the production manager. This would be repeated in the organization to the very top. In that context, *line* is used to denote a responsibility relationship, not to be confused with the ability of one postholder to influence another. So a production supervisor will interact with and has some degree of influence over the activities of other supervisors, the maintenance supervisor and so on. However they have no rights to order another supervisor to undertake (or desist from taking) particular actions. Any difficulties between, say, the maintenance supervisor and the production supervisor would have to be formally dealt with by the production manager as the line manager of the supervisor.

The second way in which the term line is used is in referring to *line and staff functions*. The distinction between line and staff functions is most easily understood in terms of the relationship with the main purposes of the organization. For example, in a major bank the *line functions* would be those associated with direct banking activities, including the branch network, commercial loans, insurance services, treasury services and debit recovery. They are the operational functions of the business. The *staff functions* refer to the activities which although necessary are supportive of the main operational functions. Examples would include personnel, marketing, computer services, finance and legal services. One potential confusion is that the definition of staff function differs between organizations and depending upon the main business. So a computer company might class the computer function as a line department, as might a bank setting up Internet banking services. The terms *line* and *staff* potentially become more confusing because employees within *staff functions* have *line managers*!

The distinction between line and staff functions is becoming less meaningful as the commercial activities of organizations diversify. All functions are now expected to add value to the organization or they become prospects for closure or outsourcing. For example, Merrick (1999) reviews the experience of Westminster City Council which outsourced most of its personnel department. The remaining in-house personnel function concentrates on strategic issues, leaving the day-to-day provision or the service to the subcontractor. In that example the outsourced personnel function is a *staff function* to the Council departments, but at the same time a *line function* within the company providing the service. The result of the outsourcing seems to have been generally successful, with just a few frustrations existing among line managers. Equally, companies can sometimes see the opportunity for turning their own staff functions into a commercial activity. For example, British Airways frequently advertises the services of Chameleon Training and Consulting, the commercial organization created from the development of customer care training for its own staff (see their advertisement in *People Management*, 1999, p 90). The distinction between line and staff functions in terms of activity is clearly blurred.

Within many organizations the distinction between line and staff functions becomes part of the power and political processes. Managers in line functions frequently accuse staff managers of not contributing any value to the organization and of simply interfering in order to protect their jobs. Staff departments are frequently said to have too much power and an ability to distract the organization away from simply meeting the needs of the customer. Managers and specialists in the staff functions frequently feel that their potential to contribute to effective operational activity is undervalued and not appreciated by line managers, unless a crisis arises. The role of personnel departments in seeking to organize training for staff is frequently a example of this resentment. Line managers under pressure to reduce numbers of employees and to raise productivity frequently demand more training as a means of creating the employee flexibility needed. However, they are frequently unwilling to release staff to attend the training provided as they would then not be able to meet current production demands. This creates a vicious circle of low-skilled employees and an inability to improve the situation with personnel frequently being blamed for not recruiting the appropriate people to begin with and not providing the training needed at the most appropriate time.

Span of control

The *span of control* refers to the number of subordinates reporting to a single boss. So a small electrical section within the maintenance department of a manufacturing company might consist of four electricians reporting to a supervisor who in turn reports to the maintenance manager. The *span of control* of the electrical supervisor would therefore be four. However, if the maintenance manager also had reporting to them a mechanical supervisor, a stores supervisor, a maintenance planner and an electronics supervisor, each with four people reporting directly to them the span of control of the maintenance manager would be five, not the entire maintenance workforce of 20 technical staff plus five supervisors (and planner). In other words, the concept of *span of control* does not jump the levels within the reporting line.

The significance of the concept of the span of control lies in its relationship with the diversity of responsibility and interaction requirements. The more people reporting to a single boss the more likely it is that the boss is responsible for a broad range of disparate activities. It is not usual for a single person to be equally knowledgeable and experienced about a wide range of issues and job functions, therefore the wider their responsibilities the more likely it is that they will underperform in some aspect of them. This also provides opportunities for subgroups and informal leaders to emerge which can lead to fragmentation of authority and other problems. Equally, the number of interaction channels increases exponentially with the number of people reporting to each boss, which means, effectively, that each person gets a smaller proportion of the time of the boss and less opportunity to contribute to group discussions etc. This can result in significant aspects of situations being missed and the potential contribution from particular specialisms being underrepresented in critical discussions.

Of course, there are also potential problems if the span of control is too narrow. For example, the boss may not have enough managerial work to do and so take over aspects of what should rightly be a subordinate's job, to the irritation of all concerned. In extreme situations the so-called one-on-one spans of control very rarely work as neither party (or other people in the company) is clear on the distinctions between the two people's responsibilities. Also there is frequently very little justification (in work responsibility or volume terms) for there to be a hierarchy in existence in such situations. There is little managerial work involved in supervising a single person and equally a senior/junior distinction often fails to reflect the needs of the situation.

Woodward (1965) undertook studies in a range of manufacturing companies to consider the impact of technology on structure. In the study she classified the organizations studied into three categories:

✦ Unit or small batch production. These organizations concentrated on the small quantities of output determined by customer needs for low volume or the creation of prototypes etc.

✦ Large batch or mass production. These organizations were the large volume producers which either made in large batches or on assembly lines.

✦ Process production. Typically, such organizations are in the business of continuous flow forms of production. Oil refineries and chemical processes would be clear examples.

Her research identified a range of findings including that those firms who structured themselves closely to the norm for their type of production technology would be most successful. Also that the span of control reflected to a significant extent the process and technology used in the organization. For example, she found that the span of control was larger at the lower levels of the organization where jobs were of a broadly similar type, but was narrower at senior levels where responsibilities between the subordinates were very different. Subsequent research has generally supported the main thrust of her arguments, although a review carried out by Collins and Hull (1986) effectively suggested that the debate has now changed from the simple alignment of technology with size and span of control because of the flexibility created through the use of new technology.

Some writers and consultants such as Urwick suggested that the span of control should be a specific number (usually five or six people) and not varied. This is perhaps unrealistic and not supported by the work of Woodward as the degree to which a manager can cope with a particular span of control depends upon a number of factors. These include the personal characteristics of the individuals concerned, the role of computer technology in the operational process, morale, motivation and other situation factors.

Scalar chain

This aspect of organizational design reflects the height dimension of an organization. It reflects the number of levels from the top to the bottom. As such it does not reflect the number of grades of staff, but the number of reporting links between the bottom level and the top level. So in the case of a production factory, a shopfloor worker might report to a supervisor, who in turn reports to the production manager, who in turn reports to the production director, who in turn reports to the chief executive. This example reflects an organization with five levels in it. Putting the span of control together with the *scalar chain* gives a common way of describing an organization as either *tall* or *flat* (see Figure 13.2).

A tall organization would be one with many levels in it (a high number for the *scalar chain*). A flat organization would be one with relatively few levels in it. In describing any organization as tall or flat it is the height relative to the breadth that allows the appropriate tag to be applied. So for example, an organization with a large span of control and say five levels would be a flatter organizational shape than one that had a smaller span of control and five levels within it.

Over the past few years many organizations have been engaging in *delayering* exercises intended to strip out levels and to reduce the scalar chain. The logic behind such moves being to reduce the number of levels of command to make the organization more responsive to its markets; reduce the levels of bureaucracy; reduce overlap between levels of responsibility; empower the staff to satisfy customers and speed up decision making. Delayering impacts on a wide range of organizations, including the trade union movement in its search for cost-effective member services. Lamb (1999) reports on a range of trade union actions in this field, including one union that cut its management overheads by half in order to achieve a closer member alignment and reduced cost of operations.

Organizational metaphors

So far in this discussion the notion of an organization has been taken for granted. In practice the way in which the *organization* finds expression in the world is limitless. The variation covers differences in size, location, product or service orientation, culture, management style, level of profit, public or private sector, number of locations etc. Therefore the umbrella term *organization* is intended to conjure up a generalized picture from which more specific meaning can be gleaned. This is a simple expression of a *metaphor*:

> Thus, metaphor proceeds through implicit or explicit assertions that A is (or is like) B. When we say 'the man is a lion,' we use the image of a lion to draw attention to the lion-like aspects of the man. The metaphor frames our understanding of the man in a distinctive yet partial way. (Morgan, 1986, p 13)

In this explanation, Morgan indicates that while there are some aspects of the man that resemble a lion, there are many that do not. What the metaphor does do is to provide an insight through an efficient form of communication: the lion conjures up a complex picture that needs few words to express it – provided that the receiver has the same understanding. To *know* that the man is like a lion provides a basis for both understanding and action towards that person without having to have a detailed knowledge of him.

In the same way, we use *organization* as a metaphor to describe individual units, to disguise difference and simplify complexity arising from the existence of individual variation. This perspective adds a dimension to the contingency approach to organization design. If

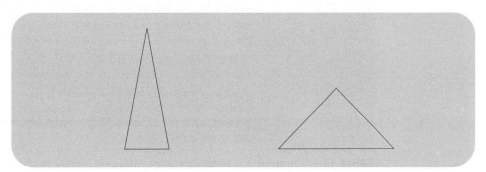

FIGURE 13.2 Tall or flat?

humans understand through the use of *metaphor* then perhaps the metaphors managers use to relate to organizations determines how they subsequently structure them. Morgan identifies a number of metaphors that illustrates the perspectives implicit in them.

Metaphor become the basis of beliefs about how organizations *should* function. The 'facts' encountered are 'fitted' into the metaphorical image. The importance of metaphor in contingency thinking is that it provides a means through which humans understand organizations and how they function in a specific context. That understanding can provide a basis for deciding how the organization could be structured.

The significance of questioning the existing metaphorical perspective of an organization is demonstrated in Management in Action 13.3. This describes how a Japanese company made several false starts before it identified its future direction. Its original perception of itself was limited by the assumptions made about its core technologies.

Stop | Consider

To what extent does the approach and eventual success in identifying ways to survive at NKK reflect organizational design and management decision making and to what extent was it due to the need to find any alternative to closure along with a willingness to invest heavily in doing so?

Could any organization achieve the same level of success given an almost blank cheque?

Justify your views.

Charting organizations

The organization chart is a means by which organizations describe the structure and reporting relationships that exist. The organization chart can also be an effective means of tracking formal lines of communication, levels of responsibility and audit trails. Reproduced as Figure 13.3 is an example of the organization chart for a hypothetical medium-sized company in the fast food industry.

There are, however, severe limitations in the ability of the organization chart to reflect

Machine	A network of parts: functional departments ... which are further specified as networks of precisely defined jobs (p 27)
Organisms	Living systems, existing in a wider environment on which they depend for the satisfaction of various needs (p 39)
Brains	Utilizes the concepts of intelligence, feedback and information processing to model organizational functioning
Culture	Directs attention to the symbolic or even 'magical' significance of even the most rational aspects of organizational life (p 135)
Politial	Managers frequently talk about authority, power and superior–subordinate relations ... Organizations as systems of the government that vary according to the political principles employed (p 142)

TABLE 13.1 Organizational metaphors (*source*: Morgan, G (1986) *Images of Organization*, Sage, Newbury Park, CA)

MANAGEMENT IN ACTION 13.3

Steelmaker that reinvented itself

The sharply rising yen following the 1985 Plaza Accord together with the decline in world ship-building created a number of problems for Japanese companies, not least of which was the potentially terminal decline in profits for NKK, Japan's second largest steelmaker. Two lessons have been learned from the NKK experience of attempting to diversify. First, the parent company was prepared to let the steelmaker take startling risks in the search for new business. Second, the financial support for the process was never in doubt. The aim, according to Mr Seigo Abe, manager of the leisure specialities department of NKK, was simply to find ways of surviving.

Mr Abe was appointed to the marine engineering department of NKK from its new business department in 1985, just after the need to diversify was identified. It took several years to identify new business that profitably makes use of the considerable skill and expertise available within the company. Initial thinking found that the key areas of skill within the company were associated with high-performance welding, the design and testing of ice breakers and the manufacture of wave pools for testing ship models.

Early attempts to diversify were into fish farming and making stretch limousines. The making of fish farms and limousines required welding technology and it was assumed that the other necessary aspects associated with those operations would fall into place. Not so. The fish farms were unproductive and the stretch limousines did not handle well on roads. This caused a review of what the core skill areas actually were within NKK. The definition of these was refined down to making ice and snow for ice-breaking test equipment and producing accurate wave formations for model wave machines. The possibility of making artificial beaches and ski slopes therefore became the focus of attention.

A prototype pool in a water park in Osaka demonstrated that NKK could make very regular surfing waves, more consistent than could be found in nature. The company also learned how to design and build water parks as a consequence of contracts for laying pipes around water slide complexes. The closure of a baseball ground as part of a cost-cutting exercise by the steel division of NKK presented the opportunity for the marine engineering unit to propose and, having been given the go-ahead, to build its own tropical beach complex. The facility is known as Wild Blue and is located in Yokohama. It lost money during its first three years of operation but Mr Abe claims that these difficulties have been addressed and that it was currently close to breakeven, with 800,000 visitors each year.

NKK also built an indoor ski resort as a contractor to the company that wanted to develop the facility. This was less of a financial risk for NKK as it was not faced with running the facility once opened. It also opened up opportunities for acting as advisers and contractors on similar projects throughout Asia. Another of the success stories for NKK was in making ice cubes for high-class Tokyo clubs. Using the company expertise in making ice to test ice-breaking equipment, NKK has been able to make ice cubes under high pressure from pure water. This produces an ice cube with similarities to an iceberg, including many air bubbles trapped inside. When the ice begins to melt in the drink it makes a crackling noise which customers like and provides a profitable opportunity for the company!

Adapted from: Dawkins, W (1995) Steelmaker that reinvented itself, *Financial Times*, 29 March, p 5.

what actually happens within an organization. Not included are the cross-functional relationships that are necessary to ensure that information flows around the organization in an appropriate way. Neither does it reflect the decision-making processes that exist. Frequently, organization charts do not reflect the levels of responsibility held by the individual posts indicated in them. For example, in Figure 13.3 the senior managers are all shown at the same level, reporting to the chief executive. But there are four directors and one manager in the job titles at that level. Does this imply that the business planning manager has less responsibility than the others or does it simply reflect that the postholder does not have a seat on the board of directors? There have been attempts to reflect the relative seniority of people within an organization chart by scaling the vertical dimension of it (see Figure 13.4).

The solid lines drawn between job titles on an organization chart reflect direct reporting and responsibility relationships. These reflect the line manager-based relationships discussed earlier in this chapter. In addition, it is not uncommon to see dotted lines between positions in a chart. These indicate high levels of influence and interaction-reporting relationships, but exclude line manager-reporting lines. For example, the production planner in a manufacturing company may report to the logistics manager as their line manager, but have a dotted-line relationship with the production manager. This would arise as a result of the need for significant level and frequency of contact between the two postholders. The production planner does not work for the production manager, but can significantly impact on the effective running of the production department, so it makes sense for the semi-formal relationship between the two to be recognized. Not all influencing forms of relationship would be recognized by a dotted line. It is only used to indicate a strong need for the working relationship to be officially recorded.

There are other ways of reflecting how an organization functions. For example, the concept of a *rich picture* provides a mechanism through which a dynamic situation can be reflected in a manner meaningful to the participants. Figure 13.5 is an example that

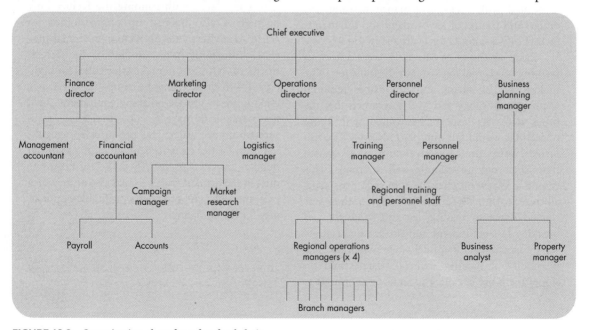

FIGURE 13.3   Organization chart for a fast food chain.

illustrates the problems and influences acting upon a particular situation. The picture is reasonably self-explanatory in that the swords represent conflict and the joined hands areas of agreement. In effect, an organization chart describes the formal appearance of an organization but a rich picture can reflect how the organization actually works. It can reflect how the processes function as well as people interaction and behaviour patterns within the organization.

Another means of reflecting activity within an organization is through an *influence diagram*. This can illustrate the relationships and influences that exist between individuals and groups within and outside the organization. Figure 13.6 is a simple influence diagram based around a village playing fields committee (the organization). The type of arrow used between elements in the diagram reflects the form and/or frequency that interaction takes.

Organizations are continually subjected to change. This can include individuals leaving or joining; jobs being declared redundant or new jobs created; promotions and changes in reporting relationships; acquisitions and divestments. Consequently, the organization chart would need to be frequently updated in order to maintain its relevance and value. Townsend (1985) goes so far as to suggest that organization charts can demoralize people as they reflect how far from the top most people actually are and the number of bosses that exist above each individual. The organization chart reflects how management think or wish the organization to look and function. This is not necessarily the same as the way the employees (and customers) think that the organization looks or functions, based on their experience, a point made by Heller (1997). The validity of an organization chart is a function of a number of factors, including:

✦   Age. The older an organization chart is, the less likely it is to reflect current structure and reporting relationships.

✦   Detail. The level of detail included in a chart reflects its value. It is not unusual to find that larger organizations have several organization charts, covering different levels and divisions within the organization.

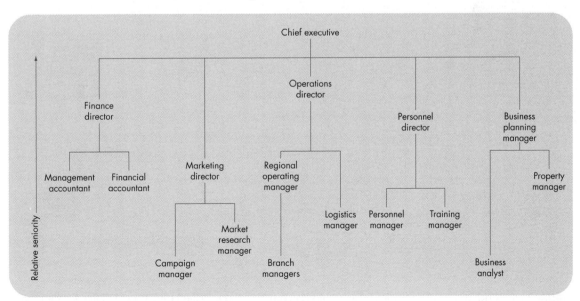

FIGURE 13.4   Organization chart scaled to show relative seniority.

◆ Purpose. The purpose for which the chart was designed also affects its value. A chart drawn up to reflect the main functional splits within the organization would be of little value in identifying who deals with customer queries.

◆ Need. Organization charts have limitations in being able to describe how an organization functions. This need might be more effectively met through the use of rich pictures and influence diagrams.

Three perspectives on determinism

There are three approaches to the issue of determinism. One view (the deterministic approach) holds that structure is a function of one of two schools of thought. First, that technology is the main basis for the determination of structure and form. The second deterministic perspective holds that it is situational or other environmental factors that determine structure. The third, non-deterministic perspective, holds that organization structure is a function of managerial choice.

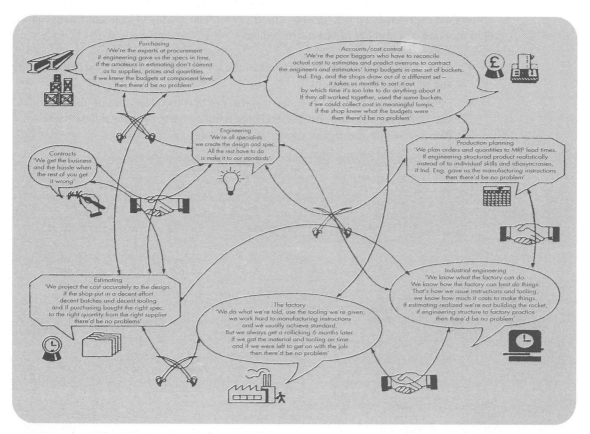

FIGURE 13.5 A rich picture of a situation in an engineering company (*source*: Checkland, P and Scholes, J (1990) *Soft Systems Methodology in Action*, John Wiley, Chichester).

Technological determinism

This holds that the production technology of an organization determines the structural frameworks that are adopted (Woodward, 1965). Woodward identified a number of tendencies among firms utilizing similar production technologies. There was a definite relationship between the technology used and a number of structural measures, including managerial span of control; length of the chain of command; relative proportion of indirect labour (support staff) and managers. Her conclusion was that those organizations that were structured in ways typical of their technological norms tended to be the most profitable. However, as indicated in the discussion on span of control more recent research tends to indicate that the technology debate has moved on from that discussed by Woodward.

Perrow (1967) proposed a slightly different view of the influence of technology. His view was that the technology utilized within an organization could vary from the routine to the non-routine. At the routine end of the spectrum everything tends to be tightly organized and follows a regular pattern, thereby limiting the amount of discretion (of action) available to the lower levels within the organization. In such organizations it is the ranks of the middle managers who actually make it function as they represent the main organizing

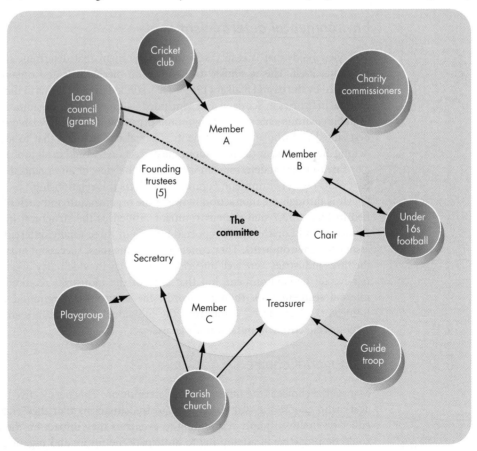

FIGURE 13.6 Influence diagram (*source*: Giles, K and Hedge, N (1994) *The Manager's Good Study Guide*, Open University, Milton Keynes).

and co-ordinating levels. Interestingly, it is the ranks of middle managers who have been most at risk of elimination in the delayering exercises of recent years. Perrow suggests that those organizations adopting the non-routine approach tend to generate high levels of discretion among front-line operational staff, as it is they who must actually take decisions and make the organization work.

It is important to recognize that both Perrow and Woodward are using the term technology to refer to the production technology used rather than the use of computers. In a low-technology environment the process would require highly skilled employees to produce small batches of product for the customer. At the other extreme, machines dominate with individuals undertaking a range of comparatively small tasks in support of mass production processes. Technology provides the opportunity for managers to make work predictable and the opportunity tightly to specify the jobs that people undertake. Also there is a greater need to introduce standard procedures to routinize the response to crises in situations where technology is more sophisticated. It was Perrow's contention that the form of structure adopted by the organization was a function of the tightness of job specification, which originated from the technology and predictability of the work. This differed from the view of Woodward in that it was her view that the technological complexity directly influenced the structural form.

Environmental determinism

This view holds that it is forces in the environment that determine how an organization structures itself. This is similar to the ideas on mechanistic and organismic organizations identified by Burns and Stalker (1961). They studied organizations in the electronics and traditional industries in Scotland and concluded that *mechanistic* organizations were best suited to stable environments and that *organismic* organizations (fluid, flexible and responsive) were best suited to turbulent environments. They also concluded that to attempt to adopt the 'wrong' framework, or to fail to adopt the correct one, would in all probability lead to failure.

Environmental determinism is based on the view of an organization as an interactive part of its own environment. Figure 13.7 reflects this relationship.

It is through the interaction between the organization and each of the groups identified in Figure 13.7 that the environment influences the structural frameworks adopted. Lawrence and Lorsch (1967) reported a study of three totally different industries and the associated environments. They concluded that the most successful organizations in each of the three industries were well integrated in the way in which they organized their activities relative to the environment, but that each of the industries required different forms of internal segmentation. In other words, the environment required different structural frameworks, but success came from the individual organization's ability to integrate its activities effectively in pursuit of its goals.

Managerial choice

Managerial choice is the other view of determinism. This perspective holds that it is managers who choose the way to respond to the situations that they encounter. This could either be reactive, simply responding to events as they impact on the organization; or it could be proactive in attempting to anticipate the future and organize in anticipation of circumstances. This latter approach is the essence of strategic thinking that is now such a dominant feature of managerial activity.

It is possible to reconcile these approaches to organizational structure in that managerial choice does not totally negate the influence of determinism. For example, it was pointed out in the discussion about the work of Woodward that there was a *tendency* for organizations to be more successful if they followed the norms for their industry and technology. This allows for some variability in structural form, a point also evident in the work of Lawrence and Lorsch. So even in the deterministic approach managers can be seen to be exercising decision making by adopting slightly different structures. However, the commercial results achieved by the organizations were found to vary with the closeness of following the norms. Perhaps, therefore, managerial choice is an intervening variable between environment and structure, with the consequences being apparent in the level of success achieved by the organization.

Socio-technical systems theory

The notion of a *system* originated in the physical sciences as a means of reflecting how a number of elements or subsystems interact within a cohesive whole. It has since been integrated into the social sciences and with particular success in the explanation of how organizations function. Some of the earlier ideas in this context were identified by Kast and Rosenzweig (1972). Figure 13.8 represents an *open systems* view of an organization.

As an *open system* the organization is in an interactive relationship with its environment. It draws its raw materials etc. from the environment, converts them into goods and services which are fed back into the environment. It is very much a cyclical and interactive process. For example, the Ford Motor Company makes motor vehicles which it sells to its

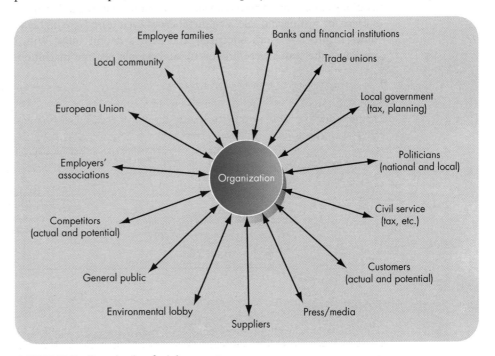

FIGURE 13.7 Organizational environments.

customers for money. The money thus obtained is recycled in the form of wages, tax payments and the purchase of raw materials. Information is also part of this process. For example, if a particular model is not selling, or is selling very quickly, the manufacturing process (or pricing policy) can be adjusted very quickly to respond to the new situation.

Within an organization there are a number of *subsystems*, each of which will have its own inputs, transformation processes and outputs, within an environmental context. For example, the transformation process of the Ford Motor Company consists of a number of separate, but integrated subsystems, including manufacturing, design, finance, marketing and personnel. Each of these functional areas will have their own links to the environment and will become involved with the other subsystems in contributing to the overall output of the organization. Management in Action 13.4 illustrates the effects of the cyclical nature of feedback between the organization and its environment as the organization grows through success.

Stop | Consider *Do you think that Femcare took the correct decision in selling the rights of Contrelle? Bearing in mind the company considered the possibility of raising additional finance and rejected it as an option, what would you have done if you were running Femcare (and why)?*

The *socio-technical* approach to an organization recognizes that it is necessary to incorporate both the social and technical aspects of work if an effective system is to be created. The first work in socio-technical systems originated in studies of coal mining in the northeast of England in the late 1940s and early 1950s. The technology of coal extraction was changing as mechanical equipment became available. Previously, teams of men had worked as groups in driving tunnels through coal seams, removing the coal and sending it to the surface for sorting and sale. The members of each team were highly dependent upon each other in order to work effectively and earn a decent wage. With the introduction of machines the teams were broken up and people became machine minders, working in

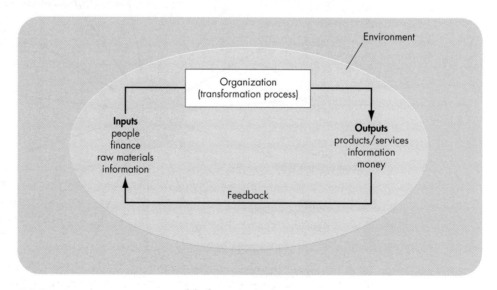

FIGURE 13.8   An open systems model of an organization.

MANAGEMENT IN ACTION 13.4

Excess of success

Small companies that achieve rapid success can be faced with very real problems. The demands of success on the business can lead to the company's resources being so stretched that it breaks. Success is every entrepreneur's dream, but it needs to be controlled and planned for, if it is not to become a nightmare.

Femcare, a Nottingham-based surgical instrument production and marketing company has been in business since 1982. One of its main products is the Filshie Clip, developed by Marcus Filshie, a consultant gynaecologist based at the Queen's Medical Centre in Nottingham. It is a device that can provide women with a potentially reversible sterilization and represents most of Femcare's sales of £3m per year.

In 1989 the company bought a new product that could assist women with incontinence difficulties following childbirth. The company acquired the rights to the product and began to both make and market Contrelle, as it is called. Unlike the other products handled by Femcare, which were sold to clinicians, Contrelle was available to women through pharmacies and could be bought as frequently as decided by the woman herself. Femcare recognized that they needed to introduce Contrelle into as many markets as possible during its protected patent life and so an extensive advertising campaign began. Sales took off rapidly, much faster than expected, and the company quickly recognized that it was getting out of its depth.

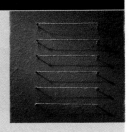

The demands on manufacturing were greater than Femcare could cope with, even if they could get the raw materials in large enough quantity, which in itself represented a problem. The option of raising money in order to expand the company quickly was considered. However, it was rejected in the belief that such a move could have threatened sales of the core medical instruments and placed the entire business at risk. Instead they searched for a global partner that could handle the anticipated level of business. Eventually most of the rights to Contrelle were sold to Coloplast, a Danish company specializing in medical equipment. A phased handover of the product was introduced, with Coloplast developing a new version of the original product and beginning production with that design.

Femcare would have preferred to have retained control of Contrelle. However, they recognized both that it had grown beyond their capability to handle it and the risk to the business. Instead the company is now concentrating on the potential of the Filshie Clip and seeking partners to work in the US market.

Adapted from: Gourlay, R (1995) Excess of success, *Financial Times*, 28 March, p 16.

much larger groups. There was a marked deterioration in a number of aspects of work, including the number of accidents, industrial disputes, absence levels and labour turnover. The Tavistock Institute, based in London, began a series of studies to try to solve the problems. Their suggestion was to change the ways of using the new equipment, to build teams back into the work and to encourage interdependence among the workers.

This work, described by Trist and Bamforth (1951) began a series of further studies into the design of organizations and the work done within them. The need being to design jobs and organizational structures that could meet the needs of both technology and people. For example, Emery and Thorsrud (1976) reviewed the manning, operation and hierarchical organization structure of bulk carriers used by the Norwegian merchant navy. This approach is the beginning of the contingency model.

The contingency model of organizational design

Scientific management produced a tendency for organizations to become broadly similar in terms of the approach to structure and the tasks to be done. If there were *one best way* to be identified then every organization would eventually discover and follow it. This approach also underestimated the ability of individual employees to manage their own working environment and job activities together with the organizational value and benefits to be gained from so doing. It assumed a managerial superiority.

The human relations movement recognized the significance of people in organizations. In performing the tasks designated to them, individuals are still people, they are not machines that can and will follow precise instructions over and over again without question. Human beings have free will and an ability to think. Based on the work of Elton Mayo and the Hawthorne Studies, it began where scientific management ended. Unfortunately, to concentrate on the people issues of an organization is to omit any technological constraint and the commercial imperative of operating within acceptable cost levels. The result was an equally limited perspective on what created an effective organization.

The *contingency* approach arose out of a realization that the earlier perspectives on structure were inherently limited. It was initially suggested that a broader range of factors influenced effectiveness, including the structural arrangement of an organization. There are two ways in which the relationship between people, task and structure can be explained:

✦ Separated. The relationship between the people, task elements and structure depend upon the impact of a range of factors from the environment surrounding that situation.

✦ Integrated. Task and people aspects within an organization are themselves part of the environmental forces acting upon the situation. It is therefore the perception and interpretation by management of these various forces that creates the basis of structural design.

Using the second approach, the design of an organization is said to be contingent or dependent on the forces acting upon the situation. This is the basis of the contingency approach to organization design. The *contingency model* postulates that the design of the organization is contingent on a number of forces acting upon the situation. Previous approaches attempted to identify universal truths or prescriptions that would provide a simple answer to the need to be able to organize. Figure 13.9 differentiates the traditional and contingency approaches in this respect.

It is clear from Figure 13.9 that the contingency approach links together the circumstances and the structure, but in a different way from the traditional view. The traditional view seeks to impose a definitive cause and effect relationship between circumstances and structure. The contingency model takes a more holistic view and suggests that structure is the result of a range of forces impacting upon the situation, management's interpretation of them and the identified business objectives. Figure 13.10 illustrates the contingency model.

Taking each element in the model illustrated in Figure 13.10 in turn:

✦   External contingency factors. There are a wide range of factors that impact on the situation. For example, the activities of competitors can influence what is done. Clearly, the industry in which the organization operates will have an impact on the structural arrangements adopted. The location in which the organization is based will also impact on the structural arrangements through the cultural norms etc. operating. Burns and Stalker (1961) developed the concepts of *mechanistic* and *organismic* to describe the way in which an organization is organized relative to its environment. *Mechanistic* refers to organizational forms that tend to emerge in stable and predictable conditions. In essence it reflects the application of clear hierarchical

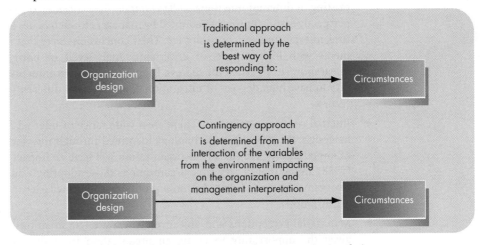

FIGURE 13.9   Traditional and contingency approaches to organization design.

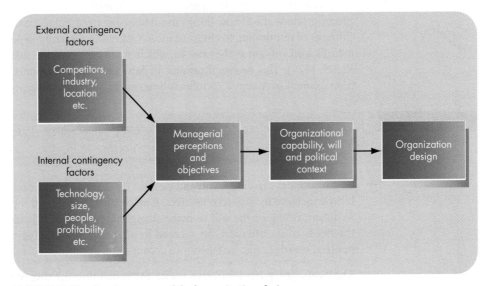

FIGURE 13.10   Contingency model of organization design.

structures, specialization of tasks, clear application of a disciplines approach to work. In that sense it holds many similarities to the bureaucratic form of organization. *Organismic* reflects an organizational form emerging in fluid and relatively unpredictable situations. It reflects the need to be capable of adapting to changing and unpredictable circumstances quickly. It is typified by a network approach to organization and control with a high level of fluidity in task definition and job responsibilities. It also incorporates a high level of technical expertise at the lower levels of the organization and a recognition of the value of individual contribution.

Lawrence and Lorsch (1967) considered the work of Burns and Stalker and sought to extend it through the consideration of what they termed integration and differentiation. *Integration* reflected the ways that co-ordination between departments was brought about. They viewed this as not so much a difference reduction process, as a mediation attempt to incorporate the genuinely different qualities and perspectives existing in different functions. *Differentiation* they considered to reflect the variety of perspectives and approaches adopted by managers to such issues as formality of structure, interpersonal relationships etc. Their conclusions were that in complex environments with high degrees of uncertainty high levels of both differentiation and integration were needed for success. In more stable environments, while it was necessary to have high degrees of integration, lower levels of differentiation could produce success.

✦ Internal contingency factors. There are a wide range of internal forces that influence its design, the production technology identified through the work of Woodward, for example. Clearly, the size of the organization will have an impact on its design. Child (1988) argues that in very large organizations those adopting a bureaucratic approach to organizing were likely to be more profitable and grow faster than less bureaucratic organizations.

✦ Managerial perceptions and objectives. There are few situations where a manager is given the opportunity to create an organization from first principles. It usually involves changing an existing organization. This can involve adapting to circumstances such as a new product introduction or competitive threat. Personal preference and preconceptions about how things should be organized influence the *metaphors* used as the basis of responding to circumstances. Culturally determined perspectives and preferences also influence the way in which managers exercise their roles (Child and Kieser, 1979). This has implications for how they might respond to perceived forces. Management in Action 13.5 reflects how one organization *interpreted* its situation.

Stop | Consider	*What might the contingency approach to organizational design suggest that the future holds for IKEA?*

✦ Organizational capability, will and politics. The organization needs to have the capability to achieve its desired objectives. If an organization does not possess the expertise to do something or the will to make changes happen then it is likely to fail to match the needs of its situation. To succeed in adapting or changing an organization the political realities must be taken into account and appropriate strategies developed.

The contingency model is very useful for explaining the diversity in organizational design that is found to exist. It provides for the forces external to the organization to be

MANAGEMENT IN ACTION 13.5

Struggle to save the soul of IKEA

The international furniture retailer IKEA began over 50 years ago in the small railway town of Smaland in Sweden. Since then its founder, Ingvar Kamprad, has seen it grow into an international company with over 125 stores in 26 countries, with sales in 1994 of $4.7bn. As it has grown in size and complexity the company has vigorously attempted to retain the company principles set out by Ingvar Kamprad and enshrined in the 'testament of a furniture dealer' written by him in 1976.

The company headquarters in Smaland remains the hub of the business, although for tax reasons they long ago moved the legal base. The IKEA retail business is owned by a foundation established in the Netherlands and the legal headquarters is in Denmark. The family interests of the founder incorporate Inter IKEA, which owns the brand name and controls the franchise operations (a minority of the stores), and Ikano, a separate company with banking and finance industry interests. The company remains a privately owned business and retains a high level of secrecy about its trading position and profitability. As a policy they prefer to avoid having to raise public money or borrow from the banks in order to retain control of the business.

The style of management within the company attempts to retain the informal approach adopted from its early beginnings. Employees are referred to as co-workers, offices in headquarters are open plan, suits are non-existent as a sign of status and even ties are rarely worn. Everyone in the company travelling on business is required to follow the example set by the chief executive of travelling economy class and using public transport rather than taxis. The trading policy of the company (from the testament) is to sell a basic high-quality product range that is typically Swedish and at a price that the majority of people could afford, wherever it operates in the world. Remarkably as a company it has achieved

success without formal market research and adapting to local differences in taste. As indicated by Jan Kjellman, head of the Swedish division which incorporates the design team: 'We don't ask so many questions before we start up new things. Last year we launched the "Swedish Cottage" range without any market research – but the customer liked it very much.'

However, things are having to change within IKEA in response to the consequences of market pressure for the financial performance of the company. Some of the forces acting upon the company include:

✦ Over recent years recession in some of its main markets have hit turnover hard.

✦ In the USA the company began operations in 1985, but found profit very difficult to achieve. For example, sales of beds and bedding were very poor in the USA and it was only following market research that it was discovered that larger beds and bedding were the norm in that country. Consequently when larger sizes were introduced sales improved considerably.

✦ With rapid expansion the structure and operation of the company had become more cosmopolitan and its original values and 'Swedishness' was under threat.

✦ The cost of operations had risen from around 30% of sales to around 37% over 10 years. This placed financial strain on a company whose margins were already tight.

✦ The distribution system required almost 90% of goods to be funnelled through the 12 distribution centres, causing delay and customer frustration. Already some 30% has been moved to direct store delivery from suppliers and plans are in hand to raise that to 50%.

✦ The inability to adapt products to local tastes restricts sales opportunities and some concessions are having to be made. For example, leather sofas in Belgium and corner sofas in Austria have been introduced.

The company is facing the twin pressure of attempting to retain the essential basis of success along with its Swedish origins while at the same time maximizing the turnover and revenue from its international operations. Many of the interna-

tional markets have dramatically different requirements. For example plans exist for a new store to be opened in China where house sizes are considerably smaller than in the West and so the product range will need further modification. The battle is engaged, only time will tell which 'side' of IKEA dominates!

Adapted from: Carnegy, H (1995) Struggle to save the soul of IKEA, *Financial Times*, 27 March, p 12.

mixed with forces internal to the company. These are interpreted by managers and filtered through capability etc. to produce a structure that will be specific to that organization at a particular point in time.

It was during the 1960s that the Industrial Administration Research Unit emerged at Aston University as a leading multidisciplinary research group. They developed a research approach which examined three elements (Pugh and Hickson, 1989, pp 9–15):

✦ Change and complexity. Because of the degree of change to which organizations are subjected, it is necessary to develop theories that are incremental rather than discrete. The structure of an organization is the result of a number of forces acting upon (and interacting with) the situation.

✦ Institutional arrangements. These include the control, hierarchical and work arrangements that exist. In many organizations these arrangements exist before employees join and will be there after they leave. Consequently, individuals are slightly detached from total ownership as they are in practice custodians of these features during their employment.

✦ Multiple perspectives. In order to create a full understanding it is necessary to consider more than one point of view. Different perceptions of an organization might exist among the different stakeholder groups. One way of illustrating this necessity is to consider the notion of perspective illustrated in Figure 13.11.

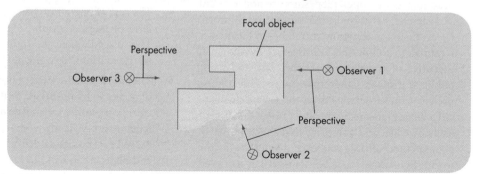

FIGURE 13.11 Multiple perspectives of an object.

Each one of the individual observers sees only part of the shape and each view is different. Consequently, each can only be considered a partial reflection of the whole. For a realistic description of the object it would be necessary to integrate the three individual reports into a cohesive framework. The approach of identifying multiple perspectives is much more complex for social entities such as organizations.

The use of the concept of a contingency model does not imply that there is only one approach to explaining the links between organization and environment. For example, Burns and Stalker attempted to reflect the degree of fit between organization and the industrial environment; Perrow considered aspects of technology, as did Woodward; Lawrence and Lorsch considered the influences of internal factors such as degree of differentiation and integration. The Aston studies brought together a number of these approaches in attempting to reflect the dynamics of the process.

The contingency model has been the subject of a number of criticisms. These include the fact that it assumes a relationship between organization and performance. The achievement of organizational performance is assumed to be a function of the structure and degree of fit with the environmental forces acting upon the situation. This ignores the ability and performance of managers at a personal level together with a range of other factors independent of structure. For example, an incompetent sales person is unlikely to win many orders irrespective of the structure of the sales department. Legge (1978) suggests that the contingency model is intuitively attractive because it contains powerful *normative* connotations. It encourages the view that effectiveness could be achieved if only the context could be interpreted properly. It also avoided the one best way approach of scientific management, while retaining the basis of a formula of the if–then type.

To suggest that it is necessary to incorporate social as well as technical aspects into organizational design does not prescribe the possible effects of this. The contingency model does not take account of the exercise of power or control in dynamic work relationships. In addition, technology, for example, is not a neutral force within an organization. Managers decide that they will utilize a particular form of technology, they decide upon its use and application in order to achieve particular objectives, including control over operational processes. They therefore determine to a significant extent how a range of factors will impact on the process of organizing.

The viable systems model

Another approach to the notion of how an organization should be structured is the *viable systems model*. It is based upon cybernetic and systems principles and adopts a radical view of organizational design. Cybernetics is a term that originated from the study of control and communications in system functioning (Wiener, 1948).

The viable systems model takes a totally different view of an organization compared with that reflected in the traditional organization chart. The viable systems model begins with the notion of an organization as being an open system (Figure 10.6), made up of a number of subsystems. Each subsystem has a part to play in ensuring that the organization is optimally organized to interact with its environments. Beer (1979) defines an organizational viable systems model as containing the following systems:

✦ System 1. The purpose of the activities that fall within this system are the achievement of organizational goals. For example, in a large international airline business the system 1 elements would be the operational divisions within the group. This could include a passenger division, cargo division and perhaps a travel agency division. Within a large manufacturing group it would be the manufacturing units. There would be as many system 1 elements as there are separate operational activities present in the system as a whole.

✦   System 2. The purpose of this system is to co-ordinate the activities of the system 1 elements. In the viable systems model each system 1 element is a separate entity and therefore capable of pursuing its own interests. While this may be of benefit, it needs to be co-ordinated if such actions are not to be detrimental to the whole organization. This is the purpose of system 2. System 2 is a link between the operational parts of the organization and the control parts of the organization.

✦   System 3. This system is concerned with the control aspects of company policy. Policy for the system as a whole is determined by the systems yet to be discussed and it is the purpose of system 3 to ensure that the operational components (system 1 elements) are adhering to the established policies. To achieve this system 3 would act as a focal point for information from the other systems. The head office-based accounting function in a large multinational company would be a typical example of a system 3 activity.

✦   System 3*. This is designated system 3 star and refers to the audit activities within the system as a whole. Its function is to enable system 3 to find out directly what is going on in the system 1 elements. The most obvious example of system 3* is the internal audit activities of the organization. However, it could incorporate a broad range of special initiatives intended to monitor a broad range of activity, for example an employee attitude survey.

✦   System 4. This system is oriented towards the development of the organization. It has direct links with the environment and is in a position to be able to capture for the organization as a whole the environmental information necessary for designing future policy and operational activity. It acts as the switch for information passing from systems 1–3 to system 5 and from system 5 to the other systems. Typical examples of system 4 activity would be market research and corporate planning.

✦   System 5. This system is intended to be responsible for the policy formulation for the whole organization. It has the responsibility for ensuring that the other systems are integrated into a cohesive whole and that the organization is effectively represented in the systems of which the organization is a part.

The viable systems model can be represented as a diagram (see Figure 13.12). There are a number of conventions used in charting in this approach to describing organizations and these will be introduced following the diagram.

The first point to note is that the diagram should not be seen in the same terms as an organization chart. It is not hierarchical for example. System 5 is not senior to system 4, which in turn is not superior to system 3 and so on. Each system has its own responsibilities and functions that need to be integrated into an effective whole if success is to be achieved. Indeed, Beer has suggested that the most senior managers within the organization should be in charge of the system 1 elements, because that is where the ultimate responsibility for the achievement of operational objectives rests.

The second point concerns the identification of activity to be classified into the appropriate system. It is important in the application of the model to avoid the assumption that system equates with function. It is tempting to categorize functions as the systems, indeed in the earlier descriptions of each of the systems a functional example was given to illustrate the activity involved. This approach works as long as it is a very large, multidivisional organization that is being modelled. It becomes increasingly difficult to sustain this approach in smaller organizations.

Beer refers to one common problem for organizations as *autopiesis*, a tendency to over-elaborate and for support systems to seek to become viable systems in their own right. Clearly, this is not possible. An accounting department cannot become an organization in its own right unless it fundamentally changes its purpose and becomes an accounting organization.

The channels of communication are shown as passing from one system to another. This is acceptable as long as a crisis does not develop. For example, imagine that there is a

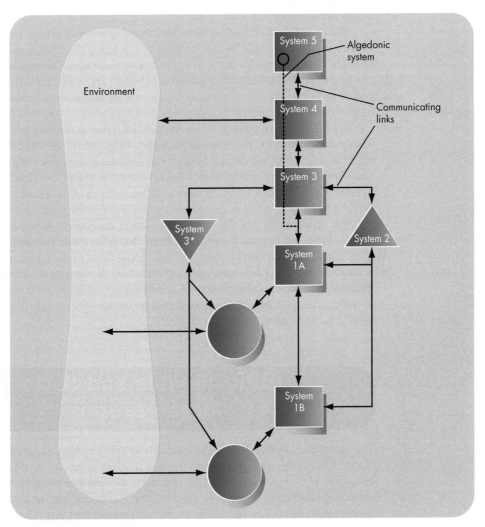

FIGURE 13.12 Viable systems model (*adapted from*: Beer, S (1985) *Diagnosing the System for Organizations*, John Wiley, Chichester).

major fire at one of the company manufacturing units. There would clearly be a number of significant events and consequences that followed. The model recognizes this through the inclusion of communication channels that can in special circumstances circumvent the normal routes. This Beer referred to as an *algedonic* system.

Consideration of the model should suggest that system 3 is about stability and order as prerequisites for control. The view of the organization held within system 3 is that of a rational entity. System 4, contrariwise, is interested in change and adaptation to market demands and therefore would tend to see control as a hindrance. The conflict between these two perspectives needs to be balanced if the organization is not to become dangerously oriented one way or the other. This is a key function of system 5. If an organization is lead by system 4, it will tend to be very fluid in approach to its business, frequently change its products and never gain the benefits possible through consolidation of its position. An organization that is lead by system 3 will tend to be overly conservative, resistant to change and may not see that the world and its markets are changing. In other words, it will become introverted.

The model as described so far relates to a single organization. In terms of the viable systems model this would be called the *system in focus*. The notion of *recursion* was introduced to describe the idea that every system was made up of subsystems and was also part of a larger system. To illustrate the notion of being part of a larger system, imagine that the system in focus (organization under study) was an international airline. In turn it would be part of the larger airline industry, which in turn would be part of the transport industry. This is recursion on a larger scale. Within the system in focus, there would be a number of operating divisions (for example passenger, cargo, travel agents, caterers, maintenance, pilot training) all of which could operate as separate companies if they were to be broken away from the parent group. This is the notion of recursion at a lower level. It is possible to reflect this idea of recursion in a more elaborate form of the viable systems diagram (see Figure 13.13).

The approach to describing an organization and how it functions within the viable systems approach is radically different from that reflected in the traditional organization chart. There is a considerable degree of additional detail in the viable systems model and it is based on a theoretical framework (cybernetics). It captures a considerable amount of information and is a useful means of reviewing the rationale associated with operational decision making. It has also been used to contribute to the introduction of initiatives such as total quality management (Flood, 1993).

BPR, flexible and flatter organizations

The significance of structure lies in its ability to achieve organizational objectives and efficiency. Business process re-engineering is a modern approach to this which requires an organization to *organize* around the necessary processes in the search to meet customer needs and continually to improve productivity. It assumes that the application of *scientific management* principles can support the achievement of organizational objectives. In essence, the structure of an organization should be a function of its objectives, technology and environmental forces – a form of contingency model. There is a wealth of research data

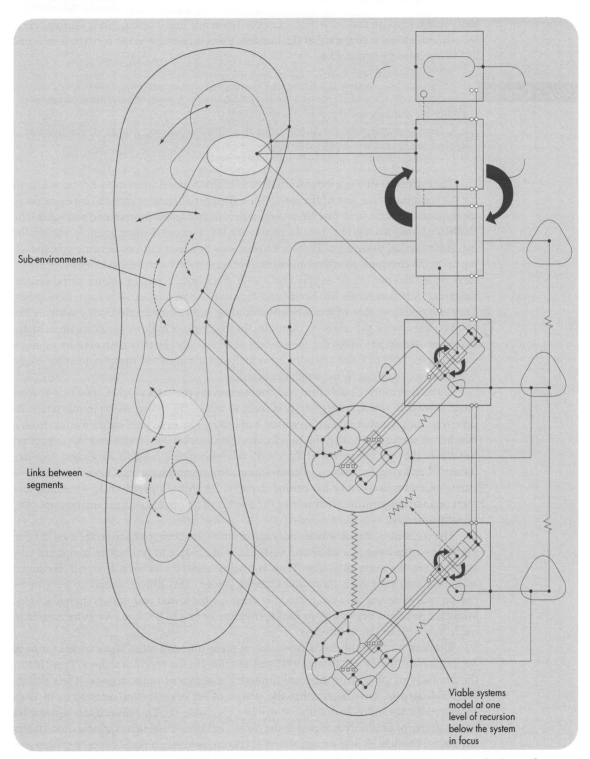

FIGURE 13.13 Viable systems model indicating recursion (*adapted from*: Beer, S (1985) *Diagnosing the System for Organizations*, John Wiley, Chichester).

that would support this view (for example Lawrence and Lorsch, 1967; Perrow, 1979; Woodward, 1970). A summary of the business process re-engineering concept is included as Management in Action 13.6.

To what extent does BPR consist of the application of scientific management techniques and/or the contingency approach to organizing?

Does it simply reflect a fashion that is doomed to failure, just as earlier formula approaches have done? Justify your views.

The essence of BPR is a move from the traditional hierarchy towards a horizontal focus for the organization as part of the search for a stronger alignment with the core process of meeting customer need. In that sense every aspect of an organization should add value. The challenge facing managers is how to emphasize the horizontal while accommodating the inevitable vertical dimension. There are many ways in which this can be achieved depending upon the company objectives and form. This can involve developing matrix type structures or, 'integration of the supply chain with disciplines acting as centres of excellence. Examples … in companies like Kodak and Ericsson' (Armistead and Rowland, 1996, p 52). They also point out that BPR can be about finding ways of more effectively managing the boundaries between processes to, 'minimise the disconnects in flows of information, materials or people' (p 53). However, the concept of BPR is heavily criticized, even by its originators, as the level of failed applications is high and it can be too complex to apply easily. The costs can significantly outweigh the benefits.

The notion of the flexible firm was discussed in the previous chapter. It reflects a broad range of ways in which an organization seeks to move and change shape in relation to its experience of the environments in which it operates. The need for flexibility arises from a number of sources including the rapidly changing market conditions and the impact on survival of the cost of operations. In today's relatively global markets with rapid and easy transport and communication infrastructures, any organization that cannot respond to events quickly is likely to be left behind. Equally, the cost of operations is something that plays an increasingly important role in the success of an organization as margins are continually squeezed.

The economies of Asia which once captured manufacturing jobs from the west in large numbers on the basis of a ready and vast supply of cheap and productive labour are now experiencing the same difficulty. They are being undercut as even less well-developed economies can offer even more and cheaper labour. This process seems to be a never ending cycle of seeing who can outbid the other for the lowest cost of operational activity. Whatever its origin, organizations find themselves having to become ever more flexible in order to be able to stay in business.

The need for flexibility finds expression in many different ways. There are the forms of flexibility identified by Atkinson (1984) and described in the previous chapter. There is also the flexibility in job activity achieved through the design of organizations. It has already been indicated in this chapter that the design of an organization determines in large measure what the individuals within it will be expected to do. Therefore, it can also impact on the degree of flexibility achieved in the use of that labour resource. Organization creates structures, boundaries and demarcations. It encourages certain types of co-operation and inhibits other forms. Any structure needs to have added into it a variety of integrative practices to overcome the barriers and constraints that are created. The upshot of this is that

MANAGEMENT IN ACTION 13.6

Business process re-engineering

There have been many attempts over the years to find the most effective way to improve the productivity and customer service levels within organizations. It has been suggested that business process re-engineering (BPR) is either the key to achieving that in the modern organization or it is little more than a reworking of the ideas of FW Taylor and scientific management.

The term BPR emerged around 1990 following the work of two distinct sets of authors. Management consultant Mike Hammer wrote an article in the *Harvard Business Review* titled 'Reengineering work: don't automate, obliterate'. This article talked about the need to re-engineer at both the business and process level. At about the same time an article appeared in the *Sloan Management Review* with the title 'The new industrial engineering: information technology and business process redesign'. Written by Thomas Davenport and James Short it talked of business process redesign, but not of re-engineering as such. The Hammer approach tended to suggest a fundamental review and change process whereas Davenport and Short adopted a more cautious and structured approach through the application of technology and industrial engineering principles. In practice the term business process re-engineering was not used by either set of writers and appeared only after the publication of both articles.

There are a number of definitions of BPR but that offered by Hammer and Champey in a 1993 publication is a useful starting point:

The fundamental rethinking and radical redesign of business processes to achieve dramatic improvements in critical contemporary measures of performance, such as cost, quality, service and speed.

Some organizations claim to have made considerable savings and improvements through the application of BPR. For example:

♦ Ford Motor Company reduced the number of people in the accounts payable department by 75%, with no reduction in service level.

♦ The Bank of America and Italy reduced cashier closing time by 91%, opened 50 new branches and doubled revenue without any increase in staff.

♦ Kodak reduced new product development time by 50% and reduced tool and manufacturing costs by 25%.

However, not all companies that attempt BPR achieve the success intended. Hammer estimates that 70% of organizations that attempt BPR do not achieve any benefits. BPR is about every aspect of the business, not just the manufacturing processes. It involves changing the structures, attitudes, culture, management style and values. It implies a fundamental re-evaluation of the purpose of the business and of developing the 'best way' of achieving that objective, taking nothing that currently exists for granted. Hammer uses the analogy of a 'paved cowpath' to describe the process that normally exists in an organization. Just as cows will tread familiar paths around the fields and to the milking parlours, organizations tend to accept the familiar as necessary and so change becomes a process of adaptation. Hammer argues that the only givens are the inputs and outputs and that between the two lies the possibility completely to redesign new ways of doing things.

The usual organization structure gets in the way of effective working as it compartmentalizes activity and creates the need to hand over work and split responsibility. Hammer and Champey illustrate this notion through the example of IBM Credit Corporation. In arranging finance on behalf of customers five steps were necessary (each in a different department) and the processing time for each application was about six days, although it could take two weeks. After 'walking the process' it became apparent that the actual work time for each application was about 1.5 hours. The whole operation was re-engineered with a new job of 'deal structurer' being created to process each application from beginning to end. Supported by new technology and database systems the turnaround time fell to four hours with a small reduction in staff numbers and the capability to handle many more transactions.

Adapted from: Patching, D (1994) Business process re-engineering: getting to the heart of the matter, *Management Services*, June, pp 10–13; and Patching, D (1994) Business process re-engineering: what's in a name? *Management Services*, November, pp 8–11.

particular levels and forms of flexibility will be created as a consequence of the structure that is adopted by an organization and therefore this needs to be actively considered in the search for ever greater levels of flexibility and control of cost.

Flatter organizations are those with relatively few levels in the hierarchy. The intended and assumed benefits of this have already been discussed in relation to the concept of the *scalar chain*. The intention is to improve the rapidity of response and to reduce the levels of bureaucracy in the organization. However, it can also have unintended consequences for the organization and the people who work within it.

It is usually the middle ranks of manager and specialist within the organization who are removed from the structure in the *delayering*, *downsizing* or *rightsizing* of an organization. These terms for the attempt to create a flatter organization have negative connotations to them, implying cutting back and removing people. In creating a flatter organization it is necessary to recognize that more needs to be changed than simply the removal of layers of management. Systems, procedures and working practices need to adapted to the new situation as well if it is to work. Simply taking people and levels out of the organization and expecting the remaining employees and managers to absorb the consequences is unrealistic and a recipe for disaster. Such an approach effectively suggests that the jobs removed did not contribute anything to the organization or duplicated what others did and can safely be eliminated.

If a flatter organization removes slack from the system there will be less spare capacity to deal with any crises or emergency situations that arise. Everyone can become so busy concentrating on the immediate task that they do not communicate with others above, below or alongside themselves. This can mean that jobs do not get done, questions are not asked or if asked remain unanswered etc. It also means that the steps between levels of management become greater. One implication of this is that managers do not develop the experience of taking decisions in a way consisting of a number of relatively small steps with many levels above them checking before organizations commit to the decision. In a flatter organization this safety process is absent and so there is a greater risk of inappropriate or wrong decisions being made.

In flattened organizations managers who feel that the organization cannot be trusted to look after them will take the initiative and look after their own interests. This in turn weakens the commitment of an individual to the organization. It introduces the danger of an instrumental approach to work emerging among the people who are charged with seeking to motivate and lead the rest of the employees within the organization (Gretton, 1993).

Organizational design: an applied perspective

From a manager's point of view contingency theory offers a *richer* vehicle for considering the issues surrounding organization design. The earlier views about the determinants of structure assume a restricted *metaphor* on the nature of organizations and how they operate. At the simplest level, the existence of the organizational hierarchy created by the structure creates the very conditions that make it difficult for organizations to meet the needs of their customers. The creation of a hierarchy emphasizes the need for everyone inside the organization to focus on the boss, their needs and interpretation of events. Continued employment, promotion and performance assessment are dependent on the views of superiors. Therefore, in practice, what the boss does not see, does not exist. Inevitably this directs the attention of employees inwards and upwards, not in the direction of the customer.

The customer experiences any organization horizontally, not vertically. Consider your experiences of a bank, supermarket, university, church or any other organization. You are very unlikely to meet anyone other than the lower levels of the organization as it is they who meet you and deal with your transaction. The senior levels frequently see their role as running the organization, not dealing with the customers. Figure 13.14 seeks to reflect this position in terms of the conflicting forces originating from customer and hierarchical needs acting on any organization. Because of this fundamental clash between the verticality and horizontalness of focus it is hardly surprising that senior managers become detached from an understanding of the real needs of customers. Everything on which they base their decisions is processed and filtered for them.

The appeal of contingency ideas is the potential to determine the significance and number of relationships acting on the situation and therefore to account for them (at least superficially) in the design of the organization. This emphasis on a *normative* perspective

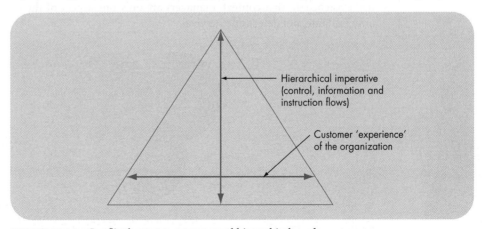

FIGURE 13.14 Conflict between customer and hierarchical needs.

delivers high levels of usability benefit to managers but perhaps offers little by way of fundamental explanation of what it is that creates structure (Legge, 1978). Organizations are composed of a number of smaller groups or departments and these can have very different perspectives and interactions with the environment around them. For example, the personnel department will interact with a number of the same groups and individuals as the production department, but a largely different set to those appropriate to the research and development function. This view of an organization is reflected in the overlapping shapes in Figure 13.15.

The implication of Figure 13.15 is that an organization does not just have one single environment, but many internal and external environments. This is a complexity that the viable systems model (Figure 13.13) is capable of reflecting. The discussion so far has concentrated on what can be described as organizational adaptation to environmental forces. The need for managers to integrate both the formal and informal elements within the organization is a point made in Management in Action 13.7.

Stop | Consider

To what extent does MiA 13.7 imply that an organization needs to undergo an evolutionary process to change itself, just as with every living thing in nature?

If that is so, how might managers seek to respond to the need for change in organizational design other than through managerial intervention?

Another way of considering how organizations evolve over time has been the use of population ecology approaches to the process. Using what can be described as Darwinian theories this approach emerged in the late 1970s, but it has not yet produced a significant alternative explanation. It attempts to utilize the notion of *selection* to the way in which structure evolves over time. The most appropriate organizations are 'selected' for survival based on environmental fit and adaptation (Thompson and McHugh, 1990, p 98).

While it may be an interesting academic debate to consider the nature of structure, its determinants and evolutionary forces, managers function in real time in a dynamic context. Consequently, the advantages of models such as displayed in Figures 13.10 and 13.12 can provide them with an improved opportunity to influence design and perhaps increase the probability of survival. The notion of *selection* in ecology would imply that the environments are in some way choosing the most effectively adapted *specimens* for continued existence. In that context, managers are only one aspect of the environment and can only facilitate, not determine survival.

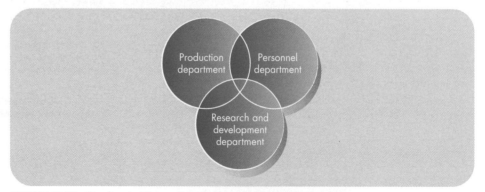

FIGURE 13.15 Overlapping interactions between organizational activity.

MANAGEMENT IN ACTION 13.7

A mesh of the formal and the flexible

That every organization consists of a formal set of frameworks, systems, procedures and policies would not be denied. It is the existence of such architecture that provides the skeleton that holds the organization together and provides the outline shape. However, that is only part of the 'beast'. Also within every organization are the informal aspects that ensure that the formal frameworks actually do what they are supposed to do. Continuing the metaphor, it could be argued that the informal aspects of the organization represent the flesh and muscle of the 'beast' that creates the three-dimensional manifestation of it, as well as allowing movement and thought.

Most practising managers are only too well aware of the existence of the informal organization. They must live and work with and through it every day. It provides the networking, power and political dimensions within any organization. The informal is primarily about relationships not structures. That is why it is the informal that makes an organization work (or not as the case may be). The structure and systems can only provide the potential for future action to happen. It is among the academic and book-writing community that this reality of organizational life is somewhat ignored when the latest fashion or fad is promulgated as the best way to design an organization.

Lorenz discusses this in relation to the work of Nitin Nohria and James Berkley, who argue that the formal aspect of organization has been underplayed in the search for 'better' formal models. Nohria and Berkley go as far as to reject the notion of the concept of a new paradigm, arguing instead for a shifting action perspective as a more helpful metaphor. This view of an

organization is as an organism, where many different things are happening at once which are constantly in flux. This can often be as a result of low-level action within the organization.

To illustrate the need for informal aspects of an organization to be included in design change, Nohria and Berkley draw attention to the experiences of three divisions within Allen-Bradley. The company, which makes high-tech industrial control devices, opted to introduce a flat, team-based 'concentric' structure in 1990. However, within months the old hierarchy had reasserted itself. Business teams were formed to oversee the operational teams, and an executive council was formed to oversee the work of the business teams. Within a year the work of the teams was severely restricted and by 1992 much of the concentric structure was disbanded. A multidivisional structure was reintroduced.

Some of the benefits of the attempts to restructure were retained within Allen-Bradley. The two major benefits retained and which were necessary for a changed informal structure were IT systems that spanned the whole organization together with broader performance measures. In essence it is as necessary to change the informal structure within an organization as it is to change the formal if 'doing things differently' is to have any real meaning and to stand any chance of long-term success.

Adapted from: Lorenz, C (1994) A mesh of the formal and the flexible, *Financial Times*, 4 November, p 11.

Structure is the means of organizing within the enterprise. It is the vehicle for ensuring that the necessary work can be done without overloading individuals. It allows specialization to be introduced in order to reduce the skill and training required within the organization. However, it also provides the simplified and repetitive tasks that can create alienation and a lack of commitment to the objectives being sought. It is a double-edged sword, providing benefits and disadvantages. It is in an attempt to offset some of the disadvantages arising from structural forms that the alternative organizations introduced in the previous chapter are important. It is tempting to assume that the only structural forms that exist are the large private and public sector organizations that are the most apparent examples. This is simply not the case. Many different forms of organization exist and they can provide lessons for anyone who is prepared to study them.

It should also be apparent that there are few occasions in which managers have the opportunity to design an organization from first principles. Managers are usually faced with a number of situations in organizationanl design terms, each of which adds particular constraints to the process. At the simplest level an entrepreneur may create a new organization. However, as such, it is likely to be small in scale, requiring only the simplest of structures. In another context, a manager may be faced with a crisis and need to reshape an existing organization to cut cost or refocus the business. Again, a manager may be faced with rapid growth and need to expand quickly. A merger may be proposed that would need the integration and reshaping of two or more overlapping organizations. An organization may seek to develop new product lines (or close existing ones) the implications of which need to be integrated into an existing framework. A new manager may decide that a reorganization is necessary in order that they might strengthen their own position relative to a group of long-serving subordinates. These all reflect examples of situations where changes to an existing structure is likely to occur.

In essence, managers are usually faced with changing an existing organizational design and not the opportunity to create something from a blank sheet of paper. With the need (or desire) to change an existing structure comes a range of factors that need to be taken into account which are not present in creating something for the first time. For example, existing staff will be familiar, experienced and comfortable with the status quo and may well resent and resist any imposed changes. Equally, procedures and systems may need to be redesigned to accommodate the proposed changes. Even customers and suppliers may not be happy with the impact of proposed changes. The various stakeholder groups may have opinions that are necessary to take into account in the design process. They will certainly have an expectation that their opinions and needs should be taken into account in the process. All of this adds up to a much more complex process of adapting an organizational design to changed circumstances than a design for a new company. Management in Action 13.8 outlines the process adopted when two very large insurance companies merged.

Stop | Consider

To what extent does the process described in MiA 13.8 indicate the application of a contingency approach to organizational design and what extent the application of a means of smoothing or avoiding the potential problems associated with the merger?
   Does this distinction matter?

MANAGEMENT IN ACTION 13.8

Premium bonding

In February 1998 Commercial Union and General Accident, both general insurance businesses on a global scale merged, forming the £18 billion insurance company CGU Insurance. One of the key features of the process was the heavy involvement of staff in creating the design of the combined organization. Cees Schrauwers, managing director of Commercial Union indicated when he announced the merger:

> We wanted to avoid the infighting that is so often associated with takeovers, especially as the two companies were of almost equal size. We have all seen examples of mergers where the internal warfare has carried on for years after the event. That was something we wanted to avoid.

The merger was announced on 25 February 1998. All local managers were contacted by telephone overnight and asked to be in their office by 7 am the next morning to receive a faxed briefing document. Presentation materials were delivered to each branch by 9 am that morning. Included in the briefing was a commitment to design the new organization according to a set of principles:

✦ Structures will have the fewest possible number of levels (maximum of 5).

✦ Decision making will be delegated to the lowest appropriate level.

✦ Positions will have clear accountabilities, outputs and measures.

It was some four months before the legal and financial merger was completed. In between the initial briefing and formal merger both companies worked hard to retain the loyalty of existing staff. Research was conducted during this time to identify what the new company (CGU) needed to do in order to maintain the high levels of contribution from the staff. This was followed by the

creation of a 'Discovery' programme. Large groups of first-line supervisors and technical specialists were nominated by staff in both companies to be trained to undertake a culture survey. First-line supervisors were chosen as the people to undertake the culture survey because they were close to staff, management and customers. Each person on the Discovery programme was paired up with someone from the other company in order to allow a cross-examination of each others organization. In effect a 'visitors' eye view was created of each company and its way of doing things.

The second stage followed in June 1998, shortly after the Discovery process, when the two trade unions represented within CGU Insurance helped to support and organize a two-day conference for about 500 junior managers and technical specialists. It was the employees who nominated their first-line supervisors for inclusion in the process, which was given the title 'Being One'. The 500 delegates and trade union representatives were split into four smaller cohorts within the conference hall and asked to work on one aspect of the programme, in addition an employee survey and brand research was undertaken. This was all seeking to answer the basic question: 'What would make CGU Insurance the best place to work for employees?'

Each of the four cohorts within the conference worked on a sub-set of the main topic which were:

✦ Getting the work done.

✦ Leading and managing people.

✦ Developing and rewarding people.

✦ Working atmosphere and environment.

The activity in the hall was constantly televised on huge screens around the hall in order to give the two days the vibrancy, atmosphere and feeling of a major sporting event. During the latter part of the two days three-quarters of the delegates would circulate around the hall finding out what the other groups were deciding as part of developing their own group's work. The remaining quarter would stay behind and answer questions from the other groups seeking information. Strong feelings were surfaced over the course of the event. For example there was anger at the lack of an engaging style of leadership in both companies and the acceptance by managers of poor performance.

At the end of the event the directors undertook a commitment to build the type of organization that would meet the mandate emerging from the two-day conference. The areas of the commitment undertaken were:

✦ To incorporate an empowered branch network, with appropriate support processes and profit accountability.

✦ To create high-performing teams that recognize success based on a 'can-do' attitude and supported by training, multiskilling and rewards

✦ To develop an appropriate supportive, open, relaxed and performance-oriented management style based on competence.

✦ To encourage staff through personal development, succession planning and provision of open access to opportunity.

✦ To value staff through consultation and a recognition of individuality. Support staff through valuing their contribution and rewarding it through performance pay.

The next (third) stage was to use a series of focus groups among senior managers in order to translate the directors commitments into what became known as 'the best place to work blueprint'. This contained three main strands:

✦ Alignment of employee aspiration and company practice in terms of issues such as

key result areas and knowing where each person fitted into the organization.

✦ Performance management practice to include issues such as managerial support for fair dealing and acknowledgement of success, along with customer-focused teams and well-trained managers.

✦ Support from leaders who inspire confidence and trust; provide the technical and administrative support for front-line staff; provide an informal working environment and a respect for home and work life separation.

This blueprint now forms the basis for an annual employee survey to monitor employee expectation and company performance. The third stage created the basis for the fourth major involvement exercise, which took place in September 1998 and involved about 80 people from the trade unions, technical specialists and all levels of management. They were brought together to undertake an organizational design process. To aid in this they had the output from a small team that had spent several months collecting data from around the group on aspects of best practice and operational effectiveness. At the end of the four-day design process the group had provided an outline of the new organization in terms of its relationship with its customers, its services and cost drivers. The main structural frameworks were also designated at that time including the size of business units (between 30–50 people), the size of work teams (between 10–12 people) and which locations would remain and which would be closed.

The result of the design process was piloted in a number of offices that were converted into CGU Insurance locations during April 1999. The final touches were put on the design framework during that pilot experience. It was at this stage that outside management support was introduced to the change process when Pricewaterhouse-Coopers provided members for a programme management team. The new structures were then

MANAGEMENT IN ACTION 13.8 continued

rolled out to the other locations within the new company and the process of integration gathered pace. It also initiated the beginning of an attempt to continue to capture the potential of all employees in making the company a leader through employee involvement in decision making.

Adapted from: Clarry, T (1999) Premium bonding, *People Management*, 2 September, pp 34–9.

Conclusions

The design and structure of an organization is an area in which managers make choices. The form of the organization is not something that occurs by chance, or as a result of some dictat from the government. It is appropriate to view an organization as something over which people have stewardship for a period of time. They are therefore constrained by a number of forces in moulding the organization. These constraints include the industry, size, history, technology, markets, legal constraints, profitability, the will and ability of individuals within the organization.

The notion of a direct cause and effect link between a number of environmental forces and the structure of an organization is overly simplistic. It ignores the interactive nature of external and internal forces and managerial responses. The use of metaphor was introduced as a means of accounting for the understanding that managers have of what an organization is and how it should function relative to its circumstances. It is not the intention to suggest that contingency or systems approaches offer perfect explanations and applied options for understanding organization design. They do, however, offer a richer means of attempting to understand the processes involved together with a basis for future research.

Discussion questions

1. Define the following key terms used in this chapter:

Recursion	*Span of control*	*Organization chart*
Variety	*Centralization/decentralization*	*Metaphor*
System in focus	*System*	*Mechanistic/organismic model*
Autopiesis	*Contingency*	*Influence diagram*
Algedonic system	*Scalar chain*	*Determinism*
Rich picture l		

2. Describe how the contingency approach to organizational design emerged.

3. What is the viable systems model? Explain each of the systems within the model and describe the significance of the algedonic system.

4. Is it inevitable that centralization and decentralization will be cyclical trends in organizational design? Why or why not?

5. In what ways does the concept of a metaphor as described by Morgan (1986) contribute to understanding of how organizations are structured?

6. Describe the contingency approach to designing an organization. How does it differ from the traditional views on structure?

7. Assess the contribution of the Aston studies to the understanding of the contingency view of organizations.

8. Does the distinction between line and staff functions as described in this chapter offer anything of value in understanding organizational design, or does it simply reflect the normal political behaviour and conflict that might be expected to exist in any human situation? Justify your answer.

9. Describe the approaches to determinism described in this chapter. Why do they offer a restricted view of organizational design?

10. What is a flexible firm and how does it reflect the contingency ideas described in this chapter?

Research activities

1. Identify an organization with which you are familiar. Find out as much as you can about the organization, its size, products or services etc. Attempt to redesign the organization using the principles of the contingency model. In undertaking this exercise you should make whatever assumption you find necessary about the organization, its environments and the people within it. You will not be able to collect enough information to make this a real exercise, but it should allow you to consider the implications of the model.

2. Consider the viable systems model. Using the organization identified in activity 1 undertake a review of the organization using the viable systems model. What conclusions do you draw about this model compared to the contingency approach?

3. In a group of four fellow students, seek out a number of unusual organizations. If you find real examples near to where you are based make an attempt to speak to some of the members or senior representatives. For all examples you find, describe the structure of the organization together with some of the objectives that the designers were attempting to achieve. Make an assessment of how successful they have been, together with the differences in structure compared with conventional organizations.

Key reading

From Clark, H, Chandler, J and Barry, J (1994) *Organization and Identities: Text and Readings in Organizational Behaviour*, International Thomson Business Press, London:

- ✦ Burns, T and Stalker, GM: Mechanistic and organic systems of management, p 331. The original of this seminal work on the subject.
- ✦ Baron, RD and Norris, GM: The dual labour market, p 335. An introduction to the emergence of differentiated labour markets.
- ✦ Atkinson, J: The flexible firm, p 337. The original article referred to earlier.
- ✦ Pollert, A: The flexible firm: a model in search of reality, p 343. An extract which considers some of the issues associated with the flexible firm.
- ✦ Hirst, P and Zeitlin, J: Knowing the buzz word is not enough, p 345. This reviews the experience of flexibility in the UK as compared with experience elsewhere.

Further reading

Armistead, C and Rowland, P (1996) *Managing Business Processes: BPR and Beyond*, Wiley, Chichester. This is an edited book with contributors drawn from a wide range of organizations and academic disciplines. It seeks to review the basis of process approaches to organizations and what it means to manage from that paradigm. As such it does intersect with the design of organizations at a number of levels.

Beer, S (1985) *Diagnosing the System for Organizations*, John Wiley, Chichester. This book is intended as a workbook introduction for managers intending to find out more about the viable systems model and to attempt to redesign their organizations accordingly.

Brown, H (1992) *Women Organizing*, Routledge, London. Chapter 3 is worth reading in the context of the contingency and systems approaches as it provides a detailed review of social context within which organizations function and the basis of women creating organizations for their own needs.

Espejo, R and Harnden, R (eds) (1989) *The Viable System Model: Interpretations and Applications*, John Wiley, Chichester. Provides a broad review of the viable systems model and reports several studies of its application.

Roberts, KH (1994) Functional and Dysfunctional Organizational Linkages. In (eds) Cooper, CL and Rousseau, DM *Trends in Organizational Behaviour*, Vol 1, John Wiley, Chichester. This chapter considers the notion of linkages within organizations and how they contribute to (or reduce) the risk of disaster in an environmental context.

References

Arkin, A (1999) Return to centre, *People Management*, 6 May, 34–41.

Armistead, C and Rowland, P (1996) Managing by Business Process. In Armistead, C and Rowland, P. (eds). *Managing Business Processes: BPR and Beyond*, Wiley, Chichester.

Atkinson, J. (1984) Manpower strategies for flexible organizations, *Personnel Management*, August, 28–31.

Beer, S (1979) *The Heart of Enterprise*, John Wiley, Chichester.

Bible, (The Jerusalem translation) (1966) Darton, Longman & Todd, London.

Burns, T and Stalker, GM (1961) *The Management of Innovation*, Tavistock. London.

Child, J and Kieser, A (1979) Organization and Managerial Roles in Britain and West German Companies: An Examination of the Culture-free Thesis. In (eds) Lammers, C and Hickson, D (eds) *Organizations Alike and Unlike*, Routledge & Kegan Paul, London.

Child, J (1988) *Organization: A Guide to Problems and Practice*, 2nd edn, Paul Chapman, London.

Collins, PD and Hull, F (1986) Technology and span of control: Woodward revisited, *Journal of Management Studies*, March, 143–64.

Emery, FE and Thorsrud, E (1976) *Democracy at Work*, Martinus Nijhoff, Leiden.

Flood, RL (1993) *Beyond TQM*, John Wiley, Chichester.

George, CS (1972) *The History of Management Thought*, 2nd edn, Prentice Hall, Englewood Cliffs, NJ.

Gretton, I (1993) Striving to succeed in a changing environment, *Professional Manager*, July, 15–17.

Handy, CB (1993) *Understanding Organizations*, 4th edn, Penguin, Harmondsworth.

Heller, R (1997) *In Search of European Excellence*, HarperCollins Business, London.

Heseltine, M (1999) Change the people, not the system, *Management Today*, October, p 32.

Kast, F and Rosenzweig, J (1972) General systems theory: applications for organization and management, *Academy of Management Journal*, December, 447–65.

Lamb, J (1999) UK's largest union resorts to delayering programme, *People Management*, 28 October, 19.

Lawrence, PR and Lorsch, JW (1967) *Organization and Environment*, Harvard University Press, Boston, MA.

Legge, K (1978) *Power, Innovation and Problem Solving in Management*, McGraw-Hill, London.

Marglin, SA (1974) What do bosses do? The origins and functions of hierarchy in capitalist production, *Review of Radical Political Economics*, **6**, 60–102.

Merrick, N (1999) Premier division, *People Management*, 19 August, 38–41.

Mintzberg, H (1979) *The Structuring of Organizations*, Prentice Hall, Englewood Cliffs, NJ.

Mintzberg, H (1981) Organization design: fashion or fit, *Harvard Business Review*, **59**, 103–16.

People Management (1999) Advertisement for Chameleon Training and Consulting, 28 October, 90.

Morgan, G (1986) *Images of Organization*, Sage, Newbury Park, CA.

Perrow, C (1967) *Organizational Analysis: A Sociological View*, Tavistock, London.

Perrow, C (1979) *Complex Organizations: A Critical Essay*, 2nd edn, Scott Foresman, Glenview.

Pugh, DS and Hickson, DJ (1989) *Writers on Organizations*, 4th edn, Penguin, London.

Taylor, FW (1947) *Scientific Management*, Harper & Row, New York.

Thompson, P (1989) *The Nature of Work*, 2nd edn, Macmillan, Basingstoke.

Thompson, P and McHugh, D (1990) *Work Organizations*, Macmillan, Basingstoke.

Townley, B (1994) *Reframing Human Resource Management: Power, Politics and the Subject at Work*, Sage, London.

Townsend, R (1985) *Further up the Organization*, Coronet Books, London.

Trist, EL and Bamforth, KW (1951) Some social and psychological consequences of the longwall method of goal-getting, *Human Relations*, February, 3–38.

Wiener, N (1948) *Cybernetics*, John Wiley, New York.

Woodward, J (1965) *Industrial Organizations: Theory and Practice*, Oxford University Press, London.

Woodward, J (1970) *Industrial Organizations: Behaviour and Control*, Oxford University Press, Oxford.

CHAPTER 14

Organizational culture

CHAPTER SUMMARY

This chapter considers the concept of culture and its impact on the organizational context. The chapter begins with a review of what culture means within an organization together with the general forms that it can take. The determinants of culture are then explored followed by a consideration of the notion of national culture and its links with organizational culture. This is followed by a review of the relationship between culture and globalization. The management of culture and the possibilities for changing organizational culture are then introduced. The relationship between culture and organizational design are also discussed. The chapter concludes with a management review of organizational culture.

LEARNING OBJECTIVES

After studying this chapter and working through the associated Management in Action panels, Discussion questions and Research activities, you should be able to:

✦ Explain why the concept of culture is problematic when applied to organizations.

✦ Describe the different levels of analysis used in cultural analysis.

✦ Outline the forms through which organizational culture finds expression.

✦ Understand the links between culture and organizational design.

✦ Appreciate the relationship between culture as used within an organization and as used to describe national difference.

✦ Discuss the significance of sub- and countercultures to an organization.

✦ Assess the possibilities for the management and change of organizational culture, together with the means of doing so.

✦ Detail the significance of the culture for the management of an organization.

Introduction

The concept of culture began to make an impact on organizational thinking in the late 1970s and early 1980s. However, its existence is evident in a number of the ideas from earlier writers, for example, Barnard (1938) and Jaques (1952). Culture is a difficult concept to define, being something that can easily be recognized but that is difficult to pin down in objective terms. As a concept, culture emerged from anthropological research among ethnic groups and societies. Unfortunately, from this wealth of established literature there is no dominant view of how culture should be conceptualized. According to Allaire and Firsirotu (1984) for example there are eight separate schools of thought on what the term *culture* means.

It is comparatively easy to recognize that organizations 'do things differently', or that they 'feel' different to other organizations. However, it is much more difficult to say with any degree of certainty in what ways and to what degree organizations differ. The phrase 'the way we do things around here' is frequently offered as an operational definition of culture (Deal and Kennedy, 1988). However, while that may be a useful approach to understanding the scope of the concept of *culture*, it offers little analytical power. Included in that definition are the procedural, work organization, job design and structural aspects that contribute much to 'how things are done'. These are in addition to those features of the organization that would be generally regarded as cultural dimensions. It may be that work organization and procedural issues are a reflection of the underlying culture of the organization, but the definition offered by Deal and Kennedy does not give any real clue to the parameters and scope of the concept.

Another difficulty with the concept of *culture* is the degree to which individuals, organizations or entire communities display characteristics which are consistent within it. So for example to what extent do all British people display characteristics that would be consistent with the British culture? It is apparent from even the most casual observation that there are many commonalites between people in a specific culture, but that individual differences also provide considerable variety as well. This question is also becoming increasingly difficult to answer with the evolution of multicultural societies and the encouragement of diversity within society. However, this presumption ignores the reality of history in which people moved around the world in considerable quantity as a response to economic necessity, war, invasion and the search for profit. Over time many of these migrations integrated into the local community to some extent.

If the concept of culture at a national level cannot be considered to precisely define every person that lives within it or explain their behaviour patterns, what of organizations? Does the concept of organizational culture imply anything about the people who work within it, or does it simply reflect the preferred ways of doing things as stated by Deal and Kennedy? These are questions that this chapter will seek to explore.

Defining organizational culture

The first problem in seeking to offer a definition of the term culture is the sheer diversity of meaning that it contains. As far back as 1952 Kroeber and Kluckhohn reported 164 different meanings of the concept of *culture*, a figure which must have been well exceeded in the intervening 50 years. This has led some writers to suggest that the concept has no real value because the variety of meaning is so diverse and largely contradictory that it is impossible for it to offer any value as a research idea (Kraut, 1975). However, it remains necessary for any researcher or manager seeking to understand or work in the organizational field to be able to describe those facets of human experience and behaviour that contribute to the differences and similarities in how people engage with their perceived world. In that sense culture as a concept retains its value as a meta construct which has metaphorical and some descriptive power, even if it is imprecise and problematic.

Kilman *et al.* (1985) suggest that *culture* reflects the ideologies, shared philosophies, values, beliefs, assumptions, attitudes, expectations and norms of an organization. It is also suggested to be something that emerges over time and is not specifically created. A much earlier definition offered by Jaques (1952) suggests that culture is the:

> Customary and traditional way of thinking and doing things, which is shared to a greater or lesser degree by all members, and which the new members must learn and at least partially accept, in order to be accepted into the services of the firm. (p 251)

Deal and Kennedy (1988) also offer a range of elements within culture, including the importance of symbolism and leadership as a means of achieving employee commitment. Thompson and McHugh (1990) provide an insightful review of this phenomenon, pointing out the significance of personnel management in achieving and maintaining new and more appropriate (from a management perspective) cultures. They review a considerable body of evidence to demonstrate that, as far as the *excellence* view of culture is concerned, it has little to offer by way of an explanation for the significance of culture in an organizational context.

The two definitions of culture provided so far can be seen as supportive of each other. The Kilman *et al.* (1985) view of the 'things' that compose culture can be seen to provide the basis to the earlier definition provided by Jaques (1952) and through which the learning of it could be achieved. In other words, the later definition considers content and the earlier definition process. However, the process as described by Jaques is one of acquisition by individuals. It assumes that the individuals will either possess the same culture as the organization before joining it or that they will subsequently acquire it through the various forms of training and socialization. This implies it is something that it is management's interest to design or engineer. Particular cultures will be more supportive of management's objectives than others. Interest in the so-called Japanese management phenomenon fuelled interest in this issue through the perceived need to build strong teams through what Thompson and McHugh call *compulsory sociability* (p 239). Management in Action 14.1 provides an insight into some of these Japanese management practices.

| Stop | Consider | *To what extent do you consider that the initiatives described in MiA 14.1 reflect an attempt to create organizational cultures based upon a blend of both east and west?* |

Or are they an attempt to provide more effective managerial control in a way that the host country managers and employees would find acceptable?

MANAGEMENT IN ACTION 14.1

East meets west

International operations are a fact of organizational life. Even very small companies find themselves in the position of having to trade or operate in countries other than their home base. Many large international companies have considerable experience in operating in other countries and with other cultures. However well established that experience might be it does not eliminate potential problems from the mixing of language, culture and business practice in overseas locations.

Over the past decade or so a number of Japanese companies have established manufacturing or other operational units in the UK. The need to be able to achieve operational objectives, inevitably determined by the Japanese head office, with a British workforce has provided some interesting examples of the effects of culture. For example, the Japan Travel Bureau (JTB) employs about 10,000 staff worldwide, about 400 of whom work within Europe, its European HQ being in London. Faced with rapid expansion of its market share (about 30% of Japanese travel business) the company was undergoing rapid change. In common with many international operations JTB was headed in Europe by a home country national, supported by a mixture of Japanese and European personnel. Company surveys during the late 1980s identified a number of problems. There was a lack of empathy between local staff and Japanese managers created by cultural and language differences. Also a lack of motivation and commitment among staff, together with a lack of understanding of the organization's goals and underpinning values. High labour turnover among local staff was also a problem. A lack of appropriate skill existed among many of the managers and local staff, partly as a result of the vicious circle created by the high labour turnover.

A number of initiatives were put in place to address these issues in conjunction with a carefully selected consultancy able to offer support

across the language barrier as well as a flexible approach to the change programme. The result was an educational initiative given the title *Issho-ni* or 'together'. It was to address the many issues identified

through the survey, including cultural differences, customer first values, communications, relationships and managerial competencies. The programme was based around several monthly workshops, organized hierarchically as a precursor for a later integrated approach. Not surprisingly a number of problems emerged during the running of pilot programmes, including rejection, suspicion and hostility. The programme attempted to deal with these issues and they did reduce, although not completely. Subsequently, customer service groups were established at each local office in an attempt to emphasize the local identification of issues and a local team-based resolution. The outcome of the process was positive in that labour turnover reduced and improvements in customer service occurred.

In the manufacturing sectors there has been much publicity for initiatives such as *kaizen* or the continuous improvement of an operation through small improvements to working practices. This approach was given considerable impetus through the arrival of large Japanese companies including Nissan and Toyota. Having identified the UK as an appropriate base for European operations the manufacturing units found it necessary to both compete with factory operations in Japan and ensure that the manufacturing infrastructure in the UK was compatible with their needs. A number of initiatives were introduced to achieve these objectives. For example, Toyota chose to refer to employees as 'members' in an attempt to generate a feeling of belonging. This went along with teamworking and employee involvement on a scale not usually seen in the UK (problem solving and daily briefings for example), even encouraging pre-work exercises.

Beyond that level of activity suppliers were encouraged to adopt the so-called Japanese manufacturing methods in order to ensure a continuity of supply in quantity, quality and price to whichever car manufacturers they supplied. Visits by company purchasing staff and other specialists take place in an attempt to assist the first- and then second-tier suppliers to improve their performance and to be able to meet the needs of what

are increasingly important customers. However, some suppliers are sensitive to the competing pressures of better quality and productivity leading to job security on the one hand, but potentially the need for fewer workers to produce the output on the other. Not an easy tightrope to walk in any culture or location.

Adapted from: Fitzgerald, J (1991) A Japanese lesson in European togetherness, *Personnel Management*, September, pp 45–7; and Williams, M (1993) East meets west, *Personnel Today*, 26 January, pp 34–5.

Levels of analysis

From the foregoing discussion on definitions it might appear that the concept of organizational culture is clear and easy to measure. This is not the case, particularly as the concept incorporates so many dimensions or variables (evident in the Kilman *et al.* (1985) definition). Recall also the previous discussion in terms of the complexity and confusion in the way the term *culture* is used.

It is possible to identify three levels of analysis from the literature on culture (see Figure 14.1).

Taking each level in turn:

✦ Perceived culture. This reflects the most apparent level of cultural analysis. It is based upon the 'way things get done around here' view of culture. Typically, it would incorporate the rituals, stories and ceremonies that identify the group in action.

✦ Common values, and so on. The second level of analysis attempts to get behind that

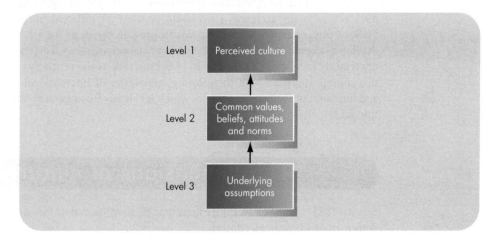

FIGURE 14.1 Levels of cultural analysis

which is observable and identify the factors that determine the perceived culture. Typically this level of analysis would incorporate the factors identified in the Kilman *et al.* definition.

✦ Underlying assumptions. Behind the common values are the underlying assumptions that individuals hold about the world and how it functions. It is often very difficult to identify these hidden assumptions as they are not directly articulated in the behaviour and attitudes that people display.

There are other ways in which approaches to the study of culture have been categorized. For example, Adler (1984) categorized studies of culture in terms of the research perspective adopted, including parochial, polycentric and synergistic. The main distinguishing features between these categories of study being the number of cultures studied and the methodology adopted within the research. Redding (1994) proposes a two-dimensional classification scheme for research in this area based upon the degree of interpretation or description in the study with the second scale being a continuum from micro to macro levels of analysis. More recently Cray and Mallory (1998) suggest that it is possible to address many of the earlier criticisms of research in this field by classifying studies according to their relationship to theory. In doing so they offer three approaches that can be identified from the literature:

✦ Naive comparative. This approach regards culture as the explanatory variable for any differences observed. The writers use the term naive to reflect the lack of any theoretical basis to the work. The emphasis in such studies being to compare issues such as how managerial functions differ between cultures.

✦ Culture free. An approach taking contingency theory as the basis of seeking to explore the differences and similarities between cultures. The notion of contingency allows the perspective of cross-cultural studies to be undertaken and the impact on a variety of structural dimensions associated with organizing and managing to be explored.

✦ Culture bound. This approach draws on a broad range of theoretical models to explore and explain the differences between cultures.

Each of these categorization approaches has its own strength and they are not automatically mutually exclusive. Each could be used for different purposes. The Cray and Mallory categorization model sets out to provide the basis for what they subsequently develop as a cognitive model of international management based on cultural concepts. This uncertainty in how to classify studies of culture reflects the relatively recent exploration of this concept, together with the growing complexity of international operational activity and human multicultural experience which inevitably frustrates any attempt to theorize in this field.

The dimensions of culture

Schein (1985) identified six dimensions that, he suggests, reflect the composition of culture within an organizational context:

+ Behavioural regularities. This reflects observable patterns of behaviour. It might include induction ceremonies, the in-group language and the ritualized behaviour patterns that reflect membership of particular groups or organizations.

+ Dominant values. These are the specific beliefs expressed by groups and organizations. For example, an organization might attempt to create a 'quality image' by adopting a number of relevant initiatives and publishing its objective to achieve 'quality' as a policy.

+ Norms. These are general patterns of behaviour that all members of a group are expected to follow. For example, many retail chains set specific behaviour standards for employees in terms of the phrases used for customer greetings and the requirement to smile and make eye contact.

+ Rules. Rules are specific instructions of what must be done, whereas norms are sometimes unwritten and informally accepted. The rules are the 'must dos' of the organization set out by management. However, because they must be followed employees may simply *comply* with them. This represents the difference between doing something because it is necessary and doing it because of a belief that it is right or because it represents a 'norm' of the particular group.

+ Philosophy. In this context these reflect the underlying beliefs that people hold about people in general, their beliefs, mentality and the basis on which they operate. Given that an *organization* is largely formed by the managers who run it, the philosophy of it naturally tends to reflect their values. Based on this philosophy managers determine the policies and practices that will guide the company and help to frame its culture and operations.

+ Climate. The physical layout of buildings, attitudes to open plan as opposed to enclosed offices, recreation facilities, management style and the design of public areas all help to create the atmosphere or climate within the company.

Each of these six dimensions of culture is a complex idea in its own right. They do, however, offer descriptive ability in beginning to tease out how culture influences organizations and how in turn organizations can influence culture. This circularity is reflected in Figure 14.2.

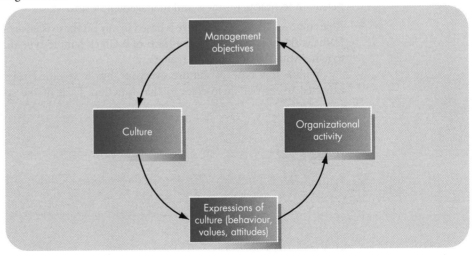

FIGURE 14.2 The cycle of culture.

The circularity displayed in Figure 14.2 indicates that culture produces particular behaviour and associated belief patterns, which in turn influences what actually happens within the organization. Actual events are then measured against management objectives and the consequences feed back into culture. The implication being that if management perceive that a particular culture achieves the objectives being pursued it will be reinforced. If it does not contribute to the achievement of objectives then management will attempt to change it.

Cultural frameworks

The previous discussion concentrated on the dimensions of culture evident at level two of the analysis model (Figure 14.1). It is now appropriate to describe how culture manifests itself at level one. In other words, how is culture experienced in an organization? How is culture observed and detected? There are a number of different approaches to this question.

Handy's four types

Based on the earlier work of Harrison (1972), Handy (1993) describes four manifestations of culture:

✦ Power culture. Typically found in small organizations, everything revolves around the focal person. All important decisions are made by them and they retain absolute authority in all matters. As a diagram Handy describes this culture as a web (Figure 14.3) and the *metaphor* of a spider's web very graphically illustrates this type of culture in operation.

   The main features of this type of culture are a single-mindedness in approach, dominated by the focal person and their personality, with a lack of bureaucracy in operations. The success of power culture depends on the capabilities of the focal person in technical, business and management terms.

✦ Role culture. This type of culture is based firmly on the existence of procedure and rule frameworks. It is typified by the form of a Greek temple-type diagram (Figure 14.4) together with the notion of bureaucracy.

   Within this type of culture everyone has a specified role to perform and is expected to restrict themselves to that function. Each of the specialist functions is

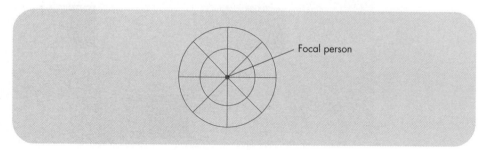

FIGURE 14.3 Power culture.

co-ordinated in its duties and activities by the overarching functions at the top of the organization. The two important attributes associated with the role culture are *predictability* and *stability*. The hierarchy dominates this type of organization with instructions coming down the organization and information going back up to the senior levels.

✦ Task culture. This culture emphasizes the need to concentrate on the work of the organization. The expertise within the organization is vested in the individuals within it and it is they who must be organized in a way that meets the needs of the business. The description used by Handy to illustrate this culture is that of a net (Figure 14.5).

This type of culture is generally supportive of a team form of organization. It requires people to concentrate on the task to be achieved and nothing else. It is a flexible approach to the needs of the organization and would emphasize adaptability as a key requirement among its members. Decision making is frequently distributed throughout the 'net' and moves dependent on the needs of the immediate task. Organizations heavily involved in project-based operations such as consultancy teams and civil engineering might be expected to utilize such cultural frameworks as the task model.

✦ Person culture. This is based upon the individual. As such it should not be confused with the power culture just described. The power culture is based around a single focal point. The person culture allows each person to be a focal point depending on the circumstances. A consultancy practice and barristers' chambers are used by Handy to illustrate this type of culture.

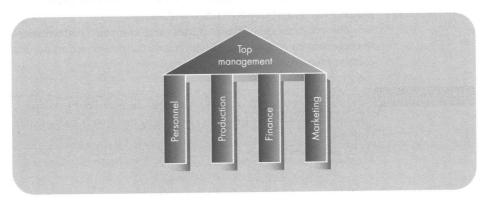

FIGURE 14.4   Role culture.

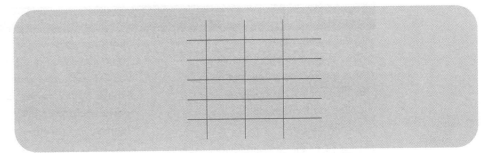

FIGURE 14.5   Task culture.

There are obvious links between the concept of culture as described here and the structural issues discussed in previous chapters. Some of the links have been made obvious, as in the case of bureaucracy, while others have only been hinted at. For example, the task culture has a number of associations with the matrix form of structure, with its emphasis on teams and dual reporting relationships.

Ouchi's type Z companies

Ouchi suggested that Japanese firms operated from a cultural base different from that of western organizations. He also introduced the notion that this originated from the societal culture in Japan and that it offered a likelihood of higher levels of productivity than cultures from the western tradition. In his 1981 work he identified a number of key differences between Japanese and American organizations (see Table 14.1).

Ouchi gave his idea the title Theory Z because it extended McGregor's Theory X and Theory Y (see Chapter 10) as a stereotypical organizational type. Ouchi suggested that some American organizations contained some of the features described in Table 14.1, but not to the extent found in Japanese organizations.

A number of the claims made by Ouchi have been brought into question by later researchers. For example, the notion of lifetime employment in Japan applies to only a small proportion of employees in a few larger organizations. It is also suggested that far from being a more participative approach to organizing work activity, the Japanese approach produces a more tightly controlled approach to work. Little personal discretion exists and employees are pitted against each other in the relentless search for ever higher productivity and quality (Garrahan and Stewart, 1992).

The relationship between culture and company performance is demonstrated in Management in Action 14.2 which reviews the drastic action needed to enable one large company to survive.

| Stop | Consider |

To what extent can the changes at Whessoe be described as changes to the culture of the business or simply changes to its commercial and business orientation driven by market forces?

Justify your answer.

Japanese organizations	American organizations
Lifetime employment	Short-term employment
Slow evaluation and promotion	Rapid evaluation and promotion
Non-specialized career paths	Specialized career paths
Implicit control mechanisms	Explicit control mechanism
Collective decision making	Individual responsibility
Holistic concern	Segmented concern

TABLE 14.1   Ouchi's cultural differences (*source*: Pugh, DS and Hickson, DJ (1989) *Writers on Organizations*, 4th edn, Penguin, London)

MANAGEMENT IN ACTION 14.2

Whessoe's culture change works wonders

Whessoe was a company with a long and proud tradition. Its roots were laid some 200 years ago at the start of the Industrial Revolution. The founder was one William Kitchin, who owned a corner ironmongery shop in Darlington in the north of England. The road outside the shop led to the tiny village of Whessoe, from where the company eventually took its name. Being located where Robert Stephenson built the first railway line, it was not surprising that Kitchin became involved in the project. Initially building steam engines for the railways, the company began to produce other forms of boiler and pressure vessels as the technology developed. For example it began to make the equipment that produced gas from coal at the turn of the century, then later equipment for the petrochemical industry and more recently nuclear power station pressure vessels and instrumentation. The company built a world-class reputation for engineering excellence in pressure vessel technology.

Older technologies were replaced and changes in the nuclear industry to pressurized water reactors (PWRs) introduced new technologies which also undermined Whessoe's position. The Chernobyl disaster in the former Soviet Union created a downturn in the whole nuclear industry. This was bad news for Whessoe which found itself in a difficult commercial position. The quality of its work was appropriate to the very high standards called for by the nuclear industry, but alternative markets were unwilling to pay for such high quality. Replacement business was therefore difficult to obtain. It was time for a fundamental rethink about the business and its future.

The relationship between Whessoe and the City was poor as a result of the unstable performance of the company, together with its ability to produce unpleasant surprises. The company had had no finance director for many years, believing

that if the quality of its engineering was good, everything else would follow. Chris Fleetwood was appointed to that position in 1987. By 1989 when the crisis hit Whessoe, Chris Fleetwood had moved up from the position of finance director to chief executive and appointed a new senior management team charged with finding ways out of the crisis. The approach adopted contained a mixture of savage surgery and overseas acquisition.

The heavy engineering plant on a 36-acre site in Darlington was closed and flattened. Making modules for the offshore oil and gas industry was also dropped. The project engineering operation, for contracts in the petrochemical and irrigation scheme businesses, was sharpened up for future sale, the belief being that such an operation exposed the company to higher levels of risk than were acceptable for its size and that the business, although sound, would be better suited to a larger company. During this process the numbers employed reduced from a high of 5000 people worldwide to about 1100, with only about 450 in the UK. Although the surgery cut the group's turnover by about 50%, it opened up opportunities for acquisition as a result of the reduced costs and cash generated from the sale of businesses. The first acquisitions were in the USA and Norway in the instrumentation and control industry. It represented a clear shift in emphasis away from heavy engineering towards the higher technology aspects of petrochemical and related instrumentation products. One of the few parts of the Darlington-based operation to survive was the small instrumentation department, which was moved to Newton Aycliffe, a few miles away, to give it the opportunity for a new start. Out went the old ways of work and troublesome industrial relations with five unions representing 60 workers. Harmonized terms and conditions of employment between staff and manual workers were introduced in return for the elimination of demarcation restrictions.

Also retained was the group's pipework business, which specialized in the highly technical area of power station and petrochemical operations. Pipework must be capable of coping with both very high pressures and temperatures in these areas and it represents a complex and specialized area of work for the company. The financial results of the dramatic business and cultural changes faced by Whessoe began almost immediately with healthy profit margins, the ability to raise capital through the City and the improved valuation placed on the company by the City.

The next phase for the company is to build on its established international base to expand into other countries and to capture the benefits of the integration of the different products across all markets. Companies in the group are encouraged to sell each others' products and to learn from each other in developing new applications and markets. The culture change achieved was from a heavy engineering company locked into the quality of its product, to an engineering company driven by profit and performance.

Adapted from: Levi, J (1993) Whessoe's culture change works wonders, *Management Today, May, pp 36–42.*

Peters and Waterman's excellence and culture

Peters and Waterman (1982) attempted to identify what it was that made some American organizations *excellent*. The research included reviews of the published data over a 25-year period on each of the 43 companies in the sample. This was supported by a range of interviews with senior executives. From this research (and in collaboration with Pascale and Athos) the McKinsey 7-S Framework was developed. It was so called because the four researchers worked for McKinsey and Company, one of the foremost management consultancy practices. The 7-S model identifies seven separate but interdependent features associated with running an organization. Each of the seven aspects begin with the letter 'S', as shown in Table 14.2.

The seventh item in the list (shared values) relates specifically to organizational culture. From the 7-S Framework emerged a set of eight features that Peters and Waterman suggest are commonly found among excellent organizations. As such, these features prescribe the cultural dimensions of an organization from the perspective of *the way things are done around here*:

Structure	organizational framework
Strategy	organizational direction
Systems	including procedures
Style	of management
Skill	company strengths
Staff	people issues
Shared values	culture

TABLE 14.2   McKinsey 7-S Framework

◆ Bias for action. Based on the recognition that to delay action can be fatal. This determines the need for managers to be action rather than analysis oriented. This reflects a belief that is necessary constantly to change things in order to stay ahead of the competition and technological development.

◆ Being close to the customer. Accepting that the market determines what will be successful drives a desire to get close to the customer in order to understand their needs. It also implies a depth of relationship within which it would be difficult to 'hurt each other', a necessary prerequisite for an effective and communal future.

◆ Autonomy and entrepreneurship. The recognition that too much control from the centre of the organization stifles creative development. Employees should be encouraged, it is argued, to contribute to company performance and take risks in pursuit of the development of products and services that effectively meet the needs of customers.

◆ Productivity through people. Acceptance that it is individual employees who deliver productivity in the dynamic, real-time world of organizations. Consequently, it is necessary for all employees to seek to perform better and all management practices should support this ideal. It also recognizes that peer group pressure can be a major stimulant to the level of delivered performance actually achieved.

◆ Hands on, value driven. The philosophy of the organization needs to be seen by all employees as a clear set of values that they can subscribe to. The hands-on perspective allows managers to experience personally all aspects of the organization through their presence where the work is done. It also allows an opportunity to reinforce the organization's values through direct and constant interaction with employees. Naturally it also allows managers to form an understanding of where changes in philosophy or policy might be needed and to exercise tighter control through direct involvement in the operational process.

◆ Stick to the knitting. By staying close to those products and services that the organization already has experience of, the degree of risk is reduced. Management will have an understanding of the supply chain from beginning to final consumption, together with the associated problems and opportunities. Moves into unfamiliar territory reduce the depth of knowledge making the risk of failure that much higher.

◆ Simple form, lean staff. The temptation to elaborate organizational design and the accompanying systems and procedures should be resisted. The search for ever more certain knowledge and reduced uncertainty as the means through which to better take decisions is ever present in organizations. Consequently there is a tendency to seek to incorporate new functions and specialisms as finance allows and perceived need dictates. In addition there is always the political temptation for managers to grow empires as a means of increasing their own status and influence. Unless organizations are careful, they run the risk of creating situations where the level of bureaucracy stifles the creative and entrepreneurial spirit that generates growth.

◆ Simultaneous loose–tight control. The ability to achieve a balance between these two competing pressures creates effectiveness in operational terms. Peters and Waterman go further by suggesting that it is necessary to provide effective control without limiting the freedom of action necessary to take advantage of the circumstances pertaining at the time.

The ideas developed by Peters and Waterman have been subjected to considerable criticism. A number of the organizations they identified as excellent very quickly ran into problems in the recessionary markets of the early to mid-1980s. Peters himself produced work which he claimed superseded these ideas. For example, in *Thriving on Chaos* (1989) he describes even more radical approaches to dealing with the turbulence from market uncertainty. However, as suggested earlier in this chapter, Thompson and McHugh (1990) claim that the excellence literature has little to offer in the debate on organizational culture. It is possible to reconcile these two positions in that the *excellence* literature reflects a number of organizational practices which in themselves do not define culture, but reflect the first level from Figure 14.1, whereas Thompson and McHugh reflect on issues pertinent to levels two and three.

Management in Action 14.3 provides an insight into the ideas of a senior manager and writer who wants to encourage radical approaches to how culture can be used to influence corporate activity.

Stop | Consider

Is the approach adopted by Semler an attempt to allow culture to develop as preferred by the employees or an attempt to impose one preferred by himself?

To what extent does the answer to the previous question matter to employees managers or customers?

To what extent do you consider that because the company culture indicated is so different from any other that particular types of people would be encouraged to join it and they therefore become highly motivated by these differences?

If more companies were to follow this example would the lack of uniqueness limit the success? What might this imply?

Deal and Kennedy's cultural profile

The work of Deal and Kennedy (1988) developed two particular aspects of organizational culture. First, they describe four types of culture based on the effects of the degree of risk and the speed of feedback from the environment on decision making:

✦ Work and play hard culture. In this form of culture people would tend to be a cohesive group that *attacked* both work and play enthusiastically. This category would be typically found in organizations with low risk but rapid feedback loops. Fast food restaurants would perhaps serve as an example of this type of organization.

✦ Process culture. The emphasis in this type of culture is on the systems and procedures associated with the organization. It is typified by a low-risk environment with a slow feedback response. Success comes from attention to detail. Local government organizations and large insurance companies might provide examples.

✦ Macho culture. This type of culture is associated with high risk and rapid feedback. It implies broadly similar features to the power and person cultures identified earlier. It is a culture based on the individual and the ability of the focal person to be able to achieve objectives. In that sense, small entrepreneurial organizations and specialized consultancies would be examples.

✦ Bet your company culture. The emphasis in this type of organization is on technical skill. The risks are very high but the feedback is slow in coming from the environment. This situation relies on the supremacy of the technical specialists to 'get it right' within the directional guidelines laid down.

MANAGEMENT IN ACTION 14.3

Secrets of the Semler effect

Semco is a company based in Brazil. Nothing special in that, it could be argued. However, the company is headed by someone very special. Ricardo Semler took over the company from his father at the beginning of the 1980s when he was just 21 years old. Since then he has taken the manufacturer of pumps, mixers and other industrial equipment to new heights, with sales growing by a factor of six and profits by 500%. In many ways the company is a vast testbed for new and different ideas in managing and organizing.

The most startling impact of Semco from the outside is that employees are able to set their own working hours, some are even able to set their own salary levels and everyone from the highest to the lowest has open access to company financial information. The intention is to create a self-sustaining organization which can carry on without an obvious leader. For example, five people share the position of chief executive officer on a six-month rotating basis. Semler takes his turn along with the others.

Semler takes the view that: 'The main goal of a company should be to create an entity which everyone involved in feels is worthwhile. That will then manifest itself in good-quality, good customer service.' He also considers that the company is an ongoing project and that change is not a once-for-all effect: 'Semco is an ongoing project and we think we are only halfway there. We need another 10–15 years to finish the job.'

In setting the approach for Semco, Semler picked aspects from many other organizations and systems: personal freedom, individualism and competition from capitalism. The control of greed and sharing of information and power from socialism. The flexibility of the Japanese was also added, although not the veneration of elders or strong ties to the company. The company was about to enter a consolidation phase in its evolution he suggested. For example, only about 25% of employees set their own salaries. Semler would like to see everyone undertaking that role as well as being involved with the financial analysis programmes. He would also like to see the level of working from home increased from the 20% of people who do so for between one and three days each week.

Clearly a sea change is under way at Semco that influences the way work is organized and managed. Many other companies, researchers and students have sought Semler's advice on how to achieve the same level of success. This advice can now be acquired from his book on his approach at Semco, but Ricardo Semler claims not to be about to become a consultant, selling his vision to others!

Adapted from: Dickson, T (1993) Secrets of the Semler effect, *Financial Times*, 25 June, p 13.

The second perspective added by the work of Deal and Kennedy is that of the existence of strong and weak cultures. A strong culture would be evident if almost all members supported it or if it were composed of deeply held value and belief sets. Table 14.3 indicates those features associated with a strong culture. A weak culture by comparison is one that is not strongly supported or rooted in the activities and value systems of the group.

From the items included in Table 14.3 there are two of particular interest. The *hero* is a person who personifies the values and actions expected of the true believer in that particular culture. They are used as role models and exemplars for the population at large. The use of *ritual* and *ceremony* as the basis of reinforcement of the desired culture is also part of the mechanisms for ensuring that it is internalized by individuals. The importance of *ritual* and *ceremony* was demonstrated in a story told by Wright (1979). Retirement parties frequently follow a predicable pattern. The purpose of such events is to provide an opportunity to say goodbye to the 'old guard' and to demonstrate allegiance to the remaining team and the firm as a whole. As such the speeches and events are usually carefully scripted to meet these demands. At one such event described by Wright a retiring GM executive broke the unwritten rules by openly criticizing a senior manager much to the visible embarrassment of the others in the room.

Managers frequently seek to inculcate a strong culture in order to achieve the simple form, lean staff type of organization (downsized or rightsized) identified by Peters and Waterman. A strong culture which is highly supportive of management's objectives makes the organization easier to manage and more profitable as more of the total effort and energy available is channelled towards meeting the business objectives. However, there is a conflict inherent in this situation in that strong cultures become difficult to change as a result of the very depth of commitment and unity created by them. This is undoubtedly one of the problems faced by British retailer Marks & Spencer in its difficulties over the last years. The company, once famous for its highly paternalistic and very strong culture which provided a solid mass of energy ploughing forward and in tune with the needs of the buying public, now appears to have lost its way and is floundering. It now gives the impression of desperately seeking to get in touch with its customers once again but finding it difficult to change fundamentally its old ways and presumptions of pre-eminence.

Trice and Beyer's organization culture

Trice and Beyer (1984) describe culture in terms of it being a device for providing common meaning for a particular group. They describe 11 elements that go to make up an organizational culture, grouped together under four categories as follows:

A. **Company communications.** The means through which culture is described, communicated to the group and continually reinforced across time:

  ✦ Stories. These reflect the past and are based on real events but elaborated in the retelling.

  ✦ Myths, sagas and legends. These include real and fictional events from the past and reinforce the 'greatness' of the group. They are often based upon activities involving its founders, heroes and other significant individuals.

  ✦ Folk tales. These tend to be fictional stories which carry meaning and reinforcement about the group and its culture to new and existing members.

  ✦ Widely shared philosophy
  ✦ Concern for individuals
  ✦ Recognition of heroes
  ✦ Belief in ritual and ceremony
  ✦ Well-understood informal rules and expectations
  ✦ Importance of individual contribution to whole

TABLE 14.3 Deal and Kennedy's strong cultural elements

♦ Symbols. These are the outward and visible signs that express the underlying values of the group. The use of slogans such as 'The customer is king' reflect the desired approach to customers which individuals are expected to uphold.

B.   **Company practice.** This category reflects the activities that organizations engage in that demonstrate the culture in operation and reinforce its importance:

♦ Rites. An activity which demonstrates that the culture is beneficial to the members and that it espouses worthy goals. Typically, it would involve the opportunity for the public reward for some noteworthy behaviour by an employee that reinforced the cultural norms.

♦ Ritual. Refers to behaviour that does not produce work-related objectives, but helps to reinforce group cohesion. A gambler may blow on the dice before throwing them, in order to bring luck. Company outings and similar extra-curricular activities can often serve the same purpose within organizations.

♦ Ceremonial. An official visit of a head of state to another country is accompanied by much ceremonial activity. This serves several functions including signifying the importance of the visit for both countries. Such ceremonial also reflects an elaborate display of the traditional forms of hospitality and culture in the countries concerned.

Similar ceremonial practices are found in most organizations when important visitors are entertained. Company milestones also offer the opportunity for much ceremonial activity. For example, celebrating 50 years of operation or the production of one million units of output.

C.   **Common language.** Every organization has its own terminology to describe events and activities. A major part of the socialization of new members into a new group involves their learning the common language for that group. The most obvious examples of this process come from professional occupational groups. For example, engineers must learn the technical terms for the area of engineering for which they are training and doctors must learn all the medical terms. This serves to separate them from non-engineers or doctors as well as providing an effective form of communication. It also serves to reinforce group cohesion in that it helps to bind together the individuals through common forms of expression. Recall the discussion in earlier chapters in relation to in-groups and out-groups in this context.

D.   **Physical culture.** This reflects the physical nature of organizations and is the tangible reflections of the culture within it.

♦ Artefacts. The equipment and facilities provided are a strong signal about the culture. For example, the presence of director-only car parking and dining rooms, as compared to single-status facilities, provides a reflection of the underlying culture.

♦ Layout. The physical layout of the buildings, open-plan offices and integrated work teams, compared to functional and separate offices provides a reflection of the aims, intentions and operating preferences prevalent within the organization.

Sub- and countercultures

In the discussion so far the notion of culture has been used in what might be described as a unifying or integrating context. It seeks to bind together the individuals within the organization. However, that is not the only view of culture. This reflects the *integration* perspective on culture and tends to take the organization as a whole as the locus of attention. It is also possible to see culture as a *differentiating* feature of organizational life. This *differentiation* view of culture concentrates its analysis at the level of the separate groups that exist within the whole entity. At this level of analysis it becomes possible to identify differences and inconsistencies in culture between individual groups and the entire organization (Meyerson and Martin, 1987). The description of culture being an *integration* process can be described as offering a limited perspective. The existence of sub- and countercultures within an organization forces consideration of disunity and even conflict as part of the cultural milieu.

The existence of *informal groups* within any organization has long been recognized. These together with the designated departments and functions officially sanctioned within the formal organization reflect social groupings that operate on the behaviour of the people within them. You will recall that this was the focus of much of the discussion of Chapters 5 and 6 in this text. It is hardly surprising therefore that the existence of subgroups within the organization (both formal and informal) would be likely to create situations in which each developed distinct cultures to some extent. While there are likely to be some common features in the cultures that exist in each of the subgroups, there will also be differences. This means that there will be differences in the cultures operating across the organization and not a single, common one. This raises several issues in relation to the notion of a single organizational culture and how layers of slightly varying culture meld together within a common context (the organization). It would not be surprising to find that the organizational culture was a blend of subgroup cultures or even the imposition of a dominant culture on a collection of surpressed minority ones.

Countercultures exist where one or more groups are disaffected and have objectives that run counter to those of the dominant group. Within an organization *countercultures* can exist in parts of the company and can create hostility and anti-management feelings. For example, when one company is taken over by another the integration process can create situations where countercultures are created. Managers feel that their previous efforts are being undermined by the acquiring company and that their careers will be blighted in the future. Such resistance is often self-perpetuating in that it begins to isolate the individuals from the main groups and increases the value of the counterculture to the deviants – as they become regarded.

Equally, where one group feels that its views or culture are being surpressed by another this can lead to revolt in some form or another. In organizational terms this can be illustrated as the classic management and workers struggle. From this perspective, managers seek to impose their values on the workers who react negatively and seek to strike and create other industrial relations problems. So a *counterculture* emerges and is reinforced through a perpetual cycle of struggle for cultural expression and dominance. For example, the UK record of industrial action has been very poor in the past, with an average of 3.2 million working days being lost each year between 1950 and 1967 due to strikes. This increased to 11.7 million days average each year between 1968 and 1980 (Salamon, 1992, p 388). This is a clear indicator of the power of countercultures as the trade union movement rejected the managerial perspective on how industry should function and the basis for the distribution of the rewards available as a result of the contribution of workers.

It can also be argued that as the culture within society changes the dominant culture within an organization comes under pressure to change. This can be described as *cultural diversity* or, perhaps more accurately, *cultural fragmentation*. One example of this type of cultural influence is indicated through the growing significance of women and ethnic groups in organizational life. Over the past few years there has been moves to integrate women and people from ethnic minority groups more effectively into mainstream organizational careers and jobs. While reflecting changes in society as a whole, this requires changes in the white male-dominated organizational cultures of the past. This can be clearly illustrated through recent reviews of the Metropolitan Police service in London and its continued lack of ability effectively to accommodate women and people from the ethnic communities into its ranks (Cooper, 2000). The report finds that appropriate policies exist but that the operationalization of them fails because of an inability to gain understanding or commitment to them at the lower levels of the organization. Another major problem was identified as training because it was not effectively tied to the achievement of the intended objectives and so failed clearly to support them or be grounded in the identified training 'gap'.

The role of human resource managers in attempting to achieve appropriate cultures is illustrated in Management in Action 14.4. Part of this process is to ensure that improvements to industrial relations practice achieve higher levels of harmony and commitment to management's objectives. In short to achieve a unity of culture in practice.

Stop | Consider

How could human resource managers contribute to the development of each of the four cultures indicated in MiA 14.4?

How could human resource managers seek to change the culture within an organization from (say) the pioneer culture to (say) the value-driven culture?

The determinants of culture

In the early days of an organization the culture is very much dependent upon the founders, their personalities and preferred ways of doing things. There are a number of parallels between this type of development of a culture and the Tuckman and Jensen (1977) stages in small group development, discussed in an earlier chapter. For example, employees must first get to know the boss and their way of doing things. This is followed by a period of adjustment as both parties become accustomed to working with each other etc. This learning or acquiring a culture Herskovitts (1948) termed as *enculturation*. In doing so it reflects a process that is similar to learning by assimilation or absorption. This could be differentiated from *socialization* as a process which involved more of a direct training dimension to it. Handy (1993) indicates a number of influences on the apparent culture of an organization:

✦ History and ownership. In a very real sense culture is something that is independent of most individuals within the organization. In all cases other than a start-up (or close-down) the company existed before particular employees joined it, and it will continue to exist after they leave it. From that perspective, the culture of an organization is more enduring than the individuals within it, but subject to accommodation as the fluid human resource flows through it and interacts with the culture that exists. The type of ownership will also have an impact on the culture of the organization. For example, a small company owned by an authoritarian figure will be managed in a totally different way from that owned by a humane bureaucrat. The corresponding cultures will also

MANAGEMENT IN ACTION 14.4

Winning ways with culture

Corporate culture has been variously described as the glue that holds an organization together or the rock on which it founders. The role of the personnel function in relation to the corporate culture can also be somewhat difficult. As potential 'guardians of the corporate culture', personnel professionals can find themselves cast in the role of the guardians of an outdated culture and therefore vulnerable to be changed along with it. In a recent research project, the Institute of Personnel and Development sought to find out how personnel professionals could function in relation to the development and change of corporate cultures within international organizations. For international organizations there are two distinct types of culture active in any given context. They are the national culture and the organizational culture. There can be very real tensions and difficulties between these two cultural frameworks.

The study was based upon 15 case study organizations each at different stages of cultural 'management'. At one extreme there was a major bank undergoing a culture change programme and at the other a French retail company attempting to retain its 'family' culture built up over 40 years of history. As a working definition of culture the study recognized that corporate culture is largely determined by the environment in which it 'exists', including national values, national, business and customer characteristics as well as economic considerations. The four main determinants of corporate culture were identified as strategy, structure and technology, values and systems and policies.

One of the key management skills in relation to the management of corporate culture or of any attempt to change it was identified as that of managing tension. Tension arises when the existing culture is being challenged during a change process or when the components within an existing culture are incompatible. Given that all the organizations studied had international elements

in their operations it was on cross-border management that the study concentrated. It was argued that the approach to cross-border management determined the corporate culture and its management within the organization to a significant extent. A four-cell matrix was created, based on the dimensions of the closeness of the relationship between home base and local site, and an organization being either people or systems driven. The four cells in the matrix were:

◆ Value driven. Being people driven and having a close relationship with the home base, this cell implied a common values approach to culture within the organization. Some common policies and practices would be dictated by the centre, but considerable influence could be expected among individual locations to adapt to local circumstances.

◆ Centralist. Based on a close relationship with a home base and systems driven, this cell implied a desire to have a corporate culture that would be based on that of the parent company. Policies and procedures determined by the home country and issued to all locations with an implication that they would be followed closely, with little local discretion.

◆ Local autonomous. Being people driven and with a loose connection with the home base, this cell implied considerable freedom to allow separate cultures to coexist within the company.

◆ Pioneer. Being systems driven and with a loose relationship with the home base, this cell implied a strong use of expatriate managers to 'take the message' out to local organizations and run them in line with centrally determined systems. In culture terms expa-

MANAGEMENT IN ACTION 14.4 continued

triates would be expected to epitomize the dominant corporate culture, but have some discretion to adapt to local conditions.

In terms of the role of personnel managers towards corporate culture the study identified several areas of initiative, including:

✦ Strategic development. The identification of appropriate cultural components and the associated personnel policies.

✦ Communication. The communication of policies and procedures in such a way that the cultural norms would be reinforced at every location and at all levels.

✦ Implementation. The encouragement of flex-

ible personnel practices and appropriate training to encourage people to cope with change and to reinforce the desired culture.

✦ Review. To keep under constant review the people management strategies, policies and practices followed to ensure that they support the desired culture.

The research concluded with the view that diversity represented an important organizational strength not a weakness and that some organizations were making effective commercial use of this.

Adapted from: Baron, A (1994) Winning ways with culture, *Personnel Management*, October, pp 64–8.

be different. Working for a US multinational company compared to a French equivalent will be different because the cultures and norms of the owners will be different. In these last examples the national cultures from the location in which the headquarters is based would tend to influence the norms, preferences, procedures and policies adopted throughout the organization.

✦ Size. Size influences culture if for no other reason than the formality required in the operation of larger organizations. This does not automatically imply that large organizations have cultures that are 'better' or 'worse' than small organizations. They are simply different as a natural function of the scale of operations.

✦ Technology. An organization that specializes in the use of high technology within its operations will emphasize the technical skills of employees in the values that govern its culture. Contrast that situation with a company in the service sector where the emphasis is on personal service in dealing with customers or clients which would value a completely different set of characteristics and values.

✦ Goals and objectives. What the organization sets out to achieve will also influence the culture. For example, the organization that seeks to become the best in customer service within its industry will seek to incorporate values inherent in that idea into the culture. The converse is also true, that culture can influence the objectives being sought. For example universities find it very difficult to balance and reconcile the need to be commercial in 'selling' educational services and at the same time to promulgate the development of individuals, pursue research excellence and encourage academic freedom.

✦ Environment. The organizational environment is made up of several independent and interdependent elements. There are the customer markets, the supplier markets, the financial markets, governmental influences, competitors and the environmental lobby, to name just a few. The way in which an organization chooses to interact with each of the elements in its environment will influence how it organizes itself and shapes its culture.

✦ People. The preferred style of work among senior managers, the preferences among employees as to how they wish to be managed both interact in the cultural dimension. If management attempt to enforce a culture that is unacceptable to employees there will undoubtedly be a reaction, examples being industrial action, sabotage, high labour turnover, low productivity, low quality and a need for tight supervision and control. Equally, employees who attempt to force management to accept their culture are also courting danger, particularly if the preference is overtly anti-managerial. Management may decide that the cost of operations in such a volatile, hostile and confrontational environment outweigh the benefits and relocate.

Management in Action 14.5 outlines some of the strategies that may be necessary if a change in culture is desired, perhaps in difficult circumstances.

Stop | Consider

It could be argued that culture should emerge naturally in any given situation over time, the purpose of culture being to create distinctiveness between organizations and common understandings based on the factors indicated earlier. Consequently, any attempt to change or manage culture represents management attempts to manipulate employees in the search for ever higher levels of control and profit.

Discuss this statement in the light of the advice given in MiA 14.5.

National culture

Organizations operate within a national setting. In that sense they are subject to the same cultural forces that act upon every other aspect of life in that situation. The majority of employees of an organization will come from the national setting into the organization bringing their culture with them. It would be natural to expect, therefore, that the culture of an organization would be based largely on the predominant local culture. That is, however, an assumption that proves very difficult to refute or substantiate in practice. This is as the result of a number of factors acting upon any given situation. For example, within any culture there exists *sub-* and *countercultures* that introduce variety, there is the growing movement of people around the world introducing cultural diversity into any particular setting. There is also the growing globalization of business which introduces another element of variety into the cultural milieu.

The *convergence* perspective on the relationship between national and organizational culture suggests that within an organization the national culture is subservient. This implies that organizations are able to identify and separate culture into two distinct forms (internal and external). Also, that they are able to manage the internal form as necessary to support business objectives as distinct from the surrounding national culture. In practice this view holds that employees leave their social culture (as it might be described) at the door when they arrive at work and automatically and naturally adopt the cultural values of the workplace without difficulty.

MANAGEMENT IN ACTION 14.5

Cultivate your culture

Egan argues that there are often two levels of culture operational in any organizational setting. The 'culture-in-use' represents the dominant culture in any particular context. Organizations would hope that this would be the culture preferred by management and intended to support business objectives. Unfortunately, this is sometimes not the case. There is often a 'culture-behind-the-culture' that represents the real beliefs, values and norms that underpin behaviour patterns within the company. These cultural norms frequently remain unnamed, undiscussed, undiscussable or even unmentionable. Egan points out that these covert cultures lie outside the normal managerial control processes. In either case, an espoused or covert culture adds cost or benefit to the organization. Cost is added if the dominant culture hinders the effective operation of the business or prevents it from changing in line with its environment. Benefit is added if the culture enables the business to function effectively.

Having audited the cultural scenario within the organization, Egan proposes a number of strategies for dealing with culture change:

1. Strategies based on business reality
    ◆ Use business strategy as a starting point. A change in business strategy can provide the necessary leverage for changing culture.
    ◆ Use contemporary approaches. The approaches over recent years associated with total quality management and business process re-engineering are just two examples of approaches that can be used to lever culture change.
    ◆ Use reorganizing as a basis. Restructuring and reorganizing work also provide opportunities for culture change.
    ◆ Turn human resource systems into levers. Obvious areas in this category include the use of training and promotion to reinforce the message and move people into other jobs as part of a culture change process.

2. Change-linked strategies
    ◆ Action-based approaches. Direct action in areas not apparently associated with culture can produce changes in culture as a consequence. For example a concentration on introducing 'lean production' into a factory might take some time but in the process many things are likely to change, including culture.
    ◆ Crisis approaches. Financial or other crisis situations are opportunities to change the culture.

    During a crisis, providing everyone accepts that one exists, people are more likely to adopt different behaviours and be willing to consider change across a broad front.

3. Frontal attacks
    ◆ The use of guerrilla tactics. During turnaround situations it is frequently possible to dislodge outdated cultural elements. The use of roving 'hit squads' (individuals with the power to turn up and ask difficult questions) can also be used to begin a culture change process.
    ◆ Programme blitz. Simply flooding the organization with training courses and other programmes to promote the new values can also be an effective (if costly) way of 'forcing' the new culture into the system by 'swamping' the old one.
    ◆ Symbolism. The use of symbols to convey powerful messages about both the demise of the old and emergence of the new can also assist in changing the culture. For example, it is reported that Lee Iacocca, former chairman of Chrysler, having turned around the company was to be presented with a car by a

grateful workforce. They duly made one ready and presented it to him, only to have him turn it down and ask for the next one off the assembly line, the symbolism being that every car produced should be capable of being presented to the chairman.

✦ Cultural dissonance. Constant pointing out that the dominant culture does not serve the business can become so annoying that people change, just to stop the constant annoyance.

✦ Critical mass. Form a critical mass of people

who can champion the new culture and encourage them to work on the others in the organization who need to be convinced.

✦ Imperial approach. Adopting a leadership stance and simply announcing 'what-will-be' might just achieve the change in culture. It is possible that others are simply waiting for positive direction.

Adapted from: Egan, G (1994) Cultivate your culture, *Management Today*, April, pp 39–42.

The *divergence* view holds that national culture takes preference and that organizational culture will adapt to local cultural patterns (Lammers and Hickson, 1979). This view holds that it is organizations that need to adapt to local circumstances otherwise the corporate culture will be out of syncronization with the local norms and will be ignored or even create problems. It is not difficult to envisage that both views could be correct in appropriate circumstances. For example, large international organizations that operate according to centralized styles could well display *convergence* characteristics, while, conversely, organizations predominantly based in a specific country are more likely to demonstrate *divergence*.

It is also possible that there will be a middle line. That organizational culture will frequently contain elements of national and company preference. In other words, adapting to meet the needs of both head office and local preferences. It has even been suggested to me by postgraduate students from many parts of the world with practice of working in companies headquartered in other countries that a form of what was described as *innocent deception* is frequently practised. This implies that local staff give the superficial appearance (officially and upwards) of complying with the requirements of head office, while in practice doing things as dictated by the local culture. This, of course, is anecdotal evidence and therefore of limited value, but it is heard frequently and it always sounds credible.

Hofstede's perspectives

Hofstede (1980, 1983) carried out an extensive series of studies over some 13 years into the subject of culture. He defines culture as mental programming on the basis that it predisposes individuals to particular ways of thinking, perceiving and behaving. That is not to say that everyone within a particular culture is identical in the way they behave. It does imply, however, that there is a tendency to produce similar patterns of behaviour. He developed four dimensions of culture from a factor analysis of his questionnaire-based research data:

✦ Individualism–collectivism. This factor relates to the degree of integration between the individuals in a society. At one extreme, individuals concentrate on looking after their own interests and those of their family. At the other extreme there are societies that emphasize collective responsibility to the extended family and the community.

✦ Power distance. The degree of centralization of authority and autocratic leadership. The higher the levels of concentration of power in a few people at the top, the higher the power distance score. In those locations with a low power distance score there is a closer link between those with power and 'ordinary' people.

✦ Uncertainty avoidance. This is described in terms of how the members of a society deal with uncertainty. Everyone lives in the present, the future remains uncertain and unpredictable as does the potential behaviour of other people. Consequently, ways need to be found that limit the potentially negative effects of this situation. Societies in which individuals are relatively secure do not feel threatened by the views of others and tend to take risk in their stride. These Hofstede classified as weak in terms of uncertainty avoidance. In strong uncertainty avoidance societies reliance is placed on policies, procedures and institutions in an attempt to control and minimize the effects of risk.

✦ Masculinity–femininity. The division of activity within a society can be based on the sex of the individual or it can be gender free. Those societies that Hofstede classified as 'masculine' displayed a high degree of social sex role division. In other words, activity tended to be gender based, stressing achievement, making money, generation of tangible outputs and largeness of scale. In those societies classified as feminine the dominant characteristics tended to be those of preferring people before money, seeking a high quality of life, helping others, preservation of the environment and smallness of scale.

Table 14.4 provides an indication of those countries that exhibit high and low levels of each of the four dimensions identified by Hofstede.

If the Hofstede classification is a valid reflection of the cultural basis of countries and consequently a reflection of the major tendencies of most individuals within them, then organizations need to take these preferences into account. Organizations from particular cultures may be more easily accommodated into locations with similar characteristics.

It is also possible that the Hofstede framework could be used to describe organizations themselves. Hofstede himself considered that power distance and uncertainty avoidance were the 'decisive dimensions' of organizational culture (1990, p 403). This view clearly links organizational and national culture by implying that the preferred ways of managing and organizing in a specific context will be based upon the national tendencies. This assumption is not, however, directly tested in his work. It is possible that organizational culture is composed of different dimensions from national culture.

The research itself can be criticized on the basis of its emphasis on description rather than analysis. Categorization of cultures is inevitably a simplification process based on frameworks and interpretation imposed by the researcher. Although there are statistical methods that can be used to identify clusters of related data (Hofstede used this approach) it is still left to the researcher to interpret the findings. By adopting this approach, Hofstede omits a more detailed consideration of how cultures form, change and are maintained (Furnham and Gunter, 1993). The categorization approach also underplays the variety found within culture. It has already been stated that culture as defined by Hofstede reflects tendencies rather than absolutes. However, as presented the dimensions give no clue as to the degree of difference that could be expected in any context (Tyson and Jackson, 1992). Hofstede tends to regard culture as relatively consistent across time, changing only slowly, a view based upon the anthropological perspectives of culture. More recent work from a sociological perspective prefers the view of culture as a much more dynamic process representing the balance between contradictory social and economic pressures and themes constantly acting on a society in real time (Alvesson, 1993).

Trompenaars' perspective

Frans Trompenaars, who is Franco-Dutch, worked for Shell in nine countries before becoming a consultant to several major multinational companies. He built up a database of the cultural characteristics of 15,000 managers and staff from 30 companies in 50 different countries. In his book *Riding the Waves of Culture* (1993) he discusses several aspects of cultural difference and its relationship with organizational life based on his large database.

His views contrast sharply with those that suggest that the world is becoming a 'global village', in that he argues firmly that what works in one culture will seldom do so in another. Included in his observations are the following examples:

✦ Performance pay. He suggests that people in France, Germany, Italy and many parts of Asia tend not to accept that 'individual members of the group should excel in a way that reveals the shortcomings of other members'.

✦ Two-way communications. Americans may be motivated by feedback sessions, Germans, however, find them, 'enforced admissions of failure'.

✦ Decentralization and delegation. These approaches might work well in Anglo-Saxon cultures, Scandinavia, the Netherlands and Germany. They are likely to fail in Belgium, France and Spain.

Trompenaars identifies seven dimensions of culture. Five deal with the way in which people interact with each other. A sixth deals with people's perspective on time and the seventh concerns the approach to moulding the environment. These combine to create different corporate cultures including:

✦ Family. Typically found in Japan, India, Belgium, Italy, Spain and among small French companies. Hierarchical in structure with the leader playing a 'father figure' within the organization. Praise can frequently be a better motivator than money in such cultures.

	Individualism	Power distance	Uncertainty avoidance	Masculinity
High	USA	Philippines	Greece	Japan
	UK	Mexico	Portugal	Australia
	Australia	India	Japan	Italy
	Canada	Brazil	France	Mexico
Low	Mexico	Australia	Denmark	Sweden
	Greece	Israel	Sweden	Denmark
	Taiwan	Denmark	UK	Thailand
	Colombia	Sweden	USA	Finland
			India	

TABLE 14.4   Illustration of Hofstede's classification

+ Eiffel Tower. Large French companies typify this culture, as might be expected from the title. It also embraces some German and Dutch companies. Hierarchical in structure, very impersonal, rule driven and slow to adapt to change are the dominant characteristics of such companies.

+ Guided missile. Typical of American companies, and to a lesser extent found in the UK. Egalitarian and strongly individualistic in nature with a measure of impersonality included for 'good measure'. Capable of adjusting the established course of action quickly but not completely.

Trompenaars advises companies to avoid a blanket approach to culture, based on the dominant head office variety. Instead he argues that a *transnational* approach should be adopted, in which the best elements from several cultures are brought together and applied differently in each country. Managers should also be trained in cross-cultural awareness and respect and how to avoid seeing other people's cultural perspective as stubbornness.

Management in Action 14.6 provides a general insight into how the national culture of Japan translates into ways of doing business as experienced by someone from a western tradition.

Stop | Consider

Consider each of the points made in MiA 14.6. How many of these could you describe as good business practice in any culture and how many would you imagine (or know) to be appropriate just in Japan?

What does that suggest to you about how culture finds expression in business practice?

What can you infer about how culture is described and understood? For example, the writer of MiA 14.6 is stated as having long experience of living and working in Japan, but does that mean he is able to describe the culture there in any meaningful way (in terms of distinction with other cultures) or is he simply reflecting business practice in that context? Is this distinction relevant to the understanding of culture?

Globalization and culture

Globalization is a term that has a relatively recent history in relation to the ways in which business operates internationally. It is a term that is frequently found in relation to strategic management and reflects process of operating internationally within a guiding framework. According to Yip (1989) globalization consists of a three-stage process as the organization evolves:

+ Developing a core strategy as the basis of competitive advantage, usually home country based. A home country-based organization.

+ Internationalization of the home country strategy. A multinational organization.

+ Globalization through integration of the largely separate country-based international strategies. The global organization.

The third stage of this model is what differentiates globalization in modern times from previous international business activity. Bartlett and Ghoshal (1989) add two other types of organization to those just listed:

MANAGEMENT IN ACTION 14.6

Bridging the divide

Japan frequently appears to outsiders to be very modern, high tech and sophisticated. Yet just under the surface lies a culture that goes back many centuries with modern society retaining many of the ancient business practices and traditions. Walter Bruderer lived in Japan for ten years and offers the following pointers to getting off to a good start when seeking to do business in that country:

+ Establish good relationships. The Japanese tend to be rather formal in the rituals associated with the start of a relationship. A slow start is regarded as a judicious way to begin a potentially long-lasting relationship. A valuable business relationship requires careful cultivation, sales calls, courtesy visits, perhaps an occasional lunch or other social event.

+ Describe your organization. As well as getting to know the individual, Japanese business people expect to get to know the companies with whom they do business. Taking time to explain the company and its aims and intentions in relation to Japan are important.

+ Meetings. Arrange a first meeting through a mutual acquaintance by letter or telephone. Once a meeting is arranged do not change it as this would be considered disrespectful. Take time and do not rush between appointments. Be prepared to offer small gifts on a first meeting, perhaps a novelty item from the home country. Do not offer a gift made by your firm as this would be seen as a paltry giveaway, not a gift.

+ Knowing how decisions are made. Decisions are frequently made by middle managers, not chief executives. Meeting the president of a company may only be for the purposes of exchanging greetings.

+ Waiting for a 'yes' or 'no'. Decisions are rarely made quickly in Japan. Having made a presentation on a business proposal it would be common to be told that the matter will be considered. This is because of a wish to avoid giving offence and also to allow a full review of the proposal, the company and the individuals. However, once a decision is taken it will be acted upon quickly.

+ Being patient, patient, patient. Traditions, customs and rituals are evident all around the business process within Japan. The most effective approach in this situation is to display patience.

+ Using the Japanese language. The use of Japanese in all literature and promotion material is essential. It creates a feeling of being serious and of wanting to belong. Make use of native Japanese speakers to ensure the accuracy of translations in order to avoid mistakes that might cause offence.

+ Speaking English. For all practical purposes the Japanese are not fluent English speakers. Equally, many people have some ability to speak English. If you have to speak English use simple words and speak slowly. Write down key words and numbers for meetings.

+ Adopting a moderate approach. The Japanese prefer foreign approaches to business to be similar to their own, moderate, low key and deliberate. The hard driving and argumentative approach is regarded as self-centred, ostentatious, confrontational and the wrong way to nurture a relationship.

+ Dressing. In Japanese companies the conventional dress is plain and conservative. People rarely wish to stand out. The same applies to their perception of foreign business people.

Adapted from: Bruderer, W (1993) Bridging the divide, *Financial Times*, 3 April, p 16.

+ International organization. Whereas the global company seeks to capitalize the advantages of the potential to function on a global scale, but in a centralized way, the international organization seeks to function more like a co-ordinated federation. In seeking this the international firm seeks an appropriate balance between the needs and contribution potential of both the centre and local units.

+ Transnational organization. According to Bartlett and Ghoshal this type of organization seeks to blend together the three major themes of global integration, local differentiation and worldwide innovation. In practice an integrated network of all available resources and products used to the best advantage of the organization as a whole.

Many companies have a long tradition of international trade in one form or another. International business on a significant scale emerged during the middle decades of the nineteenth century (Jones, 1996, p 25) but had existed in simple form for a long time prior to then. Because of the difficulty of transport prior to the nineteenth century international business was most frequently organized on the basis of sending trusted agents abroad to trade locally and subsequently to transmit the wealth back home, often after many years. The successful operations of both the Dutch and English East India Companies between the sixteenth and eighteenth centuries were notable exceptions to this rule.

One of the difficulties facing any organization operating internationally is that of culture. It is commonly understood that culture does differ around the world, but it is less clear in what way that impacts on how business should be done or how businesses should adapt themselves to local circumstances. The major difficulties involved in this process are first, the identification of the factors defining culture. Second, the misalignment of culture at a human and nation-state levels. This chapter has already explored the complexity of the concept of culture itself. But even if that can be overcome at a practical level it remains impossible to align culture with nationality in a precise way.

There are many aspects of business that are considered on a national basis, for example transport routes, distribution channels, customs regulations and legal frameworks. However, it is not possible to say the same in relation to the culture of the inhabitants of a specified country. Every country is made up of different cultural groups, with varying degrees of similarity and difference. Equally, cultural groupings frequently span national boundaries. Even today there are several major trouble spots in the world where ethnicity (as an expression of culture) is linked to attempts to break up an existing country into individual self-ruled autonomous units. So *nation* is only a poor reflection of the cultural boundaries that exist among the people who inhabit the world.

There are two basic options available to an organization in its approach to culture:

+ Polycentric. This approach encourages the view that within an organization it should be permissible for each unit within the global entity to function effectively in a decentralized way. It takes the view that it is not possible to operate in a consistent way around the world as a consequence of the cultural differences that exist and so each unit within the company should be allowed to 'do its own thing', so to speak. One illustration of this is based on the existence of bribery in some parts of the world.

Most western companies would seek to avoid any attempt to become involved in bribes as a way of doing business, but in some parts of the world this practice is a way of life. In some countries it is difficult for the government to raise enough tax to be able to pay for an effective public service. Consequently, paying money to public servants can be a form of local tax collection as they seek to make a living wage. For example, it has been reported that in Mexico it is common practice for businesses to 'tip' the local postman once a month, otherwise the post simply gets lost in the system (Stockton, 1986).

The real danger with the polycentric approach is that the organization becomes overwhelmed with the impact of the number and scale of differences that must be accommodated. Even though culture in the local environment can have a major impact on how a business should seek to interact with that environment, not every difference needs to form the basis of doing things differently across the organization.

✦   Ethnocentric. This approach reflects the opposite perspective and is based on the assumed superiority of the home-based culture. Effectively, it assumes that every other culture must be subservient to that of the globalizing organization. There are many variations on a theme for this approach to dealing with culture. For example, an organization might simply believe that a particular culture is less developed than that of the home country and over time it will 'drift' towards the more developed culture as experience and economic development improves. It is also possible to be ethnocentric as a result of believing that it is a business imperative to have worldwide consistency in policy, procedural and practice issues to make it easier to run the company.

The potential danger of this approach to culture is that it may prevent the company getting close to the local community and so lose competitive advantage. Also it is possible to experience problems with local staff who must tread a difficult balance between following orders and meeting the needs of the situation. Governments can also react negatively to organizations who appear to be operating in a heavy-handed way in relation to local ways of doing things.

In most cases companies adopt a middle position with regard to being either *polycentric* or *ethnocentric*. In many ways this issue follows the same pattern as the centralization or decentralization debate in organization structure, discussed in an earlier chapter. Organizations tend to move between the two positions over time depending upon a number of factors such as the need to cut cost, improve productivity or as part of a restructuring/change programme. In dealing with global operations there are a wide range of dimensions of organizational experience which reflect cultural issues. Table 14.5 includes many of the features that form part of this experience and about which decisions must be made.

Ulrich and Black (1999) reflect upon the process of globalization in terms of the often quoted mantra of *acting globally and thinking locally*. This they then suggest turns into the requirement to consider the capability of the organization to meet these particular demands if they are to function successfully in the global market. They suggest that six areas of capability arise from this need, included in Table 14.6.

It should be obvious from the list in Table 14.6 that each of the capabilities listed involves managing a tension. It is through this tension that culture makes its impact evident. In seeking to organize on a global scale it is necessary for senior managers to retain control and to be able to extract ever greater levels of value from the operations. This involves the inevitable and never ending search for economies of scale. In the search for control and cost effectiveness uniformity in all things is an inevitable first port of call. However, cultural (and other) differences around the world simply will not allow such simple solutions. For example, Colgate-Palmolive found that its large tubes of toothpaste were not selling well in Latin America and was forced to introduce much smaller tube sizes. The reason for this was that most people simply could not afford the price of a large tube.

Another example is when Disney had to drop its usual ban on the sale and consumption of alcohol in its theme parks in order to accommodate the cultural norms in Europe as compared to the USA. Equally, as Urlich and Black point out, global firms are in direct competition with local organizations which will know the local circumstances more intimately and will be more effectively integrated into the infrastructure. Local firms may also enjoy a strong brand loyalty and be well connected within officialdom. All of which makes it difficult for globalizing organizations to get it right and why cultural issues form an important aspect of the process.

There is another form of globalization with a direct impact on cultural issues in organizations. That is the growing tendency for organizations to experience multicultural issues within a single operational unit. With an increasing number of people from different ethnic traditions being found in most countries it is common to have to deal with cultural diversity in an organization's home territory. It is possible to adopt either a polycentric or ethnocentric approach to these issues, although European legislation in relation to equality prefers the polycentric approach.

Managing culture

Managing culture is something that automatically forms part of the remit of any manager. However, in many situations this is not specifically recognized as a need. That is usually because there is a congruence between the manager's experience and the surrounding culture. It is often only when faced with the need to manage cross-culturally its significance becomes apparent. There are many ways suggested in which culture can be managed. The

Physical attributes	There is a wide diversity in the physical characteristics of people within a cultural context even though there may also be a number of dominant characteristics
Behavioural attributes	Characteristics such as the social and subgroups to which people belong, the attitudes towards gender, age, family, work itself, self-reliance and the significance of career all impact on culture and behaviour in an organizational context. Communication conventions as well as moral, religious and related beliefs also impact on business.

TABLE 14.5   Cultural and related characteristics

1	To determine core activities and separate them from non-core activities
2	To achieve consistency while encouraging flexibility
3	To obtain leverage in the market (bigger is better) at the same time as focus (smaller is better)
4	To share learning throughout the organization and to encourage the creation of new knowledge
5	To build a global brand that respects and honours local custom
6	To engender a global perspective at the same time as ensuring local accountability

TABLE 14.6   The six global capabilities

models of organizational culture indicated earlier in this chapter all provide a means through which better to understand the concept and through that to be able to more effectively manage it. For example, the work of Hofstede proposes a number of variables that differentiate cultures and so provide the basis for knowing how people differ and therefore how to cope with (manage) the differences identified.

In seeking to address the issue of how culture impacts on behaviour in an organizational context, Cray and Mallory (1998, pp 89–112) develop a cognitive model. The essence of the model is that actual behaviour is based on many forces acting on that individual. Their model of the cognitive approach to the relationship between culture and behaviour is included as Figure 14.6.

The model is built up systematically by the writers based on a discussion of how behaviour is channelled by the forces acting upon it. Taking each element of the model briefly in turn:

✦ National culture. In each of the models of culture discussed earlier it is assumed that national culture has a direct impact on the behaviour of the individuals within it. However, this ignores the filtering mechanism of the individual themselves. While it may be true that in some situations there is an almost automatic link between culture and behaviour, that might not always be the case when new situations arise. Also the inclusion of cognitive processes within the model allows the researcher (or manager) wishing to explore the links between national culture and behaviour to identify which factors within a culture impact directly on the decisions taken by the individual.

✦ Organizational culture. The organizational culture also impacts on the behaviour of individuals either directly or through the cognitive frameworks proposed. As the organizational culture is to some extent likely to be a subset of the larger national culture it will also be influenced by it and impact on the cognitive frameworks of the individual within it.

✦ Individual cognitive framework. This hypothetical framework reflects the ability of individuals to capture phenomena, categorize it and utilize the information in decision making processes. Within the model it reflects the largely unconscious processes in which the individual experiences and has the opportunity (through free will) to determine a behavioural response.

✦ Organizational cognitive framework. There has been considerable debate on whether organizations can have a cognitive framework in the same way as people. There are those who argue that it cannot exists on the basis of an organization being an inanimate object. Others who suggest that an organization does possess a cognitive frame-

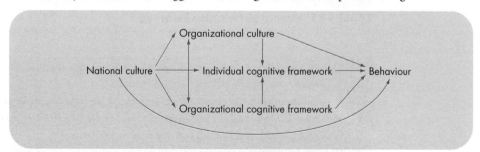

FIGURE 14.6 The impact of culture on behaviour: a cognitive model (*source*: Cray, D and Mallory, G (1998) *Making Sense of Managing Culture*, International Thomson Business, London).

work support their views by suggesting that a measure of collective consciousness must exist within the organization independent of the individuals if consistency of operational activity and direction is to be achieved. If it is assumed to exist then as a construct the organizational cognitive framework must influence the behaviours and cognitions of those who work within it.

In offering a basis for being able to manage cultural issues more effectively the model allows an improved understanding of why contrasting behaviours occur between cultural boundaries. As such it should allow those cognitive features which are deep seated and thus less amenable to change to be identified and separated out from those cognitive components that may be easier to manipulate (Cray and Mallory, 1998, p 107). The writers illustrate the potential of the model through one of the small number of studies of cognition as a comparative tool. Calori *et al.* (1992) found differences between French and British managers in their *cognitive maps* of the competitive forces and dynamics active in their organization's environment. The differences, it is argued, are based on the educational system and culture differences between the two countries. Similar differences in the cognitions of managers between the industries included in the study were also found, suggesting support for the inclusion of the *organizational cognitive framework* element in the model (Figure 14.6).

A number of tools have been developed over recent years that seek to measure aspects of culture within an organization, making it easier to manage those aspects that need attention. For example Cartwright from the University of Exeter developed a nine-factor test that seeks to measure the strength (on a scale from 1–5) of employee feelings with regard to several aspects of the way that management run the company. The nine factors are shown in Table 14.7.

Each of the nine factors indicated in Table 14.7 contains four questions, which Cartwright developed after studying the cultural similarities of 50 top-performing companies. In a case study involving this tool Littlefield (1999) describes how Kerry Foods, a large direct sales company of 500 people and a turnover of £70m per year, undertook the exercise following the rapid growth of the company. A number of problem areas were identified from the initial application of the Nine Key Factors survey, including the need to address the way in which head office initiatives were communicated and implemented, together with the style of management adopted by first-line managers. There was also a need to integrate the staff from the various merged companies (that had created the rapid growth) into one unit better. The first company-wide survey produced a mean score of 3.4 as the overall satisfaction score and the second, a year later, a score of 3.9. The considerable effort within the company during the year involving training, one-to-one meetings and the use of incentives was clearly beginning to pay off. It was felt by the senior managers of the company that it had been possible to manage the culture by beginning to understand and change it over the one year between surveys. It was intended that the survey would become an annual event in seeking to measure cultural shifts across the company.

Acceptance	Trust/agreement	Development
Fairness	Expectation	Team spirit
Respect	Balance	Ownership

TABLE 14.7 The nine key factors

Trompenaars and Woolliams (1999) elaborate on Trompenaars' earlier work on culture and link it with that of Charles Hampden-Turner who developed a methodology for reconciling apparently opposing values. In doing so they confirmed the original seven dimensions reflecting ways that the values which differ between cultures can be grouped. The seven dimensions are:

♦ Universalism v participation. This reflects the distinction between cultures which value allegiance to rules and those which value loyalty to relationships and other people.

♦ Individualism v communitarianism. This reflects the distinction between cultures that favour individual development and fulfilment as compared to those cultures which value behaviour in support of the group as a whole.

♦ Specific v diffuse. This reflects the distinction between cultures which favour sticking to the facts and impersonal business relationships as compared to those cultures which prefer to build personal relationships before doing business.

♦ Neutrality v affectivity. This reflects the differences between cultures in which it is common to hide emotions or where it is acceptable to be open with personal emotions.

♦ Inner directed v outer directed. This dimension reflects the degree to which the individuals within different cultures are in control of their environment or the degree to which the environment controls them.

♦ Achieved status v ascribed status. In some cultures it is argued that success confirms status and subsequently promotion. In other cultures status is a function of position, which subsequently motivates the individual who delivers performance.

♦ Sequential time v synchronic time. This dimension reflects the differences between cultures in orientation to the passing of time, the varying focus on timescales and ability to handle more than one thing at a time.

The writers argue that each of these dimensions reflects an aspect of managing in what they call a transcultural manner. Each of the dimensions reflects a tension between the two juxtaposed concepts that must be reconciled in some way or other by managers operating across cultures. The conflicts that arise in seeking to deal with the differences in cultural preference evident in each dimension must involve actions such as compromise, reconciliation of the different perspectives or allowing one cultural norm to dominate. It is in measuring these possibilities that the work of Hampden-Turner has relevance. In some situations their research shows that women appear to exhibit a higher ability to be able to reconcile opposing values than do their male counterparts. Also some men begin by starting from their own cultural perspective and then move towards the opposing values as they seek to resolve the dilemma. Other managers seek to approach things from the opposite direction. They have also found in their preliminary research that those managers who recognize, respect and are able to reconcile the dilemmas arising under each one of these seven dimensions perform better than those who do not.

Changing organizational cultures

The discussion so far has painted a picture of organization culture in terms of something that evolves over time and reflects the needs of human beings to interact in pursuit of collective endeavour. Adopting the definitions of culture as *mental programming* or *the way we do things around here* implies that culture is a device that should allow higher levels of efficiency to be achieved.

This view of culture depicts it as the *glue* or *cement* that holds the organization together. Turner (1986) criticizes the view that culture can be managed, suggesting that it would not be possible to manipulate it accurately because it becomes such an integral part of the organization's fabric. The definition of culture in terms that are relatively superficial also ensures that it is more amenable to change (Berg, 1985). For example, if culture were defined only in terms of the symbols used to reinforce it, changing the symbols would change the culture. A tendency to think of culture as changeable would tend to push the preferred definition of it in the direction of concepts amenable to change.

Lundberg (1985) argues that it is possible to change culture and provides a six-stage programme for achieving this objective:

+ External. Identify external conditions that may encourage a change to the existing culture.

+ Internal. Identify internal circumstances and individuals that would support change.

+ Pressures. Identify those forces pressing for change in the culture.

+ Visioning. Identify key stakeholders and create in them a vision of the proposed changes, the need and benefits.

+ Strategy. Develop a strategy for achieving the implementation of the new culture.

+ Action. Develop and implement a range of action plans based on the strategy as a means of achieving movement to the desired culture.

There are a number of problems with both of the last two views. They are equally rather simplistic in the view of culture and the nature of change. To suggest that there is only one culture within an organization is to deny the existence of *sub-* and *countercultures*. Each non-dominant culture in a specific context is likely to seek to increase its own significance. Consequently, there are political, power and control perspectives to take into account.

Equally, to suggest that culture is static understates the experience of organizational life. New products and production processes are developed; people move to other organizations and jobs; organizations change structures; competitive pressure results in takeovers and mergers. It is stability that is the exception. Perhaps, therefore, *adaptation* over time is a more realistic perspective on culture in relation to change.

Perhaps the 'problem' is not one of how to ensure that change happens, but one of ensuring that it moves in the right direction. Looked at from this point of view it is possible to reconcile the two apparently opposing perspectives concerning culture change. Perhaps culture can be described as very difficult to change in the short term, but viewed as a continually changing phenomenon, it can be manipulated in appropriate directions over time. It could also be amenable to rapid change in times of crisis when survival becomes an issue on which to focus the attention of everyone in the organization.

Management in Action 14.7 demonstrates how one service industry organization went about changing its culture.

To what extent does the change processes described in MiA 14.7 reflect cultural issues and to what extent the practice of good management?

To what extent does this imply that an effective organizational culture will automatically follow from the exercise of 'good' management?

The significance of culture for organizational design

Culture influences a number of aspects of organizational activity including how people interact in the course of their daily work. For example, the need for close supervision of activity should be reduced if the objectives to be achieved are internalized by the individuals. This is not the only type of organizational influence, there are also connections between culture and structure.

Choice is available to managers in how to compartmentalize activities in order to meet their objectives. This was reflected in the contingency approach to organizational design discussed in Chapter 13. A definition of culture in terms of *how things get done* would imply that structure is at least partly a function of culture. That is not to suggest that culture is a deciding feature in the design of an organization, but it is at least a silent partner in the process. It operates by colouring, influencing and shaping the perceptions and understanding of how things should be organized in pursuing the desired objectives.

From that perspective culture is an intervening variable. This can be more easily shown as a diagram (see Figure 14.7). It is something that acts upon the forces that are in turn determining the design of the organization.

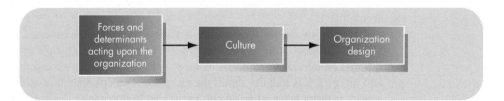

FIGURE 14.7   Culture as a design mediator.

MANAGEMENT IN ACTION 14.7

Real change dealer

Motor car dealers frequently have the reputation of being little more than rip-off merchants, only interested in getting the highest price for a poor quality car and with even worse after-sales service. One company set out to change that image and to gain a commercial advantage at the same time. Lindsay Levin took over as managing director of Whites in 1994 and became one of the few women in this traditionally male-dominated industry. The dealership is located in the south-east of England and was founded by her great-grandfather in 1908. It currently enjoys a turnover of about £82 million per year with 350 staff.

There was overcapacity in the industry generally and a heavily incentivized commission culture permeated all levels of payment, right from the deal with the manufacturer to eventual sales to a customer. Consequently, a hard 'push-at-any-cost' approach was apparent in any motor dealership. There were also clear distinctions between managers, technicians and customers within the system and a feeling that the customer was almost an intrusion into the process, not to be allowed to see or understand what was going on in the servicing or repair of their cars.

Levin began from a personal conviction in the value of developing people and teamwork. The starting point was an analysis of the attitudes of both staff and customers, including 15 hours of video interviews from customers who were less than satisfied with the service obtained from the company. A harrowing experience for staff and managers alike, who saw for the first time what people actually thought of their work and how they treated customers.

The second major tactic in seeking to change aspects of the culture within the organization was when Levin declared that she would be prepared to see a drop in revenue while the changes were being introduced, the first evidence of this being the closure of the dealership for an afternoon in order to bring people together to launch the

change programme. Volunteers were sought to train as continuous improvement facilitators and from the 50 who showed interest 20 completed the training and formed the basis of subsequent action teams.

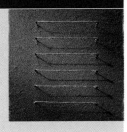

The pace of change was slow to begin with as staff were not convinced that managers actually wanted to hear what was being proposed or that they would implement the proposals. As an encouragement each team was 'given' £500 to spend on anything that they felt would benefit the business, but many teams had to be pushed into spending it. The entire process of change required a change to the existing culture in which staff (and managers) expected staff to report a problem to a manager and then wait for a decision and course of action to be cascaded down from above. The intention was to change this to a culture of expecting initiative to be shown at all levels. For example, technicians are now expected to deal directly with customers in identifying problems with cars and explaining remedial action, rather than this being a job for the customer services manager.

The other changes introduced within the company include:

✦ Self-selected multifunctional teams have been formed incorporating sales, after-sales and technical staff.

✦ A change in the pay structure for sales staff to 25% dependent upon team performance and 75% dependent upon competencies.

✦ The introduction of a shift system covering six-day working for sales staff to allow seven-day week sales cover.

✦ Technicians work 12-hour shifts over three days, followed by four days off.

✦ Introduction of salaried status for technicians.

✦ Introduction of continuous improvement groups led by the specially trained change champions.

✦ Introduction of team leader training over ten one-day sessions over the year.

✦ Technicians receive one day's training each month.

✦ Role-playing exercises on customer care have been introduced into the induction training for new employees.

One final element of the culture change process within the company was the deliberate decision not to recruit a personnel manager until the changes had begun to take hold. This was because Levin wanted everyone to take the whole process seriously and not simply pass responsibility back to personnel. Having made significant

impact on the culture of the organization a personnel manager has been appointed with the intention that line functions will demand support from the function, rather than having to be pushed into further change, thereby building on the success achieved to date.

After some three years of the change process the attention of Levin can now be turned to considering the future of the business. The motor manufacturers themselves are closely monitoring Levin's work and using it as the basis of encouraging other dealers to make change. Academic interest in Levin's achievements is also growing with the Lean Enterprise Research Centre at Cardiff Busines School suggesting that her model reflects the future of motor retailing.

Adapted from: Littlefield, D (1999) Real change dealer, *People Management.* 29 July, pp 44–6.

Organizational culture: a management perspective

From a management point of view culture occurs naturally out of the situation. It is not something that managers have to deliberately design and implement. However, that is not to say that managers should adopt a passive stance towards it. Neither does it imply that they should not, and do not, attempt to create specific cultures. Managers have influence on the form of culture within their organizations. The discussion in this chapter has taken the view that there is an active relationship between managers and culture. This is also implied by Figure 14.8, based on a description by Payne (1991), which emphasizes the *managed* nature of the process.

The culture that emerges over time within an organization may not be an appropriate one for the achievement of the identified objectives. For example, it could be that the dominant culture within an organization is hostile to management's intentions. This situation would make it very difficult for managers to achieve their goals. Of course this does assume that the goals being sought by managers are the 'right' ones and that they are the only ones worth pursuing.

It has already been established earlier in this chapter that the concept of culture provides managers with a number of opportunities. For example, a culture supportive of management's objectives should make it easier and cheaper to manage the organization as a result of the acceptance and internalization of the goals by employees. This opportunity manifests itself in three main ways:

♦ Control. The existence of a strong managerially based culture should enable control mechanisms to be audit and record oriented. Such an approach would be evident in an organization that operates a *just-in-time* approach to manufacturing. Just in time is an approach where suppliers and manufacturers are linked together in an extended process to ensure that work-in-progress stocks are minimized and that components are delivered to the user just in time for them to be used. Among the effects of this are a reduced need to check the quality and quality of components delivered. Reliance on getting everything 'right first time' is very high. Consequently, a higher level of trust in employees and suppliers 'to do what is necessary' is required. An appropriate culture helps to ensure that this can be achieved.

♦ Norms. Culture provides the norms of behaviour which underpin how individuals go about the tasks that they are expected to do. Again, a management-supportive culture should ensure that the norms in existence are favourable and automatically enforced through the dynamics among group members. An example of this would be the existence of a 'work until the job is complete' norm. The existence of such a norm among employees would allow managers to have confidence that customer orders would be despatched on time unless a real crisis occurred, as the employees would expect to stay behind until the order was complete.

♦ Commitment. This last example also serves to demonstrate the third advantage of culture for managers. That of commitment. A strong management-based culture would produce a situation where employees were generally committed to and supportive of management's aims and objectives. This would be more than simple compliance by employees, it would be active agreement with and support for management objectives.

From a managerial perspective the main problem arises in attempting to create an appropriate culture. It is too simplistic to suggest that managers can decide, design, implement and maintain particular cultures. There are many other features and processes that need to be in place as well. For example, the decision to move towards a more participative culture in which employees are given greater autonomy and authority will fail if it is not supported by appropriate training, encouragement and tolerance of mistakes. Similarly, to

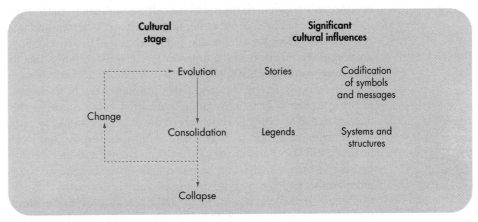

FIGURE 14.8 The development of culture (*adapted from*: Payne, R (1991) Taking stock of corporate culture, *Personnel Management*, July.

attempt to change the culture of an organization without taking into account the structural and procedural dimensions is also likely to fail.

The maintenance of a culture once installed is also problematic. It has already been suggested that culture is subject to continuous adaptation. Consequently, the question of attempting to maintain a static position with regard to culture does not arise as it will change anyway. The problem is therefore one of how to retain direction and alignment with organizational objectives. Assuming that a culture change has been made this process becomes one of preventing the new culture from slipping back towards the old or an unde-sired one. Assuming that the culture has been introduced effectively then it should not 'slip' as everyone would be convinced of the benefits to be gained from the new one. This is not always done fully or effectively however.

Watson (1994) studied one company in depth at a time when it was undergoing con-siderable change, including attempts to modify its culture. He describes a number of reac-tions to this process from people within the organization (pp 109–34):

✦ Resistance from all levels.

✦ A lack of confidence in the commitment, understanding and ability of senior man-agers.

✦ Confusion about what culture was.

✦ A cynical view of culture change being just another initiative designed by senior man-agers to further their own careers.

This reflects the political and situational reality within which culture exists and evolves. Indeed, it could be argued that culture makes the difficulty of managing worse. The creation of groups and their reinforcement through culture produces the very boundaries that differentiate them and creates separate but cohesive units. In the act of becoming a group various *out-groups* are formed. They are in practice every other group that exists. Out-groups are generally considered as different and in extreme cases regarded as the enemy. Also, anything from outside a group that seeks to impact on the way things are cur-rently done by that group represent a potential infringement of its independence and therefore something to be resisted. So management seeking to change the culture of the various work groups frequently encounter resistance These are not conducive conditions or concepts in relation to the notion of culture as a managerially supportive concept.

Reference has been made earlier to the existence of strong and weak cultures. A strong culture is one that is very noticeable and which would be actively supported by a high pro-portion of the members of the organization. A weak culture is one that is not as obvious and which would only be supported by a minority, or not actively supported by more than a few individuals. Strong cultures, if they are supportive of managers, have the advantage of being a positive benefit. A strong managerial-based culture is the easiest situation to manage in that everyone has internalized the objectives sought by managers and will there-fore function in the desired way. There is unity of purpose and intent. Having said that, however, strong cultures are less amenable to change and they develop a life of their own. Because of the internalization by individuals of the beliefs and values underpinning the group, ownership and a strong feeling of unity is dissipated throughout the population. Consequently, the level of ownership (and hence control) in the hands of managers is that much less. Therefore, the ability of managers to direct and channel the behaviour within such cultures is also reduced. It is for that reason that attempts to develop strong cultures (organizational or national) require that a figurehead dimension is incorporated. In other words, an attempt to incorporate a protection device into the culture which allows the retention of a measure of control and influence through common support for the leader.

In terms of organizational structure, culture is one of the internal contingency factors that influence the design (see Figure 14.7). This includes national as well as organizational culture elements. The cultural perspective on organization structure contains two main dimensions:

✦ Managing internationally. In one aspect this describes the need to manage across cultures as part of international operations. Once engaged in operating internationally change in the requirements from a culture by the organization arise. Distances in both time and space produce a need to manage differently, as does the increase in scale of operations. This does not take into account the increased interaction between organization culture (which will have emerged within a compatible national culture) and different national cultures being experienced as globalization develops.

✦ Accommodating cultural diversity. This aspect emerges as the result of the interaction of organizational and national culture. It is too simplistic to suggest that an effective mixing of different national and organizational culture can be achieved. Neither is it possible to suggest that such issues can be safely ignored. People's basic approach to work and organizational responsibilities are developed within a particular national culture. For an organization to superimpose its own cultural norms on that situation and expect that employees will adapt underestimates the strength of existing values and beliefs. This is evident from the work of both Hofstede and Trompenaars discussed earlier.

The developing field of cognitive mapping as a way of understanding the relationship between culture and management is one which may offer useful insights in the future. It is likely that some form of accommodation will take place and that compliance will emerge on the surface with local preference being met in the *reality* of activity. For the managers of large international organizations the need to maintain some form of company consistency in culture while at the same time recognizing local differences is a major task. It is also one which requires particular sensitivity if problems are to be avoided. Expatriate managers find it particularly difficult to adjust to local conditions and can often fail in their assignments through not being able to balance these conflicting requirements.

Management in Action 14.8 provides an overview of a number of these issues as they were facing the managers of the Channel Tunnel as they began to create operational activity.

Stop | Consider *The approach suggested in MiA 14.8 implies that exposure to different cultures is the best way to encourage understanding and therefore tolerance. Might this imply that seeking to develop a common culture from among different cultures is impossible and that tolerance of other cultures within a neutral blend of what would be acceptable is the only option for true global organizations?*

MANAGEMENT IN ACTION 14.8

Breaking the executive mould

The Channel Tunnel presents a number of unique problems for the senior managers running the company. In many international companies there is a definite cultural, policy and procedural bias towards the home country. It is also likely that there will be a distinct cultural distinction between the home country and individual locations, for example the German employees of a US company would expect to be covered by German employment law and local traditions. However, with Eurotunnel this is not practical. With train services operating between a number of countries it is necessary to have a more definite combination of cultures and approaches within a single set of organization structures and arrangements.

Yves-Noel Derenne, the director of human resources for Eurotunnel, indicated that:

> The aim is not to recruit a particular nationality for a particular post, but to get the right person for the job, whether they be British, French, German or from some other country. There are some jobs which we would expect to be filled by one nationality rather than another. The servicing of rolling stock (because this is based in France) would naturally fall into this category. Headquarters for security, on the other hand, will be based in Britain.

> The holders of some jobs, however, will need to be capable of speaking both English and French as the nature of their jobs will require them to move between the two countries and deal regularly with customers and other staff from other countries. For example, train drivers and traffic controllers are expected to be bilingual, as are customer service personnel, but to a lesser extent.

Alain Bertrand, Eurotunnel's chief executive responsible for transport operations, said:

> We do not want a competitive culture to develop, Britain versus France. Unlike other national or multinational companies, which have separate management operations for different countries, we supply a single service irrespective of which country the customer comes from. It is important, therefore, that we establish a single management structure and corporate culture in which safety and customer service are the main driving force rather than nationalism.

Considerable amounts of time and money have been put into language training for those staff who need it. Two weeks' training for front-line customer service staff and four weeks for managers and engineers. The legal and cultural frameworks across countries have also had to be taken into account in designing employment policies. Generally speaking the approach adopted reflects a 'best of both worlds' view of dealing with such difference. For example, French employees are covered by the legal requirement to have works councils and so this has been introduced for all workers. National cultural aspects involving such areas as after-work leisure activities might not be so easy to reconcile. Perhaps the exposure over time to different ways of mixing work and private life together with other aspects of cultural difference may be the only way to ensure that people get used to differences between groups of workers.

Adapted from: Taylor, A (1993) Breaking the executive mould, *Financial Times*, 4 June, p14.

Conclusions

The subject of culture is one that influences a wide range of behaviour both within society as a whole and within organizations. It is not a precisely defined concept and is capable of being misinterpreted and manipulated by the managers who must attempt to make use of it in their work activities.

Taking into account the differences in definition referred to earlier, the concept of culture is generally recognized as being a valuable notion in describing a range of activities and features that are associated with organizational life. New employees must be effectively integrated into the organization if they are to become useful members of the team (as defined by management). It is not possible to manage every person all the time that they are at work. Some internalization of responsibility and knowledge of requirements must be handed over if efficiency in management is to be achieved. This is where the concept of culture is able to deliver a meaningful way of accounting for these phenomena. However, the notion that culture, particularly strong culture, provides a conflict-free way for managers to ensure harmony and the achievement of objectives is simplistic and does not reflect experience (Thompson and McHugh, 1990, p 236).

Discussion questions

1. Define the following key terms used in this chapter:

Organizational culture	*Norms*	*Task culture*
Subculture	*Power culture*	*Ouchi's Theory Z*
Counterculture	*Role culture*	*Ritual*
Dominant values		

2. Discuss the significance of 'culture' in the context of managing an organization.

3. To what extent does corporate culture depend upon national culture?

4. 'The concept of culture is of little practical value to managers because it simply describes tendencies and ignores the variation between individuals.' Discuss this statement.

5. It has been suggested that strong organizational cultures are essential to the achievement of success. It has also been suggested that strong cultures could predispose an organization to failure. Can you find an argument that could reconcile these two positions?

6. How would you set about achieving a change in an organization's culture?

7. 'The concept of culture is intended to provide managers with an opportunity to increase the level of control without increasing the level of management.' Discuss.

8. In what ways does culture influence the design and structure of an organization?

9. The section 'Cultural frameworks' describes a number of approaches to the 'form' that culture takes. Which approach most appeals to you and why is it superior to the others?

10. 'Culture is such an imprecise term that it is not possible to measure it let alone change it within an organization.' Comment on this statement.

Research activities

1. Obtain about six annual reports from leading commercial organizations. Analyze the information contained in the reports and attempt to identify any connections between culture and structure. What conclusions can you draw about the relationship between culture and structure from the analysis?

2. Identify an organization, a long-standing group or club, for example. Use one of the models in this chapter to describe the culture of that organization. In addition, identify the major influences on the evolution of that culture and indicate its suitability for the future objectives of the organization or group.

3. For the same organization used in activity 2, identify the stories, rituals, myths, legends and ceremonials that exist within it. Attempt to identify how these help to inculcate and sustain the culture of the organization.

Key reading

From Clark, H, Chandler, J and Barry, J (1994) *Organization and Identities: Text and Readings in Organizational Behaviour*, International Thomson Business Press, London:

◆ Bell, D: Work and its discontents, p 44. Provides an insight into how organizations and society link together.

◆ Campbell, B *et al.*: The manifesto for new times, p 49. Provides a basis for considering the context of culture and change.

◆ Pascale, R and Athos, A: Corporate cultures, p 351. Illustrates the notion of corporate culture and its consequences for the management of people.

◆ Axtell, Ray C: Corporate culture as a control device, p 357. This considers culture as a control process within an organization.

◆ Höpfl, H *et al.*: Excessive commitment and excessive resentment: issues of identity, p 373. Summarizes the notion of culture in an organizational context.

Further reading

Hampden-Turner, C (1990) *Corporate Cultures: From Vicious to Virtuous Circles*, Random Century, London. Provides a readable review of culture in an organizational context.

Kotter, JP and Heskett, JL (1992) *Corporate Culture and Performance*, The Free Press, New York. Considers the general issue of culture and its relationship with organizational performance.

Martin, J (1992) *Cultures in Organizations*, Oxford University Press, New York. A well-argued and comprehensive review of the subject.

Mohrman, SA and Cummings, TG (1989) *Self-designing Organizations*, Addison-Wesley, Reading, MA. This takes into account the relationship between culture and work organization as part of the design process.

Smith, PB and Peterson, MF (1988) *Leadership, Organizations and Culture*, Sage, Newbury Park, CA. Considers the relationship between the three major concepts.

Weick, KE (1995) *Sensemaking in Organizations*, Sage, Thousand Oaks, CA. A text on an area of work with very close relationships to culture. It is about how people make sense of the events that they experience, most particularly when the events do not map onto existing schemas.

References

Adler, NJ (1984) Understanding the ways of understanding: cross-cultural management methodology reviewed, *Advances In International Comparative Management*, 1, 31–67.

Allaire, Y and Firsirotu, M (1984) Theories of organizational culture, *Organization Studies*, 5, 193–226.

Alvesson, M (1993) *Cultural Perspectives on Organizations*, Cambridge University Press, Cambridge.

Barnard, C (1938) *The Functions of the Executive*, Harvard University Press, Cambridge, MA.

Bartlett, CA and Ghoshal, S (1989) *Managing Across Borders: The Transnational Solution*, Hutchinson, London.

Berg, PO (1985) Organizational Change as a Symbolic Transformation Process. In Frost, PJ, Moore, LF, Louis, MR, Lundberg, CC and Martin, J (eds) *Organization Culture* , Sage, Beverly Hills, CA.

Calori, R, Johnson, G and Sarnin, P (1992) French and British top managers understanding of the structure and dynamics of their industries: a cognitive analysis and comparison, *British Journal of Management*, 3, 61–78.

Cooper, C (2000) The Met fails inspection on race and recruitment, *People Management*, 20 January, 11.

Cray, D and Mallory, G R (1998) *Making Sense of Managing Culture*, International Thomson Business Press, London.

Deal, T and Kennedy, A (1988) *Corporate Cultures: The Rights and Rituals of Corporate Life*, Penguin, Harmondsworth.

Furnham, A and Gunter, B (1993) Corporate Culture: Diagnosis and Change. In Cooper, CL and Robertson, IT (eds) *International Review of Industrial and Organizational Psychology*, John Wiley, Chichester.

Garrahan, P and Stewart, P (1992) *The Nissan Enigma; Flexibility at Work in a Local Economy*, Mansell, London.

Handy, CB (1993) *Understanding Organizations*, 4th edn, Penguin, Harmondsworth.

Harrison, R (1972) How to describe your organization, *Harvard Business Review*, September/October.

Herskovitts, MJ (1948) *Man and His Works: The Science of Cultural Anthropology*, Alfred A Knopf, New York.

Hofstede, G (1980) *Culture's Consequences: International Differences in Work Related Values*, Sage, London.

Hofstede, G (1983) Dimensions of National Cultures in Fifty Countries and Three Regions. In Deregowski, J, Dziurawiec, S and Annis, RC (eds) *Expectations in Cross-cultural Psychology*, Swets & Zeitlinger, Lisse.

Hofstede, G (1990) The Cultural Relativity of Organizational Practices and Theories. In Wilson, DC and Rosenfeld, RH (eds) *Managing Organizations: Text, Readings and Cases*, McGraw-Hill, London.

Jaques, E (1952) *The Changing Culture of a Factory*, Tavistock, London.

Jones, G (1996) *The Evolution of International Business: An Introduction*, Routledge, London.

Kilman, RH, Saxton, MJ and Serpa, R (1985) Introduction: Five Key Issues in Understanding and Changing Culture. In *Gaining Control of The Corporate Culture*, Jossey Bass, San Francisco, CA.

Kraut, AI (1975) Some recent advances in cross-national research, *Academy of Management Journal*, 18 538–49.

Kroeber, AL and Kluckhohn, C (1952) *Culture: A Critical Review of Concepts and Definitions*, Peabody Museum, Cambridge, MA.

Lammers, CJ and Hickson, DJ (1979) *Organizations Alike and Unlike*, Routledge, London.

Littlefield, D (1999) Kerry's heroes, *People Management*, 6 May, pp 48–50.

Lundberg, CC (1985) On the Feasibility of Cultural Intervention in Organizations. In Frost, PJ, Moore, LF, Louis, MR, Lundberg, CC and Martin, J (eds) *Organization Culture*, Sage, Beverly Hills, CA.

Meyerson, D and Martin, J (1987) Cultural change: and integration of three different views, *Journal of Management Studies*, 24, 623–47.

Ouchi, W (1981) *Theory Z: How American Business Can Meet the Japanese Challenge*, Addison-Wesley, Reading, MA.

Payne, R (1991) Taking stock of corporate culture, *Personnel Management*, July.

Peters, TJ (1989) *Thriving on Chaos*, Macmillan, London.

Peters, TJ and Waterman, RH (1982) *In Search of Excellence: Lessons from America's Best-run Companies*, Harper & Row, New York.

Redding, S G (1994) Comparative management theory: jungle, zoo or fossil bed? *Organization Studies*, 15, 323–59.

Salamon, M (1992) *Industrial Relations: Theory and Practice*, 2nd edn, Prentice Hall, Hemel Hempstead.

Schein, EH (1985) *Organizational Culture and Leadership*, Jossey Bass, San Francisco, CA.

Stockton, W (1986) Bribes are called a way of life in Mexico, *New York Times*, 25 October, p 3.

Thompson, P and McHugh, D (1990) *Work Organizations: A Critical Introduction*, Macmillan, Basingstoke.

Trice, HM and Beyer, JM (1984) Studying organizational cultures through rites and rituals, *Academy of Management Review*, **9**, 653–69.

Trompenaars, F (1993) *Riding the Waves of Culture*, Nicholas Brealey, London.

Trompenaars, F and Woolliams, P (1999) First-class accommodation, *People Management*, 22 April, 30–7.

Tuckman, B and Jensen, N (1977) Stages of small group development revisited, *Group and Organizational Studies*, **2**, 419–27.

Turner, BA (1986) Sociological aspects of organizational symbolism, *Organization Studies*, **7**, 101–15.

Tyson, S and Jackson, T (1992) *The Essence of Organizational Behaviour*, Prentice Hall, Hemel Hempstead.

Ulrich, D and Black, J S (1999) The New Frontier of Global HR. In Joynt, P and Morton, R (eds) *The Global HR Manager*, Institute of Personnel and Development, London.

Watson, TJ (1994) *In Search of Management: Culture, Chaos and Control in Managerial Work*, Routledge, London.

Wright, JP (1979) *On A Clear Day You Can See General Motors*, Wright Enterprises, Grosse Point, MI.

Yip, GS (1989) Global strategy in a world of nations, *Sloan Management Review*, Autumn.

PART VII

The management of organizations

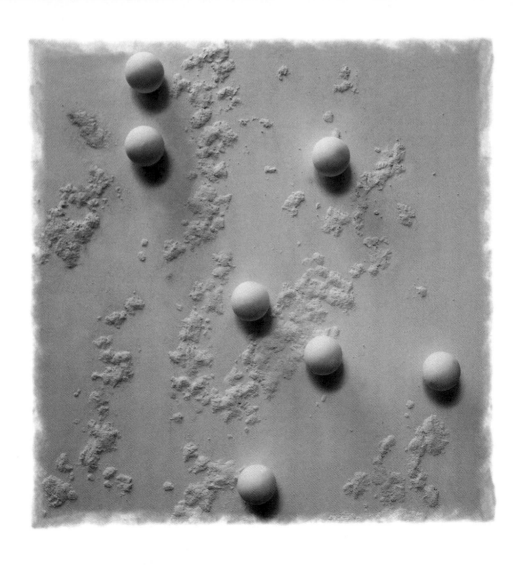

CHAPTER 15

Management within organizations

CHAPTER SUMMARY

This chapter sets out to introduce the nature of management as it is prac-tised within organizations. The chapter will begin with a consideration of what management is. This will be followed by a review of the manage-ment process and what it is that managers actually do. A number of the contextual aspects of management will then be introduced, such as the type and size of organization, culture and international aspects. The roles that managers undertake and the skills that they require form the next area for discussion. In turn this will be followed by consideration of issues such as discrimination and the effectiveness of management. Critical incident management will then be introduced as a new area for serious considera-tion. The power aspects of management will be discussed along with the impact of new organizational forms on the tasks involved. Consideration of the nature and impact of meetings and humour in management will also be discussed.

LEARNING OBJECTIVES

After studying this chapter and working through the associated Management in Action panels, Discussion questions and Research activities, you should be able to:

♦ Understand what management is within an organizational context.

♦ Describe what it is that managers actually do when carrying out their jobs.

♦ Explain the roles that managers perform and the skills that they need.

♦ Outline the significance of training managers to deal with critical inci-dents.

♦ Assess the relationship between power and management.

♦ Appreciate the significance of humour in management.

♦ Discuss contextual influences on management such as type and size of organizations as well as the cul-tural and international aspects of organizational activity.

♦ Detail the significance of gender in a management context.

Introduction

Management is a common term and almost everyone would be able to describe, at least in very general terms, what a manager does. Managers run things, they run companies, they run football clubs, they run shops and restaurants. This chapter will set out to explore just what it is that managers actually do when they run the things that they do. Some of the questions that will be examined along the way include what actually is management, what do managers do and is the job of managing the same in every type of organization?

These are not the only questions that will be addressed, because there are so many facets of the task of managing that are worthy of examination. For example, what about the role of women in management and how should managers respond to critical incidents? The job of 'running things' is complex and becoming ever more so. As a consequence this chapter reviews much of the nature and form of that complexity in order to provide a better understanding of what is required to perform the task effectively. As will become apparent during the discussion, 'running things' is a vast understatement of what the job actually involves.

One important aspect of the task of management is the question of how managers themselves are trained and developed to undertake their responsibilities. This is an area of organizational activity that is often undervalued by organizations, particularly in Britain (Harrison, 1994). However this situation is changing with the range of undergraduate and postgraduate degrees available in business and management growing every year, in line with the number of students seeking to qualify in this field. Also the volume of in-company training provision is also expanding rapidly as organizations recognize that they also need to make provision for the development of their own managers. Frequently, in-company training programmes for managers have been validated by university management departments to improve content credibility and impact. Management in Action 15.1 provides an insight into the issues associated with the training and development of a special group of managers – directors. The directors of any company have particular responsibilities to ensure that the organization for which they hold legal responsibility is managed in accordance with the law and also that it is directed appropriately as a trading entity.

Stop | Consider

Should the training of directors (and managers in general) be made a legally required process for all organizations?

Should this requirement apply to all sizes and types of organization?

Justify your answer examining some of the problems and difficulties involved if training were to be legally required.

What is management?

The introduction to this chapter has already given a simple clue to what management is. It is about 'running things'. However, that explanation of itself carries very little real meaning and communicates very little of what management actually involves. The *Pocket Oxford Dictionary* (1969) defines the term 'manage' as comprising the following connotations: 'Conduct the working of, have effective control of, bend to one's will, cajole … find a way … contrive to get along … bring about, secure … deal with … skilful handling'.

MANAGEMENT IN ACTION 15.1

Business class

Invariably the staff who might be expected to identify training needs and provide training for senior managers and directors are lower in status than the managers targeted. There is also a degree of reluctance among directors to admit that they need training. To admit a training need might be seen to undermine their credibility. A survey by the Industrial Society found that one in six organizations provided no training for its directors. The personnel department determined training for board members in only 10% of cases and the board itself in 20%. Individual board members decided their own training needs in the majority of cases.

John Harper, professional development director for the Institute of Directors, indicated that the situation was changing rapidly. The most obvious lack of training for directors was when they first took up a board-level appointment. Only 11% of organizations automatically review the training needs of new directors and one-third of organizations rarely or never do so.

To meet the needs of board-level leaders of organizations a number of courses have been developed over recent years. Most involve the Institute of Directors and a university in some form of collaborative endeavour. The Institute developed a diploma programme in company direction aimed at providing delegates with a solid basis in the duties and responsibilities of a director. There are also master's degree

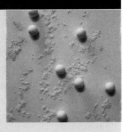

programmes that are becoming available and which aim to provide delegates with the skills necessary to perform at board level. The first one of these was offered by Leeds Metropolitan University in 1994.

One of the difficulties facing board members is the distinction between the responsibilities of directors and those of managers. For example, Judith Barras, course leader for the master's course at Leeds Metropolitan University, suggested that directors who were appointed to the board after being managers within the same company sometimes had a limited vision of the needs of the firm as a whole. Work done in this area by Henley Management College produced a number of 'standards' such as organizing and running a board of directors, vision, strategy and responsibility to stakeholders. A number of personal competencies for directors have also been identified including integrity, decisiveness, the ability to listen and a willingness to adopt a 'helicopter' perspective. The provision of training for both newly appointed and more experienced directors is aimed at addressing these and similar issues.

Adapted from: Hall, L (1994) Business class, *Personnel Today*, 3 May, pp 31–2; and Merrick, N (1994) Taking training to the top, *Personnel Management*, December, pp 51–2.

The term *manage* can be applied to many different situation. For example, an individual could *manage* to lose 20 kilograms in weight over the course of three months by dieting and taking more exercise. Equally, they could *manage* to balance their budget over the course of a year so that they did not spend more than they earned in salary. Also, using the term in a negative sense, an individual could *manage* to make a complete mess of a do-it-yourself project on their home and be forced to call in a builder to repair the damage and complete the project properly. Each of these situations, together with the many possibilities for the association with the term *manage* that have not been included, is interesting and has something to offer in terms of understanding the concept. However, they do not specifically relate to the organizational context which is the primary focus of this text.

To *manage* within an organizational context carries with it several connotations that are based on the dictionary definition already indicated, but which also incorporate other implications. To understand the nature of management within an organizational context it is first necessary to understand the concept of an organization. Any organization is established by someone, or a group of people to achieve particular objectives, including providing benefits to the 'owners' who established it. This generalized view can be applied to almost any type of organization, including those found in the private sector, the public sector, charities, residents associations, the not-for-profit and commercial companies etc. In the commercial sector the clear objective of the founders is to make profit from an enterprise, through the manufacture of goods or the delivery of a service into the marketplace. In the public sector the government (or ruler) establishes a government department or public utility on behalf of the people to enhance the quality of life in society or to make the functioning of government more effective. In the case of the charity and not-for-profit sectors, organizations are established by groups of people who wish to contribute something to the improvement of standards of living for disadvantaged or excluded groups of people. The main point to recognize is that the benefit are created through an organization, even if it is not measured in financial terms, to the founders.

In the early days of any organization it can usually be *managed* by the founders, largely because of the limited size and scale of the operation. However, once it is established and begins to grow, then it needs to have other people brought into the organization. These are, first, worker level personnel but, eventually, other managers are required to assist in *managing* the organization. Naturally in the public sector as a result of the nature of the way that government works *managers* would be involved in the process right from the start. That aside, *managers* are appointed by the beneficial owners to act on their behalf. In principle, it does not matter whether this is a small company with the owners heavily involved and assisted by professional managers, or a large company owned predominantly by institutional investors through the stock market. *Managers* are appointed by the beneficial owners to act on their behalf in realizing the objectives of the owners.

Managers are in a unique position within an organization in that they are appointed to achieve the objectives set for them and to act *in loco parentis* for the beneficial owners, and yet they are employees. They do not, in most cases, own the company that they manage, although they may in some cases be granted significant blocks of the share capital, yet they are expected to act is if they were the owners. This introduces an element of the complexity in the job of management. Managers are predominantly employees, with the same rights and contract-based relationship with the company as other workers. However, they are expected to act and function as if they were the beneficial owners, on whose behalf they are employed.

In effect they are one of a number of *stakeholders* linked to the organization. A stakeholder is generally defined as falling into one of two categories 'someone who has an interest' (Lynch, 1997, p 427):

✦ Those involved in the carrying out of the organization's mission and objectives. For example, managers and employees.

✦ Those involved in the outcome of the mission and objectives of the organization. For example, shareholders, customers, government, suppliers, financial institutions etc.

To this a third category can be added, those groups and individuals with an interest in the byproducts of the mission and objectives of the organization. For example, trade unions, the local community, family members of the employees, local shops etc. These groups may have some interest in the outcomes of the organization's mission and objectives. For example, local shops are keenly interested in the volume of money in the local community, as without money to spend people do not visit shops. It does not matter to the local shopkeeper that a particular company is prospering and as a result will move to new premises 500 miles away. What matters is that the employees in the local community will be made redundant and have less money to spend. A generalized model of the *stakeholders* surrounding any organization is shown as Figure 15.1.

The value of the *stakeholder* concept is in offering a means of recognizing the range of groups and individuals with a vested interest in an organization. However, it also provides a means of recognizing the possibly different consequences for each category. This allows managers to prioritize and channel appropriate actions for each category. Not all *stakeholders* have equal power when it comes to influence on the organization and its actions. The level of power held by any particular stakeholder group can also change depending upon the circumstances. For example, the print unions and employees held considerable power in newspaper publishing on Fleet Street, London over many decades. They had the power to stop production instantly and not infrequently did so in pursuit of higher wages and improved working conditions. However, with the introduction of computer-based technologies much of that power evaporated very quickly.

As companies develop it is possible that managers will develop interests different from those of the owners or shareholder of the business. Shareholders are primarily interested in a financial return on their investment. Managers frequently have an interest in growth and reinvestment as with increased size comes professional development, reputation and enhanced salary and benefit levels. Holl (1977) for example suggests that unless managers of large organizations are threatened by takeover or rewarded in particular ways, they may well take a broader view of the organization and its objectives than the shareholders. This trend to separate ownership from control was detected as far back as the 1930s and can be seen in many corporate battles of today. For example, the recent attempts by some

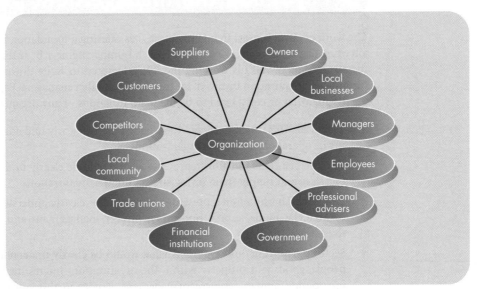

FIGURE 15.1   Stakeholder map of an organization.

members (the owners) of Standard Life, a very large mutual insurance company, to force the company to demutualize and so realize their 'locked-in wealth' was fiercely (and expensively) resisted by the senior managers of the organization (Moore, 2000). Managers won the battle (having spent some £10m on the project) on that occasion, but perhaps not for long, at least in the opinion of some investors.

In another perspective on the complexity of management, Cook and Emler (1999) explored the perceptions of subordinate and superior managers in the evaluation of candidates for a middle manager vacancy. This type of research is interesting from many perspectives, including the exploration of who might make a 'good' manager and why. The researchers predicted that senior managers (future boss of the candidate) would evalute candates differently to the subordintes of the applicants. The same candidates were evaluated by both groups of evaluators and they used the same criteria (moral, technical and social qualities) to do so. The moral qualities appeared to give the greatest degree of difference, being more significant to subordiantes than superiors. This led the researchers to suggest that those being managed want the people with power over them to have high 'moral' characteristics.

This discussion adds weight to the view expressed earlier that management represents a complex process. Clearly, form the foregoing discussion managing an organization involves achieving objectives. However, it also involves managing the *stakeholder environment*, managing the power balance between stakeholder groups and harnessing the resources available (including money, equipment, facilities, systems and employees) in pursuit of the desired objectives. There is also more than a suspicion emerging from some of the literature in this area that managers are beginning to exert more influence than the owners of the business in deciding what the organization's objectives should be. It is now appropriate to consider some of the theoretical perspectives on the topic in order to begin to tease out just what management involves.

Fayol and the management process

The work of Fayol is most frequently quoted as offering a foundation in what it is that the job of managing involves. Fayol was a French mining engineer by training and worked for the same company all his working life. He attempted to write down his views on what running an organization involved, for the benefit of other managers. Fayol (1916) began by identifying what he considered to be the main functions of any organization:

✦ Technical. This function represents what would be clearly understood as manufacturing or operations in today's organizations.

✦ Commercial. This function represents what would be clearly understood as purchasing, sales and supply chain or logistics in today's organizations.

✦ Financial. This function represents what would be clearly understood as the provision of financial funds, capital budgeting, project management and risk assessment in today's organizations.

✦ Security. This function represents what would be clearly understood as protection of people, goods and property within the organization. Interestingly, Fayol would also incorporate human resource management activity in this category in the sense of avoiding strikes etc.

- ✦ Accounting. This function represents what would be clearly understood as the management accounting function together with stocktaking, costing, and statistical analysis in today's organizations.

- ✦ Administrative. This function represents what would be clearly understood as the management responsibilities in today's organizations.

The management of organizations (administrative functions in Fayol's words) were said to consist of the following activities. In this list of activities Fayol was describing what has become known as the *management process*. In essence, the process that manager's must go through in order to manage:

- ✦ Forecasting. This stage in the management process involves predicting or attempting to foresee the future.

- ✦ Planning. Having foreseen the future it is then necessary to make provision for dealing with it. This, along with the term forecasting comes from the single French word *prevoyance*, used by Fayol it means to both predict and prepare for the future.

- ✦ Organizing. Having developed a plan for the future it is then necessary to provide and organize the resources required for the achievement of the plan.

- ✦ Co-ordinating. This stage of the process is about ensuring that all of the resources available are arranged appropriately, function effectively and are in harmony (co-ordinated) in order that the plan can be realized.

- ✦ Commanding. This function is about ensuring that everything works as it is intended to in order to achieve the plan. This involves giving instruction to employees and ensuring that performance of every person is appropriate to the objectives.

- ✦ Controlling. This function is about ensuring that the plan has been followed. It is about ensuring that everything is done in proper order and in sequence to ensure the achievement of the objectives established in the plan.

Fayol also proposed a set of 14 principles of management, which he argued would help to ensure that the process of management was successful. He pointed out that these principles should be used with some flexibility and adapted to the circumstances prevailing at the time for the organization. His 14 principles are included in Table 15.1.

Fayol is not the only person to have a view on the nature of management, although he may be the most widely quoted. FW Taylor (1947), as part of his *scientific management* approach for example, suggested that the work of the general foreman should be broken down into eight separate functions, each undertaken by a different person. This approach he termed *functional foremanship*. The type of activity identified by Taylor provides a very different feel from the job of management than the functions indicated by Fayol. However, it must be recognized that Taylor was making these suggestions about the functions of a particular management job, whereas Fayol was describing management in general and from a top-down perspective. The eight functions identified by Taylor as comprising *functional foremanship* are included in Table 15.2.

Managing in a social world

Managers do not manage in isolation from the forces acting upon society as a whole and, in particular, the reactions to their attempts to control and organize from those being managed. For example, Montgomery (1979) makes the point that the direct challenge to the power and conditions of work for craft level employees, led directly to their rejection on practical and ethical grounds of scientific management-based attempts at management

1	Authority and responsibility. Authority cannot exist without responsibility. The exercise of authority ensures that the right things are done
2	Unity of command. Each worker should have only one boss
3	Division of work. Breaking the work down into small sets of tasks allows the worker to develop high levels of specialization and efficiency
4	Discipline. This is necessary for efficiency to exist. The manager must exercise appropriate discipline in maintaining order
5	Subordination of individual interest to that of the organization. The organization must be placed above personal or group interest if it is to succeed
6	Equity. Each person should be treated with equity as far as it is possible to do so
7	Scalar chain. There should be a proper hierarchy of grades and responsibilities from the bottom to the top of the organization
8	Remuneration. Payment methods should be fair and benefit both employer and employee
9	Centralization. The degree of centralization appropriate in any organization depends upon the circumstances
10	Order. Material and social order is necessary for the avoidance of loss in goods and people efficiency
11	Esprit de corps. Harmony and unity should be encouraged among the workforce to ensure that everyone works together in the interests of the organization
12	Initiative. This should be encouraged in all levels as a soruce of strength for the organization
13	Stablility of tenure. Where possible organizations should avoid the 'hire and fire' approach to managing people. With security of employment comes commitment and efficiency
14	Unity of direction. There should be one head and one plan controlling the overall direction of the organization

TABLE 15.1   Fayol's 14 principles of management

Inspector	Repair boss
Time and cost clerk	Instruction card clerk
Gang boss	Order of work and route clerk
Shop disciplinarian	Speed boss

TABLE 15.2   Functional foremanship

control. This reaction emerged originally in the USA when the government attempted to introduce scientific management methods into the arsenals during World War I. However, as Montgomery also points out, most of the opposition to Taylor's ideas was overcome by the mid-1920s, with some of the unions in the USA supporting its application in return for recognition and union involvement in collective bargaining etc. (Nadworny, 1955).

Much of the criticism of the methods of management implied by approaches developed by writers such as Fayol and Taylor are that they are inflexible. They imply that managers should be able to apply a *formula* and in doing so effectivemes and efficiency will be achieved. This is not the case. Management reflects a two-way dynamic between the manager and the managed, it is a social process. Figure 15.2 reflects the story of one incident that makes this very clear.

Willmott (1984) also reminds us that management as a reflection of the husbandry of resources must not be confused with managers as individuals who are responsible for controlling the work of other people within an organizatinal framework. For example, corporate planners develop many of the plans to be subsequently approved by managers in a process of selection betweeen options through interactive, but directed activity. In this type of process managers are effectively exercising selection between options through interactive, but directed activity. In such processes it is not the managers themselves who plan or forecast as indicated in the Fayol conception of the management process, they arrange for it to be done, subject to their approval.

Management in Action 15.2 suggests that, based on the example of a number of very large groups, the practice of management is about doing what others in the City expect, rather than to manage per se.

| Stop | Consider | *Identify what the implications for organizations, managers, employees, customers and society might be of the pressure on senior managers to keep producing the big deals in order to satisfy City expectations as suggested in MiA 15.2.* |

It was during the early years of the twentieth century that management began to emerge as a distinct occupational catagory. During that period organizations were growing

On the door-hanging section last year, the Superintendent instructed the men to work to their man assignments (i.e. job specifications). Their written instructions were that they were to do 14 two-door cars, 14 estates, and 21 four-door saloon cars. The men accepted – but management couldn't get the cars into correct rotation. The result was chaos, as the workers did just what they had been told to do. Two-door cars wer coming down the line with doors for four-cars – 7 inches too short … estate car doors were being smashed into position on whatever car turned up next! The superintendent begged the men to return to their own patterns of working. But the men insisted on working strictly to their instructions for the rest of the shift. The result of this was that management allowed us to work to our own patterns. They left it to us. The situation is the same today.

FIGURE 15.2   Managers always know best (*source: Red Notes* (1976)).

MANAGEMENT IN ACTION 15.2

The importance of being active

Searjeant suggests that fund managers who look after the very large investment funds on behalf of clients become desperate for corporate action simply when there has been little of it for a while. In short the need to sell unit trust and other funds to retail clients results in a demand for action in the City to provide ever greater interest, share movement and growth potential which is then used as a marketing tool.

One example given to illustrate this point is the announcement from Diageo that it intends to sell its international BurgerKing chain. One of the reasons given for this is the fundamental conflict between the requirement for successfully running BurgerKing operations through the motivation of large numbers of part-time young people, as compared to the core competencies of Diageo in whisky distilling and brewing. However, this is not a new problem. It existed when BurgerKing was originally acquired as part of the acquisition of the Pillsbury food manufacturing group, which was itself also somewhat away from the Diageo core business strengths at the time it was purchased and is also rumoured to be available for sale.

Searjeant suggests that the current sale would be justified by Diageo on the basis of a strategic

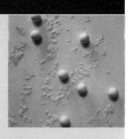

analysis of current and future requirements. However, he also points out that the perception in the City is that Diageo is selling BurgerKing because it has not done a big deal for quite a while and is under pressure to do so in order to justify its reputation and that of its senior managers. Similar examples are quoted from organizations such as Bass and tobacco giants BAT and Philip Morris.

Pointing out that most big companies operate in markets that do not grow any faster than the underlying economies, Searjeant indicates that this inevitably creates problems. Over recent years actuarial projections of investment returns have reduced considerably to around 5–7% per year, while fund managers are chasing projections of around 11–13% average growth in earnings per share over the next few years. Corporate activity is demanded in order to try and bridge the gap between projected returns and required returns for the benefit of fund managers' sales figures.

Adapted from: Searjeant, G (2000) The importance of being active, *The Times Weekend Money*, 1 July, p 54.

---

in scale as they were able to capture the benefits of the then emerging technology to make and distribute goods and services in vast quantities. Accordingly, as society was changing, so were the organizations within them in terms of size and complexity. This encouraged the *professionlization of management* as an occupational category and the emergence of models underpining its practice. It was Child (1969, p 225) who pointed this out, by suggesting that management's claim to be a profession could only be plausible if it were supported by a generalized body of knowledge. Therefore *principles of management* began to emerge as claims to be such a basis.

With the suggestion of the existance of management as profession a number of writers suggested that a post-capitalist society was emerging with the consequential lack of need to consider the political conflict between owners and labour (see, for example, Dahrendorf, 1959). Such views, however were not universal, or held across Europe. Fores and Glover (1976), for example, indicate that although the specialist nature of executive jobs was recognized across Europe, the collective category of manager in such activity was not recognized in every country.

A more recent sociological perspective on management is provided by Reed (1989). He brings together much of the earlier sociological thinking on management and in doing so identifies four themes on what it is about, including:

✦ Technical perspective. Management as, 'a rationally designed and operationalized tool for the realization of predominantly instrumental values concerned with the systematic co-ordination of social action on a massive scale' (pp 2–3).

✦ Political perspective. Management as, 'a social process geared to the regulation of interest group conflict in an environment characterized by considerable uncertainty over the criteria through which effective organizational performance is assessed' (p 6).

✦ Critical perspective. Management as, 'a control mechanism that functions to fulfil the economic imperatives imposed by a capitalist mode of production and to disseminate the ideological frameworks through which these structural realities can be obscured' (p 10).

✦ Practice perspective. Management as, 'a process or activity aimed at the continual recoupling or smoothing over of diverse and complex practices always prone to disengagement and fragmentation' (p 21).

The *practice perspective* on management attempts to bring together elements from the other three perspectives into a more holistic framework. What managers actually do is therefore regarded a function of the dominant perspective in any given situation.

What managers do

There is such a wide diversity of management work that it is not possible to specify what range of duties every manager will undertake. There have been a number of reports produced over the years that consider the nature, training and exercise of management responsibilities. Two of these from relatively recent times are summarized in Management in Action 15.3.

Stop | Consider

Earlier in this chapter it was suggested that managment is carried out within a social context. To what extent do the views expressed in MiA 15.3 reflect the natural adaptaion of management practice within a changing social context, or simply the improved practice of management itself?

Justify your views.

The explanation of management in MiA 15.3 offers very little detail of what it is that managers actually do while at work. Most studies of what it is that managers actually do reflect a view of management not at all like that implied by the Fayol model. They describe a fragmented, hectic job with frequent switches in activity. Handy (1993) summarizes a

MANAGEMENT IN ACTION 15.3

Whither management?

Collins reports two studies carried out during 1993 and 1994 on different aspects of the future of management. The first report by Cannon found that there were hopeful signs following the original Handy and Constable reports. For example, the commitment to developing managers had not been as seriously hit in the recession during the early 1990s as had been feared by many. More people were studying for undergraduate business and management degrees than had been set as targets in the original report. More organizations claimed an awareness of the importance of developing people at work and progress on the accreditation of in-company learning was growing. Perhaps more important, the study also found that the majority of managers who could affect the performance of their organizations during the first years of the new millennium were already in post.

The second report by Taylor identified a number of interesting features associated with management in the future including:

+ Managing the paradoxes between various competing pressures will remain an important aspect of organizational life. For example, long-term planning versus short-term performance.

+ Although fewer managers will be needed in manufacturing industry, new managerial activities will emerge in the healthcare industry and in non-traditional situations such as school management.

+ A recognition that people management is an important aspect of line management activity, not restricted to a specialist department.

+ A growth in generalist management and a decline in functional specialisms.

+ The development of teamworking in a variety of forms. This will by itself change the nature of management into a facilitation or indirect management activity.

+ The creation of many short-life teams with an increase in the short time allowed for the 'forming', 'storming', etc. process of acclimatization.

+ The development of new management techniques to manage the remote workforce. Homeworking and other forms of telecommuting require different forms of management to be exercised leading to changes in the 'command and control' aspects of management.

+ University education is intended to encourage individuals to enquire and challenge the status quo. Given the emphasis in much of the earlier organizational training on becoming 'good' employees this could lead to traditional authority being challenged or even ignored, respect and credibility being based much more upon the 'youth culture' views of situations, people and their capabilities.

+ More work still needed to be done to assist managers to make the jump from functional to general management levels within their organizations.

Adapted from: Collins, P (1995) Whither management?, *Management Services*, July, pp 16–18.

number of studies (Chapter 11) into the job of managers that clearly demonstrate this, including:

✦ Supervisors. Guest found that each one averaged 583 separate events that required the supervisor to 'do' something in every working day.

✦ Managers. Stewart found that on average each manager enjoyed only nine 30-minute periods without interruption over a four-week period.

✦ Chief executives. Mintzberg found that many activities for this category of senior manager fitted into ten-minute bursts of time. Meetings were also short, lasting one hour on average.

✦ Organization size. Mintzberg reported differences in activity between the chief executives of large and small organizations.

Mackenzie (1972) categorizes the time activity of managers as either *managing* or *operating* and describes the changing balance between these two categories at different levels of the managerial hierarchy. Figure 15.3 illustrates this changing balance of activity classification between hierarchical levels.

The specific nature, range and pattern of work undertaken by any manager will depend upon a wide range of factors. Stewart (1985) identifies a number of these, including:

✦ Industry. The job of a personnel manager in a national retail chain employing 1000 people would be different to the same job carried out in a heavy engineering company with the same number of employees on one site.

✦ Role. The figurehead role of the senior manager in a large bureaucracy carries with it implications about a difference in activity pattern compared to that of an entrepreneur at the head of a rapidly growing diverse group of companies.

✦ Pattern of work. Most management jobs (as with many others) contain a degree of cyclicality, perhaps weekly, monthly, quarterly or annually. For example, the job of a budget accountant is largely determined by the monthly budget cycle. However, a chief executive would focus on the quarterly and annual results reported to investors. Also, project-based jobs are different in activity pattern to line management positions.

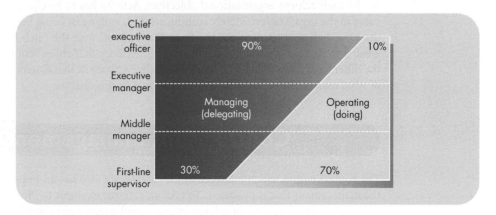

FIGURE 15.3 Managerial activity (© Alec MacKenzie. *Source*: MacKenzie, RA (1972) *The Time Trap: How to Get More Done in Less Time*, McGraw-Hill, New York).

- ✦ Level. The level within the hierarchy clearly influences the tasks performed by the manager. The chief executive generally does different things to the first-line manager.

- ✦ Exposure. This aspect of activity reflects the degree of visibility and representation of the organization in the execution of a manager's job. For example, a sales manager is highly exposed (visible) in that much of their time would be spent in contact with customers. This can be compared to the job of a management accountant which would be largely focused on activity within the organization.

- ✦ Contacts. The nature of interaction with other people is a key factor in work activity. For example, the job of a public relations manager would be expected to be completely different in activity from that of a personnel manager.

- ✦ Personal factors. Individual difference and preferences encourage variation in work activity to take place at any level within an organization. For example, one manager may prefer to stay in their office and manage through sending memos and e-mail, another may prefer to walk the job and deal with people in person.

Luthans (1995) describes four general types of management activity, along with the approximate proportion of time devoted to it extracted from the 'Real Managers Study'. However this model does not take account of the range of different types and level of management jobs that exists. Luthans' four types of management activity are as follows:

- ✦ Traditional management. Planning, decision making and controlling. This accounts for 32% of management time.

- ✦ Routine communication. Exchanging information and handling paperwork. This accounts for 29% of management time.

- ✦ Networking. Interacting with outsiders, socializing and politicking. This accounts for 19% of management time.

- ✦ Human resource management. Managing conflict, motivating, discipline, staffing and development. This accounts for 20% of management time.

There is another aspect associated with activity to be considered in this discussion. There is a vast difference between *activity* and *effectiveness*. Simply *doing something* does not by itself achieve organizational objectives. Activity has to be effective before it has any value to the organization. Merely rushing around, looking or being busy is not enough. To use a football analogy, it is not the team that runs all over the pitch for 90 minutes that wins, it is the team that scores the most goals. Activity that either scores goals or prevents the other team from doing so is the only *effective* activity in that situation. This is an aspect of what managers do that will be discussed later in this chapter.

Context and management

The context within which management is carried out also has an impact on the nature of the management that is practised. To take an extreme example to illustrate this point, the job of the chief executive of a large international organization would be expected to be completely different from the job of the owner of a small manufacturing company employing five people in total. There are many aspects of the context within which management is carried out that could be explored. Figure 15.4 illustrates a number of the more significant aspects of the context that might be expected to impact on how management is practised within an organization.

Taking each element within Figure 15.4 for further discussion:

✦ Public/private sector organizations. There are a number of differences between public sector organizations and those in the private sector. It might immediately be assumed that the major distinction lies in the fact that public sector organizations are bureaucratic and do not have the profit motive as the rationale for their existance. While this is undoubtedly true to a significant extent, reality is much more complex than that implies. The public sector is now subjected to many variations on the theme of market testing (and charging for services) in an attempt to ensure efficiency and cost minimization. For example, tuition fees have been introduced for students attending English and Welsh universities. This will inevitably change the relationship between institutions, students, staff and govenment over time. It will in turn also influence the management of universities as they attempt to respond to this changing dynamic. University managers will have to become more commercially aware, rather than simply being the group to allocate resources and account for their use.

Equally, many very large commercial organizations have bureaucratic tendencies and do not match the private sector notional model of 'lean and fit'. The banking sector might serve as an example of bureaucratic organizations in the sense of very large institutions seeking to dominate and dictate to the customer. Ashworth (2000) illustrates this through a discussion of the behaviour of large banks in seeking to enforce disloyalty charges on their own customers for using the cash dispensers of other banks, as well as to continue to pay very low interest rates on current acounts. This has now changed or is being put under severe pressure as a result of consumer reaction, government pressure and the growth in the number of telephone or elec-

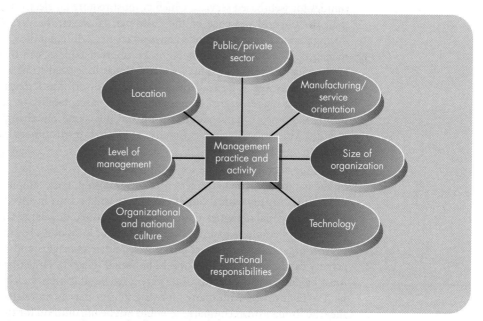

FIGURE 15.4 Contextual influences on management.

tronic bank accounts paying relatively high rates of interest, thereby forcing the banks to become more customer responsive or lose significant business.

Management in the public sector was regarded as a process of ensuring that the centrally determined policies and procedures were being applied, along with the inevitable checking of the work of subordinates. At a senior level, the job of public sector management was regarded as dealing with the political interface. In local as well as national government elected politicians inevitably seek to carry out what they regard as their electoral mandate. This inevitably requires public servants to develop new policies and procedures that will impact on the delivery of the public services to the general population. In the private sector it is generally assumed that senior managers must interpret the desires of the owners of the business (often the City) as well as the customers in seeking to achieve the best financial return. However, as has already been discussed, this relationship is perhaps more complex and subject to change than this assumption implies.

As with many stereotypes these images hide as much as they reveal about the nature of work and management in both types of organization. Often people work in the public sector because they wish to be involved in some form of public service. People do not only seek to work in the private sector because it pays more money. There are many differences between the public and private sectors, but there are also many similarities (Farnham and Horton, 1996).

◆ Manufacturing/service orientation. The nature of manufacturing and service organizations are fundamentally different. Pure manufacturing operations do not require the presence of the customer during the process of making something. However, the customer must inevitably be present in some guise during the provision of a service. Of course, there are many examples of mixed approaches. For example, providing designer-made clothes requires the customer to be present for fittings etc., but it also contains a manufacturing aspect in making the clothes. Equally, there are many opportunities for web-based services which at most require an electronic interaction rather than the physical presence of the customer. However, the presence of a customer during part of the organization's activities creates a different dimension to the work of managers. The flow of customers can be unpredictable as can their requirements in any service environment. This inevitably leads to a need to be able to manage that uncertainty as well as be available to deal with any crisis as it develops. Service operations have a higher degree of immediacy and susceptability to customer complaint during the process than manufacturing and this alone can change the nature of the way in which management functions in that environment (Fitzsimmons and Fitzsimmons, 1994).

◆ Size of the organization. The scale of the operation will also have a significant impact on the nature of the management activtiies within it. For example, the chief executive of a small company with about 50 employees will become involved in a much broader set of managerial activities than the chief executive of a large company with many thousands of employees spread over a number of locatioons. For the chief executive of a small organization there are many fewer other managers and specialists to whom activity can be delegated than would be found in a very large organization, and so it must be done personally. Also in a very large organization the chief executive would tend to be involved with many more 'significant players' in related fields than would the CEO from a small company. It would not be uncommon for the CEO of very large organizations to mix with senior banking, City and political figures on a regular basis.

The CEO of a small company might meet the local member of parliament and bank manager if they are lucky.

✦ Functional responsibilities. The functionl responsibilities of a manager will also influence the work they become involved with. For example, the activities of an engineering manager would be different to some extent to the activities of the human resource manager in the same organization. There would be some degree of similarity in these two jobs. Both managers would have to comply with common company procedures and policies, they would both have to attend similar meetings and might become involved in joint projects. However, the emphasis of the two jobs would differ and the expertise and level of general contact might also be different. The engineer would be expected to have a high technical knowledge across the engineering disciplines and also to manage stores and maintenance employees, in many ways a specialized line management function. The human resource manager could have to manage thier own department, but the staff within it would be at different levels of the organization to the maintenance personnel. Also, the human resource manager might act as a high level adviser and facilitator to the management team in terms of assisting in their personal and professional development, particularly in the area of developing management capabilities.

✦ Technology. The level of technology used within the organization is another feature which would be expected to impact on the practice of management. For example, in an organization in which computer technology undertakes much of the actual processing of work, then management becomes focused much more strongly on managing the people interface with both the technology and the customer. It is also likley that management will emphasize the creation of novel ways of using the technology available and of developing new applications. Management in Action 15.4 considers one new innovation in this field, the emergence of shared services in human resource management delivery.

Stop | Consider

To what extent might the management of the HR service centres described in MiA 15.4 differ from managing in other contexts?
To what extent might this be as a result of the call centre and intranet technology used?

✦ Location, organizational and national culture. The topic of culture is explored in Chapter 14 and so will not be developed here. Suffice it to say that in this context the cultural context within which management is practised would be expected to have a significant impact on the work of the managers themselves.

There are inevitably tensions inherent in international management that do not arise in a single country context. Adler (1991) describes the 'tensions between one's immediate national concerns and the broader interests of humanity and the future' (p 148). She quotes the work of Levinson on the impact of early culture experience which predisposes individuals to particular ways of relating to other people and expectations of power-based relationships. It is suggested that this in turn conditions particular ways of managing or being led in an organizational context. Managers running international operations must, of necessity, be able to reconcile these issues across international borders.

MANAGEMENT IN ACTION 15.4

Centre of attention

Re-engineering has been applied to the provision of human resource (HR) management within a number of large organizations. The provision of centralized services is not new, but what is new about the current wave of HR service centre development is, first, the opportunity for the customer (or client) to take as much or as little of the service as they feel necessary and, second, the application of technology to the process.

Research by the Institute for Employment Studies (IES) shows that there are a number of different models that are used for the provision of shared HR services. However, most organized the provision of HR services into three distinct categories. First, the retention of a corporate HR group dealing with high-level strategy, governance and policy. Second, the provision of HR business partners/advisers to work within individual business units, supporting operational managers on issues such as development, change and organizational design. Third, the creation of a shared services unit providing a range of HR advice and support to operational managers via a call centre or intranet. This last category covers the practical, day-to-day HR activity that can take up so much time, particularly when linked to the inevitable administration that occurs with managing people. For example, the paperwork necessary to record employee benefit choices or to advertise a job vacancy.

The IES study identified three main reasons for the introduction of shared services approaches to HR provision:

✦ Cost reduction. Reducing the number of HR specialists by centralizing activity, saving on accommodation costs and exploiting common purchasing power.

✦ Improving quality. The approach encourages specialization, consistency through the technology and the development of expertise through repetition. Individual shared service

staff become more aware of best practice through involvement and exposure to issues. They also become more focused and sensitive to customer needs (the business units forming the client base of the service). Managers are also more able to monitor the quality of service provision effectively.

✦ Responding to (and leading) organizational change. This means being able to flex the provision of HR services as the business develops and changes and also to be able to segregate the different client needs appropriately to concentrate on areas of business need.

The development and availability of appropriate technology was an important element in the opportunity to create shared services centres. Some organizations rely heavily on the use of call centre-type operations to deliver the service. For example, IBM has established an 'AskHR' service covering Europe, the Middle East and Africa from a common base just outside Portsmouth. Although it might appear to be like any other call centre, it employs people who speak 11 different languages and who are conversant with HR practice in their respective countries. Also, unlike most call centres, staff are taken away from the phone desks for about 20% of their time to work on projects. Higher category staff in the centre spend a greater proportion of their time on project work. It is envisaged that employees will progress through the two levels of job within the 'AskHR' operation, before moving into individual business units at a strategic level.

Although a number of organizations have followed this type of route, not all have. For example, PowerGen, a power utility in the UK, has gone down a totally different route in adopting the service centre principle. Splitting the existing HR function into the three categories suggested above, the service centre was located in the same head office building as most of the client business units. This enabled a high degree of human interaction between client and service centre staff and therefore less reliance of communication and computer technology. Customers can actually walk into the service centre and speak to staff face to face, a point which the manager of the unit feels is important to its success.

From a management perspective the issues in running these service centres are described as being of attracting and retaining appropriate staff, selling the services to the business units and ensuring a high quality of service provision. There is a danger that in a call centre-type of environ-

ment staff would not envisage career progression and may become bored quickly. The example from IBM indicated above demonstrates both the opportunity to a ensure career path for such staff and the development of the high-level skills needed to deal with HR work of this type. Even within the PowerGen example, where technology does not feature so heavily, the provision of career routes through the service centre are regarded as an important aspect of maintaining an effective service. The manager of one such operation described the service centre as the 'nursery for the development of future HR consultants within the company'.

Adapted from: Reilly, P (2000) Called into question, *People Management*, 6 July, pp 26–30; and Pickard, J (2000) Centre of attention, *People Management*, 6 July, pp 30–6.

Fenby (2000) reports a study by one overseas employment specialist that suggested that 88% of companies viewed a period spent overseas on assignment as useful for career prospects. This result is particularly important considering the number of organizations, even relatively small ones that now engage in international operations in some form or another. He also quotes a former head of Ford, Alex Trotman as saying:

> Think global, be prepared to work in several different cultures. You'll never get on staying in one place. Speak more than one language; get used to the idea of intensive competition. Be nimble, be courageous and always expect the unexpected.

Adler also quotes an interesting report by Oh (1976) reflecting the application of Theory X and Theory Y to management in China after the 1949 revolution. It identified that managers allied with the communist ideology tended to adopt the Theory Y perspectives in the belief that they were closely aligned with the philosophy of Chairman Mao. Managers with less skill in the ideological areas tended to adopt Theory X principles. This provides an indication that leadership approach may be influenced by political and economic as well as cultural perspectives.

A US-owned company with a subsidiary in South America is likely to face different management scenarios and pressures from those of an indigenous organization. Equally, a foreign organization in any country in the world led by a national from the host country is likely to face different leadership scenarios and pressures from one managed by a parent country expatriate. Figure 15.5 reflects the interaction between the variables active in the international context.

✦ Levels of management. This aspect of the context has already been alluded to on a number of occasions. It is inevitable that the level of a particular manager will impact on their activities. A branch manager in a bank will become invovled in a range of activities different from the regional manager, who will also become involved in different activities from the branch operations director. Moving up the levels within a large organization requires the individual to become involved in less immediate operational issues and to focus on corporate performance and longer term planning. This point is illustrated clearly in Figure 15.3 in the context of the balance between *managing* and *operating*. A junior line manager will spend more time actually joining in the operational work of the organization than would the chief executive. The junior line manager in becoming involved in the work of their subordinates inevitably engages with the basic operations of the organization. However, a chief executive who becomes involved in the work of their subordinates becomes engaged with senior management activity, a different form of *managing*, not *operating*.

Management roles and skill

Role theory originated from the theatre where it is obvious that the actors are performing *roles* as written by the author and as interpreted by the director. The requirements of the part that each actor is performing are set out in the script. There is a requirement that each player will behave (perform) as expected for the whole performance to work as intended. Extending this analogy out from the theatre implies that there is a web of expectation that everyone in an organization will perform as expected in the specific role that they are performing. The application of this *metaphor* in practice creates stability and predictability in work activity and relationships within organizations.

The application of role theory provides individuals with an outline (or model) of what is expected of them in undertaking a particular job or function. The use of *role play* is common in many management training courses as a way of getting the participants to practise (rehearse) behaviour repetoires for use in their daily work. How to tackle 'problem

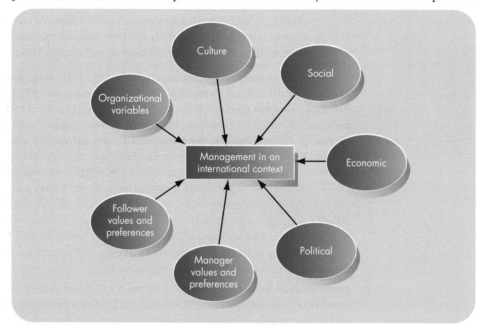

FIGURE 15.5 Management in an international context.

employees' would be one such example, where individuals are often provided with the opportunity to *role play* particular events and explore appropriate behaviour patterns. The observation that someone is a good (or bad) *role model* is another indication of the value of the concept in *shaping* behaviour.

Zimbardo carried out a famous experiment in which students took part in the role play of a prison over two weeks. Students were screened for emotional stability and maturity before being randomly allocated to the role of guard or prisoner. A basement was transformed into a prison and the volunteers were dressed appropriately. Guards were instructed to maintain order during their shift and left to arrange things on that basis. Within six days the experiment had to be called off. Both sets of *players* became so integrated into their roles that the safety and well-being of the 'prisoners' was being put at risk. Several explanations have been put forward for this result including the significance of the concept of a role and the attendant expectations in relation to the behaviour patterns on all concerned. Knowledge of the role of a particular person communicates to other people what behaviour patterns to expect from that person. Also the direct and powerful influence of the concept of a role on *shaping* the behaviour of *players* could explain the result (Haney *et al.*, 1973).

Considering the notion of role in formal terms there are a number of concepts that need to be examined:

✦ Role set. The name given to the group of people with whom a particular person might interact in a particular context. Figure 15.6 is the role set of a personnel manager.

✦ Role definition. The sum of behavioural expectations from the role set surrounding a focal person in a specific context.

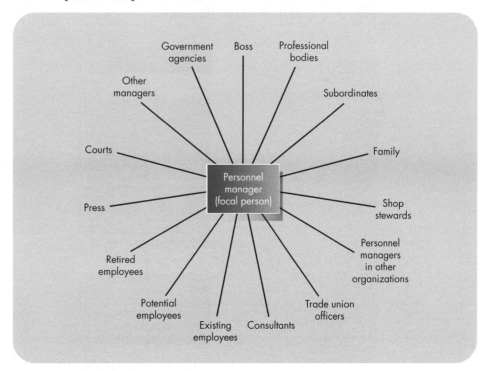

FIGURE 15.6　Role set of a personnel manager.

✦ Role ambiguity. Refers to the existence of uncertainty among the role set about the precise role that each is expected to play in a specific context.

✦ Role incompatibility. Where expectations of members of the role set differ with the focal person's view of their role. For example, employees may have been used to an open informal style of management. The subsequent appointment of a manager with an authoritarian style is likely to produce incompatibility in the expectations of both parties in terms of the most appropriate management style to be adopted.

✦ Role conflict. Arises with the dilemmas between the roles that individuals are expected to perform in the same situation. In performance appraisal reviews there is often scope for role conflict as a result of the performance and salary requirements of the system. Managers are expected to 'help' the individual improve their performance at the same time acting as 'judge' in assessing the level of pay rise to be awarded. In a court context it is the equivalant of attempting to be the defence barrister and trial judge at the same time, hence the role conflict!

✦ Role stress and strain. Pressure is placed on individuals as a result of the roles that they are required to undertake in a specific context. For example, where there is role conflict present the individual will inevitably experience stress and feel under pressure. Pressure is not of itself a bad thing, but too much (or too little) can be harmful. This was demonstrated by Weiman (1977) who found that individuals who were at either the low or high end of the stress range displayed more significant medical problems than those who experienced medium stress.

Mintzberg (1973) describes a number of roles undertaken by managers (see Figure 15.7). Each of the roles indicated acts in a co-ordinated way to produce a whole job, effectively creating a role profile for the position.

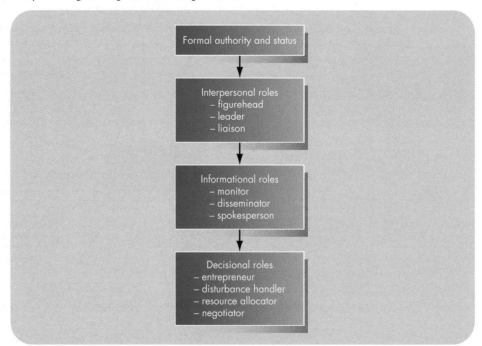

FIGURE 15.7 Mintzberg's management roles.

Each of the three classes of role indicated in the Mintzberg model is oriented as follows:

◆ Interpersonal roles. These roles reflect the form that the interaction with other people takes as a consequence of the status and type of managerial job held by a particular manager. For example, the industrial relations manager of a company would be expected to act as a figurehead in representing the company to the employees, the leader of the management–union negotiation body and a liaison between managers and the trade unions. This represents a different role pattern than might be expected to apply to the director of human resource management in the same company.

◆ Informational roles. These roles reflect the nature of the way that information is used in the job of the manager. These are heavily dependent on the dictates of the interpersonal roles of the postion. For example, the industrial relations manager indicated here would find it necesary to disseminate particular types of information in particular ways to particular people as a result of their interpersonal roles.

◆ Decisional roles. These roles reflect the nature of decision-making requirements within a particular managerial job. They are heavily dependent on the previous two categories of role indicated. For example, the industrial relations manager would be expected to play a leading role as a disturbance handler in the company as a consequence of their status and information networks.

More recent studies have introduced different role titles, including *visioning* and *motivator*. There has been some support for the use of these more recent concepts and their impact on organizational performance (Hart and Quinn, 1993). However, it has also been suggested that much of this is a reflection of a 'pop culture' in management – in other words a transient, shallow perspective offering little of substance.

It has already been suggested that the training and development of managers is often undervalued by organizations. One approach to the development of appropriate skills among managers is that based on the framework proposed by Pedler *et al.* (1994). This framework identifies 11 capabilities, grouped under three levels, that differentiate successful from unsuccessful managers. They are:

◆ Basic knowledge and information. This level includes those things necessary for taking decisions such as the possesion of a relevant professional understanding, an awareness of events and a command of the basic facts.

◆ Skills and attributes. This level reflects the necessary ability to function as a manager in the specific context. It includes analytical and problem solving skills, social skills, emotional resilience and an ability to be proactive in situations.

◆ Meta qualities. This level reflects the ability that some managers have to bring together the other skills and abilities in novel ways in dealing with situations. It includes such capabilities as being creative, displaying mental agility, having a balanced approach to learning and a sound self-knowledge.

Another approach to identifying the skills needed by managers at any level of an organization are proposed through the Management Charter Initiative (MCI). The MCI, established in 1988, is an independent body established with the aim of improving the performance of managers in the UK. One of the objectives of the MCI has been to develop national Management Standards, based on best practice, as a framework for developing managers who are capable of performing effectively. The Management Standards proposed by the scheme fall into seven key roles, each containing a number of units which form the basic competency blocks for being able to perform the role effectively (HMSO, 1997). The seven key roles are indicated in Table 15.3. However, not everyone would support the MCI initiative as reflecting the full range of competencies required of all management jobs.

Management and discrimination

This topic could cover a wide range of perspectives. It is managers who take many of the decisions within organizations, and discrimination in an organizational context is in many instances about inappropriate decision making. It is about issues such as selecting an individual to do a job on the basis of the colour of their skin, gender or physical capacity, rather than on the basis of the qualification and skills of the person in relation to the job for which they are being considered. It is about bringing into a decision-making process factors that are irrelevant to the needs of the situation and considering factors that would not impact on the ability of the individual to perform effectively.

The example of selection was used earlier as a means of illustrating this point. It is not, however, the only area in which discrimination occurs. It can occur in promotion decisions, it can arise in areas such as granting access to development and training opportunities or even in the way in which managers speak or deal with other people. For example, the words used by a superior to evaluate the performance of a female subordinate was

Key role	Example of units within the role
Manage activities	Manage activities to meet customer requirements Contribute to improvements at work Establish strategies to guide the work of your organization
Manage resources	Manage the use of physical resources Manage the use of financial resources Secure financial resources for your organizational plans
Manage people	Manage yourself Create effective working relationships Select personnel for activities
Manage information	Facilitate meetings Chair and participate in meetings Use information to take critical decisions
Manage energy	Promote energy efficiency Identify improvements to energy efficiency
Manage quality	Promote the importance and benefits of quality Manage continuous quality improvement Carry out quality audits
Manage projects	Co-ordinate the running of projects Plan and prepare projects Manage the running of projects

TABLE 15.3 MCI management standards

demonstrated to be different from that used to describe the performance of a man (Thomas, 1987). The findings showed that women were described as less competent, logical and mature than men and their performance attracted fewer recommendations and only very general levels of praise as compared to males.

This last research finding reflects the vast majority of discrimination studies in that it is focused on gender. However, it is reasonably safe to assume that much the same would be found with the other forms of discrimination that can arise. Wilson (1995) reviews many aspects of organizational behaviour in terms of the gender issues that arise, including management. She points out that:

> Sex-role identity, which seems to be more of a result of socialization than of basic sex differences, seems to have a substantial effect on the formation of occupational aspirations and expectations. Men are going to aspire to, and succeed in, more male-intensive occupations. (p 115)

Clearly this view, based on research findings, has significant implications for the number of women who would seek to become managers in the first place and who would subsequently achieve the opportunity to function in that capacity.

On pages 172–5 Wilson establishes the case for claiming that men and women bring different qualities to the role of management, quoting a wide variety of research sources in the process. Many of the studies reviewed by Wilson suggest that women display what could be described as 'people' orientation in their practice of management, whereas men tend to display a 'task' focus in their management style. While this vastly oversimplifies the discussion, it has been suggested that it might also be a function of laboratory studies of management practice, rather than a function of real gender difference at the workplace (p 175). She concludes with the view that there is much more to learn about how the social world is constructed to the advantage (in terms of pre-eminence) of men, and the ways in which this is perpetuated in both management research and practice.

Gardiner and Tiggemann (1999) suggest that women face different pressures from men in industries that are male dominated. Also, that in male-dominated industries they face different pressures from both men and women in industries dominated by women. In male-dominated industries women report adopting more male characterized management styles. Research from the Centre for Developing Women Business Leaders at Cranfield University suggests that the strength of the informal organizational culture is what effectively holds women back from reaching the top jobs (Vinnicombe and Harris, 2000). For example, the authors surveyed 100 international organizations and found that in many 'closed informal' systems existed for selection and promotion, involving nomination without candidates' knowledge and appointments being agreed after discussion between line managers and central personnel. Only between 2 and 15% of overseas postings are held by women, indicated elsewhere in this chapter as a key requirement for senior management appointments these days. Another study reported by Vinnicombe and Harris suggests that *success* as measured by organizations tends to reflect the male view rather than how women might define it. Another study demonstrated also that the concept of commitment is defined differently by both men and women and that as a consequence of the male domination of senior levels, again it is that definition that tends to be recognized and valued.

Management and organizational effectiveness

To be effective the manager needs to take account of their own preferences, the preferences of the group being lead, the task to be achieved and the context within which it is being carried out. John Adair (1983) describes what a manager has to do in terms of a three-circle model. He emphasizes the notion of leaderhip rather than the notion of management in his approach, which became known as *action-centred leadership*. Each circle represents a major part of the process of exercising management responsibilities. These are the principle responsibilities for which the leader will be held accountable.

✦ Achieving the task.

✦ Developing the individual.

✦ Building and maintaining the team.

In this model achieving the task is self-evident as a significant aspect of management. Adair also suggested that to be successful a leader would need to recognize that it was as important to be able to distinguish between the needs of the individual and the work group. He argued that it would be very rare when the needs and requirements of all three componenets were matched. Therefore, it was necessary for the leader to manage the tensions between the three components using a mixture of eight elements of a functional approach to management. These elements are indicated in Table 15.4.

Luthans (1995) also describes two research-based attempts to link *success* and *effectiveness* (pp 384–6), defining *success* as speed of promotion, networking activities correlated most strongly with it and traditional/human resource management activity the least. The implication of this finding being that promotion depends on socializing and politicking rather than task activity effectiveness. In terms of *effectiveness*, measured by quality, quantity, employee satisfaction and commitment, communication and human resource management activities were most strongly correlated with it. One implication of this finding is that achieving results does not advance careers! There are a number of other implications that arise from this work including the difficulties inherent in how to measure effectiveness and success.

There has been some research support for the view that conscientiousness (as a personality construct) plays a significant part in the achievement of job performance (Barrick and Mount, 1991). Robertson *et al.* (2000) explored this further and found no statistically significant relationship between conscientiousness and current job performance or promotability. They do, however, suggest that conscientiousness does have some links with specific aspects of job performance such as the need for an individual who is organized, and quality driven. In terms of promotability, the significant factors appeared to be articulate, decisive, flexible,

Defining the task	Evaluating
Planning	Motivating
Briefing	Organizing
Controlling	Setting an example

TABLE 15.4 Adair's eight functional principles of leadership

innovative, motivated and persuasive, but these same factors were negatively correlated with conscientiousness. The authors suggest the need for a broader view of both personality and what determines job performance. Management in Action 15.5 considers another aspect of this, the effects of having an uncaring manager within the organization.

Stop | Consider   *Consider the views expressed in MiA 15.5 and seek to reconcile these in terms of the view of management suggested by both Fayol and Taylor.*

Critical incident management

One aspect of management that is just beginning to develop as a result of a number of very high-profile events is that of *crisis management*. Everyone faces the occasional crisis in their lives from time to time. For example, a car tyre bursting while travelling along a motorway at high speed, a thief breaking into your house and stealing all your possessions, being sacked from your job without any warnings represent just some of the difficulties that can erupt and create problems. However, there are some jobs in which the exposure to crisis forms an integral aspect of what might be expected every, or at least most days. For example, members of the police, fire and ambulance services are frequently called upon to deal at very short notice with a crisis of some description. A police officer might seek to arrest a thief, only to be faced with a person holding a gun and threatening to kill a hostage. A fire officer may attend a house fire only to be told that people are trapped inside the building. An ambulance crew may attend the scene of a horrific traffic accident and have to deal with terribly mutilated bodies.

These are not the only examples of jobs in which crises can arise. For example, an airline pilot must be prepared for engine failure or other disaster and know how to cope. The senior manager of an oil refinery must have anticipated (and prepared for) a wide range of possible disasters so that if one happens everyone on site knows what to do. This last example indicates the key theme of this section, that of the management role in preparing for and leading the efforts should a critical incident arise. There is very little literature available on this subject and in terms of the management of critical incidents, Flin (1996) is the first to bring a number of relevant themes together.

The Home Office (1994), the government department in the UK which is responsible for emergency services, established a three-level incident command structure which has generally been adopted by the relevant services. The three levels within the incident command and control structure are included as Table 15.5.

In many emergency situations it would be the operational level of command who would arrive on the scene first and therefore take initial responsibility. Flin (1996. p 13), quoting Home Office manuals, suggests that the exercise of effective control needs the incident commander to work through the following list of requirements:

✦   Prepare.

✦   Assess.

✦   Plan.

✦   Resources.

✦   Implement.

MANAGEMENT IN ACTION 15.5

Same indifference

The Corporate Advisory Board of Washington DC estimates that the cost of replacing a technical expert in IT, project management or marketing as 1.75 times the individual's salary. Not a cheap process! Even front-line service staff can cost up to 50% of annual salary to replace and train. With some call centres reporting staff turnover in excess of 50% per year, some organizations are spending vast sums of money on replacing staff. Not surprisingly, under such circumstances, it makes sense to find out what makes staff stay put and to try to ensure that they do so.

There are many reasons why staff leave organizations. Better opportunities can present themselves, relocation of either the individual or partner, downsizing, re-engineering and merger activity represent just some of them. Among these many reasons some originate from within organizations themselves and add to any insecurity felt by people, encouraging them to take personal responsibility for their careers. However, one significant reason for people leaving an organization is poor management. Buckingham suggests that people do not leave organizations, they leave particular managers. He goes on to report research in one large retail company showing that one in six employees rated their supervisor or manager as the most disliked aspect of the job, a not uncommon result in large organizations.

Buckingham reports the results of research carried out by the Gallup Organization, based on 200,000 employees across 12 industries. This demonstrated that those organizations that demonstrated (through employee survey) high scores on four factors all had higher productivity, profit and customer satisfaction levels and lower staff turnover. The four factors on which managers scored highly in these 'successful' organizations were:

✦ Having a manager who shows care, interest and concern for each individual.

✦ That each employee knows what is expected of them.

✦ That each employee has a role that fits their abilities.

✦ That each employee regularly receives positive feedback and recognition for work well done.

Buckingham indicates that expectation in organizations is usually shaped by the emphasis on process conformity rather than on the existence of clearly defined objective results for employees to achieve. Also that in recruitment and career planning, emphasis is placed on employee skill and experience, not on natural talent and personal qualities. In addition, recognition and reward for individual employees is usually left to individual managers, leading to inconsistency in the treatment of subordinates. In a recent study it was found that a statistically significant correlation between management talent and level of employee engagement with the work of the organization existed. Managers with the highest levels of talent all scored highly on the answer to the question from their subordinates: 'At work I have the opportunity to do what I do best every day?' This seems to suggest that management should be viewed as the facilitation of employee contribution, not in terms of command and control.

Adapted from: Buckingham, G (2000) Same indifference, *People Management*, 17 February, pp 44–6.

+ Control.
+ Evaluate.

Similar responsibilities exist within commercial organizations, However, there has been criticism by the Heath and Safety Executive and others of the unclear planning and organization for managing critical incidents following rail and other major accidents. One of the difficulties faced by managers of commercial organizations is that the concept of *command*, particularly in an emergency situation, is very different from the practice of *management* (Larken, 1992, p 31):

> But when time is at a premium and when danger immediately threatens, command has to encompass a whole range of extra skills, mostly concerned with the rapid assessment of people who have changed under pressure and of things which have failed to operate or activate as they might have been expected. Management is predominantly objective and consultative. …An important subsidiary conclusion is that the application of conventional management techniques can ironically be quite dangerous in an emergency. (quoted in Flin, 1996, pp 20–1)

Flin (p 42) goes on to suggest that the necessary personality charcteristics for an incident commander are:

+ Willingness to accept leadership role.
+ Emotional stability.
+ Stress resistance.

Command	Level	Management function
Bronze	Operational	This corresponds to the normal operational response provided by the emergency services where the management is of routine tasks. The initial response to most incidents is at this level. In a major incident the bronze commanders are likely to be in charge of the front-line teams
Silver	Tactical	Their command objective is to determine priority in allocating resources, to plan and co-ordinate actions. At a major incident the silver commander is likely to be the incident commander and located at the incident control post
Gold	Strategic	Their purpose is to formulate the overall policy for the incident response, ensuring that priorities for demands from the tactical commanders are met. They are responsible for government and media liaison. The gold commanders are chief or senior officers, who are likely to be located at a headquarters incident room rather than at the scene. They do not take tactical decisions

TABLE 15.5 Incident command and control structure (*source*: Home Office (1994) *Dealing with Disaster*, 2nd edn, HMSO, London, Crown copyright reproduced with the permission of the Controller of Her Majesty's Stationery Office)

- ✦ Decisiveness.
- ✦ Controlled risk taking.
- ✦ Self-confidence.
- ✦ Self-awareness.

She also identifies (p 44) the skills profile required of an incident commander:

- ✦ Leadership ability.
- ✦ Communication skills (especially briefing and listening).
- ✦ Delegating.
- ✦ Team management.
- ✦ Decision making under pressure.
- ✦ Situation awareness.
- ✦ Planning and implementing actions.
- ✦ Calm and able to manage stress in self and others.
- ✦ Preplanning for possible emergencies.

Management in Action 15.6 considers another aspect of critical activity within management, that of dealing with the need for care when processing dangerous material on a regular basis.

Stop | Consider

The view of the personnel director in MiA 15.6 suggests that the process workers were reponsible for the scandal for 'not doing what was expected of them'.

To what extent can management delegate accountability and responsibility in any organization, not just in those with critical processes? Is it possible to delegate responsibility but not accountability? Can managers ever abdicate from their accountability for what happens in organizations?

If there are boundaries around the delegation of responsibility and accountability, can employees ever become fully engaged with the work of their organization?

Management, power and delegation

Another approach to understanding the nature of management is through an examination of the skills and abilities required to undertake the task. Hellriegel *et al.* (1989, pp 267–71) describe management as a set of activities based on the following characteristics, one of which is power:

- ✦ Relationships. The quality of the relationship between the manager and subordinates is a major determinant of the ability of the manager to function effectively.
- ✦ Skills. The skills of self-understanding, visioning, effective communication and empowerment are necessary to achieve effectiveness in group activity.
- ✦ Power. (originally based on French and Raven, 1958) Power is what allows the manager

MANAGEMENT IN ACTION 15.6

Management blasted at nuclear plant

Following a spate of scares and scandals at the Sellafield nuclear power plant (which employs 10,000 people) the government safety watchdog claimed that a lack of management skills such as communication, motivation and supervision were responsible. The personnel director admitted that there had 'probably not been enough investment in training' but blamed the process workers for not doing what was expected of them. The scandals at the plant caused a number of orders to be lost, very large compensation payments to be made, the return of nuclear material from Japan and the resignation of the chief executive.

The latest scandal came to light when it was found that process workers had falsified records involving the measurement of batches of fuel pellets. The report of the Nuclear Installations Inspectorate (NII) identified that the nature of the job, lack of supervision and poor training had contributed in no small measure to the subsequent procedural failures. The inspectors said that the workers' actions were 'not at all surprising' given the 'tedious' nature of the tasks involved. The local trade union representative, John Kane, describes middle managers in terms of a 'treacle layer who, although highly qualified in certain tasks, have very few people management skills.'

The task at the centre of the latest problem required process workers to measure the dimensions of fuel pellets hundreds of centimetre long by using the following procedure:

✦ Put their hands into protective gloves set in a glass case containing the fuel pellets.

✦ Pick up a single fuel pellet using a pair of tweezers already in the glass case.

✦ Present the individual fuel pellet at three different angles to a laser measuring device inside the glass compartment.

✦ The individual process worker carrying out this range of tasks called out the three laser readings to another process worker.

✦ The second process worker entered those figures onto a computer spreadsheet.

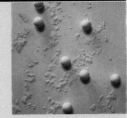

This sequence of tasks was repeated at regular intervals as dictated by the quality-control procedures.

The process workers regarded the recording of these data as boring and meaningless and some simply copied previous records into the computer spreadsheet to avoid having to do the job. There was apparently little or no supervision of the checking procedure and the process workers were not trained in understanding the significance of the task. The NII inspectors said that while the result of the failure correctly to measure was not a danger in itself, it represented an approach to work and management that could lead to serious problems in the future.

The NII inspectors blamed a wide range of management situations for the problems, including reductions in staff numbers to prepare the company for partial privatization, safety managers were overworked and safety arrangements unclear, safety training was poor and the organizational structure was confusing. The board of directors was not based on the site and this resulted in a mixture of business and operational managers running aspects of it. Accountability was therefore widely distributed and generally confused throughout the site. It was recommended that there should be someone placed in overall charge of the location.

Fundamental change was demanded and management training was said to be underway. Three process workers were dismissed as a result of their part in the failure to undertake the quality checks as required. The design of process work was also being reviewed as part of the exercise.

Adapted from: Cooper, C (2000) Management blasted at nuclear plant, *People Management*, 16 March, pp 16–7.

to carry out the function. In the case of management situations these sources of power include:

✦ Legitimate. Subordinates accept that the manager has the right to be obeyed.

✦ Reward. The manager controls access and allocation of rewards valued by the subordinates.

✦ Coercive. The manager controls punishment including disciplinary action, withholding pay or demotion.

✦ Referent. The personal characteristics of the manager produce in subordinates the desire to follow directions.

✦ Expert. Subordinates believe that the manager has expertise over and above the others in the team.

Each of these sources of power has a number of qualities. First, power in general does not exist as an absolute entity. With the exception of coercive power it is the gift of the subordinate to accept the power sought by the manager. For example, if the subordinate does not believe that the manager can deliver desired rewards then that form of power will not function effectively. Even in the case of coercive power the manager does not usually have the power to use force and may not have the freedom to sack the employee without recourse to formal procedures and appeals. Second, effective managers use most of the sources of power indicated, but the particular one applied at any time would depend on the prevailing circumstances.

Pfeffer (1992) explores a wide range of aspects of the use of power and influence within organizations. In his analysis he suggests that managing with power involves the following:

✦ Recognizing different interests. Inevitably, there are a range of *stakeholders* within any organization and each will have different interests, perspectives and objectives in relation to the business and how things should be done. It is necessary to understand the *political landscape* involving the various coalitions and interest groups in order to understand which might be supportive and which hostile.

✦ Identify the views of the various stakeholder individuals and groups. This is not just about understanding their views but why they hold them. This is particularly important for those groups and individuals that we do not like personally, as they are the most difficult to take seriously as a threat.

✦ Understand the need for power to achieve results. Power is needed to overcome opposition and it is necessary to understand where it comes from and how to develop greater levels of power held.

✦ Understand the strategies and tactics through which power is developed. Also understand issues such as timing, the use of structure, commitment and interpersonal influence.

✦ Being prepared to use power. It is of no value to understand power if the manager is not prepared (or able) to use it to achieve the desired end result.

The discussion so far presents a very rational and practical view of power in relation to management activtiy. However, it is one that might be suggested to imply that power is something that is neutral or which can only exist if all parties agree to it. For example, the French and Raven conception of it implies that employees accept or reject particular forms of power 'against' them. While there may be some truth in this view, life is never that simple. Employees need the income that jobs (and therefore managers) provide and so the balance of power immediately shifts. Townley (1994) explores the work of Michael Foucault in relation to the practice of human resource management and in doing so examines the concept of power within organizations. One of the conclusions reached in Townley's analysis is that: 'Panopticism is an exercise of power based on analysis and distribution. It operates through hierarchy, surveillance, observation and writing. In this sense power is not located in a person but in practices' (p 139).

Panopticism originates from the design of prisons with a central control tower, from which the guards can observe and control the prisoners in the individual cell blocks radiating from the central hub. A number of people (including Foucault) have likened this design to that of an organization. This incorporates management's attempts to exercise control over the workforce through a wide range of structural, procedural and observational devices. It could be argued that such approaches are an attempt to move the ability to exercise of power away from acquiescence by employees in the direction of the 'right of managers to manage'.

Many of the *participatory* and *involvement*-based managemant practices found in organizations today can be viewed through this same lens. Perhaps they function at the level of socializing employees into the ways of thinking preferred by managers? Getting employees involved or engaged in the business encourages workers to see themselves as partners rather than simply employees. As partners they might be expected to adopt patterns of thinking and behaving more like those of managers. By adopting this *frame of reference*, employees reduce the need for managers to exercise power as employees automatically self-regulate by engaging in approved behaviour patterns.

One of the difficult practical problems faced by managers is how much responsibiity they should retain and how much they should *delegate* to subordinates. This 'problem', or more accurately dilemma, also relates to the issue of power. Many managers feel that in delegating some of their responsibilities they are actually giving away some of their power. In the bureaucratic organizational design great emphasis is placed on the heirarchy and decision making being carried out at the appropriate level. Exceptions to the standard or normal sphere of responsibility are required to be 'pushed up' the heirarcy for resolution. Inevitably, this can lead to managers becoming overloaded with relatively minor issues and, therefore, not having the time to exercise managerial reponsibility. One natural response to this is to increase the number and levels of management, which runs counter to the current trends in *downsizing* and *delayering*. These initiatives inevitably reduce the number of levels within an organization because they are grounded in the notion that real effectiveness in operational activity comes from pushing decision making, responsibility and accountability down to the lowest levels possible, that is, *delegation*. It is also argued that giving workers more responsibility increases the quality of the work experience for the individual and, as they are the ones who deal directly with customers, enhance the level of customer service.

Delayering and downsizing are both initiatives that can fall within the approach called *business process re-engineering* described by Hammer and Champy (1995). Essentially, the authors claim (p 53) that the 'old system' of organizing work was based on the assumptions that the workers did not have the time, inclination to monitor and control work, neither did they have the skills and knowledge to be able to take decisions, therefore managers and many of the specialist functions developed as a response to this. Hammer and Champy argue that these assumptions are now invalid and, moreover, the traditional response creates inefficiency, delay, additional cost and lower levels of customer service. Hence, they argue the need fundamentally to re-engineer based on process, not function and as a result (among other things) to compress the vertical dimension of organizations, achieved through delegation.

However, not everyone agrees with this view. For example, McCabe and Knights (2000) argue that Hammer and Champy fail to recognize:

> How power relations in contemporary organizations are bound up with managerial identity. More importantly it [BPR] ignores the way in which power relations are intrinsic to capitalist organizations: heirarchy has not just arisen by accident, it has purpose, being essential to management's control over labour. (p 647)

McCabe and Knights go on to argue that in their view the hierarchy will continue to remain intact because management will be unable to absolve themselves from control through delegation and empowerment. This is because power is relational and inherently part of a capitalist organizational life. They also make the point that in delegating authority and responsibility, managers are not seeking to give away actual control and power. They are simply seeking to ensure that the functioning of the organization more effectively meets customer needs and hence the objectives of management. This, they argue is simply another form of control.

From this perspective, delegation and empowerment suggest a 'neat trick' perpetrated by senior management on the workers. Delegation under this model seeks to integrate workers within the *frame of reference* determined by managers, thereby allowing middle and junior managers (and the associated cost) to be eliminated from the organization through delayering, downsizing or re-engineering through the *socialization* of employees into the 'new paradigms' maintaining the same overall balance of power and control, while claiming that the quality of work has been improved as well as the level of customer service. It is control achieved through more acceptable social means than the exercise of direct power; covert rather than overt means. Of course, reduced cost and improved profit levels are also likely byproducts of these initiatives and so the investors are also likely to be satisfied with the outcome.

Meetings and humour in management

Meetings are an inevitable aspect of management. The need to involve other people in decision making as well as persuading them to co-operate in specific courses of action are just two of the reasons for their existence. Other reasons for holding meetings include:

✦ Habit. Holding the regular Monday production meeting, simply because it has always been held, rather than for a specific purpose.

✦ Political. For example, it is possible for managers to convene a meeting simply to be able to say at some future time that everyone was (or had the opportunity to be) involved in (or comment on) a particular project or decision.

✦ Courage and risk aversion. Managers can lack the courage to take a particular decision on their own. This can be a strategy adopted if the decision is risky in business, political or personal terms as it allows the manager to say (if things go wrong) that it was the meeting that decided to take a particular decision. This approach allows the *diffusion of responsibility* to be used as a defence if necessary. This might be expected to occur more frequently in organizations in which a *blame culture* existed. A *blame culture* describes an organization in which every error (or something not going exactly to the wishes of senior people) must be the fault of an individual or group. Usually the 'blamed' individual or group must be made to 'pay' for their faults as an example to others and to ensure compliance in the future. Not surprisingly, such cultures encourage a 'cover your ass at all costs' approach to work at all levels.

Meetings can therefore be held for rational business-oriented purposes, routine purposes and even defensive or offensive reasons. Just because a meeting is called does not imply that the reason for it is automatically apparent. There may be an agenda which is quite clear, although it is not uncommon to find games being played in terms of what can be included and when etc. Such events can provide a clear indicator of a *hidden agenda* at work. This term implies that someone is seeking to manipulate a meeting for some purpose that they do not wish to reveal. However, the existence of a *hidden agenda* for a meeting can frequently only be guessed at and may only be apparent once the meeting is underway or from comments made (or events that occur) afterwards. The reasons for a *hidden agenda* freuently fall into the political or courage headings indicated earlier.

In addition to formal meetings that have been the focus of the discussion so far, there are vast numbers of informal discussions that take place in corridors and over coffee that serve much the same purpose as formal meetings. They can create alliances, sound out opinion and prepare the arguments for a formal meeting. In many large organizations, particularly the public sector, it is common to hold pre-meetings. These are relatively informal meetings held prior to a formal meeting which in practice allow all the arguments to take place away from the formal setting and so allow the formal meeting simply to ratify the decisions already made. Mackenzie (1972) suggests that many middle managers spend up to 80% of their time in meetings and that approximately 50% of that time may be wasted (p 98).

Humour is a topic that is not formally part of organizational functioning and has therefore been regarded as something incidental to management. It is suggested that organizations are places of rationality and that humour has no place in them. Levity could be a signal that business is not being taken seriously, that there is a lack of respect for the products or senior managers. Humour is generally considered a trivializing process. However, that is not the only purpose of humour. Consider for example the use of satire as a means of making political points; such insights are frequently far from trivial.

Barsoux (1993) in a book devoted to a consideration of the links between humour, management and culture, suggests that humour in the workplace, 'is rarely neutral, trivial or random. It is deployed for the achievement of quite specific purposes to do with self-preservation, getting things done or getting one's way' (p vii). Barsoux identifies the three main purposes of humour as being:

✦ Sword. The *action* aspect of humour. From this perspective it can persuade individuals to particular points of view. It can allow individuals to say those things which otherwise could not be said without causing offence and damage to relationships within the organizational setting.

✦ Shield. The *defensive* aspect of humour. It can be used to make criticism more acceptable (by making a joke out of it) and to enable individuals and groups to cope more easily with failure.

✦   Values. This aspect provides the basis for *conditioning* individuals into a particular role and contributes to the *reinforcement* of organizational values. The use of practical jokes and the use of 'in-jokes' – only understandable to the in-group – are the means by which groups can be formed and bonded into cohesive units.

In his book based on a participative research project, Watson (1994) describes a number of aspects of humour during his interviews and observations of managers. In addition to the functions of humour outlined, he describes the role of humour in relation to communication and control. He describes the facilitation of communication provided through a touch of humour in the conversation: 'They [the listener] get something back for giving the speaker their attention' (p 187).

Management: an applied perspective

The variables associated with the practice of management that have been discussed in this chapter include:

✦   The manager. There are a number of personal variables that influence the approach to management. They include the personality characteristics of the individual together with the training and experience that they have undergone during their lives and careers. Managers' perceptions about the situation and their subordinates (frequently based on past expereince) also influence how they respond to situations. It should be remembered that managers are also subordinates, with the exception of those that own their organizations. As such they do not have complete freedom to practice management as they might wish to do. They are constrained by the presence of other and more senior managers as well as company culture and policy. Even the board of directors has to present itself to its shareholders for evaluation and re-election at regular intervals.

✦   The managed. The factors relevant to this aspect of management are generally mirror images of the factors indicated earlier. For example, the personality factors of the subordinates will to some extent predispose them to prefer to be managed in particular ways. Inevitably over time there is a degree of *fit* that emerges between individual and job/organization. Individuals that do not fit into a particular situation either because they think or behave differently tend to leave or are pushed out of the group. However, managers can only manage by consent. A manager who seeks to operate in ways totally unacceptable to their subordinates will be unlikely to achieve their objectives and may even find themselves being replaced.

✦   The context. The industry and organization itself will carry some degree of influence on the nature of management practised within it. For example, a context which has been highly confrontational in the past in terms of relationships between managers and workers is unlikely to change quickly to one that could support a participative approach.

✦   The situation. The objectives being sought are a feature of the management process. A military leader seeking to win a battle is faced with a different situation to the manager seeking to process thousands of customer accounts. Consequently there will be differences in the way management would be exercised because of these situations. However, situations can change very quickly, requiring changes to the way in which management operates. A competitor may introduce a new product innovation, a price war may break out and competition from cheap labour economies are an ever present threat in every country. These situations require what existed to be changed in order for the organization to be able to survive, this in turn requires managers to be proactive in 'managing' the organization.

✦   The task. The work of professional or technical specialists requires different approaches to management than work in a factory. The name *professional* implies a level of capability and an approach to work that implies that management is less to do with the content of the work than employee development and the monitoring of performance. Such professional employees frequently resent (and resist) direct supervision and control. The importance of the task as well as the technology involved are also variables that could be expected to impact on the practice of management activities. Importance in this context refers to significance for the organization or individuals within it. The more significant the task for the organization, the more likley it is that it will be closley managed.

Figure 15.8 reflects the linkages between these main variables.

Management is still a problematic concept to understand and define. For example, which of the variables identified in Figure 15.8 are the most important and which the least?

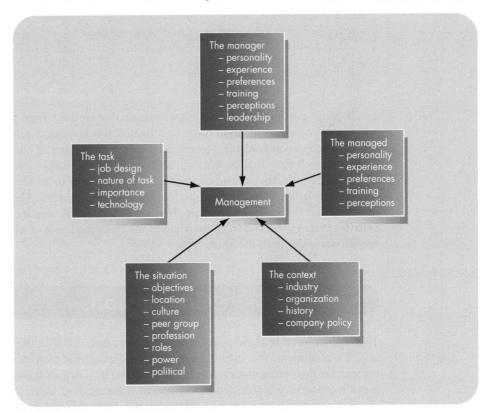

FIGURE 15.8   The factors influencing management.

How do the variables interact and how do they influence the approach adopted by particular individuals in particualr situations? Would the variation in one variable in Figure 15.8 automatically produce a difference in the way that management is practised? If so, to what degree? Another interesting question, ignored in this chapter, reflected the degree of similarity (or dissimilarity) between the concepts of management as defined in this chapter and leadership. This question will be reviewed in the next chapter.

To the practising manager these issues are very real as they attempt to practice the art and science of management in real time and in real organizations. Senior managers have a responsibility to ensure that their organizations are effectively managed, but before they can make provision for that they need to understand the processes involved. That need created part of the intuitive attraction for initiatives such as business process re-engineering. Senior managers also need to be able to make provision for the selection and development of more junior managers. However, if management reflects a situation-specific set of competencies, then a completely different set of criteria apply to the selection, training and careers of managers in every situation. If true, this would seem to fly in the face of much experience common to many management jobs, decision making, working with groups for example, and present insurmountable training problems.

Management in Action 15.7 considers aspects of the ways in which managers learn how to become a manager.

Stop	Consider

To what extent does the view of how managers learn contained in MiA 15.7 demonstrate that it is necessary to have both formal training in management as well as mentored support during the early years of a career in management?

Is it possible to function effectively as a manager without formal training? Why or why not?

It is not possible to offer definitive models that would ensure that the best match between manager and situation could be provided. It is reasonably safe to assume that the degree of adaptation available through the inherent capabilities of human beings provides a basis for believing that people can learn many of the skills associated with being a manager. Also, that they can adapt their behaviour patterns to achieve at least a workable compromise between anarchy and perfection in specific contexts. The difficulty remains, however, that individuals learn inappropriate habits or become locked into particular behaviour repertoires and so fail to adapt to the changing needs of what is required to be an effective manager in the future.

Conclusions

This chapter has considered many of the variables associated with the subject of the practice of management. The chapter began by considering what management actually is and some of the theoretical models developed to explain its function. It also considered what it is that managers actually do and the contextual influences such as the type and size of organization, the culture and international issues that inevitably impact on how management goes about its tasks. The roles that managers adopt while performing their duties was also

MANAGEMENT IN ACTION 15.7

Who taught you to do what you do?

Every manager must learn how to carry out the tasks associated with the job. But how? Ballin and Vincent carried out some research in the steel industry that involved 19 separate businesses and a sample of 245 managers to seek answers to this question. Their research involved a three-stage process. The first was a questionnaire about the experience of the managers in relation to training. The second was a structured 45-minute interview about the experiences of managers in relation to the timing and relevance of training received. The third was another interview process aimed at identifying future training needs and the attitude of managers to training in general.

The results emphasize the role of training in the development of managers rather than specifically who they learn from. It indicated that the training received by most managers was well timed but that learning about people management should come before experiencing it for the first time. There was a general feeling of a lack of structure to the training and development received by managers and that some of the training was too general in content. Equally, managers do not generally place much effort into self-development, although they do have some influence over what training they receive. They tend to emphasize formal training courses rather than experiential training for both themselves and subordinates.

Pearn, Honey and Clutterbuck used 250 delegates attending their presentation at the Institute of Personnel and Development annual conference to address the issue of how managers learn. Among the findings of their survey were:

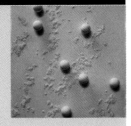

♦ Peers within the organization were the most popular choice of 'who it was easy to learn from'. This was followed by the line boss and a mentor. Off-line mentors, by way of contrast, were seen as having the most potential for managers to learn from.

♦ In terms of the learning cycle, most respondents found that 'experiencing' was the easiest part of learning with the 'concluding' aspect being the most difficult.

♦ Making mistakes represented an important learning opportunity, but the language of talking about mistakes was unpleasant and difficult. It was generally thought that from an organizational perspective the two biggest causes of mistakes were 'blinkered thinking' and 'defining goals'. From an individual perspective the most likely causes of mistakes were 'pressure to act' and 'generalization' (working on partial, untested information and assumption).

Adapted from: Ballin, M and Vincent, R (1995) Who taught you to do what you do?, *People Management*, 30 November, pp 32–3; and Pearn, M, Honey, P and Clutterbuck, D (1995) Learning from the good, the bad – and the ugly mistakes, *People Management*, 30 November, p 43.

considered. Discrimination and gender issues were introduced into the discussion as a key feature of managerial responsibility. Critical incident management was discussed as it forms part of the major responsibilities of some management positions. Power in relation to management was discussed next and shown to be a major aspect of what management is about and how it can achieve its objectives. The chapter ended with a brief consideration of humour in management and the function of meetings which account for much management time.

Discussion questions

1. Define the following key terms used in this chapter:

   Management

   Discrimination

   MCI competency roles

   Fayol's management process

   Taylor's functional foremanship

   Organization

   Fayol's 14 principles of management

   Mintzberg's role model

   Professionalization of management

   Role ambiguity

   Role set

   Stakeholder

2. What is management?

3. Compare and contrast the views on the management process as outlined by Fayol and the four themes on what management is about described by Reed.

4. 'Successful management is about acquiring power and using it to ensure that you achieve your objectives.' Based on the material introduced in this chapter to what extent could this viewpoint be justified?

5. 'Meetings are a complete waste of everyone's time; they are a major source of inefficiency in any organization.' Discuss this statement and in doing so review the possible benefits to be achieved through meetings. How could meetings be made more meaningful to the participants and organizations?

6. To what extent might the context play a more significant part in determining what it is that managers do than the wishes of the managers themselves?

7. Does humour have any part to play in management? Justify your answer.

8. 'True equality can never occur in organizations until managers are forced to recruit and promote people not like themselves.' Discuss this statement.

9. To what extent can role theory contribute to an understanding of what management is about?

10. Discuss what it is that managers spend their time doing.

Research activities

1. Arrange to interview about six different managers from a range of organizations and job functions. Talk to them about their own approach to management. Identify what they actually do in their jobs. Analyze the information collected and see if you can detect any differences in activity or purpose between the different types and levels of management job. Also see if the material collected reflects a view of management as presented by any of the theorists and models presented in this chapter. Seek to explain why some models might be represented in your research and others not.

2. As an individual see if you can arrange to shadow a manager for a couple of days. This

could be from any type of organization and could be arranged through a family member, friend of the family, or even by observing a university/college manager. Observe what they spend their time doing and how they operate. During and after the shadowing activity make a record of what happened so that you can compare notes with fellow students. In discussing your observations with fellow students see if you can interpret your notes in the light of material presented in this chapter. If that is not possible, see if you can explain why that might be so.

3. Conduct a library search on the subject of management. From that research, what issues do you think are relevant to understanding management that have (or have not) been introduced in this chapter and why might that be so?

Key reading

From Clark, H, Chandler, J and Barry, J (1994) *Organization and Identities: Text and Readings in Organizational Behaviour*, International Thomson Business Press, London:

♦ Kanter, RM: Men and women of the corporation, p 152. Considers the nature of organizations and the impact on the people that work in them.

♦ Nichols, T and Beynon, H: The labour of superintendence: managers, p 192. This considers the reality of management in an organization.

♦ Roethlisberger, FJ and Dickson, R: Group restriction of output, p 247. Although emphasizing the significance of groups, it also reviews the relationship between managers and subordinates.

♦ Coch, L and French, JRP: Overcoming resistance to change using group methods, p 260. Considers a number of aspects of change management, including the strategies adopted by managers.

♦ Fiedler, FE: Leadership: a contingency model, p 272. Part of the original work from this particular writer on the first of the contingency models.

♦ Needham, P: The 'autonomous' work group, p 310. Discusses the nature and role of management within this form of work organization.

Further reading

Berkeley Thomas, A (1993) *Controversies in Management*, Routledge, London. This text concentrates on attempting to understand the complexities associated with the study of management.

Heller, R (1985) *The Naked Manager: Games Executives Play*, McGraw-Hill, New York. The behaviours that managers adopt and the political and business reasons that motivate it are the focus of attention.

Luecke, R (1994) *Scuttle Your Ships Before Advancing and Other Lessons from History on Leadership and Change for Today's Managers*, Oxford University Press, New York. This book takes a look back into history at a number of major events involving management, leadership and change. It then attempts to draw lessons from those episodes that can be of value to managers of today.

Saeed, SM (1986) *Managerial Challenges in the Third World*, Prager, New York. This book is not widely available, but might be in an academic library. It considers from a practical point of view what managing in the third world involves, including the differences in operating conditions, ethical value systems and standards of education among the workforce. It presents an interesting comparison with much of the western-developed approaches to management, based on particular contextual conditions, but which are assumed to have universal applicability.

Stewart, R and Barsoux, J-L (1994) *The Diversity of Management: Twelve Managers Talking*, Macmillan, Basingstoke. This book is based around interviews with practising managers. Drawn from a wide range of middle- and senior-level jobs in diverse industries the interviewees provide an introspective account of the nature of their work.

Turner, RV (1988) *Men Raised from the Dust: Administrative Service and Upward Mobility in Angevin England*, University of Pennsylvania Press, Philadelphia. This is an interesting review of the lives and work of six historical figures from the late twelfth and early thirteenth century-England. At that time the life of the king was becoming much more complex and there was a need for a new breed of able administrators who could run the burgeoning government machine. The people who rose to these positions were often not from traditional noble families, a situation that created resentment and problems. However, such administrators were able to acquire much power and manipulate the situation to their own advantage, gaining land, wealth and social standing. In that sense this historical review has much in common with the practice of management today and is worth exploring.

References

Adair, J (1983) *Effective Leadership: A Self-development Manual*, Gower, Aldershot.

Adler, NJ (1991) *International Dimensions of Organizational Behaviour*, 2nd edn, Wadsworth, Belmont, CA.

Ashworth, A (2000) Hoist on their own cash dispensers, *The Times, Weekend Money*, 8 July, p 53.

Barrick, MR and Mount, MK (1991) The big five personality dimensions and job performance: a meta-analysis, *Personnel Psychology*, **44**, 1–26.

Barsoux, J-L (1993) *Funny Business: Humour, Management and Business Culture*, Cassell, London.

Child, J (1969) *British Management Thought*, Allen & Unwin, London.

Cook, T and Emler, N (1999) Bottom-up versus top-down evaluations of candidates' managerial potential: an experimental study, *Journal of Occupational and Organizational Psychology*, **72**, 4, December, 423–39.

Dahrendorf, R (1959) *Class and Class Conflict in Industrial Society*, Routledge & Kegan Paul, London.

Farnham, D and Horton, S (eds) (1996) *Managing the New Public Services*, 2nd edn, Macmillan, London.

Fayol, H (1916) *General and Industrial Administration*, trans by C Storrs, Sir Isaac Pitman, London.

Fenby, J (2000) Make that foreign posting your ticket to the boardroom, *Management Today*, July, pp 48–53.

Fitzsimmons, JA and Fitzsimmons, MJ (1994) *Service Management for Competitive Advantage*, McGraw-Hill, New York.

Flin, R (1996) *Sitting in the Hot Seat: Leaders and Teams for Critical Incident Management*, Wiley, Chichester.

Fores, M and Glover, I (1976) The real work of executives, *Management Today*, September.

French, J and Raven, B (1958) The Bases of Social Power. In Cartwright, D (ed.) *Studies in Social Power*, Institute for Social Research, Ann Arbor, Michigan.

Gardiner, M and Tiggemann, M (1999) Gender differences in leadership style, job stress and mental health in male- and female-dominated industries, *Journal of Occupational and Organizational Psychology*, **72**, 301–15.

Hammer, M and Champy, J (1995) *Reengineering the Corporation: A Manifesto for Business Revolution*, Nicholas Brealey, London.

Handy, C (1993) *Understanding Organizations*, 4th edn, Penguin, Harmondsworth.

Haney, C, Banks, C and Zimbardo, P (1973) A study of prisoners and guards in a simulated prison, *Naval Research Reviews*, Office of Naval Research, Department of the Navy, Washington, September, pp 1–17.

Harrison, R. (1994) *Employee Development*, IPD, London.

Hart, SL and Quinn, RE (1993) Roles executives play: CEOs, behavioural complexity, and firm performance, *Human Relations*, May, 543–75.

Hellriegel, D, Slocum, JW and Woodman, RW (1989) *Organizational Behaviour*, 5th edn, West Publishing, St Paul, MN.

HMSO (1997) April. *What Are Management Standards? An Introduction*, HMSO, London.

Holl, P (1977) Control type and the market for corporate control in large US corporations, *Journal of Industrial Economics*, **25**, 259–73.

Home Office (1994) *Dealing With Disaster*, 2nd edn, HMSO, London.

Larken, J (1992) The Command Requirement and OIM Qualification. In *Collected Papers of the First Offshore Installation Management Conference: Emergency Command Responsibilities*, Robert Gordon University.

Luthans, F (1995) *Organizational Behaviour*, 7th edn, McGraw-Hill, New York.

Lynch, R (1997) *Corporate Strategy*, Pitman Publishing, London.

Mackenzie, RA (1972) *The Time Trap: How to Get More Done in Less Time*, McGraw-Hill, New York.

McCabe, D and Knights, D (2000) Such Stuff as Dreams are Made on: BPR Up Against the Wall of Functionalism, Heirarchy and Specializism. In Knights, D and Willmott, H (eds) *The Reengineering Revolution: Critical Studies of Corporate Change*, Sage, London.

Mintzberg, H (1973) *The Nature of Managerial Work*, Harper & Row, New York.

Montgomery, D (1979) The past and future of workers' control, *Radical America*, **13**, 6.

Moore, J (2000) Mutual distrust, *The Times, Weekend Money*, 1 July, p 54.

Nadworny, M (1955) *Scientific Management and the Unions*, Harvard University Press, Cambridge, MA.

Oh, TK (1976) Theory y in the People's Republic of China, *California Management Review*, **19**, 77–84.

Pedler, M, Burgoyne, J and Boydell, T (1994) *A Manager's Guide to Self-Development*, 3rd edn, McGraw-Hill, Maidenhead.

Pfeffer, J (1992) *Managing with Power: Politics and Influence in Organizations*. Harvard Business School Press, Boston.

Pocket Oxford Dictionary (1969) Compiled by Fowler, FG and Fowler, HW, 5th edn. Oxford University Press, London.

Reed, M (1989) *The Sociology of Management*, Harvester Wheatsheaf, Hemel Hempstead.

Robertson, IT, Baron, H, Gibbons, P, MacIver, R and Nyfield, G (2000) Conscientiousness and managerial performance, *Journal of Occupational and Organizational Psychology*, **73**, 171–80.

Stewart, R. (1985) *The Reality of Management*, 2nd edn, Pan Books, London.

Taylor, F W (1947) *Scientific Management*, Harper & Row, New York.

Thomas, P J (1987) Appraising the Performance of Women: Gender and the Naval Officer. In Gutek, BA and Larwood, L (eds) *Women's Career Development*, Sage, London.

Townley, B (1994) *Reframing Human Resource Management: Power, Ethics and the Subject at Work*, Sage, London.

Vinnicombe, S and Harris, H (2000) A gender hidden, *People Management*, 6 January, pp 28–9.

Watson, TJ (1994) *In Search of Management: Culture, Chaos and Control in Managerial Work*, Routledge, London.

Weiman, C (1977) A study of occupational stressors and the incidence of disease/risk, *Journal of Occupational Medicine*, February, pp 119–22.

Willmott, H (1984) Images and ideals of managerial work, *Journal of Management Studies*, **21**, 3, 349–68.

Wilson, F (1995) *Organizational Behaviour and Gender*, McGraw-Hill, Maidenhead.

CHAPTER 16

Leadership and organizations

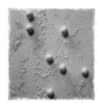

CHAPTER SUMMARY

This chapter sets out to introduce the nature of leadership and its relationship with management. The main theoretical perspectives on the subject of leadership will then be introduced. A number of the different trait, style and contingency perspectives will be discussed, followed by a review of a number of other views on the subject of leadership. For example, attribution theory, the vertical dyad model and action-centred leadership. The alternatives to conventional forms of leadership will also be discussed, as will the symbolic dimension to its function and relationship to the stages in an organizational lifecycle. The nature of leadership in creating entrepreneurial and visionary direction will be introduced as will the relationship with power and success. The chapter will conclude with a review of the applied perspectives associated with leadership.

LEARNING OBJECTIVES

After studying this chapter and working through the associated Management in Action panels, Discussion questions and Research activities, you should be able to:

+ Understand the distinction between leadership and management.

+ Describe the relationship between leaders and followers.

+ Explain the significance of the symbolic aspect of leadership.

+ Outline the trait approach to leadership.

+ Assess the contribution to understanding leadership of the various style approaches.

+ Appreciate the significance of the contingency approaches to the study of leadership.

+ Discuss the contribution of the 'other' approaches to leadership.

+ Detail the approaches to leadership identified as related to the organizational lifecycle.

Introduction

Management is a topic that is taken for granted within an organizational context. Managers run things, they organize, they plan and control etc. They are the category of employee specifically tasked with ensuring that the organization achieves its objectives and flourishes on behalf of the stakeholder groups, predominantly the beneficial owners. So far so good, but there is another term which is often associated with management which also incorporates a number of different connotations that render it worthy of detailed consideration in its own right. That concept is *leadership*.

Consider for a moment the two terms *management* and *leadership*. Are they equivalent, simply reflecting alternative words to describe the same job or activity? Do they represent completely different ideas about the task of being in charge of organizational activity? Is it possible for a manager not to be a leader or is every leader automatically a manager? These are just two of the questions that are not easy to answer directly or simply in relation to establishing the relationship between *management* and *leadership*. However, they are fundamental in seeking to establish what it is that *leadership* is and its value as a concept worthy of study in an organizational context. The starting point for this chapter is to consider these two terms and to draw out the differences and similarities between them.

Leadership and management

The terms *management* and *leadership* are frequently used interchangeably. But are they the same? Is a manager automatically a leader and do leaders always manage? The study of management and leadership has covered many different aspects of the activity. Most of this work has attempted to identify what it is that managers have to do or the skills and personal qualities that they should display in order to achieve success. Success in this context is usually assumed to reflect benefit to the organization, although there is usually a heavy hint of personal success and career advancement for those who apply the right formula (or have the right characteristics). For example, Rothman (1987) light-heartedly concluded that birthdates formed a key variable in selecting future successful leaders. This emerged because it was found that the senior managers of a number of large organizations shared the same birthday as their predecessors!

The terms *management* and *leadership* tend to be used interchangeably on many occasions. They clearly involve groups of people and specific functions in relation to the group and its activities. It would be unusual, however, to describe a group of people as having a manager, unless the group was in a specific context. That context invariably lies within an organization and, specifically, a formal part of the structure. An informal or friendship or trade union group would not usually be described as having a manager, but there would inevitably be a formal or informal leader of such groups. A department would, however, have a manager as the formal leader of that particular group. This situation can be made more complex because of the modern company practice of terming many formal group leaders as *team leaders*. An attempt perhaps to recognize that the term (and practice of) *leadership* has certain advantages over the term *management*, particularly at the first-line supervisor level. However, it would also be possible to argue that managers are simply seeking to restrict the use of the term *management* to the more senior levels and that the introduction of the *team leader* description gets away from the connotations of the *supervisor* label, without admitting that such individuals are part of *management*. The two terms of *management* and *leadership* therefore have aspects in common, but are synonymous only up to point. Management in Action 16.1 provides an indication of some of the current thinking on the nature of leadership.

Stop | Consider

To what extent do the views expressed in MiA 16.1 suggest that leadership represents a subset of management skills?

Do the views expressed in MiA 16.1 imply that the leadership ability of an individual is a factor on which management performance should be judged?

Leadership and management are two topics that between them generate a vast quantity of published material, training courses and seminars. This material frequently claims to provide a means of delivering increased performance to the organization through the more effective leadership of teams. The assumption underpinning much of this material is that leadership reflects a set of characteristics that can be learned and that ensure that *leaders* stand out from the ranks of *managers,* who are defined as not so successful. For the organization this effort (it is claimed) can lead to enhanced commercial success in an increasingly hostile environment. The perspective of much of this vast output of developmental material is that leaders *lead*, but managers only *manage*. Leaders are said to be the ones with vision who are capable of getting the best performance out of the team, whereas managers are the ones who simply organize, plan and control activity, but who are unable to get the best out of other people. It simplifies to the view that management equates to bad, inefficient, bureaucratic corporate activity; compared with leadership which equates to good visionary and charismatic approaches, which motivate staff to scale unimaginable heights of performance and contribution to the organization and its objectives.

However, there is little hard evidence of the sustained gain for any particular *formula* for identifying leadership (or management) approaches that would guarantee success in every context. The number and complexity of variables active in the organizational environment and therefore involved in achieving success requires an equally complex set of responses in order to *lead, manage* and *achieve* it. This is the basis of the law of *requisite variety* identified by Ashby (1956). This postulates that complexity in the environment can only be managed through equally complex response strategies within the organization. Figure 16.1 attempts to provide an indication of the range and complexity of variables impacting on individuals and organizations. Figure 16.1 demonstrates that leadership (and indeed management) while significant are not enough of themselves to provide the *requisite variety* to achieve success through overcoming environmental complexity.

One of the chief difficulties in measuring organizational success is the meaning of the term success itself. Success is frequently a relative term in that for any organization it is often taken to reflect performance in comparison to other organizations. It is often taken to reflect level of profit or market share compared to competitors, but these are not the only ways in which success could be measured. Survival and contribution to society in some way are other possible measures of success, but are not often used as the financial markets tend to dominate thinking about such matters and act as the ultimate arbiter. An organization not considered to be successful in terms acceptable to the financial markets will be punished in terms of its share price and perhaps be subjected to takeover and reorganization

MANAGEMENT IN ACTION 16.1

Taking the lead in leadership

The distinction between leadership and management is explored in a book by Stuart Levine and Michael Crom, of Dale Carnegie & Associates, called *The Leader in You*. It identifies a number of distinctions between management and leadership. For example:

> A leader is a person who can communicate with and motivate people. A manager is someone who doesn't spend enough time recognizing people through a sincere appreciation of what they do. A leader understands that the way to motivate a person is not with a bullwhip and chair – the lion tamer's style of management – but with appreciation.

Leadership is about listening to people, supporting and encouraging them and involving them in decision-making and problem-solving processes, they say. Management involves telling people, what to do, and how, when and where to do it, and then closely supervising their performance. Levine and Crom suggest that no individual can assimilate all the information available to them, so leaders have to start building teams and relying on members of those teams to make the most of what is available and achieve the goals.

In their work they quote Sir Christopher Hogg, chairman of Reuters, as saying:

> Leadership is about getting the best out of people. It is about communicating a vision, and persuading, rather than compelling people. Management, on the other hand, is about an effective performance within an institutional framework, which secures the obedience of a lot of people.

Robert Waterman in his book, *The Frontiers of Excellence,* argues that top-performing companies are better able to meet the needs of their people. Looking after the needs of the people within the organization helps to attract better people in the first place and motivates them to place the needs of the organization and its customers above other interests. In meeting the needs of one's own people it is necessary to understand what motivates them and to have an effective alignment between culture, systems, procedures and leadership. This is far removed from the old idea of manager as one who tells people what to do.

Adapted from: Gretton, I (1995) Taking the lead in leadership, *Professional Manager*, January, pp 20–2.

as a result. Of course, not all organizations are publicly quoted and therefore these *rules* do not apply universally.

Most of the factors indicated in Figure 16.1 are self-explanatory. However, the *non-specific forces* identified would benefit from some explanation. They include:

✦ Random factors. This category reflects those things for which it is difficult to anticipate and plan. For example, an employee being in a bad mood on a particular day or the failure of a supplier to deliver on time can significantly influence events and so impact on the relative success of the organization.

✦ Time and repetitive influences. These reflect experiential influences that impact on activity. Over time behaviour patterns change and influence future actions. Alternatively, behaviour patterns can remain consistent for too long and become outdated and problematical. The simplest illustration is the story about the little boy who cried wolf once too often and as a result failed to protect the sheep for which he was responsible. Response behaviours to situations need to change over time in order to remain appropriate, but this needs to be planned if it is to have any measure of success in an organizational context.

✦   Interactive forces. This reflects the *action and reaction* nature of experience. An initiative to increase market share is likely to lead to a response from competitors seeking to protect their business. Subordinates are not passive in responding to their experience of being led, thereby creating a dynamic between leader and led. This interactive chain of events leads to situations in which there is an ever present degree of uncertainty in being able to control or shape events in the future.

Leadership and management are complex processes. Simplistic attempts to explain them or train individuals to use a formula are doomed. This view is apparent in Management in Action 16.2

Stop | Consider   *What does the view expressed in MiA 16.2 imply about the distinction between management and leadership in the future?*

What then provides the distinction between management and leadership? The following list of topics provides some indication of and summarizes the areas that differentiate between them:

✦   Role. Watson (1994) defines management as a process of ensuring that the resources under control are appropriately directed. Leadership, by the same token, is described in terms of people skills and performance. Torrington and Hall (1991) describe the

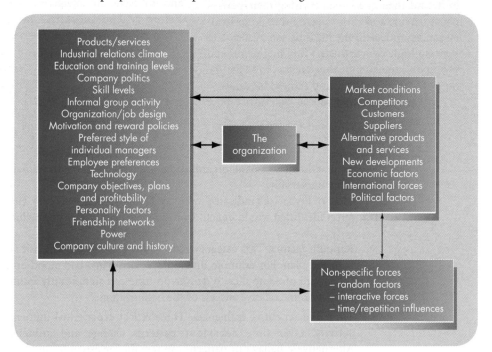

FIGURE 16.1   The complexity of the management environment.

MANAGEMENT IN ACTION 16.2

The manager's dilemma

The key features of managing in the new millennium include, according to Heller:

✦ Managers will be concerned with unleashing the potential all around them.

✦ Managers will need to listen to the messages coming to them from below about what needs to be 'facilitated' to achieve objectives. Those who don't listen will find their basis of authority eliminated.

✦ Old-style authority frameworks will crumble in an age when success and progress depend on breaking the rules.

✦ The view of an organization as a 'system of interrelated parts' will grow and the complexity will be dealt with by outsourcing as many of the non-core activities as possible and networking more effectively.

✦ Success in management will be defined in terms of the ability to work effectively with colleagues from other companies to achieve results for the organization. The distinction between the management and consultancy modes of operation will become blurred.

✦ The tasks carried out by individual managers will be subject to frequent change in line with the changing perception of customer needs and how those needs should be met through the resources available. Predictable career paths and functional specialisms will erode significantly.

✦ With the emphasis on task groups and multi-disciplinary teamworking' and as a consequence of the delayering of recent years, the opportunity for frequent promotion will largely disappear. Beyond the year 2000 managers will progress in status and reward terms by the successful achievement of assignments, rather than vertical progression and changing job titles.

✦ 'Theory Y' motivation perspectives will dominate the thinking and approaches of managers as they seek to involve as many people as possible in assignments.

✦ The effective integration of both 'hard' and 'soft' perspectives into their work will also be a characteristic of the next generation of successful manager.

✦ The ability to 'live the vision' as expressed in corporate values, rather than just pay 'lip service' to them, will also define the new manager.

✦ Future commercial wars are going to be won with ideas, not whips and chains. As a consequence, managers will not plan, organize, control, etc. They will advise, facilitate, encourage self-management and ensure that adequate resources are available for the groups that actually achieve objectives for the organization.

✦ The comprehensive growth in various forms of strategic alliance will blur the boundaries between organizations. The consequences are vast for the management of ambiguity and boundary management in the job of the new manager. They become very aware of the true nature of the 'open' organization and job.

Adapted from: Heller, R (1994) The manager's dilemma, *Management Today*, January, pp 42–7.

'role that members of the organization take on in order to exercise formal authority and leadership' (p 129). From this perspective, leadership is to be understood as a subset of management. Something that managers do in order to be effective. However, leadership as part of a group activity may not be part of the formal structure. The leader of a group designing a new computer system may not be a manager but would be expected to lead the team. There are also informal groups within an organization which will have some form of leadership but not a manager. Management can be suggested to be an outwardly focused activity in the sense of formally representing the organization within the work group. Leadership, by way of contrast, represents an inwardly focused activity intended to optimize performance and maintain cohesion within the group itself to address the externally determined requirements.

◆ Situation. A manager is appointed and would hold that position irrespective of most changes in the situation. Leaders, however, are suggested to be much more situation specific. John Adair illustrates this with examples of shipwreck survivors appointing leaders depending upon the group needs at the time: the soldier for defence, the farmer for food and the builder for shelter (1983, p 15). Situational leadership makes best use of the specialized knowledge available to the group from among the members. For example, the *company doctor* is an individual frequently brought in to replace a senior manager not considered capable of saving a company in time of crisis. Such individuals usually stay for a very short period of time. Their leadership approach is invariably based upon the 'do it my way or out' philosophy, an approach which can achieve the desired results in the short term, albeit with much blood on the office carpets.

◆ Context. The military context is one in which considerable emphasis is laid on leadership rather than management. Constant training and drill leads to a highly capable military *machine*. There is an interesting contradiction in this situation involving such close and directive management with an emphasis on leadership as the dominant ideology. Much of this can be explained by reference to two unique circumstances peculiar to military activity. First, the chaos and horror of war itself. Second, the need to motivate subordinates to undertake actions which are ultimately life threatening to the individual. Large bureaucratic organizations, conversely, tend to emphasize management rather than leadership. This is inevitably the result of the need to mobilize large quantities of resource in predictable and planned ways over the long term in support of the organization's objectives.

◆ Purpose. Traditionally jobs and organizations were considered to have permanence into the foreseeable future. Therefore the role of management becomes a routinized and largely symbolic process. In times of turbulence and instability this inevitably and fundamentally changes. This need to change is responsible for the shift in emphasis towards leadership as the dominant ideology in organizations during times of crises. In times of crisis there is a need to mobilize people to action but in a controlled way. Military and war metaphors and terminology frequently emerge as dominant themes and common forms of expression at such times. Over recent years company trainers find themselves providing training for leadership more than for other aspects of management (Rowe, 1993, p 65). Scase and Goffee (1989) reported their survey of managers in which 69% of men and 82% of women indicated a need for more human relations and leadership training (p 68).

◆ Scope. The usual differentiation between management jobs is between senior, middle and junior management positions. This distinction is a very poor indicator of the type of job involved. For example, a junior manager in a very large organization may have a budgetary responsibility larger than a senior manager in a very small one. Stewart (1976) identified other bases for the classification of management jobs:

✦ Hub. Jobs that have considerable contact with subordinates, peers and superiors.
✦ Peer dependent. These jobs contain a high degree of needing to persuade others to undertake specific actions. Consequently, they are frequently found on the boundaries between groups.
✦ People management. Such jobs emphasize the traditional boss–subordinate types of responsibilities.
✦ Solo. Jobs that require the individual to work alone on assignments but which also require a high level of seniority to do so.

Although the Stewart framework provides a clear indication of the nature of different types of management job, it does not provide any information about the level or seniority in the hierarchy. More than one dimension is therefore required to describe management jobs. Figure 16.2 links together the traditional and Stewart views of management work in such a matrix. This classification suggests that perhaps there are some management jobs in any organization that naturally contain a higher degree of leadership than others.

Leaders or followers?

In the foregoing discussion about the relationship between management and leadership it was apparent that management reflects a formal position within an organization with particular responsibilities. Leadership, by the same token seems to reflect more of the personal qualities and abilities of the individual as a prerequisite to the enhanced performance of the

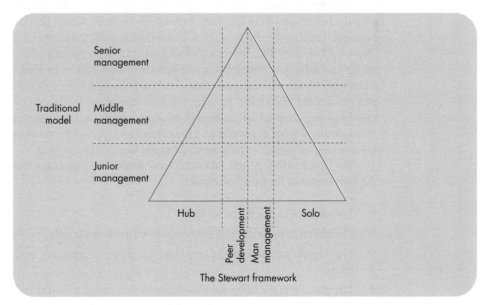

FIGURE 16.2 The management job matrix.

rest of the group. One of the interesting questions about the topic of leadership to emerge from this discussion reflects the degree to which leaders have to be accepted by their followers.

The view of management embraced by the previous discussion implies that management is in effect an imposed form of leadership. Managers are appointed by more senior managers to undertake particular responsibilities in relation to a formal group within the organization. The process of appointment (or even confirmation in a more democratic process) still creates an imposition. It is the company that appoints the person who will manage. The group, or the followers in that sense, have little influence or alternative, other than to abide by the decision. Leaders by comparison are able to capture the imagination of the group and harness that in the pursuit of organizational objectives. A view which begs the question about whether this could be achieved if the followers did not fully support the leader. In short, can a leader lead unless the followers are prepared to accept the leader?

A manager can manage to a significant degree against the wishes of the employees through force and direction. Such managers may not achieve the best results, but they can enforce certain standards of performance. The existence of the disciplinary procedures within the company, recruitment procedures and the need for employees to earn a living all ensure, as a minimum response, a *compliance* with managerial dictates. However, the question is can a leader lead under circumstances where resistance exists? Mazlish (1990) identifies a number of characteristics associated with leadership, several of which throw some light on this issue. He points out (pp 251–2) that there is no *leader* for all situations and that the potential leader must find the right circumstances and the right group to lead. He illustrates his point with the comment that General Ulysses Grant would have remained a failed army officer working in his family's leather business if the American Civil War had not broken out. Mazlish also points out that a specific leader is *formed* during interaction with the followers, 'discovers a self, forms and takes on an identity as a particular kind of leader, in the course of interacting with the chosen group' (p252). From that perspective, leadership is as much a function of the followers as it is of the leader.

Leadership appears, therefore, to be a social process in which the leader is able to influence the behaviour of the followers, but only once the followers have accepted their relative position. To integrate this basic view of leadership with the perspective of Mazlish, leadership would seem to describe a mutual adaptation and acceptance process. One in which the leader and followers contribute a willingness to lead and to be lead within an adaptable framework in formulating processes which will lead effectively to jointly acceptable styles and the desired end result. In brief, the followers allow the leader to exercise power and influence over then under conditions of acceptability and a degree of co-operation, provided a mutual benefit is available. There is also an aspect of power evident in this approach to leadership, a topic to which we shall return later in this chapter.

McGregor (1960, p 182) takes this view further by suggesting that leadership reflects the interaction of four main variables:

✦   The characteristics of the leader.

✦   The characteristics of the followers, as well as their attitudes and needs.

✦   The organizational context including its purpose, structure and tasks to be undertaken.

✦   The broader environmental context including social, political and economic forces.

These influences are most easily reflected as a diagram (see Figure 16.3).

Having set the scene in terms of what leadership is and how it might be considered to relate to the concept of management, it is now appropriate to explore the major theoretical themes on it, beginning with the trait perspective.

Trait theories of leadership

For much of history it was assumed that leadership was a set of qualities that someone was born with. Adair (1983) quotes from a lecture given to students of St Andrew's University in 1934:

> It is a fact that some men possess an inbred superiority which gives them a dominating influence over their contemporaries, and marks them out unmistakably for leadership. This phenomenon is as certain as it is mysterious. It is apparent in every association of human beings in every variety of circumstances and on every plane of culture. In a school among boys, in a college among the students, in a factory, shipyard, or a mine among the workmen, as certainly as in the church and in the Nation, there are those who, with an assured and unquestioned title, take the leading place, and shape the general conduct. (p 7)

It is being argued that good leaders naturally display those characteristics that are required by the position that they hold. The significance of this approach is that leaders cannot be *trained* and therefore must be *selected*. It also implies that successful leaders will be situation specific. This view originated from the aptly named *great man* (as at that time they were all men) view of leadership which suggested that in every situation (particularly in times of crisis) the best leader would emerge from the crowd and lead in such a way that the difficulties would be overcome. As a natural extension of this view future successful leaders could be identified by seeking out people with the same characteristics as existing successful leaders.

Handy (1993) suggests that by 1950 there had been over 100 studies attempting to identify appropriate traits. Unfortunately, little commonality was identified, with only

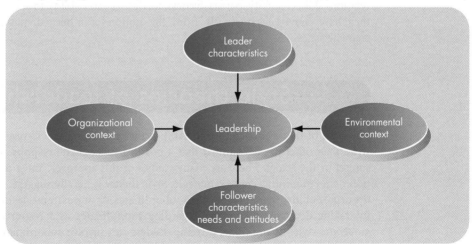

FIGURE 16.3 Leadership determinants.

about 5% of the traits being common. Those traits found to have some association with successful leadership include:

◆ Intelligence. A high level of intelligence and good at solving abstract, complex problems.

◆ Initiative. The ability to identify a need for action and to actually initiate courses of action.

◆ Self-assurance. Confidence in one's ability to do things and to be successful.

◆ Overview. The ability to stand back and take a broader view of situations.

◆ Health. To be of good health.

◆ Physique. To be above average weight and height, alternatively to be significantly below average physique.

◆ Social background. To be born into the higher socio-economic groups within society.

To find a leader with every characteristic (not just those listed here) would seem to be an impossible task. Many successful leaders do not fit the profile implied by the characteristics. There are simply too many exceptions to the rules to imply that they are essential for success. The terms used to describe the traits themselves are also imprecise and require judgement rather than allowing absolute measurement. For example, socio-economic grouping is a relative term, peculiar to each generation and society.

Although now largely discredited as an approach to leadership theory, trait approaches are used in the design of many *assessment centres* for the purposes of recruitment and career development for managers. Assessment centres involve a range of tasks to be undertaken with the behaviour and performance of testees being recorded and evaluated by a team of assessors. The justification for the use of traits in this way is based on the view that there are personal characteristics and behaviour patterns that impact on the effectiveness with which managers will perform their duties. Consequently, identifying individuals with those characteristics will allow improved managerial and organizational performance. The concept of traits has not disappeared from management and leadership thinking, they now appear as skill-based characteristics such as technical skill, conceptual skill and human relations skill, creativity, persuasiveness, tactfulness and ability to speak well. In that sense they have moved away slghtly from the notion of inherited, natural or untrainable characteristics.

Style theories of leadership

The basis of this approach to leadership is that subordinates will respond better to some *styles* than others. It is assumed that a positive subordinate response creates the success sought by the leader. There are many studies of this approach, most capable of classification on an *autocratic–democratic* scale. Style theory generally suggests that leaders vary in the degree of involvement allowed to subordinates. At one extreme, leaders can direct activity, taking decisions themselves regarding subordinates as a resource to be used – an *autocratic* style. At the other extreme, leaders can involve subordinates in planning and undertaking work, delegating some of their responsibility – a *democratic* style. It is appropriate to consider style theories in chronological sequence, providing an opportunity to reflect on the evolution of knowledge.

The University of Iowa studies

These were carried out in boys' clubs during the late 1930s by Lippitt and White to study the consequences of leadership differences on aggressive behaviour among 10 year olds. They varied leadership style as follows:

✦ Authoritarian. The leader was directive and did not allow participation among the boys. A friendly or impersonal style was adopted, hostile approaches were avoided.

✦ Democratic. Discussion and group decision making was encouraged. The leader attempted to be objective but tried to avoid becoming 'one of the group'.

✦ *Laissez faire*. The leader gave complete freedom to the group of boys. This reflected a lack of leadership rather than a particular style.

It was the group of boys subjected to the democratic leadership style that contained the lowest levels of aggression and apathy and should therefore have been the most successful. The management parallel being that a democratic style should produce similar beneficial results. However, there is a vast difference between clubs for boys and the management of complex formal organizations. It is unfortunate that the original studies did not report other measures of success such as productivity or achievement. The studies are criticized as not specifically organizational based and being experimentally weak. They were, however, the first serious examination of different styles of leadership.

The Ohio State University studies

The Ohio State University studies began in 1945 and used a questionnaire to examine leadership. Those questioned included officers, other ranks and civilian staff in the army and navy, manufacturing company supervisors, college administrators, teachers and student leaders.

The results were subjected to factor analysis and two factors emerged. They were called:

✦ Consideration. Indicating a concern by the leader for subordinate welfare, respect and rapport with them.

✦ Initiating structure. Reflects the degree to which the leader is task focused, emphasizing the achievement of objectives.

These studies are of prime importance in establishing the importance of the task and people dimensions of success. It has been argued that these studies do not necessarily identify actual leader behaviour but reflect the perceptions of those completing the form. For example, leaders could answer on the basis of how they think they behave, or how they would like to behave, rather than how they actually behave. Equally a subordinate might complete the questions on the basis of personal feelings towards their boss rather than actual behaviour experienced.

Likert's four systems of management

Likert developed this approach from the many years of work by a team at the University of Michigan. The four systems (or styles) of leadership identified through the research are:

✦ System 1. Exploitative autocratic. The leader has no confidence or trust in subordinates and does not seek or get ideas from them on work problems.

✦ System 2. Benevolent autocratic. The leader has some confidence and trust in subordinates. Occasionally the leader will seek ideas and opinions on work problems from subordinates. Their style is paternalistic.

✦ System 3. Participative. There is significant confidence and trust in subordinates by the leader. However, the leader still seeks to ultimately control decision making but frequently seeks the opinions of subordinates and makes use of them in the process.

✦ System 4. Democratic. The leader completely trusts subordinates in all areas associated with the activity. The leader actively seeks the opinions of subordinates and always makes use of them.

Research into successful and unsuccessful teams was based on asking thousands of managers about the teams with which they had experience. The most successful departments were described in terms of systems 3 and 4 while the least successful were associated with systems 1 and 2 (Likert, 1967).

However, his work has not been without its critics. It was based on questionnaires and is subject to the criticisms common to such approaches. Also there may be circumstances where it is not appropriate to adopt democratic processes. For example, in a crisis there may not be the time to consult and seek opinion. Muczyk and Reimann (1987) also argue that not every organization has the skill or quality of support to enable participation to be undertaken effectively.

The Tannenbaum and Schmidt continuum

Tannenbaum and Schmidt (1973) utilize concepts of *boss-centred leadership* and *subordinate-centred leadership* to describe the essential differences in the style of leadership expressed in the continuum that they use as the basis of their model. In this model they express the exercise of a balance between managerial authority and freedom for subordinates in any given context. Figure 16.4 reflects this approach to leadership.

It should be noted that within the model the use of authority or access to freedom never completely disappears. Even at the *freedom for subordinates* extreme of the continuum the boss still retains the power to say no and to require something to be done in a particular way. However, at the other extreme, employees also retain some freedom, even if it is only the opportunity to display token resistance. Although there are a number of different styles that can be identified within the model (Figure 16.4 indicates seven of them) there are four main categories that are most frequently described:

✦ Tells. The leader identifies appropriate solutions to problems and the appropriate courses of actions and thereafter tells the subordinates what they are supposed to do.

✦ Sells. The leader still decides upon the appropriate course of action in any given situation but attempts to overcome disagreement and resistance among the workforce by selling the decision to them. Often this involves justifying the decision (determined by the boss) as the best course of action in the circumstances.

✦ Consults. The leader allows time for subordinates to discuss the problem and present ideas and solutions to the boss. These are then used by the leader to make decisions which are then announced to, and actioned by, the subordinates.

✦ Joins. The leader defines the nature of the issue to be decided along with any constraints and presents these to the group. The leader then becomes part of the group in finding and implementing acceptable solutions.

The form of leadership that would be appropriate in a particular context depends upon leader preferences, subordinate preferences and situational variables. This model leans towards the contingency approach to leadership in recognizing that success in any particular context depends upon a range of factors, effectively creating the need for an appropriate match between situational need, employee expectation and preferred style of the leader.

Blake and Mouton's grid

This approach emerged during the late 1960s and is based on the idea that differences in leadership approach are a function of two factors:

✦ Concern for people.
✦ Concern for production.

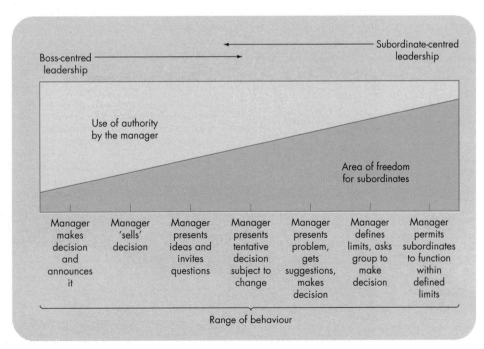

FIGURE 16.4 Continuum of leadership behaviour (*source*: Luthans, F (1995) *Organization Behaviour*, 7th edn, McGraw-Hill, New York).

These ideas were not new, being similar to work from the Ohio State University studies discussed earlier. However, Blake and Mouton produced a more systematic approach to the identification of generic styles. A grid is the usual way to represent the relationship between the two factors used in the model. Since it was originally published in 1964, the work has been revised several times, most recently as The Leadership Grid (Blake and McCanse, 1991). Figure 16.5 illustrates this latest version of the model with the five main leadership styles indicated within it.

The term *concern* is used in this context as reflecting *emphasis-in* something rather than implying the welfare-based perspective of the term. The score for individuals along each scale would be identified through an analysis to the responses to a questionnaire. Looking at the five leadership style stereotypes indicated in the model:

✦ Impoverished management. This style would be typified by a low concern for both people and production. Such a leader would be considered as remote from their sub-

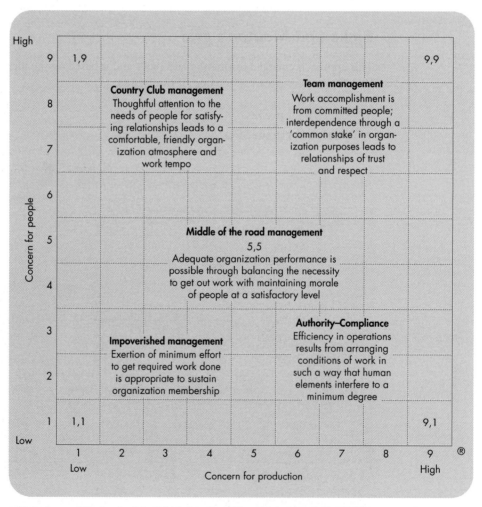

FIGURE 16.5 The Leadership Grid ® (*source*: Blake, RR and McCanse, AA (1991) *Leadership Dilemmas – Grid Solutions*, Gulf Publishing, New York. All rights reserved).

ordinates and with little interest in achieving the business goals set for their department or section.

✦ Authority–compliance management. This style would be typified through a very high concern for production but very low concern for people. Such a leader would rely on the application of standard procedures and policies to determine action rather than the possible contribution from staff. They would be considered to be *drivers* of staff in the search for the achievement of objectives.

✦ Country club management. This style would be typified by a very high concern for people but with low levels of concern for production. Such a leader would be concerned with the need to create harmony and avoid conflict thereby allowing subordinates to get on with the job. They would tend to be regarded as *one of the workers* by subordinates. They tend to seek a comfortable working environment in relationship terms, often in the belief that this ensures that production will follow automatically.

✦ Middle of the road management. This style is typified through a medium level of concern for both people and production. Keeping everyone happy is a typical approach of such individuals. Unfortunately, because they are not strong on either index, they tend to underachieve on both, achieving neither good levels of production nor highly integrated work teams.

✦ Team management. This style is typified by an equally very high concern for both people and production. Managers with this profile seek to create teams in which both the needs of individuals and the search for output become integrated.

Blake and Mouton found that managers tend to have one dominant style but that many have a back-up style if the first proves unsuccessful. They also found that many managers could vary their dominant style to some degree. The factors that influence the style adopted by an individual are shown in Figure 16.6.

Hersey and Blanchard's situation approach

This approach was developed by Hersey and Blanchard (1982) and is based on the existence of two different sets of leader behaviour:

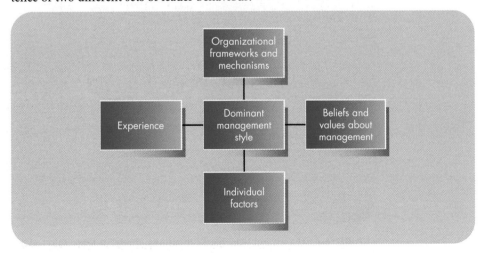

FIGURE 16.6 Management style determinants.

✦ Task behaviour. This approach is based on the degree to which the leader provides an output-focused perspective for the group.

✦ Relationship behaviour. This approach is based on the amount of support, encouragement and two-way communication that the leader engages in.

There are similarities between this approach and that of Blake and Mouton. The Hersey and Blanchard situation approach adds to the ideas from Blake and Mouton by incorporating additional variables, based on the work of Fiedler. However, not all the situation variables suggested by Fiedler are included, only those related to the *readiness* of the subordinates to be willing and able to achieve a particular task. From the two basic styles (task and relationship behaviour) emerge four actual styles when the situation variable of subordinate *readiness* is added to the model (Figure 16.7).

The four actual styles of leadership are:

✦ Telling. If the subordinates display a low level of readiness to be willing and able to achieve the task then the leader should adopt a task-oriented style by *telling* subordinates what is expected from them.

✦ Selling. This style would be most appropriate where the subordinates display moderate levels of *readiness* towards the task to be achieved.

✦ Participating. Where medium levels of subordinate *readiness* towards the task are found it is possible for the leader to lean towards the relationship aspects of the situation in terms of style.

✦ Delegating. With high levels of subordinate *readiness* there is an opportunity to delegate much of the responsibility for both task and relationship dimensions. The leadership role then becomes facilitation rather than managerial.

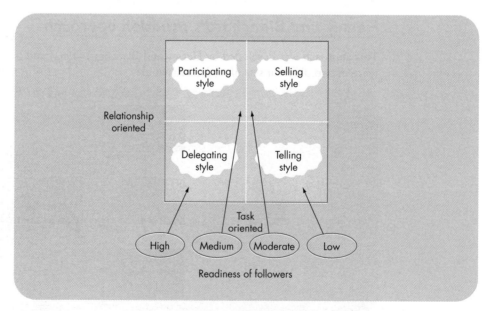

FIGURE 16.7 Hersey and Blanchard's situational model of leadership (*adapted from*: Hersey, P and Blanchard, K (1982) *Management Organizational Behaviour*, Prentice Hall, New York).

There are also similarities between the styles suggested here and those from Tannenbaum and Schmidt described earlier. In practice, this model builds on the work of the three sets of earlier writers indicated.

There have been a number of criticisms of this model. For example, the theoretical underpinning was argued to be weak because the provision of a rationale for the underlying relationships was neglected. The questionnaire used to determine leader effectiveness was also heavily criticized. Nicholls (1985) argues that the model breaks the three principles of consistency, continuity and conformity. A revised model is offered by Nicholls which, it is suggested, does not break these principles. Naturally Hersey and Blanchard do not agree with the Nicholls' perspective and defended their work in a later publication.

The Hersey and Blanchard model spans the borderline between style and contingency theories of leadership. It emphasizes leadership style but it also introduces situational aspects into the model as being important factors in the determination of which style would be most successful in particular situations.

Artists, craftsmen and technocrats

In her research Pitcher (1997) describes three styles of leadership, each with two further subdivisions. In these she describes the differing styles, 'not as rigid categories, abstract concepts, or neat little boxes, but as central tendencies of individual human beings people are predominantly one style with some minor elements of another' (p 140).

Table 16.1 identifies the main characteristics of the three major styles of artist, craftsman and technocrat.

An outline of the nine categories of style from this model are as follows:

✦ Pure technocrat. Such a style reflects an individual who is cerebral, uncompromising, stiff, hard-headed and detail oriented. Individuals displaying this style lack humour, will brook no opposition and remain calmly superior.

✦ Plodding technocrat. Such a style reflects an individual who is rigid, dogmatic, uncompromising and hard-headed. The major distinction with the pure technocrat is that the plodding technocrat is not as bright!

✦ Flashy technocrat. Such a style reflects an individual who is brilliant in the sense of being able to argue for their point of view and the use of 'experts' to support it.

Artist	Craftsman	Technocrat
Unpredictable	Well balanced	Cerebral
Funny	Helpful	Difficult
Imaginative	Honest	Uncompromising
Daring	Sensible	Stiff
Intuitive	Responsible	Intense
Exciting	Trustworthy	Detail oriented
Emotional	Realistic	Determined
Visionary	Steady	Fastidious
Entrepreneurial	Reasonable	Hard-headed
Inspiring	Predictable	No-nonsense

TABLE 16.1   Characteristics of artist, craftsman and technocrat

However, their ideas are not new or original, they are not the true entrepreneur or innovator, they are simply quick witted at being conventional.

✦ Pure craftsman. Such a style reflects an individual who is steady, realistic, trustworthy, calmly intelligent, reflective, tolerant of human error and gives people the benefit of the doubt. It reflects someone who other people love to work with because they genuinely value the contribution from other people.

✦ Regimental craftsman. Such a style reflects an individual who is very methodical, analytical, conservative and controlled. Very similar to the pure craftsman they change their minds more slowly and need more convincing to do so.

✦ Creative craftsman. Such a style reflects an individual who is rather like the gentle artist (described later) but also has the characteristics of the realistic, sensible team player. They also differ from the gentle artist because they prefer to develop new ideas as evolutions from what already exists as opposed to revolutionary innovations. Also, they can deliver more effectively than the gentle artist through their ability to generate team commitment.

✦ Pure artist. Such a style reflects an individual who is unpredictable, imaginative daring, intuitive and exciting. They are the type of individual who is full of nervous energy, constantly on the move, throwing out an idea every minute.

✦ Authoritarian artist. Such a style reflects an individual who is hard to get along with, a poor listener, but brilliant, very determined and analytical. Generally lacking an attractive personality, they are able to take people long with them through the force of their ideas.

✦ Gentle artist. Such a style reflects an individual who is softly spoken, self-effacing, warm, easy-going and people oriented. Like the pure artist they prefer to develop the big project and lots of them, but they do not have the big ego, do not blame others for failure and do not take themselves too seriously.

Pitcher recognizes that an organization will inevitably consist of many leaders, each of whom will fall into one of the nine categories indicated in her model. Therefore every style will be found in any organization. She also suggests that for any organization its ability to survive and prosper depends to a significant extent on the power struggles carried out between the styles in the dynamic of everyday organizational life. That is not to suggest that open warfare exists between these styles, but a recognition that tension and conflict exists between people who are in leadership positions and who possess different styles.

The view that Pitcher puts forward is that the technocrat has dominated management thinking and practice over the past few decades. In turn, this has stifled both the opportunity for the artist to create and the ability of the craftsman to deliver the products and services provided by organizations to the benefit of society. It is her view that it is the artist who should be the overall leader, with the other two categories having specific roles to play in support and delivery of the vision.

Contingency theories of leadership

Contingency theory attempts to *add value* by incorporating a wider range of variables into the equation. They suggest that the most appropriate style of leadership is *contingent* on a range of variables from the context within which the leadership will be exercised. These circumstances could include the expectations of the subordinates, the nature of the task to be achieved or the atmosphere. Management in Action 16.3 reflects the most difficult contingency situation imaginable, a commercial organization attempting to operate during a civil war.

Is the situation described in MiA 16.3 so extreme as to be irrelevant as a set of contingency factors? Justify your views.

Could leadership in such situations ever be taught to managers or is it something that they would have to experience in order to develop their own approach? Why or why not?

Fiedler's contingency model

This model attempts to identify situational influences on leadership within a framework that also incorporates the notion of effectiveness in achieving success. Fiedler (1967) brought together three situational aspects for determining the most effective style of leadership. Style was defined as an expression of the leader's personality preferences for either a task or relationship approach. The three situational variables are:

✦ Leader–member relationships. It would be reflected in the degree of trust between the parties and a willingness to follow the leader's direction on the part of the subordinates.

✦ Task structure. Tasks are either *structured* or *unstructured* in the degree to which the task is capable of being achieved through standard procedures. This is similar to the concept of programmed and non-programmed approaches to decision making as described by Simon.

✦ Position power. This construct reflects the degree of authority held by the leader.

The two levels possible for each of these three constructs produces eight situational combinations. These Fiedler combined into three levels of situational favourableness, each linked with either *task* or *relationship* approaches in the behaviour of the leader (Figure 16.8). Figure 16.8 shows that when the situation is either very favourable or very unfavourable to the leader then a *task style* would be most effective. When the situation is

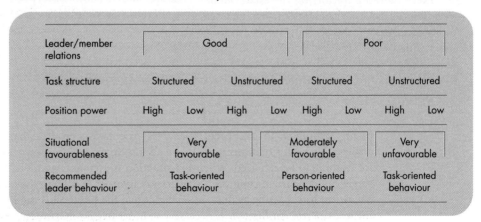

FIGURE 16.8 Fiedler's contingency model of leadership.

MANAGEMENT IN ACTION 16.3

When managers carry guns

The civil war in Mozambique lasted for 17 years until the signing of a peace accord in October 1992. This deal was largely instigated by 'Tiny' Rowland who arranged the first meeting between the president and the rebel leader. Rowland was at the time head of Lonrho, Mozambique's biggest foreign investor. Lonrho, which had a £53m investment in cotton estates and other businesses, was an obvious target for the rebels during the civil war. In response, the company recruited a private army of 1400 men commanded by Gurkhas in order to protect their estates, staff and the flow of cotton. The cost of this was enormous, absorbing up to 30% of the cost of the Mozambique operation.

The rebel forces had crippled much of the economy of Mozambique by blowing up electricity pylons, railway sabotage, the planting of land mines, burning villages and marching men away into the bush. Lonrho organized its own security. For example, in the Limpopo Valley, triple stacks of wire, watchtowers and tanks guarded the perimeter of the company cotton farm. The main buildings were fortresses. John Hewlett, managing director of the Mozambique operation, said: 'All our managers were used to farming with a gun on their back. They were mostly Boers or white Rhodesians, and they were excellent at their jobs.'

Every morning tractors on the estate would leave for the fields in columns of five, guarded by 50 members of the security force. Farming was planned with military precision. Routines were changed daily to foil surprise attacks and a constant radio link with headquarters

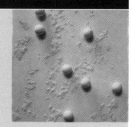

was maintained. Hewlett recalled that several full-blown battles occurred, one resulting in 16 fatalities among the rebel forces.

It was one very large and brutal attack on the farms by the rebels that changed Hewlett's mind about the feasibility of running such operations in the middle of a civil war. About 200 rebels herded cattle at the perimeter fence at dawn one day, raising clouds of dust. A tree was used to fell the barbed wire and the cattle stampeded into the compound, followed by the rebels. In a very short period afterwards the rebels blew up about $500,000 of chemicals and irrigation pipes and set fire to offices and vehicles. The radio operator was burned to death at his transmitter. It was at that point the Hewlett reported back to 'Tiny' Rowland that the war had to be stopped.

In the resulting peace Lonrho made use of its resources in Mozambique to help rebuild the country. It provided former rebels with trucks and office equipment as they attempted to become a respectable political party. The Gurkhas were used as sappers in clearing land mines. Estimates of how many land mines were laid during the civil war ranged from several hundred thousand to millions. Main routes had to be cleared first to allow delivery of humanitarian aid to the stricken population.

Adapted from: Crawford, L (1994) When managers carry guns, *Financial Times*, 25 May, p 18.

highly favourable to the leader then task orientation ensures that the objectives are achieved. In such situations it would be all too easy for a 'good time to be had by all' but for nothing to be achieved. When the situation is very unfavourable to the leader then a single-minded, driving approach is necessary in order to achieve the objectives against the balance of forces acting against the leader. When the situation is moderately favourable to the leader a *relationship style* is necessary in order to gain maximum employee support for the achievement of the objectives.

In determining the orientation of the leader in terms of *task* or *relationship* behaviour Fiedler developed a test which he called the Least Preferred Co-worker scale (LPC). Fiedler suggests that these two concepts of task or relationship preference reflect personality characteristics and are therefore relatively stable leader features. There has been criticism of the research studies that were used to support the development of the model. However, there has also been some support for the methodology (Strube and Garcia, 1981).

Fiedler's work reflects the view that success is a function of the interaction between the relationships in the workplace, the task to be achieved, the relative power balance between leader and led and the preferred style of the leader. Fiedler suggests that in attempting to optimize effectiveness, organizations should allow managers to maximize the fit between their preferred style and the other variables. This could be achieved through action plans for improving relationships or perhaps by moving key individuals. This approach has attracted some criticism on the basis that they are not consistent with the original model (Jago and Ragan, 1986).

Fiedler subsequently developed his work into a Cognitive Resource Theory (CRT) (Fiedler, 1986). This model attempts to identify the situational circumstances which interact with the cognitive characteristics of the leader and which impact on group performance. As with all research this approach has not been without its critics (Vecchio, 1992). However, it does offer a broader understanding of the interacting variables involved in leadership.

House's path–goal leadership theory

The path–goal model of leadership links leader behaviour with subordinate motivation, performance and satisfaction (House and Mitchell, 1974). This approach is similar to the expectancy theory of motivation. It postulates that subordinate motivation will be improved if the expectation that positive rewards will be forthcoming is likely to be realized. House identified four styles of leader behaviour:

✦ Directive leadership. Under this style the leader is expected to provide precise instruction on what is required and how it is to be achieved.

✦ Supportive leadership. This reflects a style that adopts a friendly, concerned approach to the needs and welfare of subordinates.

✦ Participative leadership. This reflects a style in which the leader would seek opinions and suggestions from subordinates before making a decision.

✦ Achievement-oriented leadership. This reflects a style in which the leader is task oriented and sets challenging goals for subordinates.

This contingency approach is based on the notion that individual leaders are capable of changing their style to match the needs of the situation. The two situational factors are:

✦ Subordinate characteristics. Leader acceptability depends to a significant extent on the degree to which subordinates perceive leader behaviour as a source of present or future satisfaction.

✦ Demands facing subordinates. Leader behaviour would motivate performance in subordinates if the satisfaction of subordinate need were dependent on their performance in the work itself and/or other aspects of the work environment.

The path–goal model reflects the influence of leader behaviour on subordinate activity within a directional flow of activity towards the goal to be achieved (Figure 16.9)

There have been some attempts to substantiate the model, with mixed results. A paper which reviewed 48 studies demonstrated mixed levels of support for aspects of the model and suggested the continued testing of it (Indvik, 1986).

The Vroom, Yetton and Jago model of leadership

This model was introduced in 1973 by Vroom and Yetton and expanded by Vroom and Jago (1988). Like the other contingency models, it attempts to identify styles of leadership appropriate in particular situations. It presupposes that leaders can vary their style of behaviour and that only some aspects of the situation are relevant to the type of leadership that would be most effective in that context. The model postulates that it is the degree of subordinate involvement in the decision-making process that is the major variable in leader behaviour. The model is managerial in orientation in that it attempts to offer ways to provide a means of determining a high-quality decision in relation to the task itself, but at the same time ensure that subordinates will actively support the decision.

There are four decision trees offered by the model, two for group problems and two for individual problems. Each pair contains a decision tree for emergency (or time-pressured) situations and one for less time-sensitive events. The latter variation also allows managers to develop subordinate decision making through their involvement in the process. The decision tree does not provide the answer to the problem itself, but offers a suggestion for a leader style that *should* generate the *best* decision in the circumstances, based on levels of subordinate involvement.

There is a potential difficulty in this model for leaders in that changing style dependent on the situation could lead to them being thought inconsistent in their style by subordinates. Equally, for a leader to change style may create conflict, confusion or lower morale and productivity among subordinates. Subordinates may become accustomed to being involved in decision making or become unsure of the degree of involvement that they will enjoy at any given time. That said, there is some research evidence that decisions consistent with the model are more effective than those not consistent with it.

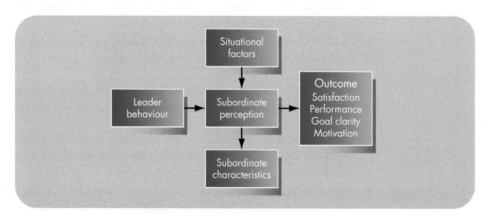

FIGURE 16.9 Path–goal model of leadership.

Other approaches to leadership

The vertical dyad linkage model

This approach to leadership was developed by Dansereau *et al.* (1975). It suggests that leaders behave differently with different subordinates. Between the leader and each subordinate is an individual relationship, referred to as a vertical dyad. The model postulates that leaders create an *in-group* and an *out-group* around themselves and that these groups receive different treatments from the leader. The *in-group* is made up of a few special individuals, more trusted, given preferential treatment and special privileges than those not in that elite. Figure 16.10 reflects the basis of the vertical dyad linkage model.

Transactional and transformational model

This model was originally developed by Burns (1978) and refined by Kuhnert and Lewis (1987) who suggested that there are two types of management activity, each demanding different skills:

✦ Transactional. This includes the allocation of work, making routine decisions, monitoring performance and interacting with other functions within the organization.

✦ Transformational. This is about having the skills and personal qualities to be able to recognize the need for change and being able to identify appropriate courses of action. See for example Avolio *et al.* (1999) who suggest that there are a number of sub-components to the concept including charisma, intellectual stimulation and individualized consideration.

Bass (1990) identified the characteristics of both types of leader (Table 16.2). He suggests that transactional leaders are a hindrance to change and they foster a climate of mediocrity. Transformational leads, by the same token, can produce improved performance in situations of uncertainty and change.

Tepper (1993) found transformational leaders more frequently adopted legitimating tactics than transactional leaders in explaining their decisions and selected courses of action. They were also able to achieve higher acceptance of objectives among subordinates than were transactional leaders. The problem highlighted through this model is that most

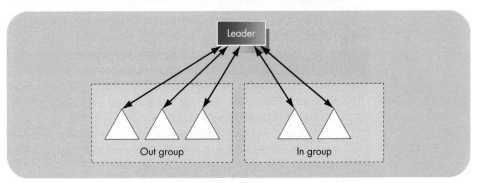

FIGURE 16.10 The vertical dyad model of leadership.

leaders are required to engage in both transactional and transformational leadership as part of the exercise of their responsibilities.

Charismatic leadership

House (1977) characterized charismatic leaders as full of self-confidence, with a high level of confidence in subordinates and high expectations for results. They also have a clear vision of the goal to be achieved, are able to communicate this effectively and lead by example. Charismatic leaders can, however, create problems for organizations. They may not fully understand the business or its environment and so may lead it in the wrong direction. Equally, if they do not make effective provision for succession to the leadership position when they wish to relinquish control the organization can flounder. This eventuality is illustrated in Management in Action 16.4.

Stop | Consider

To what extent would it be possible for a charismatic leader to plan for their successor to be another charismatic leader?

To what extent is it likely that a future charismatic leader would become a threat to the current leader and so be resented and possibly removed from the company?

It has been argued that charismatic leadership could be a function of both leader traits and situational variables (Conger and Kanungo, 1988). Personal traits that may produce a charismatic approach include self-confidence, skills in impression management and social sensitivity. Contextual variables that could encourage the emergence of a charismatic leader include crisis situations and high levels of subordinate dissatisfaction with the current leadership. Howell and Avolio (1992) introduce an ethical perspective to the discussion, pointing out that it is possible for charismatic individuals to abuse their capabilities in order to achieve an unquestioning following and hence a leadership position.

Transactional leaders
1 Contingent reward: Contracts exhange of rewards for effort, promises rewards for good performance, recognizes accomplishments
2 Management by exception (active): Watches and searches for deviations from rules and standards, takes corrective action
3 Management by exception (passive): Intervenes only if standards are not met
4 *Laissez faire*: Abdicates repsonsibilities, avoids making decisions

Tranformational leaders
1 Charisma: Provides vision and sense of mission, instils pride, gains respect and trust
2 Inspiration: Communicates high expectations, uses symbols to focus efforts, expresses important purposes in simple ways
3 Intellectual stimulation Promotes intelligence, rationality, and careful problem solving
4 Individual consideration: Gives personal attention, treats each employee individually, coaches, advises

TABLE 16.2   Characteristics of transactional and transformational leaders (*source*: Bass, BM (1990) From transactional to tranformational leadership: learning to share the vision, *Organizational Dynamics*, Winter)

MANAGEMENT IN ACTION 16.4

The man at the top is king

What happens when the top manager either dies or leaves the company suddenly? This is an issue that faced the senior executives of Argentine oil giant YPF in 1995 when the light aircraft carrying the company president José Estenssoro crashed into the Andes. It is a particularly difficult situation when the leader is charismatic and the dominant force in the company, as was the case with José Estenssoro. After taking over as company president he saw the state-owned company privatized in 1993 and began the turnaround of the loss-making company into a profitable and expanding business. Employee numbers were cut dramatically from 50,000 to about 6000, yet it managed to achieve membership of the top ten private oil companies measured by reserves through his leadership approach.

Michael J Wolf of management consultants Booz Allen & Hamilton in New York has made a study of charismatic leaders in the media industry. His studies suggest that an inspired succession is crucial, particularly in industries where flair and leadership are key factors for success. However, according to Wolf: 'One of the problems for companies with visionary leaders is that it is often difficult for that person to build a pipeline of talented managers – it's one of the things they tend to ignore.' He goes on to explain that such individuals are frequently reluctant to share their corporate 'gameplan' with the next level of management down. They are often self-obsessed and difficult to work with. 'One of the big questions that companies are facing these days is: do they have a model that relies on stars, or do they have a pipeline of talent?' he asks.

Ben Morgan of Kleinwort Benson in Buenos Aires said of the situation facing YPF:

I think they've suffered an enormous shock

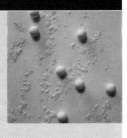

and they're a little bit directionless as a consequence. Because he was so much the front man and had articulated the strategy so well, there is a worry among institutional investors about whether the business can be made to work without someone of his character.

Two options face a company in this situation. First, attempt to create a team to take over at the top and develop the management talent lower down the organization while holding the situation stable in the short term. Alternatively, some analysts advise, for example Christopher Ecclestone, a broker with Interacciones in Buenos Aires, that an international search should be made for a 'heavyweight' appointment that could step into the vacant position. Someone who could articulate the company strategy and act as front man. This is thought to be particularly important for YPF in Argentina where the corporate hierarchy tends to be more autocratic than in other countries. The argument for this approach being that the day-to-day running of the company was effectively handled by the lower levels of management and that this had not changed as a result of the death of José Estenssoro. Morgan agreed with this view saying that it was difficult to get collective responsibility right, the squabbling could be destructive and that someone with natural authority was needed to keep the company moving along.

Adapted from: Pilling, D (1995) The man at the top is king, *Financial Times*, 15 September, p 12.

Conger (1999) suggests that many skills associated with charisma can be developed. For example, speaking skills as part of developing the ability to communicate effectively, and learning how to think critically about the status quo and what could be improved in it. It is also possible to learn how to stage events that send powerful messages to other people. For example, Jim Dawson the newly appointed head of Zebco (the largest fishing tackle producer in the world) quickly recognized the problems with employee relations in the company and abolished managers' reserved parking spaces (he got all their secretaries to park in them before their bosses arrived one day) and also personally smashed all the time clocks on the shopfloor (used for employees to record arrival and departure times). Both actions sent out very clear signals about the future style of leadership. It is also possible for the aspiring charismatic leader to learn how to motivate the team on a day-to-day basis. What Conger suggests it is not possible to learn is how to be passionate about what you do, that has to be discovered at a personal level. Passion about what they are doing is a great driver of charismatic leaders and creates enthusiasm in the followers for achieving the vision. It also suggests that it takes courage to become unconventional and a risk taker, the other major skills of a charismatic leader.

Attribution theory

Attribution theory suggests that individuals observe the behaviour of others and then *attribute* causes to it. In a leadership context, the leader observes the behaviour of subordinates, imputes causes to it, and reacts on the basis of those interpretations (Martinko and Gardner, 1987). For example, an employee who is frequently late for work and who will not work overtime may be classified as lazy and not interested in the job. One major problem that can be created by this view of leadership is that assumptions made by the leader may be wrong. In the example of the employee being late, it may be that domestic difficulties mean that the employee is unable to arrive at work any earlier or stay late, not that they are lazy and do not want to work. In addition, the *attribution* of causes of behaviour does not automatically result in behavioural responses. For example, a leader might interpret the cause of employee behaviour as poor working conditions and seek to address those issues rather than change their leadership behaviour.

Action-centred leadership

The basis of this approach as developed by John Adair and propounded in many books (see, for example, Adair, 1983). Essentially he views leadership as a function of three separate, but linked ideas:

✦ Achieving the task. This includes activities such as planning the work to be done, allocating resources and duties, checking performance and reviewing progress.
✦ Building and maintaining the team. This includes activities such as building team spirit and maintaining morale, maintaining discipline and the training of the group. It also includes establishing subgroups and appointing section leaders.
✦ Developing the individual. This includes activities such as dealing with the personal problems of subordinates, reconciling the needs of the group and the individual and the training of individuals.

Although these three areas of leadership are distinct in themselves they do interact with each other in that actions (or inaction) in one area will influence events in the other two. So, for example, a leader who overemphasizes the task aspects of the model at the expense of the team and individual elements is likely to find that morale drops and that individuals become progressively alienated. Adair uses a three-circle model to illustrate the integrated and interdependent relationship between these three aspects of leadership (see Figure 16.11).

Adair suggests that the development of leaders comes through exposure to each of the three aspects of the model. In essence, being required to take *action* related to each of the dimensions of leadership and to gain the experience and ability to balance all three dimensions at the same time. Training course have been developed to promote personal development in each of the three aspects of the model. Adair also suggests that leaders need the skill to be *aware* of what is going on within the groups for which they are responsible and the *understanding* of which of the components of the leadership process is dominant in any given situation.

Alternatives to leadership

Kerr and Jermier (1978) suggest three areas where substitution for leadership is possible:

✦ Subordinate characteristics. Situations where employees are professionally qualified, highly experienced and very able to undertake the duties expected of them do not need leadership in the conventional sense of the term. Also, where a particular subordinate is indifferent to the rewards that the leader can offer for co-operating and acceptance of a subordinate position there is little scope for the practice of leadership.

✦ Task characteristics. Where the work is highly routine and contains immediate feedback on performance and achievement there is little scope for the exercise of leadership. The employee is effectively controlled by the job that they undertake and feedback on performance etc. is automatically and quickly received through the work

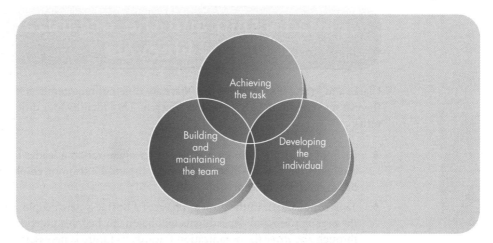

FIGURE 16.11   What a leader has to do (*source*: Adair, J (1983) *Effective Leadership: A Self-development Manual*, Gower, Aldershot).

itself. Leadership in such situations becomes restricted to ensuring that work is provided to the employee and that it is taken away when it is complicated.

✦ Organizational characteristics. An organization that is highly routinized with little flexibility will have limited need for leader activity as it will almost run itself.

Research suggests that these factors do substitute for leadership in certain situations. However, there may be other factors in existence that can influence the level of contribution from a leader. For example an architectural consultancy may have a high number of individuals within it that are highly experienced and capable of doing what is required of them. However, the practise may still benefit from a leader who is capable of acting as a spokesperson and representing the practice to the wider community.

There are groups that attempt to operate without a formal leader. For example, workers' co-operatives and autonomous work teams. A form of democracy would be likely to exist in such groups, replacing the traditional leadershhip role. These groups tend to abolish the *functions* that would be carried out by a leader. They redistribute the activities and functions in order to create greater involvement for every member and encourage more effective contribution from everyone. In addition, such groups frequently have a strong desire to practise democracy within an organizational context and therefore seek alternative ways of *organizing*.

Leadership as symbolism

It has been argued that it is the symbolism associated with the leadership role that influences subordinate behaviour (Griffin *et al.*, 1987). For example, the head of state of any country has several official duties to perform, signing new laws, opening parliament, welcoming official visitors etc. In doing so they act as a symbol representing the entire country and its institutions. In a work context individuals take a lead from the behaviour of their managers. If a leader is thoughtful, caring, concerned and works hard, subordinates will tend to respect that individual and work in a similar manner. The converse is also true.

Leadership and the organizational lifecycle

Clarke and Pratt (1985) suggest that there are different requirements from a leader during the various stages in the organization's lifecycle. They identify four different leadership patterns:

✦ Champion. In the formation stages of an organization a leader is required who can *champion* the new business, win orders, organize a team of employees and display a broad spectrum of leadership ability.

✦ Tank commander. In the growth phase of a business new people will be brought into the organization and departments will be established. An individual to *bulldoze* ideas through and *drive* the organization towards its future is necessary during this stage of evolution.

♦ Housekeeper. The maturity phase tends to require an emphasis on the achievement of cost effectiveness. This is the phase when much activity surrounds the development and application of standard procedures to activity, the careful husbandry of what already exists.

♦ Lemon squeezer. Decline can either result in demise or rejuvenation. A tough leader is required in order to *squeeze* the maximum out of the situation and attempt to inject new life into the organization at this stage in its evolution.

A variation on this approach is that proposed by Rodrigues (1988). This version is based on the premise that the real variation in experience for most organizations is in attempting to continue to function in constantly dynamic context. This carries with it implications for problem solving, implementation and stability in a constantly changing environment. This reflects a different form of lifecycle to that just described and so leaders are needed who can cope with the ever changing demands of this type of organizational experience. Alternatively, leaders should be changed at regular intervals if they cannot adapt to changes in situation.

Leaders, entrepreneurs and vision

It is generally accepted that entrepreneurs create things, new organizations, new products and services and develop new ways of doing existing things. It has been argued that entrepreneurial behaviour is characterized by a high achievement motivation, with the need for power and affiliation at work (Thompson, 1990). Ettinger (1983) goes further by suggesting that there are two types of entrepreneur:

♦ Independent entrepreneurs. Such individuals are more concerned with independence than power and therefore are more likely to create, develop and seek to retain control over their own organizations.

♦ Organization makers. Such individuals have a stronger need to exercise power than to search for independence. Consequently, they tend to search for growth opportunities as this yields both size and power. This form of entrepreneurial activity seeks to take control of organizations with growth potential, develop them. The result for the individual entrepreneur being to float to the top of an ever larger organization as they drive it forward, thereby obtaining ever greater amounts of power.

Clearly, there are two different approaches to leadership evident in Ettinger's work. Drucker (1985) links together the ideas of innovation and entrepreneurship and suggests that the sources of innovation, on which entrepreneurs depend, include:

♦ The unexpected. For example, the development of computer games subsequently led to the development of opportunities to develop computer systems and programs that would function in a home environment.

♦ Incongruous events. Differences between what is actually provided and what consumers feel should be provided can lead to the development of more appropriate offerings. For example, the general dissatisfaction with low rates on bank accounts has led many organizations to establish lower cost telephone and Internet banks in order to offer better rates of interest and attract more customers.

✦ Improvement and development. Existing products and services can always be improved upon. For example, the development of digital photography is a development of the traditional film-based technologies.

✦ Changes in industry and market structures. The opening of the railway links between England and France through the Channel Tunnel have fundamentally changed the cross-channel ferry business. Volume has reduced on the ferries and they must seek other ways of retaining some form of profitable business in competition with the trains.

✦ Demographic changes. The population demographics of many countries is changing and this provides opportunities for new products and services. For example, people are generally living longer and many have both time and money to spend. Consequently, holidays and leisure facilities for such people are developing fast.

✦ Changes in consumer mood and perceptions. The general mood among many people for healthier eating and physical fitness provides many opportunities for gymnasium equipment, food supplements and organic food for the entrepreneur to develop.

✦ Creation of new knowledge. Research and invention can provide new opportunities for entrepreneurs to convert ideas into new products and services.

✦ Inspiration. This category reflects the bright idea that turns out to be a winner. Examples include the development of the ballpoint pen and the Post-it Note.

Mintzberg *et al.* (1998) describe the entrepreneurial organization as a very flat structure with a very small number of top managers, one of whom (the entrepreneur) predominates through the need to lead the others. The basic description of such an organization is one of simplified form and without elaboration. Everything is determined by the small number of senior people and therefore the middle management and support staff numbers are very small. It is the vision and leadership capabilities of the entrepreneur that enables and energizes the organization.

The concept of the visionary leader is also discussed by Mintzberg *et al.* (1998) and draws on earlier work carried out by Frances Westley at McGill University. Westley sought to explain visionary leadership in terms of two analogies:

✦ Hypodermic needle. This analogy is based on the notion of the vision being the active ingredient loaded into the syringe, which is then injected into the employee by the leader in order to create an energized and directed response.

✦ Drama. This analogy of visionary leadership is about creating the equivalent of a stage play in which *repetition*, *representation* and *assistance* combine to create a magical moment when fiction and life harmonize. Westley adds a fourth aspect, that of *integrity* to this basic model. The four key terms represent:
    ✦ Repetition. The inspiration of the visionary stems from a depth of experience in a particular context obtained through repetition over an extended period of the needs and practices required to function effectively within it.
    ✦ Representation. This reflects the ability of the visionary to be able to articulate the vision in a way which makes it alive and real for the followers. It is the ability to get others to buy into the vision through language and communication skills.

✦ Assistance. Leaders need followers. Actors respond to the feedback that they receive from the audience. Westley argues that leaders become visionary because what they communicate appeals to specific stakeholder groups at particular times. They are therefore given the opportunity to lead by that group, as long as their vision holds and benefits that group.

✦ Integrity. The problem with the concept of drama is that a play is a particular form of reality, it is a representation or an interpretation of it for the benefit of the audience. An organization, contrariwise, represents a different form of reality. Its function and purpose relative to the principle *stakeholders* is not only for entertainment or enlightenment, the audience are also the actors, writers, set designers and directors at the same time. Therefore, Westley argues that a leader who only relies upon the first three notions will fail. It is the integrity that the followers feel lies behind what the leader says (and does) that allows leadership to become visionary and not just a performance.

Management in Action 16.5 illustrates how one organization (the Body Shop) set about encouraging the development of entrepreneurial activity as a part of a redundancy exercise. In doing so it not only encouraged the setting up of new organizations, but also helped the local community, redundant employees, the Body Shop itself and a number of employees who would otherwise have stayed within the organization.

Stop | Consider

MiA 16.5 does not mention leadership or vision. Might this imply that these factors are not relevant in entrepreneurial activity or might it imply that the Body Shop was seeking to achieve certain commercial objectives and make the best out of a difficult situation? Justify your views.

Leaders and power

The notion of power as part of the management of organizations was introduced in the previous chapter. There is also an element of power associated with the exercise of leadership so many of the points made there are also relevant in this discussion. Power reflects the ability to influence other people and events. Leadership reflects the ability of one person to direct and control the activities of others, albeit from a slightly different perspective from that of management. It still reflects the process of influence and therefore the exercise of power.

Power is an interesting concept in that it is invisible and largely intangible. Equally, it cannot be felt, tasted or heard. In effect, it exists only in the minds of the people subjected to its effects. It is they who acknowledge that another person holds power over them. Of course, there are situations in which power is obvious and can be easily detected. For example, a thief holding a club and threatening to use it unless you hand over your money is obviously exerting power over you. However, as the French and Raven (1958) model (introduced in Chapter 15) suggests leaders and managers have many levers available to use, not all of which incorporate the blatant use of force to achieve influence.

Power in leadership is the achievement of a willing subjugation of subordinates to the will of the leader. The leader is largely given the ability to influence by the followers

MANAGEMENT IN ACTION 16.5

Giving support in all the right places

In January 1999 the Body Shop found itself having to make 300 people redundant as part of a cost-reduction programme. In the process the management established an outplacement scheme to assist the individuals find alternative work. Part of this scheme was the setting up of an entrepreneurs' club to assist those people who wanted to create their own businesses. This action was intended to lessen the negative impact of large-scale job losses on the local community in West Sussex, England.

Jim McNeish, head of global learning and development with the company, said: 'We asked people what we could do to support them, and started a dialogue. The real power kicked in when they began to ask the Body Shop for support here, training there and sponsorship for different groups and projects.' Support offered has included one-to-one advice sessions on how to develop a business plan and locate other support services; six months' use of a business centre with appropriate IT and administrative back-up; the provision of training grants; and mentoring opportunities with Body Shop managers.

One-day training events have been held to encourage networking between the start-up organizations and the establishment of common purchasing and marketing support. They were also encouraged to explore ways in which they could use each other's services. Banks and other support service providers also attend these events to offer advice and support. Applications for financial support are screened by a management committee from the Body Shop and given final approval by Gordon Roddick, the chairman. The company actively seeks to make use of the fledgling organizations as suppliers and will assist with cashflow in the early days, for example paying invoices up front rather than on normal commercial terms.

The new organizations are discouraged from

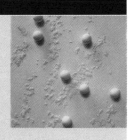

being totally dependent on the Body Shop for business. For example, interest-free loans of up to £20,000 were available, but only if the new venture were capable of sustaining itself without Body Shop business. In addition, the new business had to be run using the same values as guided the Body Shop. However, not every proposal has been accepted for support. There are some aspects of company business that Body Shop wish to retain internal control over. The company allows employees to spend two days each week during their last three months of employment on developing their own career and business planning.

Body Shop managers hope that this process will encourage employees within the company to see opportunities and come forward with ideas for developing and spinning off new business opportunities. One or two have sought to disengage from the company through this route. For example, Lisa Denison was a community action manager with the company but could see an opportunity to become a freelance community development consultant and convinced her manager to support the transition process.

The benefits to the company from this entrepreneurial process are that they can outsource non-core aspects of the business, while retaining loyalty and commitment from suppliers, but without an exclusive relationship. Its links with the local community have been strengthened. The entrepreneurs have been helped to make the transition which should make the chance of establishing a secure long-term business that much more likely. It might even inspire more people to become entrepreneurs.

Adapted from: Johnson, R (1999) Body Shop: giving support in all the right places, *People Management*, 2 September, p 46.

themselves. This is unlike the position in management when the manager has the right (as a result of their formal organizational role) to demand compliance with their wishes, ultimately through the threat of punishment. The style theories of leadership discussed earlier were generally said to be based on a continuum running from autocratic to democratic. It would be those styles at the autocratic end of the spectrum that would be least likely to be able to generate a willing response from the followers and therefore be more likely to make use of the overt forms of power indicated in the French and Raven model.

Of course the French and Raven model requires that employees actually believe that the leader has the ability to deliver the rewards and/or punishments implied by their use of power. For example, a leader who seeks to exercise power through the allocation of rewards, but in a context where the subordinates do not believe that the leader can deliver them, is unlikely to be able to exercise power over that group of followers.

It could be argued that recent trends in management in which the emphasis has been on leadership reflects a move to find ways of sharing power that is acceptable to both managers and subordinates. It was Likert (1967) who identified that leaders who engaged and shared responsibility and power with their subordinates achieved the best levels of productivity. The results of his research were developed into the four systems of management discussed in this chapter.

So far the discussion has ignored those leaders who do not form part of the formal organization. Leadership reflects the ability to lead others and that simply does not occur only within the formal organization. Many companies have sports and social clubs as part of the welfare and support facilities offered to employees. Such organizations are not usually part of the formal organization and the leaders of such facilities are frequently non-management employees who have a particular desire and wish to run such facilities. Management may have representatives on the management committee of the club but will not run it on a day-to-day basis. These facilities provide opportunities for people who would not otherwise have the opportunity to display leadership capabilities.

In addition, there are trade union groups, friendship groups and special interest groups all of which will or may seek to influence managers in some way or other and which must be led by people who can represent their constituencies effectively. Frequently, the degree of power that such leaders are able to exert over the formal organization is a direct consequence of their leadership qualities and capabilities within the group for which they act as leader. A trade union representative with strong leadership qualities is more likely to be able to achieve and demonstrate solidarity among the members and so achieve greater concessions from management than someone who is simply an effective negotiator.

Leadership and success

So far in this discussion about leadership the issue of level of leadership has been ignored. The term leader implies a single person at the head of an organization. This may be true for small or entrepreneurial orgnizations, but many organizations contain large numbers of people and also have many possible leaders at a significant number of levels. There will be the chief executive officer of the organization, supported by the other executive directors and senior managers. Below those levels will be the departmental and functional managers, with reporting to them section heads, middle managers and technical specialists. Then below that level will be the numerous supervisory and junior management positions that make up the bulk of the 'management' jobs within any large organization. It would be highly improbable that any organization could be successful on the strength of a single leader at the top of the managerial hierarchy.

By implication, therefore, it is necessary for an organization to have leaders at every level if maximum utility is to be achieved from the notion of leadership as compared to the concept of management. This sounds sensible enough, but it does raise several interesting questions that are not easy to answer. For example, if every manager within an organization were also a leader would there be a danger that this would detract from the ability of the top leader to differentiate themselves and so function effectively as the focal point for organizational direction and vision? The conventional response to this being that if such circumstances were to occur (not highly likely) then the organization would be so successful that because of the unity of effort and performance the question would be irrelevant.

What this question does raise, however, is the issue of leadership as a reflection of the personal qualities of the individual together with the resultant impact on the group for which the leader is responsible, compared to the process of managing an organization. For an organization to be maximally effective is it necessary to have a mixture of managers and leaders, leaders in the sense of the visionary who can, to use the analogy from Westley just introduced, use drama to energize employees and managers who can adopt an appropriate style to ensure the delivery of performance at the operational level? Such a view would bring the discussion back to the results of the Michigan studies led by Likert discussed earlier which found that participatory styles generated the highest levels of productivity.

In the case of leaders who achieve that position through charisma a different set of questions arise. For example, how does charisma develop within the individual? Does it reflect natural abilities which the individual is born with or do they develop over time? If they develop over time, how does that happen, is it guaranteed to happen and does it have a natural limit that might be different between individuals? Given that charismatic leaders make most impact at the very top of whichever organization they inhabit, these are not minor questions. Since the most commonly held view of charisma is that it reflects the ability to lead through the force of personality, this might imply that it develops as the individual's personality forms. Assuming that charismatic leaders do not simply emerge at the top of the organization overnight it is interesting to speculate how they function within an organization. Consider an organization with a highly charismatic middle manager – could the more senior managers (who may not be charismatic) cope with such a potential threat to their position within their ranks? Such a person may be able to work wonders within their own sphere of responsibility but what of the rest of the organization? Would such a person rise through the ranks very quickly as their ability to achieve results pushes them ever upwards? Or would they be seen as a threat to the existing leadership, as creating an organization within an organization through their attractiveness as a leader to all below them?

What all these questions raise in general terms is how is leadership managed within an organization? Many would argue that leadership qualities can be developed through training and experience. For example, the Blake and Mouton model discussed earlier assumes that having identified the current leadership style as reflecting the balance between concern for people or production, appropriate training can move the individual towards the ideal 9,9 position. However, Pitcher (also discussed earlier) suggests that training, at least as currently undertaken, is unlikely to be successful in moving people's underlying style. Experience suggests that the most likely scenario is that training can provide understanding and experience in different leadership styles, but that the individual may or may not enact them in the normal course of their work. Actually achieving changes in the leadership approach of the individual depends upon a wide range of factors including how they are managed by their own boss, past experience willingness to experiment, organizational context and feedback on performance. Figure 16.12 reflects a number of these factors.

Another way to consider the issue of success within an organization is in terms of *key result areas*. Success is one of those terms that can mean different things to different people, therefore it is not always easy to precisely determine the relationship of leadership to it. However, one model that seeks to do just that is the one that underpins the European Quality Award, introduced in 1992. Established by the European Foundation for Quality Management (EFQM) which was established in 1988 by 14 leading western European companies to encourage quality-based achievements. The essence of the model is that leadership should drive business policy, strategy, people management and resource deployment in the search for business results. The model is shown in Figure 16.13.

The nine elements within the model are classified as either:

✦   Enablers. These include those aspects reflecting how the organization is achieving its results. They include the style of leadership and how managers drive quality and continuous improvement, people management policies and practices for energizing staff to improve quality etc.

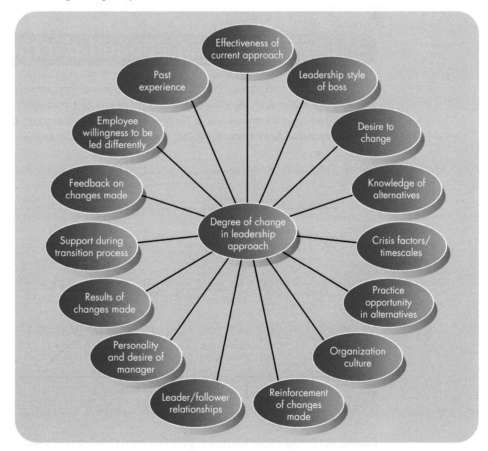

FIGURE 16.12   Factors influencing likelihood of changing leadership approach.

✦ Results. These areas in the model reflect what the company is achieving in the particular areas indicated. For example, people satisfaction reflects what employees actually think about the company and customer satisfaction reflects the customer perspective on the offerings of the company.

The nine elements in the model are scored by a visiting panel of assessors and the company ranked against others in the competition for the award of the prize. However, it is the relationship of leadership to the achievement of the key performance results for the business that is of prime importance in this discussion. The basis of the model is that leadership is a key driver of activity, but that the effects of this are mediated through many other factors before success can be judged. In other words, it is leadership linked to the context that provides the opportunity to achieve success, not leadership itself. Management in Action 16.6 reflects two cases in which attempts at achieving continuous improvement through leadership had very different outcomes.

Stop | Consider

In the light of the material contained in MiA 16.6 how useful is the EFQM model (Figure 16.13) as a basis of measuring the links between leadership and achieving success?
Is it that the model has good descriptive but little analytical power?

Leadership: an applied perspective

That leadership and management are not the same has already been established. Management is the exercise of formal authority in an organizational context, leadership is more to do with performance. It is hardly surprising that managers have for a long time been interested in leadership. Gone are the days when leadership could be assumed as a

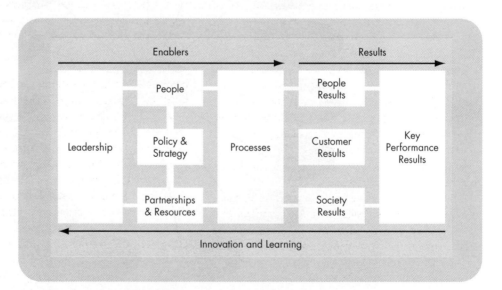

FIGURE 16.13 The EFQM Excellence Model (© EFQM 1999. *Source*: European Foundation for Quality Management, 1999).

MANAGEMENT IN ACTION 16.6

Measuring business excellence

Baxter and MacLeod review the leadership aspect of the EFQM model in some detail and in doing so introduce two case studies that demonstrate different end results, but with similar leadership evaluations from assessors using the model. The first case is based in an aerospace service company. The senior manager (pseudonym Martin Simpson) was responsible for a site that employed 900 people working a four-shift system on the service and repair of jet engines. It was an operation that suffered significant variation in workload demand and had been owned by four different companies in a ten-year period.

In order to reinforce the strength and position of the site in what was a precarious business position, Martin sought to be proactive by actively promoting quality improvement. He introduced a total quality initiative with the title Air Care which began with a four-month diagnostic study intended to profile the company culture and related aspects. The intention was to deliver jet engine overhaul based on a partnership between customers, employees and suppliers, utilizing a framework which measured the cost of quality. Martin recognized that this would need commitment from senior managers and the exercise of leadership qualities. Accordingly, a continuous people involvement process was undertaken which involved training in total quality management (TQM) being cascaded down the organization and also some of the facilitators for the subsequent continuous improvement programme were chosen from the shopfloor.

Some success was reported from the initial stages of the Air Care process, but many of the expectations raised during the training had not been met. For example, adequate financial and other support had not been provided for the cross-functional projects that had been identified. As a consequence, Martin decided that it was necessary to train all employees in TQM. Out of this process came the setting up of improvement

teams. These were empowered employee groups that met weekly and could choose their own projects. Results were again patchy, partly because management had been excluded from the process (at the employees' request) and so failed to give full support to some of the changes proposed. To re-energize the process Martin decided that he would introduce a re-engineering programme (running alongside the other activities) to reduce the turnaround time for an engine from 75 days to 35.

Four project teams were set up and they were able to reduce the turnaround time to 42 days. However, another takeover happened at this time and Martin left the company. No further work was undertaken on the turnover reduction timescales and it stayed at 42 days. Progress came to a standstill.

The second case involved Neil MacFarlane, personnel manager at the cement-making site of a global conglomerate. The site was thought to be earmarked for closure and two previous attempts to introduce TQM in recent years had failed. Neil decided to give it one more try and to position himself as the facilitator of an employee-empowered process. He encouraged people to become involved, tried to make things fun (even using the local zoo for meetings), encouraged workers themselves to make presentations and implement their ideas. The approach adopted was that individuals were encouraged to implement their ideas themselves (the title of the programme was Do It!) – only if they needed help did they call on the team for assistance or if this did not work the facilitator was approached or ultimately the total quality steering group.

In cement making the kiln is the key piece of equipment and so a multidisciplinary team was established to examine stoppages over the previous two years, the idea being to create an action plan to prevent repetition of the causes identified. A new kiln reporting system was developed and a number of sub-groups established to explore different aspects of the overall kiln process. Dramatic improvements in kiln performance were reported as a result of these actions. Neil was moved to another job but the momentum was so strong that improvements continued to be made after he left. In that sense this was unlike the previous example when progress stopped when the main champion left the scene.

In both cases the leadership offered to the programmes was strong and based around the charisma of the sponsoring person. However, because of the circumstances the effect was not the same. In the first case, progress ceased when Martin left, in the second, it had developed a life of its own and continued after Neil's departure.

Baxter and MacLeod make the point that, in the first case, Martin relied too heavily on himself to be the driving force, whereas, in the second example, Neil encouraged others to take the lead and engaged in a higher degree of sharing of information and power as part of the TQM process. That it seems made the difference in the level of ongoing success achieved. These cases demonstrate that leadership of itself does not guarantee success; it is mediated through other elements, the basis of the EFQM model. However, recognition of this does not make it any easier to measure how the elements in the model interact to create success.

Adapted from: Baxter, LF and MacLeod, A (1999) Measuring business excellence: the case of leadership, *Management Services*, July, pp 14–7.

right of birth – at least in many situations. Managers have an interest in the study of the subject from many perspectives. First, to protect their position. Second, managers have an interest in understanding leadership to increase operational effectiveness. Third, it might provide them with a means of dealing more effectively with other managers. Fourth, it could provide managers with an improved means of controlling the organization. Taking each of these points in turn:

✦ Protecting their position. Consider the choice between a manager or someone with obvious leadership qualities (but with the same technical skills as the manager) who both applied for a particular vacancy that you were seeking to fill. Which would you choose? Given the material discussed in this chapter the answer should be obvious, at least for most situations. Therefore, at a personal level the person who can demonstrate the leadership qualities to achieve better results and higher levels of effectiveness from subordinates is more commercially attractive. Such people are more likely to be promoted and rise to senior positions within organizations more rapidly than those without such qualities. That is, all things being equal. Life within organizations is not always as rational or certain, however. If that were the case then this discussion in itself would be irrelevant. Other factors do interfere with the process of career progression, politics, nepotism, opportunity, personal antagonism, favouritism, discrimination and jealousy all play a part. However, in seeking to overcome some of these factors self-interest can be served through acquiring appropriate leadership qualities as well as technical skills.

✦ Increasing operational effectiveness. Managers are always seeking to achieve higher levels of operational effectiveness. Simple cost reduction and reductions in unit labour cost are ever present imperatives among managers. The ever present threat of the availability of cheaper labour from somewhere else in the world seems to be a never ending process. Technical capability can achieve so much, but it cannot achieve everything on a continuous basis. It is people who achieve results, predominantly non-managers. It is the workers who actually deliver the goods and services to the organization and its customers who deliver real performance and effectiveness. The human being is the most effective of computer-based technologies, if it chooses to be so. It is through the qualities of leadership that the choice process can be influenced in favour of management. Employees can be captured, energized and directed through leadership, leading to greater levels of effectiveness in operational activity.

✦ Dealing with colleagues. This raises the issues about the scope of leadership. Does leadership reflect a set of characteristics that only function in a vertical direction? Much of the literature discussed in this chapter assumes that to be the case. It is described in terms of being something that operates between leaders and followers. But what about leader-to-leader interaction? A considerable proportion of the activity of leaders involves interacting with other leaders for some purpose. For example, the leader of a trade union group will spend a great deal of time representing members and their interests to management and in so doing be interacting and seeking to influence other leaders. This inevitably raises the question about the impact of leadership qualities on those interactions. Pitcher (1997) believes that it is the interaction between the styles of technocrat, artist and craftsman in a team of management that significantly impacts on the well-being of the organization. For example, the artist is bored with detail and so needs the craftsman and technocrat around them to look after detail and realism. Technocrats, by way of contrast, find it very difficult to do anything other than concentrate on the detail and cannot tolerate the caveats and qualification insisted upon by the other two styles. She suggests (p 166) that, 'the trick is to have the right people in the right place at the right time and to make sure that the technocrat has loads of influence and not a shred of power'. One implication of this quotation being that technocrats should not run organizations. Success (or failure) comes from the type of leadership provided relative to the circumstances and the dynamic between the styles within the organizational context. That is the essence of the EFQM model discussed earlier.

✦ Increased control. Leadership can also enhance the ability to control. Management has the right to control as a result of the organizational responsibilities given to the role. However, holding that right to control does not automatically achieve it in full measure. Employees may comply with the requirements placed on them by managers for many reasons, some may enjoy their work; some may see the opportunity for advancement as a result of co-operation; others may need the income that the job provides. Yet others may simply go along with whatever is demanded of them because they are still within their *zone of indifference* – the demands of the manager do not disturb them enough to create a reaction against the requirement to comply. However, when a leader is directing events then there should be a greater degree of willingness among employees to acquiesce to the requirements dictated by the leader. In that sense whatever style or form through which the leader leads they should find it easier (than a manager) to achieve a more effective control over employees. More effective in that context refers to the existence of willingness, co-operation, enhanced performance and general support for the leader-determined objectives. Even in the democratic styles indicated above the leader plays a significant part as one of the team in shaping the group norms and activities and so is influential in determining control mechanisms and behaviour patterns.

Atkinson (1999) suggests that without leadership there can be no change and that organizations that do not implement strategies for continued and sustained improvement will not recruit the best people and will be more likely to fail. He argues for a strong blend of transactional and transformational style within the leader and that this should be developed by training and development. In his discussion, he also makes the point that employees inevitably watch their boss, making judgements about their behaviour and the honesty of their leadership style. He uses the expression: 'Do what you say and say what you do.' This makes the point that these judgements are critical in establishing trust among the employees and developing a consistent management style. Management in Action 16.7 sets out some of his views in relation to leadership.

Stop | Consider
To what extent does the material presented by Atkinson reflect the underlying theme of this chapter?
Justify your views.

Conclusions

This chapter has considered many of the variables associated with the subject of leadership. The major theoretical approaches to the study of leadership have been introduced and critically evaluated. In addition, we have discussed a number of other approaches to the subject and related these to features of management activity where appropriate. We have considered alternative approaches to the subject of leadership including charismatic leadership and action-centred leadership. Also considered were the symbolic aspects of leadership and the relevance of it during different stages of the organizational lifecycle. Entrepreneurship and vision and their relationship to leadership were discussed as was the relationship with power and success. The chapter ended with a brief consideration of some of the leadership implications that emerge within the dynamic of organizational experience.

Discussion questions

1. Define the following key terms used in this chapter:

Charismatic leadership	Contingency	Blake and Mouton's leadership grid
Leadership	Vroom, Yetton and Jago's model	Hersey and Blanchard's model
Style	House's path–goal model	Pitcher's model of leadership
Trait	Likert's four systems of management	Fiedler's model

2. Discuss the differences and similarities between the concepts of management and leadership.

MANAGEMENT IN ACTION 16.7

Without leadership there is no change

Atkinson suggests that the following benefits can be achieved from introducing a strong leadership development programme:

+ Behaviours will be clarified which will immediately lead to improved team performance.

+ Leadership style will exist by design rather than through default and will signal the preferred ways of leading.

+ Development activities will improve as they will be designed and targeted at managers as they undergo the transition.

+ Clear signals will be provided to new recruits and newly promoted managers.

+ Team morale will improve as new leadership styles transform the old control-based model to new trust based perspectives.

+ Performance management will be taken seriously and cultural measures become measurable and therefore changeable.

+ The early adopters of the new styles (first through the training etc.) will be able to help the later and slower paced leaders to adapt to the new styles.

+ The organizational focus will be on achieving the best from teams.

+ The ability to attract and retain top talent will be enhanced through the improved psychological contract with leaders and their newly defined role within the organization.

Atkinson goes on to offer his suggestions as to the main characteristics of effective leaders (he describes them as the top 5 Es):

+ Energy. The leader must be able to offer high energy levels to demonstrate resilience, ability and stamina in the demanding businesses of

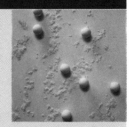

the future. Energy in that sense means being positive and able to keep going under pressure.

+ Enthusiasm. High levels of self-confidence and self-esteem are important to effective leadership. The main block to personal achievement is that individuals do not believe that they can do more. People with low self-esteem are difficult to move from their comfort zone and will usually not challenge the traditional ways of doing things.

+ Energize. This involves the ability to energize others. It is the leader who can pass on their own enthusiasm and energy who achieves the highest levels of effectiveness within their teams.

+ Execute. Actually getting on with things is another key aspect of effectiveness for any leader. Forever asking for clarification, more information and greater detail or discussion never produced anything. It is only when a decision is made and acted upon that things change. So prevarication is out for the effective leader. Related to this of course is the need to be able to learn from experience. Making decisions quickly is one thing, but they need to be good ones. Learning from past mistakes is one important aspect of making better decisions quickly.

+ Edge. Living on the edge by always seeking new ways and challenging the traditional ways of doing things. Never being satisfied with what exists is the key characteristic here.

Adapted from: Atkinson, P (1999) Without leadership there is no change, *Management Services*, August, pp 8–11.

3. Is an attempt to identify the most appropriate leadership style simply another attempt to identify a formula which is doomed to failure? Justify your answer.

4. Describe Likert's four systems of management and attempt to make a case for system 1 being the most appropriate style in a particular context. What might this imply about the concept of effectiveness in leadership?

5. 'Come the hour, come the leader.' Discuss this statement in the light of the approaches to leadership discussed in this chapter.

6. 'Leaders need to find the right group and context before they are able to exercise their leadership.' Discuss this statement.

7. Do the concepts of artist, craftsman and technocrat reflect leadership styles or personality characteristics? Justify your answer.

8. Fiedler's contingency model suggests that if the situation is very unfavourable to the leader then it is necessary to drive the subordinates towards the objectives by adopting a task-oriented style of leadership. Do you agree with this view? Justify your answer.

9. To what extent is leadership simply a means of expressing management in a way that employees would find more acceptable and therefore work harder?

10. 'Charismatic leaders are not appropriate in the middle ranks of managerial jobs because they could provide the basis for an organization within an organization to develop.' Discuss this statement.

Research activities

1. Arrange to interview about six different managers from a range of organizations and job functions. Talk to them about their own approach to management. Identify what they consider to be the differences and similarities between management and leadership. Do they consider that management and leadership are skills that can be taught or are they natural talents possessed by some people but not everyone? Do they have a particular style of operation or do they change approach to fit the circumstances? Consider the results of the interviews and draw lessons from it with what you have studied in this chapter.

2. For a number of famous business, military or political leaders obtain a copy of their biography or autobiography. What does it tell you about their views of leadership. Can you reconcile the different views expressed and does the material presented in this chapter accommodate their views (and if not why)?

3. Conduct a library search on the subject of leadership. What issues do you think that are relevant to topics that have (or have not) been introduced in this chapter?

Key reading

From Clark, H, Chandler, J and Barry, J (1994) *Organization and Identities: Text and Readings in Organizational Behaviour*, International Thomson Business Press, London:

- ✦ Kanter, RM: Men and women of the corporation, p 152. Considers the nature of organizations and the impact on the people that work in them.
- ✦ Nichols, T and Beynon, H: The labour of superintendence: managers, p 192. This considers the reality of management in an organization.
- ✦ Roethlisberger, FJ and Dickson, R: Group restriction of output, p 247. Although emphasizing the significance of groups, it also reviews the relationship between managers and subordinates.
- ✦ Coch, L and French, JRP: Overcoming resistance to change using group methods, p 260. Considers a number of aspects of change management, including the strategies adopted by managers.
- ✦ Fiedler, FE: Leadership: a contingency model, p 272. Part of the original work from this particular writer on the first of the contingency models.
- ✦ Needham, P: The 'autonomous' work group, p 310. Discusses the nature and role of management within this form of work organization.

Further reading

de la Billière, P Sir (1994) *Looking for Trouble: SAS to Gulf Command, the Autobiography*, HarperCollins, London. A book which considers leadership from a personal perspective and from the very particular context of the military and special operations.

Fallon, I (1988) *The Brothers: The Rise and Rise of Saatchi and Saatchi*, Hutchinson, London. This book considers the careers of the two Saatchi brothers and the empire that they created from nothing. Naturally it is limited by its date of publication and much has happened since then. However, it serves as a starting point for considering leadership in a more complete context.

Heller, R (1985) *The Naked Manager: Games Executives Play*, McGraw-Hill, New York. The behaviours that managers adopt and the political and business reasons that motivate it are the focus of attention.

Hersey, P and Blanchard, KH (1988) *Management of Organizational Behaviour*, 5th edn, Prentice Hall, Englewood Cliffs, NJ. This contains a reply to the Nicholls' criticisms of their original model.

Luecke, R (1994) *Scuttle Your Ships Before Advancing and Other Lessons from History on Leadership and Change for Today's Managers*, Oxford University Press, New York. This book takes a look back into history at a number of major events involving management, leadership and change. It then attempts to draw lessons from those episodes that can be of value to managers of today.

Nicholls, JR (1985) A new approach to situational leadership, *Leadership and Organization Development Journal*, 6, 2–7. This offers another view of the Hersey and Blanchard model of management style. It claims to identify major weaknesses in the original and suggests how these can be overcome.

References

Adair, J (1983) *Effective Leadership: A Self-development Manual*, Gower, Aldershot.
Ashby, WR (1956) *An Introduction to Cybernetics*, Methuen, London.

Atkinson, P (1999) Without leadership there is no change, *Management Services*, August, pp 8–11.

Avolio, BJ, Bass, B and Jung, DI (1999) Re-examining the components of transformational and transactional leadership using the multifactor leadership questionnaire, *Journal of Occupational and Organizational Psychology*, **72**, 4, 441–62.

Bass, BM (1990) From transactional to transformational leadership: learning to share the vision, *Organizational Dynamics*, Winter, 19–31.

Blake, RR and McCanse, AA (1991) *Leadership Dilemmas – Grid Solutions*, Gulf Publishing, New York.

Burns, JM (1978) *Leadership*, Harper & Row, New York.

Clarke, C and Pratt, S (1985) Leadership's four-part progress, *Management Today*, March, 84–6.

Conger, J (1999) Charisma and how to grow it, *Management Today*, December, pp 78–81.

Conger, JA and Kanungo, RM (1988) Behavioural Dimensions of Charismatic Leadership. In Conger, JA and Kanungo, RM (eds) *Charismatic Leadership: The Elusive Factor In Organizational Effectiveness*, Jossey Bass, San Francisco, CA.

Dansereau, F, Graen, G and Haga, WJ (1975) A vertical dyad linkage approach to leadership within formal organizations: a longitudinal investigation of the role-making process, *Organizational Behaviour and Human Performance*, **15**, 46–78.

Drucker, PF (1985) *Innovation and Entrepreneurship*, Heinemann, London.

Ettinger, JC (1983) Some Belgian evidence on entrepreneurial personality, *European Small Business Journal*, **1**, 2.

Fiedler, FE (1967) *A Theory of Leadership Effectiveness*, McGraw-Hill, New York.

Fiedler, FE (1986) The contribution of cognitive resources to leadership performance, *Journal of Applied Social Psychology*, **16**, 532–48.

French, J and Raven, B (1958) The Bases of Social Power. In Cartwright, D (ed.) *Studies in Social Power*, Institute for Social Research, Ann Arbor, Michigan.

Griffin, RW, Skivington, KD and Moorhead, G (1987) Symbolic and interactional perspectives on leadership: an integrative framework, *Human Relations*, **40**, 199–218.

Handy, C. (1993) *Understanding Organizations*, 4th edn, Penguin, Harmondsworth.

Hersey, P and Blanchard, KH (1982) *Management of Organizational Behaviour*, 4th edn, Prentice Hall, Englewood Cliffs, NJ.

House, RJ (1977) A 1976 theory of charismatic leadership. In Hunt, JG and Larson, LL (eds) *Leadership: The Cutting Edge*, Southern Illinois University Press, Carbondale, IL.

House, RJ and Mitchell, TR (1974) Path–goal theory of leadership, *Journal of Contemporary Business*, Autumn, 81–97.

Howell, JM and Avolio, BJ (1992) The ethics of charismatic leadership: submission or liberation?, *Academy of Management Executive*, May, 43–54.

Indvik, J (1986) Path-goal theory of leadership: a meta-analysis, *Academy of Management Best Papers Proceedings*, 189–92.

Jago, AG and Ragan, JW (1986) The trouble with leader match is that it doesn't match Fiedler's contingency model, *Journal of Applied Psychology*, **71**, 555–59.

Kerr, S and Jermier, JM (1978) Substitutes for leadership: their meaning and measurement, *Organizational Behaviour and Human Performance*, **22**, 375–403.

Kuhnert, KW and Lewis, P (1987) Transactional and transformational leadership: a constructive/developmental analysis, *Academy of Management Review*, October, 648–57.

Likert, R (1967) *The Human Organization*, McGraw-Hill, New York.

McGregor, D (1960) *The Human Side of Enterprise*. McGraw Hill, New York.

Martinko, MJ and Gardner, WL (1987) The leader/member attribution process, *Academy of Management Review*, April, 235–49.

Mazlish, B (1990) *The Leader, the Led and the Psyche*, University Press of New England, Hanover, NH.

Mintzberg, H, Quinn, JB, Ghoshal, S (1998) *The Strategy Process*, Prentice Hall, Hemel Hempstead.

Muczyk, JP and Reimann, BC (1987) The case for directive leadership, *The Academy of Management Executive*, November.

Nicholls, JR (1985) A new approach to situational leadership, *Leadership and Organization Development Journal*, **6**, 2–7.

Pitcher, P (1997) *The Drama of Leadership*, John Wiley, New York.

Rodrigues, CA (1988) Identifying the right leader for the right situation, *Personnel*, September, 43–6.

Rothman, A (1987) Maybe your skills aren't holding you back: maybe it's a birthday, *Wall Street Journal*, 19 March, 35.

Rowe, C (1993) *The Management Matrix*, Alfred Waller, London.

Scase, R and Goffee, R (1989) *Reluctant Managers: Their Work and Lifestyles*, Unwin Hyman, London.

Stewart, R (1976) *Contrasts in Management*, McGraw-Hill, Maidenhead.

Strube, MJ and Garcia, JE (1981) A meta-analytic investigation of Fiedler's contingency model of leadership effectiveness, *Psychological Bulletin*, September, 307–21.

Tannenbaum, R and Schmidt, WH (1973) How to choose a leadership pattern, *Harvard Business Review*, May-June, 178–80.

Tepper, BJ (1993) Patterns of downward influence and follower conformity in transactional and transformational leadership, *Academy of Management Best Papers Proceedings*, 267–71.

Thompson, JL (1990) *Strategic Management: Awareness and Change,* Chapman & Hall, London.

Torrington, D and Hall, L (1991) *Personnel Management: A New Approach*, 2nd edn, Prentice Hall, Hemel Hempstead.

Vecchio, RP (1992) Cognitive resource theory: issues for specifying a test of the theory, *Journal of Applied Psychology*, 77, 375–6.

Vroom, VH and Jago, AG (1988) *The New Leadership*, Prentice Hall, Englewood Cliffs, NJ.

Watson, TJ (1994) *In Search of Management: Culture, Chaos and Control in Managerial Work,* Routledge, London.

CHAPTER 17

Ethical perspectives in organizational behaviour

CHAPTER SUMMARY

This chapter begins with the consideration of the links between ethics and moral philosophy before going on to discuss different approaches to the subject. This will be followed by the consideration of a number of aspects of ethics as associated with organizational behaviour. For example, researching into human behaviour within an organization, cultural issues and social responsibility are aspects associated with ethical dilemmas. There are also many ethical issues associated with the employment of people within an organization that managers need to consider including privacy, working beyond the contract and whistleblowing. The areas to be considered next are the links between ethics and employee participation, concluding with an applied review of the topic.

LEARNING OBJECTIVES

After studying this chapter and working through the associated Management in Action panels, Discussion questions and Research activities, you should be able to:

+ Understand the basis of ethics and its links with moral philosophy.

+ Describe the nature and significance of corporate governance.

+ Explain the different classifications of ethical perspective.

+ Outline the links between culture and ethics.

+ Assess some of the ethical dilemmas facing managers.

+ Appreciate the ethical implications that arise from the managerial imperative to achieve value for money through the employment of people.

+ Discuss the different approaches that managers might take to resolving the ethical difficulties that they face.

+ Detail the issues surrounding whistleblowing and the many forms of antisocial behaviour that occur within an organizational context.

Introduction

Ethics influences both the process involved in making decisions and the criteria used to judge between options. It also influences many other aspects of business activity such as approaches to social responsibility, business tactics and the treatment of whistleblowers. The involvement of employees in decision making also contains ethical perspectives linked to the purpose, form, degree and impact of such participation. It is not only managers that face ethical dilemmas. Employees frequently have to make judgements which contain an ethical dimension. For example, what should an employee do when they consider that their organization is cheating customers? There are also situations where both managers and employees can collude to defraud other people. Management in Action 17.1 illustrates one such situation, collusion in defrauding the state benefit system. Clearly the ethical and legal implications are being ignored by the individuals involved.

Stop | Consider   *To what extent is the situation described in MiA 17.1 an ethical problem or a simple desire on the part of government and individuals to minimize expenditure and maximize income?*

What might your views in relation to the first question imply about the nature and relevance of ethics to society in general and organizations in particular?

The employment of people within an organization automatically creates difficulties for managers. Employees are human beings and are unlike the other resources available to the organization. Most resources are automatically malleable at the whim of management. Money will go where it is channelled. Raw material will be worked on and change appearance until it is part of the finished product or scrapped. These forms of resource have no choice in how they are used. Human beings do have choice, they can react, interact and are of the same species as managers. There are moral, political, legal and practical reasons for treating employees differently from the other resources available.

To begin with humans decide which organizations to seek to be associated with. They decide when to leave – unless that decision is taken out of their hands through death, illness, accident, retirement or termination of employment by management. While at work there are also many choices available to the human resource. How hard to work; how much effort to put into the job; how conscientious to be in looking after the general interests of the employer; how hard to resist employer demands for more work; how hard to push in seeking to meet their own aspirations for higher pay or shorter hours etc. These reflect just some of the ways in which human beings can influence events associated with their work experiences.

Managers seek to find ways to *manipulate* the resources under their control in the interests of their objectives. More efficient ways of making products, reductions in waste and higher productivity are just some of the *manipulations* engaged in. *Manipulation* is frequently regarded as having negative connotations and that can be so in some situations. By way of contrast, a wood carver can create something of great beauty as a result of the *manipulation* of tools and pieces of wood. The managerial imperative to manipulate is, according to the rational view, intended to harness and direct resources in pursuit of objectives and does not contain a negative connotation. Unfortunately, life is not always so clear and there are frequently hidden agendas being pursued in the dynamic context of an organization. The *manipulations* encountered within an organizational setting can, broadly

MANAGEMENT IN ACTION 17.1

Employers 'helping workers to claim dole'

The so-called 'black economy' provides opportunities for individuals to earn money that is hidden from the state and, therefore, not liable to taxation. This increases the earnings levels of the individuals in receipt of the money and 'starves' the government of income. It is also a process that allows the employer to save money by not having to pay any company taxation to the state as a result of having someone on the payroll. In addition, it is possible to pay the employee a lower wage because they will not have to pay tax on that income. As a process, the black economy works at many different levels. Individual householders may ask a friend with plumbing skills to put in a new shower unit in the bathroom of their house and pay the friend for doing the work. At another level an individual may work for a company at the same time as claiming state benefit for being unemployed.

In the UK the various civil service departments that have a responsibility for paying state benefit to unemployed people have become increasingly aware of the attempts of some unscrupulous people to defraud the system. In a relatively recent trend it has also been found that some employers are actively colluding with employees to allow them to claim unemployment pay as well as wages. This has become so

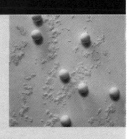

significant that special fraud units have been established to find and prosecute claimants and employers found engaging in these practices. In the year 1992–3, 55 employers were prosecuted and another 71 cases were pending. A total of 264,616 investigations of individuals were carried out which resulted in 2602 prosecutions and another 61,129 people withdrew claims for benefit without being prosecuted.

In some cases employers were found to be allowing employees time off work to claim benefit. In a small number of cases employers actually drove the employee to the benefit office to sign on as unemployed. Typically, such employers were very small, with fewer than 15 workers in total. They also tended to be in the service sector such as mini-cab firms, hotels, catering, casual farm work and amusement arcades. A government minister claimed that such practices were 'an example of how the black economy corrodes the fabric of our society' and that 'this behaviour gives unscrupulous employers an unfair advantage over their competitors'.

Adapted from: Bennett, W (1993) Employers 'helping workers to claim dole', *The Independent*, 11 August, p 4.

speaking, include attempts to enhance commercial advantage by *slanting events against the opposition*. This can lead to many forms of antisocial behaviour, market manipulations, bullying and bending of the conventional rules. This defines the field of interest for ethics within organizational behaviour.

Philosophy and ethics

Ethics is about doing the right thing. Philosophy is about, 'the critical evaluation of assumptions and argument' (Raphael, 1994, p 1). Moral philosophy is a branch of philosophy that takes as its sphere of interest a, 'philosophical inquiry about norms or values, about ideas of right and wrong, good or bad, what should and what should not be done' (Raphael, 1994, p 8). Clearly, therefore, there are close associations between the study of ethics and that of moral philosophy. Both have an interest in right and wrong behaviour.

Moral philosophy as an approach is able to tease out the underlying assumptions in ethical situations and critically evaluate them. Ethics takes as its focus of interest behaviour that contains rightness, goodness, correctness or appropriateness in a particular context. Another way of considering the distinction is that ethics is related to aspects of interpersonal behaviour whereas moral philosophy covers a broader range of experiences in the human condition, including beauty and feelings.

The evaluation of behaviour as either good or bad is judged by reference to the norms or values that are generally accepted within a particular context. There are four major approaches to the basis of moral decision making that have emerged over the years, including:

✦ Naturalism. This view holds that morality can be judged on the basis of human tendencies to adopt a *self-interest* view of behaviour. It posits the view that any particular morality will be situation specific. Being grounded in the species nature of human beings, this approach to morality would be variable depending upon the forces active in a particular context.

✦ Rationalism. This view suggests that there is an absolute truth which underpins ethical standards. The level of knowledge and understanding available in a particular context are a function of the application of reason and logic. Expressed morality can be viewed as an approximation to its real form. As knowledge and understanding develop through logic and reason the expression of morality is refined and therefore comes closer to the ultimate.

✦ Utilitarianism. This perspective proposes that doing what is *right* promotes happiness. Consequently, the higher the level of practised morality the greater the level of experienced happiness. In that context, morality can be equated with the concept of *goodness*. There are different perspectives on this view of morality. Bentham was the leading nineteenth-century classical utilitarian who claimed that individuals always act on the basis of achieving maximum personal levels of happiness. The view that all will ultimately benefit from downsizing is an organizational version of this concept and is reflected in Management in Action 17.2.

| Stop | Consider | *Is it possible to reconcile the views expressed in MiA 17.2 with those of Bentham when he suggests that individuals will always act to achieve maximum personal happiness? Consider the perspectives of each of the major stakeholder groups in this review.* |

One of the major difficulties for this approach is that of operationalizing the definition of *goodness*. Goodness (or happiness) are terms that can have multiple meanings and selective impacts at the same time. For example, flogging individuals convicted of theft might create a feeling of *happiness* among victims, but at the same time create pain and *unhappiness* for the criminal and their family. Remember that the family of the thief may have benefited from the crime in a monetary sense but were not necessarily directly involved in the crime itself. So should the majority rule in the

MANAGEMENT IN ACTION 17.2

The cold war is over and the bosses won

The cold war created many political and military problems for those countries engaged in it. However, it also brought with it a number of benefits. In the USA it allowed bosses to demonstrate that America had the highest standard of living and lowest levels of unemployment. Bosses were encouraged, as a consequence of the bloated cold war economy, to inflate their payrolls and boast about how many staff they employed. That has all changed.

In the global competition for jobs, first with China and then Russia, US industry is hard pressed. Automation has cut jobs in every industry including banking and finance. Most companies are being downsized, rightsized or re-engineered. The current boast of bosses is of how many people they have fired, forced into retirement before their due date or turned into part-time or contract staff with no fringe benefits at all. Nicholas von Hoffman termed the boss of today as the 'bizbrute'.

The truth behind much of the unemployment faced by today's blue- and white-collar workers is not that poor performance or incompetence causes redundancy. It is the high cost of health insurance, pension plans and the fact that young people will do the job for half the money that lies behind much of it. For example over the six years prior to 1994 inflation in the USA increased by 27%, but wages increased by only 19%. Manufacturing employees now work 320 hours more than their European counterparts. Over a ten-year period they have added a total of 17 days to the normal work year. Many are burned out as well as disillusioned.

Science PhDs feel the changes more than

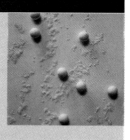

many. During the 1980s they could expect to walk straight into an affluent lifestyle with an income over $50,000. Indeed, students were actively encouraged to follow this path. With many science and technical jobs moving (with the assembly work) to the location offering the cheapest labour, this is no longer the case. Many well-qualified science and technology students are now lucky to find jobs washing test tubes rather than work as research or development specialists. Prospects for law graduates are the worst for ten years, with one in six being unemployed six months after graduating in the summer of 1992.

Pringle suggests in a rather cynical way that: 'The key to protecting your job during downsizing is to keep your income low, refuse all raises and other forms of additional compensation. Also, if you're over 40, lie about it.' Pringle illustrates his views with reference to a US sitcom called 'The Larry Sanders Show', which reflects the backstage reality of the late-night talk show. In doing so it also depicts many of the problems facing US employees. Employees harassed by the show's directors are pressured into spending more and more time at work and are castigated for attempting to deal with the inevitable personal problems that arise from this stress. The show draws a picture of the experience of life within the modern organization being nothing more than work and ruthless bosses. A caricature for sure, but with a high degree of reflection of the real life experience for many people.

Adapted from: Pringle, P (1995) The cold war is over and the bosses won, *The Independent*, 2 January, p 11.

application of rightness? To accept this view could be considered as the basis of justifying the horrors of war, the Holocaust and that most recent version of it, ethnic cleansing.

The difficulties faced by *utilitarianism* in providing an effective basis for understanding morality produced a number of alternative approaches. One of them, referred to as *intuitionism*, proposed a number of values that stand the test of time and therefore reflect underlying and unchanging principles. Although there are variations in the nature of the principles proposed within this approach, Raphael (1994) identifies eight that cover those most frequently proposed (see Table 17.1).

✦ Formalism. It was Kant who described a distinction between categorical and hypothetical imperatives in reaching moral decisions. The hypothetical imperative is based on the pragmatic approach to situations. It considers that actions should be designed to meet some self-interest function of the decision maker. Kant argued that this approach did not explain all circumstances relating to moral decisions and that categorical imperatives reflected circumstances where the means-to-an-end perspective did not apply. For example, giving to charity can be seen in terms of goodness for its own sake and not as a means of providing a direct or indirect benefit to the giver. This provides a *formalized* approach to deciding between courses of action. It requires the individual to apply three filters to the decision (see Table 17.2).

It should be apparent that the perspective adopted in Table 17.2 implies a democratic approach to moral decisions. It can be argued that this approach produces a basis for the regulation of society through the legislative, political and procedural frameworks that are established to provide structure and order. Similar parallels have been suggested to hold in an organizational context. For example, the development of rules and bureaucratic forms of organization as a basis for decision making. Hosmer

✦ Promoting the happiness of other people
✦ Refraining from harm to other people
✦ Treating people justly
✦ Telling the truth
✦ Keeping promises
✦ Showing gratitude
✦ Promoting one's own happiness
✦ Maintaining and promoting one's own virtues

TABLE 17.1 Principles of intuitionism (*source*: Raphael, DD (1994) *Moral Philosophy*, 2nd edn, Oxford University Press, Oxford)

1	Consider you are attempting to create a rule for every individual to follow
2	Consider that the human beings involved are ends in themselves and not a means to some personal gratification
3	Consider that everyone else in society has the same rights and freedoms to act as they see fit and that they should act on the basis of 1 and 2 above

TABLE 17.2 A simplified form of Kantian ethics (*adapted from*: Raphael, DD (1994) *Moral Philosophy*, Oxford University Press, Oxford)

(1987) describes an approach to management decision making that reflects this ethical perspective (Figure 17.1).

Another way of thinking about the approach adopted by Hosmer is that of a decision-making process influenced by the elements contained in Figure 17.1. The ideas contained in Figure 17.1 can be accommodated into that process as filters for the variables involved. Figure 17.2 attempts to represent this view by reflecting the impact of ethics on the process.

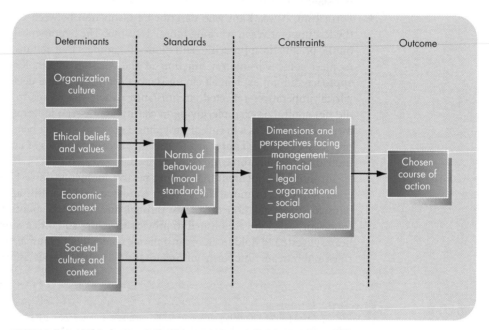

FIGURE 17.1   Ethical perspectives in management decision making (*adapted from*: Hosmer, ET (1987) Ethical analysis and HRM, *Human Resource Management*, 23).

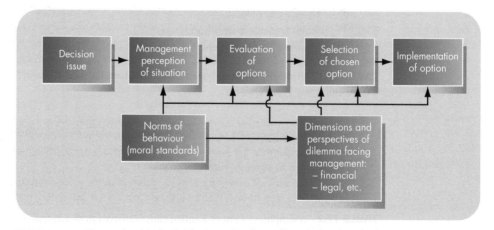

FIGURE 17.2   Hosmer's ethical model applied to a rational decision-making process.

Ethical perspectives in organizations

Ethical issues are about *rightness*, *wrongness*, *good* and *bad*. This is as much applicable within the sphere of organizational activity as it is in the field of politics or behaviour in society as a whole. Deciding the right thing to do in any particular context can be a demanding task. Consider for example the position of a subordinate who finds out that their manager is falsifying expenses claims. What would be the proper and right course of action for the subordinate to adopt? The choices include:

✦ Do nothing.

✦ Report the manager to a more senior manager.

✦ Let the manager know that they have been found out.

✦ Send an anonymous letter to the chief executive.

✦ Report the manager to the subordinates' trade union.

✦ Write a letter to the press.

✦ Write a letter to the largest shareholder.

✦ Report the manager to their professional association (if they belong to one).

Each of these options has a range of costs and benefits for the individuals involved in the situation. In weighing up the most appropriate course of action the subordinate can adopt one of two approaches. First, they could take the decision based on their judgement of the fundamental rightness or wrongness of the act that they have encountered. In doing so they would be acting irrespective of any consequences for the manager involved, themselves or the organization. Second, they could form a judgement based on the possible consequences for the principle *stakeholders*. For example, if they had an extremely good working relationship with the manager and felt a high degree of personal loyalty towards that individual then an approach that ran counter to that would be likely to cause distress to the subordinate and so be less likely to be adopted.

Cederblom and Dougherty (1990) use the ideas introduced earlier as the basis for deciding between alternative courses of action. They refer to the two approaches as *utilitarianism* and *contractarianism*. Utilitarian approaches are summarized as *benevolence* and contract approaches are about *fairness*. Within each model there are two versions, giving four different options from which to form the basis of choosing an appropriate course of action.

Utilitarian approach

This approach is grounded in the concept of *utility* or *usefulness*. In determining the right course of action in any given context a key feature should be the level of valued results produced. The approach to be adopted is one of *benevolence* towards the needs of others in determining one's own behaviour. This approach looks forward in assessing the ethical perspectives on any particular situation. It requires an evaluation of options on the basis of the future impact on those that are likely to effected by the consequences.

Act utilitarianism   This version suggests that every dilemma should be regarded on its own merits. For example, telling a lie could be justified if it created happiness for the people involved. It would appear to run contrary to all the norms of society to be able to justify actions such as lying, cheating and even murder under some circumstances. Given the rise in criminal acts experienced by many people over the past few years it would be possible to argue that to allow citizens to murder individuals who threaten them with criminal acts would both save money by simplifying the legal system and make ordinary people feel happier – but are these reasons adequate by themselves to make such actions right?

Rule utilitarianism   This approach takes the view that applying the principles of *act utilitarianism* might be a good thing to do in that instance, but still wrong according to the need to operate society in a consistent way. The rule approach to utilitarianism implies that it is necessary to create rule frameworks that would serve as the basis for individuals to identify appropriate courses of action in specific contexts.

Contract approach

This approach to deciding between conflicting courses of action and resolving ethical dilemmas is grounded in the notion that agreements whether they be explicit or tacit should be honoured. In general terms, it considers that by virtue of the social environment within which human beings function co-operation is a major imperative. As a consequence of the web of interaction formed as a result of co-operative activity engaged in by human beings many mutual obligations are created. In the execution of these *contractual* relationships individuals are required to apply the general test of *fairness* to their behaviour. However, circumstances can create an inequality in the balance of power between the parties to any agreement and so true *fairness* is difficult to achieve. For example, the scarcity of a particular commodity pushes up the price irrespective of the ability (or willingness) of customers to pay.

Equally, information can tip the balance one way or the other. Inside knowledge of an impending takeover bid could allow certain individuals to buy shares before they rise sharply when the announcement is made. This would not be fair to those selling shares as they will not gain the benefit that they would have otherwise had. The major difficulty with the *contract* approach is that it is difficult to create a fair set of *rules* on which to determine them. Individuals designing the *rules* would be required to have no vested interest in the outcome of the decision. Cutting a cake is frequently used to illustrate this principle. To be equally fair to all involved the person cutting the cake should either be the last person to select a piece to eat or not have a piece at all. A *contract* view is one that looks backward at the obligations that have been entered into and assesses the implications of these for future behaviour.

Restricted contractarianism   This approach takes the view that every agreement entered into should be assessed through the *veil of ignorance* (Rawls, 1971). This forces an individual to consider the *rightness* of any arrangement without knowing the impact of the outcome on themselves.

Libertarian contractarianism   This approach holds that the parties should be bound by any agreement voluntarily entered into as long as it does not conflict with the broader rules of a just society or cause harm to others. It is an approach that accepts the limitations on the concept of fairness in the dynamic nature of the social world in which human beings operate. It implies that once a contract is entered into, individuals have an obligation to abide by the terms of that relationship and not to take precipitated action to terminate (or change) the contract.

It has already been suggested in many of the chapters in this text that much management activity is associated with making choices or taking decisions. The same is true of many of the non-managerial jobs that exist within organizations. Manual workers on an assembly line have to make decisions about the quality of work that they are undertaking, administrative employees have decisions to make with regard to dealing with customer queries or complaints and so on. Many of these situations contain ethical dimensions. Leys (1962) produced a diagram in which a number of moral standards are identified and in which conflict with the standards in the opposite side of the model (see Figure 17.3).

This model is useful in identifying many of the conflicts and dilemmas associated with decision making. For example, an employee faced with a boss who is attempting to increase efficiency and reduce the cost of operations will span the dilemmas of loyalty and institutional trends at one side of the model and integrity/self-respect at the opposite side. In such a situation an employee may well feel that *loyalty* to the organization is important and that increased efficiency represents an *institutional trend* that cannot be stopped. At the same time, however, these feelings are likely to be in conflict with the need for personal *integrity* in performing a good job to high standards of quality and *self-respect* in not being simply a creature of management, subject to every whim of the boss.

This model does not provide a basis for identifying a course of action to resolve the moral dilemma facing the individual. It simply helps to identify some of the conflicting areas of experience. In addition, there are situations which span more than two opposite forces in the model. At best this model should be regarded as a simplification of the complexity of situations involving ethical conflicts. It is, however, a useful starting point for thinking about the issues involved in a specific situation.

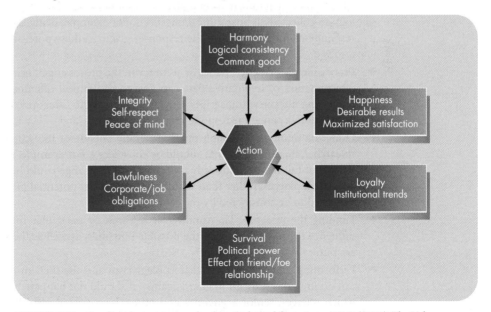

FIGURE 17.3 Conflicts between moral values (*adapted from*: Leys, WAR (1962) *The Value Framework of Decision Making*, Prentice Hall, Englewood Cliffs).

Ethics and research

Ethics is not just about how people should behave within an organizational context. There are ethical issues associated with the development of knowledge and understanding about organizations and the people who work within them. There is a considerable volume of research carried out each year in the business and management areas. The objectives of such activity is to further the stock of knowledge on aspects of human and organizational behaviour in its many guises. This applies whether it is intended to better describe how the financial markets function or how groups form and act within particular contexts or how managers make decisions. Whatever the form of research there are potential ethical issues to consider. Indeed, some writers go as far as to suggest that the use of the scientific method in pursuit of knowledge based on western conceptions and dominance provides a privileged position for it in terms of both epistemology and ethics (Brown, 1992, pp 71–2). A view which has in practice elevated the natural sciences to a form of civil religion in the USA according to another writer quoted by Brown. Hornsby-Smith (1993, p 62) describes the role of codes of practice in this field as a means of seeking, 'to control unethical methods of investigation … by professional bodies'.

Remenyi *et al.* (1998) devote an entire chapter to the issues of ethics in business research as part of their introductory text on the subject. In doing so they identify a number of issues that need to be thought through in terms of the ethical considerations (Chapter 13). Some of the central issues that they identify include:

✦ What should be researched. For example, there are issues that might be commercially sensitive or that might impact on how employee performance is manipulated by managers that might be difficult to justify ethically or be difficult to access in practice.

✦ How the research should be conducted. Issues such as the ways that evidence is collected, how much information is given to respondents and the cross-checking of information collected all pose ethical questions. For example, being completely open with respondents might influence the responses given, so these potential conflicts must be resolved.

✦ Processing the evidence. Issues of accuracy in the processing of numerical data and the interpretation of qualitative data can give rise to ethical dilemmas. For example, in processing interview transcripts it may be necessary to categorize responses and in so doing subtly change the respondents' actual views.

✦ Using the findings. Although this is generally outside of the scope of the individual researcher, it is an aspect that should be considered. For example, research identifying successful mechanisms for reducing resistance to change could be used by managers against employees, rather than with employees. It has potential negative connotations that need to be considered by the researcher.

✦ Funding the research. The funding of research by particular interest groups could influence the research design, the possible outcomes as well as the uses to which they are put.

✦ Performing the work. Issues such as plagiarism and the theft of other people's ideas can occur and is difficult to guard against. It should not happen, but there are cases in which referees, senior academics and others have passed off other people's ideas as their own. Sample selection and the fabrication of results are other possible occurrences that can arise and which naturally have an impact on the research.

✦ Responsibility to the greater community. There may be occasions in which a researcher comes across a range of unacceptable or even illegal practices. In such situations the researcher has to take a position and decide what to do. To 'go public' with such information may limit or stop the research altogether. To do nothing may endanger individual employees or customers or allow some form of exploitation to continue.

One very revealing discussion about the ethics of trust between subjects and respondents is that of Finch (1993). She points out that in her research experience it is easy for a woman researcher to establish a meaningful rapport with women respondents and therefore gain access to deeply personal opinions and views. This she suggests provides, 'a real exploitative potential in the easily established trust between women, which makes women especially vulnerable as subjects of research' (p 174).

Fielding (1993, p 169) highlights the ethical dilemma facing those researchers engaging in ethnographic studies by referring to the earlier work of Rosenhan. The research led by Rosenhan required that 'pseudo-patients' be placed in mental hospitals as a way of checking on the diagnosis activities of medical staff. When they arrived at the hospital each 'pseudo-patient':

Feigned hearing voices, but once admitted they ceased simulating any symptoms. All but one was admitted with a diagnosis of schizophrenia. Not one was caught out. ... Nor were their diagnoses changed when they switched to normal behaviour, despite many of their fellow patients guessing.

This research demonstrated the unreliability of psychiatric diagnosis as well as the institutional and professional consequences of 'labelling' patients. A different outcome would be very likely to have emerged had informed consent by the medical staff been required as part of the research process. Indeed Rosehan adopted such a policy in a subsequent study, resulting in 23 out of 193 admissions being 'listed' as 'pseudo-patients' when none had been sent to that particular hospital. These studies, important as they are, clearly highlight aspects of the ethical difficulties facing researchers in seeking to advance knowledge. There are obvious dangers for the perceived competence of medical staff among patients, as well as access to and modes of treatment. It is not possible to know the impact on the models and theories used within organizational behaviour of the particular ethical standards adopted by researchers. It does, however, reflect the need to be aware of ethical aspects of research as well as in management practice in seeking to explain and understand behaviour.

Business ethics and corporate governance

Mahoney (1997) identifies a number of reasons why businesses take an interest in ethics. They include:

✦ Following fashion. This approach perhaps regards ethics as something that is useful in the short term, but may pass like many other fashions. So complying with the current fashion represents something that would be adopted as a means of not falling behind or being open to criticism but is not really integrated into business operations or management thinking. Consequently, it would soon fall by the wayside as the next fashion emerged.

✦ Response to pressure. There are many pressure groups that seek to influence business activities. By adopting ethical codes and policies these can be kept at arm's length because management will be generally more proactive in dealing with the environment, local communities, customers and suppliers

✦ Pursuit of profit. Being ethical can be profitable, or so it would be argued by some. It is possible that by being ethical in pursuit of business goals 'things' would be 'got right first time' more often and customers would be attracted to doing business with such organizations. However, being ethical can also be expensive, particularly if pressure groups or the press form the view that the business is being cynical in search of profit and seek to expose its shortcomings.

✦ Stakeholders consider that it is right. Such individuals would probably behave and manage organizations in an ethical way irrespective of other considerations as a matter of personal belief. Therefore the cost or benefit to be gained becomes irrelevant to such business leaders. However, if such a business made huge losses it would still go bankrupt. Banks, the city, other investors and other creditors are not renowned for accepting ethical policies in lieu of money.

✦ Mixture of the reasons already given. In many cases, the reasons that businesses engage in ethical activity is for a mixture of the reasons indicated, the proportion of each reason active in the specific context depending upon the situation.

Although there are many ways of defining corporate governance, the Cadbury Committee (1992) defined it in terms of the systems through which companies are directed and controlled. The need for a review of corporate governance arose as the result of number of high profile scandals in the business world involving fraud and the abuse of power by senior managers and directors in the UK and USA. In the UK the Cadbury

The board of directors should have separate audit and remuneration committees, comprised only of independent directors

The audit committee should meet with the external auditors of the company at least once each year and without any executive director present

The total remuneration package of directors should be fully disclosed in the annual report of the company

The term of office for a director should be no more than three years in between shareholder votes on appointment to the office held

Non-executive directors must have funds available to them to pay for independent professional advice

The board must meet at regular intervals

Non-executive directors should be appointed through a formal process

Non-executive directors should enjoy a standing in society or the business community that ensures that their views carry weight

Non-executive directors should be completely independent of the company other than in relation to their fees and any shareholdings

No one person should have total power at the top of the company. The jobs of chief executive and chairman of the board should be split wherever possible.

TABLE 17.3 Major recommendations of the Cadbury Committee

Committee produced a number of recommendations (the main ones are listed in Table 17.3) and received a mixed response. The general reaction was that it should have incorporated a broader set of recommendations including environmental and social responsibility aspects of business activity. This has subsequently been developed to some extent as a result of the work of the Hample Committee, established to review and report during 1998 on corporate governance.

Codes of practice

In an attempt to provide individuals with guidance on ethical standards and behaviour many organizations and professional bodies have produced codes of practice. These can be written in many different forms, but most attempt to establish what the approved courses of action are in particular circumstances, for example, what to do if faced with a demand for a bribe. They also attempt to provide an indication of the procedure to be adopted if a breach of the code is suspected as a result of someone not following established procedures.

The codes of practice for professional bodies only direct themselves to issues associated with that particular area of work and how it should be conducted. There can be occasions when the code of practice for a professional body is in conflict with the practices within the organization employing the member. Such eventualities pose difficulties for the individual in deciding which to follow. For example, a medical practitioner employed by a company may interpret their professional standards as a duty to provide the highest standards of care for employees, but the company may interpret its requirement is to provide the most cost-effective level of care.

Social responsibility

The notion of *social responsibility* stems from thinking about the role of business in society. It emerges from asking just what should the responsibility of any business be to society as an entirety? In asking this apparently simple question there are many problems that immediately arise. The two main ones being what does *responsibility* mean and what defines *society*? Responsibility is generally taken to imply a duty of care or a set of obligations. Society, however, is a much more difficult concept to define, particularly in relation to a specific business. At one level of interpretation it could simply imply the government of the country or region in which the business is located. At a broader, more general level it implies the *stakeholders* linked with a particular business. There are benefits from taking the broader definition as any business impacts on each of the stakeholder groups in different ways. The notion of *social responsibility* allows both the positive and negative impact of business activity to be identified and assessed. For example, taking such a view allows the relative benefits to all parties to be evaluated in the desire of a company to provide cheaper goods and services while allowing levels of pollution of the environment to increase.

Johnson and Scholes (1993, p 192) discuss a report produced in 1981 which identifies ten roles that seek to reflect the underlying functions of organizations. It ranges from those organizations that seek to maximize profit and function accordingly, to those that engage with the social and political aspects of the environments within which they operate. Of course, this engagement does not disbar interest in making profit if the organization is commercially based. However, not all organizations are commercially based, some being created to create jobs or to otherwise serve the public interest in some way. This classification process can assist in identifying the different attitudes among organizations towards social responsibility, but it does not provide a basis for condoning particular expressions of it. Johnson and Scholes go on (p 195) to identify some of the internal and external aspects of social responsibility that impact on organizations:

✦ Internal aspects. These include issues such as employee welfare provision, working conditions and job design.

✦ External aspects. These include issues such as 'green policies', product design and possible use/abuse, marketing and advertising standards and placements, dealing with suppliers, employment policies and community activity.

There are, of course, many other aspects of *social responsibility* that can be identified. For example, which locations (and why) to enter in operational and selling terms and the degree of political influence sought and exercised in them. The difficulty associated with establishing, maintaining and enforcing *social responsibility* within the business and management community lies in the very nature of the *stakeholder* concept. Each stakeholder group has a particular relationship with the organization. This is perhaps more accurately described as a *web of relationships* as it is very rarely a single element relationship. For example, employees can be assumed in general terms to want interesting work that does not damage their health and with high pay (among other things). Governments seek high levels of employment, high taxation income, industrial relations (and social) stability, international prestige and a low cost of social support to the population. Even in these two simple examples it is possible to identify the conflicts that could exist between elements of the 'desires' of the individual stakeholders. If employees and governments cannot be relied upon to naturally seek the common good, how much less could business leaders in search of the best financial return be expected to follow such an emphasis? Therefore the role of pressure groups, investigative journalists, professional bodies and individuals is crucial in pursuit of *social responsibility* among organizations.

A recent survey found that, among other features associated with social responsibility, 87% of respondents felt that business decision makers had a responsibility to take into account the impact of decisions on the local communities; 77% felt that directors should set an example as responsible and involved members of their local communities; 87% of respondents felt that organizations could differentiate themselves in marketing terms through their social responsibility activities, 73% felt that organizations should encourage the development of employees so that they can easily find alternative employment as it is not guaranteed (Butcher and Harvey, 1999, p 39). However just because such strong feelings exist, that does not ensure that appropriate polices will emerge or be effectively implemented. It takes time to organize a synthesis between society and business, especially when there is little tradition of social responsibility in general.

Cross-cultural perspectives on ethics

The starting point for understanding ethics in an international context is, according to Stewart and White (1995), to understand the major religious and philosophical teachings. These writers suggest that such reviews identify a common thread in the concepts of *mutuality* and the *common good*. However, as the economic development of regions and individual countries evolve then the nature of ethical problems also changes. It is, they suggest, much too simplistic to contemplate the standards applied in western developed countries as the ideal to be achieved by developing countries. The developed economies of the west do not offer an *ideal*, they experience new situations requiring different ethical discussions and solutions to those relevant in other cultures.

Leisinger (1995) quotes the earlier work of Goodpaster in identifying the following 'moral common sense' rules:

+ Avoid harming others.
+ Respect the rights of others.
+ Do not lie or cheat.
+ Keep promises and contracts.
+ Obey the law.
+ Prevent harm to others.
+ Help those in need.
+ Be fair.
+ Reinforce these imperatives in others.

He goes on to explore the difficulties in applying such standards in the largely unequal world in which we all live, unequal being measured in terms of the small proportion of the world's population responsible for the unsustainable lifestyle and use of resources. These are major ethical issues across the global environment for business and governments to deal with. Another aspect of ethical concern on a global scale is that of bribery and extortion. Mahoney (1995) discusses several aspects associated with these phenomena and the impact on commodity and financial markets as well as the diversion of resources away from more effective use within society. He describes several initiatives under the auspices of the United Nations and individual governments to limit the occurrence of such behaviour through the policing of business activity and company reporting requirements.

Mahoney discusses the difficult issue of the degree to which companies should engage with cultures in which corruption is rife and offers a number of suggestions, the essence of the discussion being that there is more than one ethical response to an unethical situation. This is achieved using the apartheid era in South Africa and the widespread bribery found in Italy prior to the 1990s as examples. He argues that it is the justification for engagement with a particular unethical practice as well as the stance adopted by the organization that changes situations. Working in such environments can be justified providing:

+ It is unavoidable, at least in the short term.
+ The reason for so doing is grounded in good business and social reasons.
+ The business endeavours to change the unethical features of the particular culture.

The ability to influence events in a particular location depend upon the opportunity for an individual company to do so and a willingness within the society to change. In seeking this change official complaints, the use of the media to publicize such activity or even providing opportunities for local people that would not otherwise be available can all begin to move a situation on from its current state. Other measures include the need for education of the general public, the creation of specific legal frameworks penalizing such behaviour and requiring company self-regulation. In some cases (Russia being one example) even allowing the government to engage in what would otherwise be regarded as unethical behaviour in order to create order from chaos. However, at the end of the day success in controlling bribery and corruption can only be achieved if individuals have the moral courage to follow through with courses of action that change the situation.

Ethics and antisocial behaviour

The previous discussion touched on bribery and extortion as unethical practices and these are examples of what could be described as antisocial behaviour. There are, however, many other occurrences that would fall into this category. Giacalone and Greenburg (1997) identify a number of events that they classify as falling, at least potentially, within the classification of antisocial behaviour (see Table 17.4).

Some of the items in Table 17.4 have already been discussed and some have an obvious ethical dimension, for example lying and theft. However, some are not so obvious and need further consideration. For example, the threat of lawsuits can be a good thing in improving the standards of ethical behaviour within a company, say following the occurrence of an episode of sexual harassment. However it can also be a process that is used unethically. For example, a dismissed employee threatening to go to court to sue the employer as a way of obtaining a 'buy-off' settlement, because they know that it would be cheaper for the company to pay money rather than defend their case. Equally, whistleblowing can be used maliciously to cause trouble if the grounds for so doing are not well founded or truthful.

Espionage is another rather shady area of activity which few organizations would admit to being involved with. The equipment to enable espionage to be carried out exists and there have been numerous examples of computer hacking, but it is not clear as to the true extent of the potential problem. It is, however, an area that certainly carries with it ethical dimensions. It is certainly possible for the government of most countries to arrange for listening devices to be placed on telephones etc. providing they (sometimes) follow strict guidelines. Countries make a practice of collecting information on other countries as part of the international diplomacy process. Companies also collect information on markets, competitors, customers, suppliers, potential and actual employees etc. In the commercial world it is not a large step from collecting information otherwise in the public domain and going one step further and seeking information that would not otherwise be available – this is espionage. Croft (1994) provides an interesting look at a range of information sources available as well as the bugging and other devices that can be used to engage in 'corporate cloak and dagger', as his book is titled.

Arson	Fraud	Sabotage
Blackmail	Interpersonal violence	Sexual harassment
Bribery	Kickbacks	Theft
Discrimination	Lawsuits	Violation of confidentiality
Espionage	Lying	Whistleblowing
Extortion		

TABLE 17.4   Examples of antisocial behaviour

Punch (1996) explores another aspect of antisocial behaviour which he terms 'dirty business', 'corporate misconduct' or 'organizational deviance'. His range of interest spans examples ranging from nuns in a Belgian convent diverting approximately $5 million from a hospital project to build an indoor swimming pool and place TV sets in each cell of a new convent (p i), to the global BCCI and Maxwell scandals (pp 5–15). His work claims that misconduct is endemic to business and that to understand such behaviour it is necessary to understand, 'the nature of business, the realities of organizational life, the dilemmas of management, and the manners and morals of managers in their daily working lives' (p 213). In seeking to explain why it is that managers engage in deviant practices, Punch identifies three categories of variable:

✦ Structure. This category covers such features as the competitive nature of the markets that businesses engage in; that the size and complexity on businesses can create 'obfuscation of authority' (p 222); the emphasis placed on goals with the associated opportunity structures and rewards available.

✦ Culture. The opportunity for deviance to become ingrained in corporate culture is ever present.

✦ Personality/identity. The depersonalization of corporate activity can result in managers feeling removed from the consequences of their actions or seeking to rationalize them through denial, claiming that business is an analogy for war, following a role model or simply for the fun or excitement. It is even possible that companies have a need at times for 'dirty work' to be undertaken and that some managers are willing to undertake such duties. It is even suggested that the huge rewards that can be achieved by people at the top of business encourages both them and others to cut corners and take risks to achieve promotion and success.

Much of this antisocial behaviour depends upon individual people being willing to engage in it. It was Kohlberg who first proposed a model of the stages of moral reasoning in humans (see, for example, Kohlberg and Ryncarz, 1990). This model contained six stages which each person was claimed to go through in a fixed sequence over time. The model states that a person operates at each stage until progression in moral reasoning occurs and that propels the individual on to the next stage. Snell (1995) reviews this model and proposes his own version of it, based on research among practising managers. The six stages in the development of ethical reasoning in Snell's model are (pp 148–9):

✦ Avoid punishment; obey those in authority.

✦ Seek personal gain; avoid losing out.

✦ Earn the approval of others around you or attached to you by being nice to them and by fitting in with their expectations.

✦ Conform to rules, laws, codes and conventions.

✦ Follow principles based on respect for people and their rights, other organisms, the greater good, a strong sense of empathy and compassion for the human condition (strangers included) etc.

✦ Continually question your own actions and principles.

Snell argues, based on his research, that there are four 'psychic prisons' (incorporating one of the *metaphors* identified by Morgan (1986) that restrict the ability of managers to deal effectively with ethical dilemmas. The first two are within the individual and the second are based in the environment. They are:

✦ Being in possession of a limited ethical reasoning capacity.

✦ Having stereotypical assumptions about the nature of organizational structures, responsibilities and power relationships.

✦ Holding restricted levels of organizational responsibility or power.

✦ Being constrained in the actions possible by a particular moral ethos dominant in a particular context.

Among the implications of this research is that an individual chooses to act in particular ways either as a consequence of their own internal cognitive processes and/or as a result of external, contextual forces. This view generally supports the ideas of Punch in his view that organizational and personal factors can influence the occurrence of antisocial behaviour.

Whistleblowing and ethics

Whistleblowing is an act on the part of an employee to bring into the public arena acts that an organization would prefer to keep hidden. Such individuals frequently try unsuccessfully to use internal methods to bring about change within the organization and stop the unethical or illegal activities. In frustration at what they see as the intransigence and wrongdoing of individuals within the organization they find themselves having to go public and *blow the whistle* on the situation. Whistleblowing has generally been thought of as an ethical issue, but Rothschild and Miethe (1994) prefer to place it into a broader context as an aspect of political resistance. They define whistleblowing as, 'the disclosure of illegal, unethical or harmful practices in the workplace to parties who might take action' (p 254). This definition invariably implies that the 'issues' are taken to a higher level within the organization and/or outside it. This distinguishes it from other forms of worker protest which might be horizontal, by involving colleagues or family members in listening to explanations of the 'problem'.

In whistleblowing the individuals often leave themselves open to retaliation on the part of managers and other employees who think that their job and profit levels might be at risk. They are often dismissed, subjected to abuse and threats of violence to themselves their families or property. When the employer is the government it can also lead to imprisonment for revealing secrets. Lynn (1998) describes the totally different experience of two people who found themselves in whistleblowing situations. The first individual worked in marketing at the Abbey National (a large bank) and discovered that his boss was putting false invoices through the system. He collected the information, left the company for another job and then gave his information to the board of the company. They investigated the allegations, found them to be true and involved the police. The individual was given £25,000 as a reward for the stress and invited back to the company with a promotion. The second individual was the managing director of an advertising agency and sought to 'straighten out' a few financial irregularities. Five months later he was sacked for incompetence. The parent group would not investigate his claims that a more senior executive within the group was fiddling and that this was the cause of his dismissal. It took the next five years of his life to collect enough evidence to prove his case, eventually winning large sums of money in compensation and an apology.

This and the fact that blowing the whistle is intended to change something within the organization allows Rothschild and Miethe to describe it as a political process. Codes of practice have been seen as a way of institutionalizing whistleblowing, allowing senior managers to take action on problems as they emerge. However, it is not only employers who try to prevent the truth from coming into the public domain. Rothschild and Miethe describe a case in which one employee was fired because she began to ask questions about the chemicals she worked with, only to find that she was suffering life-threatening conditions as a consequence of her work. Yet other employees tried to keep her quiet and 'turned their backs on her' because their jobs were at risk (p 263). They also point out, as do Giacalone and Greenburg earlier, that whistleblowing can be abused for purely political reasons and so become a different type of ethical problem.

Ethics and the management of people

The role of people in an organization is somewhat ambiguous. Although the job that people are expected to do is frequently written down in a job description such documents very rarely include everything that is expected of the person. Many managers insist on the inclusion of a clause in a job description along the lines of 'undertake any other duties as required by management'. Such clauses recognize that in order to achieve the objectives of the organization (and managers) flexibility is required and that if every employee literally worked to their job description inefficiency would result. What is expected of employees by the organization and what they as individuals and groups should expect from the organization is based on a complex wheel of interdependent factors. Figure 17.4 reflects the interaction between these influences and the role of people within the organization.

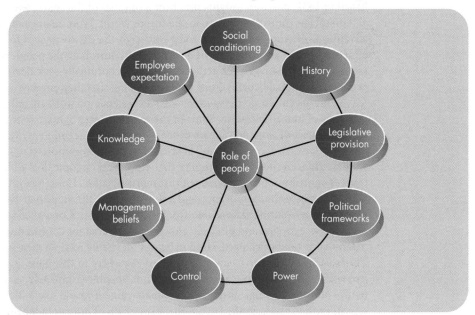

FIGURE 17.4 The wheel of people role determinants within organizations.

Another way to consider the role of people within an organization is through the concept of employee involvement. People are primarily employed by organizations to perform tasks that cannot otherwise be done by machines. As much as technology has developed in recent years it is not yet possible for organizations to function without people to do some of the jobs. Taking the job as the basic reason for the existence of employees, it follows that managers seek to make effective use of them. Employee involvement has a part to play in blurring the distinction between the basic job of employees and the degree of engagement with the objectives being sought by managers. In much of the modern approach to human resource management there is a theme apparent of finding mechanisms that will encourage (or require) employees to *go beyond the contract* in contributing to the organization. This view is represented in the discussion by Townley (1994, pp 13–5) of a Foucaultian analysis of the essence of the employment contract and the practice of human resource management.

The major advantage to organizations from the employment of people over machines is the flexibility that they provide. They are cheaper to acquire (no capital costs); can be dispensed with quickly and more cheaply if necessary; and they are adaptable and can solve problems in a dynamic environment. However, there are disadvantages with the employment of people: they are not as consistent in work output or quality as machines; they cannot work every hour that exists without a break; and maintenance costs (wages and benefits) are high. In addition, the major difficulty involved with the employment of people is that they have free will and expectations. Seeking to achieve the desired output from people in a work context therefore inevitably raises many ethical issues, most of which are never satisfactorily resolved.

People are not completely malleable to the will of others. Even in the most difficult of circumstances individuals will find ways of expressing individuality and freedom from total domination. The story of Lomax (1995 – identified in the Further reading) demonstrates how prisoners of war can maintain some measure of independence even in the most hostile of conditions. Also from literature, the classic *Brave New World* by Huxley, first published in 1932, provides insights into how a number of the characters are able to resist the all embracing control of society in the future world. From management's perspective the advantages of employing people must outweigh the disadvantages for it to be worth the effort and cost. Therefore, ways of directing and controlling the people resource are important aspects of management activity. Managers continually seek devices or techniques to generate additional benefits from the *social capital* that they employ.

From an employee perspective their experience of work includes the ever growing demands of industrialization. Some of these include ever tighter control, reduced ability to adjust the pace of work and subservience to the needs of technology. Mills (1959) described most work experience as a number of *traps*, a theme common to many later sociological studies. *Traps* in this context implies that employees become 'locked into' particular patterns of contribution and reward within an organization. Consequently, employees actively seek to increase the significance and value obtained through their work responsibilities. Managers seek *controlled behaviour* from their employees. Controlled in this context means predictable, expected and directed. However, the search for control does not automatically mean that it can be achieved. Human beings inevitably retain a measure of independence. The existence of *negative power* introduced elsewhere in this book is just one example of *free will* in an organizational context. It is not possible completely to control the essential nature of human beings simply because management would like to do so.

Alienation was identified as another expression of human independence. Management cannot force labour to join in and become part of the system. Compliance is not the same as commitment. The *Fordist* approach was an early twentieth century attempt to provide control, building upon the principles of *scientific management*. The human dimension of the organization was something that Ford actively discouraged in the work context: 'A big business is really too big to be human. It grows so large as to supplant the personality of the man' (Ford, 1923, p 263). Because this approach was largely unsuccessful, attempts at what has been described as *social engineering* replaced it. One aspect of social engineering is to persuade employees to subscribe to the same values as managers through becoming involved in the business. Goffee and Scase (1995) review a number of features of the *Fordist* and the *post-Fordist* approaches to the management paradigm associated with work. Table 17.5 identifies some of the major distinctions between these two paradigms.

The more enlightened management approaches recognize that it is not possible to force or restrict the human qualities that employees possess naturally. Indeed, it might even be possible to harness (or manipulate) those very qualities to provided added value to the organization. One manager described this as recognizing that with every pair of hands recruited came a free brain. Among the strategies designed to address these issues are those intended to increase employee involvement in the running of the business. Management in Action 17.3 reflects the industrial democracy processes in the John Lewis Partnership, a co-ownership organization in which every employee part owns the business.

| Stop | Consider |

Is it reasonable to assume that the approach to participation outlined in MiA 17.3 would be enough to engage employees with the business? Justify your views.
What ethical dilemmas could you envisage arising in such an environment and how would you deal with them?

It is important to recognize that not every employee would wish to become involved with the running of their organization. Some individuals would be happy to simply sell their labour and achieve self-actualization and personal meaning though other routes. For example, a young person may view a job as providing the money to allow them to take a year out subsequently to travel the world. Involvement in areas of running a business can

From: Fordist	To: Post-Fordist
Precisely defined job roles	Broadly-defined job roles
Specialist skills	Transferable skills
Tight control	Loose control
Bounded responsibilities	Autonomy and discretion
Rules and procedures	Guidelines for behaviour
Closed communication	Open/fluid communication
High status differences	Low status differences
Low-trust relationships	High-trust relationships
Prevailing custom and practice	Innovation and change
Colleagues as individuals	Colleagues as team members
Invisible management	Visible leadership

TABLE 17.5 Paradigm shifts in management (*source*: Goffee, R and Scase, R (1995) *Corporate Realities*, Routledge, London)

MANAGEMENT IN ACTION 17.3

Writing wrongs with democracy

The Gazette is the staff newspaper of the John Lewis Partnership and it plays a key role in the way in which democracy functions within the organization. Marion Scott, its editor, indicated that it had won an award from the Campaign for Freedom of Information for its contribution to 'free and open debate about both policy and personnel issues of a kind that most companies go out of their way to prevent'.

The history of *The Gazette* goes back to the early days of the John Lewis Partnership when in 1918 John Spedan Lewis set it up as a means of improving communication within the company. The organization is owned by the employees and they expect a significant say in how it is run. All permanent employees, including part-time staff, are co-owners of the business and entitled to influence the policy and direction of the company as well as share in the profits. Referred to as 'partners' the co-owners are not able to elect managers or interfere with day-to-day operational issues, but they can call into question the actions of managers through the letters pages of *The Gazette*. Only on rare occasions does a letter not appear in print. This decision can only be made by the partnership chairman and its non-appearance must be justified in *The Gazette*.

Letters published can be anonymous and some contain pointed complaints about the behaviour of senior managers. For example, recent examples have included a complaint about the 'pathetic use of rudeness and sarcasm' by a senior manager and an observation about the chairman's membership of the Freemasons. Where a letter requires a reply senior managers are expected to do so. It provides a very tangible

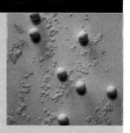

measure of the accountability of managers to those whom they manage.

The Gazette is not the only form of democracy within the company. Other forms of democracy and involvement engaged in by the John Lewis Partnership include:

✦ The central council. A consultative body that has the ultimate power to remove the partnership's chairman from office.

✦ Branch councils. These function rather like the works councils in Germany and scrutinize management decisions and actions at local level.

✦ Committees for communication. These are the oldest representative bodies. Only open to non-management partners, they meet about six times each year.

✦ Partners' counsellor. An ombudsman role within the structure to represent the interest of ordinary partners.

The various representative bodies publish the minutes of meetings to all staff, a virtual plethora of information for all to see, should they wish to do so. One issue of potential difficulty for 'open communication' is that of the commercial sensitivity of some information. This does not appear to have had an adverse effect on the organization in practice or profit levels over the years.

Adapted from: Arkin, A (1994) Writing wrongs with democracy, *Personnel Management Plus*, April, pp 22–3.

at best meet the needs and expectations of some employees and therefore should be available rather than compulsory. In doing so it can improve the *quality of working life* and provide managers with the potential for better results. Forcing people to become involved simply introduces another form of direct control and is unlikely to have any positive result.

There are number of other areas of ethical dilemma that emerge from the need for organization and control within a business and which face both employees managers in their operational activities.

The role of work in society

Work plays a number of important roles in society. It provides the economic basis for individuals to be able to earn money and thereby purchase the goods and services necessary for life and recreation. There are the indirect benefits of work through the payment of taxes so that common services such as healthcare can be provided. Work also provides individuals with social meaning in their lives through the careers and work activities that they engage in. For example, those with appropriate creative talents could become artists and find ways of expressing their individual identity through their work. It also provides an opportunity for social encounters with other people as employees interact with other human beings.

Should work and the organizations that provide it be seen as the dominant force within society? Should any organization have the power to dictate to the members of a society how they should live and work. Is work a basic human right in society? How much time should be devoted to work, how much payment should be received and so on? In short, should we as humans work to live or live to work? There are a number of organizations who have an income larger than many of the poorer countries of the world. This could provide opportunities for big business to *arrange* society in a way that supports business objectives, rather than to the benefit of society. These and many other aspects of the role of work in society create ethical dilemmas that are not easy to resolve, yet politicians and business leaders must develop policies and practices which match the expectations of society to some degree if social conflict is to be avoided.

Corporate and public interest

There is a fundamental conflict between organizations and the public at large. In very crude terms, all organizations would like to sell cheap products at a very high prices. Consumers, by the same token, would like very expensive products at very low prices. This is a vast simplification of a complex process associated with purchase and ownership. It is well known among marketing people that there are circumstances in which charging low prices actually undervalues the product or service in the eyes of potential customers and therefore make them less likely to buy. This form of conflict can frequently lead to ethical conflicts arising as organizations seek to maximize their profits.

One of the illustrations that can be used to describe potential conflicts in this area is contained in Management in Action 17.4. The conflicts between corporate and public interest in this example are associated with the company need for cheap labour in order to reduce the cost of operations and customer preference for a reasonably priced toy. There are many 'factors' at work in this type of situation. The moral issues include the deliberate payment of low wages (by European standards) as a management policy. There are also issues of customers purchasing products that have not created jobs within their own society and therefore encouraging cheap labour. Countering this is the provision of economic development in areas that desperately need it. There is also the issue of profit export from, and technology/skill transfer to, areas of cheap labour. This begins to open up economic arguments that are well beyond the scope of this text. Goldsmith (1995) puts forward a spirited defence of his views that by not protecting jobs and production at home, countries are sowing the seeds of their own destruction.

MANAGEMENT IN ACTION 17.4

Poverty pay of Barbie doll workers

A report produced by the World Development Movement, the Catholic Institute for International Relations and the Trades Union Congress show that poverty wages are frequently paid to workers in Asia making toys for sale in the west.

The findings of the research indicated that many leading toy companies use subcontracted factories in Asia which fail to meet basic internationally agreed standards. The average person works a shift of at least ten hours each day for six days per week. For example, Chinese workers were paid less than £2 per day to make Barbie dolls. The Mattel company which makes the Barbie doll spends about £1.80 per doll sold on advertising, about the same as the daily wage for each factory worker.

In Bangkok the research team interviewed factory workers and reported the following comments:

> Barbie doll is more expensive than our wages. We lost a lot of sweat to produce those dolls.

Another worker explained that overtime was compulsory,

> We have to do it otherwise we would

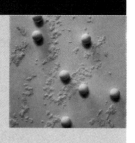

be dismissed.... One month the management gives 60 dolls for one worker to produce but when we finish the 60 dolls per month they will increase it another 10 to 70 dolls; if we finish 70 dolls they will increase it again.

The group sponsoring the research pressed the British Toy and Hobby Association, which represents companies responsible for 90% of all sales of these products in the UK market, to adopt a new charter in this area. It seeks to establish an independently monitored code of practice for the safe production of toys. It would require companies to undertake spot checks on subcontractors and to take action if any violations were found.

Mattel, as a leading maker of toys, welcomed the proposed charter and suggested that it would enhance its own existing code of practice which required subcontractors to comply with local labour and safety laws. It also required staff to report any violation of the laws.

Adapted from: Garner, C (1995) Poverty pay of Barbie doll workers, *The Independent*, 23 December, p 2.

Stop | Consider   *Based on your reading of MiA 17.4 and this chapter to what extent do you think (and why) that ethical considerations should outweigh economic and market forces?*

Obligations at work

There are a number of areas of obligation that impact on employees. Figure 17.5 attempts to reflect many of these.

Not all of the groupings identified in Figure 17.5 will apply to every employee and there are categories not represented. The ethical dilemmas arising from obligations at work arise as a result of the potential conflicts in demands placed on the individual from the various groupings. For example, balancing the demands of organization and family can create problems in many situations, as can the demands of ever higher productivity on the self-respect of the individual.

Privacy

The right to privacy for the individual has been eroded in a number of areas over recent years and in turn raises a number of ethical dilemmas. For example, the use of information technology has created an opportunity to collect and retain more information about employees than was previously possible. The organization is able to *know* its employees more fully. However, this should not be overstated as large bureaucracies such as the civil service have had effective and comprehensive personnel files on staff for many years.

Another aspect of privacy in today's world is that associated with medical screening. Testing for drug use and for the existence of HIV are just two of the more recent areas to emerge. How far medical screening should be allowed to go before it moves from being necessary to being intrusive is a difficult balance to strike.

Working at home and work/life balance

There are many situations that arise which require the individual to take work home with them. A report may be required at short notice and it may be necessary for a manager to finish it at home in the evening. An employee working on an assembly line may not be able to stop themselves thinking about work when they are at home after management announce that the number of employees is to be reduced.

The ethical issues surrounding the practice of working at home are many and depend on the circumstances creating the situation. The dilemmas and issues involved in the two examples just quoted are different. In the first case, they surround the rights and obligations of both parties. Does a manager have the right to expect subordinates to put in more

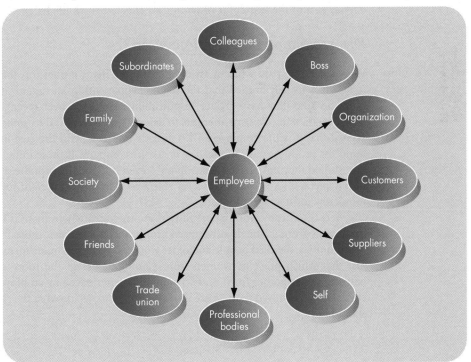

FIGURE 17.5 Employee obligation map.

hours than contractually agreed, particularly at short notice? Equally, does an employee in a senior position have an obligation to 'do what is necessary' in pursuing corporate objectives? In the second case, the ethical issues are of a completely different nature as the employee is not being required to think about work at home, it is a result of the threat of redundancy and the relative opportunity of alternative work.

Where additional work is required of an employee a wide range of ethical issues are involved in addition to those implied in the previous discussion. For example, to refuse to take work home could be regarded as an act of disloyalty and have implications for the career and promotion prospects of the individual concerned. There could also be a number of other employees only too willing to take advantage of the situation as a means of attempting to advance their own careers and promotion. For managers not to accept that they should 'do what is necessary' has implications for their right to be considered leaders and might have a detrimental impact on the well-being of all members of the organization.

The demands of work in terms of the balance with other aspects of life have long been recognized as a major problem for women with caring roles at home as well as careers. Equally, in many organizations there is a phenomenon which has become known as 'presentism' that impacts on both women and men employees. Presentism is simply a reflection of the usually unstated expectation of being 'in the office' for long periods of time as proof of commitment and hard work. One survey in 1998 among BT's senior managers found that 38% would not accept promotion because of the perceived damage to home lives (Cooper, 2000, p 35). Cooper also shows that a number of large organizations are beginning to recognize the need for employees to balance life and work responsibilities and are introducing more flexible policies as a result. BT, for example, uses a mixture of longer but fewer working days each week, working from home, or combinations of long and short days as part of the search for providing an effective work life balance.

Pay, promotion and discrimination

Who should be paid what in an organization? This is a question that also raises ethical issues. It is usually argued that the senior people within an organization should be paid more because they have greater responsibility. However, over recent years organizations have been making strident attempts to delayer themselves and to *empower* employees. It is argued that it is the employees who directly interface with the customer or who actually build the product who can *make or break* the company. If these individuals are so important should they not be paid accordingly – even if it does disrupt the conventional wisdom of pay hierarchies? If the lower level employees do not get *it* right today there will be no tomorrow for managers to plan.

Access to promotion opportunity is another area where there is unequal access for a number of groups. The disadvantaged groups include females, those from ethnic minority communities, disabled people and older workers. There are many forms of *glass ceiling*, not just that which prevents women from gaining access to the more senior posts. Sexual harassment is another form of discrimination experienced by employees. Again, there are ethical issues involved in these areas in attempting to decide what the right course of action should be.

Ethics and employee involvement

The function with a particular interest in employee involvement is the human resource department. As such these specialists tend to believe in the value of involving people at work as intrinsically good, providing the basis for an ethical approach to management. It is also frequently assumed and argued to provide a means of increasing motivation, tapping into higher levels of commitment and making best use of the human qualities available to the organization.

There are many different views about the nature of human resource management within an organization. Hyman and Mason (1995, Chapter 4) provide a comprehensive review of the distinction between the terms *personnel* and *human resource* activities in the context of employee involvement. Among the conclusions is an indication that organizational level employee participation may be intended to impact on (effectively reduce) employee representation through trade unions. This in turn raises other ethical dilemmas in relation to the rights of employees to *free association*, the role of work in society and the rights of managers to demand unquestioning loyalty.

Marchington *et al.* (1992) suggest that there are four types of involvement:

✦ Downward communication. Top down in nature and intended to better inform employees. The purpose being to ensure that employees are aware of what is going on within the organization and their part within that *drama*, the rationale being that if employees understand the situation they will be willing to play their part more effectively.

✦ Upwards problem solving. To make more direct use of the skill, ability and ideas of employees in helping managers to solve problems, based on the view that employees directly involved in the finding of solutions will be more likely to make them work effectively. They may also be able to find other ways to contribute to the smooth running of the organization through improved work methods and work organization.

✦ Financial participation. To give employees a direct stake in the financial performance of their organization, the rationale being that employees who benefit from the performance of the organization will be motivated to search out ways of more effectively meeting customer need and reducing operating costs. However, it has been argued by some trade unions that employees already have a financial stake in the running of the company through continued employment and their wages. To put more of their financial income at risk through company financial performance is a form of double jeopardy and not something that should be encouraged.

✦ Representative participation. Not everyone can become fully involved in practice (ability, numbers of people, the time and cost involved) neither would some employees want to become involved (partly through a lack of interest and the traditional role of workers not being involved). Consequently, it is often the case that a number of representatives from among the workforce become involved with management on behalf of all employees.

There are a number of ethical consequences that arise from the involvement of employees in areas that have been traditionally considered the sole prerogative of managers. Some of the issues include:

+ Degree of involvement. Changes to the degree of involvement will disturb existing arrangements. Senior managers and shareholders may have to become accustomed to sharing power with a new group who may have different objectives for the business. Shareholders may want high dividends; managers seek to grow the company to provide career opportunities and status; while employees seek secure employment and reinvestment of profit. Any form of involvement would therefore need to be accepted by the existing stakeholders.

+ Role of management. Whatever the form of involvement adopted employees will have expectations of increased influence over events in the future. This could be interpreted by managers as an erosion of their traditional function and rights within the organization.

+ Role of trade unions. A trade union might suddenly find itself not the only voice representing employee interest if employees become actively involved in decision making. If a trade union were to consider that it was being marginalized either deliberately or unintentionally it could resist the effective introduction and operation of the selected approach.

+ Management's right to manage. While the term *right* can be questioned in this context and it may not be clear who bestows (or agrees to) that *right*, managers operate on the basis that they are able to exercise it. However, it would not be unusual to find situations where participation exists in which some employees develop links with senior managers over the heads of their immediate superiors. Under such circumstances it is possible to undermine the position of the superior by threats, real or implied, to go over their head. Employees who become involved in the running of an organization may become party to information that is not available to managers, again a potential source of problems.

+ Rights of involved employees. Do employees become equal partners with the stock owners of the company? Is the limit of their involvement to solve operational problems and to support management in the day-to-day running of the organization? Having experienced minor forms of involvement employees may seek greater levels of it. Employees may think that involvement gives them a greater say in the running of the company than was intended by management or provided by the scheme.

+ Responsibilities of involved employees. Managers would argue that with involvement comes responsibility. Employees may consider the main benefits of participation are to offset ineffective management and enhance their own circumstances. Should involved employees only expect to change the things that other *stakeholders* do, or should they be expected to change themselves as well? Are there responsibilities associated with involvement that require an introspective consideration, not automatically present among uninvolved employees?

If involvement were to be beneficial in significantly improving operational performance then employees would absorb much of the need for management activity. In so doing involvement could influence the design and structure of an organization. Management in Action 17.5 reflects the experience of two businesses in attempting to deal with these issues.

MANAGEMENT IN ACTION 17.5

The bumpy road to devolution

Microsoft's attempt to empower its workforce was launched with great razzamatazz. It was, however, a one-day wonder and collapsed. Employee surveys showed that people did not understand what it meant to them and many dismissed it as yet another management fad. Shaun Orpen, director of marketing services for Microsoft, suggested that: 'There was a genuine feeling in certain areas of the company that people had been given responsibility but not control. They did not know how far their authority went.'

This led the company to rethink what empowerment meant within the organization. The second time there was no high-profile launch. Managers concentrated on how they could realistically devolve both responsibility and authority to staff. For example, the finance director told his staff they no longer needed his authority to take time off, as long as colleagues knew about it and how to contact them. The next phase involved the empowerment of teams and providing people with the necessary skills to exercise discretion.

Linda Holbeche, director of research at Roffey Park Management Institute, suggests that a lack of clarity over roles and responsibilities is one of the major reasons why attempts to empower employees fail. Equally, many managers are unwilling to delegate significant amounts of power to employees. Much of the delegated power remains at the 'ordering of paper clips' level. The existence of a 'blame culture' will quickly discourage the use of initiative and the exercise of judgement.

Holbeche illustrates the effective empowerment of employees in Thresher, the major UK drinks retailer. The company prefers to use the term 'enabling' rather than empowerment. It is about people being given the support to carry out their responsibilities, not simply management

abdicating its responsibilities. The exercise began with a combined personnel and operations review of the key operational roles. Having identified what people were expected to do and whether they had the skills to do it, the company set about reviewing the rules and procedures within which people worked. This was followed by structural reorganization at the top of the organization and increased training of the people lower down the organization.

The introduction of self-managed teams in the local areas of the food and drinks section of the company encouraged more initiative in running the business to be taken, for example, the development of new staff working models and the local use of incentives. Groups of branch managers meet regularly to share ideas and develop best practice. This also has the benefit of giving shop staff the experience of having to take responsibility in the absence of their boss.

An analysis of the company performance showed that in the areas where these changes had been made, performance had improved. Surveys of store and area managers also indicated that they considered the company to be more open, informal and participative. The results have encouraged the company to plan to roll out the process to the rest of the organization. This is anticipated to last about 18 months. It is also anticipated to be a 'bumpy road' by the senior managers as resistance to change is anticipated at all levels. The approach adopted will be one of talking about where the senior managers want the business to go rather than empowerment as such.

Adapted from: Arkin, A (1995) The bumpy road to devolution, *People Management*, 30 November, pp 34–6.

Stop | Consider

Could an organization introduce a successful employee involvement scheme for unethical reasons? What might such reasons be? What does this imply about ethics in an organizational context?

At the most basic level, all employees are automatically involved with the organization as a result of the work that they do. The work that employees do needs to be acceptable to management in a range of ways or they will be dismissed. If the company is not successful then it will fail and they will lose their jobs. In addition, there are many informal processes that exist for employee involvement. For example, the *grapevine* is usually the quickest way for information to circulate around the company. Gossip and rumour frequently have a higher credibility than formal channels of communication because they are not subject to editing and filtering by managers.

Downward communication

Downward communication is intended to inform, to lead opinion and form attitudes that would be considered favourable to management. There are potential ethical problems to be faced in the use each of the forms of downward communication available. For example, the degree of management bias in the content and the perhaps unstated intention of the communication itself. Employees may interpret the content as a deliberate attempt to manipulate their views and adopt a totally different set of attitudes to those intended.

Among the main forms of downward communication are:

✦ Section or departmental meetings. A production department may hold regular weekly meetings to discuss problems and plans surrounding the current production cycle. As part of that process the senior manager may feed back to their subordinates information from the last senior management meeting.

✦ Team briefing. The cascade concept of communicating downwards. The senior management team would determine what should form the central core of each briefing session. Each senior manager would brief their immediate team using the core material supported by local information as necessary. Each person would then take the core brief and repeat the process for their own subordinates, repeated throughout the organization. Ramsey (1992) notes general satisfaction with this approach, but points out that success is highly dependent upon contextual features and that commitment to the process needs to be maintained.

✦ In-house journal. Company newspapers, journals, magazines and booklets have been in existence for many years. It is also common to find special employee versions of the annual report to shareholders being produced in larger companies. The major difficulties with these forms of journalism are the quality of the publication, generating enough copy to keep the content interesting and preventing the propaganda inclinations of some managers becoming overly assertive.

✦ Roadshow. Over the past few years the notion of senior managers going out to meet employees has developed. The three most common forms of this approach are to have a cycle of senior management visits, have senior managers host breakfast (or lunch) meetings or to arrange theatrical-style shows at which employees come together in large numbers to experience a *show* put on by management. This last form can be very expensive, involving, lighting, sound, large screen video, fireworks and a well-known personality to lead the presentation.

✦ Electronic. In these days of electronic communication the use of e-mail, video and multimedia approaches to communicating form a real possibility. The use of video conferencing provides opportunities for many groups of individual to receive information and interact with others.

Upwards problem solving

This approach allows employees to utilize their skills and knowledge in the search for increased productivity, quality and commitment. The potential ethical issues in this approach tend to revolve around the intention of the process as one of encouraging employees to *go beyond the contract*, but within a defined boundary. The contract reflects the essential rights and responsibilities of both employer and employee in relation to the job undertaken by the employee. Just as with any commercial contract it establishes the boundaries and scope of the relationship. Technically, neither party can deviate from the contract terms without the agreement of the other. Contribution through the various forms of empowerment can be argued as encouraging a partial deviation from the contract, without requiring a formal renegotiation of the terms or *quid pro quo* in return. There are clearly ethical perspectives impacting on this decision area. The forms of upwards problem solving can include:

✦ Suggestion schemes. This involves employees identifying ways to improve things and putting forward the suggestion to a committee for consideration. Employees must identify what the problem is, how it can be solved, what the benefits would be expected to be and any problems. If adopted then the person making the suggestion is usually rewarded with a percentage of the saving. It has occasionally been suggested that ideas have been turned down, only to see them implemented a few months later as part of a *normal* change. Managers can feel threatened if it is implied that they should have been able to solve the problem earlier. In most cases the employee only receives a small amount in comparison to the potential saving generated.

✦ Quality circles. These originated in Japan after World War II. They were developed by American consultants as a means of improving quality and productivity through employee problems solving (Clutterbuck and Grainer, 1990). Quality circles are voluntary groups of between six and ten employees from a common work area. Members are trained in problem-solving techniques and encouraged to identify difficulties in their own work areas and to find workable solutions. The group presents their solution to the management team, which then implements it. If management decide not to implement the solution they are required to explain their reasons to the circle. Management in Action 17.6 reflects a similar initiative using project improvement groups.

Stop | Consider   *To what extent does the approach represented in MiA 17.6 reflect the need for managers to solve problems that they find themselves unable to solve as compared with a real desire to involve employees?*

How would you try to carry out research into this difficult question as managers are unlikely to tell the truth if they are seeking to manipulate employees? What ethical issues might arise in relation to your research in this area?

MANAGEMENT IN ACTION 17.6

The green shoots of improvement

Jardinerie Garden Centre was started in Cheshire about 12 years ago by three people, Ken Allen, Jon Kitching and Peter Ulyatt. Ken Allen, the chairman of the company, said that: 'We believe that if you get people working together, then profits will come from that energy.' The company quickly grew over ten years from a single garden centre to ten garden centres, an interior landscaping business and a staff of about 200 people.

As the organization grew and spread geographically so did the problems of communication. Early in the 1990s Ken Allen met John Teire of Charlbury Consultants, specialists in team-working and communication training. A senior manager attended one of the programmes provided by Teire and identified ways in which the company could move forward. The programme was made available to the remainder of the management team and adapted for delivery inside the company to members of staff.

The result of the involvement in the programme was that the company was able to use volunteers to set up a project initiation group (or Pig), to find ways of establishing active involvement among employees. A number of 'Piglets' (or project improvement groups) of between four and eight people were set up among employee groups and encouraged to find ways of improving their work. Members of the original Pig toured the sites talking to staff and explaining that the Piglets were intended to provide a means of getting things done right first time, making full use of individuals' talents and giving all staff a chance to develop. Staff were encouraged to come up with their own ideas for improvement which in turn were classified under five separate headings:

✦ Customer care.

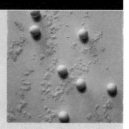

✦ Security.
✦ Frontage.
✦ Training.
✦ Information.

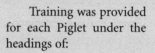

Training was provided for each Piglet under the headings of:

✦ Learning how to manage the project.
✦ Learning how to manage the team.
✦ Learning how to manage the learning so that it became the way things were done in the company.

Unlike many other involvement initiatives, the company has not adopted a 'top-down' approach. It allowed employees to decide for themselves what structures and systems were necessary to be able to deliver teamwork. For example one of the problems faced by the interior landscaping division was that clients moved the plants around within their own premises. This means that it can be difficult for Jardinerie's staff to find the plants that they are supposed to be caring for when they go to the client's premises. This is even more difficult during holiday periods when substitute staff are sent to client premises. The Piglet examined this problem and developed a simple system of ensuring that information was kept in a way that everyone could access. Another Piglet developed a security system to eliminate pilferage of plants and other garden material. This area is sensitive as it can involve staff being accused of theft. In this case the staff willingly accepted the system developed by their own members.

Adapted from: Arkin, A (1994) The green shoots of improvement, *Personnel Management Plus*, May, pp 18–19.

There was enthusiastic support for this form of employee involvement in the UK in the early 1980s, but problems and difficulties quickly began to emerge (Brennan, 1991; Collard and Dale, 1989). Some first-line managers interpreted quality circles as a threat. Some employees were seen as *rising stars*, effectively more able than existing managers. Trade unions sometimes interpreted the establishment of circles as a deliberate attempt to undermine their position and as a means of getting more from workers without extra reward. Circles also found that some of the problems that they attempted to solve were too complex or that for unclear reasons solutions were not implemented.

✦ Total quality management (TQM). It has been suggested that TQM is a philosophy rather than a technique. Flood (1993, p xiii) argues that: 'In reality TQM means a long-term, deep involvement of management in partnership with the workforce.' This implies a different approach to managing an organization to that traditionally experienced. The essence of TQM is that the need to pursue excellence and improvement are continual processes. Holden (1994, p 585) provides a useful summary of TQM in relation to employee involvement. TQM is frequently tied into other initiatives such as culture change, worker flexibility and customer care programmes. In that context the emphasis in TQM becomes a management led initiative which, 'with top-down overtones suggests a system whereby worker empowerment is restricted very much within the boundaries set by management' (Holden, p 584).

Also described are increases in worker control and accountability through the increased monitoring and automation of recording and testing procedures. These points are reinforced by other writers (see for example Kerfoot and Knights, 1994). Garrahan and Stewart (1992) describe processes requiring employees to *report* the work failings of others or risk being held accountable themselves. Holden describes evidence that reflects the weaknesses associated with the running of TQM programmes, many of which are similar to those described in relation to quality circles.

✦ Group working. It is only in recent years that group working has been systematically developed. The involvement of employees can be increased through the effective delegation to the group of what would otherwise be management responsibilities. Work allocation, pace of work, job rotation and work scheduling are examples of the responsibility that can be given to the team. They can become self-managed teams agreeing to deliver a certain end result in return for a particular wage, but being *relatively free* to function in the execution of the process.

✦ Project teams. Project teams represent a slightly different form of work group. They provide involvement through involvement in specific exercises. Typical examples of project team activities include the development of a new product, the design of a new workplace layout or the development of a new disciplinary procedure.

Financial participation

Financial participation provides involvement through a monetary stake in the activities of the organization. The main variations are:

✦ Co-operatives. This represents a particular approach to the design, structure and ownership of an organization. Essentially, the employees own the organization and are therefore directly involved in its financial performance through their decision making.

In many of these types of organization the pursuit of profit would not be the main motivation for individuals becoming involved. However, as the owners of the organization they are participating in the financial aspects of the organization as well as the decision making, policy formulation and work.

✦ Profit share. This has a long history and there are many examples from the nineteenth century (Church, 1971). The basic model for profit share schemes is that a nominated percentage of the profit generated by the organization would be shared out to employees in the form of a bonus. This form of participation was given a boost during the 1980s in the UK as a result of the beneficial tax treatment for payments resulting from schemes approved by the Inland Revenue. Profits can be distributed either in the form of money or as shares in the company. One of the difficulties associated with profit share is that profit, hard work and effort are not always directly linked. It is difficult to maintain motivation and commitment when that which is intended to facilitate it does not materialize.

✦ Share options. Forms of share option include executive schemes and Save-As-You-Earn (SAYE) schemes. The employee is free to keep or sell the shares once the SAYE scheme allows the shares to be purchased. The executive share option allocates shares to an executive perhaps equal in value to a year's salary. The actual involvement is restricted to the channels open to all shareholders, but only once the shares become the property of the individual. At an individual level each shareholding might be small, but taken as a whole they could form a significant block. Over time this could provide the basis for a real power shift within the organization. If a takeover battle occurred it would be possible for the employee shares to play a critical role in deciding the outcome. Management in Action 17.7 describes an employee share ownership scheme introduced in the bus industry.

Stop | Consider   *Can you identify any potential ethical dilemmas in the situation described in MiA 17.7? How might they be resolved?*

Representative participation

This approach to involvement does not provide involvement for each individual employee. It is a means of becoming involved through some form of representative arrangement. Forms of representative involvement include:

✦ Collective bargaining. This can be considered a form of employee involvement because it provides the opportunity for employee representatives to explore plans, ideas and options with managers as part of the process. The commonly held view of collective bargaining is that it is intended to provide wage rises for employees. However, it also provides an opportunity for a much broader level of involvement. Trade unions are not able to represent their members effectively during pay negotiations if they do not have an appreciation of management intentions and the financial background to company performance. There are instances in which the level of involvement provided through this medium is prescribed in law. Information required for the interpretation of redundancy proposals must be provided to employee representatives before consultation begins.

MANAGEMENT IN ACTION 17.7

Bus employees take the wheel

In South Yorkshire, a progressive public transport policy was operated for ten years prior to 1986. The major aspect of this policy was that bus prices were heavily subsidized. In 1986 the Conservative government in London forced a change in that policy, bus fares rose by 250% and a process began which led to the management buyout of the company and a major experiment in employee involvement. The bus company involved in this example employed 2490 people, leased 832 vehicles and had four main garages.

Glasman describes how the new company came into existence thus:

> On 16 November 1993 South Yorkshire Transport Ltd sold all its shares in Mainline Group Ltd to a new company, Mainline Partnership Ltd, for a nominal £1.
>
> To set up Mainline Partnership Ltd, Mainline Group gave £40,000 to two trusts – Employee Benefit Trust One (EBT1) and Employee Benefit Trust Two (EBT2) – which subscribed for four million shares at the nominal price of one pence per share. Employees received 74% of the shares on the basis of 114 shares for each year of service (with a minimum qualification of two years' service) – the remaining 26% were held in trust by EBT1.
>
> The new board consists of four executive directors, led by Peter Sephton, who is both chief executive and chairman. There are four non-executive employee directors, two non-executive community directors (who are district councillors appointed by the management and employee directors) and a non-executive business director (nominated by management and approved by the employee directors).
>
> On some issues, such as a proposal to close a bus garage or to sell the company, the employee directors effectively have a veto. To complicate matters further, the four executive directors have special voting shares which can be used to outvote the ordinary shares, but may not be used for items on which the employee directors have the controlling vote.

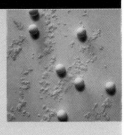

One of the issues identified early in the changeover process was the remuneration level for managers. In the resulting adjustment 60 senior managers in the company were offered a share-based bonus scheme. The scheme was based around the allocation of phantom shares to each manager. These are not real shares in the company: their value reflects the market price of the company's actual shares but they do not convey voting rights. After holding the phantom shares for seven years up to 50% can be cashed in at the prevailing value, the rest only when the manager leaves the company. Obviously the higher the market value of the real shares the larger the bonus. The purpose of the scheme is to attract, retain and motivate senior managers through a loyalty payment process. Managers judged not to be performing could be removed from the scheme.

The possibility of the introduction of a profit-share scheme for other employees which would be intended to allow the payment of an additional sum of money each week was also under discussion. In this case a number of ownership and incentive arrangements have been applied to involve and encourage employees and managers to co-operate in the effective delivery of an important public service.

Adapted from: Glasman, D (1994) Bus employees take the wheel, *Personnel Management Plus*, May, pp 20–1.

✦ Joint consultation. This implies a regular forum in which managers and employee representatives can meet to discuss issues of common concern. The major difference with negotiation is that management does not have to agree a course of action with employees. The process allows employee opinion and experience to be provided to managers. Managers can then incorporate these into decisions. A Confederation of British Industry (CBI) survey in 1989 reported that 47% of companies had some form of joint consultation. However, it was more likely to be found in the larger organizations. It is not unusual to find joint consultative arrangements falling into disuse if the management do not take them seriously and listen to the views of employee representatives. Management frequently claim that commercial sensitivity restricts what can be included in joint consultation, the argument being that competitors are liable to find out what is being planned.

There are many different approaches and experiences associated with employee involvement around the world. Holden (1994) and Hyman and Mason (1995) provide examples from the experiences gained in other countries in this area of work.

Ethics: an applied perspective

A considerable proportion of management activity is about taking decisions. Implicit in that view is the notion that managers are faced with options and choices. In many situations facing managers there are dilemmas and conflicts between aspects of the decision facing them. For example, offering a bribe to a potential customer may be against company policy, but it may help to provide jobs in an area of high unemployment, may prevent a company from losing money (if the market is tight) and the product may be the best on the market. Also, competitors may offer bribes to be able to sell inferior products. In addition, just because it is against company policy does not mean that it is against the principles and practices of every country.

This example is just one form of ethical dilemma faced by managers. How should they decide what it is right to do in this and similar circumstance? Equally, it is not only managers that are faced with ethical dilemmas. Employees are also exposed on occasions to decisions that are difficult. What should employees do when they find that an organization has been cheating its customers? How significant should the cheating be before something is done? There is no single approach that will allow individuals to resolve these types of decision dilemma. This chapter introduced some of the distinctive approaches based on moral philosophy that exist to guide decision making. Each approach offers a particular view of what defines right and wrong in any particular context and against which decisions should be judged. Elliott (1998) makes the point that there are both internal and external organizational forces that impact on any individual at the time that they are faced with an ethical dilemma and which will impact on the decision made. He uses the example (p 22) in which: 'An Operations Manager has to decide on a sensitive staffing issue, at a time when there is internal competition for his/her job, some family trauma, he/she feels rather demotivated by the reward system and there is the threat of law if things go wrong!' Clearly, the balance of particular forces impacting on the individual is likely to influence their decision to some degree, even if it should not.

One area of ethical dilemma for managers relates to the degree and form of involvement that employees should be allowed to have in the running and direction of the business. For at the heart of all capitalist systems is a contradiction, 'the need to achieve both control *and* consent of employees, in order to secure not just the extraction, but the realization of their surplus value' (Legge, 1995, p 175). In most organizations involvement is not undertaken because it is an intrinsically good thing to do. It is done because managers see that it has advantage in helping them to achieve their objectives. The control over both the production process and the people provided by *scientific management* has not been able to deliver the desired levels of control and benefits over the people, process and end result. Consequently, the management focus has moved in the search to find ways of social control that more effectively *manipulate* the people resource in the search for more effective organizations and higher returns on capital employed. Efforts begun under the human relations umbrella have now become more sophisticated in response to the prevailing circumstances.

At one extreme it could be argued that employees are a resource to be used and that they are paid to do management's bidding. That view, however, is grounded in the *scientific management* view that managers 'decide' and workers 'do'. As a consequence it misses out on the potential to make use of the mental and intellectual capabilities of employees to contribute to the more effective running of the business. To be able to get employees involved in the business could actually make management activities easier, generate higher profits, improve quality and generally improve operational effectiveness. The general delayering of organizations over recent years has taken out many of the middle and junior management positions that previously sought to ensure that 'workers' did in fact work and follow the management agenda. However, without those managerial positions in place senior managers face the potential of being seriously overloaded. Consequently, it could be argued that involvement allows managers to delegate work to the lower levels, protecting themselves from overload. Involvement from this perspective is no more than a pragmatic and self-interested approach to coping with cost reduction.

The difficulty facing managers is how to identify the most effective means of achieving the objective without creating more problems. The difficulties with employee involvement in practice has been the commitment of managers to make it work. It is easy to understand from a manager's perspective that any form of employee involvement might threaten the position and status of managers. If there were few problems and employees were committed to the aims of the organization to the extent that they were able to organize themselves, what would become of the job of management?

Equally, not all employees would wish to become involved in an organization beyond the contractual obligations associated with their job. Consequently, dual levels of involvement have to be catered for. Not all approaches to involvement offer equally effective results, which also complicates the process. As far back as 1975 Poole identified that the intended purpose of involvement would determine which method would be likely to be most effective. On page 164 he indicates that in deciding the form of involvement provided by legislation, lower level forms would be more appropriate if the purpose was to improve efficiency rather than to extend the rights of workers. Deciding what the right thing to do is in this respect an ethical problem as well as a managerial one.

Conclusions

The material included in this chapter provides a basis on which ethical dilemmas can be resolved. It considered the different approaches that have emerged over the years and how they might link to organizational activity. A number of the more common areas of conflicting moral obligation were discussed. Just as important in this light are the areas that have been omitted. For example, giving to political parties and charity by organizations is an area that can create difficulties which must be resolved in a coherent way.

Employees are involved in their organizations as soon as they are recruited. There is no perfect approach to employee involvement and managers are faced with different views about what the right thing to do is. The concepts of power and control also have a significant degree of interaction with both ethics and involvement in organizational activity and will be covered in later chapters.

Discussion questions

1. Define the following key terms used in this chapter:

Utilitarianism	*Total quality management*	*Restricted contractarianism*
Whistleblowing	*Profit share*	*Act utilitarianism*
Formalism	*Employee involvement*	*Fordism*
Ethics	*Contractarianism*	*Social responsibility*
Rule utilitarianism	*Libertarian contractarianism*	*Snell's model of ethical*
Financial participation		*reasoning*

2. 'Ethics has no part to play in managerial activities.' Discuss this statement.

3. Discuss employee rights to privacy in the light of management's need to maintain good public and customer relations.

4. The primary responsibility of employees is to the organization that pays their wages. Whistleblowing should therefore result in the dismissal of the employee. Discuss.

5. 'Profit share schemes are an attempt to turn employees into capitalists and so be sympathetic to management control.' Discuss this statement.

6. Employees put their livelihood at stake by becoming involved with an organization and should not be subjected to additional financial risk as a result of other forms of financial participation. Discuss

7. 'Business is about making money and anything lawful and within reason that achieves that objective is ethical.' Discuss.

8. Consider the stages of moral development proposed by Snell. To what extent can you recognize these developmental stages in yourself and others?

9. Do you think that a code of practice could provide adequate guidance for individuals in deciding upon the right course of action in any particular situation? Justify your answer.

10. How would you persuade a manager who thought that their job was at risk from an employee involvement initiative not to attempt to undermine the benefits from the programme?

Research activities

1. Obtain a number of ethics codes of practice from sources open to you. They may be from professional institutions, commercial organizations or government. Compare the approach taken by each example that you find. How similar are they? Do you consider that they offer definite advice on how to resolve dilemmas in the context that they are intended to apply. If not, why? How would you undertake the task of drawing up a code of practice if you were asked to do so?

2. Interview a manager and ascertain their views on aspects of ethics in an organizational context. Repeat the exercise with a trade union representative, an employee and a shareholder. How do the different views compare? Seek to reconcile any differences and similarities that you find.

3. Search the newspapers and magazines for examples of claimed unethical behaviour on the part of managers or others within an organization. Analyze the information that you have collected and seek to explain what the ethical issues actually are, how the behaviour described is actually unethical, how it could be justified by the individuals concerned and how the situation could have been prevented or handled better. What does this analysis tell you about ethics within an organizational context?

Key reading

From Clark, H, Chandler, J and Barry, J (1994) *Organization and Identities: Text and Readings in Organizational Behaviour*, International Thomson Business Press, London:

- ✦ Friedman, AL: Marx's framework, p 25. This summarizes the Marxist view of aspects of capitalism as the creator of the work organizations within which labour is expressed.
- ✦ Foucault, M: Docile bodies and panopticism, p 35. This introduces one aspect of the basis of power and control in a social context.
- ✦ Foucault, M: The subject and power, p 43. Another extract from the genius of this writer on the nature and basis of power relationships in society.
- ✦ Bell, D: Work and its discontents, p 44. Considers the interaction between politics, ideology and work organization in social evolution.
- ✦ Whyte, WH: The organization man, p 149. This considers the relationship between careers and the level of ownership of the individual by the organization.
- ✦ Canter, RM: Men and women of the corporation, p 152. This introduces the idea that work and organizations impact upon the lives of employees and their families in different ways.
- ✦ Tiger, L: The possible biological origins of sexual discrimination, p 165. Considers discrimination as a function of biology rather than social forces.
- ✦ Oakley, A: Myths of women's place, p 169. Takes a strongly opposite point of view to that of Tiger and describes the labelling of women's work as an attempt to maintain male control.

✦ Coch, L and French, JRP: Overcoming resistance to change using group methods, p 260. Looks at one form of employee involvement.

✦ Brunsson, N: The virtue of irrationality – decision making, action and commitment, p 294. This considers the rationality of some decision making within organizations and how this relates to an action orientation.

✦ Höpfl, H *et al.*: Excessive commitment and excessive resentment: issues of identity, p 373. Considers the impact of attempts to change culture on commitment and related concepts.

Further reading

Alatas, SH (1991) *Corruption: Its Nature, Causes and Functions*, S Abdul Majeed, Kuala Lumpur, in association with Gower, London. As the title suggests, this book reviews the history and causes of corruption. It is set primarily within an Asian context and so provides a less usual reflection on aspects associated with ethics.

Cotton, JL (1993) *Employee Involvement: Methods for Improving Performance and Work Attitudes*, Sage, London. This text provides a comprehensive review of many of the techniques and practices associated with employee involvement. As the title suggests it is firmly rooted in the belief that by providing involvement employees will become more committed to the organization and its goals and that this in turn will create better service and profits.

Hyman, J and Mason, B (1995) *Managing Employee Involvement and Participation*, Sage, London. The text provides a comprehensive review of the basis of employee involvement. It also introduces recent initiatives in this field together with the typical responses by employees, employers and trade unions. It also incorporates experience and examples from Europe and America.

Jamieson, KM (1994) *The Organization of Corporate Crime: Dynamics of Antitrust Violation*, Sage, London. An American review of the illegal and anti-competitive activities of some executives. The writer attempts to place these findings into a theoretical framework.

Lomax, E (1995) *The Railway Man*, Jonathan Cape, London. The true story of a British army officer captured in the fall of Singapore and his subsequent treatment by the Japanese on the infamous Burma railway. It is the story of how the Japanese authorities reacted, the immediate and long-term consequences for the people involved and the ultimate reconciliation of captor and captive.

Maclagan, P (1998) *Management and Morality: A Developmental Perspective*, Sage, London This text is concerned with the realization of individual moral potential and the development of ethically responsive organizations.

References

Brennan, B (1991) Mismanagement and quality circles: how middle managers influence direct participation, *Employee Relations*, **13**, 5.

Brown, C (1992) Organization Studies and Scientific Authority. In Reed, M and Hughes, M (eds) *Rethinking Organization: New Directions in Organization Theory and Analysis*, Sage, London.

Butcher, D and Harvey, P (1999) Be upstanding, *People Management*, 30 June, pp 37–42.

Cadbury Committee (1992) *The Financial Aspects of Corporate Governance*, Stock Exchange Council, London.

Cederblom, J and Dougherty, CJ (1990) *Ethics at Work*, Wadsworth, Belmont, CA.

Church, R (1971) Profit sharing and labour relations in England in the nineteenth century, *International Review of Social History*, No. 14.

Clutterbuck, D and Grainer, S (1990) *Makers of Management: Men and Women Who Changed the Business World*, Macmillan, London.

Collard, R and Dale, B (1989) Quality circles. In Sisson, K (ed.) *Personnel Management in Britain*, Blackwell, Oxford.

Confederation of British Industry (1989) *Employee Involvement: Shaping the Future Business*, CBI, London.

Cooper, C (2000) Choose life, *People Management*, 11 May, pp 35–6.

Croft, J (1994) *Corporate Cloak and Dagger: Inside the World of Industrial Espionage*, HarperCollins, London.

Elliott, BBR (1998) Ethical considerations in the operations mix, *Management Services*, July, pp 20–3.

Fielding, N (1993) Ethnography. In Gilbert, N (ed.) *Researching Social Life*, Sage, London.

Finch, J (1993) It's Great to Have Someone to Talk to: Ethics and Politics of Interviewing Women. In Hammersley, M (ed.) *Social Research: Philosophy, Politics and Practice*, Sage, London.

Flood, RL (1993) *Beyond TQM*, John Wiley, Chichester.

Ford, H (1923) *My Life and Work*, Heinemann, London.

Garrahan, P and Stewart, P (1992) *The Nissan Enigma: Flexibility at Work in a Local Economy*, Mansell, London.

Giacalone, RA and Greenburg, J (1997) *Antisocial Behaviour in Organizations*, Sage, Thousand Oaks, CA.

Goffee, R and Scase, R (1995) *Corporate Realities: The Dynamics of Large and Small Organizations*, Routledge, London.

Goldsmith, J (1995) *The Response*, Macmillan, London.

Holden, L (1994) Employee involvement. In Beardwell, I and Holden, L (eds) *Human Resource Management: A Contemporary Approach*, Pitman, London.

Hornsby-Smith, M (1993) Gaining Access. In Gilbert, N (ed.) *Researching Social Life*, Sage, London.

Hosmer, LT (1987) Ethical analysis and human resource management, *Human Resource Management*, **26**, 313–30.

Huxley, A (1932) *Brave New World*, Chatto & Windus, London.

Hyman, J and Mason, B (1995) *Managing Employee Involvement and Participation*, Sage, London.

Johnson, G and Scholes, K (1993) *Exploring Corporate Strategy: Text and Cases*, 3rd edn, Prentice Hall, Hemel Hempstead.

Kerfoot, D and Knights, D (1994) Empowering the 'Quality Worker': The Seduction and Contradiction of the Total Quality Phenomenon. In Wilkinson, A and Willmott, H (eds) *Making Quality Critical*, Routledge & Kegan Paul, London.

Kohlberg, L and Ryncarz, RA (1990) Beyond Justice Reasoning: Moral Development and Consideration of a Seventh Stage. In Alexander, D and Langer, M (eds) *Higher Stages of Human Development*, Oxford University Press, Oxford.

Legge, K (1995) *Human Resource Management: Rhetorics and Realities*, Macmillan, Basingstoke.

Leisinger, KM (1995) Corporate Ethics and International Business: Some Basic Issues. In Stewart, S and Donleavy, G (eds) *Whose Business Values? Some Asian and Cross-Cultural Perspectives*, Hong Kong University Press, Hong Kong.

Leys, WAR (1962) The Value Framework of Decision Making. In Mailick, S and Van Ness, EH (eds) *Concepts and Issues in Administrative Behaviour*, Prentice Hall, Englewood Cliffs, NJ.

Lynn, M (1998) The whistleblower's dilemma, *Management Today*, October, pp 54–61.

Mahoney, J (1995) Ethical Attitudes to Bribery and Extortion. In Stewart, S and Donleavy, G (eds) *Whose Business Values? Some Asian and Cross-Cultural Perspectives*, Hong Kong University Press, Hong Kong.

Mahoney, J (1997) *Mastering Management*, Financial Times Pitman Publishing, London.

Marchington, M, Goodman, J, Wilkinson, A and Ackers, P (1992) New Developments in Employee Involvement. Manchester School of Management, Employment Department Research Series No. 2.

Mills, CW (1959) *The Sociological Imagination*, Oxford University Press, New York.

Morgan, G (1986) *Images of Organization*, Sage, Newbury Park, CA.

Poole, M (1975) *Workers' Participation in Industry*, Routledge & Kegan Paul, London.

Punch, M (1996) *Dirty Business: Exploring Corporate Misconduct, Analysis and Cases*, Sage, London.

Ramsey, H (1992) Commitment and Involvement. In Towers, B (ed) *The Handbook of Human Resource Management*, Blackwell, Oxford.

Raphael, DD (1994) *Moral Philosophy*, 2nd edn, Oxford University Press, Oxford.

Rawls, J (1971) *A Theory of Justice*, Harvard University Press, Cambridge, MA.

Remenyi, D, Williams, B, Money, A and Swartz, E (1998) *Doing Research in Business and Management: An Introduction to Process and Method*, Sage, London.

Rothschild, J and Miethe, TD (1994) Whistleblowing as Resistance in Modern Work Organizations: The Politics of Revealing Organizational Deception and Abuse. In Jermier, JM, Knights, D and Nord, WR (eds) *Resistance and Power in Organizations*, Routledge, London.

Snell, R (1995) Psychic Prisoners? Managers Facing Ethical Dilemmas: Cases from Hong Kong. In Stewart, S and Donleavy, G (eds) *Whose Business Values? Some Asian and Cross-Cultural Perspectives*, Hong Kong University Press, Hong Kong.

Stewart, S and White, W (1995) Conclusion: Whose Business Values? In Stewart, S and Donleavy, G (eds) *Whose Business Values? Some Asian and Cross-Cultural Perspectives*, Hong Kong University Press, Hong Kong.

Townley, B (1994) *Reframing Human Resource Management: Power, Ethics and the Subject at Work*, Sage, London.

CHAPTER 18

Managing change

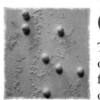

CHAPTER SUMMARY

This chapter will start by considering the nature and impact of change on organizations and the people who are employed within them. This will be followed by a consideration of the major triggers of change within an organizational setting. A number of the major models informing the management of the change process will then be discussed. The chapter will then introduce some of the forms that resistance to change can take, as well as some of the reasons for it. Following this will be a consideration of the role of innovation as a change strategy. This chapter will conclude with a consideration of change from an applied perspective.

LEARNING OBJECTIVES

After studying this chapter and working through the associated Management in Action panels, Discussion questions and Research activities, you should be able to:

✦ Understand the range of forces that impact on an organization and which can require change to be made.

✦ Describe the major change models, reflecting the wide diversity in approach to the management of it.

✦ Explain the difference between and significance of planned and unplanned change.

✦ Outline the association and implication between politics, power and change.

✦ Assess the value of managing innovation as part of a change strategy.

✦ Appreciate why people frequently resist change.

✦ Discuss the mechanisms through which managers attempt to control change.

✦ Detail the contingency and systems approaches to change management.

Introduction

The world in which we live is changing, as are the organizations within which we work and the work that we undertake within them. The world has always changed and people, plants and animals have evolved and adapted to new environmental circumstances that arise. The failure to adapt effectively to new circumstances has been punished very severely with the death or demise of the individual or species. However, the rate of change that is being experienced now is much greater than ever before. To demonstrate this rate of change together with some of the ways in which it can influence the working environment Table 18.1 has been extracted from Pritchett (1996).

There is always a danger in using the benefit of hindsight in looking back and claiming that the world was a 'better and simpler' place in times gone by. It is not possible to put ourselves in exactly the same position as our forebears. Life was probably just as complex and difficult for them as it is for people today, but in different ways. Problems and situations that we think of as easy to deal with today might have appeared much more complex in years gone by. The present level of technology and understanding was simply not available in history to assist or support people in their lives. For example, imagine trying to run a business in nineteenth-century Holland. This company bought porcelain goods in Japan for sale across Europe and orders took three months to get to Japan and the goods might not return for another three months, if they ever arrived at all (as the ship might sink while travelling in either direction). The speed of communication, pattern of business and transport technology might be vastly different today, which solves some of the problems alluded to, but it also creates new ones. The speed with which change must be accommodated is undoubtedly growing compared to that experienced in history. However, the difficult question to answer is what impact that has on organizations and people, when compared to experience in the past.

Given that change has always existed and that it requires adaptation among those exposed to it, it should be a feature of life that humans can easily cope with. However, this does not appear to be the case. Resistance and reluctance to adapt to change appear to be a common reaction among adult human beings within an organizational environment. There would appear to be a desire, if not a predisposition among significant numbers of humans to remain with the familiar and to avoid the ambiguity or uncertainty that accompanies change.

Predictability in life appears to be a valued condition for many people. There are likely

1 The number of mobile telephones sold was zero in 1982 and 4 million in 1995
2 The cost of computing power drops approximately 30% every year and microchips are doubling in performance power every 18 months
3 The first industrial robot was introduced during the 1960s. By 1982 there were approximately 32,000 in use in the USA. Today there are over 20 million
4 Of the largest 100 UK companies in 1965 only 32 remained on that list in 1995
5 In 1954, 45% of UK employees worked in manufacturing. Now it accounts for less than 22%

TABLE 18.1 Five changes over recent years (*source*: Pritchett, P (1996) *The Employee Handbook of New Work Habits for a Radically Changing World*, Pritchett & Rummler–Brache, London)

to be many reasons underlying this response. It is, however, a different reaction from that evident among young children. Young children are very keen to learn and acquire new skills and, once learned, they become desperate to demonstrate them to adults who will probably applaud and positively reward such behaviour. For example, consider the joy and pleasure on a child's face when it has just learned to walk and it stumbles about seeking (and achieving) the attention of its parents and other adults who all watch and offer praise etc. This willingness to change the current behaviour capabilities in children is something that disappears by the time most people reach adulthood or at least when they work in an organization.

It is interesting to contemplate why this reluctance to change emerges or should be so. Is it 'taught out' of people as a result of formal education; or because of the natural slowing of the cognitive processes underlying learning; or as a result of the organizational experiences encountered? Change in an organizational context invariably means having to take on more work, stress or even losing one's job, hardly positive reward for accepting change. It is because of the dilemma created by the requirement to change within an organization and a general reluctance to willingly embrace it by people that managers must pay special attention to the subject.

Pressure for change

For organizations there are particular *events* and *experiences* that are the instigators of change. Some of these forces arise from outside the organization and some from inside it. These forces can be changes by the organization or events to which the organization must respond by making changes. However, it is somewhat misleading to talk of *organizations* in this context, because organizations as such cannot do anything. It is the managers who run organizations who must first of all recognize events and then determine the courses of action to be followed. Management in Action 18.1 illustrates that some changes originate among the political, cultural and fashion connotations of management.

| Stop | Consider |

One implication of the views contained in MiA 18.1 is that organizational change is a self-inflicted problem to a significant extent. It is not required as a result of the real needs of society, product and service development or technology. It simply occurs because it is described as a good thing in the conventional wisdom of senior managers and, therefore, a necessary thing.

To what extent and why do you support this view of change? In addition, what might this imply about the ways that society should seek to control (if at all) organizational and managerial activity?

Change within an organization can affect many different aspects of it. For example an individual might find that a change to the technology used might impact on their traditional methods of work or might eliminate the need for their job altogether. Change can affect a group through, say, the introduction of teamwork. Change could also affect the entire organization. For example, the development and introduction of a new product range might involve the building of a new factory in a location with cheaper labour and the

MANAGEMENT IN ACTION 18.1

Off with their overheads

Cutting the number of employees may be a necessary course of action in difficult situations but it has the potential to damage future prospects. As Trapp says: 'It is not a lesson that British or US managers have yet fully learned. The cut, cut, cut mentality is now deeply embedded in Anglo-Saxon corporate culture – every company says people are its greatest asset, but when life starts to get tough, again and again those "assets" are unceremoniously heaved over the side.'

Fortune magazine suggested in the early 1990s that companies were caught in the grip of 'wee-ness envy', an envy and desire to emulate other companies that were smaller than themselves. Russell Baker commented that the scale of dismissals by a manager was a measure of the right to membership of the CEO club. Two examples of the cut, cut, cut mentality identified by Trapp include:

✦ During 1995 British Gas experienced 150% increase in complaints. At the same time it was in the process of shedding 25,000 jobs.

✦ Ever Ready the battery manufacturer was acquired by Hanson in the early 1980s. It shed 900 of the 2900 jobs at the R & D centre. This began what one commentator described as an attempt to make the decline of the company as long and profitable as possible. When it was sold in 1993 its market share had dropped from 80% to 30%. Its technology was by then ten years behind the industry.

Professor Gary Hamel, visiting professor of international and strategic management at London Business School, compiled a 'Downsizing Hall of Fame' which included such names as Westinghouse, Kodak, General Motors, Union Carbide and DuPont, all of which had aggressively reduced the numbers employed over recent years. In the UK, companies such as Hanson, GEC, British Coal (which cut itself out of existence) and the clearing banks would all appear on the list. This has produced a generation of what

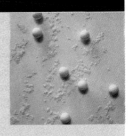

Hamel describes as 'lowest common denominator managers' in the USA and the UK. Managers who are able to delayer, downsize, declutter and divest better than managers in other countries. As evidence of this, from 1987 to 1991 (a period of economic growth) more than 85% of the *Fortune* 500 companies reduced the size of their white-collar staff. Hamel describes the process as one of 'corporate anorexia' – leaner companies are not necessarily fitter.

Business process re-engineering (BPR) has most frequently been linked with downsizing and has largely been discredited as a consequence. It has been suggested that some 75% of all attempts to apply BPR fail. The main intention behind BPR to focus the business on what it should be attempting to achieve has been overshadowed by it potential to cut cost and numbers of employees. Surveys in the USA have shown that only 22–34% of companies that restructure increase productivity to their satisfaction. This invariably leads to a downward spiral of cutting and failure to achieve success. Similar results on profitability have also been observed. In a survey of 210 companies not one reported a post-redundancy profit performance that matched previous figures.

Hamel suggests that companies continue to adopt the cutting approach because it has become an organizational norm. Organizations are 'forced' by various means to follow the conventional wisdom of the day. This includes pressure from institutional shareholders, following the fashions of the moment, pressure from City analysts, a desire to be like other organizations and a wish to follow the lead of those organizations that are regarded as the most prestigious in their industry. It does not, however, guarantee commercial success or benefit for customers or society.

Adapted from: Trapp, R (1995) Off with their overheads, *Independent on Sunday,* Business section, 10 December, pp

reallocation of work across existing locations, as well as structural and other changes to the organization.

There are also changes that impact on society and which in turn cascade back into organizations. For example, the taxation levels applied to products such as alcohol and tobacco by governments are often designed to influence consumption rates in a downwards direction. Consequently, the organizations producing these products experience reductions in business. Also, with products such as tobacco there is an attempt to influence the health of the population through taxation levels and so impact on the need for public health provision and other government spending. This invariably also impacts on the public sector in a variety of ways.

There is another factor to be taken into account when considering the nature of, and complexity inherent in, change. That is the occurrence of random or chance factors. For example, in some parts of the world earthquakes and storms are natural hazards occurring on an annual basis. An earthquake could physically destroy buildings and disrupt communications in seconds, the effects of which could last for months. The high probability and severity of such factors can cause sudden and dramatic change and also they require mechanisms to be developed that can more easily tolerate these factors and when they occur, recover more easily. This enters the fields of risk assessment along with emergency and recovery planning, all of which are beyond the scope of this chapter.

Forces acting on organizations

There are many and varied forces acting on organizations which create, directly or indirectly, the need for change. There are many ways that these forces can be classified; one is to categorize them as originating from either outside or inside the organization. Table 18.2 represents some of the external sources of pressure for change (Open University, 1990).

In addition to these sources of change, Hellriegel *et al.* (1989) identify the following:

◆ Rapid product obsolescence. This refers to the increasing rapidity of product change necessitated by fashion and technology etc. It reflects the pace of change in what

Source of change	Examples
Market demand	Decline in demand for particular products/services, for example, monochrome television sets
Market supply	Mergers in retail companies
Economic	Overall fall in retail companies; changes in exchange rates
Social	Changes in taste, for example, increase in health consciousness in 1980s
Technological	Increased availability of new production technologies and information systems
Political	Change in leadership of local authority or government
Chance	Earthquake, fire, flood, storm

TABLE 18.2 External pressure for change (*source*: *Managing Change*, Book 9, B784, The effective manager, Open University)

organizations can offer to the marketplace and what customers demand by way of products and services.

 ✦ Knowledge explosion. Information and knowledge are rapidly becoming commodities in their own right. This creates both new organizations and also impacts on those not directly involved in the *creation of information*. This knowledge explosion can influence an organization in many different ways. For example, the growth of the internet allows potential customers to find and compare a range of possible suppliers much more easily than would have been possible without that technology. Another trend among organizations is to *benchmark* themselves against other organizations as a means of judging their performance against nominated targets. This requires the collection and analysis of large quantities of data; usually on a reciprocal basis between organizations or through management consultancies. Management in Action 18.2 reflects a number of aspects associated with this trend.

Stop | Consider   *MiA 18.1 suggested that much change resulted from managers seeking to follow the practices of other senior managers. Taking that perspective into account, to what extent is benchmarking a necessary management tool or simply a means of justifying management preferred strategies?*

 ✦ Demographics. The demographics and nature of both customers and the workforce is changing which inevitably impacts on many aspects of organizational functioning. Education levels are generally rising, with more people now entering higher and further education than ever before. Whatever else advanced education achieves it appears to significantly influence expectations about the role of work in people's lives. Individuals with more qualifications develop an expectation that their work experience will reflect that achievement and the delayed start to their working life. In economic terms they seek a return for their investment of staying later in the educational system. Also, the growth of the dual career family along with the emergence of an older population with disposable wealth has created opportunities for new products and services to be developed.

The internal forces for change that arise within an organization include:

 ✦ Efficiency. There is an ever present drive for *minimalism* in organizations. The increased level of competition evident today forces every organization to enter a spiral of cost reduction. The finance markets seek ever higher profit levels on behalf of investors. Managers themselves have careers to *manage* through being *better* than their peer group. Better in this context implies being able to demonstrate that they can deliver that which more senior managers expect – minimalism!

 ✦ Fashion. Change for the sake of change is another force acting upon internal change processes. There are organizations (and managers) who pride themselves on being *cutting edge* in this respect. This creates a pressure for change as others follow and adopt yesterday's innovation.

 ✦ Control. New managers frequently make changes simply to demonstrate that the previous incumbent has gone, thereby allowing the new manager to be seen as the one in control. Employees frequently refer to, 'the way it has always been'. This might be accurate, but it also represents an attempt to socialize the new manager into employee-

MANAGEMENT IN ACTION 18.2

A measure of success

Benchmarking is a process intended to provide a basis for comparison. It allows an organization to identify others against which it can measure its own performance and from which it can learn new ways of improving its effectiveness. For example:

♦ South-West Airlines in the USA studied the performance of the pit crews at the Indy 500 motor car race and learned how to reduce the turnaround time of its aircraft at an airport gate from 30 minutes to 15.

♦ The Granite Rock Company studied the use of ATMs in banking. Its own loading procedures required accurate figures and records along with simple and convenient use. The upshot was that the company introduced a system of ATM-like cards for its drivers to make the weighing and record keeping simpler, faster and more reliable.

Benchmarking is not new; it has, however, taken off as a necessary management technique over the past few years. It could be argued that it was Walter Chrysler who began the idea many years ago when he bought and stripped down an Oldsmobile. He was intent in finding out what went into the competitor's car, how it was made and how much it cost to make. It was during the early 1990s that renewed and large-scale interest in the technique emerged. It is frequently seen alongside business process re-engineering and total quality management as a trilogy of efficiency improvement techniques. The British government also uses the technique as part of its market-testing programme for public sector efficiency.

In a survey of the top 10,000 UK companies

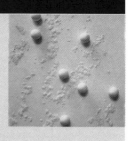

by Coopers & Lybrand and the Confederation of British Industry it was revealed that 66% of the respondents across all sectors practised bench-marking and that 85% felt that it had been successful.

Of the *Fortune* 500 companies, 80% use the technique and 60% intended to increase investment in its application. In the early 1980s it was Xerox that began to use benchmarking to seek ways of combating competition from the Far East in copier products. In doing so it recognized that to identify the best ways of doing things it was not essential to copy from one company. It is possible to identify parallels in other sectors and companies against which to measure oneself and as a basis to learn from their experience.

In recent times the emphasis in benchmarking has moved away from performance measurement and concentrated on what gives leading companies their competitive edge. The emphasis should not be 90% on the development of measurements and 10% on change, but the other way around, according to Victor Luck, head of commerce and industry consulting services at Coopers & Lybrand. Arthur Andersen, an international accounting and consultancy firm, has invested over £6.4m in developing the Global Best Practices Knowledge Base. This represents its proprietary benchmarking database, built up from a wide variety of sources and intended for use by its consultants in helping clients. Clearly benchmarking as a technique is likely to be around for some considerable time to come.

Adapted from: Dickson, T (1993) A measure of success, *Financial Times*, 5 May, p 14.

preferred work practices. Employees have the upper hand in such situations as they inevitably know the established ways better than the new manager. If the new manager changes everything around then it neutralizes that potential benefit, allowing the new manager to demonstrate that they are 'in control'.

✦ Internal pressure. Change can be forced on an organization as a result of the internal pressure from various stakeholder groups. For example, changes to the wage structure and working practices could be brought about as a result of industrial action by the workforce. The social pressure from women and ethnic minority groups for a greater degree of equality at work has forced organizations to respond by changing previously white male- (at least in the western world) dominated employment and work practices.

Stewart (1991) identifies a number of changes that specifically influence managerial careers in addition to any other aspects of organizational life. They include, in addition to the points already made:

 ✦ Business structure. This category would include more frequent changes in business ownership; growth in multinational and foreign ownership; privatization of the public sector and the globalization of business activity. These changes inevitably impact on the ways that predominantly middle and junior managers can progress their careers. For example, the takeover of one company by another inevitably creates overlap in many areas. Inevitably as a consequence a number of positions (and therefore people) will be surplus to requirements at the same time as new career opportunities are created for others.

 ✦ Business functioning. This factor reflects the growth of flexibility as a means of matching resources to requirement through self-employment, contracting and the need to seek new business opportunities. More and more aspects of company activity are being 'contracted out' to other organizations in the search for cost reduction and efficiency. The house building industry in the UK provides a clear example of this. Years ago each building company would directly employ the joiners, bricklayers, plumbers and other craftspeople needed to build the houses. Today they directly employ only a very small number of workers, the bricklaying, plumbing, joinery and electrical work being subcontracted to independent companies or teams of self-employed people. Consequently, the opportunities for people to work their way up from worker to manager within the same company are much reduced and the job of site managers is one of project management rather than the direct control of workers.

This discussion has demonstrated that a wide range of forces act upon organizations and directly or indirectly result in change. It is now appropriate to consider how these are experienced within an organization. There are four different ways in which change can be experienced by an organization, dependent on the scale of change and the degree of planning involved. Figure 18.1 illustrates these through the name of each of the four categories on the two axes.

Each of the four cells in Figure 18.1 reflects different response scenarios to the experienced situation. As such they provide a basis for identifying management strategies. The axes of the model will be discussed in the following subsections, but it is appropriate to consider each of the cells in turn briefly at this point:

✦ Surprise. This reflects situations that are both unplanned and relatively minor in nature. For example, interest rates might unexpectedly change and require the finance managers of a company to adjust loan repayment schedules.

✦ Incremental. This could reflect situations which are anticipated and are relatively minor in nature. For example, the implementation of quality circle recommendations may require that small changes be made to the design of a particular component to make it easier to fit during the assembly operations. However, this will be only one of a series of changes planned by the circle to make the production process more effective.

◆ Crisis. This represents both the unexpected and the serious. An extreme example might be the destruction of a factory as the result of a gas explosion or terrorist attack. It contains the potential to destroy the organization unless the response is appropriate and effective.

◆ Strategic. This represents major planned events that attempt to position the organization more effectively in relationship to its environment. For example, a company making manual typewriters anticipating the growth of computer-based systems may seek to acquire a business systems or computer division. Management in Action 18.3 reflects another form of strategic and fundamental change, based on the desire for organizational survival.

Stop | Consider   *To what extent would the situation described in MiA 18.3 be more accurately described as a crisis rather than strategic change?*
    What difference, if any, does such a distinction make?

Adaptive change

The vertical axis of Figure 18.1 represents a scale of change impact. Those changes categorized as adaptive are relatively small in scale and which as a consequence can be accommodated without major disruption and danger to the organization. It represents the many thousands of small *adaptive* movements in absorbing and responding to day-to-day events, balancing and integrating operations with the environment within which they take place. However, small in scale as such changes may be in organizational terms, that does not mean that they will be small in impact for individual employees or managers.

There are many possible examples of this type of change that exist. For example, a flu epidemic occurs and the level of sickness absence suddenly and unexpectedly rises. This type of change can be accommodated relatively easily, but not without some measure of

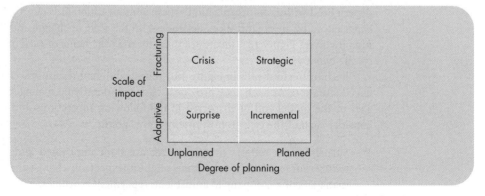

FIGURE 18.1   The change matrix.

MANAGEMENT IN ACTION 18.3

Launching a new tradition in a Clyde shipyard

The shipbuilding industry in the UK once led the world in its field but had the reputation of poor management and conflictual industrial relations. Working practices were inflexible and investment was very low. Not surprisingly, shipyards in Asia soon overtook the UK in terms of delivery, cost and innovation.

Of the few remaining shipyards, Kvaerner Govan, owned by a Norwegian shipping and engineering group and located on the river Clyde, is a notable exception. Showing losses of £45m in 1988 when it was taken over by Kvaerner it turned in a profit of £1m in 1994 and had forward orders for at least two years. In the past the company suffered a serious lack of investment and poor working practices. For example, absenteeism was running at 23% and productivity was low, taking 2.5 times as many hours to build a ship as its competitors. The turnaround in the company fortunes had been achieved through several initiatives running in parallel:

✦ £31m investment in new plant and machinery.
✦ Recognition that 35% of costs were associated with 'making' each ship and it was therefore an added value company.
✦ Identification of 'lost time' of 240,000 hours per year. The major reasons being:
  ✦ Average working week of around 29 hours compared with the paid hours of 39, the causes being concessions to the workforce on breaks, stopping and starting times to encourage new work practices.
  ✦ 60,000 hours each year spent by union representatives on union business.
  ✦ 70,000 hours lost each year through accidents and injuries.
  ✦ Inefficient shift pattern organization and restrictive practices also accounted for a high number of hours lost.
  ✦ Absenteeism accounted for 440 of the yard's 2000 employees being off work at any one time.
✦ The unions were told of the findings and that

if the company were to survive it had to become profitable. It was also made clear that the processes to be changed would be agreed and that training would be provided for employees to enable them to work in the ways required.

✦ New welding techniques were needed for an order and so training was begun and a bonus of 5% paid to those who passed the course.
✦ The absence problem was tackled head-on. Employees were visited at home to find out if they were fit to return to work. Individuals were told that their sick pay would be stopped and their jobs were in jeopardy. The absence rate fell sharply to 10% and then again to 5% when overtime pay was restricted to those who had worked 37 hours or more in a week.
✦ The changes were introduced in two phases. The working week was reduced to 37 hours but the various concessions were eliminated. The number of shop stewards was cut to 20 and they were allowed one hour each day for union duties. Petty demarcations between jobs were eliminated. The second phase followed a year later. It involved the changing of shift patterns. Shopfloor resistance to these changes led to a strike as shiftwork had previously been optional and controlled by the unions. The strike ended when the company sent letters to all employees telling them that they would be sacked the following week if they did not return to work. Several layers of management and supervisory jobs were also eliminated during this phase.

The result of these changes brought the number of hours to build a ship down to almost the same as its competitors and returned the yard to profit.

Adapted from: Hodges, C (1994) Launching a new tradition in a Clyde shipyard, *Personnel Management Plus*, April, pp 20–1.

increased cost. Employees at work could be asked to stay behind and work overtime. Alternatively, temporary labour could be hired to cover for the absent employees. Allowing production to fall behind schedule is another option. These represent the tactical levels of decision that line managers engage in all the time in responding to the ever changing circumstances that they are exposed to.

Other *adaptive* changes are more permanent, but nevertheless minor in scale. For example, minor modifications to the external features of product design on an annual basis. The intention being to keep it fresh in appearance and to respond to marketing initiatives among competitors. The introduction of a new computer package for personnel records would serve as another example. The new system might require changes to the design of a number of personnel forms and procedures as well as the transfer of much existing data from one computer system to another. Overall however, important as such systems are they represent changes that are relatively small in comparison to everything that the organization does.

Fracturing change   – large change

This scale of change impact (Figure 18.1) represents the major events that occur within the experience of all organizations. The scale of change represented by this category is very large and of such significance that could seriously damage or destroy the organization. In other words, it has the potential to *fracture* or break it.

Products and services are all designed to meet particular needs among their consumers. There is always a danger that these needs can be met in different ways and thus eliminate the market for a particular product. In recent years the changes to political structures have fundamentally changed the military balance that existed for the previous 40 years. The so-called *peace dividend* has produced a number of major changes, including the possibility for a massive reduction in business for those companies making military equipment. Such organizations have had to adjust rapidly to this dangerous situation (for their survival and profit) or face severe contraction in size or even their demise.

Another example of the possibility of fracturing change would be the natural disasters that can strike any organization at any time. For example, a gas explosion could destroy a building and so potentially destroy the company. A major area of managerial responsibility over recent years has been the field of risk and disaster planning in an attempt to minimize the consequence of such events.

There is a scale of magnitude reflecting the level of real or potential threat to an organization. Equally, some issues which might be major in one context may be considered minor in another. For example, in a company with a poor industrial relations record frequent strikes may be the norm. Therefore, it may be part of the management planning process to build an allowance into their operations, schedules and costs to reduce the impact. Also, there are situations in which relatively minor events can slip out of control and become life threatening if they are not handled effectively. For example, the new computerized personnel system referred to in the previous subsection could be inappropriate or faulty in some respect. Its introduction could also be resisted by personnel staff. Employees might also interpret its introduction as an attempt by managers to tighten control and intrude into their lives. The consequences of any of these could be a slide into a major disaster for the organization if they were not effectively managed.

Planned change

The horizontal axis of Figure 18.1 reflects the degree of planning that can be brought to bear on the situation. It is about the level of anticipation concerning the events which are forcing change to occur. Planned change represents those events that management intend to occur and for which they can provide a predetermined response.

There are many examples of planned change. Management may identify that its ability to retain market share is being threatened by competitors with much lower labour costs. Consequently, a package of measures could be developed including the introduction of automation and high technology; the development of flexibility and teamwork practices among the workforce; the linking of wages to performance; the redesign of the product to make it more attractive to the customer; along with the development of a range of customer inducements and support measures.

It also represents the strategic moves made by organizations in order to position themselves to minimize the overall impact of declining markets and to capture the potential of expanding businesses. This refers to the merger, acquisition and divestment strategies that many large organizations engage in as they search for higher returns, market dominance and growth. Planning for the many small changes that occur is also part of normal managerial experience. For example, the introduction of total quality management initiatives are an attempt to capture and routinize the process of continuous improvement.

Unplanned change

This category represents the unexpected events that arise and which can never be completely eliminated from an organization's environment. Parts of California are known to be subject to earthquakes as they lie along faults in the earth's crust. Knowing this, measures can be taken to minimize the consequences through building design and emergency planning. However, it is not yet possible to predict with any certainty when or how strong a particular tremor will be. They remain random factors and so when they occur preprepared recovery plans must be activated. It can be argued that it is one of the primary responsibilities of management to anticipate events and to minimize the possibility of the unexpected arising. Also they have a responsibility for the development of plans for dealing with such eventualities that cannot be eliminated or totally controlled. This contingency planning approach to change attempts to scan the internal and external environment and develop response scenarios for what might be expected to occur.

Over recent years many organizations have engaged a reductionist approach to managing. The ability to cut back the numbers of employees and to rationalize operational activity has been a much prized skill. This was the point made earlier in Management in Action 18.1. This is achieved by eliminating *slack* from the system as a whole and by concentrating on *doing* rather than *thinking*. One of the potential dangers of this *minimalist* approach is that it removes the ability to *anticipate* and *plan* as a result of the emphasis on producing to standardized plans in the current and future time periods. The inherent risk in this approach is that there is a higher potential to miss intelligence and important signals from the environment, which in turn creates the risk of more unplanned events arising with the consummate risk of *crisis* being higher. Crisis in Figure 18.1 being the least desirable and most dangerous cell in the matrix naturally carries with it the greater risk for the survival of the organization.

Approaches to organizational change

It has already been established that change is both endemic to management and an issue which can generate resistance from a wide range of sources. The major responsibility of managers is to enable the organization to function effectively and so it is they who have a prime responsibility for both creating change and responding to it in pursuit of their objectives. Management in Action 18.4 illustrates that not all large-scale change can be planned and that even senior managers have to respond to the situations that they find themselves in.

Stop | Consider

How would you classify the changes described in MiA 18.4 in terms of the change matrix proposed in Figure 18.1?
  Justify your choices.

Leavitt's organizational variables and change

One model of a company, the work of Leavitt (1965), reflects the major constituent parts of an organization within its environment. This can be used as the basis for change management initiatives to be identified as well as the consequences of change to be considered (see Figure 18.2).

Leavitt argues that change can affect any (or all) of these variables. Alternatively, they can be changed individually in an attempt to influence other elements within the organization. So for example, the technology used by a company could be changed in order to impact on the structure, people, and task aspects of it. Because of the integrated nature of these elements changes to one of them will have consequential effects on the others. As another example, the change of some of the key managers in an organization could well create a number of subsequent changes to the structure of the organization, its technology and some of the tasks to be undertaken.

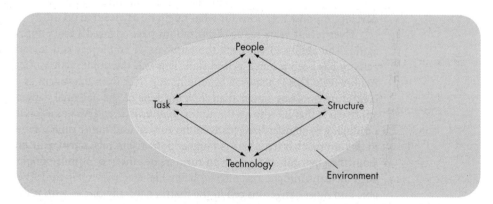

FIGURE 18.2   Leavitt's organization variables (*source*: Huczynski, A and Buchanan, D (1991) *Organizational Behaviour*, Prentice Hall, Hemel Hempstead).

MANAGEMENT IN ACTION 18.4

Shake-up inspires new state of mind

On 5 July 1995 the UK government decided to merge the employment and education departments. The justification for this move was that the overlap between education and training provision was not effectively served by the separation of the two main civil service departments responsible for them. The scale of the integration was to bring together two distinctly different organizations with vastly different traditions and functions and, as a consequence, create a single entity that could improve services to the nation. The numbers employed by these two departments of state were employment 50,000 people and education 1700. Many of the employment department's staff (45,000) were engaged in front-line duties associated with the employment service (job centres, etc.). The education department was much more policy based in its function and many of its staff worked through public bodies such as the Further Education Funding Council.

The merger, for that is what it was, was always going to be difficult and complex. There were a number of sub-departments that would not easily fit into the new structure. For example, the division that dealt with industrial relations policy development was transferred to the Department of Trade and Industry. The Health and Safety Executive (about 4300 staff) was transferred to the Department of the Environment. The merger was extraordinary for three principle reasons:

◆ Speed. The two secretaries of state responsible for the departments (the senior politicians) and the two permanent secretaries (the senior civil servants) did not know of the planned change until one hour before it was announced.

◆ Culture. The cultures of the two organizations were completely different.

◆ Leadership. It was initially decided that both senior civil servants would be retained.

Since then, however, one of them (Sir Tim Lankester) left to take up the position as director of the School of Oriental and African Studies.

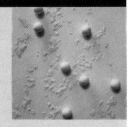

The senior managers quickly determined that they would adopt a holistic approach by focusing on the five ingredients necessary for success:

◆ Clarity of values.

◆ Clarity of aims and objectives.

◆ A structure that facilitated the achievement of values, aims and objectives.

◆ Processes that supported the achievement of values, aims and objectives.

◆ People who felt comfortable with the values and who had the necessary skills.

A transitional board was established to develop the mechanisms for integration and by mid-September an integrated set of aims for the new Department for Education and Employment was published. They were to:

> Support economic growth and improve the nation's competitiveness and quality of life by raising standards of educational achievement and skill and by promoting an efficient and flexible labour market.

By Christmas 1995 the senior 110 positions had been filled and work began on other aspects of the change. This involved restructuring the work of the departments and of introducing common systems of recruitment, appraisal, training and promotion. Communication was used constantly to keep staff informed and involved in the change process. Bichard explained that he tried to ensure that information was honest, never hiding bad news, ensuring that fairness would be a key criterion and wherever possible seeking an outcome with which the staff would be comfortable. The next stage was to move people's attention from looking backwards to looking towards the future.

Adapted from: Bichard, M (1996) Shake-up inspires new state of mind, *People Management*, 8 February, pp 22–7.

Mergers, acquisition and change

Already introduced in this discussion are the opportunities to achieve change within an organization through adaptations to aspects of it such as structure, technology etc. Another major creator of change within an organization is the merger and acquisition activity commonly found as part of the strategic planning intended to achieve growth and/or cost reduction. Johnson and Scholes (1993, p 233) suggest that development by acquisition tends to occur in waves. They quote such periods of high acquisition activity in the UK as 1898–1900, 1926–29, 1967–73 and 1985–87. They also point out that each of these periods showed a tendency for particularly high activity in specific industries. For example, between 1985–87 there was a considerable volume of high street retailing takeover activity taking place in the UK.

Whether the purpose of the acquisition, merger or takeover is growth or cost reduction, change is an inevitable consequence. Two or more sometimes very different organizations must be brought together and from that total pool of capability, a new unified organization must be forged with the potential to return greater shareholder wealth, growth and/or cost reduction. It is the task of the managers in that situation to realize that potential. Among the many problems of duplication of resources, product range, customer lists and procedural/systems incompatibilities that must be resolved, often the major difficulties lie among the people and organizational culture areas.

Organizational culture is discussed in detail in an earlier chapter in this text and much of that material is relevant to this discussion. Johnson and Scholes explore (Chapter 11) the process of managing strategic change, including the cultural dimensions. They suggest that the important cultural blockages to change can be:

✦ Routines. By this term they refer to the, 'ways that things get done around here'. It reflects the normal ways of operating and functioning, which inevitably differ to some degree between any two organizations.

✦ Control systems. These refer to the reporting and procedural ways of working within the organization.

✦ Structures. This reflects the arrangement of tasks and jobs into sections, departments and a hierarchy of responsibility.

✦ Symbols. This they define as the, 'symbolic acts and artefacts of an organization [that] help to preserve the paradigm' (p 401). This reflects those aspects of an organization that help to create its identity and sense of difference from other organizations. Inevitably, therefore, these symbols can become a major source of difficulty for achieving cultural change following a merger or takeover.

✦ Power and dependency relationships. The ways in which power and political activity finds expression in the separate organizations will inevitably be disturbed by attempts to combine them. New relationships, alliances and power structures will have to be formed and inevitably this gives rise to new political activity as integration takes place. It is commonplace to hear stories in such situations about the old days, references to us and them and how the other lot are not as good as we were. In some ways this reflects a process of establishing a new 'pecking order', as found among chickens and other animals when forming a flock or group.

Johnson and Scholes suggest that the role of the change agent is vital in seeking to achieve success in changing culture. They suggest that the options offered by Kotter and Schlesinger (1979) (indicated in Table 18.4) are available and that each has advantages and disadvantages to be considered. Success in achieving change in the culture of the organizations depends in getting the style of the change agent to match the needs of the situation. Management in Action 18.5 reflects some recent research into change following merger and acquisition activity.

Stop | Consider

To what extent do you consider that the ideas put forward by Johnson and Scholes offer a means of achieving the, 'careful and sensitive management' of integration, suggested as necessary in MiA 18.5?

Re-engineering and quality approaches to change

Business process re-engineering became popular during the early 1990s. It was an approach to the design of organizational activity that required managers to go back to first principles and recreate the organization with a complete emphasis on meeting the needs of customers. Most organizations are organized vertically. Reports are created and transmitted upwards to more senior managers, instructions are determined at a senior level and communicated downwards. Careers are developed in a vertical direction as promotion takes the individuals up the organization. However, the customer experience of any organization is horizontal. Very few customers of an organization ever meet or deal with people at a senior level. Consequently, it is hardly surprising to find that much human effort within any organization is directed at meeting the needs of the hierarchy, rather than being totally focused on the needs of the customer. Hammer and Champy (1995) took this idea one stage further and proposed that any company should be organized around the notion of a *process* and that each process should be re-engineered so that it added maximum value and contained minimal non-value adding support activity. This they termed *business process re-engineering* (often shortened to BPR).

The concept of a *process* is fundamental to BPR. A process in this context refers to a series of actions or proceedings used in the manufacturing, creation or achievement of something (Malhotra, 1998). Harrington (1991, p 9) defines a process as any activity that adds value to an input in converting it into an output for an internal or external customer. However a process is defined, the message from BPR is clear, only things that add value to the customer requirement should be considered important. Hammer and Champy describe re-engineering as an approach to change and efficiency that capitalizes on the American strengths of, 'individualism, self-reliance, a willingness to accept risk and a propensity for change' (p 3). They also describe it as an approach which requires discontinuous thinking in challenging existing thinking and ways of undertaking business operations. In short, a revolutionary way to identify and implement change. The essential approach being to rapidly identify change and then equally quickly implement it.

This rapid, revolutionary and top-down driven approach to change can be compared with approaches that emerge out of thinking about quality and how to maximize it. For example, total quality management (TQM) is one such approach and according to Slack *et al.* (1998, p 763) evolved from the earlier inspection approach to quality as the dominant paradigm. TQM is an approach to quality which they suggest stresses the following:

MANAGEMENT IN ACTION 18.5

Executive action for acquisition success

Angwin describes a number of changes that surround the takeover process. He suggests that as many as one in seven executives will experience a takeover during their working lives and that this might be expected to be higher for MBA-qualified managers. He also points out that most takeovers fail (about 44% subsequently split up) and that many of those involved find it a negative experience. In America consultants recommend a formal grieving period for staff in the acquired company, including mock funerals and coffins on occasions!

The research conducted by Angwin suggests that immediately following the takeover a high level of change-related initiatives occur and that this quickly tails off. He reports levels of 500 changes initiated in the first month following a takeover dropping steadily to fewer than 50 changes by month 19. This process reflects the new owners being seen to 'take control' and making everyone in the company see that they 'mean business'. The speed of making such changes is a little surprising given that the new owners cannot know everything about the acquired company before they take charge. It might be expected that extensive pre-takeover planning would identify what changes were to be made following acquisition. Angwin's research, carried out in conjunction with Ernst & Young, did not find this in practice. Many executives described the process as running into a 'wall' as senior managers who instigated the deal frequently go on to complete new deals and the running of the acquired company falls to executives not involved in the negotiations.

Some of the immediate change can be accounted for as a result of the need to introduce standardized procedures and practice in the finance areas. Equally there is the 'expectation' on senior executives that change will be made and so already planned or considered change might be implemented when this was not possible under the old regime. If a senior executive is appointed from outside to run the company then they will wish to 'stamp' their authority on both the old and new companies. Doing nothing was not regarded as a realistic option by the respondents in Angwin's study.

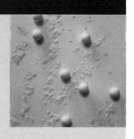

The research shows that not all changes are introduced in the relatively short time after a takeover. This is noticeable at the end of the first year with the initial thrust on finance and marketing being replaced by human resource issues coming to the fore. This was suggested to be a necessary refinement on what inevitably was a crude process immediately following a takeover. The subsequent changes also tend to be more complex and difficult to achieve. Perhaps the skeletons in the cupboard of the acquired company have finally come to light and need to be dealt with. The post-takeover period is highly stressful for everyone concerned, particularly because job security is always at risk. It is not uncommon to find that companies put together teams of opposite numbers from each company to integrate activity. Over the period of the integration it becomes apparent which of the pair will be 'released'.

After an acquisition there can be strong feelings of 'winners and losers', but it is frequently forgotten that it can be a two-way process. The acquiring company can also be changed as a result of exposure to the purchased one. This interactive development is the very best possibility to emerge from a takeover and can be a driver for strategic renewal. However, for this to be achieved, takeovers must be change processes and that means careful, sensitive management.

Adapted from: Angwin, D (1996) Executive action for acquisition success, *Warwick Nexus*, Spring, pp 4–5.

✦ Meeting the needs and expectations of customers.

✦ Covering all parts of the organization.

✦ Including every person in the organization.

✦ Examining all costs associated with quality (especially the cost of failure).

✦ Emphasizing 'right first time' in quality.

✦ Developing the systems and procedures that support quality improvement.

✦ Developing continuous improvement.

Dale (1999, p 231) suggests that it can take up to ten years to implement TQM fully through the: 'Fundamental principles, practices, procedures and systems, [to] create an organizational culture that is conducive to continuous improvement and [to] change the values and attitudes of its people.' Clearly there are a number of major differences in the approach to change offered between BPR and TQM. BPR is intended to be revolutionary, rapid, top-down driven and a single-shot process. TQM, conversely, is slow, evolutionary, bottom up in emphasis and incremental in its approach to change. Indeed, Hammer and Champy argue (p 216) that TQM should be used in between the major upheavals created through a BPR exercise.

Both BPR and TQM are about change although the methods of achieving it are radically different. However, Hammer and Champy admit in subsequent work (as do many other writers) that most BPR initiatives failed to work or deliver the sustained benefits intended by senior managers. The disruption perhaps being just too much to be able to cope with effectively without creating organizational collapse. The time distinction for the implementation of change between these two initiatives is interesting in that BPR argues that very rapid change is most easily accommodated. In effect, frenetic periods of disruption each time the processes are revisited and redesigned (causing changes to occur) followed by the relative quiet and stable periods when TQM approaches may be followed. TQM, however, claims that perfection can never be completely achieved and that the search for it reflects a journey not an end state. Consequently, an incremental approach to continuous improvement is most beneficial as the journey progresses. It also posits that it is the people who carry out the work of the organization who know what creates the difficulties and they should be the ones to drive change in order to raise the level of quality achieved and solve the operational problems.

The approach adopted in TQM is that a problem once resolved has disappeared forever, but there are always more problems to tackle. However, TQM takes such a long time to become truly integrated within an organization's fabric and culture that it too can fail, particularly if people think that it does not deliver results or improve operational activity. Being driven by its bottom-up philosophy it contains a very heavy demand on the time of many ordinary employees which can cost significant sums of money if it is done in company time. One of the criticisms of TQM has been that some companies have tried to make involvement in it voluntary and in private rather than company time, so avoiding the cost of its operation.

Having discussed some of the major organizational variables and initiatives that can create change, it is now appropriate to consider the approaches and models that have been proposed as reflecting the change process itself.

Lewin's forcefield model of change

Lewin (1951) developed a change model which states that any situation exists as the result of a balance between the forces acting upon it. These forces occur in opposing directions, some *driving* for change while others are *restraining* that change by pressing in the opposite direction. It is known as the *forcefield analysis model*, intended to guide the identification of the forces acting upon the situation (see Figure 18.3).

The model is very simple to understand and can easily be applied to a wide range of situations. For example, assume the current level of absence within a company to be 500 hours per month. An analysis of the situation might reveal the *driving* and *restraining* forces indicated in Table 18.3.

The absence level of 500 hours per month is the balance point between the sum of driving and restraining forces. It follows that if a change is desired in that situation then either the magnitude of the driving forces needs to be increased and/or the magnitude of the restraining forces reduced.

Lewin identified three stages of change associated with his forcefield analysis model:

♦ Stage 1 Unfreezing. The first stage requires the current situation to be *unfrozen*. The current level of absence is frozen at 500 hours as a result of the balance between the

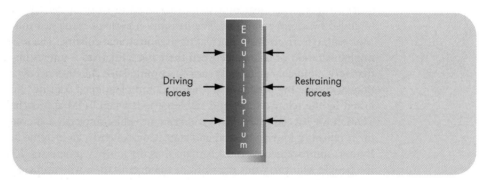

FIGURE 18.3   Lewin's forcefield analysis model.

Driving forces	Restraining forces
Management need for higher productivity	Laziness
Need to reduce high levels of payment for sickness absence	Past practice
Management desire for control	Boring and monotonous work
Employee commitment to the company	Lack of car ownership
Employee travel to work distance	Poor public transport
Employee loss of income	Road congestion
Employee desire to do a good job	Domestic difficulties
Career development and promotion desire	Illness
	Inconvenient work starting time
	Habit

TABLE 18.3   Examples of driving and restraining forces acting on absence levels

cause dissatisfaction two opposing forcefields. A desire to change that requires the current situation to be unfrozen in preparation for change to be made. It is a difficult period in any change process as the intentions for the future become clear and when resistance to that intention surfaces. In the example used, this could involve a statement by management of the problems associated with absence and the beginning of negotiations with the trade unions on how to deal with the problem.

✦ Stage 2 Changing. Having unfrozen the situation it is then time to make appropriate *changes*. This could involve introducing mandatory counselling after every period of absence; changing the working hours; introducing flexitime; introducing nursery provision and many more initiatives. These changes could be in either or both of the driving and restraining force categories. The level of absence should be seen to reduce if the changes have been successful.

✦ Stage 3 Refreezing. The change process is one of movement. The third stage of the Lewin model requires the changes to be *refrozen* or consolidated in a new state of balance. If this is not done then the balance will not be fixed and it will *slip* back to its previous position. Refreezing implies that the changes made become the new norms for that particular situation.

Organizational development and change

Organizational development (OD) can be defined as, 'a systematic application of behavioural science knowledge to the planned development and reinforcement of organizational strategies, structures, and processes for improving an organization's effectiveness' (Cummings and Worley, 1993, p 2). The strands of theory and practice within OD include:

✦ T-groups. Small unstructured groups meet and, by exploring the interactive behaviour of the group, learn about their own behaviour.

✦ Survey feedback. The findings from attitude or similar surveys need to be communicated to the participants in a way that creates learning opportunities.

✦ Action research. This reflects an active and iterative approach to research and change. It is based upon a cyclical process beginning with research into identified problems. This in turn leads to conclusions and the development of action plans. Opportunities for further study and problem solving are also identified, and so the cycle begins again.

✦ Quality of working life. The quality of working life (QWL) movement has already been discussed in an earlier chapter and it has now been incorporated into the OD practitioner's toolkit.

✦ Strategic change. An attempt to integrate all organizational variables into a common purpose. A vision or strategy is needed for this and the change perspective arises through the consequence of the integration of all activity into a cohesive (*strategic*) whole.

The basis and practice of OD has been criticized for a number of reasons. It is a practice that assumes incrementalism as the best way to achieve change. This is fine as long as the organization is at a high level of effectiveness to begin with. Dunphy and Stace (1988) argue that not all situations allow for the slow process of evolutionary change. Time and the political climate may be against the approach. This debate also reflects the distinction between the BPR and TQM approaches discussed earlier. OD as a process requires participation which, as Stephenson (1985) suggests, is not the panacea often claimed. Individuals or groups intent on resisting change, perhaps as a consequence of being disadvantaged by the outcome, may not be persuaded by involvement and might slow down the process itself. Involvement can expose but not necessarily solve problems. Compromise may not be the best option and changing opinions may not deliver the results sought and intended. For example, Management in Action 18.6 reflects a situation where the attempts at involvement did not work to the advantage of any of the stakeholders. Also a company faced with a competitor's product that serves as a replacement for their own may not have the time or financial resource to allow an OD approach to finding a solution.

Stop | Consider

Do the events contained in MiA 18.6 suggest that employee involvement in change:
✦ *is not a good idea*
✦ *may only work in certain situations*
✦ *cannot be separated from the political and power structures that exist,*
✦ *should be used only as a means of manipulating opinion and attitudes to a management desired perspective or*
✦ *should be used because ultimately all stakeholders have to accept some responsibility for the circumstances that they create?*
Justify your views.

Figure 18.5 makes specific reference to the notion of power as part of the change process. This is lacking in the classic OD approach. Recognizing this weakness Schein (1985) makes several suggestions for including a power and political perspective to OD interventions. Identifying with powerful stakeholders and attempting small projects first to gain credibility before tackling the more complex and risky projects, for example.

Power, politics and change

There are two major ways in which power and politics interact with change:

✦ Process. If change is to be successful support and commitment must be maximized while resistance and opposition are minimized. Power and politics can be used to facilitate this. For example, offering to provide help in the future in return for support now would constitute a recognition of the political dimension to decision making.

✦ Purpose. There is a saying about not getting mad but getting even as a means of extracting revenge. Change can therefore be used as the means to achieve another purpose. For example, the management of a company might 'engineer' the need for a redundancy in order to be able to dismiss particular employees. The implication being that it would be possible to 'create' a reduction in the number of employees and then to 'engineer' the means of selecting particular employees classified as undesirable.

Stephenson (1985) identifies the following tactics useful in the introduction of change:

✦ Simple first. 'Nothing succeeds like success.' Beginning with small projects that are

MANAGEMENT IN ACTION 18.6

Involvement and failure

This example reflects the experience of the operations director of the company indicated as it was told to me. It has not been independently verified, neither is it certain that the other stakeholders would agree with the views expressed. The company within which the story is set employed about 300 people, mostly women in the manufacture of fabric containers. The production process involved the cutting of rolls of polypropylene fabric to particular lengths and sewing them together to make large sacks and single-trip industrial containers. The work was physically demanding.

Prior to the operations director joining the company some attempt at increasing factory productivity had been made through the introduction of work measurement-based incentive schemes. The production manager of the company when this was being done had agreed that it would be cheaper to estimate the job times and then to negotiate these with the trade union representatives. This would, he argued, also allow some degree of participation of employees in the process. In practice it produced a situation in which the job times were very generous and an effective employee veto existed on attempts to raise productivity. If a job time could not be agreed then average earnings were paid until agreement was reached, resulting in significant delays in implementing true incentive conditions. Inevitably, over a couple of years employee earnings rose steeply and productivity dropped. For example, on some jobs, employees could earn what would be classed as a week's wage in one day. On other jobs it was a struggle for employees to make a decent wage. This also led to some supervisors taking bribes from employees for allocating them jobs with the highest earnings potential.

Clearly this situation could not continue and the production manager was sacked. The operations director telling this story was appointed with the remit of sorting the problems out and

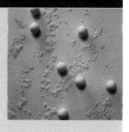

restoring a sound basis for factory operations. He began by reviewing the current situation and as a result he came to the conclusion that a fundamental change was needed as the company was losing money. The employees also considered the existing scheme unfair and inequitable. Also they wanted better benefits generally. All parties accepted that fundamental change was necessary if the company were to survive. The operations director considered that as a consequence the basis existed for a joint management–employee approach to finding a solution.

A joint management–employee group was established and agreed that a completely new way of determining a fair day's work for a fair day's pay was needed. A professionally qualified work study engineer with considerable experience in the same industry was brought to remeasure the jobs in the factory and to act as a consultant to the group. It was after the consultant had carried out his remeasurement of the jobs in the factory that problems began to emerge. When the real level of productivity was established through conventional work measurement techniques the employees on the joint group began to realize the degree of change that was going to be required. They expressed concern that the times were wrong and that no human being could be expected to work at the rate implied by the figures. It became clear that this perception would be a major sticking point in achieving change, but the operations director was determined to maintain the involvement of employees in finding a solution.

Meetings were held over a period of eight months in an attempt to find ways around the problems identified by the work study exercise. A number of options were considered involving many different wage structures and transitionary arrangements (to give employees time to adjust to the new requirements as well as allow them to

MANAGEMENT IN ACTION 18.6 continued

maintain their earnings levels). Essentially the new arrangements required that employees raise average productivity by 25% over a two-year period in order to retain current earnings levels. Of course that average figure hid a wide range of individual job variation. Also some employees would be more significantly affected than others. For example, the wife of one of the supervisors was always among the highest earners, as was one of the shop stewards, because they had been 'bought off' in the past with easy jobs that paid a high bonus.

Over time it became apparent to the operations director that the employees on the group were not really interested in finding a solution. They were simply seeking to prolong their involvement in the process in order to maintain the status quo. A comprehensive package was put together by management which included elements of transitionary protection for one extra year, profit-share payments, improved holidays, the introduction of a company pension scheme and other benefits, in return for agreeing to the new work study arrangements. The employee group did not feel that they could support this package as they admitted that it would create problems for them personally with their colleagues. The package was therefore put formally to the trade union for negotiation but was rejected. The trade union representatives said that

it was completely unacceptable as it required them to work harder for the same money. They wanted to retain the current wage system but to accept the other benefits in the proposed package. Naturally this was unacceptable to management. The trade union would not negotiate with managers on any other basis and so management called a factory meeting and put the plan to all employees. The proposals were noisily shouted down and rejected in a mass vote.

Management had one more attempt at negotiating with the trade union over the proposed package, even suggesting a longer phasing in of the new work study arrangement, but this, too, was rejected. The events were reported to the board of the holding group at its next meeting and the decision was taken to close the company down. When the closure was announced to the factory a small group of people (not trade union representatives) approached the operations director representing many of the workers and said that they had not realized that it would end in closure. They also said that they had not been serious in rejecting the company proposals, they simply wanted to retain the status quo as long as possible and that if management had said that it was accept the deal or the factory would close, then they would have accepted. The factory closed three months later and everyone lost their jobs.

successful creates confidence and encouragement to go on and tackle more difficult problems.

+ Adaptation. Being flexible and adaptable in modifying planned changes improves the chances of success. It provides a means of meeting unplanned events and of dealing with resistance.

+ Incorporation. People feel less threatened and more comfortable with minor change. Consequently incorporating as much as possible from an existing situation in a change programme gives the appearance of continuity and stability.

+ Structure. Political persuasion can be used to influence attitude through the structural and physical aspects of change. Product and service quality ultimately comes down to employee commitment. This reflects underlying attitudes to a significant extent. By changing working practices through training, reward systems etc. quality is addressed directly and changes in attitude brought about over time. Eventually the changed attitude supports the higher quality without the need for *structural props*.

◆ Ceremony. The use of ceremonial events provide a clear signal of what defines success in a particular context. It also has the effect of institutionalizing change through the ceremonies attached to it. The razzamatazz around new product launches are as much about rewarding the changes in bringing them about as they are marketing initiatives.

◆ Assurances. How people perceive that they will be treated as the result of change is important to how they react to it. Previous experience of the value of assurances (on say fair treatment) are an important part of creating future responses.

◆ Timescales. As a general rule the more time available to make change the more likely it is to be successful. However, there are situations in which time is not available and rapid change must take place. Crises can become a focus for successful change.

◆ Support. Adapting to change causes stress and individuals often feel threatened. This requires support in order to maintain momentum and to avoid encouraging resistance.

◆ Transition. There are three different contexts active at the same time in change processes. The existing situation, the desired situation and the transitional situation. They are not discrete categories of event. This creates uncertainty, ambiguity and complexity, all of which must be managed.

◆ Unexpected. Unexpected things can and will occur. Some preparation for these situations can be done and not all are hostile to change.

Another way of considering the political and power dynamics associated with change were identified by Nadler and Tushman (1988). In this view there are three mechanisms required to manage the problems associated with the power, anxiety and transitional situations found in all change situations:

◆ Mobilizing political support. This mechanism is all about preparing the ground for the change process. It involves gaining the support of key sponsors and of forming supportive alliances with those likely to be influential in or affected by the process. It is about attempting to maximize support and minimize resistance to the proposed changes.

◆ Encouraging supportive behaviour. This mechanism uses a variety of devices to build support among those more directly involved with the change. For example, the participation of employees in designing changes to working practices might help them understand existing problems and identify appropriate alternatives.

◆ Managing the transitional process. Having identified what is to be done, it then has to be achieved in practice. The difficulties associated with transition are the uncertainty of the new state – because it has not yet arrived; the familiarity of the old – because it has not yet gone; and the complexity of temporary arrangements – designed to facilitate movement from one situation to another. The transition period is a dangerous one for any change process as things can go horribly wrong and threaten the achievement of the ultimate objective.

While power and politics are very important aspects of any change process they do not provide the only basis for managing them. Indeed, it could be argued that by acting in an overtly political way management could be encouraging others to act in a similar way, creating a deteriorating cycle of behaviour into a pit of intrigue and politics. In this situation power and politics become the masters not the servants.

Contingency approaches to change

Contingency approaches to change incorporate a broader range of elements into the process than political or OD perspectives. They represent a directly managerial approach to the subject of change compared with OD, which tends to be directed at incremental and self-directed methods. However, under the OD methodology managers still retain control of the agenda and context. It could therefore be argued that it also represents a manipulative device intended to find ways of achieving acceptance of managerial perspectives.

Kotter and Schlesinger's model

One of the earlier approaches to the contingency view of change is reflected in the work of Kotter and Schlesinger (1979). They identified a number of change management strategies along with the contexts to which they could be applied (see Table 18.4).

Taking each of the strategies for change in turn:

✦ Education plus communication. This strategy represents an approach to change based on understanding and rationality. If employees can be shown the reason behind a proposed change they are more likely to accept the need for it and support the programme. It is a slow process and can provide potential opposition through access to information.

✦ Participation plus involvement. This strategy is based on the notion that if people are actively involved in change they will go along with it. It can be useful where resistance is likely to exist. Also by working together improvements to interpersonal relationships could occur and the ground prepared for more effective change in the future. There is a danger of participation producing inappropriate outcomes if a new power balance emerges.

✦ Facilitation plus support. This would be suitable in situations where the difficulty was one of being able to cope with the change process or the new situation. It is an approach in which the strategy is one of providing an opportunity to come to terms with the change and to grow in confidence during the transition.

✦ Negotiation plus agreement. Negotiation is a strategy aimed at resolving difference though agreement. It is usually associated with problem solving and situations in which a trade-off possibility exists. Changing working patterns in return for higher pay, for example.

✦ Manipulation plus co-option. The political aspects of change provide a clear indication of situations in which some form of *arranging* of events and alliances are undertaken in order to make more certain a particular outcome. In a very real sense this represents a *manipulation* of events. Co-option can be used as a means of diverting resistance through direct involvement. For example, the promotion of an active trade union representative to a supervisory position might reduce conflict and allow a more moderate individual to take over the trade union position. The major problems with manipulation and co-option are in being discovered or misinterpreted.

◆ Explicit plus implicit coercion. This strategy towards change is all about force and threat. It is not intended to create commitment, it is intended to achieve compliance. It is a 'take it or else' approach. As an example it is the strategy that makes it quite clear that the company will relocate to areas of cheap labour unless the workforce accept lower wages and higher output targets. Implicit coercion is a more subtle form of that force. As a strategy this can offer success for a while – as a result of the compliance achieved. For example, the threat to close a factory if employees do not accept low pay might work for a while but as soon as higher paid work becomes available they will leave. The quality and quantity of output might also be expected to drop or if the spending power of the employees becomes very low they may call the bluff of managers and strike.

Approach	Commonly used in situations	Advantages	Drawbacks
Education + communication	Where there is a lack of information or inaccurate information or inaccurate information and analysis	Once persuaded, people will often help with the implementation of change	Can be very time consuming if many people are involved
Participation + involvement	Where the initiators do not have all the information they need to design the change, and where others have considerable power to resist	People who participate will be committed to implementing change, and any relevant information they have will be integrated into the change plan	Can be very time consuming if participators design an inappropriate change
Facilitation + support	Where people are resisting because of adjustment problems	No other approach works as well with adjustment problems	Can be time consuming, expensive and still fail
Negotiation + agreement	Where someone or some group will clearly lose out in a change, and where that group has considerable power to resist	Sometimes it is a relatively easy way to avoid major resistance	Can be too expensive in many cases if it alerts others to negotiate for compliance
Manipulation + co-option	Where other tactics will not work or are too expensive	It can be a relatively quick and inexpensive solution to resistance problems	Can lead to future problems if people feel manipulated
Explicit + implicit coercion	Where speed is essential and the change initiators possess considerable power	It is speedy and can overcome any kind of resistance	Can be risky if it leaves people mad at the initiators

TABLE 18.4 Methods of managing change (*source*: Kotter, JP and Schlesinger, CA (1979) Choosing strategies for change, *Harvard Business Review*, March/April)

Dunphy and Stace's model

Dunphy and Stace (1990) introduce a two-dimensional matrix as another way of identifying strategies for the management of change. One axis describes the *scale of change* involved and the other the *style of change management* in the situation (Figure 18.4).

The four change strategies in Figure 18.4 are as follows:

♦ Participative evolution. This strategy involves relatively small changes achieved through involvement.

♦ Forced evolution. This strategy forces change onto the participants, but the changes themselves are relatively small.

♦ Charismatic transformation. This strategy is used for large-scale change of a one-off nature. Frequently such changes are initiated and driven by a charismatic leader or sponsor.

♦ Dictatorial transformation. This strategy relies on force or coercion to make large-scale changes of a one-off nature. This could be most successful as a one-time emergency response to a crisis. Here time is of the essence and significant resistance might be expected.

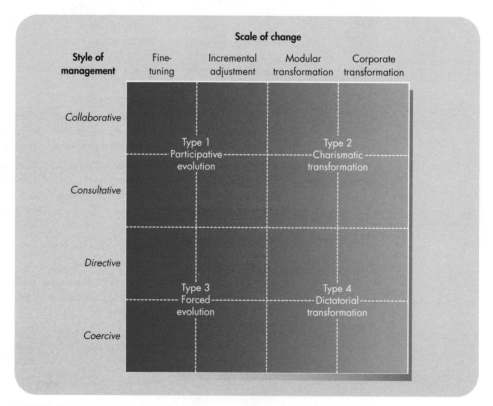

FIGURE 18.4 Dunphy and Stace's change strategies (*source*: Dunphy, D and Stace, D (1990) *Under New Management: Australian Organizations in Transition*, McGraw-Hill, Sydney).

Plant's model

In seeking to manage change Plant (1987) advocates *key relationship mapping* in attempting to identify appropriate change strategies. The model requires consideration of four key elements associated with change: winners, losers, power and information (see Figure 18.5).

Winners would not normally be expected to resist proposed changes, whereas losers would. If a company reorganizes its wage structures those employees who receive a pay rise are likely to consider it a good scheme and those who are likely to lose money under the new scheme would consider it a bad one. In this type of situation the power balance between management and trade unions might be important in the identification of likely courses of action. For example, a company with a seasonal product cycle would be at a political disadvantage if it sought to introduce this type of change at the time of peak production. Also those who hold or have access to information have the potential to help or hinder change. In considering these four elements it is possible to identify the *key relationships* between them and to plan networking strategies in support of the change process.

Kanter, Stein and Jick's 'big three' model

This model of change (Kanter *et al.* 1992) proposes that change is multidirectional and continuous. Stability as it is usually experienced within organizations does not reflect the absence of change. It reflects levels of change that are not noticed by the participants; or it reflects change that goes unchallenged by them. From that perspective stability is regarded as a state of predictability and when the interests of the various stakeholder groups are broadly in alignment.

Change as conceived by this model occurs when there is a lack of predictability or harmony within the situation at any one or more of the major themes that exist within an organization. For example, the organization may lose its close connection with the environment if it becomes complacent and does not monitor its competitors or customer needs. Equally, the organization may need to change radically if its physical structure is no longer able to organize the delivery of goods and services in ways that more effectively meet the customer needs. In that sense this model of change offers an attempt to capture a very broad concept of change tied into human experience within an organizational setting. The authors suggest that at the societal level it is macro evolutionary forces that act upon the situation, emerging from other organizations and social change generally. At the organizational level the authors argue that it is micro evolutionary forces emerging from factors

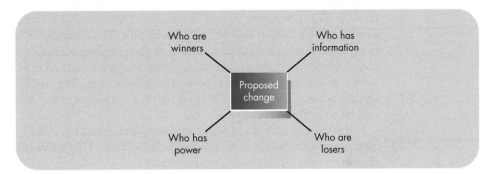

FIGURE 18.5 Key relationship map (*source*: Plant, R (1987) *Managing Change and Making It Stick*, Fontana, London).

such as the stage in the organizational lifecycle, age, history etc. that influence change. At the individual level of an organization, it is suggested that it is the political forces associated with power and control that influence the change process. Change as experienced within the organization will depend on the balance of each of the individual forces acting upon the situation at any particular moment.

Although this model offers an attempt to describe change as a complex social process, it is difficult to identify how it could be used to manage the process. It suggests that there are many possible forces acting upon the situation at many different levels, but that simply identifies potential change forces and does not offer clues or explanation in any particular context. An analyst or manager seeking to use the model is left to identify the particular forces acting upon the situation for themselves, and so different interpretations are possible between people. The big picture may be useful in identifying general trends, but is of little value to the specific manager or employee seeking to deal with their own situation.

Each of the contingency models reflect a *simplification* of the complex circumstances that exist at the time of change. Simplification represents a mechanism for aiding understanding and therefore the ability to control. It is searching for and imposing the familiar onto stimuli to create meaning. In doing so the signals can be misinterpreted, clues missed and inaccurate interpretations made. Inevitably, if this happens as part of a change programme there is a danger of a failure in the process, or in the ability to generate the result intended.

The potential limitations in contingency models have been recognized by a number of writers and Dunford (1992) reviews some of them in relation to the Dunphy and Stace model outlined earlier. Examples include the complexity of the organization and environment relationship and the political nature of managerial self-interest. Managers have particular ways of relating to organizations, workers and the rights and responsibilities of the other stakeholder groups. This leads to the creation of particular *interpretative schemes*, the existence of which play a determining role in strategy formulation. So as with all aspects of management, caution is necessary in accepting any model of change management.

Systems perspectives on change

There are a number of systems approaches that have something to offer as a basis for problem solving. One approach is specifically worthy of mention in the context of managing change. *Total systems intervention* (TSI) is grounded in the philosophy of *critical systems thinking*. This philosophy is itself based upon three principles: complementarism, social awareness, and human well-being/emancipation. These principles reflect the view that techniques should be selected according to their appropriateness, that the social context plays a major part in determining the approach adopted and that the human dimension to work should contribute to the process of problem solving. The original source for this perspective is Flood and Jackson (1991). A more recent review of this subject (Flood, 1996) is referenced as Further reading.

The TSI approach is a problem-solving approach and has a wider application than the management of change. It is included here because of its relevance to managing some change processes. TSI comprises three phases:

✦ Creativity. 'The task during the creativity phase is to use systems metaphors as organizing structures to help managers think creatively about their enterprises' (p 50).

+ Choice. 'The task during the choice phase is to choose an appropriate systems-based intervention methodology (or set of methodologies) to suit particular characteristics of the organization's situation as revealed by the examination conducted in the creativity phase' (p 51).

+ Implementation. 'The task during the implementation phase is to employ a particular systems methodology (systems methodologies) to translate the dominant vision of the organization, its structure, and the general orientation adopted to concerns and problems, into specific proposals for change' (p 52).

Although there are three stages to the TSI methodology it is intended to function as an iterative process with movement back and forth through reference to earlier and later stages during the process. Within the TSI approach there is the opportunity to utilize one or more specific systems methodologies. Each of the systems methodologies available is claimed to be of benefit in particular contextual conditions.

The benefits of the systems approaches are that a range of techniques can be accessed that offer the opportunity to tailor actions to locally defined analysis. It offers the ability for wide involvement in creating a creative picture of the situation and of finding mechanisms for resolving the competing points of view about those situations, in the process finding ways of surfacing and managing the power and political aspects of change.

Chaos and change

There is a widespread view in human society that advancing knowledge is about seeking to impose order from chaos. From that perspective, chaos is regarded as something that is random, of no value, with no order or apparent pattern evident. Indeed the *Pocket Oxford Dictionary* (1969) defines chaos as: 'Formless welter of matter conceived as preceding creation; utter confusion … utterly without order or arrangement.' Clearly chaos is something to be avoided and the role of science and research has generally been seen as the main mechanism through which knowledge can be created and so order imposed on what would otherwise be simply a chaotic mess. However, a relatively recent branch of science has begun to develop an interest in what has become known as chaos and complexity theory. The point of interest in essence lies largely in the distinction between unpredictability and chaos. The weather is frequently quoted as an example in this context. The weather patterns are largely unpredictable, but that does not mean that they are chaotic in the broadest sense of the term. They are unpredictable systems, but they are quite ordered in a very complex way. Another analogy is that of the so-called butterfly effect. A butterfly flaps its wings in Australia and this sets in motion a chain of events that creates a tidal wave on the east coast of South America. Most times this does not happen, but it might under the right circumstances. The same can be said of much of the reality of organizational experience. There exists a massive array of variables in an equally complex dynamic environment impacting on every organization. This forms the basis of the study of chaos theory to the organizational situation.

Waldrop (1992, pp 9–10) summed these issues up when he wrote:

Why did the Soviet Union's forty year hegemony over eastern Europe collapse within a few months in 1989? Why did the stock market crash more than 500 points on a single Monday in October 1987? … If evolution (or free-market capitalism) is really just a matter of the survival of the fittest, then why should it ever produce anything other than ruthless competition among individuals? In a world where nice guys all too often finish last, why should there be any such thing as trust and cooperation?

Marion (1999) suggests that:

Mathematically, Chaos happens when equations used to describe seemingly simple systems just won't behave as expected. They will not yield a stable response, or the answers they give jump wildly when the quantity of an input variable is even lightly perturbed. These equations are called 'nonlinear' because their inputs are not predictably related to their output. (p 15)

Hopefully, the potential for such models to be of value in an organizational context begins to become apparent with this quotation. Managing within an organizational environment would be seen to qualify as falling within the chaotic concept as described by Marion.

The point to emerge from the work of Marion and others is that any organization is essentially a complex adaptive system (CAS). As such, it forever perched on the edge of change, susceptible to the 'slightest breath of wind [which] can topple them. Most breezes – even gales – have no effect, however, because CAS are, by definition, vast networks of interdependent structures, and such interdependency gives strength to a structure' (p 270). However because of the relationships between the elements within the CAS, change has the potential to reverberate throughout the system, providing the impact is in the right place, at the right time, with the right force and the system itself is in the right state. This is again where the butterfly analogy makes sense within an organizational context.

The change agent

Another feature of the management of change touched on earlier is the role of *change agents* in the process. A change agent is someone who plays a leading part in sponsoring the need for change or in its implementation. There have been a number of frameworks describing the forms of change agent activity. One of the more recent is that of Ottaway (1982) who produced a taxonomy linked to a particular model of change – that of Lewin (1951). However, in general terms has a much broader relevance than its grounding in one model. Three types of change agent are identified:

✦ Change generators. These are linked with the unfreezing process. They are the individuals or groups who identify areas of potential change and convince others of the need to take action. This could include a charismatic leader who is able to create a movement willing to adopt the changes expressed in the leader's vision. It could also include a special project team who are give the task of reviewing a particular aspect of company operations.

✦ Change implementors. These deliver actual change to the organization. They can be charismatic leaders who are able to persuade subordinates to accept change. They can be sponsors from senior management who lend their position to the call for change and so encourage others to see it as important or inevitable. They can be industrial relations specialists who have the task of making agreements with employee representatives and thereby operationalize change proposals.

◆ Change adopters. These represent the *refreezing* stage of the Lewin model. They are the individuals who make the changes work in practice and by so doing ensure that they become the norms within that particular context. They are inevitably the line managers, supervisors and employees who get on with the job and make sure that it does not slip back to what existed before.

Resistance to change

The starting point for considering *resistance to change* is the image conjured up by the phrase itself. It implies that an individual or group has determined to frustrate the intentions of another to implement a particular course of action. In a managerial context, that inevitably reflects the decision of the employer to *change* some aspect of the organization and in so doing influence the work activities and/or employment of workers. Kahn (1982) suggests that resistance behaviour during times of change is frequently indistinguishable from normal behaviour patterns. The difference being a function of the perspective of the person classifying the behaviour rather than the behaviour itself.

The following material has been compiled from a number of sources including Armstrong (1995), Hellriegel *et al.* (1989), Kanter (1983), Kotter and Schlesinger (1979), Moorhead and Griffin (1992), Mullins (1996) and Plant (1987).

Individual resistance to change

Individuals resist change for a number of reasons, including those indicated in Figure 18.6.

Many of the reasons indicated in Figure 18.6 are self-explanatory and easily understood. For example, fear of the unknown infers that the individual would prefer to remain with existing arrangements. Change can be a negative experience for many employees. Organizational experience soon indicates that managers do not always have the best interests of employees at heart, particularly when cutbacks are the norm! However, some of the reasons identified in Figure 18.6 need further explanation:

◆ Symbolic meaning. The entitlement to benefits such as a company car or the use of a private office rather than an area separated by partitions all provide symbols of status within the organization. Changes which impact on such visible signs can be fiercely resisted even if they are incidental.

◆ Change shock. The previous routine will have been familiar, individuals will have known instinctively what they were supposed to do. Change can destroy that level of familiarity and create situations in which predictability reduces, thus creating an experience of shock for the individual.

◆ Selective attention and retention. Individuals define *reality* for themselves based upon their understanding of the world as they experience and understand it. Change can call into question these *frames of reference* and as a consequence be rejected. Individuals have a tendency to only pay attention and retain that information which supports their existing world views which can also lead to resistance.

◆ Dependence. Students are dependent upon lecturers for their intellectual development. However, taken to extreme, dependence can become a force which resists change as security is threatened. Dependence can also place significant power in the hands of those who are relied upon. Management in Action 18.7 reflects how ICL communicated in order to minimize the possibility of negative dependence and at the same time raised awareness of the positive side of change.

◆ Security and regression. The need for security can lead to a search for the past when

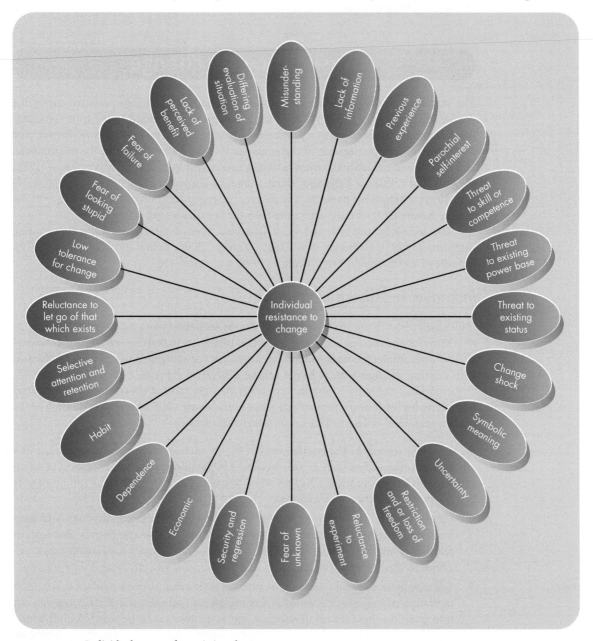

FIGURE 18.6   Individual reasons for resisting change.

MANAGEMENT IN ACTION 18.7

Network support

ICL, the computer company transformed itself in 1990 from making and selling its own hardware to offering a wide range of value added services. As a consequence the company had to develop completely new ways of operating and of communicating with employees. Half of the staff within the company now work for subsidiaries and the head office has been reduced in size from 750 people to just 50.

Any change that is planned by management should be communicated as quickly and thoroughly as possible was the view expressed by Mr David Wimpress, the group personnel director for the UK. These principles were applied when the company needed to tell its employees that a pay freeze was being implemented and that the staff numbers would have to be reduced by 4% in 1993. The information was quickly cascaded throughout the company by management using the established mechanisms.

Subsidiary companies have their own management teams and their first line of responsibility is to that organization and its performance. However, the personnel specialists of each company also meet with Wimpress each month to discuss items of 'common interest'. In addition each of the head office directors sits on the board of subsidiary companies. For example, Wimpress acts as chairman of the training and office design companies in the group. The breadth and depth of involvement resulting from these links helps to bind together the separate aspects of the business.

A number of different forms of communication are used by the company. They include:

✦ Team briefing. Each manager collects their staff together and 'briefs' them on whatever is to be communicated. Questions are asked and answered within the meeting. The essential message is then used as the basis of subsequent briefings by each subordinate to brief their own staff. Information, reactions and responses can also be communicated back up

the line within this framework.

✦ E-mail is used by the company to cascade information throughout the organization quickly. Being a computer organization almost everyone has access to a terminal and so this option becomes feasible.

✦ Audio cassette-based briefings on specific aspects of company policy are issued to staff on a regular basis.

✦ An annual company attitude and opinion survey is undertaken across the whole company. There is a common set of questions but subsidiaries are allowed to incorporate specific issues if necessary. Topics include an evaluation of management effectiveness, team-briefing processes and the setting and clarity of objectives.

✦ A company handbook of policies is common to all subsidiaries.

✦ A document called *The Management Framework* sets out the commitment to customer care and issues such as how to word a job offer letter. It is intended to communicate to managers how to act in order to provide a consistently high-quality outward appearance of the company.

✦ Investing in People is a scheme within the company which, among other things, encourages managers to engage effectively in performance pay, regular staff appraisals, objective setting and career-planning issues. These processes encourage the effective use of the people resource within the company and provide a two-way dialogue on what is happening and how it will impact on the individuals concerned.

Adapted from: Williams, M (1993) Network support, *Personnel Today*, 23 March, p 41.

Stop | Consider *Consider the extent to which the approach described in MiA 18.7 could be explained either as a form of communication in order to ease the process of change or an attempt to create a form of dependence among employees supportive of the new management approach?*

Does this distinction matter? Justify your views.

things appeared simpler and more familiar. This *regression* on the part of such individuals is a clear force for resisting change.

Group and organizational resistance to change

Resistance to change at a group or organizational level comes in many forms (see Figure 18.7).

Most of the categories of resistance identified in Figure 18.7 are self-explanatory, but a few could benefit from some explanation:

✦ Misinformation. Control over communication provides opportunities for a group to impart particular interpretations to information and so engineer resistance.

✦ Organization structure. The bureaucratic form of organization was designed to deliver consistency and predictability of operations. Consequently, it is a structure that does not cope easily with change.

✦ Previous agreements. Arrangements entered into with another group or organization

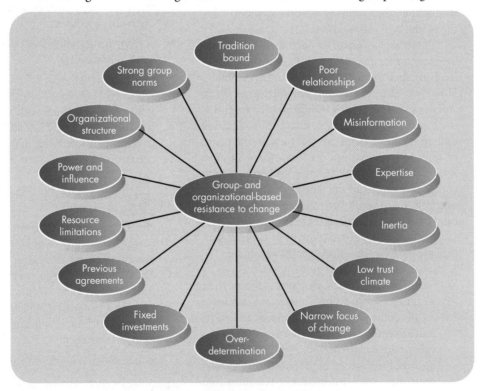

FIGURE 18.7 Group and organizational reasons for resisting change.

are designed to control events in the future. This restricts the ability to make changes in the interaction between these groups over the period of such agreements.

✦ Fixed investments. The investments that an organization makes in buildings, land and equipment place considerable restriction on what can be done in the future. In practice, they limit the ability to change because they represent assets that are not easy to liquidate in the short term.

✦ Overdetermination. The systems and procedures that organizations create to provide control can also restrict the ability to introduce change.

✦ Narrow focus of change. In considering change an organization very often takes the immediate zone of impact into account. It is possible for situations to arise in which groups not immediately affected by change resist involvement and so limit the benefits ultimately gained. For example, in addressing the production problems in one department management may introduce team working and in the process replace supervisors with team leaders. Supervisors in other departments may see this as an attempt to erode their status and indeed job security. If they are not involved in the original exercise and supportive of the changes, then they may well resist any attempts to introduce change in the future.

Innovation as a change strategy

Innovation and change are areas of activity that are strongly tied together. One dictionary definition of innovation is to bring in novelties and to make changes. This conveys a feeling of something that is frivolous, not to be taken seriously and of little importance. Nothing could be further from the truth about the experience of innovation in many organizations. The need to be able to stay ahead in an increasingly competitive world is something that many management writers draw attention to. Tom Peters, for example, has produced a stream of books that began with *Thriving On Chaos* published in 1988. All were intended to drive a message home about the need for continual revolution in responding to the operating environment, the basic message being innovate or die.

It is in this context that innovation and change are strongly linked together. The degree of innovation demanded by such writers as Peters requires nothing less in the running of organizations than a total and complete revolution on a continuous basis. Change on a large scale, permanently. The line of argument being that competition poses such a dramatic and global threat that if western companies do not completely revolutionize their strategies and operational activities they will not be able to compete with companies that make those changes and operate from a base with natural advantages.

Innovation carries with it a measure of risk because it involves doing things differently. Consider the decision to innovate through the introduction of high technology. The equipment will be expensive; it may not have been used for that particular application before; employees may see it as a threat to their future employment; and it will take time to commission the equipment to an acceptable standard of reliability. Each of these features carries with it a measure of risk which when combined produce an even greater danger of failure. There are some industries that are particularly prone to the risks associated with innovation. For example, restaurants and clothing are subjected to rapid and frequent changes in fashion and taste. Unless they continually innovate and update their offerings to the market they will lose trade. The risk for these organizations is that their offerings will not be found *attractive* by potential customers.

Just as with change itself, innovation is an issue that finds resistance in many organizations for a number of reasons. There is a significant degree of inertia built into most organizations. Control and operational effectiveness comes from the predictability, repeated practice and consistency available through standardized products and services. Changing anything can create uncertainty, unfamiliarity and problems. Pascale (1990) points to a number of organizational features that restrict the ability to innovate and change (see Table 18.5). These arose from a comparison between Honda and General Motors.

There are different forms that innovation can take. Betz (1987) identifies three levels of innovative activity:

✦ Radical. This represents the invention of something new. This is frequently the application of fundamental science. It carries with it the greatest level of risk, highest cost and longest timescale for development.

✦ Systems. This level represents the application of existing science and technology in a novel way. It tends to be the combination of radical level innovations once they become established and less vulnerable to failure. The combination of the internal combustion engine and carriage-building technologies to create the motor car for example. The timescales involved in the introduction of innovations at this level are shorter.

✦ Incremental. This level of innovation represent the adaptation of existing technologies and products etc. It is the fine tuning of that which already exists. It is the easiest form of innovation to make use of, along with being the cheapest and least vulnerable to failure.

In parallel with the risks, costs and timescales associated with each of these three levels of innovation the scale of benefit runs conversely. The possible returns from the radical level of innovation are much higher than at the incremental level. Risk and return are

Finances hegemony	the pre-eminence of one function (finance) with a resistricted perspective
Learned helplessness	simultaneous pressure to show initiative while undermining examples of it by senior managers
Rituals of humiliation	the socialization process of conformity as the basis of promotion
Rituals of avoidance	the internal company realities of how conflict and difference are dealt with
Privilege and reward	the rights and rewards of senior executives in comparison with the lower levels and the history of compliance with authority
Empowerment	the lack of any real delegation of power and decision-making ability
Reinforcing folklore	the traditions and usual ways of doing things are continually passed down and reinforced in stories

TABLE 18.5 Examples of the restrictions on innovation and change (*source*: Pascale, R (1990) *Managing on the Edge: How Successful Companies Use Conflict to Stay Ahead*. Penguin, London)

strongly correlated: the higher the risk the higher the potential return. This dilemma makes innovation management such a problematic issue. The upgrading of existing technologies can more easily demonstrate a return, whereas the return from R&D is at best at some unspecified time in the future.

There is no aspect of an organization that is not amenable to innovative activity. The Leavitt model of an organization identified in Figure 18.2 identifies the four defining features of an organization as *people, technology, task* and *structure*, surrounded by the *environment*. Each of these features can sustain innovation in one form or another. Innovation is a process that is only dependent on the ingenuity of the human resource within the organization. It is limited only by their creativity and willingness to engage in it. Creativity in this context is what Morgan (1993) sought to encourage in his book, *Imaginization: The Art of Creative Management*. This text looks at how people think and seeks to capture ways in which this can be turned into a means of coping with a fluid and unstable future.

Another way of conceptualizing an organization is the model that has become known as the *7-S framework*. Originally developed for use by the McKinsey consulting firm in 1979 by individuals such as Richard Pascale, Anthony Athos, Robert Waterman and Tom Peters it attempts to capture the most important features of activity for managers (see Figure 18.8).

Pascale (1990) revisits this model in the context of a discussion of stagnation and renewal as a cyclical process. Innovation and change are not single events that can be adopted once and then forgotten. They represent dynamic processes in which change is followed by a period of stagnation as the benefits are harvested. This in turn produces a resistance to seek continuous change and so a disjointed process is generated. The *7-S framework* provides a basis for managers to consider each of the important elements of the organization on a regular basis and so limit the negative effects of stagnation.

Having identified that innovation is an important part of the change process it is useful to consider how it is harnessed to the benefit of the organization. Schermerhorn (1993) identifies five elements of the innovation process:

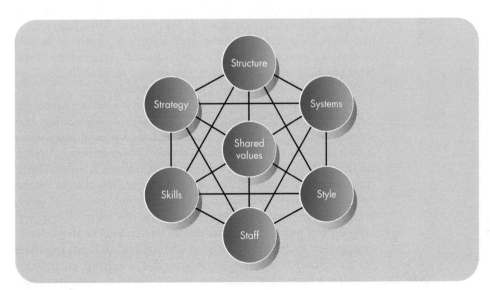

FIGURE 18.8 The McKinsey 7-S framework (*source*: Peters, TJ and Waterman, RH (1982) *In Search of Excellence*, HarperCollins, New York).

✦ Internal organizational sensitivity. Reflects the ability to be aware of the need for innovation and how to harness effort in support of it.

✦ Idea creation. This stage involves generating new ideas and finding ways of adapting existing methods and procedures.

✦ Initial experimentation. This reflects the development of prototypes and testing the ideas generated in the previous stage.

✦ Feasibility determination. The determination of the practicality of an innovation involves checking the financial viability, practicality and operational benefits to be gained.

✦ Final application. This stage represents the commercialization of ideas and their adoption within the organization. In a perfect world it would lead to further ideas creation as a consequence of the internal sensitivity to the need for innovation.

Change: an applied perspective

It was suggested earlier that management and change are closely linked and that change is an ongoing feature of organizational life. That must be the starting point for any consideration of a management perspective on change. It can be argued that management is a process of seeking a balance between change and stability. Stability is necessary in order to achieve the economies of scale in mass production and services. Change, by the same token, is necessary because of the need to keep ahead of the competition and to ensure constantly reducing cost. It can be argued that the success of Japanese management methods is in being able to provide the means of effectively harnessing these conflicting requirements.

Too much change, it can be argued, is bad for operations, leads to confusion and reduces efficiency, quality and morale. Too little change results in stagnation with no ability to adapt to changing circumstances. Many recent developments in management practice have been designed to allow ever greater levels of change to be adopted without loss of control over operations: just in time, teamwork, empowerment, quality circles and the other planning and control techniques all offer some ability to adapt operational activity to changes in product, technology or environment.

Another way of looking at change is that it is a natural part of life. The problems arise from stability, not from change. The changing seasons, weather, ageing, birth and death, sickness and health and family responsibilities represent just some of the ways in which change manifests itself in the life experience of human beings. Consider the changes in the range of skills and abilities of a human being between the ages of three and 12. Under these circumstances it is not stability that is the norm, it is change. Yet there is something that happens to human beings when they become adult and part of an organization that seeks to create security, stability and predictability. This resists change. Perhaps it is the human experience of organizations that creates this 'change' in people? It is the responsibility of management to develop the structural, procedural and cultural arrangements that encourage the expression of human talents desirable in a change environment. It is this complexity that is reflected in the chaos theory approaches to understanding change as a process.

What to change is one of the major difficulties faced by management. Everything and continuously would appear to be the advice offered by many of the writers on the topic.

But for practising managers knowing what to change is frequently a difficult decision. How far change should go is another difficult decision area, as resistance and cost inevitably increase with the degree of change. The process of change is another area with a number of dangers attached to it. The end result, once achieved, may not meet the expectations predicted and fail to deliver the intended benefits. This exposes management to additional cost and loss of credibility as they seek to remedy the deficiency. So from a management perspective change is a dangerous practice that it is not possible to avoid and yet it carries all manner of personal, professional and organizational risks. As indicated in the section on chaos theory, organizations are forever on the edge of change and from which even the slightest breath of wind might topple. Truly an exciting aspect of management!

Conclusions

This chapter has analyzed the nature of change and assessed the ways in which it impacts on organizations and management. The reasons for change were examined as were the forms of resistance to it. Change management approaches were evaluated as was innovation as part of the change process. Every aspect of an organization is subject to and involved with change in some way or other. From that perspective every other chapter in this book contains some aspect of change, its origins, impact and interacting variables. It is for that reason that change is a suitable linking theme for this book.

Discussion questions

1. Define the following key terms used in this chapter:

Forcefield analysis model	*Fracturing and adaptive change*	*Innovation*
Planned and unplanned change	*Organizational development*	*Change agent*
Leavitt's organizational variables	*Individual resistance to change*	*Chaos theory*
Dunphy and Stace's change strategies		

2. Describe the McKinsey 7-S framework and explain how it could be used to inform a change management programme.

3. Outline the links between power, politics and change and explain why they are necessary to the management of a change programme.

4. Provide a brief explanation for each of the individual reasons for resisting change identified in Figure 18.6.

5. Distinguish between planned and unplanned change, adaptive and fracturing change. What are the consequences of these distinctions?

6. What are the main reasons for resistance to change and how can they be overcome?

7. Describe the contingency approach to organizational change and distinguish it from the OD approach.

8. Provide a brief explanation for each of the group and organizational reasons for resisting change identified in Figure 18.7.

9. 'The true skill in management is to keep change happening so that everyone has to pay attention to what they are doing and they do not have any spare time to cause trouble for managers.' Discuss this statement.

10. Describe the stages of innovation from creating the climate to implementation. What are the risks associated with change and how do they link with the levels of innovation identified?

Research activities

1. In small groups of five, seek out an organization that has just gone through a major change of some description. This might be the introduction of a new product, a significant reduction in the number of employees or the amalgamation with another company. Arrange to discuss the changes made with a cross-section of managers and employees. Identify how the need to change was detected, how it was planned and implemented and if it has been successful. Compare what you find in terms of the different opinions expressed and methods used with the material introduced in this chapter. Explain the differences and similarities that you find.

2. Conduct a forcefield analysis of a situation in your life. It could be the number of times that you miss lectures or the number of times that you phone parents or friends. Attempt to identify factors that might drive you to attend lectures (or phone) more frequently and those that encourage you to do it less frequently. Draw a diagram of this particular forcefield. Attempt to identify a change programme for the situation using the three stages in the Lewin model. Attempt to implement your analysis and after two months' review if you were able to refreeze your behaviour at the desired level. Explain why or why not. What does this teach you about managing change?

3. Trawl through books and magazines for examples of change that were successful and examples that failed. Attempt to identify what created the conditions for success and failure in the examples that you find. Reconcile the findings of your work on this with the material contained in this chapter.

Key reading

From Clark, H, Chandler, J and Barry, J (1994) *Organization and Identities: Text and Readings in Organizational Behaviour*, International Thomson Business Press, London:

✦ Campbell, B *et al.*: The manifesto for new times, p 49. This considers the changes facing Britain as a capitalist society entering the 1990s.

✦ Cockburn, C: Male dominance and technological change, p 197. Considers the impact of changing technology in the printing industry on the work of both men and women.

✦ Roethlisberger, FJ and Dickson, WJ: Group restriction of output, p 247. Part of the famous

Hawthorne Studies, this demonstrates that change is endemic to organizations and that employees do not always react to it in ways anticipated by managers.

♦ Coch, L and French, JRP: Overcoming resistance to change using group methods, p 260. This is a research-based examination of change and its consequences within one manufacturing establishment.

♦ Hobsbawm, EJ and Rudé, G. Early forms of worker resistance – swing riots, p 317. This attempts to reflect the experience of workers attempting to influence (change) aspects of their working life.

Further reading

Cummings, TG and Worley, CG (1993) *Organization Development and Change*, 5th edn, West Publishing, St Paul, MN. A text dedicated to the review of the subjects indicated in the title and how they impact on organizational activity and functioning. In that sense it is a standard textbook in this field.

Flood, RL (1996) *Solving Problem Solving*, John Wiley, Chichester. This text takes a new look at a number of systems approaches to problem solving and updates the approach to the TSI perspective introduced earlier. In that context problem solving is being equated with the management of change. It should be recognized that there are distinctions between these two concepts in particular situations.

Mabey, C and Mayon-White, B (1993) *Managing Change*, 2nd edn, Paul Chapman Publishing, London. This book is intended to be a reader for one of the Open University courses that deals with managing change. It brings together a wide range of research-based perspectives on change and how to manage it, as well as examples of it in practice.

McCalman, J and Paton, RA (1992) *Change Management: A Guide to Effective Implementation*, Paul Chapman, London. As the title suggests, this book is about how to manage change processes. In doing so it concentrates on the two approaches to managing change, the systems approach and the organizational development model.

Morgan, G (1993) *Imaginization: The Art of Creative Management*, Sage, London. Although not about change directly, this book provides a whole set of ways to develop new perspectives on thinking about organizations and management. In practice this represents an invitation to change our thinking about organizations and what we do within them. If this approach is to be of any value then it should also change organizations as a consequence.

Oswick, C and Grant, D (eds) (1996) *Organization Development: Metaphorical Explorations*, Pitman, London. This text attempts to provide a basis for the critical evaluation of organizational development, rather than the more usual practitioner perspective. It also uses the metaphor as a basis of enhancing understanding of organizational development in general and specific terms.

References

Armstrong, M (1995) *A Handbook of Personnel Management Practice*, 5th edn, Kogan Page, London.
Betz, F, (1987) *Managing Technology*, Prentice Hall, Englewood Cliffs, NJ.
Cummings, TG and Worley, CG (1993) *Organization Development and Change*, 5th edn, West Publishing, St Paul, MN.
Dale, BG (1999) Quality Costing. In Dale, BG (ed.) *Managing Quality*, 3rd edn, Blackwell, Oxford.
Dunford, RW (1992) *Organizational Behaviour: An Organizational Analysis Perspective*, Addison-Wesley, Sydney.
Dunphy, D and Stace, D (1988) Transformational and coercive strategies for planned organizational change: beyond the OD model, *Organization Studies*, 9, 317–34.

Dunphy, D and Stace, D (1990) *Under New Management: Australian Organizations in Transition*, McGraw-Hill, Sydney.

Flood, RL and Jackson, MC (1991) *Creative Problem Solving: Total Systems Intervention*, John Wiley, Chichester.

Hammer, M and Champy, J (1995) *Reengineering the Corporation: A Manifesto for Business Revolution*, Nicholas Brealey, London.

Harrington, HJ (1991) *Business Process Improvement: The Breakthrough Strategy for Total Quality, Productivity and Competitiveness*, McGraw-Hill, New York.

Hellriegel, D, Slocum, JW and Woodman, RW (1989) *Organizational Behaviour*, 5th edn, West Publishing, St Paul, MN.

Johnson, G and Scholes, K (1993) *Exploring Corporate Strategy: Text and Cases*, 3rd edn, Prentice Hall, Hemel Hempstead.

Kahn, EF (1982) Conclusion: Critical Themes in the Study of Change. In PS Goodman and Associates (eds), *Change in Organizations*, Jossey Bass, San Francisco, CA.

Kanter, RM (1983) *The Change Masters*, Allen & Unwin, London.

Kanter, RM, Stein, BA and Jick, TD (1992) *The Challenge of Organizational Change: How Organizations Experience it and Leaders Guide it,* The Free Press, New York.

Kotter, JP and Schlesinger, LA (1979) Choosing strategies for change, *Harvard Business Review*, March/April.

Leavitt, HL (1965) Applied Organizational Change in Industry: Structural, Technological and Humanistic Approaches. In March, JG (ed.) *Handbook of Organizations*, Rand McNally, Chicago, IL.

Lewin, K (1951) *Field Theory in Social Science*, Harper & Row, New York.

Malhotra, Y (1998) Business process redesign: an overview, *IEEE Engineering Management Review*, **26**, 3, Fall.

Marion, R (1999) *The Edge of Organization: Chaos and Complexity Theories of Formal Social Systems*, Sage, Thousand Oaks, CA.

Moorhead, G and Griffin, RW (1992) *Organizational Behaviour*, 3rd edn, Houghton Mifflin, Boston, MA.

Morgan, G (1993) *Imaginization: The Art of Creative Management*, Sage, Newbury Park, CA.

Mullins, LJ (1996) *Management and Organizational Behaviour*, 4th edn, Pitman, London.

Nadler, D and Tushman, M (1988) *Strategic Organizational Design*, Scott, Foresman, Glenview, CO.

Open University (1990) Book 9, *Managing Change*. Course B784 The Effective Manager, Open Business School, Milton Keynes.

Ottaway, RN (1982) Defining the Change Agent. In Evans, B, Powell, JA and Talbot, R (eds) *Changing Design* , John Wiley, Chichester.

Pascale, R (1990) *Managing on the Edge: How Successful Companies Use Conflict to Stay Ahead*, Penguin, London.

Peters, TJ (1988) *Thriving on Chaos*, Random House, New York.

Plant, R (1987) *Managing Change and Making it Stick*, Fontana, London.

Pocket Oxford Dictionary (1969) 5th edn, Oxford University Press, Oxford.

Pritchett, P (1996) *The Employee Handbook of New Work Habits for a Radically Changing World*, Pritchett Rummler-Brache, London.

Schein, VE (1985) Organizational realities: the politics of change, *Training and Development Journal*, February, 37–41.

Schermerhorn, JR (1993) *Management for Productivity*, 4th edn, John Wiley, New York.

Slack, N, Chambers, S, Harland, C, Harrison, A and Johnston, R (1998) *Operations Management*, 2nd edn, Pitman, London.

Stephenson, T (1985) *Management: A Political Activity*, Macmillan, Basingstoke.

Stewart, R (1991) *Managing Today and Tomorrow*, Macmillan, Basingstoke.

Waldrop, MM (1992) *Complexity: The Emerging Science at the Edge of Order and Chaos*. Simon & Schuster, New York.

PART VIII

The dynamics of the work environment

CHAPTER 19

Power and control

CHAPTER SUMMARY

This chapter will begin by considering the related concepts of power, influence and authority. There are a variety of perspectives on the subject of power which form the next area for discussion. This is followed with an examination of what it is that generates power as used by individuals and groups within an organization. Power is frequently described as an influence on decision making and this is the next focus of the chapter. The forms and characteristics of control are then explored before the strategies for using it are introduced. The relationship between aspects of power and control as they are encountered within an organizational context are then discussed. Reactions to control such as resistance and compliance are considered and the chapter concludes with a consideration of the applied perspectives on the topics discussed.

LEARNING OBJECTIVES

After studying this chapter and working through the associated Management in Action panels, Discussion questions and Research activities, you should be able to:

✦ Understand the nature of power as experienced within an organization.

✦ Describe the sources of power within an organization.

✦ Explain the relationship between power and decision making.

✦ Assess the differences and similarities between the concepts of power, influence and authority.

✦ Detail the positive and negative aspects of power and control in the running of an organization.

✦ Appreciate the nature and impact of control within organizations.

✦ Outline the characteristic features of control systems.

✦ Discuss some of the forms that power and control can take within an organization.

Introduction

The notion of power is endemic in organizational relationships. Managers exercise *power* over subordinates in directing their endeavours towards the objectives being sought. Industrial relations activity within organizations is largely directed towards a redistribution of the prevailing power balance between managers and employees. For example, the annual negotiation over wages is an attempt to influence the otherwise unilateral management determination of the distribution of company finances.

A concept that has strong association with power is that of *control*. This can be used to refer to a range of actions, including the procedures associated with the control of machine processes. It can also refer to the management of the organization on behalf of the principle stakeholders. However, it can also be used to reflect more sinister processes. It can be taken to reflect the *manipulation* of employee behaviour by managers. There are for example, many examples where managers resort to bullying tactics in order to force subordinates to comply with their wishes. These intentions may not only reflect the need to provide job instruction and achieve high productivity, but also the desire of some individuals to exercise control (or domination) over others in its broadest sense (Adams, 1992).

Both of the concepts of power and control can contain positive aspects as well as negative connotations. For example, an effective power balance between capital and labour should allow both to function effectively without damage to the interests of either. That is in essence the basis of a free market. Controlled activity within an organization can also be of benefit to the various stakeholders. For example if through the *control* of the production process within the organization, product changes are brought about which in turn provide commercial advantage, then it could be argued that such activity was advantageous and of benefit to customers, employees and shareholders. The difficulty with both concepts however is that very often the positive and negative aspects function in parallel, or they are not used solely for the benefit of the stakeholder groups. In other words they can be used for personal advantage or for political reasons by individuals or groups. Politics is a subject to which we shall return in the next chapter.

Power, influence and authority

Power is a concept related to ideas of manipulation and providing the means through which objectives are realized. In that sense it reflects a mobilizing and energizing force. For example, managers have the *power* to require subordinates to follow their instructions, the ultimate sanction being dismissal if they refuse. The rational view of the role of management, holding that managers do the thinking and act in the best interests of the organization, whereas employees are there to follow orders in doing the work considered necessary. This view has predominated throughout history and has been reinforced through such approaches as scientific management.

Power also reflects a process of being able to *influence* the behaviour of others. Influence being generally viewed as a soft expression of power. For example, a manager exercising power could order an employee to do something. A manager exercising influence may, through recruitment, training, reward and socialization practices encourage employees to align their working habits and attitudes to those of management, therefore avoiding the need to give orders. The same end result is achieved, but through different mechanisms.

Power is also something that is an accompaniment to the concept of *authority*. Generally, those in authority would be expected to have power. However, this is only relatively accurate as there are those who hold power irrespective of their position. The elected prime minister of a country has considerable *power* by virtue of their electoral mandate. With a large parliamentary majority they are able to ensure that particular legislation is enacted and enforced. However, they are also at the whim of the population when it comes to election time. The *victims* of the power displayed by politicians (the population) hold the power to take away from the prime minister the position that is the source of their power. At election time the ordinary voter holds considerable power over those in authority under normal circumstances. At the time of writing (September 2000) British road hauliers, taxi drivers, farmers and fishermen had all but brought the country to a standstill by slow-driving protests and blockading petrol stations and oil refineries in protest at high fuel costs. It was reported that about 80% of the price of fuel is tax and that 90% of filling stations had run out of petrol after three or four days of blockade. The government rejected any suggestion of concession on taxation levels and demanded that the oil companies and police ensure that supplies get through. A number of politicians complained bitterly about the drivers' action, stating that people should accept government decisions over fuel prices. This view is interesting as it was only a few months earlier that the same government encouraged citizens to stop buying from companies that charged high prices and enacted legislation to force car manufacturers to lower prices, even using the phrase 'rip-off Britain' in the process! This example clearly demonstrates the *power* of the people in an attempt to *influence* those in *authority*! It also demonstrates the way in which *power* and *politics* are linked.

Management in Action 19.1 outlines how influence is becoming more important than power in an organizational context as a means of achieving commercial success. It also explores ways in which influence can be achieved and used to advantage when formal authority and power is absent.

Stop | Consider

To what extent does influence as described in MiA 19.1 reflect a recognition that traditional ways of exercising power no longer work effectively and therefore its application needs to be appropriate to the dominant social conditions?
Justify your views.

Power has been defined in many different ways. Perhaps the most effective definition is that provided by Pfeffer (1992) who brings together a number of views on it as, 'the potential ability to influence behaviour, to change the course of events, to overcome resistance, and to get people to do things that they would not otherwise do' (p 30). In this definition the linkage between *power*, *influence* and *authority* is evident.

Within an organizational context it is easy to envisage the hierarchical linkage between power, influence and authority. There is no purpose to the position of a line manager unless it is the exercise of authority over others. However, some management positions exist because of the high technical skill and status necessary to undertake the job and the direct management of others may not be a major activity. However, by virtue of the position within the hierarchy of such positions, authority and the ability to influence others will still exist.

MANAGEMENT IN ACTION 19.1

Influence without authority

Cohen and Bradford describe that 'the crutch of authority' is missing from modern organizations. However, that does not mean that management action is unnecessary – things still have to be done. The inhabitants of modern organizations need to be able to influence others. This not only applies in top-down situations, where managers may have larger spans of control as a consequence of delayering and may be responsible for areas in which they have no personal expertise. It can include the need for subordinates to influence superiors and/or equals who may be busy and not have the time or inclination to offer assistance. Managers who are under considerable pressure to achieve results may show a marked reluctance to take actions involving more work for themselves or adding more change to an already overburdened system.

Influence is not a new organizational skill. Cohen and Bradford remind us that it was the snake in the Garden of Eden that first demonstrated the possibility of gaining advantage through it. The eating of the apple by Eve and then her influence on Adam speaks volumes for the significance of the concept in organizational terms.

Northrop, an American aircraft manufacturer, decided that manufacturing specialists should be involved from the beginning of the design process, the intention being to improve the ability to build aircraft more efficiently and with fewer problems. The cost and time involved in making engineering changes while in production were excessive and reduced the commercial viability of the company. The ability of the manufacturing people to veto the design engineer's specifications at first caused some problems and resentment. However, when the benefits became obvious in the form of fewer in-process problems it began to function more easily. The results speak for themselves in that 97% of all parts fitted perfectly first time (the previous best was 50%) and

engineering changes were reduced to one-sixth of their previous levels and implemented five times faster. The same applies in many service sector companies, including banks, which must share information between separate parts of the organization to target customers more effectively. In the days of electronic information flows it is less easy for managers to control access to information. Restricting its availability is less practical, thus encouraging co-operation-based control processes.

Effective influence begins with the ways in which individuals think about the people that they must influence. Regarding them as a partner or strategic ally involves a different approach to working relationships. It moves away from the old win–lose approach to interpersonal relationships with an emphasis on obligations and exchange. After all the person who wants help from you today might be in a position to help you next week. It matters little if they are your boss or a subordinate, the network of relationships is about mutual benefit. Cohen and Bradford make the following suggestions for individuals seeking to achieve influence over others:

+ Mutual respect. Assume that others are competent and smart.
+ Openness. It is not possible to know everything, so sharing information helps you as well as 'them'.
+ Trust. Assume that individuals will not purposely hurt or undermine you and so there is no reason to hold back information.
+ Mutual benefit. Plan win–win strategies.

Adapted from: Cohen, AR and Bradford, DL (1993) Influence without authority, *World Executives Digest*, December, pp 28–32.

There are also many positions within an organization that do not have any formal authority yet the individuals concerned are able to exercise considerable influence. The secretary or personal assistant to a chief executive is frequently in such a position. *Having the ear* of the person with formal authority allows them a considerable degree of influence beyond their formal status. In a very real sense they are *gatekeepers* and the power behind the throne. The *gatekeeper* role within an organization is very important in that, as the title suggests, such a postholder can grant or restrict access. For example, the secretary to the personnel manager has the power to make and prioritize appointments, pass on messages and direct enquiries to lower status personnel staff. To a real extent they are in a position to shape the work experience of their boss, as well as the access granted (and hence fortunes of) people wanting to engage with the boss for some purpose. Many salespeople and consultants make a point of getting to know the secretaries of appropriate managers and departments in client organizations for just this reason.

Authority has been described as the legitimate expression of power (Handy, 1993, p 124). In this context, it reflects power used by someone who is accepted as having the legitimate right to exercise it in that context. Employees generally accept the rights of managers to exercise authority over their activities and behaviour by virtue of the position conveyed formally by the organization. The work of Milgram (1965), introduced in an earlier chapter, is important in this context. His experiments with fake electric shocks demonstrated just how far people can be pushed and how easy it is for individuals in authority to achieve compliance with their wishes.

It was Chester Barnard who was among the first to write about the notion of authority in an organizational context. In 1938 he describes authority in the following terms:

> The character of a communication (order) in a formal organization by virtue of which it is accepted by a contributor to or 'member' of the organization as governing the action he contributes; that is, as governing or determining what he does or is not to do so far as the organization is concerned. (p 163)

Barnard goes on to explain that a requirement to act in a particular way is evaluated by the recipient in terms of its legitimacy. Acceptance of the requirement to follow the order also acknowledges the authority of the giver of that order. Conversely, denial of the order also denies the legitimacy of the giver to issue it. So, much as those in authority might deny it, the classification of an order as legitimate or otherwise is not in their gift, it is for the recipient to decide. This is what Luthans (1995) describes as an *acceptance theory* of authority intended to support group cohesion and goals.

The inability of those in authority to guarantee that subordinates accept every instruction as legitimate remains a potential source of difficulty for them. This is well demonstrated through the example given earlier of the reaction of the British politicians to blockades of petrol stations and oil refineries by drivers. There have also been many disciplinary cases within organizations based on the refusal of an employee to carry out what was classified by managers as a reasonable instruction. Inevitably, whatever the context, the refusal to obey a reasonable instruction (as defined by management) would be regarded as a threat to the established order and as such something to be dealt with severely.

Influence is an interesting word in English and Handy (1993) introduces it as both noun and verb to explain some of the confusion with power. He attempts to clarify its use by restricting it to use as a verb in the sense of, 'the use of power' (p 124). In that connection *power* is but one of the sources of the ability to influence others. Influence can therefore be regarded as a *broader* concept than power. Influence is also a *softer* term than power. It implies a willing acquiescence on the part of the subject and more subtle processes at work than would be expected if power was being applied. Influence implies persuasion, co-oper-ation and relationship-based mechanisms for achieving the desired behaviour. In essence a two-way process as compared to power which is unidirectional and predominantly top down. However, power is not only top down as is demonstrated through the actions of the British drivers indicated earlier!

It would be tempting to restrict the distinction between *power* and *influence* to this rather cosy view based around the notion of persuasion. However, these terms are more complex than that would allow. Overt attempts to use power and force are likely to be met with *resistance*. Consequently, it is not uncommon to find more subtle mechanisms being used in order to obtain *compliance* with the will of another. For example, as a result of man-agement encouraging employees to become shareholders of the company they might find it easier to accept the management-preferred perspectives on issues such as flexible working and lower pay rises. Thus, encouraging shareholding could be interpreted as a cynical attempt to manipulate employees into a position where the exercise of naked power by managers became unnecessary. Rothschild and Miethe (1994) (quoting Forsyth, 1993) identify, in the context of *whistleblowing*, a number of influence strategies that they suggest are used in order to obtain *compliance* from employees. These are identified in Table 19.1.

Eight of these nine tactics, bullying being the odd one out, represent the indirect applica-tion of practices intended to persuade the individual to offer compliance to the will of the per-petrator. In each of these cases it could be suggested that a deliberate attempt to avoid resistance is being attempted and hence the underlying notion of power is being hidden or dis-guised. For example, the person initiating a negotiation is seeking to move the other person (or group) towards their position, recognizing that they may not get all they wish for, but it will represent some movement and possibly the exercise of power disguised as compromise.

Where power is a feature of a particular relationship there is also *dependency*. Power can be exercised if there is no dependency present but it achieves *compliance* at best. In an organization for example, if an individual employee does not value money, promotion or any of the other 'benefits' provided there is little *dependency* present and the opportunity for power to be used as a source of influence is strictly limited. In effect managers have few *levers* (influencing tactics) with which to control and direct the behaviour of the individ-ual. Employees that need the job and/or the money for some or a number of reasons are dependent and thus amenable to the exercise of power. Management in Action 19.2 provides one illustration which demonstrates the impact of a lack of dependency.

Promising	to do something for the individual in the future
Bullying	the use of threat (real or implied)
Discussion	the use of rational argument and explanation
Negotiation	making compromises
Manipulation	the use of lies and deceit
Demand	insistence on compliance
Claiming expertise	reliance on superior knowledge or skill
Ingratiation	reliance on flattery
Evasion	avoidance of revealing aspects of the situation

TABLE 19.1 Influencing tactics (*source*: Forsyth, GDR (1993) *Group Dynamics*, Brooks/Cole Publishing Company, Pacific Grove, CA)

MANAGEMENT IN ACTION 19.2

You know what you can do with the job!

This story was told to me by the person who was the driver in the situation described. He had been a middle manager within the public sector for about 30 years before taking the early retirement package offered as part of a government scheme to reduce public spending. He found himself with plenty of time on his hands after he retired and thought that it would be a good idea to get a part-time job to give himself an interest and to enhance his pension. He looked around and eventually found a job as the driver for a medical practice. The job involved working two nights each week driving a doctor to visit patients who had asked to see someone urgently in their home as they could not wait until the normal surgery next day.

The driver, who was in his mid-50s, knew his area well and was soon able to get quickly from one patient to another. However, he was quite a lot older than many of the doctors he was transporting around. He indicated that some of the doctors were very friendly and liked to chat as the night passed, while others were remote and viewed themselves as distinctly superior to a humble driver. On one occasion a particular young doctor who on previous occasions had shown himself to be arrogant and not interested in getting to know the driver was to be particularly obnoxious.

The pair had been driving around the list of patients for about two hours and the doctor was clearly in a bad mood. Among other instances of

rudeness he insisted that the driver take him home as he wanted to pick up a book to read in between visits. This done he demanded that the driver speed up to the next visit so that they could make up for lost time. The driver said yes, but that he was not prepared to break the speed limit as he would have to pay a fine if he was caught by the police. The doctor told him to shut up and drive as instructed or he would report him to the manager for insubordination. The driver lost his temper somewhat at this and stopped the car. He asked the doctor who he thought he was talking to in such a way. The doctor replied that he was only a driver and such people needed the job and the money so he had better keep driving. His last words being: 'What would you do if I threatened you with dismissal for not following orders. You need the money don't you?

The driver replied that, he did not need the money. Also that he would drive out into the countryside near to his own home, stop the car, get out and throw the keys into a field. Then he would walk home to bed. The doctor was lost for words. He had obviously never been spoken to like that before and had assumed that the driver was dependent upon the job and wage that it provided. His reaction after a couple of minutes of embarrassed silence was to laugh and say that he had only been joking and could they go now. He was never rude or hostile to the driver after that, although he never became friendly either.

Stop | Consider

To what extent would it be an impossible task to manage employees who are not dependent upon the job or the organization for an income or meaning in their lives?
How might you attempt to manage such employees?

Perspectives on power

The study of power within organizations has generally been neglected by the mainstream disciplines. It is in the field of organization theory that it has gained most prominence as part of the fundamental relationships between organizations and the social structures of which they form part. Ackroyd (1994, p 287) points out that:

> The dominant view in the UK has emphasized the place of organization in the social structure and so makes power and authority central to the analysis. Social structures are structures of power and the organization is a vital part of the mechanism sustaining and perpetuating the social structure.

Much of the emphasis within organization theory therefore has explored the nature of power relationships and on the ways in which organizations interact with other organizations within a social context. The other major focus for the study of power has been that of its association with resistance within the notion of the agency concept of organization. This debate forms much of the basis for the development of *labour process theory* (Braverman, 1974). In subsequent sections some of the major themes associated with the study of *power* will be explored.

Traditional perspectives on power

Within much of the traditional management literature power was assumed to reflect the nature of the hierarchical relationships endemic to organizations. Management was described as an activity that involved the determination of what needed to be done and then the direction of the necessary resources to meeting that objective. Within that *paradigm* management had the power to ensure that what was necessary was actually done. Non-management people within the organization existed solely to provide the means of achieving the objectives, there to have *power* exercised over them. In that sense power is a reflection of the natural social order and processes and as such only a minor element within the study of leadership and control processes.

This view of power was also evident in the views of the early trade unions. For example, during the great building dispute of 1859–60, when carpenters, masons and bricklayers struck in London for (among other things) the right to a nine-hour working day, the trade unions told the Central Master Builders Association:

> That our society shall be governed by laws, and that the members shall be requested to conform to those laws is but natural, and we believe that such is the case in all corporations and every club among the upper classes in Pall Mall and St James's. (quoted in Briggs, 1955, pp 176–7)

They accepted without question that the rule of law in both society and organizations was 'natural' and that if individuals did not follow the 'rules' they could not expect the support of the trade union.

Some of the models used within the literature, particularly that of leadership, capture aspects of power as a normal dimension to be used by managers in the determination of appropriate courses of action. For example, Likert's (1967) four systems of management contain at one extreme an approach titled 'exploitative autocratic' and at the other 'democratic' the distinction between them largely being grounded in the way in which power is used by the leader concerned. At the autocratic end of the spectrum, leadership is purely top down, akin to the giving and acting upon orders. At the other end, democracy is based on trust on the part of the leader that subordinates can effectively contribute through involvement (in management-approved ways) to the achievement of management-determined objectives. Also managers retain the ultimate right to say 'no' even in a democratic process.

Fiedler (1967) developed his contingency model of leadership which specifically incorporated a power dimension into his work. Through the leader 'position power' concept Fiedler was reflecting the degree of authority held by the leader. It was scaled as either high or low, reflecting the degree to which the group would follow the leaders wishes. This model is interesting in that it only recognizes the possibility of 'low' as the smallest amount of power held by a leader. Yet in MiA 19.2 a specific example was given whereby, assuming that the example can be generalized, it might be possible for the ultimate sanction of dismissal to carry little weight in supporting the conventional conception of hierarchical power. The conventional views of power in management do not generally acknowledge the possibility that a leader may not hold power or influence in a particular situation.

The conception of power within an organization in this way is generally based on the existence of three features:

✦ Humans with needs, wants and desires that can only be met through the individual engaging with an organization.

✦ The existence of resources through which these needs and wants can be met.

✦ The existence of a manager who is prepared to act as the go-between in facilitating the 'deal' between the individual and the organization and subsequently managing its realization in practice.

At least one of the models of power within an organization introduced in a following section (that of French and Raven (1968)) is based on the existence of resources that are valued by the organization. These resources are not just physical resources such as position or money, they can include personal characteristics such as expertise.

A slightly broader view of power emerges from the work of Pfeffer (1992) when it is linked to the concept of politics (the topic of the next chapter). Pfeffer essentially argues that power is a *commodity* for managers and that political activity is the means through which it is obtained. He suggests that power within the organization is needed if a particular manager is to gain influence and advance their department; function; professional capabilities; significance (to the organization); and personal standing; wealth and career. In that context power is not just a top-down concept, it reflects a 360° process endemic to the experience of managers and non-managers alike.

Lower level employees can also gain and exercise power in a number of ways. Strikes and other forms of industrial action are intended to demonstrate that employees can force management to concede to the demands if they will not willingly agree to them. Also within the economy of any country a scarcity of labour or particular skills will cause wage rates to rise as companies compete for scarce resources, reflecting a different form of power. Management in Action 19.3 reflects one example of this diffuse concept of power as it can actually function within an organizational context.

MANAGEMENT IN ACTION 19.3

Promoting the function?

This story was told to me by the human resource director involved in the situation. The company employed about 4000 people and was a medium-sized bank with the usual branch network and range of head office functions. Up to the late 1980s the personnel function had been a small department led by a senior manager (not director level). Below that level were a personnel manager and training manager who looked after the entire company. In turn they were supported by a personnel manager for the branches, one for the head office functions and a couple of training officers. There were also a small number of personnel officers and clerical support staff. The department employed a total of about 17 people. The head of the department reported directly to the chief executive, although he did not sit on the board of the company.

Clearly in this situation the department was regarded as a support function, with no board level responsibility or automatic influence on its deliberations. This was not an uncommon situation at the time as many companies had been downsizing and support functions such as personnel had been hard hit and marginalized. The emphasis, and hence power, lay with the value adding operational departments. However, the finance sector was changing rapidly by the late 1980s and many companies began to develop new business strategies to take advantage of the new opportunities available. In the company concerned a major firm of business consultants was retained to assist in the development of new strategies and the subsequent reorganization of the company to enable it to realize its objectives. Clearly a major part of this process involved reorganizing the jobs that people did, training, the development of new pay structures etc., all of which fell into the sphere of influence of the personnel department.

Not surprisingly under these circumstances the head of personnel argued that major changes

were also required within his function. He argued that a range of things should change, including a rebranding of the function under the title of human resource department, that he should be elevated to director status (to better advise the board of people issues) and that more staff were needed to operationalize the people strategies needed within the new business plan. This view was supported by the retained consultants. This was agreed by the board of directors and the department was totally transformed.

The senior manager became director of human resource management. Integrated into the function were the salary administration and pensions functions and a number of new sections were created. A reward management department was established as was an employee relations and safety unit. The training function was expanded and a number of regional human resource managers were recruited. In total the number of people employed in the new human resource management department grew to about 70, approximately 30 of whom were new to the company at senior specialist or manager level.

The payroll cost of the department jumped by considerably more than the rise in numbers might suggest. The number of people in the department rose from about 17 to about 70 suggesting a rise of just over four times. However, the new posts accounted for about 30 positions in the new department, the rest being transfers from other functions within the company. This might suggest an additional payroll cost to the company of about double its original cost. However, the new positions were predominantly at the senior specialist and manager levels and so the new cost was that much higher. The total new cost to the company was an increase in salary and benefits of approximately seven times its previous magnitude. A massive jump by anyone's standards. It should also be noted that this additional cost did not include any company employee-based taxes, training, equipment or other costs. It only reflected salary and benefit costs.

From the now director of human resource management's perspective the changes contained a number of benefits. He now had a seat on the board. That gave him the power to influence strategy and policy more easily, at the same time as giving him the status to influence other managers more directly. Personnel activity in the company increased dramatically because there were more people carrying it out. However, it was said that company performance in terms of the bottom line did not improve as a consequence of this additional activity. But the main advantage to the director was that as a consequence of his elevation to the board and the growth in size of his department he personally trebled his salary because he was became responsible for a much bigger (and more significant) department!

The director was a truly happy man and effectively brought forward his retirement by several years as a result of his increased ability to save along with the pension enhancement following his meteoric salary and benefit increases.

Stop | Consider

To what extent does the outcome of MiA 19.3 reflect either the exercise of politics as a way of gaining power within an organization, or simply opportunism in taking advantage of circumstances (for personal gain) as they arise?

Does this distinction matter? Why or why not?

Foucault and power

For Foucault, power represented something different from the idea of a commodity or a property. He considered that power was a *condition* that existed within society as a whole. It fundamentally existed in the language that is used and so created the knowledge accepted by a particular society as reflected in its social practices (Linstead, 1993, p 63). Power in this context uses discourse to create the rules which in turn creates and classifies the knowledge available in particular ways. In an organizational context this allows the classification of activity (and people, jobs skill etc.) into differentiated packages of management and non-management classes and so allows the hierarchical framework to be perpetuated as legitimate.

Foucault reminds us in his work that the boundaries around the 'things' that we 'see, understand and take for granted' are in fact artificial and socially created. In that sense our stock of knowledge is created for us out of the discourses that exist within society. By creating these boundaries and compartments our attention is channelled in certain directions and it is automatically directed away from other things. We are effectively *socialized* into seeing and understanding the world in which we live through the discourses that we experience and this is a reflection of power as conceived by Foucault. For example, one aspect of the existence of power is evident in the ways in which business and management are taught within a university context.

There are a number of specialist disciplines taught to students, such as management accounting, financial accounting, human resource management, marketing, organizational behaviour etc. However this does not match the experience of managing an organization.

Although many organizations are compartmentalized along functional lines these must be integrated if success is to be achieved. The chapters in this text dealing with organization structure should have made it clear that one of the major difficulties facing modern organization is how to become more horizontal and less perpendicular in an attempt to break down the artificial boundaries of function and hierarchy and better serve the customer. In terms of the provision of central government services through the diverse range of civil service departments one British prime minister (Tony Blair) has been frequently reported as wanting to encourage 'joined-up government' to blur these boundaries. (See, for example, Brooks *et al.* (2000, p 10) for one instance of just how difficult this can be to achieve in practice, demonstrating the power of dominant organizational forces.)

Foucault demonstrates the association between power and knowledge through a number of examples. In one (Foucault, 1975) outlined in Townley (1994, p 5) he describes how the authorities define an individual accused of murdering his mother, sister and brother through the reports of the police, doctors and presiding judge. These reports are then used by the authorities as the means of *knowing* the accused and then deciding his fate, thereby exercising *power* over him. Similar arguments are made in terms of the nature of power within an organizational setting. He suggested that factories have many similarities to other institutions such as prisons, monasteries, the military, schools and hospitals. In each of these institutions the prime objective was to *know* the subject effectively and fully as a basis for being able to ensure, 'that they operate as one wishes' Foucault (1977, p 138). O'Neill (1986, pp 51–2) describes the outcome of power as a form of *socialization* in social institutions (including organizations) as, 'places where the system can project its conception of the disciplinary society in the reformed criminal, the good worker, student, loyal soldier and committed citizen'.

Labour process theory and Lukes' views on power

Labour process theory originated from the Marxist tradition and attempts to explain the nature of work. It has been defined as, 'the means by which raw materials are transformed by human labour, acting on the objects with tools and machinery: first into products for use and, under capitalism, into commodities to be exchanged on the market' (Thompson, 1989, p xv). As an area of study it began with Braverman, who in 1974 published *Labour and Monopoly Capital,* which stimulated the rediscovery of the earlier Marxist material on the nature of labour. Within this tradition there is the view that management protects itself from the consequences arising from excessive use of authority by allowing practices such as collective bargaining and the legal definition of workers rights to develop, thereby retaining the pre-eminence of capital over labour (Burawoy, 1979). By so allowing some of its power to be dissipated, capital retains effective control over labour activity and use, leading some writers to talk of the *manufacture of consent*. This describes how workers are encouraged to continue to support (to give their consent) to the relative imbalance of power in a capitalist society.

Lukes (1982) attempts to provide a more radical perspective on power. He develops a three-dimensional model which seeks to explain a wider view of its function within an organizational context. The first dimension is suggested to reflect the nature of power as it would be commonly described in much of the literature. In that sense it is a view of power based on its observable and measurable effects. In such it is detected in the behaviour of individuals, who are analyzed in terms of the relative degrees of power that they hold in a particular context. Decision making and conflict are common examples of situations that are interpreted and dissected for the relative quantities of power evident.

The second dimension according to Lukes, reflects the exercise of power over what might be classed as the *agenda*. For example, the management of a company may recognize a trade union as the representative body for shopfloor employees. However, the scope of involvement for the trade union (and hence employees) in the decision making and running of the company will be governed by the recognition agreement. Management, therefore, have a mechanism to retain control over the agenda for employee involvement. Brannen (1983), for example, describes how worker–director schemes such as that run by British Steel in the 1970s were effectively manipulated through careful scheme design, adulteration of the rule of engagement and the socialization of the representatives involved. As a consequence the rights and power of management over the agenda and activity were never seriously challenged. In this example, the *socialization* process effectively shaped the views, attitudes and desires of those subjected to it. This reflects covert activity intended to retain the status quo in terms of the relative power balance and its associated structures rather than introducing a different conception of the underlying concept. However, this second dimension of power has been challenged as still requiring it to be defined in observable terms.

The third dimension in Lukes' model suggests that concepts of hegemony, incorporation, dependency and inaction underpin power. In that context it reflects the essential structural inequalities that exist between groups. For example, management have in their gift the jobs that provide economic and other necessities for the workers, so there is an inevitable asymmetrical basis to the employment relationship. The major problem with Lukes' model is that it requires the unseen to be incorporated into the analysis. For example, to what extent is power being used and what are its consequences in a situation where a company receives 150 applications for five jobs? Clearly, there is an element of power implicit is such situations as management must choose the lucky five and the remaining 145 will be rejected. A wide range of forces could impact on these decisions. Managers could take bribes in appointing particular individuals, they may also pick (or reject) people with certain physical characteristics or people from a particular ethnic group or gender. But, having done so what are the likely consequences for the relationship in the future? Managers would like to ensure subsequent *compliance*, but it is not guaranteed. These represent fundamental difficulties that Lukes does not effectively address.

Sources of organizational power

In practical terms *power* is invisible. It has never been seen, unless that is, someone points a gun at you and demands that you hand over your money or that you do as instructed. It cannot be held, touched and it is not detectable by any mechanical or electronic sensor. However, as apparent from the previous discussion, power is a very real and potent force in any organization. It is important to distinguish between power and the associated trappings which are detectable. For example, wealth is frequently associated with power. Stereotypical assumptions lead to implying that an individual holds power simply because they dress in expensive clothing or behave as if they were superior. False claims to power through such outward signs if uncovered can leave the individual concerned subject to ridicule or marginalization. Equally, of course, the opposite is also true. There are individuals and groups who are not obviously powerful and yet in practice they might be described as the power behind the throne. The people with the real power to influence, decide, direct events and other people.

Power is something that only lives in the minds, attitudes, behaviours, expectations and perceptions of individuals. Once established in society the prevailing forms of power are supported by a wide range of structural devices. The laws, culture, status, work and educational systems are aligned in support and reinforcement of a particular power framework. However, individuals and groups who for various reasons do not wish to accept the prevailing power framework can seek to democratically change the situation or if all else fails seek to overturn it through revolution. Of course, these situations where direct force (or the threat of it) is used to obtain results, represent the application of a particular form of power.

Revolution can also occur within an organizational environment. If enough shareholders consider that the management is failing then they could be removed and changed. Equally, a management that becomes disaffected with its position relative to the owners may seek to leave or achieve a buyout in order to gain more power over events. It is also employee acceptance of the fact that managers have the *power* to direct endeavours that allows managers to exercise it. If the employees were not willing to accept management direction then managers would have no ability to influence events, other than by changing the entire workforce. This is the *dependency* aspect of power described earlier.

If power is not a tangible entity and is dependent upon the recipients to create its significance where does it originate? French and Raven (1968) identified a number of sources of power within a social context. These are based on the commodity or resource dependency view of power indicated earlier. The sources identified include:

✦ Coercive power. This form is based on the ability of the power holder to enforce the threat of direct control. In the mind of the receiver of this form of power is the fear that they may be punished if they do not comply with the directions of the power holder. An organizational example of this is provided in Management in Action 19.4, which illustrates the power of frozen food manufacturers over small shops.

Stop | Consider

To what extent and how might the consumer benefit from forcing frozen food manufacturers to abandon the provision of free freezers?

What does the previous answer imply about commercial power within society and the ways in which it should be controlled?

In any organization there is a degree of coercive power implied in the managerial relationship with subordinates. Historically, this power source was much stronger than it is today. The emergence of trade unions, improved management practices and employment legislation have all provided counterbalancing to the freedom of managers to take unilateral action. However, as was indicated earlier, by accepting these limited restrictions managers are able to effectively retain their *relative power advantage*.

✦ Reward power. Managers have the power to award pay increases, promote and otherwise reward individuals who perform as desired. In most organizations there are limitations on the opportunity for individual managers to control a broad range of rewards. For example, individual managers do not have total freedom on issues such as promotion. Company procedures are designed to limit the ability of individual managers to create inconsistencies in reward allocation across the organization.

MANAGEMENT IN ACTION 19.4

Ice-cream makers caught in cold war

The provision of freezers to shops by ice-cream and frozen-food makers has been used over the years to provide a means of controlling the market. Essentially, a large frozen-food manufacturer would agree to give the shopkeeper a freezer cabinet as long as only that company's products were kept in it. Sales staff from the manufacturer would check the cabinets during their regular calls on each shop. From the shopkeeper's perspective the advantage was access to a 'free' freezer that was designed to house particular products. The advantage to the frozen-food manufacturer was that they were able to restrict consumer access to their competitors' products – the size of many small shops prevents the use of a wide range of display cabinets.

Another side effect of this practice was the restriction of access to the market by small manufacturers who could not afford to subsidize shops as a means of acquiring vital shelf space. Pendleton's Ices in Merseyside was one such company. After a year of financial problems, closure, insolvency and industrial action by employees, new hope of it remaining in business arose. Grants were made available from the government and the local council. Nestlé (which bought the factory) donated equipment worth £500,000 and a local businessman invested

£150,000. These actions allowed the company to restart operations. Fifty one per cent of the shares in the company were held by the employees.

The troubled history of the plant had not daunted the will of the employees to keep the business afloat. However only about 27 of the company's 75 member workforce had been re-employed by the summer of 1993. This was due in no small part to the 20% shortfall in revenue compared to that anticipated in the business plan. This shortfall was largely due to the inability of the company to find outlets for its products as a result of freezer cabinet restrictions. However, Co-operative supermarkets had agreed to take the product and other potential customers were being pursued with high quality products. The company was also intent on complaining to the Monopolies and Mergers Commission about the freezer practice. Employees and managers were hopeful of improvements in sales despite the restrictions imposed as a result of restrictive practices by the large manufacturers.

Adapted from: (para. 1) Rice, I (1993) Whiff of controversy hangs in the air, *Financial Times*, 16 November, p 14; (paras 2 and 3) Foster, J (1993) Ice-cream makers caught in cold war, *The Independent*, 10 August, p 5.

However, such requirements do not automatically remove favouritism, it simply requires it to be justified in terms acceptable to the system. In that sense it could drive the use of reward power underground, cloaked in a veil of half-truth and thinly disguised justification.

Managers can easily send the wrong signals about what behaviours are valued by inadvertently rewarding inappropriate behaviours. Paying considerable attention to difficult or troublesome employees can indicate to good employees that it does not *pay* to be well behaved. Managers who occasionally allow poor quality work to be despatched clearly indicate that good quality is not always important. In general terms such inadvertent rewarding of undesirable behaviour reinforces the idea that individuals should *play the system*, taking an instrumental view of work.

✦ Legitimate power. In any organization most people accept that managers have legitimate authority to exercise power. There are three main sources of this form of authority (Luthans, 1995, p 323). First, the accepted social structures within a society provide certain groups with a legitimate basis for exercising power. It might be a ruling family or a class of people that perform that role. Second, cultural values can also create a basis for claiming *legitimate power* through the veneration of particular classes or individuals. For example, old people often become significant leaders, or men play a dominant role in society. Third, *legitimate power* can be delegated. Managers are acting on behalf of the owners of an organization in running the business on their behalf. In doing so they hold delegated power from the owners.

Handy (1993) suggests that holding *legitimate power* provides automatic access to three invisible assets. First, information, which as a commodity can be directed, channelled and traded by power holders. Second, rights of access to a number of different networks. The significance of networking cannot be underestimated. Heald (1984) examines many different networks along with the principles and practices that guide them. The value and growth of women-only networks (using the Internet) is described by Ashley (2000). Third, the right to organize. With legitimate power comes the right to decide what and how things should be done. Management in Action 19.5 illustrates some of the implications of legitimate power in the sometimes uneasy relationship between academics and the organizations that fund jobs within universities.

Stop | Consider	*What are the ethical issues raised by MiA 19.5 and how would you deal with them? What does your previous answer imply about the role of ethics in relation to power?*

+ Expert power. This originates from the knowledge, skill and expertise of the holder. The pilot of an aeroplane is the one with the appropriate skills to fly it and consequently everyone goes where the pilot decides. Within management, technical specialists often have greater knowledge than the line managers that they are supposed to be supporting and so have considerable influence. Claims to be an expert are however subject to validation by the group over whom the expertise is being claimed. Failure to deliver the results of claimed expertise can be dealt with severely by the group who will feel that their trust has been violated, that they have been conned and let down badly.

+ Referent power. This is about the characteristics of an individual. It could be that the individual is of celebrity status and so attracts others to join them and follow their wishes. Religious and political leaders are frequently charismatic and so attract many follows only too willing to follow every word and instruction. Advertisers continually utilize this perspective in using models, stars and personality figures to sell products through association and/or emulation.

There is also a sixth form of power that is different in nature from the others, but can have a significant impact on events (Handy, 1993, p 131):

+ Negative power. This form of power impacts through not doing something that should be done. For example, a post room employee who is dissatisfied with their job could quickly cause confusion throughout the organization by deliberately misdirecting the post for a few days. It is the ultimate revenge of the *little people* within the organization.

These sources of power provide the basis of the ability to influence the behaviour and

MANAGEMENT IN ACTION 19.5

Dons learn that 'freedom' has a bottom line

It is common practice for academic posts to be sponsored by commercial organizations. Most of the time this does not pose a problem for any of the parties involved: university, sponsor, the individual academic or the wider community. However, there have been occasions when this set of relationships has been put at risk for various reasons. Perhaps not surprisingly this has been most keenly observed among accounting academics. Jack provides several examples of what can happen when 'the world outside intersects with university life'.

In one example Mr Prem Sikka, from the University of East London, wrote to the Chartered Association of Certified Accountants questioning the voting procedures for an election in which he was unsuccessful. The correspondence between the two grew to an amazing half-inch thick. However, most significantly the Association wrote to the vice-chancellor seeking to find out if the university endorsed Mr Sikka's views. This was seen by Mr Sikka as an attempt to put pressure on him from above. Mr Anthony Booth, director of standards for the Association, explained that, had the institution endorsed Mr Sikka's views then a review of the accreditation of courses offered by the university might have taken place, as these depended to a significant extent on trust between the parties.

Another case described by Jack was that of David Cooper, one time Price Waterhouse professor of accounting at UMIST. In 1984, during the year-long national miners' strike in the UK, he published an article alleging 'misinformation' in the National Coal Board's assessment of the viability of its coal mines. One member of the board expressed indignation and the editorial practice of the journal in question was reviewed. Cooper

also claims to have been telephoned by one of the partners at Price Waterhouse (they had also been appointed sequestrators to the National Union of Mineworkers). Cooper recalls the conversation with the partner thus: 'He screamed at me about causing the firm severe embarrassment and how could we bite the hand that fed us and how Price Waterhouse would continue to fund the chair over his dead body.' The partner concerned (by now retired) was asked for a response by Jack and he said: 'I did have words. It was an irritation. We were just concerned that he didn't start impinging on our activities. We were trying to keep a low profile.'

This is not a problem unique to the UK. In the USA Abe Briloff, emeritus professor of accounting at Baruch College in New York, faced a defamation suit brought against him in 1976 by Saul Steinberg. The professor had written a critical article about Steinberg's work as a corporate raider. Most academics would claim to adopt a responsible attitude to such matters. For example, Christopher Nobes, Coopers & Lybrand professor of accounting at Reading University, indicated:

> Maybe sometimes a professor might feel constrained from saying things because they are worried what the firm or its clients might think, or the professor doesn't like what the firm says. I have sometimes not done things because of my link with Coopers. I have never said something I don't believe. Sometimes I have not said things I do believe. That's merely being responsible.

Adapted from: Jack, A (1993) Dons learn that 'freedom' has a bottom line, *Financial Times*, 9 December, p 14.

actions of others. What they do not do is provide an indication of how that power is converted into influence. It is the mechanisms or tactics described in Table 19.1 that provide the operationalization of power.

Power and decision making

Decision making and politics are inextricably entwined within organizational activity. Many decision-making approaches assume rational behaviour on the part of the participants. Politics also influences the ability to implement a solution. Former President of the United States of America Richard Nixon wrote in 1982: 'It is not enough for a leader to *know* the right thing. He must be able to *do* the right thing. … The great leader needs … the capacity to achieve' (p 5).

Being able to ensure that a particular course of action is followed requires both power and political expertise. This is most clearly identified in the sphere of national and local politics. The hugely successful British television series and books under the title of 'Yes, Minister' and 'Yes, Prime Minister' found much of their appeal in illustrating the political management of the elected politicians by civil servants. After the British election campaign of May 1997 much debate centred on the ability of the newly elected Labour government to implement its election promises irrespective of opposition through the scale of its majority in the House of Commons. This despite any experience of real political power for the previous 18 years while they were in opposition.

Pfeffer (1992) identifies three aspects of decision making that provide for the concept of power to be incorporated into the processes. They are:

+ Decisions change nothing. Taking a decision does not automatically imply that it will be acted upon. New Year resolutions are a clear example of decisions to take actions in one's own life which invariably last about one week. In addition to a *decision science* it is necessary to understand *implementation science*.

+ Decision quality requires retrospective assessment. It is not possible to judge the value of a decision until after the event. It is only with the benefit of hindsight that any realistic evaluation can be made.

+ Significance duration. Pfeffer points out that the impact of any decision invariably lasts longer than the time taken to reach the decision in the first place. This perspective has led some psychologists to suggest that human beings are *rationalizing* rather than *rational* (Aronson, 1972). It also provides a link with *cognitive dissonance* as discussed in an earlier chapter.

One of the consequence of this perspective on decision making is that it reflects a stream rather than discrete processes. A decision is taken and then implemented. Consequences then flow from that. Some of the results will be desired, others will be undesirable or were not anticipated and so further decisions are required. In addition, circumstances around the decision could also change, or the decision could have been wrong in the first place. Whatever the cause, there are many reasons which require decision making to be regarded a continuous process. It also allows for power to influence the three aspects of decision making indicated earlier.

So far this discussion has been about *decision science* aspects and has largely ignored the *implementation* issues. Within commercial organizations it is largely assumed that power is directly correlated with level in the hierarchy. While that may be true to some extent it reflects a vast oversimplification of the nature of organizational power and its practice. The trade union representatives in some organizations hold more power than many of the line managers, at least reflected in the ability to influence employees. The other sources of power identified earlier also form part of the dynamic of organizational behaviour and its influence on decision making. For example, managers rarely work in isolation, it is necessary for other people to be involved on many occasions. For instance, an accounting department may create a policy on expense claims, but it is other individuals who must comply with the system if it is to work. Management in Action 19.6 illustrates this and the use of negative power with regard to the completion of expense claims within one large organization.

Is MiA 19.6 about negative power, or is about incompetent management, or does it reflect a group of staff seeking to retain a practice that was able (unfairly) to provide them with high levels of expense allowance?
Does this distinction matter? Why or why not?

Managers must engage in co-operative behaviour in ensuring that their decisions are acted upon. The personnel department of a company would find it hard to implement a new remuneration system if other managers refused to allow employees time to write job descriptions or attend meetings to evaluate jobs. Competing priorities are frequently cited as the reason for one department or manager not being able to help another, the net result being that a particular decision may not be implemented, irrespective of the intentions of senior managers. An opposing view is that managers should always follow orders, as in the military. However, what if the *orders* are deficient? The danger in highly centralized structures in which real power is restricted to a few people at the top of the organization is that it can be abused. The late Robert Maxwell was an illustration of the ability of one individual to use various forms of power and bullying to centralize control for their own purposes.

Pfeffer (1992) identifies seven decision issues that should be considered as part of the process of decision making (see Table 19.2). Of course, not every decision requires the exercise of power in order to be successfully implemented. If the contributors are actively in favour of the decision or even if it is within their *zone of indifference* it is unlikely to require much application of power to influence events. The zone of indifference refers to an area of impact on an individual below the threshold at which they will respond negatively.

There have been attempts to create a contingency model of power by bringing together the work of French and Raven as already described and the work of Kelman. Luthans (1995) brings together these ideas in a model, to which has been added the levels of analysis perspective of Fincham (1992). The resulting contingency model is reflected in a simplified form in Figure 19.1.

In the contingency approach to power there exists a relationship between the sources of power and the responses generated as a consequence of specific conditions and motivation to respond in particular ways. For example, with a power source based on reward, a compliance reaction is likely to be created if the target person seeks to avoid punishment or to make a favourable impression. To be successful the power holder must have the ability to deliver the reward as well as the punishment for failure.

It was argued in Chapter 17 that empowerment and other forms of involvement

MANAGEMENT IN ACTION 19.6

Reasonable expenses

This is a true story that has been changed slightly to protect both the organization and its employees. The essential facts, however, remain the same. The company concerned was in the service sector and employed several hundred field-based staff. The primary duties of these staff involved travelling to client organizations and carrying out work at those locations. This could involve a short visit of about two hours or anything up to two weeks of travelling daily to the same location. Clearly this process involved considerable amounts of travelling and high levels of expense claim.

The company concerned paid staff a mileage allowance for each mile travelled on company business. The distance used as the basis of payment was the smaller of either the actual distance travelled or the distance to the visit from the office at which the member of staff was based. This was generally regarded as a fair system by staff as it allowed for the normal travel to work distance each day.

In an attempt to save money senior management decided that any distance travelled to visit a client which involved the individual travelling over part of the normal route to the office would also be discounted for expense purposes. This was

seen as both complex and unfair by the staff concerned. It also involved keeping more records of distance and routes travelled.

As a consequence staff adopted a number of strategies in response to this instruction. One of the most effective was to find and use minor roads when visiting clients in areas near to the normal route to the office. Another involved changing visiting routines to find reasons to attend the office when visits involved distances which would be longer than if done directly from home. Managers became confused about the new rules and would sign expense claims only to have them rejected by the accounts department on a technicality. This led to severe delays in payment as queries were resolved.

Very quickly it was recognized that the cost of administration of the scheme was increasing rapidly, as was the level of expense claim. Eventually the old rule was reinstated. In other words, by following the new scheme and using some ingenuity employees were able to exercise negative power and frustrate the intentions of senior management.

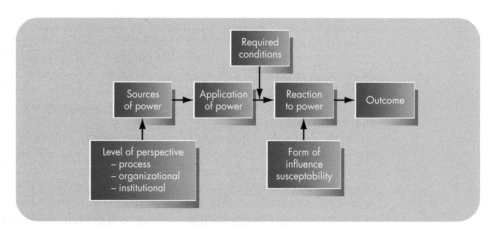

FIGURE 19.1 Contingency model of power.

contain elements of power and control. One possibility in situations where power is an obvious element within the employment relationship is that employees will simply comply or conform. In Etzioni's (1975) terms they might adopt an *alienative* or *calculative* (instrumental) response. Clearly in today's world of lean, delayered and high-performing organizations these responses are not desirable. Empowering and otherwise involving employees can be a way of encouraging them to *buy into* or *adopt* the underlying values of management. Employees with the same value set as managers would be easier to manage and would think in the same terms as managers. This can be thought of as eliminating the need for power in the employment relationship. Equally, it can be described in terms of substituting internalized forms of self-control for the less effective outward forms. In effect, relying on covert rather than overt forms of power application – power by socialization.

Power as part of the decision-making process is frequently associated with political behaviour. Individual managers frequently seek power as a means to further their careers and enhance the position of their departments. This relationship was also identified in the work of McClelland on motivation. This was reviewed in an earlier chapter when the nPow concept associated with the need for power within the individual was discussed. The acquisition of power is something that some managers seek and is associated strongly with a tendency to function politically.

Control within organizations

There are many definitions of control. One of the simplest is that provided by Dunford (1992), in which it is described as a process which, 'involves attempts to bring about desired outcomes' (p 243). This definition should immediately suggest a connection with the subject of power. Power is frequently used as the means through which to be able to exercise control over something or someone. Within an organization there are two distinct and opposite aspects to the existence of control. First, it provides the basis of order and predictability in operational activity. Processes need to be *under control* if the product or service is to be delivered consistently to the customer with acceptable quality and at a realistic price. This is the view of control which defines the responsibilities of senior managers as suggested in Management in Action 19.7.

1	Decide what your goals are, what you are trying to accomplish
2	Diagnose patterns of dependence and interdependence; what individuals are influential and important in your achieving your goal?
3	What are their points of view likely to be? How will they feel about what you are trying to do?
4	What are their power bases? Which of them is more influential in the decision?
5	What are your bases of power and influence? What bases of influence can you develop to gain more control over the situation?
6	Which of the various strategies and tactics for exercising power seem most appropriate and are likely to be effective, given the situation you confront?
7	Based on the above, choose a course of action to get something done

TABLE 19.2 Power and decision making (*source*: Pfeffer, J (1992) *Managing with Power*, Harvard Business School Press, Boston, MA)

MANAGEMENT IN ACTION 19.7

Tightening the reins on risk

The collapse of Barings Bank resulting from the actions of one trader in an office on the other side of the world is every manager's nightmare. It was an event which forced the issue of control and risk assessment to the forefront of management thinking. There have been a number of committees that have considered the issue of corporate control and most have suggested (among other things) that its review and development should form part of the board's responsibility on a regular basis. In these days of flatter and leaner organizations, however, it is not uncommon to find managers seeking to replace formal control systems with a reliance on 'appropriate' and 'responsible' forms of employee behaviour.

Following downsizing activity over the last few years there are not as many people actually working within organizations. Generally speaking, control systems are not regarded as 'added value' activities and so come to be regarded as a potential source of saving. It is sometimes argued that if employees and managers had the 'right' values and attitudes (whatever they may be) then they would effectively self-control. For example, some surveys have shown that the morale of managers could have a material impact on the level of fraud within a company. If this 'appropriate behaviour' could be achieved and assuming that the form of self-control achieved was in align-

ment with what management wanted, the need for formal control systems would be eliminated or at least severely reduced. However, a number of people argue that this is not practical or viable as a basis for protecting the organization against fraud or simple bad decision making. Sensible control processes are needed which balance the need for employees to be able to apply common sense with the need to protect the business.

Risk assessment is the emerging discipline which specializes in the identification and evaluation of the possible dangers that exist in and around the organization. The application of scenario planning which asks the question 'What would happen if …?' is the basis of this approach. However, to apply it effectively needs a thorough understanding of the business and its operations. It also needs to be applied across all aspects of the business, not just at the level of 'What would happen if the electricity supply to the computers was interrupted?' It also requires directors to question what they are told and not just assume that everything is as it appears.

Adapted from: Atkins, R (1995) Tightening the reins on risk, *Financial Times*, 22 March, p 12.

Stop | Consider

An old saying common within the field of management consultancy is: 'Believe nothing of what you are told and only half of what you see!' How might this philosophy be built into a management control system?

This saying suggests that managers should not trust anyone or anything within an organization. How can this position be reconciled with the view that suggests that people are an organization's greatest asset?

Second, there is the opposing perspective that control is restrictive, lacks flexibility, is manipulative and greedy with regard to the abolition of personal freedom. It could be argued that many initiatives on employee involvement and participative management are covert attempts to find ways of retaining control within an illusion of freedom for the individual. These initiatives are frequently expressed as an encouragement to go beyond the contract and enjoy a new partnership with managers in developing a mutually prosperous and fulfilling future. The net effect, however, being the exercise of more subtle forms of control intended to minimize the risk of conflict and maximize contribution. This is related to the view of power indicated earlier which suggested that by allowing some controlled erosion of total power, effective control is retained by management.

It has been suggested by Huczynski and Buchanan (1991, p 579) that control has three connotations. First, it is necessary as an *economic* activity, critical to the success of the organization. Second, it represents a *psychological* necessity in order to eliminate the ambiguity, unpredictability and disorder that would prevent individuals from operating effectively within the organization. Third, it represents a *political* process in which some individuals and groups are able to exercise control over less fortunate groups. It possible to identify a fourth purpose that control serves in addition to the three just identified, that is its *physical* connotations. A brief description of each is provided below:

✦ Physical. At the detailed control level jobs, processes and machines need to be organized and controlled effectively if they are to combine to produce the goods and services required (Edwards, 1986). Frequently, the physical level of control involves record keeping, measuring activity and checking actual performance against that intended.

✦ Economic. As an economic process control is geared towards achieving the financial objectives of the organization. It is not just the detailed control described above. It represents the micro level co-ordination and planning of activity along with the macro level directional planning necessary to achieve the financial returns to ensure that investors and other stakeholders remain satisfied.

✦ Psychological. This process represents both the need among individuals to function within a predictable environment and the inherent need that some individuals have to either control or be controlled. In its broadest sense management can be described as a controlling activity. That some individuals seek elevation to these positions can be taken as evidence of their desire to exercise control over resources. There are individuals who for many reasons do not gain promotion within organizations. Some do not have the opportunity, others do not have the confidence or the inclination. Still others perceive promotion as selling out to the owning 'classes' or perhaps they achieve fulfilment through other aspects of their life. Whatever the reason subordinates psychologically accept the right to be controlled by others.

✦ Political. Control provides the means by which existing structures and social conditions can be reinforced. Owners of capital insist on their pre-eminent right to ultimate determination of organizational existence. If an organization does not make money then the owners, creditors and banks retain the right to liquidate the assets irrespective of the impact on the non-owning stakeholders. That represents the ultimate political control. Of course accountants would argue that an uneconomic business must fail, but this represents the exercise of a particular perspective and the case could be argued otherwise. A different economic picture might emerge if the social costs of closure were to be taken into account, for example.

There are other political perspectives to control. For example, through the exercise of political skill a departmental manager may be able to increase their own significance and importance within an organization, thereby being able to exercise control over a greater

MANAGEMENT IN ACTION 19.8

Thou shalt not cook the books

The finances of English cathedrals provides a fascinating opportunity to study accountancy practice. The Cathedrals Measure of 1963 required the accounts of the 42 Anglican cathedrals to be published each year. However, it provided little guidance on the form that the accounts should take and the Church Commissioners do not examine them in any detail. Most cathedrals operate as charities and need considerable sums of money to maintain them. But as Mr Malcolm Hoskins of Touche Ross suggested: 'Like any other charity, if anything the incentive is not to appear too financially healthy.' He should know, he has audited cathedral accounts and serves on a working party set up by the Association of English Cathedrals to identify how to present financial information fairly and consistently.

One member of a commission set up in 1992

by the Archbishop of Canterbury to examine the management of church resources said: 'Cathedral accounting is disgraceful. It's a fascinating aspect of medieval life. They get up to every trick in the book.'
He described the use of off-balance sheet finance and undeclared trusts as ways to conceal the true wealth of cathedrals from the church hierarchy. Deans and canons are in an impregnable position in a cathedral as, once appointed, they become a 'corporation spiritual' and immune to any earthly power but God. Perhaps, that is, until the controlling power of the accounting profession reaches out and lays its hand on them!

Adapted from: Jack, A (1993) Thou shalt not cook the books, *Financial Times,* 17 December, p 9.

range of resources. Management in Action 19.8 illustrates this and other aspects of control within an unusual context.

Stop | Consider

To what extent do the accounting practices of cathedrals as described in MiA 19.8 raise ethical issues about power and control, or do they simply reflect shrewd management practice in seeking to maximize income?
Does the answer to the previous question matter and if so in what ways?

Form and characteristics of control

Control and organization are inextricably linked. It has been argued (Thompson, 1989) that it was a desire for increased control by owners that formed a significant part of the movement towards the factory system of production in the eighteenth century. Under the *putting-out* system owners could not directly and closely control the activities of workers and the development of the factory system was intended to change that situation. Table 19.3 reflects some of the major levers of control that functioned under the putting-out system. It can be seen from that information that although the owners had considerable power in the process, it tended to be retrospective. So, for example, they could withhold work, but this would only be done if there was a reason, such as a lack of orders or the quality of work was poor. But by the time that action had been taken the owner would have given out raw material and perhaps machines etc. so incurring cost and delay. Equally if the quality of finished work was poor and the owner rejected it, refusing to pay for raw material would have been used and time lost. The factory system was designed to provide greater levels of control and predictability in the production process and in a way which minimizes loss and cost of operations.

So although the control *levers* indicated in Table 19.3 would appear to provide a sound basis for the effective operation of a business this is not so compared with factory-based systems of production. A factory system provided the owners with an opportunity to exercise an immediate *in-process* level of control. For example, it became possible to break the manufacturing process down into small parts and to create jobs requiring low skill levels. Lower skill levels are directly associated with cheaper labour and reduced unit labour costs. Equally, the pace and methods of work could be directly controlled in a factory, increasing the output per worker and further reducing labour costs. The factory system also increased the level of *dependency* of the workers on the owners, so providing greater social control as well. The factory as a building provided what Foucault describes as an opportunity for managers to observe, know and therefore control, effectively creating the reality within which the workers should work and live.

Very little control takes the overt form of force or pressure. It is usually incorporated into the fabric of the organization, management practice and indeed society. Becoming part of the experience of what would be considered *normal* it is not subjected to question by those to whom it is being applied. If control is defined in terms of the ability to determine the behaviour of others it makes sense to exercise it in such a way that obviates the likelihood of conflict. Creating an acceptance of the normality and necessity for control mechanisms is one way of achieving this. The main forms of organizational control are now discussed.

Output control

This is based on the premise that if the output achieved is as predicted, then the *system* is under control. It is the *management-by-exception* process that posits that managers should function on the basis of defining in advance what should occur, provide the resource to deliver that requirement and subsequently manage the deviations from that intention. It is argued that it is a waste of valuable time and resource to monitor and review things that are going according to plan. The difficulty is that reports can be falsified or presented in such a way as to disguise the true situation. That is partly the message carried in Management in Action panels 19.7 and 19.8.

Allocation	the ability to allocate or withhold work
Price	the ability to reduce the price paid to workers in order to pressure them into producing more in order to maintain earnings
Quality	the ability to reject (and therefore not pay) for work not of an acceptable standard
Machine	in some instances owners provided workers with the equipment necessary to perform the tasks and so controlled production methods

TABLE 19.3 Control under the 'putting-out' system

Process control

This form of control reflects the mirror image of the previous approach in that it relies on monitoring and controlling the *means rather than the ends*. It is premised on the view that it is necessary to control the detail and process aspects of operational activity in order to ensure that the objectives are achieved. It represents the traditional bureaucratic approach to organizational activity. Procedures determine in detail what should be done within the *system* and yet more procedures determine and report on events as they occur. In practice this can be an expensive approach to control and it provides fertile ground for business process re-engineering and other techniques to eliminate what is seen as non-value adding activity.

Work design

In terms of the ability to control activity in the workplace the design of jobs is a key determinant. The way that the tasks to be undertaken are clustered together into jobs reflects a major feature of organizational life. However, it is also a reflection of the intentions of management in relation to how they view the business and the need to *control* activity in relation to the desired objectives. For example, the specialization of work in a hospital into such categories as nursing, physiotherapy, hotel services and administration allows high skill levels to be developed across a relatively narrow range of tasks. Thereby productivity can be achieved in a *factory*-type of hospital configuration. As such it provides the possibility of tighter control of the overall process and its associated cost. The *paradigm* adopted by management significantly determines the approach to issues of control and work organization according to writers such as Morgan (1986).

Structure

Much of the work design issues follow from and contribute to the way in which the organization is structured. It is the approach to compartmentalization of activity that provides the opportunity to control through specialization. It also allows managers to be able to simplify complex activity into meaningful and understandable units. For example, the creation of an accounting department provides the opportunity for the development of efficient, specialized accounting control systems as a consequence of grouping together experts in a particular field. It also provides the more senior managers with the knowledge that accounting issues are the responsibility of that department and that they have (in theory) no bias towards other functions in reporting accounting data. The *compartments* provide a clarity in relating to the complexity of organizational activity, particularly from a *top-down* perspective. Consider the difficulty of attempting to understand and manage a university if it were not compartmentalized into student records, library, teaching etc. Unfortunately, as effective as this top-down perspective might be for the senior people within the organization, they are not the customers. Tighter and more effective vertical control can therefore be achieved at the cost of customer experience and satisfaction. These two often conflicting requirements represent a difficult balance to achieve.

Hierarchy and authority

The owners of the capital are held to be the people who have the ultimate right to determine what happens within an organization. Much of that right is delegated to the board of directors. In large organizations some form of delegation must be introduced. In practice a power-sharing process must be entered into in order to define the relationships between the principle players. As a consequence of these processes a hierarchical arrangement of responsibility and control is introduced into the organization. Individuals explicitly acquiesce to these arrangements when they agree to join the organization. Managers know that they have certain rights to exercise control over their subordinates, again subject to policies and procedures. They are part of a complex web of hierarchy and authority that allows control over activity to be exercised in support of the objectives being sought. This view is reflected in the description of activity in Management in Action 19.9.

Stop	Consider	*To what extent are the concepts of power, control and ethical behaviour mutually exclusive?*
		Justify your views.

It has long been recognized that the direct exercise of authority is not always the most effective way to achieve the desired result. It can create a *compliance*- and *dependency*-based cultural environment. Being *conditioned* to expect that someone in authority will direct every move can result in individuals failing to exercise discretion and common sense in performing their duties. An employee who continued to produce faulty components knowing them to be substandard because they had not been told to stop would serve as an example.

Unless it is a specific requirement then the exercise of direct authority is likely to be resented by subordinates and produce a compliance response (or conflict). It is therefore desirable from a management point of view to avoid these undesirable consequences by softening the application of authority-based control. There are many ways of attempting to achieve this, for example the use of training courses allows managers to inculcate employees with the *preferred value and attitude sets*, thereby seeking to internalize among employees the managerial norms that underpin control. Employees consequently become self-regulating (if the process is successful). Only if employees show dissent would it be likely that formal authority (direct control) becomes the means of achieving the desired result.

In commercial organizations it is increasingly being claimed that with *every pair of hands recruited comes a free brain*, and that this represents the most valuable of the human assets. To capitalize on this managers need to ensure that individuals are liberated from constraint and prepared to contribute to the maximum of their capability. This was introduced in Chapter 17 as employee involvement. Under such operational situations the direct application of control is likely to be counterproductive. It is hardly surprising that middle managers have not been enthusiastic supporters of employee empowerment as it can be described as undermining their traditional authority base. It is also possible that increased control can be achieved by accident. If employees push for greater involvement and as a consequence become more understanding and amenable to management perspectives, greater managerial influence (control) over events will have been achieved (Fells, 1989).

Skill

There are many jobs in which skill or professional status provides an opportunity to exercise control in one form or another. To *know more* than others in the same context is a basis

MANAGEMENT IN ACTION 19.9

Employers cast as partners in crime

Lorenz reports on an article in the *Harvard Business Review* (March/April, 1994) on the nature of ethical behaviour in organizations. It was titled 'Managing for organizational integrity' and was written by Professor Lynn Sharp Paine from Harvard. In the article she argues that corporate misconduct is not usually the result of individual flaws or problems. Unethical business practice, she argues, more frequently reflects the values, attitudes, language and behavioural patterns that define an organization's operating culture.

Paine describes a rush towards 'compliance-based ethics programmes' in order to meet the requirements of US legislation. The magnitude of fines for unlawful conduct partly reflects the degree to which companies have tried to prevent such misconduct. The provision of a rulebook, a code of ethics and training is unlikely to be sufficient on its own to prevent such practices, according to Paine. She suggests that appropriate behaviour will only be encouraged when organizations take an 'integrity-based' approach to ethics. This approach encourages the development of guiding values, aspirations and patterns of thought which support ethically sound

behaviour; in addition a sense of shared account-ability between employees is needed.

One example given by Paine which demonstrates the lack of an integrity-based ethics approach is that involving a car service offshoot of Sears Roebuck in America. The company was accused of misleading customers and selling them unnecessary parts and services. Sears' chief executive accepted management's responsibility for the problem as a result of introducing pay and target-setting processes which encouraged overselling.

This is contrasted with the case of Johnson & Johnson in which all levels of the company quickly and automatically withdrew a particular painkiller from the market after batches were found to have been poisoned. Paine suggests that without a shared set of values and the guiding principles that were ingrained throughout the organization the response would not have been the same.

Adapted from: Lorenz, C (1994) Employers cast as partners in crime, *Financial Times*, 4 March, p 14.

---

for acquiring power and exercising control. Only chartered accountants are able to sign the audit of a set of company accounts. This requirement is intended to provide confidence to investors that the accounts are a true and realistic reflection of the financial position of the company. Such auditors hold considerable power. The degree to which this is a double-edged sword in practice is evident from the number of major accounting practices that are being sued for large sums of money when events come to light not previously identified through an audit.

Technology

Machines can work at a predictable and stable pace until they break down or are switched off. People are not so programmable. As a consequence of the desire of managers to justify the introduction of technology humans are frequently relegated to second place in consideration. It is the technology that *determines* (controls) the human participation in the production process. The work that humans undertake is determined by what the technology cannot tackle and by what is needed to service the ability of the technology to maintain continuous production. This is very real form of control over human endeavour.

It is not just factory work that has been subjected to the influence of control through technology. Clerical, administrative, technical and managerial work has all been influenced and are therefore subject to different forms of control than in the past. For example, in customer service teams it is common to find that the technology providing improved ability to serve the customer also provides the opportunity to manage the performance of staff more effectively. Telephone calls are recorded for subsequent analysis, call rates and queue waiting statistics are automatically generated.

Social control

There are many forms of *social control*, including those institutions provided by the state, the police, law and other government agencies. In addition, and of particular relevance to an organizational setting are institutions such as the education system which is intended to prepare children and young people for the world of work. Within an organization there are the induction, training, development, performance appraisal, pay, promotion and career development activities which all provide a basis for shaping behaviour patterns in management preferred ways.

Clegg and Dunkerley (1980) describe the impact of control as provoking a *vicious circle* reinforcing the need for ever tighter means of control. This arises as a consequence of the continually constricting influence of control on employees and of their reaction in terms of increased dissatisfaction thereby reinforcing the perception of managers and creating the need for more direct control. Figure 19.2 reflects the essence of their model.

It is the danger of creating the downward spiral of ever tighter control leading to less real or meaningful contribution from employees that leads to organizations attempting to introduce involvement strategies. The hope being that involved employees would internalize the need for the control being sought by managers and so respond positively.

Power, control and resistance

Resistance to the exercise of power is not new. It was Marx who linked the ideas of revolution and the overthrow of capitalism as the natural response of workers to the

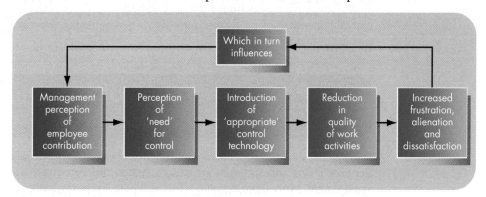

FIGURE 19.2 Vicious cycle of control (*adapted from*: Clegg, S and Dunkerley, D (1980) *Organizational Class and Control*, Routledge & Kegan Paul, London)

unequal power and levels of control inherent in it. The exploitation of labour in the capitalist system of production would inevitably result in revolution as the workers sought to resist and achieve a socialist state. Conflict as a concept will be covered in the next chapter and so will not be fully developed here. However, it represents only one form of resistance found within any organization.

It has already been suggested that overt forms of control and attempts to exert power would be likely to be met with some form of resistance. However, resistance is not something that might find expression immediately. Braverman (1974, p 151) suggested in the context of developing the *labour process theory*, that the reaction of workers to the degradation of work forced upon them would, 'continue[s] as a subterranean stream that makes its way to the surface when employment conditions permit, or when the capitalist drive for a greater intensity of labor oversteps the bounds of physical and mental capacity'.

In short, the workers will pick their time for reacting to the exercise of power and control. When that will be depends either on the existence of the right economic conditions (e.g. low unemployment levels or an urgent order needing special treatment) or if the level of pressure gets too great. Of course this view of resistance is based upon the existence of what Marx and others call *class consciousness*. In other words, a natural working-class reaction to their exploitation under capitalist forms of production once they become aware of it. There are other forms of resistance reflecting the day-to-day reactions of employees and managers to their experience of work.

There are many apocryphal as well as true stories of resistance in many forms and in many organizations, some of which enter the realms of folk history and legend. For example just about everyone who has worked in an office must have been told of the secretary of the rude and difficult boss who sought revenge by spitting in his (they usually were male) coffee and smiling sweetly at the praise for its being made perfectly! More formally, managers can resist the implementation of instructions from more senior managers by claiming that they don't have the necessary resources or other tasks have a higher priority. Workers can strike or even leave an organization if they do not like the way it is run or the way in which power and control are exercised. Sabotage and whistleblowing are other forms of resistance to the effects of how power and control are being exercised within the organization.

LaNuez and Jermier (1994) review episodes of sabotage by managers and technocrats and suggest that it could be significantly linked to reduced levels of power and privileges in managerial and technical specialist types of work. In essence they argue that such job holders are moving away from alignment with the objectives of the capital owners who are generally in search of profit maximization, whereas managers want security, career progression and growth.

Power and control: an applied perspective

The way in which power and control functions within an organizational context is very complex. Power and authority are closely aligned concepts and are integral to aspects of management. With organizational status and position in the hierarchy comes the right to have others follow your instructions. Managers without power are likely to have little influence on the organization for which they work. It is the close relationship between power and influence within a management context that provides a perfect breeding ground for the political behaviour that forms a major theme in the next chapter.

Etzioni (1975) first provided a categorization for the basis of power as normative (based on legitimacy of authority), utilitarian (based on the payment of inducements) or coercive (based on the ability to apply sanction). It is through the application of the last two categories that the potential for the misuse of power and political behaviour is created.

However, it is also important to recognize that there are three caveats to the use of power in an organization. They are:

✦ Balance. Only on very rare occasions is there a complete imbalance in the power held between the parties to a particular situation. Pushed too hard employees may feel that they have nothing to lose, withdrawing their labour by going on strike or seeking alternative work. The degree of care and attention that an employee pays to their work is largely a matter for them to decide. Managers are not in a position to control every aspect of work all of the time. Employees who feel they have no meaningful stake in an organization are likely to become *alienated*, to *resist* and to apply *negative power* to the disadvantage of management.

✦ Domain. Few sources of power are likely to be valid across time and in every context. For example, an employer may be able to force down the price of labour when there is little alternative work for employees. However, employers are generally unable to restrict the movement of jobs into areas that have cheap labour available. As a result, labour costs will inevitably rise and employees will the apply classic economic principle of going to the highest bidder by moving employers.

✦ Relativity. The application of power is only possible if the source is of value to the target person or group. For example, an organization that does not value personnel management skills is unlikely to listen to the advice offered by such specialists and therefore the function would have little power in that situation.

Kotter (1977) identified a number of characteristics shared by those managers who were able to use and manage power effectively, including:

✦ Sensitivity. They are able to understand the feelings of others as to how power is obtained and used.

✦ Intuitive. They have an intuitive feel for how to acquire and use power across a wide range of contexts. They also recognize that in making use of power that it is people that are influenced by it, not just objects.

✦ Repertoire. They have a wide repertoire of power sources on which to call.

✦ Career. Some jobs are naturally more powerful than others and they gravitate towards these positions by actively seeking them out.

✦ Investment. Managers who are able to make effective use of power tend to regard it as an investment. It is not a static resource, it can be grown, harvested and squandered. Through careful husbandry all the resources available to an individual can be used to grow the power available to them.

✦ Maturity. The naked use of power and crude attempts to acquire it are quickly transparent to most, who then resist it. To be most effective power needs some support (or at least little resistance – *the zone of indifference*) from those exposed to it and so a mature approach to it is more likely to produce positive results for the individual practising it.

It has been argued (Braverman, 1974) that the organizational history of the twentieth century can be described in terms of increasing management control and the potential for conflict and *alienation* that flows from it. This neatly encapsulates the fundamental dilemma that exists from a management perspective. The scale of international business, the level of competition, the differential costs of operations around the world and many other forces all create conditions in which there is continual pressure for improved organizational performance. Inevitably, this dynamic leads managers to seek ever greater levels of control over every aspect of the enterprise in order to achieve greater added value from it. Braverman makes it clear that the price for this increased control is that employees experience greater levels of *alienation*. They are increasingly treated as just one of the resources available to managers and, consequently, subject to manipulation.

For managers, control contains different connotations depending upon such factors as the seniority and job function of the individual. For example, a chief executive should not be concerned with control over the purchase of pens. They should, however, assure themselves that someone is exercising control over the purchase and use of consumables. A production supervisor would be expected to exercise detailed control over day-to-day production activities. They would not be expected to opine on the strategic direction of the business, that would be regarded the preserve of senior managers. Control in an organization is a fragmented function, distributed across the members according to level and function. This could be taken to imply a rational and planned process, determined by some all-seeing and omnipotent senior manager applying appropriate models to achieve effective control. Such models do indeed exist. Figure 19.3 is representative of this view, based upon Dent and Ezzamel (1995).

However, even within models such as included as Figure 19.3 there is limited recognition of the realities of organizational life. The data essential for control purposes may not exist; even if they do exist they may not be accurate or available at the appropriate time.

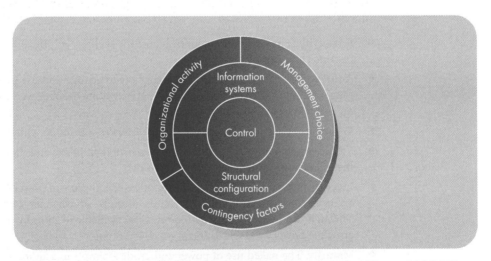

FIGURE 19.3 The organizational control 'onion' (*adapted from*: Dent, J and Ezzamel, M (1987) Organizational control and management activity. In Ezzamel, M and Hart, H (eds) *Advanced Management Accounting: An Organizational Emphasis*, Cassell, London.

The style of management and decision making are also variables that influence control activities. In addition, there are the power and political processes that operate and which can influence both the control processes themselves and the interpretation of the data emerging from them. Like all aspects of management the design of control systems, the interpretation of data and the subsequent actions following from the analysis are social processes. As a consequence they are subject to all of the foibles, idiosyncrasies and other influences associated with individual and collective human behaviour. Management in Action 19.10 describes one such situation in which there were a number of forces, not all rational, acting upon a particular situation.

Stop | Consider

To what extent does MiA 19.10 imply that it is not possible to control through numbers and systems, but that it reflects a social process involving shared frames of reference? What might this imply about the process of management within organizations?

Drawing on the earlier work of Edwards (1986), Blyton and Turnbull (1994) identify a major problem for employers in relation to the *wage–work* bargain with employees. It is the last vestige of the ability of employees to resist the attempts of employers to exercise absolute control and to be able to adjust the level of effort expended in the service of the master. The extended tea break, pace and diligence of work are some of the variables at the disposal of the employee in demonstrating independence from total subjugation to the will of another. Recent managerial approaches can be categorized as attempts to delegate control in such a way as to provide the illusion of independence and encourage self-control. Torrington and Hall (1991) use a hierarchical model of discipline in an organizational context to describe the level of responsibility for ensuring appropriate behaviour (see Figure 19.4).

There are many implications that emerge from considering the nature of discipline as described in Figure 19.4. Defined in terms of behaving in expected ways, discipline can be seen as a means of control. Management discipline is behaviour control achieved through a superior, team discipline is achieved through group norms and influence and self-discipline is achieved through accepting and internalizing the desired behaviours. At the self-

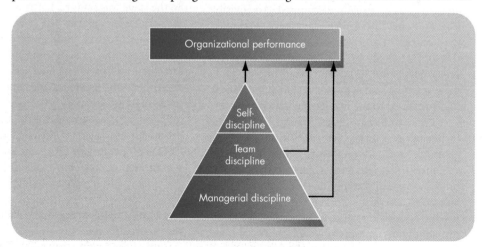

Organizational performance

Self-discipline

Team discipline

Managerial discipline

FIGURE 19.4   The discipline hierarchy (*adapted from*: Torrington, D and Hall, L (1991) *Personnel Management: A New Approach*, 2nd edn, Prentice Hall, Hemel Hempstead).

MANAGEMENT IN ACTION 19.10

Controlling the invisible

This story describes real events that occurred; only the names and location have been changed to protect the individuals concerned. The process involved the preparation of pig carcasses into pork joints and for curing as bacon. The management accountant was responsible for the determination of product costing and required a full breakdown of material and labour data for each process. The work study department were tasked with the job of obtaining and collating the wide variety of data needed for this. A number of studies were undertaken to determine the time taken to perform the work and product weight was checked at each stage of the process. The data collection phase of this exercise lasted for several weeks.

The data were collated and among the various findings was the rather surprising one that each carcass lost weight at each stage of the process. Each carcass was weighed before each process and all processed meat was also weighed (including the small trimmings, bones, etc.). There was always a slight difference between the after-processed weight and the original weight. When this was first discovered it was thought to be due to careless weighing. Considerable effort was made to tighten up on the weighing process and this was eventually discounted. An invisible loss as it became known had been identified. Everyone on the project team was satisfied that this loss (of about 4% of total weight on average) was probably due to moisture leaching out as the meat was being cut. This was included in the findings presented to the management accountant.

The accountant was not happy with the idea of having something that could not be properly accounted for and, even worse, with no physical evidence to see. This went against every belief and professional training for the accountant and he refused to accept the work as the basis of costing product. Something had to be wrong. Meat did not simply become invisible. Of course, the fact that meat is a valuable commodity and the temp-

tation to steal it is an ever present risk in the trade was another factor in the thinking of the accountant. He was being asked to price the company product on the basis that some 4% was disappearing. Over a full year that represented a considerable volume and value of meat. The accountant created a scene within the senior management of the company and demanded that the data be rejected and more tests be done. He even refused to believe the evidence of his own eyes when he was present at a demonstration of the effect.

Clearly, there was a problem associated with the ability to control the processing of meat within this factory that needed to be addressed. It was at this stage that the politics and relative power of the key players began to influence events. The management accountant was not popular as an individual and had upset the production director in the past. He was considered to be pedantic, rude, unhelpful and not part of the senior management team. And that was on a good day! The finance director was a quiet individual who did not have high level of charisma or other natural or status sources of power and influence. So the stage was set for a battle of who would win the argument about the invisible loss. The accountants had a natural advantage in this situation as they had to satisfy the board of directors that the company was being well run. They also determined the product costing upon which sales prices and production costs depended. But the management accountant was in a difficult political position as he had alienated the key players from the operational functions and did not have strong support from his own superior.

After considerable lobbying by all concerned and discussion with various other organizations in the meat industry the management accountant was overruled and the invisible loss became a feature of the costing process.

discipline level of the hierarchy very little management effort is required as employees effectively *police* themselves by delivering that which is expected of them automatically. If this level of the hierarchy can be achieved then the benefits to managers in terms of the reduced cost of management, an improved performance from employees and reduced levels of conflict are considerable. From this perspective, it is hardly surprising that managers have made considerable efforts to ensnare employees into adopting self-managed practices across a wide range of facets of employment. It also leads to the accusation of deceit and manipulation by those who interpret such events as a cynical attempt to take advantage of employees in the pursuit of higher profit levels.

Conclusions

Power and control are important aspects of organizational behaviour. They are inseparable from the needs of organization and the needs, aspirations and inclinations of the individuals that work within them. Power is endemic to the employment relationship. Employers have jobs, individuals need to work for economic, psychological and social reasons. Interestingly, managers are also employees and subject to these same pressures, but within the particular context of acting for the largely absent owners of the organization. Control is needed to ensure that objectives are met. However, as with most other aspects of organizational behaviour they contain the seeds of danger and risk that can cause damage to either individuals or the organization if they are not handled carefully and with respect.

Discussion questions

1. Define the following key terms used in this chapter:

Zone of indifference	*Vicious cycle of control*	*Expert power*
Power	*Control*	*Referent power*
Authority	*Socialization*	*Legitimate power*
Influence	*Forms of control*	*Reward power*
Coercive power	*Negative power*	*Wage–work bargain*

2. Can compliance as an employee response to power and control ever form a basis for the creation of an effective organization? Justify your answer.

3. 'Ultimately everyone has free will and can resist control by others. Consequently power does not exist in reality. Control is therefore a device that provides at best the illusion of order and structure.' Discuss.

4. It is suggested that there is an inevitable power imbalance in the employment relationship and that this can lead to the development of self-defence groupings such as trade unions. Why might this power imbalance exist, is it inevitable and how might it be limited?

5. Describe the main sources of organizational power and provide examples of each from an organization with which your are familiar.

6. 'Employee participation is nothing more than the worst type of confidence trick, played on people who have no opportunity to resist by those who have everything to gain.' Discuss this statement in the light of the material presented in this chapter.

7. Identify the differences and similarities between the concepts of power and influence.

8. Why is the 'zone of indifference' important to the notion of how power and control operate within an organization? Justify your answer.

9. 'The trick in management is to find ways of control that are socially acceptable.' Discuss.

10. Management is ultimately about acquiring and using power successfully. The best leaders are successful politicians. Reconcile these two statements.

Research activities

1. Interview a cross-section of people from different levels of a particular organization. Attempt to incorporate individuals from manual, clerical, administrative, specialist/technical as well as a range of management jobs. Attempt to identify how each group views power and control; which functions are most powerful and why. Is the exercise of power and control in that context beneficial or harmful to the individuals, organization and/or customers? Compare and contrast the views of each group and draw any general conclusions from the results. How do your results compare with the material contained in this chapter?

2. Seek to interview a cross-section of practising managers and trade union officers about the subject of power and control. How do these groups see the concepts and issues differently and what divergence of opinion is there within each group? Attempt to explain these differences in terms of the material covered in this chapter.

3. Identify a range of journals and books from disciplines that might be expected to have some views about power and control. These might include management, sociology, psychology, criminology, politics, military studies and law. How does each of these disciplines treat these concepts and what are the differences and similarities between them? What organizational and managerial implications exist from the range of views identified?

Key reading

From Clark, H, Chandler, J and Barry, J (1994) *Organization and Identities: Text and Readings in Organizational Behaviour*, International Thomson Business Press, London.

✦ Foucault, M: Docile bodies and panopticism, p 35. This offers insight into the forms of social control employed by managers to achieve their objectives.

✦ Foucault, M: The subject and power, p 43. This short extract considers the relationship between power and freedom.

- Bell, D: Work and its discontents, p 44. Time as money, which can be wasted, are examples of how control is related to the experience of capitalism.
- Nichols, T and Beynon, H: The labour of superintendence: managers, p 192. Considers how the social construction of working relationships and the attitudes taken by members of the hierarchy influences the freedom to act.
- Illich, I: Disabling professions, p 207. Reflects on control associated with the existence of professional groups.
- Thompson, EP: Time and work – discipline, p 216. Considers the nature of time and its ability to control much human experience of work.
- Taylor, FW: Scientific management, p 231. Introduces some of Taylor's ideas on the way that work should be organized and controlled.
- Roethlisberger, FJ and Dickson, WJ: Group restriction of output, p 247. This identifies the way that employees manipulate events in an attempt to ensure that they are not at the whim of management.
- Hobsbawm, EJ and Rudé, G: Early forms of worker resistance – swing riots, p 317. This extract demonstrates that those subjected to direct forms of control are liable to resist if they feel that they have nothing to lose.
- Taylor, L and Walton, P: Industrial sabotage, p 321. Sabotage can take many forms, all disruptive, some dangerous or humorous (usually to colleagues or outsiders).
- Höpfl, H *et al.*: Excessive commitment and excessive resentment: issues of identity, p 373. This attempts to reflect on how the concept of commitment was used by one very large organization as a means of introducing change across a wide range of work aspects.
- Braverman, H: The degradation of work, p 385. This considers the effects of control and conflict on individuals through the emergence of degradation.
- Marx, K: Alienated labour, p 387. Introduces some of Marx's views on alienation and its roots in the capitalist nature of work.
- Fromm, E: Alienation, p 391. This introduces another perspective on how work is managed. Implicit are the notions of control and conflict underpinning much management practice.
- Wright Mills, C: The cheerful robot, p 396. This material considers the concept of freedom of the individual in the context of the needs of organization.

Further reading

Adams, A (1992) *Bullying At Work: How to Confront and Overcome It*, Virago, London. This review of the experiences of individuals at work being bullied provides an insight into the darker side of control. The book is written as a guide to the subject and also offers some advice on how to deal with the subject of being bullied at work.

Jay, A (1987) *Management and Machiavelli*, revised edn, Hutchinson Business, London. A humorous text which considers many aspects associated with power and authority in management. It does not take Machiavelli's work specifically as its basis, but his spirit is evident. A translation of Machiavelli's original work, which is very accessible and available as a 1981 Penguin book, is also well worth reading.

Jermier, JM, Knights, D and Nord, WR (eds) (1994) *Resistance and Power in Organizations*, Routledge, London. Provides a review of how attempts to use power as a basis of control inevitably leads to resistance in one form or another. It is grounded in the labour process perspective and attempts to interpret the arguments from the perspectives implied by that model.

Matthews, R (1989) *Power Brokers: Kingmakers and Usurpers Throughout History*, Facts On File, Oxford. Although not a business or management book this text provides a brief insight into the way that power, its acquisition and use has been used by those who would aspire to be political leaders.

Monks, RAG and Minow, N (1991) *Power and Accountability*, HarperCollins, London. This book attempts to show some of the consequences of power when large organizations can operate without the effective means of holding them accountable for their actions. As such it is a chilling reminder of the many ways that power can be abused and trust violated.

Pfeffer, J (1992) *Managing With Power: Politics and Influence in Organizations*, Harvard Business School Press, Boston, MA. This text provides a comprehensive review of the use of power and politics within modern organizations. It considers the organizational, personal and career aspects of these concepts as well as their association with decision making.

References

Ackroyd, S (1994) Re-Creating Common Ground: Elements for Post-Paradigmatic Organization Studies. In Hassard, J and Parker, M (eds) *Towards a New Theory of Organizations*, Routledge, London.

Adams, A (1992) *Bullying At Work: How to Confront and Overcome It*, Virago, London.

Aronson, E (1972) *The Social Animal*, WH Freeman, San Francisco, CA.

Ashley, J (2000) The new girls' network, *Management Today*, September, 72–5.

Barnard, CI (1938) *The Functions of the Executive*, Harvard University Press, Cambridge, MA.

Blyton, P and Turnbull, P (1994) *The Dynamics of Employee Relations*, Macmillan, Basingstoke.

Brannen, P (1983) *Authority and Participation in Industry*, Batsford, London.

Braverman, H (1974) *Labour and Monopoly Capital: The Degradation of Work in the Twentieth Century*, Monthly Review Press, New York.

Briggs, A (1955) *Victorian People: A Reassessment of Persons and Themes 1851–67*, Penguin, Harmondsworth.

Brooks, R, Chittenden, M and Prescott, M (2000) The guilt zone, *Sunday Times*, 10 September.

Burawoy, M (1979) *Manufacturing Consent: Changes in the Labour Process under Monopoly Capitalism*, University of Chicago Press, Chicago.

Clegg, S and Dunkerley, D (1980) *Organization, Class and Control*, Routledge & Kegan Paul, London.

Dent, J and Ezzamel, M (1987) Organizational Control and Management Activity. In Ezzmel, M and Hart, H (eds) *Advanced Management Accounting: An Organizational Emphasis*, Cassell, London.

Dunford, RW (1992) *Organizational Behaviour: An Organizational Analysis Perspective*, Addison-Wesley, Sydney.

Edwards, PK (1986) *Conflict at Work: A Materialist Analysis of Workplace Relations*, Basil Blackwell, Oxford.

Etzioni, A (1975) *A Comparative Analysis of Complex Organizations*, The Free Press, New York.

Fells, RE (1989) The employment relationship, control and strategic choice in the study of industrial relations, *Labour and Industry*, **2**, 470–92.

Fiedler, FE (1967) *A Theory of Leadership Effectiveness*, McGraw-Hill, New York.

Fincham, R (1992) Perspectives on power: processual, institutional and internal forms or organizational power, *Journal of Management Studies*, **29**, 6.

Forsyth, GDR (1993) *Group Dynamics*, 3rd edn, Brooks/Cole, Pacific Grove, CA.

Foucault, M (ed.) (1975) *I Pierre Rivière, having Slaughtered my Mother, my Sister, and my Brother: A Case of Parricide in the 19th Century*, trans F Jellinek, University of Nebraska Press, Lincoln.

Foucault, M (1977) *Discipline and Punish: The Birth of the Prison*, Allen Lane, London.

French, JRP and Raven, B (1968) The Bases of Social Power. In Cartwright, D and Zander, AF (eds) *Group Dynamics: Research and Theory*, 3rd edn, Harper & Row, New York.

Handy, CB (1993) *Understanding Organizations*, 4th edn, Penguin, Harmondsworth.

Heald, T (1984) *Old Boy Networks: Who We Know and How We Use Them*, Ticknor & Fields, New York.

Huczynski, AA and Buchanan, DA (1991) *Organizational Behaviour: An Introductory Text*, 2nd edn, Prentice Hall, Hemel Hempstead.

Kotter, J (1977) *Power, Dependence and Effective Management*, The Free Press, New York.

LaNuez, D and Jermier, JM (1994) Sabotage by Managers and Technocrats: Neglected Patterns of Resistance at Work. In Jermier, JM, Knights, D and Nord, WR (eds) *Resistance and Power in Organizations*, Routledge, London.

Likert, R (1967) *The Human Organization*, McGraw-Hill, New York.

Linstead, S (1993) Deconstruction in the Study of Organizations. In Hassard, J and Parker, M (eds). *Postmodernism and Organizations*, Sage, London.

Lukes, S (1982) *Power: A Radical View*, Macmillan, London.

Luthans, F (1995) *Organizational Behaviour*, 7th edn, McGraw-Hill, New York.

Milgram, S (1965) Some conditions of obedience and disobedience to authority, *Human Relations*, **18**, 57–76.

Morgan, G (1986) *Images of Organization*, Sage, Newbury Park, CA.

Nixon, RM (1982) *Leaders*, Warner, New York.

O'Neill, J (1986) The disciplinary society: from Weber to Foucault, *British Journal of Sociology*, 37, 1, 42–60.

Pfeffer, J (1992) *Managing With Power: Politics and Influence in Organizations*, Harvard Business School Press, Boston, MA.

Rothschild, J and Miethe, TD (1994) Whistleblowing as Resistance in Modern Work Organizations: The Politics of Revealing Organizational Deception and Abuse. In Jermier JM, Knights, D and Nord, WR (eds) *Resistance and Power in Organizations*, Routledge, London.

Thompson, P (1989) *The Nature of Work: An Introduction to Debates on the Labour Process*, 2nd edn, Macmillan, Basingstoke.

Torrington, D and Hall, L (1991) *Personnel Management: A New Approach*, 2nd edn, Prentice Hall, Hemel Hempstead.

Townley, B (1994) *Reframing Human Resource Management: Power, Ethics and the Subject at Work*, Sage, London.

CHAPTER 20

Conflict and organizational politics

CHAPTER SUMMARY

This chapter begins with an introduction to the concepts of conflict and organizational politics. Conflict then becomes the focus of attention in attempting to identify its sources and the forms through which it finds expression. This is followed by consideration of the consequences of conflict within an organizational context. The next topic for review is the major perspectives on the subject of conflict, including the traditional view, labour process theory and resistance. Political behaviour is then examined in relation to is existence within an organization and its relationship with power, control and conflict. This is followed by an exploration of how politics could be used by managers and others. The next section of the chapter considers how political behaviour might be managed. The chapter then concludes with a consideration of the applied perspectives on the topics discussed.

LEARNING OBJECTIVES

After studying this chapter and working through the associated Management in Action panels, Discussion questions and Research activities, you should be able to:

✦ Understand the different perspectives on the concept of conflict.

✦ Describe the sources of conflict within an organization.

✦ Explain the relationship between politics and decision making.

✦ Outline the concept of organizational politics.

✦ Assess the view conflict is not automatically negative in its impact.

✦ Appreciate how political behaviour is used by individuals within organizations.

✦ Discuss how political behaviour can be managed within an organization.

✦ Detail the major conflict handling strategies used within organizations.

Introduction

Conflict frequently arises when the *differences* between two or more groups or individuals become apparent. In industrial relations situations this might occur if a trade union makes a demand for a 10% pay increase and management make an equally forceful case for a 2% increase. However, the existence of *differences* such as these do not automatically lead to *open conflict*. It depends what happens. The large difference in the pay claims of the trade union and the management would be subject to *negotiation* between the parties in an attempt to reach an agreement or acceptable compromise. Only if open argument, disagreement or some form of industrial action resulted would it be said that real *conflict* existed. However, some writers would argue that *latent conflict* is inherent in the use of labour within a capitalist sytem of production.

Therefore, normal use of the term conflict implies a negative and openly hostile situation. Indeed, the first definition of the term in the *Pocket Oxford Dictionary* (1968) is, 'trial of strength between opposed parties or principles'. In an organizational context it is perhaps more appropriate to consider conflict in terms of its *potential* or as a *scale of activity*. In industrial relations terms the need to take into account the potential for conflict in the relationships between managers and employees requires anticipatory behaviour in seeking to develop strategies and practices that minimize the risk. This requirement often leads to forms of partnership and involvement being developed as a means of avoiding the *open conflict* which could lead to strikes and other industrial action intended to force a change in behaviour in the other party. A full discussion of employee involvement has been introduced in a number of previous chapters in relation to ethics, power and control for example.

Concepts that have strong associations with *conflict* are those of *power*, *control* and *politics*. Control can be used to refer to a range of actions, including the mechanistic procedures associated with the control of machine processes. However, it can also refer to the management of the organization on behalf of the principle stakeholders. It can also be used to reflect more sinister processes. It can be taken to reflect the *manipulation* of employee behaviour by managers – *social control*. In that same context control can also be sought through the acquisition of power perhaps through political activity. It might be argued in some situations that this was being done as a means of reducing the likelihood of conflict. For example, employee involvement in the decision-making processes of a company might be introduced because the managers believe in the approach. By the same token, it may be introduced for political reasons because it might be thought of as a means of socializing employees into management preferred attitudes and ways of thinking; thereby reducing the potential for strikes and other forms of conflict. Such managers may anticipate that this approach will enable commercial benefit to be achieved through higher productivity or general employee co-operation with management-determined decisions.

Politics reflect processes found in the behaviour of individuals in the workplace. *Politicking* is frequently described as behaviour outside the accepted procedures and norms, intended to further the position of an individual or group at the expense of others. As such it is frequently identified with undesirable behaviour not intended to advance the interests of the organization. It is most often associated with the attempts of individuals to advance their own careers or to undermine the status and reputation of other departments and people to their personal advantage.

Both concepts of conflict and politics do however contain positive dimensions. For example, the resolution of conflict can allow for genuine differences to be resolved in a dynamic which strengthens the working relationship. Political activity can also be of benefit to the organization. If through the *politicking* of the marketing manager product changes are brought about which in turn provide commercial gains for the organization, then it could be argued that such behaviour was of benefit. It is the 'Janus-faced' nature of both conflict and politics that encourages some writers to describe a *shadow organization* or *shadow themes* within an organization as the point of fusion between the legitimate and the illegitimate in human behaviour. (See for example, Stacey (2000, pp 386–7).)

Sources of organizational conflict

Conflict can be considered as something that disrupts the normal and desirable states of stability and harmony within an organization. Under this definition it is something to be avoided and if possible eliminated from the operation. However, it is also possible to consider conflict as an inevitable feature of human interaction and perhaps something that if managed constructively could offer positive value in ensuring an effective performance within the organization.

There are six major areas within an organization that can give rise to conflict (see Figure 20.1). Each of these sources of conflict will be discussed in the following subsections.

Intrapersonal

This represents the conflicts that arise within the individual. There are many forms in which this can arise, but essentially stems from the choices or decisions that each individ-

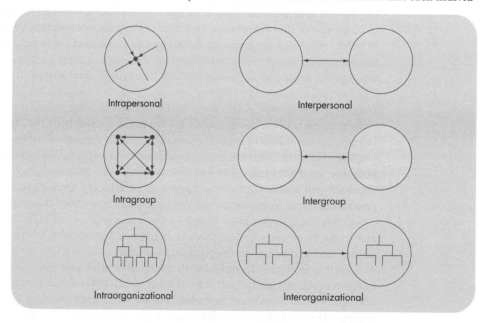

FIGURE 20.1 The major sources of conflict.

ual must make. For example, the ethical dilemmas facing individuals in their work were discussed in Chapter 17. These represent one potential area of conflict for the individual to resolve within themselves. Others internal conflicts are of a less complex nature, for example, to go to work or stay at home when feeling unwell, how much effort to put into the job etc.

Interpersonal

Whetten and Cameron (1991) identify four sources of interpersonal conflict. They are:

+ Personal difference. No two people are exactly alike. It is not possible to like everyone with whom one works and personalities frequently clash.

+ Role incompatibility. The functional nature of work activity creates very real potential for interpersonal conflict. For example, a personnel manager may seek to organize training courses for employees. However, an operations manager with tight production schedules to meet and with no spare labour may resent the efforts of the personnel manager. There exists a high probability of conflict between the two managers in this type of situation.

+ Information deficiency. An individual with access to information is better able to perform more effectively. They also *know* more in Foucault's (1975) terms and are therefore better able to exercise power over the situation and other people. Consequently, information can provoke conflictual relationships between individuals. At a less political level the quality of information provided to a computer system designer could easily become the subject of conflict if subsequently the system does not meet user expectations.

+ Environmental stress. Conflict can become more likely in times of severe competitive pressure. Most organizations have been going through significant periods of downsizing, re-engineering and change over the past decade. As a consequence individuals can find that their ability to retain a job and career is continually under threat. If individuals within the organization feel such threat the environmental conditions exist for fractious relationships and *open conflict*.

Intragroup

One particular context within which interpersonal conflict can be found occurs within a group. The models proposed by Belbin and Margerison and McCann, discussed in the chapters dealing with groups, claim to offer a basis for minimizing the potential for harmful conflict between group members. These models argue that careful selection should provide balance between the necessary skills and personal qualities among group members to allow the task to be achieved effectively without unnecessary friction or conflict. Group activity inevitably brings the characteristics, attitudes and opinions of individual members into focus. The interaction of these variables on the group process and conflict can be reflected in a diagram (Figure 20.2).

Intergroup

Many different groups exist within an organization and inevitably they will experience differences and conflict at some point in time. Employees seek to earn as much money as possible, employers, of course, want labour to be as cheap as possible. There is an inherent basis for conflict in this situation. Marketing departments may press hard for a diversified product range with regular changes in order to compete in turbulent markets. The production department may demand stability in order to achieve economies of scale. Again there is the potential for interdepartmental friction and conflict in this type of situation, created by the functional nature of organizational structure.

Intraorganizational

Individuals and groups play such a significant part in organizational activity that they inevitably account for much of the incidence of conflict. However, there are other features of organization that favour the emergence of conflict (see Figure 20.3).

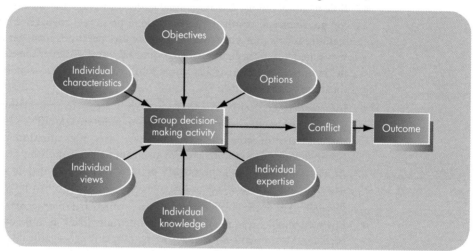

FIGURE 20.2   Group decision making and conflict.

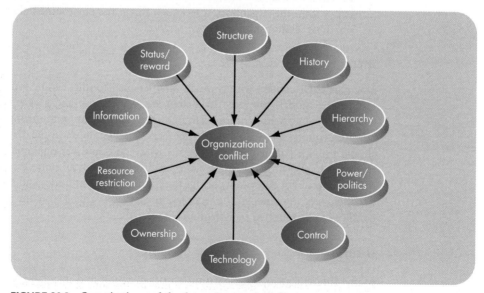

FIGURE 20.3   Organization and the determinants of conflict.

The physical realization of an organization in terms of structure, hierarchy, information flows, together with career development, rewards, information flows are all ways of *compartmentalizing* activity. Link these with the inevitable limitations of resource availability and a basis for competition is created. There is a very narrow line between competition and conflict. If one party considers that it has not been fairly treated in the competitive process or attempts to influence outcomes in its favour then conflict can arise. There are also propensities to conflict in the nature of organizational ownership and the relative exclusion of employees. The impact of technology on jobs linked to the concepts of power, control and politics are other endemic features of organizational functioning that allow conflict to emerge.

Interorganizational

Markets provides a scenario in which organizations are inevitably in conflict with each other. All of the competitors in a particular industry attempt to meet the needs of the customer in such ways as to maximize profit and market share for themselves. The unfair use of state subsidy can support otherwise uneconomic organizations to the disadvantage of organizations that do not have access to those funds. There is considerable unease in some quarters at the potential for *conflict of interest* to exist within the large accountancy practices which offer a wide range of services. The essence of this debate is reflected in Management in Action 20.1.

Stop | Consider
Based on the views expressed in MiA 20.1, should there be restrictions on the range of products and services that a company can offer? Justify your views.
What might your answer suggest abut the nature of a free market economy?
How would you ensure compliance with any restriction requirement?

Forms of organizational conflict

This section explores how conflict finds expression within an organizational setting. Disagreement that escalates to the level of conflict could become apparent in many forms including arguments, adversarial attitudes, antagonistic and other forms of hostile behaviour for example. Within an organization there are two distinct levels for differentiating the form that conflict can take. They are the individual and group levels of analysis.

Conflict from a managerial perspective has the potential to create disruption within the organization and hence lower output levels, quality and profit. As a result most organizations attempt to institutionalize the mechanisms for seeking to minimize the risk of its occurring and dealing with it quickly if it should arise. These forms of conflict are now discussed further, taking each level of conflict expression in turn. However, this is not the only way of thinking about conflict within an organization and some of the other perspectives will be discussed in a later section.

Individual

Some of the ways in which conflict can find its way into observable behaviour include:

MANAGEMENT IN ACTION 20.1

For what we are about to receive

Many large accounting practices have a range of services they offer to clients. Such firms claim that there are 'Chinese walls' between the various component parts of the practice, particularly in the sensitive areas of audit, support and insolvency. However, not everyone is convinced that the inevitable tensions are dealt with as they should be. This situation becomes even more complex when the role of bankers in company financial management is taken into account.

Jack describes one case that illustrates some of these potential conflicts. It involves a north London textile company, a bank, the accountants that it hired and the eventual fall into receivership of the business. In 1992 the company lost its largest customer. The bank pressed the owner of the business to consider the implications of this loss of revenue and he agreed to pay £18,000 to a large firm of accountants to write a report on the viability of the company. As a result of the report all parties agreed that the company should stay in business, but that the position should be reviewed six months later. During that time the business paid the accountants £3000 each week to monitor the financial health of the company.

At the end of the six months the company overdraft had been reduced to within a few thousand pounds of the owner's forecast. The owner and his independent auditors made repeated proposals for the restructuring of the company which were turned down by the bank and the accountants. Instead the bank appointed the firm of accountants as receivers and closed the business down. The underlying issue from this case (and many others) is the probity of banks using the same accountants to investigate troubled companies as would be appointed as receivers should the company fail. The potential conflict of interest that arises in these situations emerges from the pressure on the accountants to generate fee-earning opportunities. There is a danger that the information on a company may be 'slanted' to

'encourage' its closure in order to gain the additional fees for the accountants were they appointed as receiver.

Not all firms of accountants undertake insolvency work as some believe that the potential for a conflict of interest does not serve their clients well. Mr Michael Snyder, senior partner at accountants Kingston Smith indicated that they did not conduct any insolvency work because he believed that it did not sit happily with its work as investigating accountants. He went on to say: 'What is required is a wholly independent review. The investigators appointed [from large firms] are most likely to be insolvency experts with the prospect of a future receivership in their minds.'

However, not surprisingly, these claims are vigorously denied by the large firms. Allan Griffiths, a partner with Grant Thornton and vice-president of the Society of Practitioners of Insolvency, said: 'It's a bit hard to stomach people doubting my professional integrity. I get my enjoyment from saving companies, not closing them down.' He also suggested that most of the companies that he is asked to investigate emerge intact with existing management in place and with the creditors none the wiser. He also pointed out that to appoint another firm as receivers would add to the cost as they would have to learn about the business. Word would spread and the value of the remaining assets would drop further. The banks are also divided on the issue. The Royal Bank of Scotland has taken positive steps to control the situation by reducing the number of people who can approve receivership from 300 to three. By this action, and by deliberately not appointing investigating accountants as receivers, it claims to have greatly reduced the number of companies put into receivership.

Adapted from: Jack, A (1994) For what we are about to receive, *Financial Times*, 24 June, p 18.

+ Sabotage. The deliberate interruption of company operations is the broad definition of sabotage (Brown, 1977). At one extreme, it involves causing machines to breakdown by deliberately causing a malfunction. At the other extreme, it is simply not working as effectively as would be considered reasonable by management. Sabotage arises through the deliberate intent to damage the interests of another by an individual who considers that they have some reason to feel aggrieved by the actions of that party. Sabotage is not part of the conflict itself, but it reflects an attitude and an attempt to *get even* with the target. LaNuez and Jermier (1994, p 221) define sabotage to be, 'deliberate action or inaction that is intended to damage, destroy or disrupt some aspect of the workplace environment, including the organization's property, product, processes or reputation, with the net effect of undermining [the] goals of capital elites'. Management in Action 20.2 illustrates one aspect of sabotage in a factory.

Stop | Consider

Does MiA 20.2 demonstrate sabotage, or does it reflect alienation, frustration, resistance, boredom or bad job design? Justify your views.

In MiA 20.2 it is suggested that the supervisors might have known what was happening. Why do you think that they may have known but chosen to ignore it?

How would you have dealt with the situation if you had been the production manager responsible for the machine?

+ Ethical dilemmas. The existence of an ethical dilemma is an example of a conflict, usually between alternative courses of action. For example, should an individual *whistleblow* on their boss who has been deliberately over claiming expenses? Miceli and Near (1997) suggest that in some situations the main purpose of whistleblowers can be to further their own position at the expense of others. One measure of the antisocial use of whistleblowing is suggested as the use of the concept of *net harm*. In other words, the balance between the proportion of people helped or harmed by the process.

+ Interpersonal disputes. It is just not possible for all human beings to live in peace and harmony all of the time. Much as we might strive for such an ideal and even function as if it were the norm, the weight of history and human nature would suggest otherwise. For example, a manager may *perceive* that a subordinate is lazy and inefficient. The manager may as a result of that perception make life difficult for the individual as an encouragement to them to leave. This would inevitably create a conflictual and antagonistic relationship between them.

+ Work manipulation. It is not unknown for new work procedures to be followed to the letter by those onto whom they have been forced, even though they recognize that problems will occur. The intention being to exact a measure of revenge on the managers concerned. Thompson (1989, p 137) quotes an example from Chrysler in which the assembly line operators had been given precise instructions on what sequence of car doors to hang. Unfortunately, management could not provide the correct sequence of cars. The workers continued to do exactly as they had been instructed and chaos resulted. Managers begged the workers to go back to the ways of working that the workers themselves had developed – they had in practice used the skills that they had developed in knowing what job to do next as well as a measure of common sense. The workers, however refused and insisted on following the way of working demanded by management for the rest of the shift. Management then withdrew the new job instructions and allowed the workers some discretion.

MANAGEMENT IN ACTION 20.2

Time for a break

This story was told to me by the factory industrial engineer who was a member of the task force charged with solving the problem, only to find that the real problem was completely different from what had been expected.

The particular factory in question made large quantities of fibreboard ceiling panels. These were made in sizes of approximately 3 metres by 2 metres and then cut down to smaller panels as dictated by the specific customer order. It was possible to have a number of textured finishes pressed into the surface of the panels and all would then be finished off with several paint coatings as dictated by the order. These panels would be used in offices, banks, retail outlets or any number of similar buildings.

Not surprisingly, being fibreboard there was a significant quantity of dust in the atmosphere and more was created by the cutting and sanding processes in the factory. Much of the dust was removed by the dust extraction and air conditioning systems, but some still found its way into the factory environment.

The machine in question was the final painting and packing line which was about 100 metres in length with a normal crew of 24. This allowed for the machine to run continuously during the production shift. Each employee took turns on a rota to have a break and so the machine only actually required about 18 people to operate it at any point in time. The other six people were on a break lasting about 20 minutes at a time.

The machine was loaded with ceiling panels cut, pressed and primed as required by the order and a final coat of paint was applied automatically in a spray booth. The panels then went through a drying oven, to be followed by a quality check before being packed into boxes at the packing stations. The finished boxes were then stacked on pallets and moved into the finished goods warehouse.

The process was not technically complex,

consisting of conveyor belts; spray booths with moving arms, fed by paint pumped from large containers; drying ovens, which were heated by gas; a cooling section with cold air circulated by fans. The quality checks were done on a large flat conveyor and the boxes were packed by picking tiles off the same conveyor belt. This brief description conjures up an image of a large, relatively simple production process, with a number of elements that needed to be co-ordinated if the end product were to be acceptable. For example, if the spray heads were not cleaned regularly they tended to clog and if the oven temperature was not appropriate burnt or wet paint resulted. The machine had a bad record of inconsistent production and stopped for unspecified reasons a number of times each shift.

This pattern evolved over a considerable period of time and so the production manager set up a task force to explore what was happening and to find solutions to the problem. Many weeks of investigation by the industrial engineer, maintenance engineer, quality inspector etc., all produced minor changes to the process but not the significant improvement sought. During the investigation it was noticed that mechanical breakdowns began to increase. The safety trips on the motors driving the conveyor belts began to cut in and stop the motors from working. By the time the electricians were called out to examine the motors they had stopped. They were very hot to the touch, but once cooled down they started OK and worked as expected. No electrical or mechanical fault could be found either on the equipment or as a result of the way in which operators were using it. A complete mystery.

This lasted for several weeks and neither cause nor solution seemed any clearer. Until that is, one day, purely by chance, the industrial engineer appeared by the machine and found the cause. A pile of dust had built up around one of the conveyor belt motors. An investigation followed. It transpired that the operators had been building piles of dust around the electric motors, effectively insulating them and allowing the heat to build up to the extent that the safety trip cut in and switched them off. When the electricians were called in the operators quickly disposed of the dust, leaving a very hot motor to be examined by the electricians.

The operators claimed the jobs they did were so boring that 'playing this game' added a bit of interest to their daily routine and gave them more time in the mess room chatting to their friends and playing cards etc. The management view was that this represented sabotage and formal disciplinary hearings were held. No employee was actually dismissed as a result, partly because it was not clear just how much the supervisors had known about this 'game'. However, it was made clear that if it happened again dismissal would result. Productivity on the machine did improve after this situation was dealt with. However, the jobs were not changed in any way in an attempt to improve job satisfaction.

✦ Misuse of resources. The appropriating of resources for personal use can be rationalized by individuals on the basis of correcting a perceived injustice and by so doing reduce the possibility of conflict. Examples include making private phone calls at work, use of the Internet and e-mail systems at work and taking pens and paper clips home. Many organizations now consider such theft as a major cost and attempt to clamp down on it. The procedures involved have included random searches of people and property, which can create new opportunities for conflict to emerge!

✦ Choice. Virtually limitless opportunities for choice exists within an organization. Promotion; access to career development opportunities; pay increases; interesting work; the giving or withholding or friendship; co-operation and assistance are just some of the more obvious. For example, to fall out with a boss may result in open conflict over duties, or it may result in certain opportunities not being made available. Discrimination in all its forms falls clearly into this type of behaviour.

✦ Politicking and power. There is an ability to experience conflict through power and political behaviour. For example, the personal conflict between two managers could lead to an attempt by one to undermine the position and authority of the other through political activity.

✦ Rumour and gossip. This can be regarded as a milder form of political behaviour and power. That is not to suggest that rumour and gossip in themselves are mild. There are occasions when they form very powerful and damaging weapons in their own right. The creating and spreading of rumours about someone with whom one is in conflict can represent effective ways of undermining their position and credibility. Management in Action 20.3 describes the impact of one such situation.

Stop | Consider

Imagine that you had been brought in from outside the company and put in charge of the department described in MiA 20.3. How would you deal with the situation?

Justify your intended plan of action and outline any contingency plans that you would develop?

MANAGEMENT IN ACTION 20.3

Getting rid of the boss

This event was described to me by the personnel director of the organization concerned. It is a real story and only names and incidental details have been changed.

There was one small department within a large company that dealt with a single product for a particular market. This department was for all practical purposes independent of other activities within the company. Over the years it had gained the reputation for being a problem area, containing difficult staff, and ineffective management. The standard of service was continually slipping downwards. Eventually the manager was moved sideways and replaced by one of the staff who up to that point had enjoyed a good reputation for attempting to do things correctly.

Unfortunately, this action created a number of additional and unforeseen problems within the department. The previous boss resented being moved to another job. The staff began to see that change was about to be forced upon them and began to side with the old boss. The new manager was not experienced, neither did he receive any training. Senior managers did not make any obvious attempt to ensure that everyone would take the new situation seriously. The result was an

escalating cycle of resentment, frustration and a sense of grievance and unresolved conflict at a personal and job level.

Eventually, rumours began to spread about the new boss and staff would not talk directly to the individual. In short, life became difficult, a hostile (bad) atmosphere developed and work began to suffer even more. After some time anonymous letters were sent to senior managers purporting to demonstrate the wild excesses in behaviour and general lack of ability of the boss. Investigations failed to reveal the source of these letters but the situation continued to deteriorate. Eventually, after about a year, the boss asked to be moved to another job and this was done. After another three months the boss resigned and left the company altogether.

A new boss was recruited from outside the organization but he was not given the resources necessary to change the situation. Things did not deteriorate much further but neither did they get any better. The department did not develop the full potential of its product and market and was eventually closed down.

✦ Attitude. It is possible to identify how attitudes can be influenced by conflict and indeed vice versa. Individuals who experience conflict and for whom it is not effectively resolved retain a sense of grievance and hostility towards the other party. It is against that background that attitudes towards and about other people are formed.

✦ Absence and leaving. In extreme instances conflict can result in one or more party withdrawing from the situation. This can result in absenteeism or in leaving the company, as was the case in Management in Action 20.3.

Group

Some of the forms of conflict identified under the *individual* classification can also find expression at the *group* level. For example, if bad attitudes develop between workers and management, strikes and other forms of industrial action will become more likely as *trust* and *mutual respect* diminish. The major forms of group conflict include:

✦ Strikes and lock-outs. The withdrawal of labour by employees or the prevention of work activity by management are two sides of the same coin. During a collective dispute between managers and trade unions the final lever that either party hold is to restrict the activities of the other. If all employees go on *strike* they effectively prevent management from running the business. If managers *lock out* the workers they prevent them from working or earning any wages. The intention of both courses of action is to force one side to concede to the demands of the other or at least to negotiate further to find an acceptable compromise.

✦ Work to rule. The loss of income can be significant during a strike even if it is only for a brief period. It is clearly more effective to attempt to find ways of putting pressure on an employer without the consequent loss of income. One way of achieving this is through the notion of a *work to rule*. The rationale of such a course of action is that managers inevitably encourage employees to *go beyond the contract* in work activities. Although extending the contract is claimed to be a feature that distinguishes human resource management from personnel management (Legge, 1995), it has a long history in practice. If it were not so then the practice of *working to rule* would not have carried any weight or had any impact in practice. To go beyond the contract is an attempt to obtain more value for money from the labour resource than the current balance of the *wage–work bargain* would imply. It reflects an intention to avoid the need to renegotiate the contract through persuasion, socialization and other forms of encouragement. As such it represents an attempt to exploit, or to gain an advantage. However, given the complexity of organizational activity it is impossible to specify in great detail every element of the work relationship between management and worker with all its rights, responsibilities and obligations. Many forms of seeking to *go beyond the contract* represent one-way processes, rather than attempts to seek true and balanced flexibility from the labour resource. In other words, management expect the right to *go beyond the contract*, but do not expect (or allow) employees to claim the same right.

  Even unskilled workers hold the power to frustrate the efficiency and profitability of the organization by failing to co-operate actively in the work process. The required level of co-operation needs to go beyond mere compliance with rules if work is to be performed efficiently. Indeed, a common form of worker insubordination is *working to rule*, whereby employees are able to undermine the manufacturing process or quality or service provided merely by doing exactly and precisely as they are required (rather than exercising a level of discretion not covered by the rules). Essentially, then, management want workers to follow the spirit, not the letter of the rules (Blyton and Turnbull, 1994, p 31). One example of the consequences of doing this was indicated in our earlier example of what happened to door fitting on the assembly line at Chrysler.

  It is interesting to contemplate why it is that organizations are making themselves increasingly vulnerable to this form of action through delayering and empowering employees. Clearly, the greater responsibility that is delegated to employees the greater the risk of susceptibility to action of this type should conflict erupt. This is perhaps why many organizations seek to adopt what have been described as progressive personnel policies in an attempt to reduce (through *socialization, empowerment* and *association*) the divergence of attitude between managers and workers. It is a trend that parallels (but in the opposite direction) the diminution in the power to influence events of the trade union movement since the late 1970s as a result in political and economic forces.

✦ Work restriction. Groups are capable of determining the level of effort that they are prepared to invest on the employers behalf. A frustrated group of employees who feel some sense of grievance with an employer are not likely to perform at their best.

✦ Factionalism. There are a wide range of means by which groups can affect some degree of expression of conflictual relationships with other groups. The circumstances that gave birth to the British tradition of trade unions being occupationally based also gave rise to strategies that attempted to protect the interests of those groups against the interests of others. This created a number of opportunities to display factional behaviour including demarcation disputes between unions and employers and membership disputes between unions.

The consequences of conflict

There are a number of consequences that arise from the existence of conflict. The potential for conflict between individuals and groups in the work context produces a situation in which co-operation cannot be taken for granted. Everyone within the organization must work on the quality of relationships or conflict is likely to arise. In essence where *trust* is absent or at a very low level, conflict is almost inevitable. For example, Sheppard and Tuchinsky (1996, pp 153–61) reflect on the role of negotiation as a means of building *trust* within an organization through its ability to reconcile difference and build partnerships. One of the outcomes of such approaches would be to reduce the level of open hostility or conflict present in a particular situation.

That is not to suggest that conflict can be eliminated completely. There will always be individuals who do not get along at a personal level. For example, Lewicki and Bunker (1996, pp 126–8) develop a model which reflects the possible outcomes for a relationship in which *trust* has been violated. Included among the active variables are the possible responses by the violator, one of which is disagreement with the violated person's perceptions. Clearly under such circumstances repair to the relationship will be impossible and conflict or a rupture will result. Equally, the motivations that cause one group to act in a particular way are subject to different perceptions and interpretations by another. However, to minimize conflict (assuming that represents a desirable state) is something that requires positive action rather than passivity.

Conflict is a concept that, it can be argued, is either a negative or positive force. Interpreted as a negative force and therefore something to be driven out (or at least minimized) conflict is regarded as something that disrupts effective relationships or company operations. It follows, therefore that if employees can be persuaded, or forced, to see things as managers do then conflict would largely disappear. As a positive force, it can be described as a means of challenging the status quo and any other forms of ineffectiveness within the system. Thereby forcing all parties within an organization to seek the most effective compromises in making full use of all available resources in pursuit of objectives. This is the basis of the *pluralist* perspective to be discussed later.

Another viewpoint suggests that conflict represents a force that can either be negative or positive depending upon the circumstances. Too much or too little conflict is harmful. However, just the right amount of conflict can actually aid in optimizing performance. This view is represented in Figure 20.4.

Essentially in this view, conflict is being defined as a pressurizing force. Using the analogy of a domestic water pipe, too little pressure in the system and no water will come out of the tap. Too much pressure and the pipe is likely to burst. Just the right amount of pressure is needed in order to make the system function effectively as intended.

Conflict in this model is regarded as a force that can be harnessed to ensure that *slackness* is kept out of the workings of the organization. For example, if management cannot take for granted the loyalty and commitment of employees they will find it necessary to ensure that they keep in touch with the thinking and aspirations of the workers. In so doing a continual reassessment of the working relationship will be undertaken and the potential for major conflict minimized.

With no conflict in existence a form of amnesia would result. People and groups would begin to act as if they were operating on *automatic pilot*, simply going through the motions at work without thinking about them. In this view such a organization would become *slack* and *desensitized* to the activities going on around it. Equally, at the other extreme, excessive conflict, for example a protracted labour stoppage, would bring the organization to a standstill and thereby reduce performance to zero.

In practice there are a number of consequences of conflict within an organization. They range from the harmful to the beneficial. Not all would be active in every situation. They include the items identified in Figure 20.5.

Most of the consequences identified in Figure 20.5 are self-explanatory, but some need further elaboration. Items such as stress, high labour turnover and difficult relationships can easily be understood as a direct consequence of conflict. However, items such as training and involvement would be better understood if they are considered further:

✦ Training. Where conflict is a real possibility training and other *exposure* activities can be effective means of exploring and resolving the difficulties. Training can therefore emerge as a direct consequence of the perceived conflict. Conflict can be reduced through many training initiatives. For example, *socialization* training could help to integrate groups by pushing a common framework and culture as the basis of the relationship. Equally, forming *joint problem solving* types of group can encourage formally conflicting groups to work together and find new ways of co-operating towards a common goal.

✦ Autocratic leadership. There is a view that conflict represents an unwillingness to compromise and a direct challenge to authority. Therefore, one consequence could be to become more autocratic in management style, thereby eliminating the opportunity and desire to compromise. This view can be based on the assumption that conflict

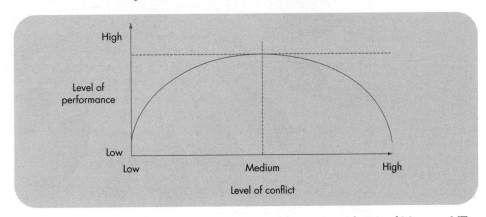

FIGURE 20.4 Conflict impact on performance (*adapted from*: Ivancevich, JM and Matteson, MT (1993) *Organizational Behaviour and Management*, 3rd edn, Irwin, Homewood, IL).

emerges as a result of perceived weakness and willingness to compromise under pressure. Making the leadership position clear and strong eliminates conflict as subordinates recognize that it is pointless. The counter argument is that such approaches *bottle up* resentments that always find expression at some point in time and in a form damaging to the organization.

✦ Low-quality staff. There are organizations who have a reputation for autocratic management and conflictual working relationships. Consequently, in a local labour market potential employees tend to regard such employers as a last resort and only remain until something better comes along. High labour turnover, poor quality products and services typify such organizations.

✦ Less communication. When people are in conflict the level and quality of communication drops. This can be seen in any industrial dispute, or even a family argument. There are also consequences such as the emergence of strong subgroups along with increased political behaviour among the groups and individuals concerned. As a consequence of this there is a tendency to attempt to institutionalize the procedures and process by which conflict is resolved.

Many of the items incorporated into Figure 20.5 reflect negative consequences of con-

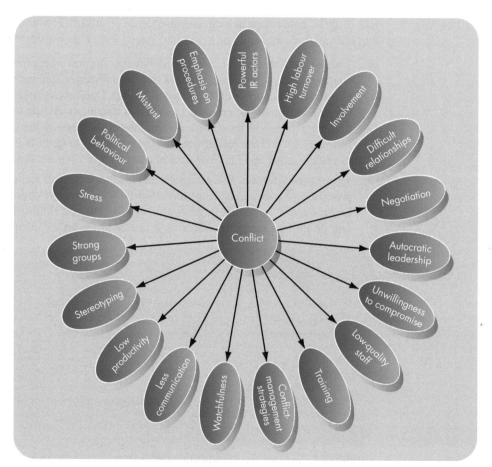

FIGURE 20.5 Some consequences of conflict.

flict and it might be argued that this should be taken to imply that the view represented in Figure 20.4 is invalid. If there are very few positive consequences of conflict it cannot be helpful to performance. This need not be so as it should be possible to achieve medium levels of conflict overall through handling strategies such as *negotiation* and *socialization*. Offsetting the negative consequences of conflict should also improve performance through the removal of barriers to performance. The process of conflict resolution should also provide greater levels of unity within the organization thereby improving performance. One potential weakness implied by Figure 20.4 is that to be effective organizations should encourage a certain degree of conflict. This is not a view that would sit comfortably with many managers, who usually prefer to see performance achieved through more conventional mechanisms.

Having discussed a number of views on conflict which would generally be classified as pluralist, or unitarist in nature. It would now be useful to reflect on these terms and consider the main perspectives on the subject.

Perspectives on conflict

There are a number of perspectives on the topic of conflict and this section will begin by reviewing the traditional points of view. Then the labour process theory perspectives will be discussed. Labour process theory has already been introduced in this text and so will not be fully developed in this chapter.

Traditional views

The traditional views on conflict were encapsulated by Fox (1966) who describes three major perspectives on organizations, each of which having a different underpinning based on the nature of conflict:

✦ Pluralism. *Pluralism* holds that an organization comprises a collection of groups each with their own objectives, aspirations and agenda to follow. Inevitably, the diversity of groups involved will have divergent interests in some areas, but convergent views in other areas. Employees seek to maximize earnings and organizations seek the lowest labour costs. These different perspectives are irreconcilable and are therefore a basis for *conflict* between the groups involved. However, such differences do not automatically result in a failure of the ability of the organization to function. All of the groups recognize that compromise is essential if they are to stand any chance of partially achieving their objectives. For example, if the cost of labour becomes too expensive the company may become uncompetitive and close down, resulting in everyone losing their jobs. So the *wage–work bargain* becomes a major area of potential conflict and agreement in the search for balance between these conflicting interests.

In the *pluralist* model conflict provides an indication of the issues on which there are fundamental differences between the various *stakeholders*. In effect, it provides a relationship regulation mechanism, surfacing problems while preventing major fracture (through the recognition of the need to compromise) which would be to every group's disadvantage. However, as Management in Action 20.4 shows there are situations in which the opportunity to bridge the gap in seeking a resolution simply does not exist.

MANAGEMENT IN ACTION 20.4

A boss's life at the sharp end

Life for Alberto Morales, general manager of the Gillette manufacturing subsidiary near Seville in Spain, changed completely on 18 March 1994 when he told the works council that the company had decided to close the factory. Since then his home has been put under 24-hour guard, he is always accompanied by two bodyguards and he no longer leaves his office to walk around the factory.

About 250 people are employed at the factory, but the parent company wants to concentrate European razor-blade manufacture in England and Germany. Reaction to the proposed closure was strongly hostile at a number of levels. The regional government challenged the decision in the courts and the industry minister for the country described the move as 'a provocation' for example. Even a boycott of Gillette products was suggested in reaction to the closure. Spanish labour law allows for collective redundancy on certain grounds, including the reorganization of production. However, these were intended to cover situations within Spain, not the cross-border transfers of work. Globally, Gillette was seeking to realign its operations, which involved the loss of about 2000 jobs, mostly outside the USA, and the creation of new jobs in countries such as China, Russia and Poland where new ventures were planned. The justification for the

factory closure, according to Morales, 'is not that it is unprofitable, but that it is superfluous'.

To avoid lengthy administrative procedure, Spanish employers frequently offer the maximum redundancy compensation of 45 days' pay for each year of service. Morales suggested that the company might even go beyond that level in order to achieve a negotiated settlement. The works council at the Seville factory would not listen to the initial offer from management for two months. This consisted of a retirement plan, outplacement services and a range of resettlement policies. Future negotiations were also likely to be 'conflictual' in nature. The future for Morales at a personal level was also bleak. He was 54 and had been at the factory for 20 years, the last six as general manager. He felt that there were not many suitable alternative positions for him within the company. As a factory manager, the possible locations were likely to be India or somewhere else in the world. Not a prospect that he relished, so once the factory was closed down he expected to be out on the street just like the other workers.

Adapted from: White, D (1994) A boss's life at the sharp end, *Financial Times*, 8 June, p 20.

Stop | Consider

To what extent could the gap between the conflicting views of employees and the government on one hand and the company on the other be reconciled?

To what degree might the reactions of the workers be a recognition of the inevitable and therefore an attempt to increase the 'price of going quietly'? Could you ever determine if this was actually the case? How?

What would you do if you were the general manager of the factory trying to deal with the situation?

✦ Unitarianism. This suggests that the whole organization is the natural unit of consideration. The organization is frequently likened to a family unit in which different branches and factions might exist but the family unit is the unit of concern for all members. Conflict in that sense is something that reflects a major breakdown in the *normal* and desirable state of affairs. From that perspective conflict is suggested to reflect something that should be avoided if possible and if it arises eliminated. It is viewed as emanating from members classed as deviant, so they should be dealt with severely as they put at risk the overall harmony of the group.

✦ Marxist. The *Marxist* or *radical* perspective as it is sometimes called suggests that conflict is an inevitable function of capitalism. Under this view, employees are fundamentally exploited by the controllers of the means of production. One of the consequences of this is *resistance* to the will of management in the form of *conflict*. Not only is this inevitable but desirable in the Marxist tradition as it assists the breakdown of capitalism in the revolutionary creation of socialism.

Labour process theory

The concept of the *labour process* developed out of the Marxist tradition and has been defined in the following terms:

> The means by which raw materials are transformed by human labour, acting on the objects with tools and machinery: first into products for use and, under capitalism, into commodities to be exchanged on the market. (Thompson 1989, p xv)

As an area of study it began with Braverman, who in 1974 published *Labour and Monopoly Capital* which stimulated the rediscovery of the earlier Marxist material on the nature of labour.

Labour process theory, therefore, seeks to explore the nature of work relations within a specific system of production. In most analyses this is reflected in the way in which capitalism acquires labour as a commodity and uses it to produce other commodities to the benefit of the capital owners. Within this analysis *conflict* between workers and managers (or more accurately capital owners represented by managers) is inevitable as more and more control is exercised in the search for increased efficiency in the value extracted from the labour process. Of course, the workers are not passive in this process and are well able to resist this search for ever more profitable use of their labour. Thompson and McHugh (1995) indicate that the twin fundamental pressures on any capitalist organization of market competition and conflict within the employment relationship require them to continually reappraise their production capabilities. This inevitably places more pressure in the system, resulting in ever greater conflict potential.

Thompson and McHugh (1995, pp 373–4) also identify a number of consequences that flow from the capitalist nature of the labour process, including:

✦ Work organizations are distinct from other organizations and can only be understood within a theory of capital accumulation and labour process.

✦ Organizations are structures of control in the broadest sense of the term. The concept of *management agency* as the means of achieving control develops in this context.

✦ In advanced capitalist societies large scale organizations act as mechanisms which integrate economic, political, administrative and ideological structures.

✦ Organizational structures and processes involve political issues, decisions and choices on such matter as job design, control systems etc.

◆ Organizations do not embody a universal rationality, but rather a contested rationality arising from the antagonistic and conflictual relationships between capital and labour.

◆ Organizational change reflects the balance between control and resistance expressed in the daily dynamic of experience.

There would appear to be five core elements to a theory of labour process and which are identified by Thompson (1989). They are:

◆ Labour as a unique commodity. In seeking to create profit capitalists acquire a number of resources which they control in pursuit of bringing the goods and services to market. Many of the resources are totally malleable at the discretion of the owner. For example, raw material will allow itself to be moulded and worked into any shape or product for which it has a capacity to become.

   However, the human resource has a high degree of restriction in level of malleability. Humans have *free will*, they can answer back, they have understanding and communication abilities and, most important, they can *resist* management's direction. Many of these human capacities are of potential value to the capitalist. The vast majority of managers are paid employees and are paid to organize, take decisions and use what have been described as the higher level human qualities in support of capitalist objectives. Humans employed to produce the goods and services, however, have generally been regarded as little more than a flexible machine.

   Because human labour has the qualities necessary for the achievement of capitalist intentions it is an essential part of the process of converting the other resources into the goods and services intended for sale. However, it is a mixed blessing as it automatically brings with it other undesirable qualities and obligations (from a capitalist point of view). For example, a surplus of cash within a capitalist organization has a very different set of connotations and ramifications compared with a surplus of people. It is the range and nature of these relative contrasts between the human and other resources that give it the unique qualities in capitalism.

◆ Labour is a special focus of attention in capitalism. It is the nature of capitalism to create surplus. The notion of profit is a surplus – the extra obtained through the market system over the cost of production. From that perspective every resource used within the capitalist organization must provide an opportunity for a contribution to the surplus obtained. This is the basis of the concept of added value used in accounting. In the Japanese management approach anything that does not add value represents waste and should be eliminated. Consequently, there is a requirement for labour to create surplus as its basis for existence. In short, labour value must be higher than its cost for it to be viable as a resource. It is argued that this predisposes the participants to a *conflictual* relationship.

◆ Capitalism forces minimization. It should be apparent from the previous discussion that there are two pressures in a capitalist system. The first is the notion of surplus as the objective of the whole process. The second is the volatility and unpredictability of the market system. In a truly free market there is no possibility of an individual being able to dictate prices. It is simple economics that high profits attract new supplies and hence price reductions. The converse is also true, the result being that it is not possible to opt out of the process, once begun it is ongoing.

It is the unpredictability of markets that has created attempts to *fix* them in one form or another. Cartels, restraint of trade clauses in employment contracts and holding back supplies are some of the manipulations used to control risk (and keep prices high). The other side of this particular coin is to minimize the cost of operations so that it is possible to achieve the maximum surplus from a particular market price. This is more directly amenable to management action than some of the other options. It also provides a differentiating feature between organizations. Market price affects all suppliers equally, but internal costs influence only one organization. It is also possible to use this approach as the basis of price reduction to force out some of the rivals and achieve a stronger position over market conditions. This invariably forces capitalist organizations into a perpetual search for lower costs and the minimization of disruption to the will of management. Once begun it is a competitive process and functions in a way reminiscent of the concept of perpetual motion; competition forces everyone to minimize or demise.

✦ Control is an imperative. There are several perspectives to this feature of the *labour process theory*. First, in order to ensure that profit is obtained the process must be controlled. If the capitalist does not control the process then one of the other *stakeholders* will. Second, because there are conflicting objectives between the stakeholders in an organization, *control* is the means by which these are regulated. Third, *control* is something that is associated with *power* and the ability to have other people do what the controller wants. It is something that people seek in order to be able to exercise it at a personal level. Fourth, there are differences between operational and strategic control. Because of the size and complexity of most large organizations the owners of capital delegate much of the operational control decisions to employees designated as managers. By giving employees a financial stake in the performance of the business it is argued that they will be more committed to the objectives of management. However, the proportion of ownership divested in this way tends to be very small in comparison to the total. Consequently, the degree of control devolved is also of little real significance.

✦ Institutionalized conflict. The classic Marxist view of the class struggle is also part of the *labour process*. Much of the foregoing discussion has created a picture of the exploitation of workers. It can be argued that because of the notion of a requirement for added value from every aspect of the resource base it is by nature an exploitative process. Employees are paid less in wages than the true value of their labour. This is the basis of the *wage–work bargain* much beloved of industrial relations specialists. Managers are permanently attempting to seek better value from the employee resource and employees are attempting to balance the contribution with the reward achieved. This is a low-*trust* approach to organizing.

Employees are dependent upon the owners of capital for the ability to earn money and acquire the necessities of life. It is therefore a relationship that includes a degree of *mutual dependence* as well as control. Capitalists need workers to supply their profit. The goods and services produced are sold in a market. But there must be someone to purchase them. Inevitably the goods produced are consumed in some degree by the workers that produce them. It is a feature of modern capitalist organization that as part of the search for minimization much production is carried out in locations remote from consumption. But even in these situations consumerism is beginning to emerge in developing countries to fuel the cycle of dependence.

As Thompson readily admits, there are many who would argue with the views put forward by labour process theorists. They include those who would see it as moving away from a traditional Marxist view of the common ownership and those who would prefer to see an emphasis on management study as a traditional social science. It does, however, provide a way of considering the nature of labour in capitalist organizations and perhaps placing *conflict* into a broader context. It is also an inescapable fact that not all organizations are capitalist, even in a predominately capitalist society. There are the public services, voluntary organizations and charities. Each of these institutions makes use of modern management techniques and would be indistinguishable from capitalist organizations apart from the profit motive. So perhaps the labour process approach is fundamentally flawed as a means of being able to provide an all-embracing perspective on every type of organization.

Conflict and resistance

The previous chapter discussed the nature of *resistance* within the context of power and control. This chapter has touched on the nature of *resistance* within the concept of conflict and perspectives such as the labour process theory. Resistance has been described in this chapter as a reaction by workers to the attempt by managers to exercise control as part of the capitalist search for domination of the labour resource. Equally, resistance can be seen as a cause of conflict as workers reject management attempts to create their *reality* and *frame of reference* in management preferred terms. In short, if workers always agreed with managers there would be no conflict because it is the worker resistance to that control that creates it – at least that is what many managers would like to believe! But as we have already seen there are other points of view about the nature and role of resistance in relation to power, control and conflict.

Traditionally within the field of management, resistance has been studied as a reaction by labour to the exploitation of labour within a capitalist system which is subject to both economic and political control (Hyman, 1987). There are also perspectives on resistance as a cultural issue (for example, Clarke *et al.* (1976), Willis (1990)), all of which are based on the view encapsulated by Salaman (1979, p 145):

> Despite the major efforts of senior executives to legitimize the activities, structures and inequalities of the organization and to design and install 'foolproof' and reliable systems of surveillance and direction, there is always some dissension, some dissatisfaction, some effort to achieve a degree of freedom from hierarchical control – some resistance to the organization's domination and direction.

Collinson (1994) identifies two distinct and very different forms of resistance, both of which he illustrates through case study examples. The first is described as *resistance through distance*. This reflects the strategies adopted by workers to escape control and the demands of authority through physical or symbolic distance form the existing power structures. The second is described as *resistance through persistence*. This reflects resistance through the dogged and persistent demanding of employees to become better informed. therefore being better equiped to challenge management decision making. It is the opposite strategy to *resistance through distance*, because it holds management to account, whereas the former strategy holds firm to the absolute position of managers as responsible for everything.

Resistance through distance is a form of resistance as it seeks to, 'deny any involvement in or responsibility for the running of the organization' (p 37). It is an approach to work which recognizes a clear distinction between work and non-work lives as totally separate spheres and also refuses to accept the dilution of the capital/labour split in responsibility and role. In that sense it resists the attempts of managers to achieve control through involvement and integration. However, as the discussion by Collinson shows, such approaches can create *conflict* among colleagues as it can be regarded as simply complying with management intentions. As a perspective *resistance through distance* accepts the managerial prerogative in a wide range of areas including decision making and technical expertise, therefore adherents simply respond to management's intended actions.

Resistance through persistence, by way of contrast, challenges the managerial prerogative at every opportunity. As the title suggests it *persists* in pushing managerial decision making and information flows as a way of *resisting* the imposition of a management created agenda and frame of reference. By constantly challenging the management perspective ultimately the underlying assumptions, prejudices, inconsistencies and irrationalities are exposed. This can lead to changes in management intentions and a better deal for workers. However, it is possible that such approaches can create *conflict* between workers, as well as the conflict that naturally arises with the managers who are being persistently challenged. Not all workers will support such persistence, for example those who believe in *resistance through distance* will not support such engagement. Also colleagues who fear that they have something to lose as a result of the engagement may become conflictual in attitude. For example, they may fear that persistently questioning the financial data released by the company during annual negotiations may make management hostile to the entire factory and lead to its being closed down.

Conflict-handling strategies

There are a number of ways in which conflict can be managed within an organizational setting. They include:

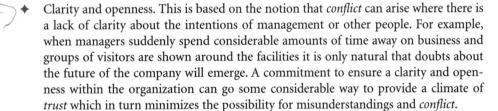

+ Clarity and openness. This is based on the notion that *conflict* can arise where there is a lack of clarity about the intentions of management or other people. For example, when managers suddenly spend considerable amounts of time away on business and groups of visitors are shown around the facilities it is only natural that doubts about the future of the company will emerge. A commitment to ensure a clarity and openness within the organization can go some considerable way to provide a climate of *trust* which in turn minimizes the possibility for misunderstandings and *conflict*.

+ Signals. The signals that managers and other individuals within the organization give also contribute to the likelihood of conflict breaking out. For example, if managers only speak to employees when there is a real threat of industrial action taking place, then they are sending out a clear signal of what they think about the workers. It becomes apparent that the only way to attract the attention of management is to threaten to take industrial action. Appropriate signals can be used to encourage different behaviour patterns. For example, it would be possible to encourage openness and discussion by involving employees on a regular basis. This would also signal that it was not necessary to threaten conflict in order to gain attention.

◆ Training and socialization. The development of training courses can help to reinforce a management perspective. For example, a training course on customer care is a signal that managers are interested in customers, as well as providing an opportunity to explain why managers adopt those views and thereby providing staff with an opportunity to internalize those same views. This provides an opportunity for employees to be *socialized* into particular behaviour patterns and beliefs as defined by management, thereby reducing the potential for conflict.

Employees who display inappropriate behaviours are less likely to be allowed to develop their careers or gain access to training. Consequently, career development and promotion depends upon delivering appropriate behaviours and generally meeting management expectations. Part of this involves not engaging in behaviours that would be classed as undesirable, including conflictual or questioning orientations.

◆ Style and structure. Autocratic managers with dictatorial styles are more likely to create resentment and hostility. Employees inevitably seek the means to deal with this and collective action may be the result. The structure of an organization can also encourage conflict if there are unclear boundaries between work and decision-making responsibilities. For example, if it is not clear that the sales department must agree any urgent delivery orders with the production department before they are confirmed then a basis for departmental conflict exists.

◆ Procedure. There are many different forms of procedural mechanism that can be utilized to either prevent conflict from arising or to minimize its potential for disruption and negative effects. Among the more common procedural devices used are:

   ◆ Operating policy and procedures. Every organization requires policy and procedural frameworks to guide its functioning. The purpose being to provide clarity of operational responsibility, prevent duplication of effort and to establish *ground rules* for activity. In many large, complex organizations such policies and procedures would be committed to writing in the form of procedures manuals. However, in smaller companies they may be more informal and reflected in the organization structure, job descriptions and the normal ways of carrying out the work required.

   Communication and consultation procedures. Conflict can arise through a lack of knowledge or the misunderstanding of the actions and intentions of others. Communication and consultation between the various groups that exist within an organization should facilitate an improved level of understanding and knowledge which in turn should reduce the prospect of conflict.

   ◆ Decision-making practices. The processes adopted with regard to decision making can also be used to reduce the opportunity for conflict and assist with its resolution. For example, a department that is involved in a decision will have little scope for subsequently engaging in conflictual behaviour with regard to the outcome. Of course, this point of view assumes that the decision-making process is both rational and fair. In most organizational decision-making situations there is a degree of power and political behaviour present and if not kept in check these in themselves can create scope for parties feeling aggrieved and conflict arising.

   ◆ Negotiation. This was a topic covered in detail in Chapter 11 (along with decision making). Negotiation provides a process by which individuals and groups can directly resolve their differences. It is a process of reaching an accommodation that is acceptable to all parties to the process. However, it assumes that all parties are prepared to negotiate and reach a compromise which although less than ideal would be acceptable.

✦ Discipline and grievance procedures. Torrington and Hall (1991) introduce the notion of *organizational justice* in relation to discipline and grievance procedures (p 542). The employment contract determines the duties and responsibilities to which both employer and employee commit themselves during the employment relationship. The discipline and grievance procedures are the vehicles through which both parties have the opportunity to ensure satisfaction with the execution of the contract. For example, if an employee arrives late for work the employer is not receiving the input of time required by the contract. One way to redress this conflict is through the application of the disciplinary procedure by management. Equally, if an employee feels that they are being discriminated against by a manager (perhaps not being given an opportunity for promotion to a more senior position) they have the grievance procedure through which to seek redress for this conflict.

✦ Industrial relations procedures. One definition of industrial relations is that it, 'is concerned with the formal and informal relationships which exist between employers and trade unions and their members' (Armstrong, 1991, p 667). The same source (p 665) indicates that: 'The primary aims of [industrial relations] policies and procedures are to improve co-operation, to minimize unnecessary conflict, to enable employees to play an appropriate part in decision making, and to keep them informed on matters that concern them.'

Disputes between employers and trade unions are a major reflection of the existence of a state of conflict within an organization. However, to retain an ability to continue operations and earnings levels both parties need to achieve a workable compromise. It is in this area that the process of negotiation plays a part. If it is not possible to achieve a resolution of the conflict through direct negotiation there is the opportunity to invoke the services of the Advisory, Conciliation and Arbitration Service (ACAS) who have at their disposal specialists in dealing with conflict situations. The aim of ACAS is to assist the parties to find solutions to what are very often intractable and deep-rooted conflictual situations.

All these strategies provide an indication of the devices that are available through which to manage conflict but not how to respond to it in behavioural terms. Equally, they do not specifically take into account alternative perspectives on conflict such as the *labour process* or *Marxist* views on capital and labour. Thomas (1976) identified five generic conflict-handling styles based on the balance between two dimensions of the need to satisfy the concerns of the *self*, 'self-assertion' and the *other party*, 'co-operation' involved. This model is reflected in Figure 20.6

The five conflict-handling styles identified in Figure 20.6 are:

✦ Smoothing or accommodating. This approach reflects a style that would allow the other party to achieve what they desire from the situation. It is an attempt to maintain unity and harmony though subjugating one's own wishes. This could be as a consequence of indifference towards any needs other than those of the other party. It could also reflect a degree of fear of the consequences of failing to allow the other party to have their way.

✦ Avoidance. This style reflects a minimalist approach to the situation. It constitutes a desire to ignore the problem and hope that it will go away. Common responses include ignoring the problem, evading specific attempts to deal with it and elongating any procedural devices invoked to deal with it. This is the active avoidance of any open confrontation or hostility.

✦ Collaboration and problem solving. This approach represents the *maximize* approach to conflict situations. It reflects the *win–win* approach to negotiation and problem solving (Fisher and Ury, 1986). This style gives equal recognition to the need to resolve conflict through meeting the objectives and desires of both parties if a lasting settlement is to be achieved. Leaving one party disadvantaged is a recipe for future conflict. That is not to say that every party can expect to achieve everything desired as a result of conflict resolution.

✦ Competitive or authoritarian. This style reflects the *win-at-all-costs* approach to conflict resolution. It contains no consideration of the other parties' interests in the situation and simply concentrates on the desires of the *self* in the process. In negotiation terms it represents the view that anything conceded is something lost.

✦ Compromise. This is the search for the *acceptable*. It represents the *satisficing* approach to conflict resolution. It is the search for the acceptable middle ground between two points of view so that no one completely wins or loses.

The style adopted in a particular conflict situation will be a reflection of a number of forces. For example, the preferences of the individuals will play a part. Prior experience will also create a tendency towards a particular style. For example, a trade union which encountered an aggressive manager during previous negotiations is more likely to begin meetings using the same style in future. Also in an emergency situation, where little time is available

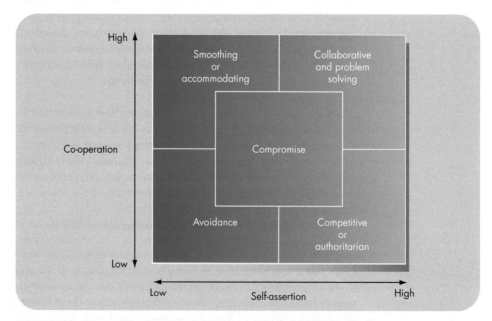

FIGURE 20.6   Five conflict-handling styles (*source*: Thomas, K (1976) Conflict management. In Dunnette, MD (ed.) *Handbook of Industrial and Organizational Psychology*, Rand McNally, New York).

to seek mutually acceptable solutions, it is more likely that a directive/authoritarian style would be adopted.

Politics within organizations

The quotation from Richard Nixon used in the previous chapter indicated that an effective leader must be able to implement the decisions made as well as know what should be done. In doing so the significance of political perspectives become apparent. There are two different perspectives on organizational *politics*. One views politics as a negative process that actively inhibits the effective running of an organization. The other views it in a more positive light, viewing politics as an inevitable mechanism of conflict resolution and a process geared to reaching compromise.

It is not possible to offer a definitive view of all political behaviour, it can only be judged on a case-by-case basis. For example, managers who seek to advance their own careers by engaging in *politicking* might engage in some unpleasant tactics. However, assuming that they subsequently perform very well as senior managers, how should they be judged? Of course there are a range of criteria that could be used to evaluate this situation and the material on ethics in a previous chapter has relevance to this. One of the major difficulties in assessing political activity is that it is not possible to know what might have happened in the same situation but under different circumstances in order to create a basis for evaluation.

One of the earliest works on the subject of politics was that of Machiavelli on the subject of serving princes and other rulers. His work titled *The Prince* was written in the period of fifteenth-century Renaissance Italy when politics was frequently a life-or-death business. Essentially, the argument put forward by Machiavelli was that the ends justified the means and anything was acceptable in the pursuit of the protection of the state. In short, it reflected on the mechanisms and strategies necessary to obtain and hold onto power through political activity.

The negative view of politics imposes a definition that considers it to be outside normal practice, used to enhance existing power or to offset the power of another, the purpose being to increase the certainty that a particular and preferred course of action (as defined by the person engaging in politics) will be followed (Mayes and Allen, 1977). The difficulty in practice is that it is not always possible to categorize acts of political behaviour as clearly as this definition might imply. Imagine a situation in which a manager attempts to influence a forthcoming decision by lobbying for support for their preferred plan. Just how far this should go before it would be considered wrong or political is a difficult matter to judge, particularly if the result were beneficial to the organization.

The more positive view of political behaviour regards it as an inevitable part of the need for individuals and groups to function in a collective context. Organizations are run by a mixture of individuals, departments and interest groupings. Whatever the nature of a job it involves interaction with other people and politics is a means of achieving collaboration between them and other sub-units within the organization. Every individual is part of a number of formal and informal groups within the organization. There are professional as well as friendship and departmental groups to identify just some of the more obvious. Each of these *levels* and *collections* within the organization will have objectives to achieve and preferences for how the organization should function. For example, the marketing department frequently finds itself in conflict with the production department because of the different perceptions on product design and, how best to prioritize, sequence and process customer orders. However, co-operation is needed between these groups when it comes to production planning and so a political balance must be struck, with each side seeking the greater degree of influence on the process.

Split departments are another form of grouping within organizations that can become part of the political process. The manufacturing division of a company might include a personnel department which is technically separate from the head office personnel function. It is not uncommon in these situations to find that a divisional personnel department identifies more strongly with the plans and objectives of its manufacturing division than with its professional grouping in head office.

As a positive process, politics allows for these groupings to find ways of accommodating each other's perspective in a competitive framework which limits real damage to relationships, the individuals, groups or the organization. Underlying this model of political behaviour is its association with success and failure. Imagine a situation in which a manager presses for a preferred course of action which is then followed but which is not successful. The perceived status if not the actual job and status of the individual concerned would be severely reduced.

Most managers recognize the dual nature of politics within an organization. They intuitively understand that it contains elements of both good and bad and that it can be an important, indeed inevitable part of the experience of work. Gandz and Murray (1980) carried out a survey among over 400 managers in an attempt to identify how managers perceived politics in their working lives. Table 20.1 reflects some of the more interesting findings from this research.

It is clear from the findings illustrated in Table 20.1 that politics is regarded as common, more prevalent in senior positions and linked with success and promotion. It is

Statement	Strong or moderate agreement %
(a) The existence of workplace politics is common to most organizations	93.2
(b) Successful executives must be good politicians	89.0
(c) The higher you go in organizations, the more political the climate becomes	76.2
(d) Only organizationally weak people play politics	68.5
(e) Organizations free of politics are happier than those where there is a lot of politics	59.1
(f) You have to be political to get ahead in organizations	69.8
(g) Politics in organizations are detrimental to efficiency	55.1
(h) Top management should try to get rid of politics within the organization	48.6
(i) Politics help organizations function effectively	42.1
(j) Powerful executives don't act politically	15.7

TABLE 20.1 Perceptions about politics among managers (*source*: Gandz, J and Murray, V (1980) The experience of workplace politics, *Academy of Management Journal*, June)

also regarded as something that individuals undertake if they have no other source of power and that it is the cause of inefficiency and unhappiness. These findings reflect the duality of politics in its positive and negative connotations. These findings have broadly been confirmed by later studies (Ashforth and Lee (1990), for example).

The positive view of organizational politics suggests that it will be rewarded if it is linked to success for the organization in some way. Imagine that a marketing manager were to set out to change the existing power balance of the organization from one which favoured the production department to one which favoured marketing. The strategies adopted might include attempting to *get close* to the chief executive, using every opportunity to make adverse comment about problems in production and indicating how competitors were gaining market share through the adoption of marketing strategies. Strengthening alliances with departments that might be favourable to the cause of marketing would also be another likely strategy. As a consequence of these strategies further imagine that a change in the power of the production department occurred as the company became marketing driven. If as a result the company found its reputation, market share and profits rose then it is likely that the company would pay more attention to advice from the marketing department in the future and less attention to the needs of production. That is until the marketing department succumbed to the political activity of other departments or failed to deliver success. This can be reflected in diagrammatic form (see Figure 20.7).

The point made by Figure 20.7 is that from an organizational point of view rewarding political behaviour (if it delivers success) encourages functions to compete in this way without harming the whole. In effect this approach allows for a process of providing an effective match between the needs of the market and the capability of the organization. Political activity that helps the organization ultimately benefits everyone and should be allowed free rein or so it would be argued within this conception of it. It is the harsh world of the market that is the ultimate judge of politics, not the impact on particular individuals or groups. If the market reacts badly to the consequences of political behaviour then one way or another *punishment* of the perpetrators will follow.

This view of political behaviour would be criticized because it ignores the personal and ethical perspectives on why people engage in it. It is clear from the negative perspective on politics that there are individuals who use it for their own ends, rather than for the benefit of the organization. It can be used to help or harm individuals just as it can be a process of attempting to acquire power to enable decisions to be implemented that could be beneficial to everyone.

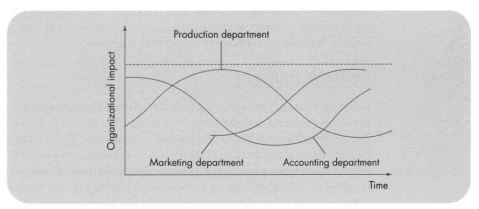

FIGURE 20.7   Organizational politics: impact and success.

Political strategies

The use of power within an organizational setting involves adopting one of three strategies. They will be discussed in the subsections that follow.

Offensive strategies

These political strategies are effectively initiating behaviours. They represent the attacking behaviours that are intended to gain advantage over another individual or group. In military terms these are the equivalent of one army going on the offensive and attacking another before it has time to marshal its defences. An example of this form of political behaviour is described in Management in Action 20.5.

Stop | Consider

How could James have reacted to the situation other than by resigning and what might the consequences of that have been?

What does this tell you about political behaviour among managers?

Frequently political behaviour contains a high degree of *normal* or *allowable* behaviour but applied in ways that produce a particular end result. In Management in Action 20.5 it can be reasonably inferred that James' manager wanted rid of him as he was perceived to be a threat to the manager's position. However, prioritizing work and reallocating resources are all perfectly legitimate practices in running a department. It is the intent behind such actions that indicates a political motive. In reality, James was set up to fail by his boss who used political strategies and company procedures in a way which cloaked the real intention and allowed it to take place.

There is another type of offensive strategy based on the view that: 'If it is not possible to look good oneself, then make the others look bad.' This is an *undermining* strategy. It covers many different types of behaviour all intended to weaken the position of another individual or group. Examples include making disparaging comments about the target at either a personal or professional level. It can involve recalling with gusto any past mistakes as evidence of continued weakness. This can also lead to *whispering campaigns*. The spreading of rumour without evidence can be a very effective means of undermining other people without the need for evidence to support the assertions.

Defensive strategies

Defensive strategies are those that are not intended to harm others but are destined to prevent harm being done by them. In Management in Action 20.5 James decided not to defend himself as such but to find another job and leave. He could have attempted to fight fire with fire and engage in a range of political behaviours to protect himself. For example, he could have made a number of alliances with more senior managers who may have been prepared to defend him against his boss. He could have set out to undermine the position of his boss with other managers. James could also have attempted to set his manager up for a fall by deliberately doing something wrong that would directly reflect on his boss. It

Getting rid of a subordinate

This is a true story, according to the individual who told it to me during an interview. Only the details and names have been changed to protect the individuals and the organization.

James was an experienced manager and had a particular expertise in personnel management, having worked for a number of years with one of the large consultancies. He was recruited by a large manufacturing company to act as deputy manager in the personnel department in preparation for the departmental manager's promotion about six months later. The existing departmental manager had not worked in any other organization since leaving university some 15 years earlier.

Shortly after James joined the company it became apparent that it was entering a difficult period and that restructuring was a real possibility. It was at that time that the departmental manager began to adopt an offensive political campaign against a number of people including James. James had been recruited to take over from his manager and it was becoming apparent that

this would not happen. The department manager was not going to be promoted in the restructuring. James was therefore a potential threat to his manager's position.

The political campaign included deliberately holding back the start date for jobs that James was to undertake and reallocating staff and other resources away from supporting him. Performance was, however, still to be judged against the original objectives and timescales for the work allocated to James. Eventually, after about seven months, it was time to review James' salary. His manager produced an annual report that claimed that James was under-performing, incompetent and should be down-graded, perhaps even dismissed. Such performance certainly did not justify receiving any pay increase that year. James, having suspected what was to happen, had found another job and so tendered his resignation on the spot.

should not be inferred that defensive political behaviour is weak or less aggressive than the offensive form. It can be just as effective and equally nasty in execution. It is the intention, not the content that differentiates it.

Neutral strategies

This approach to political behaviour reflects a stance that does not actively engage in it for either of the two purposes so far described. It reflects an actively protectionist approach to politics. It is an approach that attempts to keep out of political battles but one which will defend itself if absolutely necessary. It is an appeasing approach to the existence of politics. It is easiest to use offensive politics against a neutral strategy as it takes considerable pressure to begin to force the other party to retaliate. James could be described as adopting a neutral strategy in response to his manager's attack. He did not defend himself other than by attempting to do the best job that he could and by attempting to be considered as a non-threatening subordinate by his manager. In the end rather than *take on* his manager in a battle, he side-stepped the problem by leaving the organization.

Some of the tactics that are used politically within an organization are identified in Table 19.1 (from the previous chapter) as influencing tactics. Behaving politically is a process of attempting to influence other people towards a decision, viewpoint or course of action favoured by the initiator. Consequently, many of the strategies adopted can be categorized under the headings in that table. Other researchers have identified categories that are framed slightly differently. For example, Yukl and Falbe (1990) identified the tactics described in Table 20.2.

Using political behaviour

It can be seen by comparing Tables 19.1 (influencing tactics) from the previous chapter and 20.2 (political tactics) from this chapter that although the terms used are different, they are broadly similar in flavour and content. These behaviours refelct the purpose of much political behaviour as an intention to influence other people in some way or another. Moorhead and Griffin (1992) bring together the work of a number of other writers in order to identify the main techniques associated with political behaviour. Table 20.3 lists the main techniques identified.

The following sections consider each technique briefly.

Control of information

There is a saying that information is power. The ability to determine who has access to what information provides a particularly powerful opportunity to influence events. Decision

Tactics	Description
Pressure tactics	The use of demands, threats, or intimidation to convince you to comply with a request or to support a proposal
Upward appeals	Persuading you that the request is approved by higher management or appealing to higher management for assistance in gaining your compliance with the request
Exchange tactics	Making explicit or implicit promises that you will receive rewards or tangible benefits if you comply with a request or support a proposal or reminding you of a prior favour to be reciprocated
Coalition tactics	Seeking the aid of others to persuade you to do something or using the support of others as an argument for you to agree also
Ingratiating tactics	Seeking to get you in a good mood or making you think favourably of the influence agent before asking you to do something
Rational persuasion	Using logical arguments and factual evidence to persuade you that a proposal or request is viable and likely to result in the attainment of task objectives
Inspirational appeals	Making an emotional request or proposal that arouses enthusiasm by appealing to your values and ideals or by increasing your confidence that you can do it
Consultation tactics	Seeking your participation in making a decision or planning how to implement a proposed policy, strategy or change

TABLE 20.2 Political tactics (*adapted from*: Yukl, G and Falbe, CM (1990) Influence tactics and objectives in upward, downward and lateral influence attempts, *Journal of Applied Psychology*, 75)

making requires information. The individual with access to the best range and quality of information is the one most likely to be in a strong position to plan effective strategies for the future. In relation to the stock market, access to inside information on company plans could make anyone privy to it rich as they could either buy or sell shares at the most advantageous price. That is why *insider dealing*, as it is called, is regarded as a serious offence and market authorities are constantly monitoring market activity in order to detect and prevent it.

Control of communication channels

The control of who has access to whom, who communicates with whom etc. can significantly influence events. During the 1960s, 1970s and early 1980s most trade unions regarded communication with employees as their prerogative. In situations where particularly militant trade union representatives were present threats of strike action would be used if managers proposed addressing their workforce directly. In such situations whoever actually communicated with the workforce was likely to put their particular perspective on the message being communicated. This trade union control over the communication channels within organizations is now rare as more joint or parallel processes now exist. However, there are many examples that can be found within the management levels of an organization. Simple examples include who is invited to attend particular meetings and who might be left off the distribution list for a report.

Use of outside specialists

The use of external specialists can be a powerful lever to ensuring that one's point of view is favoured. The selection of a particular consultant or expert is a difficult process as there are many thousands of potential candidates available. It is relatively easy to select one who might be expected (or told) to support a particular point of view. Even the large practices have an interest in repeat business. The careful selection and briefing of consultants ensures that they are able to deliver an *appropriate* report and recommendations. The question is 'appropriate' from whose perspective? This can reflect a process that adds weight to the position of those insiders who also lean towards that proposed viewpoint, as outside experts are *supposed/assumed* to be independent, and expert.

Control over work and meeting agendas

Being able to influence events directly is another useful political technique. The individual who determines the agenda for a meeting determines what can (and frequently of more

♦ Controlling information
♦ Control of communication channels
♦ Using outside specialists
♦ Control of the work and/or meetings agenda
♦ Game playing
♦ Impression and image management
♦ Creating coalitions
♦ Control of decision-making criteria

TABLE 20.3 Political techniques (*adapted from*: Moorhead, G and Griffin, RW (1992) *Organizational Behaviour*, 3rd edn, Houghton Mifflin, Boston, MA)

significance what cannot) be discussed. This allows the direction of decision making to be determined and channelled to the advantage of the person setting the agenda. A related political technique is to accept responsibility for writing the minutes of a meeting. Very few meeting records are verbatim and so the writer has considerable discretion over what is recorded and more importantly how the content of the record should be phrased. Naturally it is usual for the minutes to be verified at a subsequent meeting but a skilled political operator would not find that a particular problem.

Game playing

There are individuals who appear to enjoy the 'sport' of playing politics just to see what happens and to demonstrate their ability to control events. Management in Action 20.5 described the events surrounding James and his eventual departure from the organization. The department manager in that situation was playing games in that he was using established procedure and practice to achieve a particular objective that would not have been officially sanctioned. As an individual he also enjoyed engaging in political activity as he tried similar 'games' with other people and his colleagues.

Impression and image management

This represents a less direct approach to politics as it involves creating an image that in turn could be expected to influence events. Simple examples include attempting to become associated with successful projects or to distance oneself from failing ones. It is not unusual for a manager to sit on the sidelines of a particular programme of work and to suddenly seek to take a high profile near to completion when success is more certain. Claiming major involvement in particular projects is another common example of overstating reality in order to enhance one's reputation. Of course, this must be done carefully as a number of people will know the truth on such claims. Once exposed as false claims they can undermine every other claim made by that individual. Bromley (1993) provides an analysis of many aspects of impression management which collectively demonstrate the complexity of these psychological constructs.

Creating coalitions

Political alliances are another means of achieving desired objectives. Imagine a situation in which a personnel manager wishes to introduce a new payment system into a company. The sales manager may not see any benefit or problems with such a scheme and so may be neutral towards it. The production manager may be in favour if higher productivity and reduced cost is possible. The finance director may be openly hostile towards the idea as it would create additional work for his department. The employees may also be against the idea because higher productivity may result in job losses and having to work harder. Clearly the personnel manager needs to ensure that all the managers are supportive of the plan before attempting to convince the employees of its merits. The finance director is presumably more senior to the other managers and as a result would carry 'more weight' in collective decision making. Perhaps if the sales manager could be persuaded actively to support the scheme and ways could be found to lessen the burden on the finance department then open hostility might be reduced. The personnel manager would probably begin to lobby the sales manager for support, perhaps using the argument that the higher productivity achieved would benefit the sales department through pricing and delivery benefits. This together with a scheme redesign might be enough to sway the finance director in a meeting.

Taken to extreme this approach to political behaviour can be little more than horse trading. Attempting to operate on the basis of buying co-operation for past favours or seeking support in return for promises of future help on matters of value to the courted individual. At an organizational level this approach reflects the cartel approach to fixing markets in favour of particular suppliers.

Control over decision-making criteria

It is sometimes possible for a manager to set down the criteria against which decisions will be made and in so doing they do not have to be directly involved in order to influence events. It is not uncommon for industrial relations specialists facing the annual negotiation round with the trade unions to initially hold meetings with other managers to determine the negotiating strategy. In doing so it can happen that a chief executive will set out in very clear terms what they expect to happen and in effect to write the script for the negotiators. Clearly, in this situation very little scope is available to the negotiation team to respond creatively to the dynamics of the situation and create a settlement acceptable to all sides. The 'dead hand' of the chief executive rests over the situation and effectively controls events in absentia. In a more general context such approaches can allow a leader to claim non-involvement in a situation while in reality controlling events. They are able to distance themselves from events both physically and psychologically while retaining control in reality.

Managing political behaviour

The degree to which it is possible to manage political behaviour in others is difficult to specify. It depends on so many factors. For example, the style of management within the organization can determine the level and volume of politicking that takes place. The personality of the individual is also likely to influence their predisposition for playing games and other forms of politics. The skill level and networks of the individuals concerned can also influence events.

Managers are inevitably in competition with each other for resources and power. There are never enough resources to meet every possible demand within an organization. Every manager would like to feel that they could make a positive contribution to the organization given a completely free hand in spending unlimited amounts of money. However, it is just not possible for any organization to be in that position and therefore a process of *rationing* must exist. Rationing implies deciding between competing options for allocating scarce resource and finding ways to *prioritize* alternative options. This creates a context where managers must justify proposed actions and find ways to gain support for their plans. Politicking can be used to influence these processes and increase the probability of success.

In order to attempt to control and minimize the harmful effects associated with politics it is necessary to find ways to encourage competition without allowing hidden agendas to flourish. Specifying in advance how decisions will be made and by not allowing power to become a means of acquiring resources are just some of the ways that this can be encouraged. By separating the evaluation of resource allocation from issues associated with performance evaluation and promotion some control of politics can also be achieved. The sending of very clear signals that politicking will not be tolerated by dealing severely with obvious cases and encouraging examples to be openly discussed are other means of minimizing its impact.

Conflict and politics: an applied perspective

In the previous chapter it was pointed out that Braverman (1974) considered that the organizational history of the twentieth century could be described in terms of increasing management control and the potential for *conflict* and *alienation* that flowed from that situation. Workers are increasingly treated as just one of the resources available to managers and consequently subject to their attempts at manipulation. It is against that background that the concept of *resistance* is an important counterbalance to the domination of capital. However, it is also interesting to remember that managers also are workers, they are not the real owners of capital, and as such are subjected to many of the same constraints as workers. They are of course in a privileged position and, acting in *loco parentis* for the absent owners, are able to pass on down the line attempts to achieve ever tighter control and manipulation, perpetuating the potential for *control* and *politics* to function within an organization.

There are different views about the impact of the existence of *conflict* within an organization. The response to the existence of real or potential conflict would depend in part on the view of the dominant stakeholders about its role within the organization. Against this backdrop much management activity over the past few years has been an attempt to *reframe organizational reality* for employees so that effective (and tighter) control can be exercised but in ways that minimize the risk and consequences of conflict. The complex interlinkage between power, politics, conflict and control in an organizational context are reflected in the example described in Management in Action 20.6.

Stop | Consider

If you had been the senior manager of the new newspaper Reforma *how would you have dealt with the need to sell you paper? What tactics would you use and why?*

What probability of success and problems might you expect and how would you deal with them?

Conflict is regarded by most managers as something to be avoided within their organization. It is thought to be a distraction; a sign of dissension or disloyalty; an indication that their 'message' is not getting through; even an indication that their capabilities as a manager are being challenged or questioned. It is also thought by many managers to be a reflection of the natural attitudes of workers to work and the role of management. The views of such managers are neatly summed up in the often told story resulting from the visit of chairman of British Coal to a coal mine in the north-east of England in the early 1960s. The particular pit visited had a high absence level even by industry standards and the chairman asked one miner why he only worked four days each week. The answer came back without hesitation: 'Because I can't earn enough in three days!' In other words, I only work here because of circumstances and the money that it provides. Many managers think that represents how most, if not all, workers think. Consequently the risk of conflict is ever near as managers seek to drive for productivity, quality, commitment etc.

MANAGEMENT IN ACTION 20.6

Mexican union cries foul at paper's tactics

The Union of Newspaper Hawkers has 17,000 members in Mexico City along with the exclusive rights to sell newspapers in the city. However, even with a population of about 8 million people only around 500,000 daily newspapers are sold. There are 32 different daily newspapers in Mexico city and nearly all charge the same price (60 US cents) per copy. Into the fray a new newspaper (*Reforma*) has emerged and it wants to dictate when and how its papers are sold. The union does not want to go along with that and sees it as a direct challenge to its position.

It is the Union of Newspaper Hawkers that dictates where and when all of the newspapers are sold. News stands do not open before 8 am and they are invariably loaded down with papers that will not be sold. The publishers of about half the daily papers are not too concerned about volume of sales as most of their income is derived from flat-fee government advertising. Private advertising, which is dependent upon volume of sales, does not contribute much to the income of most of the publishers. *Reforma* has been in a continuous battle with the union since it sought to control where and when its papers would be available. It wanted to target the more affluent areas,

but could not do so through the union distribution system.

The distribution of *Reforma* was done through a motley salesforce of journalists, students, politicians and housewives who suffered violent attacks and theft over the initial weeks of its existence. In a twist of tactics, the publishers of *Reforma* sent its own vendors out onto the streets on the Sunday that Mexico celebrates its revolution. It is one of only five days in the year when the union does not work and so newspapers are not normally available. Union leaders claim that *Reforma* is attempting to destroy the union, which, it argues, provides a service to many publications. The government also regards the union in a friendly light having used it in the past as a last stand against renegade or independent publications. However, the publishers of *Reforma* have appealed to the Federal Competition Commission to be allowed to distribute the paper themselves, and have ignored negotiations at the Interior Ministry which is responsible for regulating the media.

Adapted from: Bardacke, T (1994) Mexican Union cries foul at paper's tactics, *Financial Times*, 22 November, p 22.

Conversely, some workers regard managers as the enemy and as deliberately seeking to take advantage at any opportunity. Consequently a lack of trust can exist and form fertile ground for conflict to erupt. Many practising managers and writers would subscribe to the *pluralist* or *unitarist* perspective on conflict discussed earlier. They would argue that attempts at employee *involvement* and *participation* over recent years have represented attempts to move away from what has been described as the old-style confrontational basis to the employment relationship. Cynics might argue that such approaches do not represent a new paradigm in management. They simply represent a recognition that the social conditions within which work is carried out have changed and that managers have found it necessary to soften their approach in order to find more convenient ways to continue to enact the ongoing struggle between capital and labour.

The use of political behaviour can enhance the relative level of power and influence held by an individual or group, thereby increasing their status and perhaps their ability to exercise control and avoid conflict. Or alternatively, increased power relative to an adversary might provide a basis for winning if conflict actually erupts into hostility, strike or other industrial action. Of course, *resistance* reflects another major concept that forms part of the *latent conflict* within an organization. As indicated in the earlier discussion it can find expression in many ways, going slow, withholding effort and sabotage all reflecting ways that workers can engage in forms of conflict without open hostility.

Politics, by way of contrast, can be seen as a means of sharing power among a number of interested groups and individuals. At an organizational level it can provide a mechanism for allowing the relative power of the various departments and subsidiary companies to rise and fall without adversely effecting the structure and performance of the overall organization. It is, however, possible for political behaviour to be misused to the personal advantage of those perpetrating it. In such situations it is not uncommon to find the existence of special interest groups that are informal, perhaps temporary, but definitely outside the formal organizational framework.

Cliques are one form of group whose prime motivation is the defence of the members against the interests of other groups and individuals. Trade unions exist to advance and protect the interests of members against the inevitable power imbalance in the employment relationship. Another example would be a coffee break group that attempted to provide member support against the behaviour of a dictatorial and inconsistent boss. *Cabals* are another form of group that attempt to take the initiative within an organization to the positive advantage of its members (Burns, 1955). The phrase *young Turks* is frequently use to describe the activities of young executives who attempt to force the organization to adopt policies supportive of their wishes. In that sense it represents a proactive approach to the acquisition and use of power through political means.

Political behaviour is encouraged to exist in situations where the formal roles and authority are unclear. If the designated roles and lines of authority are clearly specified then it is easy for breaches and deviations to be identified. In addition it is also easy to appeal to the formal structural mechanisms as ways of combating the politicking. There are a number of issues that emerges from this view of political behaviour and organizational informality or lack of clarity. A number of new structural forms of organization attempt to take out the formality and rigidity of structure originating from *bureaucracy*. The informality and lack of clear role definition implied by these recent innovations could provide the very basis on which political behaviour flourishes. It is possible that without very clear attempts to manage out these aspects of organizational activity they could offset the advantages available through the informality and ability to respond rapidly to market conditions.

There are also managerial benefits from being political. Over the past few years organizations have been delayering and downsizing, all of which impacts directly on the number of management jobs available. This has had a major impact on management careers and job opportunity. No longer can managers expect to be protected from the harsh realities that have faced many other occupational groups. As a consequence they find it necessary to take a more active role in managing their own careers and survival. This can lead to political behaviour as a means of influencing decisions about job security and career development. Being considered a good employee is now as important for every manager as it is for every other employee. Politics can be used to enhance the probability of success by tipping the balance one way rather than another. Trust and loyalty between employer and employee has always been part of this non-political equation and yet in the emerging world of personal careers writers such as Charles Heckscher suggest that it should be eliminated. This view is outlined in Management in Action 20.7.

MANAGEMENT IN ACTION 20.7

The importance of stamping out loyalty

In a book review of *White Collar Blues: Management Loyalties in an Age of Corporate Restructuring* by Charles Heckscher (1995), published by HarperCollins, Jackson identifies some interesting ideas. In the USA, middle managers account for 8% of the workforce, yet between 1988 and 1993 they accounted for 19% of the job losses. The old middle-class ethos of commitment to the organization was based on a two-way commitment. In return for security, managers worked extra hours, took risks and allowed inroads into their personal lives. Heckscher suggests (as have others) that this two-way commitment has been broken by employers and so they cannot expect middle managers to continue to support a one-sided deal.

The existence of communal trust and loyalty between the members of an organization developed as a means of allowing the bureaucratic forms of organization to function effectively. However, Heckscher argues that this is now too rigid and does not allow change to happen at the necessary rate. Heckscher goes on to argue that it should not be a question of how to regain the loyalty of middle managers, but how to stamp it out once and for all. While managers cling to the debris of the old order, fundamental change cannot happen and continuous decline becomes inevitable. This creates a cycle of yet more drudgery, further resentment and less likeli-

hood that change will be successful.

Some of Heckscher's work has revealed that change was least successful in organizations in which loyalty was strongest and managers were most over-worked. Conversely, change was most effective in those organizations in which the level of loyalty was the weakest. A different form of loyalty is proposed by Heckscher, that of loyalty not to the organization, but to the project on which the individual is working. This may last for three to five years and then the individual moves on to another project, perhaps even with a different company.

There are, of course, many implications of this form of working. Individuals would have to accept greater levels of responsibility for their own career, job networking and training. Equally, organizational issues such as pension portability and commitment to making individuals more marketable on a wider scale would need to be introduced. But for those organizations and individuals who have been able to make this change the benefits in being more relaxed and confident about the future and their place in it are available.

Adapted from: Jackson, T (1995) The importance of stamping out loyalty, *Financial Times*, 30 March, p 18.

Stop | Consider   *Reflect on the implications of the views of Heckscher on the nature and form of trust as it should be developed. What implications might this approach to trust have for conflict and political activity within organizations?*

There is also a link between the type of organization and the form that politics takes within it. For example, in bureaucratic organizations it is the audit functions that enjoy a high degree of power and influence. The predominance of rules and procedures encourages the policing role in an attempt to prevent fraud. In organic types of organization it is the advisory functions that have most power as they attempt to maintain consistency of operation across a range of relatively segregated operating units. In this type of situation the organizational politics would tend to be aimed at holding or changing the power balance between line and staff functions.

Conclusions

This chapter has attempted to consider the related topics of conflict and politics. These subjects have strong links with negotiation, power and control which were introduced in previous chapters. Both conflict and politics can be argued to be endemic to organizational life. There are also individuals who introduce an element of game playing intended to enhance their power base and as a means of making work more interesting. Politics and conflict can also introduce a source of fun and enjoyment to the observers of this behaviour in others. However, there is a danger of trivializing these concepts if this aspect is overplayed. Being the subject of political activity is no joke for most people and conflict can only result in a dissipating effect on corporate and individual performance. The difficulty is that, following the Marxist and labour process perspectives, and much common experience, they are ever present within the employment situation.

Discussion questions

1. Define the following key terms used in this chapter:

Conflict	*Cabals*	*Politics*
Resistance	*Unitarism*	*Conflict-handling styles*
Political strategies	*Pluralism*	*Sabotage*
Compliance culture	*Political strategies*	*Forms of conflict*
Sources of conflict	*Labour process*	*Cliques*

2. What are the major forms of conflict that might be expected to arise in a group context? How do these differ from individual expressions of conflict?

3. Managers must compete for scarce resources. Political behaviour can influence decisions. In what ways might it be possible to encourage competition while minimizing the potentially harmful effects of political behaviour?

4. What does the term resistance mean and how does it relate to the concepts of power, control and conflict? Illustrate your ideas with examples from organizations with which you are familiar.

5. Describe the various sources of conflict that exist within an organizational context. To what extent can any of them be eliminated?

6 Compare and contrast the influencing tactics identified in Table 19.1 (previous chapter) with the political techniques identified in Table 20.3 (this chapter).

7. Identify and provide an analysis of the procedural devices that can be used to minimize and resolve conflict within an organization.

8. 'Conflict management represents the biggest challenge for every manager.' To what

extent and why do you agree with this statement?

9. Outline the labour process theory and explain how it can inform an understanding of the concept of conflict within an organizational context.

10. 'Politics is a process which cannot be eliminated from an organization therefore it should be ignored in running a business.' Discuss this statement.

Research activities

1. In the library find six different journal articles associated with conflict and politics. What are the different points of view expressed in these papers about these concepts and how do they support or contradict the discussion in this chapter? In addition, attempt to find any books on the subject of how managers should use politics and/or conflict. How do the views expressed in these books differ if compared with the academic papers that you identified?

2. Speak to a number of practising managers about the subjects of conflict and politics. How do they describe these terms and how significant do they consider them to be in practical management activities? Do the different types of organization or industry have an impact on the perception of the managers about these subjects? Do the interviewees consider that politics can be controlled, if so how?

3. Examine the national press, magazines and journals for as much information as you can find on a particular industrial dispute. Put together an analysis of the situation in terms of the material presented in this chapter and the previous one (power and control). In your analysis specifically consider how the dispute arose and developed; could it have been resolved earlier and why was it not handled in that way; who stood to gain most from the situation being handled in the way that it was and why; how have events developed since the dispute was resolved?

Key reading

From Clark, H, Chandler, J and Barry, J (1994) *Organization and Identities: Text and Readings in Organizational Behaviour*, International Thomson Business Press, London.

✦ Kanter, RM: Men and women of the corporation, p 152. This considers issues associated with experience within an organization that contain examples of power, conflict and control.

✦ Cockburn, C: Male dominance and technological change, p 197. This extract considers how male dominance can be reaffirmed through the application of technology.

✦ Roethlisberge, FJ and Dickson, WJ: Group restriction of output, p 247. This identifies the way that employees manipulate events in an attempt to ensure that they are not at the whim of management.

✦ Hobsbawm, EJ and Rudé, G: Early forms of worker resistance – swing riots, p 317. This extract demonstrates that conflict is liable to erupt if those subjected to direct forms of control feel that they have nothing to lose.

✦ Taylor, L and Walton, P: Industrial sabotage, p 321. This provides another example of employee reaction to strong control.

- ◆   Hyman, R: The power of collective action, p 322. Reflects on the role and value of collective action as a means of resolving conflict.
- ◆   Braverman, H: The degradation of work, p 385. This considers the effects of control and conflict on individuals through the emergence of degradation.
- ◆   Marx, K: Alienated labour, p 387. Introduces some of Marx's views on alienation and its roots in the capitalist nature of work.
- ◆   Fromm, E: Alienation, p 391. This introduces another perspective on how work is managed. Implicit are the notions of control and conflict underpinning much management practice.
- ◆   Wright Mills, C: The cheerful robot, p 396. This material considers the concept of freedom of the individual in the context of the needs of organization.

Further reading

Caws, P (ed.) (1989) *The Causes of Quarrel: Essays on Peace, War, and Thomas Hobbes*, Beacon Press, Boston, MA. This book provides a philosophical and political review of many aspects associated with conflict and control in an international context. Although not directly intended as an organizational text, it does incorporate a wide range of parallels.

Edelmann, RJ (1993) *Interpersonal Conflicts at Work*, British Psychological Society, Leicester. This small book is intended to help the reader to understand the causes of a range of interpersonal conflicts that can arise in a work setting and to be able to develop strategies to cope with them more effectively.

Gunn, C (1992) *Nightmare on Lime Street: Whatever Happened to Lloyd's of London*, Smith Gryphon, London. This book is based in the world of the insurance market. In describing and analyzing the events surrounding three years of disastrous losses for the investors of Lloyd's it becomes clear that there are many issues associated with conflict, politics and control.

Heller, R (1985) *The Naked Manager: Games Executives Play*, McGraw-Hill, New York. Considers a broad range of the games that are played within organizations. They are not directly political in the negative sense of the term. Nevertheless it is possible to gain a flavour of the complexity and subtlety of much of this activity.

Jay, A (1987) *Management and Machiavelli*, revised edn, Hutchinson Business, London. A humorous text which considers many aspects associated with power and authority in management. It does not take Machiavelli's work specifically as its basis, but his spirit is evident. A translation of Machiavelli's original work, which is very accessible and available as a 1981 Penguin book, is also well worth reading.

Kolb, DM and Bartunek, JM (eds) (1992) *Hidden Conflict in Organizations: Uncovering Behind-the-Scenes Disputes*, Sage, Newbury Park, CA. This book provides an insight into a wide range of dispute and conflict situations that are not at first glance formally part of organizational life. The book surfaces many otherwise hidden or cloaked features of conflict and its resolution.

Pascale, RT (1991) *Managing on the Edge: How Successful Companies Use Conflict to Stay Ahead*, Penguin, London. This book takes the view that conflict is an aspect of human behaviour which is to be welcomed within an organizational setting. It encourages a healthy tension between the individuals and functional groupings which can be used to the benefit of the business through the synergy generated.

References

Armstrong, M (1991) *A Handbook of Personnel Management Practice*, 4th edn, Kogan Page, London.

Ashforth, BE and Lee, RT (1990) Defensive behaviour in organizations: a preliminary model, *Human Relations*, July, 621–48.

Blyton, P and Turnbull, P (1994) *The Dynamics of Employee Relations*, Macmillan, Basingstoke.

Braverman, H (1974) *Labour and Monopoly Capital: The Degradation of Work in the Twentieth Century*, Monthly Review Press, New York.

Bromley, DB (1993) *Reputation, Image and Impression Management*, John Wiley, Chichester.

Brown G (1977) *Sabotage: A Study of Industrial Conflict*, Spokesman Books, Nottingham.

Burns, T (1955) The reference of conduct in small groups, *Human Relations*, **8**, 467–86.

Clarke, J, Hall, S, Jefferson, T and Roberts, B (eds) (1976) Subculture, Cultures and Class: A Theoretical Overview. In *Resistance Through Rituals: Youth Subcultures in Post-War Britain*, Hutchinson, London.

Collinson, D (1994) Strategies of Resistance: Power, Knowledge and Subjectivity in the Workplace. In Jermier, JM, Knights, D and Nord, WR (eds) *Resistance and Power in Organizations*, Routledge, London.

Fisher, R and Ury, W (1986) *Getting to Yes: Negotiating Agreement Without Giving In*, Penguin, New York.

Foucault, M (ed.) (1975) *I Pierre Rivière, having Slaughtered my Mother, my Sister, and my Brother: A Case of Parricide in the 19th Century*, trans F Jellinek, University of Nebraska Press, Lincoln.

Fox, A (1966) Industrial Sociology and Industrial Relations. Royal Commission Research Paper No. 3, HMSO, London.

Gandz, J and Murray, V (1980) The experience of workplace politics, *Academy of Management Journal*, June, 237–51.

Hyman, R (1987) Strategy or structure? Capital, labour and control, *Work, Employment and Society*, **1**, 1, 25–55.

LaNuez, D and Jermier, JM (1994) Sabotage by Managers and Technocrats: Neglected Patterns of Resistance at Work. In Jermier, JM, Knights, D and Nord, WR (eds) *Resistance and Power in Organizations*, Routledge, London.

Legge, K (1995) *HRM, Rhetorics and Reality*, Macmillan, London.

Lewicki, RJ and Bunker, BB (1996) Developing and Maintaining Trust in Work Relationships. In Kramer, RM and Tyler, TR (eds) *Trust in Organizations: Frontiers of Theory and Research*, Sage, Thousand Oaks, CA.

Mayes, BT and Allen, RW (1977) Toward a definition of organizational politics, *Academy of Management Review*, **2**, 672–7.

Moorhead, G and Griffin, RW (1992) *Organizational Behaviour*, 3rd edn, Houghton Mifflin, Boston, MA.

Miceli, MP and Near, JP (1997) Whistle-Blowing as Antisocial Behaviour. In Giacalone, RA and Greenburg, J (eds) *Antisocial Behaviour in Organizations*, Sage, Thousand Oaks, CA.

Pocket Oxford Dictonary (1968) Compiled by Fowler, FG and Fowler, HW, 5th edn Oxford University Press, Oxford.

Salaman, G (1979) *Work Organizations: Resistance and Control*, Longman, London.

Sheppard, BH and Tuchinsky, M (1996) Micro-OB and the Network Organization. In Kramer, RM and Tyler, TR (eds) *Trust in Organizations: Frontiers of Theory and Research*, Sage, Thousand Oaks, CA.

Stacey, RD (2000) *Strategic Management and Organisational Dynamics: The Challenge of Complexity*, 3rd edn Pearson Education, Harlow.

Thomas, K (1976) Conflict Management. In Dunnette, MD (ed.) *Handbook of Industrial and Organizational Psychology*, Rand McNally, New York.

Thompson, P (1989) *The Nature of Work: An Introduction to Debates on the Labour Process*, 2nd edn, Macmillan, Basingstoke.

Thompson, P and McHugh, D (1995) *Work Organizations: A Critical Introduction*, 2nd edn, Macmillan, Basingstoke.

Torrington, D and Hall, L (1991) *Personnel Management: A New Approach*, 2nd edn, Prentice Hall, Hemel Hempstead.

Whetten, DA and Cameron, KS (1991) *Developing Management Skills*, 2nd edn, HarperCollins, New York.

Willis, P (1990) Masculinity and Factory Labour. In Alexander, J and Seidman, S (eds) *Culture and Society: Contemporary Debates*, Cambridge University Press, Cambridge.

Yukl, G and Falbe, CM (1990) Influence tactics and objectives in upward, downward, and lateral influence attempts, *Journal of Applied Psychology*, **7**, 132–40.

CHAPTER 21

Stress

CHAPTER SUMMARY

This chapter will consider the nature of stress in the work environment. It will begin with a review of what stress is together with the consideration of a number of related concepts. This will be followed by a review of the sources of stress before moving on to introduce the effects that it can have on both the individual and organization. There is a growing recognition of the potentially negative effects of stress on individual and organizational performance and therefore the next section considers the most commonly found mechanisms and approaches to dealing with it. The chapter will conclude with a number of managerial perspectives and insights on the topic.

LEARNING OBJECTIVES

After studying this chapter and working through the associated Management in Action panels, Discussion questions and Research activities, you should be able to:

✦ Understand the distinction and similarities between stress and concepts such as burnout and pressure.

✦ Describe the physiological effects of stress and the consequent impact on the behaviour of individuals.

✦ Explain some of the coping mechanisms for dealing with stress.

✦ Outline the sources of stress that have relevance to an organizational context.

✦ Assess the impact of stress on the management and performance of an organization.

✦ Appreciate the effects that stress can have on the individual at work and how coping strategies can assist in minimizing the potentially harmful effects.

✦ Discuss a range of managerial perspectives on the nature, consequences and coping strategies associated with stress.

✦ Detail the theoretical underpinnings of stress and its management.

Introduction

Everyone experiences stress at various points in their life. Students about to take a university entrance examination the result of which could determine the direction of the rest of their lives would be a classic example. There are, however, many other examples such as starting a new job, facing up to a potentially serious illness and the effects of a fear of flying are just some of the more obvious. The common effects of stress are also well known and familiar to most human beings. They include a feeling of helplessness and of not being able to cope, sweating, shortness of breath and an inability to concentrate.

One of the first questions that is asked in relation to stress is that if it is a phenomenon that produces negative consequences for the individual why does it exist? Evolution, so it is argued should have surely *dropped* this aspect of human physiology many generations ago. Well it has not, it is still with us and it is suggested that it is becoming a major problem for individuals, organizations and society. For example in Japan there is now a cause of death known as *karoshi*, or sudden death from overwork that claims the lives of an estimated 10,000 people each year (Dawkins, 1993). The results of a survey carried out in the UK during 1994 revealed that 67% of respondents claimed overwork caused stress, 55% were fearful of being made redundant and suffered stress as a consequence and 54% claimed that they did not get enough support at work which also caused stress. Outside work 88% of respondents claimed that financial pressure was stressful and 84% replied that relationships were also stressful (Hall, 1994).

Stress – a preliminary review

There are a number of features associated with stress that can help to protect the individual from overloading themselves physically, mentally or emotionally. It is frequently suggested that the reactions to stress are part of the *fight or flight* response capability that humans have in common with many other species. In order to protect itself (and frequently survive) an animal must be able to distinguish between situations in which it is appropriate to stay and fight or in which it is more sensible to withdraw and avoid the direct confrontation with a competitor for territory or a predator seeking its next meal. The physiological response to stress in humans effects the sympathetic nervous system (a subsystem of the autonomic nervous system) in ways that would prepare and predispose the *flight* response to occur if necessary.

However, the present-day living experience of many humans does not provide obvious opportunities for the individual to run away from whatever causes them stress. For example, a student under pressure before an exam is not totally able to withdraw from the situation and hence remove the stress. To do so would require a complete change of lifestyle. Human life patterns and experience are now so complex and with so many interrelated facets that to respond on the basis of single episodes is frequently inappropriate. For example parental and teacher expectation of a child's performance is interlinked with family and school life and job opportunities are linked to school and examination performance. The initial earnings levels in most jobs are rarely adequate in providing an opportunity for a new worker to become independent of family support at an early age. So the individual is effectively *locked into* a situation which is potentially stressful, being both dif-

MANAGEMENT IN ACTION 21.1

Managers working more than before

A survey of 1250 managers was carried out by the Institute of Management and DHL International (UK) in 1994. It sought to identify the amount of time that managers were at work and the reasons for it. Among the findings were:

✦ Almost 50% of managers indicated that their workloads had increased 'greatly' over the previous two years.

✦ The workloads of 20% of managers had increased by more than 15 hours each week over the previous two years.

✦ Over 40% of respondents worked more than 10 hours extra each week.

✦ 80% of managers said that they worked more than 6 hours each week in excess of their official working time.

✦ Almost 50% said that work took priority over everything else in their lives.

✦ The majority of respondents wanted to spend more time with family and friends.

✦ More managers than ever did their own typing and basic office tasks that might previously have been done by a secretary.

✦ Most of the additional workload arose from company restructuring.

✦ Most managers have fewer staff to support them.

Adapted from: Donkin, R (1995) Managers 'working more than before', *Financial Times*, 6 March, p 9.

ficult to escape from and difficult to live with. From an organizational point of view this situation is reflected in Management in Action 21.1 which describes the changing patterns of managerial experience of their workload, one of the major causes of stress for the individuals concerned.

| Stop | Consider

Can you think of any other possible explanations for the results of the survey reported in MiA 21.1 besides the 'fact' that everyone is actually working much harder?

How might you test out your ideas?

Having described stress in ways that might suggest an inevitability about its existence, a number of people do escape from it by running away from home or dropping out from a situation. There are many parallels in this with the way in which many adults responding to stress by removing themselves from the situation either physically or psychologically in an attempt to deal with the consequences of it. Some 23% of the 118 chief executives (from major British and European companies) who responded to a questionnaire-based survey carried out by Cooper and Sutherland were actively thinking of resigning as a result of the stress levels (Arkin, 1991).

Within an organizational context stress can originate from events and circumstances inside or outside that work setting. The effects of stress can also be felt both inside or outside the organization. In simplified form this produces a four-cell matrix (Figure 21.1) of stress contexts that can be used to categorize the events involved and identify appropriate forms of coping strategy.

Taking each of the four cells in turn:

✦ Contextual. With both the origins of the stress and the effects of it being within the organization it is the context and what is within it that should be the focus of attention. For example, one of the Further reading texts identified at the end of this chapter is about bullying at work. One of the consequences of this might be high labour turnover as those subjected to it leave at the earliest opportunity. So, in reviewing this situation management have both the problem and its solution under their direct sphere of influence.

✦ Personal. Where the source of the stress lies outside the organization but the repercussions are experienced within it different response modalities are necessary. For example, an employee experiencing domestic problems is unlikely to be reliable or effective while at work. The requirement to perform as a reliable employee can place additional levels of stress on the individual. Consequently, counselling might be one option that could assist the individual to identify ways to deal with the domestic problems and to cope more easily with the job requirements and thus reduce the level of stress.

✦ Insidious. Where the stress originates inside the organization but the primary effects on the individual lie outside it there are very real problems for the organization. Consider the subject of bullying once again. It is likely that the perpetrator would be more senior than the victim and that they would be at pains to mask their behaviour from those able to take action against them. So, it is not uncommon to find that acts of bullying come as a surprise and shock to more senior managers who see completely different personality and character aspects of the bully than does the victim. Victims who seek to complain about bullying can easily find themselves subjected to even more retaliation as inappropriate responses by senior managers alert the bully to the complaint. It is not surprising that victims often keep quiet and seek to withdraw from the situation as quickly as possible rather than *make waves*. Again, in such situations, it would not be unexpected to find that the major effects of stress are noticed outside work in the private life of the victim. Family, behavioural, health and other problems could be the result. In such situations it is difficult for an organization to identify the causes of the stress unless all managers are particularly sensitive to employee behaviour. Of course, if that were the situation it would be less likely that bullying would exist in the first place.

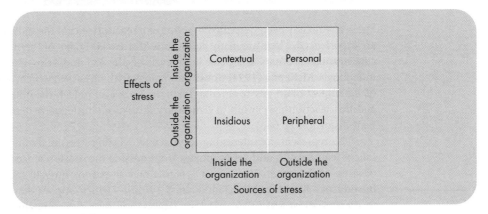

FIGURE 21.1   The stress context.

✦ Peripheral. This cell in the matrix represents circumstances in which both the source of the stress and its effects lie outside the organization. As such it is *peripheral* to the functioning of the organization and many managers would argue that it represents an irrelevance to them. However, an alternative view would hold that a caring employer should offer support to employees in attempting to improve the overall quality of life experienced by individuals. In more pragmatic terms, there are few circumstances in which there would be no organizational impact (however small) as a result of stress arising from an outside context.

Something that is a stressor for the individual may be completely outside work (say, the threat of losing a place on a local sports team to a very keen enthusiast) may result in sleeping problems and hence a tired employee at work. So, in the search for ever higher performance from employees, it would be of benefit to treat the existence this cell of the matrix with some scepticism. There are however some situations in which both cause and effect remain firmly outside the workplace. To escape from a more stressful situation at home into the predictable world of work can provide a form of escape (a form of the flight response) for some people for some of the time. However, even in this situation there will always be a risk of events becoming so stressful that this form of coping strategy breaks down.

One other aspect of stress is important to introduce. That is that individuals vary in their response to stressful situations. What is stressful for one person another can cope with easily and may not be regarded as even mildly stressful by them. The stress response is something that occurs within each individual and every individual has a personal view of events and a personal tolerance level for the pressures that are experienced. For example, some people are afraid of spiders and find being near them or even just looking at pictures of them distressing. Some people, however, keep spiders as pets and find them loveable creatures to be played with and held whenever possible.

So far this discussion has been about the subject of stress and has introduced it at a common sense level. It is now appropriate to consider the concept in a more structured and systematic manner, beginning with an attempt to define stress.

Stress – what is it?

Stress has already been described in terms of a reaction within the individual to events that are experienced. There are many definitions of stress and most of them consider it to be the consequence of events that place high levels of physical and/or psychological demand on individuals. McKenna (1994) draws the analogy with physics in which, 'stress arises because of the impact of an environmental force on a physical object; the object undergoes strain and this reaction may result in temporary distortion, but equally it could lead to permanent distortion' (p 585).

This represents an interesting approach to defining stress in that it reflects many of the salient features of it and yet originates from outside the social sciences. It links the origins of stress to environmental forces – events and situations outside the individual. It also introduces a term that is related to stress – *strain* – which implies that stress can be linked to pressure in one of its many forms. The notion of a *distortion* also alludes to a consequential change in the stressed object and, perhaps more significantly, that the effect can be either temporary or permanent. However, what this particular definition does not incorporate is a recognition that the effects of the stressor on the individual are to a significant extent dependent upon individual differences and experience. In physical terms the *distortion* is a function of the characteristics of the object under strain. For example some individuals find the thought of flying very stressful irrespective of the number of occasions that they do it. Other individuals find that having flown a number of times the level of stress experienced reduces and they can cope with it more easily.

In relation to the related concepts of *pressure* and *strain*, Handy (1993) offers the distinction that *pressure* represents stimulating stress and that *strain* reflects harmful stress. In practice, therefore, both represent types of stress. This distinction has a long tradition and originated from work in the 1930s by Selye (see Thompson and McHugh (1995, p 273)). It does have the benefit of providing the opportunity for considering the consequences of stress for the individual. The basis for this differential view of the effects of stress is that a certain level of it is necessary for generating performance, but that too much stress can reduce performance and be harmful to the individual. This perspective is frequently reflected in a diagram (see Figure 21.2).

The view of stress implied in diagrams such as Figure 21.2 are a useful way of linking many of the foregoing ideas, such as the relationship with physiological arousal. In *useability* terms it does, however, contain one major weakness. The levels of both stress and performance used in the model are not defined. In short what does *high* levels of stress and performance mean? It was suggested earlier in this chapter that the effects of stress are dependent on individual difference and experience. This would imply that every individual would have a different curve for each different stress-inducing situation. The model is therefore of general relevance but of limited predictive value. It would not, for example, help managers to determine the optimal level of stress in any specific work context. It could, however, lead them to explore how the variables could be measured and what they mean in that particular context. Even without precise definition to hold a debate in any specific context about what defines stress and performance could produce a very useful

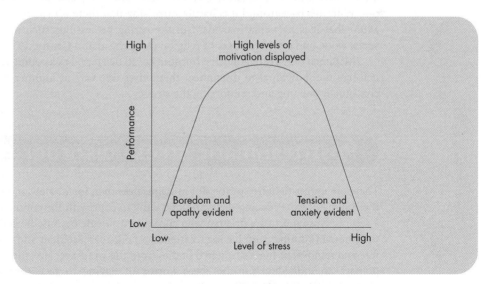

FIGURE 21.2 Stress and performance (*adapted from*: Moorhead, G and Griffin, RW (1992) *Organizational Behaviour*, 3rd edn, Houghton Mifflin, Boston, MA).

learning experience for the individuals and the organization, particularly if it produced action plans that were beneficial to both employees and organization.

Having explored the term stress in some depth and the links with the two related concepts of pressure and strain it would be useful to introduce two other concepts that are closely associated with it. McKenna (1994) discusses the concepts of burnout and post-traumatic stress disorder in this context and it is to a discussion of these that we now turn.

Burnout

Burnout is a term that has originated over the last decade or so to describe the situation in which some individuals literally are unable to keep going in their jobs. It was typified by a lack of performance, poor decision making, negative attitudes and exhaustion. It is the equivalent of a fire burning itself out or a engine running out of petrol and simply coming to a complete standstill.

Clearly, the consequences for both the individual and organization are serious in these situations. Burnout has been described as a form of stress (Ganster and Schaubroeck, 1991) and characterized as emotional exhaustion, depersonalization and diminished personal accomplishment (Cordes and Dougherty, 1993, quoted in Luthans 1995, pp 297–8). Jackson *et al.* (1986) suggest that burnout is more likely among individuals who display high aspirations and who are highly motivated. It is also more likely in situations where the organization restricts the individual's opportunity to use their own initiative while insisting on particular goals being achieved in a particular way.

It is the constant stress of attempting to achieve all of the personal and organizational objectives identified and the inability to do so effectively that has been suggested to lead to burnout. The individual is constantly being frustrated in being able to achieve all that they feel that they are capable of and all that they seek. This ongoing frustration places them in a continual spiral of increasing levels of stress until they exhaust themselves by burning out. With this background it is hardly surprising that there is evidence (Evans and Fisher, 1993) that it is particularly evident in the caring professions such as nursing, teachers, social work, and even ministers of religion (Moorhead and Griffin, 1992, p 467).

McKenna (1994) suggests that burnout could be viewed as a coping mechanism in that it forces the individual to disconnect themselves one way or another from the situation continually creating and reinforcing the stress.

Post-traumatic stress disorder (PTSD)

There are events that are so stressful in themselves that, fortunately, most of us are spared the trauma of experiencing them and of having to cope with the consequences. There was a recent press report of a fireman who committed suicide because he could not cope with the trauma resulting from having to attend a major road accident and assist in the cutting free and removal of five decapitated bodies from the wreckage. No amount of training can prepare an individual for the sheer horror of having to face such a situation. The Dobschiner book included in the Further reading has been included with the intention of providing an insight into just this type of event, although from a completely different context. There are many similar books demonstrating the range of traumatic events some people must face in their lives. Also relevant in this context is the notion of critical incident management discussed in Chapter 15.

The psychological effects arising from major traumatic events such as already described or a war or an accident at work are classified as PTSD. Frost (1990, described in McKenna, 1994) identifies a number of the features of this disorder, including the individual having nightmares and/or flashbacks about the events, sleeplessness, edginess and outbursts of anger. It can also lead to alcohol and drug abuse in an attempt to lessen the anguish involved and to help blank out remembrances of the experience.

The consequences for the lives, work and relationships of individuals suffering from PTSD could be considerable. It is a condition that is beginning to be taken seriously by both the medical profession and employers. Employers have a duty of care towards employees and there are health and safety at work issues that arise from the occurrence of PTSD as a result of events experienced at work. Employers have found themselves being sued for damages when an employee has claimed that the condition resulted from something for which management could be held accountable. It has also lead to the establishment of specialist medical units in an attempt to provide effective treatment for sufferers.

Sources of stress

Figure 21.1 identified stress as originating from either inside or outside the organization. While this is generally true it is not comprehensive. Breaking that two-level classification down into greater detail can allow for improved analysis and subsequently the development of more effective coping strategies. The most common sources of stress that could be expected to have a measure of impact on organizational activity include:

✦ Environmental. Forces in the environment in general could be expected to create stress for the individuals within an organization. The actual process of getting to work can be stressful for many people. Many people claim to be at their best in the evening and for such individuals having to get up to go to work and perform at a satisfactory level can be a chore. Equally, driving through crowded streets, finding somewhere to park, travelling on a crowded bus or train or simply waiting at a bus stop wondering if it will arrive on time are all generators of stress before work has begun. Air pollution and climatic conditions are other sources of stress from the general environment. Management in Action 21.2 reflects some of the sources of stress acting upon aid agency workers. Clearly such people work in very difficult situations with much of the stress originating from the circumstances within which they must operate.

Stop | Consider *Should every organization be required to undertake a risk analysis of the stress factors that exist within it and implement similar programmes to those indicated in MiA 21.2? Or is it simply not necessary or too costly?*
Justify your views.

✦ Competitive. The competitive conditions that exist around all organizations represents a particular form of environmental stressor. In the harsh world of competitive reality

MANAGEMENT IN ACTION 21.2

Stopping disaster from ruining lives

Over recent years the number of natural, political, military and other disasters has been proliferating. In parallel to this so have the number and size of the aid agencies that attempt to alleviate the worst effects for the populations caught up in these situations. The 1994 war in Rwanda was a crisis both for the people caught up in it and the aid agencies as they struggled to cope with the scale of events. In Rwanda some 200 non-governmental agencies (NGOs) were at work at an estimated cost of $1.4 billion. It involved the movement of around 1.5 million refugees into four neighbouring countries and the genocide of between 500,000 and 800,000 people. Tens of thousands more died of dehydration and illness. Clearly, this represented a stressful situation for all those exposed to it, including aid workers. A five-volume report published by 36 of the countries and international bodies involved helped to examine some of the problems and highlight the need for better aid agency work in the field.

Ann Smith was in charge of a Red Cross feeding station at Huambo in Angola when it was attacked by rebel forces. In her words:

> They were firing off their guns into the air. They took everything from passports and toilet rolls to cars and we were left with nothing but the clothes we had on and our radio. We somehow managed to persuade them that it was in their interests not to destroy the radio, but they wouldn't let us use it so we lost contact with head office.
>
> We ended up sleeping on the floor for several days hoping that someone would rescue us. Planes were apparently sent in, but were unable to land because the airport was bombed. we felt really desperate. It was a terrifying experience.

A few days later, government troops reached Huambo and released the aid workers trapped

there. Ann continues: 'We were packed off in a lorry and squeezed into a cargo plane with no seats and sent to Luanda.'

The debriefing of Ann and her colleagues by the Red Cross was very thorough. The 30 Red Cross staff were allowed to stay in the same hotel for a few days and talk to each other about their experiences. The group then went to Red Cross headquarters in Geneva for further debriefing before returning home to Britain. Back home Smith was given a few weeks off to relax and was offered counselling before being given a medical and psychological examination. She was full of praise for the approach of the Red Cross. Since her experiences in Angola she has been to Chechnya assessing the needs of field hospitals and constantly crossing the front lines between Russian and Chechen troops: a very stressful life full of hair-raising experiences.

A number of initiatives have been set up by people like Paul Emes, overseas personnel manager for the British Red Cross. For example, a research programme by a number of the agencies into the causes of stress in aid work identified that it had many causes, including:

✦ The witnessing of suffering.

✦ Poor communications and conflict with expatriate colleagues.

✦ Poor management in the field.

✦ Poor selection practices.

✦ Lack of career development.

✦ Insufficient training for field staff.

✦ Poor appraisal of individual performance and needs.

In response a number of initiatives were established. This included a code of practice about the use of human resource practices in all aspects of the employment of people in aid work.

The British Red Cross has opted for a one-day assessment centre for prospective field staff, it being recognized that a one-hour interview was not enough time to evaluate an individual's ability to cope with life among disasters. The pre-departure training has also been increased to incorporate teamworking and stress management. Post-attachment counselling is now the norm, with only 1% refusal being experienced. Other initiatives are being planned to move the situation forward in terms of being able to manage the human aspect of aid work more effectively. This includes reviewing management training and inter-agency co-operation to develop improved standards of field training and staff recruitment.

Adapted from: Pickard, J (1996) Stopping disaster from ruining lives, *People Management*, 25 July, pp 32–4.

no organization is safe from being required to continually improve its performance in an attempt to fight off the threat of loss of business or even closure. Competitors are continually seeking product improvements and introducing marketing-based initiatives to attract new business and attempt to enhance the chances of higher profit levels and survival. Business-related activities such as these can also be used defensively and in response to the activities of others in an attempt to protect existing levels and types of business.

In the public sector there are also number of initiatives such as privatization and market testing which are intended significantly to influence the running of the organizations required to undergo such change. This process is invariably driven by the political masters of public service organizations in pursuit of political and economic objectives.

The net result of all of this activity in the competitive environment of organizations is an instability, uncertainty and unpredictability, in turn leading to a pressure for shorter planning and decision-making horizons. This in itself creates a stressful background to the operating environment. However, when this is linked to cost reduction and efficiency drives, such as *business process re-engineering* and *delayering*, additional stress is created as a result of the lower levels of slack available within an organization. Increasing efficiency can only be achieved in one of two ways, either producing more output with the same resource or by holding the output constant while reducing the resource required to produce it. It is, of course, possible to combine these approaches and seek to produce more output with less resource. However an efficiency gain is achieved the result is a greater utilization of resource. Consequently, there is a reduced ability to absorb additional activity – at just the time when competitive pressure requires a more dynamic, urgent and flexible response from the organization. This inevitably places additional stress on those people left within the organization and who have to cope.

✦ Organizational. The act of having to work in an organization is in itself a stress creating experience. Earlier chapters in this book have examined many features associated with the nature of an organization and the complexity of this form of social structure should be obvious as a consequence. The structure of the organization can create frustration in that hierarchy and compartmentalization introduce a measure of artificial constraint on work activity. Many of the more recent innovations in organizational design evolved as an attempt more closely to arrange organizational activity to customer experience and requirement.

The rules, procedures and policies adopted by organizations are another source of stress and frustration. Employees who have significant caring responsibilities outside work frequently find that company rules on attendance, timekeeping, time off, and crèche facilities are far from helpful. The needs of such individuals to balance the competing demands of the various component parts of their life are a major source of stress.

Even work-related rules and procedures can be unclear and create ambiguity and stress. For example, deciding who has the authority to sign for goods received or to authorize deviations from a standard specification can create difficulties. This can lead to problems in dealing effectively with suppliers and customers, additional cost as well as stress for all concerned. Management in Action 21.3 provides an insight into some of the tensions that exist within the health service between doctors and managers as they attempt to cope with new ways of organizing and working.

Stop | Consider

Should hospital care be left to doctors, or is it possible to 'manage' the process? Is the search for management in this context simply an attempt to ration resources? Or is it a deliberate attempt by politicians to introduce stress (pressure) into the situation so that something has to give forcing services to become more effective?

Justify your views.

✦ Job. The work that individuals do is also a major source of stress for many of them. The job may be boring and involve many repetitive, short cycle tasks. Many jobs are complex and full of uncertainty with little support and assistance in performing the necessary tasks. Handy (1993) identifies a number of role- (job-) related aspects that can lead to stress for the individual (see Table 21.1).

Role ambiguity	Lack of clarity in what the job entails in terms of evaluation, responsibility, advancement and expectations of performance
Role incompatability	Lack of clarity in expectation of job content between job holder and other people. Perhaps differences between job demands and personal ethics would be an example
Role conflict	The requirement to perform more than one role in the same situation
Role overload	An extreme form of role conflict in which too many roles are expected from one person
Role underload	The opposite of role overload when the role expected is well below that which the individual perceives themselves capable
Responsibility for others	To rely on others to do what is necessary. Achieving results through others
Boundary roles	Those jobs that co-ordinate or integrate two or more groups. Salespeople are a typical example, being the customer representative within the organization
Career uncertainty	Lack of clarity in the future direction of work or career

TABLE 21.1 Job-related sources of stress (*source*: Handy, CB (1985) *Understanding Organisations*, 3rd edn, Penguin, Harmondsworth)

MANAGEMENT IN ACTION 21.3

Hospital staff suffer unhealthy tension

The reforms of the National Health Service in the UK over the last few years have brought many changes, among them an attempt to increase the application of 'management' to the running of hospitals. This inevitably introduced a new tension into a world previously run by doctors. Summing up the two stereotypes of the positions, Kuper suggests that hospital managers claim that: 'Doctors attending hospital meetings turn up late, noisily crumple packets of crisps and arrange for their bleepers to go off halfway through.'

The doctors' view of the situation is given by Dr James Johnson, chairman of the British Medical Association's Consultants' Committee:

Doctors spend too much time doing paperwork and attending meetings. Managers were trying to make them take commercial factors into account when treating patients. Patients were demanding ever more care and were also complaining more – partly inspired by the Patient's Charter.

These views represent a scenario in which it would be difficult not to detect tension between the parties involved.

Another facet of the tensions between hospital managers and doctors is the need for record

keeping. Professor Cyril Chantler, dean of the combined medical schools of Guy's and St Thomas's, indicated that more efficiency and evidence of effectiveness were being demanded. This required additional record keeping and the evaluation of treatment plans.

The payment for hospital work by general practitioners (GPs) was for a period done under a contract negotiated between the hospital managers and fund-holding GP practices. The payment allowed doctors outside the hospital system to determine the work of those employed within it. This was completely different from the days when hospital doctors decided for themselves what treatments they undertook. Equally the payment for 'consultant episodes' resulted in pressure for more minor operations and fewer of the major resource-demanding activities. Dr Johnson described the situation thus: 'Trying to manage consultants is like trying to herd cats.' Each side regards the other as hostile and unlikely to assist its cause. This leads to open hostility and stress for all concerned.

Adapted from: Kuper, S (1995) Hospital staff suffer unhealthy tension, *Financial Times*, 16 May, p 10.

Job insecurity is another major source of stress for many individuals. There have been many surveys over recent years which show that a significant proportion of individuals feel insecure in their jobs and are fearful that they may be made redundant in the near future. This creates stress as well as reducing confidence and a willingness to take on long-term commitments. There is also the *survivor syndrome* which reflects the stress experienced by those individuals who do not lose their jobs and yet mirror the responses among those who have (Hall, 1995), perhaps originating from a feeling of guilt about being 'spared' compared to colleagues and friends.

✦ Personal. There are some individuals who appear to be natural worriers. They seem to be pessimistic about most things in life and subject themselves to additional stress as a result. For example, worrying about being punctual for appointments or if a job will be finished on time, while laudable objectives in themselves, to some people they become major causes of concern. This perspective takes us into the area of *personality* characteristics and *individual difference*. In addition there are also *perceptual* and experience differences that influence the ways that stress impacts on the individual. For example, some individuals see proposed change to a job as a threat while others might seek the opportunity to advance themselves through the changes being made. In the first illustration, stress could result from the fear of change while the second person might be expected to take the change in their stride. Of course, the individual who welcomed the changes to their job as an opportunity might subject themselves to high stress levels as they seek to capitalize on the situation.

✦   Interpersonal. The quality of interpersonal relationships that exist within the organization can also become major sources of stress. This can arise in all directions and between all groups and individuals. Superiors can become difficult and bully subordinates. Subordinates can also be problematic in relationship terms and increase the stress experienced by their boss. Peer groups can be difficult and not co-operate effectively by delaying work or decisions and thereby frustrating the intentions of other people, also increasing the levels of stress.

✦   Professional. Professional bodies frequently have codes of practice and standards to which members are expected to subscribe and adhere in their work activities. There can be occasions when these standards are in conflict with the personal standards of the individual, the requirement of the organization for which they work or those of some other business associate. This can create stress for the individual in reconciling or living with the discrepancy.

Each of these major sources of stress can operate together in different groupings to create a dynamic and ever changing context within which the individual must function and respond. Figure 21.3 attempts to reflect this dynamic relationship.

The sources of stress impact on the individual and that person responds to the experienced stress in ways largely determined by a number of mediators. The consequences of that stress follow from that interpretation of the stressful situation and, as was suggested by the physics-based analogy used by McKenna introduced earlier, it could either be of temporary or permanent effect. The mediators identified in Figure 21.3 are the major determinants of the individual's response to the stress experience, and include:

✦   Personality. The *personality* characteristics of the individual can influence how the person responds to what happens to them, including the experience of stress. Features such as the determination to succeed and level of ambition in the individual might be generally considered to reflect personality characteristics. In addition, there are many

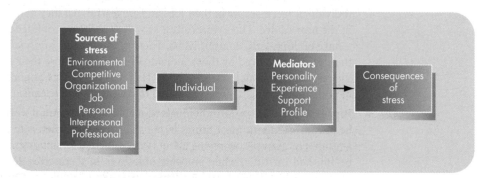

FIGURE 21.3   Stress and the individual.

other personality traits that might be expected to influence the reaction to stress inducing situations.

✦ Experience. Previous experience of situations can raise the tolerance threshold for stress. For example, driving over the same route to work every working day for ten years could be expected to produce less stress than driving over the same route for the first time.

✦ Profile. The profile of the individual in terms of age, degree of physical fitness, education level and gender could also play a part in determining the way in which stress is dealt with by that person.

✦ Support. The support networks surrounding the individual can also influence the ability to cope with stress. An individual working in an organization that provided easy access to counselling facilities and other forms of social support could be expected to have a higher tolerance for stress. In such organizations as a result of the higher profile of stress together with an understanding of the potentially negative consequences lower levels of it could be expected. Contrariwise, a manipulative employer could attempt to engender higher levels of stress within the organization on the basis that the support mechanisms provided create a higher tolerance for coping with the effects.

Having discussed the causes of stress it is now appropriate to consider the effects that stress can have for both individuals and organizations.

Effects of stress

There are a number of consequences associated with stress. Clearly, it would be expected to influence the individual in a number of ways. In addition, as a consequence of the impact on the individual it would be expected to produce effects on the people around that person and the organization itself. For example, imagine that an individual reacts to the stress they experience by becoming bad tempered and irritable. The changes in their normal behaviour pattern under such circumstances could be expected to create strains in the family, friendship and work relationships surrounding the stressed person. Table 21.2 demonstrates some of the effects of stress on the absence levels within organizations.

For the organization employing the individual the presence of a bad-tempered and irritable employee could have the effect of turning customers away and also there is a strong possibility that the individual concerned would not be effective in their job in other ways. Figure 21.4 reflects these zones of impact for stress. Primarily the consequences impact on the individual themselves, the people around them and with whom they come

20% of medium-sized companies report up to 50% of all sick days as being stress related
100 million working days lost each year due to stress (UK only)
30 times as many days lost due to stress as from industrial disputes
Stress-related absence has increased by 500% since the mid-1950s

TABLE 21.2 Sample statistics on the effects of stress (*source*: Ward, T (1996) *The Stress Factor*, Institute of Management, Humberside, Newsletter)

into contact, the organization for which they work and possibly other organizations. This much should be apparent from the discussion so far.

The examples just described also provide the basis for suggesting that the effects of stress are interactive, self-reinforcing and cumulative.

+ Interactive. The behaviour of any individual could be expected to produce responses in the behaviour patterns of those with whom they interact, thereby creating stress for other people and influencing their own behaviour patterns.

+ Self-reinforcing. The experience of stress and the changes in behaviour that it can produce in the individual and those around them creates a stressful situation in its own right. This effectively reinforces the experience of stress in that context.

+ Cumulative. It is not just that a particular aspect of work is stressful, the experience of work in total becomes stressful. The effects of the two previous features of stress (interactive and self-reinforcing) produces a situation in which the level of experienced stress begins to rise and feed on itself for everyone involved.

Moorhead and Griffin (1992) identify six areas of the consequences of stress, categorized as either *individual* or *organizational* factors. In terms of the model described in Figure 21.4 the effects of stress on the people and organizations with whom the focal person would come into contact would find expression in the ways identified in the Moorhead and Griffin classification scheme.

Individual consequences of stress

There are three main areas in which stress would impact on the individual; *psychological*, *behavioural* and *medical*. Each of these areas is in practice interactive in that the symptoms and behavioural consequences are not mutually exclusive. A person under stress could be expected to display a range of all three categories. However, the range of symptoms displayed would not be the same for each person and not everyone would display the full range of symptoms. In the discussion that follows no distinction will be drawn between stress, burnout and PTSD. The distinctions and similarities associated with these three concepts were discussed earlier and they can all create some or all of the following consequences. Briefly considering each category in turn:

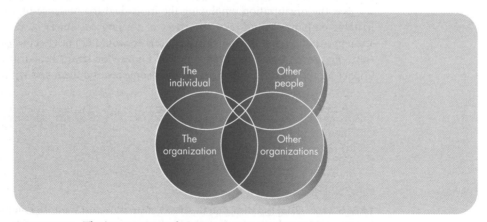

FIGURE 21.4   The impact zones of stress.

◆ Psychological. There are a wide range of psychological consequences of stress. They can include anxiety, depression, nervousness, irritability, tension, moodiness and boredom. Cox (1978) identifies apathy, low self-esteem, poor decision making, short attention span, hypersensitivity to criticism and mental blocks in addition to the more usual factors.

◆ Behavioural. The behavioural consequences are the observable features of the individual's response to stress. For example, being bad tempered. However, as with all features of human nature and behaviour it is not the actual existence of bad temper that indicates stress. Every individual is different in the ways that they behave and may be short tempered normally as part of their psychological make-up. This is also true of all of the psychological factors just indicated as well as the medical conditions to follow. It is changes in normal behaviour patterns etc. that perhaps provide the most reliable indicator of the effects of stress. However, changes in the normal profile of an individual can also be the result of many other causes, for example, the onset of disease.

Some of the more common behavioural influences arising from stress identified include smoking, drinking, drug abuse, violent outbursts, general aggression, moodiness, going absent from work, sickness, demanding perfection from subordinates. In addition to these, Cox (1978) identifies impulsive behaviour, emotional outbursts, excessive eating and nervous laughter as typical examples. Other examples identified by Hogg (1988) include increased smoking, caffeine and alcohol use as well as drug abuse.

◆ Medical. The medical consequences of stress are related to the physical effects of it on the individual and resulting medical conditions. These include heart disease, stroke, high blood pressure, headaches, back problems, ulcers, intestinal disorders and skin conditions (Quick and Quick, 1984). Cox (1978) also identifies sweating, dryness of the mouth as well as the effects of alcohol and drug abuse as medical conditions resulting from stress. Hogg (1988) also identifies links with cancer, allergies, rheumatoid arthritis, diabetes, asthma, sleep and sexual disorders.

Organizational consequences of stress

The organizational effects of stress can also be categorized under three headings *attitude, performance* and *withdrawal.* Once again these three terms should not be regarded as mutually exclusive. Taking each in turn:

◆ Attitude. The attitudes of the employee towards aspects of the organization could be expected to change as a result of the stress experienced. For example, they may begin to hate the job that they do, or express feelings of hostility towards particular individuals, departments, customers or suppliers. They may also express disparaging comment about the effectiveness and other job-related abilities of those same categories of contact people or groups. *Attitudes* can have significant influence on behaviour, and in this context could be expected to influence *motivation* and willingness to function as an effective employee (at least from a management perspective). In short, the attitudes of employees (at any level or the organization) suffering from stress could be expected to become hostile to the desires and expectations of managers.

◆ Performance. Figure 21.2 provides an indication of the relationship between levels of stress and performance. It is clear from that discussion that too little stress can reduce operational performance as can too much stress. The difficulty is in identifying the appropriate levels of stress in order to achieve a positive result. Too much stress on an individual begins to adversely effect the attitudinal, psychological, behavioural and medical aspects of their overall well-being. Clearly, under these circumstances employees are less likely to be working with high levels of efficiency or effectiveness. Attention to detail is likely to suffer as is the desire to do the job right and take an active interest in the employers interests. Quality is likely to reduce and the general level of efficiency will drop as employees find it necessary to cope with the additional burdens caused by the stress.

Things within the organization could gradually be expected to deteriorate as a general lethargy and unwillingness to become proactive settled upon the employees. Of course, not everyone within the organization would be suffering the same levels of stress and also the responses to it would vary among employees. However, over time as stress takes its toll on everyone it poses the danger of a gradual of diminution in performance that even drags down those not originally affected by it. It is a potentially debilitating state within the organization that can insidiously whittle away at its very fabric and foundations. This danger poses a very real threat, as modern organizations attempt to drive up performance and cut costs.

Another aspect associated with organizational performance and stress are illness and accident rates. The effect of stress on the individual has already been suggested to create medical, relationship and psychological problems. These in turn also influence the performance of an organization through increased sickness and absence levels as well as placing employees at a higher risk of accidents at work. Essentially, more people are needed on the payroll to cover those people off work ill, thereby increasing the cost of operations. The alternative being either to leave the work of absent employees undone or to put extra pressure on those still at work to do more work, thereby increasing the likelihood of more stress and even higher levels of absence.

In addition, there are other costs associated with illness and accident. For example, the cost of providing health screening and life insurance cover for employees is rising rapidly, as are pension and other benefit costs. There is also the very real risk of an employer being taken to court and sued for damages by an employee incapacitated in some way because of stress. Welch (1996) reports a record payment (at that time) of £175,000 to a social worker forced to retire on health grounds after two nervous breakdowns brought on by an impossible workload. These facets of managing the consequences of stress effectively reduce the overall performance of the organization by increasing the cost of running it.

✦ Withdrawal. This organizational consequence of stress can take one of two forms, physical or psychological. Psychical withdrawal includes temporary absence due either to sickness or to simply staying away from work. It can be for short or extended periods, anything up to two years or longer in extreme cases. It can also include what would generally be called *skiving*. That is, finding ways of avoiding work while at work. This includes such sanctions as going slow or deliberately restricting the output produced; sabotaging machines to make them break down and thereby 'earn' a rest from the pace of work; going to the toilet for a 'rest' or staying longer than necessary when there. Another form of physical withdrawal is to permanently leave the organization. An individual may seek another job because they see it as too stressful to continue in the one that they have.

Psychological withdrawal involves action short of physically doing things to absent oneself from work. It could involve not making an effort to consider the organization's interests or caring about customer views. 'Letting something go' (perhaps a quality defect) instead of doing something positive to correct it would be a typical response in this category. It involves not putting oneself out on behalf of the employer's interests. It is indicating that although still at work and working while there, the individual does not really care about the organization or its future.

Having identified many of the effects of stress it is now appropriate to consider how to deal with it in order to minimize the consequences.

Dealing with stress

There are many sources that can provide support or offer help in developing coping strategies for dealing with stress. However, prevention is inevitably more effective than cure and so some of the techniques have anticipatory or tolerance enhancing dimensions to them. There is a specific managerial responsibility of minimizing the possible effects of harmful stress on employees. This arises as a result of legislative requirements to provide a safe working environment as well as through the moral obligations to care for the employees *at work*.

It should not be forgotten that managers are themselves susceptible to stress, just as any other employee. By ensuring that effective stress management strategies are adopted managers should be considering every person within the organization, not just themselves or the other employees. It is easiest to consider the strategies most frequently encountered as falling into either an *individual* or *organizational* classification.

In considering the forms of strategy that can be used to deal with stress the implications of Figure 21.1 in classifying it should be kept in mind. The actual strategies adopted to meet the needs of particular individuals and situations should be targeted at both *source* and *effect* if the intervention is to be successful.

Individual stress management strategies

There are many strategies that individuals can use either on their own or as part of a formal programme in order to combat the negative effects of excessive stress. Some approaches such as time management can be totally up to the individual to decide upon and implement. Others such as stress counselling may involve making use of an organizationally (or community health service) provided resource. Almost invariably, access to this latter type of stress management approach is directed either by medical practitioner or by someone within the organization. Management in Action 21.4 demonstrates that a wide range of approaches to provide individuals with the ability to cope with and overcome the effect of stress are being used by organizations.

Stop | Consider   *Do the approaches described in MiA 21.4 offer an effective response, or should managers be required to find ways of reducing the causes of stress within the organization instead? Justify your views.*

MANAGEMENT IN ACTION 21.4

Alternative ways to take out stress

Many companies offer staff access to a free phone enquiry line and a limited number of free counselling sessions as a way of dealing with stress. Cable Midlands wanted to go further than that. Their business provides cable TV, telephone and information services in the Midlands region of the UK. It had a staff of about 600 in mid-1996, expected to grow to about 700 by the end of that year. A recent merger with the largest cable operator in the UK as well as constant changes in technology and working practices brought with it rising levels of stress for all employees.

Steve Miller, a training consultant with the company, had previous experience of running stress management workshops and was keen to develop similar initiatives within Cable Midlands. His advice was that in addition to topics like time management and assertiveness training as ways to combat stress a number of complementary therapies could offer benefits. The first workshop was titled 'Managing Pressure to Maximise Performance'. It was available only to managers as a pilot programme. Reaction was favourable and so it was made generally available and runs regularly twice each month.

Other pilot programmes developed include a two-day programme to allow managers to assess their own stress levels, the symptoms and the exploring of strategies to manage it more effectively in the future. Other approaches tried or planned within the company include:

+ Sessions in clinical hypnosis to teach practical relaxation techniques.

+ Aromatherapy advice is offered at lunchtimes and in workshops It emphasizes the use of massage and aromatic oils to reduce muscular tension.

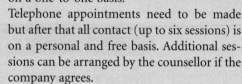

+ Reflexology. Employees are instructed how to use pressure points in the feet to relieve stress.

+ Confidential counselling is also available on a one-to-one basis. Telephone appointments need to be made but after that all contact (up to six sessions) is on a personal and free basis. Additional sessions can be arranged by the counsellor if the company agrees.

+ Technical awareness training. It was recognized that in a rapidly changing environment stress arises from not being able to keep up to date and so sessions that aim to keep staff abreast of technical developments were provided.

+ The company plans to offer yoga and exercise classes.

+ A second generation of stress courses is also planned to focus on the psychological aspects of managing stress.

+ The managing of perception and general avoidance of negative thought processes as well as maintaining creativity are other areas under consideration for future programmes.

The cost of the initiatives was around £10,000 which, it was hoped, will be recovered through reduced sickness levels and labour turnover. Initial results were positive with about 1% drop in absence being reported and lower labour turnover also being reported by some departments.

Adapted from: Butler, S (1996) Alternative ways to take out stress, *People Management*, 16 May, pp 43–4.

The definition of an individual stress management strategy used here is that it represents an approach in which the individual takes some action regarding their own life, behaviour or work. The approach being intended to either reduce the impact of stress upon them or make the individual more able to cope with it if the stress cannot be reduced. The more common strategies in this category include:

+ Time management. It has been suggested many times that much stress in a work-related context arises as a result of poor time management skills on the part of individual managers and employees. There are many courses and self-help books available on the subject of how to manage time more effectively. Although each one of these sources represents a slightly different approach to the subject, they all contain some form of daily goal setting, prioritization of work and delegation, the argument being that if the main goals and priorities can be achieved than the outstanding issues that may not be completed that day are of little consequence and so unlikely to produce much by way of stress on the individual.

  Stress at work can originate from the level of constraint and routine in a job, or from the relative freedom to prioritize and regulate one's own activities. It is in this last type of work that time management would have some ability to offer constructive support. From the material on leadership and management in this book it should be apparent that many managers' experience is one of frequent and competing short cycle activities. Under those circumstances it is easy to lose sight of the main objectives being sought and to fall into the trap of always responding to the last *event*. In so doing, the manager can quickly become swamped with minute detail and begin to feel that they are being managed by events and in control of nothing – the beginning of stress. Goal setting, prioritization and delegation are the recognition that not everything that lands on one's desk has to be dealt with or if it cannot be ignored then it does not require a response immediately. This provides the means by which control over events can be achieved and stress levels managed.

+ Relaxation and meditation. These two approaches come in many forms from the active pursuit of hobbies and activities outside of work to the formality of learning forms of meditation or practising yoga. The logic behind these approaches being that stress can become a constant companion of the individual and consequently overwhelm them. By engaging in some from of relaxation activity it breaks the continual feeling of stress and helps to provide balance in the life of the individual. It is rather like attempting to keep in mind the old adage that individuals work to live not live to work! Relaxation can involve simply leaving the desk or work area for a while to have lunch or a chat with colleagues as well as the pursuit of hobbies or vacations.

+ Behaviour control. This approach to stress management involves attempting to manage more effectively the situations that generate stress. It requires the individual to recognize their own behaviour patterns and to be able to anticipate those situations which lead to stress and to develop strategies to deal with them more effectively next time they arise.

  For example, one senior management team I observed in action were having a particularly stressful time as their company was losing money and they could not find ways of reducing costs or increasing sales. During a particularly stressful series of meetings with the trade union representing the employees the management team would hold post mortem meetings after each negotiation session. A routine soon developed in which one of the managers would make a comment based on an event from the meeting and someone else would turn it into a joke and laughter to the point of hysteria and tears streaming down everyone's face would break out. Usually the event starting the joke and the joke itself were of a very poor standard and the reaction was out of all proportion to the actual humour. The individuals concerned agreed that the jokes were not funny outside the immediate context. Even managers not present at the negotiations could not understand the joke.

In this example, the managers were not able to manage events and eliminate the stress in that they could not avoid the negotiation meetings. Neither could they manage the process or outcome completely. The behaviour that they could control was after the event and the humour provided a means of relieving the levels of stress generated by the process.

♦ Counselling. The provision of counselling facilities for employees is another mechanism by which individuals can be encouraged to explore their feelings and other emotions surrounding the events creating stress. There are many different reasons why stress arises within an organization and having the opportunity to talk provides an opportunity for the individual to develop ways of dealing with them in the future. Employees who have been subjected to traumatic events at work often find it difficult to go back into that same situation without fear or panic attacks. For example the emergency services who must deal with road accident situations and bank employees who have been subjected to armed robbery at work can all experience these difficulties. Counselling can provide a means by which the individual can come to terms with their experiences and cope more easily with the normal work and life experiences. Management in Action 21.5 illustrates a number of aspects of counselling in a stress management context.

Stop | Consider

In the EAP described in MiA 21.5 management of the company are told of the volume of use of the system. Should they also be given information on the type of problems etc. so that action can be taken to impact on the casuses of stress? Why or why not?

♦ Role management. Table 21.1 identifies a number of job-related sources of stress. Role management attempts to manage the stress arising from each of these. For example, managing the stress created from role conflicts might involve an employee with significant domestic responsibilities saying no to the organization when a more senior manager demands that a job be completed immediately. Each of the job-based sources of stress can be managed more effectively if the individuals concerned take the time and trouble to make an assessment of what creates the stress and what alternatives exist to the usual response patterns. Situations involving role overload may involve delegation or the compartmentalization of work responsibilities. For those individuals in boundary roles recognizing that ultimate loyalty lies with one party helps to clarify the orientation towards the job without destroying the ability to facilitate the relationship between the groups around the individual.

♦ Biofeedback. Stress creates a number of physiological changes in the body such as heart rate, electrical patterns in the brain and temperature. It is possible to display physical representations of these changes for the individual and by doing so train them to control particular responses. For example, by concentrating on the frequency of the 'bleep' sound from a heart monitor when exposed to stress an individual can

MANAGEMENT IN ACTION 21.5

Cheers all round for employee counselling

Employee assistance programmes (EAPs) are not new. Whitbread introduced its version called Person to Person in response to the large-scale rationalizations taking place in the late 1970s and early 1980s. Those people being made redundant were offered specialist redundancy counselling. However, it was also found that the degree of change in the business caused stress and other effects among those who stayed with the company. The Person to Person programme was introduced to help individuals through the traumatic change process. The company recognized that stress and tension are common occurrences in everyday organizational life. It posed a very real threat to mental, emotional and physical well-being. It can have consequences for both the work and private lives of the individuals concerned as well as family, friends and colleagues. Equally, problems at home can have knock-on consequences for an individual at work.

Parts of the Whitbread business are vulnerable to criminal activity and assault so there is crisis management support and training for managers available through the occupational health team. The EAP offered by Whitbread is provided on an 'arms' length' basis in that counselling is provided by independent specialists who do not work for the company. The company lays down the standard of service required and monitors the delivery of those services, but does not become involved with the process itself. Complete anonymity is guaranteed by the process. The company receives general information about how many people have made use of the facilities but not who they are. It could be a pub manager or the chief executive, that is not revealed.

It is a process available 365 days a year from 7.30 every morning until midnight. It is available to the employee and immediate family living at home. Telephone contact is made initially by the employee or their family and after a discussion a meeting can be arranged at a location selected by the employee. This can be home, work or a hotel

for example. Three personal sessions are available through the company, more must be paid for by the employee if they are needed.

Between 5 and 7% of employees use the system each year. Figures for 1994 show that 56% of all problems were discussed and settled on the phone, the remaining 44% receiving one-to-one counselling. Problems fall into four main groups:

- ✦ Work related, 33%.
- ✦ Legal, 22%.
- ✦ Family/marital, 14%.
- ✦ Emotional, 12%.

The calls received were:

- ✦ 84% directly from employees.
- ✦ 8% management referrals.
- ✦ 3% from employee's partner.
- ✦ 5% referrals from the occupational heath team.

The scheme is promoted on a regular basis so that employees know that they have access to it. Among the benefits from the EAP at Whitbread the following are indicated as the most significant:

- ✦ Reduced number of grievances.
- ✦ Enables better decisions to be made.
- ✦ Reduced accidents.
- ✦ Assisted positive approach to drug and alcohol problems.
- ✦ Demonstrates a caring attitude to employees and their families.
- ✦ Helps recruitment and retention.
- ✦ Raised efficiency.
- ✦ Enhanced the quality of service.
- ✦ Enable the management to monitor and improve employee well-being.
- ✦ Provided a good financial investment.

Adapted from: Anderson, I (1996) Cheers all round for employee counselling, *Professional Manager*, January, pp 8–10.

attempt to slow it down. The frequency of the sound 'bleep' reflects their success in doing so. By concentrating on such biofeedback individuals can learn more effectively to manage the physiological consequences of stress.

◆ Exercise. The use of regular exercise can produce a number of benefits in addition to the weight loss and fitness improvement that are the most obvious gains. Someone who takes regular exercise is more likely to be fit and less prone to a wide range of medical conditions such as heart disease and back problems. Additionally, exercise can provide an opportunity to work off some of the aggression and frustration built up during stress. The physical tiredness created by exercise can also encourage better sleeping patterns and create a form of relaxation. It effectively breaks the cycle of stress creating more stress by providing a balancing element into the life of the individual. Management in Action 21.6 shows how one company attempted to use exercise to improve the general health of its employees and provide them with stress management opportunities.

Stop | Consider

To what extent are the initiatives indicated in MiA 21.6 about health and stress reduction or about public relations, personnel administration and commercial advantage? Does this distinction matter?

◆ Networking. The use of networks and other support groups can provide another way of dealing with stress. When under stress the individual tends to feel isolated, think that they are the only one in that position and turn their focus of attention inwards. The value of a network or support group is in providing an outward focus for the individual. It is rare to find that only one individual is 'suffering' stress at any one time or as the result of a particular combination of circumstances. The ability to realize this and to talk with professional colleagues, friends and other support providers (family being the most significant and most frequently forgotten example) creates an opportunity to externalize the problems and seek ways of dealing with them. The opportunity to occasionally confide in other significant people is a necessary part of everyone's life and never more so when the individual is under stress and could benefit from positive support.

In professional as opposed to social support networks appropriate assistance for the individual might come in the form of learning new ways to tackle particular job-related problems. It might involve professional updating in new techniques or other forms of career development. It might even involve recognizing that many people suffer the same problem and that no one else has been able to deal with it more effectively. The recognition that as an individual you are not a complete failure and that many others have just as many problems can be a great stress reliever. It is not unusual to find that we place ourselves under considerable levels of stress because we think that we should do more than we can actually do. Figure 21.5 reflects the advice given by one anonymous writer on the subject (and benefits) of accepting personal limitations.

That view contained in Figure 21.5 provides a note of recognition that life and our role in it are far from perfect. The suggestion that balance in working and other aspects of life is also important in managing stress as an individual. It is now appropriate to consider the organizational stress management strategies available.

MANAGEMENT IN ACTION 21.6

Healthy worker, healthy office

The notion of organizations providing fitness programmes for employees arrived formally in Britain in 1992 with the creation of the Wellness Forum. The founder members included Glaxo, Marks & Spencer and J Sainsbury. By the beginning of 1995 the Forum had 40 member companies and promotes healthy eating, keep fit classes and anti-smoking campaigns. Tim Biggs of the Wellness Forum said:

> Our work is not just a question of occupational health but trying to improve people's lifestyles so they are happier in themselves, which will reflect in their working lives. Enlightened organizations are looking to improve healthcare to improve their profits.

Two companies that undertake an active approach to worker health include:

✦ Unipart. The car parts company has spent £1m helping its 2500 employees feel and look good. Its sports facilities include squash courts, an aerobics studio and a centre for alternative health therapies. Called the Lean Machine, it is an attempt to combat stress while staying ahead of the competition. John Neil, group chief executive said:

> We're told that change will be ten times faster this decade than in the past. This rapid pace of change means that employees are facing more and more stress which can manifest itself in physical and mental problems.
> In the Lean Machine, they can not only get fit so that they can cope with stress, and receive treatment to deal with some of the problems created by stress, they can also learn how to manage stress through exercise and therapies to avoid problems.

✦ Du Pont. The chemicals and fabrics company first introduced a scheme in Northern Ireland in 1989. Northern Ireland has one of the highest incidence of coronary heart disease in the world. The company invests a lot of money in the training and development of its staff and did not want to see it wasted through an early death. The company has an established pre-recruitment medical screening procedure, but it was felt that further action was necessary after people joined the company. The company offers free private medical insurance and spends about £154 per year on occupational heath for all 1000 employees at the Northern Ireland plant. Every three years each employee undergoes a routine medical screening and a lifestyle examination. The assessment assesses the employee's chances of developing heart disease over the following ten years.

Research at Harvard Medical School suggests that stress reduction programmes by companies reduces the level of visits to doctors by between 35 and 50%. However, Nigel Watson, principle lecturer in sociology at Sunderland University, suggests that the benefits to employers are not just health related. It shows that they are caring employers and may therefore allow them to become the 'employer of first choice' among potential employees. In the service sector there is also a feeling that staff who feel cared for and loved will pass on those values in their customer dealings.

Adapted from: Wolffe, R (1995) Healthy worker, healthy office, *Financial Times*, 27 January, p 13.

Organizational stress management strategies

There are a number of reasons why organizations as institutions should take a positive approach to the management of stress. Morally (and legally) if stress is created within an organizational context then there is an obligation to deal with it if it is harmful to those exposed to it. It also makes commercial sense. The notion in Figure 21.2 that stress is linked with performance suggests that organizations deliberately attempt to increase levels of stress to their own advantage in seeking higher performance. However, because it is a relationship that cannot be precisely quantified there is a danger of creating excessive amounts of stress. What is not clear is what level of stress is detrimental to human health and well-being. So it could be that the level of stress necessary to create optimal performance is, at a human level, detrimental to the individual. Under such circumstances the organization could be creating grounds for legal action concerning the health and safety of its workers and make itself liable in the courts for damages and other prosecution.

More specifically the strategies adopted by organizations in an attempt to manage stress include the following. It will be apparent that many of the following issues have been discussed previously in this book:

✦ Job design. Careful attention to the design of the jobs to be undertaken within the organization can provide a means of minimizing stress for the individuals doing them. Ensuring that jobs are not, wherever possible, boring with very small cycle times, or otherwise overloaded would be examples. Also the relationship between technology and work activities has a significant bearing on the levels of stress within an organization.

✦ Involvement and communication. Employees who are involved in the decision-making aspects of work, and who are well informed about what is happening, are more likely to be able to understand their own position in relation to the overall picture. Consequently, as a result of a lower level of ambiguity in the way that the organization functions and what is going on some of the stress-creating possibilities are eliminated and those that remain lessened through the increased understanding of context. In addition employees are enabled through the involvement and communication processes to articulate the existence of stress and its causes and have them dealt with by management.

✦ Awareness programmes. Sensitivity training is a process of making people aware of the existence of stress, its causes and mechanisms for dealing with it. It is a process of bringing stress out into the open so that it can be dealt with. Individuals who become more aware of the nature of stress and how to deal with it are better able to make informed choices in relation to it and their own lives. They have the opportunity

> From tomorrow I will welcome rejection and failure with open arms. I will accept that I am GLORIOUSLY inadequate for the challenges that life places before me. HOWEVER, fortunately or unfortunately, as the case may be, I am the best person currently available!

FIGURE 21.5 Anonymous reflection on personal limitations.

presented to them to form action plans to influence their quality of life and can choose to adopt a positive response or continue in established patterns.

- ✦ Health programmes. Health screening and the development of a range of improvement strategies are the intention of this approach. The identification of individuals who are overweight, drink or smoke to excess together with the development of exercise, diet and giving up smoking plans are all part of this strategy, the idea being to provide for an improved medical ability to withstand stress and to introduce a more effective balance into the life of the individual.

    In the context of improving employee health there is an issue about the introduction of drug and alcohol screening tests. A number of organizations have introduced a range of tests from the perspective of safety at work. For example imagine the possible consequences of a train driver being under the influence of alcohol or drugs while at work. The results of such tests can be used to identify employees with problems (perhaps as a result of stress) and as a basis of providing assistance to them. However, they can also be used to identify the behaviour patterns of employees and as a possible basis for disciplinary action. As a consequence number of trade unions and other bodies are reluctant to unilaterally endorse them (Turner, 1995).

- ✦ Organizational design. Much of the stress within any organization comes from the physical and social arrangements within the organization itself. Customers experience an organization *horizontally* while most organizations function *vertically*. It is hardly surprising that such situations create stress for those that experience them. Departments frequently have functional responsibilities which clash with the requirements placed on individual employees to meet the needs of customer groups. Conflicting loyalty to the work and functional groups and the difficulties in persuading other functions to co-operate are just two of the areas that create stress. Therefore, attention to the physical structuring of the organization could be a means of reducing the stress experienced within it.

- ✦ Personal development. The encouragement of individuals to seek self-development opportunities is another strategy that can be used by organizations to manage stress levels. The provision of job and professional training courses is one form of this provision. The more proficient an individual feels the less stress in doing their normal job will be experienced. However, it is also possible to encourage individuals to see development in broader terms than organizationally based. The encouragement to develop new skills such as learning another language, drawing or playing a musical instrument all provide an opportunity to relax, and provide a balance in life that allows stress creating situations to be placed in context and the effects reduced.

- ✦ Personnel policies. There are many personnel policy areas that can be used to influence the experienced levels of stress by employees. The provision of crèche facilities and flexible working arrangements are aspects that can help some people balance work commitments and other significant parts of their life. The consequence being a happier employee who is less stressed.

- ✦ Procedural frameworks. Procedures are intended to guide activity within the organization. If they are ambiguous or in conflict with each other then they are not effective. The result is stress for the people affected by them. For example, if it is not clear under what circumstances the sales department can take an emergency order from a valued customer and change the production schedule then the potential for conflict and confusion between all the people involved will exist. It is likely that conflict and hostility will exist between the production and sales departments and the front-line staff in both departments will become stressed every time such an order is placed. Equally, general levels of stress will rise whenever the two departments must make contact. The review and design of more effective operational procedures is intended to reduce stress from these sources.

✦   Conflict management. The existence of conflict is endemic to organizational life. There are many possible sources of conflict that exist and a number have already been introduced in this section. The inclusion of conflict management in this section is not intended to imply that it can be completely eliminated, only that it can be reduced and managed more effectively. One of the conflict management techniques identified in and earlier chapter was to recognize the distinction between competition and conflict and to institutionalize competition. Bringing competition into the open as part of the natural decision-making processes within the organization while at the same time restricting conflict is a difficult balance to strike, particularly when organizational politics and power are incorporated into the picture. However, in attempting to do so the levels of stress could be reduced for all concerned.

✦   Planning. The actual organization of work and planning for the future is a means of reducing ambiguity and of providing clarity and predictability into the working life of employees. As a consequence a number of sources of stress should be reduced.

✦   Culture design. If a supportive culture can be created as opposed to one based on politics and power employees are more likely to help and support each other. The consequence of the supportive type of organizational culture is that co-operation would create less opportunity for stress arising from compartmentalization or friction and it would provide the environment for supporting those individuals who were experiencing particular stress situations.

Management in Action 21.7 provides an example of the ways that Glaxo Research and Development attempted to utilize a range of options for dealing with stress following a merger with Wellcome.

Having introduced a wide range of perspectives on the management of stress it must be remembered that the research links between many of them are weak if not ambiguous. At a common sense level all of these issues should have a beneficial effect on the level of stress in an organization and the ability of individuals to cope with it. However, organizational life is much more complex than implied by that simplistic relationship. There are too many intervening variables between stress, work and the individual to be able to make trite statements that it can be reduced by simple actions. There are no perfect, guaranteed solutions in attempting to manage stress. Every person is different and responses to stress management strategies will differ, just as with the reaction to the original stress-creating situation. (For an indication of the difficulties involved in attempting to tease out the variables and the relationships between them in stress research refer to Semmer *et al.*, 1996.)

Stress: an applied perspective

Stress is an interesting phenomenon from a management perspective. It has already been demonstrated in this chapter that it is both necessary in order to create high performance

MANAGEMENT IN ACTION 21.7

Coping with uncertainty

The following quotation comes from John Hume, human resource director of Glaxo Research and Development, following the merger of the R&D facilities from Glaxo and Wellcome:

> Any large-scale change involves leading people into the unknown, and the Glaxo-Wellcome merger is probably the largest ever in our industry. Employees will be uncertain about who will do what and where, whether they'll get a job they like, whether their long-term projects will continue. It's bound to be stressful.

Within Glaxo the R&D workforce had a young average age (about 33 years) and from a total workforce of about 3700 some 2500 have degrees, about 500 have PhDs. The work produces a high 'feel-good' factor because it is associated with the search for cures for diseases. Although Glaxo bought Wellcome it was not an asset-stripping exercise. The best of both organizations were to be brought together to create a new company. Glaxo had a strong history of stress management. Managers are trained in how to identify and manage stress and consultants also run lunchtime sessions on handling it. There is an occupational heath presence on each of the R&D sites as well as fitness centres. Personnel staff are trained in counselling through attendance on appropriate courses. There is also a well-publicized confidential employee counselling assistance programme provided by an external organization.

After the merger stress levels rose as people realized the possible implications for their own careers. The level of stress appeared in a number of ways. The 'rumour machine' went into overtime, a slight increase in the number of people using the external counselling service was detected and more people began to talk to personnel and occupational health staff about issues indirectly related to the merger such as career plans. The response of the company has included a number of elements:

+ Staff have been reminded about the employee assistance programme.

+ Stress awareness programmes have been relaunched.

+ Managers and supervisors have been trained in change management programmes.

+ Managers have also been trained on how to give staff 'bad news'.

+ Managers have been trained on how to select people for the new structures.

+ Across the company staff have been given interview training and an outplacement service has been established.

+ Considerable effort has gone into the process of communicating the company's severance compensation scheme.

+ A 'survivor syndrome' package has been developed for managers to deal with the employees that remain. It also provides advice on issues from organizational design and development to performance management. The pack includes ideas for training courses and a book called *Healing the Wounds*, by David Noer, on the aftermath of downsizing etc.

+ A general communication process to provide as much information as possible to staff (to remove uncertainty) was developed. It included a fortnightly bulletin and special weekly newsletters. There are also weekly face-to-face briefings from line managers and regular briefings from senior managers.

+ Focus groups provide a means of managers keeping in touch with the concerns and interests of employees which in turn provide issues that can be addressed through the communication channels. The various staff committees provide another means of channelling information in both directions.

MANAGEMENT IN ACTION 21.7 continued

Hume identified the lessons from his experience of the merger:

♦ Ensure that the management team is aware of the issues and trained to manage them.

♦ Communication is crucial and face-to-face communication is a must wherever possible.

♦ Ensure that the personnel, occupational health and any other specialist support staff are equipped to cope with the situation in advance.

♦ If possible use outside counselling or other help to deal with the stress.

♦ Monitor everything that you do.

Adapted from: Crabb, S (1995) Coping with uncertainty, *People Management*, 29 June, pp 23–4.

and yet in excessive quantity can be harmful to both individual and organization. In research terms it has been studied since the beginning of the twentieth century as a cognitive and medical or physiological phenomenon. Thompson and McHugh (1995) provide a brief but very readable summary of the evolution of stress research over this period of time (pp 273–8).

Stress appears to be an aspect of organizational functioning that is necessary and yet cannot be effectively measured or controlled at an appropriate level for all concerned. It effects everyone in the organization from the most senior executive to the most junior employee. It is also such a complex feature of human existence that it is not possible to state with any certainty which jobs and particular individuals are most vulnerable to it.

There are so many potential sources of stress and different jobs are susceptible to different forms of it. Equally, individuals vary in their response propensity to it. It has been suggested that one major determinant of individual response to stress is personality type. McKenna (1994) provides a summary of the Type A personality profile (p 601) and indicates the tendency of such people to display behaviours making them more prone to a range of conditions including coronary heart disease. It is further suggested that such individuals are prone to suffer excessive levels of stress. The behaviours characterizing a Type A personality are indicated in Table 21.3.

By contrast, the individual with Type B personality characteristics does not display these behaviours and is therefore less liable to suffer the effects of stress. It has also been argued that those individuals that display an external *locus of control* are more susceptible to the effects of stress. The argument being that such individuals tend to interpret events as being *outside* their control. The less control that an individual has over their lives and the

Haste
Aggressiveness
Restlessness
Extreme competitiveness
Impatience
Under pressure
Preoccupied with deadlines

TABLE 21.3 Some of the Type A personality behaviour patterns

events that they encounter the more they will be stressed by the necessity to respond and deal with them (McKenna, 1994, p 602).

There are a number of reasons why managers take an interest in stress within their organizations. It is not too much of an exaggeration to suggest that this probably is for reasons of self-interest in one form or another. The reasons include:

✦ Performance. In attempting to find ways of improving corporate performance managers are taking an interest in stress as something that is necessary. If through the more effective management of stress among employees (by reducing it or increasing tolerance capabilities) higher productivity can be achieved then a commercial advantage is gained. From this perspective, the management approach is about pushing back the boundaries of understanding and controlling stress in the search for higher profit.

✦ Cost. Absence in one form or another as a result of stress is a significant cost to organizations. It has been suggested that between 50 and 75% of all illness is stress related (Brenner, 1978). Some estimate stress-related costs associated with absence and people changing jobs at around £1.3 billion (Summers, 1990). Clearly, changes in productivity as a result of improved stress control, providing reductions in cost of this magnitude would significantly improve corporate performance. The statistics used in these estimates are from the 1980s and current levels are likely to be significantly higher as the trend was rapidly rising at that time (see, for example, Table 21.2) there is not much reason to suspect that the levels will have significantly reduced since then.

✦ Protection. Managers are seeking to protect their organizations from the negative consequences of stress. The most obvious being protection from the threat of litigation and claims for damages from employees who suffer the consequences of stress. In addition to the financial costs associated with such claims there are the public relations issues to be taken into account. Management in Action 21.8 reflects the attitude of the insurance industry in monitoring stress issues in order to manage claims and premium levels. Not surprisingly, the level of premium charged will be significantly influenced by the company record in minimising the risk of claim.

Stop | Consider

What do you make of the apparent irony in the situation where one set of commercial organizations (insurance companies) are seeking to reduce cost and increase profits by forcing other companies to adopt stress management policies?

Organizations are invariably very conscious of public image and the possibility of being shown in public as wanting in the care of employees. Allowing stress to reach excessive levels might suggest to customers that their interests are not being cared for effectively. In addition, the signal to existing and potential employees could make it more difficult to attract and retain good quality staff.

✦ Personal. Stress is no respecter of person and position. It can effect anyone. This includes managers. It is managers who make decisions on behalf of organizations and they are in a position to determine the level of priority given to particular issues. It would not be unreasonable to suggest that issues that might be expected to impact on managers would be prioritized more highly than issues that do not. Stress is an issue that could have a significant effect on managers, therefore it could be expected to be an issue which they would be prepared to take more active interest in.

MANAGEMENT IN ACTION 21.8

Insurers keep watch against stress attacks

The insurance industry has a vested interest in monitoring the levels of stress within the world of work. Should employees fall victim to stress and be forced to give up work then they may attempt to hold the employer liable in law for the damages that they have suffered. Recent claims by police officers, other emergency services and military personnel over incidents of 'post-traumatic stress disorder' are finding their way into the courts. The essence of such claims (according to Ian Walker, of law firm Russell Jones & Walker) is that, to quote from the basis of the claim of a number of police officers that they were exposed to: 'Wholly unreasonable sights, sounds and experiences that were far beyond what would normally be regarded as part of their everyday activities.'

Similar cases are beginning to appear from the non-uniformed/emergency services areas. For

example, in 1994 a social worker successfully sued his employer for negligence after claiming that his workload had damaged his health. David Rogers, head of the personal injury department for lawyers Davies Arnold Cooper said: 'Unless employers take steps in the next few years then, yes, these claims will start to rise.'

David Thomas, liability insurance expert at Willis Corroon, the insurance broker said: 'We will start to see insurers discriminate more efficiently between companies with good health and safety practices and those with less good practices.' Insurance premiums will surely follow that split.

Adapted from: Kuper, S and Atkins, R (1995) Insurers keep watch against stress attacks, *Financial Times*, 28 March, p 12.

+ Fashion. There are many organizations who consider that they are industry leaders and who have pride in being the first to adopt particular techniques or strategies. For such organizations to be known generally to be at the forefront of dealing with the effects of stress is a matter of pride. There are other organizations who rather than innovate themselves follow the trend set by others. These *followers of fashion* simply do things for the sake of appearance rather than having a positive motivation. The only thing that such organizations are keen to avoid is not introducing something after everyone else, they hate being last. Now, of course, it is not organizations that adopt these strategies but the managers within them. Such approaches can be used politically within an organization to push particular ideas or functions to advantage.

+ Reputation. This category represents the first group referred to in the fashion section. They are the innovators and attempt to be the leader in particular industries in developing novel approaches to products and the application of management techniques.

+ Morality. There are managers who adopt a moral position in relation to issues associated with stress (and many other aspects of management). Ethics and the issues raised in that chapter are all pertinent to this discussion. The moral view of stress would take the approach that as it has the potential to be harmful to employees it should be controlled and minimized. Furthermore, as it can be harmful then employees should be offered the opportunity to cope with it more effectively and thereby minimize the consequences.

+ Legislation. Legislation surrounding health and safety at work is becoming ever tighter. Employers are being increasingly required to identify the areas of risk to employee health and to put in place effective measures to reduce or eliminate them as far as possible. This approach also places a requirement on employers to provide employees with the opportunity to offset any consequences of these risks for themselves. Stress is increasingly being regarded as a risk factor to the health aspects associated with work and therefore liable to control. Many mangers are simply recognizing this and anticipating events by adopting appropriate control mechanisms.

Conclusions

This chapter has introduced the subject of stress, what it is in relation to similar concepts and what creates it. This was followed by a discussion on the effects of stress on the individual and the organization and then how they can attempt to manage the effects of it. A number of the management perspectives on stress concluded this chapter. Throughout this chapter indicators of the complexity of stress were identified as was the integrated nature of it with other material in this book. It would appear that some measure of stress is an inevitable byproduct of working in an organization, and indeed it has been suggested that it is essential to securing high performance. However, too much stress is considered detrimental to those exposed to it and so the problem associated with it from a managerial point of view is one of achieving an effective balance.

Many of the causes of stress have already been identified in earlier chapters in this book as have many or the mechanisms for dealing with it. Consequently, it provides a useful point at which to end this book and demonstrate the integrated nature of all organizational behaviour activity. It is also a useful theme on which to draw the reader's attention of the need to consider issues in the round and not just as discrete elements linked to individuals, or groups etc. Organizations are complex whole units not simple elements linked together but retaining an essentially discrete nature. The reader could do worse than begin to read the book again bearing that in mind!

Discussion questions

1. Define the following key terms used in this chapter:

Stress	*Locus of control*	*Role ambiguity*
Pressure	*Type A and B personality*	*Individual stress management*
Strain	*Role conflict*	*Organizational stress management*
Burnout	*Role overload*	*Effects of stress*
PTSD		

2. What are the main sources of stress and how might they be controlled?

3. 'Stress is a necessary part of life and work and cannot be eliminated.' Discuss this statement.

4. 'Managers only think they are stressed. It is the factory and office workers tied to

boring and monotonous jobs and with low pay who really experience stress.' To what extent do you agree with this statement? Justify your answer.

5. Outline the main effects of stress on the organization.

6. Describe the distinction, if any, between stress, burnout, pressure and PTSD.

7. Outline the main effects of stress on the individual.

8. Describe the main options available to an individual in attempting to deal with the effects of stress.

9. Some organizations, particularly in the Far East, make all employees do a short period of physical exercise before starting work each day. What general benefits do you think that this might have and to what extent do you think that it would help in managing stress?

10. Describe the main options available to an organization in attempting to deal with the effects of stress.

Research activities

1. First, attempt to identify how you might measure the level of stress present in jobs. Second, identify about six different jobs and list them in rank order based on your subjective view on how stressful they might be. Using the stress-measuring device that you identified in the first part of this activity attempt to measure the stress levels in a small sample of people from each job that you have identified. Compare the rank order of stress that you first identified and that obtained from your research and explain any differences between them. What does your research activity tell you about research into stress and stress at work generally?

2. It has been suggested that education is a preparation for life and that examinations are a preparation for the stress encountered in a work context. Individuals who cannot cope with the stress of examinations are unlikely to be able to cope with the pressure of senior management positions. Think about the issues implied by this viewpoint and attempt to find any research or other evidence that would support of discredit it.

3. Interview a small sample of people about the stress that they experience in their lives. Attempt to identify those factors that cause stress in a work context and those that originate from outside a work context. Explain your findings in terms of your reading of this chapter and other material on stress.

Key reading

From Clark, H, Chandler, J and Barry, J (1994) *Organization and Identities: Text and Readings in Organizational Behaviour*, International Thomson Business, London:

✦ Selye, H. Stress: the general adaptation syndrome and dissonances of adaptation, p 398. This extract considers stress from a medical perspective and attempts to explain it in terms of the need/ability of an organizm to adapt to its experienced environment.

✦ Eyer, J and Sterling, P: Stress-related mortality and social organization, p 400. This reading represents a social/political approach to understanding the subject of stress. It attempts to draw out the association between work as experienced in a capitalist-dominated organizational framework and its human consequences.

✦ Cooper, CL: Stress and industry: altruism or big business?, p 414. This extract shows the directions being taken by some organizations in attempting to deal with stress and the effects that it generates. It also suggests that this is largely driven by managerial self-interest and not an altruistic desire to improve the health of workers.

✦ Clark, H: Patriarchy, alienation and anomie: new directions for stress research, p 416. This reading attempts to bring together some of the issues raised in the readings on alienation and stress. It then suggests new directions for future research into the causes and effects of stress.

Further reading

Adams, A (1992) *Bullying At Work: How To Confront and Overcome It,* Virago, London. One of the major forms of stress at work originates from the experience of being managed. It is not an unusual experience to find subordinates at any level being forced to do things or being bullied in other ways. This book attempts to explore this experience and to offer readers an understanding of the root causes and ways to deal with it.

Cooper, C, Liukkonen, P and Cartwright, S (1996) *Stress Prevention in the Workplace: Assessing the Costs and Benefits to Organizations*, European Foundation for the Improvement of Living and Working Conditions, Office for Official Publications of the European Communities, Luxembourg. This report considers three case studies on how particular organizations have attempted to identify the sources and costs of stress. It also details the subsequent actions taken by these organizations and how they attempted to identify the benefits obtained from the interventions taken.

Dobschiner, J-R (1969) *Selected To Live*, Pickering & Inglis, London. Not a business text, this book is a very personal and moving real life reflection of Jewish experience during the Second World War. It demonstrates the stress that can arise from events around the individual and which impact on every other aspect of life. It demonstrates how under extreme circumstances individuals can develop ways to cope with considerable levels of stress.

Gabriel, Y and Lang, T (1995) *The Unmanageable Consumer*, Sage, London. Organizations do not exist in a vacuum and must meet the needs of their customers more effectively than competitors if they are to stay in business. It is generally recognized that trading conditions for most organizations are becoming more complex and difficult and this text attempts to explore one aspect of this: the nature of consumerism and its effect on organizations. The reality of attempting to meet the ever-changing demands of customers is a source of considerable pressure and stress within any organization and this text helps to provide an insight into these issues.

Kramer, RM and Tyler, TR (1996) *Trust In Organizations*, Sage, London. Much stress originates from the existence of uncertainty and unpredictability in being able to cope with all that needs to be done and the inevitable pressures in working within an organization. This text considers the subject of trust from a multidisciplinary perspective. It is relevant to the study of stress in that high trust environments are more likely to be supportive of the individuals within them and consequently less stressful.

Levi, L and Lunde-Jensen, P (1997) *Socio Economic Costs of Work Stress in Two EU Member States: A Model for Assessment of the Costs of Stressors at National Level*, European Foundation for the Improvement of Living and Working Conditions, the Office for Official Publications of the European Communities, Luxembourg. As the title suggests this report attempts to identify a model for the determination of the macro-level costs of stress at work. It also attempts to consider the issues surrounding what causes job stress and how it can be dealt with.

Newton, T with Handy, J and Fineman, S (1995) *Managing Stress: Emotion and Power at Work*, Sage, London. This text takes a different view of stress, seeking to place into a wider discourse on emotion, power, gender and subjectivity within an organization. In the process a historical review of stress research is undertaken as is an attempt to place the concept into such frameworks as labour process theory and Foucaultian philosophy.

References

Arkin, A (1991) When high-flyers turn their backs on stress, *PM Plus*, April, p 20.

Brenner, MH (1978) The stressful price of prosperity, *Science News*, March, p 166.

Cordes, CL and Doughtery, TW (1993) A review and an integration of research on job burnout, *Academy of Management Review*, October, pp 621–24.

Cox, T (1978) *Stress*, University Park Press, Baltimore, MD.

Dawkins, W (1993) More than the job's worth, *Financial Times*, 16/17 October, p 9.

Evans, BK and Fisher, DG (1993) The nature of burnout: a study of the three-factor model of burnout in human service and non-human service samples, *Journal of Occupational and Organizational Psychology*, March, pp 29–38.

Ganster, DC and Schaubroeck, J (1991) Work stress and employee health, *Journal of Management*, **17**, pp 235–71.

Hall, L (1994) Pressure gauge, *Personnel Today*, 17 May, p 29.

Hall, L (1995) Breakdown service, *Personnel Today*, 28 February, p 25.

Handy, CB (1993) *Understanding Organizations* 4th edn, Penguin, Harmondsworth.

Hogg, C (1988) Stress Management. Personnel Management Factsheet No. 7, Institute of Personnel Management, London.

Jackson, SE, Schwab, RL and Schuler, RS (1986) Towards an understanding of the burnout phenomenon, *Journal of Applied Psychology*, **71**, pp 630–40.

Luthans, F (1995) *Organizational Behaviour*, 7th edn, McGraw-Hill, New York.

McKenna, E (1994) *Business Psychology and Organizational Behaviour*, Lawrence Erlbaum Associates, Hove.

Moorhead, G and Griffin, RW (1992) *Organizational Behaviour*, 3rd edn, Houghton Mifflin, Boston, MA.

Quick, JC and Quick, JD (1984) *Organisational Stress and Preventive Management*, McGraw-Hill, New York.

Semmer, N, Zapf, D and Greif, S (1996) Shared job strain: a new approach for assessing the validity of job stress measurements, *Journal of Occupational and Organizational Psychology*, **69**, September, pp 293–310.

Summers, D (1990) Testing for stress in the workplace, *Financial Times*, December 7.

Thompson, P and McHugh, D (1995) *Work Organisations: A Critical Introduction*, 2nd edn, Macmillan, Basingstoke.

Turner, M (1995) To test recruits or test at random?, *People Management*, 30 November, pp 22–7.

Ward, T. (1996) The stress factor. Institute of Management Humberside Branch Newsletter, Institute of Management, Corby.

Welch, J (1996) Stress ruling ups the stakes for employers, *People Management*, 16 May, p 13.

Index